2020

Income Tax FUNDAMENTALS

GERALD E. WHITTENBURG

STEVEN L. GILL

San Diego State University

∴ CENGAGE

Australia • Brazil • Mexico • Singapore • United Kingdom • United States

Income Tax Fundamentals, 2020 Edition
Gerald E. Whittenburg and Steven L. Gill

Senior Vice President, Higher Ed Product, Content, and Market Development: Erin Joyner

Product Director: Jason Fremder

Associate Product Manager: Jonathan Gross

Senior Content Manager: Tricia Hempel

Product Assistant: Margaret Russo

Marketing Manager: Chris Walz

Senior Digital Project Manager: Tim Richison

Production Service: MPS Limited

Designer: Chris Doughman

Cover Images:

   donatas1205/Shutterstock.com;
   iStock.com/gerenme

Special page images:

   Zhukov Oleg/Shutterstock.com;
   ILYA AKINSHIN/Shutterstock.com

Intellectual Property

   Analyst: Ashley Maynard
   Project Manager: Carly Belcher

For product information and technology assistance, contact us at
Cengage Customer & Sales Support, 1-800-354-9706.

For permission to use material from this text or product,
submit all requests online at **www.cengage.com/permissions.**
Further permissions questions can be emailed to
permissionrequest@cengage.com.

Tax forms reproduced courtesy of the Internal Revenue Service (**www.irs.gov**).

Library of Congress Control Number: 2019916757

ISBN: 978-0-357-10823-9

Cengage
200 Pier 4 Boulevard
Boston, MA 02210
USA

Cengage is a leading provider of customized learning solutions with employees residing in nearly 40 different countries and sales in more than 125 countries around the world. Find your local representative at **www.cengage.com.**

Cengage products are represented in Canada by Nelson Education, Ltd.

To learn more about Cengage platforms and services, visit **www.cengage.com**.

To register or access your online learning solution or purchase materials for your course, visit **www.cengage.com**.

Printed in the United States of America
Print Number: 01   Print Year: 2019

ProConnect™ Tax Online

Work like a pro.

Get the #1 cloud-based professional tax software for free.[1,2]

Go beyond the basics and connect with the modern tools you need to work efficiently.

- **Work with confidence.**
  Get returns done right the first time with access to all the forms you need, backed by industry-leading calculations and diagnostics.

- **Work smarter.**
  Save time with logical data-entry worksheets instead of traditional forms-based methods. Plus, get quick training resources so it's easy to stay up to speed.

- **Work from anywhere.**
  It's all online, so there's nothing to install or maintain. And whether you're on your mobile phone or laptop, PC or Mac – you're always good to go.

Visit TaxEducation.Intuit.com to get started.

Only one sign-up per student. No special code required. If you have trouble accessing or using the software, reach out to us at taxeducation_support@intuit.com anytime for help.

CONCISE, CURRENT, & PRACTICAL!

Income Tax Fundamentals'
Winning Forms Approach Is Time-Tested

*I*ncome Tax Fundamentals 2020 Edition* is designed as a self-contained book for an introductory course in individual income taxation. We take pride in the concise, current, and practical coverage of the income tax return preparation process. *Income Tax Fundamentals* continues to be the **market-leading textbook** with a tax forms-based approach that is a reliable choice, with an experienced author team that offers a commitment to accuracy. The workbook format of the textbook presents materials in practical sections with multiple examples and review problems. The presentation of the material does not assume that the reader has taken a course in accounting, making it appropriate for use as a self-study guide to federal income tax. *Income Tax Fundamentals* adopters tell us:

> Great text. I have used it for years mostly because of its simple and straightforward approach to the basic income tax elements.
>
> — Jerold K. Braun, Daytona State College

> This text provides an excellent overview for community tax classes. The software gives these students good hands-on experience with the concepts.
>
> — Jay Wright, New River Community College

> I love this book with all its comprehensive problems that progress from easy to difficult.
>
> — LoAnn Nelson, PhD, CPA, Lake Region State College

> The layout of the chapters is well-thought out.
>
> — James Hromadka, San Jacinto College

> I enjoy using the Whittenburg text...it is the best I have found.
>
> — Jana Hosmer, Blue Ridge Community College

Whittenburg and Gill's hallmark **"Forms Approach"** allows students to practice filling out tax returns right in the book while also having the option to download tax forms online. *Income Tax Fundamentals* has been redesigned to follow the new Form 1040 and supporting Schedules 1 through 3. Every attempt to align the concepts with the schedules has been made so students can follow from the detailed form to the schedule and eventually to Form 1040.

Each individual tax form required to complete the problems in the textbook is included within *Income Tax Fundamentals* and within the complimentary Intuit ProConnect Online. ProConnect Online is an industry-leading tax preparation software that is hosted on the cloud and provides robust tax content and easy navigation. The Intuit website offers community and knowledge-based content, view alerts, and FAQ articles. All of the 2019 individual income tax return problems in the textbook may be solved using the Intuit software, or students may prepare the tax returns by hand.

Evolves Each Year to Benefit You

NEW TO THIS EDITION

The Tax Cuts and Jobs Act (TCJA) of 2017

Although most of the new tax law became effective at the start of 2018, a significant amount of administrative tax guidance has followed in the last 24 months. New IRS notices, revenue rulings, and procedures have been reviewed and analyzed with the new material being included in this edition when appropriate. Improved clarity on the qualified business income deduction and the lapse of the individual shared responsibility for health care are notable changes that are covered.

A New Form 1040 and Schedules (again)

Never leave well enough alone. The postcard-size Form 1040 and six schedules have been replaced by a more sizable Form 1040 and three schedules. In addition, a new Form 1040-SR has been introduced for taxpayers age 65 and older. All of these form changes, plus new qualified business income deduction forms, are covered in the same seamless forms-based approach in previous editions.

Introduction of additional real-life source documents

We continue to include commonly used source documents in the exercises and tax return problems such as Form W-2, a myriad of Forms 1099, Form 1095-A, and additional accounting schedules such as trial balances and income statements in an effort to replicate the tax return preparation process more closely. Information that is not relevant to the problem is included to encourage students to use analytical and critical-thinking skills to deal with less structured problems.

Latest Tax Law is included

Compared to 2018, the degree of tax law changes has been small, but *Income Tax Fundamentals* continues to monitor all changes through October 2019. Recent guidance on the qualified business income deduction and bonus depreciation is covered in this edition.

UPDATED CUMULATIVE SOFTWARE PROBLEM

The cumulative software problem included as Group 5 questions at the end of Chapters 1–8 have been updated to include more source documents (Form W-2s, 1099s, etc.) and include extraneous information to encourage students to think more critically about the relevance of certain items when preparing tax returns.

A COMPLETE LEARNING SYSTEM—CENGAGENOWv2

CengageNOWv2 for Taxation takes students from motivation to mastery. It elevates thinking by providing superior content designed with the entire student workflow in mind. Students learn more efficiently with the variety of engaging assessments and learning tools. For instructors, CengageNOWv2 provides ultimate control and customization and a clear view into student performance that allows for the opportunity to tailor the learning experience to improve outcomes.

Motivation

Many instructors find that students come to class unmotivated and unprepared. To help with engagement and preparedness, CengageNOWv2 for Whittenburg offers the following feature:

Self-Study Questions based on the information presented in the textbook help students prepare for class lectures or review prior to an exam. Self-Study Questions provide ample practice for the students as they read the chapters, while providing them with valuable feedback and checks along the way, as the solutions are provided conveniently in Appendix E of the textbook.

Application

Students need to learn problem-solving skills in order to complete taxation problems on their own. However, as students try to work through homework problems, sometimes they become stuck and need guidance. To help reinforce concepts and keep students on the right track, CengageNOWv2 for Whittenburg offers the following:

- **End-of-chapter homework: Group 1 and 2 problems**
- **Algorithmic versions** of end-of-chapter homework are available for at least 10–15 problems per chapter.

- **Detailed feedback for each homework question.** Homework questions include enhanced, immediate feedback so students can learn as they go. Levels of feedback include an option for "check my work" prior to submission of an assignment. Then, after submitting an assignment, students receive even more extensive feedback explaining why their answers were incorrect. Instructors can decide how much feedback their students receive and when, including providing the full solution, if they wish.
- Built-in **Test Bank** for online assessment.

For students who need additional support, CengageNOWv2's **Adaptive Study Plan** is complete with quizzes, an eBook, and more.

- It is designed to help give students additional support and prepare them for the exam.

Mastery

Finally, students need to make the leap from memorizing concepts to critical thinking. They need to be able to connect multiple topics and master the material. To help students grasp the big picture of taxation, tax return preparation, and achieve the end goal of mastery, CengageNOWv2 for Whittenburg offers the following:

Comprehensive Problems allow students to complete the tax return problems by entering the relevant information on tax forms and schedules in the Intuit ProConnect Online tax software or by manually preparing the tax forms and schedules provided within each chapter.

Cengage Learning Testing Powered by Cognero®

Cognero® is a flexible, online system that allows instructors to:

- author, edit, and manage test bank content from multiple Cengage Learning solutions
- create multiple test versions in an instant
- deliver tests from your LMS, your classroom or wherever you want

Cognero® possesses the features necessary to make assessment fast, efficient, and effective:

- <u>Simplicity at every step</u>. A desktop-inspired interface features drop-down menus and familiar, intuitive tools.
- <u>Full-featured test generator</u>. Choose from 15 question types (including true/false, multiple choice, and essay). Multi-language support, an equation editor, and unlimited metadata help ensure your tests are complete and compliant.
- <u>Cross-compatible capability</u>. Import and export content into other systems.

CL Testing Powered by <u>Cognero</u>® is accessible through the instructor companion site, **www.cengage.com/login.**

Key Terms

Key Terms with page references are located at the end of all of the chapters and reinforce the important tax terms introduced in each chapter.

Key Points

Following the Key Terms is a brief summary of the learning objective highlights for each chapter to allow students to focus quickly on the main points of each chapter.

RELIABLE INSTRUCTOR RESOURCES ARE CONVENIENT

Solutions Manual

The manual contains detailed solutions to the end-of-chapter problems in the textbook, Chapter Outlines and Suggested Minimum Assignments, and the Additional Comprehensive Problems that are located in Appendix D.

Comprehensive Instructor Companion Website

This password-protected site contains instructor resources: the Solutions Manual, the Test Bank, Cognero® testing tools, Solutions to the Cumulative Tax Return Problems, Intuit ProConnect Online software solutions and instructions, PowerPoints, and more: **www.cengage.com/login.**

AS WE GO TO PRESS

To access tax law information after the publication of this textbook, please visit **www.cengage.com**. At the home page, input the ISBN of your textbook (from the back cover of your book). This will take you to the product page where free companion resources are located.

Step-by-Step Format
Builds Student Confidence

The practical, step-by-step format in *Income Tax Fundamentals 2020 Edition* builds from simple to complex topics. The authors are careful to lead students down a path of understanding rather than overwhelming them with excessive detail and multiple Internal Revenue Code references.

- Helpful examples within each chapter provide realistic scenarios for students to consider.

EXAMPLE Scott provides all of the support for an unrelated family friend who lives with him for the entire tax year. He also supports a cousin who lives in another state. The family friend can qualify as Scott's dependent, but the cousin cannot. The family friend meets the member of the household test. Even though the cousin is not considered a relative, he could have been a dependent if he met the member of the household part of the test. ♦

- The short Learning Objective sections within each chapter offer numerous examples, supported by the "Self-Study Problems" throughout. The Self-Study Problems encourage students to answer a series of short questions in a fill-in-the-blank or multiple-choice format. The solutions to the Self-Study Problems are provided at the end of the textbook, offering immediate solutions to students to help build confidence.

- The Quick Tax Reference Guide on the inside of the back cover of the textbook includes the Tax Equation.

MARRIED FILING JOINTLY OR QUALIFYING WIDOW(ER)	
$0	
$19,400	$19,400
$78,950	$78,950
$100,000	$100,000
$168,400	$168,400
$321,450	$321,450
$408,200	$408,200
$612,350	$612,350

10% of taxable income *
$1,940.00 + 12% of the excess over $19,400 *
$9,086.00 + 22% of the excess over $78,950 *
$9,086.00 + 22% of the excess over $78,950 *
$28,765.00 + 24% of the excess over $168,400
$65,497.00 + 32% of the excess over $321,450
$93,257.00 + 35% of the excess over $408,200
$164,709.50 + 37% of the excess over $612,350

MARRIED FILING SEPARATELY	
$0	
$9,700	$9,700
$39,475	$39,475
$84,200	$84,200
$100,000	$100,000
$160,725	$160,725
$204,100	$204,100
$306,175	$306,175

10% of taxable income *
$970.00 + 12% of the excess over $9,700 *
$4,543.00 + 22% of the excess over $39,475 *
$14,382.50 + 24% of the excess over $84,200 *
$14,382.50 + 24% of the excess over $84,200 *
$32,748.50 + 32% of the excess over $160,725
$46,628.50 + 35% of the excess over $204,100
$82,354.75 + 37% of the excess over $306,175

HEAD OF HOUSEHOLD

10% of t

LEARNING OBJECTIVES

After completing this chapter, you should be able to:

LO 1.1 Explain the history and objectives of U.S. tax law.

LO 1.2 Describe the different entities subject to tax and reporting requirements.

LO 1.3 Apply the tax formula for individuals.

LO 1.4 Identify individuals who must file tax returns.

LO 1.5 Determine filing ... understand the calculation of tax according to filing ...

- Learning Objectives help organize information and are referenced by the end-of-chapter exercises.

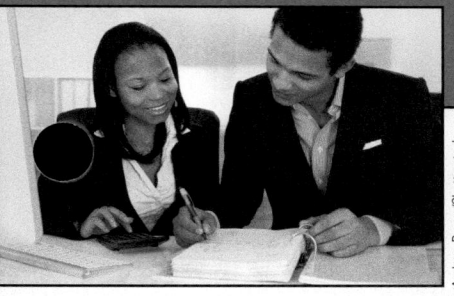

Real-World Applications Keep Students Engaged

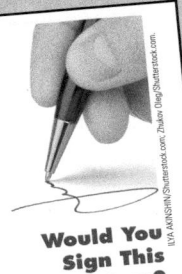

Would You Sign This Tax Return?

Your client, William Warrant, was hired for a management position at an Internet company planning to start a website called "indulgedanimals.com" for dogs, cats, and other pets. When he was hired, William was given an incentive stock option (ISO) worth $500,000, which he exercised during the year. Exercise of the ISO creates a tax preference item for alternative minimum tax (AMT) and causes him to have to pay substantial additional tax when combined with his other tax items for the year. He is livid about the extra tax and refuses to file the AMT Form 6251 with his tax return because the AMT tax is "unfair" and "un-American" according to him. Would you sign this tax return?

- The "Would You Sign This Tax Return?" feature places readers in the office of a tax preparer with interesting and sometimes humorous real-world tax ethics questions that will intrigue students. Many of these features are inspired by the authors' own experiences working with various clients in tax preparation. As part of each scenario, students decide if they would sign the tax return. The instructor can use the cases to spark group discussions on basic tax preparation ethics.

- Real-world examples within Tax Break segments provide actual, effective examples of tax-planning strategies that clearly illustrate the concepts discussed throughout the book and cover nearly every basic tax-planning technique used by tax preparers.

TAX BREAK

Divorcing couples may save significant taxes if one or both of the spouses qualify as an "abandoned spouse" and can use the head of household filing status. The combination of head of household filing status for one spouse with married filing separately filing status for the other spouse is commonly seen in the year (or years) leading up to a divorce. In cases where each spouse has custody of a child, the separated taxpayers may each claim head of household status.

Would You Believe?

The following quotation is often attributed to Albert Einstein: "The hardest thing in the world to understand is the income tax."

- Interesting tax facts within "Would You Believe?" sections grab students' attention with interesting asides, including captivating facts and stories about tax laws and preparation.

- New Tax Law boxes throughout the textbook draw students' attention to specific areas affected by new tax legislation.

New Tax Law!

The TCJA made no direct changes to the accumulated earnings tax or the personal holding company tax; however, the significant decrease in the corporate tax rate makes deferring income without distributing the earnings and profits of a corporation considerably more attractive from a tax planning perspective. Undoubtedly, this will increase both the use of this strategy and the IRS' sensitivity to this matter.

Income Tax Fundamentals
Delivers Proven End-of-Chapter Strengths

- The pages are perforated, allowing students to complete end-of-chapter problems and submit them for homework. Students can also tear out tax forms as needed.
- Several question types ensure a variety of assignment options:
  - Multiple-Choice Questions
  - Problems
  - Writing Assignments
  - Comprehensive Problems
  - The Cumulative Software Problem provided in Chapters 1–8 gives students the flexibility to use multiple resources, such as the tax forms within the book, Intuit ProConnect Online or alternative tax preparation software.

Digital Tools Enhance Student Understanding

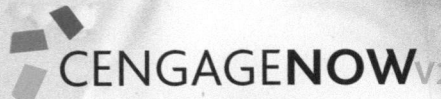

CengageNOWv2 is a powerful online homework tool. This online resource includes an interactive eBook, end-of-chapter homework, detailed student feedback and interactive quizzing, that covers the most challenging topics, a lab guide for using the Intuit ProConnect Online software, flashcards, and much more.

The student companion website offers—*at no additional costs*—study resources for students. Go to **www.cengage.com**, and input the ISBN number of your textbook (from the back cover of your book). This will take you to the product page where free companion resources are located.

Intuit ProConnect Online access is included with each textbook. A detailed reference lab guide will help the student use the software for solving end-of-chapter problems.

For students who are new to the Intuit ProConnect product, we have placed tips throughout the textbook providing guidance to assist students with the transition from a paper form to using the tax software.

Marc Romanelli/Getty Images

Note to Students: Maximize Your Reading Experience

This book includes many examples to help illustrate learning objectives. After reading each section, including the examples, answer the corresponding Self-Study Problems. You can find the solutions to the Self-Study Problems at the end of the textbook in Appendix E to check your accuracy. Use your performance to measure your understanding, and re-read the Learning Objectives section if needed. Many key tax terms are defined in each chapter, which will help improve your overall comprehension.

USING TAX SOFTWARE

Numerous tax return problems in the textbook can be solved using either tax preparation software or hand preparation. The popular software, Intuit ProConnect Online, is available with the textbook. Helpful tips for using ProConnect have been placed throughout the book so that students can more easily train on the software and prepare the tax returns included in each of the first eight chapters. A student guide to Intuit ProConnect Online is provided at the companion website. Your college may offer additional tax preparation software, such as Intuit's ProSeries®, but remember that you can always prepare the solutions manually on the chapter-provided tax forms, schedules and worksheets.

USING THE FEATURE "WOULD YOU SIGN THIS TAX RETURN?"

A practitioner who knows when to say "I cannot sign this tax return," even if it means losing a client, is exercising the most basic ethical wisdom. Most chapters contain a "Would You Sign This Tax Return?" case reflecting a common client issue. Each issue corresponds to an obvious concept illustrated in the previous section. However, the approach to advise the client is not obvious. The art of explaining tax rules to a client who does not understand them, or, worse, wants to break them, requires not only a good understanding of the rules, but also good interpersonal skills and sometimes the gift of persuasion. The news in the last several years has shown reports of respected CPA firms with members who failed to say the simple words, "I cannot sign this tax return," demonstrating that simple ethical practice is not always easy. We hope instructors will use these cases to spark group discussions or contemplation, and, perhaps, add examples from their own experience.

USING THE CUMULATIVE SOFTWARE PROBLEM

The Cumulative Software Problem can be found at the end of Chapters 1–8. The case information provided in each chapter builds on the information presented in previous chapters, resulting in a lengthy and complex tax return by the conclusion of the problem in Chapter 8. Your instructor may have you work in groups to prepare each of the tax returns. The groups can follow the real-world accounting firm model using a preparer, a reviewer, and a firm owner who takes responsibility for the accuracy of the return and signs it. All of the issues in the problem are commonly seen by tax preparers and are covered in the textbook. The full return is difficult to prepare by hand, so tax software is recommended. If the problem is prepared using tax software, the data should be saved so the additional information in the succeeding chapters can be added without duplicating input from previous chapters.

About the Authors

Gerald E. Whittenburg On March 8, 2015, we unexpectedly lost our dear friend and co-author Gene Whittenburg. As the original author of *Income Tax Fundamentals*, Gene was critical in designing the forms-based approach that the book has used successfully for over two decades. Gene started his life in a small town in Texas, entered the Navy, served his country in Vietnam, earned a Bachelor's, Master's, and PhD degrees, and served as a distinguished faculty at San Diego State University for almost 40 years. We intend to continue to honor Gene by committing to uphold his standard of publishing excellence.

Steven L. Gill is an associate professor of accounting and taxation in the Charles W. Lamden School of Accountancy at San Diego State University. He also serves as the Director of Graduate Programs at the Fowler College of Business at SDSU. Steve received a BS in Accounting from the University of Florida, an MS in Taxation from Northeastern University, and a PhD in Accounting from the University of Massachusetts. Prior to entering academia, he worked for almost 12 years in the field of tax and accounting, including roles in public accounting, internal audit, corporate accounting, and, ultimately, vice president of finance. Although currently in inactive status, Steve holds a Certified Public Accountant designation. He has published a wide variety of articles in various academic and practitioner journals, and has taught at both the undergraduate and graduate levels, including taxation and financial and management accounting. Steven also serves as an author on Cengage's Federal Tax Research series.

Reviewers

Janice Akao, *Butler Community College*

Sandra Augustine, *Hilbert College*

George Barbi, *Lanier Technical College*

Lydia Botsford, *DeAnza College*

Mike Bowyer, *Montgomery Community College*

Jerold Braun, *Daytona State College*

Lindy Byrd, *Augusta Technical College*

Greg Carlton, *Davidson County Community College*

Diana Cescolini, *Chaffey College*

John Chappell, *Northland Community and Technical College*

Marilyn Ciolino, *Delgado Community College*

Diane Clugston, *Cambria-Rowe Business College*

Tonya Coates, *Western Piedmont Community College*

Thomas Confrey, *SUNY Orange*

Amy Conley, *Genesee Community College*

Eric DaGragnano, *Western Governors University*

Geoffrey Danzig, *Miami Dade College – Hialeah Campus*

Richard Davis, *Susquehanna University*

Susan Davis, *Green River Community College*

Vaun Day, *Central Arizona College*

Ken Dennis, *San Diego City College*

Kerry Dolan, *Great Falls College Montana State University*

Vicky C. Dominguez, *College of Southern Nevada*

Lisa Farnam, *College of Western Idaho*

John Fasler, *Whatcom Community College*

Brian Fink, *Danville Area Community College*

Brenda Fowler, *Central Carolina Community College*

George Frankel, *San Francisco State University*

Alan Fudge, *Linn-Benton Community College*

Gregory Gosman, *Keiser University*

Nancy Gromen, *Blue Mountain Community College*

Jeffery Haig, *Copper Mountain College*

Tracie Hayes, *Randolph Community College*

Michael Heath, *River Parishes Community College*

Cindy Hinz, *Jamestown Community College*

Rob Hochschild, *Ivy Tech Community College*

Japan Holmes, Jr., *Savannah Technical College*

Jana Hosmer, *Blue Ridge Community College*

James Hromadka, *San Jacinto College*

Carol Hughes, *Asheville Buncombe Technical Community College*

Norma Hunting, *Chabot College, Hayward, California*

Adrian Jarrell, *James Sprunt Community College*

Paul Johnson, *Mississippi Gulf Coast Community College*

Jessica Jones, *Mesa Community College*

Dieter Kiefer, *American River College*

Christopher Kinney, *Mount Wachusett Community College*

Angela Kirkendall, *South Puget Sound Community College*

Mark Klamrzynski, *Phoenix College*

Raymond Kreiner, *Piedmont College*

William Kryshak, *University Wisconsin-Stout*

Linda Lane, *Walla Walla Community College*

Christie Lee, *Lanier Technical College*
Anna Leyes, *Ivy Tech Community College*
Jeannie Liu, *Rio Hondo College*
Susan Logorda, *Lehigh Carbon Community College*
Heather Lynch, *Northeast Iowa Community College*
Diania McRae, *Western Carolina University*
Deanne Michaelson, *Pellissippi State Community College*
Jennifer Morton, *Ivy Tech Community College*
Sharon O'Reilly, *Gateway Technical College*
Mike Prockton, *Finger Lakes CC*
John Ribezzo, *Community College of Rhode Island*
Lance Rodrigues, *Ohlone College*
Hanna Sahebifard, *Golden West College*
Larry Sayler, *Greenville University*
James Shimko, *Jackson Community College*
Barry Siebert, *Concordia University–Saint Paul*
Kimberly Sipes, *Kentucky State University*
Amy Smith, *Pearl River Community College*
Thomas Snavely, *Yavapai College*

Joanie Sompayrc, *UT-Chattanooga*
Barbara Squires, *Corning Community College*
Todd Stowe, *Southwest Florida College*
Gracelyn Stuart-Tuggle, *Palm Beach State College*
Robert L. Taylor, *C.P.A. Lees-McRae College*
Teresa Thamer, *Brenau University*
Craig Vilhauer, *Merced College*
Stan Walker, *Georgia Northwestern Technical School*
Teresa Walker, *Greensboro College*
Joe Welker, *College of Western Idaho*
Jean Wells, *Howard University*
Mary Ann Whitehurst, *Southern Crescent Technical College*
Sharon Williams, *Sullivan University*
Douglas Woods, *Wayne College*
Patty Worsham, *Chaffey College*
Jay Wright, *New River Community College*
Douglas Yentsch, *South Central College*
James Zartman, *Elizabethtown PA College*
Jane Zlojutro, *Northwestern Michigan College*

ACKNOWLEDGMENTS

The authors wish to thank all of the instructors who provided feedback for the 2020 edition via surveys as well as the following supplement authors and verifiers for their most valuable suggestions and support:

D. Elizabeth Stone Atkins—*High Point University, High Point, NC*
David Candelaria—*Mt. San Jacinto College, Menifee, CA*
Jim Clarkson—*San Jacinto College South, Houston, TX*

Pennie Eddy—*Appalachian Technical College, Jasper, GA*
Paul Shinal—*Cayga Community College, Auburn, NY*
Lisa Swallow—*University of Montana, Missoula, MT*

In addition, gratitude is expressed to Susan Gill, Kathleen Smith, and Steve Smith for their expert assistance reviewing chapters of this textbook. We would also like to thank Janice Stoudemire, and Wendy Shanker on their work of reviewing and verifying the content in CengageNOWv2 including the end-of-chapter items and Test Bank problems. We would also like to extend our thanks to the Tax Forms and Publications Division of the Internal Revenue Service for their assistance in obtaining draft forms each year.

We appreciate your continued support in advising us of any revisions or corrections you feel are appropriate.

Steven L. Gill

THE ANNOTATED 1040 MAP

The annotated 1040 map is an expanded tax formula, illustrating where each piece of the tax formula is covered in the textbook. The 1040 map helps you understand how all of the elements of the textbook and the tax formula fit together. Use this as a reference and bookmark this page.

Form 1040 Department of the Treasury—Internal Revenue Service (99)
U.S. Individual Income Tax Return **2019** OMB No. 1545-0074 IRS Use Only—Do not write or staple in this space.

Filing Status
Check only one box.
☐ Single ☐ Married filing jointly ☐ Married filing separately (MFS) ☐ Head of household (HOH) ☐ Qualifying widow(er) (QW) **LO 1-5**

If you checked the MFS box, enter the name of spouse. If you checked the HOH or QW box, enter the child's name if the qualifying person is a child but not your dependent. ▶

Your first name and middle initial	Last name	Your social security number
If joint return, spouse's first name and middle initial	Last name	Spouse's social security number

Home address (number and street). If you have a P.O. box, see instructions. | Apt. no.

Presidential Election Campaign
Check here if you, or your spouse if filing jointly, want $3 to go to this fund. Checking a box below will not change your tax or refund. ☐ You ☐ Spouse

City, town or post office, state, and ZIP code. If you have a foreign address, also complete spaces below (see instructions).

LO 1-7

Foreign country name | Foreign province/state/county | Foreign postal code

If more than four dependents, see instructions and ✓ here ▶ ☐

Standard Deduction
Someone can claim: ☐ You as a dependent ☐ Your spouse as a dependent
☐ Spouse itemizes on a separate return or you were a dual-status alien

LO 1-6, 7-1

Age/Blindness You: ☐ Were born before January 2, 1955 ☐ Are blind Spouse: ☐ Was born before January 2, 1955 ☐ Is blind

Dependents (see instructions):

(1) First name Last name	(2) Social security number	(3) Relationship to you	(4) ✓ if qualifies for (see instructions):	
			Child tax credit	Credit for other dependents
			☐	☐
			☐	☐
			☐	☐
			☐	☐

Standard Deduction for—
- Single or Married filing separately, $12,200
- Married filing jointly or Qualifying widow(er), $24,400
- Head of household, $18,350
- If you checked any box under *Standard Deduction,* see instructions.

1	Wages, salaries, tips, etc. Attach Form(s) W-2			1	LO 2-2
2a	Tax-exempt interest	2a	LO 2-10	b Taxable interest. Attach Sch. B if required	2b	LO 2-9
3a	Qualified dividends	3a	LO 2-9	b Ordinary dividends. Attach Sch. B if required	3b	LO 2-9
4a	IRA distributions	4a	LO 5-3	b Taxable amount	4b	LO 5-3
c	Pensions and annuities	4c	LO 2-7	d Taxable amount	4d	LO 2-7
5a	Social security benefits	5a	LO 2-16	b Taxable amount	5b	LO 2-16
6	Capital gain or (loss). Attach Schedule D if required. If not required, check here ▶ ☐			6	LO 4-1 to 4-6
7a	Other income from Schedule 1, line 9			7a	
b	Add lines 1, 2b, 3b, 4b, 4d, 5b, 6, and 7a. This is your **total income** ▶			7b	
8a	Adjustments to income from Schedule 1, line 22			8a	
b	Subtract line 8a from line 7b. This is your **adjusted gross income** ▶			8b	
9	**Standard deduction or itemized deductions** (from Schedule A)	9	LO 1-7, 5-6 to 5-10		
10	Qualified business income deduction. Attach Form 8995 or Form 8995-A	10	LO 4-10		
11a	Add lines 9 and 10			11a	
b	**Taxable income.** Subtract line 11a from line 8b			11b	

For Disclosure, Privacy Act, and Paperwork Reduction Act Notice, see separate instructions.   Cat. No. 11320B   Form **1040** (2019)

Form 1040 (2019)   Page **2**

12a	**Tax** (see inst.) Check if any from Form(s): **1** ☐ 8814 **2** ☐ 4972 **3** ☐ _____	12a	LO 1.5, 2.9, 4.4, 6.4		
b	Add Schedule 2, line 3, and line 12a and enter the total ▶			12b	
13a	Child tax credit or credit for other dependents	13a	LO 1-7, 7-1		
b	Add Schedule 3, line 7, and line 13a and enter the total ▶			13b	
14	Subtract line 13b from line 12b. If zero or less, enter -0-			14	
15	Other taxes, including self-employment tax, from Schedule 2, line 10			15	
16	Add lines 14 and 15. This is your **total tax** ▶			16	
17	Federal income tax withheld from Forms W-2 and 1099			17	LO 2-2, 9-1
18	Other payments and refundable credits:				
a	Earned income credit (EIC)	18a	LO 7-2		
b	Additional child tax credit. Attach Schedule 8812	18b	LO 7-1		
c	American opportunity credit from Form 8863, line 8	18c	LO 7-5		
d	Schedule 3, line 14	18d			
e	Add lines 18a through 18d. These are your **total other payments and refundable credits** ▶			18e	
19	Add lines 17 and 18e. These are your **total payments** ▶			19	

• If you have a qualifying child, attach Sch. EIC.
• If you have nontaxable combat pay, see instructions.

Refund

Direct deposit? See instructions.

20	If line 19 is more than line 16, subtract line 16 from line 19. This is the amount you **overpaid**	20	
21a	Amount of line 20 you want **refunded to you.** If Form 8888 is attached, check here ▶ ☐	21a	
▶ b	Routing number ⬚⬚⬚⬚⬚⬚⬚⬚⬚ ▶ **c** Type: ☐ Checking ☐ Savings		
▶ d	Account number ⬚⬚⬚⬚⬚⬚⬚⬚⬚⬚⬚⬚⬚⬚⬚⬚⬚		
22	Amount of line 20 you want **applied to your 2020 estimated tax** ▶	22	

Amount You Owe

23	**Amount you owe.** Subtract line 19 from line 16. For details on how to pay, see instructions ▶	23	
24	Estimated tax penalty (see instructions) ▶	24	

Third Party Designee

(Other than paid preparer)

Do you want to allow another person (other than your paid preparer) to discuss this return with the IRS? See instructions.   ☐ **Yes.** Complete below.   ☐ **No**

Designee's name ▶   Phone no. ▶   Personal identification number (PIN) ▶ ⬚⬚⬚⬚⬚⬚

Sign Here

Joint return? See instructions. Keep a copy for your records.

Under penalties of perjury, I declare that I have examined this return and accompanying schedules and statements, and to the best of my knowledge and belief, they are true, correct, and complete. Declaration of preparer (other than taxpayer) is based on all information of which preparer has any knowledge.

Your signature	Date	Your occupation	If the IRS sent you an Identity Protection PIN, enter it here (see inst.) ⬚⬚⬚⬚⬚⬚
Spouse's signature. If a joint return, **both** must sign.	Date	Spouse's occupation	If the IRS sent your spouse an Identity Protection PIN, enter it here (see inst.) ⬚⬚⬚⬚⬚⬚
Phone no.		Email address	

Paid Preparer Use Only

Preparer's name	Preparer's signature	Date	PTIN	Check if: ☐ 3rd Party Designee ☐ Self-employed
Firm's name ▶			Phone no.	
Firm's address ▶			Firm's EIN ▶	

Go to *www.irs.gov/Form1040* for instructions and the latest information.   Form **1040** (2019)

DRAFT AS OF JULY 11, 2019 DO NOT FILE

SCHEDULE 1
(Form 1040 or 1040-SR)

Department of the Treasury
Internal Revenue Service

Additional Income and Adjustments to Income

▶ Attach to Form 1040 or 1040-SR.
▶ Go to *www.irs.gov/Form1040* for instructions and the latest information.

OMB No. 1545-0074

2019

Attachment
Sequence No. **01**

Name(s) shown on Form 1040 or 1040-SR

Your social security number

Part I	Additional Income		
1	Taxable refunds, credits, or offsets of state and local income taxes	1	LO 5-7
2a	Alimony received	2a	LO 2-13
b	Date of original divorce or separation agreement (see instructions) ▶		
3	Business income or (loss). Attach Schedule C	3	Chapter 3
4	Other gains or (losses). Attach Form 4797	4	LO 8-8
5	Rental real estate, royalties, partnerships, S corporations, trusts, etc. Attach Schedule E	5	LO 4-7, 4-8
6	Farm income or (loss). Attach Schedule F	6	
7	Unemployment compensation	7	LO 2-15
8	Other income. List type and amount ▶	8	LO 2.6, 2.12
9	Combine lines 1 through 8. Enter here and on Form 1040 or 1040-SR, line 7a	9	
Part II	Adjustments to Income		
10	Educator expenses	10	LO 5-5
11	Certain business expenses of reservists, performing artists, and fee-basis government officials. Attach Form 2106	11	LO 5-5
12	Health savings account deduction. Attach Form 8889	12	LO 5-1
13	Moving expenses for members of the Armed Forces. Attach Form 3903	13	LO 5-5
14	Deductible part of self-employment tax. Attach Schedule SE	14	LO 6-6
15	Self-employed SEP, SIMPLE, and qualified plans	15	LO 5-4
16	Self-employed health insurance deduction	16	LO 5-2
17	Penalty on early withdrawal of savings	17	LO 2-9
18a	Alimony paid	18a	LO 2-13
b	Recipient's SSN ▶		
c	Date of original divorce or separation agreement (see instructions) ▶		
19	IRA deduction	19	LO 5-3
20	Student loan interest deduction	20	LO 5-8
21	Reserved for future use	21	
22	Add lines 10 through 21. These are your **adjustments to income.** Enter here and on Form 1040 or 1040-SR, line 8a	22	

For Paperwork Reduction Act Notice, see your tax return instructions.   Cat. No. 71479F   Schedule 1 (Form 1040 or 1040-SR) 2019

SCHEDULE 2
(Form 1040 or 1040-SR)

Department of the Treasury
Internal Revenue Service

Additional Taxes

▶ Attach to Form 1040 or 1040-SR.
▶ Go to *www.irs.gov/Form1040* for instructions and the latest information.

OMB No. 1545-0074

2019

Attachment
Sequence No. **02**

Name(s) shown on Form 1040 or 1040-SR

Your social security number

Part I	Tax		
1	Alternative minimum tax. Attach Form 6251	1	LO 6-5
2	Excess advance premium tax credit repayment. Attach Form 8962	2	LO 7-4
3	Add lines 1 and 2. Enter here and include on Form 1040 or 1040-SR, line 12b	3	
Part II	Other Taxes		
4	Self-employment tax. Attach Schedule SE	4	LO 6-6
5	Unreported social security and Medicare tax from Form: a ☐ 4137 b ☐ 8919	5	
6	Additional tax on IRAs, other qualified retirement plans, and other tax-favored accounts. Attach Form 5329 if required	6	
7a	Household employment taxes. Attach Schedule H	7a	LO 6-7
b	Repayment of first-time homebuyer credit from Form 5405. Attach Form 5405 if required	7b	
8	Taxes from: a ☐ Form 8959 b ☐ Form 8960		
c	☐ Instructions; enter code(s)	8	LO 6-8
9	Section 965 net tax liability installment from Form 965-A	9	
10	Add lines 4 through 8. These are your **total other taxes.** Enter here and on Form 1040 or 1040-SR, line 15	10	

For Paperwork Reduction Act Notice, see your tax return instructions.   Cat. No. 71478U   Schedule 2 (Form 1040 or 1040-SR) 2019

SCHEDULE 3
(Form 1040 or 1040-SR)

Department of the Treasury
Internal Revenue Service

Additional Credits and Payments

▶ **Attach to Form 1040 or 1040-SR.**
▶ **Go to** *www.irs.gov/Form1040* **for instructions and the latest information.**

OMB No. 1545-0074

2019

Attachment
Sequence No. **03**

Name(s) shown on Form 1040 or 1040-SR

Your social security number

Part I	Nonrefundable Credits		
1	Foreign tax credit. Attach Form 1116 if required	**1**	LO 7-6
2	Credit for child and dependent care expenses. Attach Form 2441	**2**	LO 7-3
3	Education credits from Form 8863, line 19	**3**	LO 7-5
4	Retirement savings contributions credit. Attach Form 8880	**4**	LO 7-9
5	Residential energy credit. Attach Form 5695	**5**	LO 7-8
6	Other credits from Form: **a** ☐ 3800 **b** ☐ 8801 **c** ☐ _____	**6**	
7	Add lines 1 through 6. Enter here and include on Form 1040 or 1040-SR, line 13b	**7**	

Part II	Other Payments and Refundable Credits		
8	2019 estimated tax payments and amount applied from 2018 return	**8**	LO 9-2
9	Net premium tax credit. Attach Form 8962	**9**	LO 7-4
10	Amount paid with request for extension to file (see instructions)	**10**	LO 1-4
11	Excess social security and tier 1 RRTA tax withheld	**11**	
12	Credit for federal tax on fuels. Attach Form 4136	**12**	
13	Credits from Form: **a** ☐ 2439 **b** ☐ Reserved **c** ☐ 8885 **d** ☐ _____	**13**	
14	Add lines 8 through 13. Enter here and on Form 1040 or 1040-SR, line 18d	**14**	

For Paperwork Reduction Act Notice, see your tax return instructions.   Cat. No. 71480G   Schedule 3 (Form 1040 or 1040-SR) 2019

DRAFT AS OF July 11, 2019 DO NOT FILE

TABLE OF CONTENTS

Glow Images/Getty Images

Andy Dean Photography/Shutterstock.com

Pgiam/iStock Unreleased/Getty Images

QUESTIONS

Please contact the Cengage Learning Taxation publishing team if you have any questions:

Jonathan Gross, Associate Product Manager: jonathan.gross@cengage.com
Chris Walz, Marketing Manager: chris.walz@cengage.com
Tricia Hempel, Senior Content Manager: patricia.hempel@cengage.com

CHAPTER 1

The Individual Income Tax Return

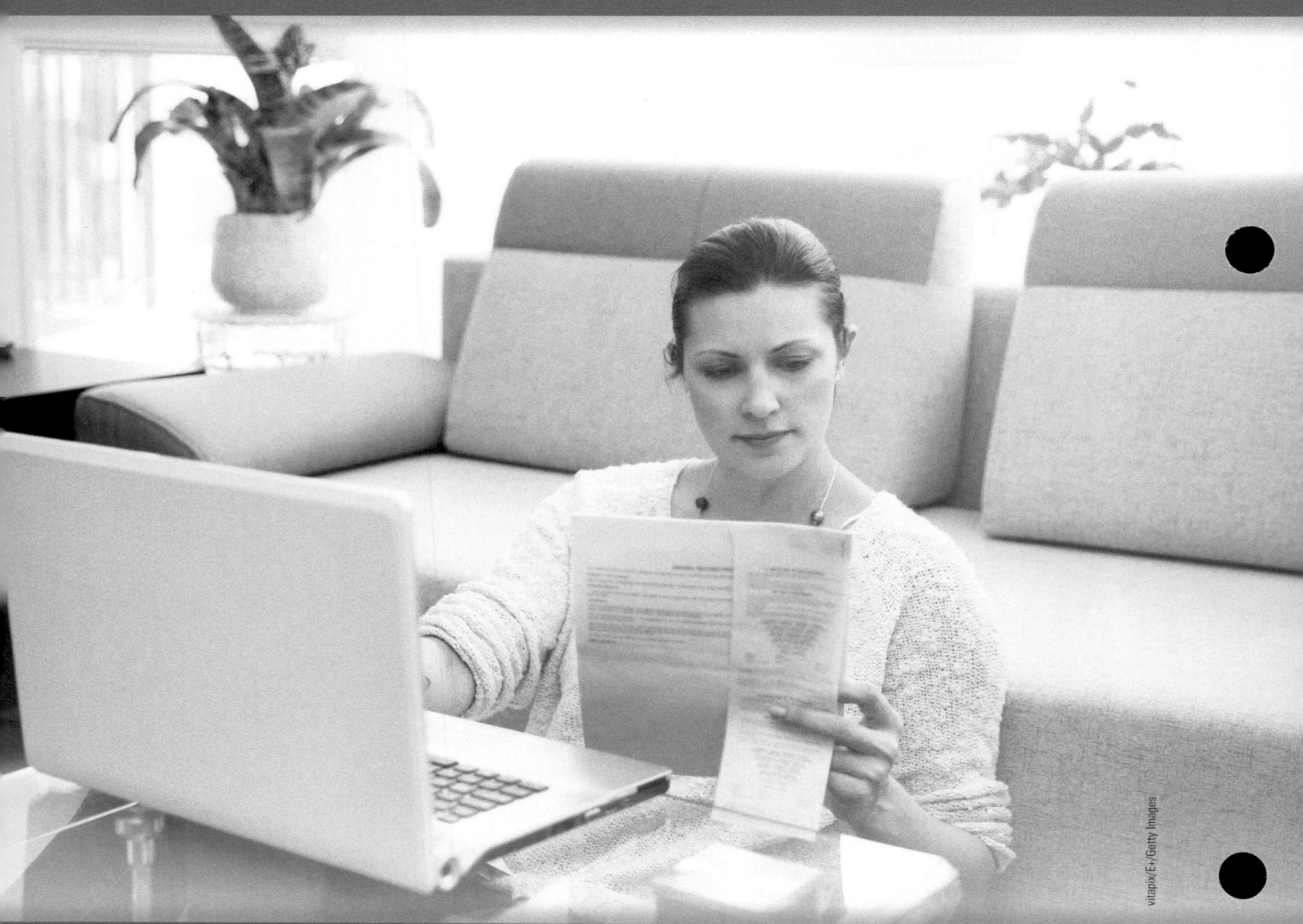

After completing this chapter, you should be able to:

LO 1.1   Explain the history and objectives of U.S. tax law.

LO 1.2   Describe the different entities subject to tax and reporting requirements.

LO 1.3   Apply the tax formula for individuals.

LO 1.4   Identify individuals who must file tax returns.

LO 1.5   Determine filing status and understand the calculation of tax according to filing status.

LO 1.6   Define qualifying dependents.

LO 1.7   Calculate the correct standard or itemized deduction amount for taxpayers.

LO 1.8   Compute basic capital gains and losses.

LO 1.9   Access and use various Internet tax resources.

LO 1.10   Describe the basics of electronic filing (e-filing).

OVERVIEW

This chapter introduces the U.S. individual income tax system. Important elements of the individual tax formula are covered, including the tax calculation, who must file, filing status, and the interaction of itemized deductions and the standard deduction. The chapter illustrates all the steps required for completion of a basic Form 1040. Also included is a discussion of reporting and taxable entities.

An introduction to capital gains and losses is included to provide a basic understanding of capital transactions prior to the detailed coverage in Chapter 4. An overview of tax information available at the Internal Revenue Service (IRS) website and other helpful tax websites is also included. A discussion of the process for electronic filing (e-filing) of an individual tax return completes the chapter.

Learning Objective 1.1

Explain the history and objectives of U.S. tax law.

1-1 HISTORY AND OBJECTIVES OF THE TAX SYSTEM

1-1a Tax Law History and Objectives

The U.S. income tax was established on March 1, 1913 by the Sixteenth Amendment to the Constitution. Prior to the adoption of this amendment, the U.S. government had levied various income taxes for limited periods of time. For example, an income tax was used to help finance the Civil War. The finding by the courts that the income tax law enacted in 1894 was unconstitutional eventually led to the adoption of the Sixteenth Amendment. Since adoption of the amendment, the constitutionality of the income tax has not been questioned by the federal courts.

Many people inaccurately believe the sole purpose of the income tax is to raise sufficient revenue to operate the government. The tax law has many goals other than raising revenue. These goals fall into two general categories—economic goals and social goals— and it is often unclear which goal a specific tax provision was written to meet. Tax provisions have been used for such economic motives as reduction of unemployment, expansion of investment in productive (capital) assets, and control of inflation. Specific examples of economic tax provisions are the limited allowance for expensing of capital expenditures and the bonus depreciation provisions. In addition to pure economic goals, the tax law is used to encourage certain business activities and industries. For example, an income tax credit encourages businesses to engage in research and experimentation activities, the energy credits encourage investment in solar and wind energy businesses, and a special deduction for soil and water conservation expenditures related to farm land benefits farmers.

Social goals have also resulted in the adoption of many specific tax provisions. The child and dependent care credit, the earned income credit, and the charitable contribution deduction are examples of tax provisions designed to meet social goals. Social provisions may influence economic activities, but they are written primarily to encourage taxpayers to undertake activities to benefit themselves and society.

An example of a provision that has both economic and social objectives is the provision allowing the gain on the sale of a personal residence up to $250,000 ($500,000 if married) to be excluded from taxable income. From a social standpoint, this helps a family afford a new home, but it also helps achieve the economic goal of ensuring that the United States has a mobile workforce.

The use of the income tax as a tool to promote economic and social policies has increased in recent years. Keeping this in mind, the beginning tax student can better understand how and why the tax law has become so complex.

1-1b The Tax Cuts and Jobs Act of 2017

Although the tax laws often change in some way each year, significant overhauls of the tax code are actually quite rare. However, in December 2017, The Tax Cuts and Jobs Act or TCJA (PL 115-97) was signed into law. For budgetary reasons, many of the provisions of the tax law are set to expire over the next decade. Many of the more important expiring provisions are listed below along with the chapter in this textbook in which they are discussed.

Summary of Major Tax Provisions Scheduled to Expire

TCJA Provision	Expires	Chapter
Reduction of individual tax rates	2025	1
Increased standard deduction	2025	1
Suspension of personal exemptions	2025	1
Qualified business income deduction	2025	4
Suspension of itemized deduction phase-out	2025	5
Temporary cap on state and local taxes	2025	5
Suspension of miscellaneous itemized deductions subject to 2 percent floor	2025	5
Suspension of moving expense deduction	2025	5
Reduced limits on mortgage interest deduction	2025	5

TCJA Provision	Expires	Chapter
Restrictions on personal casualty losses	2025	5
Increased AMT exemption and phase-out	2025	6
Changes to kiddie tax	2025	6
Increased child tax credit	2025	7
100 percent bonus depreciation	Phases out starting 2023	8

It remains uncertain if these provisions will be either extended or made permanent; however, when appropriate, the textbook includes background on the pre-TCJA law in the event those provisions return.

Also, Form 1040 underwent additional changes since the 2018 design change and a new Form 1040-SR for taxpayers over age 65 has been introduced. As a "forms-based" textbook, the design changes have been implemented throughout the textbook.

Most taxpayers know they can deduct contributions of cash to qualified charities but may not deduct the value of their time or services. However, taxpayers may be able to deduct mileage ($0.14 per mile) associated with the provision of services to a qualified charity.

TAX BREAK

Self-Study Problem 1.1 *See Appendix E for Solutions to Self-Study Problems*

Which of the following is not a goal of the income tax system?

a. Raising revenue to operate the government.

b. Providing incentives for certain business and economic goals, such as higher employment rates, through business-favorable tax provisions.

c. Providing incentives for certain social goals, such as charitable giving, by allowing tax deductions, exclusions, or credits for selected activities.

d. All the above are goals of the income tax system.

1-2 REPORTING AND TAXABLE ENTITIES

1.2 Learning Objective

Describe the different entities subject to tax and reporting requirements.

Under U.S. tax law, there are five basic tax reporting entities. They are individuals, corporations, partnerships, estates, and trusts. The taxation of individuals is the major topic of this textbook; an overview of the taxation of partnerships and corporations is presented in Chapters 10 and 11, respectively. Taxation of estates and trusts is a specialized area not covered in this textbook.

1-2a The Individual

The most familiar taxable entity is the individual. Taxable income for individuals generally includes income from all sources such as wages, salaries, self-employment earnings, rents, interest, and dividends. Most taxpayers will file Form 1040. The Form 1040 has been redesigned again for 2019. A small number of the items that were relegated to Schedules 1 through 6 in 2018 are back on the face of the Form 1040 in 2019 (e.g., capital gains and losses from Schedule D). Although the Form 1040 does not fill an entire page, it also is no longer "postcard" sized. There is a new Form 1040-SR for taxpayers over the age of 65.

Form 1040-SR is almost identical to Form 1040 except for larger print size and some additional disclosure on the standard deduction presented on the face of the form.

The number of schedules has been reduced to three (Schedules 1, 2, and 3) by combining many of the elements of the previous six schedules:

Schedule	Primary Purpose
1	Additional forms of income other than wages, interest, dividends, distributions from qualified retirement plans such as IRAs and pensions, Social Security benefits, and capital gains and losses. Schedule 1 also reports many of the deductions for adjusted gross income.
2	Additional taxes beyond the basic income tax such as the alternative minimum tax, repayments of excess advance premium tax credit, self-employment taxes, and household employment taxes.
3	Credits and payments other than withholding including education credits, the credit for child and dependent care expenses, residential energy credit, estimated tax payments, excess Social Security taxes withheld, and the net premium tax credit.

In addition to Schedules 1–3, certain types of income and deductions must be reported on specific schedules that are included with the Forms 1040 or 1040-SR.

Schedule	Primary Purpose
A	Itemized deductions such as medical expenses, certain taxes, certain interest, charitable contributions, and other miscellaneous deductions
B	Interest income (over $1,500) or ordinary dividend income (over $1,500)
C	Net profit or loss from a sole proprietor trade or business, other than farm or ranch activities
D	Capital gains and losses
E	Rental, royalty, and pass-through income from partnerships, S corporations, estates, and trusts
F	Farm or ranch income

These tax forms and schedules and some less common forms are presented in this textbook.

The origin of the Form 1040 has been rumored to be associated with the year 1040 B.C. when Samuel warned his people that if they demanded a king, the royal leader would be likely to require they pay taxes. However, in the early 1980s, the then-Commissioner of the IRS, Roscoe Eggers indicated that the number was simply the next one in the control numbering system for federal forms in 1914 when the form was issued for taxpayers for the tax year 1913. About 350,000 people filed a 1040 for 1913. All the returns were audited. In 2018, less than 1 percent of the approximately 150 million individual tax returns were audited.

1-2b **The Corporation**

Corporations are subject to the U.S. income tax and must report income annually on Form 1120. Corporations are taxed at a flat rate of 21 percent for all corporations regardless of income level.

Some corporations may elect S corporation status. An S corporation does not generally pay regular corporate income taxes; instead, the corporation's income passes through to the shareholders and is included on their individual returns. S corporations must report tax information annually on Form 1120S. Chapter 11 covers the basics of corporate taxation, including a discussion of S corporations.

1-2c **The Partnership**

The partnership is not a taxable entity; instead it is a reporting entity. Generally, all income or loss of a partnership is included on the tax returns of the partners. However, a partnership must file Form 1065 annually to report the amount of the partnership's total income or loss and show the allocation of the income or loss to the partners. The partners, in turn, report their share of ordinary income or loss on their tax returns. Other special gains, losses, income, and deductions of the partnership are reported and allocated to the partners separately, since these items are given special tax treatment at the partner level. Capital gains and losses, for example, are reported and allocated separately, and the partners report their share on Schedule D of their income tax returns. See Chapter 10 for a discussion of partnerships, including limited partnerships and limited liability companies.

SUMMARY OF MAJOR TAX FORMS AND SCHEDULES

Form or Schedule	Description
1040	Individual income tax return
Schedule 1	Additional income and adjustments to income
Schedule 2	Additional taxes
Schedule 3	Additional credits and payments
Schedule A	Itemized deductions
Schedule B	Interest and dividend income
Schedule C	Profit or loss from business (sole proprietorship)
Schedule D	Capital gains and losses
Schedule E	Supplemental income and loss (rent, royalty, and pass-through income from Forms 1065, 1120S, and 1041)
Schedule F	Farm and ranch income
1041	Fiduciary (estates and trusts) tax return
1120	Corporate tax return
1120S	S corporation tax return
1065	Partnership information return
Schedule K-1 (Form 1065)	Partner's share of partnership results

All of the forms listed here, and more, are available at the IRS website (**www.irs.gov**).

Self-Study Problem 1.2 *See Appendix E for Solutions to Self-Study Problems*

Indicate which is the most appropriate form or schedule(s) for each of the following items. Unless otherwise indicated in the problem, assume the taxpayer is an individual.

ITEM	Form or Schedule
1. Bank interest income of $1,600 received by a taxpayer who itemizes deductions	_____
2. Capital gain on the sale of AT&T stock	_____
3. Income from a farm	_____
4. Estate income of $850	_____
5. Partnership reporting of an individual partner's share of partnership income	_____
6. Salary of $70,000 for a taxpayer under age 65 who itemizes deductions	_____
7. Income from a sole proprietorship business	_____
8. Income from rental property	_____
9. Dividends of $2,000 received by a taxpayer who does not itemize deductions	_____
10. Income of a corporation	_____
11. Partnership's loss	_____
12. Charitable contribution deduction for an individual who itemizes deductions	_____
13. Single individual, age 67, with no dependents whose only income is $18,000 (all from Social Security) and who does not itemize deductions or have any credits	_____

Learning Objective 1.3

Apply the tax formula for individuals.

1-3 THE TAX FORMULA FOR INDIVIDUALS

Individual taxpayers calculate their tax in accordance with a tax formula. Understanding the formula is important, since all tax determinations are based on the result. The formula is:

> Gross Income
> − Deductions for Adjusted Gross Income
> = Adjusted Gross Income
> − Greater of Itemized Deductions or the Standard Deduction
> − Qualified Business Income Deduction
> = Taxable Income
> × Tax Rate (using appropriate tax tables or rate schedules)
> = Gross Income Tax Liability and Additional Taxes
> − Tax Credits and Prepayments
> = Tax Due or Refund

The IRS released data in mid-2019 that reflects 2018 individual tax returns filed by mid-May (any extended but unfiled tax returns are not included). The data show that on average, taxpayers had lower effective tax rates than in 2017 for all income brackets. Taxpayers with incomes over $1 million represented less than 1 percent of the returns filed, about 7 percent of the taxable income, and about 14 percent of the tax liability.

1-3a **Gross Income**

The calculation of taxable income begins with gross income. Gross income includes all income, unless the tax law provides for a specific exclusion. The exclusions from gross income are discussed in Chapter 2. Gross income from wages, interest, dividends, pensions, Social Security, and capital gains and losses are reported directly on Form 1040 (interest and dividends and capital gains and losses may first flow through Schedules B and D, respectively). All other forms of income are reported on Schedule 1.

1-3b **Deductions for Adjusted Gross Income**

The first category of deductions includes the deductions for adjusted gross income. These deductions include certain trade or business expenses, certain reimbursed employee business expenses paid under an accountable plan, pre-2019 alimony payments, student loan interest, the penalty on early withdrawal from savings, contributions to qualified retirement plans, and certain educator expenses. Later chapters explain these deductions in detail. Deductions for gross income are reported on Schedule 1.

1-3c **Adjusted Gross Income (AGI)**

The amount of adjusted gross income is sometimes referred to as the "magic line," since it is the basis for several deduction limitations, such as the limitation on medical expenses. A taxpayer's adjusted gross income is also used to determine limits on certain charitable contributions and contributions to certain individual retirement accounts.

Talk Show Host Stephen Colbert's Tax Tip: Be extremely wealthy … all kinds of breaks for guys like that!

Colbert Report, April 3, 2006

Would You Believe?

1-3d **Standard Deduction or Itemized Deductions**

Itemized deductions are personal expense items that Congress has allowed as tax deductions. Included in this category are medical expenses, certain interest expenses, certain taxes, charitable contributions, certain casualty losses, and a small number of miscellaneous items. Taxpayers should itemize their deductions only if the total amount exceeds their standard deduction amount. The following table gives the standard deduction amounts for 2019.

Filing Status	Standard Deduction
Single	$ 12,200
Married, filing jointly	24,400
Married, filing separately	12,200
Head of household	18,350
Qualifying widow(er)	24,400

Taxpayers who are 65 years of age or older or blind are entitled to an additional standard deduction amount. For 2019, the additional standard deduction amount is $1,650 for unmarried taxpayers and $1,300 for married taxpayers and surviving spouses. Taxpayers who are both 65 years of age or older and blind are entitled to two additional standard deduction amounts. See LO 1.7 for a complete discussion of the basic and additional standard deduction amounts.

1-3e **Exemptions**

Prior to the TCJA, taxpayers received a deduction called an exemption for themselves, spouse (if married filing jointly), and dependents. Exemptions were suspended by the TCJA starting in 2018. The suspension is scheduled to expire at the end of 2025.

1-3f **The Gross Tax Liability**

A taxpayer's gross tax liability is obtained by reference to the tax table or by use of a tax rate schedule. Tax credits and prepayments are subtracted from gross tax liability to calculate the net tax payable to the government or the refund to the taxpayer.

TAX BREAK

Taxpayers may provide information with their individual tax return authorizing the IRS to deposit refunds directly into their bank account. Taxpayers with a balance due may also pay their tax bill with a credit card, subject to a fee.

Self-Study Problem 1.3   *See Appendix E for Solutions to Self-Study Problems*

Bill is a single taxpayer, age 27. In 2019, his salary is $29,000 and he has interest income of $1,500. In addition, he has deductions for adjusted gross income of $2,200 and he has $6,500 of itemized deductions. Calculate the following amounts:

1. Gross income $_____
2. Adjusted gross income $_____
3. Standard deduction or itemized deduction amount $_____
4. Taxable income $_____

Learning Objective 1.4

Identify individuals who must file tax returns.

1-4 **WHO MUST FILE**

Several conditions must exist before a taxpayer is required to file a U.S. income tax return. These conditions primarily relate to the amount of the taxpayer's income and the taxpayer's filing status. Figures 1.1 through 1.3 summarize the filing requirements for taxpayers in 2019. If a taxpayer has any nontaxable income, the amount should be excluded in determining whether the taxpayer must file a return.

Taxpayers are also required to file a return if they have net earnings from self-employment of $400 or more, or owe taxes such as Social Security taxes on unreported tips. When a taxpayer is not required to file but is due a refund for overpayment of taxes, a return must be filed to obtain the refund.

A taxpayer who is required to file a return should mail the return to the appropriate IRS Campus Processing Site listed on the IRS website (**www.irs.gov**) or electronically file the return as discussed in LO 1.10. Generally, individual returns are due on the fifteenth day of the fourth month of the year following the close of the tax year. For a calendar year individual taxpayer, the return due date is generally April 15. If the 15th falls on a weekend or holiday, returns are due the next business day. However, there are two exceptions: (1) In Maine and Massachusetts, Patriots' Day is celebrated on the third Monday of April. When Patriots' Day is on April 15 or the first business day after April 15, the tax filing deadline is deferred for an additional day for residents of Maine and Massachusetts. (2) The second exception is a result of Emancipation Day, a holiday observed in the District of Columbia.

FIGURE 1.1 WHO MUST FILE

Chart A—For Most People

IF your filing status is . . .	AND at the end of 2019 you were* . . .	THEN file a return if your gross income** was at least . . .
Single	under 65 65 or older	$12,200 13,850
Married filing jointly***	under 65 (both spouses) 65 or older (one spouse) 65 or older (both spouses)	$24,400 25,700 27,000
Married filing separately	any age	$5
Head of household	under 65 65 or older	$18,350 20,000
Qualifying widow(er)	under 65 65 or older	$24,400 25,700

*If you were born on January 1, 1955, you are considered to be age 65 at the end of 2019. (If your spouse died in 2019 or if you are preparing a return for someone who died in 2019, see Pub. 501.)

**Gross income means all income you received in the form of money, goods, property, and services that isn't exempt from tax, including any income from sources outside the United States or from the sale of your main home (even if you can exclude part or all of it). Don't include any social security benefits unless (a) you are married filing a separate return and you lived with your spouse at any time in 2019, or (b) one-half of your social security benefits plus your other gross income and any tax-exempt interest is more than $25,000 ($32,000 if married filing jointly). If (a) or (b) applies, see the instructions for lines 5a and 5b to figure the taxable part of social security benefits you must include in gross income. Gross income includes gains, but not losses, reported on Form 8949 or Schedule D. Gross income from a business means, for example, the amount on Schedule C, line 7, or Schedule F, line 9. But, in figuring gross income, don't reduce your income by any losses, including any loss on Schedule C, line 7, or Schedule F, line 9.

***If you didn't live with your spouse at the end of 2019 (or on the date your spouse died) and your gross income was at least $5, you must file a return regardless of your age.

FIGURE 1.2

Chart B—For Children and Other Dependents (See *Who Qualifies as Your Dependent*, later.)

If your parent (or someone else) can claim you as a dependent, use this chart to see if you must file a return.

In this chart, **unearned income** includes taxable interest, ordinary dividends, and capital gain distributions. It also includes unemployment compensation, taxable social security benefits, pensions, annuities, and distributions of unearned income from a trust. **Earned income** includes salaries, wages, tips, professional fees, and taxable scholarship and fellowship grants. **Gross income** is the total of your unearned and earned income.

Single dependents. Were you **either** age 65 or older **or** blind?

☐ **No.** You must file a return if **any** of the following apply.
- Your unearned income was over $1,100.
- Your earned income was over $12,200.
- Your gross income was more than the **larger** of—
  - $1,100, or
  - Your earned income (up to $11,850) plus $350.

☐ **Yes.** You must file a return if **any** of the following apply.
- Your unearned income was over $2,750 ($4,400 if 65 or older **and** blind).
- Your earned income was over $13,850 ($15,500 if 65 or older **and** blind).
- Your gross income was more than the **larger** of—
  - $2,750 ($4,400 if 65 or older **and** blind), or
  - Your earned income (up to $11,850) plus $2,000 ($3,650 if 65 or older **and** blind).

Married dependents. Were you **either** age 65 or older **or** blind?

☐ **No.** You must file a return if **any** of the following apply.
- Your unearned income was over $1,100.
- Your earned income was over $12,200.
- Your gross income was at least $5 and your spouse files a separate return and itemizes deductions.
- Your gross income was more than the **larger** of—
  - $1,100, or
  - Your earned income (up to $11,850) plus $350.

☐ **Yes.** You must file a return if **any** of the following apply.
- Your unearned income was over $2,400 ($3,700 if 65 or older **and** blind).
- Your earned income was over $13,500 ($14,800 if 65 or older **and** blind).
- Your gross income was at least $5 and your spouse files a separate return and itemizes deductions.
- Your gross income was more than the **larger** of—
  - $2,400 ($3,700 if 65 or older **and** blind), or
  - Your earned income (up to $11,850) plus $1,650 ($2,950 if 65 or older **and** blind).

FIGURE 1.3

Chart C—Other Situations When You Must File

You must file a return if any of the seven conditions below apply for 2019.

1.	You owe any special taxes, including any of the following.
a.	Alternative minimum tax.
b.	Additional tax on a qualified plan, including an individual retirement arrangement (IRA), or other tax-favored account. But if you are filing a return only because you owe this tax, you can file **Form 5329** by itself.
c.	Household employment taxes. But if you are filing a return only because you owe this tax, you can file **Schedule H** by itself.
d.	Social security and Medicare tax on tips you didn't report to your employer or on wages you received from an employer who didn't withhold these taxes.
e.	Write-in taxes, including uncollected social security and Medicare or RRTA tax on tips you reported to your employer or on group-term life insurance and additional taxes on health savings accounts. See the instructions for Schedule 2, line 8.
f.	Recapture taxes. See the instructions for line 12a and Schedule 2, lines 7b and 8.
2.	You (or your spouse, if filing jointly) received health savings account, Archer MSA, or Medicare Advantage MSA distributions.
3.	You had net earnings from self-employment of at least $400.
4.	You had wages of $108.28 or more from a church or qualified church-controlled organization that is exempt from employer social security and Medicare taxes.
5.	Advance payments of the premium tax credit were made for you, your spouse, or a dependent who enrolled in coverage through the Marketplace. You or whoever enrolled you should have received Form(s) 1095-A showing the amount of the advance payments.
6.	Advance payments of the health coverage tax credit were made for you, your spouse, or a dependent. You or whoever enrolled you should have received Form(s) 1099-H showing the amount of the advance payments.
7.	You are required to include amounts in income under section 965 or you have a net tax liability under section 965 that you are paying in installments under section 965(h) or deferred by making an election under section 965(i).

Emancipation Day is observed on April 16; however, when the 16th is a Saturday, the holiday is celebrated on the prior Friday and when the 16th is Sunday, the holiday is celebrated on the following Monday. In 2020, April 15 is a Wednesday, Patriots' Day is Monday the 20th and Emancipation Day is Thursday the 16th, thus the filing deadline will be Wednesday, April 15th.

April 15, 2020 will be the first time since 2015 that all individual taxpayers will be required to file on April 15. Going back to the 2016 filing season (for 2015 tax returns), either the Emancipation Day or Patriots' Day holidays affected all or some taxpayers and provided a day or two delay in the filing deadline. Procrastinators take notice!

A six-month extension of time to file may be requested on Form 4868 by the April due date. Regardless of the original filing deadline, the extension is until October 15 unless that day falls on a weekend or holiday in which case the extended due date is the following business day. However, all tax due must be paid by the April due date or penalties and interest will apply.

Self-Study Problem 1.4 *See Appendix E for Solutions to Self-Study Problems*

Indicate by a check mark whether the following taxpayers are *required* to file a return for 2019 in each of the following independent situations:

	Filing Required?	
	Yes	**No**
1. Taxpayer (age 45) is single with income of $10,000.	_____	_____
2. Husband (age 67) and wife (age 64) have an income of $25,000 and file a joint return.	_____	_____
3. Taxpayer is a college student with a salary from a part-time job of $6,500. She is claimed as a dependent by her parents.	_____	_____
4. Taxpayer has net earnings from self-employment of $4,000.	_____	_____
5. Taxpayers are married with income of $15,900 and file a joint return. They expect a refund of $600 from excess withholding.	_____	_____
6. Taxpayer is a waiter and has unreported tips of $450.	_____	_____
7. Taxpayer is a qualifying widow (age 48) with a dependent son (age 18) and income of $22,800.	_____	_____

1-5 FILING STATUS AND TAX COMPUTATION

1.5 Learning Objective

Determine filing status and understand the calculation of tax according to filing status.

An important step in calculating the amount of a taxpayer's tax is the determination of the taxpayer's correct filing status. The tax law has five different filing statuses: single; married filing jointly; married filing separately; head of household; and qualifying widow(er). A tax table that must be used by most taxpayers, showing the tax liability for all five statuses, is provided in Appendix A. The tax table must be used unless the taxpayer's taxable income is $100,000 or more or the taxpayer is using a special method to calculate the tax liability. If taxpayers cannot use the tax table to determine their tax, a tax rate schedule is used. Each filing status has a separate tax rate schedule as presented in Appendix A.

1-5a Single Filing Status

A taxpayer who does not meet the definition of married, qualifying widow(er), or head of household status must file as single. This status must be used by any taxpayer who is unmarried or legally separated from his/her spouse by divorce or separate maintenance decree as of December 31 of the tax year. State law governs whether a taxpayer is married, divorced, or legally separated. If a taxpayer's spouse dies during the year, the taxpayer's status is married for that year.

1-5b Married Filing Jointly

Taxpayers are considered married for tax purposes if they are married on December 31 of the tax year. Also, in the year of one spouse's death, the spouses are considered married for the full year. In most situations, married taxpayers pay less tax by filing jointly than by filing separately. Married taxpayers may file a joint return even if they did not live together for the entire year.

TAX BREAK — Head of Household is a filing status that can be difficult to understand but comes with some substantial tax benefits if a taxpayer qualifies. Single parents should carefully analyze their situation since Head of Household provides lower tax rates and higher standard deductions than Single filing status. This benefit is not just limited to single parents. All unmarried taxpayers that maintain a household and provide support for another person should consider whether they qualify for this tax-advantageous status.

1-5c Married Filing Separately

Married taxpayers may file separate returns and should do so if it reduces their total tax liability. They may file separately if one or both had income during the year. If separate returns are filed, both taxpayers must compute their tax in the same manner. For example, if one spouse itemizes deductions, the other spouse must also itemize deductions. Each taxpayer reports his or her income, deductions, and credits and is responsible only for the tax due on his or her return. If the taxpayers live in a community property state, they must follow state law to determine community income and separate income. The community property states include Arizona, California, Idaho, Louisiana, Nevada, New Mexico, Texas, Washington, and Wisconsin. See Chapter 2 for additional discussion regarding income and losses from community property.

A legally married taxpayer may file as head of household (based on the general filing status rules) if he or she qualifies as an abandoned spouse. A taxpayer qualifies as an abandoned spouse only if *all* of the following requirements are met:

1. A separate return is filed,
2. The taxpayer paid more than half the cost (rent, utilities, etc.) to maintain his or her home during the year,
3. The spouse did not live with the taxpayer at any time in the last 6 months of the year, and
4. For over 6 months during the year the home was the principal residence for a dependent child, stepchild, or adopted child. Under certain conditions, a foster child may qualify as a dependent.

In certain circumstances, married couples may be able to reduce their total tax liability by filing separately. For instance, since some itemized deductions, such as medical expenses and casualty losses, are reduced by a percentage of adjusted gross income (discussed in Chapter 5), a spouse with a casualty loss and low separate adjusted gross income may be better off filing separately.

1-5d Head of Household

If an unmarried taxpayer can meet special tests or if a married taxpayer qualifies as an abandoned spouse, he or she is allowed to file as head of household. Head of household rates are lower than rates for single or married filing separately. A taxpayer qualifies for head of household status if both of the following conditions exist:

1. The taxpayer was an unmarried or abandoned spouse as of December 31 of the tax year, and
2. The taxpayer paid more than half of the cost of keeping a home that was the principal place of residence of a dependent child or other qualifying dependent relative. An unrelated dependent or a dependent, such as a cousin, who is too distantly related, will not qualify the taxpayer for head of household status. If the dependent is the taxpayer's parent, the parent need not live with the taxpayer. In all cases other than dependent parents, who may maintain a separate residence, the qualifying dependent relative must actually live in the same household as the taxpayer. A divorced parent who meets the above requirements, but has signed an IRS form or a qualifying legal agreement shifting the dependency deduction to his or her ex-spouse, may still file using head of household status.

Divorcing couples may save significant taxes if one or both of the spouses qualify as an "abandoned spouse" and can use the head of household filing status. The combination of head of household filing status for one spouse with married filing separately filing status for the other spouse is commonly seen in the year (or years) leading up to a divorce. In cases where each spouse has custody of a child, the separated taxpayers may each claim head of household status.

TAX BREAK

1-5e Qualifying Widow(er) with Dependent Child

A taxpayer may continue to benefit from the joint return rates for 2 years after the death of his or her spouse. To qualify to use the joint return rates, the widow(er) must pay over half the cost of maintaining a household where a dependent child, stepchild, adopted child, or foster child lives. After the 2-year period, these taxpayers often qualify for the head of household filing status.

1-5f Tax Computation

For 2019, there are seven income tax brackets (10 percent, 12 percent, 22 percent, 24 percent, 32 percent, 35 percent, and 37 percent). Individuals with taxable income below $100,000 are required to use the tax tables presented in Appendix A. Taxpayers with income equal to or more than $100,000 use the tax rate schedules (also presented in Appendix A). An example of the single tax rate schedule is presented below. Certain high-income taxpayers are subject to additional taxes discussed in Chapter 6.

Single Tax Rate Schedule

If taxable income is over—	But not over—	The tax is:
$ 0	$ 9,700	10% of taxable income
9,700	39,475	$970.00 + 12% of the excess over $9,700
39,475	84,200	$4,543.00 + 22% of the excess over $39,475
84,200	160,725	$14,382.50 + 24% of the excess over $84,200
160,725	204,100	$32,748.50 + 32% of the excess over $160,725
204,100	510,300	$46,628.50 + 35% of the excess over $204,100
510,300	----------	$153,798.50 + 37% of the excess over $510,300

The tax rates applicable to net long-term capital gains currently range from 0 percent to 31.8 percent depending on the taxpayer's tax bracket and the kind of capital asset. The calculation of the tax on capital gains is discussed in detail in Chapter 4, and the applicable tax rates are discussed in LO 1.8 of this chapter.

The tax rates for qualifying dividends, discussed in detail in Chapter 2, range from 0 percent to 23.8 percent in 2019.

EXAMPLE Carol, a single taxpayer, has adjusted gross income of $120,000 and taxable income of $105,000 for 2019. Her tax is calculated using the 2019 tax rate schedule from Appendix A as follows:

$19,374.50 = $14,382.50 + [24% × ($105,000 − $84,200)] ♦

EXAMPLE Meg is a single taxpayer during 2019. Her taxable income for the year is $27,530. Using the tax table in Appendix A, her gross tax liability for the year is found to be $3,109. ♦

TAX BREAK

Taxpayers considering marriage may be able to save thousands of dollars by engaging in tax planning prior to setting a wedding date. If the couple would pay less in taxes by filing as married rather than as single (which will frequently happen if one spouse has low earnings for the year), they may prefer a December wedding. They can take advantage of the rule that requires taxpayers to file as married for the full year if they were married on the last day of the year. On the other hand, if filing a joint return would cause the couple to pay more in taxes (which frequently happens if both spouses have high incomes), they may prefer a January wedding.

Self-Study Problem 1.5   *See Appendix E for Solutions to Self-Study Problems*

Indicate the filing status (or statuses) in each of the following independent cases, using this legend:

A – Single
B – Married, filing a joint return
C – Married, filing separate returns
D – Head of household
E – Qualifying widow(er)

Case	Filing Status
1. The taxpayers are married on December 31 of the tax year.	_____
2. The taxpayer is single, with a dependent child living in her home.	_____
3. The taxpayer is unmarried and is living with his girlfriend.	_____
4. The taxpayer is married and his spouse left midyear and has disappeared. The taxpayer has no dependents.	_____
5. The unmarried taxpayer supports her dependent mother, who lives in her own home.	_____
6. The taxpayer's wife died last year. His 15-year-old dependent son lives with him.	_____

TIP

In ProConnect, much of the input is controlled by the left-hand margin. Filing status is part of Client Information under the General heading. By clicking on Filing Status, a dropdown appears in the main window to allow the preparer to select the taxpayer's filing status. For married filing jointly and separately statuses, the Live With Spouse box should be checked if it applies.

Learning Objective 1.6

Define qualifying dependents.

1-6 QUALIFYING DEPENDENTS

1-6a Dependents

Prior to 2018, taxpayers were able to deduct approximately $4,000 each for themselves, their spouse (if married filing jointly), and any dependents. The TCJA eliminated the personal and dependency exemptions in lieu of a larger standard deduction; however, dependents remain important for other reasons. For example, head of household filing status, the child tax credit, and the earned income tax credit all depend on having a qualified dependent. Lastly, the suspension of personal and dependency exemptions is scheduled to expire after 2025 which means, exemptions may yet return. A dependent is an individual who meets the tests discussed on the following page to be considered either a *qualifying child* or a *qualifying relative*.

1-6b Qualifying Child

For a child to be a dependent, he or she must meet the following tests:

1. **Relationship Test**
   The child must be the taxpayer's child, stepchild, or adopted child, or the taxpayer's brother or sister, half-brother or half-sister, or stepsibling, or a descendant of any of these. Under certain circumstances, a foster child can also qualify. The child must be younger than the person claiming him or her unless the child is permanently disabled.

2. **Domicile Test**
   The child must have the same principal place of abode as the taxpayer for more than half of the taxable year. In satisfying this requirement, temporary absences from the household due to special circumstances such as illness, education, and vacation are not considered.

3. **Age Test**
   The child must be under age 19 or a full-time student under the age of 24. A child is considered a full-time student if enrolled full-time for at least 5 months of the year. Thus, a college senior graduating in May or June can qualify in the year of graduation.

4. **Joint Return Test**
   The child must not file a joint return with his or her spouse. If neither the spouse nor the child is required to file, but they file a return merely to claim a refund of tax, they are not considered to have filed a return for purposes of this test.

5. **Citizenship Test**
   The dependent must be a U.S. citizen, a resident of the United States, Canada, or Mexico, or an alien child adopted by and living with a U.S. citizen.

6. **Self-Support Test**
   A child who provides more than one-half of his or her own support cannot be claimed as a dependent of someone else. Support includes expenditures for items such as food, lodging, clothes, medical and dental care, and education. To calculate support, the taxpayer uses the actual cost of the above items, except lodging. The value of lodging is calculated at its fair rental value. Funds received by students as scholarships are excluded from the support test.

In the event that a child satisfies the requirements of dependency for more than one taxpayer, the following tie-breaking rules apply:

- If one of the individuals eligible to claim the child is a parent, that person will be allowed to claim the dependent.
- If both parents qualify (separate returns are filed), then the parent with whom the child resides the longest during the year prevails. If the residence period is the same or is not ascertainable, then the parent with the highest AGI (Adjusted Gross Income) prevails.
- If no parents are involved, the taxpayer with the highest AGI prevails.

EXAMPLE Bill, age 12, lives in the same household with Irene, his mother, and Darlene, his aunt. Bill qualifies as a dependent of both Irene and Darlene. Since Irene is Bill's mother, she has the right to claim Bill as a dependent. The tie-breaking rules are not necessary if the taxpayer who can claim the dependent does not claim the dependent. Hence, Darlene can claim Bill as a dependent if Irene does not claim him. ♦

In the case of divorced or legally separated parents with children, the ability to claim a qualifying child belongs to the parent with whom the child lived for more than 6 months out of the year. The opportunity to claim the child as a dependent can be shifted to the noncustodial parent if the custodial parent signs IRS Form 8332, and the form is attached to the noncustodial parent's tax return.

Figure 1.4 illustrates the interaction of the qualifying child dependency tests described on the previous page.

1-6c Qualifying Relative

A person who is not a qualifying child can be a qualifying relative if the following 5-part test is met. A child of a taxpayer who does not meet the tests to be a qualifying child can still qualify as a dependent under the qualifying relative tests described below.

1. **Relationship or Member of Household Test**
   The individual must either be a relative of the taxpayer or a member of the household. The list of qualifying relatives is broad and includes parents, grandparents, children, grandchildren, siblings, aunts and uncles by blood, nephews and nieces, "in-laws," and adopted children. Foster children may also qualify in certain circumstances. If the potential dependent is a more distant relative, additional information is available at the IRS website (**www.irs.gov**). For example, cousins are not considered relatives for this purpose.

   In addition to the relatives listed, any person who lived in the taxpayer's home as a member of the household for the entire year meets the relationship test. A person is not considered a member of the household if at any time during the year the relationship between the taxpayer and the dependent was in violation of local law.

   EXAMPLE Scott provides all of the support for an unrelated family friend who lives with him for the entire tax year. He also supports a cousin who lives in another state. The family friend can qualify as Scott's dependent, but the cousin cannot. The family friend meets the member of the household test. Even though the cousin is not considered a relative, he could have been a dependent if he met the member of the household part of the test. ♦

2. **Gross Income Test**
   The individual cannot have gross income equal to or above the exemption amount ($4,200 in 2019). Although exemptions are no longer deductible, the exemption amount will continue to be updated by the IRS. Gross income does not include any income exempt from tax (for example, tax-exempt interest or exempt Social Security benefits).
3. **Support Test**
   The dependent must receive over half of his or her support from the taxpayer or a group of taxpayers (see multiple support agreement below). Unlike the gross income test, income exempt from tax and earned by the potential dependent is considered for the support test.
4. **Joint Return Test**
   The dependent must not file a joint return unless it is only to claim a refund of taxes.
5. **Citizenship Test**
   The dependent must meet the citizenship test discussed above.

   EXAMPLE A taxpayer has a 26-year-old son with gross income less than the exemption amount who receives more than half his support from his parents. The son fails the test to be a qualifying child based on his age, but passes the test to be a dependent based on the qualifying relative rules. ♦

Figure 1.5 illustrates the qualifying relative tests described above.

As long as the dependency tests are met, a person who was born or died during the year, such as a baby born before or on December 31, can be claimed as a dependent. Taxpayers must provide a Social Security number for all dependents.

If a dependent is supported by two or more taxpayers, a multiple support agreement may be filed. To file the agreement, the taxpayers (as a group) must provide over 50 percent of the support of the dependent. Assuming that all other dependency tests are met, the group may give the dependent to any member of the group who provided over 10 percent of the dependent's support.

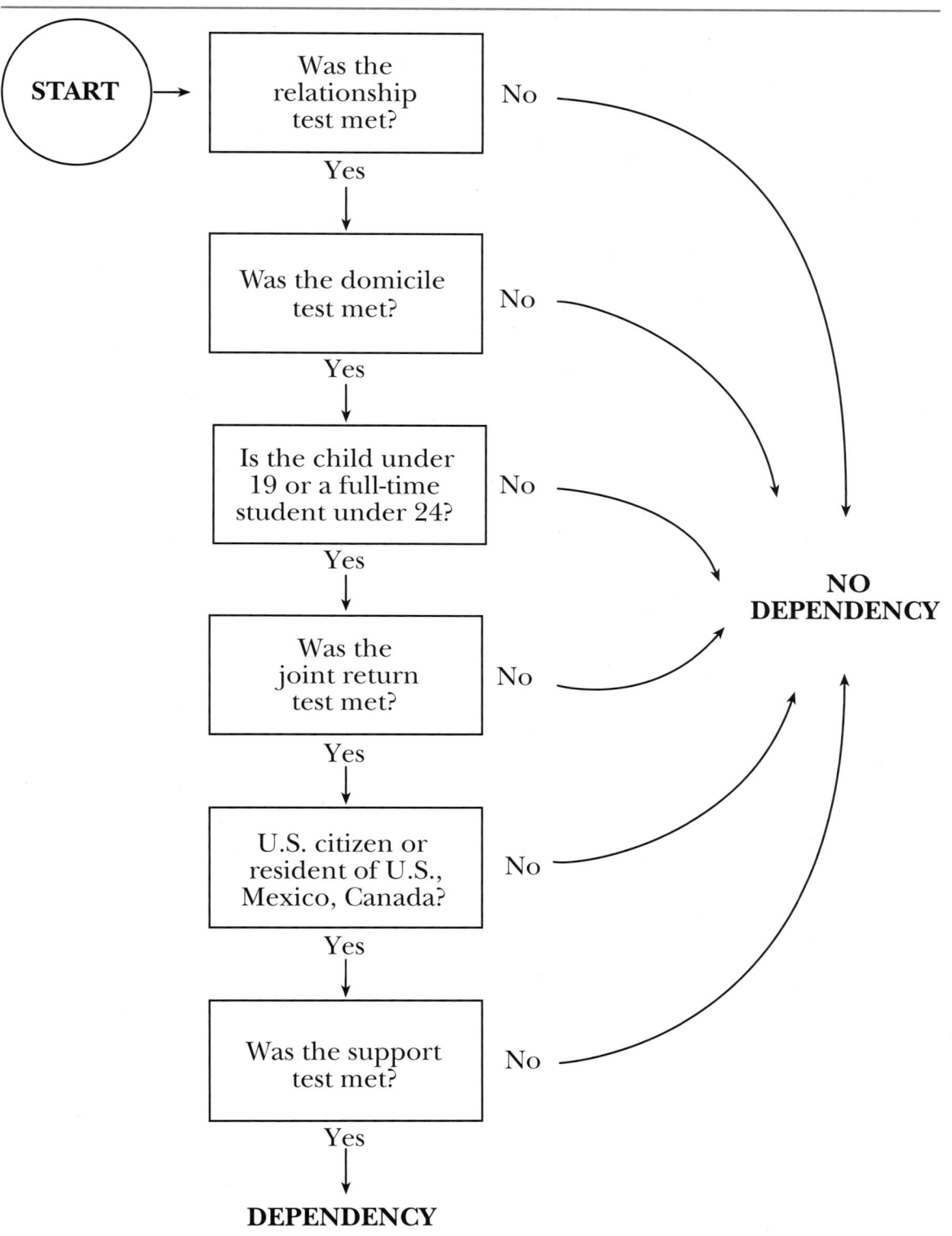

FIGURE 1.4   DEPENDENCY TESTS FLOW CHART FOR QUALIFYING CHILD

START

Was the relationship test met? — No

Yes

Was the domicile test met? — No

Yes

Is the child under 19 or a full-time student under 24? — No

Yes

Was the joint return test met? — No

Yes

U.S. citizen or resident of U.S., Mexico, Canada? — No

Yes

Was the support test met? — No

Yes

NO DEPENDENCY

DEPENDENCY

FIGURE 1.5 DEPENDENCY TESTS FLOW CHART FOR QUALIFYING RELATIVE

Spouse information is entered under Client Information and is just under Taxpayer Information on the left-hand margin. Dependents are a new category under General. Be sure and input date of birth and other fields. Typically, the Child Tax Credit and the Earned Income Credit should be set to When Applicable to permit the software to make the correct determination based on input. New dependents can be added by clicking the [+] tab at the top of the main window for Dependents.

1-6d **Credits for Dependents**

Although deductions for personal exemptions are no longer permitted from 2018 through 2025, dependent status is important for claiming a number of individual tax credits such as the child tax credit, the credit for other dependents, and the earned income tax credit. Many of these tax credits are covered in Chapter 7; however, due to the relatively large number of taxpayers that are eligible for the child tax credit and the credit for other dependents, an overview is provided here.

A tax credit differs from a tax deduction. A tax deduction serves to lower the taxable income of the taxpayer.

EXAMPLE   Emily's adjusted gross income is $50,025. She is eligible for a $12,200 standard deduction. This lowers her taxable income to $37,825 ($50,025 − $12,200). If Emily is single, her 2019 tax liability is $4,345. ♦

A tax credit lowers the tax liability dollar for dollar. A credit is generally more advantageous than a deduction.

EXAMPLE   Emily (from the previous example) is also eligible for a $500 tax credit. Rather than reduce her taxable income, the tax credit reduces the tax itself to $3,845 ($4,345 − $500). ♦

In 2019, the child tax credit is $2,000 per child. To qualify for the credit, the child must be a qualifying child under the age of 17 and have a Social Security number at the time the tax return is filed. Additional requirements are covered in Chapter 7.

The credit for other dependents is $500 per dependent. An "other dependent" need not be a child but must qualify as either a qualifying child or qualifying dependent. Additional requirements are covered in Chapter 7.

EXAMPLE   Bruce and Demi Mehr have two children, Anna (age 12) and Clark (age 18). Both Anna and Clark qualify as qualifying children under the dependent rules. Assuming all other requirements are met, the Mehrs may claim a $2,000 child tax credit for Anna and a $500 other dependent credit for Clark (as he is not under age 17). ♦

ProConnect is designed to automatically compute the child tax credit and other dependent credit based on the information input in the Dependent window. If no such credit is being shown, it could be due to missing information (for example, birthdate) or the credits were inadvertently suppressed in the Dependent window. The child tax credit and other dependent credit can be overridden under Credits/EIC, Residential Energy, Oth Credits in the left-hand margin but this is generally not a good idea.

Self-Study Problem 1.6   *See Appendix E for Solutions to Self-Study Problems*

Indicate in each of the following situations whether the taxpayer has a dependent in 2019.

	Yes	No
1. Betty and Bob, a married couple, had a new baby in December 2019.	_____	_____
2. Charlie, age 25, supports his 26-year-old brother, who is not a full-time student. His brother lives with Charlie all year. His brother's gross income is $4,500 from a part-time job.	_____	_____
3. Donna and her sister support their mother and provide 60% of her support. If Donna provides 25% of her mother's support and her sister signs a multiple support agreement, can Donna claim the mother as a dependent?	_____	_____
4. Frank is single and supports his son and his son's wife, both of whom lived with Frank for the entire year. The son (age 20) and his wife (age 19) file a joint return to get a refund, reporting $2,500 ($2,000 earned by the son) on gross income. Both the son and daughter-in-law are full-time students.	_____	_____
5. Gary is single and provides $5,000 toward his 19-year-old daughter's college expenses. The remainder of her support is provided by a tax-exempt $9,500 tuition scholarship. The daughter is a full-time student.	_____	_____
6. Helen is 50 years old and supports her 72-year-old mother, who is blind and has $5,000 of Social Security benefits that are not taxable.	_____	_____

Would You Sign This Tax Return?

Sign Here	Under penalties of perjury, I declare that I have examined this return and accompanying schedules and statements, and to the best of my knowledge and belief, they are true, correct, and complete. Declaration of preparer (other than taxpayer) is based on all information of which preparer has any knowledge.			
	Your signature	Date	Your occupation	If the IRS sent you an Identity Protection PIN, enter it here (see inst.)
Joint return? See instructions. Keep a copy for your records.	Spouse's signature. If a joint return, **both** must sign.	Date	Spouse's occupation	If the IRS sent your spouse an Identity Protection PIN, enter it here (see inst.)
	Phone no.		Email address	
Paid Preparer Use Only	Preparer's name	Preparer's signature		Date / PTIN / Check if: ☐ 3rd Party Designee ☐ Self-employed
	Firm's name ▶			Phone no.
	Firm's address ▶			Firm's EIN ▶

Your clients, Adam and Amy Accrual, have a 21-year-old daughter named April. April is single and is a full-time student studying for her bachelor's degree in accounting at California Poly Academy (CPA) in Pismo Beach, California, where she lives with her roommates year-round. Last year, April worked at a local bar and restaurant four nights a week and made $18,000, which she used for tuition, fees, books, and living expenses. Her parents help April by sending her $300 each month to help with her expenses at college. This is all of the support given to April by her parents. When preparing Adam and Amy's tax return, you note that they claim April as a dependent for tax purposes. Adam is insistent that they can claim April because of the $300 per month support and the fact that they "have claimed her since she was born." He will not let you take April off his return as a dependent. Would you sign the Paid Preparer's declaration (see example above) on this return? Why or why not?

1-7 THE STANDARD DEDUCTION

The standard deduction was placed in the tax law to provide relief for taxpayers with few itemized deductions. The amount of the standard deduction is subtracted from adjusted gross income by taxpayers who do not itemize their deductions. If a taxpayer's gross income is less than the standard deduction amount, the taxpayer has no taxable income. The 2019 standard deduction amounts are presented below:

Filing Status	Standard Deduction
Single	$ 12,200
Married, filing jointly	24,400
Married, filing separately	12,200
Head of household	18,350
Qualifying widow(er)	24,400

1-7a Additional Amounts for Old Age and Blindness

Taxpayers who are 65 years of age or older or blind are entitled to an additional standard deduction amount. For 2019, the additional standard deduction amount is $1,650 for un-married taxpayers and $1,300 for married taxpayers and qualifying widows or widowers. Taxpayers who are both at least 65 years old and blind are entitled to two additional stan-dard deduction amounts. The additional standard deduction amounts are also available for the taxpayer's spouse, but not for dependents. An individual is considered blind for pur-poses of receiving an additional standard deduction amount if:

1. Central visual acuity does not exceed 20/200 in the better eye with correcting lenses, or
2. Visual acuity is greater than 20/200 but is limited to a field of vision not greater than 20 degrees.

EXAMPLE John is single and 70 years old in 2019. His standard deduction is $13,850 ($12,200 plus an additional $1,650 for being 65 years of age or older). ◆

EXAMPLE Bob and Mary are married in 2019 and file a joint return. Bob is age 68, and Mary is 63 and meets the test for blindness. Their standard deduction is $27,000 ($24,400 plus $1,300 for Bob being 65 years or older and another $1,300 for Mary's blindness). ◆

1-7b Individuals Not Eligible for the Standard Deduction

The following taxpayers cannot use the standard deduction, but must itemize instead:

1. A married individual filing a separate return, whose spouse itemizes deductions
2. Most nonresident aliens
3. An individual filing a short-period tax return because of a change in the annual accounting period

EXAMPLE Ann and Ed are married individuals who file separate returns for 2019. Ann itemizes her deductions on her return. Ed's adjusted gross income is $12,000, and he has itemized deductions of $900. Ed's taxable income is calculated as follows:

Adjusted gross income	$ 12,000
Itemized deductions	(900)
Taxable income	$ 11,100

Since Ann itemizes her deductions, Ed must also itemize deductions and is not entitled to use the standard deduction amount. ◆

1-7c Special Limitations for Dependents

The standard deduction is limited for the tax return of a dependent. The total standard deduction may not exceed the greater of $1,100 or the sum of $350 plus the dependent's earned income up to the basic standard deduction amount in total (e.g., $12,200 for single taxpayers), plus any additional standard deduction amount for old age or blindness. The standard deduction amount for old age and blindness is only allowed when a dependent files a tax return. It is not allowed to increase the standard deduction of the taxpayer claiming the dependent.

EXAMPLE   Penzer, who is 8 years old, earned $17,000 as a child model during 2019. Penzer is claimed as a dependent by his parents on their tax return. Penzer is required to file a tax return, and his taxable income will be $4,800 ($17,000 less $12,200, the standard deduction amount). If Penzer had earned only $9,000, his standard deduction would be $9,350 [the greater of $1,100 or $9,350 ($9,000 + $350)], and he would not owe any tax or be required to file a return. ♦

EXAMPLE   Geoffrey, who is 4 years old and claimed as a dependent on his parents' tax return, earned $6,500 of interest income on a large bank account left to him by his grandmother. He had no earned income. His standard deduction is $1,100 (the greater of $1,100 or $350). His taxable income will be $5,400 ($6,500 less $1,100, the standard deduction amount). Dependent children may be taxed at trust income tax rates when their taxable income is made up of unearned income, such as interest. The special "kiddie tax" calculations are covered in Chapter 6. ♦

Self-Study Problem 1.7   *See Appendix E for Solutions to Self-Study Problems*

Indicate in each of the following independent situations the amount of the standard deduction the taxpayers should claim on their 2019 income tax returns.

_____ 1. Adam is 45 years old, in good health, and single.

_____ 2. Bill and Betty are married and file a joint return. Bill is 66 years old, and Betty is 60.

_____ 3. Charlie is 70, single, and blind.

_____ 4. Debbie qualifies for head of household filing status, is 35 years old, and is in good health.

_____ 5. Elizabeth is 9 years old, and her only income is $3,600 of interest on a savings account. She is claimed as a dependent on her parents' tax return.

_____ 6. Frank and Frieda are married with two dependent children. They file a joint return, are in good health, and both of them are under 65 years of age.

Learning Objective 1.8

Compute basic capital gains and losses.

1-8 A BRIEF OVERVIEW OF CAPITAL GAINS AND LOSSES

When a taxpayer sells an asset, there is normally a gain or loss on the transaction. Depending on the kind of asset sold, this gain or loss will have different tax consequences. Chapter 4 of this textbook has detailed coverage of the effect of gains and losses on a taxpayer's tax liability. Because of their importance to the understanding of the calculation of an individual's tax liability, a brief overview of gains and losses will be discussed here.

The amount of gain or loss realized by a taxpayer is determined by subtracting the *adjusted basis* of the asset from the *amount realized*. Generally, the adjusted basis of an asset is its cost less any depreciation (covered in Chapter 8) taken on the asset. The amount realized is generally what the taxpayer receives from the sale (e.g., the sales price less any cost of the sale). The formula for calculating the gain or loss can be stated as follows:

Gain (or loss) realized = Amount realized − Adjusted basis

Most gains and losses realized are also recognized for tax purposes. Recognized gains and losses are those that are included in the taxpayer's taxable income. The exceptions to this general tax recognition rule are discussed in Chapter 4.

EXAMPLE   Lisa purchased a rental house a few years ago for $100,000. Total depreciation to date on the house is $25,000. In the current year she sells the house for $155,000 and receives $147,000 after paying selling expenses of $8,000. Her gain on the sale is $72,000, calculated as follows:

Amount realized ($155,000 − $8,000)	$ 147,000
Adjusted basis ($100,000 − $25,000)	(75,000)
Gain realized	$ 72,000

This gain realized will be recognized as a taxable gain. ♦

1-8a **Capital Gains and Losses**

Gains and losses can be either *ordinary* or *capital*. Ordinary gains and losses are treated for tax purposes just like other items of income such as salaries and interest, and they are taxed at ordinary rates. Capital gains and losses receive special tax treatment.

A capital gain or loss arises from the sale or exchange of a capital asset. In general, a capital asset is any property (either personal or investment) held by a taxpayer, with certain exceptions as listed in the tax law (see Chapter 4). Examples of capital assets held by individual taxpayers include stocks, bonds, land, cars, boats, and other items held as investments or for personal use. Typical assets that are not capital assets are inventory and accounts receivable.

The tax rates on long-term (held more than 12 months) capital gains are summarized as follows:

Income Level	2019 *Long-term capital gains rate**
Married filing jointly	
$0–$78,750	0%
$78,751–$488,850	15%
>$488,850	20%
Single	
$0–$39,375	0%
$39,376–$434,550	15%
>$434,550	20%
Head of household	
$0–$52,750	0%
$52,751–$461,700	15%
>$461,700	20%
Married filing separately	
$0–$39,375	0%
$39,376–$244,425	15%
>$244,425	20%

*Special higher rates for "high-income" taxpayers are covered in Chapter 6.

Gain from property held 12 months or less is deemed to be short-term capital gain and is taxed at ordinary income rates. Capital gains from the sale of assets that have been depreciated, or capital gains from "collectibles," may be taxed at higher rates as discussed in Chapter 4.

EXAMPLE   In the current year, Chris, a single taxpayer, sells AT&T stock for $25,000. He purchased the stock 5 years ago for $15,000, giving him an adjusted basis of $15,000 and a long-term gain of $10,000. Chris' taxable income without the sale of the stock is $140,000, which puts him in the 24 percent tax bracket. The tax due on the long-term capital gain would be $1,500 (15% × $10,000) instead of $2,400 (24% × $10,000) if the gain on the stock were treated as ordinary income. ♦

When calculating capital gain or loss, the taxpayer must net all capital asset transactions to determine the nature of the final gain or loss (see Chapter 4 for a discussion of this calculation). If an individual taxpayer ends up with a net capital loss (short-term or long-term), up to $3,000 per year can be deducted against ordinary income. The net loss not used in the current year may be carried forward and used to reduce taxable income in future years (see Chapter 4 for a discussion of capital losses). Losses from capital assets held for personal purposes, such as a nonbusiness auto or a personal residence, are not deductible, even though gains on personal assets are taxable.

TAX BREAK   Taxpayers may wish to postpone the sale of capital assets until the holding period is met to qualify for the preferential long-term capital gains rate. Of course, there is always the risk that postponing the sale of a capital asset such as stock may result in a loss if the price of the stock decreases below its cost during volatile markets. The economic risks of a transaction should always be considered along with the tax benefits.

EXAMPLE   Amy purchased gold coins as an investment. She paid $50,000 for the coins. This year she sells the coins to a dealer for $35,000. As a result, Amy has a $15,000 capital loss. She may deduct $3,000 of the loss against her other income this year. The remaining unused loss of $12,000 ($15,000 − $3,000) is carried forward and may be deducted against other income in future years. Of course, the carryover is subject to the $3,000 annual limitation in future years. ♦

TAX BREAK

Volunteer Income Tax Assistance (VITA) Program

The Volunteer Income Tax Assistance (VITA) program offers free tax help to people who generally make $55,000 or less, persons with disabilities, the elderly and limited English-speaking taxpayers who need assistance in preparing their own tax returns. IRS-certified volunteers provide free basic income tax return preparation with electronic filing to qualified individuals. VITA sites are generally located at community and neighborhood centers, libraries, schools, shopping malls, and other convenient locations across the country.

Many universities and colleges operate VITA sites in conjunction with their accounting programs. This is a small but vital part of the VITA program run by the IRS. The majority of the VITA sites are not run by schools, but rather by community groups, such as churches, senior groups (AARP), military bases, etc. If a student has a chance to participate in a VITA program, he or she should do so if at all possible. The experience provides valuable insight into preparing tax returns for others. Please see the IRS website **www.irs.gov** to locate the nearest VITA site and for more information.

Self-Study Problem 1.8 *See Appendix E for Solutions to Self-Study Problems*

Erin purchased stock in JKL Corporation several years ago for $8,750. In the current year, she sold the same stock for $12,800. She paid a $200 sales commission to her stockbroker.

1. What is Erin's amount realized? $_____
2. What is Erin's adjusted basis? $_____
3. What is Erin's *realized* gain or loss? $_____
4. What is Erin's *recognized* gain or loss? $_____
5. How is the gain or loss treated for tax purposes (if any)?

_____

_____

_____

TAX BREAK

The IRS recommends considering the following when getting married:

- Social Security numbers on the tax return need to match the Social Security Administration's (SSA) records. Be sure and report any name changes to the SSA.
- Taxpayers may want to consider changing their withholding, especially if both spouses work.
- Marriage is likely to trigger a "change in circumstance" if a taxpayer is receiving advance payments on the premium tax credit. The appropriate health insurance marketplace should be notified.
- Change of address with the U.S. Postal Service (online) and with the IRS (Form 8822).
- Change in filing status to married filing jointly or separately should be considered.

1-9 TAX AND THE INTERNET

1.9 Learning Objective

Access and use various Internet tax resources.

Taxpayers and tax practitioners can find a substantial amount of useful information on the Internet. Government agencies, businesses, organizations, and groups (e.g., the IRS, AICPA, and Cengage) maintain sites that contain information of interest to the public.

The information available on various websites is subject to rapid change. Discussed below are some current Internet sites that are of interest to taxpayers. Taxpayers should be aware that the locations and information provided on the Internet are subject to change by the site organizer without notice.

1-9a The IRS Website, www.irs.gov

One of the most useful websites containing tax information is the one maintained by the IRS. The IRS site has a search function to assist users in locating information. A number of common tasks are available at the home page such as refund status or making a tax payment. The Forms and Publications search function is particularly useful and allows the user to locate and download almost any tax form, instructions, or publication available from the IRS. A Help function is available to aid users of the IRS website. Online and telephone assistance from the IRS is provided for users who have questions or want to communicate with the IRS. The IRS has also launched a YouTube video channel, an iTunes podcast, and a Twitter, Tumblr, and Facebook page. The YouTube channel has numerous educational videos covering a number of tax-related topics, including how to check on a refund and how to file a tax return extension. The IRS news feed on Twitter, @IRSnews, is also a good source of tax information. The IRS also offers IRS2GO—a mobile phone application.

A 2019 screenshot of the IRS website (**www.irs.gov**) is presented in Figure 1.6.

FIGURE 1.6   IRS WEBSITE

Source: Internal Revenue Service

1-9b   Intuit's ProConnect Tax Online

Intuit offers a line of tax preparation products such as ProConnect Tax, Lacerte, and the well-known Turbo Tax. Many of the Intuit products have training and support available online at no charge. You can find ProConnect help at **http://accountants-intuit.com /proconnect-tax-online-us-en** and more general tax help at **http://blog.turbotax.intuit .com/**.

Would You Believe?

The IRS issues warnings to taxpayers each year about identity theft scams via e-mail known as "phishing" scams. The e-mails look official and may even have a link to a bogus website that looks almost identical to **www.irs.gov** (and may even mention USA.gov or IRS.gov). The fake e-mails may also appear to have been sent by the IRS Taxpayer Advocate's Office. Taxpayers who get these messages should not respond to the e-mail or click on the links. Although the IRS maintains Twitter and Facebook accounts, the IRS does not initiate contact with taxpayers by e-mail, texting, or any social media.

Self-Study Problem 1.9 — *See Appendix E for Solutions to Self-Study Problems*

Indicate whether the following statements are true or false by circling the appropriate letter.

T F 1. Taxpayers can download tax forms and IRS publications from the IRS website.

T F 2. A help function is available to aid users of the IRS website.

T F 3. The IRS has a mobile phone app.

1-10 ELECTRONIC FILING (E-FILING)

1.10 Learning Objective

Describe the basics of electronic filing (e-filing).

Electronic filing (e-filing) is the process of transmitting federal income tax return information to the IRS Service Center using a device with Internet access. For the taxpayer, electronic filing offers faster processing and generally a faster refund. The fastest refund can be obtained through a direct deposit to the taxpayer's bank account (however, the taxpayer can also choose to be paid by check). IRS statistics show an error rate of less than 1 percent on electronically filed returns, compared with more than 20 percent on paper returns.

Two methods of e-filing of individual income tax returns are available with the IRS. The first e-filing method is using a personal computer device and tax preparation software such as Intuit's ProConnect Tax Online, which is included as part of this textbook. Individual taxpayers may transmit their returns from their homes, workplaces, libraries, retail outlets, or, in some limited situations, a mobile phone app. The IRS website contains detailed information on this process as the IRS is constantly working to make e-filing more user-friendly and widely available. The IRS provides free tax preparation and e-filing software to individuals with income below certain thresholds (see **www.irs.gov/freefile**). Individuals with higher income may still e-file free, using IRS fill-in forms (see **www.freefilefillableforms.com**). The fillable forms program performs calculations but will not provide the tax preparation guidance that standard tax software programs provide.

The second e-filing option is to use the services of a tax professional, including certified public accountants, tax attorneys, IRS-enrolled agents, and tax preparation businesses qualifying for the IRS tax professional e-filing program.

Electronic filing represents a significant growth area in computerized tax services. More than 90 percent of all individual taxpayers now e-file. Mandatory electronic filing is currently in the process of being phased in for the professional tax return preparation industry. In the future, electronic filing will likely be required for most tax returns filed.

In 2006, General Electric Co. (GE) electronically filed their corporate tax return. If printed, it was estimated at 24,000 pages and expected to stack up to 8 feet tall. In 2010, GE enjoyed a 7 percent effective tax rate but filed a federal income tax return estimated at a whopping 57,000 pages or 19 feet tall.

Self-Study Problem 1.10   *See Appendix E for Solutions to Self-Study Problems*

Indicate whether the following statements are true or false by circling the appropriate letter.

T   F   1.   Compared to paper returns, electronic filings significantly reduce the error rate for tax returns filed.

T   F   2.   Individuals may not use electronic filing for their own personal tax returns, but must engage a tax professional if they wish to e-file.

T   F   3.   Taxpayers who e-file generally receive faster refunds.

T   F   4.   Taxpayers who e-file can only request their refund in the form of a check.

KEY TERMS

Individual, 1-3	itemized deductions, 1-7	qualifying child, 1-15
Form 1040, 1-3	exemptions, 1-8	qualifying relative, 1-16
Corporation, 1-5	single filing status, 1-11	tax deduction, 1-19
Partnership, 1-5	married filing jointly, 1-11	tax credit, 1-19
tax formula for individuals, 1-6	married filing separately, 1-12	capital assets, 1-23
gross income, 1-7	head of household, 1-12	capital gains and losses, 1-23
adjusted gross income, 1-7	qualifying widow(er), 1-13	e-filing, 1-27
standard deductions, 1-7	dependent, 1-14	

KEY POINTS

Learning Objectives	Key Points
LO 1.1: Explain the history and objectives of U.S. tax law.	• The income tax was established on March 1, 1913 by the Sixteenth Amendment to the Constitution. • In addition to raising money to run the government's programs, the income tax is used as a tool for enacting economic and social policies. • Examples of economic tax provisions are the limited allowance for expensing capital expenditures and bonus depreciation provisions. The charitable contribution deduction is an example of a social tax provision. • The Tax Cuts and Jobs Act (TCJA) has a number of significant individual tax provisions that expire in 2025.
LO 1.2: Describe the different entities subject to tax and reporting requirements.	• Individual taxpayers file Form 1040 or 1040-SR (if age 65 or older) and any supplemental schedules required. • Corporations must report income annually on Form 1120 and pay taxes. • An S corporation generally does not pay regular corporate income taxes; instead, the corporation's income or loss passes through to its shareholders and is included in their individual tax returns. S corporations file on Form 1120S. • A partnership files Form 1065 to report the amount of partnership income or loss and to allocate the items of income, loss, deduction, and credit to the partners. Generally, all income or loss of a partnership is included in the tax returns of the partners.

LO 1.3: Apply the tax formula for individuals.	• AGI (adjusted gross income) is gross income less deductions for adjusted gross income. • AGI less the larger of itemized deductions or the standard deduction and less the qualified business income deduction equals taxable income. • Appropriate tax tables or rate schedules are applied to taxable income to calculate the gross tax liability. • The gross income tax liability plus additional taxes less credits and prepayments equals the tax due or refund.
LO 1.4: Identify individuals who must file tax returns.	• Conditions relating to the amount of the taxpayer's income must exist before a taxpayer is required to file a U.S. income tax return. • Taxpayers are also required to file a return if they have net earnings from self-employment of $400 or more, or owe taxes such as Social Security taxes on unreported tips.
LO 1.5: Determine filing status and understand the calculation of tax according to filing status.	• There are five filing statuses: single; married filing jointly; married filing separately; head of household; and qualifying widow(er). • Tax is calculated using the appropriate tax table or tax rate schedule for the taxpayer's filing status.
LO 1.6: Define qualifying dependents.	• Personal exemptions were suspended by the TCJA for tax years 2018–2025. • Dependents are still important for determining filing status and certain credits. • A dependent is an individual who is either a qualifying child or qualifying relative.
LO 1.7: Calculate the correct standard or itemized deduction amount for taxpayers.	• The standard deduction was placed in the tax law to provide relief for taxpayers with few itemized deductions. • For 2019, the standard deduction amounts are: Single $12,200; Married, filing jointly $24,400; Married, filing separately $12,200; Head of household $18,350; Qualifying widow(er) $24,400. • Taxpayers who are 65 years of age or older or blind are entitled to additional standard deduction amounts of $1,650 for unmarried taxpayers and $1,300 for married taxpayers and surviving spouses in 2019.
LO 1.8: Compute basic capital gains and losses.	• The amount of gain or loss realized by a taxpayer is determined by subtracting the adjusted basis of the asset from the amount realized. • Gains and losses can be either ordinary or capital. • Ordinary gains and losses are treated for tax purposes like other items such as salary and interest. • Capital gains and losses result from the sale or exchange of capital assets. • Common capital assets held by individual taxpayers include stocks, bonds, land, cars, boats, and other items held as investments. • Gain from property held 12 months or less is deemed to be short-term capital gain and is taxed at ordinary income tax rates. • Gain from property held more than 12 months is deemed to be long-term capital gain and is taxed at preferential income tax rates. • The long-term capital gain rates for 2019 vary between 0, 15, and 20 percent, depending on the taxpayer's income. • If an individual taxpayer ends up with a net capital loss (short-term or long-term), up to $3,000 per year can be deducted against ordinary income. Any excess capital loss is carried forward to subsequent tax years. Losses from personal-use assets are not deductible.

LO 1.9: Access and use various Internet tax resources.	• Taxpayers and tax practitioners can find a substantial amount of useful information on the Internet. • Useful websites containing tax information include the IRS (**www.irs.gov**) and the Intuit websites.
LO 1.10: Describe the basics of electronic filing (e-filing).	• Electronic filing (e-filing) is the process of transmitting federal income tax return information to the IRS Service Center using a device with Internet access. • Electronic filing offers a faster refund through a direct deposit to the taxpayer's bank account or the taxpayer can request the refund be sent by check.

QUESTIONS and PROBLEMS

GROUP 1:
MULTIPLE CHOICE QUESTIONS

LO 1.1

1. Which of the following recent tax changes is *not* scheduled to expire after 2025?
   a. Suspension of personal exemptions
   b. General lowering of individual tax rates
   c. Restrictions on the deduction of casualty and theft losses
   d. Reduction of corporate tax rates to 21 percent

LO 1.1

2. Which of the following tax forms are used by individuals in 2019?
   a. 1040A
   b. 1040-EZ
   c. 1040-SR
   d. 1120

LO 1.2

3. Partnership income is reported on:
   a. Form 1040
   b. Form 1120
   c. Form 1040X
   d. Form 1065

LO 1.2

4. On which of these would wage income be reported?
   a. Schedule 1
   b. Schedule 2
   c. Schedule 3
   d. Form 1040

LO 1.3

5. Which of the following is a deduction for adjusted gross income in 2019?
   a. Personal casualty losses
   b. Medical expenses
   c. Student loan interest
   d. Charitable contributions
   e. None of the above

LO 1.3

6. All of the following are itemized deductions in 2019 *except*:
   a. Charitable contributions
   b. Alimony payments
   c. State and local taxes
   d. Medical expenses
   e. All of the above are itemized deductions

LO 1.3

7. Ramon, a single taxpayer with no dependents, has adjusted gross income for 2019 of $98,000 and his itemized deductions total $19,000. What taxable income will Ramon show in 2019?
   a. $74,950
   b. $74,850
   c. $79,000
   d. $85,800
   e. $87,650

LO 1.4

8. Ben is a single taxpayer with no dependents and is 32 years old. What is the minimum amount of income that he must have to be required to file a tax return for 2019?
   a. $4,200
   b. $12,700
   c. $12,000
   d. $12,200
   e. None of the above

LO 1.5

9. Joan, who was divorced in 2019, had filed a joint tax return with her husband in 2018. During 2019, she did not remarry and continued to maintain her home in which her five dependent children lived. In the preparation of her tax return for 2019, Joan should file as:
   a. A single individual
   b. A qualifying widow(er)
   c. Head of household
   d. Married, filing separately
   e. None of the above

LO 1.5

10. Glenda, a single taxpayer from Kansas, paid for more than one-half of the support for her mother, Dorothy. Dorothy did not live with Glenda in Kansas, but rather has lived in a nursing home in an adjacent state since Dorothy's husband died three years ago. Glenda's filing status should be:
    a. Single
    b. Married filing separately
    c. Qualifying widower
    d. Head of household
    e. Parental dependent

LO 1.6

11. Margaret and her sister support their mother and together provide 85 percent of their mother's support. If Margaret provides 40 percent of her mother's support:
    a. Her sister is the only one who can claim their mother as a dependent.
    b. Neither Margaret nor her sister may claim their mother as a dependent.
    c. Both Margaret and her sister may claim their mother as a dependent.
    d. Margaret and her sister may split the dependency exemption.
    e. Margaret may claim her mother as a dependent if her sister agrees in a multiple support agreement.

LO 1.6

12. Margaret, age 65, and John, age 62, are married with a 23-year-old daughter who lives in their home. They provide over half of their daughter's support, and their daughter earned $4,100 this year from a part-time job. Their daughter is not a full-time student. The daughter can/cannot be claimed as a dependent because:
    a. She cannot be claimed because she is over 19 and not a full-time student.
    b. She can be claimed because she is a qualifying child.
    c. She can be claimed because she is a qualifying relative.
    d. She cannot be claimed because she fails the gross income test.

LO 1.6 13. Yasmine and her spouse Carlos, who file married filing jointly, provide all the support for their 17-year-old son, Miguel. If Miguel qualifies as a qualifying child under the dependent rules, Yasmine and Carlos will be able to claim
a. $0
b. $500
c. $1,000
d. $2,000
e. $2,500

LO 1.6 14. Robin and Howie file married filing jointly and have a 13-year-old daughter. They also provide all the support for Howie's 82-year-old mother, who lives in a nursing home nearby. The amount of the combined child tax credit and other dependent credit for Robin and Howie is:
a. $0
b. $1,000
c. $1,500
d. $2,000
e. $2,500

LO 1.7 15. Arthur is 65 years old and single. He supports his father, who is 90 years old, blind, and has no income. What is Arthur's standard deduction?
a. $12,200
b. $13,850
c. $15,500
d. $18,350
e. $20,000

LO 1.7 16. Taxpayers who are 65 or older get the benefit of:
a. An additional exemption
b. An additional amount added to their standard deduction
c. An additional amount added to their itemized deductions
d. None of the above

LO 1.7 17. Taxpayers who are blind get the benefit of:
a. An additional exemption
b. An additional amount added to their standard deduction
c. An additional amount added to their itemized deductions
d. None of the above

LO 1.8 18. Which of the following is *not* a capital asset to an individual taxpayer?
a. Stocks
b. A 48-foot sailboat
c. Raw land held as an investment
d. Inventory in the taxpayer's business
e. All of the above are capital assets

LO 1.8 19. Jayne purchased General Motors stock 6 years ago for $20,000. In the current year, she sells the stock for $35,000. What is Jayne's gain or loss?
a. $15,000 long-term gain
b. $15,000 short-term gain
c. $15,000 ordinary loss
d. $15,000 extraordinary gain
e. No gain or loss is recognized on this transaction

LO 1.8 20. Alexis purchased a rental house 3 years ago for $290,000. Her depreciation to date is $35,000. Due to a decrease in real estate prices, she sells the house for only $280,000 in 2019. What is her gain or loss for tax purposes?
a. $0
b. $10,000 loss
c. $10,000 gain

d. $35,000 loss

e. $25,000 gain

LO 1.8

21. Shannon, a single taxpayer, has a long-term capital loss of $7,000 on the sale of bonds in 2019 and no other capital gains or losses. Her taxable income without this transaction is $47,000. What is her taxable income considering this capital loss?

a. $40,000

b. $44,000

c. $47,000

d. $55,000

e. Some other amount

LO 1.9

22. Access the Internet and go to www.irs.gov and select "Search Forms & Instructions." Enter "4868" into the search box. What is Line 6 of the Form 4868?

a. Total payments

b. Balance due

c. Your name

d. Estimate of total tax liability

e. Your social security number

LO 1.9

23. Access the Internet and go to www.irs.gov and select "News" in the upper right hand corner (on mobile devices, select "Menu" in the upper right hand corner and select "News"). Select "IRS Guidance" (on mobile devices, hit the plus on "more News," then scroll down until you see "IRS Guidance") and then select "IRS Guidance in Plain English." Which of the following is a written statement issued to a taxpayer that interprets and applies tax laws to the taxpayer's specific set of facts?

a. Private letter ruling

b. Revenue ruling

c. Revenue procedure

d. Notice

e. Regulation

LO 1.10

24. Electronically filed tax returns:

a. May not be transmitted from a taxpayer's home computer

b. Constitute more than 90 percent of the returns filed with the IRS

c. Have error rates similar to paper returns

d. Offer larger refunds than paper returns

GROUP 2:
PROBLEMS

LO 1.1

1. List three major purposes the tax system is meant to serve:

a. _____

b. _____

c. _____

LO 1.3

2. Jason and Mary are married taxpayers in 2019. They are both under age 65 and in good health. For 2019 they have a total of $41,000 in wages and $700 in interest income. Jason and Mary's deductions for adjusted gross income amount to $5,000 and their itemized deductions equal $18,700. They have two children, ages 32 and 28, that are married and provide support for themselves.

a. What is the amount of Jason and Mary's adjusted gross income?

$ _____

b. What is the amount of their itemized deductions or standard deduction?

$ _____

c. What is their taxable income?

$ _____

LO 1.3

3. Leslie is a single taxpayer who is under age 65 and in good health. For 2019, she has a salary of $24,000 and itemized deductions of $1,000. Leslie allows her mother to live with her during the winter months (3–4 months per year), but her mother provides all of her own support otherwise.

   a. How much is Leslie's adjusted gross income?

   $ _____

   b. What amount of itemized or standard deduction(s) should she claim?

   $ _____

   c. What is the amount of Leslie's taxable income?

   $ _____

LO 1.3
LO 1.8

4. In 2019, Lou has a salary of $53,300 from her job. She also has interest income of $1,600 and dividend income of $400. Lou is single and has no dependents. During the year, Lou sold silver coins held as an investment for a $7,000 loss. Calculate the following amounts for Lou:

   a. Adjusted gross income

   $ _____

   b. Standard deduction

   $ _____

   c. Taxable income

   $ _____

LO 1.3
LO 1.5
LO 1.7

5. Diego, age 28, married Dolores, age 27, in 2019. Their salaries for the year amounted to $47,230 and they had interest income of $3,500. Diego and Dolores' deductions for adjusted gross income amounted to $2,000, their itemized deductions were $16,000, and they have no dependents.

   a. What is the amount of their adjusted gross income?

   $ _____

   b. What is the amount of their itemized deductions or standard deduction?

   $ _____

   c. What is the amount of their taxable income?

   $ _____

   d. What is their tax liability for 2019?

   $ _____

LO 1.3
LO 1.5
LO 1.7

6. Ulysses and Penelope are married and file separate returns for 2019. Penelope itemizes her deductions on her return. Ulysses' adjusted gross income was $17,400, his itemized deductions were $2,250. Neither have any dependents. Calculate Ulysses' income tax liability assuming the couple does not live in a community property state.

   $ _____

LO 1.3
LO 1.5
LO 1.7

7. Alicia, age 27, is a single, full-time college student. She earns $13,200 from a part-time job and has taxable interest income of $1,450. Her itemized deductions are $845. Calculate Alicia's taxable income for 2019. (Please note: Chapter 6 will cover the computation of tax credits for dependent college students under age 24.)

   $ _____

LO 1.3
LO 1.5
LO 1.7

8. Jonathan is a 35-year-old single taxpayer with adjusted gross income in 2019 of $46,300. He uses the standard deduction and has no dependents.
   a. Calculate Jonathan's taxable income. Please show your work.

   _____

   _____

   b. When you calculate Jonathan's tax liability are you required to use the tax tables or the tax rate schedules, or does it matter?

   _____

   c. What is Jonathan's tax liability?

   _____

LO 1.3
LO 1.5
LO 1.7

9. Jim, age 50, and Martha, age 49, are married with three dependent children. They file a joint return for 2019. Their income from salaries totals $49,500, and they received $10,125 in taxable interest, $5,000 in royalties, and $3,000 in other ordinary income. Jim and Martha's deductions for adjusted gross income amount to $3,200, and they have itemized deductions totaling $18,200. Calculate the following amounts:
   a. Gross income

   $ _____

   b. Adjusted gross income

   $ _____

   c. Itemized deduction or standard deduction amount

   $ _____

   d. Taxable income

   $ _____

   e. Income tax liability (Do not consider the alternative minimum tax covered in Chapter 6 or any credits.)

   $ _____

LO 1.3
LO 1.5
LO 1.6
LO 1.7

10. Frank, age 35, and Joyce, age 34, are married and file a joint income tax return for 2019. Their salaries for the year total $84,800 and they have taxable interest income of $3,900. They have no deductions for adjusted gross income. Their itemized deductions are $24,700. Frank and Joyce do not have any dependents.
    a. What is the amount of their adjusted gross income?

    $ _____

    b. What is their deduction for personal exemptions?

    $ _____

    c. What is the amount of their taxable income?

    $ _____

LO 1.3
LO 1.5
LO 1.7

11. Christine is a single 50-year-old taxpayer with no dependents. Her only income is $40,750 of wages. Calculate her taxable income and her tax liability. Please show your work.

    _____

    _____

    _____

LO 1.4

12. Nicoula is a server at a La Jolla restaurant. Nicoula received $1,200 in unreported tips during 2019 and owes Social Security and Medicare taxes on these tips. Her total income for the year, including the tips, is $4,300. Is Nicoula required to file an income tax return for 2019? Why or why not?

_____

_____

_____

LO 1.4

13. For each of the following situations (none of the taxpayers claim dependents), indicate whether the taxpayer(s) is (are) required to file a tax return for 2019. Explain your answer.
    a. Helen is a single taxpayer with interest income in 2019 of $8,750.

    _____

    _____

    b. Joan is a single college student who is claimed as a dependent by her parents. She earned $1,550 from a part-time job and has $1,150 in interest income.

    _____

    _____

    c. Leslie, age 64, and Mark, age 66, are married and file a joint return. They received $17,800 in interest income from a savings account.

    _____

    _____

    d. Ray, age 60, and Jean, age 57, are married and file a joint tax return. Their only income is $14,700 in interest income.

    _____

    _____

    e. Harry, a 19-year-old single taxpayer, had net earnings from self-employment of $1,500.

    _____

    _____

    _____

LO 1.5

14. Determine from the tax table in Appendix A the amount of the income tax for each of the following taxpayers for 2019:

Taxpayer(s)	Filing Status	Taxable Income	Income Tax
Allen	Single	$21,000	$_____
Boyd	MFS	24,545	$_____
Caldwell	MFJ	35,784	$_____
Dell	H of H	27,450	$_____
Evans	Single	45,000	$_____

LO 1.5

15. For each of the following cases, indicate the filing status for the taxpayer(s) for 2019 using the following legend:

    A—Single   **D**—Head of household

    B—Married filing a joint return   **E**—Qualifying widow(er)

    C—Married filing separate returns

Case	Filing Status
a. Linda is single and she supports her mother (who has no income), including paying all the costs of her housing in an apartment across town.	_____
b. Frank is single and he has a dependent child living in his home.	_____

c. Arthur is single and he supports his 30-year-old brother, _____
who lives in his own home.

d. Leslie's final decree of divorce was granted on June 18, _____
2019. She has no dependents.

e. Tom and Carry were married on December 31, 2019. _____

LO 1.5   16. Melissa and Aaron are married taxpayers with taxable income of $105,000.

a. When you calculate their tax liability, are you required to use the tax tables or the tax rate schedules, or does it matter? _____

_____

_____

b. What is their 2019 tax liability? _____

_____

LO 1.5   17. Jessica and Carl were married on July 1, 2019. What are their options for filing status for their 2019 taxes?

_____

_____

_____

LO 1.5   18. Maggie is single and supports her 85-year-old parents who have no income and live in a home rented for them by Maggie. What is Maggie's filing status and why?

_____

_____

_____

LO 1.5   19. List each alternative filing status available to unmarried individual taxpayers and the circumstances under which the alternatives can be used. _____

_____

_____

_____

LO 1.5
LO 1.6   20. Mary is single and supports her 30-year-old son who has income of $2,000 and lives in his own apartment.

a. Can she claim him as a dependent? _____

b. Can she claim head of household filing status? Why or why not? _____

_____

_____

_____

LO 1.6   21. In each of the following situations, determine whether the taxpayer(s) has/have a dependent and if so, the total amount of child tax credit and other dependent credit (assuming no limitations apply).

	Dependent? (Yes/No)	Total Child and Other Dependent Credit
a. Donna, a 20-year-old single taxpayer, supports her mother, who lives in her own home. Her mother has income of $1,350.	_____	_____
b. William, age 43, and Mary, age 45, are married and support William's 19-year-old sister, who is not a student. The sister's income from a part-time job is $4,200.	_____	_____
c. Devi was divorced in 2018 and receives child support of $250 per month from her ex-husband for the support of their 8-year-old son, John, who lives with her. Devi is 45 and provides more than half of her son's support.	_____	_____
d. Wendell, an 89-year-old single taxpayer, supports his son, who is 67 years old, lives with him, and earns no income.	_____	_____
e. Wilma, age 65, and Morris, age 66, are married. They file a joint return.	_____	_____

LO 1.6

22. What is the total dollar amount of personal and dependency exemptions which a married couple with two children (ages 11 and 14, both of which are qualified children) and $80,000 of adjusted gross income would deduct in 2019? What is the total child and other dependent credit that could be claimed (before any limitations)

_____

_____

LO 1.6

23. If Charles, a 16-year-old child model, earns $50,000 a year and is completely self-supporting even though he lives with his parents, can his parents claim him as a dependent? Why or why not?

_____

_____

_____

LO 1.6

24. Marc's brother, Phillip, who is a 20-year-old French citizen, lives in France for the full year. Marc supports Phillip while he attends college. Can Marc claim Phillip as a dependent? Why or why not?

_____

_____

_____

LO 1.7

25. Describe the difference between the standard deduction and itemized deductions. How should a taxpayer decide whether to take the standard deduction or claim itemized deductions?

_____

_____

_____

LO 1.9

26. Go to the IRS website (**www.irs.gov/newsroom**) and note the name of the most recent news release.

LO 1.9

27. Go to the IRS website (**www.irs.gov**) and print out a copy of the most recent *Schedule F* of *Form 1040*.

LO 1.9

28. Go to the Turbo Tax Blog (http://blog.turbotax.intuit.com/) and search the blog for an article on the deduction of student loan interest. What is the maximum deduction that can be taken in a year?

GROUP 3:
WRITING ASSIGNMENTS

RESEARCH

1. Jerry, age 23, a full-time student and not disabled, lives with William and Sheila Carson. Jerry is William's older brother. Jerry is single, a U.S. citizen, and does not provide more than one-half of his own support. William and Sheila are both 21 and file a joint return. Can William and Sheila claim Jerry as a qualifying child?
   Required: Go to the IRS website (**www.irs.gov**) and review Publication 501. Write a letter to William and Sheila stating if they can claim Jerry as a qualifying child.

ETHICS

2. Jason and Mary Wells, friends of yours, were married on December 30, 2019. They know you are studying taxes and have sent you an e-mail with a question concerning their filing status. Jason and Mary would each like to file single for tax year 2019. Jason has prepared their taxes both as single and married filing jointly, and he has realized that the couple will get a larger combined refund if they each file single. Jason argues "that it's not as if we were married for very long in 2019." Prepare an e-mail to respond to Jason and Mary's inquiry.

GROUP 4:
COMPREHENSIVE PROBLEMS

> **Instructions for working all Group 4 Comprehensive Tax Return Problems in the textbook are as follows:**
>
> **Birthdays:** If using the tax software, create birthdates for taxpayers and dependents. Adult taxpayers should have ages between 25 and 64 unless a different age is specified.
>
> **Wages:** Assume the wages subject to income tax in the problems are the same as Social Security wages and Medicare wages. Create employer names and other information which may be required by your tax software package.
>
> **Missing Data:** Please make realistic assumptions about any missing data. Decide whether taxpayers contribute to the Presidential Election Campaign, which does not affect tax liability.
>
> **Tax Forms:** Tax forms to complete the problems are found at the end of each chapter. Additional copies can be found on the IRS website (www.irs.gov).

1A. Patty Banyan is a single taxpayer (birthdate May 18, 1992) living at 543 Space Drive, Houston, TX 77099. Her Social Security number is 466-33-1234. For 2019, Patty has no dependents, and her W-2, from her job at a local restaurant where she parks cars, contains the following information:

a Employee's social security number 466-33-1234	OMB No. 1545-0008	Safe, accurate, FAST! Use	IRS e-file	Visit the IRS website at www.irs.gov/efile
b Employer identification number (EIN) 33-1235672		**1** Wages, tips, other compensation 20,051.12	**2** Federal income tax withheld 1,197.78	
c Employer's name, address, and ZIP code Burger Box 1234 Mountain Road Houston, TX 77099		**3** Social security wages 20,051.12	**4** Social security tax withheld 1,243.17	
		5 Medicare wages and tips 20,051.12	**6** Medicare tax withheld 290.74	
		7 Social security tips	**8** Allocated tips	
d Control number		**9**	**10** Dependent care benefits	
e Employee's first name and initial Last name Suff. Patty Banyan 543 Space Drive Houston, TX 77099		**11** Nonqualified plans	**12a** See instructions for box 12	
		13 Statutory employee Retirement plan Third-party sick pay	**12b**	
		14 Other	**12c**	
			12d	
f Employee's address and ZIP code				
15 State Employer's state ID number TX	**16** State wages, tips, etc.	**17** State income tax	**18** Local wages, tips, etc.	**19** Local income tax **20** Locality name

Form **W-2** Wage and Tax Statement   2019   Department of the Treasury—Internal Revenue Service

Copy B—To Be Filed With Employee's FEDERAL Tax Return.
This information is being furnished to the Internal Revenue Service.

These wages are Patty's only income for 2019.

Required: Complete Form 1040 for Patty Banyan for the 2019 tax year.

1B. Using the information from Problem 1A, assume Patty's birthdate is May 18, 1952 and complete Form 1040-SR for Patty Banyan for the 2019 tax year.

2A. Hardy and Dora Knox are married and file a joint return for 2019. Hardy's Social Security number is 466-47-3311 and her birthdate is January 4, 1975. Dora's Social Security number is 467-74-4451 and her birthday is July 7, 1974. They live at 143 Maple Street,

Knoxville, TN 37932. For 2019, Hardy did not work, and Dora's W-2 from her butcher's job showed the following:

a Employee's social security number 467-74-4451 OMB No. 1545-0008	Safe, accurate, FAST! Use — IRS e-file Visit the IRS website at www.irs.gov/efile

b Employer identification number (EIN) 33-0711111	**1** Wages, tips, other compensation 50,994.12	**2** Federal income tax withheld 3,067.52
c Employer's name, address, and ZIP code Grocery City 1700 Harding Valley Street Knoxville, TN 37932	**3** Social security wages 50,994.12	**4** Social security tax withheld 3,161.64
	5 Medicare wages and tips 50,994.12	**6** Medicare tax withheld 739.41
	7 Social security tips	**8** Allocated tips
d Control number	**9**	**10** Dependent care benefits
e Employee's first name and initial Last name Suff. Dora Knox 143 Maple Street Knoxville, TN 37932	**11** Nonqualified plans	**12a** See instructions for box 12
	13 Statutory employee Retirement plan Third-party sick pay	**12b**
	14 Other	**12c**
		12d
f Employee's address and ZIP code		
15 State Employer's state ID number TN	**16** State wages, tips, etc.	**17** State income tax	**18** Local wages, tips, etc.	**19** Local income tax	**20** Locality name

Form **W-2** Wage and Tax Statement   **2019**   Department of the Treasury—Internal Revenue Service

Copy B—To Be Filed With Employee's FEDERAL Tax Return.
This information is being furnished to the Internal Revenue Service.

Hardy and Dora have a 20-year-old son named Fort (Social Security number 552-52-5552), who is a dependent that lives with them, is not a full-time student, and generates $5,200 of gross income for himself.

Required: Complete Form 1040 for Hardy and Dora for the 2019 tax year.

2B. Abigail (Abby) Boxer is a single mother (birthdate April 28, 1981) working as a civilian accountant for the U.S. Army. Her Social Security number is 676-73-3311 and she lives at 3456 S Career Avenue, Sioux Falls, SD 57107. Helen, Abby's 18-year-old daughter (Social Security number 676-73-3312 and birthdate April 16, 2001), is a dependent child living with her mother, and she does not qualify for the child tax credit due to her age but does qualify for the other dependent credit of $500. Abby's Form W-2 from the U.S. Department of Defense shows the following:

a Employee's social security number 676-73-3311 OMB No. 1545-0008	Safe, accurate, FAST! Use — IRS e-file Visit the IRS website at www.irs.gov/efile

b Employer identification number (EIN) 31-1575142	**1** Wages, tips, other compensation 59,364.23	**2** Federal income tax withheld 4,996.00
c Employer's name, address, and ZIP code DFAS Cleveland Center PO Box 998002 Cleveland, OH 44199	**3** Social security wages 59,364.23	**4** Social security tax withheld 3,680.58
	5 Medicare wages and tips 59,364.23	**6** Medicare tax withheld 860.78
	7 Social security tips	**8** Allocated tips
d Control number	**9**	**10** Dependent care benefits
e Employee's first name and initial Last name Suff. Abigail Boxer 3456 S Career Avenue Sioux Falls, SD 57107	**11** Nonqualified plans	**12a** See instructions for box 12
	13 Statutory employee Retirement plan Third-party sick pay	**12b**
	14 Other	**12c**
		12d
f Employee's address and ZIP code		
15 State Employer's state ID number SD	**16** State wages, tips, etc.	**17** State income tax	**18** Local wages, tips, etc.	**19** Local income tax	**20** Locality name

Form **W-2** Wage and Tax Statement   **2019**   Department of the Treasury—Internal Revenue Service

Copy B—To Be Filed With Employee's FEDERAL Tax Return.
This information is being furnished to the Internal Revenue Service.

Abby also has taxable interest from Sioux Falls Savings and Loan of $300 and tax-exempt interest from bonds issued by the state of South Dakota of $127.

Required: Complete Form 1040 for Abigail for the 2019 tax year.

GROUP 5:
CUMULATIVE SOFTWARE PROBLEM

1. Albert Gaytor and his wife Allison are married and file a joint return for 2019. The Gaytors live at 12340 Cocoshell Road, Coral Gables, FL 33134. Captain Gaytor is a charter fishing boat captain but took 6 months off from his job in 2019 to train and study for his Masters Captain's License.

   In 2019, Albert received a Form W-2 from his employer, Coconut Grove Fishing Charters, Inc.:

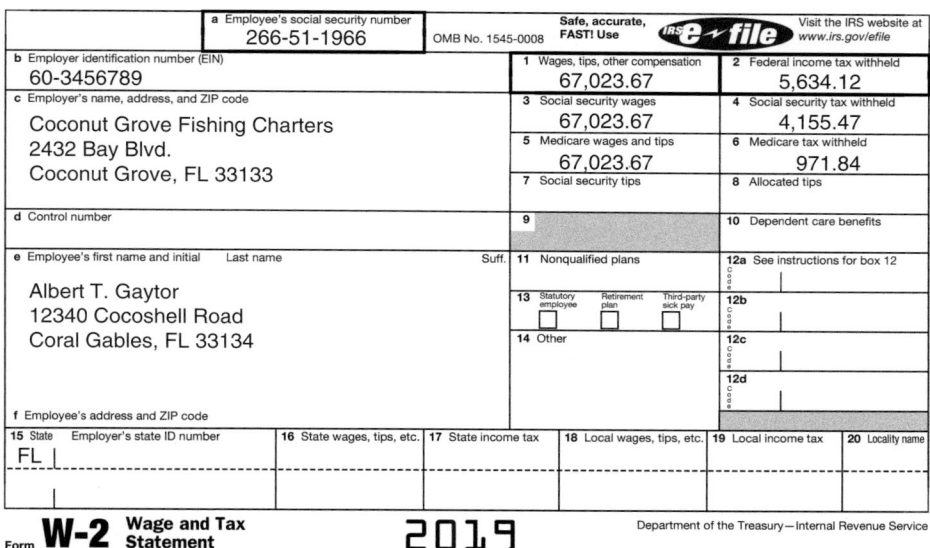

Name	Social Security Number	Date of Birth
Albert T. Gaytor	266-51-1966	09/22/1970
Allison A. Gaytor	266-34-1967	07/01/1971
Crocker Gaytor	261-55-1212	12/21/2002
Cayman Slacker	261-11-4444	03/13/2001
Sean Slacker	344-23-5656	05/01/2000

The Gaytors have a 17-year-old son, Crocker, who is a full-time freshman at Brickell State University. The Gaytors also have an 18-year-old daughter, Cayman, who is a part-time student at Dade County Community College (DCCC). Cayman is married to Sean Slacker, who is 19 years old and a part-time student at DCCC. Sean and Cayman have a 1-year-old child, Wanda Slacker (Social Security number 648-99-4306). Sean, Cayman, and Wanda all live in an apartment up the street from Albert and Allison during the entire current calendar year. Sean and Cayman both work for Sean's wealthy grandfather as apprentices in his business. Their wages for the year were a combined $50,000, which allowed them to pay all the personal expenses for themselves and their daughter.

Albert and Allison have a savings account and received the following Form 1099-INT for 2019:

☐ CORRECTED (if checked)

PAYER'S name, street address, city or town, state or province, country, ZIP or foreign postal code, and telephone no. Vizcaya National Bank 9871 Coral Way Miami, FL 33134	Payer's RTN (optional)	OMB No. 1545-0112 20**19** Form **1099-INT**	**Interest Income**
	1 Interest income $ 337.54		Copy B
	2 Early withdrawal penalty $		**Copy B**
PAYER'S TIN 60-7654321	RECIPIENT'S TIN 266-51-1966	**3** Interest on U.S. Savings Bonds and Treas. obligations $	**For Recipient**
RECIPIENT'S name Albert T Gaytor	**4** Federal income tax withheld $	**5** Investment expenses $	This is important tax information and is being furnished to the IRS. If you are required to file a return, a negligence penalty or other sanction may be imposed on you if this income is taxable and the IRS determines that it has not been reported.
Street address (including apt. no.) 12340 Cocoshell Road	**6** Foreign tax paid $	**7** Foreign country or U.S. possession	
	8 Tax-exempt interest $	**9** Specified private activity bond interest $	
City or town, state or province, country, and ZIP or foreign postal code Coral Gables, FL 33134	**10** Market discount $	**11** Bond premium $	
FATCA filing requirement ☐	**12** Bond premium on Treasury obligations $	**13** Bond premium on tax-exempt bond $	
Account number (see instructions)	**14** Tax-exempt and tax credit bond CUSIP no.	**15** State	**16** State identification no.	**17** State tax withheld $ $

Form **1099-INT**   (keep for your records)   www.irs.gov/Form1099INT   Department of the Treasury - Internal Revenue Service

Required: Use a computer software package such as Intuit ProConnect to complete Form 1040 for Albert and Allison Gaytor for 2019. Be sure to save your data input files since this case will be expanded with more tax information in later chapters. Make assumptions regarding any information not given.

Form 1040
Department of the Treasury—Internal Revenue Service   (99)
U.S. Individual Income Tax Return   **2019**   OMB No. 1545-0074   IRS Use Only—Do not write or staple in this space.

Filing Status
Check only one box.

☐ Single   ☐ Married filing jointly   ☐ Married filing separately (MFS)   ☐ Head of household (HOH)   ☐ Qualifying widow(er) (QW)

If you checked the MFS box, enter the name of spouse. If you checked the HOH or QW box, enter the child's name if the qualifying person is a child but not your dependent. ▶

Your first name and middle initial	Last name	Your social security number
If joint return, spouse's first name and middle initial	Last name	Spouse's social security number

Home address (number and street). If you have a P.O. box, see instructions.	Apt. no.	**Presidential Election Campaign**
City, town or post office, state, and ZIP code. If you have a foreign address, also complete spaces below (see instructions).		Check here if you, or your spouse if filing jointly, want $3 to go to this fund. Checking a box below will not change your tax or refund. ☐ You ☐ Spouse

Foreign country name	Foreign province/state/county	Foreign postal code	If more than four dependents, see instructions and ✓ here ▶ ☐

Standard Deduction

Someone can claim: ☐ You as a dependent   ☐ Your spouse as a dependent

☐ Spouse itemizes on a separate return or you were a dual-status alien

Age/Blindness   **You:** ☐ Were born before January 2, 1955   ☐ Are blind   **Spouse:** ☐ Was born before January 2, 1955   ☐ Is blind

Dependents (see instructions):

(1) First name Last name	(2) Social security number	(3) Relationship to you	(4) ✓ if qualifies for (see instructions):
			Child tax credit	Credit for other dependents
			☐	☐
			☐	☐
			☐	☐
			☐	☐

Standard Deduction for—
- Single or Married filing separately, $12,200
- Married filing jointly or Qualifying widow(er), $24,400
- Head of household, $18,350
- If you checked any box under *Standard Deduction*, see instructions.

1	Wages, salaries, tips, etc. Attach Form(s) W-2		**1**
2a	Tax-exempt interest **2a**	**b** Taxable interest. Attach Sch. B if required	**2b**
3a	Qualified dividends **3a**	**b** Ordinary dividends. Attach Sch. B if required	**3b**
4a	IRA distributions **4a**	**b** Taxable amount	**4b**
c	Pensions and annuities . . . **4c**	**d** Taxable amount	**4d**
5a	Social security benefits . . . **5a**	**b** Taxable amount	**5b**
6	Capital gain or (loss). Attach Schedule D if required. If not required, check here . . . . ▶ ☐		**6**
7a	Other income from Schedule 1, line 9		**7a**
b	Add lines 1, 2b, 3b, 4b, 4d, 5b, 6, and 7a. This is your **total income** . . . . ▶		**7b**
8a	Adjustments to income from Schedule 1, line 22		**8a**
b	Subtract line 8a from line 7b. This is your **adjusted gross income** . . . . ▶		**8b**
9	**Standard deduction or itemized deductions** (from Schedule A) **9**		
10	Qualified business income deduction. Attach Form 8995 or Form 8995-A **10**		
11a	Add lines 9 and 10		**11a**
b	**Taxable income.** Subtract line 11a from line 8b		**11b**

For Disclosure, Privacy Act, and Paperwork Reduction Act Notice, see separate instructions.   Cat. No. 11320B   Form **1040** (2019)

Form 1040 (2019)   Page **2**

12a	**Tax** (see inst.) Check if any from Form(s): **1** ☐ 8814 **2** ☐ 4972 **3** ☐ _____		**12a**		
b	Add Schedule 2, line 3, and line 12a and enter the total . . . . . . ▶			**12b**	
13a	Child tax credit or credit for other dependents	**13a**			
b	Add Schedule 3, line 7, and line 13a and enter the total . . . . . . ▶			**13b**	
14	Subtract line 13b from line 12b. If zero or less, enter -0-			**14**	
15	Other taxes, including self-employment tax, from Schedule 2, line 10 . . .			**15**	
16	Add lines 14 and 15. This is your **total tax** . . . . ▶			**16**	
17	Federal income tax withheld from Forms W-2 and 1099			**17**	
18	Other payments and refundable credits:				
a	Earned income credit (EIC)	**18a**			
b	Additional child tax credit. Attach Schedule 8812	**18b**			
c	American opportunity credit from Form 8863, line 8 . . .	**18c**			
d	Schedule 3, line 14	**18d**			
e	Add lines 18a through 18d. These are your **total other payments and refundable credits** . . . ▶			**18e**	
19	Add lines 17 and 18e. These are your **total payments** . . . . ▶			**19**	

*   If you have a qualifying child, attach Sch. EIC.
*   If you have nontaxable combat pay, see instructions.

Refund

Direct deposit?
See instructions.

20	If line 19 is more than line 16, subtract line 16 from line 19. This is the amount you **overpaid**		**20**	
21a	Amount of line 20 you want **refunded to you.** If Form 8888 is attached, check here . . . ▶ ☐		**21a**	
▶ **b**	Routing number ⬚⬚⬚⬚⬚⬚⬚⬚⬚ ▶ **c** Type: ☐ Checking ☐ Savings			
▶ **d**	Account number ⬚⬚⬚⬚⬚⬚⬚⬚⬚⬚⬚⬚⬚⬚⬚⬚⬚			
22	Amount of line 20 you want **applied to your 2020 estimated tax** . . . . ▶	**22**		

Amount You Owe

23	**Amount you owe.** Subtract line 19 from line 16. For details on how to pay, see instructions . . . ▶		**23**	
24	Estimated tax penalty (see instructions) . . . . ▶	**24**		

Third Party Designee

(Other than paid preparer)

Do you want to allow another person (other than your paid preparer) to discuss this return with the IRS? See instructions.   ☐ **Yes.** Complete below.   ☐ **No**

Designee's name ▶	Phone no. ▶	Personal identification number (PIN) ▶ ⬚⬚⬚⬚⬚

Sign Here

Joint return?
See instructions.
Keep a copy for your records.

Under penalties of perjury, I declare that I have examined this return and accompanying schedules and statements, and to the best of my knowledge and belief, they are true, correct, and complete. Declaration of preparer (other than taxpayer) is based on all information of which preparer has any knowledge.

Your signature	Date	Your occupation	If the IRS sent you an Identity Protection PIN, enter it here (see inst.) ⬚⬚⬚⬚⬚⬚
Spouse's signature. If a joint return, **both** must sign.	Date	Spouse's occupation	If the IRS sent your spouse an Identity Protection PIN, enter it here (see inst.) ⬚⬚⬚⬚⬚⬚
Phone no.		Email address	

Paid Preparer Use Only

Preparer's name	Preparer's signature		Date	PTIN	Check if:
					☐ 3rd Party Designee
Firm's name ▶			Phone no.		☐ Self-employed
Firm's address ▶				Firm's EIN ▶	

Go to *www.irs.gov/Form1040* for instructions and the latest information.   Form **1040** (2019)

Form 1040-SR Department of the Treasury—Internal Revenue Service (99)

U.S. Tax Return for Seniors **2019** OMB No. 1545-0074 IRS Use Only—Do not write or staple in this space.

Filing Status
Check only one box.

☐ Single ☐ Married filing jointly ☐ Married filing separately (MFS)
☐ Head of household (HOH) ☐ Qualifying widow(er) (QW)

If you checked the MFS box, enter the name of spouse. If you checked the HOH or QW box, enter the child's name if the qualifying person is a child but not your dependent. ▶

Your first name and middle initial	Last name	Your social security number
If joint return, spouse's first name and middle initial	Last name	Spouse's social security number

Home address (number and street). If you have a P.O. box, see instructions. | Apt. no.

Presidential Election Campaign
Check here if you, or your spouse if filing jointly, want $3 to go to this fund. Checking a box below will not change your tax or refund. ☐ You ☐ Spouse

City, town or post office, state, and ZIP code. If you have a foreign address, also complete spaces below (see instructions).

Foreign country name | Foreign province/state/county | Foreign postal code

If more than four dependents, see inst. and ✓ here ▶ ☐

Standard Deduction

Someone can claim: ☐ You as a dependent ☐ Your spouse as a dependent
☐ Spouse itemizes on a separate return or you were a dual-status alien

Age/Blindness **You:** ☐ Were born before January 2, 1955 ☐ Are blind
Spouse: ☐ Was born before January 2, 1955 ☐ Is blind

Dependents (see instructions):

(1) First name Last name	(2) Social security number	(3) Relationship to you	(4) ✓ if qualifies for (see inst.): Child tax credit	Credit for other dependents
			☐	☐
			☐	☐
			☐	☐
			☐	☐

Attach Schedule B if required.

1	Wages, salaries, tips, etc. Attach Form(s) W-2	**1**	
2a	Tax-exempt interest . . **2a**	**b** Taxable interest . . . **2b**	
3a	Qualified dividends . . . **3a**	**b** Ordinary dividends . . **3b**	
4a	IRA distributions **4a**	**b** Taxable amount . . . **4b**	
c	Pensions and annuities . **4c**	**d** Taxable amount . . . **4d**	
5a	Social security benefits . . **5a**	**b** Taxable amount . . . **5b**	
6	Capital gain or (loss). Attach Schedule D if required. If not required, check here . ▶ ☐	**6**	
7a	Other income from Schedule 1, line 9	**7a**	
b	Add lines 1, 2b, 3b, 4b, 4d, 5b, 6, and 7a. This is your **total income** . . . . . ▶	**7b**	
8a	Adjustments to income from Schedule 1, line 22	**8a**	
b	Subtract line 8a from line 7b. This is your **adjusted gross income** . . . . . ▶	**8b**	

Standard Deduction
See *Standard Deduction Chart* below.

9	**Standard deduction or itemized deductions** (from Schedule A)	**9**	
10	Qualified business income deduction. Attach Form 8995 or Form 8995-A	**10**	
11a	Add lines 9 and 10	**11a**	
b	**Taxable income.** Subtract line 11a from line 8b	**11b**	

Standard Deduction Chart

Don't use this chart if someone can claim you (or your spouse if filing jointly) as a dependent, your spouse itemizes on a separate return, or you were a dual-status alien. Instead, see instructions.

Add the number of boxes checked in the "Age/Blindness" section of *Standard Deduction* . . . . ▶

IF your filing status is. . .	AND the number of boxes checked is. . .	THEN your standard deduction is. . .	IF your filing status is. . .	AND the number of boxes checked is. . .	THEN your standard deduction is. . .
Single	0	$12,200	Head of household	0	$18,350
	1	13,850		1	20,000
	2	15,500		2	21,650
Married filing jointly or Qualifying widow(er)	0	24,400	Married filing separately	0	12,200
	1	25,700		1	13,500
	2	27,000		2	14,800
	3	28,300		3	16,100
	4	29,600		4	17,400

For Disclosure, Privacy Act, and Paperwork Reduction Act Notice, see separate instructions. Cat. No. 71930F Form **1040-SR** (2019)

DRAFT AS OF July 11, 2019 DO NOT FILE

Form 1040-SR (2019)   Page **2**

12a	**Tax** (see instructions). Check if any from:	
	1 ☐ Form(s) 8814 **2** ☐ Form 4972 **3** ☐ _____	**12a**
b	Add Schedule 2, line 3, and line 12a and enter the total . . . . ▶	**12b**
13a	Child tax credit or credit for other dependents	**13a**
b	Add Schedule 3, line 7, and line 13a and enter the total . . . . ▶	**13b**
14	Subtract line 13b from line 12b. If zero or less, enter -0-	**14**
15	Other taxes, including self-employment tax, from Schedule 2, line 10 . . .	**15**
16	Add lines 14 and 15. This is your **total tax** . . . . ▶	**16**
17	Federal income tax withheld from Forms W-2 and 1099	**17**
18	Other payments and refundable credits:	
a	Earned income credit (EIC)	**18a**
b	Additional child tax credit. Attach Schedule 8812 . . .	**18b**
c	American opportunity credit from Form 8863, line 8 . . .	**18c**
d	Schedule 3, line 14	**18d**
e	Add lines 18a through 18d. These are your **total other payments and refundable credits** ▶	**18e**
19	Add lines 17 and 18e. These are your **total payments** . . . . . . ▶	**19**

> • If you have a qualifying child, attach Sch. EIC.
> • If you have nontaxable combat pay, see instructions.

Refund	**20** If line 19 is more than line 16, subtract line 16 from line 19. This is the amount you **overpaid**	**20**
	21a Amount of line 20 you want **refunded to you.** If Form 8888 is attached, check here ▶ ☐	**21a**
Direct deposit? ▶ See instructions. ▶	**b** Routing number	▶ **c** Type: ☐ Checking ☐ Savings
	d Account number	
	22 Amount of line 20 you want **applied to your 2020 estimated tax** ▶	**22**
Amount You Owe	**23** **Amount you owe.** Subtract line 19 from line 16. For details on how to pay, see instructions ▶	**23**
	24 Estimated tax penalty (see instructions) . . . . . . ▶	**24**

Third Party Designee
(Other than paid preparer)

Do you want to allow another person (other than your paid preparer) to discuss this return with the IRS? See instructions.   ☐ **Yes.** Complete below.   ☐ **No**

Designee's name ▶	Phone no. ▶	Personal identification number (PIN) ▶	

Sign Here

Under penalties of perjury, I declare that I have examined this return and accompanying schedules and statements, and to the best of my knowledge and belief, they are true, correct, and complete. Declaration of preparer (other than taxpayer) is based on all information of which preparer has any knowledge.

Joint return? See instructions. Keep a copy for your records.

Your signature	Date	Your occupation	If the IRS sent you an Identity Protection PIN, enter it here (see inst.)
Spouse's signature. If a joint return, **both** must sign.	Date	Spouse's occupation	If the IRS sent your spouse an Identity Protection PIN, enter it here (see inst.)
Phone no.		Email address	

Paid Preparer Use Only

Preparer's name	Preparer's signature	Date	PTIN	Check if: ☐ 3rd Party Designee ☐ Self-employed
Firm's name ▶			Phone no.	
Firm's address ▶			Firm's EIN ▶	

Go to *www.irs.gov/Form1040SR* for instructions and the latest information.   Form **1040-SR** (2019)

Student Name _____

Class/Section _____

Date   _____

KEY NUMBER TAX RETURN SUMMARY

CHAPTER 1

Comprehensive Problem 1A

Adjusted Gross Income (Line 8b)   _____

Taxable Income (Line 11b)   _____

Total Tax (Line 16)   _____

Tax Refund (Line 21a)   _____

Comprehensive Problem 1B

Adjusted Gross Income (Line 8b)   _____

Standard Deduction or Itemized Deductions (Line 9)   _____

Total Tax (Line 16)   _____

Tax Refund (Line 21a)   _____

Comprehensive Problem 2A

Adjusted Gross Income (Line 8b)   _____

Standard Deduction or Itemized Deductions (Line 9)   _____

Tax (Line 12b)   _____

Amount Overpaid (Line 20)   _____

Comprehensive Problem 2B

Adjusted Gross Income (Line 8b)   _____

Standard Deduction or Itemized Deductions (Line 9)   _____

Credit for Other Dependents (Line 13a)   _____

Total Tax (Line 16)   _____

Amount Overpaid (Line 20)   _____

Gross Income and Exclusions

LEARNING OBJECTIVES

After completing this chapter, you should be able to:

LO 2.1 Apply the definition of gross income.

LO 2.2 Describe salaries and wages income reporting and inclusion in gross income.

LO 2.3 Explain the general tax treatment of health insurance.

LO 2.4 Determine when meals and lodging may be excluded from taxable income.

LO 2.5 Identify the common employee fringe benefit income exclusions.

LO 2.6 Determine when prizes and awards are included in income.

LO 2.7 Calculate the taxable and nontaxable portions of annuity payments.

LO 2.8 Describe the tax treatment of life insurance proceeds.

LO 2.9 Identify the tax treatment of interest and dividend income.

LO 2.10 Describe the tax treatment of municipal bond interest.

LO 2.11 Identify the general rules for the tax treatment of gifts and inheritances.

LO 2.12 Describe the elements of scholarship income that are excluded from tax.

LO 2.13 Describe the tax treatment of alimony and child support.

LO 2.14 Explain the tax implications of using educational savings vehicles.

LO 2.15 Describe the tax treatment of unemployment compensation.

LO 2.16 Apply the rules governing inclusion of Social Security benefits in gross income.

LO 2.17 Distinguish between the different rules for married taxpayers residing in community property states when filing separate returns.

OVERVIEW

This chapter starts with the definition of gross income. Tables 2.1 and 2.2 list the common inclusions in and exclusions from gross income. Detailed coverage is provided for inclusions and exclusions that may present unique issues for taxpayers. The coverage includes the special tax treatment for interest and dividends, alimony, prizes and awards, annuities, life insurance proceeds, and gifts and inheritances. Coverage of exclusions from gross income includes scholarships, accident and health insurance benefits, certain meals and lodging, municipal bond interest, and the special treatment of Social Security benefits. The elements of gross income discussed here represent much of what is included in the first line of the individual tax formula.

Learning Objective 2.1

Apply the definition of gross income.

2-1 THE NATURE OF GROSS INCOME

Gross income is the starting point for calculating a taxpayer's tax liability. The tax law states that gross income is:

... all income from whatever source derived, including (but not limited to) the following items:

- Compensation for services, including fees, commissions, fringe benefits, and similar items
- Gross income derived from business
- Gains derived from dealings in property
- Interest
- Rents
- Royalties
- Dividends
- Annuities
- Income from life insurance and endowment contracts
- Pensions
- Income from discharge of indebtedness
- Distributive share of partnership gross income
- Income in respect of a decedent
- Income from an interest in an estate or trust

The definition of gross income as **"all income from whatever source derived"** is perhaps the most well-known definition in the tax law. Under this definition, unless there is an exception in the law, the U.S. government considers all income taxable. Therefore, prizes and awards, cash and noncash payments for goods and services, payments made in trade or *barter* (such as car repairs traded for tax preparation services), and illegal income not generally reported to the IRS are all still taxable income.

Table 2.1 provides an expanded list of items that are included in gross income. When in doubt, the general rule is that everything a taxpayer receives must be included in gross income unless specifically excluded. Any noncash items must be included in gross income at the fair market value of the items received.

The tax law provides that certain items of income are exempt from taxation; these items are referred to as *exclusions*. The exclusions include items such as life insurance proceeds, gifts, and veterans' benefits. A more complete list of exclusions from gross income is provided in Table 2.2.

In 2016, the Chicago Cubs won the Major League Baseball World Series for the first time in 108 years. Interestingly, a large number of betting slips were never turned in. Reports indicated that Cubs fans preferred to keep the uncashed slips as souvenirs of the long-awaited occasion. Once the slip expires, it has no value for redemption and so taxpayers do not have any taxable income in spite of winning. If the souvenir is later sold at a gain, income would be recognized.

TABLE 2.1	2019 INCLUSIONS IN GROSS INCOME—PARTIAL LIST

Alimony (excluded after 2018)
Amounts recovered after being deducted
   in prior years
Annuities
Awards
Back pay
Bargain purchase from employer
Bonuses
Breach of contract damages
Business income
Clergy fees and contributions
Commissions
Compensation for services
Contributions received by members
   of the clergy
Damages for nonphysical personal injury
Death benefits
Debts forgiven
Directors' fees
Dividends
Embezzled funds
Employee awards (except certain service awards)
Employee benefits (except certain fringe benefits)
Employee bonuses
Employee stock options
Estate and trust income
Farm income
Fees
Gains from illegal activities

Gains from sale of property
Gambling winnings
Group-term life insurance premiums paid by
   employer for coverage over $50,000
Hobby income
Incentive awards
Interest income
Jury duty fees
Living quarters, meals (unless furnished for employer's convenience, etc.)
Military pay (unless combat pay)
Notary fees
Partnership income
Pensions
Prizes
Professional fees
Punitive damages
Rents
Retirement pay
Rewards
Royalties
Salaries
Scholarships (room and board)
Severance pay
Strike and lockout benefits
Supplemental unemployment benefits
Tips and gratuities
Unemployment compensation
Virtual currency (such as Bitcoin) paid for services
Wages

TABLE 2.2	2019 EXCLUSIONS FROM GROSS INCOME—PARTIAL LIST

Accident insurance proceeds
Alimony (excluded after 2018)
Annuities (to a limited extent)
Bequests
Casualty insurance proceeds
Child support payments
Damages for physical personal injury
   or sickness
Disability benefits (generally,
   but not always)
Gifts
Group-term life insurance
   premiums paid by employer
   (coverage not over $50,000)
Health insurance proceeds

Inheritances
Life insurance proceeds
Meals and lodging (furnished for
   employer's convenience, etc.)
Military allowances (including G.I. bill benefits)
Minister's dwelling rental value allowance
Municipal bond interest
Olympic medals and cash awards given
   to athletes
Relocation payments
Scholarships (tuition and books)
Social Security benefits (with limits)
Veterans' benefits
Welfare payments
Workers' compensation

Self-Study Problem 2.1   *See Appendix E for Solutions to Self-Study Problems*

Indicate whether each of the items listed below should be included in gross income or excluded from gross income in 2019.

	Included	*Excluded*
1. Prizes and awards	_____	_____
2. Embezzled funds	_____	_____
3. Child support payments	_____	_____
4. Alimony	_____	_____
5. Pensions	_____	_____
6. Inheritances	_____	_____
7. Welfare payments	_____	_____
8. Bequests	_____	_____
9. Jury duty fees	_____	_____
10. Royalties	_____	_____
11. Life insurance proceeds paid at death	_____	_____
12. Hobby income	_____	_____
13. Rewards	_____	_____
14. Partnership income	_____	_____
15. Casualty insurance proceeds	_____	_____
16. G.I. Bill benefits	_____	_____
17. Scholarships for room and board	_____	_____
18. Business income	_____	_____
19. Gifts	_____	_____

Learning Objective 2.2

Describe salaries and wages income reporting and inclusion in gross income.

2-2 SALARIES AND WAGES

Serving as an employee of a company is the most common way to earn income in the United States. More than 80 percent of all individual income tax returns include some amount of wage income, and wages represent approximately 70 percent of the adjusted gross income reported. Payments in almost any form, including salaries and wages, from an employer to an employee are considered income. The primary form of reporting wages to an employee is through Form W-2. An employee should receive a Form W-2 from an employer providing information about the wages paid to that employee during the year (the employer's responsibilities with Form W-2 are examined in Chapter 9). Figure 2.1 presents a Form W-2 for 2019.

Box 1 of Form W-2 is where employers should report taxable wages, salary, bonuses, awards, commissions, and almost every other type of taxable compensation. In most instances, the amount in Box 1 is reported directly on Line 1 of Form 1040, Wages, salaries, tips, etc. If a taxpayer receives more than one Form W-2 or is jointly filing with a spouse having their own Form W-2, the amounts in Box 1 are combined before entering on Line 1 of Form 1040.

EXAMPLE   Bonnie and Clyde are married and file jointly. In 2019, Bonnie received two Forms W-2 from two separate employers reporting $34,000 of wages on one and $16,500 on the other. In addition, Clyde also received a Form W-2 reporting wages of $23,000 in Box 1. Bonnie and Clyde should report $73,500 ($34,000 + $16,500 + $23,000) on Line 1 of Form 1040 (or Form 1040-SR, if Bonnie or Clyde are age 65 or older). ♦

FIGURE 2.1	**FORM W-2**

a Employee's social security number 791-51-4335	OMB No. 1545-0008	Safe, accurate, FAST! Use IRS e-file	Visit the IRS website at www.irs.gov/efile

b Employer identification number (EIN) 12-3456789		**1** Wages, tips, other compensation 134,627.00	**2** Federal income tax withheld 15,184.00
c Employer's name, address, and ZIP code Ivy Technologies Inc. 436 E. 35 Ave. Gary, IN 46409		**3** Social security wages 132,900.00	**4** Social security tax withheld 8,239.80
		5 Medicare wages and tips 142,627.00	**6** Medicare tax withheld 2,068.09
		7 Social security tips	**8** Allocated tips
d Control number		**9**	**10** Dependent care benefits 5,000.00
e Employee's first name and initial Last name Suff. Eric Hayes 555 E. 81st Street Merrillville, IN 46410		**11** Nonqualified plans	**12a** See instructions for box 12 C	127.00
		13 Statutory employee ☐ Retirement plan ☒ Third-party sick pay ☐	**12b** D	8,000.00
		14 Other	**12c** DD| 12,345.00
			12d	
f Employee's address and ZIP code			

15 State Employer's state ID number IN	00122231001	**16** State wages, tips, etc. 134,627.00	**17** State income tax 4,956.00	**18** Local wages, tips, etc. 134,627.00	**19** Local income tax 987.00	**20** Locality name LAKE

Form **W-2** Wage and Tax Statement   **2019**   Department of the Treasury—Internal Revenue Service

Copy B—To Be Filed With Employee's FEDERAL Tax Return.
This information is being furnished to the Internal Revenue Service.

Box 2 of Form W-2 reports the amount of federal income tax withheld from the taxpayer's wages by the employer for the year. This amount is reported in a fashion similar to that of Box 1 except on Line 17 of Forms 1040 and 1040-SR.

Boxes 3 through 6 report information related to the amount of wages subject to Social Security and Medicare taxes and the related taxes withheld. The amounts generally do not impact the income tax reporting by a taxpayer, although as discussed in Chapter 9, when a taxpayer has multiple employers and the amount of Social Security tax withheld exceeds the annual limits of Social Security taxable wages, the excess is treated as an additional tax payment. Note that the amounts in Box 1 and Boxes 3 and 5 often agree but they are not always the same for all taxpayers. For example, if an employee contributes part of their salary to a qualified retirement plan such as a 401(k) plan, the contribution is not generally subject to income tax but is subject to employment taxes. The amount of taxable wages in Box 1 would be lower than the amounts reported in Boxes 3 and 5 by the retirement plan contribution amount. In addition, wages are subject to Social Security tax up to a limit ($132,900 in 2019) and therefore, Box 3 will not exceed the annual limit.

Box 8 reports allocated tips for amounts not included in Box 1 taxable wages. Box 10 is where flexible spending contributions to a dependent care program are reported (see LO 2.5 for more information). Box 12 is for reporting a variety of different forms of compensation such as reimbursed parking, health care premiums paid by the employer, and other fringe benefits. The type of compensation is identified by the code provided adjacent to the amount in Box 12, as described in the instructions to the Form W-2. Commonly used codes are:

Code	Explanation
C	Taxable group life insurance
D	Elective deferral into 401(k) plans
E	Elective deferral into 403(b) plans
G	Elective deferral into 457(b) plans
V	Income from nonstatutory stock options
W	Contributions to a health savings account
DD	Cost of employer-sponsored health care

The retirement plan box in Box 13 will be checked if the taxpayer is eligible to participate in a retirement plan [and thus may limit the amount of deductible IRA (individual retirement account) contributions]. Box 14 is designated to report other forms of compensation as needed.

State and local tax information is reported at the bottom of Form W-2 in Boxes 15 through 20. This includes the taxable wages for state tax purposes and the amount of state income tax withheld which is generally part of the state and local tax itemized deduction (see Chapter 5).

Self-Study Problem 2.2   See Appendix E for Solutions to Self-Study Problems

a Employee's social security number 232-11-4444	OMB No. 1545-0008	Safe, accurate, FAST! Use	IRS e~file	Visit the IRS website at www.irs.gov/efile

	1 Wages, tips, other compensation 56,000.00	2 Federal income tax withheld 3,456.00
b Employer identification number (EIN) 12-9876543		
c Employer's name, address, and ZIP code	3 Social security wages 61,000.00	4 Social security tax withheld 3,782.00
QBI Company	5 Medicare wages and tips 61,000.00	6 Medicare tax withheld 884.50
4512 Lake Drive	7 Social security tips	8 Allocated tips
Grand Rapids, MI 49503		
d Control number	9	10 Dependent care benefits
e Employee's first name and initial Last name Suff.	11 Nonqualified plans	12a See instructions for box 12 D | 5,000.00
Summer Sandborne	13 Statutory employee ☐ Retirement plan ☒ Third-party sick pay ☐	12b DD | 8,700.00
134 Bostwick Ave NE	14 Other	12c
Grand Rapids, MI 49503		12d
f Employee's address and ZIP code		

15 State Employer's state ID number	16 State wages, tips, etc.	17 State income tax	18 Local wages, tips, etc.	19 Local income tax	20 Locality name
MI |	56,000.00	1,145.00			

Form **W-2** Wage and Tax Statement   **2019**   Department of the Treasury—Internal Revenue Service

Copy B—To Be Filed With Employee's FEDERAL Tax Return.
This information is being furnished to the Internal Revenue Service.

Based on Summer's Form W-2, determine the following amounts:

a.   Taxable wages to report on Line 1   _____

b.   Federal tax payments withheld to report on Line 17   _____

c.   The amount that Summer contributed to her company's 401k plan   _____

TIP

Entering wages from a Form W-2 is one of the most common data entry points for a tax preparer. Predictably, wages are entered under the Income section, more specifically, under Wages, Salaries, Tips (W-2). When selecting the Wages subheading, the entire entry screen for the W-2 is presented in the main window. The subheadings on the left-hand margin slide the entry form up and down for easier entry. Any additional W-2s can be added using the [+] tab at the top of the main window. Although the fictional textbook employers do not have import access, using ProConnect, many W-2s can be imported directly from an employer's payroll system. Enter the employer's identification number and click the circular arrow to import wages data.

2-3 ACCIDENT AND HEALTH INSURANCE

Many taxpayers are covered by accident and health insurance plans. These plans pay for the cost of medical care of the taxpayer and any dependents who are insured under the plan. The taxpayer may pay the total premiums of the plan, or his or her employer may pay part or all of the premiums. Taxpayers are allowed liberal exclusions for payments received from these accident and health plans. The taxpayer may exclude the total amount received for payment of medical care. This exclusion applies to any amount paid for the medical care of the taxpayer, his or her spouse, or dependents. The payment may be made to the doctor, the hospital, or the taxpayer as reimbursement for the payment of the expenses. In addition, any premiums paid by a taxpayer's employer are excluded from the taxpayer's income, and the premium payments may be deducted by the employer.

Most accident and health care policies also pay fixed amounts to the insured for loss of the use of a member or function of the body. These amounts may also be excluded from income. For example, a taxpayer who receives $25,000 because he or she is blinded in one eye may exclude the $25,000 from income.

EXAMPLE Bob is a married taxpayer. His employer pays a $750 per month premium on a policy covering Bob and his family. Jean, Bob's wife, is sick during the year and her medical bills amount to $6,500; the insurance company paid $6,000 for the bills. Bob and Jean may exclude from income the $750 per month premium paid by Bob's employer and the $6,000 paid by the insurance company. The $500 not paid by the insurance company is deductible on Bob and Jean's return, subject to the medical expense deduction limitations (see Chapter 5). ◆

Self-Study Problem 2.3 *See Appendix E for Solutions to Self-Study Problems*

Marjorie, a single taxpayer, is an employee of Big State Corporation. Big State Corporation pays premiums of $3,000 on her health insurance for the current year. Also, during the current year, Marjorie has an operation for which the insurance company pays $5,000 to her hospital and doctor. Of the above amounts, how much must Marjorie include in her gross income?

$_____

2-4 MEALS AND LODGING

If certain tests are met, employers may exclude the value of meals and lodging from an employee's taxable income. The exclusion is granted for any meals and lodging furnished by the employer for the convenience of the employer, but only if:

1. The meals are furnished on the business premises of the employer during working hours because the taxpayer must be available for emergency calls or the employer limits the employee to short meal periods, and
2. The lodging is on the business premises and must be accepted as a requirement for employment.

To exclude the value of lodging provided by the employer, the employee must be required to accept the lodging to perform the duties of the job properly. For example, a taxpayer who receives lodging on an offshore oil rig may exclude the value of the lodging from income, since the employee cannot go home at night. The exclusion for lodging also includes the value of utilities such as electricity, water, heat, gas, and similar items that make the lodging habitable.

The value of meals or lodging provided by the employer in other situations, and cash allowances for meals or lodging, must be included in the employee's gross income. Starting in 2018, the business that pays the costs for meals provided for the convenience of an employee may only deduct 50 percent of those costs (the deduction is eliminated after 2025).

Self-Study Problem 2.4   *See Appendix E for Solutions to Self-Study Problems*

In each of the following independent cases, indicate whether the value of the meals or lodging should be included in or excluded from the taxpayer's income.

	Included	Excluded
1. A waiter is required to eat lunch, furnished by his employer, on the premises during a busy lunch hour.	_____	_____
2. A police officer receives a cash allowance to pay for meals while on duty.	_____	_____
3. A worker receives lodging at a remote construction site in Alaska.	_____	_____
4. A taxpayer manages a motel and, although the owner does not require it, she lives at the motel rent free.	_____	_____
5. A bank teller is furnished meals on the premises to limit the time she is away during busy hours.	_____	_____

Learning Objective 2.5

Identify the common employee fringe benefit income exclusions.

2-5 EMPLOYEE FRINGE BENEFITS

The tax law provides that all fringe benefits must be included in the employee's gross income, unless specifically excluded by law. The primary types of fringe benefits that may be excluded from gross income are described below.

2-5a Flexible Spending Accounts

Many employers create formal plans that allow employees to contribute pre-tax money to a special account from their wages to pay for one or more of the expenses listed below. If all the requirements of the plan are met and the employee provides receipts for the expenses incurred, the full amount of expenses reimbursed out of the employee's account will be treated as a tax-free reduction in salary. These accounts may provide significant tax savings for employees, with only a small administrative cost to employers.

EXAMPLE   In 2019, Dina has wage income of $43,000 and elects to defer $2,000 into a health care flexible spending account. She uses all $2,000 of the money for qualifying medical expenses in 2019. Dina's taxable income will be $41,000. The $2,000 is excluded from her income as long as she uses the funds for qualifying medical expenses. ◆

Employees must be aware, however, of the "use-it-or-lose-it" rule for flexible spending accounts (e.g., any balance remaining in the employee's account at December 31 is lost). For health care flexible spending accounts, employers have the option to allow $500 of the unused medical spending account to carry over to the next year or to offer a $2\frac{1}{2}$-month grace period after year-end to incur additional medical expenses before the employee loses the balance in the account.

Dependent Care Flexible Spending Accounts

Employers may offer dependent care flexible spending accounts (FSAs) in which employees may set aside up to $5,000 of their salary each year to cover the costs of caring for a dependent child or aging parent. Such costs may include day care, day camp, in-home care and preschool. Dependent care benefits paid will be reported in Box 10 of Form W-2 and are reported on Form 2441 with the Child and Dependent Care Credit. See Chapter 7 for more information.

Health Care Flexible Spending Accounts

Employers may offer health care flexible spending accounts in which employees can set aside up to $2,700 from their 2019 salary to cover medical expenses that they anticipate incurring during the year. These expenses may include eyeglasses, laser-eye surgery, necessary dental work, and health insurance copayments. Amounts used from a health care FSA may not also be deducted as an itemized deduction for medical expenses (see Chapter 5). Health care FSAs should not be confused with Archer medical spending accounts (MSAs) or health savings accounts (HSAs) which are covered in Chapter 5.

Public Transportation, Parking at Work, and Bicycle Commuting

Employees can exclude from gross income payments from employers of up to $265 per month in 2019 (the maximum exclusion is adjusted for inflation) to cover the cost of public transportation to, or parking for, work. However, starting in 2018, employers may not deduct these payments to the extent they are excluded from the employee's income; thus effectively removing transportation and parking as a qualified fringe benefit. In cases where the employee is being reimbursed transportation or parking costs that are necessary to ensure the safety of the employee, those costs remain deductible. The bicycle commuter fringe is suspended until 2025. Employers may continue to establish a plan whereby an employee's own pre-tax salary is used to pay for public transportation costs and parking up to the exclusion limits. By doing so, these costs are paid for by the employee using pre-tax dollars as the withheld wages used to cover these costs are not subject to income or employment taxes.

2-5b Group Term Life Insurance

Employers may pay for up to $50,000 of group term life insurance for employees as a tax-free fringe benefit. Providing group term life insurance to employees must not favor officers, shareholders, or highly compensated personnel.

Internal Revenue Code §79 was first passed in 1964 and provided the exclusion of employer paid group term life insurance premiums up to $50,000. The $50,000 limit has not been adjusted since originally passed into law. In today's dollars, you would need almost $400,000 to equal $50,000 in 1964. The National Funeral Directors Association estimated the average cost of a funeral in 1965 as $790 and almost $7,400 in 2017.

2-5c Education Assistance Plans

Employers may provide up to $5,250 of excludable annual tuition assistance under an educational assistance plan. The exclusion requires an employer to have a written plan and the educational assistance can be paid to an employee or former employee. Assistance over $5,250 is included in the taxpayer's wages unless otherwise excludable as a working condition benefit that would have been deductible as a business expense (see Chapter 3).

Section 127 of the Code introduced the education assistance plan in 1979. In 1985, the $5,000 exclusion limit was increased to $5,250. According to the College Board, average tuition and fees for a public four-year college in the 1985–1986 school year was $1,318. In 2018–2019, that amount had increased to $9,980. Today's exclusion is unlikely to pay for even a single year of college tuition. Source: **www.collegeboard.org**

2-5d No-Additional-Cost Services

This category of fringe benefits includes services that are provided to employees and their families at little or no additional cost to the employer, and which would otherwise have remained unused. An airline employee who is allowed to fly at no cost on a standby basis is an example. The value of the airfare may be excluded from the employee's gross income.

Employees are only allowed to receive tax-free services in the major line of business in which they are employed. For example, if an airline company also owns a rental car agency, the employees working in the airline division would not be entitled to the tax-free use of rental cars.

2-5e Qualified Employee Discounts

The value of employee discounts may be excluded from gross income if the discounts are available on a nondiscriminatory basis. That is, the discounts must be available to substantially all full-time employees. The item being discounted must be from the line of business in which the employee is engaged. The discount exclusion also does not apply to discounts on real estate or personal property held for investment. For services provided at a discount, the exclusion is limited to 20% of the typical customer price. For merchandise, the exclusion is limited to the employer's gross markup on the goods.

EXAMPLE   R.J. works for an auto parts store chain. R.J. purchases a new water pump for her car at the employee discounted price of $26. Normally, the part would be sold for $41. R.J.'s employer's cost for the part is $26. Because R.J.'s cost is not less than the cost of the part to her employer, the discount is within the exemption and is not taxable to R.J. ♦

2-5f Working Condition Fringe Benefits

An employee may exclude the value of property or services provided by an employer to the extent that the cost of the property or services would be a deductible expense of the employee. Examples of this type of exclusion include the use of a company car for business (not personal) purposes and a subscription to a tax journal paid for by a CPA firm. The working condition fringe benefit rules also allow several expenses which would not be deductible if paid by the employee. These include the value of certain employer-provided education and certain use of demonstrator autos by automobile salespeople.

2-5g De Minimis Fringe Benefits

The value of small fringe benefits may be excluded from an employee's gross income if accounting for the benefits would be impractical. Examples of this type of exclusion include occasional personal use of an office copy machine, personal letters typed by a company administrative assistant, a company picnic for the employees, and small non-cash holiday gifts provided to employees (e.g., a Christmas turkey).

If an employer provides a subsidized lunchroom for its employees, the value of the meals may be excluded from the employees' income if (1) the facility is on or near the employer's place of business, (2) the revenue from the lunchroom normally exceeds direct operating costs, and (3) the meals are provided without discrimination to all employees. Starting in 2018, the tax law limits the employer's deduction related to the eating facility to only

50 percent of the cost. Upon the expiration of the provision in 2025, the tax law permits no deduction for such costs.

Cell phones provided to employees primarily for business purposes are considered tax-free de minimis fringe benefits. Examples of cell phones which qualify include those provided to allow employees to communicate with clients, or to allow employers to contact employees in the field or at home.

2-5h **Tuition Reduction**

All employees of educational institutions may exclude from their income the value of a tuition reduction, if the plan is for an undergraduate education and available to all employees. The exclusion applies to the employees, their spouses, and their dependents. The value of a graduate education tuition reduction plan may only be excluded by graduate students of the institution who are teaching or doing research at that institution.

2-5i **Athletic Facilities**

Employees may exclude from gross income the value of the use of an athletic facility located on the premises of their employer. The facility must be used primarily by employees.

2-5j **Retirement Planning Fringe Benefit**

Qualified retirement planning services constitute a fringe benefit that is excluded from income. This change was made to encourage employers to provide retirement planning services for their employees to assist them in preparing for retirement. Qualified retirement planning services are any retirement planning services provided to an employee and his or her spouse by an employer maintaining a "qualified employer plan." The exclusion also applies to advice and information on retirement income planning for an individual and his or her spouse, including how the employer's plan fits into the individual's overall retirement income plan. The exclusion, however, does not apply to services that may be related to tax preparation, accounting, legal, or brokerage services.

EXAMPLE As part of its qualified plan, Linda's employer provides retirement planning services. Linda has a meeting with a financial planner to review her retirement plan. The cost of the meeting ($600) is paid for by her employer's qualified plan. The $600 is not income to Linda and is deductible to the employer. ◆

A summary of various fringe benefits is provided in Table 2.3.

Self-Study Problem 2.5   *See Appendix E for Solutions to Self-Study Problems*

Indicate in each of the following cases whether the value of the employee fringe benefit is included (I) in or excluded (E) from the employee's gross income.

_____ 1. An employee of a railroad receives a free train-trip pass.

_____ 2. An employee of a department store receives a 25 percent discount on a shirt. The department store's markup is 15 percent.

_____ 3. An employee attends a New Year's party paid for by her employer.

_____ 4. An employee of a stock brokerage firm receives a subscription to a financial newsletter paid for by his employer.

_____ 5. An employee's wife regularly uses a company car to go shopping.

_____ 6. An airline employee receives a 50 percent discount at a hotel chain owned by her employer while traveling on vacation.

_____ 7. An employee uses the company's employee fitness room.

TABLE 2.3   SUMMARY OF FRINGE BENEFITS

Type of Fringe	Summary of Treatment	Learning Objective
Accident and Health Benefits	Exempt except for long-term care provided through a flexible spending arrangement	2.3, 2.5
Achievement Awards	Exempt up to $1,600 for qualified plan awards ($400 for nonqualified)	2.6
Adoption Assistance	Exempt up to $14,080	7.7
Athletic Facilities	Exempt if substantially all use is by employees and families and operated on employer's premises	2.5
De Minimis Benefits	Exempt if property or service provided to employee has so little value that accounting for it would be unreasonable or administratively impracticable (never cash and cash equivalents)	2.5
Dependent Care Assistance	Exempt up to $5,000	2.5
Educational Assistance	Exempt up to $5,250	2.5
Employee Discounts	Exempt with certain limits	2.5
Employee Stock Options	Beyond scope of textbook	
Employer-provided cell phones	Exempt if primarily for business purposes	2.5
Group-term Life Insurance	Exempt up to $50,000	2.5
Health Savings Accounts (HSA)	Exempt up to certain limits	5.1
Lodging on Business Premises	Exempt if for convenience as a condition of employment	2.4
Meals	Exempt if furnished on premises for convenience or de minimis	2.4
Moving Expenses	Exempt if otherwise deductible and related to military service	5.5
No-additional-cost Services	Exempt	2.5
Retirement Planning Services	Exempt	2.5
Transportation (Commuting) Benefits	Exempt up to $265 per month for parking and transit passes and exempt if de minimis	2.5
Tuition Reduction	Exempt if undergraduate or if graduate and employee performs teaching or research	2.5
Working Condition Benefits	Exempt	2.5

Source: Adapted from IRS Publication 15-B.

2-6 PRIZES AND AWARDS

Determine when prizes and awards are included in income.

Prizes and awards are taxable income to the recipient. Winnings from television or radio shows, door prizes, lotteries, and other contest winnings are income to taxpayers. In addition, all other awards are generally taxable, even if they are awards given for accomplishments and with no action on the part of the taxpayer. Even a Nobel prize is taxable. If the prize or award is received in property instead of cash, the fair market value of the property is included in the taxpayer's income. For example, the gift bags given to the attendees at the Academy Awards include items such as expensive jewelry and vacations worth more than $100,000. The value of these gift bags is included in taxable income. Taxpayers may refuse a prize and exclude its value from income.

An exception is provided for certain employee achievement awards in the form of tangible personal property, such as a gold watch for 25 years of service. If the award is made in recognition of length of service or safety achievement, the value of the property may be excluded from income. Generally, the maximum amount excludable is $400. However, if the award is a "qualified plan award," the maximum exclusion is increased to $1,600. The definition of tangible personal property with respect to employee achievement awards excludes cash, cash equivalents, gift cards, gift coupons, gift certificates, vacations, meals, lodging, tickets to theater or sporting events, stocks, bonds, other securities, and other similar items.

In late 2013, a Washington state resident won the largest single-day game show prize—an Audi R8 sports car valued at $157,000. Assuming a California tax rate of 9.3 percent (the show is filmed in Los Angeles, and Washington state has no individual income tax) and a federal rate of 26 percent (adjusted for state taxes), the income tax bill alone is over $55,000. The estimate to pay taxes to register the car in her home town are almost $15,000 for a total tax bill of $70,000. The taxes can make the price feel not quite so right!

Would You Believe?

EXAMPLE Van enters a drawing and wins a new automobile. The automobile has a sticker price of $20,200. The fair market value of the prize should be included in Van's gross income, but the fair market value is probably not the sticker price; instead, it is the price at which a similar car normally would be sold. ♦

Self-Study Problem 2.6 *See Appendix E for Solutions to Self-Study Problems*

For each of the following independent cases, indicate the amount of gross income that should be included on the taxpayer's return.

Gross Income

1. Helen enters a radio contest and wins $2,000. $_____

2. Professor Deborah wins an award of $10,000 for a book on literature she published 4 years ago. The award was presented in recognition of her past literary achievements. $_____

3. Bill is a professional baseball player. Because he has hit 50 home runs this season, he was given a new wrist watch worth $2,500. $_____

4. John is an employee of Big Corporation. He is awarded $5,000 for a suggestion to improve the plant layout. $_____

5. Martha received a desk clock worth $350 from her employer in recognition of her 15 years of loyal service as an employee. $_____

2-7 ANNUITIES

2.7 Learning Objective

Calculate the taxable and nontaxable portions of annuity payments.

When taxpayers consider retirement, they often purchase annuities. An annuity is a type of investment in which the taxpayer purchases the right to receive periodic payments for the remainder of his or her life. The amount of each periodic payment is based on the annuity purchase price and the life expectancy of the annuitant. Standard mortality tables, based on the current age of the annuitant, are used to calculate the annuity amount.

2-7a **The Simplified Method**

Individual taxpayers generally must use the "simplified" method to calculate the taxable amount from an annuity for annuities starting after November 18, 1996. Nonqualified plan annuities and certain annuitants age 75 or older must still use the general rule discussed below.

To calculate the excluded amount, the IRS provides the following worksheet.

SIMPLIFIED METHOD WORKSHEET

1. Enter total amount received this year.   1. _____

2. Enter cost in the plan at the annuity starting date.   2. _____

3. Age at annuity starting date

	Enter
55 or under	360
56–60	310
61–65	260
66–70	210
71 or older	160

3. _____

4. Divide line 2 by line 3.   4. _____

5. Multiply line 4 by the number of monthly payments this   5. _____
   year. If the annuity starting date was before 1987, also
   enter this amount on line 8, and skip lines 6 and 7.
   Otherwise, go to line 6.

6. Enter the amount, if any, recovered tax free in prior years.   6. _____

7. Subtract line 6 from line 2.   7. _____

8. Enter the smaller of line 5 or 7.   8. _____

9. Taxable amount this year: Subtract line 8 from line 1. Do   9. _____
   not enter less than zero.

Note 1: The denominators provided in step 3 above are effective for annuity starting dates after November 18, 1996. For annuity starting dates prior to November 18, 1996, see the IRS website.

Note 2: When annuity benefits with starting dates after 1997 are paid over two lives (joint and survivor annuities), a different set of denominators must be used in step 3.

Combined Age of Annuitants	**Number of Payments**
110 or under	410
111–120	360
121–130	310
131–140	260
141 or older	210

EXAMPLE   Joey, age 67, began receiving benefits under a joint and survivor annuity to be paid over the joint lives of himself and his wife Jody, who is 64. He received his first annuity payment in March of the current year. Joey contributed $38,000 to the annuity and he had no distributions from the plan before the current year. The monthly payment to Joey is $1,700.

Joey must use the simplified method to calculate his taxable amount. Using the worksheet, Joey's taxable amount for the current year would be:

SIMPLIFIED METHOD WORKSHEET

1. Enter total amount received this year.   1. _$17,000.00_

2. Enter cost in the plan at the annuity starting date.   2. _$38,000.00_

3. Combined age at annuity starting date

	Enter
110 or under	410
111–120	360
121–130	310
131–140	260
141 or older	210

3. _____260_____

4. Divide line 2 by line 3.   4. $ ___146.15___

5. Multiply line 4 by the number of monthly payments this year.   5. $ _1,461.50_

6. Enter the amount, if any, recovered tax free in prior years.   6. $ ___0.00___

7. Subtract line 6 from line 2.   7. _$38,000.00_

8. Enter the smaller of line 5 or 7.   8. $ _1,461.50_

9. Taxable amount this year: Subtract line 8 from line 1. Do not enter less than zero. ◆   9. _$15,538.50_

The exclusion ratio (the result on line 4 of the Simplified Method Worksheet) is calculated at the start of the annuity and remains constant. For annuities starting after 1986, the maximum amount excludable is limited to the taxpayer's investment in the annuity. After the taxpayer's investment is recovered, all additional amounts received are fully taxable. If the taxpayer dies before the entire investment is recovered, any unrecovered amount is permitted as a miscellaneous itemized deduction (not subject to the 2 percent floor) at the time of the annuitant's death. For annuities starting before 1987, the exclusion ratio is used for the life of the annuitant, even after full recovery of the investment. For these earlier annuities, if the annuitant dies prior to recovering the entire investment, the unrecovered portion is lost.

2-7b The General Rule

Prior to implementation of the Simplified Method discussed above, the General Rule was used for most annuities. Rather than use the denominators provided in Step 3 of the Simplified Method Worksheet, the life expectancy of the annuitant was determined based on mortality tables provided by the IRS. The excluded amount under the general rule can be calculated as follows:

$$\text{Amount Excluded} = \frac{\text{Investment in Contract}}{\text{Annual Payment} \times \text{Life Expectancy}} \times \text{Amount Received}$$

2-7c **Employee Annuities**

Many employees participate in retirement plans organized by their employers. Employers generally make periodic payments to the plans on behalf of their employees. If the payments are made to qualified retirement plans, contributions by the employer are not taxable to the employees in the current year. Since the contributions are not taxable when made, they are not considered part of the employee's investment in the contract when calculating the exclusion ratio.

Self-Study Problem 2.7   *See Appendix E for Solutions to Self-Study Problems*

Part a

Phil retired in January 2019 at age 63. His pension is $1,500 per month from a retirement plan to which Phil contributed $42,500. Phil's life expectancy is 21 years, and this year he received eleven payments for a total pension income of $16,500. Calculate Phil's taxable income from the annuity in the current year, using the general rule.

$_____

Part b

Calculate Phil's taxable income using the following Simplified Method Worksheet.

SIMPLIFIED METHOD WORKSHEET

1. Enter total amount received this year.   1. _____

2. Enter cost in the plan at the annuity starting date.   2. _____

3. Age at annuity starting date

	Enter
55 or under	360
56–60	310
61–65	260
66–70	210
71 or older	160

3. _____

4. Divide line 2 by line 3.   4. _____

5. Multiply line 4 by the number of monthly payments this year. If the annuity starting date was before 1987, also enter this amount on line 8, and skip lines 6 and 7. Otherwise, go to line 6.   5. _____

6. Enter the amount, if any, recovered tax free in prior years.   6. _____

7. Subtract line 6 from line 2.   7. _____

8. Enter the smaller of line 5 or 7.   8. _____

9. Taxable amount this year: Subtract line 8 from line 1. Do not enter less than zero.   9. _____

2-8 **LIFE INSURANCE**

2.8 Learning Objective

Describe the tax treatment of life insurance proceeds.

Life insurance proceeds are excluded from gross income based on the premise that it would be inappropriate in a time of need to tax the proceeds from a life insurance policy. Therefore, a major exclusion from gross income is provided for life insurance proceeds. To be excluded, the proceeds must be paid to the beneficiary by reason of the death of the insured. If the proceeds are taken over several years instead of a lump sum, the insurance company pays interest on the unpaid proceeds. The interest is generally taxable income.

Early payouts of life insurance, also called accelerated death benefits or viatical settlements, are excluded from gross income for certain terminally or chronically ill taxpayers. The taxpayer may either collect an early payout from the insurance company or sell or assign the policy to a viatical settlement provider. A terminally ill individual must be certified by a medical doctor to have an illness which is reasonably expected to cause death within 24 months. A chronically ill individual must be certified by a medical doctor as unable to perform daily living activities without assistance. Chronically ill taxpayers may only exclude gain on accelerated death benefits to the extent proceeds are used for long-term care.

If an insurance policy is transferred to another person for valuable consideration, all or a portion of the proceeds from the life insurance policy may be taxable to the recipient. For example, taxable proceeds result when a policy is transferred to a creditor in payment of a debt. When a transfer for value occurs, the proceeds at the death of the insured are taxable to the extent they exceed the cash surrender value of the policy at the time it was transferred, plus the amount of the insurance premiums paid by the purchaser. There is an exception to the rule that policies transferred for valuable consideration result in taxable proceeds. Transfers to a partner of the insured, a partnership in which the insured is a partner, or a corporation in which the insured is an officer or a shareholder do not cause the policy proceeds to be taxable.

EXAMPLE   Howard dies on January 15, 2016, and leaves Wanda, his wife, a $50,000 insurance policy, the proceeds of which she elects to receive as $10,000 per year plus interest for 5 years. In the current year, Wanda receives $12,200 ($10,000 + $2,200 interest). She must include the $2,200 of interest in income. ◆

EXAMPLE   David owns a life insurance policy at the time he is diagnosed with a terminal illness. After his diagnosis, he sells the policy to Viatical Settlements, Inc., for $100,000. David is not required to include the gain on the sale of the insurance in his gross income. ◆

EXAMPLE   Amy transfers to Bill an insurance policy with a face value of $40,000 and a cash surrender value of $10,000 for the cancellation of a debt owed to Bill. Bill continues to make payments, and after 2 years Bill has paid $2,000 in premiums. Amy dies and Bill collects the $40,000. Since the transfer was for valuable consideration, Bill must include $28,000 in taxable income, which is equal to the $40,000 total proceeds less $10,000 value at the time of transfer and $2,000 of premiums paid. If Amy and Bill were partners in the same partnership, the entire proceeds ($40,000) would be tax free. ◆

Self-Study Problem 2.8   *See Appendix E for Solutions to Self-Study Problems*

On March 19, 2014, Karen dies and leaves Larry an insurance policy with a face value of $100,000. Karen is Larry's sister, and Larry elects to take the proceeds over 10 years ($10,000 plus interest each year). This year Larry receives $13,250 from the insurance company. How much income must Larry report for the current year?

$_____

2-9 INTEREST AND DIVIDEND INCOME

Identify the tax treatment of interest and dividend income.

Any interest or dividend income a taxpayer receives or that is credited to his or her account is taxable income, unless it is specifically exempt from tax such as state or municipal bond interest (discussed further in LO 2.10). If the interest or dividends total more than $1,500, the taxpayer is required to file Schedule B of Form 1040, which instructs the taxpayer to list the amounts and sources of the income.

The fair market value of gifts or services a taxpayer receives for making long-term deposits or opening accounts in savings institutions is also taxable interest income. Interest is reported in the year it is received by a cash basis taxpayer.

TAX BREAK

Taxpayers may defer reporting interest income on a bank certificate of deposit (CD) if the CD has a maturity of 1 year or less and there is a substantial penalty for early withdrawal. For example, assume an investor purchases a 6-month CD on September 1, 2019, which matures on March 1, 2020, and the bank charges a penalty equal to 2 months of interest in the event of early withdrawal. In this case, the 4 months of interest earned on the account during 2019 will not have to be reported until the investor's 2020 tax return is filed.

When a taxpayer withdraws funds early from a CD and must pay a penalty as described above, the full amount of the interest is reported as income and the penalty may be deducted on Form 1040 as a deduction for adjusted gross income.

2-9a U.S. Savings Bonds

The U.S. government issues three basic types of savings bonds to individuals: Series EE Bonds, Series HH Bonds, and Series I Bonds. Series EE Bonds, whether sold at a discount (before 2012) or at face value, increase in value over their life, and the increase in redemption value is generally taxable when the bond is redeemed and the interest is paid. The second type of savings bond, Series HH Bond, was issued at face value and pays interest twice a year. Interest on Series HH Bonds is reported in the year received by a cash basis taxpayer. (Note: As of August 31, 2004, the Treasury stopped issuing Series HH bonds. HH bonds sold before August 31, 2004, are still outstanding and paying interest.) Series I Bonds, like Series EE Bonds, do not pay interest until maturity, but earnings are adjusted for inflation on a semiannual basis.

Cash basis taxpayers report the increase in redemption value (interest) on a Series EE Bond or a Series I Bond using one of the following methods:

1. The interest may be reported in the year the bonds are cashed or in the year they mature, whichever is earlier (no election is required to use this method), or
2. The taxpayer may elect to report the increase in redemption value each year.

If the taxpayer wants to change from method (1) to method (2), he or she may do so without the permission of the IRS. In the year of change, all interest earned to date and not previously reported must be reported on all Series EE Bonds and Series I Bonds held by the taxpayer. Once method (2) is selected, the taxpayer must continue to use it for all Series EE Bonds currently held or acquired in the future. Taxpayers cannot change back to method (1) without permission of the IRS.

Schedule B of Form 1040 has been around for a long time—the first version appeared as part of the Form 1040 in 1950. The dollar threshold of interest or dividends to require a Schedule B was at $400 in 1974. It was changed to $1,500 in 2002 and remains at that same amount today. Using the Consumer Price Index Inflation Calculator (**www.bls.gov/data/inflation_calculator.htm**), you would need about $2,100 to equal the purchasing power of $400 in 1974.

2-9b Dividends

Dividends are a type of distribution paid to a shareholder by a corporation. Taxpayers may receive the following types of distributions from a corporation:

1. Ordinary and qualified dividends
2. Nontaxable distributions
3. Capital gain distributions

Ordinary dividends are by far the most common type of corporate distribution. They are paid from the earnings and profits of the corporation. Ordinary dividends are also qualifying dividends if the stock is held for a certain amount of time (generally 60 days) and the dividend is issued by a U.S. corporation. If the ordinary dividends are not qualifying dividends, then instead of being taxed at the lower long-term capital gains rate, they will be taxed at the ordinary income rate. Corporations issuing dividends and brokerage companies holding stock investments for taxpayers are required to classify and report the amount of qualifying dividends to investors.

Nontaxable distributions are a return of invested capital and are not paid from the earnings and profits of the corporation. They are considered a return of the taxpayer's investment in the corporation and are not included in the taxpayer's income. Instead, the taxpayer's basis in the stock is reduced by nontaxable distributions until the basis reaches zero.[1] After the stock has reached a zero basis, distributions that represent a return of capital are taxed as capital gains. Capital gain distributions are reported on Line 6 of Forms 1040 or 1040-SR or Schedule D, Line 13 (if required otherwise).

2-9c Current Tax Rates for Dividends

For years, experts have argued that corporate dividends are taxed twice, once when the corporation pays tax on profits, and once when the dividend is received by the shareholder. To provide some tax relief for individual taxpayers who receive corporate dividends, the tax rates on qualifying dividends are lower than the rates for ordinary income.

Income level	Qualified dividends and long-term capital gains rates*
Married filing jointly	
$0–$78,750	0%
$78,751–$488,850	15%
>$488,850	20%
Single	
$0–$39,375	0%
$39,376–$434,550	15%
>$434,550	20%
Head of household	
$0–$52,750	0%
$52,751–$461,700	15%
>$461,700	20%

*An additional 3.8 percent Medicare tax on net investment income, including qualifying dividends, applies to high-income taxpayers with income over certain thresholds. Please see Chapter 6 for further details.

[1]A taxpayer's basis in an investment is usually the cost of the investment. The basis is used to determine the gain or loss when the investment is sold.

Note that the break points between 0 and 15 percent for qualified dividends and long-term capital gains rates are similar to but not the same as the ordinary rate brackets for the same filing status. For example, the single ordinary income rate bracket breaks between 12 and 22 percent at $39,475; whereas the dividend/capital gain rate breaks at $39,375.

EXAMPLE   Sandra is a single taxpayer with wage income of $42,000 and qualified dividends of $1,000 in 2019. Assume Sandra has no other deductions or income except the standard deduction. Sandra's taxable income is:

Wage income	$42,000
Qualified dividends	1,000
Standard deduction	(12,200)
Exemption (suspended by TCJA)	0
Taxable income	$30,800

Sandra's income now must be separated into the ordinary and qualified dividends portions:

Taxable income	$30,800
Qualified dividends	(1,000)
Ordinary income	$29,800

The 2019 tax on $29,800 of ordinary income is $3,385. As Sarah's taxable income of $30,800 including the long-term gain is below $39,375, the threshold for 0 percent qualified dividend and long-term capital gains for a single taxpayer in 2019, her dividend tax rate is 0 percent and thus her total tax liability is $3,385. ◆

EXAMPLE   Dee is a single taxpayer with wage income of $44,000 and qualified dividends of $8,000 in 2019. Assume Dee has no other deductions or income except the standard deduction. Dee's taxable income is

Wage income	$44,000
Qualified dividends	8,000
Standard deduction	(12,200)
Exemption (repealed by TCJA)	0
Taxable income	$39,800

Dee's income now must be separated into the ordinary and qualified dividend and long-term capital gain portions:

Taxable income	$39,800
Qualified dividends	(8,000)
Ordinary income	$31,800

The 2019 tax on $31,800 of ordinary income is $3,625. Dee's taxable income without the qualified dividends is below the 15 percent threshold of $39,375 for a single taxpayer in 2019, but her taxable income with qualified dividends of $39,800 is above the threshold; thus a part of the qualified dividend will be taxed at 0 percent and a part at 15 percent. Of her $8,000 qualified dividends, $7,575 is below the $39,375 threshold and is taxed at 0 percent while $425 is above the $39,375 threshold and is taxed at 15 percent for an additional tax of $64 to bring Dee's total tax liability to $3,689. The treatment of Dee's ordinary and qualified dividend income is presented in Figure 2.2.

FIGURE 2.2 **TAX RATES FOR QUALIFIED DIVIDENDS AND LONG-TERM CAPITAL GAINS**

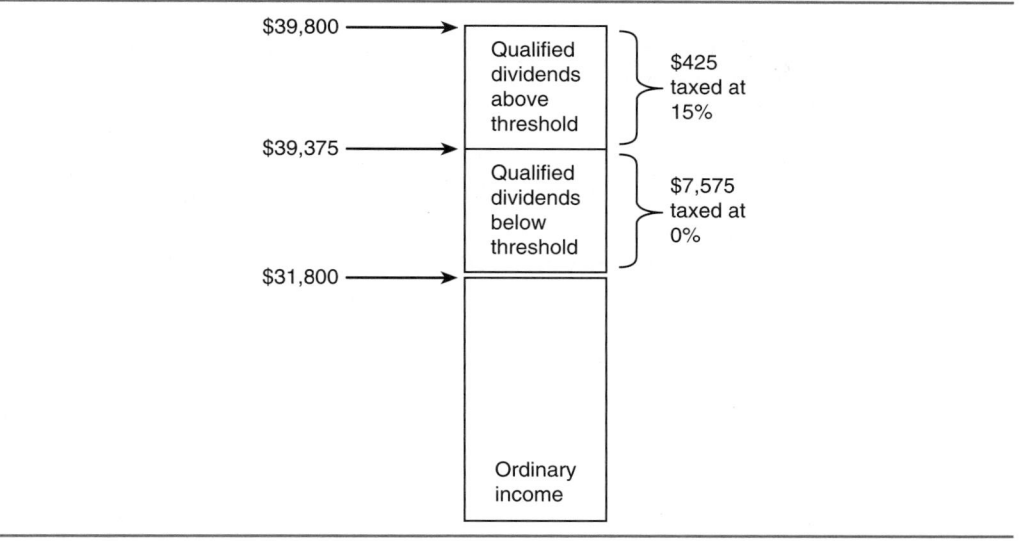

In order to assist with the calculation of preferential taxes on qualified dividends and long-term capital gains, the IRS provides the Qualified Dividends and Capital Gain Tax Worksheet as part of the Form 1040 instructions. This worksheet is presented on Page 2-24. ♦

2-9d Reporting Interest and Dividend Income

Generally, interest or dividend income in amounts greater than $10 must be reported by the payor to the recipient on a Form 1099-INT or Form 1099-DIV. These two forms are presented as part of Self-Study Problem 2-9.

On the Form 1099-INT, most taxable interest is reported in Box 1. The penalty for early withdrawal from a deposit account is reported in Box 2 and is generally deductible as a for AGI deduction (see Chapter 5). Because states may not tax interest from U.S. government obligations such as Treasury Bills, Treasury Bonds, and U.S. savings bonds, interest from these items is reported in Box 3. Tax-exempt interest is reported in Box 8 and to the extent the payor withheld income tax, that amount is reported in Box 4 and should be included with the total withholding on Line 17 of Form 1040. Taxable interest from each payor is reported on Schedule B (shown on Page 2-23) if interest totals more than $1,500 or is simply totaled on Line 2b of Form 1040. Tax-exempt interest is reported on Line 2a of Form 1040 (but not on Schedule B).

Form 1099-DIV reports total ordinary dividends in Box 1a. Box 1b reports the amount of qualified dividends included in Box 1a. These amounts are entered on to Schedule B (if more than $1,500 in total) or directly on to Lines 3a and 3b of Form 1040. Mutual fund investments, and to a lesser degree, corporate stock investments, can also pay capital gain dividends, which are reported in Box 2a of Form 1099-DIV. Unlike ordinary and qualified dividends which are reported by the taxpayer on Schedule B or Form 1040 as described above, capital gain dividends are reported on Schedule D of Form 1040 (see Chapter 4) or if a taxpayer has *only* capital gain distributions reported on Form 1099-DIV, the amount can be reported on Line 6 of Form 1040.

Self-Study Problem 2.9   *See Appendix E for Solutions to Self-Study Problems*

Victor and Grace Alito received the following Forms 1099-INT and 1099-DIV during 2019:

☐ CORRECTED (if checked)

PAYER'S name, street address, city or town, state or province, country, ZIP or foreign postal code, and telephone no. Mango Savings and Loan 600 Tausick Way Walla Walla, WA 99362	Payer's RTN (optional)	OMB No. 1545-0112 20**19** Form **1099-INT**	**Interest Income**
	1 Interest income $ 1,780.00		
	2 Early withdrawal penalty $		Copy B
PAYER'S TIN 13-2122333 RECIPIENT'S TIN 313-44-5454	**3** Interest on U.S. Savings Bonds and Treas. obligations $		For Recipient
RECIPIENT'S name Victor Alito	**4** Federal income tax withheld $	**5** Investment expenses $	This is important tax information and is being furnished to the IRS. If you are required to file a return, a negligence penalty or other sanction may be imposed on you if this income is taxable and the IRS determines that it has not been reported.
Street address (including apt. no.) 1112 Constitution Ave, NW	**6** Foreign tax paid $	**7** Foreign country or U.S. possession	
	8 Tax-exempt interest $	**9** Specified private activity bond interest $	
City or town, state or province, country, and ZIP or foreign postal code Washington, DC 20224	**10** Market discount $	**11** Bond premium $	
FATCA filing requirement ☐	**12** Bond premium on Treasury obligations $	**13** Bond premium on tax-exempt bond $	
Account number (see instructions)	**14** Tax-exempt and tax credit bond CUSIP no.	**15** State **16** State identification no. **17** State tax withheld $ $	

Form **1099-INT**   (keep for your records)   www.irs.gov/Form1099INT   Department of the Treasury - Internal Revenue Service

☐ CORRECTED (if checked)

PAYER'S name, street address, city or town, state or province, country, ZIP or foreign postal code, and telephone no. Grape Large Cap Index Fund 21251 Stevens Creek Road Cupertino, CA 95014	**1a** Total ordinary dividends $ 1,658.00	OMB No. 1545-0110 20**19** Form **1099-DIV**	**Dividends and Distributions**
	1b Qualified dividends $ 1,600.00		
	2a Total capital gain distr. $ 200.00	**2b** Unrecap. Sec. 1250 gain $	Copy B For Recipient
PAYER'S TIN 24-1234567 RECIPIENT'S TIN 313-44-5454	**2c** Section 1202 gain $	**2d** Collectibles (28%) gain $	
RECIPIENT'S name Victor and Grace Alito	**3** Nondividend distributions $	**4** Federal income tax withheld $	This is important tax information and is being furnished to the IRS. If you are required to file a return, a negligence penalty or other sanction may be imposed on you if this income is taxable and the IRS determines that it has not been reported.
	5 Section 199A dividends $	**6** Investment expenses $	
Street address (including apt. no.) 1112 Constitution Avenue, NW	**7** Foreign tax paid $	**8** Foreign country or U.S. possession	
City or town, state or province, country, and ZIP or foreign postal code Washington, DC 20224	**9** Cash liquidation distributions $	**10** Noncash liquidation distributions $	
FATCA filing requirement ☐	**11** Exempt-interest dividends $	**12** Specified private activity bond interest dividends $	
Account number (see instructions)	**13** State **14** State identification no. **15** State tax withheld $ $		

Form **1099-DIV**   (keep for your records)   www.irs.gov/Form1099DIV   Department of the Treasury - Internal Revenue Service

In addition, the Alitos also received $400 of tax-exempt interest. The Alitos file jointly and have taxable income, including interest and dividends of $42,000.

Complete Schedule B of Form 1040 and the Qualified Dividends and Capital Gain Tax Worksheet on Pages 2–23 and 2–24 for the Alito's 2019 tax year.

Self-Study Problem 2.9

SCHEDULE B
(Form 1040 or 1040-SR)

Department of the Treasury
Internal Revenue Service (99)

Interest and Ordinary Dividends

▶ Go to *www.irs.gov/ScheduleB* for instructions and the latest information.
▶ Attach to Form 1040 or 1040-SR.

OMB No. 1545-0074

20**19**

Attachment
Sequence No. **08**

Name(s) shown on return

Your social security number

DRAFT AS OF July 24, 2019 DO NOT FILE

Part I

Interest

(See instructions and the instructions for Forms 1040 and 1040-SR, line 2b.)

Note: If you received a Form 1099-INT, Form 1099-OID, or substitute statement from a brokerage firm, list the firm's name as the payer and enter the total interest shown on that form.

1 List name of payer. If any interest is from a seller-financed mortgage and the buyer used the property as a personal residence, see the instructions and list this interest first. Also, show that buyer's social security number and address ▶

	Amount
1	

2 Add the amounts on line 1 . . . . | **2** | |

3 Excludable interest on series EE and I U.S. savings bonds issued after 1989. Attach Form 8815 . . . | **3** | |

4 Subtract line 3 from line 2. Enter the result here and on Form 1040 or 1040-SR, line 2b . . . . ▶ | **4** | |

Note: If line 4 is over $1,500, you must complete Part III.

Part II

Ordinary Dividends

(See instructions and the instructions for Forms 1040 and 1040-SR, line 3b.)

Note: If you received a Form 1099-DIV or substitute statement from a brokerage firm, list the firm's name as the payer and enter the ordinary dividends shown on that form.

5 List name of payer ▶

	Amount
5	

6 Add the amounts on line 5. Enter the total here and on Form 1040 or 1040-SR, line 3b . . . . ▶ | **6** | |

Note: If line 6 is over $1,500, you must complete Part III.

Part III

Foreign Accounts and Trusts

Caution: If required, failure to file FinCEN Form 114 may result in substantial penalties. See instructions.

You must complete this part if you **(a)** had over $1,500 of taxable interest or ordinary dividends; **(b)** had a foreign account; or **(c)** received a distribution from, or were a grantor of, or a transferor to, a foreign trust.

		Yes	No

7a At any time during 2019, did you have a financial interest in or signature authority over a financial account (such as a bank account, securities account, or brokerage account) located in a foreign country? See instructions . . . .

If "Yes," are you required to file FinCEN Form 114, Report of Foreign Bank and Financial Accounts (FBAR), to report that financial interest or signature authority? See FinCEN Form 114 and its instructions for filing requirements and exceptions to those requirements . . . . . .

b If you are required to file FinCEN Form 114, enter the name of the foreign country where the financial account is located ▶

8 During 2019, did you receive a distribution from, or were you the grantor of, or transferor to, a foreign trust? If "Yes," you may have to file Form 3520. See instructions . . . . . .

For Paperwork Reduction Act Notice, see your tax return instructions.   Cat. No. 17146N   **Schedule B (Form 1040 or 1040-SR) 2019**

Self-Study Problem 2.9

Qualified Dividends and Capital Gain Tax Worksheet—Line 12a

Before you begin: ✓ See the earlier instructions for line 12a to see if you can use this worksheet to figure your tax.
✓ Before completing this worksheet, complete Form 1040 or 1040-SR through line 11b.
✓ If you don't have to file Schedule D and you received capital gain distributions, be sure you checked the box on Form 1040 or 1040-SR, line 6.

1. Enter the amount from Form 1040 or 1040-SR, line 11b. However, if you are filing Form 2555 (relating to foreign earned income), enter the amount from line 3 of the Foreign Earned Income Tax Worksheet .... **1.** _____

2. Enter the amount from Form 1040 or 1040-SR, line 3a* .... **2.** _____

3. Are you filing Schedule D?*
    ☐ **Yes.** Enter the **smaller** of line 15 or 16 of Schedule D. If either line 15 or 16 is blank or a loss, enter -0-.
    ☐ **No.** Enter the amount from Form 1040 or 1040-SR, line 6. **3.** _____

4. Add lines 2 and 3 .... **4.** _____

5. If filing Form 4952 (used to figure investment interest expense deduction), enter any amount from line 4g of that form. Otherwise, enter -0- .... **5.** _____

6. Subtract line 5 from line 4. If zero or less, enter -0- .... **6.** _____

7. Subtract line 6 from line 1. If zero or less, enter -0- .... **7.** _____

8. Enter:
    $39,375 if single or married filing separately,
    $78,750 if married filing jointly or qualifying widow(er),
    $52,750 if head of household. .... **8.** _____

9. Enter the smaller of line 1 or line 8 .... **9.** _____

10. Enter the smaller of line 7 or line 9 .... **10.** _____

11. Subtract line 10 from line 9. This amount is taxed at 0% .... **11.** _____

12. Enter the smaller of line 1 or line 6 .... **12.** _____

13. Enter the amount from line 11 .... **13.** _____

14. Subtract line 13 from line 12 .... **14.** _____

15. Enter:
    $434,550 if single,
    $244,425 if married filing separately,
    $488,850 if married filing jointly or qualifying widow(er),
    $461,700 if head of household. .... **15.** _____

16. Enter the smaller of line 1 or line 15 .... **16.** _____

17. Add lines 7 and 11 .... **17.** _____

18. Subtract line 17 from line 16. If zero or less, enter -0- .... **18.** _____

19. Enter the smaller of line 14 or line 18 .... **19.** _____

20. Multiply line 19 by 15% (0.15) .... **20.** _____

21. Add lines 11 and 19 .... **21.** _____

22. Subtract line 21 from line 12 .... **22.** _____

23. Multiply line 22 by 20% (0.20) .... **23.** _____

24. Figure the tax on the amount on line 7. If the amount on line 7 is less than $100,000, use the Tax Table to figure the tax. If the amount on line 7 is $100,000 or more, use the Tax Computation Worksheet .... **24.** _____

25. Add lines 20, 23, and 24 .... **25.** _____

26. Figure the tax on the amount on line 1. If the amount on line 1 is less than $100,000, use the Tax Table to figure the tax. If the amount on line 1 is $100,000 or more, use the Tax Computation Worksheet .... **26.** _____

27. **Tax on all taxable income.** Enter the **smaller** of line 25 or 26. Also include this amount on the entry space on Form 1040 or 1040-SR, line 12a. If you are filing Form 2555, don't enter this amount on the entry space on Form 1040 or 1040-SR, line 12a. Instead, enter it on line 4 of the Foreign Earned Income Tax Worksheet .... **27.** _____

If you are filing Form 2555, see the footnote in the Foreign Earned Income Tax Worksheet before completing this line.

2-10 **MUNICIPAL BOND INTEREST**

In 1913 when the Sixteenth Amendment was enacted, Congress questioned the constitutionality of taxing the interest earned on state and local government obligations. Congress provided an exclusion from taxpayers' income for the interest on such bonds. To qualify for the exclusion, the interest must be from an obligation of a state, territory, or possession of the United States, or a political subdivision of the foregoing or of the District of Columbia. For example, Puerto Rico bonds qualify for the exclusion. Federal obligations, such as treasury bills and treasury bonds, do not qualify.

The interest exclusion allows high-income taxpayers to lend money to state and local governments at lower interest rates (discounts).

EXAMPLE   Rigby is considering two different bond investments. This first option is a corporate taxable bond that yields a pre-tax return of 8.4 percent. The second option is a tax-exempt municipal bond that yields 6.5 percent. If Rigby is in the 35 percent tax bracket, the after-tax return of the taxable bonds can be computed as:

$$\text{After-tax return} = \text{Pre-tax return} \times (1 - \text{tax rate})$$
$$5.46\% = 8.4\% \times (1 - 0.35)$$

Since the tax-exempt bond is not subject to tax, the after-tax return is 6.5 percent and thus is preferable. Using a re-arranged version of the same formula can determine what the equivalent yield on a taxable bond would need to be to make Rigby indifferent between the two bonds (all other terms being equal):

$$\text{After-tax return} = \text{Tax-free return} / (1 - \text{tax rate})$$
$$10.0\% = 6.5\%/(1 - 0.35) \; \blacklozenge$$

Typically, interest rates on municipal bonds reflect the after-tax return that compensates for higher income tax rates (35 or 37 percent) and thus tax-exempt bonds will often have a lower after-tax yield than a taxable bond in the hands of a lower-income investor.

EXAMPLE   Mordecai is also considering the same bonds as Rigby in the previous example; however, Mordecai is in the 22 percent tax bracket. The after-tax return on the corporate bond is 6.55 percent [$8.4\% \times (1 - 0.22)$]. In Mordecai's situation, the after-tax return on the taxable corporate bond is greater than the tax-exempt return of 6.5 percent on the municipal bond. ◆

Taxpayers in low tax brackets are likely to find that they earn a higher overall return investing in taxable bonds rather than comparable tax-free municipal bonds. This is because the smaller tax benefit from the municipal bonds does not make up for the reduced interest rate paid on municipal bonds. Municipal bonds are also generally not appropriate investments for IRAs or other retirement accounts since income on these accounts is excluded from tax until withdrawn.

TAX BREAK

Self-Study Problem 2.10   *See Appendix E for Solutions to Self-Study Problems*

Calculate the taxable interest rate that will provide the equivalent after-tax return in the cases that follow.

1. A taxpayer is in the 24 percent tax bracket and invests in a San Diego City Bond paying 7 percent. What taxable interest rate will provide the same after-tax return?

    _____%

2. A taxpayer is in the 32 percent tax bracket and invests in a New York State Bond paying 6.5 percent. What taxable interest rate will provide the same after-tax return?

    _____%

---

intuit proconnect. TIP

Interest and dividends are both common forms of income in addition to wages. The way the two items are reported is slightly different and not always intuitive. Tax-exempt interest (which is entered on Line 2a of Form 1040) is not included as part of taxable interest (Line 2b). Qualified dividends (line 3a), however, are included as part of ordinary dividends (Line 3b). Interest and Dividends are both located in ProConnect under Income and have a Quick Entry and a 1099 entry screen (with Box numbers presented) available. Quick Entry handles most Forms 1099-INT and Forms 1099-DIV; however, should one wish to use the detailed entry screens, they will appear in the left-hand margin when Quick Entry is open. One can always return to Quick Entry using the link at the top of the detail entry form (especially if there is a need to add more 1099s).

Learning Objective 2.11

Identify the general rules for the tax treatment of gifts and inheritances.

2-11 GIFTS AND INHERITANCES

Taxpayers are allowed to exclude from income the fair market value of gifts and inheritances received, but income received from the property after such a transfer is generally taxable. Normally, the gift tax or estate tax is paid by the donor or the decedent's estate; such property is, therefore, usually tax free to the person receiving the gift or inheritance.

One tax problem that may arise concerning a gift is the definition of what constitutes a gift. The courts define a gift as a voluntary transfer of property without adequate consideration. Gifts made in a business setting are suspect since they may be disguised payments for goods or services. The courts are likely to rule that gifts in a business setting are taxable income, even if there was no obligation to make the payment. Also, if the recipient renders services for the gift, it will be presumed to be income for the services performed.

EXAMPLE   In January of the current year, Richard inherits shares of Birch Corporation stock worth $22,000. After receiving the stock, he is paid $1,300 in dividends during the current year. His gross income from the inheritance in the current year would be $1,300. The $22,000 fair market value of the stock is excluded from gross income. ♦

Self-Study Problem 2.11   *See Appendix E for Solutions to Self-Study Problems*

Don is an attorney who supplied a list of potential clients to a new attorney, Lori. This list aided in the success of Lori's practice. Lori was very pleased and decided to do something for Don. In the current year, Lori gives Don a new car worth $40,000. Lori was not obligated to give this gift to Don, and she did not expect Don to perform future services for the gift. How much income, if any, should Don report from this transaction? Explain your answer.

Income $_____

Explain _____

_____

2-12 SCHOLARSHIPS

2.12 Learning Objective

Describe the elements of scholarship income that are excluded from tax.

A scholarship is an amount paid or awarded to, or for the benefit of, a student to aid in the pursuit of his or her studies. Scholarships granted to degree candidates are taxable income, with the exception of amounts spent for tuition, fees, books, and course-required supplies and equipment. Therefore, scholarship amounts received for items such as room and board are taxable to the recipient.

EXAMPLE In 2019, Diane receives a $5,000 scholarship to study accounting at Big State University. Diane's expenses for tuition and books amount to $1,200 during the fall semester; therefore, she would have taxable income of $3,800 ($5,000 − $1,200) from the scholarship. ♦

Payments received by students for part-time employment are not excludable; they are taxable as compensation. For example, students in work–study programs must include their compensation in gross income. Some scholarships will be reported on Form 1098-T. This form is discussed further in Chapter 7.

Self-Study Problem 2.12   *See Appendix E for Solutions to Self-Study Problems*

Indicate whether each item below would be included in or excluded from the income of the recipient in 2019.

	Included	Excluded
1. A $2,000 National Merit Scholarship for tuition	_____	_____
2. A basketball scholarship for room and board	_____	_____
3. Payments under a work–study program	_____	_____
4. Salary for working at Beech Research Laboratory	_____	_____
5. A scholarship for $10,000 to cover qualified costs of $7,600.	_____	_____
6. Payment received from an employer while on leave working on a research project	_____	_____

2-13 ALIMONY

2.13 Learning Objective

Describe the tax treatment of alimony and child support.

The term alimony, for income tax purposes, includes separate maintenance payments or similar periodic payments made to a spouse or former spouse. Payments must meet certain requirements to be considered alimony.

1. The payments must be in cash and must be received by the spouse (or former spouse).
2. The payments must be made under a decree of divorce or separate maintenance or under a written instrument incident to the divorce.
3. The payor must have no liability to make payments for any period following the death of the spouse receiving the payments.
4. The payments must not be designated in the written agreement as anything other than alimony.
5. If the parties are divorced or legally separated, they must not be members of the same household at the time the payments are made.

Disguised child support payments may not be treated as alimony. Payments contingent on the status of a child, such as the age or marital status of the child, are not considered alimony.

EXAMPLE Under a 2013 divorce agreement, Sam has agreed to pay his former spouse, Silvia, $1,000 per month. The payments meet all the tests for classification as alimony, but they will be reduced to $600 per month when their child, in Silvia's custody, becomes 18 years of age. In this situation, $400 of each payment must be treated as nondeductible child support and cannot be considered alimony. ♦

Under previous tax law, alimony was deductible by the payer and includable in income by the recipient. However, the alimony provisions were repealed and these amounts are neither includable nor deductible for divorce and separation agreements entered after December 31, 2018. For alimony paid pursuant to a divorce or separation instrument executed on or before December 31, 2018, alimony is deductible by the payor and included by the recipient unless the agreement is modified and the modification expressly provides that the new tax law applies to such modification.

EXAMPLE Brad and Jen were married in 2015. The relationship did not work out and they divorced in 2016. The divorce decree required Brad to pay Jen alimony of $1,000 per month. Because this divorce was effective prior to 2019, the alimony is deductible by Brad and is gross income to Jen. ♦

EXAMPLE Miley and Liam were married in 2018. The relationship did not work out and they divorced in 2019. Miley is required to pay Liam alimony of $1,000 per month. The alimony is neither deductible to Miley nor included in Liam's gross income. ♦

2-13a Property Transfers

A spouse who transfers property in settlement of a marital obligation is not required to recognize any gain as a result of the property's appreciation. Thus, if in a divorce settlement, a wife transfers property with a fair market value of $10,000 and a tax basis of $3,000 to her husband, she will not be required to recognize the gain of $7,000 ($10,000 − $3,000). Of course, the husband would be required to assume the wife's tax basis ($3,000) in the property. The transfer of property in settlement of a divorce is not considered alimony and there is no deduction by the spouse who transfers the property, nor is it income to the recipient.

2-13b Child Support

Payments made for child support are not deductible by the taxpayer making them, nor are they income to the recipient. However, they may be an important factor in determining which spouse is entitled to claim the dependent child (see Chapter 1). Child support payments must be up to date before any amount paid may be treated as alimony. That is, if a taxpayer is obligated to pay both child support and alimony, he or she must first meet the child support obligation before obtaining a deduction for alimony payments. Payments for child support include payments designated as such in the marital settlement agreement, plus any alimony payments that are contingent upon the status of a child.

EXAMPLE Jim is required under a 2012 divorce decree to pay $400 in alimony and $250 in child support per month. Since the decree separately states that $250 is child support, only $400 per month is deductible by Jim and counts as income to his ex-wife. ♦

Income from alimony, when applicable, is reported in the Income section under SS Benefits, Alimony, Misc. Income (SS Bene., Misc. Inc.). Once this heading is clicked, Alimony and Other Income will be presented as a subheading. Deductible alimony paid, when applicable, is reported under Deductions. Once Adjustments to Income is clicked, a series of subheadings is presented including Alimony Paid.

intuit
proconnect.
TIP

Self-Study Problem 2.13   *See Appendix E for Solutions to Self-Study Problems*

A taxpayer (payor ex-spouse) is required to pay an ex-spouse (recipient ex-spouse) alimony of $12,000 per year. Determine how much alimony is deductible by the payor ex-spouse and how much alimony is recognized as income by the recipient ex-spouse based on the following information:

Details	Deductible by payor	Includable by recipient
a. The payments are made in 2019 as part of a divorce decree executed in 2018. The divorce decree is modified in 2019 to explicitly apply the provisions of the TCJA.	_____	_____
b. The payments are made in 2019 as part of a divorce decree executed in 2016.	_____	_____
c. The payments are made in 2019 as part of a divorce decree executed in 2019.	_____	_____

Sign Here	Under penalties of perjury, I declare that I have examined this return and accompanying schedules and statements, and to the best of my knowledge and belief, they are true, correct, and complete. Declaration of preparer (other than taxpayer) is based on all information of which preparer has any knowledge.			
	Your signature	Date	Your occupation	If the IRS sent you an Identity Protection PIN, enter it here (see inst.)
Joint return? See instructions. Keep a copy for your records.	Spouse's signature. If a joint return, **both** must sign.	Date	Spouse's occupation	If the IRS sent your spouse an Identity Protection PIN, enter it here (see inst.)
	Phone no.		Email address	
Paid Preparer Use Only	Preparer's name	Preparer's signature	Date	PTIN	Check if: ☐ 3rd Party Designee
	Firm's name ▶		Phone no.		☐ Self-employed
	Firm's address ▶			Firm's EIN ▶

For the last 10 years, you prepared the joint tax returns for Dominic (husband; age 40) and Dulce (wife; age 35) Divorcio. In 2018, they got a divorce and remained as your separate tax clients. Under the dissolution decree, Dominic has to pay Dulce $2,500 per month alimony, which he does for the current year. You have completed Dominic's tax return for the current year and you deducted the required alimony payments to Dulce on Dominic's Form 1040. Dulce came in to have you prepare her tax return and refused to report her alimony received as income. She stated, "I am not going to pay tax on the $30,000 from Dominic." She views the payments as "a gift for putting up with him for all those years of marriage." Dulce will not budge on excluding this alimony from income. Would you sign the Paid Preparer's declaration (see example above) on this return? Why or why not?

Would You Sign This Tax Return?

2-14 **EDUCATIONAL INCENTIVES**

Explain the tax implications of using educational savings vehicles.

2-14a **Qualified Tuition Programs (QTP)**

A Qualified Tuition Program (more commonly referred to as a Section 529 tuition plan) allows taxpayers (1) to buy in-kind tuition credits or certificates for qualified higher education expenses (a prepaid tuition plan) or (2) to contribute to an account established to meet qualified higher education expenses (a savings-type plan). Such Qualified Tuition Programs may be sponsored by a state government or a private institution of higher learning. Section 529 plans permit tax-free distributions if the distribution is used for qualified higher education expenses. Qualified higher education expenses include tuition, fees, books, supplies, and equipment required for the enrollment or attendance at an eligible educational institution. In addition, reasonable room and board costs, subject to certain limitations, are also qualified expenses allowed to be paid from the Section 529 tuition plan. Qualified higher education expenses also include tuition in connection with enrollment or attendance at an elementary or secondary public, private, or religious school. The use of the specific term "tuition" excludes other types of qualifying education expenses such as books, supplies, and equipment for elementary or secondary students. The maximum exclusion for elementary or secondary education (i.e., K-12) is $10,000 per beneficiary per year.

EXAMPLE   Walt and Skyler Blanco have two children, Jesse and Jane, and established 529 plans for each of them many years ago. Jesse is now in his second year of college at Albuquerque Community College and Jane is a junior at Albuquerque High School for Math and Science, a private high school. In 2019, the Blancos have $3,500 distributed from the 529 plan with Jesse as the named beneficiary to pay for his community college tuition, books, and course-related supplies. Jane's private school tuition is much higher and the Blancos distribute $12,000 from the 529 plan for which she is the beneficiary. $11,000 of the distribution is used to pay for tuition, $550 for books, and $450 for her private school uniforms. The Blancos may exclude $13,500 of the distributions. Jesse's $3,500 distribution meets the definition of qualified higher education expenses. Only $10,000 of Jane's distribution meets the definition of qualified higher education expenses. The remaining $1,000 of tuition is in excess of the annual limit and the books and uniform costs do not qualify. ♦

The earnings portion of QTP distributions that are not used for qualified tuition expenses are includable in the distributee's gross income under the annuity income rules and are subject to a 10 percent early withdrawal penalty.

Unlike Educational Savings Accounts, discussed later in this section, there is no income limit on the amount of contributions to a Qualified Tuition Program. Like an Educational Savings Account, however, the contributions are not deductible. Any contributions are gifts, and thus subject to the gift tax rules. In addition, most programs impose some form of overall maximum contribution for each beneficiary based on estimated future higher education expenses.

EXAMPLE   Bill has AGI of $275,000 and has two children. He chooses to contribute $9,000 (he is allowed to contribute any amount up to the limit imposed by his state's law) to a QTP for each of his children in 2019, even with his high AGI. The $18,000 is not deductible to Bill. Any earnings on the contribution accumulate tax free and are excluded from gross income if used for future qualified higher education expenses. ♦

A taxpayer may claim an American Opportunity credit or lifetime learning credit (discussed in detail in Chapter 7) for a tax year and exclude from gross income amounts distributed (both the principal and the earnings portions) from a qualified tuition program on behalf of the same student. This is true as long as the distribution is not used for the same expenses for which a credit was claimed. However, the amount of qualified higher education expenses for a tax year for purposes of calculating the exclusion from income must be reduced by scholarships, veterans' benefits, military reserve benefits, employer-provided educational assistance amounts, and the tuition amounts used to generate the American Opportunity and lifetime learning credits.

EXAMPLE In 2019, Sammy receives $15,000 from a qualified tuition program. He uses the funds to pay for his college tuition and other qualified higher education expenses. Sammy also claims an American Opportunity credit of $1,500 for the year, using the expenses paid from the QTP funds. For purposes of the QTP exclusion calculation, the $15,000 must be reduced to $13,500 ($15,000 − $1,500). ◆

The tax law provides that if the total distributions from a qualified tuition program and from an educational savings account exceed the total amount of qualified higher education expenses, the taxpayer will have to allocate the expenses among the distributions for purposes of determining how much of each distribution is excludable.

There are billions of dollars invested in the increasingly popular Section 529 Qualified Tuition Programs across the country. The plans offered by different states vary significantly and it is possible for a taxpayer to invest in the plan of a state other than the state that he lives in. The following two websites offer information comparing state plans and answers to questions regarding plan operations: **www.collegesavings.org** and **www.savingforcollege.com**.

TAX BREAK

2-14b Educational Savings Accounts

Taxpayers are allowed to set up educational savings accounts, also known as Coverdell Education Savings Accounts, to pay for qualified education expenses. The maximum amount a taxpayer can contribute annually to an educational savings account for a beneficiary is $2,000. Contributions are not deductible and are subject to income limits. Contributions cannot be made to an educational savings account after the date on which the designated beneficiary becomes 18 years old. In addition, contributions cannot be made to a beneficiary's educational savings account during any year in which contributions are made to a qualified state tuition program on behalf of the same beneficiary. The educational savings account exclusion for distributions of income is available in any tax year in which the beneficiary claims the American Opportunity credit or the lifetime learning credit (see Chapter 7), provided the distribution is not used for the same expenses for which the credit was claimed.

Contributions to educational savings accounts are phased out between AGIs of $95,000 and $110,000 for single taxpayers and $190,000 and $220,000 for married couples who file a joint return (these limits are not adjusted annually for inflation). Like regular and Roth IRAs, contributions applied to the current tax year must be made by April 15 (or the next business day, if April 15 falls on a weekend or holiday) of the following year.

EXAMPLE Joe, who is single, would like to contribute $2,000 to an educational savings account for his 12-year-old son. However, his AGI is $105,000, so his contribution is limited to $667, calculated as follows:

$$\frac{(\$110,000 \text{ upper limit} - \$105,000 \text{ AGI})}{\$15,000} \times \$2,000 = \$667 \text{ contribution}$$

$15,000 is the difference between the upper ($110,000) and lower ($95,000) phase-out limits. ◆

TAX BREAK For parents with income above the allowable limit, a gift may be made to a child and the child may make the contribution to an educational savings account. There is no requirement that the contributor have earned income as there is for IRAs.

Amounts received from an educational savings account are tax free if they are used for qualified education expenses. Qualified education expenses include tuition, fees, books, supplies, and related equipment for private, elementary, and secondary school expenses as well as for college. Room and board also qualify if the student's course load is at least 50 percent of the full-time course load. If the distributions during a tax year exceed qualified education expenses, part of the excess is treated as a return of capital (the contributions), and part is treated as a distribution of earnings. The distribution is presumed to be pro rata from each category. The exclusion for the distribution of earnings is calculated as follows:

$$\frac{\text{Qualified education expenses}}{\text{Total distribution}} \times \text{Earnings} = \text{Exclusion}$$

EXAMPLE   Amy receives a $2,000 distribution from her educational savings account. She uses $1,800 to pay for qualified education expenses. Immediately prior to the distribution, Amy's account balance is $5,000, $3,000 of which are her contributions. Because 60 percent ($3,000/$5,000) of her account balance represents her contributions, $1,200 ($2,000 × 60%) of the distribution is a tax-free return of capital and $800 ($2,000 × 40%) is a distribution of earnings. The excludable amount of the earnings is calculated as follows:

$$\frac{\$1,800}{\$2,000} \times \$800 = \$720 \text{ is excludable (thus, the amount taxable is \$80,}$$
$$\text{or } \$800 - \$720).$$

Amy's adjusted basis for her savings account is reduced to $1,800 ($3,000 − $1,200). ♦

2-14c Higher Education Expenses Deduction

Please note that at the time we go to print, the higher education expense deduction has expired and is no longer available. Because this deduction has previously been extended a number of times, a summary of the 2017 material remains in this textbook. Be sure and check the textbook companion website or www.irs.gov for changes.

In 2017, taxpayers were allowed a for AGI or "above-the-line" deduction for qualified tuition and related expenses incurred during the tax year. The deduction was allowed for qualified tuition and related expenses for enrollment at an institution of higher education during the tax year. In addition, the deduction was allowed for qualified expenses paid during a tax year if those expenses are in connection with an academic term beginning during the tax year or during the first 3 months of the next tax year. The tuition expense deduction is currently expired.

EXAMPLE   Jerry pays $2,000 for his son's college tuition in November 2017 for the spring 2018 term. The spring term starts in January 2018. The $2,000 is deductible in 2017, even though it is for education provided in a later tax year. ♦

The deduction cannot exceed a specified annual amount. The deduction was $4,000 for single and head of household taxpayers with modified AGI below $65,000 and for married filing jointly taxpayers with modified AGI below $130,000. The amount was $2,000 for single taxpayers with modified AGI between $65,000 and $80,000 and for married joint filers with modified AGI between $130,000 and $160,000. Taxpayers with AGI exceeding the limits were not allowed a deduction.

Self-Study Problem 2.14   *See Appendix E for Solutions to Self-Study Problems*

a. Abby has a distribution of $10,000 from a qualified tuition program, of which $3,000 represents earnings. The funds are used to pay for her daughter's qualified higher education expenses. How much of the $10,000 distribution is taxable to the daughter?

$_____

b. During 2019, Henry (a single taxpayer) has a salary of $85,000 and interest income of $4,000. Henry has no other income or deductions. Calculate the maximum contribution Henry is allowed for an educational savings account.

$_____

2-15 UNEMPLOYMENT COMPENSATION

2.15 Learning Objective

Describe the tax treatment of unemployment compensation.

Unemployment compensation payments are fully taxable. Unemployment compensation is generally reported on a Form 1099-G.

EXAMPLE Genny was unemployed for several months during 2019 and received unemployment compensation of $4,000. The $4,000 is included in Genny's taxable income for 2019. ◆

Self-Study Problem 2.15   *See Appendix E for Solutions to Self-Study Problems*

Anthony was unemployed during part of 2019 and received the following Form 1099-G:

☐ CORRECTED (if checked)

PAYER'S name, street address... Florida Dept of Econ Opportunity, 107 E. Jefferson St., Tallahassee, FL 32399	1 Unemployment compensation $ 3,000.00	OMB No. 1545-0120 20**19** Form **1099-G**	Certain Government Payments
	2 State or local income tax refunds, credits, or offsets $		
PAYER'S TIN 12-7654321 RECIPIENT'S TIN 313-22-1212	3 Box 2 amount is for tax year	4 Federal income tax withheld $ 0.00	Copy B For Recipient
RECIPIENT'S name Anthony Starky	5 RTAA payments $	6 Taxable grants $	This is important tax information...
Street address 103 Brickell Ave.	7 Agriculture payments $	8 If checked, box 2 is trade or business income ▶ ☐	
City Miami, FL 33101	9 Market gain $		
Account number	10a State 10b State identification no.	11 State income tax withheld $ $	

Form **1099-G**   (keep for your records)   www.irs.gov/Form1099G   Department of the Treasury - Internal Revenue Service

How much unemployment compensation is included in Anthony's gross income?

$_____

Learning Objective 2.16	2-16 **SOCIAL SECURITY BENEFITS**

Apply the rules governing inclusion of Social Security benefits in gross income.

Some taxpayers may exclude all of their Social Security benefits from gross income. However, most middle-income and upper-income Social Security recipients may have to include up to 85 percent of their benefits in gross income. The formula to determine taxable Social Security income is based on *modified adjusted gross income* (MAGI). Generally, MAGI is the taxpayer's adjusted gross income (without Social Security benefits) plus any tax-free interest income. On rare occasions, taxpayers will also have to add back unusual items such as the foreign earned income exclusion, employer-provided adoption benefits, or interest on education loans. If MAGI plus 50 percent of Social Security benefits is less than the base amount shown below (base amounts are not adjusted for inflation), benefits are excluded from income.

Base Amounts	Applies To
$32,000	Married filing jointly
0	Married taxpayers who did not live apart for the entire year and still filed separate returns
25,000	All other taxpayers

The formula for calculating the taxable amount of Social Security is complex and time-consuming. Many taxpayers rely on tax-preparation software to perform the calculation. For preparation by hand, the Form 1040 Instructions include a full-page worksheet that takes taxpayers through the calculation one step at a time.

EXAMPLE   For the 2019 tax year, Nancy, a single taxpayer, receives $7,000 in Social Security benefits. She has adjusted gross income of $20,000, not including any Social Security income, and receives $10,000 of tax-exempt municipal bond interest. Nancy must include $3,500 of her Social Security benefits in income. The amount included in gross income is determined as follows:

SIMPLIFIED TAXABLE SOCIAL SECURITY WORKSHEET (FOR MOST PEOPLE)

1. Enter the total amount of Social Security income.	1. $ 7,000
2. Enter one-half of line 1.	2. 3,500
3. Enter the total of taxable income items on Form 1040 except Social Security income.	3. 20,000
4. Enter the amount of tax-exempt interest income.	4. 10,000
5. Add lines 2, 3, and 4.	5. 33,500
6. Enter all adjustments for AGI except for student loan interest, the domestic production activities deduction, and the tuition and fees deduction.	6. –0–
7. Subtract line 6 from line 5. If zero or less, stop here, none of the Social Security benefits are taxable.	7. 33,500
8. Enter $25,000 ($32,000 if married filing jointly; $0 if married filing separately and living with spouse at any time during the year).	8. 25,000
9. Subtract line 8 from line 7. If zero or less, enter –0–.	9. 8,500

Note: *If line 9 is zero or less, stop here;* **none of your benefits are taxable.** *Otherwise, go on to line 10.*

10. Enter $9,000 ($12,000 if married filing jointly; $0 if married filing separately and living with spouse at any time during the year). 　　　10.   9,000

11. Subtract line 10 from line 9. If zero or less, enter –0–. 　　　11.   –0–

12. Enter the **smaller** of line 9 or line 10. 　　　12.   8,500

13. Enter one-half of line 12. 　　　13.   4,250

14. Enter the **smaller** of line 2 or line 13. 　　　14.   3,500

15. Multiply line 11 by 85% (.85). If line 11 is zero, enter –0–. 　　　15.   –0–

16. Add lines 14 and 15. 　　　16.   3,500

17. Multiply line 1 by 85% (.85). 　　　17.   5,950

18. **Taxable benefits.** Enter the **smaller** of line 16 or line 17. 　　　18. $ 3,500

                                                                   ◆

EXAMPLE   Linda, a widow, is retired and receives Social Security benefits of $14,000 in 2019. She has MAGI of $47,000. Linda must include $11,900 of her Social Security benefits in income. The amount included in income is determined as follows:

SIMPLIFIED TAXABLE SOCIAL SECURITY WORKSHEET (FOR MOST PEOPLE)

1. Enter the total amount of Social Security income. 　　　1. $14,000

2. Enter one-half of line 1. 　　　2.   7,000

3. Enter the total of taxable income items on Form 1040 except Social Security income. 　　　3.   47,000

4. Enter the amount of tax-exempt interest income. 　　　4.   –0–

5. Add lines 2, 3, and 4. 　　　5.   54,000

6. Enter all adjustments for AGI except for student loan interest, the domestic production activities deduction, and the tuition and fees deduction. 　　　6.   –0–

7. Subtract line 6 from line 5. If zero or less, stop here, none of the Social Security benefits are taxable. 　　　7.   54,000

8. Enter $25,000 ($32,000 if married filing jointly; $0 if married filing separately and living with spouse at any time during the year). 　　　8.   25,000

9. Subtract line 8 from line 7. If zero or less, enter –0–. 　　　9.   29,000

Note: *If line 9 is zero or less, stop here;* **none of your benefits are taxable.** *Otherwise, go on to line 10.*

10. Enter $9,000 ($12,000 if married filing jointly; $0 if married filing separately and living with spouse at any time during the year).	10.	9,000
11. Subtract line 10 from line 9. If zero or less, enter –0–.	11.	20,000
12. Enter the **smaller** of line 9 or line 10.	12.	9,000
13. Enter one-half of line 12.	13.	4,500
14. Enter the **smaller** of line 2 or line 13.	14.	4,500
15. Multiply line 11 by 85% (.85). If line 11 is zero, enter –0–.	15.	17,000
16. Add lines 14 and 15.	16.	21,500
17. Multiply line 1 by 85% (.85).	17.	11,900
18. **Taxable benefits.** Enter the **smaller** of line 16 or line 17.	18.	$11,900

◆

A summary of the tax treatment of Social Security benefits is presented in Table 2.4.

TABLE 2.4   **SOCIAL SECURITY INCOME INCLUSION FORMULAS**

Filing Status	MAGI + 50% SS	Amount of SS That Is Included in Taxable Income
Single, HOH, Surviving Spouse, MFS (Living apart)	Under $25,000	No SS benefits included in taxable income
	$25,000–$34,000	The lesser of: 50% of SS benefits, or 50% of (MAGI + 50%SS, over $25,000)
	Over $34,000	The lesser of: 85% of SS benefits, or (lesser of box above or $4,500) + 85% of (MAGI + 50%SS, over $34,000)
Married Filing Jointly	Under $32,000	No SS benefits included in taxable income
	$32,000–$44,000	The lesser of: 50% of SS benefits, or 50% of (MAGI + 50%SS, over $32,000)
	Over $44,000	The lesser of: 85% of SS benefits, or (lesser of box above or $6,000) + 85% of (MAGI + 50%SS, over $44,000)

Note: The Social Security income inclusion formulas in the table above are shown for information only. No problems in the textbook will require the use of these formulas.

intuit
proconnect.
TIP

Social Security benefits are entered under the same heading in Income as alimony discussed in LO 2.13.

Self-Study Problem 2.16   *See Appendix E for Solutions to Self-Study Problems*

For the 2019 tax year, Kim and Edward are married and file a joint return. They have Social Security benefits of $13,000 and their adjusted gross income is $20,000, not including any Social Security income. They also receive $30,000 in tax-free municipal bond interest. How much, if any, of the Social Security benefits should Kim and Edward include in gross income? Use the worksheet below to compute your answer.

$ _____

SIMPLIFIED TAXABLE SOCIAL SECURITY WORKSHEET (FOR MOST PEOPLE)

1. Enter the total amount of Social Security income.   1. $ _____

2. Enter one-half of line 1.   2. _____

3. Enter the total of taxable income items on Form 1040 except Social Security income.   3. _____

4. Enter the amount of tax-exempt interest income.   4. _____

5. Add lines 2, 3, and 4.   5. _____

6. Enter all adjustments for AGI except for student loan interest, the domestic production activities deduction, and the tuition and fees deduction.   6. _____

7. Subtract line 6 from line 5. If zero or less, stop here, none of the Social Security benefits are taxable.   7. _____

8. Enter $25,000 ($32,000 if married filing jointly; $0 if married filing separately and living with spouse at any time during the year).   8. _____

9. Subtract line 8 from line 7. If zero or less, enter –0–.   9. _____

Note: *If line 9 is zero or less, stop here;* **none of your benefits are taxable.** *Otherwise, go on to line 10.*

10. Enter $9,000 ($12,000 if married filing jointly; $0 if married filing separately and living with spouse at any time during the year).   10. _____

11. Subtract line 10 from line 9. If zero or less, enter –0–.   11. _____

12. Enter the **smaller** of line 9 or line 10.   12. _____

13. Enter one-half of line 12.   13. _____

14. Enter the **smaller** of line 2 or line 13.   14. _____

15. Multiply line 11 by 85% (.85). If line 11 is zero, enter –0–.   15. _____

16. Add lines 14 and 15.   16. _____

17. Multiply line 1 by 85% (.85).   17. _____

18. **Taxable benefits.** Enter the **smaller** of line 16 or line 17.   18. $ _____

| Learning Objective 2.17 | 2-17 **COMMUNITY PROPERTY** |

Learning Objective 2.17

Distinguish between the different rules for married taxpayers residing in community property states when filing separate returns.

When married couples file separate income tax returns, a special problem arises. Income derived from property held by a married couple, either jointly or separately, as well as wages and other income earned by a husband and wife, must be allocated between the spouses. State law becomes important in making this allocation.

The law in nine states is based on a community property system of marital law. In these states, the property rights of married couples differ from the property rights of married couples residing in the remaining common law states. The nine states that are community property states are:

Arizona	Louisiana	Texas
California	Nevada	Washington
Idaho	New Mexico	Wisconsin

Note: In Alaska, spouses may elect to treat income as community income.

Under the community property system, all property is deemed to be either separate property or community property. Separate property includes property acquired by a spouse before marriage or received after marriage as a gift or inheritance. All other property owned by a married couple is presumed to be community property. For federal income tax purposes, each spouse is automatically taxed on half of the income from community property.

The tax treatment of income from separate property depends on the taxpayer's state of residence. In Idaho, Louisiana, Texas, and Wisconsin, income from separate property produces community income. Thus, just as each spouse is taxed on half of the income from community property, each spouse is also taxed on half of the income from separate property. In the other five community property states, income on separate property is separate income and is reported in full on the tax return of the spouse who owns the property. Income such as nontaxable dividends or royalties from mineral interests assumes the classification of the asset from which the income is derived. Capital gains also retain their classification based on the classification of the property from which the gain arises.

EXAMPLE   John and Marsha are married and live in Texas. John owns, as his separate property, stock in AT&T Corporation. During the year, John receives dividends of $4,000. Assuming John and Marsha file separate returns, each of them must report $2,000 of the dividends. On the other hand, if John and Marsha lived in California, John would report the entire $4,000 of the dividends on his tax return and Marsha would not include any of the dividend income on her tax return. ◆

In all of the community property states, income from salary and wages is generally treated as having been earned one-half by each spouse.

EXAMPLE   Robert and Linda are married but file separate tax returns. Robert receives a salary of $30,000 and has interest income of $500 from a savings account which is in his name. The savings account was established with salary earned by Robert since his marriage. Linda collects $20,000 in dividends on stock she inherited from her father. The amount of income which Linda must report on her separate income tax return depends on the state in which Robert and Linda reside. Three different assumptions are presented below:

State of Residence

Linda's Income:	Texas	California	Common Law States
Salary	$15,000	$15,000	$ 0
Dividends	10,000	20,000	20,000
Interest	250	250	0
Total	$25,250	$35,250	$20,000

◆

2-17a **Spouses Living Apart**

To simplify problems that could arise when married spouses residing in a community property state do not live together, the tax law contains an exception to the above community property rules. Under this special provision, a spouse will be taxed only on his or her actual earnings from personal services. For this provision to apply, the following conditions must be satisfied:

1. The individuals must live apart for the entire year,
2. They must not file a joint return, and
3. No portion of the earned income may be transferred between the spouses.

EXAMPLE   Bill and Betty, both residents of Nevada, are married but live apart for the entire year. Bill has a salary of $30,000 and Betty has a salary of $35,000. Normally, Bill and Betty would each report $32,500. However, if the required conditions are met, Bill and Betty would each report their own salary. If Bill and Betty had any unearned income, such as dividends or interest, the income would be reported under the general community property rules. The special provision applies only to earned income of the spouses. ♦

Another provision addresses the problem of spouses who fail to qualify for the above special exception because they do not live apart for the entire year. In certain cases, a spouse who fails to include in income his or her share of community income, as required by the community property laws, may be relieved of any liability related to this income. To be granted relief, the taxpayer must not know of or have reason to know of the omitted community property income.

Self-Study Problem 2.17   *See Appendix E for Solutions to Self-Study Problems*

Tom and Rachel are married and living together in California. Their income is as follows:

Tom's salary	$40,000
Rachel's salary	30,000
Dividends (Tom's property)	5,000
Dividends (Rachel's property)	3,000
Interest (community property)	4,000
Total	$82,000

a. If Rachel files a separate tax return, she should report income of:

$_____

b. If Tom and Rachel lived in Texas, what should Rachel report as income?

$_____

KEY TERMS

gross income, 2-2
barter, 2-2
inclusions – gross income, 2-3
exclusions – gross income, 2-3
employee fringe benefits, 2-8
flexible spending accounts, 2-8
dependent care flexible spending
   accounts, 2-9
health care flexible spending
   accounts, 2-9
group term life insurance, 2-9
education assistance plans, 2-9
no-additional-cost services, 2-10
qualified employee discounts, 2-10
working condition fringe benefit, 2-10

de minimis fringe benefits, 2-10
tuition reduction, 2-11
retirement planning fringe
   benefit, 2-11
qualified plan award, 2-12
annuities, 2-13
the simplified method, 2-14
the general rule, 2-15
employee annuities, 2-16
accelerated death benefits, 2-17
viatical settlements, 2-17
interest income, 2-18
Schedule B, 2-18
U.S. savings bonds, 2-18
dividends, 2-19

municipal bond interest, 2-25
gift, 2-26
scholarship, 2-27
alimony, 2-27
property transfers, 2-28
qualified tuition programs
   (Section 529 tuition plan), 2-30
educational savings account
   (Coverdell Education Savings
   Accounts), 2-31
modified adjusted gross income
   (MAGI), 2-34
community property, 2-38
separate property, 2-38

KEY POINTS

Learning Objectives	Key Points
LO 2.1: Apply the definition of gross income.	• Gross income means "all income from whatever source derived." • Gross income includes everything a taxpayer receives unless it is specifically excluded from gross income by the tax law.
LO 2.2: Describe salaries and wages income reporting and inclusion in gross income.	• The primary form of reporting wages to an employee is through Form W-2. • Employers should report the employee's taxable wages, salary, bonuses, awards, commissions, and almost every other type of taxable compensation in Box 1 of the Form W-2. • If a taxpayer receives more than one Form W-2 or is jointly filing with a spouse having their own Form W-2, the amounts in Box 1 are combined before entering the total on Line 1 of the Form 1040. • Other Form W-2 information such as federal taxes paid will also be reported by the taxpayer on the Form 1040.
LO 2.3: Explain the general tax treatment of health insurance.	• Taxpayers may exclude health insurance premiums paid by their employer. • Taxpayers are allowed an exclusion for payments received from accident and health plans. The taxpayer may exclude the total amount received for payment of medical care, including any amount paid for the medical care of the taxpayer, his or her spouse, or dependents.
LO 2.4: Determine when meals and lodging may be excluded from taxable income.	• Meals and lodging are excluded from gross income provided they are for the convenience of the employer and they are furnished on the business premises. Lodging must be a condition of employment to be excluded.
LO 2.5: Identify the common employee fringe benefit income exclusions.	• Certain fringe benefits provided to employees may be excluded from the employees' gross income. These include dependent care and health care flexible spending accounts, group term life insurance (up to $50,000), education assistance plans, and others.

LO 2.6: Determine when prizes and awards are included in income.	• Amounts received from prizes and awards are normally taxable income unless refused by the taxpayer. • Certain small prizes (generally under $400) for length of service and safety achievement are excluded from gross income. If the award is a "qualified plan award," then up to $1,600 of the value of the award may be excluded.
LO 2.7: Calculate the taxable and nontaxable portions of annuity payments.	• Annuity payments received by a taxpayer have an element of taxable income and an element of tax-free return of the original purchase price. • The part of the payment that is excluded from income is the ratio of the investment in the contract to the total expected return. • The total expected return is the annual payment multiplied by the life expectancy of the annuitant, based on mortality tables provided by the IRS. • Individual taxpayers generally must use the "simplified" method to calculate the taxable amount from a qualified annuity starting after November 18, 1996.
LO 2.8: Describe the tax treatment of life insurance proceeds.	• Life insurance proceeds are generally excluded from gross income. If the proceeds are taken over several years instead of in a lump sum, any interest on the unpaid proceeds is generally taxable income. • Early payouts of life insurance are excluded from gross income for certain terminally or chronically ill taxpayers. • All or a portion of the proceeds from a life insurance policy transferred to another person for valuable consideration may be taxable to the recipient.
LO 2.9: Identify the tax treatment of interest and dividend income.	• Interest income is taxable except for certain state and municipal bond interest. • Interest or dividend income exceeding $1,500 per year must be reported in detail on Schedule B of Form 1040. • Series EE and Series I Savings Bond interest is taxable in the year the bonds are cashed unless a taxpayer elects to report the interest each year as it accrues. • Series HH Savings Bond interest is taxable each year as it is paid to the taxpayer. • Ordinary dividends are taxable in the year received. • Qualified dividends are taxed at rates ranging from 0 percent to 20 percent and possibly included in the 3.8 percent net investment income tax.
LO 2.10: Describe the tax treatment of municipal bond interest.	• Interest from an obligation of a state, territory, or possession of the United States, or of a political subdivision of the foregoing, or of the District of Columbia, is excluded from gross income.
LO 2.11: Identify the general rules for the tax treatment of gifts and inheritances.	• The receipt of gifts and inheritances is usually excludable from gross income. Income received from the property after the transfer may be taxable to the recipient.
LO 2.12: Describe the elements of scholarship income that are excluded from tax.	• Scholarships granted to degree candidates are excluded from gross income if spent for tuition, fees, books, and course-required supplies and equipment. Amounts received for items such as room and board are taxable to the recipient.
LO 2.13: Describe the tax treatment of alimony and child support.	• Alimony paid in cash is taxable to the person who receives it and is deductible to the person who pays it, for divorce agreements dated prior to January 1, 2019. • Child support is not alimony and therefore is not taxable when received, nor deductible when paid. • A spouse who transfers property in settlement of a marital obligation is not required to recognize any gain as a result of the property's appreciation. The receiving spouse assumes the tax basis of the property. • The TCJA repealed the alimony provisions and these amounts are neither included nor deducted in taxable income beginning with divorce or separation agreements after December 31, 2018.

LO 2.14: Explain the tax implications of using educational savings vehicles.	• A Qualified Tuition Program (Section 529 plan) allows taxpayers (1) to buy in-kind tuition credits or certificates for qualified higher education expenses or (2) to contribute to an account established to meet qualified higher education expenses. Distributions from the account are not taxable if the account is used for qualified higher education expenses. • Qualified higher education expenses include tuition, fees, books, supplies, and equipment required for the enrollment or attendance at an eligible educational institution. In addition, taxpayers are allowed reasonable room and board costs, subject to certain limitations. • The maximum exclusion for elementary or secondary education (K-12) for tuition only, is $10,000 per beneficiary per year. • The maximum amount a taxpayer can contribute annually to an educational savings account for a beneficiary is $2,000. The contribution is not deductible, and if the amounts received are used for qualified education expenses, the distributions are not taxable.
LO 2.15: Describe the tax treatment of unemployment compensation.	• Unemployment compensation is taxable.
LO 2.16: Apply the rules governing inclusion of Social Security benefits in gross income.	• Taxpayers with income under $25,000 ($32,000 for Married Filing Jointly) exclude all of their Social Security benefits from gross income. • Middle-income and upper-income Social Security recipients, however, may have to include up to 85 percent of their benefits in gross income. • Calculating the taxable amount of Social Security is complex and most easily done using a worksheet, such as the one provided in this chapter, or a tax program such as Intuit ProConnect Tax Online.
LO 2.17: Distinguish between the different rules for married taxpayers residing in community property states when filing separate returns.	• Income derived from community property held by a married couple, either jointly or separately, as well as wages and other income earned by a married couple, must be allocated between the spouses, if filing separately. • Nine states use a community property system of marital law. These states are Arizona, California, Idaho, Louisiana, Nevada, New Mexico, Texas, Washington, and Wisconsin. In Alaska, spouses may elect to treat income as community property. • In general, in a community property state, income is split one-half (50 percent) to each spouse. There are exceptions for certain separate property (e.g., property owned prior to marriage, etc.).

QUESTIONS and PROBLEMS

GROUP 1:
MULTIPLE CHOICE QUESTIONS

LO 2.1   1. The definition of gross income in the tax law is:
  a. All items specifically listed as income in the tax law
  b. All cash payments received for goods provided and services performed
  c. All income from whatever source derived
  d. All income from whatever source derived unless the income is earned illegally

LO 2.1   2. Which of the following is not taxable for income tax purposes?
  a. Prizes
  b. Severance pay
  c. Gifts
  d. Partnership income
  e. All of the above are taxable

LO 2.1

3. All of the following items are taxable to the taxpayer receiving them, *except*:
   a. Life insurance proceeds
   b. Unemployment compensation
   c. Embezzled funds
   d. Prizes
   e. Gambling winnings

LO 2.1

4. Which of the following types of income is tax exempt?
   a. Unemployment compensation
   b. Income earned illegally
   c. Dividends from foreign corporations
   d. Municipal bond interest
   e. Dividends from utility corporations' stock

LO 2.1

5. Which of the following is included in gross income?
   a. Loans
   b. Scholarships for room and board
   c. Worker's compensation
   d. Health insurance proceeds
   e. None of the above

LO 2.3
LO 2.4
LO 2.11
LO 2.12

6. Which of the following items would be included in the gross income of the recipient?
   a. Insurance payments for medical care of a dependent child
   b. Insurance payments for loss of the taxpayer's sight
   c. Season tickets worth $2,000 given to a son by his father
   d. Payments to a student for working at the student union food court
   e. Lodging provided to a worker on a remote oil rig

LO 2.3

7. Malin is a married taxpayer and has three dependent children. Malin's employer offers health insurance for employees and Malin takes advantage of the benefit for her entire family (her spouse's employer also offers health insurance but they opt out). During the year, Malin paid $1,200 toward her family's health insurance premiums through payroll deductions while the employer paid the remaining $9,200. Malin's family visited health care professionals numerous times during the year and made total co-payments toward medical services of $280. Malin's daughter had knee surgery due to a soccer injury and the insurance company paid the hospital $6,700 directly and reimbursed Malin $400 for her out-of-pocket health care expenses related to the surgery. How much gross income should Malin recognize related to her health insurance?
   a. $0
   b. $9,200
   c. $14,020 ($9,200 + $6,700 − $1,200 − $280 − $400)
   d. $8,000 ($9,200 − $1,200)
   e. None of the above

LO 2.4

8. George works at the Springfield Nuclear Plant as a nuclear technician. The plant is located 15 miles from the town of Springfield. George likes to eat his lunch at the plant's cafeteria because he is required to be available for nuclear emergencies during his shift. Unsurprisingly, there are no other eating establishments located near the plant. George estimates the value of the meals he was provided during the current year as $1,300. He estimates the cost for him to have prepared those lunches for himself as about $560. The cost of the meals to the power company was $470. How much income does George need to recognize from the meals?
   a. $1,300
   b. $560
   c. $470
   d. $830 ($1,300 − $470)
   e. None of the above

LO 2.5

9. Which of the following is a fringe benefit excluded from income?
   a. A mechanic at Denise's employer, a car rental company, provides $1,000 of repair services to Denise's personal car for free
   b. Alfa-Bet, a high-tech corporation, pays for each employee's membership at the 24 Hour Biceps Gym closest to each Alfa-Bet office
   c. Quickchat Inc. gives each employee a $10 giftcard to the local coffee shop on National Coffee Day
   d. Hedaya, a doctoral student at Ivy University, receives a full tuition waiver while serving as research assistant

LO 2.5

10. Which of the following will result in the recognition of gross income?
    a. Gail's employer allows her to set aside $4,000 from her wages to cover the cost of daycare for Gail's four-year-old daughter. Gail's daycare costs are $4,300 for the year.
    b. Hannah purchases a new sofa from her employer, Sofas-R-Us, for $1,200. The cost of the sofa to the furniture store is $1,100 and the sofa normally sells for $1,700.
    c. Jayden's employer purchases her commuting pass for the subway at a cost of $225 per month.
    d. Havana is a lawyer. The law firm she works for pays for her subscription to Lawyer's Weekly, a trade magazine for attorneys.
    e. None of the above will result in recognition of gross income.

LO 2.6

11. Which of the following prizes or awards is taxable?
    a. Professional sports awards
    b. Prizes from a television game show
    c. Awards for superior performance on the job
    d. A one-acre lot received as a prize
    e. All of the above are taxable

LO 2.6

12. Huihana receives a watch for achieving 20 years of employment with her employer. The watch cost the employer $225 and has a market value of $250 on the date awarded. Huihana is in the highest tax bracket for single taxpayers. How much gross income will Huihana recognize on the receipt of the watch?
    a. $250
    b. $200
    c. $25
    d. $0
    e. $50 or $59.50 including the net investment income tax

LO 2.7

13. A 64-year-old taxpayer retires this year and receives the first payment on an annuity that was purchased several years ago. The taxpayer's investment in the annuity is $97,500, and the annuity pays $1,000 per month for the remainder of the taxpayer's life. Based on IRS mortality tables, the taxpayer is expected to live another 20 years. If the taxpayer receives $4,000 in annuity payments in the current year, the nontaxable portion calculated using the simplified method is:
    a. $0
    b. $1,500
    c. $1,400
    d. $4,000
    e. None of the above

LO 2.7

14. Amara has an annuity and over time has recovered her entire investment but it continues to pay her $450 per month. Amara should recognize how much of each monthly payment as gross income?
    a. $0
    b. Some amount greater than $450
    c. Some amount between $0 and $450
    d. $450

LO 2.8   15. Which of the following might result in life insurance proceeds that are taxable to the recipient?

    a. A life insurance policy in which the insured is the son of the taxpayer and the beneficiary is the taxpayer

    b. A life insurance policy transferred by a partner to the partnership

    c. A life insurance policy transferred to a creditor in payment of a debt

    d. A life insurance policy purchased by a taxpayer insuring his or her spouse

    e. A life insurance policy purchased by a corporation insuring an officer

LO 2.8   16. Harry's wife Lila passes away in January of the current year. Fortunately, Lila had a $1 million life insurance policy. Harry elects to receive all $1 million in the current year and spends $200,000 of it on a luxury around-the-world trip with his new girlfriend. Harry's gross income from the life insurance is:

    a. $0

    b. $200,000

    c. $800,000

    d. $1,000,000

LO 2.9   17. Nomi is in the highest individual tax bracket and receives $500 in qualified dividends from Omega Corp. Nomi's tax liability (not including any net investment income tax) with respect to these dividends is:

    a. $0

    b. $277.20

    c. $100.00

    d. $75.00

    e. $50.00

LO 2.9   18. Rebecca, a single taxpayer, owns a Series I U.S. Savings Bond that increased in value by $46 during the year. She makes no special election. How much income must Rebecca recognize this year?

    a. $0

    b. $46

    c. $23

    d. $0 if in first 5 years or $46 thereafter

LO 2.10   19. Interest from which of the following types of bonds is included in federal taxable income?

    a. State of California bond

    b. City of New Orleans bond

    c. Bond of the Commonwealth of Puerto Rico

    d. U.S. Treasury Bond

    e. All of the above are excluded from income

LO 2.11   20. Which of the following gifts would probably be held to be taxable to the person receiving the gift?

    a. One thousand dollars given to a taxpayer by his or her father

    b. An acre of land given to a taxpayer by a friend

    c. A car given to a loyal employee by her supervisor when she retired to recognize her faithful service

    d. A Mercedes-Benz given to a taxpayer by his cousin

    e. An interest in a partnership given to a taxpayer by his or her uncle

LO 2.12   21. Kelly receives a $40,000 scholarship to Ivy University. She uses $30,000 on tuition and books, $5,000 for a used car, and $5,000 for rent while at school. Kelly will recognize _____ gross income.

    a. $0

    b. $5,000

    c. $10,000

    d. $30,000

    e. $40,000

LO 2.13

22. Hillary gets divorced in 2016 and is required to pay her ex-spouse $200 per month until her son reaches 18 years of age in 7 years and $120 per month thereafter. How much of her 2019 payments are deductible as alimony?
    a. $0
    b. $2,400
    c. $1,440
    d. $960

LO 2.13

23. Ivanka and Jared are divorced in the current year. As part of the divorce settlement, Ivanka transfers a plot of land in Long Island, NY to Jared. Ivanka's basis in the property was $20,000 and the market value of the property was $250,000 when transferred. Jared holds the property through the end of the year and in hopes of building a residence on it. How much income do Ivanka and Jared recognize in the current year?
    a. $0 for Ivanka and $20,000 for Jared
    b. $230,000 for Ivanka and $20,000 for Jared
    c. $230,000 for Ivanka and $0 for Jared
    d. $0 for both Ivanka and Jared
    e. $0 for Ivanka and $250,000 for Jared

LO 2.14

24. Gina receives a $2,900 distribution from her educational savings account. She uses $1,500 to pay for qualified higher education expenses and $1,400 on a vacation. Immediately prior to the distribution, Gina's account balance is $5,000, $3,000 of which is her contributions. What is Gina's taxable income (after any exclusion) from the distribution?
    a. $1,400
    b. $560
    c. $840
    d. $0
    e. Some other amount

LO 2.14

25. Which of the following is correct for Qualified Tuition Programs?
    a. Contributions are deductible, and qualified educational expense distributions are tax free.
    b. Contributions are not deductible, and qualified educational expense distributions are tax free.
    c. Contributions are deductible, and qualified educational expense distributions are taxable.
    d. Contributions are not deductible, and qualified educational expense distributions are taxable.

LO 2.14

26. In 2019, Amy receives $8,000 (of which $3,000 is earnings) from a qualified tuition program. She does not use the funds to pay for tuition or other qualified higher education expenses. What amount is taxable to Amy?
    a. $0
    b. $8,000
    c. $3,000
    d. $11,000

LO 2.14

27. For married taxpayers filing a joint return in 2019, at what AGI level does the phase-out limit for contributions to Qualified Tuition Programs start?
    a. $110,000
    b. $190,000
    c. $220,000
    d. There is no phase-out limit on QTP contributions

LO 2.14   28. Which of the following is *not* true with respect to education incentives?
a. The contributions to qualified tuition programs (Section 529 plans) are not deductible.
b. The contributions to educational savings accounts (Coverdell ESA) are not deductible.
c. Tuition paid by a taxpayer earning $300,000 of income is not deductible.
d. Married taxpayers must have income less than $100,000 to contribute to a qualified tuition program (Section 529 plan).

LO 2.14   29. During 2019, Carl (a single taxpayer) has a salary of $91,500 and interest income of $11,000. Calculate the maximum contribution Carl is allowed for an educational savings account.
a. $0
b. $400
c. $1,000
d. $2,000
e. Some other amount

LO 2.14   30. George receives a $1,500 distribution from his educational savings account. He uses $1,200 to pay for qualified higher education expenses. Immediately prior to the distribution, George's account balance is $5,000, $3,000 of which is his contributions. What is George's tax-free return of capital from the distribution?
a. $1,500
b. $1,200
c. $900
d. $750
e. $600

LO 2.15   31. Alicia loses her job part way through 2019. Her employer pays her wages of $15,450 up through her date of termination. After that, she received $3,400 of unemployment compensation from the state until she gets a new job for which she is paid wages of $3,000 through year end. Based on this information, Alicia's gross income for 2019 is:
a. $0
b. $3,000
c. $6,400
d. $18,450
e. $21,850

LO 2.16   32. For 2019, the minimum percentage of Social Security benefits that could be included in a taxpayer's gross income is:
a. 0%
b. 25%
c. 50%
d. 75%
e. 85%

LO 2.16   33. Generally, modified adjusted gross income (MAGI) is adjusted gross income (without Social Security benefits):
a. Less tax-exempt interest
b. Less personal and dependency exemptions
c. Less itemized deductions
d. Less tax-exempt interest plus any foreign income exclusion
e. Plus tax-exempt interest income

LO 2.17

34. Dana and Larry are married and live in Texas. Dana earns a salary of $45,000 and Larry has $25,000 of rental income from his separate property. If Dana and Larry file separate tax returns, what amount of income must Larry report?
    a. $0
    b. $22,500
    c. $25,000
    d. $47,500
    e. None of the above

LO 2.17

35. Which of the following conditions need *not* be satisfied in order for a married taxpayer, residing in a community property state, to be taxed only on his or her separate salary?
    a. The husband and wife must live apart for the entire year.
    b. A minor child must be living with the spouse.
    c. The husband and wife must not file a joint income tax return.
    d. The husband and wife must not transfer earned income between themselves.
    e. All of the above must be satisfied.

GROUP 2:
PROBLEMS

LO 2.1

1. Indicate whether each of the items listed below would be included (I) in or excluded (E) from gross income for the 2019 tax year.
    _____ a. Welfare payments
    _____ b. Commissions
    _____ c. Hobby income
    _____ d. Scholarships for room and board
    _____ e. $300 set of golf clubs, an employee award for length of service
    _____ f. Severance pay
    _____ g. Ordinary dividend of $50
    _____ h. Accident insurance proceeds received for personal bodily injury
    _____ i. Inheritances
    _____ j. Gifts
    _____ k. Tips and gratuities

LO 2.1

2. Jane is a roofing contractor. Jane's friend needed a new roof but did not have the cash to pay. Jane's friend instead paid with a used truck that Jane could use in her roofing business. The truck had originally cost the friend $17,500 but it was gently used and only worth $6,000. Jane did not actually need the truck and ended up selling it to a used car dealer for $5,200 a few months later. Explain what amount of gross income Jane must recognize as a result of the truck payment and why. _____
    _____
    _____
    _____

LO 2.1

3. Larry is a tax accountant and Sheila is a hairdresser. Larry prepares Sheila's tax return for free and Sheila agrees to style Larry's hair six times for free in return for the tax return. The value of the tax return is approximately $300 and the hair styling work is approximately $300.
    a. How much of the $300 is includable income to Larry? Why? _____
    _____
    _____
    b. How much of the $300 is includable income to Sheila? Why? _____
    _____
    _____

LO 2.1

4. Kerry and Jim have a successful marijuana farm in the woods around Humboldt County, California. Growing marijuana is illegal for federal purposes. Are Kerry and Jim required by law to report the income from their farm on their tax return? Why? _____
_____
_____

LO 2.2

5. Kristen, a single taxpayer, receives two 2019 Forms W-2 from the two employers she worked for during the year. One Form W-2 lists her wages in Boxes 1, 3, and 5 as $18,700. Her other employer's Form W-2 has $43,000 in Box 1 but only $46,500 in both Box 3 and Box 5. Kristen participated in the second employer's 401(k) plan. She also received health care from her second employer. Lastly, her second employer provided $30,000 of group term life insurance to Kristen.
   a. What amount should Kristen report as taxable wages in 2019?
   b. What could explain the difference between Box 1 wages and Boxes 3 and 5 on her second employer's W-2?

LO 2.3

6. Skyler is covered by his company's health insurance plan. The health insurance costs his company $9,500 a year. During the year, Skyler is diagnosed with a serious illness and health insurance pays $100,000 for surgery and treatment. How much of the insurance and treatment payments are taxable to Skyler? _____
_____

LO 2.3

7. Ellen is a single taxpayer. Ellen's employer pays $150 per month ($1,800 this year) for her health insurance. During the year, Ellen had medical expenses of $3,500 and the insurance company paid $2,000 of the expenses. How much of the above amounts, if any, must be included in Ellen's gross income?

$ _____

   Why? _____
_____

LO 2.4

8. a. Milton is a nurse whose employer provided meals for him on the employer's premises, since he is given only 30 minutes for lunch. Is the value of these meals taxable income to Milton?
   Explain _____
_____

   b. Mary is a San Diego ambulance driver. The city provides Mary with meals while she is working so she will be available for emergencies. Is the value of these meals taxable income to Mary?
   Explain _____
_____

   c. Indigo is the head of security at a casino. The casino operator frequently provides meals from the casino buffett to Indigo as a gesture of goodwill for the great job she is doing. Is the value of these meals taxable income to Indigo?
   Explain _____
_____

LO 2.5

9. Linda and Richard are married and file a joint return for 2019. During the year, Linda, who works as an accountant for a national airline, used $2,100 worth of free passes for travel on the airline; Richard used the same amount. Linda and Richard also used $850 worth of employee discount coupons for hotel rooms at the hotel chain that is also owned by the airline. Richard is employed at State University as an accounting clerk. Under a tuition reduction plan, Richard saved $4,000 in tuition fees during 2019. He is studying for a master's degree in business at night while still working full-time. Richard also had $30 worth of personal typing done by his administrative assistant at the University. What is the amount of fringe benefits that should be included in Linda and Richard's gross income on their 2019 tax return?

$ _____

LO 2.5

10. Ellen's tax client, Tom, is employed at a large company that offers health care flexible spending accounts to its employees. Tom must decide at the beginning of the year whether he wants to put as much as $2,700 of his salary into the health care flexible spending account. He expects that he will have to pay for at least $8,000 of medical expenses for his family during the year since his wife is seeing a psychiatrist every week and his daughter and son are both having their teeth straightened. Tom does not itemize deductions. Should Ellen recommend that Tom put the maximum amount in his health care flexible spending account, and if so, why? _____

_____

_____

LO 2.6

11. How much of each of the following is taxable?
   a. Cheline, an actress, received a $6,400 gift bag for attending the Academy Awards Ceremony during 2019.
   b. Jon received a gold watch worth $660 for 25 years of service to his accounting firm (not a qualified award).
   c. Kerry won $1,000,000 in her state lottery.
   d. Deborah is a professor who received $30,000 as an award for her scientific research from the university that employs her.

LO 2.6
LO 2.12

12. For each of the following independent cases, indicate the amount of gross income that must be included on the taxpayer's 2019 income tax return.
   a. Malchia won a $4,000 humanitarian award.

$ _____

   b. Rob won a new automobile (with a sticker price of $15,700 and a market value of $14,500) for being the best junior tennis player in 2019.

$ _____

   c. George received a $3,500 tuition and fees scholarship to attend Western University.

$ _____

LO 2.7

13. Lola, age 67, began receiving a $1,000 monthly annuity in the current year upon the death of her husband. She received seven payments in the current year. Her husband contributed $48,300 to the qualified employee plan. Use the Simplified Method Worksheet below to calculate Lola's taxable amount from the annuity.

SIMPLIFIED METHOD WORKSHEET

1. Enter total amount received this year.   1. _____

2. Enter cost in the plan at the annuity starting date.   2. _____

3. Age at annuity starting date

	Enter
55 and under	360
56–60	310
61–65	260
66–70	210
71 and older	160

3. _____

4. Divide line 2 by line 3.   4. _____

Group 2, Problem 13 continued on Page 2-51.

5. Multiply line 4 by the number of monthly payments this year. If the annuity starting date was before 1987, also enter this amount on line 8, and skip lines 6 and 7. Otherwise, go to line 6.

5. _____

6. Enter the amount, if any, recovered tax free in prior years.

6. _____

7. Subtract line 6 from line 2.

7. _____

8. Enter the smaller of line 5 or 7.

8. _____

9. Taxable amount this year: Subtract line 8 from line 1. Do not enter less than zero.

9. _____

LO 2.8

14. Sharon transfers to Russ a life insurance policy with a cash surrender value of $27,000 and a face value of $100,000 in exchange for real estate. Russ continues to pay the premiums on the policy until Sharon dies 7 years later. At that time, Russ has paid $12,000 in premiums, and he collects the $100,000 face value. How much of the proceeds is taxable to Russ?

$ _____

Why? _____

_____

LO 2.8

15. Greg died on July 1, 2019, and left Lea, his wife, a $45,000 life insurance policy which she elects to receive at $9,000 per year plus interest for 5 years. In the current year, Lea receives $9,500. How much should Lea include in her gross income?

$ _____

LO 2.8

16. David is certified by his doctor as terminally ill with liver disease. His doctor certifies that he cannot reasonably be expected to live for more than a year. He sells his life insurance policy to Viatical Settlements, Inc., for $250,000. He has paid $20,000 so far for the policy. How much of the $250,000 must David include in his taxable income? _____

_____

LO 2.8

17. Helen receives a $200,000 lump sum life insurance payment when her friend Alice dies. How much of the payment is taxable to Helen? _____

_____

LO 2.9

18. How are qualified dividends taxed in 2019? Please give the rates of tax which apply to qualified dividends, and specify when each of these rates applies. _____

_____

_____

LO 2.9

19. Describe the methods that an individual taxpayer that holds Series I Bonds can use to recognize interest.

_____

_____

LO 2.9

20. Sally and Charles Heck received the following Form 1099-DIV in 2019:

☐ CORRECTED (if checked)			
PAYER'S name, street address, city or town, state or province, country, ZIP or foreign postal code, and telephone no.	**1a** Total ordinary dividends $ 850.00	OMB No. 1545-0110 **2019** Form **1099-DIV**	**Dividends and Distributions**
Devona Corporation 33133 Hilltop Drive Alpine, CA 91901	**1b** Qualified dividends $ 694.00		
	2a Total capital gain distr. $	**2b** Unrecap. Sec. 1250 gain $	**Copy B**
PAYER'S TIN **RECIPIENT'S TIN** 27-1234567 313-13-1313	**2c** Section 1202 gain $	**2d** Collectibles (28%) gain $	**For Recipient**
RECIPIENT'S name Sally Heck	**3** Nondividend distributions $	**4** Federal income tax withheld $ 0.00	This is important tax information and is being furnished to the IRS. If you are required to file a return, a negligence penalty or other sanction may be imposed on you if this income is taxable and the IRS determines that it has not been reported.
	5 Section 199A dividends $	**6** Investment expenses $	
Street address (including apt. no.) 1420 Pasadena Blvd.	**7** Foreign tax paid $	**8** Foreign country or U.S. possession	
City or town, state or province, country, and ZIP or foreign postal code Carrollton, TX 75007	**9** Cash liquidation distributions $	**10** Noncash liquidation distributions $	
	FATCA filing requirement ☐	**11** Exempt-interest dividends $	**12** Specified private activity bond interest dividends $
Account number (see instructions)	**13** State **14** State identification no.	**15** State tax withheld $ $	

Form **1099-DIV**   (keep for your records)   www.irs.gov/Form1099DIV   Department of the Treasury - Internal Revenue Service

The Hecks also received the following dividends and interest in 2019 (Forms 1099-DIV not shown):

	Sally	Charles	Jointly
Qualifying dividends:			
Altus Inc.	$2,000		
Buller Corp.		$350	
Gene Corporation			$3,100
Interest:			
Porcine Bank			1,245
River Bank			650
City of New York Bonds		100	

    Assuming the Hecks file a joint tax return, complete Schedule B of Form 1040 (on Page 2-53) for them for the 2019 tax year. Do not attempt to complete the Qualified Dividends and Capital Gain Tax Worksheet.

LO 2.10

21. Vandell is a taxpayer in the 25 percent tax bracket. He invests in Otay Mesa Water District Bonds that pay 4.5 percent interest. What interest on a taxable bond would provide the same after-tax return to Vandell?

_____%

LO 2.10

22. Karen is a wealthy retired investment advisor who is in the 35 percent tax bracket. She has a choice between investing in a high-quality municipal bond paying 5 percent or a high-quality corporate bond paying 7 percent. What is the after-tax return of each bond and which one should Karen invest in? Explain your answer.

_____

_____

_____

LO 2.11

23. In June of 2019, Kevin inherits stock worth $125,000. During the year, he collects $5,600 in dividends from the stock. How much of these amounts, if any, should Kevin include in his gross income for 2019?

$ _____

Why? _____

_____

SCHEDULE B
(Form 1040 or 1040-SR)

Department of the Treasury
Internal Revenue Service (99)

Interest and Ordinary Dividends

▶ Go to *www.irs.gov/ScheduleB* for instructions and the latest information.
▶ Attach to Form 1040 or 1040-SR.

OMB No. 1545-0074

2019

Attachment
Sequence No. **08**

Name(s) shown on return

Your social security number

			Amount
Part I	**1**	List name of payer. If any interest is from a seller-financed mortgage and the buyer used the property as a personal residence, see the instructions and list this interest first. Also, show that buyer's social security number and address ▶	
Interest			
(See instructions and the instructions for Forms 1040 and 1040-SR, line 2b.)			**1**
Note: If you received a Form 1099-INT, Form 1099-OID, or substitute statement from a brokerage firm, list the firm's name as the payer and enter the total interest shown on that form.			
	2	Add the amounts on line 1	**2**
	3	Excludable interest on series EE and I U.S. savings bonds issued after 1989. Attach Form 8815	**3**
	4	Subtract line 3 from line 2. Enter the result here and on Form 1040 or 1040-SR, line 2b . . . . ▶	**4**

Note: If line 4 is over $1,500, you must complete Part III.

			Amount
Part II	**5**	List name of payer ▶	
Ordinary Dividends			
(See instructions and the instructions for Forms 1040 and 1040-SR, line 3b.)			**5**
Note: If you received a Form 1099-DIV or substitute statement from a brokerage firm, list the firm's name as the payer and enter the ordinary dividends shown on that form.			
	6	Add the amounts on line 5. Enter the total here and on Form 1040 or 1040-SR, line 3b . . . . ▶	**6**

Note: If line 6 is over $1,500, you must complete Part III.

			Yes	No
Part III		You must complete this part if you **(a)** had over $1,500 of taxable interest or ordinary dividends; **(b)** had a foreign account; or **(c)** received a distribution from, or were a grantor of, or a transferor to, a foreign trust.		
Foreign Accounts and Trusts	**7a**	At any time during 2019, did you have a financial interest in or signature authority over a financial account (such as a bank account, securities account, or brokerage account) located in a foreign country? See instructions		
		If "Yes," are you required to file FinCEN Form 114, Report of Foreign Bank and Financial Accounts (FBAR), to report that financial interest or signature authority? See FinCEN Form 114 and its instructions for filing requirements and exceptions to those requirements		
Caution: If required, failure to file FinCEN Form 114 may result in substantial penalties. See instructions.	**b**	If you are required to file FinCEN Form 114, enter the name of the foreign country where the financial account is located ▶		
	8	During 2019, did you receive a distribution from, or were you the grantor of, or transferor to, a foreign trust? If "Yes," you may have to file Form 3520. See instructions		

For Paperwork Reduction Act Notice, see your tax return instructions.   Cat. No. 17146N   **Schedule B (Form 1040 or 1040-SR) 2019**

LO 2.11

24. Gwen is a tax accountant who works very hard for a large corporate client. The client is pleased and gives her a gift of $10,000 at year-end. How much of the gift is taxable to Gwen? _____

LO 2.11

25. Charlene receives a gift from her boyfriend of $10,000. He knows she is having financial problems and wants to help her. How much of the gift is taxable to Charlene? _____

LO 2.12

26. Robbie receives a scholarship of $20,000 to an elite private college. $8,000 of the scholarship is earmarked for tuition, and $12,000 covers his room and board. How much of the scholarship, if any, is taxable to Robbie? _____

LO 2.13

27. Answer the following questions:

a. Under a 2017 divorce agreement, Joan is required to pay her ex-husband, Bill, $700 a month until their daughter is 18 years of age. At that time, the required payments are reduced to $450 per month.

   1. How much of each $700 payment may be deducted as alimony by Joan?
      $ _____

   2. How much of each $700 payment must be included in Bill's taxable income?
      $ _____

   3. How much would be deductible/included if the divorce agreement were dated 2019?
      $ _____

b. Under the terms of a property settlement executed during 2019, Jane transferred property worth $450,000 to her ex-husband, Tom. The property has a tax basis to Jane of $425,000.

   1. How much taxable gain must be recognized by Jane at the time of the transfer?
      $ _____

   2. What is the amount of Tom's tax basis in the property he received from Jane?
      $ _____

LO 2.13

28. Arlen is required by his 2019 divorce agreement to pay alimony of $2,000 a month and child support of $2,000 a month to his ex-wife Jane. What is the tax treatment of these two payments for Arlen? What is the tax treatment of these two payments for Jane?

   Arlen _____

   Jane _____

LO 2.13

29. As part of the property settlement related to their divorce, Cindy must give Allen the house that they have been living in, while she gets 100 percent of their savings accounts. The house was purchased for $90,000 20 years ago in Southern California and is now worth $700,000. How much gain must Cindy recognize on the transfer of the house to Allen? What is Allen's tax basis in the house for calculating tax on any future sale of the house?

   Cindy _____

   Allen _____

LO 2.14

30. Jose paid the following amounts for his son to attend Big State University in 2019:

Tuition	$6,400
Room and board	4,775
Books	772
A car to use at school	1,932
Student football tickets	237
Spending money	4,000

How much of the above is a qualified higher education expense for purposes of his Qualified Tuition Program?

$ _____

LO 2.14

31. In 2019, Van receives $20,000 (of which $4,000 is earnings) from a qualified tuition program. He uses the funds to pay for his college tuition and other qualified higher education expenses. How much of the $20,000 is taxable to Van?

$ _____

LO 2.15

32. Lydia, a married individual, was unemployed for a few months during 2019. During the year, she received $3,250 in unemployment compensation payments. How much of her unemployment compensation payments must be included in gross income?

$ _____

LO 2.16

33. During the 2019 tax year, Brian, a single taxpayer, received $7,400 in Social Security benefits. His adjusted gross income for the year was $14,500 (not including the Social Security benefits) and he received $30,000 in tax-exempt interest income and has no for-AGI deductions. Calculate the amount of the Social Security benefits that Brian must include in his gross income for 2019.

SIMPLIFIED TAXABLE SOCIAL SECURITY WORKSHEET (FOR MOST PEOPLE)

1. Enter the total amount of Social Security income.   1. _____

2. Enter one-half of line 1.   2. _____

3. Enter the total of taxable income items on Form 1040 except Social Security income.   3. _____

4. Enter the amount of tax-exempt interest income.   4. _____

5. Add lines 2, 3, and 4.   5. _____

6. Enter all adjustments for AGI except for student loan interest, the domestic production activities deduction, and the tuition and fees deduction.   6. _____

7. Subtract line 6 from line 5. If zero or less, stop here, none of the Social Security benefits are taxable.   7. _____

8. Enter $25,000 ($32,000 if married filing jointly; $0 if married filing separately and living with spouse at any time during the year).   8. _____

9. Subtract line 8 from line 7. If zero or less, enter –0–.   9. _____

Note: If line 9 is zero or less, stop here; **none of your benefits are taxable.** Otherwise, go on to line 10.

10. Enter $9,000 ($12,000 if married filing jointly; $0 if married filing separately and living with spouse at any time during the year).   10. _____

11. Subtract line 10 from line 9. If zero or less, enter –0–.   11. _____

12. Enter the **smaller** of line 9 or line 10.   12. _____

13. Enter one-half of line 12.   13. _____

14. Enter the **smaller** of line 2 or line 13.   14. _____

15. Multiply line 11 by 85% (.85). If line 11 is zero, enter –0–.   15. _____

16. Add lines 14 and 15.   16. _____

17. Multiply line 1 by 85% (.85).   17. _____

18. **Taxable benefits**. Enter the **smaller** of line 16 or line 17.   18. _____

LO 2.16

34. Please answer the following questions regarding the taxability of Social Security:

a. A 68-year-old taxpayer has $20,000 in Social Security income and $100,000 in tax-free municipal bond income. Does the municipal bond income affect the amount of Social Security the taxpayer must include in income? _____
_____

b. A 68-year-old taxpayer has $20,000 in Social Security income and no other taxable or tax-free income. How much of the Social Security income must the taxpayer include in taxable income? _____
_____
_____

c. A 68-year-old taxpayer has $20,000 in Social Security income and has significant other taxable retirement income. What is the maximum percentage of Social Security that the taxpayer might be required to include in taxable income? _____
_____
_____

GROUP 3:
WRITING ASSIGNMENT

RESEARCH

1. Vanessa Lazo was an amazing high school student and so it was no great surprise when she was accepted into Prestige Private University (PPU). To entice Vanessa to attend PPU, the school offered her a reduced tuition of $13,000 per year (full-time tuition would typically be $43,000 per year). PPU also has a scholarship program thanks to a large donation from William Gatos. Vanessa was the Gatos Scholarship winner and will receive a scholarship for $20,000. Vanessa is required to use the scholarship first to pay her $13,000 tuition and the remainder is to cover room and board at PPU. Lastly, PPU also offered Vanessa a part-time job on the PPU campus as a student lab assistant in the Biology Department of PPU for which she is paid $1,500.

Required: Go to the IRS website (**www.irs.gov**) and locate Publication 970. Review the section on Scholarships. Write a letter to Vanessa Lazo stating how much of the PPU package for Vanessa is taxable.
(An example of a client letter is available at the website for this textbook, located at **www.cengage.com**.)

GROUP 4:
COMPREHENSIVE PROBLEMS

1. Beverly and Ken Hair have been married for 3 years. Beverly works as an accountant at Cypress Corporation. Ken is a full-time student at Southwest Missouri State University (SMSU) and also works part-time during the summer at Cypress Corp. Ken's birthdate is January 12, 1993 and Beverly's birthdate is November 4, 1995. Bev and Ken's earnings and income tax withholdings are reported on the following Form W-2s:

a Employee's social security number		
465-74-3321	OMB No. 1545-0008	Safe, accurate, FAST! Use IRS e-file Visit the IRS website at www.irs.gov/efile

b Employer identification number (EIN) 31-1238967	1 Wages, tips, other compensation 51,000.00	2 Federal income tax withheld 4,790.00
c Employer's name, address, and ZIP code Cypress Corp. 1234 E. Chestnut Parkway Springfield, MO 65802	3 Social security wages 51,000.00	4 Social security tax withheld 3,162.00
	5 Medicare wages and tips 51,000.00	6 Medicare tax withheld 739.50
	7 Social security tips	8 Allocated tips
d Control number	9	10 Dependent care benefits
e Employee's first name and initial Last name Suff. Beverly Hair 3567 River Street Springfield, MO 63126	11 Nonqualified plans	12a See instructions for box 12
	13 Statutory employee ☐ Retirement plan ☐ Third-party sick pay ☐	12b
	14 Other	12c
		12d
f Employee's address and ZIP code		

15 State Employer's state ID number	16 State wages, tips, etc.	17 State income tax	18 Local wages, tips, etc.	19 Local income tax	20 Locality name
MO	51,000.00	680.00			

Form **W-2** Wage and Tax Statement   **2019**   Department of the Treasury—Internal Revenue Service

Copy B—To Be Filed With Employee's FEDERAL Tax Return.
This information is being furnished to the Internal Revenue Service.

a Employee's social security number		
465-57-9934	OMB No. 1545-0008	Safe, accurate, FAST! Use IRS e-file Visit the IRS website at www.irs.gov/efile

b Employer identification number (EIN) 31-1238967	1 Wages, tips, other compensation 2,700.00	2 Federal income tax withheld 0.00
c Employer's name, address, and ZIP code Cypress Corp. 1234 E. Chestnut Parkway Springfield, MO 65802	3 Social security wages 2,700.00	4 Social security tax withheld 167.40
	5 Medicare wages and tips 2,700.00	6 Medicare tax withheld 39.15
	7 Social security tips	8 Allocated tips
d Control number	9	10 Dependent care benefits
e Employee's first name and initial Last name Suff. Ken Hair 3567 River Street Springfield, MO 63126	11 Nonqualified plans	12a See instructions for box 12
	13 Statutory employee ☐ Retirement plan ☐ Third-party sick pay ☐	12b
	14 Other	12c
		12d
f Employee's address and ZIP code		

15 State Employer's state ID number	16 State wages, tips, etc.	17 State income tax	18 Local wages, tips, etc.	19 Local income tax	20 Locality name
MO	2,700.00	0.00			

Form **W-2** Wage and Tax Statement   **2019**   Department of the Treasury—Internal Revenue Service

Copy B—To Be Filed With Employee's FEDERAL Tax Return.
This information is being furnished to the Internal Revenue Service.

The Hairs have interest income of $1,000 on City of St. Louis bonds. Beverly and Ken also received the following Form 1099-INT and 1099-DIV:

☐ CORRECTED (if checked)

PAYER'S name, street address, city or town, state or province, country, ZIP or foreign postal code, and telephone no.	Payer's RTN (optional)	OMB No. 1545-0112	**Interest Income**
Boatman's Bank 300 City Avenue Springfield, MO 63126	**1** Interest income $ 651.76	20**19** Form **1099-INT**	

			Copy B
		2 Early withdrawal penalty $	
PAYER'S TIN 33-1234566	RECIPIENT'S TIN 465-74-3321	**3** Interest on U.S. Savings Bonds and Treas. obligations $	For Recipient
RECIPIENT'S name Beverly and Ken Hair		**4** Federal income tax withheld $	**5** Investment expenses $	This is important tax information and is being furnished to the IRS. If you are required to file a return, a negligence penalty or other sanction may be imposed on you if this income is taxable and the IRS determines that it has not been reported.

Street address (including apt. no.) 3567 River Street	**6** Foreign tax paid $	**7** Foreign country or U.S. possession
City or town, state or province, country, and ZIP or foreign postal code Springfield, MO 63126	**8** Tax-exempt interest $	**9** Specified private activity bond interest $
	10 Market discount $	**11** Bond premium $
FATCA filing requirement ☐	**12** Bond premium on Treasury obligations $	**13** Bond premium on tax-exempt bond $
Account number (see instructions)	**14** Tax-exempt and tax credit bond CUSIP no.	**15** State	**16** State identification no.	**17** State tax withheld $ $

Form **1099-INT**   (keep for your records)   www.irs.gov/Form1099INT   Department of the Treasury - Internal Revenue Service

☐ CORRECTED (if checked)

PAYER'S name, street address, city or town, state or province, country, ZIP or foreign postal code, and telephone no.	**1a** Total ordinary dividends $ 300.00	OMB No. 1545-0110	**Dividends and Distributions**
Green Corporation 900 South Orange Ave. Springfield, MO 63126	**1b** Qualified dividends $ 300.00	20**19** Form **1099-DIV**	

	2a Total capital gain distr. $	**2b** Unrecap. Sec. 1250 gain $	Copy B
PAYER'S TIN 33-11223344	RECIPIENT'S TIN 465-57-9934	**2c** Section 1202 gain $	**2d** Collectibles (28%) gain $	For Recipient
RECIPIENT'S name Ken Hair	**3** Nondividend distributions $	**4** Federal income tax withheld $	This is important tax information and is being furnished to the IRS. If you are required to file a return, a negligence penalty or other sanction may be imposed on you if this income is taxable and the IRS determines that it has not been reported.
	5 Section 199A dividends $	**6** Investment expenses $	
Street address (including apt. no.) 3567 River Street	**7** Foreign tax paid $	**8** Foreign country or U.S. possession	
City or town, state or province, country, and ZIP or foreign postal code Springfield, MO 63126	**9** Cash liquidation distributions $	**10** Noncash liquidation distributions $	
FATCA filing requirement ☐	**11** Exempt-interest dividends $	**12** Specified private activity bond interest dividends $	
Account number (see instructions)	**13** State	**14** State identification no.	**15** State tax withheld $ $	

Form **1099-DIV**   (keep for your records)   www.irs.gov/Form1099DIV   Department of the Treasury - Internal Revenue Service

Ken is an excellent student at SMSU. He was given a $1,750 scholarship by the university to help pay educational expenses. The scholarship funds were used by Ken for tuition and books.

Last year, Beverly was laid off from her former job and was unemployed during January 2019. She was paid $1,825 of unemployment compensation until she started work with her current employer, Cypress Corporation.

Ken has a 4-year-old son, Robert R. Hair, from a prior marriage that ended in divorce in 2014. During 2019, he paid his ex-wife $300 per month in child support. Robert is claimed as a dependent by Ken's ex-wife.

During 2019, Ken's aunt died. The aunt, in her will, left Ken $15,000 in cash. Ken deposited this money in the Boatman's Bank savings account.

Required: Complete the Hairs' federal tax return for 2019 on Form 1040, Schedule 1, and the Qualified Dividends and Capital Gain Tax Worksheet.

2A. Ray and Maria Gomez have been married for 3 years. Ray is a propane salesman for Palm Oil Corporation and Maria works as a city clerk for the City of McAllen. Ray's birthdate is February 21, 1991 and Maria's is December 30, 1993. Ray and Maria's earnings are reported on the following Form W-2s:

a Employee's social security number 469-21-5523	OMB No. 1545-0008	Safe, accurate, FAST! Use *e-file*	Visit the IRS website at www.irs.gov/efile

b Employer identification number (EIN) 21-7654321	1 Wages, tips, other compensation 30,415.00	2 Federal income tax withheld 3,070.00
c Employer's name, address, and ZIP code Palm Oil Corporation 11134 E. Pecan Blvd. McAllen, TX 78501	3 Social security wages 30,415.00	4 Social security tax withheld 1,885.73
	5 Medicare wages and tips 30,415.00	6 Medicare tax withheld 441.02
	7 Social security tips	8 Allocated tips
d Control number	9	10 Dependent care benefits
e Employee's first name and initial Last name Suff. Ray Gomez 1610 Quince Avenue McAllen, TX 78701	11 Nonqualified plans	12a See instructions for box 12
	13 Statutory employee ☐ Retirement plan ☐ Third-party sick pay ☐	12b
	14 Other	12c
		12d
f Employee's address and ZIP code		

15 State Employer's state ID number TX	16 State wages, tips, etc.	17 State income tax	18 Local wages, tips, etc.	19 Local income tax	20 Locality name

Form **W-2** Wage and Tax Statement   **2019**   Department of the Treasury—Internal Revenue Service

Copy B—To Be Filed With Employee's FEDERAL Tax Return.
This information is being furnished to the Internal Revenue Service.

a Employee's social security number 444-65-9912	OMB No. 1545-0008	Safe, accurate, FAST! Use *e-file*	Visit the IRS website at www.irs.gov/efile

b Employer identification number (EIN) 23-4444321	1 Wages, tips, other compensation 32,402.00	2 Federal income tax withheld 2,654.00
c Employer's name, address, and ZIP code City of McAllen 1300 W. Houston Ave. McAllen, TX 78501	3 Social security wages 32,402.00	4 Social security tax withheld 2,008.92
	5 Medicare wages and tips 32,402.00	6 Medicare tax withheld 469.83
	7 Social security tips	8 Allocated tips
d Control number	9	10 Dependent care benefits
e Employee's first name and initial Last name Suff. Maria Gomez 1610 Quince Ave. McAllen, TX 78701	11 Nonqualified plans	12a See instructions for box 12
	13 Statutory employee ☐ Retirement plan ☐ Third-party sick pay ☐	12b
	14 Other	12c
		12d
f Employee's address and ZIP code		

15 State Employer's state ID number TX	16 State wages, tips, etc.	17 State income tax	18 Local wages, tips, etc.	19 Local income tax	20 Locality name

Form **W-2** Wage and Tax Statement   **2019**   Department of the Treasury—Internal Revenue Service

Copy B—To Be Filed With Employee's FEDERAL Tax Return.
This information is being furnished to the Internal Revenue Service.

Ray and Maria have interest income as reported on the following 1099-INT:

☐ CORRECTED (if checked)		
PAYER'S name, street address, city or town, state or province, country, ZIP or foreign postal code, and telephone no. McAllen State Bank 3302 N. 10th Street McAllen, TX 78501	Payer's RTN (optional) **1** Interest income $ 673.12	OMB No. 1545-0112 20**19** Form **1099-INT**	**Interest Income**
	2 Early withdrawal penalty $		**Copy B**
PAYER'S TIN 34-7657651 RECIPIENT'S TIN 444-65-9912	$ **3** Interest on U.S. Savings Bonds and Treas. obligations $		**For Recipient**
RECIPIENT'S name Maria Gomez	**4** Federal income tax withheld $ **5** Investment expenses $		This is important tax information and is being furnished to the IRS. If you are required to file a return, a negligence penalty or other sanction may be imposed on you if this income is taxable and the IRS determines that it has not been reported.
Street address (including apt. no.) 1610 Quince Avenue	**6** Foreign tax paid $ **7** Foreign country or U.S. possession		
	8 Tax-exempt interest $ **9** Specified private activity bond interest $		
City or town, state or province, country, and ZIP or foreign postal code McAllen, TX 78701	**10** Market discount $ **11** Bond premium $		
FATCA filing requirement ☐	**12** Bond premium on Treasury obligations $ **13** Bond premium on tax-exempt bond $		
Account number (see instructions)	**14** Tax-exempt and tax credit bond CUSIP no.	**15** State **16** State identification no. **17** State tax withheld $ $	

Form **1099-INT**   (keep for your records)   www.irs.gov/Form1099INT   Department of the Treasury - Internal Revenue Service

In addition, they own U.S. Savings bonds (Series EE). The bonds had a value of $10,000 on January 1, 2019, and their value is $10,700 on December 31, 2019. They have not made an election with respect to these bonds.

Ray has an ex-wife named Judy Gomez. Pursuant to their January 27, 2014 divorce decree, Ray pays her $450 per month in alimony. All payments were made on time in 2019. Judy's Social Security number is 566-74-8765.

During 2019, Ray was in the hospital for a successful operation. His health insurance company reimbursed Ray $4,732 for all of his hospital and doctor bills.

In June of 2019, Maria's father died. Under a life insurance policy owned and paid for by her father, Maria was paid death benefits of $25,000. She used $7,800 to cover a portion of the funeral costs for her father.

Maria bought a Texas lottery ticket on impulse during 2019. Her ticket was lucky and she won $4,025. The winning amount was paid to Maria in November 2019, with no income tax withheld.

Palm Oil Corporation provides Ray with a company car to drive while he is working. The Corporation spent $5,000 to maintain this vehicle during 2019. Ray never uses the car for personal purposes.

Required: Complete the Gomez's federal tax return for 2019 on Form 1040 and Schedule 1.

2B. Carl Conch and Mary Duval are married and file a joint return. Carl works for the Key Lime Pie Company and Mary is a homemaker after losing her job in 2018. Carl's birthdate is June 14, 1974 and Mary's is October 2, 1974. Carl's earnings are reported on the following Form W-2:

a Employee's social security number 835-21-5423		OMB No. 1545-0008	Safe, accurate, FAST! Use	IRS **e-file**	Visit the IRS website at www.irs.gov/efile

b Employer identification number (EIN) 61-7654321	**1** Wages, tips, other compensation 67,894.88	**2** Federal income tax withheld 6,650.00

c Employer's name, address, and ZIP code Key Lime Pie Company 223 Key Deer Blvd.	**3** Social security wages 67,894.88	**4** Social security tax withheld 4,209.48
	5 Medicare wages and tips 67,894.88	**6** Medicare tax withheld 984.48
	7 Social security tips	**8** Allocated tips

d Control number	**9**	**10** Dependent care benefits

e Employee's first name and initial Last name Suff.	**11** Nonqualified plans	**12a** See instructions for box 12 C 240.00
Carl Conch 1234 Mallory Square, Apt. #64 Key West, FL 33040	**13** Statutory employee ☐ Retirement plan ☐ Third-party sick pay ☐	**12b**
	14 Other Parking $1,680.00	**12c**
		12d

f Employee's address and ZIP code

15 State Employer's state ID number FL	**16** State wages, tips, etc.	**17** State income tax	**18** Local wages, tips, etc.	**19** Local income tax	**20** Locality name

Form **W-2** **Wage and Tax Statement**   **2019**   Department of the Treasury—Internal Revenue Service

Copy B—To Be Filed With Employee's FEDERAL Tax Return.
This information is being furnished to the Internal Revenue Service.

Carl and Mary received the following Forms 1099:

☐ CORRECTED (if checked)

PAYER'S name, street address, city or town, state or province, country, ZIP or foreign postal code, and telephone no. Coral Reef Bank 3102 Simonton Street Key West, FL 33040	Payer's RTN (optional)	OMB No. 1545-0112 2019	**Interest Income**
	1 Interest income $ 369.91	Form **1099-INT**	
	2 Early withdrawal penalty $		**Copy B**
PAYER'S TIN 31-1234444 RECIPIENT'S TIN 633-65-7912	**3** Interest on U.S. Savings Bonds and Treas. obligations $		**For Recipient**
RECIPIENT'S name Mary Duval and Carl Conch	**4** Federal income tax withheld $	**5** Investment expenses $	This is important tax information and is being furnished to the IRS. If you are required to file a return, a negligence penalty or other sanction may be imposed on you if this income is taxable and the IRS determines that it has not been reported.
Street address (including apt. no.) 1234 Mallory Sq. Apt 64	**6** Foreign tax paid $	**7** Foreign country or U.S. possession	
	8 Tax-exempt interest $	**9** Specified private activity bond interest $	
City or town, state or province, country, and ZIP or foreign postal code Key West, FL 33040	**10** Market discount $	**11** Bond premium $	
FATCA filing requirement ☐	**12** Bond premium on Treasury obligations $	**13** Bond premium on tax-exempt bond $	
Account number (see instructions)	**14** Tax-exempt and tax credit bond CUSIP no.	**15** State **16** State identification no.	**17** State tax withheld $ $

Form **1099-INT**   (keep for your records)   www.irs.gov/Form1099INT   Department of the Treasury - Internal Revenue Service

☐ CORRECTED (if checked)

PAYER'S name, street address, city or town, state or province, country, ZIP or foreign postal code, and telephone no.	1a Total ordinary dividends	OMB No. 1545-0110	Dividends and Distributions
Southwest Corporation PO Box 36611 Dallas, TX 75235	$ 234.00	20**19**	
	1b Qualified dividends		
	$ 0.00	Form **1099-DIV**	
	2a Total capital gain distr. $	2b Unrecap. Sec. 1250 gain $	Copy B For Recipient
PAYER'S TIN: 74-1536241 RECIPIENT'S TIN: 835-21-5423	2c Section 1202 gain $	2d Collectibles (28%) gain $	
RECIPIENT'S name Carl Conch	3 Nondividend distributions $	4 Federal income tax withheld $	This is important tax information and is being furnished to the IRS. If you are required to file a return, a negligence penalty or other sanction may be imposed on you if this income is taxable and the IRS determines that it has not been reported.
	5 Section 199A dividends $	6 Investment expenses $	
Street address (including apt. no.) 1234 Mallory Square #64	7 Foreign tax paid $	8 Foreign country or U.S. possession	
City or town, state or province, country, and ZIP or foreign postal code Key West, FL 33040	9 Cash liquidation distributions $	10 Noncash liquidation distributions $	
FATCA filing requirement ☐	11 Exempt-interest dividends $	12 Specified private activity bond interest dividends $	
Account number (see instructions)	13 State	14 State identification no. $ $	15 State tax withheld

Form **1099-DIV**   (keep for your records)   www.irs.gov/Form1099DIV   Department of the Treasury - Internal Revenue Service

Mary is divorced and she pays her ex-husband (Tom Tortuga) child support. Pursuant to their 2016 divorce decree, Mary pays Tom $500 per month in child support. All payments were made on time in 2019.

In June 2019, Mary's father gave her a cash gift of $75,000. Mary also received unemployment compensation as shown on the following Form 1099-G:

☐ CORRECTED (if checked)

PAYER'S name, street address, city or town, state or province, country, ZIP or foreign postal code, and telephone no.	1 Unemployment compensation	OMB No. 1545-0120	Certain Government Payments
Florida Dept of Econ Opportunity 107 E. Jefferson St. Tallahassee, FL 32399	$ 2,989.00	20**19**	
	2 State or local income tax refunds, credits, or offsets $	Form **1099-G**	
PAYER'S TIN: 21-5556666 RECIPIENT'S TIN: 3633-65-7912	3 Box 2 amount is for tax year	4 Federal income tax withheld $ 170.00	Copy B For Recipient
RECIPIENT'S name Mary Duval	5 RTAA payments $	6 Taxable grants $	This is important tax information and is being furnished to the IRS. If you are required to file a return, a negligence penalty or other sanction may be imposed on you if this income is taxable and the IRS determines that it has not been reported.
Street address (including apt. no.) 1234 Mallory Sq. #64	7 Agriculture payments $	8 If checked, box 2 is trade or business income ▶ ☐	
City or town, state or province, country, and ZIP or foreign postal code Key West, FL 33040	9 Market gain $		
Account number (see instructions)	10a State	10b State identification no.	11 State income tax withheld $ $

Form **1099-G**   (keep for your records)   www.irs.gov/Form1099G   Department of the Treasury - Internal Revenue Service

Mary won a $775 prize in a women's club raffle in 2019. No income tax was withheld from the prize.

The Key Lime Pie Company provides Carl with a company car to drive while he is working. The Company spent $6,475 to maintain this vehicle during 2019. Carl never uses the car for personal purposes. The Key Lime Pie Company also provides a cafeteria for all employees on the factory premises. Other restaurants exist in the area and so Carl is not required to eat in the cafeteria, but he typically does. The value of Carl's meals is $650 in 2019.

Required: Complete Carl and Mary's federal tax return for 2019 on Form 1040 and Schedule 1.

GROUP 5:
CUMULATIVE SOFTWARE PROBLEM

1. The following additional information is available for the family of Albert and Allison Gaytor.

   In 2019, Albert received a Form W-2 from his employer, Coconut Grove Fishing Charters, Inc. (hint: slightly modified from Chapter 1):

a Employee's social security number 266-51-1966	OMB No. 1545-0008	Safe, accurate, FAST! Use	IRS e-file	Visit the IRS website at www.irs.gov/efile

b Employer identification number (EIN) 60-3456789	**1** Wages, tips, other compensation 67,023.67	**2** Federal income tax withheld 5,634.12
c Employer's name, address, and ZIP code	**3** Social security wages 67,023.67	**4** Social security tax withheld 4,155.47
Coconut Grove Fishing Charters 2432 Bay Blvd. Coconut Grove, FL 33133	**5** Medicare wages and tips 67,023.67	**6** Medicare tax withheld 971.84
	7 Social security tips	**8** Allocated tips
d Control number	**9**	**10** Dependent care benefits
e Employee's first name and initial Last name Suff.	**11** Nonqualified plans	**12a** See instructions for box 12 DD | 8,400.00
Albert T. Gaytor 12340 Cocoshell Road Coral Gables, FL 33134	**13** Statutory employee ☐ Retirement plan ☐ Third-party sick pay ☐	**12b**
	14 Other	**12c**
	Parking $1,440	**12d**
f Employee's address and ZIP code		

15 State Employer's state ID number	**16** State wages, tips, etc.	**17** State income tax	**18** Local wages, tips, etc.	**19** Local income tax	**20** Locality name
FL |					

Form **W-2** Wage and Tax Statement   **2019**   Department of the Treasury—Internal Revenue Service

Copy B—To Be Filed With Employee's FEDERAL Tax Return.
This information is being furnished to the Internal Revenue Service.

In addition to the interest from Chapter 1, Albert and Allison also received three Forms 1099:

☐ CORRECTED (if checked)

PAYER'S name, street address, city or town, state or province, country, ZIP or foreign postal code, and telephone no.	Payer's RTN (optional)	OMB No. 1545-0112	Interest Income
Florida Electric Company 100 Palm Boulevard Jupiter, FL 33458	**1** Interest income $ 682.41	2019 Form **1099-INT**	
	2 Early withdrawal penalty $		Copy B
PAYER'S TIN 59-0247776	RECIPIENT'S TIN 266-51-1966	**3** Interest on U.S. Savings Bonds and Treas. obligations $	For Recipient
RECIPIENT'S name Albert T. Gaytor		**4** Federal income tax withheld $	**5** Investment expenses $	This is important tax information and is being furnished to the IRS. If you are required to file a return, a negligence penalty or other sanction may be imposed on you if this income is taxable and the IRS determines that it has not been reported.
Street address (including apt. no.) 12340 Cocoshell Road		**6** Foreign tax paid $	**7** Foreign country or U.S. possession	
		8 Tax-exempt interest $	**9** Specified private activity bond interest $	
City or town, state or province, country, and ZIP or foreign postal code Coral Gables, FL 33134		**10** Market discount $	**11** Bond premium $	
	FATCA filing requirement ☐	**12** Bond premium on Treasury obligations $	**13** Bond premium on tax-exempt bond $	
Account number (see instructions)		**14** Tax-exempt and tax credit bond CUSIP no.	**15** State **16** State identification no.	**17** State tax withheld $ $

Form **1099-INT**   (keep for your records)   www.irs.gov/Form1099INT   Department of the Treasury - Internal Revenue Service

☐ CORRECTED (if checked)

PAYER'S name, street address, city or town, state or province, country, ZIP or foreign postal code, and telephone no.	1a Total ordinary dividends	OMB No. 1545-0110	
Everglades Bank Corporation 1500 S. Krome Avenue Homestead, FL 33034	$ 1,031.00	**20**19	**Dividends and Distributions**
	1b Qualified dividends		
	$ 1,031.00	Form **1099-DIV**	

		2a Total capital gain distr. $	2b Unrecap. Sec. 1250 gain $	**Copy B**
PAYER'S TIN 57-4443344	RECIPIENT'S TIN 266-34-1967	2c Section 1202 gain $	2d Collectibles (28%) gain $	**For Recipient**

RECIPIENT'S name Allison Gaytor	3 Nondividend distributions $	4 Federal income tax withheld $ 0.00	This is important tax information and is being furnished to the IRS. If you are required to file a return, a negligence penalty or other sanction may be imposed on you if this income is taxable and the IRS determines that it has not been reported.
	5 Section 199A dividends $	6 Investment expenses $	
Street address (including apt. no.) 12340 Cocoshell Road	7 Foreign tax paid $	8 Foreign country or U.S. possession	
City or town, state or province, country, and ZIP or foreign postal code Coral Gables, FL 33134	9 Cash liquidation distributions $	10 Noncash liquidation distributions $	
	FATCA filing requirement ☐	11 Exempt-interest dividends $	12 Specified private activity bond interest dividends $
Account number (see instructions)	13 State	14 State identification no.	15 State tax withheld $ $

Form **1099-DIV**   (keep for your records)   www.irs.gov/Form1099DIV   Department of the Treasury - Internal Revenue Service

☐ CORRECTED (if checked)

PAYER'S name, street address, city or town, state or province, country, ZIP or foreign postal code, and telephone no.	1a Total ordinary dividends	OMB No. 1545-0110	
Grapefruit Mutual Fund 1500 S. Orange Blossom Trail Orlando, FL 32809	$ 160.00	**20**19	**Dividends and Distributions**
	1b Qualified dividends		
	$	Form **1099-DIV**	

		2a Total capital gain distr. $	2b Unrecap. Sec. 1250 gain $	**Copy B**
PAYER'S TIN 51-3334433	RECIPIENT'S TIN 266-34-1967	2c Section 1202 gain $	2d Collectibles (28%) gain $	**For Recipient**

RECIPIENT'S name Allison Gaytor	3 Nondividend distributions $	4 Federal income tax withheld $ 0.00	This is important tax information and is being furnished to the IRS. If you are required to file a return, a negligence penalty or other sanction may be imposed on you if this income is taxable and the IRS determines that it has not been reported.
	5 Section 199A dividends $	6 Investment expenses $	
Street address (including apt. no.) 12340 Cocoshell Road	7 Foreign tax paid $	8 Foreign country or U.S. possession	
City or town, state or province, country, and ZIP or foreign postal code Coral Gables, FL 33134	9 Cash liquidation distributions $	10 Noncash liquidation distributions $	
	FATCA filing requirement ☐	11 Exempt-interest dividends $	12 Specified private activity bond interest dividends $
Account number (see instructions)	13 State	14 State identification no.	15 State tax withheld $ $

Form **1099-DIV**   (keep for your records)   www.irs.gov/Form1099DIV   Department of the Treasury - Internal Revenue Service

The Gaytors also received interest of $751 from bonds issued by the Miami-Dade County Airport Authority (Form 1099 not shown).

Albert went to the casino on his birthday and won big, as reflected on the following Form W-2G:

☐ CORRECTED (if checked)			OMB No. 1545-0238

PAYER'S name, street address, city or town, province or state, country, and ZIP or foreign postal code	1 Reportable winnings	2 Date won	OMB No. 1545-0238
Mikkosukee Resort and Gaming 1321 Tamiami Hwy. Miami, FL 33194	$6,022.00		20**19** Form **W-2G** Certain Gambling Winnings
	3 Type of wager	4 Federal income tax withheld $1,600.00	
	5 Transaction	6 Race	
	7 Winnings from identical wagers $	8 Cashier	
PAYER'S federal identification number 22-7777777	PAYER'S telephone number 305-555-1212	9 Winner's taxpayer identification no. 266-51-1966	10 Window	This information is being furnished to the Internal Revenue Service
WINNER'S name Albert Gaytor		11 First I.D.	12 Second I.D.	
Street address (including apt. no.) 12340 Cocoshell Rd.		13 State/Payer's state identification no. DF124562	14 State winnings $	**Copy B** Report this income on your federal tax return. If this form shows federal income tax withheld in box 4, attach this copy to your return.
City or town, province or state, country, and ZIP or foreign postal code Coral Gables, FL 33134		15 State income tax withheld $	16 Local winnings $	
		17 Local income tax withheld $	18 Name of locality	

Under penalties of perjury, I declare that, to the best of my knowledge and belief, the name, address, and taxpayer identification number that I have furnished correctly identify me as the recipient of this payment and any payments from identical wagers, and that no other person is entitled to any part of these payments.

Signature ▶   Date ▶

Form **W-2G**   www.irs.gov/FormW2G   Department of the Treasury - Internal Revenue Service

Albert had no other gambling income or losses for the year.

In February, Allison received $50,000 in life insurance proceeds from the death of her friend, Sharon.

In July, Albert's uncle Ivan died and left him real estate (undeveloped land) worth $72,000.

Five years ago, Albert and Allison divorced. Albert married Iris, but the marriage did not work out and they divorced a year later. Under the July 1, 2015 divorce decree, Albert pays Iris $11,500 per year in alimony. All payments were on time in 2019 and Iris' Social Security number is 667-34-9224. Three years ago, Albert and Allison were remarried.

Coconut Fishing Charters, Inc. pays Albert's captain's license fees and membership dues to the Charter Fisherman's Association. During 2019, Coconut Fishing paid $1,300 for such dues and fees for Albert.

Allison was laid off from her job on January 2, 2019. She received a Form 1099-G for unemployment benefits:

☐ CORRECTED (if checked)			

PAYER'S name, street address, city or town, state or province, country, ZIP or foreign postal code, and telephone no.	1 Unemployment compensation	OMB No. 1545-0120	
Florida Dept of Econ Opportunity 107 E. Jefferson St. Tallahassee, FL 32399	$ 4,050.00	20**19**	Certain Government Payments
	2 State or local income tax refunds, credits, or offsets $	Form **1099-G**	
PAYER'S TIN 21-5556666	RECIPIENT'S TIN 266-34-1967	3 Box 2 amount is for tax year	4 Federal income tax withheld $ 155.00	**Copy B** For Recipient
RECIPIENT'S name Allison Gaytor		5 RTAA payments $	6 Taxable grants $	This is important tax information and is being furnished to the IRS. If you are required to file a return, a negligence penalty or other sanction may be imposed on you if this income is taxable and the IRS determines that it has not been reported.
Street address (including apt. no.) 12340 Cocoshell Rd		7 Agriculture payments $	8 If checked, box 2 is trade or business income ▶ ☐	
City or town, state or province, country, and ZIP or foreign postal code Coral Gables, FL 33134		9 Market gain $		
Account number (see instructions)		10a State	10b State identification no.	11 State income tax withheld $ $	

Form **1099-G**   (keep for your records)   www.irs.gov/Form1099G   Department of the Treasury - Internal Revenue Service

Albert and his family are covered by an employee-sponsored health plan at his work. Coconut Fishing pays $700 per month in premiums for Albert and his family. During the year, Allison was in the hospital for appendix surgery. The bill for the surgery was $10,100 of which the health insurance reimbursed Albert the full $10,100.

Coconut Fishing also pays for Albert's parking at the marina. The monthly cost is $120.

Required: Combine this new information about the Gaytor family with the information from Chapter 1 and complete a revised 2019 tax return for Albert and Allison. Be sure to save your data input files since this case will be expanded with more tax information in later chapters.

Form **1040**
Department of the Treasury—Internal Revenue Service   (99)
U.S. Individual Income Tax Return | 20**19** | OMB No. 1545-0074 | IRS Use Only—Do not write or staple in this space.

Filing Status
Check only one box.

☐ Single ☐ Married filing jointly ☐ Married filing separately (MFS) ☐ Head of household (HOH) ☐ Qualifying widow(er) (QW)

If you checked the MFS box, enter the name of spouse. If you checked the HOH or QW box, enter the child's name if the qualifying person is a child but not your dependent. ▶

Your first name and middle initial	Last name	Your social security number

If joint return, spouse's first name and middle initial	Last name	Spouse's social security number

Home address (number and street). If you have a P.O. box, see instructions.	Apt. no.	**Presidential Election Campaign**

Check here if you, or your spouse if filing jointly, want $3 to go to this fund. Checking a box below will not change your tax or refund. ☐ You ☐ Spouse

City, town or post office, state, and ZIP code. If you have a foreign address, also complete spaces below (see instructions).

Foreign country name	Foreign province/state/county	Foreign postal code

If more than four dependents, see instructions and ✓ here ▶ ☐

Standard Deduction
Someone can claim: ☐ You as a dependent ☐ Your spouse as a dependent
☐ Spouse itemizes on a separate return or you were a dual-status alien

Age/Blindness **You:** ☐ Were born before January 2, 1955 ☐ Are blind **Spouse:** ☐ Was born before January 2, 1955 ☐ Is blind

Dependents (see instructions):

(1) First name Last name	(2) Social security number	(3) Relationship to you	(4) ✓ if qualifies for (see instructions): Child tax credit	Credit for other dependents
			☐	☐
			☐	☐
			☐	☐
			☐	☐

Standard Deduction for—
- Single or Married filing separately, $12,200
- Married filing jointly or Qualifying widow(er), $24,400
- Head of household, $18,350
- If you checked any box under *Standard Deduction,* see instructions.

1	Wages, salaries, tips, etc. Attach Form(s) W-2		**1**
2a	Tax-exempt interest **2a**	b Taxable interest. Attach Sch. B if required	**2b**
3a	Qualified dividends **3a**	b Ordinary dividends. Attach Sch. B if required	**3b**
4a	IRA distributions **4a**	b Taxable amount	**4b**
c	Pensions and annuities . . . **4c**	d Taxable amount	**4d**
5a	Social security benefits . . . **5a**	b Taxable amount	**5b**
6	Capital gain or (loss). Attach Schedule D if required. If not required, check here . . . . ▶ ☐		**6**
7a	Other income from Schedule 1, line 9 . . . . ▶		**7a**
b	Add lines 1, 2b, 3b, 4b, 4d, 5b, 6, and 7a. This is your **total income** . . . ▶		**7b**
8a	Adjustments to income from Schedule 1, line 22		**8a**
b	Subtract line 8a from line 7b. This is your **adjusted gross income** . . . ▶		**8b**
9	Standard deduction or itemized deductions (from Schedule A)	**9**	
10	Qualified business income deduction. Attach Form 8995 or Form 8995-A . . .	**10**	
11a	Add lines 9 and 10		**11a**
b	**Taxable income.** Subtract line 11a from line 8b		**11b**

For Disclosure, Privacy Act, and Paperwork Reduction Act Notice, see separate instructions.   Cat. No. 11320B   Form **1040** (2019)

Form 1040 (2019) Page **2**

12a	**Tax** (see inst.) Check if any from Form(s): **1** ☐ 8814 **2** ☐ 4972 **3** ☐ _____	**12a**		
b	Add Schedule 2, line 3, and line 12a and enter the total . . . . ▶		**12b**	
13a	Child tax credit or credit for other dependents	**13a**		
b	Add Schedule 3, line 7, and line 13a and enter the total . . . . ▶		**13b**	
14	Subtract line 13b from line 12b. If zero or less, enter -0-		**14**	
15	Other taxes, including self-employment tax, from Schedule 2, line 10		**15**	
16	Add lines 14 and 15. This is your **total tax** . . . . ▶		**16**	
17	Federal income tax withheld from Forms W-2 and 1099		**17**	
18	Other payments and refundable credits:			
a	Earned income credit (EIC)	**18a**		
b	Additional child tax credit. Attach Schedule 8812	**18b**		
c	American opportunity credit from Form 8863, line 8	**18c**		
d	Schedule 3, line 14	**18d**		
e	Add lines 18a through 18d. These are your **total other payments and refundable credits** . . . . ▶		**18e**	
19	Add lines 17 and 18e. These are your **total payments** . . . . ▶		**19**	

• If you have a qualifying child, attach Sch. EIC.
• If you have nontaxable combat pay, see instructions.

Refund	**20**	If line 19 is more than line 16, subtract line 16 from line 19. This is the amount you **overpaid**	**20**
	21a	Amount of line 20 you want **refunded to you.** If Form 8888 is attached, check here . . . ▶ ☐	**21a**
Direct deposit? See instructions.	▶ **b**	Routing number |_____| ▶ **c** Type: ☐ Checking ☐ Savings	
	▶ **d**	Account number |_____|	
	22	Amount of line 20 you want **applied to your 2020 estimated tax** . . . . ▶	**22**
Amount You Owe	**23**	**Amount you owe.** Subtract line 19 from line 16. For details on how to pay, see instructions . . ▶	**23**
	24	Estimated tax penalty (see instructions) . . . . ▶	**24**

Third Party Designee (Other than paid preparer)	Do you want to allow another person (other than your paid preparer) to discuss this return with the IRS? See instructions.	☐ **Yes.** Complete below. ☐ **No**
	Designee's name ▶ _____	Phone no. ▶ _____	Personal identification number (PIN) ▶ |_____|

Sign Here

Joint return?
See instructions.
Keep a copy for your records.

Under penalties of perjury, I declare that I have examined this return and accompanying schedules and statements, and to the best of my knowledge and belief, they are true, correct, and complete. Declaration of preparer (other than taxpayer) is based on all information of which preparer has any knowledge.

Your signature	Date	Your occupation	If the IRS sent you an Identity Protection PIN, enter it here (see inst.) |_____|
Spouse's signature. If a joint return, **both** must sign.	Date	Spouse's occupation	If the IRS sent your spouse an Identity Protection PIN, enter it here (see inst.) |_____|
Phone no.		Email address	

Paid Preparer Use Only	Preparer's name	Preparer's signature	Date	PTIN	Check if:
					☐ 3rd Party Designee
	Firm's name ▶		Phone no.		☐ Self-employed
	Firm's address ▶			Firm's EIN ▶	

Go to *www.irs.gov/Form1040* for instructions and the latest information.

Form **1040** (2019)

SCHEDULE 1
(Form 1040 or 1040-SR)

Department of the Treasury
Internal Revenue Service

Additional Income and Adjustments to Income

▶ **Attach to Form 1040 or 1040-SR.**
▶ Go to *www.irs.gov/Form1040* for instructions and the latest information.

OMB No. 1545-0074

2019

Attachment
Sequence No. **01**

Name(s) shown on Form 1040 or 1040-SR

Your social security number

Part I	Additional Income		
1	Taxable refunds, credits, or offsets of state and local income taxes	1	
2a	Alimony received	2a	
b	Date of original divorce or separation agreement (see instructions) ▶		
3	Business income or (loss). Attach Schedule C	3	
4	Other gains or (losses). Attach Form 4797	4	
5	Rental real estate, royalties, partnerships, S corporations, trusts, etc. Attach Schedule E	5	
6	Farm income or (loss). Attach Schedule F	6	
7	Unemployment compensation	7	
8	Other income. List type and amount ▶		
		8	
9	Combine lines 1 through 8. Enter here and on Form 1040 or 1040-SR, line 7a	9	
Part II	Adjustments to Income		
10	Educator expenses	10	
11	Certain business expenses of reservists, performing artists, and fee-basis government officials. Attach Form 2106	11	
12	Health savings account deduction. Attach Form 8889	12	
13	Moving expenses for members of the Armed Forces. Attach Form 3903	13	
14	Deductible part of self-employment tax. Attach Schedule SE	14	
15	Self-employed SEP, SIMPLE, and qualified plans	15	
16	Self-employed health insurance deduction	16	
17	Penalty on early withdrawal of savings	17	
18a	Alimony paid	18a	
b	Recipient's SSN ▶		
c	Date of original divorce or separation agreement (see instructions) ▶		
19	IRA deduction	19	
20	Student loan interest deduction	20	
21	Reserved for future use	21	
22	Add lines 10 through 21. These are your **adjustments to income.** Enter here and on Form 1040 or 1040-SR, line 8a	22	

For Paperwork Reduction Act Notice, see your tax return instructions.   Cat. No. 71479F   Schedule 1 (Form 1040 or 1040-SR) 2019

Qualified Dividends and Capital Gain Tax Worksheet—Line 12a

Before you begin:	✓ See the earlier instructions for line 12a to see if you can use this worksheet to figure your tax.
	✓ Before completing this worksheet, complete Form 1040 or 1040-SR through line 11b.
	✓ If you don't have to file Schedule D and you received capital gain distributions, be sure you checked the box on Form 1040 or 1040-SR, line 6.

1. Enter the amount from Form 1040 or 1040-SR, line 11b. However, if you are filing Form 2555 (relating to foreign earned income), enter the amount from line 3 of the Foreign Earned Income Tax Worksheet .... **1.** _____

2. Enter the amount from Form 1040 or 1040-SR, line 3a* .... **2.** _____

3. Are you filing Schedule D?*
   ☐ **Yes.** Enter the **smaller** of line 15 or 16 of Schedule D. If either line 15 or 16 is blank or a loss, enter -0-.
   ☐ **No.** Enter the amount from Form 1040 or 1040-SR, line 6. } **3.** _____

4. Add lines 2 and 3 .... **4.** _____

5. If filing Form 4952 (used to figure investment interest expense deduction), enter any amount from line 4g of that form. Otherwise, enter -0- .... **5.** _____

6. Subtract line 5 from line 4. If zero or less, enter -0- .... **6.** _____

7. Subtract line 6 from line 1. If zero or less, enter -0- .... **7.** _____

8. Enter:
   $39,375 if single or married filing separately,
   $78,750 if married filing jointly or qualifying widow(er),
   $52,750 if head of household. } .... **8.** _____

9. Enter the smaller of line 1 or line 8 .... **9.** _____

10. Enter the smaller of line 7 or line 9 .... **10.** _____

11. Subtract line 10 from line 9. This amount is taxed at 0% .... **11.** _____

12. Enter the smaller of line 1 or line 6 .... **12.** _____

13. Enter the amount from line 11 .... **13.** _____

14. Subtract line 13 from line 12 .... **14.** _____

15. Enter:
    $434,550 if single,
    $244,425 if married filing separately,
    $488,850 if married filing jointly or qualifying widow(er),
    $461,700 if head of household. } .... **15.** _____

16. Enter the smaller of line 1 or line 15 .... **16.** _____

17. Add lines 7 and 11 .... **17.** _____

18. Subtract line 17 from line 16. If zero or less, enter -0- .... **18.** _____

19. Enter the smaller of line 14 or line 18 .... **19.** _____

20. Multiply line 19 by 15% (0.15) .... **20.** _____

21. Add lines 11 and 19 .... **21.** _____

22. Subtract line 21 from line 12 .... **22.** _____

23. Multiply line 22 by 20% (0.20) .... **23.** _____

24. Figure the tax on the amount on line 7. If the amount on line 7 is less than $100,000, use the Tax Table to figure the tax. If the amount on line 7 is $100,000 or more, use the Tax Computation Worksheet .... **24.** _____

25. Add lines 20, 23, and 24 .... **25.** _____

26. Figure the tax on the amount on line 1. If the amount on line 1 is less than $100,000, use the Tax Table to figure the tax. If the amount on line 1 is $100,000 or more, use the Tax Computation Worksheet .... **26.** _____

27. **Tax on all taxable income.** Enter the **smaller** of line 25 or 26. Also include this amount on the entry space on Form 1040 or 1040-SR, line 12a. If you are filing Form 2555, don't enter this amount on the entry space on Form 1040 or 1040-SR, line 12a. Instead, enter it on line 4 of the Foreign Earned Income Tax Worksheet .... **27.** _____

If you are filing Form 2555, see the footnote in the Foreign Earned Income Tax Worksheet before completing this line.

Student Name _____

Class/Section _____

Date   _____

KEY NUMBER TAX RETURN SUMMARY

CHAPTER 2

Comprehensive Problem 1

Adjusted Gross Income (Line 8b)   _____

Taxable Income (Line 11b)   _____

Total Tax (Line 16)   _____

Amount Overpaid (Line 20)   _____

Comprehensive Problem 2A

Adjusted Gross Income (Line 8b)   _____

Taxable Income (Line 11b)   _____

Total Tax (Line 16)   _____

Amount Overpaid (Line 20)   _____

Comprehensive Problem 2B

Adjusted Gross Income (Line 8b)   _____

Taxable Income (Line 11b)   _____

Total Tax (Line 16)   _____

Amount Overpaid (Line 20)   _____

Business Income and Expenses

Hero Images/Getty Images

After completing this chapter, you should be able to:

LO 3.1   Complete a basic Schedule C (Profit or Loss from Business).

LO 3.2   Describe the tax treatment of inventories and cost of goods sold.

LO 3.3   Identify the requirements for deducting transportation expenses.

LO 3.4   Identify the requirements for deducting travel expenses.

LO 3.5   Determine the requirements for deducting meals.

LO 3.6   Identify the requirements for claiming business education expenses.

LO 3.7   Identify the tax treatment of dues and subscriptions.

LO 3.8   Determine which clothing and uniforms may be treated as tax deductions.

LO 3.9   Explain the special limits for business gift deductions.

LO 3.10   Explain the tax treatment of bad debt deductions.

LO 3.11   Ascertain when a home office deduction may be claimed and how the deduction is computed.

LO 3.12   Apply the factors used to determine whether an activity is a hobby, and understand the tax treatment of hobby losses.

OVERVIEW

This chapter covers Schedule C, "Profit or Loss from Business (Sole Proprietorship)," and many of the common business expenses allowed as deductions in arriving at net taxable business income. Schedule C is filed by self-employed taxpayers, such as accountants, doctors, lawyers, architects, consultants, small manufacturers, restaurateurs, store owners, gardeners, event planners, bookkeepers, and other small businesses. This form is one of the most commonly used tax forms and, for many taxpayers, the net income reported on Schedule C is the primary component in their adjusted gross income. With the TCJA's introduction of the qualified business income (QBI) deduction, the sole proprietorship, along with income from rental properties (Chapter 4), partnerships (Chapter 10), and S corporations (Chapter 11), enjoy a reduction in tax rate in an attempt to match the new 21 percent corporate rate also introduced in 2018. The QBI deduction is covered in detail in Chapter 4.

The business expenses discussed in this chapter include travel, transportation, bad debts, inventory, home office, meals and entertainment, business education, dues, subscriptions, publications, special clothing, uniforms, and business gifts. While these expenses are often associated with Schedule C (sole proprietorship income), they may also be reported with rental and royalty income on Schedule E, or farm and ranch income on Schedule F. In addition, some of these expenses might be incurred by employees in connection with their employment. Employee business expenses are covered in Chapter 5.

| **Learning Objective 3.1** | 3-1 **SCHEDULE C** |

Complete a basic Schedule C (Profit or Loss from Business).

A taxpayer who operates a trade or business or practices a profession as a sole proprietorship must file a Schedule C with the Form 1040, reporting his or her taxable income or loss from the activity. Schedule C is similar to the income statement in financial accounting. Taxable income from a business or profession is reported on either Schedule C or Schedule F (a specialized version of Schedule C for farmers and ranchers).

3-1a **Trade or Business**

The term *trade or business* is not formally defined, although the term is used often in the Internal Revenue Code (the Code). For example, Section 162 of the Code states that a taxpayer is allowed to deduct all the ordinary and necessary expenses in carrying on a trade or business. Generally, a "trade or business" for tax purposes is any activity engaged in for profit. Note that a taxpayer does not have to actually make a profit, but he or she should be seeking to make a profit through regular and continual effort. Intermittent activities (e.g., casual craft sales) or leisure pursuits (e.g., wine making) do not always rise to the level of a trade or business and may require reporting under the hobby loss rules discussed later in this chapter.

3-1b **Tests for Deductibility**

Expenses must meet several general tests to qualify as a tax deduction. Listed below are three common tests for deductibility. These tests give guidelines for deductibility, but often in practice it is a matter of judgment as to whether an expense is considered a deductible business expense. Taxpayers and IRS agents frequently disagree as to whether specific expenses pass the following tests, and many court cases have been devoted to resolving these disagreements. The tests below overlap and an expense may fail more than one test.

- **The Ordinary and Necessary Test:** Under the tax law, for trade or business expenses to be deductible they must be ordinary and necessary. Generally, this means that the expense is commonly found in the specific business, and is helpful and appropriate in running the business. For example, Rob is a CPA who goes to a "tax boot camp" which offers intensive training on tax return preparation every year. Rob also hires a trainer at his local gym to work out with him to help him maintain the strength and endurance needed to handle the rigors of tax season. The cost of the "tax boot camp" would be deductible. The cost of the personal trainer is not a common or ordinary expense of CPA firms and is not necessary for preparing tax returns and therefore would not be deductible.

- **The Business Purpose Test:** Expenses must have a legitimate business purpose to be considered deductible. Larry is an independent consultant who maintains an office in his home, although he always meets with clients at their place of business. He spent $75,000 upgrading his office to include a large attached glass sunroom and a display area for his orchid collection. This home office upgrade would likely be considered to serve no business purpose, so the expenses related to the improvements would not be allowed.
- **The Reasonableness Test:** The tax law requires that deductions be reasonable to be deducted. For example, Derek owns a small business and takes one of his clients, who is also a friend, to an expensive business dinner every week. They enjoy a variety of restaurants and fine wines, and always spend some time talking about their joint business interests. The yearly cost of the meetings and meals is $20,000, and Derek generates $15,000 of fees from his friend each year. This lavish and extravagant business entertainment would likely not be considered reasonable given the circumstances. If they had met for pizza and a business discussion every week, the expense would likely be considered reasonable and deductible.

The IRS and courts have taken a fairly permissive perspective on the deduction of business expenses; however, the Code does restrict the deduction of certain expenses such as the following:

- Personal, living, and family expenses (although see itemized deductions in Chapter 5)
- Capital expenditures (see Chapter 7)
- Expenses related to tax-exempt income
- Expenditures related to the sale of illegal drugs
- Illegal bribes and kickbacks
- Fines, penalties, and other payments to governments related to the violation of law
- Lobbying and political expenditures
- Settlement or attorney fees related to sexual abuse or harassment if subject to a non-disclosure agreement

Taxes are specifically excepted from the restriction on fines and penalties as are payments made to bring the taxpayer into compliance with the law or as restitution.

EXAMPLE   Maria owns and operates a small pizza shop in the city. The City Council is considering new zoning laws that would permit the creation of a large hotel and theme park next to Maria's restaurant which she expects would increase her business significantly. She pays $10,000 to have a study prepared to show the economic benefits of the new zoning to the City Council at a future meeting. Maria also has been a Republican since she was old enough to vote and makes a $1,000 contribution to the Republican National Committee. The $10,000 fee and her contribution to the RNC are not deductible. ♦

Much has been made of the Supreme Court's Citizens United decision in 2010 which allowed for unlimited corporate spending on political activities. Those opposed to the decision can take some comfort knowing that most of such expenditures will not be tax deductible.

3-1c **Schedule C**

Schedule C is used by sole proprietors to report profit or loss from their businesses (Schedule C-EZ is no longer available). The first section (lines A to J) of Schedule C requires disclosure of basic information such as the business name and location, the accounting method (cash, accrual, or other, as covered in Chapter 6), material participation in the business (for passive activity loss classification purposes, see Chapter 4), and whether the business was started or acquired during the year.

   Schedule C requires the taxpayer to provide a principal business or professional activity code (see Figure 3.1). These codes are used to classify sole proprietorships by the type of business activity. For example, a full-service restaurant is code 722511, as shown in Figure 3.1.

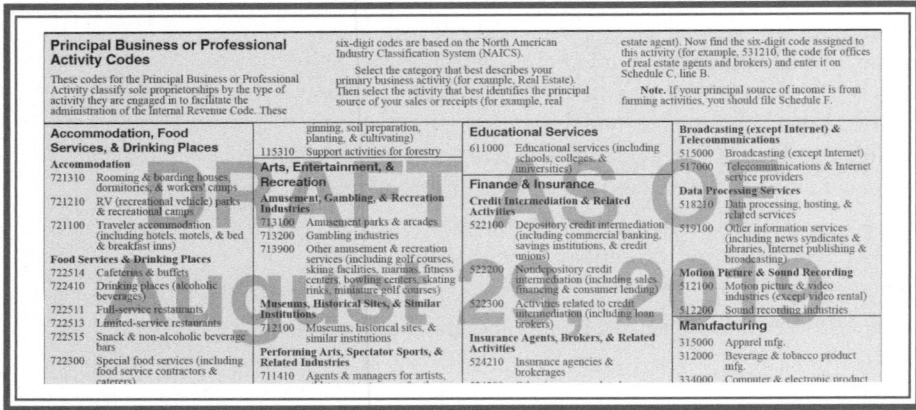
3-1d Schedule C Income (Part I)

Part I of Schedule C (Figure 3.2) contains the calculation of the taxpayer's gross income from the business or profession. The calculation starts with gross receipts or sales (line 1). Returns and allowances (line 2) and cost of goods sold (line 4) are subtracted to arrive at the gross profit from the activity. Other related income from the business (line 6) is added to the gross profit to produce the Schedule C gross income (line 7).

FIGURE 3.2   SCHEDULE C INCOME (PART I)

Part I	Income		
1	Gross receipts or sales. See instructions for line 1 and check the box if this income was reported to you on Form W-2 and the "Statutory employee" box on that form was checked . . . . ▶ ☐	1	
2	Returns and allowances	2	
3	Subtract line 2 from line 1	3	
4	Cost of goods sold (from line 42)	4	
5	**Gross profit.** Subtract line 4 from line 3	5	
6	Other income, including federal and state gasoline or fuel tax credit or refund (see instructions)	6	
7	**Gross income.** Add lines 5 and 6 . . . . ▶	7	

3-1e Schedule C Expenses (Part II)

The taxpayer reports the expenses from his or her business or profession in Part II of Schedule C (Figure 3.3). Expenses such as advertising, insurance, interest, rent, travel, wages, and utilities are reported on lines 8 through 27. Some expenses such as depreciation may require additional supporting information from another schedule. The expenses are totaled on line 28 and subtracted from gross income (line 7) to arrive at the tentative profit from the activity (line 29). An expense for business use of a taxpayer's home (see LO 3.11) is computed on Form 8829 or using the simplified method. The deductible portion of home office expenses is entered on line 30 and subtracted from tentative profit, resulting in the net profit or loss (line 31) from the activity. Common business expenses are covered in detail later in this chapter.

FIGURE 3.3   SCHEDULE C EXPENSES (PART II)

Part II	**Expenses.** Enter expenses for business use of your home **only** on line 30.					
8	Advertising	8		18	Office expense (see instructions)	18
9	Car and truck expenses (see instructions)	9		19	Pension and profit-sharing plans	19
10	Commissions and fees	10		20	Rent or lease (see instructions):	
11	Contract labor (see instructions)	11		a	Vehicles, machinery, and equipment	20a
12	Depletion	12		b	Other business property	20b
13	Depreciation and section 179 expense deduction (not included in Part III) (see instructions)	13		21	Repairs and maintenance	21
				22	Supplies (not included in Part III)	22
				23	Taxes and licenses	23
14	Employee benefit programs (other than on line 19)	14		24	Travel and meals:	
15	Insurance (other than health)	15		a	Travel	24a
16	Interest (see instructions):			b	Deductible meals (see instructions)	24b
a	Mortgage (paid to banks, etc.)	16a		25	Utilities	25
b	Other	16b		26	Wages (less employment credits)	26
17	Legal and professional services	17		27a	Other expenses (from line 48)	27a
				b	**Reserved for future use**	27b
28	**Total expenses** before expenses for business use of home. Add lines 8 through 27a . . . . . . ▶					28
29	Tentative profit or (loss). Subtract line 28 from line 7					29
30	Expenses for business use of your home. Do not report these expenses elsewhere. Attach Form 8829 unless using the simplified method (see instructions). **Simplified method filers only:** enter the total square footage of: (a) your home: _____ and (b) the part of your home used for business: _____ . Use the Simplified Method Worksheet in the instructions to figure the amount to enter on line 30					30
31	**Net profit or (loss).** Subtract line 30 from line 29. • If a profit, enter on both **Schedule 1 (Form 1040 or 1040-SR), line 3** (or **Form 1040-NR, line 13**) and on **Schedule SE, line 2.** (If you checked the box on line 1, see instructions). Estates and trusts, enter on **Form 1041, line 3.** • If a loss, you **must** go to line 32.					31
32	If you have a loss, check the box that describes your investment in this activity (see instructions). • If you checked 32a, enter the loss on both **Schedule 1 (Form 1040 or 1040-SR), line 3** (or **Form 1040-NR, line 13**) and on **Schedule SE, line 2.** (If you checked the box on line 1, see the line 31 instructions). Estates and trusts, enter on **Form 1041, line 3.** • If you checked 32b, you **must** attach **Form 6198.** Your loss may be limited.				**32a** ☐ All investment is at risk. **32b** ☐ Some investment is not at risk.	

3-1f Schedule C Cost of Goods Sold (Part III)

The calculation of cost of goods sold is reported in Part III (Figure 3.4) of Schedule C. In Part III lines 33 and 34, taxpayers must answer questions about the methods used to calculate inventory. Cost of goods sold (line 42) is equal to the beginning inventory (line 35) plus purchases (line 36), labor (line 37), materials and supplies (line 38), and other costs (line 39) less ending inventory (line 41). Please see LO 3.2 for a more detailed discussion of inventories.

3-1g Schedule C Vehicle Information (Part IV)

If a taxpayer uses a car or truck in his or her sole proprietorship, then Part IV of Schedule C (Figure 3.5) must be completed to provide the IRS with supplemental vehicle information. In Part IV, a taxpayer should provide the date the vehicle was placed in service for business use, (line 43), the business miles driven (line 44a), the commuting miles driven (line 44b), and other miles driven (line 44c). On lines 45 to 47 of Part IV, taxpayers must answer questions relevant to obtaining a deduction for business use of a vehicle.

3-1h Schedule C Other Expenses (Part V)

The expenses section of Schedule C (Part II), line 27 contains an entry for other miscellaneous expenses. These other expenses must be itemized in Part V of Schedule C and include deductible items which do not have specific lines already assigned in the expenses section (Part II). Expenses for business gifts, education, professional dues, and consulting fees are commonly listed.

FIGURE 3.4   COST OF GOODS SOLD (PART III)

Part III   Cost of Goods Sold (see instructions)

33	Method(s) used to value closing inventory: **a** ☐ Cost **b** ☐ Lower of cost or market **c** ☐ Other (attach explanation)
34	Was there any change in determining quantities, costs, or valuations between opening and closing inventory? If "Yes," attach explanation . . . . ☐ Yes ☐ No
35	Inventory at beginning of year. If different from last year's closing inventory, attach explanation . . . **35**
36	Purchases less cost of items withdrawn for personal use **36**
37	Cost of labor. Do not include any amounts paid to yourself **37**
38	Materials and supplies **38**
39	Other costs **39**
40	Add lines 35 through 39 . . . . **40**
41	Inventory at end of year **41**
42	**Cost of goods sold.** Subtract line 41 from line 40. Enter the result here and on line 4 . . . . . **42**

DRAFT AS OF August 7, 2019 DO NOT FILE

FIGURE 3.5   VEHICLE INFORMATION (PART IV)

Part IV   Information on Your Vehicle. Complete this part **only** if you are claiming car or truck expenses on line 9 and are not required to file Form 4562 for this business. See the instructions for line 13 to find out if you must file Form 4562.

43	When did you place your vehicle in service for business purposes? (month, day, year) ▶ ___ / ___ / ___
44	Of the total number of miles you drove your vehicle during 2019, enter the number of miles you used your vehicle for:
a	Business _____ **b** Commuting (see instructions) _____ **c** Other _____
45	Was your vehicle available for personal use during off-duty hours? . . . . ☐ Yes ☐ No
46	Do you (or your spouse) have another vehicle available for personal use?. . . . . ☐ Yes ☐ No
47a	Do you have evidence to support your deduction? . . . . ☐ Yes ☐ No
b	If "Yes," is the evidence written? . . . . ☐ Yes ☐ No

3-1i Self-Employment Tax

Self-employed taxpayers, sole proprietors, and independent contractors with net earnings of $400 or more, many of whom report income on Schedule C, must pay a self-employment tax calculated on Schedule SE with their Form 1040. For new business owners, the self-employment tax may come as a particularly unpleasant and costly surprise if they are not aware of its existence.

The self-employment tax is made up of two taxes, the Social Security tax, which is meant to fund old age and disability insurance payments, and the Medicare tax. For 2019, the Social Security tax rate of 12.4 percent applies to the first $132,900 of net self-employment income, while the Medicare tax rate of 2.9 percent applies to all net self-employment income, with no ceiling. Half of the self-employment tax is allowed as a deduction on Line 14 of Schedule 1 of Form 1040 in arriving at adjusted gross income. A similar tax is levied on employees partly through payroll withholding and partly through employer contributions, so it is not actually paid with Form 1040 as it is for self-employed taxpayers. Self-employed Social Security and Medicare taxes, including the 0.9 percent additional Medicare tax, are covered in detail in Chapter 6.

To report profits from a sole proprietorship in ProConnect, Under Income use Business Income (Schedule C) to enter information. Additional businesses can be added using the [+] tab at the top of the main window.

intuit proconnect
TIP

Self-Study Problem 3.1 *See Appendix E for Solutions to Self-Study Problems*

Teri Kataoka is self-employed as a professional golf instructor. She uses the cash method of accounting and her Social Security number is 466-47-8833. Her principal business code is 812990. Teri's business is located at 1234 Pinecrest Dr., Kennesaw, GA 30152. During 2019, Teri had the following income and expenses:

Fees from golf lessons	$40,125
Expenses:	
Car mileage (5,234 business miles)	3,036
Business liability insurance	475
Office expense	660
Rent on office space	2,700
City business license	250
Travel expense	3,000
Meals (deductible portion)	985
Utilities	1,015

Teri bought her car on January 1, 2019. In addition to the business miles listed above, she commuted 1,200 miles and she drove 5,000 miles for nonbusiness purposes.

Complete Schedule C on Pages 3-8 and 3-9 for Teri showing her net income from self-employment. Make realistic assumptions about any missing data.

3-2 INVENTORIES

Inventory is the stock of goods or materials that a business holds for the purpose of resale to generate a profit. The cost of inventory a taxpayer owns has a significant impact on the taxable income of the taxpayer. The deduction for the cost of goods sold of a retail business is a direct function of the amount of the beginning and ending inventories. Cost of goods sold, which is the largest single deduction for many businesses, is calculated as follows:

Beginning inventory	$ 75,000
Add: purchases	250,000
Costs of goods available for sale	325,000
Less: ending inventory	(100,000)
Cost of goods sold	$ 225,000

Self-Study Problem 3.1

SCHEDULE C **(Form 1040 or 1040-SR)** Department of the Treasury Internal Revenue Service (99)	**Profit or Loss From Business** (Sole Proprietorship) ▶ Go to *www.irs.gov/ScheduleC* for instructions and the latest information. ▶ **Attach to Form 1040, 1040-SR, 1040-NR, or 1041; partnerships generally must file Form 1065.**

OMB No. 1545-0074

2019

Attachment
Sequence No. **09**

Name of proprietor

Social security number (SSN)

A Principal business or profession, including product or service (see instructions)

B Enter code from instructions
▶

C Business name. If no separate business name, leave blank.

D Employer ID number (EIN) (see instr.)

E Business address (including suite or room no.) ▶
City, town or post office, state, and ZIP code

F Accounting method: **(1)** ☐ Cash   **(2)** ☐ Accrual   **(3)** ☐ Other (specify) ▶

G Did you "materially participate" in the operation of this business during 2019? If "No," see instructions for limit on losses . ☐ Yes ☐ No

H If you started or acquired this business during 2019, check here . . . . ▶ ☐

I Did you make any payments in 2019 that would require you to file Form(s) 1099? (see instructions) . ☐ Yes ☐ No

J If "Yes," did you or will you file required Forms 1099? . . . . ☐ Yes ☐ No

Part I   Income

1	Gross receipts or sales. See instructions for line 1 and check the box if this income was reported to you on Form W-2 and the "Statutory employee" box on that form was checked . . . . ▶ ☐	**1**	
2	Returns and allowances	**2**	
3	Subtract line 2 from line 1	**3**	
4	Cost of goods sold (from line 42)	**4**	
5	**Gross profit.** Subtract line 4 from line 3	**5**	
6	Other income, including federal and state gasoline or fuel tax credit or refund (see instructions) . .	**6**	
7	**Gross income.** Add lines 5 and 6 . . . . ▶	**7**	

Part II   Expenses. Enter expenses for business use of your home **only** on line 30.

8	Advertising	**8**		18	Office expense (see instructions)	**18**	
9	Car and truck expenses (see instructions)	**9**		19	Pension and profit-sharing plans .	**19**	
				20	Rent or lease (see instructions):		
10	Commissions and fees .	**10**		**a**	Vehicles, machinery, and equipment	**20a**	
11	Contract labor (see instructions)	**11**		**b**	Other business property . . .	**20b**	
12	Depletion	**12**		21	Repairs and maintenance . . .	**21**	
13	Depreciation and section 179 expense deduction (not included in Part III) (see instructions).	**13**		22	Supplies (not included in Part III) .	**22**	
				23	Taxes and licenses	**23**	
				24	Travel and meals:		
14	Employee benefit programs (other than on line 19) . .	**14**		**a**	Travel	**24a**	
				b	Deductible meals (see instructions)	**24b**	
15	Insurance (other than health)	**15**		25	Utilities	**25**	
16	Interest (see instructions):			26	Wages (less employment credits) .	**26**	
a	Mortgage (paid to banks, etc.)	**16a**		27a	Other expenses (from line 48) . .	**27a**	
b	Other	**16b**		**b**	**Reserved for future use** . . .	**27b**	
17	Legal and professional services	**17**					

28	**Total expenses** before expenses for business use of home. Add lines 8 through 27a . . . . . ▶	**28**	
29	Tentative profit or (loss). Subtract line 28 from line 7	**29**	
30	Expenses for business use of your home. Do not report these expenses elsewhere. Attach Form 8829 unless using the simplified method (see instructions). **Simplified method filers only:** enter the total square footage of: (a) your home: _____ and (b) the part of your home used for business: _____ . Use the Simplified Method Worksheet in the instructions to figure the amount to enter on line 30	**30**	
31	**Net profit or (loss).** Subtract line 30 from line 29. • If a profit, enter on both **Schedule 1 (Form 1040 or 1040-SR), line 3** (or **Form 1040-NR, line 13**) and on **Schedule SE, line 2.** (If you checked the box on line 1, see instructions). Estates and trusts, enter on **Form 1041, line 3.** • If a loss, you **must** go to line 32.	**31**	
32	If you have a loss, check the box that describes your investment in this activity (see instructions). • If you checked 32a, enter the loss on both **Schedule 1 (Form 1040 or 1040-SR), line 3** (or **Form 1040-NR, line 13**) and on **Schedule SE, line 2.** (If you checked the box on line 1, see the line 31 instructions). Estates and trusts, enter on **Form 1041, line 3.** • If you checked 32b, you **must** attach **Form 6198.** Your loss may be limited.	32a ☐ All investment is at risk. 32b ☐ Some investment is not at risk.

For Paperwork Reduction Act Notice, see the separate instructions.   Cat. No. 11334P   Schedule C (Form 1040 or 1040-SR) 2019

Schedule C (Form 1040 or 1040-SR) 2019
Page **2**

Part III Cost of Goods Sold (see instructions)

33 Method(s) used to
value closing inventory: **a** ☐ Cost   **b** ☐ Lower of cost or market   **c** ☐ Other (attach explanation)

34 Was there any change in determining quantities, costs, or valuations between opening and closing inventory?
If "Yes," attach explanation . . . . ☐ Yes   ☐ No

35 Inventory at beginning of year. If different from last year's closing inventory, attach explanation . . .	**35**	
36 Purchases less cost of items withdrawn for personal use	**36**	
37 Cost of labor. Do not include any amounts paid to yourself	**37**	
38 Materials and supplies	**38**	
39 Other costs	**39**	
40 Add lines 35 through 39	**40**	
41 Inventory at end of year	**41**	
42 **Cost of goods sold.** Subtract line 41 from line 40. Enter the result here and on line 4	**42**	

Part IV Information on Your Vehicle. Complete this part **only** if you are claiming car or truck expenses on line 9 and are not required to file Form 4562 for this business. See the instructions for line 13 to find out if you must file Form 4562.

43 When did you place your vehicle in service for business purposes? (month, day, year) ▶ _____ / _____ / _____

44 Of the total number of miles you drove your vehicle during 2019, enter the number of miles you used your vehicle for:

a Business _____ **b** Commuting (see instructions) _____ **c** Other _____

45 Was your vehicle available for personal use during off-duty hours? . . . . ☐ Yes   ☐ No

46 Do you (or your spouse) have another vehicle available for personal use? . . . . ☐ Yes   ☐ No

47a Do you have evidence to support your deduction? . . . . ☐ Yes   ☐ No

b If "Yes," is the evidence written? . . . . ☐ Yes   ☐ No

Part V Other Expenses. List below business expenses not included on lines 8–26 or line 30.

_____	
_____	
_____	
_____	
_____	
_____	
_____	
_____	
48 **Total other expenses.** Enter here and on line 27a	**48**

Schedule C (Form 1040 or 1040-SR) 2019

DRAFT AS OF August 7, 2019 DO NOT FILE

Valuation of inventories used in calculating the cost of goods sold is necessary to clearly reflect the income of the taxpayer.

To calculate cost of goods sold, the taxpayer must value the beginning and ending inventories of the business. He or she must determine the cost of the items on hand. This process is not as easy as it seems, since the taxpayer will often have paid different prices during the year for the same item. There are two common methods of inventory valuation used by taxpayers: first in, first out (FIFO) and last in, first out (LIFO). The FIFO method is based on the assumption that the first merchandise acquired is the first to be sold. Accordingly, the inventory on hand consists of the most recently acquired goods. Alternatively, when the taxpayer uses the LIFO method, it is assumed that the most recently acquired goods are sold first and the inventory on hand consists of the earliest purchases. FIFO and LIFO are simply calculation assumptions; the goods that are actually on hand do not have to correspond to the assumptions of the method selected. In addition to the LIFO and FIFO methods which are commonly used by taxpayers in valuing beginning and ending inventories, taxpayers may specifically identify the goods that are sold and the goods that are in ending inventory. However, the process of specifically identifying items sold and on hand is not a practical alternative for most taxpayers.

EXAMPLE   Paige made the following purchases of a particular inventory item during the current year:

March 1	50 units at $120 per unit	$ 6,000
August 1	40 units at $130 per unit	5,200
December 1	25 units at $140 per unit	3,500
Total		$14,700

If the ending inventory is 60 units, it is valued under the FIFO method as illustrated below:

25 units at $140 each	$3,500
35 units at $130 each	4,550
Ending inventory	$8,050

Assuming that Paige had no beginning inventory of the item, the same ending inventory (60 units) would be valued using the LIFO method as follows:

50 units at $120 each	$6,000
10 units at $130 each	1,300
Ending inventory	$7,300

The cost of goods sold for both the FIFO and LIFO methods are presented below:

	FIFO	LIFO
Beginning inventory	$ 0	$ 0
Add: purchases	14,700	14,700
Cost of goods available for sale	$14,700	$14,700
Less: ending inventory	(8,050)	(7,300)
Cost of goods sold	$ 6,650	$ 7,400

Notice that taxable income will be $750 more when the FIFO method is used instead of the LIFO method. During periods of rising inventory prices, taxpayers have lower taxable income and pay less tax if they use the LIFO inventory valuation method. ◆

A taxpayer may adopt the LIFO method by using it in a tax return and attaching Form 970 to make the election. Once the election is made, the method may be changed only with the consent of the IRS. Also, if the LIFO election is made for reporting taxable income, taxpayers must use the same method for preparing their financial statements. In other words, a taxpayer may not use LIFO for his or her tax return and use FIFO for financial statements presented to a bank. This rule is strictly enforced by the IRS.

Generally, if a taxpayer produces, purchases, or sells merchandise as part of the business, inventory must be kept and the accrual method for purchases and sales of merchandise must be used. However, taxpayers with gross receipts of less than $25 million (calculated over 3 years) are not required to keep inventory on the accrual method. In addition, a "safe-harbor" is provided if the business either treats inventory as non-incidental materials and supplies or treats inventory the same as on the business' financial statements or books and records. The tax accounting rules for non-incidental materials and supplies permit a taxpayer to deduct the cost of such supplies in the tax year in which the supplies are first used or paid for, whichever is later.

Additionally, prior tax law required the capitalization of certain indirect costs into inventory under Section 263A, sometimes known as the UNICAP rules. Businesses with gross receipts of no more than $25 million are not required to apply the UNICAP rules. The details of the UNICAP rules are beyond the scope of this textbook.

Self-Study Problem 3.2   *See Appendix E for Solutions to Self-Study Problems*

Kelly owns a small retail store. During the year, Kelly purchases $180,000 worth of inventory. Her beginning inventory is $62,500 and her ending inventory is $68,400. Also, she withdrew $1,250 in inventory for her personal use during the year. Use Part III of Schedule C below to calculate Kelly's cost of goods sold for the year.

Part III	**Cost of Goods Sold** (see instructions)	
33	Method(s) used to value closing inventory: **a** ☐ Cost **b** ☐ Lower of cost or market **c** ☐ Other (attach explanation)	
34	Was there any change in determining quantities, costs, or valuations between opening and closing inventory? If "Yes," attach explanation . . . . ☐ Yes ☐ No	
35	Inventory at beginning of year. If different from last year's closing inventory, attach explanation . . .	35
36	Purchases less cost of items withdrawn for personal use	36
37	Cost of labor. Do not include any amounts paid to yourself	37
38	Materials and supplies	38
39	Other costs	39
40	Add lines 35 through 39	40
41	Inventory at end of year	41
42	**Cost of goods sold.** Subtract line 41 from line 40. Enter the result here and on line 4	42

3-3 TRANSPORTATION

3.3 Learning Objective

Identify the requirements for deducting transportation expenses.

Certain transportation expenses for business purposes are deductible by taxpayers. Deductible expenses include travel by airplane, rail, and bus, and the cost of operating and maintaining an automobile. Meals and lodging are *not* included in the transportation expense deduction; those expenses may be deducted as travel expenses (see LO 3.4). Transportation expenses may be deducted even if the taxpayer is not away from his or her tax home.

Deductible transportation costs do not include the normal costs of commuting. Commuting includes the expenses of buses, subways, taxis, and operating a private car between home and the taxpayer's principal place of work, and is generally a nondeductible personal expense. The cost of transportation between the taxpayer's home and a work location is generally not deductible, except in the three sets of circumstances described below:

1. A taxpayer is allowed to deduct daily transportation expenses incurred in going between the taxpayer's residence and work locations outside the metropolitan area where the taxpayer lives and normally works.
2. If the taxpayer has a regular place of business, daily expenses for transportation between the taxpayer's home and temporary work locations are deductible.
3. A taxpayer may deduct daily expenses for transportation between the taxpayer's home and other regular or temporary work locations if the taxpayer's residence is the taxpayer's principal place of business, based on the home office rules, which are discussed later in this chapter.

In all cases, the additional costs of hauling tools and instruments are deductible. For example, the cost of renting a trailer to haul tools to a job site is deductible.

If the taxpayer works at two or more jobs during the same day, he or she may deduct the cost of going from one job to the other or from one business location to another. The deductible expense is based on the cost of travel by the shortest, most normally traveled route, even if the taxpayer uses another route. If the taxpayer works at a second job on a day that he or she does not work at the first job, the commuting expenses to the second job are not deductible.

EXAMPLE   Walter is a self-employed CPA working full-time Monday through Friday. On Tuesday night he teaches an accounting class at a local university. Walter leaves the office at 5:30 p.m. on his class day and, after dinner at a local cafe, teaches his class from 7:00 p.m. to 10:00 p.m. The distance from Walter's home to his office is 12 miles, the distance from his office to the university is 15 miles, and the distance from the university to his home is 18 miles. If Walter teaches the class thirty-two times a year, his mileage deduction is based on 480 miles (32 × 15 miles). While he is traveling from home to the office (12 miles) and from the university to home (18 miles), he is commuting and the mileage is not deductible. If Walter taught the class in the afternoon and returned to his regular job before going home, he could claim a deduction based on the round-trip mileage from his office to and from the university, 30 miles (2 × 15 miles). Alternatively, if he taught the course on a day (Saturday) when he did not work at his full-time job, Walter would not be entitled to any mileage deduction. ◆

Taxpayers may deduct the actual expenses of transportation, or they may be entitled to use a standard mileage rate to calculate their deduction for transportation costs. The standard mileage rate for 2019 is 58 cents per mile. Most costs associated with the operation of an automobile, such as gasoline, oil, insurance, repairs, and maintenance, as well as depreciation, are built into the standard mileage rate. The deduction for parking and toll fees related to business transportation (not commuting) and the deduction for interest on car loans and state and local personal property taxes on the automobile are determined separately. Self-employed taxpayers deduct the business portion of the state and local personal property taxes and interest on automobile loans on Schedule C or F. To use the standard mileage method, the taxpayer must:

1. own or lease the automobile,
2. not operate a fleet of automobiles, using five or more at the same time,
3. not have claimed depreciation on the automobile using any method other than straight-line depreciation, and
4. not have claimed Section 179 (expense election) depreciation or bonus depreciation on the automobile (see Chapter 8 for a complete discussion of depreciation).

If the taxpayer is entitled to use either the actual cost or the standard mileage method, he or she may select the method that results in the largest tax deduction for the first year. If the taxpayer does not use the standard mileage method in the first year, the method is not available for any subsequent year. A change to the actual cost method can be made any year. If, after using the standard mileage method, the taxpayer uses actual costs to determine the automobile expense deduction, depreciation on the automobile must be calculated using straight-line depreciation (see Chapter 8). The standard mileage method may be used for a car for hire, such as a taxi, if the automobile meets the other requirements for use of this method.

Taxpayers who use the actual cost method to calculate their transportation deductions must keep adequate cost records. The deductible portion of the total automobile expenses is based on the ratio of the number of business miles driven during the year to the total miles driven during the tax year multiplied by the total automobile expenses for the year. The business-use percentage is applied to the total automobile expenses for the year, including depreciation, but excluding any expenses which are directly attributable to business use of the automobile, such as business parking fees and tolls. The deduction for interest and personal property taxes is also separately computed.

EXAMPLE T.J. is a new salesman who drove his automobile 22,500 total miles during the 2019 tax year. The business use of the automobile was 80 percent of the total miles driven. The actual cost of gasoline, oil, repairs, depreciation, and insurance for the year was $10,000. The automobile expense deduction is calculated as follows:

1. Standard mileage method:
   Business mileage = 18,000 miles (22,500 miles × 80%)
   18,000 miles × 58 cents/mile $10,440

2. Actual cost method:
   80% × $10,000 (total actual cost) $8,000

   Since the deduction is larger using the standard mileage method, T.J. should deduct that amount. ◆

Vehicle expenses are reported on Form 2106 and are carried over to Schedule C or other forms. To enter deductions associated with a business vehicle, go to Vehicle/Employee Business Expense (2106) under the general Deductions item in the left margin. The deduction can be connected to the appropriate Schedule C or other business using a dropdown box.

TIP

Self-Study Problem 3.3   *See Appendix E for Solutions to Self-Study Problems*

Marc Lusebrink, sole proprietor of Oak Company, bought a used automobile and drove it 13,120 miles for business during 2019 and a total (including business miles) of 16,000 miles. His total expenses for his automobile for the year are:

Gasoline	$2,061
Oil changes	92
Insurance	1,030
Tires	225
Repairs	620
Total	$4,028

The automobile cost $20,000 on January 1, and depreciation expense for the year, including business use, was $4,000. His business parking and toll fees for business amount to $327. Calculate Marc's transportation expense deduction for the year.

Learning Objective 3.4

Identify the requirements for deducting travel expenses.

3-4 TRAVEL EXPENSES

Travel expenses are defined as ordinary and necessary expenses incurred in traveling away from home in pursuit of the taxpayer's trade or business. These expenses are deductible as long as they can be substantiated and are not lavish or extravagant. Transportation expenses incurred while not away from home such as business gifts are not included as travel expenses, although these items may be separately deductible, subject to certain limitations. Expenses included as part of the travel deduction include the cost of such items as meals, lodging, taxis, tips, and laundry. Most travel expenses are fully deductible, but Congress decided that a portion of the cost of meals is a personal expense. Therefore, only 50 percent of the cost of meals is deductible. If an employer reimburses an employee for the cost of meals, then the 50 percent limitation applies to the employer so that the employer can deduct only 50 percent of the expense.

To deduct travel expenses, a taxpayer must be away from home "overnight." Overnight does not literally mean 24 hours; it is a period of time longer than an ordinary work day in which rest or relief from work is required. Also, the taxpayer must be away from his or her "tax home" to be on travel status. A tax home is the taxpayer's principal place of business or employment, and not necessarily the same location as his or her family residence. If the taxpayer has two or more places of business, the taxpayer's tax home is at the principal place of business. Factors that determine the principal place of business include total time spent in each location, the degree of business activity, and the relative amount of income from each location.

Expenses of a temporary assignment are deductible if it is not practical to return home at the end of each day's work or if the employer requires the employee's attendance at a business meeting, training activity, or other overnight business function. If the assignment is for a long period of time or indefinite (generally more than 1 year), the new location may be considered the taxpayer's new tax home and he or she may lose the travel deduction. If the travel deduction is lost, an employee must include as income any reimbursements of travel expenses.

Taxpayers who make a combined business and pleasure trip within the United States may deduct all of the costs incurred in traveling to and from the business destination (for example, airfare) provided the trip is primarily for business. Once at the destination, only the business portion of the travel costs for meals, lodging, local transportation, and incidental expenses may be deducted; any costs which are not associated with the taxpayer's business are not deductible. If a taxpayer makes a trip which is primarily for pleasure, the travel expenses to and from the destination are not deductible even though the taxpayer engages in some business activity while at the destination. Although the traveling expenses to and from the destination are not deductible, any expenses incurred while at the destination that are related to the taxpayer's business are deductible.

Special rules and limitations apply to combined business and pleasure travel outside the United States. Even though a trip is primarily for business, if the trip has any element of pleasure, the cost of traveling to and from the destination must be allocated between the business and personal portions of the trip. The travel expenses for transportation to and from the destination must be allocated based on the number of business days compared to the total number of days outside the United States. The rules for travel costs to and from the destination where the trip is primarily for pleasure are the same as the rules for travel within the United States; none of the travel costs are deductible. Once at the destination, the taxpayer's expenses directly related to the taxpayer's business are deductible. For a complete explanation of travel outside the United States, see IRS Publication 463.

No deduction for travel expenses is allowed unless the taxpayer keeps proper expense records. Taxpayers must substantiate the following:

1. The amount of each separate expenditure, such as airfare and lodging. Expenses such as meals and taxi fares may be accumulated and reported in reasonable categories. As an alternative to reporting actual expenses, a per diem method may be used in certain circumstances.

2. The dates of departure and return for each trip and the number of business days on the trip.
3. The destination or locality of the travel described by the name of the city or town.
4. The business reason for the travel or the business benefit expected to be gained from the travel.

EXAMPLE   During 2019, Susan travels from Los Angeles to Hawaii for a 3-day business trip and pays $450 for the airfare. While in Hawaii, Susan spends 3 days on business and an additional 2 days on vacation. The lodging and meal costs are $300 and $120, respectively, for the business portion of the trip. The total cost of meals and lodging for the personal portion of the trip is $260. Susan may deduct $450 for the airfare, $300 for the business lodging, and $60 (50 percent of $120) for the business meals. None of the $260 of personal expenses is deductible. ♦

3-4a Per Diem Substantiation

Instead of requiring actual expense records, employers who reimburse employees for travel expenses can choose a per diem method of substantiation. The primary advantage of using a per diem method to substantiate expenses is that it eliminates much of the record keeping usually associated with travel expenses. The IRS has approved two per diem methods to substantiate travel expenses: (1) the standard per diem method and (2) the high-low per diem method. Employers can use per diem for all travel expenses including lodging, meals, and incidentals or an employer can use per diem for only meals and incidentals. Self-employed taxpayers may only use per diem for meals and incidentals.

1. *The Standard Federal Rate Method.* Under this method, the employee is allowed a per diem amount for travel equal to the current federal per diem rate which varies based on the travel location. A complete list of the regular per diem rates in effect for each area of the United States is available at the U.S. General Services Administration website (**www.gsa.gov**). The GSA also offers a downloadable app.
2. *The High-Low Method.* The high-low method provides a simplified way of computing the federal per diem rate for travel within the United States. This method avoids the need to keep a current list of the per diem rates for all localities in the United States. Under this method a small number of locations are designated as high-cost localities and all other locations are deemed to be low-cost areas. In 2019, the high-cost allowance is $287 per day and the low-cost amount is $195 per day. If an employer uses this method to reimburse an employee any time during a calendar year, this method must be used for all travel for that employee in the same calendar year.

Under either the standard method or the high-low method, the employee can use a current per diem amount for M&IE only. Actual cost records are required for lodging expenses. The M&IE rate may be taken from the standard per diem rate tables or the high-low method may be used. For 2019, the M&IE allowance using the high-low method is $71 per day for high-cost localities and $60 per day for low-cost localities. Employees and self-employed taxpayers who do not incur meal expenses when traveling are allowed an incidental expense allowance of $5 per day.

Per diem rates are revised on October 1 every year with additional revisions made for specific locations throughout the year. For purposes of illustration and problems, the rates above are assumed to be chosen for the full year. Different rates than those shown above may apply.

Self-Study Problem 3.4   *See Appendix E for Solutions to Self-Study Problems*

Byron is a certified public accountant who is self-employed. He is required to make a 5-day business trip to Salt Lake City for an audit. Since he is going to be in Utah, Byron decides to stay for the weekend and go skiing. His expenses for the trip are as follows:

Airfare to Salt Lake City and return	$ 480
Hotel while on the audit (5 nights at $165 per night)	825
Deductible portion of meals while on the audit	168
Laundry in Salt Lake City	22
Taxi fares in Salt Lake City	72
Transportation from Salt Lake City to and from Park City ski resort	100
Lodging at Park City ski resort	380
Lift tickets	99
Ski rental	89
Meals at Park City	182
Total	$2,417

If Byron has proper records to substantiate the above expenses, how much may he deduct as travel expenses for the 7-day trip?

$ _____

Learning Objective 3.5

Determine the requirements for deducting meals.

3-5 MEALS AND ENTERTAINMENT

Starting in 2018, there is no deduction for (1) an activity generally considered to be entertainment, amusement, or recreation, (2) membership dues for any club organized for business, pleasure, recreation, or other social purposes, or (3) a facility used in connection with any of the above items. Entertainment costs related to a recreation, social, or similar activities for the benefit of employees remain deductible.

EXAMPLE   Dee Skotech operates a small business and hosted two parties at a local night club during 2019. The first was a party for all of her clients to celebrate a great year and to thank them for their loyalty. The second party was a holiday celebration for all the employees in Dee's company. The costs associated with the client party are nondeductible entertainment costs. The costs for the employee holiday party are 100 percent deductible. ◆

Because meals and entertainment are often closely aligned, taxpayers should be cautious in attempting to deduct meals associated with an entertainment event. Client meals in which business is conducted (and the taxpayer or taxpayer's employee is present) and which are not lavish or extravagant remain 50 percent deductible. An entertainment-related meal such as one associated with a cocktail party, theatre, golf outing, or other entertainment event is only deductible if the meal is purchased separately.

EXAMPLE   Beau Gee is a salesperson for Hamilton Company. Beau has a meeting with an important customer at a local diner. Business is conducted at the meal as Beau and the customer discuss pricing, delivery dates, and other particulars, although no sale is actually closed. After the meal, Beau suggests they play a round of golf at the local golf course. After playing a round of golf, Beau and the customer stop in the golf club's "19th hole" and have a drink or two and some appetizers. Because business was conducted at the diner, the cost of the first meal is 50 percent deductible; however, the golf is entertainment and is not deductible. If the drinks and appetizers are separately purchased, the cost is 50 percent deductible. ♦

In addition to celebratory meals such as holiday parties and company picnics, other meals remain either 50 or 100 percent deductible:

Type of meal	Deductible
Meals for the convenience of the employer	50 percent (see Chapter 2) until after 2025 and then not deductible
Water, coffee, and other office snacks	50 percent deductible
Meals provided for in-office meetings with employees	50 percent deductible
Meals during business travel	50 percent deductible
Meals offered for free to the public (e.g., a free seminar)	100 percent deductible

Although entertainment-related club dues are nondeductible, dues paid to professional organizations, such as bar or medical organizations, are deductible. Dues paid to civic or public organizations, such as Chambers of Commerce, Kiwanis, and Rotary, are also allowed as legitimate business deductions. These clubs do public service work and are not organizations like country clubs which are entertainment or pleasure driven. Many business people belong to clubs such as Kiwanis or Rotary to network, meet potential clients, and increase their visibility in the community, but the club must do significant service work for the members' dues to qualify as deductions.

Self-Study Problem 3.5   *See Appendix E for Solutions to Self-Study Problems*

Milly operates a small business and incurs the following expenses:

Annual dues Tampa Bay Golf Club	$2,000
Meals with clients after golf	500
Meals with clients at the Club's dining room where business was conducted	600
Greens fees (personal and with clients)	700
Meals (personal)	250
Total	$4,050

Calculate the portion of the $4,050 that Milly can deduct.

$ _____

3-6 EDUCATIONAL EXPENSES

3.6 Learning Objective

Identify the requirements for claiming business education expenses.

Please note: Educational incentives such as qualified tuition programs and educational savings accounts are discussed in LO 2.14. The deduction for education loan interest is discussed in LO 5.7. Education tax credits are discussed in LO 7.5. Because there are numerous education incentives, the tax law in this area has become very complex. There may be more than one tax option for treating a particular education

expense. **This section deals primarily with the deduction of continuing education expenses incurred by self-employed taxpayers. The suspension of the deduction for miscellaneous expenses subject to 2 percent of AGI has effectively eliminated the deduction of unreimbursed educational costs for employees.**

There are two tests related to the deduction of educational expenses, at least one of which must be met to deduct the expenses. The tests are:

1. the educational expenses must be paid to meet *the requirements of the taxpayer's employer or the requirements of law or regulation* for keeping the taxpayer's salary, status, or job, or
2. the educational expenses must be paid to *maintain* or *improve existing skills* required in performing the duties of the taxpayer's present work.

Educational expenses meeting one of the above tests, which have a bona fide business purpose, may be deducted even if the education leads to a college degree.

Educational expenses are not deductible, even if one of the above tests is met, if (1) the education is required to meet the minimum requirements for the taxpayer's current job, or (2) the education is part of a program that will lead to a new trade or business even if the taxpayer does not intend to enter that new trade or business.

3-6a Education Required by Employer or Law

Taxpayers who are required to meet educational standards beyond minimum requirements may deduct the expenses of the education. However, the expenses must be paid for education to maintain the taxpayer's current job, not to meet the minimum requirements for that job. If the education qualifies the taxpayer for a new trade or business, the expenses are not deductible.

EXAMPLE　Jenny is a high school teacher working under a temporary teaching certificate. The state in which she teaches requires a master's degree to receive a permanent certificate, and Jenny only has a bachelor's degree. Her expenses to obtain a master's degree are not deductible even though the degree is required by her school district, since she has not yet met the minimum educational requirements to be a permanent teacher.

　　However, Jenny may qualify for the lifetime learning credit discussed in LO 7.5. ◆

3-6b Maintaining or Improving Existing Skills

Expenses that are paid by a taxpayer for education to maintain or improve existing skills are deductible. Expenses deductible under this category include the costs of continuing education courses and academic work at a college or university. However, the education must not lead to qualification in a new trade or business. The deduction of a review course for the CPA exam and bar exam is consistently disallowed by the IRS.

EXAMPLE　John is a certified public accountant (CPA) in practice with a CPA firm. He decides a law degree would be helpful to him in his present job since he does a lot of income tax planning for clients. He enrolls in a night program at a local law school. John's educational expenses are not deductible since the program leads to a new trade or business, the practice of law. Whether or not John plans to practice law is not relevant. However, John may qualify for the lifetime learning credit discussed in LO 7.5. ◆

EXAMPLE　Kenzie recently completed her degree in accounting and went to work for a local CPA firm. She spends $1,000 for a CPA exam review course to help her pass the exam. The $1,000 is not deductible since passing the CPA exam leads to a new trade or business, that of being a licensed CPA as opposed to an accountant. Depending on whether Kenzie takes this course at a qualified institution of higher education, and other circumstances, she may qualify for the lifetime learning credit discussed in LO 7.5. ♦

3-6c Expenses of Travel for Educational Purposes

Travel expenses incurred while away from home for trips that are primarily to obtain qualifying education are also deductible. For example, a taxpayer may deduct travel expenses for attending a continuing education course in a distant city. Whether a trip is primarily personal or primarily educational depends on the relative amount of time devoted to each activity. If the trip qualifies as primarily for educational purposes, the cost of transportation to and from the destination is fully deductible. The lodging and meal expenses directly connected with the educational activity are also deductible. As is the case with travel expenses, the cost of meals is only 50 percent deductible. Expenses for "travel as a form of education" are not deductible.

EXAMPLE   Jay is a doctor who attended a continuing education seminar in New York. His expenses related to attendance at the program are as follows:

Lodging in New York	$ 350
Transportation	700
Meals	150
Fee for the course	250
Total	$1,450

Jay's educational expense deduction for the seminar would be $1,375 including lodging of $350, transportation of $700, meals of $75 (50 percent of the cost of the meals), and the course fee of $250. ♦

EXAMPLE   Natalie is an instructor of Japanese at Big State University. She spends the summer traveling in Japan to improve her understanding of the Japanese language and culture. Although Natalie arranges her trip to improve her ability to teach the Japanese language, no education deduction is allowed for the travel expenses. ♦

Self-Study Problem 3.6   *See Appendix E for Solutions to Self-Study Problems*

Nadine is a self-employed attorney. Her expenses for continuing legal education are as follows:

Lodging in Tempe, Arizona	$1,200
Transportation	350
Meals	200
Books	175
Tuition	550
Weekend trip to the Grand Canyon	175
Total	$2,650

Calculate Nadine's educational expense deduction for the current year. Assume Nadine's household income is too high for her to qualify for the lifetime learning credit discussed in LO 7.5.

$ _____

Learning Objective 3.7

Identify the tax treatment of dues and subscriptions.

3-7 DUES, SUBSCRIPTIONS, AND PUBLICATIONS

Doctors, lawyers, accountants, engineers, teachers, and other professionals who are self-employed or are employers may deduct certain dues and the cost of certain subscriptions and publications. Included in this category of deductions are items such as membership to the local bar for a lawyer, dues to the American Institute of Certified Public Accountants (AICPA) for an accountant, and the cost of subscriptions to any journal that is directly related to the taxpayer's profession. Due to the suspension of miscellaneous deductions subject to 2 percent of AGI through 2025, only self-employed taxpayers can deduct dues and subscriptions. Employees can no longer deduct these costs; however, if the dues or subscription costs are reimbursed by the employer, the employer can deduct those costs.

EXAMPLE   Hal is a federal law enforcement officer who pays $200 per year for a subscription to the official agency work manual. The agency provides a manual in the office for its employees, but Hal spends a lot of time on the road away from the office. As an employee, Hal may not deduct the cost of the subscription. If Hal were self-employed, the cost would be deductible. ◆

Self-Study Problem 3.7   *See Appendix E for Solutions to Self-Study Problems*

Indicate which of the following dues, subscriptions, and publications are deductible (D) and which are not deductible (ND) by circling the correct answer.

1. Dues to the American Medical Association paid by a self-employed   D   ND
   physician.
2. A subscription to a tax journal paid for by an accounting professor.   D   ND
3. Dues to a health spa paid by a lawyer.   D   ND
4. Union dues paid by a carpenter that works for a large construction   D   ND
   company.
5. Subscription to *Motor Trend* magazine paid for by a registered   D   ND
   nurse.

Learning Objective 3.8

Determine which clothing and uniforms may be treated as tax deductions.

3-8 SPECIAL CLOTHING AND UNIFORMS

Self-employed individuals are allowed a deduction for the costs of special work clothing or uniforms. The deduction is not allowed for the general cost and upkeep of normal work clothes; the clothing must be specialized. To be deductible, the clothing or uniforms must (1) be required as a condition of employment, and (2) not be suitable for everyday use. Both conditions must be met for the deduction to be allowed. It is not enough that the taxpayer is required to wear special clothing if the clothing can be worn while the taxpayer is not on the job. The costs of protective clothing, such as safety shoes, hard hats, and rubber boots, required for the job are also deductible. If the clothing or uniforms qualify, the costs of purchase, alterations, laundry, and their maintenance are deductible. Any uniforms purchased by an employer for its employees are deductible by the employer.

The suspension of miscellaneous deductions subject to 2 percent of AGI has severely limited the deduction of uniforms and related costs by employees. In the past, uniforms worn by police officers, firefighters, nurses, and letter carriers would have qualified as an unreimbursed employee business expense. Because of the suspension of these miscellaneous deductions, taxpayers that serve in these roles as an employee are no longer permitted to deduct uniform costs. To the extent they serve as an independent contractor or are self-employed, qualifying uniform costs may be deducted. Similar to dues and subscriptions, if the employer reimburses the employee for qualifying uniform costs, the employer may deduct the costs. Self-employed taxpayers deduct special clothing and uniforms on Schedule C.

In his book, Bjorn Ulvaeus, one of the founders of 1970s megahit band Abba, states that the costumes that the band wore were intended to be so outrageous that they could not be considered suitable for general attire and thus garner a Swedish tax deduction (the tax laws are very similar to those in the U.S. on uniforms). Lady Gaga's "meat dress" worn at the 2010 Video Music Awards was likely to qualify for a deduction as well.

Would You Believe?

Self-Study Problem 3.8   *See Appendix E for Solutions to Self-Study Problems*

Steve has his own business as an installer for the light company, and he wears regular work clothes that cost $400 during the year. Also, Steve must wear safety shoes and an orange neon vest on the job that cost $650 this year, and he purchased pole-climbing equipment, spikes, and a safety belt that cost $275. What is Steve's deduction on Schedule C for these items.

$ _____

3-9 BUSINESS GIFTS

3.9 Learning Objective

Explain the special limits for business gift deductions.

Within limits, taxpayers are allowed a deduction for business gifts. Salespersons and other taxpayers may deduct up to $25 per year per donee. For purposes of this limitation, a husband and wife count as one donee. Thus, the maximum that a taxpayer could deduct for gifts to a client or potential client and his or her spouse is a total of $25 per year, unless the spouse is also a client, in which case the spouse may receive a separate $25 gift. Incidental expenses such as gift wrapping and shipping may be excluded from the limitation and are fully deductible.

There is no limitation for small business gifts costing up to $4 each that have the taxpayer's name or company name imprinted on them, such as pencils and calendars, and no limitation on promotional materials, such as signs and display racks. Also, the cost of gifts of tangible personal property made to employees for length of service on the job and safety achievement may be deducted up to a limit of $400 per employee per year. If the gift is made in conjunction with a "qualified plan," the limit is raised to $1,600. Gifts made to a taxpayer's supervisor (or individuals at a higher employment level) are not deductible. Those gifts are considered nondeductible personal expenses.

EXAMPLE   Marc is a salesperson who gives gifts to his clients. During the year, Marc gives Mr. Alford a gift costing $20 and Mrs. Alford (not a client) a gift costing $15. He also gives Ms. Bland a gift that cost $24 plus $2 for wrapping. Marc may deduct a total of $25 for the two gifts to Mr. and Mrs. Alford, and $26 for the gift to Ms. Bland. The $2 gift-wrapping charge is not included as part of the $25 limitation on the gift to Ms. Bland. ♦

3-9a **Substantiation Requirement**

To deduct meals and business gifts, taxpayers must be able to substantiate the deduction. The four items that must be substantiated to deduct meals expenses and gifts are the:

1. Amount of the expense,
2. Date and description,
3. Business purpose, and
4. Business relationship.

If any of the above information is not available, the IRS will disallow the deduction for meals expenses or gifts.

Self-Study Problem 3.9   *See Appendix E for Solutions to Self-Study Problems*

Carol makes the following business gifts during the tax year:

Donee	Amount	Deduction
1. Mr. Jones (a client)	$ 20	$_____
2. Mr. Brown (a client)	32	_____
3. Mrs. Green (a client)	15	_____
4. Mr. Green (the nonclient husband of Mrs. Green)	18	_____
5. Ms. Gray (Carol's supervisor)	45	_____
6. Mr. Edwards (a client receiving a display rack with Carol's company name on it)	75	_____
7. Various customers (receiving ball point pens with the company name on them)	140	_____
Total business gift deduction		$_____

Calculate Carol's allowed deduction for each business gift and her total allowed deduction.

3-10 **BAD DEBTS**

When a taxpayer sells goods or services on credit and the accounts receivable subsequently become worthless (uncollectible), a bad debt deduction is allowed to the extent that income arising from the sales was previously included in income. Taxpayers must use the specific charge-off method and are allowed deductions for bad debts only after the debts are determined to be partially or completely worthless.

A taxpayer who uses the specific charge-off method must be able to satisfy the IRS requirement that the debt is worthless and demonstrate the amount of the worthlessness. For a totally worthless account, a deduction is allowed for the entire amount of the taxpayer's basis in the account in the year the debt becomes worthless. The taxpayer's basis in the debt is the amount of income recognized from the recording of the debt, or the amount paid for the debt if it was purchased.

EXAMPLE   Todd owns a small retail store. During the current tax year, Todd has $8,500 worth of uncollectible accounts receivable. Assuming he reported $7,800 in sales income from the accounts, that amount is his basis in the accounts receivable. Therefore, Todd's deduction for bad debts is limited to $7,800 for the year. ◆

Business and Nonbusiness Bad Debts

Bad debts fall into two categories, business bad debts and nonbusiness bad debts. Debts that arise from the taxpayer's trade or business are classified as business bad debts, while all other debts are considered nonbusiness bad debts. The distinction between the two types of debts is important, since business bad debts are ordinary deductions and nonbusiness bad debts are short-term capital losses. Short-term and long-term capital gains may be offset by short-term capital losses. If there are net capital losses, only $3,000 of net capital losses may be deducted against ordinary income in any one tax year. Unused short-term capital losses are carried forward and may be deductible in future years, subject to the $3,000 annual limitation. The treatment of capital gains and losses is discussed in Chapter 4.

EXAMPLE   Robert loaned his friend, Calvin, $5,000 to start a business. In the current year, Calvin went bankrupt and the debt became completely worthless. Since the debt is a nonbusiness debt, Robert may claim only a $3,000 short-term capital loss deduction this year (assuming no other capital transactions). The $2,000 unused deduction may be carried forward to the next year. This is not a business bad-debt deduction, because Robert is not in the business of loaning funds. ◆

Nonbusiness bad debts are treated as short-term capital losses. To report these items, use the Schedule D/4797/etc., item under Income. Drill down into the Schedule D entry form and select the Nonbusiness Bad Debt button after entering the other relevant information.

TIP

Self-Study Problem 3.10   *See Appendix E for Solutions to Self-Study Problems*

Indicate whether the debt in each of the following cases is a business or nonbusiness debt.

	Business	Nonbusiness
1. Accounts receivable of a doctor from patients	_____	_____
2. A father loans his son $2,000 to buy a car	_____	_____
3. A corporate president personally loans another corporation $100,000	_____	_____
4. Loans by a bank to its customers	_____	_____
5. A taxpayer loans her sister $15,000 to start a business	_____	_____

Sign Here	Under penalties of perjury, I declare that I have examined this return and accompanying schedules and statements, and to the best of my knowledge and belief, they are true, correct, and complete. Declaration of preparer (other than taxpayer) is based on all information of which preparer has any knowledge.				
	Your signature	Date	Your occupation		If the IRS sent you an Identity Protection PIN, enter it here (see inst.)
Joint return? See instructions. Keep a copy for your records.	Spouse's signature. If a joint return, **both** must sign.	Date	Spouse's occupation		If the IRS sent your spouse an Identity Protection PIN, enter it here (see inst.)
	Phone no.		Email address		
Paid Preparer Use Only	Preparer's name	Preparer's signature		Date	PTIN	Check if: ☐ 3rd Party Designee ☐ Self-employed
	Firm's name ▶			Phone no.	
	Firm's address ▶			Firm's EIN ▶	

Would You Sign This Tax Return?

Your clients, Tom (age 48) and Teri (age 45) Trendy, have a son, Tim (age 27). Tim lives in Hawaii, where he studies the effects of various sunscreens on his ability to surf. Last year, Tim was out of money and wanted to move back home and live with Tom and Teri. To prevent this, Tom lent Tim $20,000 with the understanding that he would stay in Hawaii and not come home. Tom had Tim sign a formal note, including a stated interest rate and due date. Tom has a substantial portfolio of stocks and bonds and has generated a significant amount of capital gains in the current year. He concluded that Tim is a deadbeat and the $20,000 note is worthless. Consequently, Tom wants to report Tim's bad debt on his and Teri's current tax return and net it against his other capital gains and losses. Tom is adamant about this. Would you sign the Paid Preparer's declaration (see example above) on this return? Why or why not?

3-11 OFFICE IN THE HOME

Ascertain when a home office deduction may be claimed and how the deduction is computed.

Some taxpayers operate a trade or business in their homes and qualify for home office deductions. The tax law imposes strict limits on the availability of the deduction. In fact, the deduction for an office in the home is allowed by exception. The general rule for a home office deduction states that a taxpayer will not be allowed a deduction for the use of a dwelling unit used by the taxpayer as a residence. The law provides four exceptions to the general rule under which a deduction may be allowed.

Under the first exception, a deduction is allowed if the home office is used on a regular basis and exclusively as the self-employed taxpayer's principal place of business. To meet the exclusive use test, a specific area of the home must be used only for the trade or business. If the area is used for both business and personal purposes, no home office deduction is allowed. With the suspension of miscellaneous deductions subject to 2 percent of AGI, employees may no longer deduct home office expenses.

A second exception states that a deduction is allowed if the home office is used exclusively and on a regular basis by patients, clients, or customers in meetings or dealings with the taxpayer in the normal course of a trade or business. This exception allows doctors and salespeople to deduct home office expenses even though they maintain another office away from their residence, and even though the office is not the self-employed taxpayer's principal place of business.

Under the third exception, the deduction of home office expenses is allowed if the home office is a separate structure not attached to the dwelling unit and is used exclusively and on a regular basis in the taxpayer's trade or business.

The fourth and final exception to the rule allows a deduction of a portion of the cost of a dwelling unit if it is used on a regular basis for the storage of business inventory or product samples held for use in the self-employed taxpayer's trade or business of selling products. Under this fourth exception, the taxpayer's home must be the taxpayer's sole place of business.

3-11a **The Income Limitation**

The home office deduction may not reduce the net income from the business below zero, except for mortgage interest and property taxes allocable to the office, which are generally tax deductible anyway. The other costs of operating a home, which are included in the home office allocation, include rent, home insurance, repairs, cleaning, utilities and other services, homeowners' association dues, and depreciation on the cost of the home. Depreciation expense is considered only after all other expenses have been allowed. These expenses are typically allocated to the home office on the basis of the square footage of the office to the total square footage of the home. Any unused deductions may be carried over to offset income in future years.

EXAMPLE   Jane, an accounting professor, maintains an office in her apartment where she conducts a small tax practice. Jane properly allocates $1,500 in rent to the home office, and during the year she collects $1,400 in fees from various clients. Assuming Jane has no other expenses associated with her practice, only $1,400 of the rent may be claimed as a home office deduction, since she may not show a loss from the practice due to the gross income limitation. The unused portion is carried over to the next taxable year. ♦

EXAMPLE   Assume the same facts as those in the previous example, except Jane owns her home. She has real estate taxes of $100, mortgage interest of $600, maintenance expenses of $200, and depreciation of $1,000 attributable to the home office. Her deduction for home office expenses is calculated as follows:

Gross income from tax practice	$1,400
Less: mortgage interest and real estate taxes	(700)
Balance	700
Less: maintenance expense	(200)
Balance	500
Depreciation (maximum allowed)	(500)
Net income from tax practice	$ 0

Please note that the only way the home office can generate an overall business loss for Jane is if her home office mortgage interest and taxes exceed her gross business income. The unused portion of depreciation is carried over to the next taxable year. ♦

If a home office is used for both business and personal purposes, no deduction is allowed. For example, Professor Jane in the previous example would not be allowed a deduction for any expenses associated with the office in her home if the office was also used for personal activities, such as watching television.

3-11b **The Home Office Allocation**

The calculation of home office expenses involves the allocation of the total expenses of a self-employed taxpayer's dwelling between business and personal use. This allocation is usually made on the basis of the number of square feet of business space as a percentage of the total number of square feet in the residence, or on the basis of the number of rooms devoted to business use as a percentage of the total number of rooms in the dwelling.

EXAMPLE Lois operates a hair-styling salon in her home. The salon occupies 400 square feet of her residence, which has a total of 1,600 square feet. Her expenses for her residence are presented below and allocated as shown.

Expenses	Total Amount	Business Percentage*	Business Portion
Rent	$10,000	25%	$2,500
Utilities	4,000	25%	1,000
Cleaning	2,000	25%	500

*400 sq. ft./1,600 sq. ft. ♦

Self-employed taxpayers filing Schedule C and claiming a deduction for home office expenses are required to file Form 8829, Expenses for Business Use of Your Home.

3-11c Optional Safe Harbor Method

In an effort to reduce the complexity of the home office deduction, the IRS has introduced a simplified method. Under the simplified method, the self-employed taxpayer may deduct home office expenses at the applicable rate ($5 in 2019) multiplied by the number of square feet used in the home office, up to a maximum of 300 square feet, thus limiting the home office deduction to $1,500 in 2019. The deduction is still limited to the net profit from the business. Any deduction in excess of the income limit may not be carried forward. The same home office qualifications apply but no allocations are required. A taxpayer that uses the simplified method may deduct mortgage interest and property taxes as itemized deductions (see Chapter 5) without having to allocate a portion to the home office.

intuit proconnect. TIP   Similar to auto expenses, the home office deduction is not entered into Schedule C directly, but rather under Deductions and then Business Use of the Home. The interaction between the cap on taxes (Chapter 5) and the allocation of property taxes can create complexity in this area for certain taxpayers.

EXAMPLE Martha operates a business that generates $6,700 of income before the home office deduction. She has a qualifying home office of 350 square feet in her home. She properly allocates $1,200 of household expenses to her home office. Under the safe harbor method, Martha's home office deduction is $1,500 ($5 per square foot × maximum 300 square feet). Martha probably elects the larger safe harbor home office deduction. ♦

TAX BREAK The simplified method may hold advantages that extend beyond ease of use. One possible advantage is that no depreciation is deducted from the basis of a taxpayer's home and thus "depreciation recapture" (see LO 8.8) can be avoided and the exclusion of the gain on the sale of a principal residence (see LO 4.6) can still apply. A second advantage is that the property taxes and interest allocated to the small business can still be deducted on Schedule A as an itemized deduction (Chapter 5).

3-11d **Home Office Deduction for an Employee**

Under certain circumstances, an employee was eligible to take a home office deduction. One of the most important requirements was that the use of the home office was for the convenience of the employer. The TCJA, however, suspended unreimbursed employee business expenses as an itemized deduction through 2025.

Self-Study Problem 3.11   *See Appendix E for Solutions to Self-Study Problems*

Terry is a self-employed lawyer who maintains an office in her home. The office is used exclusively for client work, and clients regularly visit her home office. The mortgage interest and real estate taxes allocated to the business use of the home amount to $2,100, and maintenance, utilities, and cleaning service allocable to the business use of the home total $1,400. If gross billings of Terry's practice are $2,900 for this year and Terry has no other expenses allocable to the business, calculate the net income or loss she may report from the practice.

$ _____

3-12 **HOBBY LOSSES**

3.12 Learning Objective

Apply the factors used to determine whether an activity is a hobby, and understand the tax treatment of hobby losses.

If a taxpayer enters into an activity without a profit motive, the tax law limits the amount of tax deductions available. Under the hobby loss provisions, a taxpayer may not show a loss from an activity that is not engaged in for profit. For example, the breeding of race horses is an activity which might not be considered a trade or business when carried on by a full-time dentist. The IRS might contend that the activity was for personal enjoyment and disallow any loss for tax purposes. Despite the limitation on losses, any profits from hobbies must be included in taxable income. Hobby income is reported on Line 8, Other Income on Schedule 1 of Form 1040.

3-12a **Operational Rules**

Individual taxpayers (or S corporations) can avoid the hobby loss rules if they can show that the activity was conducted with the intent to earn a profit. To determine whether the activity was engaged in for profit, the IRS will look at the following factors:

1. carrying on the activity in a businesslike manner,
2. the time and effort put into the activity indicate an intent to make it profitable,
3. dependence on the income for the taxpayer's livelihood,
4. whether the losses are due to circumstances beyond control (or are normal in the startup phase of this type of business),
5. attempts to change methods of operation to improve profitability,
6. the taxpayer or advisors have the knowledge needed to carry on the activity as a successful business,
7. success in making a profit in similar activities in the past,
8. the activity makes a profit in some years, and
9. the activity is expected to make a future profit from the appreciation of the assets used in the activity.

The tax law provides a rebuttable presumption that if an activity shows a profit for 3 of the 5 previous years (2 of the 7 previous years for activities involving horses), the activity is engaged in for profit. For example, if an activity shows a profit for 3 of the previous 5 years, it is presumed to be a trade or business, and the IRS has the burden to prove that it is a hobby.

3-12b **Loss Limitations**

Historically, the deduction of hobby expenses have been limited. Hobby expenses were deductible to the extent of hobby income (unless otherwise deductible such as mortgage interest and property taxes) and claimed as a miscellaneous itemized deduction subject to the 2 percent of AGI floor. Thus, they were only available to deduct if the taxpayer itemized deductions.

The miscellaneous expense deduction for items subject to the 2 percent of AGI floor is suspended through 2025; thus, no miscellaneous hobby expenses are deductible. Hobby expenses associated with other allowable itemized deductions (e.g., taxes or interest) are deductible subject to the limitations on those items (see Chapter 5). The income, net of cost of goods sold, must still be reported as other income on Schedule 1, Line 8.

EXAMPLE   Fred, the president of a bank, decides that he wants to be a famous wine maker. He has the following expenses related to this activity:

Costs attributable to the wine sold	$2,000
Personal property taxes on equipment	2,500
Advertising costs	4,600

During the year, Fred sells 200 cases of wine for $7,500. If the activity is not a hobby, then Fred may take a loss, against his other income, of $1,600 ($7,500 − $2,000 − $2,500 − $4,600). However, if the activity is deemed to be a hobby, Fred would potentially be allowed to deduct the property taxes of $2,500 as an itemized deduction. The cost of the wine sold can be netted against the revenue. The remaining advertising expenses are not deductible. ◆

TIP

Hobby income can be entered under Income and then Alimony and Other Income. Be sure and net the cost of goods sold against gross income when reporting this amount. Hobby expenses are not deductible.

Self-Study Problem 3.12   *See Appendix E for Solutions to Self-Study Problems*

Kana is a CPA who loves chinchillas. She breeds chinchillas as pets (she currently owns thirteen of them) and every so often sells a baby chinchilla to a suitable family to keep as a pet. In the current year, she sells $250 worth of chinchillas and incurs the following expenses:

Chinchilla cages	$ 300
Advertising for chinchilla sales	$2,500

This activity is considered a hobby. Kana has adjusted gross income of $72,000. What is the amount of income and expense Kana recognizes (assume she itemizes deductions) associated with her chinchilla hobby?

Income $ _____

Deduction $ _____

KEY TERMS

Schedule C, 3-2
trade or business, 3-2
cost of goods sold, 3-5
self-employment tax, 3-6
inventories, 3-7
first in, first out (FIFO), 3-10
last in, first out (LIFO), 3-10

standard mileage rate, 3-12
standard mileage method, 3-12
actual cost method, 3-13
tax home, 3-14
per diem substantiation, 3-15
standard federal rate method, 3-15
high-low method, 3-15

business gifts, 3-21
business and nonbusiness bad
   debts, 3-23
home office, 3-24
hobby losses, 3-27

KEY POINTS

Learning Objectives	Key Points
LO 3.1: Complete a basic Schedule C (Profit or Loss from Business).	• Taxpayers who operate a business or practice a profession as a sole proprietorship must file a Schedule C to report the net profit or loss from the sole proprietorship. • Deductions taken on Schedule C must be ordinary and necessary, reasonable, and have a business purpose. • Schedule C filers such as sole proprietors and independent contractors with net earnings of $400 or more must pay a self-employment tax calculated on Schedule SE with their Form 1040.
LO 3.2: Describe the tax treatment of inventories and cost of goods sold.	• Cost of goods sold, which is the largest single deduction for many businesses, is calculated as follows: beginning inventory + purchases − ending inventory. • There are two common methods of inventory valuation used by taxpayers: first in, first out (FIFO) and last in, first out (LIFO).
LO 3.3: Identify the requirements for deducting transportation expenses.	• Deductible transportation expenses include travel by airplane, rail, bus, and automobile. Normal commuting costs to and from the taxpayer's place of regular employment are not deductible. • If the taxpayer works at two or more jobs during the same day, he or she may deduct the cost of going from one job to the other or from one business location to another. • The standard mileage rate for 2019 is 58 cents per mile.
LO 3.4: Identify the requirements for deducting travel expenses.	• Travel expenses are defined as ordinary and necessary expenses incurred in traveling away from home in pursuit of the taxpayer's trade or business. • Deductible travel expenses include the cost of such items as meals, lodging, taxis, tips, and laundry. • A taxpayer must be away from home "overnight" in order to deduct travel expenses. Overnight is a period of time longer than an ordinary work day in which rest or relief from work is required. Also, the taxpayer must be away from his or her "tax home" to be on travel status. • Taxpayers must substantiate the following: the amount of each separate expenditure, the dates of departure and return for each trip and the number of business days on the trip, the destination or locality of the travel, and the business reason for the travel. • As an alternative to reporting actual expenses, a per diem method may be used in certain circumstances.

LO 3.5: Determine the requirements for deducting meals.	• Self-employed taxpayers and employees are allowed deductions for 50 percent of the cost of meals at which business is conducted. • Generally, entertainment costs are not deductible. • Certain meals and entertainment costs are deductible when celebratory for all employees.
LO 3.6: Identify the requirements for claiming business education expenses.	• To be deductible as a business expense, education expenditures must be paid to meet the requirements of the taxpayer's employer or the requirements of law or regulation for keeping the taxpayer's salary, status, or job, or the expenses must be paid to maintain or improve existing skills required in performing the duties of the taxpayer's present work.
LO 3.7: Identify the tax treatment of dues and subscriptions.	• Self-employed professionals may deduct dues and the cost of subscriptions and publications. Included are items such as membership to the local bar for a lawyer, dues to the AICPA for an accountant, and the cost of subscriptions to any journal that is directly related to the self-employed taxpayer's profession. Employees may no longer deduct these costs due to the suspension of miscellaneous deductions subject to the 2 percent of AGI through 2025.
LO 3.8: Determine which clothing and uniforms may be treated as tax deductions.	• In order to be deductible, clothing or uniforms must (1) be required as a condition of employment, and (2) not be suitable for everyday use.
LO 3.9: Explain the special limits for business gift deductions.	• Taxpayers are allowed a deduction for business gifts up to $25 per year per donee. For purposes of this limitation, a husband and wife count as one donee, unless the husband and wife are both clients.
LO 3.10: Explain the tax treatment of bad debt deductions.	• Bad debts are classified as either business bad debts or nonbusiness bad debts. Debts arising from a taxpayer's trade or business are classified as business bad debts, while all other debts are considered nonbusiness bad debts. • Business bad debts are treated as ordinary deductions and nonbusiness bad debts are treated as short-term capital losses, of which only $3,000 can be deducted against ordinary income each year.
LO 3.11: Ascertain when a home office deduction may be claimed and how the deduction is computed.	• A home office is generally not deductible. However, there are four exceptions to the general rule. • A home office deduction is allowed if the home office is used on a regular basis and exclusively as the self-employed taxpayer's principal place of business. • A home office deduction is allowed if the home office is used exclusively and on a regular basis by patients, clients, or customers in meetings or dealings with the self-employed taxpayer in the normal course of a trade or business. • The deduction of home office expenses is allowed if the home office is a separate structure not attached to the dwelling unit and is used exclusively and on a regular basis in the taxpayer's trade or business. • A home office deduction of a portion of the cost of a dwelling unit is allowed if it is used on a regular basis for the storage of business inventory or product samples. • The home office deduction is limited by the amount of net income from the associated trade or business. • Employees may no longer deduct a home office, even when at the convenience of his or her employer, due to the TCJA suspension of the miscellaneous business expense deduction. • A simplified home office deduction is also available at $5 per square foot up to a maximum of $1,500 in 2019.

LO 3.12:

Apply the factors used to determine whether an activity is a hobby, and understand the tax treatment of hobby losses.

- Under the hobby loss provisions, a taxpayer may not show a loss from an activity that is not engaged in for profit.
- To determine whether the activity was engaged in for profit, the IRS will look at numerous factors including whether the activity is conducted like a business.
- Hobby expenses are no longer deductible due to the TCJA suspension of miscellaneous itemized deductions subject to the 2 percent of AGI floor.

QUESTIONS and PROBLEMS

GROUP 1:
MULTIPLE CHOICE QUESTIONS

LO 3.1

1. Which of the following is *not* a test for the deductibility of a business expense?
   a. Ordinary and necessary test
   b. Expectation of profit test
   c. Reasonableness test
   d. Business purpose test

LO 3.1

2. In the current year, Mary started a profitable housekeeping business as a sole proprietor. She has ten housekeepers working for her and spends her time selling their services and coordinating her employees' time. Mary made $50,000 in her first year of operations. In addition to filing a Schedule C to report her business earnings, Mary *must* also file
   a. Schedule A
   b. Schedule F
   c. Schedule B
   d. Schedule SE
   e. None of the above

LO 3.1
LO 3.3
LO 3.4
LO 3.5

3. Daniel is a self-employed consultant. Until this year he was always an employee. He comes to discuss his new business with you. As his tax accountant, you should:
   a. Discuss setting up a good record-keeping system for his new business
   b. Discuss the substantiation requirements for meals
   c. Discuss the self-employment tax, as well as the income tax, on business earnings in order to help Daniel estimate what he might owe in taxes for the year
   d. Discuss the rules for deducting automobile expenses
   e. Discuss all of the above

LO 3.2

4. Which of the following formulas represents the proper method of calculating cost of goods sold?
   a. Beginning inventory + Ending inventory − Purchases
   b. Ending inventory − Purchases − Beginning inventory
   c. Purchases − Beginning inventory − Ending inventory
   d. Beginning inventory + Purchases − Ending inventory
   e. None of the above

LO 3.2

5. If a taxpayer has beginning inventory of $45,000, purchases of $175,000, and ending inventory of $25,000, what is the amount of the cost of goods sold for the current year?
   a. $155,000
   b. $180,000
   c. $175,000
   d. $195,000
   e. None of the above

LO 3.3

6. Which of the following taxpayers may use the standard mileage method of calculating transportation costs?
   a. A taxi driver who owns a fleet of six cars for hire
   b. A taxpayer who used accelerated depreciation on his automobile
   c. A business executive who claimed bonus depreciation in the first year she used the car
   d. An attorney who uses his European sports car for calling on clients
   e. None of the above

LO 3.3

7. Heather drives her minivan 953 miles for business purposes in 2019. She elects to use the standard mileage rate for her auto expense deduction. Her deduction will be
   a. $510
   b. $515
   c. $519
   d. $553
   e. $953

LO 3.4

8. Which of the following taxpayers is entitled to a travel expense deduction?
   a. An employee, who worked in the Salt Lake City plant of a company, who is assigned to the Denver plant of the company for 4 years
   b. An employee who travels between several business locations within the same city each day
   c. A manager of a chain of department stores who works in the main store 3 weeks out of every month and visits distant branch locations on overnight trips during the remainder of the month
   d. An employee who resigns from his current job and accepts a new job in a city 500 miles away from his current residence
   e. A bank employee who travels to a branch office for a couple of hours of work and decides to stay overnight to attend a play

LO 3.4

9. Which of the following expenses incurred while the taxpayer is away from home "overnight" is not included as a travel expense?
   a. Laundry expenses
   b. Transportation expenses
   c. Meal expenses
   d. Business gifts
   e. Lodging expenses

LO 3.4

10. Under the high-low method, the federal per diem amount is
    a. The same in every city in the U.S.
    b. Different for every city in the U.S.
    c. The same for most cities but higher in certain locations
    d. An average of the highest and lowest costs for that city
    e. The boundary for expenses incurred in a city (never higher than the high amount but never lower than the low amount)

LO 3.4

11. Joe is a self-employed information technology consultant from San Francisco, CA. He takes a week-long trip to Chicago primarily for business. He takes two personal days to go to museums and see the sights of Chicago. How should he treat the expenses related to this trip?
    a. One hundred percent of the trip should be deducted as a business expense since the trip was primarily for business.
    b. Fifty percent of the trip should be deducted as a business expense since the IRS limits such business expenses to 50 percent of the actual cost.

    c. The cost of all of the airfare and the business days should be deducted, while the cost of the personal days are not deductible.

    d. None of the expenses are deductible since there was an element of personal enjoyment in the trip.

LO 3.5

12. Which of the following expenses is deductible as an entertainment expense?

    a. The depreciation on an airplane used to entertain customers

    b. The cost of a hunting camp used to entertain customers

    c. The dues of a racquet club used to keep in shape

    d. The cost of a paintball party for clients paid for by a computer salesman at a computer fair

    e. None of these are deductible

LO 3.5

13. Which of the following is *not* likely to be a deductible expense?

    a. The cost of tickets to a stage play for a client and the taxpayer.

    b. The cost for Rosa to take a potential customer to lunch to describe a new service Rosa's company is offering. Unfortunately, the customer explains that they are not interested in the service.

    c. The cost of a party for all of Dan's employees to celebrate a record-breaking profits year.

    d. The dues for Charles Coke to join the City Chamber of Commerce to generally improve the reputation of his business in the community.

    e. None of the above are deductible expenses.

LO 3.6

14. Which of the following taxpayers may *not* deduct their educational expense?

    a. A CPA who attends a course to review for the real estate agents' exam

    b. An independent sales representative who attends a customer relations course at a local university

    c. A self-employed attorney who attends a course on computing legal damages

    d. An independent real estate broker who attends a college course on real estate law

    e. All of the above are deductible

LO 3.6

15. Which of the following is likely a deductible business educational expense?

    a. Leah is a self-employed tax preparer. The State Board of Taxation requires Leah to attend federal and state taxation training each year to maintain her tax preparation licence.

    b. Mike is an auto mechanic. He decides he wants to be a high school math teacher but the state Department of Education requires Mike to earn a bachelor's degree in education.

    c. John teaches European History at Ridgemont High School. In order to better understand the material he teaches, John takes a summer trip with American Geographic magazine to tour Western Europe.

    d. Becca is an auto mechanic. She sees that the local community college is offering courses in jet engine repair which would prepare her to work for one of the airlines. Becca would like to work for an airline because they let employees fly for free.

LO 3.7

16. Which of the following is *not* deductible by the self-employed taxpayer?

    a. A subscription to *The CPA Journal* by a CPA

    b. A subscription to *The Yale Medical Journal* by a doctor

    c. A subscription to *Financial Management* by a financial planner

    d. A subscription to *The Harvard Law Review* by a lawyer

    e. All of the above are deductible

LO 3.8   17. Which of the following self-employed taxpayers are most likely permitted to deduct the cost of their uniform?
   a. A lawyer who wears a business suit
   b. A furnace repairman who must wear overalls while on the job
   c. A nurse who can wear casual clothes while on duty
   d. A pair of stainless steel safety gloves for a butcher

LO 3.9   18. Which of the following business gifts are fully deductible?
   a. A gift to a client that cost $35
   b. A gift to an employee, for 10 years of continued service, costing $250
   c. A gift to a client and her nonclient spouse costing $45
   d. A gift to an employee paid under a qualified plan, for not having an on-the-job injury for 25 years, costing $1,650
   e. None of the above are fully deductible

LO 3.10   19. Loren loaned a friend $9,000 as financing for a new business venture. In the current year, Loren's friend declares bankruptcy and the debt is considered totally worthless. What amount may Loren deduct on his individual income tax return for the current year as a result of the worthless debt, assuming he has no other capital gains or losses for the year?
   a. $9,000 ordinary loss
   b. $9,000 short-term capital loss
   c. $3,000 short-term capital loss
   d. $3,000 ordinary loss
   e. $6,000 short-term capital loss

LO 3.11   20. Kathy is a self-employed taxpayer working exclusively from her home office. Before the home office deduction, Kathy has $3,000 of net income. Her allocable home office expenses are $5,000 in total (includes $2,000 of allocated interest and property taxes). How are the home office expenses treated on her current year tax return?
   a. All home office expenses may be deducted, resulting in a business loss of $2,000.
   b. Only $3,000 of home office expenses may be deducted, resulting in net business income of zero. None of the extra $2,000 of home office expenses may be carried forward or deducted.
   c. Only $3,000 of home office expenses may be deducted, resulting in net business income of zero. The extra $2,000 of home office expenses may be carried forward and deducted in a future year against home office income.
   d. None of the home office expenses may be deducted since Kathy's income is too low.

LO 3.11   21. Which of the following taxpayers qualifies for a home office deduction?
   a. An attorney who is employed by a law firm and has a home office in which to read cases
   b. A doctor who has a regular office downtown and a library at home to store medical journals
   c. An accounting student who maintains a home office used exclusively for her business preparing tax returns
   d. A nurse who maintains a home office to pay bills and read nursing journals
   e. A corporate president who uses his home office to entertain friends and customers

LO 3.11

22. Carol maintains an office in her home where she conducts a dressmaking business. During the year she collects $4,000 from sales, pays $1,300 for various materials and supplies, and properly allocates $2,500 of rent expense and $500 of her utilities expense to the use of her home office. What amount of the rent and utilities expense may Carol deduct in the current year in computing her net income or loss from the dressmaking business?
    a. $0
    b. $500
    c. $2,500
    d. $2,700
    e. $3,000

LO 3.12

23. Which of the following factors is not considered by the IRS in determining whether an activity is a hobby?
    a. Whether the activity is conducted like a business
    b. The time and effort expended by the taxpayer
    c. Whether there have been changes in the methods of operation in an attempt to improve profitability
    d. Income and loss history of the activity
    e. All of the above are considered to determine if an activity is a hobby

LO 3.12

24. Stewie, a single taxpayer, operates an activity as a hobby. Brian, a different taxpayer, operates a similar activity as a bona fide business. Stewie's gross income from his activity is $5,000 and his expenses are $6,000. Brian's gross income and expenses are coincidentally the same as Stewie. Neither Stewie nor Brian itemize, but both have other forms of taxable income. What is the impact on taxable income for Stewie and Brian from these activities?
    a. Stewie will report $0 income and Brian will report a $1,000 loss.
    b. Stewie will report $5,000 income and $0 deduction and Brian will report a $1,000 loss.
    c. Stewie and Brian will report $0 taxable income.
    d. Stewie and Brian will report a $1,000 loss.
    e. Stewie will report a $1,000 loss and Brian will report $5,000 income.

GROUP 2:
PROBLEMS

LO 3.1
LO 3.3
LO 3.5
LO 3.7

1. Scott Butterfield is self-employed as a CPA. He uses the cash method of accounting, and his Social Security number is 644-47-7833. His principal business code is 541211. Scott's CPA practice is located at 678 Third Street, Riverside, CA 92860. Scott's income statement for the year shows the following:

Income Statement

Scott Butterfield, CPA
Income Statement
12/31/2019

	Current Period 1/1/2019 to 12/31/2019	Prior Period 1/1/2018 to 12/31/2018
REVENUES		
Tax Services	$ 76,123.00	$ 75,067.00
Accounting Services	49,001.00	48,860.00
Other Consulting Services	10,095.00	10,115.00
TOTAL REVENUES	135,219.00	134,042.00
COST OF SERVICES		
Salaries	32,000.00	30,100.00
Payroll Taxes	2,868.00	2,387.00
Supplies	1,391.00	1,548.00
TOTAL COST OF SERVICES	36,259.00	34,035.00
GROSS PROFIT (LOSS)	98,960.00	100,007.00
OPERATING EXPENSES		
Advertising and Promotion	300.00	350.00
Business Licenses and Permits	250.00	250.00
Charitable Contributions	425.00	275.00
Continuing Education	300.00	300.00
Dues and Subscriptions	3,500.00	3,500.00
Insurance	875.00	875.00
Meals and Entertainment	4,400.00	5,500.00
Office Expense	150.00	150.00
Postage and Delivery	50.00	50.00
Printing and Reproduction	100.00	100.00
Office Rent	14,000.00	14,000.00
Travel	865.00	865.00
Utilities	2,978.00	2,978.00
TOTAL OPERATING EXPENSES	28,193.00	29,193.00
NET INCOME (LOSS)	$ 70,767.00	$ 70,814.00

Scott also mentioned the following:

• The expenses for dues and subscriptions were his country club membership dues for the year.
• $300 of the charitable contributions were made to a political action committee.
• Scott does not generate income from the sale of goods and therefore does not record supplies and wages as part of cost of goods sold.
• Scott placed a business auto in service on January 1, 2016 and drove it 3,792 miles for business, 3,250 miles for commuting, and 4,500 miles for nonbusiness purposes. His wife has a car for personal use.

Complete Schedule C on Pages 3-37 and 3-38 for Scott showing Scott's net taxable profit from self-employment.

SCHEDULE C
(Form 1040 or 1040-SR)

Department of the Treasury
Internal Revenue Service (99)

Profit or Loss From Business
(Sole Proprietorship)

▶ Go to *www.irs.gov/ScheduleC* for instructions and the latest information.
▶ **Attach to Form 1040, 1040-SR, 1040-NR, or 1041; partnerships generally must file Form 1065.**

OMB No. 1545-0074

2019

Attachment
Sequence No. **09**

Name of proprietor

Social security number (SSN)

A	Principal business or profession, including product or service (see instructions)	**B** Enter code from instructions ▶
C	Business name. If no separate business name, leave blank.	**D** Employer ID number (EIN) (see instr.)
E	Business address (including suite or room no.) ▶	
	City, town or post office, state, and ZIP code	

F Accounting method: **(1)** ☐ Cash **(2)** ☐ Accrual **(3)** ☐ Other (specify) ▶

G Did you "materially participate" in the operation of this business during 2019? If "No," see instructions for limit on losses . ☐ Yes ☐ No

H If you started or acquired this business during 2019, check here . . . . ▶ ☐

I Did you make any payments in 2019 that would require you to file Form(s) 1099? (see instructions) . . ☐ Yes ☐ No

J If "Yes," did you or will you file required Forms 1099? . . . . ☐ Yes ☐ No

Part I   Income

1	Gross receipts or sales. See instructions for line 1 and check the box if this income was reported to you on Form W-2 and the "Statutory employee" box on that form was checked . . . . ▶ ☐	**1**	
2	Returns and allowances	**2**	
3	Subtract line 2 from line 1	**3**	
4	Cost of goods sold (from line 42)	**4**	
5	**Gross profit.** Subtract line 4 from line 3	**5**	
6	Other income, including federal and state gasoline or fuel tax credit or refund (see instructions) . .	**6**	
7	**Gross income.** Add lines 5 and 6 . . . . ▶	**7**	

Part II   Expenses. Enter expenses for business use of your home **only** on line 30.

8	Advertising	**8**		18	Office expense (see instructions)	**18**	
9	Car and truck expenses (see instructions)	**9**		19	Pension and profit-sharing plans .	**19**	
				20	Rent or lease (see instructions):		
10	Commissions and fees .	**10**		a	Vehicles, machinery, and equipment	**20a**	
11	Contract labor (see instructions)	**11**		b	Other business property . . .	**20b**	
12	Depletion	**12**		21	Repairs and maintenance . . .	**21**	
13	Depreciation and section 179 expense deduction (not included in Part III) (see instructions)	**13**		22	Supplies (not included in Part III) .	**22**	
				23	Taxes and licenses	**23**	
				24	Travel and meals:		
14	Employee benefit programs (other than on line 19) . .	**14**		a	Travel	**24a**	
15	Insurance (other than health)	**15**		b	Deductible meals (see instructions)	**24b**	
16	Interest (see instructions):			25	Utilities	**25**	
a	Mortgage (paid to banks, etc.)	**16a**		26	Wages (less employment credits) .	**26**	
b	Other	**16b**		27a	Other expenses (from line 48) . .	**27a**	
17	Legal and professional services	**17**		b	**Reserved for future use** . . .	**27b**	

28	**Total expenses** before expenses for business use of home. Add lines 8 through 27a . . . . . . ▶	**28**	
29	Tentative profit or (loss). Subtract line 28 from line 7	**29**	
30	Expenses for business use of your home. Do not report these expenses elsewhere. Attach Form 8829 unless using the simplified method (see instructions). **Simplified method filers only:** enter the total square footage of: (a) your home: _____ and (b) the part of your home used for business: _____ . Use the Simplified Method Worksheet in the instructions to figure the amount to enter on line 30	**30**	
31	**Net profit or (loss).** Subtract line 30 from line 29.		
	• If a profit, enter on both **Schedule 1 (Form 1040 or 1040-SR), line 3** (or **Form 1040-NR, line 13**) and on **Schedule SE, line 2**. (If you checked the box on line 1, see instructions). Estates and trusts, enter on **Form 1041, line 3.** • If a loss, you **must** go to line 32.	**31**	
32	If you have a loss, check the box that describes your investment in this activity (see instructions).		
	• If you checked 32a, enter the loss on both **Schedule 1 (Form 1040 or 1040-SR), line 3** (or **Form 1040-NR, line 13**) and on **Schedule SE, line 2**. (If you checked the box on line 1, see the line 31 instructions). Estates and trusts, enter on **Form 1041, line 3.** • If you checked 32b, you **must** attach **Form 6198.** Your loss may be limited.	**32a** ☐ All investment is at risk. **32b** ☐ Some investment is not at risk.	

For Paperwork Reduction Act Notice, see the separate instructions.   Cat. No. 11334P   Schedule C (Form 1040 or 1040-SR) 2019

DRAFT AS OF August 7, 2019 DO NOT FILE

Schedule C (Form 1040 or 1040-SR) 2019   Page **2**

Part III   **Cost of Goods Sold** (see instructions)

33   Method(s) used to
     value closing inventory: **a** ☐ Cost   **b** ☐ Lower of cost or market   **c** ☐ Other (attach explanation)

34   Was there any change in determining quantities, costs, or valuations between opening and closing inventory?
     If "Yes," attach explanation . . . .   ☐ **Yes**   ☐ **No**

35   Inventory at beginning of year. If different from last year's closing inventory, attach explanation . . . | 35 |

36   Purchases less cost of items withdrawn for personal use . . . . | 36 |

37   Cost of labor. Do not include any amounts paid to yourself . . . . | 37 |

38   Materials and supplies . . . . | 38 |

39   Other costs . . . . | 39 |

40   Add lines 35 through 39 . . . . | 40 |

41   Inventory at end of year . . . . | 41 |

42   **Cost of goods sold.** Subtract line 41 from line 40. Enter the result here and on line 4 . . . . . | 42 |

Part IV   **Information on Your Vehicle.** Complete this part **only** if you are claiming car or truck expenses on line 9 and are not required to file Form 4562 for this business. See the instructions for line 13 to find out if you must file Form 4562.

43   When did you place your vehicle in service for business purposes? (month, day, year)   ▶ _____ / _____ / _____

44   Of the total number of miles you drove your vehicle during 2019, enter the number of miles you used your vehicle for:

   a Business _____   **b** Commuting (see instructions) _____   **c** Other _____

45   Was your vehicle available for personal use during off-duty hours? . . . .   ☐ **Yes**   ☐ **No**

46   Do you (or your spouse) have another vehicle available for personal use?. . . . .   ☐ **Yes**   ☐ **No**

47a Do you have evidence to support your deduction? . . . .   ☐ **Yes**   ☐ **No**

   b If "Yes," is the evidence written? . . . .   ☐ **Yes**   ☐ **No**

Part V   **Other Expenses.** List below business expenses not included on lines 8–26 or line 30.

48   **Total other expenses.** Enter here and on line 27a . . . . | 48 |

Schedule C (Form 1040 or 1040-SR) 2019

LO 3.1

2. Margaret started her own business in the current year and will report a profit for her first year. Her results of operations are as follows:

Gross income	$45,000
Travel	1,000
Contribution to Presidential Election Campaign	100
Transportation 5,380 miles, using standard mileage method	?
Entertainment in total	4,200
Nine gifts at $50 each	450
Rent and utilities for apartment in total (25% is used for a home office)	10,500

What is the net income Margaret should show on her Schedule C? Show the calculation of her taxable business income.

Gross income   _____

Expenses (describe each)   _____

                                _____

                                _____

                                _____

                                _____

                                _____

Taxable business income   _____

LO 3.2

3. Lawrence owns a small candy store that sells one type of candy. His beginning inventory of candy was made up of 10,000 boxes costing $1.50 per box ($15,000), and he made the following purchases of candy during the year:

March 1	10,000 boxes at $1.60	$16,000
August 15	20,000 boxes at $1.70	34,000
November 20	10,000 boxes at $1.80	18,000

At the end of the year, Lawrence's inventory consisted of 15,000 boxes of candy.

a. Calculate Lawrence's ending inventory and cost of goods sold using the FIFO inventory valuation method.

Ending inventory $ _____
Cost of goods sold $ _____

b. Calculate Lawrence's ending inventory and cost of goods sold using the LIFO inventory valuation method.

Ending inventory $ _____
Cost of goods sold $ _____

LO 3.2

4. Kevin owns a retail store, and during the current year he purchased $610,000 worth of inventory. Kevin's beginning inventory was $67,000, and his ending inventory is $77,200. During the year, Kevin withdrew $1,780 in inventory for his personal use. Use Part III of Schedule C below to calculate Kevin's cost of goods sold for the year.

Part III	Cost of Goods Sold (see instructions)		

33 Method(s) used to
    value closing inventory: a ☐ Cost   b ☐ Lower of cost or market   c ☐ Other (attach explanation)

34 Was there any change in determining quantities, costs, or valuations between opening and closing inventory?
    If "Yes," attach explanation . . . .   ☐ Yes   ☐ No

35	Inventory at beginning of year. If different from last year's closing inventory, attach explanation . . .	35
36	Purchases less cost of items withdrawn for personal use	36
37	Cost of labor. Do not include any amounts paid to yourself	37
38	Materials and supplies	38
39	Other costs	39
40	Add lines 35 through 39	40
41	Inventory at end of year	41
42	**Cost of goods sold.** Subtract line 41 from line 40. Enter the result here and on line 4	42

LO 3.2

5. Business with gross receipts of $25 million or less may treat inventory as non-incidental materials and supplies. Find Regulation Section 1.162-3 and read paragraphs (a)(1) and (a)(2) to help answer the following:

   Frank owns an auto repair shop that serves a particular model of auto and so he tends to purchase parts in bulk. Frank is eligible to treat inventory as non-incidental materials and elects to do so. In December of 2019 he purchases 24 oil filters. He uses one to repair an auto in January 2020, and then about 2 per month and ends 2020 with 14 filters. Explain how Frank will treat his oil filter inventory.

LO 3.3

6. Teresa is a civil engineer who uses her automobile for business. Teresa drove her automobile a total of 11,965 miles during 2019, of which 80 percent was business mileage. The actual cost of gasoline, oil, depreciation, repairs, and insurance for the year was $6,440. Teresa is eligible to use the actual or standard method.
   a. How much is Teresa's transportation deduction based on the standard mileage method?

   $ _____

   b. How much is Teresa's transportation deduction based on the actual cost method?

   $ _____

   c. Which method should Teresa use to calculate her transportation deduction? _____

   Why? _____

LO 3.3

7. Art is a self-employed installer of home entertainment systems, and he drives his car frequently to installation locations. Art drove his car 15,000 miles for business purposes and 20,000 miles in total. His actual expenses, including depreciation, for operating the auto are $10,000 since he had to have the car repaired several times. Art has always used the actual cost method in the past. How much is Art's deductible auto expense for the year?

   _____

LO 3.3

8. Martha is a self-employed tax accountant who drives her car to visit clients on a regular basis. She drives her car 4,000 miles for business and 10,000 for commuting and other personal use. Assuming Martha uses the standard mileage method, how much is her auto expense for the year? Where in her tax return should Martha claim this deduction? _____

LO 3.4

9. Joan is a self-employed attorney in New York City. Joan took a trip to San Diego, CA, primarily for business, to consult with a client and take a short vacation. On the trip, Joan incurred the following expenses:

Airfare to and from San Diego	$ 478
Hotel charges while on business	340
Meals while on business	260
Car rental while on business (she drove 240 miles)	110
Hotel charges while on vacation	460
Meals while on vacation	290
Car rental while on vacation	180
Total	$2,118

Calculate Joan's travel expense deduction for the trip, assuming the trip was made in 2019.

$ _____

LO 3.4

10. Go to the U.S. General Services Administration (GSA) website. For the month of September 30, 2019, what is the per diem rate for each of the following towns:
   a. Flagstaff, AZ
   b. Palm Springs, CA
   c. Denver, CO

LO 3.4
LO 3.6

11. Bob is a self-employed lawyer and is required to take a week of continuing legal education every year to maintain his license. This year he paid $1,150 in course fees for his continuing legal education in a different city. He also paid $354 for airfare and a hotel room and paid $234 for meals. What is the total amount he can deduct on his Schedule C related to these expenses?

_____
_____
_____

LO 3.5

12. Grace is a self-employed sales consultant who spends significant time entertaining potential customers. She keeps all the appropriate records to substantiate her entertainment. She has the following expenses in the current year:

Meals where business was conducted	$5,000
Greens fees (all business)	500
Tickets to baseball games (all business)	500
Country Club dues (all business use)	6,000

What are the tax-deductible meals and entertainment expenses Grace may claim in the current year? On which tax form should she claim the deduction?

_____
_____

LO 3.5

13. Marty is a sales consultant. Marty incurs the following expenses related to the entertainment of his clients in the current year:

Dues to a country club	$4,500
(The country club was used for business	
25 days of the total 75 days that it was used.)	
Business meals at the country club	
not associated with golf or tennis	1,200
Dues to a tennis club	1,000
(The club was used 75 percent for directly	
related business.)	
Tennis fees (personal use)	260
Business meals at various restaurants	1,844

a. How much is Marty's deduction for meals and entertainment expenses for the current year?

$ _____

b. For each item listed above that you believe is not allowed as a deduction, explain the reason it is not allowed.

_____

_____

_____

_____

LO 3.6

14. a. Loren is a secretary in a lawyer's office. Since he often deals with legal matters, Loren feels that a law degree will be beneficial to him. May Loren deduct his educational expenses for law school?

_____

Explain _____

_____

b. Alicia is an employee in the sales department for an international firm. She wishes to learn Spanish to improve her ability to communicate with foreign clients. May Alicia deduct her educational expenses for language school as a miscellaneous itemized deduction?

_____

Explain _____

_____

c. Joan is a practicing lawyer. She enrolls in a local medical school and works toward a medical degree in her spare time. May Joan deduct her educational expenses for the medical classes?

_____

Explain _____

_____

LO 3.7

15. Carey opens a law office in Chicago on January 1, 2019. On January 1, 2019, Carey purchases an annual subscription to a law journal for $170 and a 1-year legal reference service for $1,500. Carey also subscribes to *Chicago Magazine* for $54 so she can find great places to take client's to dinner and review the Best 50 Lawyers in Chicago list published each year. Calculate Carey's deduction for the above items for the 2019 tax year.

$ _____

LO 3.8

16. Cooper and Brandy are married and file a joint income tax return with two separate Schedule Cs. Cooper is an independent security specialist who spent $395 on uniforms during the year. His laundry expenses for the uniforms were $175 for this year, plus $65 for altering them. Brandy works as a drill press operator and wears jeans and a work shirt on the job, which cost $175 this year. Her laundry costs were $50 for the work clothes. Brandy is also required by state regulators to wear safety glasses and safety shoes when working, which cost a total of $115.

a. How much is Cooper's total deduction on his Schedule C for special clothing and uniforms?

$ _____

b. How much is Brandy's total deduction on her Schedule C for special clothing and uniforms?

$ _____

LO 3.9

17. Sam owns an insurance agency and makes the following business gifts during the year. Calculate Sam's deduction for business gifts.

Donee	Amount	Amount Allowed
Ms. Sears (a client)	$35, plus $4 shipping	$ _____
Mr. Williams (a tennis partner, not a business prospect or client)	55	_____
Mr. Sample (a client)	22	_____
Mrs. Sample (nonclient wife of Mr. Sample)	20	_____
Various customers (calendars costing $3 each with the company name on them)	300	_____
Mr. Shiver (an employee gift, a watch, for 25 years of continuous service)	175	_____
Total business gift deduction		$ =======

LO 3.10

18. Steinar loaned a friend $9,500 to buy some stock 3 years ago. In the current year the debt became worthless.
    a. How much is Steinar's deduction for the bad debt for this year? (Assume he has no other capital gains or losses.)

    $ _____

    b. What can Steinar do with the deduction not used this year?

    _____
    _____
    _____
    _____

LO 3.10

19. Sharon is an orthopedic surgeon. She performed a surgery 2 years ago and billed $10,000 to her patient. After 2 years of attempting to collect the money, it is clear that Sharon will not be able to collect anything. Sharon reports income on her tax return on the cash basis, so she only reports the income she actually receives in cash each year. Can she claim a bad debt deduction for the $10,000?

    _____
    _____
    _____
    _____

LO 3.10

20. Carrie loaned her friend $4,500 to buy a used car. She had her friend sign a note with repayment terms and set a reasonable interest rate on the note because the $4,500 was most of her savings. Her friend left town without a forwarding address, and nobody Carrie knows has heard from her in the last year. How should Carrie treat the bad loan for tax purposes?

    _____
    _____
    _____
    _____

LO 3.11

21. Cindy operates a computerized engineering drawing business from her home. Cindy maintains a home office and properly allocates the following expenses to her office:

Depreciation	$1,500
Utilities	500
Real estate taxes	325
Mortgage interest (100 percent deductible)	500

a. Assume that Cindy earns income of $4,400 from her business for the year before deducting home office expenses. She has no other expenses associated with the business. Calculate Cindy's deduction for home office expenses.

$ _____

b. Assume that Cindy earns income of $2,600 from her business during the year before deducting home office expenses. Calculate Cindy's deduction for home office expenses.

$ _____

LO 3.11

22. Pete qualifies for a home office deduction. The amount of space devoted to business use is 300 square feet of the total 1,200 square feet in his apartment. Pete's total rent for the year is $9,600, and he pays utilities (other than telephone) of $2,500 for the year. Calculate Pete's deduction for home office expenses before the gross income limitation.

Rent	$ _____
Utilities other than telephone	_____
Total home office expenses	$ ═══════════

LO 3.11

23. Randi qualifies for a home deduction. The amount of space devoted to business use is 400 square feet of the total 2,000 square feet of her home. Randi's mortgage interest and property taxes in total are $1,600. Other deductions properly allocated to the home office total $300. In addition, Randi purchases and uses business supplies costing $200 during the year. Assume Randi earns income of $3,400 for the year before deducting any home office or supplies deduction. Calculate the largest deduction Randi can take for her home office (ignore self-employment taxes).

$ _____

LO 3.11

24. Ann is a self-employed restaurant critic who does her work exclusively from a home office. Ann's income is $25,000 before the home office deduction this year. Her office takes up 200 square feet of her 1,000-square-foot apartment. The total expenses for her apartment are $6,000 for rent, $1,000 for utilities, $200 for renter's insurance, and $800 for pest control and other maintenance. What is Ann's home office deduction? Please show your calculations.

_____

_____

_____

LO 3.12

25. Lew is a practicing CPA who decides to raise bonsai as a business. Lew engages in the activity and has the following revenue and expenses:

Sales	$ 5,000
Depreciation on greenhouse	10,000
Fertilizer, soil, pots	1,500

a. What are the factors that the IRS will consider when evaluating whether the activity is a business or a hobby?

_____

_____

_____

b. If the activity is deemed to be a regular business, what is the amount of Lew's loss from the activity?

$ _____

c. If the activity is deemed to be a hobby, what is the amount of Lew's expenses (if any) from the activity that may be deducted?

$ _____

GROUP 3:
WRITING ASSIGNMENT

ETHICS

1. Robert, a new client of yours, is a self-employed caterer in Santa Fe, New Mexico. Robert drives his personal van when delivering catered meals to customers. You have asked him to provide the amount of business miles driven using his vehicle. You are planning on using the standard mileage method to calculate Robert's deduction for transportation costs. Robert has responded by saying, "Well, I don't really keep track of my miles. I guess I drove around 3,000 miles last year for the business." What would you say to Robert?

RESEARCH

2. Your supervisor has asked you to research a potential tax deduction for a client, Randall Stevens. Randall is a bank loan officer that lives in Portland, Maine. His specialty is marine loans; in particular, loans for the renovation of classic boats. Over the years, Randall has developed a very unique expertise in valuation of classic boats and is considered a global expert in the field. In 2019, Randall is hoping to attend the North American Classic Marine Boat Show that takes place in Zihuatanejo, Mexico. Randall attends the show more or less every year in order to stay current on classic boat valuations. Interested parties from around the world attend the show in the quaint Mexican coastal town. Randall's costs to attend are $800 for show registration, $1,750 for airfare from Portland to Zihuatanejo, $2,400 for lodging. Meals are estimated at $600. Please prepare a letter for Randall that describes the issues he will face when attempting to deduct the cost of attending the show. Use IRS Publication 463 (available at **www.irs.gov**) to assist you.

(An example of a client letter is available at the website for this textbook located at **www.cengage.com.**)

1. Ken (birthdate July 1, 1988) and Amy (birthdate July 4, 1990) Booth have brought you the following information regarding their income, expenses, and withholding for the year. They are unsure which of these items must be used to calculate taxable income.

    Income:

Ken's salary (salesman)	$28,500
Amy's wages (part-time nurse)	17,500
Insurance reimbursement for repairs from an auto accident	500
Gift from Uncle George	2,000
Interest income from Lodge State Bank	840

    Federal income taxes withheld:

From Ken's salary	2,600
From Amy's wages	650

    Amy owns and operates a computer bookstore named "The Disk Drive." The store is located at 2000 Broadway Street, Menomonie, WI 54751. The business EIN is 27-1234567 and the principal business code for bookstores is 451211. During 2019, Amy had the following income and expenses:

Sales of books	$321,000
Expenses	
Store rental	16,000
Office expense	6,000
Advertising	11,700
City business license	1,020
Payroll	83,550
Payroll taxes	8,400
Utilities	8,050
Other	3,000
Cost of inventory sold	185,000

    Amy treats inventory as non-incidental materials and supplies.

    This year, Amy loaned a friend $10,000 so that he could make an investment. Instead of making the investment, the friend lost all the money gambling and left for parts unknown. Amy has no hope of ever collecting on this bad debt.

    Ken, who ordinarily never gambles, won $20,000 at a casino birthday party for one of his friends.

    The Booths provide the sole support for Ken's parents, Rod (Social Security number 124-80-9050) and Mary (Social Security number 489-37-6676) Booth, who live in their own home. Ken and Amy live at 2345 Wilson Avenue, Menomonie, WI, 54751, and their Social Security numbers are 343-75-3456 (Ken) and 123-45-7890 (Amy). Ken and Amy can claim a $500 other dependent credit for each parent.

    Required: Complete the Booths' federal income tax return for 2019 on Form 1040, Schedule 1, Schedule C, Schedule D, and Form 8949. A statement is required to be attached to a return for a nonbusiness bad debt, but this requirement may be ignored for this problem. Assume no 1099-B is filed in association with the bad debt when filling out Form 8949.

2A. Russell (birthdate February 2, 1968) and Linda (birthdate August 30, 1973) Long have brought you the following information regarding their income and expenses for the current year. Russell owns and operates a landscaping business called Lawns and Landscapes Unlimited (EIN: 32-1456789). The business is operated out of their home, located at 1234 Cherry Lane, Nampa, ID 83687. The principal business code is 561730. Russell's bookkeeper provided the following income statement from the landscaping business:

Lawns and Landscapes
Income Statement
12/31/2019

	Current Period 1/1/2019 to 12/31/2019	Prior Period 1/1/2018 to 12/31/2018
REVENUES		
Lawn maintenance	$ 82,300.00	$ 71,998.00
Lawn and plant installation	34,600.00	48,576.00
Other	17,100.00	8,001.00
TOTAL REVENUES	**134,000.00**	**128,575.00**
COST OF SERVICES		
Salaries	83,400.00	78,445.00
Payroll Taxes	6,700.00	6,432.00
Equipment Rental	12,600.00	10,651.00
Maintenance (Equipment)	8,300.00	8,435.00
Special Clothing and Safety Shoes	660.00	200.00
Contract Labor	7,780.00	6,790.00
TOTAL COST OF SERVICES	**119,440.00**	**110,953.00**
GROSS PROFIT (LOSS)	**14,560.00**	**17,622.00**
OPERATING EXPENSES		
Advertising and Promotion	1,500.00	700.00
Donations	600.00	500.00
Insurance	4,000.00	870.00
Meals and Entertainment	2,300.00	2,100.00
Subscriptions	120.00	120.00
Business Gifts	790.00	600.00
Telephone	2,015.00	1,956.00
Training	1,975.00	-
Travel	865.00	750.00
Other	1,700.00	2,724.00
TOTAL OPERATING EXPENSES	**15,865.00**	**10,320.00**
NET INCOME (LOSS)	$ **(1,305.00)**	$ **7,302.00**

The bookkeeper provided the following additional information:

- Donations expense is a $600 donation to the Campaign to Re-Elect Senator Ami Dahla.
- Training includes $575 for an educational seminar on bug control. It also includes the cost for Russell to attend an online certificate program in landscaping in order to improve his skills and advertise his designation as a certified landscaper. The tuition, fees, and books cost $1,400. He also drove his personal car 57 miles round trip to Boise to take exams three times for a total of 171 miles.
- No business gift exceeded $22 in value.
- The subscription is for a trade magazine titled Plants Unlimited.

The business uses the cash method of accounting and has no accounts receivable or inventory held for resale.

In addition to the above expenses, the Longs have set aside one room of their house as a home office. The room is 160 square feet and their house has a total of 1,600 square feet. They pay $13,200 per year rental on their house, and the utilities amount to $1,800 for the year.

The Longs also have the following interest income for the year:

Interest from Idaho Bank and Trust bond portfolio $44,000

The Longs have two dependent children, Bill (Social Security number 123-23-7654) and Martha (Social Security number 345-67-8654). Both Bill and Martha are full-time high school students, ages 17 and 18, respectively, and each can be claimed for the $500 other dependent credit. Russell's Social Security number is 664-98-5678 and Linda's is 554-98-3946. They made an estimated tax payment to the IRS of $2,500 on December 31, 2019.

Required: Complete the Longs' federal tax return for 2019 on Form 1040, Schedule 1, Schedule 3, Schedule B, Schedule C, and Form 8829. Do not complete Form 4562 (depreciation).

2B. Christopher Crosphit (birthdate April 28, 1977) owns and operates a health club called "Catawba Fitness." The business is located at 4321 New Cut Road, Spartanburg, SC 29303. The principal business code is 812190 and the EIN is 12-3456789. Chris had the following income and expenses from the health club:

Income	$216,000
Expenses:	
Business insurance	3,600
Office supplies	3,300
Payroll	98,900
Payroll taxes	9,112
Travel	2,420
Equipment & club maintenance	10,720
Cleaning service	8,775
Equipment rent	22,820
Utilities (electric, water, gas)	13,975
Telephone	2,778
Rent	32,600
Advertising	5,200
Special workout clothing and boxing gloves	780
Subscription to *Biceps Monthly* magazine	120
Educational seminar on weight training	770
Other expenses	1,830

The business uses the cash method of accounting and has no accounts receivable or inventory held for resale.

Chris has the following interest income for the year:

Upper Piedmont Savings Bank savings account	$13,000
Morgan Bank bond portfolio interest	12,075

Chris also dabbles as a broker of antique and rare books. He acquires and scavenges for books and then sells them on the Internet. He generated $4,000 of sales in 2019 and the books he sold cost $3,500. He also incurred $7,600 in travel and other expenses related to this activity. Chris has never turned a profit in the book business, but he loves books and book selling and does not mind losing money doing it.

Chris has been a widower for 10 years with a dependent son, Arnold (Social Security number 276-23-3954), and he files his tax return as head of household. Arnold (birthdate July 1, 2001) is a high school student; he does not qualify for the child tax credit but does qualify for the $500 other dependent credit. They live next door to the health club at 4323 New Cut Road. Chris does all the administrative work for the health club out of an office in his home. The room is 171 square feet and the house has a total of 1,800 square feet. Chris pays $20,000 per year in rent and $4,000 in utilities.

Chris' Social Security number is 565-12-6789. He made an estimated tax payment to the IRS of $500 on April 15, 2019.

Required: Complete Chris' federal tax return for 2019 on Form 1040, Schedule 1, Schedule 3, Schedule B, Schedule C, and Form 8829. Do not complete Form 4562 (depreciation).

GROUP 5:
CUMULATIVE SOFTWARE PROBLEM

1. The following additional information is available for the Albert and Allison Gaytor family from Chapters 1 and 2.

On September 1, Allison opened a retail store that specializes in sports car accessories. The name of the store is "Toge Pass." The store is located at 617 Crandon Boulevard, Key Biscayne, FL 33149. The store uses the cash method of accounting for everything except inventory which is kept on an accrual basis. The store's EIN is 98-7321654. Allison purchased inventory in August and thus started her business on September 1 with $40,100 of inventory. The Toge Pass accountant provided the following financial information:

Income Statement

Toge Pass Auto Parts
Calendar Year 2019

Financial Statements in U.S. Dollars

Revenue			
Gross Sales		64,050	
Less: Sales Returns and Allowances		500	
Net Sales			63,550
Cost of Goods Sold			
Beginning Inventory		40,100	
Add: Purchases		37,800	
Inventory Available		77,900	
Less: Ending Inventory		37,900	
Cost of Goods Sold			40,000
Gross Profit (Loss)			23,550
Expenses			
Advertising		3,000	
Dues and Subscriptions		-	
Gifts		180	
Insurance		805	
Interest		1,700	
Legal and Professional Fees		315	
Licenses and Fees		900	
Miscellaneous		82	
Office Expense		1,250	
Payroll Taxes		510	
Postage		-	
Rent		7,500	
Repairs and Maintenance		401	
Supplies		630	
Telephone		800	
Travel		940	
Uniforms		400	
Utilities		975	
Vehicle Expenses		-	
Wages		3,470	
Total Expenses			23,858
Net Operating Income			(308)
Other Income			
Gain (Loss) on Sale of Assets			
Interest Income			
Total Other Income			-
Net Income (Loss)			(308)

A review of the expense account detail reveals the following:

- The travel expense includes the costs Allison incurred to attend a seminar on sports car accessories. She spent $300 on airfare, $400 on lodging, $90 on a rental car, and $150 on meals. Allison has proper receipts for these amounts.
- The gift account details show that Allison gave a $30 gift to each of her six best suppliers.

- The supplies expense account detail reflects the purchase of 250 pens with the "Toge Pass" logo inscribed on each pen. Allison gave the pens away to suppliers, customers, and other business contacts before the end of the year.
- Uniforms expense reflects the cost to purchase polo shirts Allison provided for each employee (but not herself). The shirts have the Toge Pass logo printed on the front and back and are the required apparel while working but otherwise are just like any other polo shirts.
- The license and fee account includes a $600 fine Toge Pass paid to the state of Washington for environmental damage resulting from an oil spill.

Allison drove her 2011 Ford Explorer 1,700 miles for business related to Toge Pass. The Explorer was driven a total of 11,450 miles for the year. Included in the total 11,450 miles is 5,000 miles spent commuting to the store. Allison has the required substantiation for this business mileage. She uses the standard mileage method.

In July, Albert loaned a friend $7,000 so he could buy a car. Albert's friend lost his job in 2019 and stopped making payments on the loan. He plans to start making payments again, however, with additional interest as soon as he has new employment.

In late 2019, Albert started to mount and stuff some of his trophy fish to display in his "man cave" at the Gaytor's home. Some of his friends liked Albert's taxidermy work and asked him to prepare a couple of trophy fish for them as well. Although he doubts he will ever sell any more stuffed fish, he received $150 and had no expenses related to this activity in 2019.

Required: Combine this new information about the Gaytor family with the information from Chapters 1 and 2 and complete a revised 2019 tax return for Albert and Allison. Be sure to save your data input files since this case will be expanded with more tax information in later chapters.

Form **1040**

Department of the Treasury—Internal Revenue Service   (99)
U.S. Individual Income Tax Return   **2019**   OMB No. 1545-0074   IRS Use Only—Do not write or staple in this space.

Filing Status
Check only one box.

☐ Single   ☐ Married filing jointly   ☐ Married filing separately (MFS)   ☐ Head of household (HOH)   ☐ Qualifying widow(er) (QW)

If you checked the MFS box, enter the name of spouse. If you checked the HOH or QW box, enter the child's name if the qualifying person is a child but not your dependent. ▶

Your first name and middle initial	Last name	Your social security number

If joint return, spouse's first name and middle initial	Last name	Spouse's social security number

Home address (number and street). If you have a P.O. box, see instructions.	Apt. no.	**Presidential Election Campaign**

City, town or post office, state, and ZIP code. If you have a foreign address, also complete spaces below (see instructions).

Check here if you, or your spouse if filing jointly, want $3 to go to this fund. Checking a box below will not change your tax or refund.   ☐ You   ☐ Spouse

Foreign country name	Foreign province/state/county	Foreign postal code

If more than four dependents, see instructions and ✓ here ▶ ☐

Standard Deduction

Someone can claim: ☐ You as a dependent   ☐ Your spouse as a dependent

☐ Spouse itemizes on a separate return or you were a dual-status alien

Age/Blindness   **You:**   ☐ Were born before January 2, 1955   ☐ Are blind   **Spouse:**   ☐ Was born before January 2, 1955   ☐ Is blind

Dependents (see instructions):

(1) First name Last name	(2) Social security number	(3) Relationship to you	(4) ✓ if qualifies for (see instructions):	
			Child tax credit	Credit for other dependents
			☐	☐
			☐	☐
			☐	☐
			☐	☐

Standard Deduction for—
- Single or Married filing separately, $12,200
- Married filing jointly or Qualifying widow(er), $24,400
- Head of household, $18,350
- If you checked any box under *Standard Deduction,* see instructions.

1	Wages, salaries, tips, etc. Attach Form(s) W-2		**1**	
2a	Tax-exempt interest	**2a**	**b** Taxable interest. Attach Sch. B if required **2b**	
3a	Qualified dividends	**3a**	**b** Ordinary dividends. Attach Sch. B if required **3b**	
4a	IRA distributions	**4a**	**b** Taxable amount **4b**	
c	Pensions and annuities	**4c**	**d** Taxable amount **4d**	
5a	Social security benefits	**5a**	**b** Taxable amount **5b**	
6	Capital gain or (loss). Attach Schedule D if required. If not required, check here ▶ ☐		**6**	
7a	Other income from Schedule 1, line 9		**7a**	
b	Add lines 1, 2b, 3b, 4b, 4d, 5b, 6, and 7a. This is your **total income** ▶		**7b**	
8a	Adjustments to income from Schedule 1, line 22		**8a**	
b	Subtract line 8a from line 7b. This is your **adjusted gross income** ▶		**8b**	
9	**Standard deduction or itemized deductions** (from Schedule A)	**9**		
10	Qualified business income deduction. Attach Form 8995 or Form 8995-A	**10**		
11a	Add lines 9 and 10		**11a**	
b	**Taxable income.** Subtract line 11a from line 8b		**11b**	

For Disclosure, Privacy Act, and Paperwork Reduction Act Notice, see separate instructions.   Cat. No. 11320B   Form **1040** (2019)

Form 1040 (2019)   Page **2**

12a	**Tax** (see inst.) Check if any from Form(s): **1** ☐ 8814 **2** ☐ 4972 **3** ☐		**12a**		
b	Add Schedule 2, line 3, and line 12a and enter the total . . . . ▶			**12b**	
13a	Child tax credit or credit for other dependents	**13a**			
b	Add Schedule 3, line 7, and line 13a and enter the total . . . . ▶			**13b**	
14	Subtract line 13b from line 12b. If zero or less, enter -0-			**14**	
15	Other taxes, including self-employment tax, from Schedule 2, line 10			**15**	
16	Add lines 14 and 15. This is your **total tax** . . . . ▶			**16**	
17	Federal income tax withheld from Forms W-2 and 1099			**17**	
18	Other payments and refundable credits:				
a	Earned income credit (EIC)	**18a**			
b	Additional child tax credit. Attach Schedule 8812 . . .	**18b**			
c	American opportunity credit from Form 8863, line 8 . . .	**18c**			
d	Schedule 3, line 14	**18d**			
e	Add lines 18a through 18d. These are your **total other payments and refundable credits** . . ▶			**18e**	
19	Add lines 17 and 18e. These are your **total payments** . . . . ▶			**19**	

- If you have a qualifying child, attach Sch. EIC.
- If you have nontaxable combat pay, see instructions.

Refund	**20**	If line 19 is more than line 16, subtract line 16 from line 19. This is the amount you **overpaid** . . .		**20**
	21a	Amount of line 20 you want **refunded to you.** If Form 8888 is attached, check here . . . ▶ ☐		**21a**
Direct deposit? See instructions.	▶ **b**	Routing number	▶ **c** Type: ☐ Checking ☐ Savings	
	▶ **d**	Account number		
	22	Amount of line 20 you want **applied to your 2020 estimated tax** . . . . ▶	**22**	
Amount You Owe	**23**	**Amount you owe.** Subtract line 19 from line 16. For details on how to pay, see instructions . . . ▶		**23**
	24	Estimated tax penalty (see instructions) . . . . ▶	**24**	

Third Party Designee	Do you want to allow another person (other than your paid preparer) to discuss this return with the IRS? See instructions.	☐ **Yes.** Complete below. ☐ **No**	
(Other than paid preparer)	Designee's name ▶	Phone no. ▶	Personal identification number (PIN) ▶

Sign Here

Under penalties of perjury, I declare that I have examined this return and accompanying schedules and statements, and to the best of my knowledge and belief, they are true, correct, and complete. Declaration of preparer (other than taxpayer) is based on all information of which preparer has any knowledge.

Joint return?
See instructions.
Keep a copy for your records.

Your signature	Date	Your occupation	If the IRS sent you an Identity Protection PIN, enter it here (see inst.)
Spouse's signature. If a joint return, **both** must sign.	Date	Spouse's occupation	If the IRS sent your spouse an Identity Protection PIN, enter it here (see inst.)
Phone no.		Email address	

Paid Preparer Use Only

Preparer's name	Preparer's signature		Date	PTIN	Check if:
					☐ 3rd Party Designee
Firm's name ▶				Phone no.	☐ Self-employed
Firm's address ▶				Firm's EIN ▶	

Go to *www.irs.gov/Form1040* for instructions and the latest information.   Form **1040** (2019)

SCHEDULE 1
(Form 1040 or 1040-SR)

Department of the Treasury
Internal Revenue Service

Additional Income and Adjustments to Income

▶ Attach to Form 1040 or 1040-SR.
▶ Go to *www.irs.gov/Form1040* for instructions and the latest information.

OMB No. 1545-0074

2019

Attachment
Sequence No. **01**

Name(s) shown on Form 1040 or 1040-SR

Your social security number

Part I	Additional Income	
1	Taxable refunds, credits, or offsets of state and local income taxes	1
2a	Alimony received	2a
b	Date of original divorce or separation agreement (see instructions) ▶	
3	Business income or (loss). Attach Schedule C	3
4	Other gains or (losses). Attach Form 4797	4
5	Rental real estate, royalties, partnerships, S corporations, trusts, etc. Attach Schedule E	5
6	Farm income or (loss). Attach Schedule F	6
7	Unemployment compensation	7
8	Other income. List type and amount ▶	8
9	Combine lines 1 through 8. Enter here and on Form 1040 or 1040-SR, line 7a	9

Part II	Adjustments to Income	
10	Educator expenses	10
11	Certain business expenses of reservists, performing artists, and fee-basis government officials. Attach Form 2106	11
12	Health savings account deduction. Attach Form 8889	12
13	Moving expenses for members of the Armed Forces. Attach Form 3903	13
14	Deductible part of self-employment tax. Attach Schedule SE	14
15	Self-employed SEP, SIMPLE, and qualified plans	15
16	Self-employed health insurance deduction	16
17	Penalty on early withdrawal of savings	17
18a	Alimony paid	18a
b	Recipient's SSN ▶	
c	Date of original divorce or separation agreement (see instructions) ▶	
19	IRA deduction	19
20	Student loan interest deduction	20
21	Reserved for future use	21
22	Add lines 10 through 21. These are your **adjustments to income.** Enter here and on Form 1040 or 1040-SR, line 8a	22

For Paperwork Reduction Act Notice, see your tax return instructions.   Cat. No. 71479F   Schedule 1 (Form 1040 or 1040-SR) 2019

SCHEDULE 3
(Form 1040 or 1040-SR)

Department of the Treasury
Internal Revenue Service

Additional Credits and Payments

▶ Attach to Form 1040 or 1040-SR.
▶ Go to *www.irs.gov/Form1040* for instructions and the latest information.

OMB No. 1545-0074

2019

Attachment
Sequence No. **03**

Name(s) shown on Form 1040 or 1040-SR

Your social security number

Part I	**Nonrefundable Credits**		
1	Foreign tax credit. Attach Form 1116 if required	**1**	
2	Credit for child and dependent care expenses. Attach Form 2441	**2**	
3	Education credits from Form 8863, line 19	**3**	
4	Retirement savings contributions credit. Attach Form 8880	**4**	
5	Residential energy credit. Attach Form 5695	**5**	
6	Other credits from Form: **a** ☐ 3800 **b** ☐ 8801 **c** ☐ _____	**6**	
7	Add lines 1 through 6. Enter here and include on Form 1040 or 1040-SR, line 13b	**7**	
Part II	**Other Payments and Refundable Credits**		
8	2019 estimated tax payments and amount applied from 2018 return	**8**	
9	Net premium tax credit. Attach Form 8962	**9**	
10	Amount paid with request for extension to file (see instructions)	**10**	
11	Excess social security and tier 1 RRTA tax withheld	**11**	
12	Credit for federal tax on fuels. Attach Form 4136	**12**	
13	Credits from Form: **a** ☐ 2439 **b** ☐ Reserved **c** ☐ 8885 **d** ☐	**13**	
14	Add lines 8 through 13. Enter here and on Form 1040 or 1040-SR, line 18d	**14**	

For Paperwork Reduction Act Notice, see your tax return instructions.   Cat. No. 71480G   Schedule 3 (Form 1040 or 1040-SR) 2019

DRAFT AS OF
JULY 11, 2019
DO NOT FILE

SCHEDULE C
(Form 1040 or 1040-SR)

Department of the Treasury
Internal Revenue Service (99)

Profit or Loss From Business
(Sole Proprietorship)

▶ Go to *www.irs.gov/ScheduleC* for instructions and the latest information.
▶ **Attach to Form 1040, 1040-SR, 1040-NR, or 1041; partnerships generally must file Form 1065.**

OMB No. 1545-0074

2019

Attachment
Sequence No. **09**

Name of proprietor | Social security number (SSN)

A Principal business or profession, including product or service (see instructions) | **B Enter code from instructions**
▶

C Business name. If no separate business name, leave blank. | **D Employer ID number (EIN)** (see instr.)

E Business address (including suite or room no.) ▶
City, town or post office, state, and ZIP code

F Accounting method: **(1)** ☐ Cash **(2)** ☐ Accrual **(3)** ☐ Other (specify) ▶

G Did you "materially participate" in the operation of this business during 2019? If "No," see instructions for limit on losses . ☐ Yes ☐ No

H If you started or acquired this business during 2019, check here . . . . ▶ ☐

I Did you make any payments in 2019 that would require you to file Form(s) 1099? (see instructions) . . . . . ☐ Yes ☐ No

J If "Yes," did you or will you file required Forms 1099? . . . . ☐ Yes ☐ No

Part I Income

1	Gross receipts or sales. See instructions for line 1 and check the box if this income was reported to you on Form W-2 and the "Statutory employee" box on that form was checked . . . . ▶ ☐	**1**
2	Returns and allowances	**2**
3	Subtract line 2 from line 1	**3**
4	Cost of goods sold (from line 42)	**4**
5	**Gross profit.** Subtract line 4 from line 3	**5**
6	Other income, including federal and state gasoline or fuel tax credit or refund (see instructions) . .	**6**
7	**Gross income.** Add lines 5 and 6 . . . . ▶	**7**

Part II Expenses. Enter expenses for business use of your home **only** on line 30.

8	Advertising	**8**	18	Office expense (see instructions)	**18**
9	Car and truck expenses (see instructions)	**9**	19	Pension and profit-sharing plans .	**19**
10	Commissions and fees .	**10**	20	Rent or lease (see instructions):	
11	Contract labor (see instructions)	**11**	a	Vehicles, machinery, and equipment	**20a**
12	Depletion	**12**	b	Other business property . . .	**20b**
13	Depreciation and section 179 expense deduction (not included in Part III) (see instructions)	**13**	21	Repairs and maintenance . . .	**21**
			22	Supplies (not included in Part III) .	**22**
			23	Taxes and licenses	**23**
			24	Travel and meals:	
14	Employee benefit programs (other than on line 19) . .	**14**	a	Travel	**24a**
15	Insurance (other than health)	**15**	b	Deductible meals (see instructions)	**24b**
16	Interest (see instructions):		25	Utilities	**25**
a	Mortgage (paid to banks, etc.)	**16a**	26	Wages (less employment credits) .	**26**
b	Other	**16b**	27a	Other expenses (from line 48) . .	**27a**
17	Legal and professional services	**17**	b	**Reserved for future use** . . .	**27b**

28	**Total expenses** before expenses for business use of home. Add lines 8 through 27a . . . . . . ▶	**28**
29	Tentative profit or (loss). Subtract line 28 from line 7	**29**
30	Expenses for business use of your home. Do not report these expenses elsewhere. Attach Form 8829 unless using the simplified method (see instructions). **Simplified method filers only:** enter the total square footage of: (a) your home: _____ and (b) the part of your home used for business: _____ . Use the Simplified Method Worksheet in the instructions to figure the amount to enter on line 30	**30**
31	**Net profit or (loss).** Subtract line 30 from line 29. • If a profit, enter on both **Schedule 1 (Form 1040 or 1040-SR), line 3** (or **Form 1040-NR, line 13**) and on **Schedule SE, line 2.** (If you checked the box on line 1, see instructions). Estates and trusts, enter on **Form 1041, line 3.** • If a loss, you **must** go to line 32.	**31**
32	If you have a loss, check the box that describes your investment in this activity (see instructions). • If you checked 32a, enter the loss on both **Schedule 1 (Form 1040 or 1040-SR), line 3** (or **Form 1040-NR, line 13**) and on **Schedule SE, line 2.** (If you checked the box on line 1, see the line 31 instructions). Estates and trusts, enter on **Form 1041, line 3.** • If you checked 32b, you **must** attach **Form 6198.** Your loss may be limited.	32a ☐ All investment is at risk. 32b ☐ Some investment is not at risk.

For Paperwork Reduction Act Notice, see the separate instructions.   Cat. No. 11334P   Schedule C (Form 1040 or 1040-SR) 2019

DRAFT AS OF August 7, 2019 DO NOT FILE

Schedule C (Form 1040 or 1040-SR) 2019   Page **2**

| Part III | **Cost of Goods Sold** (see instructions) |

33 Method(s) used to
value closing inventory: **a** ☐ Cost   **b** ☐ Lower of cost or market   **c** ☐ Other (attach explanation)

34 Was there any change in determining quantities, costs, or valuations between opening and closing inventory?
If "Yes," attach explanation . . . .   ☐ Yes   ☐ No

35	Inventory at beginning of year. If different from last year's closing inventory, attach explanation . . .	35
36	Purchases less cost of items withdrawn for personal use	36
37	Cost of labor. Do not include any amounts paid to yourself	37
38	Materials and supplies	38
39	Other costs	39
40	Add lines 35 through 39	40
41	Inventory at end of year	41
42	**Cost of goods sold.** Subtract line 41 from line 40. Enter the result here and on line 4	42

| Part IV | **Information on Your Vehicle.** Complete this part **only** if you are claiming car or truck expenses on line 9 and are not required to file Form 4562 for this business. See the instructions for line 13 to find out if you must file Form 4562. |

43 When did you place your vehicle in service for business purposes? (month, day, year) ▶ ____ / ____ / ____

44 Of the total number of miles you drove your vehicle during 2019, enter the number of miles you used your vehicle for:

a Business _____   **b** Commuting (see instructions) _____   **c** Other _____

45 Was your vehicle available for personal use during off-duty hours? . . . . ☐ Yes   ☐ No

46 Do you (or your spouse) have another vehicle available for personal use? . . . . ☐ Yes   ☐ No

47a Do you have evidence to support your deduction? . . . . ☐ Yes   ☐ No

  b If "Yes," is the evidence written? . . . . ☐ Yes   ☐ No

| Part V | **Other Expenses.** List below business expenses not included on lines 8–26 or line 30. |

| 48 | **Total other expenses.** Enter here and on line 27a . . . . | 48 | |

SCHEDULE D
(Form 1040 or 1040-SR)

Department of the Treasury
Internal Revenue Service (99)

Capital Gains and Losses

▶ Attach to Form 1040, 1040-SR, or 1040-NR.
▶ Go to *www.irs.gov/ScheduleD* for instructions and the latest information.
▶ Use Form 8949 to list your transactions for lines 1b, 2, 3, 8b, 9, and 10.

OMB No. 1545-0074

2019

Attachment
Sequence No. **12**

Name(s) shown on return

Your social security number

Did you dispose of any investment(s) in a qualified opportunity fund during the tax year? ☐ **Yes** ☐ **No**
If "Yes," attach Form 8949 and see its instructions for additional requirements for reporting your gain or loss.

Part I **Short-Term Capital Gains and Losses—Generally Assets Held One Year or Less** (see instructions)

See instructions for how to figure the amounts to enter on the lines below. This form may be easier to complete if you round off cents to whole dollars.	**(d)** Proceeds (sales price)	**(e)** Cost (or other basis)	**(g)** Adjustments to gain or loss from Form(s) 8949, Part I, line 2, column (g)	**(h) Gain or (loss)** Subtract column (e) from column (d) and combine the result with column (g)
1a Totals for all short-term transactions reported on Form 1099-B for which basis was reported to the IRS and for which you have no adjustments (see instructions). However, if you choose to report all these transactions on Form 8949, leave this line blank and go to line 1b .				
1b Totals for all transactions reported on Form(s) 8949 with **Box A** checked				
2 Totals for all transactions reported on Form(s) 8949 with **Box B** checked				
3 Totals for all transactions reported on Form(s) 8949 with **Box C** checked				

4 Short-term gain from Form 6252 and short-term gain or (loss) from Forms 4684, 6781, and 8824 . .	**4**	
5 Net short-term gain or (loss) from partnerships, S corporations, estates, and trusts from Schedule(s) K-1	**5**	
6 Short-term capital loss carryover. Enter the amount, if any, from line 8 of your **Capital Loss Carryover Worksheet** in the instructions	**6** ( )
7 **Net short-term capital gain or (loss).** Combine lines 1a through 6 in column (h). If you have any long-term capital gains or losses, go to Part II below. Otherwise, go to Part III on the back	**7**	

Part II **Long-Term Capital Gains and Losses—Generally Assets Held More Than One Year** (see instructions)

See instructions for how to figure the amounts to enter on the lines below. This form may be easier to complete if you round off cents to whole dollars.	**(d)** Proceeds (sales price)	**(e)** Cost (or other basis)	**(g)** Adjustments to gain or loss from Form(s) 8949, Part II, line 2, column (g)	**(h) Gain or (loss)** Subtract column (e) from column (d) and combine the result with column (g)
8a Totals for all long-term transactions reported on Form 1099-B for which basis was reported to the IRS and for which you have no adjustments (see instructions). However, if you choose to report all these transactions on Form 8949, leave this line blank and go to line 8b .				
8b Totals for all transactions reported on Form(s) 8949 with **Box D** checked				
9 Totals for all transactions reported on Form(s) 8949 with **Box E** checked				
10 Totals for all transactions reported on Form(s) 8949 with **Box F** checked.				

11 Gain from Form 4797, Part I; long-term gain from Forms 2439 and 6252; and long-term gain or (loss) from Forms 4684, 6781, and 8824	**11**	
12 Net long-term gain or (loss) from partnerships, S corporations, estates, and trusts from Schedule(s) K-1	**12**	
13 Capital gain distributions. See the instructions	**13**	
14 Long-term capital loss carryover. Enter the amount, if any, from line 13 of your **Capital Loss Carryover Worksheet** in the instructions	**14** ( )
15 **Net long-term capital gain or (loss).** Combine lines 8a through 14 in column (h). Then go to Part III on the back	**15**	

For Paperwork Reduction Act Notice, see your tax return instructions.   Cat. No. 11338H   Schedule D (Form 1040 or 1040-SR) 2019

Schedule D (Form 1040 or 1040-SR) 2019   Page **2**

Part III   Summary

16   Combine lines 7 and 15 and enter the result **16**

    • If line 16 is a **gain,** enter the amount from line 16 on Form 1040 or 1040-SR, line 6; or Form 1040-NR, line 14. Then go to line 17 below.

    • If line 16 is a **loss,** skip lines 17 through 20 below. Then go to line 21. Also be sure to complete line 22.

    • If line 16 is **zero,** skip lines 17 through 21 below and enter -0- on Form 1040 or 1040-SR, line 6; or Form 1040-NR, line 14. Then go to line 22.

17   Are lines 15 and 16 **both** gains?
    ☐ **Yes.** Go to line 18.
    ☐ **No.** Skip lines 18 through 21, and go to line 22.

18   If you are required to complete the **28% Rate Gain Worksheet** (see instructions), enter the amount, if any, from line 7 of that worksheet   . . . . ▶   **18**

19   If you are required to complete the **Unrecaptured Section 1250 Gain Worksheet** (see instructions), enter the amount, if any, from line 18 of that worksheet   . . . . ▶   **19**

20   Are lines 18 and 19 **both** zero or blank?
    ☐ **Yes.** Complete the **Qualified Dividends and Capital Gain Tax Worksheet** in the instructions for Forms 1040 and 1040-SR, line 12a (or in the instructions for Form 1040-NR, line 42). **Don't** complete lines 21 and 22 below.

    ☐ **No.** Complete the **Schedule D Tax Worksheet** in the instructions. **Don't** complete lines 21 and 22 below.

21   If line 16 is a loss, enter here and on Form 1040 or 1040-SR, line 6; or Form 1040-NR, line 14, the **smaller** of:

    • The loss on line 16; or

    • ($3,000), or if married filing separately, ($1,500)   } . . . .   **21** ( )

    Note: When figuring which amount is smaller, treat both amounts as positive numbers.

22   Do you have qualified dividends on Form 1040 or 1040-SR, line 3a; or Form 1040-NR, line 10b?

    ☐ **Yes.** Complete the **Qualified Dividends and Capital Gain Tax Worksheet** in the instructions for Forms 1040 and 1040-SR, line 12a (or in the instructions for Form 1040-NR, line 42).

    ☐ **No.** Complete the rest of Form 1040, 1040-SR, or 1040-NR.

Schedule D (Form 1040 or 1040-SR) 2019

DRAFT AS OF August 30, 2019 DO NOT FILE

Form **8949**

Department of the Treasury
Internal Revenue Service

Sales and Other Dispositions of Capital Assets

▶ Go to *www.irs.gov/Form8949* for instructions and the latest information.
▶ File with your Schedule D to list your transactions for lines 1b, 2, 3, 8b, 9, and 10 of Schedule D.

OMB No. 1545-0074

2019

Attachment
Sequence No. **12A**

Name(s) shown on return

Social security number or taxpayer identification number

Before you check Box A, B, or C below, see whether you received any Form(s) 1099-B or substitute statement(s) from your broker. A substitute statement will have the same information as Form 1099-B. Either will show whether your basis (usually your cost) was reported to the IRS by your broker and may even tell you which box to check.

Part I   **Short-Term.** Transactions involving capital assets you held 1 year or less are generally short-term (see instructions). For long-term transactions, see page 2.

Note: You may aggregate all short-term transactions reported on Form(s) 1099-B showing basis was reported to the IRS and for which no adjustments or codes are required. Enter the totals directly on Schedule D, line 1a; you aren't required to report these transactions on Form 8949 (see instructions).

You *must* check Box A, B, *or* C below. Check only one box. If more than one box applies for your short-term transactions, complete a separate Form 8949, page 1, for each applicable box. If you have more short-term transactions than will fit on this page for one or more of the boxes, complete as many forms with the same box checked as you need.

☐ **(A)** Short-term transactions reported on Form(s) 1099-B showing basis was reported to the IRS (see **Note** above)
☐ **(B)** Short-term transactions reported on Form(s) 1099-B showing basis **wasn't** reported to the IRS
☐ **(C)** Short-term transactions not reported to you on Form 1099-B

1 (a) Description of property (Example: 100 sh. XYZ Co.)	(b) Date acquired (Mo., day, yr.)	(c) Date sold or disposed of (Mo., day, yr.)	(d) Proceeds (sales price) (see instructions)	(e) Cost or other basis. See the **Note** below and see *Column (e)* in the separate instructions	Adjustment, if any, to gain or loss. If you enter an amount in column (g), enter a code in column (f). See the separate instructions.		(h) Gain or (loss). Subtract column (e) from column (d) and combine the result with column (g)
					(f) Code(s) from instructions	(g) Amount of adjustment	
2 Totals. Add the amounts in columns (d), (e), (g), and (h) (subtract negative amounts). Enter each total here and include on your Schedule D, **line 1b** (if **Box A** above is checked), **line 2** (if **Box B** above is checked), or **line 3** (if **Box C** above is checked) ▶							

Note: If you checked Box A above but the basis reported to the IRS was incorrect, enter in column (e) the basis as reported to the IRS, and enter an adjustment in column (g) to correct the basis. See *Column (g)* in the separate instructions for how to figure the amount of the adjustment.

For Paperwork Reduction Act Notice, see your tax return instructions.   Cat. No. 37768Z   Form **8949** (2019)

Form 8949 (2019)   Attachment Sequence No. **12A**   Page **2**

Name(s) shown on return. Name and SSN or taxpayer identification no. not required if shown on other side	Social security number or taxpayer identification number

Before you check Box D, E, or F below, see whether you received any Form(s) 1099-B or substitute statement(s) from your broker. A substitute statement will have the same information as Form 1099-B. Either will show whether your basis (usually your cost) was reported to the IRS by your broker and may even tell you which box to check.

Part II   **Long-Term.** Transactions involving capital assets you held more than 1 year are generally long-term (see instructions). For short-term transactions, see page 1.

Note: You may aggregate all long-term transactions reported on Form(s) 1099-B showing basis was reported to the IRS and for which no adjustments or codes are required. Enter the totals directly on Schedule D, line 8a; you aren't required to report these transactions on Form 8949 (see instructions).

You *must* **check Box D, E,** *or* **F below. Check only one box.** If more than one box applies for your long-term transactions, complete a separate Form 8949, page 2, for each applicable box. If you have more long-term transactions than will fit on this page for one or more of the boxes, complete as many forms with the same box checked as you need.

- ☐ **(D)** Long-term transactions reported on Form(s) 1099-B showing basis was reported to the IRS (see **Note** above)
- ☐ **(E)** Long-term transactions reported on Form(s) 1099-B showing basis **wasn't** reported to the IRS
- ☐ **(F)** Long-term transactions not reported to you on Form 1099-B

1					Adjustment, if any, to gain or loss. If you enter an amount in column (g), enter a code in column (f). See the separate instructions.		
(a) Description of property (Example: 100 sh. XYZ Co.)	**(b)** Date acquired (Mo., day, yr.)	**(c)** Date sold or disposed of (Mo., day, yr.)	**(d)** Proceeds (sales price) (see instructions)	**(e)** Cost or other basis. See the **Note** below and see *Column (e)* in the separate instructions	**(f)** Code(s) from instructions	**(g)** Amount of adjustment	**(h)** Gain or (loss). Subtract column (e) from column (d) and combine the result with column (g)
2 Totals. Add the amounts in columns (d), (e), (g), and (h) (subtract negative amounts). Enter each total here and include on your Schedule D, **line 8b** (if **Box D** above is checked), **line 9** (if **Box E** above is checked), or **line 10** (if **Box F** above is checked) ▶							

Note: If you checked Box D above but the basis reported to the IRS was incorrect, enter in column (e) the basis as reported to the IRS, and enter an adjustment in column (g) to correct the basis. See *Column (g)* in the separate instructions for how to figure the amount of the adjustment.

Form **8949** (2019)

SCHEDULE B
(Form 1040 or 1040-SR)

Department of the Treasury
Internal Revenue Service (99)

Interest and Ordinary Dividends

▶ Go to *www.irs.gov/ScheduleB* for instructions and the latest information.
▶ Attach to Form 1040 or 1040-SR.

OMB No. 1545-0074

2019

Attachment
Sequence No. **08**

Name(s) shown on return

Your social security number

Part I **Interest** (See instructions and the instructions for Forms 1040 and 1040-SR, line 2b.) **Note:** If you received a Form 1099-INT, Form 1099-OID, or substitute statement from a brokerage firm, list the firm's name as the payer and enter the total interest shown on that form.	**1** List name of payer. If any interest is from a seller-financed mortgage and the buyer used the property as a personal residence, see the instructions and list this interest first. Also, show that buyer's social security number and address ▶	**Amount** **1**
	2 Add the amounts on line 1	**2**
	3 Excludable interest on series EE and I U.S. savings bonds issued after 1989. Attach Form 8815	**3**
	4 Subtract line 3 from line 2. Enter the result here and on Form 1040 or 1040-SR, line 2b . . . . ▶	**4**

Note: If line 4 is over $1,500, you must complete Part III.

Part II **Ordinary Dividends** (See instructions and the instructions for Forms 1040 and 1040-SR, line 3b.) **Note:** If you received a Form 1099-DIV or substitute statement from a brokerage firm, list the firm's name as the payer and enter the ordinary dividends shown on that form.	**5** List name of payer ▶	**Amount** **5**
	6 Add the amounts on line 5. Enter the total here and on Form 1040 or 1040-SR, line 3b . . . . ▶	**6**

Note: If line 6 is over $1,500, you must complete Part III.

		Yes	No
Part III **Foreign Accounts and Trusts** **Caution:** If required, failure to file FinCEN Form 114 may result in substantial penalties. See instructions.	You must complete this part if you **(a)** had over $1,500 of taxable interest or ordinary dividends; **(b)** had a foreign account; or **(c)** received a distribution from, or were a grantor of, or a transferor to, a foreign trust.		
	7a At any time during 2019, did you have a financial interest in or signature authority over a financial account (such as a bank account, securities account, or brokerage account) located in a foreign country? See instructions		
	If "Yes," are you required to file FinCEN Form 114, Report of Foreign Bank and Financial Accounts (FBAR), to report that financial interest or signature authority? See FinCEN Form 114 and its instructions for filing requirements and exceptions to those requirements		
	b If you are required to file FinCEN Form 114, enter the name of the foreign country where the financial account is located ▶		
	8 During 2019, did you receive a distribution from, or were you the grantor of, or transferor to, a foreign trust? If "Yes," you may have to file Form 3520. See instructions		

For Paperwork Reduction Act Notice, see your tax return instructions.   Cat. No. 17146N   **Schedule B (Form 1040 or 1040-SR) 2019**

Form 8829

Department of the Treasury
Internal Revenue Service (99)

Expenses for Business Use of Your Home

▶ File only with Schedule C (Form 1040 or 1040-SR). Use a separate Form 8829 for each home you used for business during the year.
▶ Go to www.irs.gov/Form8829 for instructions and the latest information.

OMB No. 1545-0074

2019

Attachment
Sequence No. **176**

Name(s) of proprietor(s)

Your social security number

Part I — Part of Your Home Used for Business

1	Area used regularly and exclusively for business, regularly for daycare, or for storage of inventory or product samples (see instructions)	**1**	
2	Total area of home	**2**	
3	Divide line 1 by line 2. Enter the result as a percentage	**3**	%
	For daycare facilities not used exclusively for business, go to line 4. All others, go to line 7.		
4	Multiply days used for daycare during year by hours used per day . . **4** hr.		
5	If you started or stopped using your home for daycare during the year, see instructions; otherwise, enter 8,760 . . . . . . **5** hr.		
6	Divide line 4 by line 5. Enter the result as a decimal amount . . . **6** .		
7	Business percentage. For daycare facilities not used exclusively for business, multiply line 6 by line 3 (enter the result as a percentage). All others, enter the amount from line 3 . . . . . ▶	**7**	%

Part II — Figure Your Allowable Deduction

8	Enter the amount from Schedule C, line 29, **plus** any gain derived from the business use of your home, **minus** any loss from the trade or business not derived from the business use of your home (see instructions)	**8**	

See instructions for columns (a) and (b) before completing lines 9–22.

		(a) Direct expenses	(b) Indirect expenses	
9	Casualty losses (see instructions)	**9**		
10	Deductible mortgage interest (see instructions)	**10**		
11	Real estate taxes (see instructions)	**11**		
12	Add lines 9, 10, and 11	**12**		
13	Multiply line 12, column (b), by line 7		**13**	
14	Add line 12, column (a), and line 13		**14**	
15	Subtract line 14 from line 8. If zero or less, enter -0-		**15**	
16	Excess mortgage interest (see instructions) . .	**16**		
17	Excess real estate taxes (see instructions) . . .	**17**		
18	Insurance	**18**		
19	Rent	**19**		
20	Repairs and maintenance	**20**		
21	Utilities	**21**		
22	Other expenses (see instructions)	**22**		
23	Add lines 16 through 22	**23**		
24	Multiply line 23, column (b), by line 7		**24**	
25	Carryover of prior year operating expenses (see instructions)		**25**	
26	Add line 23, column (a), line 24, and line 25		**26**	
27	Allowable operating expenses. Enter the **smaller** of line 15 or line 26		**27**	
28	Limit on excess casualty losses and depreciation. Subtract line 27 from line 15		**28**	
29	Excess casualty losses (see instructions)	**29**		
30	Depreciation of your home from line 42 below	**30**		
31	Carryover of prior year excess casualty losses and depreciation (see instructions)	**31**		
32	Add lines 29 through 31		**32**	
33	Allowable excess casualty losses and depreciation. Enter the **smaller** of line 28 or line 32 . . .		**33**	
34	Add lines 14, 27, and 33		**34**	
35	Casualty loss portion, if any, from lines 14 and 33. Carry amount to **Form 4684** (see instructions) .		**35**	
36	**Allowable expenses for business use of your home.** Subtract line 35 from line 34. Enter here and on Schedule C, line 30. If your home was used for more than one business, see instructions ▶		**36**	

Part III — Depreciation of Your Home

37	Enter the **smaller** of your home's adjusted basis or its fair market value (see instructions) . . .	**37**	
38	Value of land included on line 37	**38**	
39	Basis of building. Subtract line 38 from line 37	**39**	
40	Business basis of building. Multiply line 39 by line 7	**40**	
41	Depreciation percentage (see instructions)	**41**	%
42	Depreciation allowable (see instructions). Multiply line 40 by line 41. Enter here and on line 30 above	**42**	

Part IV — Carryover of Unallowed Expenses to 2020

43	Operating expenses. Subtract line 27 from line 26. If less than zero, enter -0-	**43**	
44	Excess casualty losses and depreciation. Subtract line 33 from line 32. If less than zero, enter -0- .	**44**	

For Paperwork Reduction Act Notice, see your tax return instructions.

Cat. No. 13232M

Form **8829** (2019)

DRAFT AS OF June 5, 2019 DO NOT FILE

Student Name _____

Class/Section   _____

Date   _____

KEY NUMBER TAX RETURN SUMMARY

CHAPTER 3

Comprehensive Problem 1

Adjusted Gross Income (Line 8b) _____

Standard Deduction (Line 9) _____

Taxable Income (Line 11b) _____

Total Tax (Line 16) _____

Comprehensive Problem 2A

Adjusted Gross Income (Line 8b) _____

Tentative Profit or (Loss), Schedule C (Line 29) _____

Allowable Expenses for Business Use of Your Home, Form 8829 (Line 36) _____

Total Tax (Line 16) _____

Amount Overpaid (Line 20) _____

Comprehensive Problem 2B

Adjusted Gross Income (Line 8b) _____

Tentative Profit or (Loss), Schedule C (Line 29) _____

Allowable Expenses for Business Use of Your Home, Form 8829 (Line 36) _____

Total Tax (Line 16) _____

Amount Overpaid (Line 20) _____

Additional Income and the Qualified Business Income Deduction

After completing this chapter, you should be able to:

LO 4.1   Define the term "capital asset."

LO 4.2   Apply the holding period for long-term and short-term capital gains and losses.

LO 4.3   Calculate the gain or loss on the disposition of an asset.

LO 4.4   Compute the tax on capital gains.

LO 4.5   Describe the treatment of capital losses.

LO 4.6   Apply the exclusion of gain from personal residence sales.

LO 4.7   Apply the tax rules for rental property and vacation homes.

LO 4.8   Explain the treatment of passive income and losses.

LO 4.9   Describe the basic tax treatment of deductions for net operating losses.

LO 4.10 Compute the qualified business income (QBI) deduction.

OVERVIEW

Chapter 4 covers additional important elements of income and expense which enter into the calculation of adjusted gross income (AGI). The first part of this chapter includes capital gains and other items reported through Schedule D. The second part covers the tax rules for rental properties and other business activities including limitations on passive activities reported through Schedule E. This chapter concludes with the new qualified business income deduction introduced for 2018 by the TCJA. The business income and expenses included in this chapter are all part of the calculation of a taxpayer's AGI.

| Learning Objective 4.1 | 4-1 **WHAT IS A CAPITAL ASSET?** |

Define the term "capital asset."

When taxpayers dispose of property, they must calculate any gain or loss on the transaction and report the gain or loss on their tax returns. The gain or loss realized is equal to the difference between the amount realized on the sale or exchange of the property and the taxpayer's adjusted basis in the property. How gains and losses are reported is dependent on the nature of the property and the length of time the property has been owned. Gains and losses on the sale of capital assets are known as capital gains and losses and are classified as either short-term or long-term. For a gain or loss on the sale of a capital asset to be classified as a long-term capital gain or loss, the taxpayer must have held the asset for the required holding period.

The tax law defines a capital asset as any property, whether used in a trade or business or not, other than:

1. Stock in trade, inventory, or property held primarily for sale to customers in the ordinary course of a trade or business;
2. Depreciable property or real property used in a trade or business (Section 1231 assets);
3. A patent, invention, model or design (whether or not patented), a secret formula or process, a copyright, a literary, musical, or artistic composition, a letter or memorandum, or similar property, if the property is created by the taxpayer;
4. Accounts or notes receivable; and
5. Certain U.S. government publications.

The definition of a capital asset is a definition by exception. All property owned by a taxpayer, other than property specifically noted as an exception, is a capital asset. Depreciable property and real estate used in a trade or business are referred to as Section 1231 assets and will be discussed in Chapter 8 because special rules apply to such assets.

Self-Study Problem 4.1   *See Appendix E for Solutions to Self-Study Problems*

Indicate, by circling your answer, whether each of the following properties is or is not a capital asset.

Property	*Capital*	*Asset?*
1. Shoes held by a shoe store	Yes	No
2. A taxpayer's personal residence	Yes	No
3. A painting held by the artist	Yes	No
4. Accounts receivable of a dentist	Yes	No
5. A copyright purchased from a company	Yes	No
6. A truck used in the taxpayer's business	Yes	No
7. IBM stock owned by an investor	Yes	No
8. AT&T bonds owned by an investor	Yes	No
9. Land held as an investment	Yes	No
10. A taxpayer's television	Yes	No
11. Automobiles for sale owned by a car dealer	Yes	No
12. A taxpayer's sailboat	Yes	No

4-2 HOLDING PERIOD

4.2 Learning Objective

Apply the holding period for long-term and short-term capital gains and losses.

Assets must be held for more than 1 year for the gain or loss to be considered long-term. A capital asset sold before it is owned for the required holding period results in a short-term capital gain or loss. A net short-term capital gain is treated as ordinary income for tax purposes. In calculating the holding period, the taxpayer excludes the date of acquisition and includes the date of disposition.

EXAMPLE Glen purchased stock as an investment on March 27, 2018. The first day the stock may be sold for long-term capital gain treatment is March 28, 2019. ◆

To satisfy the long-term holding period requirement, a capital asset acquired on the last day of a month must not be disposed of before the first day of the thirteenth month following the month of purchase.

EXAMPLE If Elwood purchases a painting on March 31, 2018, the first day the painting may be sold for long-term capital gain treatment is April 1, 2019. ◆

Self-Study Problem 4.2 *See Appendix E for Solutions to Self-Study Problems*

Indicate whether a gain or loss realized in each of the following situations would be long-term or short-term by putting an "X" in the appropriate blank.

Date Acquired	Date Sold	Long-Term	Short-Term
1. October 16, 2018	May 30, 2019	_____	_____
2. May 2, 2018	October 12, 2019	_____	_____
3. July 18, 2018	July 18, 2019	_____	_____
4. August 31, 2017	March 1, 2019	_____	_____

4-3 CALCULATION OF GAIN OR LOSS

A taxpayer must calculate the amount realized and the adjusted basis of property sold or exchanged to arrive at the amount of the gain or loss realized on the disposition. The taxpayer's gain or loss is calculated using the following formula:

Amount realized − Adjusted basis = Gain or loss realized

4-3a Sale or Exchange

The realization of a gain or loss requires the "sale or exchange" of an asset. The term "sale or exchange" is not defined in the tax law, but a sale generally requires the receipt of money or the relief from liabilities in exchange for property, and an exchange is the transfer of ownership of one property for another property.

EXAMPLE Maggie sells stock for $8,500 that she purchased 2 years ago for $6,000. Maggie's adjusted basis in the stock is its cost, $6,000; therefore, she realizes a long-term capital gain of $2,500 ($8,500 − $6,000) on the sale. ◆

EXAMPLE   Art owns a home which has increased in value during the tax year. If Art does not sell the home, there is no realized gain during the tax year. ◆

4-3b Amount Realized

The amount realized from a sale or other disposition of property is equal to the sum of the money received, plus the fair market value of other property received, less the costs paid to transfer the property. If the taxpayer is relieved of a liability, the amount of the liability is added to the amount realized.

EXAMPLE   During the tax year, Ted sells real estate held as an investment for $75,000 in cash, and the buyer assumes the mortgage on the property of $120,000. Ted pays real estate commissions and other transfer costs of $11,000. The amount realized on the sale is calculated as:

Cash received	$ 75,000
Liabilities transferred	120,000
Total sales price	195,000
Less: transfer costs	(11,000)
Amount realized	$ 184,000

◆

4-3c Adjusted Basis

The adjusted basis of property is equal to the original basis adjusted by adding capital (major) improvements and deducting depreciation allowed or allowable, as illustrated by the following formula:

Adjusted basis = Original basis + Capital improvements − Accumulated depreciation

The original basis of property is usually its cost. The cost is the amount paid in cash, debt obligations, other property, or services. The original basis also includes amounts you pay for the sales tax, freight, installation and testing, excise taxes, revenue stamps, recording fees, and real estate taxes if you assume the liability of the seller. If the acquired asset is real property, certain fees and other expenses are part of the cost basis in the property such as the settlement fees and closing costs you paid for buying the property but does not include fees and costs for getting a loan on the property.

The following are some of the settlement fees or closing costs included in the basis of real property:

- Charges for installing utility services
- Legal fees (including fees for the title search and preparation of the sales contract and deed)
- Recording fees
- Survey fees
- Transfer taxes
- Owner's title insurance
- Any amounts the seller owes that you agree to pay, such as back taxes or interest, recording or mortgage fees, charges for improvements or repairs, and sales commissions

The following are some of the settlement fees and closing costs that cannot be included in the basis of property:

- Amounts placed in escrow for the future payment of items such as taxes and insurance
- Casualty insurance premiums
- Rent for occupancy of the property before closing
- Charges for utilities or other services related to occupancy of the property before closing

- Charges connected with getting a loan, such as points (discount points, loan origination fees), mortgage insurance premiums, loan assumption fees, cost of a credit report, and fees for an appraisal required by a lender

Capital improvements are major expenditures for permanent improvements to or restoration of the taxpayer's property. These expenditures include amounts which result in an increase in the value of the taxpayer's property or substantially increase the useful life of the property, as well as amounts which are spent to adapt property to a new use. For example, architect fees paid to plan an addition to a building, as well as the cost of the addition, must be added to the original basis of the asset as capital improvements. Ordinary repairs and maintenance expenditures are not capital expenditures.

EXAMPLE Alan and his wife purchased a house on September 15, 2019. Their closing statement for the purchase is illustrated on Pages 4-6 and 4-7. Their original tax basis in the house is equal to the purchase price of $130,000 plus the incidental costs of the owner's title insurance (not lender's), government recording fees, and transfer taxes. Therefore, their original basis is $130,740 ($130,000 + $500 + $50 + $190). The loan origination fee represents "points" on the mortgage loan. If the house is their principal residence, the points are deductible as interest in the year of payment. The prorated interest and taxes affect their deductions for interest and taxes, as described in Chapter 5. The homeowners' insurance is a nondeductible personal expense, assuming the house is their personal residence. ♦

EXAMPLE Paul acquired a rental house 4 years ago for $91,000. Depreciation claimed on the house for the 4 years totals $14,000. Paul installed a new patio at a cost of $2,500. The adjusted basis of the house is $79,500, as calculated below:

Adjusted basis = original basis + capital improvements − accumulated depreciation
$79,500 = $91,000 + $2,500 − $14,000 ♦

If property is received from a decedent (as an inheritance), the original basis is generally equal to the fair market value at the decedent's date of death. For property acquired as a gift, the amount of the donee's basis depends on whether the property is sold for a gain or a loss by the donee. If a gain results from the disposition of the property, the donee's basis is equal to the donor's basis. If the disposition of the property results in a loss, the donee's basis is equal to the lesser of the donor's basis or the fair market value of the property on the date of the gift. When property acquired by gift is disposed of at an amount between the basis for gain and the basis for loss, no gain or loss is recognized. Note that the basis for gain and the basis for loss will be different only where the gifted property has a fair market value, on the date of the gift, that is less than the donor's adjusted basis in the property.

EXAMPLE Ron received AT&T stock upon the death of his grandfather. The stock cost his grandfather $6,000 forty years ago and was worth $97,000 on the date of his grandfather's death. Ron's basis in the stock is $97,000. ♦

EXAMPLE Jane received a gift of stock from her mother. The stock cost her mother $9,000 five years ago and was worth $6,500 on the date of the gift. If the stock is sold by Jane for $12,000, her gain would be $3,000 ($12,000 − $9,000). However, if the stock is sold for $5,000, the loss would be only $1,500 ($5,000 − $6,500). If the stock is sold for an amount between $6,500 and $9,000, no gain or loss is recognized on the sale. ♦

OMB Approval No. 2502-0265

A. **Settlement Statement (HUD-1)**

B. Type of Loan					
1. ☐ FHA 2. ☐ RHS 3. ☒ Conv. Unins.	6. File Number:		7. Loan Number:		8. Mortgage Insurance Case Number:
4. ☐ VA 5. ☐ Conv. Ins.					

C. Note: This form is furnished to give you a statement of actual settlement costs. Amounts paid to and by the settlement agent are shown. Items marked "(p.o.c.)" were paid outside the closing; they are shown here for informational purposes and are not included in the totals.

D. Name & Address of Borrower:	E. Name & Address of Seller:	F. Name & Address of Lender:
Alan & Julie Young 66 W. 2nd Street, Apt. 3F Peru, IN 46970	Chris and Fiona Everett 89 Payson Street Denver, IN 46926	2nd Farmers Bank 120 N. Broadway Peru, IN 46970

G. Property Location:	H. Settlement Agent:	I. Settlement Date:
68 W. Canal Street Peru, IN 46970	Place of Settlement:	

J. Summary of Borrower's Transaction		**K. Summary of Seller's Transaction**	
100. Gross Amount Due from Borrower		**400. Gross Amount Due to Seller**	
101. Contract sales price	$130,000.00	401. Contract sales price	$130,000.00
102. Personal property		402. Personal property	
103. Settlement charges to borrower (line 1400)	$4,354.40	403.	
104.		404.	
105.		405.	
Adjustment for items paid by seller in advance		**Adjustment for items paid by seller in advance**	
106. City/town taxes to		406. City/town taxes to	
107. County taxes 10/1/2019 to 12/31/2019	$1,000.00	407. County taxes 10/1/2019 to 12/31/2019	$1,000.00
108. Assessments to		408. Assessments to	
109.		409.	
110.		410.	
111.		411.	
112.		412.	
120. Gross Amount Due from Borrower	$135,354.40	**420. Gross Amount Due to Seller**	$131,000.00
200. Amount Paid by or in Behalf of Borrower		**500. Reductions In Amount Due to seller**	
201. Deposit or earnest money	$1,000.00	501. Excess deposit (see instructions)	
202. Principal amount of new loan(s)	$104,000.00	502. Settlement charges to seller (line 1400)	$8,240.00
203. Existing loan(s) taken subject to		503. Existing loan(s) taken subject to	
204.		504. Payoff of first mortgage loan	
205.		505. Payoff of second mortgage loan	
206.		506.	
207.		507.	
208.		508.	
209.		509.	
Adjustments for items unpaid by seller		**Adjustments for items unpaid by seller**	
210. City/town taxes to		510. City/town taxes to	
211. County taxes to		511. County taxes to	
212. Assessments to		512. Assessments to	
213.		513.	
214.		514.	
215.		515.	
216.		516.	
217.		517.	
218.		518.	
219.		519.	
220. Total Paid by/for Borrower	$105,000.00	**520. Total Reduction Amount Due Seller**	$8,240.00
300. Cash at Settlement from/to Borrower		**600. Cash at Settlement to/from Seller**	
301. Gross amount due from borrower (line 120)	$135,354.40	601. Gross amount due to seller (line 420)	$131,000.00
302. Less amounts paid by/for borrower (line 220)	( )	602. Less reductions in amounts due seller (line 520)	($8,240.00)
303. Cash ☒ From ☐ To Borrower	$30,354.40	**603. Cash** ☒ To ☐ From Seller	$122,760.00

The Public Reporting Burden for this collection of information is estimated at 35 minutes per response for collecting, reviewing, and reporting the data. This agency may not collect this information, and you are not required to complete this form, unless it displays a currently valid OMB control number. No confidentiality is assured; this disclosure is mandatory. This is designed to provide the parties to a RESPA covered transaction with information during the settlement process.

L. Settlement Charges

700. Total Real Estate Broker Fees $7,800		Paid From Borrower's Funds at Settlement	Paid From Seller's Funds at Settlement
Division of commission (line 700) as follows :			
701. $3,900.00 to ABC Realtor			
702. $3,900.00 to XYZ Realtor			
703. Commission paid at settlement			$7,800.00
704.			

800. Items Payable in Connection with Loan				
801. Our origination charge incl. origination points (1% or $1,040.00)	$1,040.00	(from GFE #1)		
802. Your credit or charge (points) for the specific interest rate chosen	$	(from GFE #2)		
803. Your adjusted origination charges		(from GFE #A)	$1,040.00	
804. Appraisal fee to Appraisers R Us		(from GFE #3)	$400.00	
805. Credit report to Equifacts		(from GFE #3)	$50.00	
806. Tax service to		(from GFE #3)		
807. Flood certification to		(from GFE #3)		
808.				
809.				
810.				
811.				

900. Items Required by Lender to be Paid in Advance				
901. Daily interest charges from 9/15/19 to 10/31/19 @ $11.40 /day		(from GFE #10)	$524.40	
902. Mortgage insurance premium for months to		(from GFE #3)		
903. Homeowner's insurance for 1 years to ($600 P.O.C.)		(from GFE #11)		
904.				

1000. Reserves Deposited with Lender					
1001. Initial deposit for your escrow account			(from GFE #9)	$250.00	
1002. Homeowner's insurance	1	months @ $ 50.00	per month $ 50.00		
1003. Mortgage insurance		months @ $	per month $		
1004. Property Taxes	2	months @ $ 100.00	per month $ 200.00		
1005.		months @ $	per month $		
1006.		months @ $	per month $		
1007. Aggregate Adjustment			-$		

1100. Title Charges				
1101. Title services and lender's title insurance		(from GFE #4)	$1,350.00	
1102. Settlement or closing fee	$ 100.00			$250.00
1103. Owner's title insurance Title Company, Inc.		(from GFE #5)	$500.00	
1104. Lender's title insurance	$ 500.00			
1105. Lender's title policy limit $ 130,000.00				
1106. Owner's title policy limit $ 130,000.00				
1107. Agent's portion of the total title insurance premium to Title Company Inc	$ 300.00			
1108. Underwriter's portion of the total title insurance premium to Underwriter	$ 75.00			
1109.				
1110.				
1111.				

1200. Government Recording and Transfer Charges				
1201. Government recording charges		(from GFE #7)	$50.00	
1202. Deed $ 25.00 Mortgage $ 25.00 Release $ 15.00				$15.00
1203. Transfer taxes		(from GFE #8)	$190.00	
1204. City/County tax/stamps Deed $ 130.00 Mortgage $				
1205. State tax/stamps Deed $ 60.00 Mortgage $				
1206.				

1300. Additional Settlement Charges				
1301. Required services that you can shop for		(from GFE #6)		
1302. Pest Inspection	$ 75.00			$75.00
1303. Home warranty	$ 100.00			$100.00
1304.				
1305.				

1400. Total Settlement Charges (enter on lines 103, Section J and 502, Section K)	$4,354.40	$8,240.00

Self-Study Problem 4.3   *See Appendix E for Solutions to Self-Study Problems*

Supply the missing information in the following blanks:

	Original Cost	Accumulated Depreciation	Capital Improvements	Adjusted Basis
1.	$15,000	$5,000	$1,000	$_____
2.	15,000	8,000	_____	9,000
3.	30,000	_____	2,000	17,000
4.	_____	9,000	4,000	18,000

Learning Objective 4.4

Compute the tax on capital gains.

4-4 NET CAPITAL GAINS

In recent years, the tax rates on long-term and short-term capital gains have become complex. Short-term capital gains are taxed as ordinary income, while there are various different preferential long-term capital gains tax rates. The 2019 capital gains tax rates are as follows:

Type of Gains	Tax Rate*
Short-Term Capital Gains	Taxed at ordinary income rates consistent with filing status
Typical Long-Term Capital Gains	Taxed at 0, 15, or 20 percent depending on level of other taxable income (see Chapter 2)
Long-Term Unrecaptured Section 1250 Gain (see Chapter 8)	Capped at 25 percent
Long-Term Collectibles Gains (Art, Gems, Coins, Stamps, etc.)	Capped at 28 percent

*The 3.8 percent Medicare tax on net investment income, including qualifying dividends, applies to high-income taxpayers with income over certain thresholds. Please see Chapter 6 for further details.

The application of the typical long-term capital gains rates of 0, 15, or 20 percent depends on the taxable income and filing status of the taxpayer. Formerly, the different rates applied to a taxpayer depending on which ordinary tax bracket the taxpayer was in (e.g., a taxpayer in the 12 percent tax bracket would pay tax on long-term gains at 0 percent since 15 percent is not preferential). The current long-term capital gains tax rates do not align perfectly with the existing ordinary income tax rates. For 2019, typical long-term capital gains (and dividends as discussed in Chapter 2) are taxed as follows:

Income level	Long-term capital gains rate*
Married filing jointly	
$0–$78,750	0%
$78,751–$488,850	15%
>$488,850	20%
Single	
$0–$39,375	0%
$39,376–$434,550	15%
>$434,550	20%

Head of household

$0–$52,750	0%
$52,751–$461,700	15%
>$461,700	20%

Married filing separately

$0–$39,375	0%
$39,376–$244,425	15%
>$244,425	20%

*Special higher rates for "high-income" taxpayers are covered in Chapter 6.

The 2019 break points between the ordinary rates and the typical long-term capital gains rates differ by minor amounts. For example, a single taxpayer moves from an ordinary income tax rate of 12 percent to 22 percent at $39,475; whereas the same taxpayer moves from a 0 percent to 15 percent long-term capital gains tax rate at $39,375.

EXAMPLE Dee is a single taxpayer with wage income of $44,000 and long-term capital gains of $8,000 in 2019. Assume Dee has no other deductions or income except the standard deduction. Dee's taxable income is

Wage income	$44,000
Long-term capital gains	8,000
Standard deduction	(12,200)
Exemption (repealed by the TCJA)	0
Taxable income	$39,800

Dee's income now must be separated into the ordinary and long-term capital gain portions:

Taxable income	$39,800
Long-term capital gains	(8,000)
Ordinary income	$31,800

The 2019 tax on $31,800 of ordinary income is $3,625. Dee's taxable income without the long-term gain is below the 15 percent threshold of $39,375 for a single taxpayer in 2019, but her taxable income with the long-term gain is above the threshold; thus a part of the long-term gain will be taxed at 0 percent and a part at 15 percent. Of her $8,000 long-term capital gain, $7,575 is below the threshold and taxed at 0 percent while $425 is above the threshold and is taxed at 15 percent for an additional capital gains tax of $64 to bring Dee's total tax liability to $3,689. The Qualified Dividends and Capital Gain Tax Worksheet introduced in Chapter 2 can be used to calculate the ordinary and long-term capital gains tax. ◆

4-4a Ordering Rules for Capital Gains

Since there are multiple kinds of capital gains on which to calculate tax, an ordering system is necessary to know which capital gains to tax at what rates. The various kinds of gains are included in taxable income in the following order:

1. Short-term capital gains
2. Unrecaptured Section 1250 gains on real estate
3. Gains on collectibles
4. Long-term capital gains

If taxpayers (or tax practitioners) have several different types of capital gains that interact with each other, the calculation may become very complex. A good tax preparation software will provide the calculation along with supporting worksheets for further review. The rules for the taxation of capital gains are exceptionally complex, and a complete discussion of them is beyond the scope of this textbook.

4-4b Calculation of a Net Capital Position

If a taxpayer has a "net long-term capital gain" (net long-term capital gain in excess of net short-term capital loss), the gain is subject to a preferential tax rate as discussed above. Thus, a taxpayer has to net all of the long-term and short-term capital transactions that take place during a year to calculate tax liability. In calculating a taxpayer's net capital gain or net capital loss, the following procedure is followed:

1. Capital gains and losses are classified into two groups, long-term and short-term.
2. Long-term capital gains are offset by long-term capital losses, resulting in either a net long-term capital gain or a net long-term capital loss.
3. Short-term capital gains are offset by short-term capital losses, resulting in a net short-term capital gain or a net short-term capital loss.
4. If Step 2 above results in a net long-term capital gain, it is offset by any net short-term capital loss (Step 3), resulting in either a net long-term capital gain (net long-term capital gain exceeds net short-term capital loss) or a net short-term capital loss (net short-term capital loss exceeds net long-term capital gain). If Step 2 above results in a net long-term capital loss, it is offset against any net short-term capital gain (Step 3), resulting in either a net long-term capital loss (net long-term capital loss exceeds net short-term capital gain) or ordinary income (net short-term capital gain exceeds net long-term capital loss).

EXAMPLE   The net capital gain computation is illustrated in the following table:

Taxpayer	Net LT Capital Gain or (Loss)	Net ST Capital Gain or (Loss)	Net Capital Position	Taxable LT Gain	Taxable ST Gain
A.	$10,000	$ 0	$ 10,000	$10,000	$ 0
B.	10,000	(4,000)	6,000	6,000	0
C.	0	20,000	20,000	0	20,000
D.	0	(20,000)	(20,000)	0	0
E.	10,000	8,000	18,000	10,000	8,000
F.	(8,000)	12,000	4,000	0	4,000
G.	(8,000)	(6,000)	(14,000)	0	0

◆

Self-Study Problem 4.4   *See Appendix E for Solutions to Self-Study Problems*

In October 2019, Jack, a single taxpayer, sold IBM stock for $12,000, which he purchased 4 years ago for $4,000. He also sold GM stock for $14,000, which cost $17,500 3 years ago, and he had a short-term capital loss of $1,800 on the sale of land. If Jack's other taxable income (salary) is $78,000, what is the amount of Jack's tax on these capital transactions?

$ _____

Learning Objective 4.5

4-5 NET CAPITAL LOSSES

Describe the treatment of capital losses.

4-5a Calculation of Net Capital Losses

The computation of an individual taxpayer's net capital loss is accomplished in a manner similar to the computation of a net capital gain. A net capital loss is incurred when the total capital losses for the period exceed the total capital gains for the period.

EXAMPLE   Connie has net long-term capital gains of $6,500 and a short-term capital loss of $8,000. The net short-term capital loss is $1,500 ($6,500 − $8,000). ◆

EXAMPLE Delvin has net long-term capital losses of $8,000 and a short-term capital gain of $4,500. The net long-term capital loss is $3,500 ($4,500 − $8,000). ♦

4-5b Treatment of Net Capital Losses

Individual taxpayers may deduct net capital losses against ordinary income in amounts up to $3,000 per year. Unused capital losses in a particular year may be carried forward indefinitely. Capital losses and capital loss carryovers first offset capital gains using the ordering rules discussed on the next page. Any remaining net capital loss may be used to offset ordinary income, subject to the $3,000 annual limitation.

EXAMPLE Carter has a net long-term capital loss of $15,000 and other taxable income for the year of $25,000. He may deduct $3,000 of the loss against the $25,000 of other taxable income. The remaining capital loss of $12,000 ($15,000 − $3,000) is carried forward to future years. ♦

When unused capital losses are carried forward, they maintain their character as either long-term or short-term. If a taxpayer has both net long-term losses and net short-term losses in the same year, the net short-term losses are deducted first.

EXAMPLE Frances has a long-term capital loss of $7,000 and a $2,000 short-term capital loss in Year 1. For that year, Frances may deduct $3,000 in capital losses, the $2,000 short-term capital loss, and $1,000 of the long-term capital loss. Her carryforward would be a $6,000 long-term capital loss. If Frances has no capital gains or losses in Year 2, she would deduct $3,000 in long-term capital losses and carry forward $3,000 ($6,000 − $3,000) to Year 3. Assuming she has no other capital gains and losses, the deduction of losses by year can be summarized as follows:

	Year 1	Year 2	Year 3
Long-term capital loss	$7,000	$6,000	$3,000
Short-term capital loss	2,000	0	0
Deduction	3,000	3,000	3,000
Long-term capital loss used	1,000	3,000	3,000
Carryforward, long-term capital loss	6,000	3,000	0 ♦

Taxpayers who have recognized a large capital loss during the year may wish to sell stock or other property to generate enough capital gains prior to year-end to use up all but $3,000 of the capital loss. This way, the capital loss in excess of $3,000 will be used in the current period rather than carried forward, and the capital gains will be fully sheltered from tax.

TAX BREAK

4-5c Personal Capital Losses

Losses from the sale of personal capital assets are not allowed for tax purposes. For instance, the sale of a personal automobile at a loss or the sale of a personal residence at a loss does not generate a tax-deductible capital loss for individual taxpayers.

EXAMPLE Rose moved to a nursing home in 2019 and sold both her personal auto and her principal residence. She originally purchased her auto for $20,000 and sold it for $10,000. She originally purchased her residence for $125,000 and sold it for $100,000. The losses on these sales are not tax deductible to Rose because the assets were personal-use assets. ♦

4-5d Ordering Rules for Capital Losses

When a taxpayer ends up with net capital losses, the losses offset capital gains using the following ordering rules:

- Net short-term capital losses first reduce 28 percent gains, then 25 percent gains, then regular long-term capital gains.
- Net long-term capital losses first reduce 28 percent gains, then 25 percent gains, then any short-term capital gains.

As with the ordering rules for capital gains, the ordering calculation may become quite complex when different classes of capital assets are present. A detailed discussion is beyond the scope of this textbook.

Self-Study Problem 4.5   *See Appendix E for Solutions to Self-Study Problems*

During 2019, Louis Winthorp, who is single, received the following Form 1099-B:

☐ CORRECTED (if checked)

PAYER'S name, street address, city or town, state or province, country, ZIP or foreign postal code, and telephone no.	Applicable checkbox on Form 8949	OMB No. 1545-0715	Proceeds From Broker and Barter Exchange Transactions
Duke Brothers Brokerage 135 S. Broad Street Philadelphia, PA 19103	Box D	20**19** Form **1099-B**	

		1a Description of property (Example: 100 sh. XYZ Co.) 100 sh. Purple Corp.	

		1b Date acquired 6/21/2010	1c Date sold or disposed 08/15/2019	

PAYER'S TIN	RECIPIENT'S TIN	1d Proceeds $ 18,000.00	1e Cost or other basis $ 12,500.00	Copy B For Recipient
34-9876543	123-44-3214	1f Accrued market discount $	1g Wash sale loss disallowed $	

RECIPIENT'S name Louis Winthorp	2 Short-term gain or loss ☐ Long-term gain or loss ☒ Ordinary ☐	3 If checked, proceeds from: Collectibles ☐ QOF ☐	This is important tax information and is being furnished to the IRS. If you are required to file a return, a negligence penalty or other sanction may be imposed on you if this income is taxable and the IRS determines that it has not been reported.
Street address (including apt. no.) 2014 Delancey Street	4 Federal income tax withheld $ 0.00	5 If checked, noncovered security ☐	
City or town, state or province, country, and ZIP or foreign postal code Philadelphia, PA 19103	6 Reported to IRS: Gross proceeds ☒ Net proceeds ☐	7 If checked, loss is not allowed based on amount in 1d ☐	
Account number (see instructions)	8 Profit or (loss) realized in 2019 on closed contracts $	9 Unrealized profit or (loss) on open contracts—12/31/2018 $	
CUSIP number	FATCA filing requirement ☐	10 Unrealized profit or (loss) on open contracts—12/31/2019 $	11 Aggregate profit or (loss) on contracts $	
14 State name	15 State identification no.	16 State tax withheld $ $	12 If checked, basis reported to IRS ☒	13 Bartering $

Form **1099-B**   (Keep for your records)   www.irs.gov/Form1099B   Department of the Treasury - Internal Revenue Service

He also received the following information (1099-B not shown):

Description	Date Acquired	Date Sold	Selling Price	Cost Basis
100 shs. Rose stock	04/18/19	12/07/19	$12,000	$19,200
50 shs. Blue stock	12/18/11	10/02/19	25,000	21,000

The basis was reported to the IRS for all sales. His taxable income is $59,000 (including gains and losses from above). Calculate Louis' net capital gain or loss and tax liability using Schedule D of Form 1040, Parts I, II, and III; Form 8949, Parts I and II; and the Qualified Dividends and Capital Gain Tax Worksheet on Pages 4-13 to 4-17.

Self-Study Problem 4.5

SCHEDULE D (Form 1040 or 1040-SR) Department of the Treasury Internal Revenue Service (99)	**Capital Gains and Losses** ▶ Attach to Form 1040, 1040-SR, or 1040-NR. ▶ Go to *www.irs.gov/ScheduleD* for instructions and the latest information. ▶ Use Form 8949 to list your transactions for lines 1b, 2, 3, 8b, 9, and 10.	OMB No. 1545-0074 20**19** Attachment Sequence No. **12**

Name(s) shown on return   Your social security number

Did you dispose of any investment(s) in a qualified opportunity fund during the tax year? ☐ **Yes** ☐ **No**
If "Yes," attach Form 8949 and see its instructions for additional requirements for reporting your gain or loss.

Part I   Short-Term Capital Gains and Losses—Generally Assets Held One Year or Less (see instructions)

See instructions for how to figure the amounts to enter on the lines below. This form may be easier to complete if you round off cents to whole dollars.	**(d)** Proceeds (sales price)	**(e)** Cost (or other basis)	**(g)** Adjustments to gain or loss from Form(s) 8949, Part I, line 2, column (g)	**(h) Gain or (loss)** Subtract column (e) from column (d) and combine the result with column (g)
1a Totals for all short-term transactions reported on Form 1099-B for which basis was reported to the IRS and for which you have no adjustments (see instructions). However, if you choose to report all these transactions on Form 8949, leave this line blank and go to line 1b .				
1b Totals for all transactions reported on Form(s) 8949 with **Box A** checked				
2 Totals for all transactions reported on Form(s) 8949 with **Box B** checked				
3 Totals for all transactions reported on Form(s) 8949 with **Box C** checked				

4 Short-term gain from Form 6252 and short-term gain or (loss) from Forms 4684, 6781, and 8824 . .	**4**	
5 Net short-term gain or (loss) from partnerships, S corporations, estates, and trusts from Schedule(s) K-1	**5**	
6 Short-term capital loss carryover. Enter the amount, if any, from line 8 of your **Capital Loss Carryover Worksheet** in the instructions	**6** ( )
7 **Net short-term capital gain or (loss).** Combine lines 1a through 6 in column (h). If you have any long-term capital gains or losses, go to Part II below. Otherwise, go to Part III on the back	**7**	

Part II   Long-Term Capital Gains and Losses—Generally Assets Held More Than One Year (see instructions)

See instructions for how to figure the amounts to enter on the lines below. This form may be easier to complete if you round off cents to whole dollars.	**(d)** Proceeds (sales price)	**(e)** Cost (or other basis)	**(g)** Adjustments to gain or loss from Form(s) 8949, Part II, line 2, column (g)	**(h) Gain or (loss)** Subtract column (e) from column (d) and combine the result with column (g)
8a Totals for all long-term transactions reported on Form 1099-B for which basis was reported to the IRS and for which you have no adjustments (see instructions). However, if you choose to report all these transactions on Form 8949, leave this line blank and go to line 8b .				
8b Totals for all transactions reported on Form(s) 8949 with **Box D** checked				
9 Totals for all transactions reported on Form(s) 8949 with **Box E** checked				
10 Totals for all transactions reported on Form(s) 8949 with **Box F** checked.				

11 Gain from Form 4797, Part I; long-term gain from Forms 2439 and 6252; and long-term gain or (loss) from Forms 4684, 6781, and 8824	**11**	
12 Net long-term gain or (loss) from partnerships, S corporations, estates, and trusts from Schedule(s) K-1	**12**	
13 Capital gain distributions. See the instructions	**13**	
14 Long-term capital loss carryover. Enter the amount, if any, from line 13 of your **Capital Loss Carryover Worksheet** in the instructions	**14** ( )
15 **Net long-term capital gain or (loss).** Combine lines 8a through 14 in column (h). Then go to Part III on the back	**15**	

For Paperwork Reduction Act Notice, see your tax return instructions.   Cat. No. 11338H   Schedule D (Form 1040 or 1040-SR) 2019

Schedule D (Form 1040 or 1040-SR) 2019   Page **2**

Part III   **Summary**

16 Combine lines 7 and 15 and enter the result **16**

- If line 16 is a **gain,** enter the amount from line 16 on Form 1040 or 1040-SR, line 6; or Form 1040-NR, line 14. Then go to line 17 below.
- If line 16 is a **loss,** skip lines 17 through 20 below. Then go to line 21. Also be sure to complete line 22.
- If line 16 is **zero,** skip lines 17 through 21 below and enter -0- on Form 1040 or 1040-SR, line 6; or Form 1040-NR, line 14. Then go to line 22.

17 Are lines 15 and 16 **both** gains?
☐ **Yes.** Go to line 18.
☐ **No.** Skip lines 18 through 21, and go to line 22.

18 If you are required to complete the **28% Rate Gain Worksheet** (see instructions), enter the amount, if any, from line 7 of that worksheet . . . . ▶ **18**

19 If you are required to complete the **Unrecaptured Section 1250 Gain Worksheet** (see instructions), enter the amount, if any, from line 18 of that worksheet . . . . ▶ **19**

20 Are lines 18 and 19 **both** zero or blank?
☐ **Yes.** Complete the **Qualified Dividends and Capital Gain Tax Worksheet** in the instructions for Forms 1040 and 1040-SR, line 12a (or in the instructions for Form 1040-NR, line 42). **Don't** complete lines 21 and 22 below.

☐ **No.** Complete the **Schedule D Tax Worksheet** in the instructions. **Don't** complete lines 21 and 22 below.

21 If line 16 is a loss, enter here and on Form 1040 or 1040-SR, line 6; or Form 1040-NR, line 14, the **smaller** of:

- The loss on line 16; or
- ($3,000), or if married filing separately, ($1,500)   } . . . . **21** ( )

Note: When figuring which amount is smaller, treat both amounts as positive numbers.

22 Do you have qualified dividends on Form 1040 or 1040-SR, line 3a; or Form 1040-NR, line 10b?

☐ **Yes.** Complete the **Qualified Dividends and Capital Gain Tax Worksheet** in the instructions for Forms 1040 and 1040-SR, line 12a (or in the instructions for Form 1040-NR, line 42).

☐ **No.** Complete the rest of Form 1040, 1040-SR, or 1040-NR.

Schedule D (Form 1040 or 1040-SR) 2019

Self-Study Problem 4.5

Form **8949**

Department of the Treasury
Internal Revenue Service

Sales and Other Dispositions of Capital Assets

▶ Go to *www.irs.gov/Form8949* for instructions and the latest information.

▶ File with your Schedule D to list your transactions for lines 1b, 2, 3, 8b, 9, and 10 of Schedule D.

OMB No. 1545-0074

2019

Attachment
Sequence No. **12A**

Name(s) shown on return	Social security number or taxpayer identification number

Before you check Box A, B, or C below, see whether you received any Form(s) 1099-B or substitute statement(s) from your broker. A substitute statement will have the same information as Form 1099-B. Either will show whether your basis (usually your cost) was reported to the IRS by your broker and may even tell you which box to check.

Part I | **Short-Term.** Transactions involving capital assets you held 1 year or less are generally short-term (see instructions). For long-term transactions, see page 2.

Note: You may aggregate all short-term transactions reported on Form(s) 1099-B showing basis was reported to the IRS and for which no adjustments or codes are required. Enter the totals directly on Schedule D, line 1a; you aren't required to report these transactions on Form 8949 (see instructions).

You *must* check Box A, B, *or* C below. Check only one box. If more than one box applies for your short-term transactions, complete a separate Form 8949, page 1, for each applicable box. If you have more short-term transactions than will fit on this page for one or more of the boxes, complete as many forms with the same box checked as you need.

- ☐ **(A)** Short-term transactions reported on Form(s) 1099-B showing basis was reported to the IRS (see **Note** above)
- ☐ **(B)** Short-term transactions reported on Form(s) 1099-B showing basis **wasn't** reported to the IRS
- ☐ **(C)** Short-term transactions not reported to you on Form 1099-B

1 **(a)** Description of property (Example: 100 sh. XYZ Co.)	**(b)** Date acquired (Mo., day, yr.)	**(c)** Date sold or disposed of (Mo., day, yr.)	**(d)** Proceeds (sales price) (see instructions)	**(e)** Cost or other basis. See the **Note** below and see *Column (e)* in the separate instructions	Adjustment, if any, to gain or loss. If you enter an amount in column (g), enter a code in column (f). **See the separate instructions.** **(f)** Code(s) from instructions	**(g)** Amount of adjustment	**(h)** Gain or (loss). Subtract column (e) from column (d) and combine the result with column (g)
2 Totals. Add the amounts in columns (d), (e), (g), and (h) (subtract negative amounts). Enter each total here and include on your Schedule D, **line 1b** (if **Box A** above is checked), **line 2** (if **Box B** above is checked), or **line 3** (if **Box C** above is checked) ▶							

Note: If you checked Box A above but the basis reported to the IRS was incorrect, enter in column (e) the basis as reported to the IRS, and enter an adjustment in column (g) to correct the basis. See *Column (g)* in the separate instructions for how to figure the amount of the adjustment.

For Paperwork Reduction Act Notice, see your tax return instructions. | Cat. No. 37768Z | Form **8949** (2019)

Form 8949 (2019)   Attachment Sequence No. **12A**   Page **2**

Name(s) shown on return. Name and SSN or taxpayer identification no. not required if shown on other side	**Social security number or taxpayer identification number**

Before you check Box D, E, or F below, see whether you received any Form(s) 1099-B or substitute statement(s) from your broker. A substitute statement will have the same information as Form 1099-B. Either will show whether your basis (usually your cost) was reported to the IRS by your broker and may even tell you which box to check.

Part II   **Long-Term.** Transactions involving capital assets you held more than 1 year are generally long-term (see instructions). For short-term transactions, see page 1.

Note: You may aggregate all long-term transactions reported on Form(s) 1099-B showing basis was reported to the IRS and for which no adjustments or codes are required. Enter the totals directly on Schedule D, line 8a; you aren't required to report these transactions on Form 8949 (see instructions).

You *must* check Box D, E, *or* F below. Check only one box. If more than one box applies for your long-term transactions, complete a separate Form 8949, page 2, for each applicable box. If you have more long-term transactions than will fit on this page for one or more of the boxes, complete as many forms with the same box checked as you need.

- ☐ **(D)** Long-term transactions reported on Form(s) 1099-B showing basis was reported to the IRS (see **Note** above)
- ☐ **(E)** Long-term transactions reported on Form(s) 1099-B showing basis **wasn't** reported to the IRS
- ☐ **(F)** Long-term transactions not reported to you on Form 1099-B

1 **(a)** Description of property (Example: 100 sh. XYZ Co.)	**(b)** Date acquired (Mo., day, yr.)	**(c)** Date sold or disposed of (Mo., day, yr.)	**(d)** Proceeds (sales price) (see instructions)	**(e)** Cost or other basis. See the **Note** below and see *Column (e)* in the separate instructions	**(f)** Code(s) from instructions	**(g)** Amount of adjustment	**(h)** Gain or (loss). Subtract column (e) from column (d) and combine the result with column (g)
2 Totals. Add the amounts in columns (d), (e), (g), and (h) (subtract negative amounts). Enter each total here and include on your Schedule D, **line 8b** (if **Box D** above is checked), **line 9** (if **Box E** above is checked), or **line 10** (if **Box F** above is checked) ▶							

Adjustment, if any, to gain or loss. If you enter an amount in column (g), enter a code in column (f). See the separate instructions.

Note: If you checked Box D above but the basis reported to the IRS was incorrect, enter in column (e) the basis as reported to the IRS, and enter an adjustment in column (g) to correct the basis. See *Column (g)* in the separate instructions for how to figure the amount of the adjustment.

Form **8949** (2019)

Self-Study Problem 4.5

Qualified Dividends and Capital Gain Tax Worksheet—Line 12a

Before you begin: ✓ See the earlier instructions for line 12a to see if you can use this worksheet to figure your tax.
✓ Before completing this worksheet, complete Form 1040 or 1040-SR through line 11b.
✓ If you don't have to file Schedule D and you received capital gain distributions, be sure you checked the box on Form 1040 or 1040-SR, line 6.

1. Enter the amount from Form 1040 or 1040-SR, line 11b. However, if you are filing Form 2555 (relating to foreign earned income), enter the amount from line 3 of the Foreign Earned Income Tax Worksheet .... **1.** _____

2. Enter the amount from Form 1040 or 1040-SR, line 3a* .... **2.** _____

3. Are you filing Schedule D?*
   ☐ **Yes.** Enter the **smaller** of line 15 or 16 of Schedule D. If either line 15 or 16 is blank or a loss, enter -0-.
   ☐ **No.** Enter the amount from Form 1040 or 1040-SR, line 6. **3.** _____

4. Add lines 2 and 3 .... **4.** _____

5. If filing Form 4952 (used to figure investment interest expense deduction), enter any amount from line 4g of that form. Otherwise, enter -0- .... **5.** _____

6. Subtract line 5 from line 4. If zero or less, enter -0- .... **6.** _____

7. Subtract line 6 from line 1. If zero or less, enter -0- .... **7.** _____

8. Enter:
   $39,375 if single or married filing separately,
   $78,750 if married filing jointly or qualifying widow(er),
   $52,750 if head of household. } .... **8.** _____

9. Enter the smaller of line 1 or line 8 .... **9.** _____

10. Enter the smaller of line 7 or line 9 .... **10.** _____

11. Subtract line 10 from line 9. This amount is taxed at 0% .... **11.** _____

12. Enter the smaller of line 1 or line 6 .... **12.** _____

13. Enter the amount from line 11 .... **13.** _____

14. Subtract line 13 from line 12 .... **14.** _____

15. Enter:
    $434,550 if single,
    $244,425 if married filing separately,
    $488,850 if married filing jointly or qualifying widow(er),
    $461,700 if head of household. } .... **15.** _____

16. Enter the smaller of line 1 or line 15 .... **16.** _____

17. Add lines 7 and 11 .... **17.** _____

18. Subtract line 17 from line 16. If zero or less, enter -0- .... **18.** _____

19. Enter the smaller of line 14 or line 18 .... **19.** _____

20. Multiply line 19 by 15% (0.15) .... **20.** _____

21. Add lines 11 and 19 .... **21.** _____

22. Subtract line 21 from line 12 .... **22.** _____

23. Multiply line 22 by 20% (0.20) .... **23.** _____

24. Figure the tax on the amount on line 7. If the amount on line 7 is less than $100,000, use the Tax Table to figure the tax. If the amount on line 7 is $100,000 or more, use the Tax Computation Worksheet .... **24.** _____

25. Add lines 20, 23, and 24 .... **25.** _____

26. Figure the tax on the amount on line 1. If the amount on line 1 is less than $100,000, use the Tax Table to figure the tax. If the amount on line 1 is $100,000 or more, use the Tax Computation Worksheet .... **26.** _____

27. **Tax on all taxable income.** Enter the **smaller** of line 25 or 26. Also include this amount on the entry space on Form 1040 or 1040-SR, line 12a. If you are filing Form 2555, don't enter this amount on the entry space on Form 1040 or 1040-SR, line 12a. Instead, enter it on line 4 of the Foreign Earned Income Tax Worksheet .... **27.** _____

If you are filing Form 2555, see the footnote in the Foreign Earned Income Tax Worksheet before completing this line.

4-6 SALE OF A PERSONAL RESIDENCE

4.6 Learning Objective

Apply the exclusion of gain from personal residence sales.

4-6a Sales After May 6, 1997

For gains on the sale of a personal residence after May 6, 1997, a seller who has owned and used a home as a principal residence for at least 2 of the last 5 years before the sale can exclude from income up to $250,000 of gain ($500,000 for joint return filers). In general, this personal residence exclusion can be used only once every 2 years. A personal residence includes single-family homes, mobile homes, houseboats, condominiums, cooperative apartments, duplexes, or row houses.

EXAMPLE Joe, a single taxpayer, bought his home 22 years ago for $25,000. He has lived in the home continuously since he purchased it. In November 2019, he sells his home for $300,000. Therefore, his realized gain on the sale of his personal residence is $275,000 ($300,000 − $25,000). Joe's recognized taxable gain on this sale is $25,000, which is his total gain of $275,000 less the exclusion of $250,000. ♦

A seller otherwise qualified to exclude gain on a principal residence who fails to satisfy the 2-year ownership and use requirements may calculate the amount of excluded gain by prorating the exclusion amount if the residence sale is due to an employment-related move, health, or unforeseen circumstances. Unforeseen circumstances include death, divorce or separation, a change in employment that leaves the taxpayer unable to pay the mortgage, multiple births from the same pregnancy, and becoming eligible for unemployment compensation. The $250,000 or $500,000 exclusion amount is prorated by multiplying the exclusion amount by the length of time the taxpayer owned and used the home divided by 2 years.

EXAMPLE John is a single taxpayer who owns and uses his principal residence for 1 year. He then sells the residence due to an employment-related move at a $100,000 gain. Because he may exclude up to one-half (1 year divided by 2 years) of the $250,000 exclusion amount, or $125,000, none of his gain is taxable. ♦

4-6b Married Taxpayers

Taxpayers who are married and file a joint return for the year of sale may exclude up to $500,000 of gain realized on the sale of a personal residence. The full $500,000 for a married couple can be excluded if:

1. Either spouse owned the home for at least 2 of the 5 years before the sale,
2. Both spouses used the home as a principal residence for at least 2 of the last 5 years, and
3. Neither spouse has used the exclusion during the prior 2 years.

EXAMPLE Don and Dolly have been married for 20 years. At the time they were married, they purchased a home for $200,000 and have lived in the home since their marriage. Don and Dolly sell their home for $800,000 and retire to Arizona. Their realized gain on the sale is $600,000 ($800,000 − $200,000), of which only $100,000 is taxable because of the $500,000 exclusion. ♦

The $500,000 exclusion for married taxpayers has been extended to spouses who sell the residence within 2 years of their spouse's death. If a portion of the sale of a residence is taxable, then it should be reported (e.g., Form 8949 using Code H and Schedule D). If no portion is taxable, then no reporting is generally required.

Beginning in 2009, Congress closed a loophole in the residence gain exclusion laws, which was used effectively by some owners of multiple rental properties. Under the residence gain exclusion laws in operation prior to 2009, taxpayers with multiple rental properties could move into a previously rented property every 2 years, reside in the property for the required 2-year period, and then sell the property using the $250,000 or $500,000 gain exclusion. Over a period of 10 years, a married couple could theoretically exclude $2.5 million of taxable gain on five separate properties. Beginning in 2009, taxpayers who rent their residence prior to their

2 years of personal use are generally limited to an exclusion smaller than the full $250,000 or $500,000 amounts. For details, examples, and exceptions to the law, visit **www.irs.gov.**

4-6c Sales Before May 7, 1997

Please note: The law below no longer applies to sales of principal residences. However, because many taxpayers still own residences with "rollover" basis determined under this law, it is important to understand how the law operated.

For sales of a personal residence before May 7, 1997, taxpayers did not have to recognize gain on the sale if they rolled the gain into a new house with a cost as high as the adjusted sales price of the old residence. The adjusted sales price was the amount realized on the sale less any qualified fixing-up expenses. Fixing-up expenses must have been incurred within 90 days prior to the date of sale and paid within 30 days after the date of sale. In addition, the purchase of the new residence had to be within 2 years of the date of sale of the old residence to qualify for nonrecognition of the gain. The adjusted basis of the new residence was reduced by any gain not recognized on the sale of the old residence.

EXAMPLE Mary sold her personal residence for $60,000 in 1994 and paid selling expenses of $3,600. Mary had fixing-up expenses of $1,400, and the basis of her old residence was $40,000. If Mary purchased a new residence within 2 years for $85,000, her recognized gain and the basis of the new residence was calculated as follows:

1. Sales price	$ 60,000
Less: selling expenses	(3,600)
Amount realized	56,400
Adjusted basis of the old residence	(40,000)
Gain realized on the sale	$ 16,400
2. Amount realized	$ 56,400
Less: fixing-up expenses	(1,400)
Adjusted sales price	55,000
Less: cost of the new residence	(85,000)
Gain recognized	$ 0
3. Gain realized	$ 16,400
Less: gain recognized	(0)
Gain not recognized (deferred)	$ 16,400
4. Cost of the new residence	$ 85,000
Less: gain deferred	(16,400)
Basis of the new residence	$ 68,600

EXAMPLE Assume instead that Mary paid only $50,000 for a new residence. The gain and basis of the new residence are calculated as follows:

1. Adjusted sales price (from above)	$ 55,000
Less: cost of new residence	(50,000)
Gain recognized	$ 5,000
2. Gain realized (from above example)	$ 16,400
Less: gain recognized	(5,000)
Gain not recognized (deferred)	$ 11,400
3. Cost of the new residence	$ 50,000
Less: gain deferred	(11,400)
Basis of the new residence	$ 38,600

The calculations on the previous page show that a taxpayer who sold one or more principal residences over a period of years and has a "rollover" basis under the old law may have a principal residence basis that is far lower than the cost of the taxpayer's residence. Because the current law does not require rollover treatment, taxpayers receive a fresh basis in a newly purchased residence which is equal to the purchase price.

Would You Believe?

The IRS has ruled that, in certain cases, a yacht may qualify as a taxpayer's principal residence.

Self-Study Problem 4.6   *See Appendix E for Solutions to Self-Study Problems*

Mike, a single taxpayer, purchased a house 20 years ago for $30,000. He sells the house in December 2019 for $350,000. He has always lived in the house.

a. How much taxable gain does Mike have from the sale of his personal residence?

$ _____

b. Assume Mike married Mary 3 years ago and she has lived in the house since their marriage. If they sell the house in December 2019 for $350,000, what is their taxable gain on a joint tax return?

$ _____

c. Assume Mike is not married and purchased the house only 1 year ago for $200,000, and he sells the house for $350,000 due to an employment-related move. What is Mike's taxable gain?

$ _____

Sign Here	Under penalties of perjury, I declare that I have examined this return and accompanying schedules and statements, and to the best of my knowledge and belief, they are true, correct, and complete. Declaration of preparer (other than taxpayer) is based on all information of which preparer has any knowledge.			
	Your signature	Date	Your occupation	If the IRS sent you an Identity Protection PIN, enter it here (see inst.)
Joint return? See instructions. Keep a copy for your records.	Spouse's signature. If a joint return, **both** must sign.	Date	Spouse's occupation	If the IRS sent your spouse an Identity Protection PIN, enter it here (see inst.)
	Phone no.	Email address		
Paid Preparer Use Only	Preparer's name	Preparer's signature	Date	PTIN	Check if: ☐ 3rd Party Designee
	Firm's name ▶		Phone no.		☐ Self-employed
	Firm's address ▶			Firm's EIN ▶	

Would You Sign This Tax Return?

Ivy Tower (age 45), a history professor at Coastal State University, recently purchased a house near the beach. In the current year, she accepted an offer from a buyer who wants to make the house into a bed and breakfast. Ivy sold her personal residence for a $100,000 gain. She owned the house 11 months as of the date of sale. After the sale closed, she discovered that the $100,000 is taxable as a short-term taxable gain (i.e., ordinary income) because she had not lived there the 2 years required for exclusion of gain on the sale of a residence. She is upset that she will have to pay substantial tax on the sale. Her best friend's husband is an M.D. who signed a letter that Ivy had to move due to the dampness and humidity at the beach. She is not a regular patient of the doctor and Ivy has no history of respiratory problems. Ivy claims she meets the medical extraordinary circumstances exception and therefore refuses to report the gain on her Form 1040. If Ivy were your tax client, would you sign the Paid Preparer's declaration (see example above) on her return? Why or why not?

Apply the tax rules for
rental property and
vacation homes.

4-7 RENTAL INCOME AND EXPENSES

The net income from rental property is taxable income to the taxpayer. In most cases, rental
income is reported with the related expenses on Part I of Schedule E. If services are provided
to the tenant beyond those customarily provided, such as cleaning and maid services, the
income is reported on Schedule C and is subject to the self-employment tax. Expenditures
deductible as rental expenses include real estate taxes, mortgage interest, insurance, commissions, repairs, and depreciation.

EXAMPLE   June Sanchez owns a house that she rents to a tenant for $600 per month.
The following are her expenses for the year:

Real estate taxes	$ 800
Mortgage interest	2,000
Insurance	200
Rent collection commissions	432
General repairs	350

June bought the property on July 1, 2003, and her original basis for
depreciation of the house is $55,000. She uses straight-line depreciation
with a 27.5 year life.

In 2019, June bought a new stove for the rental house that cost $500.
The stove has a 5-year life, and 20 percent of the stove's cost is depreciated
this year. June's net rental income for the year is calculated as follows:

Rental income ($600 × 12)		$ 7,200
Less expenses:		
Real estate taxes	$ 800	
Mortgage interest	2,000	
Insurance	200	
Commissions	432	
General repairs	350	
Depreciation:		
House ($55,000/27.5)	$2,000	
Stove ($500 × 20%)	100	
Total expenses		(5,882)
Net rental income		$ 1,318

Please note that depreciation is an advanced topic which will be covered
in detail in Chapter 8. ◆

4-7a Vacation Homes

Many taxpayers own residences which they use personally as part-year residences and rent
during the remainder of the year. Such part-year rental properties are often referred to as
"vacation homes." The tax law limits the deduction of expenses associated with the rental
of vacation homes.

EXAMPLE   Jean owns a condo in Vail, Colorado. The condo is rented for 3 months
during the year and is used by Jean for 1 month. If there were no vacation
home limitations, Jean could deduct 11 months' worth of depreciation,
maintenance, and other costs associated with the property. The resulting loss
could then be deducted against Jean's other taxable income. ◆

To prevent taxpayers from claiming a deduction for expenses effectively personal in
nature (associated with a personal residence), the tax law limits the deductions a taxpayer
can claim for expenses associated with a vacation home. Deductions attributable to

vacation homes used primarily as personal residences are limited to the income generated from the rental of the property. In general, only profit or breakeven (no loss) tax situations are allowed on the rental of vacation homes.

The expenses associated with the rental of a residence used for both personal and rental purposes are subject to three possible tax treatments. The tax treatment depends on the period of time the residence is used for personal versus rental purposes.

1. **Primarily Personal Use**

   If a residence is rented for fewer than 15 days during the year, the rental period is disregarded and it is treated as a personal residence for tax purposes. The rental income is not taxable and the mortgage interest and real estate taxes may be allowed as itemized deductions. Other expenses, such as utilities and maintenance, are considered nondeductible personal expenses.

EXAMPLE   Glenn owns a lake home. During the year he rented the home for $1,800 for 2 weeks, lived in the home for 3 months, and left the home vacant during the remainder of the year. The expenses for the lake home included $5,000 in mortgage interest, $700 in property taxes, $2,100 in utilities and maintenance, and $3,000 in depreciation. Since the lake home was rented for fewer than 15 days, Glenn would not report the $1,800 of income and would deduct only the interest and property taxes as itemized deductions on Schedule A. The other expenses are nondeductible personal expenses. ◆

2. **Primarily Rental Use**

   If the residence is rented for 15 days or more and is used for personal purposes for not more than *14 days or 10 percent of the days rented, whichever is greater*, the residence is treated as rental property. The expenses must then be allocated between the personal and rental days. If this is the case, the rental expenses may exceed the rental income, and the resulting loss would be deducted against other income, subject to the passive loss rules. (See LO 4.8 for further details.)

EXAMPLE   Assume the same facts as in the preceding example except that the $1,800 rental fee is for 20 days and Glenn uses the lake home for only 10 days during the year. Since the lake home is now rented for 15 days or more and Glenn's use of the home is not more than 14 days (or 10 percent of the days rented, if greater), the property is treated partially as rental property and partially as a personal residence. Allocation of expenses associated with the home is based on the number of days of rental or personal use compared to the total number of days of use. Glenn's personal use percentage is 33.33 percent (10 days/30 days) and the rental portion is 66.67 percent (20 days/30 days). For tax purposes, the rental income or loss is calculated as follows:

	Rental *(66.67%)*	*Personal* *(33.33%)*
Income	$ 1,800	$ 0
Interest and taxes	(3,800)	(1,900)
Utilities and maintenance	(1,400)	(700)
Depreciation	(2,000)	(1,000)
Rental loss	$(5,400)	$ 0

The interest and taxes allocable to Glenn's personal use of the property may be deductible as itemized deductions on Schedule A (see Chapter 5). The personal portion of utilities, maintenance, and depreciation are nondeductible personal expenses. ◆

3. **Rental/Personal Use**

If the residence is rented for 15 days or more and is used for personal purposes for more than *14 days or 10 percent of the days rented, whichever is greater,* allocable rental expenses are allowed only to the extent of rental income. Allocable rental expenses are deducted in three separate steps: first, the interest and taxes are deducted; second, utilities and maintenance expenses are deducted; and third, depreciation expense is deducted. For utilities, maintenance, and depreciation expenses to be deductible, there must be positive income following the deduction of items in the preceding step(s). In addition, the expenses, other than interest and taxes, are only deductible to the extent of that positive income. Expenses are allocated between the rental and personal days before the limits are applied. The IRS requires that the allocation be on the basis of the total days of rental use or personal use divided by the total days of use.

EXAMPLE   Assume Glenn rents the lake home for $2,500 for 20 days and uses it for personal purposes for 60 days. Assume Glenn has the same operating expenses as in the previous examples. Since the lake home is rented for 15 days or more and Glenn uses the home for personal purposes for more than 14 days (or 10 percent of the days rented, if greater), the property is subject to the vacation home limitations. Glenn's personal use percentage is 75 percent (60 days/80 days) and the rental portion is 25 percent (20 days/80 days). The IRS requires that the rental income or loss be calculated as follows:

Gross rental income	$ 2,500
Less: interest and taxes ($5,700 × 25%)	(1,425)
Balance	1,075
Less: utilities and maintenance ($2,100 × 25%)	(525)
Balance	550
Less: depreciation ($3,000 × 25%, limited to $550)	(550)
Net income	$ 0

The interest and taxes allocable to Glenn's personal use of the property may be deductible as itemized deductions on Schedule A (see Chapter 5). The personal portion of utilities, maintenance, and depreciation are nondeductible personal expenses. The nondeductible portion of the depreciation can be carried forward to the next tax year. ◆

It should be noted that the U.S. Tax Court has allowed taxpayers to use 365 days for the allocation of interest and taxes. Under the Tax Court rules, the interest and taxes allocable to the rental use of the property in the above example would be 5.5 percent (20 days/365 days) instead of 25 percent (20 days/80 days). The allocation of utilities and maintenance would remain unchanged, while a full $750 of depreciation (25% of $3,000) would be allowed. The remaining interest and taxes (345 days/365 days) would be included in itemized deductions.

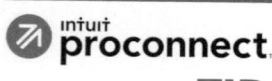

TIP   Rental activity is entered under Income and then Rental and Royalty Income (Schedule E). Key fields to consider are the Type of Property (dropdown), the number of days rented, the number of days of personal use (located below the expenses fields), and the number of days owned (if the Tax Court method is to be used).

Self-Study Problem 4.7 *See Appendix E for Solutions to Self-Study Problems*

Janet Randolf lives in a duplex that she owns at 14 Lancaster Drive, Salem, OR 97305. Janet rents one-half of her duplex and lives in the other half. Her rental income for the year is $6,000. Janet's basis for depreciation in the rental portion is $15,000, and she uses straight-line depreciation with a 27.5 year useful life. On the whole duplex, real estate taxes are $1,200, interest on the mortgage is $3,400, utilities are $1,800, and insurance is $450. Use Part I of Schedule E on Page 4-27 to report Janet's income from rental of part of the duplex.

4-8 PASSIVE LOSS LIMITATIONS

4.8 Learning Objective

Explain the treatment of passive income and losses.

Because of past abuses primarily involving tax shelters and loss deductions from rental real estate, Congress enacted legislation limiting the deduction of certain "passive" losses from other taxable income. A passive activity is a trade or business in which the taxpayer does not materially participate and most rental real estate activity. Because the most common passive loss seen on tax returns is from ordinary real estate rental activities, many taxpayers with an investment in a real estate rental property are affected by these rules. In establishing the limitations, the tax law classifies individual income into three categories. These categories are (1) active income (e.g., wages, self-employment income, and salaries), (2) portfolio income (e.g., dividends and interest), and (3) passive income and losses (e.g., rental real estate income and loss, and income and loss passed through from limited partnerships and other ventures in which the taxpayer has minimal or no involvement).

Generally, passive losses cannot be used to offset either active or portfolio income. Also, any tax credits derived from passive activities can only offset income taxes attributable to passive income. Any unused passive losses and credits are carried over and may be used to offset future passive income or taxes attributable to such income, respectively. Generally, losses remaining when the taxpayer disposes of his or her entire interest in the passive activity may be used in full; however, the taxpayer can only use remaining credits to offset the income tax arising from any gain recognized on the disposition of the activity.

EXAMPLE Mike's income items for 2019 are:

Salary	$40,000
Sales commissions	15,000
Dividends on Microsoft stock	2,000
Rental income from real estate	5,000
Loss from limited partnership	(9,000)
Interest on savings account	4,000

Mike's active income for the year is $55,000 ($40,000 + $15,000), his portfolio income is $6,000 ($2,000 + $4,000), and his passive loss is $4,000 ($5,000 − $9,000). Mike must report gross income of $61,000 ($55,000 + $6,000), since the passive loss cannot be used to offset his active or portfolio income. The net passive loss of $4,000 will be carried over to 2020. ◆

Under the passive loss rules, real estate rental activities are specifically defined as passive, even if the taxpayer actively manages the property and even if the activity is not conducted as a partnership. Individual taxpayers, however, may deduct up to $25,000 of rental property losses against other income, if they are actively involved in the management of the property and their income does not exceed certain limits. The $25,000 loss deduction is phased out when the taxpayer's modified adjusted gross income (adjusted gross income before passive losses and Individual Retirement Account deductions) exceeds $100,000. The $25,000 is reduced by 50 cents for each $1.00 the taxpayer's modified adjusted gross income exceeds that amount. Therefore, no deduction is allowed when the taxpayer's modified adjusted gross income reaches $150,000 (this threshold is not adjusted for inflation). Special limitations apply to taxpayers filing as Married, Filing Separately and claiming a deduction for real estate rental losses under this special rule.

EXAMPLE Mary has modified AGI before passive losses of $120,000. In addition, she has a rental house that she actively manages which shows a loss of $18,000 for the year. She may deduct only $15,000 ($25,000 − 50% of $20,000) of the loss because of the phase-out of the $25,000 allowance for passive rental losses where modified AGI is over $100,000. ♦

The Tax Reform Act of 1986 (TRA 86) introduced the concept of a passive loss limitation. TRA 86 also introduced the active management exception of $25,000 with a phase-out starting at $100,000 of AGI. These amounts have not been adjusted since. For tax year 1987, about 2 million individual income tax returns (about 2 percent) had adjusted gross income of $100,000 or more. In the 2016 tax year (most recent complete year released by the IRS), 18 percent of individual tax returns reported AGI of $100,000 or more. Clearly, far fewer taxpayers are eligible for the exception today.

ProConnect assumes that a rental property is actively managed and will apply the appropriate phase-out based on the modified AGI information entered elsewhere. There is a box on the General Information page of the rental property section to indicate otherwise.

4-8a Real Estate Rental as Trade or Business

Taxpayers heavily involved in real estate rental activities may qualify as having an active business rather than a passive activity. If so, the income and losses from qualified rental activities are not subject to passive loss limitations. For a real estate rental to be considered active, the taxpayer must materially participate in the activity. An individual will satisfy this requirement if both of the following are met:

1. More than 50 percent of the individual's personal service during the tax year is performed in real property trades or businesses, and
2. The individual performs more than 750 hours of service during the tax year in the real property trade or business in which he or she claims material participation.

EXAMPLE In 2019, Allan owns eighteen rental houses and spends 100 percent of his personal service time (1,800 hours in 2019) managing them. Allan spends his 1,800 hours of management time doing repairs, gardening, collecting rents, cleaning and painting vacant houses, advertising for and interviewing new tenants, doing bookkeeping, and purchasing/installing new appliances, drapes, carpets, and toilets. He keeps a log to prove how many hours he works on his property in case he is audited. Since both the above tests are met, Allan's real estate rental activity is not a passive activity. If Allan has an overall loss of $40,000 on the real estate rentals, he can deduct the entire loss on his tax return as an active business, not a passive loss. ♦

Self-Study Problem 4.7

SCHEDULE E
(Form 1040 or 1040-SR)

Department of the Treasury
Internal Revenue Service (99)

Supplemental Income and Loss

(From rental real estate, royalties, partnerships, S corporations, estates, trusts, REMICs, etc.)

▶ Attach to Form 1040, 1040-SR, 1040-NR, or 1041.
▶ Go to *www.irs.gov/ScheduleE* for instructions and the latest information.

OMB No. 1545-0074

2019

Attachment
Sequence No. **13**

Name(s) shown on return

Your social security number

Part I	**Income or Loss From Rental Real Estate and Royalties** Note: If you are in the business of renting personal property, use **Schedule C** (see instructions). If you are an individual, report farm rental income or loss from **Form 4835** on page 2, line 40.

A Did you make any payments in 2019 that would require you to file Form(s) 1099? (see instructions) . . . . . ☐ Yes ☐ No
B If "Yes," did you or will you file required Forms 1099? . . . . ☐ Yes ☐ No

1a Physical address of each property (street, city, state, ZIP code)

A	
B	
C	

1b	Type of Property (from list below)	**2** For each rental real estate property listed above, report the number of fair rental and personal use days. Check the **QJV** box only if you meet the requirements to file as a qualified joint venture. See instructions.		Fair Rental Days	Personal Use Days	QJV
A			**A**			☐
B			**B**			☐
C			**C**			☐

Type of Property:
1 Single Family Residence
2 Multi-Family Residence
3 Vacation/Short-Term Rental
4 Commercial
5 Land
6 Royalties
7 Self-Rental
8 Other (describe)

Income:	Properties:		A	B	C
3 Rents received	**3**				
4 Royalties received	**4**				
Expenses:					
5 Advertising	**5**				
6 Auto and travel (see instructions)	**6**				
7 Cleaning and maintenance	**7**				
8 Commissions.	**8**				
9 Insurance	**9**				
10 Legal and other professional fees	**10**				
11 Management fees	**11**				
12 Mortgage interest paid to banks, etc. (see instructions)	**12**				
13 Other interest.	**13**				
14 Repairs.	**14**				
15 Supplies	**15**				
16 Taxes	**16**				
17 Utilities	**17**				
18 Depreciation expense or depletion	**18**				
19 Other (list) ▶ _____	**19**				
20 Total expenses. Add lines 5 through 19 . .	**20**				
21 Subtract line 20 from line 3 (rents) and/or 4 (royalties). If result is a (loss), see instructions to find out if you must file **Form 6198**	**21**				
22 Deductible rental real estate loss after limitation, if any, on **Form 8582** (see instructions)	**22**	(	)(	)(	)

23a	Total of all amounts reported on line 3 for all rental properties	**23a**	
b	Total of all amounts reported on line 4 for all royalty properties	**23b**	
c	Total of all amounts reported on line 12 for all properties	**23c**	
d	Total of all amounts reported on line 18 for all properties	**23d**	
e	Total of all amounts reported on line 20 for all properties	**23e**	

24	**Income.** Add positive amounts shown on line 21. **Do not** include any losses	**24**	
25	**Losses.** Add royalty losses from line 21 and rental real estate losses from line 22. Enter total losses here .	**25**	( )
26	**Total rental real estate and royalty income or (loss).** Combine lines 24 and 25. Enter the result here. If Parts II, III, IV, and line 40 on page 2 do not apply to you, also enter this amount on Schedule 1 (Form 1040 or 1040-SR), line 5, or Form 1040-NR, line 18. Otherwise, include this amount in the total on line 41 on page 2	**26**	

For Paperwork Reduction Act Notice, see the separate instructions.   Cat. No. 11344L   Schedule E (Form 1040 or 1040-SR) 2019

Income from passive activities can be used by taxpayers to absorb passive losses that would otherwise be disallowed. The passive loss limitations are very complex. Certain oil and gas investments are not subject to the passive loss limitations, and special rules apply to investments in qualified low-income housing.

> Rental real estate is a common form of passive income and is input through the Rental and Royalty Income (Sch E) window. Another source of passive income is from partnerships, LLCs or S corporations. As discussed in Chapters 10 and 11, these entities report income to individual owners through a Schedule K-1. K-1 income is input under Income in the left margin and the applicable Partnership K-1 or S Corporation K-1 input.

Self-Study Problem 4.8   *See Appendix E for Solutions to Self-Study Problems*

Sherry Moore has a limited partnership investment in a commercial rental project in which she has no personal involvement. During 2019, her share of the partnership loss equals $15,000. Sherry also has a rental house that she actively manages, and this activity generated a $21,000 loss for 2019. Sherry had no passive loss carryover from prior years. If Sherry's modified adjusted gross income before passive losses is $102,000, calculate the deduction amounts for Sherry's 2019 tax return using Form 8582 on Page 4-32.

4-9 NET OPERATING LOSSES

4.9 Learning Objective

Describe the basic tax treatment of deductions for net operating losses.

Under the U.S. tax law, taxpayers are required to file an annual tax return. The pattern of a taxpayer's income, however, can lead to inequities among taxpayers with the same total amount of taxable income over a number of years. To alleviate this problem, Congress enacted the Net Operating Loss (NOL) provision.

The NOL provision is primarily designed to provide relief for trade or business losses. Generally, only losses from the operation of a trade or business and casualty and theft losses can generate a net operating loss. Thus, individual taxpayers with only wages, itemized deductions (except casualty losses), and personal exemptions (although currently suspended) cannot generate a net operating loss.

The tax law is designed to permit individuals to deduct business NOLs and prevent the deductions of nonbusiness NOLs. Thus, the NOL computation for individual taxpayers requires the categorization of items of income, deductions, gains, and losses as either business or nonbusiness related. The NOL is not simply the total taxable loss shown on page 1 of Form 1040. In general, when calculating a current net operating loss, the following tax items should be considered:

- No personal or dependency exemptions (exemptions are suspended after 2017)
- No deduction for an NOL from a different year
- Capital losses in excess of capital gains are not allowed
- "Nonbusiness" capital losses (those arising outside of a trade or business, or employment) can only be used against "nonbusiness" capital gains. Excess capital losses cannot increase the NOL
- "Business" capital losses can only be used against "business" capital gains, except that they can be used to offset a net nonbusiness capital gain if one exists
- "Nonbusiness" deductions (e.g., charitable donations, deductible medical expenses, mortgage interest, alimony, etc.) can only be used against "nonbusiness" income (interest, dividends, etc.). However, if nonbusiness capital gains exceed nonbusiness capital losses (see above), "excess" nonbusiness deductions can be offset against these gains. (Note that casualty losses are treated as "business deductions" for NOL purposes.)

EXAMPLE   Yujian, a single taxpayer, has completed her 2019 Schedule C and her net loss is $70,000. She also has wages of $45,000 and interest income from her savings of $500. Her business sold property during the year and generated a $3,000 ordinary gain and a separate $5,000 long-term capital gain. Yujian also had several capital gains and losses from the sale of stock investments. Her net results are a $17,000 short-term capital gain and a $6,000 long-term capital loss from these stock sales. Yujian itemizes her deductions and her Schedule A reports the following:

Taxes paid	$ 8,500
Mortgage interest	6,000
Charitable gifts	500
Casualty loss (federal disaster area loss)	2,500
Total itemized deductions	$ 17,500

Yujian calculates her taxable income as follows:

Wages	$ 45,000
Interest income	500
Business loss	(70,000)
Capital gains[1]	16,000
Other gains	3,000
Total income (loss) and AGI	(5,500)
Itemized deductions	(17,500)
Taxable income (loss)	$(23,000)

To compute Yujian's NOL, we need to categorize business and non-business items:

	Business	Nonbusiness
Wages	$ 45,000	
Interest income		$ 500
Business loss	(70,000)	
Capital gains	5,000	11,000
Other gains	3,000	
Itemized deductions	(2,500)	(15,000)
Total	$(19,500)	$ (3,500)

Using the above information, we can modify taxable income to compute the NOL.

Step 1: Excess nonbusiness capital losses cannot exceed nonbusiness capital gains.

Since the $6,000 nonbusiness capital losses do not exceed $17,000 of nonbusiness capital gains, no adjustment is required. In addition, we can use the $11,000 "excess" nonbusiness capital gain to absorb any nonbusiness deductions in the next step.

Step 2: Nonbusiness deductions cannot exceed nonbusiness income.

Nonbusiness deductions $15,000 − Nonbusiness income $500 = Net nonbusiness deductions $14,500

However, as previously mentioned, net nonbusiness deductions can also offset any net nonbusiness capital gains. Thus $11,000 of the nonbusiness deductions can be used; however, the remaining $3,500 ($14,500 − $11,000) are not deductible and must be added back to the tentative NOL $(23,000) + $3,500 = $(19,500).

---

[1] $1,000 long-term capital loss ($5,000 long-term capital gain from business less $6,000 long-term capital loss from stocks) netted against $17,000 short-term capital gain from stocks.

Step 3: The business capital (casualty) loss of $2,500 can only be offset by
business capital gains of $5,000. There is no excess loss and thus no
adjustment is needed.

This agrees to the business category total loss of $19,500 above which
is consistent with the NOL representing only business losses.

Yujian may carryforward (or under previous tax law, carryback) the NOL
of $19,500 to offset future income. ♦

4-9a **NOL 80 Percent Limitation**

The use of an NOL generated after December 31, 2017 is limited to 80 percent of the
current year's taxable income (without regard to the NOL deduction) when used (NOLs
generated prior to January 1, 2018 continue to be used 100 percent necessitating tracking
of different NOL periods). In addition, the carryback provisions are repealed and NOLs
may only be carried forward; however, the carryforward period is now indefinite. The
previous 2 year carryback and 20 year forward rules continue to apply to NOLs generated
prior to January 1, 2018. Unlike many other recent changes, the changes to NOLs are not
subject to expiration in 2025.

EXAMPLE   In 2017, Desiree has a net operating loss of $10,000. She elects to
forego any carryback and instead carries the NOL forward to 2018. In
2018, Desiree generates taxable income of $1,000 eligible to be offset by
her 2017 NOL without regard to the new 80 percent of taxable income
limitation. Desiree's 2018 taxable income is $0 and she has $9,000 of NOL
to carryforward into 2019. If her 2019 taxable income is $12,000, she
can utilize the entire NOL (again, without regard to the 80 percent limitation
since the NOL was created prior to 2018). ♦

EXAMPLE   In 2019, Rusty has a net operating loss of $10,000. He is not eligible
to carry the loss back and must carry it forward to 2020. In 2020, Rusty
generates taxable income of $12,000. Rusty's use of the 2019 NOL is limited
to 80 percent of his 2020 taxable income or $9,600 ($12,000 × 80%).
Rusty's 2020 taxable income after NOL is $2,400 ($12,000 − $9,600).
Rusty may carryforward the remaining $400 NOL indefinitely. ♦

4-9b **Overall Business Loss Limitation**

To reduce the potential for large business losses being claimed in a single year, the tax law
places a $510,000 annual limitation on noncorporate business losses for married filing jointly
taxpayers ($255,000 for all others) in 2019. The loss limitation is indexed for inflation. Any
excess business loss limited under these rules becomes part of the NOL for future years.

EXAMPLE   Bettina is a single taxpayer with wages of $20,000 and a business with
income of $5,000. In addition, Bettina is disposing of a passive loss activity
for which she has accumulated suspended losses of $280,000 (including
her share of the current year loss). Bettina's excess business loss is $275,000
($280,000 − $5,000) less the single threshold for 2019 of $255,000
yielding an excess loss of $20,000. This amount will become part of Bettina's
net operating loss and subject to the NOL limitation and carryforward rules. ♦

When a taxpayer creates a net operating loss (NOL), no specific entry is required
by the preparer. Instead, supplemental schedules that track the NOL will be created
automatically by the software.

TIP

Self-Study Problem 4.8

Form **8582**	**Passive Activity Loss Limitations**	OMB No. 1545-1008
	▶ See separate instructions.	**2019**
Department of the Treasury Internal Revenue Service (99)	▶ Attach to Form 1040, Form 1040-SR, or Form 1041. ▶ Go to *www.irs.gov/Form8582* for instructions and the latest information.	Attachment Sequence No. **88**

Name(s) shown on return   Identifying number

Part I   **2019 Passive Activity Loss**

Caution: Complete Worksheets 1, 2, and 3 before completing Part I.

Rental Real Estate Activities With Active Participation (For the definition of active participation, see **Special Allowance for Rental Real Estate Activities** in the instructions.)

1a	Activities with net income (enter the amount from Worksheet 1, column (a)) .	**1a**	
b	Activities with net loss (enter the amount from Worksheet 1, column (b)) . .	**1b** ( )	
c	Prior years' unallowed losses (enter the amount from Worksheet 1, column (c))	**1c** ( )	
d	Combine lines 1a, 1b, and 1c		**1d**

Commercial Revitalization Deductions From Rental Real Estate Activities

2a	Commercial revitalization deductions from Worksheet 2, column (a) . . .	**2a** ( )	
b	Prior year unallowed commercial revitalization deductions from Worksheet 2, column (b)	**2b** ( )	
c	Add lines 2a and 2b		**2c** ( )

All Other Passive Activities

3a	Activities with net income (enter the amount from Worksheet 3, column (a)) .	**3a**	
b	Activities with net loss (enter the amount from Worksheet 3, column (b)) . .	**3b** ( )	
c	Prior years' unallowed losses (enter the amount from Worksheet 3, column (c))	**3c** ( )	
d	Combine lines 3a, 3b, and 3c		**3d**

4	Combine lines 1d, 2c, and 3d. If this line is zero or more, stop here and include this form with your return; all losses are allowed, including any prior year unallowed losses entered on line 1c, 2b, or 3c. Report the losses on the forms and schedules normally used		**4**

If line 4 is a loss and: • Line 1d is a loss, go to Part II.

• Line 2c is a loss (and line 1d is zero or more), skip Part II and go to Part III.

• Line 3d is a loss (and lines 1d and 2c are zero or more), skip Parts II and III and go to line 15.

Caution: If your filing status is married filing separately and you lived with your spouse at any time during the year, **do not** complete Part II or Part III. Instead, go to line 15.

Part II   **Special Allowance for Rental Real Estate Activities With Active Participation**

Note: Enter all numbers in Part II as positive amounts. See instructions for an example.

5	Enter the **smaller** of the loss on line 1d or the loss on line 4		**5**
6	Enter $150,000. If married filing separately, see instructions	**6**	
7	Enter modified adjusted gross income, but not less than zero. See instructions	**7**	
	Note: If line 7 is greater than or equal to line 6, skip lines 8 and 9, enter -0- on line 10. Otherwise, go to line 8.		
8	Subtract line 7 from line 6	**8**	
9	Multiply line 8 by 50% (0.50). **Do not** enter more than $25,000. If married filing separately, see instructions		**9**
10	Enter the **smaller** of line 5 or line 9		**10**

If line 2c is a loss, go to Part III. Otherwise, go to line 15.

Part III   **Special Allowance for Commercial Revitalization Deductions From Rental Real Estate Activities**

Note: Enter all numbers in Part III as positive amounts. See the example for Part II in the instructions.

11	Enter $25,000 reduced by the amount, if any, on line 10. If married filing separately, see instructions .	**11**	
12	Enter the loss from line 4	**12**	
13	Reduce line 12 by the amount on line 10	**13**	
14	Enter the **smallest** of line 2c (treated as a positive amount), line 11, or line 13	**14**	

Part IV   **Total Losses Allowed**

15	Add the income, if any, on lines 1a and 3a and enter the total	**15**	
16	**Total losses allowed from all passive activities for 2019.** Add lines 10, 14, and 15. See instructions to find out how to report the losses on your tax return	**16**	

For Paperwork Reduction Act Notice, see instructions.   Cat. No. 63704F   Form **8582** (2019)

Self-Study Problem 4.9   *See Appendix E for Solutions to Self-Study Problems*

Indicate whether the following statements are true or false by circling the appropriate letter.

T F 1. 2019 NOL deductions are first carried back 2 years and then forward 20 years.

T F 2. The itemized deduction for home mortgage interest can generate an NOL for an individual taxpayer.

T F 3. An individual taxpayer's NOL is equal to the net taxable loss from page 1 of Form 1040.

T F 4. Individual taxpayer's total business losses can be limited.

T F 5. There is no limitation for using a 2019 NOL against the taxable income of the following year.

ILYA AKINSHIN/Shutterstock.com; Zhukov Oleg/Shutterstock.com.

Would You Sign This Tax Return?

Sign Here	Under penalties of perjury, I declare that I have examined this return and accompanying schedules and statements, and to the best of my knowledge and belief, they are true, correct, and complete. Declaration of preparer (other than taxpayer) is based on all information of which preparer has any knowledge.				
	Your signature	Date	Your occupation		If the IRS sent you an Identity Protection PIN, enter it here (see inst.)
Joint return? See instructions. Keep a copy for your records.	Spouse's signature. If a joint return, **both** must sign.	Date	Spouse's occupation		If the IRS sent your spouse an Identity Protection PIN, enter it here (see inst.)
	Phone no.		Email address		
Paid Preparer Use Only	Preparer's name	Preparer's signature		Date	PTIN	Check if: ☐ 3rd Party Designee ☐ Self-employed
	Firm's name ▶			Phone no.	
	Firm's address ▶			Firm's EIN ▶	

Mark (age 44) and Mary (age 41) Mower are your tax clients. They have two children, Matthew (age 20) and Mindy (age 17), who live at home. Mindy is a senior in high school and Matthew commutes to a local college where he is studying soil management. Mark owns and operates a successful lawn maintenance and landscaping business. He has 6 employees and 3 pick-up trucks used for transportation to the job sites. The business has a credit card in its name for use by the employees and Mark, who fills the trucks with gas almost daily. Mark gave a business credit card to Mary, Matthew, and Mindy and told them to use it to buy gas for their automobiles used for shopping, going to school, and short trips. In the current year, his wife and children put $5,210 of gasoline in their automobiles using the business credit card. Mark is adamant that the $5,210 be deducted on his Schedule C. He feels the amount is small compared to the business gas purchases of approximately $28,000. Mark says the amounts charged are spread throughout the credit card statements and would be very difficult for the IRS to detect in an audit. Would you sign the Paid Preparer's declaration (see example above) on this return? Why or why not?

Learning Objective 4.10

Compute the qualified business income (QBI) deduction.

4-10 QUALIFIED BUSINESS INCOME (QBI) DEDUCTION

The Qualified Business Income (QBI) deduction was introduced in 2018 and applies to tax years through 2025. The QBI deduction is a deduction for individual taxpayers reporting business income from a passthrough entity such as a sole proprietorship, partnership, limited liability company, or S corporation. It is also referred to as the Section 199A deduction, the passthrough deduction, or the QBI deduction. The QBI deduction requires no additional outlay or investment of funds but is simply granted as a function of legislative grace. A discussion of the QBI deduction related specifically to partnerships and S corporations is covered in Chapters 10 and 11, respectively.

The QBI deduction is available to individual taxpayers as a "below the line" deduction (after adjusted gross income) and is also available to taxpayers who take the standard deduction. The deduction is generally 20 percent of a taxpayer's qualified business income (QBI) from a partnership (including LLC if so treated), S corporation, or sole proprietorship.

4-10a Definition of Qualified Business Income

Qualified business income for a tax year is the net amount of qualified items of income, gain, deduction, and loss relating to any qualified trade or business of the taxpayer in the United States (foreign income is not considered). QBI excludes the following:

- Short-term capital gain, short-term capital loss, long-term capital gain, or long-term capital loss
- Dividend income
- Interest income other than interest income that is properly allocable to a trade or business
- Commodity transaction income or foreign currency gain or loss
- Any item of income, gain, deduction, or loss relating to certain notional principal contracts
- Amounts received from an annuity that is not received in connection with the trade or business
- Any item of deduction or loss properly allocable to an amount described in any of the preceding items in this list (e.g., interest expense associated with investment income)

Reasonable employee compensation paid to the taxpayer by the qualified trade or business and guaranteed payments to a partner are not QBI and therefore the QBI deduction is not applicable to such income.

EXAMPLE   Princess is a single taxpayer and operates a small business as a sole proprietor. In 2019, her business generates $80,000 of gross business income, $50,000 of business expenses, $3,000 of interest income, and a $2,000 capital gain. Princess' QBI is $30,000 ($80,000 − $50,000). The interest and capital gains are excluded from QBI. ♦

With respect to the QBI deduction, the term "*qualified* trade or business" means any trade or business other than a specified service trade or business, or the trade or business of performing services as an employee. Unfortunately, "trade or business" is not defined in the tax law. The regulations interpret trade or business to be consistent with the same phrase in Internal Revenue Code Section 162 related to the deduction of trade or business expenses. This does not provide an exceptional level of guidance for many businesses but certainly hobby activities (Chapter 3) would not qualify. The tax law provides a safe-harbor under which income from rental real estate (even if treated as passive) can qualify as qualified business income. The requirements are:

1. 250 hours or more are spent by the taxpayer with respect to the rental activity
2. Contemporaneous records of the time are maintained
3. Separate books and records for the rental activity are maintained

Note that 250 hours per year amounts to an average of over 20 hours per month. Time spent related to the rental activity on advertising, negotiating with tenants, verifying applications, daily operation, repair and maintenance, purchase of materials, and supervision of employees all count toward the required 250 hours. Time spent purchasing or financing the acquisition of the property and time spent traveling to and from the property do not generally qualify.

4-10b QBI Deduction Taxable Income Limitation

The QBI deduction is subject to a number of limitations and exceptions. A limitation that applies to all taxpayers is that the QBI deduction cannot exceed 20 percent of the taxpayer's taxable income (excluding net long-term capital gains and qualified dividend income).

EXAMPLE Alice operates a small accounting business that generates $60,000 of qualified business income. She also operates a separate investment advising business that focuses on providing crypto-currency investment advice that lost $20,000. Both of Alice's businesses are sole proprietorships. Her pre-limitation QBI deduction is $8,000 [($60,000 − $20,000) × 20%]. Alice also earned $5,000 in net capital gains but had no other forms of income and elects the standard deduction. In 2019, Alice's taxable income subject to the 20 percent limit is $27,800 ($40,000 of business income less her standard deduction of $12,200; capital gains are excluded from this calculation). Her QBI deduction is limited to $5,560 ($27,800 × 20%). ◆

4-10c Wage Limitation

The two additional limitations on the QBI deduction are (1) the wage limitation and (2) the specified service business limitation. These limitations apply to taxpayers that have taxable income (*total* taxable income not just *business* income and including long-term capital gains or qualified dividends) above the threshold amounts, which in 2019 are $321,400 for married filing jointly $160,725 for married filing separately, and $160,700 for all other taxpayers. These threshold amounts are indexed for inflation each year. The limitations are computed before considering the QBI deduction.

For taxpayers with income below the thresholds, the QBI deduction is as described above. For taxpayers with taxable income above the threshold amounts, the two limitations apply and subject to a complex phase-out.

The wage limit is the greater of:

- 50 percent of the allocable share of W-2 wages with respect to the business (the "wage limit") or
- 25 percent of the allocable share of W-2 wages with respect to the business plus 2.5 percent of the unadjusted basis of all qualified business property (the "wage and capital limit")

W-2 wages are defined as wages paid to employees (not independent contractors) including deferrals into Section 401(k) plans and the like. The term allocable share pertains to the allocation of wages similar to that associated with the allocation of partnership income (see further discussion of allocation of wages in Chapter 10). Because the tax law was designed to encourage investment in employees and business capital investment, the wage and capital limit includes a percentage of the unadjusted basis (basis prior to any depreciation) of business property.

EXAMPLE Pat operates a sole proprietorship which generates $200,000 of qualified business income that includes the deduction for wages of $66,000 that Pat pays to employees. Pat's business has invested $20,000 in qualified business property. Pat has no other sources of income and files as a single taxpayer and elects the standard deduction. Pat's initial QBI deduction is $200,000 × 20% or $40,000 which is limited to 20 percent of Pat's taxable income [$187,800 ($200,000 − standard deduction of $12,200) × 20% = $37,560]. Furthermore, since Pat's income exceeds the $160,700 threshold, the wage limits apply. The wage limit is the greater of 50 percent of the wages ($66,000 × 50% = $33,000) or the wage and capital limit of 25 percent of the wages ($66,000 × 25% = $16,500) plus 2.5 percent of the unadjusted basis of qualified business property ($20,000 × 2.5% = $500) which totals $17,000. The greater of the two wage limit amounts applies and thus Pat's QBI deduction is limited to $33,000. Pat's final taxable income will be $154,800 ($200,000 − $33,000 − $12,200). Recall that the wage limit applies if the taxpayer's taxable income *before* the QBI deduction exceeds the threshold. ◆

Qualified business property for purposes of the wage and capital limit is defined as tangible property subject to depreciation (i.e., not inventory or land) for which the depreciable period has not ended before the close of the taxable year, held by the business at year end, and used at any point during the year in the production of QBI. If the "depreciation period" for a property ended in any prior tax year, that property is not included in the calculation of tangible property. The depreciable period is defined as starting when the property was placed in service and ending on the later of (1) 10 years or (2) the last day in the last year of the property's regular depreciation.

EXAMPLE Josh, a single taxpayer, operates a sole proprietorship. He qualifies for the QBI deduction and his taxable income subjects him to the wage and capital limitations. Josh has purchased and placed in service the following property (all of which is currently being used in 2019):

Year	5-year recovery period	39-year recovery period
2008	$20,000	$600,000
2009	0	0
2010	4,000	0
2011	0	0
2012	0	0
2013	0	0
2014	25,000	0
2015	0	0
2016	10,000	0
2017	2,000	0
2018	50,000	0
2019	13,000	0
Total	$124,000	$600,000

☐ Qualified business property still within recovery period

In determining qualified business property for purposes of the QBI wage limit in 2019, Josh's property must still be within the depreciable period which ends on the later of the last full year of the recovery period or 10 years. The 2008–2014 five-year property is fully depreciated BUT only the property placed in service before 2010 is no longer qualified; thus Josh has $104,000 of qualified five-year property. In spite of being placed in service more than 10 years ago, all of the building in the 39-year category is qualified as it is still being depreciated. Josh's total qualified property under the wage and capital limit for the QBI deduction is $704,000 ($104,000 + $600,000). ◆

Recall that the wage limitations apply only if the taxpayer's taxable income exceeds the threshold amount ($321,400 or $160,700). As is typical in the tax law, a taxpayer's opportunity to use the QBI deduction does not cease entirely if the threshold is exceeded. Instead, the QBI deduction is subject to a phase-out up to an excess of $100,000 for married filing jointly taxpayers and $50,000 for all others. First, the QBI deduction is computed as if no wage limitation applies. The next step is to compute the QBI deduction including the wage limitation. The excess of the QBI deduction with no limitation over the QBI deduction with limitation is known as the "excess amount." The excess amount is subject to a pro rata phase-out based on the taxpayer's income over the threshold amount.

EXAMPLE   Phil is a single taxpayer with a QBI eligible small business and his taxable income as measured for the QBI deduction is $177,500 and thus exceeds the $160,700 threshold. Phil's QBI is $150,000 and his business paid wages of $42,000 in 2019 and has qualified business property of $660,000.

Phil's QBI deduction with no limitation = $30,000 ($150,000 × 20%)
Wage limitation is $27,000 which is the greater of:

$21,000 ($42,000 wages × 50%) or

$27,000 [($42,000 × 25%) + ($660,000 × 2.5%)]

Phil's QBI deduction is limited to $27,000; however, Phil is not subject to the entire wage limitation as his income is not $50,000 or more over the threshold amount. Thus, the wage limitation is "phased-in."

Phil's taxable income for QBI deduction purposes	$177,500
Phil's threshold amount (single taxpayer)	160,700
Excess	$ 16,800
Excess divided by the phase-out range	$16,800/$50,000 = 33.6%

Thus Phil will lose 33.6 percent of his "excess amount" of $3,000 ($30,000 QBI deduction without limit less $27,000 QBI deduction with limit) or $1,008. Phil's QBI deduction is $28,992 ($30,000 − $1,008). ◆

To summarize thus far, the QBI deduction is 20 percent of qualified business income, which is the income of a business held in any form but corporate form. QBI excludes forms of "portfolio" income such as interest, dividends, and gains. For taxpayers below the income thresholds ($321,400 married filing jointly and $160,700 for single and head of household), there are no explicit limitations other than the taxable income limit. For those with taxable income above the thresholds, the QBI deduction is limited by the wage limitation and also by the specified service business limitation (which is covered below).

4-10d Specified Service Business Limitation

For taxpayers with income in excess of the threshold, certain types of businesses are not eligible for the QBI deduction:

1. a taxpayer whose business is being an employee, and
2. a specified service trade or business.

A specified service trade or business is defined as any trade or business involving the performance of services in the fields of health, law, accounting, actuarial science, performing arts, consulting, athletics, financial services, brokerage services, or any trade or business where the principal asset of such trade or business is the reputation or skill of one or more of its owners or employees. Also, specified service businesses include those involved in investing and investment management, trading, or dealing in securities, partnership interests, or commodities.

To be clear, recall that a taxpayer in a specified service business is not necessarily prohibited from the QBI deduction but rather is not eligible for the QBI deduction if the taxpayer's taxable income exceeds the aforementioned thresholds. The same phase-out for the wage limitation also applies to a specified service business (i.e., the with and without comparison of the QBI deduction and pro-rata reduction of the excess amount). However, the phase-out applies in a two-step process that is almost certainly better left to tax software.

EXAMPLE   Jenny and Jason file jointly in 2019. Jenny is a physician and works for her pass-through business that has QBI of $310,000 in 2019. The S corporation paid Jenny wages of $80,000 and her employee wages of $40,000 in 2019. Jenny and Jason's taxable income before any QBI deduction is $385,000. Jenny's S corporation has qualified business property of $300,000.

Jenny's QBI without any limits would be $62,000 ($310,000 × 20%). However, Jenny and Jason exceed the threshold income by $63,600 ($385,000 − $321,400). The excess income of $63,600 is 63.6 percent of the phase-out range of $100,000 for married filing jointly taxpayers and thus Jenny is eligible for only 36.4 percent of the benefits from the deduction. This eligible share is applied to each of the limits as follows:

QBI is $310,000 × 36.4% = $112,840

W-2 wages of $120,000 × 36.4% = $43,680

Qualified business property $300,000 × 36.4% = $109,200

Using this information, Jenny's tentative QBI deduction under the general rules is

20% of QBI: $22,568 ($112,840 × 20%)

Or the greater of

Wages limit: $21,840 ($43,680 × 50%) or

Wages and capital limit: $13,650 [($43,680 × 25%) + $109,200 × 2.5%]

Under the first step, the QBI deduction would be $21,840. But now, the phase-out associated with income over the threshold must be applied based on these amounts. Jenny's QBI would be $22,568 with no limitation and $21,840 with limitation or an excess QBI deduction of $728. As previously calculated, Jenny and Jason's income exceeds the threshold by $63,600 or 63.6 percent of the phase-out range of $100,000. Thus, Jenny is going to lose $463 of the QBI deduction (63.6% of the excess QBI deduction of $728).

As a result of the above steps, Jenny's QBI deduction for 2019 is $22,105 ($22,568 − $463). ◆

If a taxpayer has net QBI from one or more businesses that is less than zero, no QBI deduction is permitted and the QBI loss is carried over to the following year.

EXAMPLE   Alice operates a small business that generates $20,000 of qualified business income. She also operates a separate business that lost $60,000. Both of Alice's businesses are sole proprietorships. Alice's total net QBI is less than $0 ($40,000 net loss). As a result, Alice is not permitted a QBI deduction in the current year and will carry the QBI loss forward in next year. ◆

The regulations that cover the QBI deduction are complex and the calculation of the QBI deduction can become unwieldy when a taxpayer subject to the limitations has multiple businesses eligible for the QBI deduction and some of these businesses operate at a loss and others generate income. These computations are beyond the scope of this textbook.

4-10e   Reporting the QBI Deduction

In 2019, the IRS introduced Forms 8995 and 8995-A for reporting the QBI deduction. Form 8995 is for taxpayers whose taxable income before the QBI deduction does not exceed the phase-out thresholds ($321,400 for married filing jointly and $160,700 for single and head of household in 2019). Otherwise, taxpayers must use Form 8995-A. As the complexity of the QBI deduction increases, taxpayers may also need to use four schedules (A–D) that are part of Form 8995-A. These are beyond the scope of this textbook.

Self-Study Problem 4.10   *See Appendix E for Solutions to Self-Study Problems*

Determine whether the following taxpayers are eligible for the QBI deduction and the deduction amount, if any.

Taxpayer	Eligible for QBI deduction (Y/N)?	QBI deduction amount
a. Aretha is a married taxpayer filing jointly and a shareholder in Soul Corporation (not an S corporation). She owns 10 percent of the outstanding stock and the corporation generates $700,000 of taxable income from its business operations and distributes a $70,000 dividend to Aretha. Her total taxable income before the QBI deduction is $92,000.	_____	$_____
b. Barbara Jones is a single taxpayer and sole proprietor that operates a small chain of hair salons called The Bee Hive that specialize in obscure hair colors. Her business has no employees since all the stylists operate as independent contractors. The taxpayer identification number of the Bee Hive is 317-65-4321. Barbara's business generated business income of $120,000 in 2019. Her taxable income before any QBI deduction is $132,500. Use Form 8995 on Page 4–41 to determine her QBI deduction.	_____	$_____
c. Alice Delvecchio is married and files a joint return with her spouse, Chris Delvecchio. Alice operates a small family restaurant called D's Pizza as a sole proprietor (taxpayer identification number 565-22-4321). She pays wages of $36,000, has qualified property with a basis of $67,000, and the QBI from the restaurant is $100,000. Chris has wages of $250,000 and their joint taxable income before the QBI deduction is $364,000 and includes $12,000 of qualified dividends. Use Form 8995-A on Pages 4–42 and 4-43 to determine their QBI deduction amount.	_____	$_____

TIP

All of the different entry points for information for a tax return are located on the left-hand margin of ProConnect. At the top of that list are two tabs: All and In Use. The All tab shows all of the possible data entry points and aids in the prevention of overlooking a tax item while preparing the return. For reviewing a return, the In Use tab hides the areas not in use and can be very useful.

Self-Study Problem 4.10b

Form **8995**

Department of the Treasury
Internal Revenue Service

Qualified Business Income Deduction
Simplified Computation

▶ Attach to your tax return.

▶ Go to *www.irs.gov/Form8995* for instructions and the latest information.

OMB No. XXXX-XXXX

2019

Attachment
Sequence No. **55**

Name(s) shown on return

Your taxpayer identification number

DRAFT AS OF July 25, 2019 DO NOT FILE

1	(a) Trade, business, or aggregation name	(b) Taxpayer identification number	(c) Qualified business income or (loss)
i			
ii			
iii			
iv			
v			

2	Total qualified business income or (loss). Combine lines 1i through 1v, column (c)	2	
3	Qualified business net (loss) carryforward from the prior year	3 ( )	
4	Total qualified business income. Combine lines 2 and 3. If zero or less, enter -0-	4	
5	Qualified business income component. Multiply line 4 by 20% (0.20)		5
6	Qualified REIT dividends and publicly traded partnership (PTP) income or (loss) (see instructions)	6	
7	Qualified REIT dividends and qualified PTP (loss) carryforward from the prior year	7 ( )	
8	Total qualified REIT dividends and PTP income. Combine lines 6 and 7. If zero or less, enter -0-	8	
9	REIT and PTP component. Multiply line 8 by 20% (0.20)		9
10	Qualified business income deduction before the income limitation. Add lines 5 and 9		10
11	Taxable income before qualified business income deduction	11	
12	Net capital gain (see instructions)	12	
13	Subtract line 12 from line 11. If zero or less, enter -0-	13	
14	Income limitation. Multiply line 13 by 20% (0.20)		14
15	Qualified business income deduction. Enter the lesser of line 10 or line 14. Also enter this amount on the applicable line of your return ▶		15
16	Total qualified business (loss) carryforward. Combine lines 2 and 3. If greater than zero, enter -0-		16 ( )
17	Total qualified REIT dividends and PTP (loss) carryforward. Combine lines 6 and 7. If greater than zero, enter -0-		17 ( )

For Privacy Act and Paperwork Reduction Act Notice, see instructions.

Cat. No. 37806C

Form **8995** (2019)

Self-Study Problem 4.10c

Form **8995-A**	**Qualified Business Income Deduction**	OMB No. XXXX-XXXX
Department of the Treasury Internal Revenue Service	▶ Attach to your tax return. ▶ Go to *www.irs.gov/Form8995A* for instructions and the latest information.	**2019** Attachment Sequence No. **55A**

Name(s) shown on return	Your taxpayer identification number

Part I   Trade, Business, or Aggregation Information

Complete the schedules for Form 8995-A, (A, B, C, and/or D), as applicable, before starting Part I. Attach additional worksheets when needed. See instructions.

1	(a) Trade, business, or aggregation name	(b) Check if specified service	(c) Check if aggregation	(d) Taxpayer identification number	(e) Check if patron
A		☐	☐		☐
B		☐	☐		☐
C		☐	☐		☐

Part II   Determine Your Adjusted Qualified Business Income

			A	B	C
2	Qualified business income from the trade, business, or aggregation. See instructions	2			
3	Multiply line 2 by 20% (0.20). If your taxable income is $160,700 or less ($160,725 if married filing separately; $321,400 if married filing jointly), skip lines 4 through 12 and enter the amount from line 3 on line 13	3			
4	Allocable share of W-2 wages from the trade, business, or aggregation	4			
5	Multiply line 4 by 50% (0.50)	5			
6	Multiply line 4 by 25% (0.25)	6			
7	Allocable share of the unadjusted basis immediately after acquisition (UBIA) of all qualified property	7			
8	Multiply line 7 by 2.5% (0.025)	8			
9	Add lines 6 and 8	9			
10	Enter the greater of line 5 or line 9	10			
11	W-2 wage and qualified property limitation. Enter the smaller of line 3 or line 10	11			
12	Phased-in reduction. Enter amount from line 26, if any. See instructions	12			
13	Qualified business income deduction before patron reduction. Enter the greater of line 11 or line 12	13			
14	Patron reduction. Enter the amount from Schedule D (Form 8995-A), line 6, if any	14			
15	Qualified business income component. Subtract line 14 from line 13	15			
16	Total qualified business income component. Add all amounts reported on line 15 ▶	16			

For **Privacy Act and Paperwork Reduction Act Notice, see separate instructions.**   Cat. No. 71661B   Form **8995-A** (2019)

Form 8995-A (2019)   Page **2**

Part III   Phased-in Reduction

Complete Part III only if your taxable income is more than $160,700 but not $210,700 ($160,725 and $210,725 if married filing separately; $321,400 and $421,400 if married filing jointly) and line 10 is less than line 3. Otherwise, skip Part III.

			A	B	C
17	Enter amounts from line 3	**17**			
18	Enter the amounts from line 10	**18**			
19	Subtract line 18 from line 17	**19**			
20	Taxable income before qualified business income deduction	**20**			
21	Threshold. Enter $160,700 ($160,725 if married filing separately; $321,400 if married filing jointly)	**21**			
22	Subtract line 21 from line 20	**22**			
23	Phase-in range. Enter $50,000 ($100,000 if married filing jointly)	**23**			
24	Phase-in percentage. Divide line 22 by line 23	**24** %			
25	Total phase-in reduction. Multiply line 19 by line 24	**25**			
26	Qualified business income after phase-in reduction. Subtract line 25 from line 17. Enter this amount here and on line 12, for the corresponding trade or business	**26**			

Part IV   Determine Your Qualified Business Income Deduction

27	Total qualified business income component from all qualified trades, businesses, or aggregations. Enter the amount from line 16	**27**	
28	Qualified REIT dividends and publicly traded partnership (PTP) income or (loss). See instructions	**28**	
29	Qualified REIT dividends and PTP (loss) carryforward from prior years	**29** ( )	
30	Total qualified REIT dividends and PTP income. Combine lines 28 and 29. If less than zero, enter -0-	**30**	
31	REIT and PTP component. Multiply line 30 by 20% (0.20)	**31**	
32	Qualified business income deduction before the income limitation. Add lines 27 and 31 ▶	**32**	
33	Taxable income before qualified business income deduction	**33**	
34	Net capital gain. See instructions	**34**	
35	Subtract line 34 from line 33. If zero or less, enter -0-	**35**	
36	Income limitation. Multiply line 35 by 20% (0.20)	**36**	
37	Qualified business income deduction before the domestic production activities deduction (DPAD) under section 199A(g). Enter the smaller of line 32 or line 36 ▶	**37**	
38	DPAD under section 199A(g) allocated from an agricultural or horticultural cooperative. Don't enter more than line 33 minus line 37	**38**	
39	Total qualified business income deduction. Add lines 37 and 38 ▶	**39**	
40	Total qualified REIT dividends and PTP (loss) carryforward. Combine lines 28 and 29. If zero or greater, enter -0-	**40** ( )	

Form **8995-A** (2019)

KEY TERMS

capital asset, 4-2
capital gain or loss, 4-2
Section 1231 assets, 4-2
holding period, 4-3
"sale or exchange," 4-3
adjusted basis, 4-4
capital improvements, 4-5
net capital gains, 4-8

net capital losses, 4-10
capital loss carryovers, 4-11
personal residence exclusion, 4-19
vacation homes, 4-22
primarily personal use, 4-23
primarily rental use, 4-23
passive activity, 4-25
passive income and losses, 4-25

net operating loss (NOL), 4-29
business loss limitation, 4-31
qualified business income (QBI)
   deduction, 4-34
wage limitation, 4-36
wage and capital limit, 4-36
qualified business property, 4-37
service business limitation, 4-38

KEY POINTS

Learning Objectives	Key Points
LO 4.1: Define the term "capital asset."	• A capital asset is any property, whether or not used in a trade or business, except: (1) inventory, (2) depreciable property or real property used in a trade or business, (3) patents, inventions, models or designs, secret formulas or processes, copyrights, literary, musical, or artistic compositions, letters or memorandums, or similar property if the property is created by the taxpayer, (4) accounts or notes receivable, and (5) certain U.S. government publications.
LO 4.2: Apply the holding period for long-term and short-term capital gains and losses.	• Assets must be held for more than 1 year for the gain or loss to be considered long-term. • A capital asset held 1 year or less results in a short-term capital gain or loss. • A net short-term capital gain is treated as ordinary income. • In calculating the holding period, the taxpayer excludes the date of acquisition and includes the date of disposition.
LO 4.3: Calculate the gain or loss on the disposition of an asset.	• The taxpayer's gain or loss is calculated using the following formula: amount realized − adjusted basis = gain or loss realized. • The amount realized from a sale or other disposition of property is equal to the sum of the money received, plus the fair market value of other property received, plus any liabilities relieved, less the costs paid to transfer the property. • The adjusted basis of property = the original basis + capital improvements − accumulated depreciation. • In most cases, the original basis is the cost of the property at the date of acquisition, plus any costs incidental to the purchase, such as title insurance, escrow fees, and inspection fees. • Capital improvements are major expenditures for permanent improvements to or restoration of the taxpayer's property.
LO 4.4: Compute the tax on capital gains.	• Short-term capital gains are taxed as ordinary income, while there are various different preferential long-term capital gains tax rates. • Net long-term capital gains may be subject to rates ranging from 0 percent to 28 percent (an additional 3.8 percent Medicare tax on net investment income applies to high-income individuals). • Special rates apply to long-term gains on collectibles (e.g., art, stamps, gems, coins, etc.) and depreciation recapture on the disposition of certain Section 1250 assets.

LO 4.5: Describe the treatment of capital losses.	• Individual taxpayers may deduct net capital losses against ordinary income in amounts up to $3,000 per year with any unused capital losses carried forward indefinitely. • When a taxpayer ends up with net capital losses, the losses offset capital gains as follows: (1) net short-term capital losses first reduce 28 percent gains, then 25 percent gains, then regular long-term capital gains, and (2) net long-term capital losses first reduce 28 percent gains, then 25 percent gains, then any short-term capital gains. Personal capital losses are not deductible for tax purposes.
LO 4.6: Apply the exclusion of gain from personal residence sales.	• Taxpayers who have owned their personal residence and lived in it for at least 2 of the 5 years before the sale can exclude from income up to $250,000 of gain ($500,000 for joint return filers).
LO 4.7: Apply the tax rules for rental property and vacation homes.	• Rental income and related expenses are reported on Schedule E. • Rental expenses include real estate taxes, mortgage interest, insurance, commissions, repairs, and depreciation. • If a residence is rented for fewer than 15 days during the year, the rental income is disregarded and the property is treated as a personal residence for tax purposes. • If the residence is rented for 15 days or more and is used for personal purposes for not more than 14 days or 10 percent of the days rented, whichever is greater, the residence is treated as a rental property. • If the residence is rented for 15 days or more and is used for personal purposes for more than 14 days or 10 percent of the days rented, whichever is greater, allocable rental expenses are allowed only to the extent of rental income.
LO 4.8: Explain the treatment of passive income and losses.	• The tax law defines three categories of income: (1) active income, (2) portfolio income, and (3) passive income and losses. • Normally, passive losses cannot be used to offset either active or portfolio income. Passive losses not used to offset passive income are carried forward indefinitely. • Generally, losses remaining when the taxpayer disposes of his or her entire interest in a passive activity may be used in full. • Under the passive loss rules, real estate rental activities are specifically defined as passive, even if the taxpayer actively manages the property. • Individual taxpayers may deduct up to $25,000 of rental property losses against other income, if they are actively involved in the management of the property and their income does not exceed certain limits. • Taxpayers heavily involved in real estate rental activities may qualify as running an active trade or business rather than a passive activity and fully deduct all rental losses.
LO 4.9: Describe the basic tax treatment of deductions for net operating losses.	• Net operating losses (NOL) allow taxpayers to "smooth out" their income. • Computation of an individual taxpayer NOL requires classification of income and deductions as business and nonbusiness. • An NOL generated after 2017 may only be carried forward and its use is limited to 80 percent of the future year's taxable income. • An NOL generated in 2017 or before may be carried back 2 years and forward 20 years. • Total business losses are limited after 2017.
LO 4.10: Compute the qualified business income (QBI) deduction.	• Flow-through entities are eligible for a deduction of 20 percent of QBI subject to limitations. • QBI is business income only and generally does not include interest, dividends, or capital gains. • Tax law provides a safe-harbor under which income from rental real estate can qualify as QBI if it meets the necessary requirements. • The QBI deduction may not exceed 20 percent of taxable income. • If taxable income exceeds $321,400 (MFJ) or $160,700 (single and head of household), the QBI deduction is limited by the wage limitation or the wage and capital limitation, whichever is greater. • QBI from service-related business may also be subject to limitation if income thresholds are surpassed.

QUESTIONS and PROBLEMS

GROUP 1:
MULTIPLE CHOICE QUESTIONS

LO 4.1

1. All of the following assets are capital assets, *except*:
   a. A personal automobile
   b. IBM stock
   c. A child's bicycle
   d. Personal furniture
   e. Used car inventory held by a car dealer

LO 4.1

2. Which of the following is a capital asset?
   a. Account receivable
   b. Copyright created by the taxpayer
   c. Copyright (held by the writer)
   d. Business inventory
   e. A taxpayer's residence

LO 4.2

3. Yasmeen purchases stock on January 30, 2018. If she wishes to achieve a long-term holding period, what is the first date that she can sell the stock as a long-term gain?
   a. January 20, 2019
   b. January 31, 2019
   c. February 1, 2019
   d. July 31, 2018
   e. July 30, 2018

LO 4.3

4. Vijay sells land and receives $5,000 cash, a motorcycle worth $1,600, and two tickets to the Super Bowl with a total face value (cost) of $800 but worth $1,200. In addition, the buyer assumes the mortgage on the land of $12,000. What is Vijay's amount received in this transaction?
   a. $5,000
   b. $7,800
   c. $8,200
   d. $19,800
   e. $20,200

LO 4.3

5. Bob sells a stock investment for $35,000 cash, and the purchaser assumes Bob's $32,500 debt on the investment. The basis of Bob's stock investment is $55,000. What is the gain or loss realized on the sale?
   a. $10,000 loss
   b. $10,000 gain
   c. $12,500 gain
   d. $22,500 loss
   e. $22,500 gain

LO 4.4

6. In 2019, what is the top tax rate for individual long-term capital gains and the top tax rate for long-term capital gains of collectible items assuming that the Medicare tax does not apply.
   a. 10; 20
   b. 20; 28
   c. 15; 25
   d. 25; 28

LO 4.4

7. In November 2019, Ben and Betty (married, filing jointly) have a long-term capital gain of $54,000 on the sale of stock. They have no other capital gains and losses for the year. Their ordinary income for the year after the standard deduction is $72,500, making their total taxable income for the year $126,500 ($72,500 + $54,000). In 2019, married taxpayers pay 0 percent on long-term gains up to $78,750. What will be their 2019 total tax liability assuming a tax of $8,315 on the $72,500 of ordinary income?
   a. $8,322
   b. $15,717
   c. $15,478
   d. $19,712

LO 4.4

8. Harold, a single taxpayer, has $30,000 of ordinary income after the standard deduction, and $10,000 in long-term capital gains, for total taxable income of $40,000. For 2019, single taxpayers pay 0 percent on long-term gains up to $39,375. Assuming a tax of $3,409 on the $30,000 of ordinary income, what is Harold's tax?
   a. $3,413
   b. $3,503
   c. $3,623
   d. $4,094
   e. $4,815

LO 4.4
LO 4.5

9. In 2019, Tim, a single taxpayer, has ordinary income of $29,000. In addition, he has $2,000 in short-term capital gains, long-term capital losses of $10,000, and long-term capital gains of $4,000. What is Tim's AGI for 2019?
   a. $26,000
   b. $27,000
   c. $29,000
   d. $32,000

LO 4.6

10. Oscar, a single taxpayer, sells his residence of the last 10 years in January of 2019 for $190,000. Oscar's basis in the residence is $45,000, and his selling expenses are $11,000. If Oscar does not buy a new residence, what is the taxable gain on the sale of his residence?
   a. $145,000
   b. $134,000
   c. $45,000
   d. $9,000
   e. $0

LO 4.6

11. Jim, a single taxpayer, bought his home 20 years ago for $25,000. He has lived in the home continuously since he purchased it. In 2019, he sells his home for $300,000. What is Jim's taxable gain on the sale?
   a. $0
   b. $25,000
   c. $125,000
   d. $275,000

LO 4.6

12. Susan, a single taxpayer, bought her home 25 years ago for $30,000. She has lived in the home continuously since she purchased it. In 2019, she sells her home for $200,000. What is Susan's taxable gain on the sale?
   a. $0
   b. $20,000
   c. $250,000
   d. $170,000

LO 4.6

13. Kevin purchased a house 20 years ago for $100,000 and he has always lived in the house. Three years ago Kevin married Karen, and she has lived in the house since their marriage. If they sell Kevin's house in December 2019 for $425,000, what is their taxable gain on a joint tax return?
    a. $0
    b. $75,000
    c. $125,000
    d. $250,000

LO 4.6

14. Gene, a single taxpayer, purchased a house 18 months ago for $350,000. If Gene sells his house due to unforeseen circumstances for $550,000 after living in it for a full 18 months, what is his taxable gain?
    a. $0
    b. $12,500
    c. $50,000
    d. $200,000

LO 4.7

15. Which of the following is true about the rental of real estate?
    a. Depreciation and maintenance expenses for an apartment complex are deductible.
    b. A vacation home is a home that is rented for 15 days or more and is used by the taxpayer for personal use for more than the greater of 14 days or 10 percent of the days it is rented for fair value during the year.
    c. If a home is rented for less than 15 days a year, the rent is not taxable.
    d. Repairs on rental property are deductible by the taxpayer.
    e. All of the above.

LO 4.7

16. John owns a second home in Palm Springs, CA. During the year, he rented the house for $5,000 for 56 days and used the house for 14 days during the summer. The house remained vacant during the remainder of the year. The expenses for the home included $5,000 in mortgage interest, $850 in property taxes, $900 for utilities and maintenance, and $3,500 of depreciation. What is John's deductible rental loss, before considering the passive loss limitations?
    a. $200
    b. $875
    c. $2,500
    d. $3,200
    e. $0

LO 4.8

17. Helen, a single taxpayer, has modified adjusted gross income (before passive losses) of $126,000. During the tax year, Helen's rental house generated a loss of $15,000. Assuming Helen is actively involved in the management of the property, what is the amount of Helen's passive loss deduction from the rental house?
    a. $0
    b. $3,000
    c. $10,000
    d. $12,000
    e. $15,000

LO 4.8

18. Which of the following is *not* classified as portfolio income for tax purposes?
    a. Interest income on savings accounts
    b. Dividends paid from a credit union
    c. Net rental income from real estate partnership
    d. Dividend income from stock
    e. All of the above are classified as portfolio income

LO 4.8   19. Which of the following types of income is passive income?
- a. Net rental income from real estate limited partnership investments
- b. Dividends from domestic corporations
- c. Wages
- d. Interest income from certificates of deposit
- e. None of the above

LO 4.8   20. Which of the following is classified as active income?
- a. Self-employment income from a small business
- b. Interest income
- c. Limited partnership income
- d. Dividend income from a mutual fund
- e. a. and d.

LO 4.8   21. Nancy has active modified adjusted gross income before passive losses of $75,000. She has a loss of $5,000 on a rental property she actively manages. How much of the loss is she allowed to take against the $75,000 of other income?
- a. None
- b. $2,500
- c. $5,000
- d. $10,000

LO 4.8   22. Ned has active modified adjusted gross income before passive losses of $250,000. He has a loss of $15,000 on rental property he actively manages. How much of the loss is he allowed to take against the $250,000 of other income?
- a. $15,000
- b. $10,000
- c. $5,000
- d. None

LO 4.8   23. Norm is a real estate professional with a real estate trade or business as defined in the tax law. He has $80,000 of business income and $40,000 of losses from actively managed real estate rentals. How much of the $40,000 in losses is he allowed to claim on his tax return?
- a. $40,000
- b. $25,000
- c. $20,000
- d. None

LO 4.9   24. Bonita earns $31,000 from her job, and she has $1,000 of interest income. She has itemized deductions of $35,000. There are no casualty or theft losses in the itemized deductions. What is Bonita's net operating loss for the current year?
- a. $0
- b. $1,000
- c. $3,000
- d. $4,000
- e. Some other amount

LO 4.9   25. Jim has a net operating loss in 2019. If he does not make any special elections, what is the first year to which Jim carries the net operating loss?
- a. 2015
- b. 2016
- c. 2017
- d. 2018
- e. 2020

LO 4.10 26. The qualified business income deduction is unavailable to which of the following businesses:
   a. A sole proprietor dental practice that generates about $70,000 in income each year
   b. An incorporated small tools manufacturer
   c. A partnership operated by a husband and wife that sells wood carvings over the Internet
   d. A S corporation that owns and operates a restaurant. The S corporation has six different owners.
   e. The QBI deduction is available to all of the above.

LO 4.10 27. Qualified business income does not include which of the following:
   a. Income from sales of goods
   b. Deductions related to cost of goods sold
   c. Deductions for business expenses such as rent
   d. Interest income from an investment in bonds

LO 4.10 28. In 2019, Tracy generates a $10,000 loss from an otherwise qualified business activity. Fortunately, she also works as an employee and has taxable income of $40,000. Tracy's 2019 QBI deduction is
   a. $0
   b. $2,000
   c. $8,000
   d. $6,000

GROUP 2:
PROBLEMS

LO 4.1
LO 4.2
LO 4.3
1. Martin sells a stock investment for $26,000 on August 2, 2019. Martin's adjusted basis in the stock is $15,000.
   a. If Martin acquired the stock on November 15, 2018, calculate the amount and the nature of the gain or loss.

   $_____

   b. If Martin had acquired the stock on September 10, 2017, calculate the amount and nature of the gain or loss.

   $_____

LO 4.1
LO 4.2
LO 4.3
LO 4.5
2. During 2019, Tom sold Sears stock for $10,000. The stock was purchased 4 years ago for $13,000. Tom also sold Ford Motor Company bonds for $35,000. The bonds were purchased 2 months ago for $30,000. Home Depot stock, purchased 2 years ago for $1,000, was sold by Tom for $2,500. Calculate Tom's net gain or loss, and indicate the nature of the gain or loss.

   $_____

LO 4.1
LO 4.2
LO 4.3
LO 4.5
3. Charu Khanna received a Form 1099-B showing the following stock transactions and basis during 2019:

Stock	Date Purchased	Date Sold	Sales Price ($)	Cost Basis ($)
4,000 shares Green Co.	06/04/08	08/05/19	12,000	3,000
500 shares Gold Co.	02/12/19	09/05/19	54,000	62,000
5,000 shares Blue Co.	02/04/09	10/08/19	18,000	22,000
100 shares Orange Co.	11/15/18	07/12/19	19,000	18,000

   None of the stock is qualified small business stock. The stock basis was reported to the IRS. Calculate Charu's net capital gain or loss using Schedule D and Form 8949 on Pages 4-51 through 4-54.

SCHEDULE D
(Form 1040 or 1040-SR)

Department of the Treasury
Internal Revenue Service (99)

Capital Gains and Losses

▶ Attach to Form 1040, 1040-SR, or 1040-NR.
▶ Go to *www.irs.gov/ScheduleD* for instructions and the latest information.
▶ Use Form 8949 to list your transactions for lines 1b, 2, 3, 8b, 9, and 10.

OMB No. 1545-0074

2019

Attachment
Sequence No. **12**

Name(s) shown on return

Your social security number

Did you dispose of any investment(s) in a qualified opportunity fund during the tax year? ☐ **Yes** ☐ **No**
If "Yes," attach Form 8949 and see its instructions for additional requirements for reporting your gain or loss.

Part I   **Short-Term Capital Gains and Losses—Generally Assets Held One Year or Less** (see instructions)

See instructions for how to figure the amounts to enter on the lines below. This form may be easier to complete if you round off cents to whole dollars.	(d) Proceeds (sales price)	(e) Cost (or other basis)	(g) Adjustments to gain or loss from Form(s) 8949, Part I, line 2, column (g)	(h) Gain or (loss) Subtract column (e) from column (d) and combine the result with column (g)
1a Totals for all short-term transactions reported on Form 1099-B for which basis was reported to the IRS and for which you have no adjustments (see instructions). However, if you choose to report all these transactions on Form 8949, leave this line blank and go to line 1b .				
1b Totals for all transactions reported on Form(s) 8949 with **Box A** checked				
2 Totals for all transactions reported on Form(s) 8949 with **Box B** checked				
3 Totals for all transactions reported on Form(s) 8949 with **Box C** checked				

4 Short-term gain from Form 6252 and short-term gain or (loss) from Forms 4684, 6781, and 8824 . .	**4**	
5 Net short-term gain or (loss) from partnerships, S corporations, estates, and trusts from Schedule(s) K-1	**5**	
6 Short-term capital loss carryover. Enter the amount, if any, from line 8 of your **Capital Loss Carryover Worksheet** in the instructions	**6** ( )	
7 **Net short-term capital gain or (loss).** Combine lines 1a through 6 in column (h). If you have any long-term capital gains or losses, go to Part II below. Otherwise, go to Part III on the back	**7**	

Part II   **Long-Term Capital Gains and Losses—Generally Assets Held More Than One Year** (see instructions)

See instructions for how to figure the amounts to enter on the lines below. This form may be easier to complete if you round off cents to whole dollars.	(d) Proceeds (sales price)	(e) Cost (or other basis)	(g) Adjustments to gain or loss from Form(s) 8949, Part II, line 2, column (g)	(h) Gain or (loss) Subtract column (e) from column (d) and combine the result with column (g)
8a Totals for all long-term transactions reported on Form 1099-B for which basis was reported to the IRS and for which you have no adjustments (see instructions). However, if you choose to report all these transactions on Form 8949, leave this line blank and go to line 8b .				
8b Totals for all transactions reported on Form(s) 8949 with **Box D** checked				
9 Totals for all transactions reported on Form(s) 8949 with **Box E** checked				
10 Totals for all transactions reported on Form(s) 8949 with **Box F** checked.				

11 Gain from Form 4797, Part I; long-term gain from Forms 2439 and 6252; and long-term gain or (loss) from Forms 4684, 6781, and 8824	**11**	
12 Net long-term gain or (loss) from partnerships, S corporations, estates, and trusts from Schedule(s) K-1	**12**	
13 Capital gain distributions. See the instructions	**13**	
14 Long-term capital loss carryover. Enter the amount, if any, from line 13 of your **Capital Loss Carryover Worksheet** in the instructions	**14** ( )	
15 **Net long-term capital gain or (loss).** Combine lines 8a through 14 in column (h). Then go to Part III on the back	**15**	

For Paperwork Reduction Act Notice, see your tax return instructions.   Cat. No. 11338H   Schedule D (Form 1040 or 1040-SR) 2019

Schedule D (Form 1040 or 1040-SR) 2019   Page **2**

Part III   **Summary**

16	Combine lines 7 and 15 and enter the result	**16**

- If line 16 is a **gain,** enter the amount from line 16 on Form 1040 or 1040-SR, line 6; or Form 1040-NR, line 14. Then go to line 17 below.
- If line 16 is a **loss,** skip lines 17 through 20 below. Then go to line 21. Also be sure to complete line 22.
- If line 16 is **zero,** skip lines 17 through 21 below and enter -0- on Form 1040 or 1040-SR, line 6; or Form 1040-NR, line 14. Then go to line 22.

17   Are lines 15 and 16 **both** gains?
☐ **Yes.** Go to line 18.
☐ **No.** Skip lines 18 through 21, and go to line 22.

18   If you are required to complete the **28% Rate Gain Worksheet** (see instructions), enter the amount, if any, from line 7 of that worksheet . . . . ▶   **18**

19   If you are required to complete the **Unrecaptured Section 1250 Gain Worksheet** (see instructions), enter the amount, if any, from line 18 of that worksheet . . . . ▶   **19**

20   Are lines 18 and 19 **both** zero or blank?
☐ **Yes.** Complete the **Qualified Dividends and Capital Gain Tax Worksheet** in the instructions for Forms 1040 and 1040-SR, line 12a (or in the instructions for Form 1040-NR, line 42). **Don't** complete lines 21 and 22 below.

☐ **No.** Complete the **Schedule D Tax Worksheet** in the instructions. **Don't** complete lines 21 and 22 below.

21   If line 16 is a loss, enter here and on Form 1040 or 1040-SR, line 6; or Form 1040-NR, line 14, the **smaller** of:

- The loss on line 16; or
- ($3,000), or if married filing separately, ($1,500)   } . . . .   **21** ( )

Note: When figuring which amount is smaller, treat both amounts as positive numbers.

22   Do you have qualified dividends on Form 1040 or 1040-SR, line 3a; or Form 1040-NR, line 10b?

☐ **Yes.** Complete the **Qualified Dividends and Capital Gain Tax Worksheet** in the instructions for Forms 1040 and 1040-SR, line 12a (or in the instructions for Form 1040-NR, line 42).

☐ **No.** Complete the rest of Form 1040, 1040-SR, or 1040-NR.

Schedule D (Form 1040 or 1040-SR) 2019

Form **8949**

Department of the Treasury
Internal Revenue Service

Sales and Other Dispositions of Capital Assets

▶ Go to *www.irs.gov/Form8949* for instructions and the latest information.
▶ File with your Schedule D to list your transactions for lines 1b, 2, 3, 8b, 9, and 10 of Schedule D.

OMB No. 1545-0074

2019

Attachment
Sequence No. **12A**

Name(s) shown on return	Social security number or taxpayer identification number

Before you check Box A, B, or C below, see whether you received any Form(s) 1099-B or substitute statement(s) from your broker. A substitute statement will have the same information as Form 1099-B. Either will show whether your basis (usually your cost) was reported to the IRS by your broker and may even tell you which box to check.

Part I **Short-Term.** Transactions involving capital assets you held 1 year or less are generally short-term (see instructions). For long-term transactions, see page 2.

Note: You may aggregate all short-term transactions reported on Form(s) 1099-B showing basis was reported to the IRS and for which no adjustments or codes are required. Enter the totals directly on Schedule D, line 1a; you aren't required to report these transactions on Form 8949 (see instructions).

You *must* check Box A, B, *or* C below. Check only one box. If more than one box applies for your short-term transactions, complete a separate Form 8949, page 1, for each applicable box. If you have more short-term transactions than will fit on this page for one or more of the boxes, complete as many forms with the same box checked as you need.

☐ **(A)** Short-term transactions reported on Form(s) 1099-B showing basis was reported to the IRS (see **Note** above)
☐ **(B)** Short-term transactions reported on Form(s) 1099-B showing basis **wasn't** reported to the IRS
☐ **(C)** Short-term transactions not reported to you on Form 1099-B

1 (a) Description of property (Example: 100 sh. XYZ Co.)	(b) Date acquired (Mo., day, yr.)	(c) Date sold or disposed of (Mo., day, yr.)	(d) Proceeds (sales price) (see instructions)	(e) Cost or other basis. See the **Note** below and see *Column (e)* in the separate instructions	Adjustment, if any, to gain or loss. If you enter an amount in column (g), enter a code in column (f). See the separate instructions.		(h) Gain or (loss). Subtract column (e) from column (d) and combine the result with column (g)
					(f) Code(s) from instructions	(g) Amount of adjustment	
2 Totals. Add the amounts in columns (d), (e), (g), and (h) (subtract negative amounts). Enter each total here and include on your Schedule D, **line 1b** (if **Box A** above is checked), **line 2** (if **Box B** above is checked), or **line 3** (if **Box C** above is checked) ▶							

Note: If you checked Box A above but the basis reported to the IRS was incorrect, enter in column (e) the basis as reported to the IRS, and enter an adjustment in column (g) to correct the basis. See *Column (g)* in the separate instructions for how to figure the amount of the adjustment.

For Paperwork Reduction Act Notice, see your tax return instructions.   Cat. No. 37768Z   Form **8949** (2019)

Form 8949 (2019)   Attachment Sequence No. **12A**   Page **2**

Name(s) shown on return. Name and SSN or taxpayer identification no. not required if shown on other side	Social security number or taxpayer identification number

Before you check Box D, E, or F below, see whether you received any Form(s) 1099-B or substitute statement(s) from your broker. A substitute statement will have the same information as Form 1099-B. Either will show whether your basis (usually your cost) was reported to the IRS by your broker and may even tell you which box to check.

Part II   **Long-Term.** Transactions involving capital assets you held more than 1 year are generally long-term (see instructions). For short-term transactions, see page 1.

Note: You may aggregate all long-term transactions reported on Form(s) 1099-B showing basis was reported to the IRS and for which no adjustments or codes are required. Enter the totals directly on Schedule D, line 8a; you aren't required to report these transactions on Form 8949 (see instructions).

You *must* check Box D, E, *or* F below. **Check only one box.** If more than one box applies for your long-term transactions, complete a separate Form 8949, page 2, for each applicable box. If you have more long-term transactions than will fit on this page for one or more of the boxes, complete as many forms with the same box checked as you need.

☐ **(D)** Long-term transactions reported on Form(s) 1099-B showing basis was reported to the IRS (see **Note** above)

☐ **(E)** Long-term transactions reported on Form(s) 1099-B showing basis **wasn't** reported to the IRS

☐ **(F)** Long-term transactions not reported to you on Form 1099-B

1 (a) Description of property (Example: 100 sh. XYZ Co.)	(b) Date acquired (Mo., day, yr.)	(c) Date sold or disposed of (Mo., day, yr.)	(d) Proceeds (sales price) (see instructions)	(e) Cost or other basis. See the **Note** below and see *Column (e)* in the separate instructions	(f) Code(s) from instructions	(g) Amount of adjustment	(h) Gain or (loss). Subtract column (e) from column (d) and combine the result with column (g)

2 Totals. Add the amounts in columns (d), (e), (g), and (h) (subtract negative amounts). Enter each total here and include on your Schedule D, **line 8b** (if **Box D** above is checked), **line 9** (if **Box E** above is checked), or **line 10** (if **Box F** above is checked) ▶

Note: If you checked Box D above but the basis reported to the IRS was incorrect, enter in column (e) the basis as reported to the IRS, and enter an adjustment in column (g) to correct the basis. See *Column (g)* in the separate instructions for how to figure the amount of the adjustment.

Form **8949** (2019)

LO 4.3

4. Jocasta owns an apartment complex that she purchased 6 years ago for $750,000. Jocasta has made $50,000 of capital improvements on the complex, and her depreciation claimed on the building to date is $128,700. Calculate Jocasta's adjusted basis in the building.

$_____

LO 4.3

5. Chrissy receives 200 shares of Chevron stock as a gift from her father. The stock cost her father $9,000 10 years ago and is worth $10,500 at the date of the gift.
   a. If Chrissy sells the stock for $12,500, calculate the amount of the gain or loss on the sale.

   $_____

   b. If Chrissy sells the stock for $4,600, calculate the amount of the gain or loss on the sale.

   $_____

LO 4.4
LO 4.5

6. In 2019, Michael has net short-term capital losses of $1,500, a net long-term capital loss of $27,000, and other ordinary taxable income of $45,000.
   a. Calculate the amount of Michael's deduction for capital losses for 2019.

   $_____

   b. Calculate the amount and nature of his capital loss carryforward.

   $_____

   c. For how long may Michael carry forward the unused loss?

   _____

LO 4.6

7. Larry Gaines, a single taxpayer, age 42, sells his personal residence on November 12, 2019, for $151,200. He lived in the house for 7 years. The expenses of the sale are $9,072, and he has made capital improvements of $10,150. Larry's cost basis in his residence is $86,750. On November 30, 2019, Larry purchases and occupies a new residence at a cost of $150,000. Calculate Larry's realized gain, recognized gain, and the adjusted basis of his new residence.
   a. Realized gain $_____
   b. Recognized gain $_____
   c. Adjusted basis of new residence $_____

LO 4.6

8. On July 1, 2019, Ted, age 73 and single, sells his personal residence of the last 30 years for $368,000. Ted's basis in his residence is $48,776. The expenses associated with the sale of his home total $22,080. On December 15, 2019, Ted purchases and occupies a new residence at a cost of $175,000. Calculate Ted's realized gain, recognized gain, and the adjusted basis of his new residence.
   a. Realized gain $_____
   b. Recognized gain $_____
   c. Adjusted basis of the new residence $_____

LO 4.7

9. Dick owns a house that he rents to college students. Dick receives $800 per month rent and incurs the following expenses during the year:

Real estate taxes	$1,250
Mortgage interest	1,500
Insurance	425
Repairs	562
Association dues	1,500

Dick purchased the house in 1979 for $48,000. The house is fully depreciated. Calculate Dick's net rental income for the year, assuming the house was rented for a full 12 months.

Rental income $_____
Expenses:

_____   _____
_____   _____
_____   _____
_____   _____
_____   _____

Net rental income $_____

LO 4.7

10. Sherry rents her vacation home for 6 months and lives in it for 6 months during the year. Her gross rental income during the year is $6,000. Total real estate taxes for the home are $950, and interest on the home mortgage is $3,000. Annual utilities and maintenance expenses total $1,800, and depreciation expense is $4,500. Calculate Sherry's net income or loss from the vacation home for this tax year.

$_____

LO 4.8

11. Walter, a single taxpayer, purchased a limited partnership interest in a tax shelter in 1993. He also acquired a rental house in 2019, which he actively manages. During 2019, Walter's share of the partnership's losses was $30,000, and his rental house generated $20,000 in losses. Walter's modified adjusted gross income before passive losses is $130,000.

a. Calculate the amount of Walter's allowable loss for rental house activities for 2019.

$_____

b. Calculate the amount of Walter's allowable loss for the partnership activities for 2019.

$_____

c. What may be done with the unused losses, if anything?

_____
_____
_____
_____

LO 4.8

12. Clifford Johnson has a limited partnership investment and a rental condominium. Clifford actively manages the rental condominium. During 2019, his share of the loss from the limited partnership was $11,000, and his loss from the rental condo was $17,000. Assuming Clifford's modified adjusted gross income is $124,000 for 2019, and he has no prior year unallowed losses from either activity, complete Form 8582 on Page 4-58.

LO 4.9

13. Tyler, a single taxpayer, generates a net operating loss of $12,000 in 2017 and elects to forego any carryback. He also generates a net operating loss of $6,000 in 2018. Finally, in 2019, Tyler's business turns a corner and he generates taxable income of $17,000.

a. How much of Tyler's 2017 NOL is carried forward to 2020?
b. How much of Tyler's 2018 NOL is carried forward to 2020?

LO 4.9

14. Julie, a single taxpayer, has completed her 2019 Schedule C and her net loss is $40,000. Her only other income is wages of $30,000. Julie takes the standard deduction of $12,200 in 2019.

a. Calculate Julie's taxable income or loss.

$_____

b. Calculate the business and nonbusiness portions of her taxable income or loss.

Business $_____
Nonbusiness $_____

c. Determine Julie's 2019 NOL.

$_____

LO 4.10 15. Sanjay is a single taxpayer that operates a curry cart on the streets of Baltimore. The business is operated as a sole proprietorship with no employees (Sanjay does everything). Sanjay's Schedule C reports income of $87,000. His taxable income is $80,000 and includes no capital gains. Compute Sanjay's QBI deduction.

$_____

LO 4.10 16. Rob Wriggle operates a small plumbing supplies business as a sole proprietor. In 2019, the plumbing business has gross business income of $421,000 and business expenses of $267,000, including wages paid of $58,000. The business sold some land that had been held for investment generating a long-term capital gain of $15,000. The business has $300,000 of qualified business property in 2019. Rob's wife, Marie, has wage income of $250,000. They jointly sold stocks in 2019 and generated a long-term capital gain of $13,000. Rob and Marie have no dependents and in 2019, they take the standard deduction of $24,400.

a. What is Rob and Marie's taxable income before the QBI deduction?
b. What is Rob and Marie's QBI?
c. What is Rob and Marie's QBI deduction?
d. Complete Form 8995-A on Pages 4-59 and 4-60 to report Rob's QBI deduction.

GROUP 3:
WRITING ASSIGNMENT

RESEARCH You recently received the following e-mail from a client and friend:

Hey Great Student,

I cannot believe it is almost year end! Only a few days before it's 2020.

As you recall, I was lucky enough to win big at the casino back on New Year's Day earlier this year (thanks for celebrating with me). I took the $3,000 I won and bought 100 shares of stock in that cool new smartphone app company, TriviaAddiction. I just love playing that game. Anyway, the stock has done well, and I am thinking of selling before year end now that the price has reached $240 per share. Since you are my tax adviser, I thought I'd ask a couple of questions:

1. Is there any reason to wait and sell later?
2. If I don't sell, the price might go down (TriviaMaster seems to be replacing TriviaAddiction as the "hot" new game). I'm thinking the price might be as low as $220 by early next year.

My taxable income this year and next year is expected to be $40,000 (not including the stock sale). I think that puts me in the 12 percent tax bracket? Any suggestions on what I should do?

Thanks!

Sue

Prepare an e-mail to your friend Sue addressing her questions. Be certain to include estimates of the different after-tax outcomes she is suggesting. Sue is a single taxpayer and not a tax expert and so your language should reflect her limited understanding of tax law and avoid technical jargon. Although Sue is your friend, she is also a client and your e-mail should maintain a professional style.

Form **8582**

Department of the Treasury
Internal Revenue Service (99)

Passive Activity Loss Limitations

▶ See separate instructions.
▶ Attach to Form 1040, Form 1040-SR, or Form 1041.
▶ Go to *www.irs.gov/Form8582* for instructions and the latest information.

OMB No. 1545-1008

2019

Attachment
Sequence No. **88**

Name(s) shown on return

Identifying number

Part I 2019 Passive Activity Loss

Caution: Complete Worksheets 1, 2, and 3 before completing Part I.

Rental Real Estate Activities With Active Participation (For the definition of active participation, see **Special Allowance for Rental Real Estate Activities** in the instructions.)

1a	Activities with net income (enter the amount from Worksheet 1, column (a))	**1a**	
b	Activities with net loss (enter the amount from Worksheet 1, column (b))	**1b** ( )	
c	Prior years' unallowed losses (enter the amount from Worksheet 1, column (c))	**1c** ( )	
d	Combine lines 1a, 1b, and 1c		**1d**

Commercial Revitalization Deductions From Rental Real Estate Activities

2a	Commercial revitalization deductions from Worksheet 2, column (a)	**2a** ( )	
b	Prior year unallowed commercial revitalization deductions from Worksheet 2, column (b)	**2b** ( )	
c	Add lines 2a and 2b		**2c** ( )

All Other Passive Activities

3a	Activities with net income (enter the amount from Worksheet 3, column (a))	**3a**	
b	Activities with net loss (enter the amount from Worksheet 3, column (b))	**3b** ( )	
c	Prior years' unallowed losses (enter the amount from Worksheet 3, column (c))	**3c** ( )	
d	Combine lines 3a, 3b, and 3c		**3d**

4	Combine lines 1d, 2c, and 3d. If this line is zero or more, stop here and include this form with your return; all losses are allowed, including any prior year unallowed losses entered on line 1c, 2b, or 3c. Report the losses on the forms and schedules normally used	**4**

If line 4 is a loss and: • Line 1d is a loss, go to Part II.

• Line 2c is a loss (and line 1d is zero or more), skip Part II and go to Part III.

• Line 3d is a loss (and lines 1d and 2c are zero or more), skip Parts II and III and go to line 15.

Caution: If your filing status is married filing separately and you lived with your spouse at any time during the year, **do not** complete Part II or Part III. Instead, go to line 15.

Part II Special Allowance for Rental Real Estate Activities With Active Participation

Note: Enter all numbers in Part II as positive amounts. See instructions for an example.

5	Enter the **smaller** of the loss on line 1d or the loss on line 4		**5**
6	Enter $150,000. If married filing separately, see instructions	**6**	
7	Enter modified adjusted gross income, but not less than zero. See instructions	**7**	
	Note: If line 7 is greater than or equal to line 6, skip lines 8 and 9, enter -0- on line 10. Otherwise, go to line 8.		
8	Subtract line 7 from line 6	**8**	
9	Multiply line 8 by 50% (0.50). **Do not** enter more than $25,000. If married filing separately, see instructions		**9**
10	Enter the **smaller** of line 5 or line 9		**10**

If line 2c is a loss, go to Part III. Otherwise, go to line 15.

Part III Special Allowance for Commercial Revitalization Deductions From Rental Real Estate Activities

Note: Enter all numbers in Part III as positive amounts. See the example for Part II in the instructions.

11	Enter $25,000 reduced by the amount, if any, on line 10. If married filing separately, see instructions		**11**
12	Enter the loss from line 4		**12**
13	Reduce line 12 by the amount on line 10		**13**
14	Enter the **smallest** of line 2c (treated as a positive amount), line 11, or line 13		**14**

Part IV Total Losses Allowed

15	Add the income, if any, on lines 1a and 3a and enter the total		**15**
16	**Total losses allowed from all passive activities for 2019.** Add lines 10, 14, and 15. See instructions to find out how to report the losses on your tax return		**16**

For Paperwork Reduction Act Notice, see instructions.   Cat. No. 63704F   Form **8582** (2019)

Form **8995-A**	**Qualified Business Income Deduction**	OMB No. XXXX-XXXX

Department of the Treasury
Internal Revenue Service

▶ **Attach to your tax return.**
▶ **Go to** *www.irs.gov/Form8995A* **for instructions and the latest information.**

2019
Attachment
Sequence No. **55A**

Name(s) shown on return

Your taxpayer identification number

Part I   **Trade, Business, or Aggregation Information**

Complete the schedules for Form 8995-A, (A, B, C, and/or D), as applicable, before starting Part I. Attach additional worksheets when needed. See instructions.

1	(a) Trade, business, or aggregation name	(b) Check if specified service	(c) Check if aggregation	(d) Taxpayer identification number	(e) Check if patron
A		☐	☐		☐
B		☐	☐		☐
C		☐	☐		☐

Part II   **Determine Your Adjusted Qualified Business Income**

			A	B	C
2	Qualified business income from the trade, business, or aggregation. See instructions	2			
3	Multiply line 2 by 20% (0.20). If your taxable income is $160,700 or less ($160,725 if married filing separately; $321,400 if married filing jointly), skip lines 4 through 12 and enter the amount from line 3 on line 13	3			
4	Allocable share of W-2 wages from the trade, business, or aggregation	4			
5	Multiply line 4 by 50% (0.50)	5			
6	Multiply line 4 by 25% (0.25)	6			
7	Allocable share of the unadjusted basis immediately after acquisition (UBIA) of all qualified property	7			
8	Multiply line 7 by 2.5% (0.025)	8			
9	Add lines 6 and 8	9			
10	Enter the greater of line 5 or line 9	10			
11	W-2 wage and qualified property limitation. Enter the smaller of line 3 or line 10	11			
12	Phased-in reduction. Enter amount from line 26, if any. See instructions	12			
13	Qualified business income deduction before patron reduction. Enter the greater of line 11 or line 12	13			
14	Patron reduction. Enter the amount from Schedule D (Form 8995-A), line 6, if any	14			
15	Qualified business income component. Subtract line 14 from line 13	15			
16	Total qualified business income component. Add all amounts reported on line 15 . . . . ▶	16			

For Privacy Act and Paperwork Reduction Act Notice, see separate instructions.   Cat. No. 71661B   Form **8995-A** (2019)

DRAFT AS OF July 25, 2019 DO NOT FILE

Form 8995-A (2019)   Page **2**

Part III   Phased-in Reduction

Complete Part III only if your taxable income is more than $160,700 but not $210,700 ($160,725 and $210,725 if married filing separately; $321,400 and $421,400 if married filing jointly) and line 10 is less than line 3. Otherwise, skip Part III.

			A	B	C
17	Enter amounts from line 3	17			
18	Enter the amounts from line 10	18			
19	Subtract line 18 from line 17	19			
20	Taxable income before qualified business income deduction	**20**			
21	Threshold. Enter $160,700 ($160,725 if married filing separately; $321,400 if married filing jointly)	**21**			
22	Subtract line 21 from line 20	**22**			
23	Phase-in range. Enter $50,000 ($100,000 if married filing jointly)	**23**			
24	Phase-in percentage. Divide line 22 by line 23	**24** %			
25	Total phase-in reduction. Multiply line 19 by line 24	**25**			
26	Qualified business income after phase-in reduction. Subtract line 25 from line 17. Enter this amount here and on line 12, for the corresponding trade or business	**26**			

Part IV   Determine Your Qualified Business Income Deduction

27	Total qualified business income component from all qualified trades, businesses, or aggregations. Enter the amount from line 16	**27**	
28	Qualified REIT dividends and publicly traded partnership (PTP) income or (loss). See instructions	**28**	
29	Qualified REIT dividends and PTP (loss) carryforward from prior years	**29** ( )	
30	Total qualified REIT dividends and PTP income. Combine lines 28 and 29. If less than zero, enter -0-	**30**	
31	REIT and PTP component. Multiply line 30 by 20% (0.20)	**31**	
32	Qualified business income deduction before the income limitation. Add lines 27 and 31 ▶		**32**
33	Taxable income before qualified business income deduction	**33**	
34	Net capital gain. See instructions	**34**	
35	Subtract line 34 from line 33. If zero or less, enter -0-		**35**
36	Income limitation. Multiply line 35 by 20% (0.20)		**36**
37	Qualified business income deduction before the domestic production activities deduction (DPAD) under section 199A(g). Enter the smaller of line 32 or line 36 ▶		**37**
38	DPAD under section 199A(g) allocated from an agricultural or horticultural cooperative. Don't enter more than line 33 minus line 37		**38**
39	Total qualified business income deduction. Add lines 37 and 38 ▶		**39**
40	Total qualified REIT dividends and PTP (loss) carryforward. Combine lines 28 and 29. If zero or greater, enter -0-		**40** ( )

Form **8995-A** (2019)

GROUP 4:
COMPREHENSIVE PROBLEMS

1. Skylar and Walter Black have been married for 25 years. They live at 883 Scrub Brush Street, Apt. 52B, Las Vegas, NV 89125. Skylar is a stay-at-home parent and Walt is a high school teacher. Skylar's Social Security number is 222-43-7690 and Walt's is 700-01-0002. Neither are age 65 or older. The Blacks provide all the support for Skylar's mother, Rebecca Backin (Social Security number 411-66-2121), who lives in a nursing home in Reno, NV and has no income. Walter's father, Alton Black (Social Security number 343-22-8899), lives with the Blacks in Las Vegas. Although Alton received Social Security benefits of $7,600 in 2019, the Blacks provide over half of Alton's support. Skylar and Walt claim a $500 other dependent credit each for Rebecca and Alton. Walt's earnings from teaching are:

a Employee's social security number	700-01-0002	OMB No. 1545-0008	Safe, accurate, FAST! Use	IRS e-file	Visit the IRS website at www.irs.gov/efile

b Employer identification number (EIN) 31-1239867	1 Wages, tips, other compensation 51,200.00	2 Federal income tax withheld 4,310.00
c Employer's name, address, and ZIP code	3 Social security wages 51,200.00	4 Social security tax withheld 3,174.40
Las Vegas School District 2234 Vegas Valley Drive Las Vegas, NV 89169	5 Medicare wages and tips 51,200.00	6 Medicare tax withheld 742.40
	7 Social security tips	8 Allocated tips
d Control number	9	10 Dependent care benefits
e Employee's first name and initial Last name Suff.	11 Nonqualified plans	12a See instructions for box 12 DD | $7,900.00
Walter Black 883 Scrub Brush Street, Apt 52B Las Vegas, NV 89125	13 Statutory employee ☐ Retirement plan ☒ Third-party sick pay ☐	12b
	14 Other	12c
		12d
f Employee's address and ZIP code		

15 State Employer's state ID number	16 State wages, tips, etc.	17 State income tax	18 Local wages, tips, etc.	19 Local income tax	20 Locality name
NV					

Form **W-2** Wage and Tax Statement   2019   Department of the Treasury—Internal Revenue Service

Copy B—To Be Filed With Employee's FEDERAL Tax Return.
This information is being furnished to the Internal Revenue Service.

The Blacks moved from Maine to Nevada. As a result, they sold their house in Maine on January 4, 2019. They originally paid $76,000 for the home on July 3, 1994, but managed to sell it for $604,000. They spent $13,000 on improvements over the years. They are currently renting in Las Vegas while they look for a new home.

The Blacks received the following 1099-DIV from their mutual fund investments:

☐ CORRECTED (if checked)

PAYER'S name, street address, city or town, state or province, country, ZIP or foreign postal code, and telephone no.			**1a** Total ordinary dividends $ 1,425.00	OMB No. 1545-0110 20**19** Form **1099-DIV**	Dividends and Distributions
Cyber Funds Equities Fund 41 Wall Street New York, NY 10005			**1b** Qualified dividends $ 1,002.00		
			2a Total capital gain distr. $ 6,540.34	**2b** Unrecap. Sec. 1250 gain $	Copy B For Recipient
PAYER'S TIN 17-1234326		RECIPIENT'S TIN 222-43-7690	**2c** Section 1202 gain $	**2d** Collectibles (28%) gain $	
RECIPIENT'S name Skylar B. Black			**3** Nondividend distributions $	**4** Federal income tax withheld $	This is important tax information and is being furnished to the IRS. If you are required to file a return, a negligence penalty or other sanction may be imposed on you if this income is taxable and the IRS determines that it has not been reported.
			5 Section 199A dividends $	**6** Investment expenses $	
Street address (including apt. no.) 883 Scrub Brush Street #52B			**7** Foreign tax paid $	**8** Foreign country or U.S. possession	
City or town, state or province, country, and ZIP or foreign postal code Las Vegas, NV 89125			**9** Cash liquidation distributions $	**10** Noncash liquidation distributions $	
		FATCA filing requirement ☐	**11** Exempt-interest dividends $	**12** Specified private activity bond interest dividends $	
Account number (see instructions)			**13** State	**14** State identification no.	**15** State tax withheld $

Form **1099-DIV**   (keep for your records)   www.irs.gov/Form1099DIV   Department of the Treasury - Internal Revenue Service

The Blacks own a ski condo located at 123 Buncombe Lane, Brian Head, UT 84719. The condo was rented for 185 days during 2019 and used by the Blacks for 15 days. The rental activity does not rise to the level to qualify for the QBI deduction. Pertinent information about the condo rental is as follows:

Rental income	$12,100
Mortgage interest reported on Form 1098	8,600
Homeowners' association dues	5,200
Utilities	1,200
Maintenance	3,800
Depreciation (assume fully depreciated)	0

The above amounts do not reflect any allocation between rental and personal use of the condo. The Blacks are active managers of the condo.

Required: Complete the Black's federal tax return for 2019. Use Form 1040, Schedule 1, Schedule D, Form 8949, Schedule E (page one only), Form 8582 (page one only) and the Qualified Dividends and Capital Gain Tax Worksheet to complete their tax return.

2A. Dr. George E. Beeper is a single taxpayer born on September 22, 1971. He lives at 45 Mountain View Dr., Apt. 321, Spokane, WA 99210. Dr. Beeper's Social Security number is 775-88-9531. Dr. Beeper works for the Pine Medical Group, and his earnings and income tax withholding for 2019 are:

a Employee's social security number 775-88-9531	OMB No. 1545-0008	Safe, accurate, FAST! Use	IRS e~file	Visit the IRS website at www.irs.gov/efile
b Employer identification number (EIN) 36-1389676		**1** Wages, tips, other compensation 133,900.00		**2** Federal income tax withheld 21,045.00
c Employer's name, address, and ZIP code Pine Medical Group 800 W. 7th Ave. Spokane, WA 92204		**3** Social security wages 132,900.00		**4** Social security tax withheld 8,239.80
		5 Medicare wages and tips 133,900.00		**6** Medicare tax withheld 1,941.55
		7 Social security tips		**8** Allocated tips
d Control number		**9**		**10** Dependent care benefits
e Employee's first name and initial Last name Suff. George Beeper 45 Mountain View Drive, Apt 321 Spokane, WA 99210		**11** Nonqualified plans		**12a** See instructions for box 12 DD| 5,800.00
		13 Statutory employee ☐ Retirement plan ☐ Third-party sick pay ☐		**12b**
		14 Other		**12c**
				12d
f Employee's address and ZIP code				
15 State Employer's state ID number WA|	**16** State wages, tips, etc.	**17** State income tax	**18** Local wages, tips, etc.	**19** Local income tax **20** Locality name

Form W-2 Wage and Tax Statement   **2019**   Department of the Treasury—Internal Revenue Service

Copy B—To Be Filed With Employee's FEDERAL Tax Return.
This information is being furnished to the Internal Revenue Service.

Dr. Beeper owns a rental house located at 672 Lake Street, Spokane, WA 99212. The house rents for $1,000 per month and was rented for the entire year. The following are the related expenses for the rental house:

Real estate taxes	$ 5,850
Mortgage interest	14,521
Insurance	2,215
Depreciation (assume fully depreciated)	0
Repairs	550
Maintenance	1,976

The house was purchased on July 5, 1984. Dr. Beeper handles all rental activities (e.g., rent collection, finding tenants, etc.) himself. He spends about 10 hours per month on the rental.

In 2019, Dr. Beeper sold his primary residence as he wished to move to an apartment to avoid the maintenance and upkeep of a single-family home. Dr. Beeper's home sold on February 12, 2019 for $345,000 net after commissions. He acquired the home on June 3, 2001 for $260,000 and had made improvements of $10,000.

Dr. Beeper was divorced on January 1, 2013. The divorce decree requires Dr. Beeper to pay his ex-wife, Meredith Gray (Social Security number 333-45-1234), $800 per month. Dr. Beeper made all his monthly alimony payments in 2019.

Required: Complete Dr. Beeper's federal tax return for 2019. Determine if Form 8949 and Schedule D are required. If so, use those forms and Form 1040, Schedule E (page one only), and Form 8582 (page one only) to complete this tax return. Do not complete Form 4562 for reporting depreciation.

2B. In 2019, Professor Patricia (Patty) Pâté retired from the Palm Springs Culinary Arts Academy (PSCAA). She is a single taxpayer and is 62 years old. Patty lives at 98 Colander Street, Apt. 206D, Henderson, NV 89052. Professor Pâté's Social Security number is 565-66-9378. In 2019, Patty had just a few months of salary from her previous job:

Wages	$9,800
Federal tax withheld	450
State tax withheld	0

Patty owns a rental condo located at 392 Spatula Way, Mount Charleston, NV 89124. The condo rented for two months of 2019 for $850 a month but a mold problem was discovered in the condo, her renters moved out, and she was unable to rent the apartment after the repairs (although she vigorously pursued new tenants). Patty actively manages the property herself. The following are the related expenses for the rental house:

Real estate taxes	$3,900
Mortgage interest	9,100
Insurance	561
Depreciation (assume fully depreciated)	0
Homeowners' Association dues	1,260
Repairs	1,195
Gardening	560
Advertising	1,200

The condo was purchased on August 31, 1980. Professor Pâté handles all rental activities (e.g., rent collection, finding tenants, etc.) herself.

In 2019, Patty sold her beloved home for almost 30 years for $380,000 on February 27, 2019. Her basis in the home was $120,000 and she acquired the home sometime in July of 1989 (she could not remember the day).

Required: Complete Professor Pâté's federal tax return for 2019. Use Form 1040, Schedule D, Form 8949, Schedule E, and Form 8582 (page one only) to complete this tax return. Also, to compute Patty's net operating loss carryforward, prepare only Schedule A of Form 1045.

GROUP 5:
CUMULATIVE SOFTWARE PROBLEM

1. The following additional information is available for the Albert and Allison Gaytor family.

The Gaytors own a rental beach house in Hawaii. The beach house was rented for the full year during 2019 and was not used by the Gaytors during the year. The Gaytors were active participants in the management of the rental house but the activity is not eligible for a QBI deduction. Pertinent information about the rental house is as follows:

Address: 1237 Pineapple St., Lihue, HI 96766

Gross rental income	$20,000
Mortgage interest	7,900
Real estate taxes	2,175
Utilities	1,500
Cleaning	2,400
Repairs	675

The house is fully depreciated so there is no depreciation expense.

Albert and Allison received the following combined statements 1099-DIV and 1099-B from their investment manager:

IMPORTANT TAX DOCUMENT
2019 Form 1099-DIV
Dividends and Distributions

RECIPIENT'S TIN: 266-51-1966

Albert T. Gaytor
Allison A Gaytor
JT TEN WROS
12340 Cocoshell Rd
Coral Gables, FL 33134

Fortress Securities

PO Box 1300
Gaithersburg, MD 20877
Copy B for Recipient

Fund Name	Total Ordinary Dividends	Qualified Dividends	Capital Gain Distrib	Unrecap 1250 Gain	Nondividend Distrib	Fed Tax Withheld	Exempt-Interest Dividends	State Tax Withheld
Peach Fund	0.00	0.00	450.00			0.00		

2019 Form 1099-B
Proceeds from Broker and Barter Exchange Transactions

Descript.	Date Acq	Date Sold	Proceeds	Cost	Fed Tax Withheld	Proceeds Reported to IRS	Basis Reported to IRS
100 shs. Orange Co	02/11/2001	04/16/2019	$3,000.00	$2,175.00	$0.00	Net	Yes
100 shs. Banana Co.	07/17/2005	07/31/2019	2,100.00	4,200.00	0.00	Net	Yes
100 shs Grape Corp	12/18/2018	09/25/2019	9,050.00	10,500.00	0.00	Net	Yes
5 $1,000 Par Value Bonds due 4/2019	12/30/2009	01/02/2019	5,200.00	5,415.00	0.00	Net	Yes
5,011.23 shs. Peach Mutual Fund	05/30/2010	10/22/2019	60,100.00	56,000.00	0.00	Net	Yes

On January 12, 2019, Albert and Allison sold their personal residence for $715,200 and purchased a new house for $725,000. This was their personal residence before and after the divorce (they have lived in it together for three years since remarrying). The old house cost $120,000 back in January of 2007 and they added on a new bedroom and bathroom a few years ago for a cost of $20,000. They also built a pool for a cost of $60,000. They moved into the new house on January 19, 2019.

Required: Combine this new information about the Gaytor family with the information from Chapters 1–3 and complete a revised 2019 tax return for Albert and Allison. Be sure to save your data input files since this case will be expanded with more tax information in later chapters.

Form **1040**	Department of the Treasury—Internal Revenue Service (99)	**2019**	OMB No. 1545-0074	IRS Use Only—Do not write or staple in this space.
	U.S. Individual Income Tax Return			

Filing Status

Check only one box.

☐ Single ☐ Married filing jointly ☐ Married filing separately (MFS) ☐ Head of household (HOH) ☐ Qualifying widow(er) (QW)

If you checked the MFS box, enter the name of spouse. If you checked the HOH or QW box, enter the child's name if the qualifying person is a child but not your dependent. ▶

Your first name and middle initial	Last name	Your social security number

If joint return, spouse's first name and middle initial	Last name	Spouse's social security number

Home address (number and street). If you have a P.O. box, see instructions.	Apt. no.	**Presidential Election Campaign**

Check here if you, or your spouse if filing jointly, want $3 to go to this fund. Checking a box below will not change your tax or refund. ☐ You ☐ Spouse

City, town or post office, state, and ZIP code. If you have a foreign address, also complete spaces below (see instructions).

Foreign country name	Foreign province/state/county	Foreign postal code	If more than four dependents, see instructions and ✓ here ▶ ☐

Standard Deduction

Someone can claim: ☐ You as a dependent ☐ Your spouse as a dependent

☐ Spouse itemizes on a separate return or you were a dual-status alien

Age/Blindness **You:** ☐ Were born before January 2, 1955 ☐ Are blind **Spouse:** ☐ Was born before January 2, 1955 ☐ Is blind

Dependents (see instructions):

(1) First name Last name	(2) Social security number	(3) Relationship to you	(4) ✓ if qualifies for (see instructions):	
			Child tax credit	Credit for other dependents
			☐	☐
			☐	☐
			☐	☐
			☐	☐

Standard Deduction for—
- Single or Married filing separately, $12,200
- Married filing jointly or Qualifying widow(er), $24,400
- Head of household, $18,350
- If you checked any box under *Standard Deduction,* see instructions.

1	Wages, salaries, tips, etc. Attach Form(s) W-2		**1**	
2a	Tax-exempt interest	**2a**	**b** Taxable interest. Attach Sch. B if required	**2b**	
3a	Qualified dividends	**3a**	**b** Ordinary dividends. Attach Sch. B if required	**3b**	
4a	IRA distributions	**4a**	**b** Taxable amount	**4b**	
c	Pensions and annuities . . .	**4c**	**d** Taxable amount	**4d**	
5a	Social security benefits . . .	**5a**	**b** Taxable amount	**5b**	
6	Capital gain or (loss). Attach Schedule D if required. If not required, check here . . . . ▶ ☐		**6**	
7a	Other income from Schedule 1, line 9		**7a**	
b	Add lines 1, 2b, 3b, 4b, 4d, 5b, 6, and 7a. This is your **total income** . . . . ▶		**7b**	
8a	Adjustments to income from Schedule 1, line 22		**8a**	
b	Subtract line 8a from line 7b. This is your **adjusted gross income** . . . . ▶		**8b**	
9	**Standard deduction or itemized deductions** (from Schedule A)	**9**		
10	Qualified business income deduction. Attach Form 8995 or Form 8995-A . . .	**10**		
11a	Add lines 9 and 10		**11a**	
b	**Taxable income.** Subtract line 11a from line 8b		**11b**	

For Disclosure, Privacy Act, and Paperwork Reduction Act Notice, see separate instructions.   Cat. No. 11320B   Form **1040** (2019)

Form 1040 (2019)   Page **2**

12a	**Tax** (see inst.) Check if any from Form(s): **1** ☐ 8814 **2** ☐ 4972 **3** ☐ _____		**12a**		
b	Add Schedule 2, line 3, and line 12a and enter the total ▶			**12b**	
13a	Child tax credit or credit for other dependents		**13a**		
b	Add Schedule 3, line 7, and line 13a and enter the total ▶			**13b**	
14	Subtract line 13b from line 12b. If zero or less, enter -0-			**14**	
15	Other taxes, including self-employment tax, from Schedule 2, line 10			**15**	
16	Add lines 14 and 15. This is your **total tax** ▶			**16**	
17	Federal income tax withheld from Forms W-2 and 1099			**17**	
18	Other payments and refundable credits:				
a	Earned income credit (EIC)		**18a**		
b	Additional child tax credit. Attach Schedule 8812		**18b**		
c	American opportunity credit from Form 8863, line 8		**18c**		
d	Schedule 3, line 14		**18d**		
e	Add lines 18a through 18d. These are your **total other payments and refundable credits**			**18e**	
19	Add lines 17 and 18e. These are your **total payments**			**19**	

• If you have a qualifying child, attach Sch. EIC.
• If you have nontaxable combat pay, see instructions.

Refund

Direct deposit?
See instructions.

20	If line 19 is more than line 16, subtract line 16 from line 19. This is the amount you **overpaid**	**20**	
21a	Amount of line 20 you want **refunded to you.** If Form 8888 is attached, check here ▶ ☐	**21a**	
▶**b**	Routing number _____ ▶**c** Type: ☐ Checking ☐ Savings		
▶**d**	Account number _____		
22	Amount of line 20 you want **applied to your 2020 estimated tax** ▶	**22**	

Amount You Owe

23	**Amount you owe.** Subtract line 19 from line 16. For details on how to pay, see instructions ▶	**23**	
24	Estimated tax penalty (see instructions)	**24**	

Third Party Designee

(Other than paid preparer)

Do you want to allow another person (other than your paid preparer) to discuss this return with the IRS? See instructions.   ☐ **Yes.** Complete below.   ☐ **No**

Designee's name ▶	Phone no. ▶	Personal identification number (PIN) ▶

Sign Here

Joint return?
See instructions.
Keep a copy for your records.

Under penalties of perjury, I declare that I have examined this return and accompanying schedules and statements, and to the best of my knowledge and belief, they are true, correct, and complete. Declaration of preparer (other than taxpayer) is based on all information of which preparer has any knowledge.

Your signature	Date	Your occupation	If the IRS sent you an Identity Protection PIN, enter it here (see inst.)
Spouse's signature. If a joint return, **both** must sign.	Date	Spouse's occupation	If the IRS sent your spouse an Identity Protection PIN, enter it here (see inst.)
Phone no.	Email address		

Paid Preparer Use Only

Preparer's name	Preparer's signature	Date	PTIN	Check if: ☐ 3rd Party Designee ☐ Self-employed
Firm's name ▶		Phone no.		
Firm's address ▶			Firm's EIN ▶	

Go to *www.irs.gov/Form1040* for instructions and the latest information.   Form **1040** (2019)

SCHEDULE 1
(Form 1040 or 1040-SR)

Department of the Treasury
Internal Revenue Service

Additional Income and Adjustments to Income

▶ Attach to Form 1040 or 1040-SR.
▶ Go to *www.irs.gov/Form1040* for instructions and the latest information.

OMB No. 1545-0074

2019

Attachment
Sequence No. **01**

Name(s) shown on Form 1040 or 1040-SR

Your social security number

Part I	Additional Income		
1	Taxable refunds, credits, or offsets of state and local income taxes	1	
2a	Alimony received	2a	
b	Date of original divorce or separation agreement (see instructions) ▶		
3	Business income or (loss). Attach Schedule C	3	
4	Other gains or (losses). Attach Form 4797	4	
5	Rental real estate, royalties, partnerships, S corporations, trusts, etc. Attach Schedule E	5	
6	Farm income or (loss). Attach Schedule F	6	
7	Unemployment compensation	7	
8	Other income. List type and amount ▶		
		8	
9	Combine lines 1 through 8. Enter here and on Form 1040 or 1040-SR, line 7a	9	
Part II	Adjustments to Income		
10	Educator expenses	10	
11	Certain business expenses of reservists, performing artists, and fee-basis government officials. Attach Form 2106	11	
12	Health savings account deduction. Attach Form 8889	12	
13	Moving expenses for members of the Armed Forces. Attach Form 3903	13	
14	Deductible part of self-employment tax. Attach Schedule SE	14	
15	Self-employed SEP, SIMPLE, and qualified plans	15	
16	Self-employed health insurance deduction	16	
17	Penalty on early withdrawal of savings	17	
18a	Alimony paid	18a	
b	Recipient's SSN ▶		
c	Date of original divorce or separation agreement (see instructions) ▶		
19	IRA deduction	19	
20	Student loan interest deduction	20	
21	Reserved for future use	21	
22	Add lines 10 through 21. These are your **adjustments to income.** Enter here and on Form 1040 or 1040-SR, line 8a	22	

For Paperwork Reduction Act Notice, see your tax return instructions.   Cat. No. 71479F   **Schedule 1 (Form 1040 or 1040-SR) 2019**

SCHEDULE D
(Form 1040 or 1040-SR)

Department of the Treasury
Internal Revenue Service (99)

Capital Gains and Losses

▶ Attach to Form 1040, 1040-SR, or 1040-NR.
▶ Go to *www.irs.gov/ScheduleD* for instructions and the latest information.
▶ Use Form 8949 to list your transactions for lines 1b, 2, 3, 8b, 9, and 10.

OMB No. 1545-0074

2019

Attachment
Sequence No. **12**

Name(s) shown on return

Your social security number

Did you dispose of any investment(s) in a qualified opportunity fund during the tax year? ☐ **Yes** ☐ **No**
If "Yes," attach Form 8949 and see its instructions for additional requirements for reporting your gain or loss.

Part I   **Short-Term Capital Gains and Losses—Generally Assets Held One Year or Less** (see instructions)

See instructions for how to figure the amounts to enter on the lines below. This form may be easier to complete if you round off cents to whole dollars.	**(d)** Proceeds (sales price)	**(e)** Cost (or other basis)	**(g)** Adjustments to gain or loss from Form(s) 8949, Part I, line 2, column (g)	**(h) Gain or (loss)** Subtract column (e) from column (d) and combine the result with column (g)
1a Totals for all short-term transactions reported on Form 1099-B for which basis was reported to the IRS and for which you have no adjustments (see instructions). However, if you choose to report all these transactions on Form 8949, leave this line blank and go to line 1b .				
1b Totals for all transactions reported on Form(s) 8949 with **Box A** checked				
2 Totals for all transactions reported on Form(s) 8949 with **Box B** checked				
3 Totals for all transactions reported on Form(s) 8949 with **Box C** checked				

4 Short-term gain from Form 6252 and short-term gain or (loss) from Forms 4684, 6781, and 8824 . .	**4**	
5 Net short-term gain or (loss) from partnerships, S corporations, estates, and trusts from Schedule(s) K-1	**5**	
6 Short-term capital loss carryover. Enter the amount, if any, from line 8 of your **Capital Loss Carryover Worksheet** in the instructions	**6**	( )
7 **Net short-term capital gain or (loss).** Combine lines 1a through 6 in column (h). If you have any long-term capital gains or losses, go to Part II below. Otherwise, go to Part III on the back	**7**	

Part II   **Long-Term Capital Gains and Losses—Generally Assets Held More Than One Year** (see instructions)

See instructions for how to figure the amounts to enter on the lines below. This form may be easier to complete if you round off cents to whole dollars.	**(d)** Proceeds (sales price)	**(e)** Cost (or other basis)	**(g)** Adjustments to gain or loss from Form(s) 8949, Part II, line 2, column (g)	**(h) Gain or (loss)** Subtract column (e) from column (d) and combine the result with column (g)
8a Totals for all long-term transactions reported on Form 1099-B for which basis was reported to the IRS and for which you have no adjustments (see instructions). However, if you choose to report all these transactions on Form 8949, leave this line blank and go to line 8b .				
8b Totals for all transactions reported on Form(s) 8949 with **Box D** checked				
9 Totals for all transactions reported on Form(s) 8949 with **Box E** checked				
10 Totals for all transactions reported on Form(s) 8949 with **Box F** checked.				

11 Gain from Form 4797, Part I; long-term gain from Forms 2439 and 6252; and long-term gain or (loss) from Forms 4684, 6781, and 8824	**11**	
12 Net long-term gain or (loss) from partnerships, S corporations, estates, and trusts from Schedule(s) K-1	**12**	
13 Capital gain distributions. See the instructions	**13**	
14 Long-term capital loss carryover. Enter the amount, if any, from line 13 of your **Capital Loss Carryover Worksheet** in the instructions	**14**	( )
15 **Net long-term capital gain or (loss).** Combine lines 8a through 14 in column (h). Then go to Part III on the back	**15**	

For Paperwork Reduction Act Notice, see your tax return instructions.   Cat. No. 11338H   **Schedule D (Form 1040 or 1040-SR) 2019**

Schedule D (Form 1040 or 1040-SR) 2019   Page **2**

Part III   **Summary**

16   Combine lines 7 and 15 and enter the result **16**

- If line 16 is a **gain,** enter the amount from line 16 on Form 1040 or 1040-SR, line 6; or Form 1040-NR, line 14. Then go to line 17 below.
- If line 16 is a **loss,** skip lines 17 through 20 below. Then go to line 21. Also be sure to complete line 22.
- If line 16 is **zero,** skip lines 17 through 21 below and enter -0- on Form 1040 or 1040-SR, line 6; or Form 1040-NR, line 14. Then go to line 22.

17   Are lines 15 and 16 **both** gains?
☐ **Yes.** Go to line 18.
☐ **No.** Skip lines 18 through 21, and go to line 22.

18   If you are required to complete the **28% Rate Gain Worksheet** (see instructions), enter the amount, if any, from line 7 of that worksheet . . . . ▶   **18**

19   If you are required to complete the **Unrecaptured Section 1250 Gain Worksheet** (see instructions), enter the amount, if any, from line 18 of that worksheet . . . . ▶   **19**

20   Are lines 18 and 19 **both** zero or blank?
☐ **Yes.** Complete the **Qualified Dividends and Capital Gain Tax Worksheet** in the instructions for Forms 1040 and 1040-SR, line 12a (or in the instructions for Form 1040-NR, line 42). **Don't** complete lines 21 and 22 below.

☐ **No.** Complete the **Schedule D Tax Worksheet** in the instructions. **Don't** complete lines 21 and 22 below.

21   If line 16 is a loss, enter here and on Form 1040 or 1040-SR, line 6; or Form 1040-NR, line 14, the **smaller** of:

- The loss on line 16; or
- ($3,000), or if married filing separately, ($1,500)   } . . . .   **21** (   )

Note: When figuring which amount is smaller, treat both amounts as positive numbers.

22   Do you have qualified dividends on Form 1040 or 1040-SR, line 3a; or Form 1040-NR, line 10b?

☐ **Yes.** Complete the **Qualified Dividends and Capital Gain Tax Worksheet** in the instructions for Forms 1040 and 1040-SR, line 12a (or in the instructions for Form 1040-NR, line 42).

☐ **No.** Complete the rest of Form 1040, 1040-SR, or 1040-NR.

Schedule D (Form 1040 or 1040-SR) 2019

Form **8949**

Department of the Treasury
Internal Revenue Service

Sales and Other Dispositions of Capital Assets

▶ Go to *www.irs.gov/Form8949* for instructions and the latest information.
▶ File with your Schedule D to list your transactions for lines 1b, 2, 3, 8b, 9, and 10 of Schedule D.

OMB No. 1545-0074

20**19**

Attachment
Sequence No. **12A**

Name(s) shown on return

Social security number or taxpayer identification number

Before you check Box A, B, or C below, see whether you received any Form(s) 1099-B or substitute statement(s) from your broker. A substitute statement will have the same information as Form 1099-B. Either will show whether your basis (usually your cost) was reported to the IRS by your broker and may even tell you which box to check.

Part I   **Short-Term.** Transactions involving capital assets you held 1 year or less are generally short-term (see instructions). For long-term transactions, see page 2.

Note: You may aggregate all short-term transactions reported on Form(s) 1099-B showing basis was reported to the IRS and for which no adjustments or codes are required. Enter the totals directly on Schedule D, line 1a; you aren't required to report these transactions on Form 8949 (see instructions).

You *must* check Box A, B, *or* C below. Check only one box. If more than one box applies for your short-term transactions, complete a separate Form 8949, page 1, for each applicable box. If you have more short-term transactions than will fit on this page for one or more of the boxes, complete as many forms with the same box checked as you need.

☐ **(A)** Short-term transactions reported on Form(s) 1099-B showing basis was reported to the IRS (see **Note** above)
☐ **(B)** Short-term transactions reported on Form(s) 1099-B showing basis **wasn't** reported to the IRS
☐ **(C)** Short-term transactions not reported to you on Form 1099-B

1 (a) Description of property (Example: 100 sh. XYZ Co.)	(b) Date acquired (Mo., day, yr.)	(c) Date sold or disposed of (Mo., day, yr.)	(d) Proceeds (sales price) (see instructions)	(e) Cost or other basis. See the **Note** below and see *Column (e)* in the separate instructions	Adjustment, if any, to gain or loss. If you enter an amount in column (g), enter a code in column (f). See the separate instructions.		(h) Gain or (loss). Subtract column (e) from column (d) and combine the result with column (g)
					(f) Code(s) from instructions	(g) Amount of adjustment	
2 Totals. Add the amounts in columns (d), (e), (g), and (h) (subtract negative amounts). Enter each total here and include on your Schedule D, **line 1b** (if **Box A** above is checked), **line 2** (if **Box B** above is checked), or **line 3** (if **Box C** above is checked) ▶							

Note: If you checked Box A above but the basis reported to the IRS was incorrect, enter in column (e) the basis as reported to the IRS, and enter an adjustment in column (g) to correct the basis. See *Column (g)* in the separate instructions for how to figure the amount of the adjustment.

For Paperwork Reduction Act Notice, see your tax return instructions.   Cat. No. 37768Z   Form **8949** (2019)

Form 8949 (2019)   Attachment Sequence No. **12A**   Page **2**

Name(s) shown on return. Name and SSN or taxpayer identification no. not required if shown on other side	Social security number or taxpayer identification number

Before you check Box D, E, or F below, see whether you received any Form(s) 1099-B or substitute statement(s) from your broker. A substitute statement will have the same information as Form 1099-B. Either will show whether your basis (usually your cost) was reported to the IRS by your broker and may even tell you which box to check.

Part II   **Long-Term.** Transactions involving capital assets you held more than 1 year are generally long-term (see instructions). For short-term transactions, see page 1.

Note: You may aggregate all long-term transactions reported on Form(s) 1099-B showing basis was reported to the IRS and for which no adjustments or codes are required. Enter the totals directly on Schedule D, line 8a; you aren't required to report these transactions on Form 8949 (see instructions).

You *must* check Box D, E, *or* F below. **Check only one box.** If more than one box applies for your long-term transactions, complete a separate Form 8949, page 2, for each applicable box. If you have more long-term transactions than will fit on this page for one or more of the boxes, complete as many forms with the same box checked as you need.

☐ **(D)** Long-term transactions reported on Form(s) 1099-B showing basis was reported to the IRS (see **Note** above)

☐ **(E)** Long-term transactions reported on Form(s) 1099-B showing basis **wasn't** reported to the IRS

☐ **(F)** Long-term transactions not reported to you on Form 1099-B

1 (a) Description of property (Example: 100 sh. XYZ Co.)	(b) Date acquired (Mo., day, yr.)	(c) Date sold or disposed of (Mo., day, yr.)	(d) Proceeds (sales price) (see instructions)	(e) Cost or other basis. See the **Note** below and see *Column (e)* in the separate instructions	Adjustment, if any, to gain or loss. If you enter an amount in column (g), enter a code in column (f). See the separate instructions. (f) Code(s) from instructions	(g) Amount of adjustment	(h) Gain or (loss). Subtract column (e) from column (d) and combine the result with column (g)
2 Totals. Add the amounts in columns (d), (e), (g), and (h) (subtract negative amounts). Enter each total here and include on your Schedule D, **line 8b** (if **Box D** above is checked), **line 9** (if **Box E** above is checked), or **line 10** (if **Box F** above is checked) ▶							

Note: If you checked Box D above but the basis reported to the IRS was incorrect, enter in column (e) the basis as reported to the IRS, and enter an adjustment in column (g) to correct the basis. See *Column (g)* in the separate instructions for how to figure the amount of the adjustment.

Form **8949** (2019)

SCHEDULE E
(Form 1040 or 1040-SR)

Department of the Treasury
Internal Revenue Service (99)

Supplemental Income and Loss

(From rental real estate, royalties, partnerships, S corporations, estates, trusts, REMICs, etc.)

▶ Attach to Form 1040, 1040-SR, 1040-NR, or 1041.
▶ Go to *www.irs.gov/ScheduleE* for instructions and the latest information.

OMB No. 1545-0074

2019

Attachment
Sequence No. **13**

Name(s) shown on return

Your social security number

Part I   **Income or Loss From Rental Real Estate and Royalties**   **Note:** If you are in the business of renting personal property, use **Schedule C** (see instructions). If you are an individual, report farm rental income or loss from **Form 4835** on page 2, line 40.

A Did you make any payments in 2019 that would require you to file Form(s) 1099? (see instructions) . . . . . ☐ **Yes** ☐ **No**
B If "Yes," did you or will you file required Forms 1099? . . . . ☐ **Yes** ☐ **No**

1a	Physical address of each property (street, city, state, ZIP code)
A	
B	
C	

1b	Type of Property (from list below)	**2**	For each rental real estate property listed above, report the number of fair rental and personal use days. Check the **QJV** box only if you meet the requirements to file as a qualified joint venture. See instructions.		Fair Rental Days	Personal Use Days	QJV
A				**A**			☐
B				**B**			☐
C				**C**			☐

Type of Property:

1 Single Family Residence   3 Vacation/Short-Term Rental   5 Land   7 Self-Rental
2 Multi-Family Residence   4 Commercial   6 Royalties   8 Other (describe)

Income:		Properties:		A	B	C
3	Rents received	**3**				
4	Royalties received	**4**				
Expenses:						
5	Advertising	**5**				
6	Auto and travel (see instructions)	**6**				
7	Cleaning and maintenance	**7**				
8	Commissions.	**8**				
9	Insurance	**9**				
10	Legal and other professional fees	**10**				
11	Management fees	**11**				
12	Mortgage interest paid to banks, etc. (see instructions)	**12**				
13	Other interest.	**13**				
14	Repairs.	**14**				
15	Supplies	**15**				
16	Taxes	**16**				
17	Utilities	**17**				
18	Depreciation expense or depletion	**18**				
19	Other (list) ▶ _____	**19**				
20	Total expenses. Add lines 5 through 19	**20**				
21	Subtract line 20 from line 3 (rents) and/or 4 (royalties). If result is a (loss), see instructions to find out if you must file **Form 6198**	**21**				
22	Deductible rental real estate loss after limitation, if any, on **Form 8582** (see instructions)	**22**	( )	( )	( )	( )

23a	Total of all amounts reported on line 3 for all rental properties	**23a**	
b	Total of all amounts reported on line 4 for all royalty properties	**23b**	
c	Total of all amounts reported on line 12 for all properties	**23c**	
d	Total of all amounts reported on line 18 for all properties	**23d**	
e	Total of all amounts reported on line 20 for all properties	**23e**	

24	**Income.** Add positive amounts shown on line 21. **Do not** include any losses	**24**	
25	**Losses.** Add royalty losses from line 21 and rental real estate losses from line 22. Enter total losses here .	**25**	( )
26	**Total rental real estate and royalty income or (loss).** Combine lines 24 and 25. Enter the result here. If Parts II, III, IV, and line 40 on page 2 do not apply to you, also enter this amount on Schedule 1 (Form 1040 or 1040-SR), line 5, or Form 1040-NR, line 18. Otherwise, include this amount in the total on line 41 on page 2	**26**	

For Paperwork Reduction Act Notice, see the separate instructions.   Cat. No. 11344L   Schedule E (Form 1040 or 1040-SR) 2019

Form **8582**	**Passive Activity Loss Limitations**	OMB No. 1545-1008
Department of the Treasury Internal Revenue Service (99)	▶ See separate instructions. ▶ Attach to Form 1040, Form 1040-SR, or Form 1041. ▶ Go to *www.irs.gov/Form8582* for instructions and the latest information.	**2019** Attachment Sequence No. **88**

Name(s) shown on return | Identifying number

Part I   2019 Passive Activity Loss

Caution: Complete Worksheets 1, 2, and 3 before completing Part I.

Rental Real Estate Activities With Active Participation (For the definition of active participation, see **Special Allowance for Rental Real Estate Activities** in the instructions.)

1a	Activities with net income (enter the amount from Worksheet 1, column (a)) .	**1a**	
b	Activities with net loss (enter the amount from Worksheet 1, column (b)) . .	**1b** ( )	
c	Prior years' unallowed losses (enter the amount from Worksheet 1, column (c))	**1c** ( )	
d	Combine lines 1a, 1b, and 1c		**1d**

Commercial Revitalization Deductions From Rental Real Estate Activities

2a	Commercial revitalization deductions from Worksheet 2, column (a) . . .	**2a** ( )	
b	Prior year unallowed commercial revitalization deductions from Worksheet 2, column (b)	**2b** ( )	
c	Add lines 2a and 2b		**2c** ( )

All Other Passive Activities

3a	Activities with net income (enter the amount from Worksheet 3, column (a)) .	**3a**	
b	Activities with net loss (enter the amount from Worksheet 3, column (b)) . .	**3b** ( )	
c	Prior years' unallowed losses (enter the amount from Worksheet 3, column (c))	**3c** ( )	
d	Combine lines 3a, 3b, and 3c		**3d**

4 Combine lines 1d, 2c, and 3d. If this line is zero or more, stop here and include this form with your return; all losses are allowed, including any prior year unallowed losses entered on line 1c, 2b, or 3c. Report the losses on the forms and schedules normally used . . . . | **4**

If line 4 is a loss and: • Line 1d is a loss, go to Part II.

• Line 2c is a loss (and line 1d is zero or more), skip Part II and go to Part III.

• Line 3d is a loss (and lines 1d and 2c are zero or more), skip Parts II and III and go to line 15.

Caution: If your filing status is married filing separately and you lived with your spouse at any time during the year, **do not** complete Part II or Part III. Instead, go to line 15.

Part II   Special Allowance for Rental Real Estate Activities With Active Participation

Note: Enter all numbers in Part II as positive amounts. See instructions for an example.

5	Enter the **smaller** of the loss on line 1d or the loss on line 4		**5**
6	Enter $150,000. If married filing separately, see instructions	**6**	
7	Enter modified adjusted gross income, but not less than zero. See instructions	**7**	
	Note: If line 7 is greater than or equal to line 6, skip lines 8 and 9, enter -0- on line 10. Otherwise, go to line 8.		
8	Subtract line 7 from line 6	**8**	
9	Multiply line 8 by 50% (0.50). **Do not** enter more than $25,000. If married filing separately, see instructions		**9**
10	Enter the **smaller** of line 5 or line 9		**10**
	If line 2c is a loss, go to Part III. Otherwise, go to line 15.		

Part III   Special Allowance for Commercial Revitalization Deductions From Rental Real Estate Activities

Note: Enter all numbers in Part III as positive amounts. See the example for Part II in the instructions.

11	Enter $25,000 reduced by the amount, if any, on line 10. If married filing separately, see instructions .	**11**	
12	Enter the loss from line 4	**12**	
13	Reduce line 12 by the amount on line 10	**13**	
14	Enter the **smallest** of line 2c (treated as a positive amount), line 11, or line 13	**14**	

Part IV   Total Losses Allowed

15	Add the income, if any, on lines 1a and 3a and enter the total	**15**	
16	**Total losses allowed from all passive activities for 2019.** Add lines 10, 14, and 15. See instructions to find out how to report the losses on your tax return	**16**	

For Paperwork Reduction Act Notice, see instructions.   Cat. No. 63704F   Form **8582** (2019)

Form 1045 (2019)   Page **3**

Schedule A—NOL (see instructions)

1	For individuals, subtract your standard deduction or itemized deductions from your adjusted gross income and enter it here. For estates and trusts, enter taxable income increased by the total of the charitable deduction, income distribution deduction, and exemption amount (see instructions) . .	**1**
2	Nonbusiness capital losses before limitation. Enter as a positive number (see instructions) **2**	
3	Nonbusiness capital gains (without regard to any section 1202 exclusion) **3**	
4	If line 2 is more than line 3, enter the difference. Otherwise, enter -0- . . **4**	
5	If line 3 is more than line 2, enter the difference. Otherwise, enter -0- **5**	
6	Nonbusiness deductions (see instructions) **6**	
7	Nonbusiness income other than capital gains (see instructions) **7**	
8	Add lines 5 and 7 . . . . **8**	
9	If line 6 is more than line 8, enter the difference. Otherwise, enter -0-	**9**
10	If line 8 is more than line 6, enter the difference. Otherwise, enter -0-. **But don't enter more than line 5** **10**	
11	Business capital losses before limitation. Enter as a positive number . . **11**	
12	Business capital gains (without regard to any section 1202 exclusion) **12**	
13	Add lines 10 and 12 . . . . **13**	
14	Subtract line 13 from line 11. If zero or less, enter -0- **14**	
15	Add lines 4 and 14 . . . . **15**	
16	Enter the loss, if any, from line 16 of your 2019 Schedule D (Form 1040 or 1040-SR). (For estates and trusts, enter the loss, if any, from line 19, column (3), of Schedule D (Form 1041).) Enter as a positive number. If you don't have a loss on that line (and don't have a section 1202 exclusion), skip lines 16 through 21 and enter on line 22 the amount from line 15 . . **16**	
17	Section 1202 exclusion. Enter as a positive number (see instructions)	**17**
18	Subtract line 17 from line 16. If zero or less, enter -0- **18**	
19	Enter the loss, if any, from line 21 of your 2019 Schedule D (Form 1040 or 1040-SR). (For estates and trusts, enter the loss, if any, from line 20 of Schedule D (Form 1041).) Enter as a positive number **19**	
20	If line 18 is more than line 19, enter the difference. Otherwise, enter -0- . **20**	
21	If line 19 is more than line 18, enter the difference. Otherwise, enter -0- .	**21**
22	Subtract line 20 from line 15. If zero or less, enter -0-	**22**
23	Domestic production activities deduction from your 2019 return (see instructions) . . .	**23**
24	NOL deduction for losses from other years. Enter as a positive number	**24**
25	**NOL.** Combine lines 1, 9, 17, and 21 through 24. If the result is less than zero, enter it here and on page 1, line 1a. If the result is zero or more, you **don't** have an NOL	**25**

Form **1045** (2019)

Qualified Dividends and Capital Gain Tax Worksheet—Line 12a

Before you begin:	✓ See the earlier instructions for line 12a to see if you can use this worksheet to figure your tax.
	✓ Before completing this worksheet, complete Form 1040 or 1040-SR through line 11b.
	✓ If you don't have to file Schedule D and you received capital gain distributions, be sure you checked the box on Form 1040 or 1040-SR, line 6.

1. Enter the amount from Form 1040 or 1040-SR, line 11b. However, if you are filing Form 2555 (relating to foreign earned income), enter the amount from line 3 of the Foreign Earned Income Tax Worksheet .... **1.** _____

2. Enter the amount from Form 1040 or 1040-SR, line 3a* .... **2.** _____

3. Are you filing Schedule D?*

    ☐ **Yes.** Enter the **smaller** of line 15 or 16 of Schedule D. If either line 15 or 16 is blank or a loss, enter -0-.

    ☐ **No.** Enter the amount from Form 1040 or 1040-SR, line 6. **3.** _____

4. Add lines 2 and 3 .... **4.** _____

5. If filing Form 4952 (used to figure investment interest expense deduction), enter any amount from line 4g of that form. Otherwise, enter -0- .... **5.** _____

6. Subtract line 5 from line 4. If zero or less, enter -0- .... **6.** _____

7. Subtract line 6 from line 1. If zero or less, enter -0- .... **7.** _____

8. Enter:

    $39,375 if single or married filing separately,
    $78,750 if married filing jointly or qualifying widow(er),
    $52,750 if head of household. .... **8.** _____

9. Enter the smaller of line 1 or line 8 .... **9.** _____

10. Enter the smaller of line 7 or line 9 .... **10.** _____

11. Subtract line 10 from line 9. This amount is taxed at 0% .... **11.** _____

12. Enter the smaller of line 1 or line 6 .... **12.** _____

13. Enter the amount from line 11 .... **13.** _____

14. Subtract line 13 from line 12 .... **14.** _____

15. Enter:

    $434,550 if single,
    $244,425 if married filing separately,
    $488,850 if married filing jointly or qualifying widow(er),
    $461,700 if head of household. .... **15.** _____

16. Enter the smaller of line 1 or line 15 .... **16.** _____

17. Add lines 7 and 11 .... **17.** _____

18. Subtract line 17 from line 16. If zero or less, enter -0- .... **18.** _____

19. Enter the smaller of line 14 or line 18 .... **19.** _____

20. Multiply line 19 by 15% (0.15) .... **20.** _____

21. Add lines 11 and 19 .... **21.** _____

22. Subtract line 21 from line 12 .... **22.** _____

23. Multiply line 22 by 20% (0.20) .... **23.** _____

24. Figure the tax on the amount on line 7. If the amount on line 7 is less than $100,000, use the Tax Table to figure the tax. If the amount on line 7 is $100,000 or more, use the Tax Computation Worksheet .... **24.** _____

25. Add lines 20, 23, and 24 .... **25.** _____

26. Figure the tax on the amount on line 1. If the amount on line 1 is less than $100,000, use the Tax Table to figure the tax. If the amount on line 1 is $100,000 or more, use the Tax Computation Worksheet .... **26.** _____

27. **Tax on all taxable income.** Enter the **smaller** of line 25 or 26. Also include this amount on the entry space on Form 1040 or 1040-SR, line 12a. If you are filing Form 2555, don't enter this amount on the entry space on Form 1040 or 1040-SR, line 12a. Instead, enter it on line 4 of the Foreign Earned Income Tax Worksheet .... **27.** _____

If you are filing Form 2555, see the footnote in the Foreign Earned Income Tax Worksheet before completing this line.

Student Name _____

Class/Section _____

Date   _____

KEY NUMBER TAX RETURN SUMMARY

CHAPTER 4

Comprehensive Problem 1

Capital Gain or (Loss) (Line 6) _____

Rental Real Estate (Schedule 1, Line 5) _____

Adjusted Gross Income (Line 8b) _____

Total Tax (Line 16) _____

Amount Overpaid (Line 20) _____

Comprehensive Problem 2A

Rental Real Estate (Schedule 1, Line 5) _____

Adjusted Gross Income (Line 8b) _____

Total Tax (Line 16) _____

Amount Overpaid (Line 20) _____

Comprehensive Problem 2B

Capital Gain or (Loss) (Line 6) _____

Rental Real Estate (Schedule 1, Line 5) _____

Adjusted Gross Income (Line 8b) _____

Total Tax (Line 16) _____

Net Operating Loss (Form 1045, Schedule A, Line 25) _____

Deductions For and From AGI

After completing this chapter, you should be able to:

LO 5.1   Explain how Health Savings Accounts (HSAs) can be used for tax-advantaged medical care.

LO 5.2   Describe the self-employed health insurance deduction.

LO 5.3   Explain the treatment of Individual Retirement Accounts (IRAs), including Roth IRAs.

LO 5.4   Explain the general contribution rules for small business and self-employed retirement plans.

LO 5.5   Describe other adjustments for adjusted gross income.

LO 5.6   Calculate the itemized deduction for medical expenses.

LO 5.7   Calculate the itemized deduction for taxes.

LO 5.8   Apply the rules for an individual taxpayer's interest deduction.

LO 5.9   Determine the charitable contributions deduction.

LO 5.10   Describe other itemized deductions.

OVERVIEW

Deductions related to a business (for example, Schedule C in Chapter 3) or the production of income or investment (for example, Schedules D and E in Chapter 4) represent deductions that are for AGI (above the line). The business deductions are generally reported on the separate schedules. However, the tax law permits additional for AGI deductions that may be associated with business activity or, in some instances like the student loan interest deduction, as simply a matter of legislative grace for individual taxpayers. These additional deductions are now reported on the bottom half of Schedule 1 of the Form 1040 and include one-half of self-employment taxes, deductible contributions to an individual retirement account, and others.

Deductions that occur after AGI (from AGI deductions) include the standard deduction discussed in Chapter 1. Chapter 5 will also introduce Schedule A itemized deductions. Itemized deductions fall into six categories: medical and dental expenses, state and local taxes, interest expenses, charitable contributions, casualty and theft losses, and miscellaneous deductions.

Recall from Chapter 1, that when calculating taxable income, individuals determine their standard deduction and their allowable itemized deductions and use the larger of the two. For example, if a taxpayer's standard deduction is $12,200 and her itemized deductions are $18,100, she would use her itemized deductions in calculating taxable income. On the other hand, if her itemized deductions were $9,500, she would use the larger standard deduction of $12,200 in computing taxable income.

Starting in 2018, a number of limitations were placed on itemized deductions. One example is the $10,000 limit on state and local taxes. For federal budget reasons, many of these limitations only suspend, rather than repeal the deduction. The suspensions are largely scheduled to end after 2025. As a result, brief explanations of the pre-limitation deductions are provided.

5-1 HEALTH SAVINGS ACCOUNTS

Explain how Health Savings Accounts (HSAs) can be used for tax-advantaged medical care.

There are four types of tax-favored medical spending plans available to taxpayers:

1. Health care flexible spending arrangements or FSAs (covered in Chapter 2) in which employees can set aside money to cover medical expenses and exclude the funds from gross income.
2. Health Reimbursements Arrangements (HRAs) in which the employer funds an account that may be used by employees for medical expenses (these do not generally affect an individual taxpayer's taxable income and thus are not covered in detail in this textbook).
3. Medical Savings Accounts (MSAs or Archer MSAs) which permit (limited) deductions for amounts contributed to an account established to cover medical expenses for small business and self-employed individuals. Effective January 1, 2008, no new MSA accounts may be established and thus these are not covered in detail in this textbook. Note that an Archer MSA can be rolled over into an HSA.
4. Health Savings Accounts (HSAs) are a type of savings account which may be established for the purpose of paying unreimbursed medical expenses by taxpayers who carry qualifying high-deductible medical insurance.

Contributions to HSAs are a deduction for AGI and are limited to certain dollar amounts depending on age and whether the high-deductible insurance covers an individual or a family. Earnings and unused contributions accumulated in an HSA are not taxed, and distributions to cover medical expenses are not taxed or penalized.

Health insurance with a high deductible is less expensive than standard health insurance since the issuing insurance company does not have to pay any of the taxpayer's medical expenses until a certain threshold (the deductible plus any other required out-of-pocket medical costs) is reached. The funds contributed to the HSA may then be used by the taxpayer to pay medical expenses not covered by health insurance. This popular combination of tax benefits and less expensive insurance is designed to encourage taxpayers to carry health insurance.

5-1a Deductions for Contributions to HSAs

The following table shows the contribution limits for HSA deductions for 2019. The table also shows the additional "catch-up" contributions allowed for individuals beginning at age 55 and ending at age 65, the age for Medicare eligibility. Individuals are not allowed to make contributions to HSAs once they attain the age of 65 and qualify for Medicare coverage. Finally, the table shows the lower and upper deductible and out-of-pocket medical expense limits (excluding the actual cost of insurance) required for insurance to qualify as a high-deductible health plan.

2019 Limits for HSAs		
	Family	*Self-Only*
Contribution limit	$ 7,000	$ 3,500
Additional catch-up contribution for taxpayer age 55 or older	1,000 per qualifying spouse	1,000
Minimum health insurance deductible	2,700	1,350
Maximum health insurance out-of-pocket	13,500	6,750

Although the out-of-pocket limits under the Affordable Care Act (ACA) are slightly higher than those listed above, the IRS limits determine tax compliance for HSAs. Contributions to HSAs must generally be made by April 15 of the year following the year for which the contribution is made. IRS Form 8889 is used to provide information to the IRS regarding HSA deductions claimed on Line 12 of Schedule 1 of Form 1040 and to compute the deduction amount.

EXAMPLE   Gary is 35 years old and carries self-only coverage in a qualifying high-deductible health insurance plan during 2019. Gary may contribute up to $3,500 to his HSA account and deduct this amount for AGI. Gary may use some or all of the contribution to pay medical expenses he has incurred. Any amount he leaves in the HSA account will accumulate earnings tax free and carry forward to be used for qualifying medical expenses in the future. ♦

5-1b Distributions

Distributions from HSAs are free of tax when used to pay for qualified medical expenses. Distributions which are not used to pay for qualified medical expenses are subject to both income tax and a 20 percent penalty. Once a taxpayer is 65 years old, distributions may be taken for nonmedical expenses and will be subject to income tax, but not the 20 percent penalty. Distributions from an HSA are reported on Form 1099-SA (see Self-Study Problem 5.1). The amount of the distribution is reported in Box 1 and codes indicating the proper treatment are provided in Box 3. A normal distribution is coded 1.

To report HSA information and complete a Form 8889, the input area can be found in the left-hand margin under Deductions/Adjustments to Income. The input area is conveniently called Health Savings Account (Form 8889).

intuit
proconnect

TIP

EXAMPLE   Debbie is 66 years old and has $30,000 in her HSA. She can withdraw the $30,000 to purchase a new car, but will have to pay income tax on the distribution. If she takes the distribution to pay medical expenses, no income tax will be due. If Debbie were 55 years old and took a distribution from her HSA to buy a car, she would owe both income tax and a 20 percent penalty on the distribution. ◆

5-1c Guidance

The rules governing HSAs are more detailed and lengthy than the summaries above. IRS Publication 969 is a good source of information on a range of additional issues related to HSAs and their operation.

Self-Study Problem 5.1   *See Appendix E for Solutions to Self-Study Problems*

a. Give the deductible HSA amount for each of the following taxpayers for 2019:

   1. Amy is 40 years old, has a qualifying high-deductible health plan, carries family coverage, and contributes the maximum amount to her family HSA. Deductible HSA amount: $_____

   2. Cary is 60 years old, has self-only health insurance with no deductible, and contributes $1,200 to an HSA. Deductible HSA amount: $_____

   3. Annabelle is 52 years old and contributes $2,000 to her HSA. She has qualifying self-only coverage in a high-deductible health plan. Deductible HSA amount: $_____

   4. Lucille is 70 years old and is covered by Medicare. She contributes $3,050 to her HSA. Deductible HSA amount: $_____

b. Alex Morton is a single taxpayer, age 34. She is part of a qualifying high-deductible health plan. In 2019, Alex made contributions of $2,700 to her HSA. Alex's employer reported making $300 of contributions to her HSA in Box 12 of her Form W-2 (code W). Alex spent $2,500 on qualified medical expenses. Alex received the following Form 1099-SA from her HSA administrator:

☐ CORRECTED (if checked)		

TRUSTEE'S/PAYER'S name, street address, city or town, state or province, country, ZIP or foreign postal code, and telephone number Heritage Health Partners PO Box 12345 Dallas, TX 75621		OMB No. 1545-1517 20**19** Form **1099-SA**	**Distributions From an HSA, Archer MSA, or Medicare Advantage MSA**
PAYER'S TIN 13-0080072	**RECIPIENT'S TIN** 213-21-3121	**1** Gross distribution $ 1,783.00	**2** Earnings on excess cont. $	**Copy B** **For**
RECIPIENT'S name Alex Morton		**3** Distribution code 1	**4** FMV on date of death $	**Recipient**
Street address (including apt. no.) 1921 S. Orange Ave.		**5** HSA ☒ Archer ☐ MSA		
City or town, state or province, country, and ZIP or foreign postal code Orlando, FL 32806		MA ☐ MSA		This information is being furnished to the IRS.
Account number (see instructions)				

Form **1099-SA**   (keep for your records)   www.irs.gov/Form1099SA   Department of the Treasury - Internal Revenue Service

Prepare Form 8889 (page 1 only) on Page 5-5 to determine Alex's HSA deduction and taxable HSA distribution.

Self-Study Problem 5.1

Form **8889**	**Health Savings Accounts (HSAs)**	OMB No. 1545-0074
Department of the Treasury Internal Revenue Service	▶ Attach to Form 1040, 1040-SR, or 1040-NR. ▶ Go to *www.irs.gov/Form8889* for instructions and the latest information.	**2019** Attachment Sequence No. **52**

Name(s) shown on Form 1040, 1040-SR, or 1040-NR	Social security number of HSA beneficiary. If both spouses have HSAs, see instructions ▶

Before you begin: Complete Form 8853, Archer MSAs and Long-Term Care Insurance Contracts, if required.

Part I   HSA Contributions and Deduction. See the instructions before completing this part. If you are filing jointly and both you and your spouse each have separate HSAs, complete a separate Part I for each spouse.

1	Check the box to indicate your coverage under a high-deductible health plan (HDHP) during 2019 (see instructions) . . . . ▶	☐ Self-only ☐ Family	
2	HSA contributions you made for 2019 (or those made on your behalf), including those made from January 1, 2020, through April 15, 2020, that were for 2019. **Do not** include employer contributions, contributions through a cafeteria plan, or rollovers (see instructions)	**2**	
3	If you were under age 55 at the end of 2019 and, on the first day of **every** month during 2019, you were, or were considered, an eligible individual with the **same** coverage, enter $3,500 ($7,000 for family coverage). **All others,** see the instructions for the amount to enter	**3**	
4	Enter the amount you and your employer contributed to your Archer MSAs for 2019 from Form 8853, lines 1 and 2. If you or your spouse had family coverage under an HDHP at any time during 2019, also include any amount contributed to your spouse's Archer MSAs	**4**	
5	Subtract line 4 from line 3. If zero or less, enter -0-	**5**	
6	Enter the amount from line 5. But if you and your spouse each have separate HSAs and had family coverage under an HDHP at any time during 2019, see the instructions for the amount to enter . .	**6**	
7	If you were age 55 or older at the end of 2019, married, and you or your spouse had family coverage under an HDHP at any time during 2019, enter your additional contribution amount (see instructions)	**7**	
8	Add lines 6 and 7	**8**	
9	Employer contributions made to your HSAs for 2019	**9**	
10	Qualified HSA funding distributions	**10**	
11	Add lines 9 and 10	**11**	
12	Subtract line 11 from line 8. If zero or less, enter -0-	**12**	
13	**HSA deduction.** Enter the **smaller** of line 2 or line 12 here and on Schedule 1 (Form 1040 or 1040-SR), line 12, or Form 1040-NR, line 25	**13**	
	Caution: If line 2 is more than line 13, you may have to pay an additional tax (see instructions).		

Part II   HSA Distributions. If you are filing jointly and both you and your spouse each have separate HSAs, complete a separate Part II for each spouse.

14a	Total distributions you received in 2019 from all HSAs (see instructions)	**14a**	
b	Distributions included on line 14a that you rolled over to another HSA. Also include any excess contributions (and the earnings on those excess contributions) included on line 14a that were withdrawn by the due date of your return (see instructions)	**14b**	
c	Subtract line 14b from line 14a	**14c**	
15	Qualified medical expenses paid using HSA distributions (see instructions)	**15**	
16	**Taxable HSA distributions.** Subtract line 15 from line 14c. If zero or less, enter -0-. Also, include this amount in the total on Schedule 1 (Form 1040 or 1040-SR), line 8, or Form 1040-NR, line 21. Enter "HSA" and the amount on the line next to the box	**16**	
17a	If any of the distributions included on line 16 meet any of the **Exceptions to the Additional 20% Tax** (see instructions), check here . . . . ▶ ☐		
b	**Additional 20% tax** (see instructions). Enter 20% (0.20) of the distributions included on line 16 that are subject to the additional 20% tax. Also include this amount in the total on Schedule 2 (Form 1040 or 1040-SR), line 8, or Form 1040-NR, line 60. Check box c on Schedule 2 (Form 1040 or 1040-SR), line 8, or box b on Form 1040-NR, line 60. Enter "HSA" and the amount on the line next to the box .	**17b**	

For Paperwork Reduction Act Notice, see your tax return instructions.   Cat. No. 37621P   Form **8889** (2019)

5-2 SELF-EMPLOYED HEALTH INSURANCE DEDUCTION

Self-employed taxpayers are allowed an above-the-line deduction for the cost of providing health insurance for themselves and their families. This deduction is meant to give self-employed taxpayers the same tax treatment available to employees who are offered health insurance as a tax-free benefit of employment. Deductible insurance includes the following:

- Medical and dental insurance paid to cover the self-employed taxpayer, spouse, and dependents;
- Medical and dental insurance paid for children under the age of 27 who are not dependents;
- Medicare premiums;
- Long-term care insurance paid for the taxpayer and the family of the taxpayer, within certain dollar limitations shown below.

EXAMPLE Joe has a barbershop and earns $60,000 in 2019 which he reports on Schedule C. Joe pays $10,000 in health and dental insurance costs for himself, his unemployed wife, and his 10-year-old daughter. The full $10,000 is a deduction for Joe's AGI. ♦

5-2a Special Rules

The following special rules limit the treatment of health insurance as a deduction for AGI:

- Other Health Care Plan Available: The self-employed health insurance deduction is not allowed for any months in which the taxpayer is eligible to participate in a subsidized health care plan offered by an employer of either the taxpayer or the spouse of the taxpayer.
- Earned Income Limitation: The deduction for self-employed health insurance is only allowed to the extent of the taxpayer's net self-employed earned income. For example, a taxpayer with a Schedule C business loss would not be allowed to claim a self-employed health insurance deduction even though he or she paid for health insurance. The deduction would instead be allowed as an itemized medical deduction subject to the limits discussed in LO 5.6.
- Long-Term Care Premium Limitation: The individual limitations on the deduction of long-term care premiums are as follows:

Attained Age Before the Close of the Taxable Year	2019 Limitation on Premiums
40 or less	$ 420
More than 40 but not more than 50	790
More than 50 but not more than 60	1,580
More than 60 but not more than 70	4,220
More than 70	5,270

- Definition of Self-Employment: Taxpayers with income reportable on Schedule C are generally considered self-employed. However, taxpayers with earnings from certain partnerships, S corporations, LLCs, and farm businesses may also be considered self-employed and may be allowed the above-the-line deduction for self-employed health insurance. Taxpayers with income from these sources sometimes present more complex health insurance deduction issues which should be researched as they appear.
- Deductible Portion: Self-employed taxpayers that receive advance premium tax credits under the ACA may deduct only the portion paid out of pocket, not the portion covered by the premium tax credit.

TIP

To enter self-employed health insurance and many of the other for-AGI deductions, go to Deductions/Adjustments to Income. There is a long input page, and a number of subheadings are available in the left-hand margin.

EXAMPLE   Candace is a 55-year-old massage therapist who earns $40,000 of net self-employment income in 2019. She pays $6,000 for medical insurance and $1,600 for long-term care insurance. Candace can take $7,580 ($6,000 + $1,580) as a deduction for AGI. ♦

Self-Study Problem 5.2   *See Appendix E for Solutions to Self-Study Problems*

During the 2019 tax year, Gwen supports her family as a physical therapist. She reports $90,000 of earned income on her Schedule C and paid the following insurance premiums:

- Family health insurance: $15,000
- Family dental insurance: $2,000
- Health insurance for her 24-year-old son who is not a dependent: $3,000
- Long-term care insurance for her 49-year-old husband: $800

What is Gwen's self-employed health insurance deduction for 2019? $_____

Learning Objective 5.3

Explain the treatment of Individual Retirement Accounts (IRAs), including Roth IRAs.

5-3 INDIVIDUAL RETIREMENT ACCOUNTS

There are two principal types of IRAs in the United States. One is the *traditional IRA* and the other is the *Roth IRA*. Generally, annual contributions to a traditional IRA are deductible, and retirement distributions are taxable. Annual contributions to a Roth IRA are not deductible, but retirement distributions are nontaxable. Earnings in both types of IRAs are not taxable in the current year.

EXAMPLE   Gene has $30,000 in his IRA in 2019. The earnings for the year on this IRA are $1,600. These earnings are not taxed to Gene in the current year. ♦

5-3a IRA Annual Contributions

There are annual contribution limits for both traditional and Roth IRAs. In 2019, the maximum annual contribution that may be made to either type of IRA is equal to the lesser of (1) 100 percent of the taxpayer's compensation or self-employment income (earned income) or (2) $6,000 (or $12,000 if an additional $6,000 is contributed to a spouse's IRA, and the spouse has no earned income). The maximum contribution to a spouse's IRA may not exceed $6,000. In 2019, an additional $1,000 annual "catch-up" contribution is allowed for taxpayers and spouses age 50 and over, increasing the maximum contribution to $7,000.

EXAMPLE   Quincy, age 31, works for Big Corporation and has a salary of $40,000 for 2019. Quincy is eligible to contribute the maximum $6,000 to his traditional or Roth IRA for 2019. If Quincy has a spouse who does not work, he could also contribute $6,000 into her IRA or Roth IRA. If Quincy is 55 years old instead of 31 years old, he could contribute $7,000 to his traditional or Roth IRA, and $6,000 or $7,000 for his spouse, depending on whether she is old enough to qualify for the $1,000 "catch-up" contribution. ♦

The IRA limitation calculations discussed below are quite complex and change every year. Most taxpayers and tax preparers use tax software to assist them in calculating allowable IRA deductions. It is a standard belief in the tax community that computer software has paved the way for the enormous complexity we see in today's tax law. Although it is important to understand the rules for calculating IRA contributions, please take solace in the fact that these calculations, as well as many others shown in this textbook, are not often done by hand in practice.

TAX BREAK

The annual deduction maximums above are reduced for traditional IRAs if the taxpayer is an active participant in another qualified retirement plan. The annual contribution allowed for a Roth IRA is reduced for all taxpayers over certain income levels, but is not affected by whether the taxpayer or spouse is an active participant in another retirement plan. In each case, the maximum annual contribution is phased out proportionately between certain adjusted gross income ranges, as shown below.

2019 AGI Phase-Out Ranges for Roth IRA Contributions	
Filing Status	*AGI Phase-Out Range*
Single or HOH	$122,000–$137,000
Married, Joint	$193,000–$203,000
Note: Active plan participation status is not relevant to the Roth IRA phase-out calculation. Special rules apply to married filing separate taxpayers.	

2019 AGI Phase-Out Ranges for Deductible Traditional IRA Contributions	
Type of Taxpayer	*Phase-Out Range*
Single or HOH, not a plan participant	No phase-out
Single or HOH, active plan participant	$64,000–$74,000
Married, Joint, both active participants	$103,000–$123,000
Married, Joint, neither active plan participants	No phase-out
Married, Joint, one an active participant:	(See Note 1 below)
Active participant spouse	$103,000–$123,000 (Joint AGI)
Nonactive participant spouse	$193,000–$203,000 (Joint AGI)
Note 1: When one spouse is an active participant in a retirement plan and the other is not, two separate income limitations apply. The active participant spouse may make a full deductible IRA contribution unless the $103,000–$123,000 phase-out range applies to the couple's joint income. The spouse who is not an active participant may make a full deductible IRA contribution unless the higher $193,000–$203,000 phase-out range applies to the couple's joint income.	

If a taxpayer contributes to both a traditional IRA and a Roth IRA, the combined contributions cannot exceed the normal annual limit ($6,000 or $7,000 if age 50 or older in 2019).

A nondeductible traditional IRA contribution may be made by taxpayers with income over the phase-out ranges shown above. Although the taxpayer cannot deduct the contribution, all income earned in the IRA account is sheltered from tax until the earnings are withdrawn. When there have been nondeductible IRA contributions, the calculation of the taxable portion of the withdrawn IRA money is calculated similar to the treatment of annuities discussed in Chapter 2. Many high-income taxpayers make nondeductible traditional IRA contributions each year because of the deferral of tax on the earnings of the IRA.

EXAMPLE Ed, age 31, is single and is covered by a retirement plan. If his modified adjusted gross income is $68,000, Ed's maximum deductible traditional IRA contribution is $3,600. With income of $68,000, his $6,000 contribution is proportionately phased out by dividing the amount remaining in his phase-out range, $74,000 − $68,000, or $6,000, by the $10,000 phase-out range (the difference between the bottom and top of the $64,000 and $74,000 phase-out range) and multiplying this by the $6,000 maximum IRA deduction as follows:

$$\frac{(\$74,000 - \$68,000)}{\$10,000} \times \$6,000 = \$3,600 \text{ allowed IRA deduction}$$

Ed may choose to contribute the $6,000 maximum to a traditional IRA, but the remaining $2,400 will not be deductible. Alternatively, he may contribute the remaining $2,400 to a Roth IRA since his income is below the phase-out range for Roth IRA contributions. He could also choose to ignore the allowed traditional IRA contribution and contribute the full $6,000 to a Roth IRA. In any event, he cannot contribute more than $6,000 in total to IRAs, and his maximum allowed tax deduction for a traditional IRA contribution will be $3,600. ◆

EXAMPLE Ann, who is 36 and single, would like to contribute $6,000 to her Roth IRA. However, her AGI is $125,000, so her contribution is limited to $4,800 calculated as follows:

$$\frac{(\$137,000 - \$125,000)}{\$15,000} \times \$6,000 = \$4,800 \text{ allowed Roth IRA}$$

The $15,000 denominator in the calculation above is the amount of the phase-out range between $122,000 and $137,000. If she were 50 or older and wanted to contribute $7,000, her contribution would be limited to $5,600. ◆

EXAMPLE Paul and Lucy are married and are both 36 years old. Lucy is covered by a retirement plan and earns $64,000. Paul is not covered by a retirement plan and earns $60,000. Lucy cannot make a deductible contribution to a traditional IRA since the income on their joint tax return is greater than the $123,000 maximum phase-out range for married couples. Paul, however, can make a fully deductible IRA contribution of $6,000 since Paul and Lucy's AGI is below the $193,000–$203,000 phase-out range used when one spouse is an active participant in a plan and the other is not. Lucy could still choose to make a $6,000 contribution to a Roth IRA since their joint income is below the Roth IRA phase-out range for married couples. Paul would have a choice between making a $6,000 deductible contribution to a traditional IRA or a contribution of $6,000 to a Roth IRA or some combination thereof, not greater than $6,000. ◆

An IRA contribution may be made at any time before the original due date of the tax return for the year in which the deduction is to be claimed. This means, for example, that an individual can contribute to an IRA as late as the filing deadline of April 15, 2020, and still deduct the amount on the 2019 tax return.

5-3b Roth IRA Conversions

Taxpayers may benefit from a rule allowing conversions of traditional IRAs into Roth IRAs. Although the income generated by the conversion is subject to current income tax, taxpayers with certain factors in their favor such as many years to retirement, a low current tax bracket, or a high expected tax bracket in retirement may wish to convert. Also, taxpayers with negative taxable income due to large personal deductions may wish to convert enough of their regular IRAs to Roth IRAs to bring taxable income to zero. This way the conversion can be done with no tax cost since deductions which would otherwise be lost are used to offset the taxable IRA income.

For tax years 2010 and beyond, a rule that required taxpayers to have $100,000 or less in AGI to convert regular IRA accounts to Roth IRA accounts was eliminated. Congress expects that many high-income taxpayers will take advantage of this opportunity and pay income tax due up-front on conversions.

5-3c Traditional IRA Distributions

Money removed from a traditional IRA is taxable as ordinary income and may be subject to a 10 percent penalty for early withdrawal. To avoid the 10 percent penalty, distributions from an IRA generally cannot begin before age 59½. However, penalty-free withdrawals from IRAs may be made by taxpayers under age 59½ who are:

1. Disabled
2. Using a special level payment option
3. Using the withdrawals for unreimbursed medical expenses in excess of 10 percent of their AGI
4. The recipients of at least 12 weeks of unemployment compensation and to the extent they are paying medical insurance premiums for their dependents
5. Paying the costs of higher education, including tuition, fees, books, and room and board for the taxpayers or their spouses, children, or grandchildren
6. Withdrawing up to $10,000 for first-time home-buying expenses
7. Beneficiaries due to the death of the IRA owner
8. Withdrawing funds due to an IRS levy
9. A qualified reservist

While withdrawals made by these taxpayers are penalty free, they are still subject to income taxes. Also, taxpayers must start taking minimum annual distributions from their IRA at age 70½. The IRS provides tables for calculating the required minimum annual distributions based on the taxpayer's life expectancy.

EXAMPLE Tomas is 48 years old and has a midlife crisis and decides he must have a red sports car. He withdraws $35,000 from his traditional IRA to purchase the car. Tomas does not qualify for any of the penalty-free withdrawals listed earlier. The $35,000 is taxable to Tomas as ordinary income and he is subject to a $3,500 (10% × $35,000) penalty for removing the funds before age 59½. ◆

5-3d Roth IRA Distributions

A taxpayer can make tax-free withdrawals from a Roth IRA after a 5-year holding period if any of the following requirements are satisfied:

1. The distribution is made on or after the date on which the participant attains age 59½.
2. The distribution is made to a beneficiary (or the participant's estate) on or after the participant's death.
3. The participant becomes disabled.
4. The distribution is used to pay for qualified first-time home-buyer's expenses.

EXAMPLE Bob establishes a Roth IRA at age 50 and contributes to the Roth each year for 10 years. The account is now worth $61,000, consisting of $35,000 of nondeductible contributions and $26,000 in earnings that have not been taxed. Bob may withdraw the $61,000 tax-free from the Roth IRA because he is over age 59½ and has met the 5-year holding period requirement. ♦

The distributions may be taxable if the taxpayer receives distributions from a Roth IRA and does not satisfy the above requirements. The part of the distributions that represents a return of capital is tax free, and the part that represents a payout of earnings is taxable. Under the ordering rules for Roth IRA distributions, distributions are treated as first made from contributions (return of capital) and then from earnings.

EXAMPLE Assume the same facts in the previous example, except that Bob is only age 56 and receives distributions of $10,000. Assume his adjusted basis for the Roth IRA is $12,000 (contributions made of $2,000 × 6 years). The distribution is tax free and his adjusted basis is reduced to $2,000 ($12,000 − $10,000). ♦

TAX BREAK   A gift to a Roth IRA for a child or grandchild with a summer job can grow into a very large gift over time. The amount that may be contributed to a child's Roth IRA is the lesser of $6,000 or the child's earnings. A child with $6,000 in a Roth IRA at age 16 will have well over $100,000 at age 65 if the Roth IRA investment earns 7 percent annually.

Self-Study Problem 5.3   *See Appendix E for Solutions to Self-Study Problems*

a. During 2019, George (a 24-year-old single taxpayer) has a salary of $46,000, dividend income of $14,000, and interest income of $4,000. In addition, he has rental income of $1,000. George is covered by a qualified retirement plan. Calculate the maximum regular IRA deduction that George is allowed.

$_____

b. During 2019, Irene (a single taxpayer, under age 50) has a salary of $115,500 and dividend income of $10,000. Calculate Irene's maximum contribution to a Roth IRA.

$_____

5-4 SMALL BUSINESS AND SELF-EMPLOYED RETIREMENT PLANS

The tax law provides employees, employers, and the self-employed with an incentive to plan for retirement through qualified retirement plans. Under the tax law, favorable tax treatment is granted to contributions, by or for employees, to qualified retirement plans. Employers may claim a deduction in the current year for contributions to qualified retirement plans on the employees' behalf, while the employees do not include the employer contributions in income until the contributed amounts are distributed (generally during their retirement years). Tax on earnings on the amounts contributed to the plan is also deferred. This deferral of income taxation is a significant benefit to most taxpayers.

EXAMPLE In the current year, Polly's employer makes a $2,000 contribution to a qualified plan for Polly's retirement. The $2,000 is deductible to the employer in the current year and is not taxable to Polly until she withdraws the money from the plan. Any earnings on the money contributed to the plan are also taxable only upon withdrawal from the plan (usually many years later). ◆

The tax code provides for a number of different types of plans for taxpayers to save for retirement. Most retirement plans have a number of requirements in order to be classified as "qualified" and thus extend the tax benefits described previously:

- Funding requirements: Most require that the benefit be extended to all employees and not favor only the highly compensated (nondiscriminatory)
- Fiduciary responsibility: Most require a separate account to hold the retirement assets, typically handled by a bank or financial institution
- Early withdrawals: Most penalize or prohibit early distributions from the plan with limited hardship exceptions
- Vesting requirement: Some require immediate "vesting" of contributions (i.e., the contributions are immediately set aside for an employee and will not be returned to the employer even if the employee leaves)

The retirement plan area has become one of the most complex areas of the tax law. Many tax accountants refer taxpayers to a specialist for help in choosing a plan and for guidance through the ongoing employee coverage, tax reporting, and contribution requirements. The coverage in this textbook is meant to give a simple overview of several common options available to taxpayers for tax-deferred retirement plans, which remain one of the best completely legal tax shelters available. Retirement plans for small businesses are covered here while large plans, which are generally operated by larger employers, are covered in Chapter 9.

5-4a Self-Employed and Small Business Retirement Plan Options

Although available to small businesses, complex retirement plans such as defined-benefit plans or employee stock ownership plans are generally used by only large companies due to their complexity and cost to operate (see Chapter 9). However, over time, the tax law has created a number of retirement plans directed at the small business owner or even a self-employed sole proprietor.

5-4b SEP or SEP IRA, SIMPLE IRA, and Payroll Deduction IRA

A Simplified Employee Pension (SEP or SEP IRA) is a retirement plan available to any employer (including a self-employed individual). These plans are simple to set up–the IRS even provides a one-page Form 5305-SEP that can be used. SEPs have flexible funding requirements in case funding the plan with consistent contribution amounts might be an issue for the underlying business. The amount of contributions can change from year-to-year and can be zero. Participants in SEPs must meet requirements for minimum age and years of service. An employer *must* cover employees if the employees meet the requirements for coverage.

SEP contributions and deductions are limited under different rules for employees versus the self-employed business owner. The maximum contribution made for an employee and the related deduction cannot exceed the lesser of 25 percent of the employee's compensation or $56,000 in 2019. For the self-employed business owner, the contribution maximum is the same as for employees; however, the deduction limit considers the net self-employment income after consideration of the deduction for the contribution to the SEP. As a result, the deduction available for the self-employed will be slightly lower than that of an employee and is derived by taking the plan contribution rate and dividing by one plus the contribution rate; thus effectively lowering the maximum contribution rate to 20 percent (0.25 ÷ 1.25).

EXAMPLE   Dan is a self-employed doctor. His net earned income (Schedule C net income less one-half of self-employment tax) from his practice is $125,000. Under the terms of his SEP plan, Dan contributes 20 percent of compensation (up to the maximum allowable) to the plan for his employees. Dan's maximum deduction is calculated as follows:

Dan's self-employed rate is 0.20 ÷ 1.20 = 0.1666 or 16.667 percent. His maximum deduction is $20,834, which is the lesser of 16.667% × $125,000 ($20,834) or $56,000. ◆

To avoid penalties, taxpayers generally may not receive distributions from a SEP prior to age 59½ and must start drawing amounts by the age of 70½.

In the past, a plan similar to a current SEP, known as a SARSEP, was available. SARSEPs could not be created after January 31, 1996 and although some plans were grandfathered in, many are no longer in operation.

A Payroll Deduction IRA is probably the easiest type of plan to offer. Contributions are withheld from an employee's pay and directed into a traditional IRA account. No plan set-up is necessary other than having the employee direct the payroll withholding to the IRA custodian. Contribution limits are the same as the traditional IRA limits.

A SIMPLE IRA is available to any employer with 100 or fewer employees (including a self-employed individual). SIMPLE IRAs are also easy to set up (Form 5304-SIMPLE or 5305-SIMPLE) and administer. Both the employee and the employer are eligible to contribute with an annual limit of $13,000 ($16,000 for taxpayers age 50 or older) in 2019. However, unlike a SEP, a SIMPLE IRA requires certain contributions *must* be made by the employer (match employees of the first 3 percent of compensation (with some flexibility) or 2 percent of each eligible employee's compensation.

5-4c Self-Employed 401(k), Solo 401(k), Safe Harbor, and Traditional 401(k) Plans

One of the more popular qualified retirement plans is the Section 401(k) plan, which permits an employee to choose to receive a direct payment of compensation in cash or to defer the amount through an employer contribution on behalf of the employee to a profit-sharing or stock bonus plan. Such a plan may be structured as a salary reduction agreement. The agreement may allow the employee to reduce his or her compensation or forgo an increase in compensation, with the amount contributed to the qualified retirement plan, thereby deferring tax on the compensation. Employees choose the percentage of their pay which will be withheld and contributed to the plan. Some employers match employee contributions up to a certain percentage in order to encourage participation.

In all 401(k) plans, contributions are limited in two ways: (1) for 2019, an employee may elect to make an annual contribution up to $19,000 ($25,000 for taxpayers age 50 or older) to a Section 401(k) plan, and (2) the amount of any contributions made to the Section 401(k) plan are also subject to the limitations applicable to all qualified plans (25 percent of compensation subject to a limit of $56,000, $62,000 if over age 50).

Any matching amount contributed to the plan by the employer on behalf of the employee is excluded from the employee's gross income. The contributions and the earnings on the amounts invested in the plan are taxable only when withdrawn.

A self-employed 401(k) or solo 401(k) is designed for self-employed individuals with no employees (spouse is permitted). Setup and maintenance of the plan are relatively inexpensive and easy.

A traditional 401(k) plan can be used by any type of company but is generally thought to be more appropriate for business with at least 20 employees due to the cost to establish and maintain the plan. An annual reporting of the plan assets is required (Form 5500) and special IRS testing is required to ensure that the plan does not favor highly-compensated employees.

The annual maximum ($19,000, or $25,000 if age 50 or over, in 2019) is reduced dollar for dollar by amounts contributed as a result of the employee's participation in other salary reduction plans of any employer. Contributions in excess of the maximum allowed may be subject to a 10 percent excise tax imposed on the employer. Also, if the excess contributions are not withdrawn within a specified time period, the plan will lose its status as a qualified arrangement.

Finally, Section 401(k) plans must meet certain requirements in addition to the general qualification requirements for all qualified plans. The amount deferred must be 100 percent vested and may be distributed only upon retirement, death, disability, or other separation from service, attainment of age 59½, or hardship.

EXAMPLE Carol, age 48, participates in a Section 401(k) plan. Carol's salary is $30,000 per year and she chooses to contribute 15 percent to the 401(k) plan. The maximum amount she may contribute on a tax-deferred basis to the Section 401(k) plan under a salary reduction agreement is $4,500 (15% × $30,000, not to exceed $19,000, in 2019). ♦

For small businesses with employees, a safe harbor 401(k) plan operates like other 401(k) plans with one important distinction: it must provide for employer contributions that are fully vested when made. These contributions may be employer-matching contributions, limited to employees who defer, or employer contributions made on behalf of all eligible employees, regardless of whether they make elective deferrals. The safe harbor 401(k) plan is not subject to the complex annual nondiscrimination tests that apply to traditional 401(k) plans.

Beginning in 2006, employers were allowed to set up Roth 401(k)s for their employees. The amounts allowed to be set aside are the same as for regular 401(k)s, but the dollars paid in do not reduce the employees' taxable income, which is similar to the tax treatment of Roth IRAs. Withdrawals, including earnings, are generally tax-free based on rules similar to those for Roth IRA withdrawals. Roth 401(k)s are popular because they allow a significantly higher Roth contribution than a Roth IRA and because there is no AGI limitation, they may be used by high-income taxpayers.

Different types of tax-advantaged retirement plans have developed over many years. Plans such as these tend to have long lifetimes as an employee may contribute early in their working career and then wait 40 years or more before reaching retirement age. The plans, once created, are slow to disappear. The result is a jumbled selection of plans to consider. In the previous few pages ten different plans were mentioned: SEP, SARSEP, SEP IRA, SIMPLE IRA, Payroll Deduction IRA, Self-Employed 401(k), Solo 401(k), Safe harbor 401(k), traditional 401(k), and Roth 401(k) plans. This list does not even consider the other "large" qualified plans such as traditional pension plans (defined contribution and defined benefit), profit-sharing plans, stock bonus plans, and Employee Stock Ownership Plans (ESOPs); not to mention the individual retirement opportunities available in an IRA or Roth IRA. If a taxpayer is confused about which retirement savings plan might be best for him or her, some solace can be taken in that there is probably a plan that will suit their individual situation!

Self-Study Problem 5.4   *See Appendix E for Solutions to Self-Study Problems*

a. Lewis, a self-employed individual, has net earned income of $50,000 in 2019. If Lewis has no employees, calculate the maximum contribution to a SEP plan that he may deduct from his adjusted gross income.

$_____

b. During 2019, Linda, age 32, has a salary of $40,000. She participates in a Section 401(k) plan and chooses to defer 25 percent of her compensation.

   i. What is the maximum amount Linda can contribute to the Section 401(k) plan on a tax-deferred basis?

$_____

   ii. If Linda's salary was $125,000, instead of $40,000, what is the maximum amount that she could contribute to the Section 401(k) plan on a tax-deferred basis?

$_____

Learning Objective 5.5

5-5 OTHER FOR AGI DEDUCTIONS

Describe other adjustments for adjusted gross income.

There are a number of other deductions for AGI available under the tax law. Because of the limited nature of these deductions, a less detailed description is provided. The deduction for one-half of self-employment tax, which affects almost all self-employed taxpayers, is described in Chapter 6.

5-5a Educator Expenses

Eligible educators may deduct up to $250 for the unreimbursed cost of classroom materials such as books, supplies, computer equipment, and supplementary materials as a deduction in arriving at AGI. An eligible educator is a kindergarten through grade 12 teacher, instructor, counselor, principal or aide for at least 900 hours a school year in a school that provides elementary or secondary education. If a married filing jointly couple are both eligible educators, the total deduction is up to $500 but not more than $250 for either spouse.

EXAMPLE   Glen and Iris Holland are a married couple that files jointly and both are high school teachers. In 2019, Glen and Iris spent $270 and $120 on various school supplies, respectively. The Hollands are eligible for a $370 ($250 + $120) educator expense deduction. ♦

5-5b Unreimbursed Business Expenses for Performing Artists and Others

As discussed later in this chapter, employees that incur business expenses typically were permitted to deduct those costs as an itemized deduction subject to a 2 percent of AGI floor. Certain employee taxpayers, however, are eligible to take a for AGI deduction for unreimbursed employee costs and thus are not required to itemize to deduct these costs. The deduction has become even more significant since the suspension of unreimbursed employee costs by the TCJA.

There are three different types of taxpayers eligible for this deduction (and the rules are different for each one):

1. Performing artists who worked for two or more employers during the year
2. National Guard or Reserve member
3. Fee-based government officials

Performing artists may deduct employee business expenses as a for AGI deduction if they meet the following qualifications:

1. The taxpayer was paid for providing performing arts as an employee for at least two employers.
2. The taxpayer received at least $200 each from any two of these employers.
3. The related performing-arts business expenses are more than 10 percent of gross income from the performance of those services, and
4. AGI is not more than $16,000 before deducting these business expenses.

Members of a reserve component of the Armed Forces of the United States that travel more than 100 miles away from home in connection with services in the reserves can deduct travel expenses. The travel expense deduction is limited to the regular federal per diem rate (for lodging, meals, and incidental expenses) and the standard mileage rate (for car expenses) plus any parking fees, ferry fees, and tolls. Per diems are discussed in Chapter 3.

Certain fee-basis officials can claim their employee business expenses. Fee-basis officials are persons who are employed by a state or local government and who are paid in whole or in part on a fee basis.

EXAMPLE   Sally is a building inspector for the city of Hickory, Indiana. Sally is compensated solely from fees paid directly to her by clients and is not considered an employee of Hickory. Sally's travel and other business expenses can be deducted as a for AGI deduction. ♦

Unreimbursed business expenses that are deductible are claimed on Form 2106.

5-5c Moving Expenses

In the past, the tax law provided a deduction for moving expenses to help relieve taxpayers of a portion of the financial burden of moving from one job location to another. The TCJA suspended the deduction for moving expenses (through 2025) for all taxpayers except members of the Armed Forces of the United States on active duty whose move is pursuant to a military order and incident to a permanent change of station.

Starting in 2018, reimbursements to an employee from an employer for qualified moving costs are no longer excluded from the employee's income.

Under the former law, taxpayers (except for those in the Armed Forces) had to meet three tests in order to deduct moving costs:

1. The taxpayer must change job sites.
2. The taxpayer must move so that the distance from the taxpayer's former residence to the new job location must be at least 50 miles more than the distance from the former residence to the former job location.
3. The taxpayer must remain at the new job location for a certain period of time, generally, 39 weeks. Taxpayers who were self-employed had to work at least 78 weeks at the new location.

Taxpayers in the Armed Forces are not required to meet the time or distance tests.

For the members of the military that qualify, moving expenses are reported on Form 3903.

Self-Study Problem 5.5   *See Appendix E for Solutions to Self-Study Problems*

For each of the following situations, determine whether a deduction for AGI is permitted for the taxpayer.

a. Professor Hill teaches at Bunker Hall Community College. In 2019, he spent $267 on supplies for his classroom and was not reimbursed.

b. Jackie Rights played the lead role in two different plays in 2019 in the local community theatre. Two different production companies sponsored the plays and so she was an employee of both in 2019 and was paid the same by both employers: $4,000 per play. Jackie spent $1,100 in business expenses such as new business cards, personal management fees, and new head-shots for her portfolio. Her 2019 AGI was $15,200 (she also generated income as a shared-ride vehicle driver).

c. Lieutenant Dan of the U.S. Army was stationed in Fort Bragg, NC. In 2019, his permanent post was moved from Bragg to Fort Jackson. The unreimbursed moving costs for he and his wife are $4,500.

Learning Objective 5.6

Calculate the itemized deduction for medical expenses.

5-6 MEDICAL EXPENSES

Medical expenses are the first itemized deduction listed on Schedule A. Taxpayers are allowed a deduction for the medical expenses paid for themselves, their spouse, and dependents. Unreimbursed medical expenses can only be deducted to the extent that they exceed 10 percent of the taxpayer's AGI. The formula for calculating a taxpayer's medical expense deduction is as follows:

Prescription medicines and drugs, insulin, doctors, dentists, hospitals, medical insurance premiums	$ xxx
Other medical and dental expenses, such as lodging, transportation, eyeglasses, contact lenses, etc.	xxx
Less: insurance reimbursements	(xxx)
Subtotal	xxx
Less: 10 percent of adjusted gross income	(xxx)
Excess expenses qualifying for the medical deduction	$ xxx

5-6a What Qualifies as a Medical Expense?

Expenses that are deductible as medical expenses include the cost of items for the diagnosis, cure, mitigation, treatment, and prevention of disease. Also included are expenditures incurred that affect any structure or function of the body. Therefore, amounts for all of the following categories of expenditures qualify as medical expenses:

Prescription medicines and drugs and insulin
Fees for doctors, dentists, nurses, and other medical professionals
Hospital fees
Hearing aids, dentures, prescription eyeglasses, and contact lenses
Medical transportation and lodging
Medical aids, such as crutches, wheelchairs, and guide dogs
Birth control prescriptions
Acupuncture
Psychiatric care
Medical insurance premiums, including Medicare premiums
Certain capital expenditures deemed medically necessary by a doctor
Nursing home care for the chronically ill (e.g., Alzheimer's disease care)

The IRS has allowed a deduction for the following unusual medical expenses:
- Long-distance phone calls made to a psychological counselor
- Hair transplants for premature baldness
- A wig prescribed by a psychiatrist for a taxpayer upset by hair loss
- A cell phone for a taxpayer who may need instantaneous medical help
- Treatments provided by a Native American medicine man

Certain medical expenses are not deductible. For example, the cost of travel for the general improvement of the taxpayer's health is not deductible. The expense of a swimming pool is not deductible unless the pool is designed specially for the hydrotherapeutic treatment of the taxpayer's illness. No deduction is allowed for the cost of weight-loss programs (unless prescribed by a doctor; diet foods do not qualify) or marriage counseling. Medical expenses for unnecessary cosmetic surgery or similar procedures are not deductible. Cosmetic surgery is considered unnecessary unless it corrects (1) a congenital abnormality, (2) a personal injury resulting from an accident or trauma, or (3) a disfiguring disease. In general, unnecessary cosmetic surgery is any procedure which is directed at improving the patient's appearance and does not meaningfully promote the proper function of the body or prevent or treat illness or disease.

Taxpayers that do not spend medical expenses greater than 10 percent can still enjoy the tax benefit associated with the deduction by using the medical flexible spending account discussed in Chapter 2. By excluding up to $2,700 from gross income, the after-tax savings is basically identical to taking the medical expense deduction for the same amount.

5-6b Medical Insurance

Medical insurance includes standard health policies, whether the benefits are paid to the taxpayer or to the provider of the services directly. In addition, the premiums paid for membership in health maintenance plans are deductible as medical insurance, as are supplemental payments for optional Medicare coverage. Insurance policies that pay a specific amount each day or week the taxpayer is hospitalized are not considered medical insurance and the premiums are not deductible. Premiums paid for qualified long-term care insurance policies are also deductible medical expenses up to specified limits which change each year and are based on the age of the taxpayer.

Self-employed taxpayers are allowed, subject to certain limitations, a deduction for adjusted gross income for the medical insurance premiums paid for themselves and their families. Long-term care insurance premiums, up to a specified amount based on the taxpayer's age, are considered health insurance for this purpose. These deductions are covered earlier in this chapter. If a deduction is taken for these items in arriving at AGI, then these same expenses are excluded from the medical expense deduction on Schedule A. However, if the self-employed insurance deduction is limited by net self-employment income, the excess medical insurance expenses can be included on Schedule A.

5-6c Medicines and Drugs

Prescription medicines and drugs and insulin are the only drugs deductible as medical expenses. No deduction is allowed for drugs purchased illegally from abroad, including Canada and Mexico. Nonprescription medicines such as over-the-counter antacids, allergy medications, and pain relievers, even if recommended by a physician, are not deductible as a medical expense.

5-6d **Capital Expenditures**

Payments for capital improvements purchased and installed in the taxpayer's home for medical reasons may also be deductible. Examples include support railings, lowering kitchen cabinets, and medically necessary swimming pools. Unlike other capital expenditures, allowable amounts are deducted fully in the year the item is purchased. If the expenditure is for an improvement that increases the value of the taxpayer's property, the deduction is limited to the amount by which the expenditure exceeds the increase in the value of the property. If the value of the property does not increase as a result of the expenditure, the entire cost is deductible. The cost of upkeep and operation of an item, the cost of which qualified as a medical expense, is also deductible, provided the medical reason for the improvement or special equipment still exists. To take advantage of this deduction, the taxpayer must show the improvement is used primarily for and directly related to medical care. A doctor's recommendation is an important factor in supporting the deduction.

EXAMPLE   A taxpayer has a heart condition and installs an elevator in his home at a cost of $6,000. The value of the home is increased by $4,000 as a result of the improvement. The taxpayer is allowed a deduction of $2,000 ($6,000 − $4,000), the excess of the cost of the equipment over the increase in the value of the taxpayer's home. ♦

5-6e **Transportation**

Transportation expenses primarily and necessary for medical care are deductible, including amounts paid for taxis, trains, buses, airplanes, and ambulances. Taxpayers may also claim a deduction for the use of their personal automobile for medical transportation. However, only out-of-pocket expenses such as the cost of gas and oil are deductible. Maintenance, insurance, general repair, and depreciation expenses are not deductible. If the taxpayer does not wish to deduct actual costs of transportation by personal automobile, the standard mileage rate for medical care purposes is 20 cents per mile for 2019. In addition to the deduction for actual automobile costs or the standard mileage amount, parking and toll fees for medical transportation are deductible medical expenses. If the transportation expenses are for the medical care of a dependent child, the amounts are deductible by the parent.

5-6f **Lodging for Medical Care**

Taxpayers may deduct the cost of lodging up to $50 per night, per person, on a trip primarily for and essential to medical care provided by a physician or a licensed hospital. The deduction is allowed for the patient and an individual accompanying the patient, such as the parent of a child. However, no deduction is allowed if the trip involves a significant element of recreation or vacation. No deduction is allowed for meal costs.

A Las Vegas dentist admitted he provided free dental work to an IRS revenue officer in exchange for reductions of his $100,000 tax debt. Both men were indicted on conspiracy and bribery charges.

Itemized deductions are located under Deductions/Itemized Deductions (Schedule A). Subheadings for each of the itemized deductions will be found in the left-hand margin.

Self-Study Problem 5.6   *See Appendix E for Solutions to Self-Study Problems*

During the 2019 tax year, Frank (age 65) and Betty (age 63) paid the following medical expenses:

Medical insurance	$ 425
Prescription medicines and drugs	364
Hospital bills	2,424
Doctor bills	725
Prescription Eyeglasses for Frank's dependent mother	75
Doctor bills for Betty's sister, who is claimed as a dependent by Frank and Betty	220

In addition, during 2019, they drove 700 miles for medical transportation in their personal automobile. Their insurance company reimbursed Frank and Betty $1,420 during the year for the medical expenses. If their adjusted gross income for the year is $25,400, calculate their medical expense deduction. Use Schedule A of Form 1040 on Page 5-23.

5-7 TAXES

5.7 Learning Objective

Calculate the itemized deduction for taxes.

Taxpayers are allowed to deduct certain state, local, and foreign taxes paid during the year. The purpose of the deduction for taxes is to relieve the burden of multiple taxation of the same income. However, the tax law distinguishes between a "tax" and a "fee." A tax is imposed by a government to raise revenue for general public purposes, and a fee is a charge with a direct benefit to the person paying the fee. Taxes are generally deductible; fees are not deductible. For example, postage, fishing licenses, and dog tags are considered fees that are not deductible as taxes.

Pre-TCJA, tax law provided for an itemized deduction for the following taxes:

- State, local, and foreign income taxes
- Sales taxes (in lieu of state and local income taxes)
- State, local, and foreign real property taxes
- State, local, and foreign personal property taxes

After the TCJA, these taxes largely remain deductible; however, foreign property taxes are only deductible if incurred in carrying on a business or for the production of income (e.g., rental activity). In addition, the aggregate amount of the deduction for state and local real property taxes, state and local personal property taxes, state and local, and foreign, income taxes, and general sales taxes (if elected) for any tax year is limited to $10,000 ($5,000 for married filing separately). But, the $10,000 aggregate limitation rule does not apply to (i) foreign income taxes; (ii) state and local, and foreign real property taxes; and (iii) state and local personal property taxes, if these taxes are paid or accrued in carrying on a business or for the production of income. In other words, taxes deductible on an individual's Schedule C, Schedule E, or Schedule F remain fully deductible and are not subject to the limitation. Note that state and local *income* taxes are not included in the business-related exclusion from the limitation as these taxes have always been deductible as an itemized deduction on an individual's Schedule A. These provisions (the loss of the foreign property tax deduction and $10,000 deduction limitation) apply through 2025.

EXAMPLE   Britney and Brad are married taxpayers filing jointly. In 2019, Britney has $7,800 in state income taxes withheld by her employer from her wages. Brad operates a sole proprietorship that owns a building and pays property taxes of $2,300. Brad also pays estimated state income tax payments on his business of $4,000. Lastly, in 2019 Brad and Britney pay property taxes on their home of $1,600. The $2,300 of property taxes associated with the business building are deductible on Schedule C as a business deduction. The $13,400 of itemized deduction for taxes includes Britney's state income taxes ($7,800), Brad's estimated tax payments ($4,000), and the property taxes on their home ($1,600). However, the itemized deduction for taxes is limited to $10,000 in 2019. ♦

The following taxes are not deductible:

- Federal income taxes
- Employee portion of Social Security taxes
- Estate, inheritance, and gift taxes (except in unusual situations not discussed here)
- Excise taxes and gasoline taxes (except when business-related)
- Foreign income taxes if the taxpayer elects a foreign tax credit

5-7a Income Taxes and Sales Taxes

Taxpayers may elect to deduct either state and local sales and use taxes or state and local income taxes as itemized deductions. The election to deduct state and local sales tax instead of income tax primarily benefits taxpayers in states with no income taxes or low income tax rates.

For taxpayers electing to deduct state and local income taxes paid during 2019, the amount of the deduction is the total amount of state and local taxes withheld from wages plus any amounts actually paid during the year, even if the tax payments are for a prior year's tax liability. If the taxpayer receives a refund of taxes deducted in a previous year, the refund must generally be included in gross income (e.g., Line 1 on Schedule 1 of the Form 1040) in the year the refund is received. Taxes which did not provide any tax benefit (reduction in taxes) in the year paid are not required to be included in income in the year received as a refund. For example, a taxpayer claiming the standard deduction in the year taxes are paid does not receive a tax benefit for the payment and is not required to include in income a tax refund received the following year.

EXAMPLE For 2019, Mary deducts state income taxes rather than state sales taxes as an itemized deduction. Mary has $1,800 of state income taxes withheld from her wages during 2019. In April of 2019, she paid an additional $250 for taxes due on her 2018 state income tax return. Mary's deduction for state income taxes is $2,050 ($1,800 + $250). Her state income tax return reflects a liability for the 2019 year of $1,650, resulting in a $150 refund ($1,800 − $1,650) that was received in 2020. The $150 refund is reported as income in the 2020 return, assuming Mary received a benefit from the state tax deduction for 2019. ♦

EXAMPLE Damone paid state income and property taxes of $10,250 in 2019. Damone claimed total itemized deductions of $12,500, including the $10,000 limit on state and local taxes. In 2020, Damone received a state income tax refund of $1,000. If Damone had deducted the actual amount of state taxes in 2019, he would have deducted on $9,250 ($10,250 paid in 2019 less $1,000 refund). His adjusted total itemized deductions would have been $11,750. As a result, Damone would have elected the standard deduction of $12,200 in 2019. The difference between his 2019 claimed itemized deductions ($12,500) and his properly adjusted standard deduction ($12,200) is $300. Thus, he received a $300 benefit from the overpayment of taxes, and Damone must include $300 in his 2020 income.

Self-Study Problems 5.6, 5.7, 5.8, 5.9, and 5.10

SCHEDULE A
(Form 1040 or 1040-SR)

Department of the Treasury
Internal Revenue Service (99)

Itemized Deductions

▶ Go to *www.irs.gov/ScheduleA* for instructions and the latest information.
▶ **Attach to Form 1040 or 1040-SR.**

Caution: If you are claiming a net qualified disaster loss on Form 4684, see the instructions for line 16.

OMB No. 1545-0074

2019

Attachment
Sequence No. **07**

Name(s) shown on Form 1040 or 1040-SR

Your social security number

Medical and Dental Expenses	**Caution:** Do not include expenses reimbursed or paid by others.	
	1 Medical and dental expenses (see instructions)	**1**
	2 Enter amount from Form 1040 or 1040-SR, line 8b	**2**
	3 Multiply line 2 by 10% (0.10)	**3**
	4 Subtract line 3 from line 1. If line 3 is more than line 1, enter -0-	**4**
Taxes You Paid	**5** State and local taxes.	
	a State and local income taxes or general sales taxes. You may include either income taxes or general sales taxes on line 5a, but not both. If you elect to include general sales taxes instead of income taxes, check this box . . . . ▶ ☐	**5a**
	b State and local real estate taxes (see instructions)	**5b**
	c State and local personal property taxes	**5c**
	d Add lines 5a through 5c	**5d**
	e Enter the smaller of line 5d or $10,000 ($5,000 if married filing separately)	**5e**
	6 Other taxes. List type and amount ▶ _____	**6**
	7 Add lines 5e and 6	**7**
Interest You Paid **Caution:** Your mortgage interest deduction may be limited (see instructions).	**8** Home mortgage interest and points. If you didn't use all of your home mortgage loan(s) to buy, build, or improve your home, see instructions and check this box . . . . ▶ ☐	
	a Home mortgage interest and points reported to you on Form 1098. See instructions if limited	**8a**
	b Home mortgage interest not reported to you on Form 1098. If paid to the person from whom you bought the home, see instructions and show that person's name, identifying no., and address . . . . . ▶ _____ _____	**8b**
	c Points not reported to you on Form 1098. See instructions for special rules	**8c**
	d Reserved	**8d**
	e Add lines 8a through 8c	**8e**
	9 Investment interest. Attach Form 4952 if required. See instructions	**9**
	10 Add lines 8e and 9	**10**
Gifts to Charity **Caution:** If you made a gift and got a benefit for it, see instructions.	**11** Gifts by cash or check. If you made any gift of $250 or more, see instructions	**11**
	12 Other than by cash or check. If you made any gift of $250 or more, see instructions. You **must** attach Form 8283 if over $500. . . .	**12**
	13 Carryover from prior year	**13**
	14 Add lines 11 through 13	**14**
Casualty and Theft Losses	**15** Casualty and theft loss(es) from a federally declared disaster (other than net qualified disaster losses). Attach Form 4684 and enter the amount from line 18 of that form. See instructions	**15**
Other Itemized Deductions	**16** Other—from list in instructions. List type and amount ▶ _____ _____	**16**
Total Itemized Deductions	**17** Add the amounts in the far right column for lines 4 through 16. Also, enter this amount on Form 1040 or 1040-SR, line 9	**17**
	18 If you elect to itemize deductions even though they are less than your standard deduction, check this box . . . . ▶ ☐	

For Paperwork Reduction Act Notice, see the Instructions for Forms 1040 and 1040-SR.   Cat. No. 17145C   **Schedule A (Form 1040 or 1040-SR) 2019**

For taxpayers electing to deduct sales taxes in 2019, the deduction is calculated by using either (a) actual sales taxes paid or (b) estimated sales taxes from IRS tables. Actual sales and use tax expenses are based on a "general sales tax," which is a tax imposed at one rate with respect to the retail sale of a broad range of classes of items. To the extent a higher sales tax rate than the general rate applies to motor vehicles, that excess amount is specifically excluded from the deduction amount.

The actual sales taxes paid method requires a taxpayer to maintain extensive records to substantiate the sales and use taxes paid during the year. To ease the burden on taxpayers, the tax law also permits taxpayers to use estimated state sales tax tables to calculate the deduction. Taxpayers using the estimation tables may add the sales taxes paid on items that include motor vehicles (car, truck, van, motor home, recreational vehicle), aircraft, boats, a home or a substantial addition or renovation to a home. The estimated state sales tax tables are based on the taxpayer's adjusted gross income modified by adding back certain tax-exempt sources of income such as tax-exempt interest, workers compensation, and the nontaxable parts of Social Security or qualified retirement plan distributions. The estimated sales tax also differs by the number of dependents a taxpayer has. The following is a portion of the sales tax estimation table:

2018 Optional State Sales Tax Tables*

Income At least	But less than	Alabama 1 (4.0000%)						Arizona 2 (5.6000%)						Arkansas 2 (6.5000%)					
		1	2	3	4	5	Over 5	1	2	3	4	5	Over 5	1	2	3	4	5	Over 5
$0	$20,000	278	325	357	382	402	430	291	318	334	346	356	370	398	436	460	478	492	511
$20,000	$30,000	389	455	499	534	562	602	430	469	493	512	526	546	589	645	680	706	727	756
$30,000	$40,000	445	520	570	609	641	687	501	546	575	596	614	637	687	752	793	824	849	882
$40,000	$50,000	491	574	629	672	708	758	562	613	645	669	688	714	770	844	890	925	952	990
$50,000	$60,000	532	621	681	728	766	820	616	672	707	733	754	783	845	925	976	1014	1044	1086
$60,000	$70,000	568	663	727	777	818	875	664	725	763	791	814	845	912	999	1054	1094	1127	1172
$70,000	$80,000	601	701	769	821	865	925	709	773	814	844	868	901	973	1066	1125	1168	1203	1251
$80,000	$90,000	631	736	807	862	908	972	750	818	861	893	919	954	1030	1128	1190	1237	1274	1324
$90,000	$100,000	659	769	843	900	948	1014	789	860	906	939	966	1003	1083	1187	1252	1301	1340	1393
$100,000	$120,000	696	812	890	951	1001	1071	840	916	964	1000	1029	1068	1154	1264	1334	1386	1427	1484
$120,000	$140,000	743	867	950	1015	1068	1143	906	989	1041	1079	1111	1153	1245	1365	1440	1496	1541	1602
$140,000	$160,000	786	918	1006	1074	1131	1210	967	1056	1111	1153	1186	1231	1330	1458	1538	1598	1646	1711
$160,000	$180,000	826	964	1056	1128	1187	1270	1024	1117	1176	1220	1255	1303	1408	1543	1629	1692	1743	1812
$180,000	$200,000	863	1007	1103	1178	1240	1327	1077	1175	1237	1283	1321	1371	1482	1624	1714	1781	1834	1907
$200,000	$225,000	901	1051	1152	1230	1295	1385	1132	1235	1301	1349	1388	1441	1558	1708	1802	1873	1929	2006
$225,000	$250,000	942	1098	1204	1285	1353	1447	1191	1300	1368	1420	1461	1517	1640	1798	1897	1971	2030	2111
$250,000	$275,000	980	1142	1252	1336	1407	1505	1246	1360	1432	1486	1529	1587	1717	1882	1986	2063	2125	2210
$275,000	$300,000	1015	1184	1297	1385	1458	1559	1299	1418	1493	1549	1593	1654	1790	1962	2070	2151	2216	2304
$300,000	or more	1222	1424	1560	1665	1752	1874	1608	1756	1849	1918	1974	2049	2219	2433	2568	2668	2749	2858

Income At least	But less than	California 3 (7.2500%)						Colorado 2 (2.9000%)						Connecticut 4 (6.3500%)					
		1	2	3	4	5	Over 5	1	2	3	4	5	Over 5	1	2	3	4	5	Over 5
$0	$20,000	355	385	405	419	431	447	150	164	173	180	185	193	335	360	376	388	397	410
$20,000	$30,000	521	566	595	616	633	656	218	239	252	262	270	281	501	539	563	581	595	614
$30,000	$40,000	606	659	692	717	737	764	253	277	292	303	313	325	587	632	661	681	698	720
$40,000	$50,000	679	738	775	803	825	856	282	309	326	339	349	363	661	712	744	768	786	811
$50,000	$60,000	743	808	849	879	904	937	308	337	356	370	381	397	727	784	819	844	865	893
$60,000	$70,000	801	871	915	948	974	1010	331	363	383	398	410	427	787	848	886	914	936	966
$70,000	$80,000	854	929	976	1011	1039	1077	353	386	408	424	437	454	842	907	948	977	1001	1033
$80,000	$90,000	903	982	1032	1069	1098	1139	372	408	431	447	461	480	893	962	1005	1037	1062	1096
$90,000	$100,000	949	1032	1084	1123	1154	1197	391	428	452	470	484	503	941	1014	1059	1092	1119	1155
$100,000	$120,000	1010	1098	1154	1195	1228	1274	415	455	480	499	514	535	1004	1082	1131	1167	1195	1233
$120,000	$140,000	1088	1184	1244	1289	1324	1373	447	489	516	537	553	575	1087	1172	1224	1263	1294	1335
$140,000	$160,000	1161	1263	1327	1375	1413	1465	476	521	550	572	589	613	1164	1255	1311	1352	1385	1430
$160,000	$180,000	1228	1336	1404	1454	1495	1550	502	550	581	604	622	647	1235	1331	1391	1435	1470	1517
$180,000	$200,000	1291	1404	1476	1529	1571	1629	527	578	610	634	653	679	1302	1403	1466	1513	1550	1600
$200,000	$225,000	1356	1476	1551	1606	1651	1712	553	606	640	665	685	713	1372	1478	1545	1594	1633	1685
$225,000	$250,000	1426	1551	1630	1689	1736	1800	581	637	672	698	720	749	1446	1559	1629	1680	1722	1777
$250,000	$275,000	1492	1623	1705	1767	1816	1883	607	665	702	730	752	782	1516	1635	1708	1762	1805	1864
$275,000	$300,000	1554	1690	1776	1840	1892	1961	632	692	731	759	782	814	1584	1707	1784	1840	1885	1946
$300,000	or more	1919	2088	2194	2273	2337	2423	776	850	897	933	961	1000	1980	2135	2231	2301	2358	2434

*The 2019 version of the Optional State Sales Tax Tables was not available as we went to print. Please check the IRS website (www.irs.gov) for updates to the instructions for Form 1040 Schedule A.

Because a number of states permit localities to also charge a general sale tax, a local sales tax table for some of the states is provided to assist with that calculation. Because the estimation method is fairly complex, the IRS provides a worksheet to assist with the deduction calculation and most tax preparation software will compute the amounts as well.

When it comes to entering state tax deduction information, much of the work will be done elsewhere. For example, income taxes withheld are generally input as part of the W-2 input. Estimated payments are input under the primary heading Payments, Penalties, and Extensions. Lastly, Intuit ProConnect has the state sales tax calculator built in and does not require the manual completion of the state and local sales tax worksheet.

intuit proconnect™

TIP

State and Local General Sales Tax Deduction
Worksheet—Line 5a

 Keep for Your Records

 Instead of using this worksheet, you can find your deduction by using the Sales Tax Deduction Calculator at IRS.gov/ SalesTax.

Before you begin: See the instructions for line 1 of the worksheet if you:

   ✓ Lived in more than one state during 2019, or
   ✓ Had any **nontaxable** income in 2019.

1. Enter your **state** general sales taxes from the 2019 Optional State Sales Tax Table .... **1.** $ _____

  Next. If, for all of 2019, you lived only in Connecticut, the District of Columbia, Indiana, Kentucky, Maine, Maryland, Massachusetts, Michigan, New Jersey, or Rhode Island, skip lines 2 through 5, enter -0- on line 6, and go to line 7. Otherwise, go to line 2.

2. Did you live in Alaska, Arizona, Arkansas, Colorado, Georgia, Illinois, Louisiana, Mississippi, Missouri, New York, North Carolina, South Carolina, Tennessee, Utah, or Virginia in 2019?

  ☐ **No.** Enter -0-.

  ☐ **Yes.** Enter your base **local** general sales taxes from the 2019 Optional Local Sales Tax Tables.

                  .... **2.** $ _____

3. Did your locality impose a **local** general sales tax in 2019? Residents of California and Nevada, see the instructions for line 3 of the worksheet.

  ☐ **No.** Skip lines 3 through 5, enter -0- on line 6, and go to line 7.

  ☐ **Yes.** Enter your **local** general sales tax rate, but omit the percentage sign. For example, if your local general sales tax rate was 2.5%, enter 2.5. If your local general sales tax rate changed or you lived in more than one locality in the same state during 2019, see the instructions for line 3 of the worksheet .... **3.** _____ . _____

4. Did you enter -0- on line 2?

  ☐ **No.** Skip lines 4 and 5 and go to line 6.

  ☐ **Yes.** Enter your **state** general sales tax rate (shown in the table heading for your state), but omit the percentage sign. For example, if your state general sales tax rate is 6%, enter 6.0 .... **4.** _____ . _____

5. Divide line 3 by line 4. Enter the result as a decimal (rounded to at least three places) .... **5.** _____ . _____

6. Did you enter -0- on line 2?

  ☐ **No.** Multiply line 2 by line 3.

  ☐ **Yes.** Multiply line 1 by line 5. If you lived in more than one locality in the same state during 2019, see the instructions for line 6 of the worksheet.

                .... **6.** $ _____

7. Enter your state and local general sales taxes paid on specified items, if any. See the instructions for line 7 of the worksheet .... **7.** $ _____

8. **Deduction for general sales taxes.** Add lines 1, 6, and 7. Enter the result here and the total from all your state and local general sales tax deduction worksheets, if you completed more than one, on Schedule A, line 5a. Be sure to check the **box** on that line .... **8.** $ _____

The IRS also provides an online sales tax deduction calculator at **www.irs.gov**.

EXAMPLE Jason and Tina Sterling are married filing jointly taxpayers and residents of Rock Hill, South Carolina (zip code 29732). They have no dependents and their AGI for 2019 is $85,000. Rock Hill has a 7 percent sales tax that includes 6 percent for the state portion and 1 percent for the local portion. The Sterlings paid no sales tax on specified items during the year.

The state sales tax table for South Carolina provides a general sales tax amount for income between $80,000 and $90,000 for married filing jointly as $964. South Carolina permits a local general sales tax, and thus the Sterlings use the Local Sales Tax Table for income between $80,000 and $90,000 with two family members to derive a local sales tax estimate of $151. Using the sales tax deduction worksheet, the local amount of $151 is multiplied by 1 to yield a total local sales tax amount of $151. Thus the total sales tax deduction is $1,115. ♦

This example uses 2018 state and local general sales tax estimates as the 2019 amounts were not available as we went to print.

When a married couple files separately, if one spouse uses the optional sales tax tables, the other spouse must use the optional sales tax tables as well.

5-7b **Property Taxes**

Taxes that are levied on state and local real property for the general public welfare are deductible. However, special assessments charged to provide local benefit to property owners are not deductible; these amounts increase the basis of the taxpayer's property. Also, service fees, such as garbage fees and homeowner association fees, are not deductible as property taxes.

If real estate is sold during the year, the taxes must be allocated between the buyer and the seller, and the division must be made according to the number of days in the year that each taxpayer held the property. The seller is generally responsible for the property taxes up to, but not including, the date the house was sold.

EXAMPLE Sally sells her home to Patty on March 3, 2019. The taxes for 2019 are paid by Patty and they total $1,825, or $5.00 per day ($1,825/365 days). The purchaser is treated as the owner on the day of sale. Sally is entitled to deduct 61 days of real property taxes or $305 (61 days × $5.00 per day). Patty deducts $1,520 (304 days × $5.00 per day). ♦

Generally, the escrow company or closing agent handling the sale of the property will make the allocation of taxes between the buyer and the seller and the result will be reflected in the settlement charges on the transfer of the title. These amounts are itemized on closing statements for the sale, which are provided to the buyer and the seller.

EXAMPLE William purchased a new residence from John in 2019. William's closing statement shows that he receives a credit for $299.80 in taxes that he will pay later in the year on behalf of the seller. Assuming that William pays $525.00 in total taxes on the property later in 2019, his property tax deduction for 2019 would be $225.20 ($525.00 − $299.80). John, the seller, would be allowed a deduction for $299.80 plus any other taxes he paid during the year prior to selling the property. ♦

5-7c **Personal Property Taxes**

To be deductible as an itemized deduction, personal property taxes must be levied based on the value of the property. Taxes of a fixed amount, or those calculated on a basis other than value, are not deductible. For example, automobile fees that are calculated on the basis of the automobile's weight are not deductible.

EXAMPLE   Rich lives in a state that charges $20 per year plus 2 percent of the value of the automobile for vehicle registration. If Rich pays $160 [$20 + (2% × $7,000)] for his automobile registration, he may deduct only $140, the amount that is based on the value of the automobile. ♦

Self-Study Problem 5.7   *See Appendix E for Solutions to Self-Study Problems*

Sharon is single, lives in Idaho, and has adjusted gross income of $21,150 for 2019. Sharon deducts state income tax rather than state sales tax. The tax withheld from her salary for state income taxes is $1,050, and in May of 2019 she received a $225 refund on her state income tax return for the prior year. Sharon paid real estate taxes on her house of $825 for the year and an automobile registration fee of $110, of which $25 is based on the weight of the automobile and the balance on the value of the property. Use the Taxes You Paid section of Schedule A on Page 5-23 to report Sharon's deduction for state and local taxes.

5-8 INTEREST

Apply the rules for an individual taxpayer's interest deduction.

Taxpayers are allowed a deduction for certain interest paid or accrued during the tax year. Interest is defined as an amount paid for the use of borrowed funds. The type and amount of the deduction depend on the purpose for which the money is borrowed. Interest on loans for business, rent, and royalty activities is deducted for adjusted gross income. Certain interest on loans for personal purposes is deductible as an itemized deduction. The following types of personal interest are deductible:

> Qualified residence interest (mortgage interest)
> Mortgage interest prepayment penalties
> Investment interest
> Certain interest associated with a passive activity

Interest on other loans for personal purposes which do not fall into one of the above categories is generally referred to as consumer interest and is not deductible. Consumer interest includes interest on any loan, the proceeds of which are used for personal purposes, such as credit card interest, finance charges, and automobile loan interest. Interest on loans used to acquire assets generating tax-exempt income is also not deductible.

The following items are not considered "interest" and, therefore, are not deductible as an itemized deduction for interest:

> Service charges
> Credit investigation fees
> Loan fees other than "points" discussed later under Prepaid Interest
> Interest paid to carry single premium life insurance
> Premium on convertible bonds

Many lenders require that home mortgage borrowers purchase private mortgage insurance (PMI) to protect the lender. Although similar to interest, PMI is not deductible in 2019.

EXAMPLE Fred and Betty Pebblestone, married filing jointly taxpayers, acquired their principal residence in 2014. At the time of the mortgage, the lender required that the Pebblestones acquire private mortgage insurance. In 2019, the Pebblestones paid PMI premiums of $1,700. The Pebblestones may not include the PMI premiums as an itemized deduction for interest in 2019. ♦

As we go to print, it is unknown whether Congress will revive the PMI deduction in 2019.

5-8a Taxpayer's Obligation

To deduct interest on a debt, the taxpayer must be legally liable for the debt. No deduction is allowed for payments made for another's obligation, where the taxpayer is not liable for payment. Also, both the lender and the borrower must intend for the loan to be repaid.

EXAMPLE Bill makes a payment on his son's home mortgage since his son is unable to make the current payment. The interest included in the mortgage payment is not deductible by Bill since the mortgage is not his obligation. Bill's son cannot deduct the interest since he did not make the payment. ♦

EXAMPLE Mary loans her daughter $50,000 to start a business. The daughter is 19 years old and unsophisticated in business. No note is signed and no repayment date is mentioned. Mary would be surprised if the daughter's business venture is a success. In all likelihood, a true debtor-creditor relationship is not created. ♦

A taxpayer who assumes the benefits and burdens of ownership, and is considered to essentially be an owner under state law, may be allowed to deduct mortgage interest on a residence even if not directly liable on the mortgage. This situation is not typical and the deduction is allowed only on a case-by-case basis.

5-8b Prepaid Interest

Cash basis taxpayers are required to use the accrual basis for deducting prepaid interest. Prepaid interest must be capitalized and the deduction spread over the life of the loan. This requirement does not apply to points paid on a mortgage loan for purchasing or improving a taxpayer's principal residence, provided points are customarily charged and they do not exceed the normal rate. Such points paid on a mortgage for the purchase or improvement of a personal residence may be deducted in the year they are paid. Points paid to refinance a home mortgage are not deductible when paid, but must be capitalized and the deduction spread over the life of the loan. Points charged for specific loan services, such as the lender's appraisal fee and other settlement fees, are not deductible.

EXAMPLE On November 1, 2019, Allen, a cash basis taxpayer, obtains a 6-month loan of $500,000 on a new apartment building. On November 1, Allen prepays $36,000 interest on the loan. He must capitalize the prepaid interest and deduct it over the 6-month loan period. Therefore, his interest deduction for 2019 is $12,000 ($36,000/6 months × 2 months). ♦

5-8c Qualified Residence, Home Equity, and Consumer Interest

No deduction is available for consumer (personal) interest, such as interest on credit cards and loans for personal automobiles. Qualified residence interest, however, is a type of personal interest specifically allowed as a deduction. The term "qualified residence interest" is the interest paid on "qualified residence acquisition debt." The term "qualified residence acquisition debt" is defined as debt secured by the taxpayer's principal or second residence in acquiring, constructing, or substantially improving that residence. Qualified residence acquisition debt can include the original mortgage, home equity debt, or refinanced debt. Refinanced debt is treated as acquisition debt only to the extent it does not exceed the principal amount of acquisition debt immediately before the refinancing.

The limit on the amount of interest has changed under the TCJA. The interest deduction pre-TCJA has been available to qualified mortgage debt up to $1 million ($500,000 married filing separately). Through 2025, the TCJA has lowered the amount of qualified mortgage debt to $750,000. For qualified mortgage debt incurred on or before December 15, 2017, the $1 million limit remains in place (thus "grandfathering" existing mortgage debt).

After 2025, the qualified mortgage debt limit returns to $1 million, regardless of the date of the mortgage. Refinancing of pre-TCJA qualified mortgage debt retains the $1 million limit as long as the refinanced debt does not exceed the debt balance at the time of the refinancing.

TAX BREAK

In order to take a home mortgage interest deduction, debt must be secured by a qualified home (primary residence or second home). A "home" includes a house, condominium, cooperative, and mobile home. A home also includes house trailer, boat, or similar property that has sleeping, cooking, and toilet facilities.

EXAMPLE Klaus and Len file jointly in 2019. They purchased their primary residence in New Jersey in January 2016 using a 30-year mortgage of $1,000,000. In 2019, Klaus and Len decide to refinance the amount of their $950,000 mortgage balance. Because the refinanced amount is the same or less than the mortgage balance at the time of the refinancing, the interest on the entire $950,000 balance will remain deductible. ◆

EXAMPLE Meredith and Scott file jointly in 2019. They purchase their primary residence in Palo Alto, CA in January 2019 using a 30-year mortgage of $1,000,000. In 2019, Meredith and Scott pay interest of $38,000 and make no payments toward loan principle and thus the average loan balance is $1,000,000. Because Meredith and Scott's 2019 mortgage exceeds $750,000, the interest deduction will be limited to $28,500 ($38,000 × $750,000/$1,000,000). ◆

The previously permitted deduction of interest on up to $100,000 of home equity debt has been suspended through 2025 (unless the home equity debt is qualified acquisition debt). Unlike the qualified mortgage debt, no provision is made for grandfathering in existing home equity loans.

EXAMPLE Michael and Jeanette Stern file jointly in 2019. In 2003, the Sterns purchased a home using a mortgage of $400,000. In 2016, when the mortgage balance was $50,000, the Sterns used a $300,000 home equity loan to build a substantial addition to their home. The home equity loan is treated as acquisition financing and thus is treated as qualified mortgage debt and the interest remains deductible. The Sterns could also have used the home equity to refinance the original mortgage debt and retained the deduction of interest. ◆

EXAMPLE   Barb is a single taxpayer. In 2019, she uses a home equity loan of $46,000 to pay for a new car and part of her nephew's college tuition. Barb may not deduct any of the interest on the home equity loan. ◆

If the sum of mortgage interest and other itemized deductions is less than the standard deduction, no tax benefit is received from the mortgage interest payments. In this case, a taxpayer may wish to pay the mortgage off as quickly as possible if the taxpayer believes its investments will generate an after-tax rate of return less than the interest rate on the home mortgage.

TAX BREAK

5-8d Education Loan Interest

Taxpayers are allowed a deduction for adjusted gross income (above the line) for certain interest paid on qualified education loans. The deduction is limited to $2,500 for 2019, and is phased out for single taxpayers with modified AGI of $70,000 to $85,000 and for married taxpayers with modified AGI of $140,000 to $170,000. Qualified higher education expenses include tuition, room and board, and related expenses.

EXAMPLE   Sam graduated from college in 2018, taking a job with a salary of $55,000 per year. During 2019, he pays $2,500 interest on qualified education loans. Because his income is below the $70,000 phase-out amount for individual taxpayers, he can deduct the full $2,500 of the interest in arriving at adjusted gross income on his 2019 tax return. If he had paid more than $2,500 in interest, the excess would be considered nondeductible consumer interest. ◆

5-8e Investment Interest

To prevent abuses by taxpayers, the Internal Revenue Code includes a provision limiting the deduction of investment interest expense. This provision limits the amount of deductible interest on loans to finance investments. The investment interest deduction is limited to the taxpayer's net investment income. Net investment income is income such as dividends and interest, less investment expenses other than interest. Special rules apply to dividends and capital gains included as investment income due to their preferential tax rates. The general rule is that they may only be included as investment income if the taxpayer chooses to calculate tax on them at ordinary income rates. Any disallowed interest expense is carried over and may be deducted in succeeding years, but only to the extent that the taxpayer's net investment income exceeds investment interest expense for the year. The investment interest deduction is reported on Form 4952.

EXAMPLE   Karen borrows $150,000 at 12 percent interest on January 1, 2019. The proceeds are used to purchase $100,000 worth of raw land and a $50,000 Certificate of Deposit (CD). During 2019, the CD pays interest of $1,500. Karen incurs expenses attributable to the investment property of $500. Of the $18,000 (12% of $150,000) interest expense incurred in 2019, $1,000 is deductible due to being limited by the total net investment income in 2019. The deduction is computed as follows:

Investment income	$1,500
Less: investment expenses	(500)
Net investment income	$1,000
Interest deductible in 2019	$1,000

The unused deduction of $17,000 ($18,000 − $1,000) is carried forward and may be used as an interest deduction in future years, subject to the net investment income limitation. ◆

Self-Study Problem 5.8   *See Appendix E for Solutions to Self-Study Problems*

Dorothie paid the following amounts during the current year:

Interest on her home mortgage (pre-12/16/17)	$9,250
Service charges on her checking account	48
Credit card interest	168
Auto loan interest	675
Interest from a home equity line of credit (HELOC)	2,300
Interest from a loan used to purchase stock	1,600
Credit investigation fee for loan	75

Dorothie's residence has a fair market value of $250,000. The mortgage is secured by the home at the time of purchase and has a balance of $180,000. Dorothie used the same home to secure her HELOC with a balance of $50,000. Dorothie used the proceeds of her HELOC to pay for college and to buy a new car. Dorothie has $1,000 of net investment income. Compute Dorothie's interest deduction in the following scenarios:

a. Use the Interest You Paid section of Schedule A on Page 5-23 to calculate Dorothie's interest deduction for 2019. $_____

b. Same as part a, and Dorothie used the HELOC proceeds to add a new bedroom to her home. $_____

c. Same as part a, but Dorothie's home is valued at $1.2 million and her mortgage balance is $900,000. $_____

Learning Objective 5.9

Determine the charitable contributions deduction.

5-9 CHARITABLE CONTRIBUTIONS

To encourage individuals to be socially responsible, the Internal Revenue Code allows a deduction for charitable contributions. To be deductible, the donation must be made in cash or property; the value of free use of the taxpayer's property by the charitable organization does not qualify. In addition, out-of-pocket expenses related to qualified charitable activities are deductible as charitable contributions. For example, a taxpayer who drives his car 200 miles during 2019 to take a church group to a meeting out of town would be allowed a charitable deduction of $28 (200 miles × 14 cents per mile).

EXAMPLE   Lucille allows the Red Cross to use her building rent-free for 8 months. The building normally rents for $600 per month. There is no deduction allowed for the free use of the building. ◆

To be deductible, the donation must be made to a qualified recipient as listed in the tax law, including:

1. the United States, a state, or political subdivision thereof, if the donation is made for exclusively public purposes (such as a contribution to pay down the federal debt);
2. domestic organizations formed and operated exclusively for charitable, religious, educational, scientific, or literary purposes, or for the prevention of cruelty to children or animals;
3. church, synagogue, or other religious organizations;
4. war veterans' organizations;
5. civil defense organizations;
6. fraternal societies operating under the lodge system, but only if the contribution is used for one or more of the charitable purposes listed in (2) above; and
7. certain nonprofit cemetery companies.

The following contributions are not deductible:

1. Gifts to nonqualified recipients, for example, needy individuals, social clubs, labor unions, international organizations, and political parties;
2. Contributions of time, service, the use of property, or blood;
3. Contributions where benefit is received from the contribution, for example, tuition at a parochial school; and
4. Wagering losses, such as church bingo and raffle tickets.

If a taxpayer has doubt as to the deductibility of a payment to a specific organization, he or she should review the IRS's online search tool called "Tax Exempt Organization Search."

If cash is donated, the deduction is equal to the amount of the cash. For donated property other than cash, the general rule is that the deduction is equal to the fair market value of the property at the time of the donation. The fair market value is the price at which the property would be sold between a willing buyer and seller. There is an exception to this general rule for property that would have resulted in ordinary income or short-term capital gain had it been sold on the date of the contribution. In that situation, the deduction for the contribution is equal to the property's fair market value less the amount of the ordinary income or short-term capital gain that would have resulted from sale of the property. If the sale of the property would have produced a long-term capital gain, the deduction is generally equal to the fair market value of the property. However, the fair market value is reduced by the amount of the potential long-term capital gain, if the donation is made to certain private nonoperating foundations or the donation is a contribution of tangible personal property to an organization that uses the property for a purpose unrelated to the organization's primary purpose.

EXAMPLE Jeano B. donates a painting acquired 5 years ago at a cost of $4,000 to a museum for exhibition. The painting's fair market value is $12,000. If Jeano had sold the painting, the difference between the sales price ($12,000) and its cost ($4,000) would have been a long-term capital gain. The deduction is $12,000, and it is not reduced by the amount of the appreciation, since the painting was put to a use related to the museum's primary purpose. If the painting had been donated to a hospital, the deduction would be $4,000, which is $12,000 less $8,000 ($12,000 − $4,000), the amount of the long-term capital gain that would have resulted if the painting had been sold. ♦

Rather than donate cash, taxpayers may wish to donate appreciated stock or other appreciated property to charity. If the gift is properly structured, a full deduction may be taken for the fair market value of the donated property, while tax on the appreciation is avoided completely.

TAX BREAK

5-9a Percentage Limitations

Generally, a taxpayer may not deduct total contributions in excess of 50 percent of the taxpayer's adjusted gross income. This 50 percent limitation applies to donations to all public charities, all private operating foundations, and private nonoperating foundations if they distribute their contributions to public charities within a specified time period. The TCJA increased the 50 percent limit to a 60 percent limit for contributions of *cash* to public charities and other 50 percent organizations. Contributions of other than cash remain subject to the 50 percent limit. Gifts to other qualified organizations, such as certain private nonoperating foundations, fraternal societies, and veterans' organizations, as well as gifts for the use of an organization, are limited to 30 percent of adjusted gross income. Special rules apply to contributions of long-term capital gain property. If the full fair market value of a gift of long-term capital gain property is deducted, and the contribution is to a 50 percent organization, the contribution is subject to the 30 percent limit. Taxpayers may avoid the 30 percent limit on contributions of long-term capital gain property by electing to reduce the value of the property by the appreciation that would otherwise be a long-term capital gain, in which case the 50 percent limitation applies. Long-term capital gain property donated to other than a 50 percent organization is subject to a 20 percent of adjusted gross income limitation.

EXAMPLE   In 2019, Tim gave $11,000 to his church. Tim's adjusted gross income is $21,000. Tim's cash donation is subject to the 60 percent limit of $12,600 and thus is deductible. ♦

EXAMPLE   Carol donates publicly traded stock worth $15,000 to a qualified 50 percent charity. The original purchase price of the stock, 10 years ago, was $10,000. Because the stock is a gift of long-term capital gain property, Carol's deduction is limited to 30 percent of her adjusted gross income. Given that Carol's AGI is $20,000, she may take a deduction for $6,000 (30% of $20,000) and may carry the remaining $9,000 ($15,000 − $6,000) forward to the following year. Alternatively, Carol may deduct the original $10,000 cost of the stock using the 50 percent of AGI rule, which would give her a $10,000 deduction in the current year. Even though she would have a larger deduction in the current year, she would lose $5,000 of her potential charitable contribution deduction by choosing this alternative. ♦

Generally, contributions to 50 percent organizations are deducted first, followed by contributions subject to the 30 percent and 20 percent limitations, respectively. Contributions subject to the 30 percent and 20 percent of adjusted gross income limitations are allowed only to the extent that they do not exceed 50 percent of adjusted gross income reduced by the amount of contributions subject to the 50 percent limitation.

In general, any contributions not allowed due to the adjusted gross income limitations may be carried forward for 5 years. The contributions may be deducted in the carryover years subject to the same percentage of income limitations which were applicable to the contributions in the year they originated. Contribution carryovers are allowed only after taking into account the current year contributions in the same category.

EXAMPLE   In March of 2019, Grace contributes $15,000 in cash to a public university. In addition, at the same time she donates $7,000 in cash to an organization subject to the 30 percent of adjusted gross income limitation. Grace has adjusted gross income in 2019 of $35,000. Her contribution deduction is determined as follows:

Adjusted gross income	$35,000
	×60%
60% limitation	21,000
Allowable 60% limitation contributions	(15,000)
Excess 60% limitation	6,000
Maximum 30% contributions:	
Lesser of $6,000 or 30% of adjusted	
gross income, $10,500	6,000
Total deductible contributions:	
60% contributions	15,000
30% contributions	6,000
Total	$21,000

$1,000 of the $7,000 subject to the 30 percent limitation can be carried forward to 2020. ♦

Another change made by the TCJA is that no charitable contribution deduction is permitted for a payment to a college or university in exchange for the right to purchase tickets or seating at an athletic event. Pre-TCJA law permitted an 80 percent deduction for such amounts.

EXAMPLE In 2017, Marco donated $5,000 to Big State University in exchange for the right to purchase 2017 season tickets to Big State football games. Marco deducted $4,000 ($5,000 × 80%) of this donation, which was subject to the 50 percent AGI limit. In 2019, Marco donates $5,000 to Big State University in exchange for the right to purchase 2019 season tickets to Big State football games. Marco may not deduct any of the $5,000 payment. ♦

A tax lawyer pleaded guilty to tax evasion in Federal District Court for substantially overstating his charitable contributions. He told an IRS agent that he put $500 in cash into the church collection basket each week. His pastor, however, said that the church never received more than $500 in currency at all of its weekly church services combined.

5-9b Substantiation Rules

Taxpayers should keep records, receipts, cancelled checks, and other proof of charitable contributions. For gifts of property, for example clothes and household goods given to the Salvation Army, totaling over $500, the taxpayer must attach a Form 8283 to his or her return giving the name and address of the donee, the date of the contribution, a description of the property, the approximate date of acquisition of the property, and certain other required information. For large gifts of property worth $5,000 or more, the donor must also obtain and submit an appraisal.

No charitable deduction is allowed for contributions of $250 or more unless the taxpayer substantiates the contributions with written acknowledgments from the recipient charitable organizations. The acknowledgments must contain this information:

- The amount of cash and a description (but not the value) of property other than cash contributed.
- Whether the charitable organization provided any goods or services in consideration, in whole or in part, for any property contributed. (If a payment is partly a gift and partly in consideration for goods or services provided to the donor, it is a "quid pro quo contribution" and special rules apply.)
- A description and good-faith estimate of the value of any goods or services provided by the donor, or, if the goods and services consist solely of intangible religious benefits, a statement to that effect. Intangible religious benefits are any benefits provided by organizations formed exclusively for religious purposes and not generally sold in a commercial setting. For example, attendance at church is considered an intangible religious benefit while attendance at a private religious school is not. Therefore, a donation made at a church service is generally considered a charitable contribution while tuition paid to a private religious school is not considered a charitable contribution.

Taxpayers donating amounts of cash smaller than the $250 limit are required to keep a bank record (cancelled check) or a written communication from the charity. Taxpayers who itemize deductions should use checks instead of cash for church and similar cash donations.

Gifts of clothing and household items (including furnishings, electronics, appliances, and linens) must be in "good" condition or better to qualify for a deduction. Also, charitable deductions may be denied for contributions of items with minimal value, such as used socks and undergarments. The rules for noncash contributions were enacted because some taxpayers significantly overstated the value of noncash contributions deducted.

No particular form is prescribed for the written acknowledgment, nor does the donor's tax identification number have to be contained on the acknowledgment. It may be a receipt, letter, postcard, or computer form. The acknowledgment must be obtained on or before the date on which the tax return for the tax year of the contribution is filed, or by the due date (plus extensions) if it is earlier than the actual filing date.

Taxpayers donating used vehicles to charity cannot claim a deduction greater than the amount for which the charity actually sells the vehicle. The charity is required to provide the resale information on Form 1098-C to taxpayers donating vehicles. The same rule also applies to boats and planes donated to charity. Taxpayers must attach Form 1098-C to their tax return to substantiate the deduction. Taxpayers may claim an estimated value for the automobile if the charity does not sell it but rather uses it or gives it to a needy individual. The charity must certify that an exception applies if no resale amount is provided on Form 1098-C.

For quid pro quo contributions (donations involving the receipt of goods or services by the donee), written statements (disclosures) are required from the charitable organization to donors making contributions of more than $75. The disclosures need not be individual letters to donors; they simply provide the donors with good-faith estimates of the value of the goods or services and inform the donors that only the amounts of the contributions in excess of the value of the goods or services are deductible for federal income tax purposes.

A charitable organization knowingly providing false written acknowledgments is subject to penalty (generally $1,000) for aiding and abetting in the understatement of tax liability. A penalty of $10 per contribution per event, capped at $5,000, may be imposed on charities failing to make the required disclosures for quid pro quo contributions.

TAX BREAK

A cash basis taxpayer may charge year-end expenses on a credit card and still deduct the expenses even when payment on the credit card is not made until the next year. Instead of paying medical bills, charitable contributions, or even property taxes by check at year-end, the taxpayer may prefer to charge the expense. Note, however, that the credit card may not be one issued by the company supplying the deductible goods or services, but must be a card issued by a third party.

Self-Study Problem 5.9   *See Appendix E for Solutions to Self-Study Problems*

In 2019, Eric gave $11,000 to his church. He donated $75 to Boy Scouts of America and $125 to the Mexican Red Cross. Eric gave the Salvation Army used clothes in good condition worth $150 (original cost $1,700). Eric donated $500 to Rhode Island State University (his alma mater) for the right to buy season tickets to the Fightin' Nutmeggers basketball games. Eric's adjusted gross income is $21,000. Use the Gifts to Charity section of Schedule A on Page 5-23 to report Eric's deduction for the current year.

5-10 OTHER ITEMIZED DEDUCTIONS

The final portion of this chapter discusses the significant changes that the TCJA made to other miscellaneous deductions and to the casualty and theft losses. In addition to these changes, the TCJA also suspended the phase-out of itemized deductions for high income taxpayers (the "Pease" phase-out).

5-10a Casualty and Theft Losses

Taxpayers are allowed deductions for certain casualty and theft losses. The deductions may be itemized deductions or, if related to a business, deductions for adjusted gross income. A casualty is a complete or partial destruction of property resulting from an identifiable event of a sudden, unexpected, or unusual nature. Examples of casualties include property damage from storms, floods, shipwrecks, fires, automobile accidents, and vandalism. For damage from weather conditions to be deductible, the condition must be unusual for the particular region. To qualify as a casualty, an automobile accident must not be caused by the taxpayer's willful act or willful negligence.

EXAMPLE   A taxpayer has an automobile that he decides is a lemon, and he wants to get rid of it. He drives the automobile to the top of a cliff and pushes it off. There is no casualty loss deduction since the act is willful. ◆

Many events do not qualify as casualties. For example, progressive deterioration from rust or corrosion and disease or insect damage are usually not "sudden" enough to qualify as casualties. The IRS has held that termite damage is not deductible as a casualty; however, several courts have in the past allowed the deduction. Indirect losses, such as losses in property value due to damage to neighboring property, also are not deductible.

If the taxpayer can establish that theft occurred, theft losses are deductible. It is important to show that the item was not simply misplaced. Theft losses are deductible in the year the theft is discovered, not in the year the theft took place. This is important in cases of embezzlement, where the theft has gone on over many years and the statute of limitations has run out on earlier years, otherwise preventing the taxpayer from amending returns for those years.

As a general rule, casualty losses are deductible in the year of occurrence, but there is an exception for federally declared disaster area losses. Taxpayers may elect to treat the losses in a disaster area as a deduction in the year prior to the year the casualty occurred. If a return has already been filed for the prior year, an amended return may be filed and a refund claimed for the prior year's taxes paid. This provision is designed to provide taxpayers with cash on a more timely basis when they have suffered severe casualties.

EXAMPLE   In May of 2019, Amy's house is damaged by flooding. Shortly thereafter, the president of the United States declared the region a disaster area. The damage to the house is $6,000 and the loss may be deducted in 2018 or 2019, even if the 2018 return has already been filed. If Amy elects to take the deduction in 2018, she may immediately file an amended tax return for that year and collect a refund of previously paid taxes. ◆

5-10b Measuring the Loss

The amount of the casualty or theft loss is measured by one of the following two rules:

Rule A—The deduction is based on the decrease in fair market value of the property, not to exceed the adjusted basis of the property.

Rule B—The deduction is based on the adjusted basis of the property.

Rule A applies to the partial destruction of business or investment property and the partial or complete destruction of personal property, while Rule B applies to the complete destruction of business and investment property. The cost of repairs is usually used for the measurement of loss from automobile damage. Repair costs may also be used to measure losses involving other types of property, but it is not controlling. Indirect costs, such as cleanup costs, are part of the loss, provided the payments do not restore the property to better than its previous condition.

EXAMPLE   A taxpayer purchased his house 15 years ago for $25,000. Today it is worth $160,000, and heavy rains cause the house to slide into a canyon and be completely destroyed. The taxpayer's casualty loss deduction under Rule A is the decrease in fair market value ($160,000 − $0) not to exceed the taxpayer's basis ($25,000). Thus, the deduction is limited to $25,000. ♦

5-10c Deduction Limitations

The TCJA suspended the allowable loss for personal casualty losses except when the loss is attributable to a federally declared disaster. Such losses are subject to a $100 floor per casualty and must exceed 10 percent of AGI to be deducted. The restriction to a federally declared disaster applies to tax years 2018 to 2025. If a taxpayer has a net casualty gain, the declared disaster restriction does not apply to the extent of the gain. If related to business property, there is no adjusted gross income limitation or dollar reduction applicable to casualty and theft losses; such losses are deductions for adjusted gross income.

EXAMPLE   In 2019, Wanda incurs a loss due to a complete destruction of her personal use car due to a casualty event not attributable to a federally declared disaster. Her adjusted basis in the car was $19,000 and the fair market value at the time of the loss was $8,000. Wanda's AGI is $55,000. Wanda was not insured for this type of loss and received no reimbursement. Wanda will not be able to deduct any of her loss as it was not attributable to a federally declared disaster.

If instead Wanda's loss was attributable to a federally declared disaster, she can deduct $8,000 less the $100 floor and also less 10 percent of her AGI:

$$\$2,400 = \$8,000 - \$100 - \$5,500 \;\blacklozenge$$

EXAMPLE   Cosmo incurs two personal losses during 2019. His car was stolen and destroyed by the thieves. His basis in the car was $22,000 and the fair market value at the time of the theft was $16,000. Cosmo also lost a family heirloom watch worth $4,000 in a different theft. Neither of these losses is attributable to a federally declared disaster. Cosmo's insurance covered the auto and reimbursed him $22,000 but the loss of the watch was not covered. Cosmo's casualty gain on the auto is $6,000 ($22,000 − $16,000) and his loss on the watch is $3,900 ($4,000 − $100 floor). Because Cosmo experienced a net casualty gain of $2,100, he may deduct the casualty loss against the gain despite the loss not being attributable to a federally declared disaster. ♦

Certain disasters can be deemed "qualified" federal disasters and were eligible for additional relief. For example, certain areas affected by Hurricanes Harvey, Irma, and Maria as well as the California wildfires were declared qualified federal disaster areas. The rules for qualified federal disasters require the taxpayer to use a $500 floor (instead of $100) but do not subject the casualty loss to the 10 percent AGI limitation. In addition, taxpayers that do not itemize were permitted to add the qualified federal disaster area loss to the standard deduction. At the time we go to print, areas affected by Hurricane Dorian were declared a federal disaster area and eligible for personal casualty losses, but were not declared *qualified* federal disaster areas extending additional loss benefits.

A casualty or theft loss is reported on Form 4684 and then the deductible amount is generally taken as an itemized deduction on Schedule A.

Entering the loss from a casualty is input on the left navigation menu. Select Income and then Schedule D/4797/etc. Scroll down to Casualties and Thefts (4868).

5-10d Miscellaneous Expenses

Miscellaneous itemized deductions are categorized into two types: (1) those subject to the 2 percent of AGI floor and (2) those not subject to the 2 percent of AGI floor.

The TCJA suspended the deduction of all miscellaneous itemized deductions subject to the 2 percent of AGI rule; thus, these items will no longer be deductible for tax years 2018 to 2025. The most common deductions subject to the 2 percent of AGI rule are:

- Unreimbursed employee business expenses and employee expenses reimbursed under a nonaccountable plan
- Investment expenses
- Other miscellaneous expenses including the all-important tax preparation fees

The most common unreimbursed employee expenses are included in the following list:

- Business bad debt of an employee.	- Malpractice insurance premiums.
- Business liability insurance premiums.	- Medical examinations required by an employer.
- Damages paid to a former employer for breach of an employment contract.	- Occupational taxes.
	- Passport for a business trip.
- Depreciation on a computer your employer requires you to use in your work.	- Repayment of an income aid payment received under an employer's plan.
- Dues to a chamber of commerce if membership helps you do your job.	- Research expenses of a college professor.
- Dues to professional societies.	- Rural mail carriers' vehicle expenses.
- Educator expenses.	- Subscriptions to professional journals and trade magazines related to your work.
- Home office or part of your home used regularly and exclusively in your work.	- Tools and supplies used in your work.
- Job search expenses in your present occupation.	- Travel, transportation, meals, entertainment, gifts, and local lodging related to your work.
- Laboratory breakage fees.	- Union dues and expenses.
- Legal fees related to your job.	- Work clothes and uniforms if required and not suitable for everyday use.
- Licenses and regulatory fees.	- Work-related education.

The repeal of miscellaneous deductions subject to the 2 percent floor could result in an employee being subject to additional tax liability when receiving reimbursement from an employer without an accountable plan. Since changing from an employee to an independent contractor is generally not possible without a significant change in the relationship between the individual and the business (this is a matter of law, not a choice by either the employee or employer), taxpayers that are employees in this situation may want to inquire if an accountable plan can be implemented by their employer going forward.

Miscellaneous itemized deductions not subject to the 2 percent floor were not affected by the TCJA. This category of expenses includes the following items:

- Amortizable premium on taxable bonds.
- Casualty and theft losses from income-producing property.
- Federal estate tax on income in respect of a decedent.
- Gambling losses up to the amount of gambling winnings.
- Impairment-related work expenses of persons with disabilities.
- Loss from other activities from Schedule K-1 (Form 1065-B), Box 2.
- Losses from Ponzi-type investment schemes.
- Repayments of more than $3,000 under a claim of right.
- Unrecovered investment in an annuity.

Gambling losses are not subject to the 2 percent limitation and are not directly limited. Because gambling losses are only deductible for taxpayers that itemize deductions and the TCJA increased the standard deduction and limited itemized deductions for many taxpayers, fewer taxpayers may itemize and therefore fewer taxpayers may be eligible to deduct gambling losses. Gambling winnings must be reported as other income on Form 1040 and losses may be deducted on Schedule A only to the extent of winnings.

5-10e Phase-out of Itemized Deductions

Prior to 2018, certain high-income taxpayers were subject to limits on the amount of itemized deductions. Certain AGI limits for different filing status triggered a reduction in itemized deductions by the lesser of 3 percent of the excess of the taxpayer's AGI over the threshold amount or 80 percent of itemized deductions excluding the deductions for medical expenses, investment interest expense, casualty and theft losses, and gambling losses to the extent of gambling income. The TCJA suspended the phase-out.

Self-Study Problem 5.10   *See Appendix E for Solutions to Self-Study Problems*

During 2019, Robert (a single taxpayer) is an employee and has AGI of $35,000. He lives in Jupiter, FL 33477.

a. Robert's community was struck with a hurricane. During the storm a tree blew over and destroyed his car. The storm was declared a federal disaster (FEMA Code EM-5566). The market value of the car on the date of destruction was $14,000. Robert purchased the car in July 2016 at a cost of $18,500. Robert's car was only partially covered for this type of loss and his insurance paid him $5,000. Calculate Robert's casualty or theft loss on Form 4684 on Page 5-41 and carry any deductible amount to the Casualty and Theft Losses section of the Schedule A on Page 5-23.

b. Robert also incurs the following expenses:

Safe-deposit box rental (for investments)	$ 25
Tax return preparation fees	450
Professional dues	175
Trade journals	125
Bank trust fees	1,055
Qualifying job hunting expenses	1,400
Total	$3,230

Robert also had a big day at the casinos and won $1,400. Over the year, he had substantiation for $1,700 in gambling losses. Assuming Robert is not self-employed, calculate any miscellaneous deductions and enter them in the Other Itemized Deductions section of Schedule A on Page 5-23.

Self-Study Problem 5.10

Form **4684**

Department of the Treasury
Internal Revenue Service

Casualties and Thefts

▶ Go to *www.irs.gov/Form4684* for instructions and the latest information.
▶ Attach to your tax return.
▶ Use a separate Form 4684 for each casualty or theft.

OMB No. 1545-0177

20**19**

Attachment
Sequence No. **26**

Name(s) shown on tax return

Identifying number

SECTION A—Personal Use Property (Use this section to report casualties and thefts of property **not** used in a trade or business or for income-producing purposes. You must use a separate Form 4684 (through line 12) for each casualty or theft event involving personal use property. **If reporting a qualified disaster loss, see the instructions for special rules that apply before completing this section.**)

If the casualty or theft loss is attributable to a federally declared disaster, check here ☐ and enter the FEMA disaster declaration number. (See instructions.) _____

1   Description of properties (show type, location (city, state, and ZIP code), and date acquired for each property). Use a separate line for each property lost or damaged from the same casualty or theft. If you checked the box and entered the FEMA disaster declaration number above, enter the ZIP code for the property most affected on the line for Property **A**.

	Type of Property	City and State	ZIP Code	Date Acquired
Property **A**				
Property **B**				
Property **C**				
Property **D**				

		Properties			
		A	**B**	**C**	**D**
2 Cost or other basis of each property	2				
3 Insurance or other reimbursement (whether or not you filed a claim) (see instructions) **Note:** If line 2 is **more** than line 3, skip line 4.	3				
4 Gain from casualty or theft. If line 3 is **more** than line 2, enter the difference here and skip lines 5 through 9 for that column. See instructions if line 3 includes insurance or other reimbursement you did not claim, or you received payment for your loss in a later tax year	4				
5 Fair market value **before** casualty or theft	5				
6 Fair market value **after** casualty or theft	6				
7 Subtract line 6 from line 5	7				
8 Enter the **smaller** of line 2 or line 7	8				
9 Subtract line 3 from line 8. If zero or less, enter -0-	9				

10 Casualty or theft loss. Add the amounts on line 9 in columns A through D	10	
11 Enter $100 ($500 if qualified disaster loss rules apply; see instructions)	11	
12 Subtract line 11 from line 10. If zero or less, enter -0-	12	

Caution: Use only one Form 4684 for lines 13 through 18.

13 Add the amounts on line 4 of all Forms 4684	13	
14 Add the amounts on line 12 of all Forms 4684. If you have losses not attributable to a federally declared disaster, see the instructions	14	

Caution: See instructions before completing line 15.

15   • If line 13 is **more** than line 14, enter the difference here and on Schedule D. **Do not** complete the rest of this section.

   • If line 13 is **equal** to line 14, enter -0- here. **Do not** complete the rest of this section.
   • If line 13 is **less** than line 14, and you have no qualified disaster losses subject to the $500 reduction on line 11 on any Form(s) 4684, enter -0- here and go to line 16. If you have qualified disaster losses subject to the $500 reduction, subtract line 13 from line 14 and enter the smaller of this difference or the amount on line 12 of the Form(s) 4684 reporting those losses. Enter that result here and on Schedule A (Form 1040 or 1040-SR), line 16, or Form 1040-NR, Schedule A, line 7. If you claim the standard deduction, also include on Schedule A (Form 1040 or 1040-SR), line 16, the amount of your standard deduction (see the Instructions for Forms 1040 and 1040-SR). Do not complete the rest of this section if all of your casualty or theft losses are subject to the $500 reduction.

	15	
16 Add lines 13 and 15. Subtract the result from line 14	16	
17 Enter 10% of your adjusted gross income from Form 1040 or 1040-SR, line 8b, or Form 1040-NR, line 35. Estates and trusts, see instructions	17	
18 Subtract line 17 from line 16. If zero or less, enter -0-. Also, enter the result on Schedule A (Form 1040 or 1040-SR), line 15, or Form 1040-NR, Schedule A, line 6. Estates and trusts, enter the result on the "Other deductions" line of your tax return	18	

For Paperwork Reduction Act Notice, see instructions.   Cat. No. 12997O   Form **4684** (2019)

KEY TERMS

Health Savings Accounts (HSAs), 5-2
traditional IRA, 5-8
Roth IRA, 5-8
annual contribution limits, 5-8
"catch-up" contribution, 5-8
nondeductible traditional IRA, 5-10
Roth IRA conversions, 5-11
early withdrawal, 5-11
distributions, 5-11
SEP IRA, 5-13
Payroll Deduction IRA, 5-14
SIMPLE IRA, 5-14
Section 401(k) plan, 5-14

Self-employed or Solo 401(k), 5-15
Safe harbor 401(k), 5-15
Roth 401(k), 5-15
tax, 5-21
fee, 5-21
estimated sales tax tables, 5-25
consumer interest, 5-28
prepaid interest, 5-29
qualified residence interest
  (mortgage interest), 5-29
qualified residence acquisition
  debt, 5-30
home equity debt, 5-30

investment interest, 5-31
charitable contributions, 5-32
qualified recipient, 5-32
nonqualified recipients, 5-33
Tax Exempt Organization Search,
  5-33
50 percent limitation, 5-33
30 percent limitation, 5-33
20 percent limitation, 5-34
substantiation rules, 5-35
casualty, 5-37
"qualified" federal disasters, 5-38

KEY POINTS

Learning Objectives	Key Points
LO 5.1: Explain how Health Savings Accounts (HSAs) can be used for tax-advantaged medical care.	• Health Savings Accounts (HSAs) are used for the purpose of paying unreimbursed medical expenses. • HSAs have an annual age-based contribution dollar limitation for deductions for individuals ($3,500) and families ($7,000). There is an additional $1,000 "catch-up" contribution allowed for individuals beginning at age 55 and ending at age 65, the age for Medicare eligibility. 3 • Distributions from HSAs are tax-exempt when used to pay for qualified medical expenses. Distributions which are not used to pay for qualified medical expenses may be subject to income tax and a 20 percent penalty. • Once a taxpayer is 65 years old, distributions may be taken for nonmedical expenses and will be subject to income tax, but not the 20 percent penalty.
LO 5.2: Describe the self-employed health insurance deduction.	• Deductible health insurance includes: (1) medical and dental insurance paid to cover the self-employed taxpayer, spouse, and dependents; (2) medical and dental insurance paid for children under the age of 27 who are not dependents; (3) Medicare premiums; and (4) long-term care insurance paid for the taxpayer and the family of the taxpayer. • Taxpayers with income reportable on Schedule C are generally considered self-employed. • Taxpayers with earnings from certain partnerships, S corporations, LLCs, and farm businesses may also be considered self-employed and may be allowed the deduction for self-employed health insurance. • The deduction for self-employed health insurance is only allowed to the extent of the taxpayer's net self-employed income.

LO 5.3: Explain the treatment of Individual Retirement Accounts (IRAs), including Roth IRAs.	• Generally, annual contributions to a traditional IRA are deductible and retirement distributions are taxable, while annual contributions to a Roth IRA are not deductible and retirement distributions are nontaxable. • Earnings in both types of IRAs are not taxable in the current year. • In 2019, the maximum annual contribution that may be made to either type of IRA is equal to the lesser of (1) 100 percent of the taxpayer's compensation or self-employment income (earned income) or (2) $6,000 (plus an additional $6,000 which may be contributed on behalf of a spouse with no earned income). An additional catch-up $1,000 annual contribution is allowed for taxpayers age 50 and over. • The tax deduction for contributions to traditional IRAs is limited for taxpayers who are active participants in qualified retirement plans and have income over certain limits. Contributions to Roth IRAs are limited for taxpayers with income over certain limits, but they are not affected by taxpayer participation in other retirement plans. • Taxpayers may benefit from a rule allowing conversions of traditional IRAs into Roth IRAs. • Generally, money distributed from a traditional IRA is taxable as ordinary income and may be subject to a 10 percent penalty for early withdrawal (before age 59½). Some types of early withdrawals may be made without penalty. • A taxpayer can make tax-free withdrawals from a Roth IRA after a 5-year holding period if the distribution is made on or after the date on which the participant attains age 59½. Other tax-free withdrawals may also apply.
LO 5.4: Explain the general contribution rules for small business and self-employed retirement plans.	• Employers may claim a deduction in the current year for contributions to qualified retirement plans on employees' behalf. The employees do not include the employer contributions in income until the contributed amounts are distributed. • For 2019, contributions to retirement plans by self-employed taxpayers are generally limited to the lesser of 20 percent of their net earned income before the contribution deduction or $56,000. • For 2019, the maximum employee contribution to a SEP is the lesser of 25 percent of compensation or $56,000. • For 2019, an employee may elect to make an annual contribution up to $19,000 ($25,000 for taxpayers age 50 or older) to a Section 401(k) plan. In addition, any matching amount contributed to the plan by the employer on behalf of the employee is excluded from the employee's gross income.
LO 5.5: Describe other adjustments for adjusted gross income.	• Eligible educators may deduct up to $250 for the unreimbursed cost of classroom materials. • Certain performing artists, reservists, and fee-based government officials can deduct unreimbursed employee expenses as a for AGI deduction. • Starting in 2018, moving expenses are only deductible for members of the Armed Forces pursuant to a military order and permanent change of station.
LO 5.6: Calculate the itemized deduction for medical expenses.	• Taxpayers are allowed an itemized deduction on Schedule A for medical expenses paid for themselves, their spouse, and their dependents. • Qualified medical expenses are deductible only to the extent they exceed 10 percent of a taxpayer's adjusted gross income. • Qualified medical expenses include such items as prescription medicines and drugs, insulin, fees for doctors, dentists, nurses, and other medical professionals, hospital fees, hearing aids, dentures, prescription eyeglasses, contact lenses, medical transportation and lodging, crutches, wheelchairs, guide dogs, birth control prescriptions, acupuncture, psychiatric care, medical and Medicare insurance premiums, and various other listed medical expenses.

LO 5.7:

Calculate the itemized deduction for taxes.

- The following taxes are deductible on Schedule A: state and local income taxes or state and local sales taxes, real property taxes (state and local), and personal property taxes (state and local).
- The itemized deduction for taxes is limited to $10,000.
- Nondeductible taxes include the following: federal income taxes, employee portion of Social Security taxes, estate, inheritance, and gift taxes (except in unusual situations), gasoline taxes, excise taxes, and foreign taxes if the taxpayer elects a foreign tax credit.
- If real estate is sold during the year, the taxes must be allocated between the buyer and seller based on the number of days in the year that each taxpayer held the property to determine each party's deductible amount.
- To be deductible, personal property taxes must be levied based on the value of the property. Personal property taxes of a fixed amount, or those calculated on a basis other than value, are not deductible.

LO 5.8:

Apply the rules for an individual taxpayer's interest deduction.

- Deductible personal interest includes qualified residence interest (mortgage interest), mortgage interest prepayment penalties, investment interest, and certain interest associated with a passive activity.
- Nondeductible consumer interest includes interest on any loan, the proceeds of which are used for personal purposes, such as credit card interest, finance charges, and automobile loan interest.
- "Qualified residence interest" is the sum of the interest paid on "qualified residence acquisition debt."
- Taxpayers are allowed a deduction for AGI for certain interest paid on qualified education loans.
- Deductible investment interest is limited to the taxpayer's net investment income, which is investment income such as dividends and interest, less investment expenses other than interest.

LO 5.9:

Determine the charitable contributions deduction.

- To be deductible, the donation must be made in cash or property.
- Donations must be made to a qualified recipient.
- The following contributions are not deductible: gifts to needy individuals, social clubs, labor unions, international organizations, and political parties; contributions of time, service, the use of property, or blood; contributions where benefit is received from the contribution, for example, tuition at a parochial school; and wagering losses, such as church bingo and raffle tickets.
- For donated property other than cash, the general rule is that the deduction is equal to the fair market value of the property at the time of the donation.
- Donations are limited to 60, 50, 30, or 20 percent of AGI in certain cases.

LO 5.10:

Describe other itemized deductions.

- Starting in 2018, a loss from a personal casualty such as property damage from storms, floods, shipwrecks, fires, automobile accidents, and vandalism is only deductible if associated with a federally declared disaster.
- For the partial destruction of business or investment property and the partial or complete destruction of personal property, the deduction is based on the decrease in fair market value of the property, not to exceed the adjusted basis of the property.
- For the complete destruction of business and investment property, the deduction is based on the adjusted basis of the property.
- The amount of each personal casualty loss attributable to a federally declared disaster, is reduced by $100 and only the excess over 10 percent of the taxpayer's AGI is deductible.
- Starting in 2018, the deduction for miscellaneous expenses subject to the 2 percent of AGI limit is suspended until 2025.
- Miscellaneous expenses not subject to the 2 percent of AGI limit such as gambling losses to the extent of gambling winnings, handicapped "impairment-related work expenses," certain estate taxes, amortizable bond premiums, and unrecovered annuity costs at death remain deductible.
- The phase-out of itemized deductions for high-income taxpayers has been suspended.

QUESTIONS and PROBLEMS

GROUP 1:
MULTIPLE CHOICE QUESTIONS

LO 5.1
1. Which of the following is a *false* statement about Health Savings Accounts (HSAs)?
   a. Taxpayers who contribute to an HSA must carry qualifying high-deductible health insurance.
   b. HSAs are available to any taxpayer using a health plan purchased through the state or federal exchange under the Affordable Care Act.
   c. Distributions from HSAs are not taxable when used to pay qualifying medical expenses.
   d. Taxpayers must contribute to the HSA by April 15 of the year following the tax year for which they want the deduction.
   e. Distributions from HSAs which are not used to pay qualifying medical expenses are generally subjected to a 20 percent penalty as well as income taxes.

LO 5.1
2. Charlene has self-only coverage in a qualifying high-deductible health insurance plan. She is 47 years old and wishes to contribute the maximum amount to her HSA. How much is she allowed to contribute and deduct in 2019?
   a. $1,000
   b. $1,300
   c. $3,450
   d. $3,500
   e. $4,600

LO 5.2
3. Which type of insurance is *not* deductible as self-employed health insurance?
   a. Medical insurance
   b. Disability insurance
   c. Dental insurance
   d. Long-term care insurance
   e. Spousal medical insurance

LO 5.2
4. Which of the following is *true* about the self-employed health insurance deduction?
   a. The deduction can be claimed when a subsidized employer health insurance plan is also available.
   b. The deduction can be claimed if the taxpayer has an overall business loss from self-employment.
   c. Long-term care premiums may not be deducted within specified dollar limitations based on age.
   d. The self-employed health insurance deduction is a for AGI deduction.
   e. Dental insurance is not included as deductible self-employed health insurance.

LO 5.3
5. Lyndon, age 24, has a nonworking spouse and earns wages of $36,000 for 2019. He also received rental income of $5,000 and dividend income of $900 for the year. What is the maximum amount Lyndon can deduct for contributions to his and his wife's individual retirement accounts for the 2019 tax year?
   a. $11,000
   b. $5,500
   c. $6,000
   d. $12,000
   e. None of the above

LO 5.3

6. Martha and Rob, a married couple, under 50 years of age, have adjusted gross income on their 2019 joint income tax return of $45,000, before considering any IRA deduction. Martha and Rob have no earned income. What is the amount of Martha's maximum deductible IRA contribution?
   a. $2,700
   b. $3,500
   c. $5,500
   d. $11,000
   e. $0

LO 5.3

7. Donna, age 42 and a single taxpayer, has a salary of $104,500 and interest income of $20,000. What is the maximum amount Donna can contribute to a Roth IRA?
   a. $5,000
   b. $3,850
   c. $6,000
   d. $5,500
   e. Some other amount

LO 5.3

8. Mary has a Roth IRA held more than 5 years to which she has contributed $30,000. The IRA has a current value of $62,000. Mary is 55 years old and she takes a distribution of $38,000. How much of the distribution will be taxable to Mary?
   a. $0
   b. $8,000
   c. $10,000
   d. $40,000
   e. Some other amount

LO 5.3

9. Marge has a Roth IRA held more than 5 years to which she has contributed $30,000. The IRA has a current value of $62,000. Marge is 65 years old and she takes a distribution of $38,000. How much of the distribution will be taxable to Marge?
   a. $0
   b. $8,000
   c. $30,000
   d. $38,000
   e. Some other amount

LO 5.3

10. Mindy has a Roth IRA held longer than 5 years to which she has contributed $30,000. The IRA has a current value of $62,000. Mindy is 55 years old and she takes a distribution of $38,000 after retiring on disability. How much of the distribution will be taxable to Mindy?
    a. $0
    b. $8,000
    c. $30,000
    d. $38,000
    e. Some other amount

LO 5.3

11. What is the deadline for making a contribution to a traditional IRA or a Roth IRA for 2019?
    a. April 15, 2020
    b. April 17, 2019
    c. December 31, 2019
    d. October 15, 2020

LO 5.4

12. Which of the following statements with respect to a qualified retirement plan is accurate?
    a. Self-employed individuals are not eligible to be members of a SEP.
    b. Contributions to SIMPLE IRAs are limited to 15 percent of the taxpayer's net earned income or $100,000, whichever is greater.
    c. "Net earned income" includes the taxpayer's wages from employment.
    d. Taxpayers must begin receiving distributions from a qualified plan by the age of 65.
    e. None of these statements are accurate.

LO 5.4

13. What is the maximum tax-deferred contribution that can be made to a Section 401(k) plan by an employee under age 50 in 2019?
   a. $19,000
   b. $20,000
   c. $18,500
   d. $18,000
   e. $56,000

LO 5.4

14. Paul, age 37, participates in a Section 401(k) plan which allows employees to contribute up to 15 percent of their salary. His annual salary is $125,000 in 2019. What is the maximum he can contribute, on a tax-deferred basis under a salary reduction agreement, to this plan?
   a. $24,000
   b. $20,500
   c. $18,500
   d. $18,000
   e. None of the above

LO 5.5
LO 5.10

15. Eliza is a kindergarten teacher for Alexander Hamilton Elementary School. Eliza decorates her classroom with new artwork, posters, bulletin boards, etc. In 2019, she spends $470 on materials and supplies for her classroom. The school reimburses her $100 (the annual reimbursement limit). Eliza can deduct _____ for AGI and _____ from AGI.
   a. $0 for and $0 from AGI
   b. $370 for and $0 from AGI
   c. $250 for and $120 from AGI
   d. $250 for and $0 from AGI
   e. $0 for and $370 from AGI

LO 5.5

16. Jessica is a U.S. Army Reservist and in 2019 traveled 130 miles each way to serve duty at a local military installation. She was required to report four times in 2019. Her normal route from home to the base included a $1.75 toll each way. Jessica's for AGI deduction for these costs is:
   a. $0
   b. $617.20
   c. $122.00
   d. $566.80
   e. $580.80

LO 5.6

17. The cost of which of the following expenses is *not* deductible as a medical expense on Schedule A, before the 10 percent of adjusted gross income limitation?
   a. A psychiatrist
   b. Botox treatment to reduce wrinkles around eyes
   c. Acupuncture
   d. Expense to hire and train a guide dog for a visually-impaired taxpayer

LO 5.6

18. The cost of which of the following is deductible as a medical expense?
   a. Travel to a warm climate
   b. Birth control pills
   c. A disability insurance policy that pays $200 for each day the taxpayer is in the hospital
   d. Liposuction to reduce waist size

LO 5.6

19. Which of the following is not considered a deductible medical expense?
   a. Once daily multivitamin
   b. Prescription eyeglasses
   c. Acupuncture
   d. Filling a tooth cavity

LO 5.7

20. Which of the following taxes may be deducted as itemized deduction?
    a. State gasoline taxes
    b. Local property taxes
    c. Federal income taxes
    d. Social Security taxes
    e. Medicare taxes

LO 5.7

21. In April 2019, Fred paid $60 of state income tax that was due when he filed his 2018 income tax return. During 2019, Fred's employer withheld $1,500 of state income tax from his pay. In April 2020, Fred determined that his 2019 state tax liability was on $1,200 and received his state income tax refund of $300 in May 2020. Assuming Fred itemizes, how much state income tax deduction should he report on his 2019 federal income tax return?
    a. $1,200
    b. $1,260
    c. $1,500
    d. $1,560
    e. $900

LO 5.7

22. Antonio is a small business owner and files jointly with his spouse. In 2019, he generates $100,000 of net profits from his business. His spouse, Maria, has $4,000 of state income tax withheld from her wages in 2019. They also pay $4,500 in property taxes on their home. Antonio determines that their state income taxes associated with his business are about $5,600 and makes estimated state income tax payments of that amount in 2019. How much should Antonio and Maria deduct for state taxes?
    a. Itemized deductions of $9,500 and deduct $5,600 for taxes on Antonio's Schedule C for his business
    b. Itemized deductions of $10,000 and deduct $5,100 for taxes on Antonio's Schedule C for his business
    c. Itemized deductions of $10,000
    d. Itemized deductions of $4,000 and deduct $5,600 for taxes on Antonio's Schedule C for his business

LO 5.7

23. The itemized deduction for state and local taxes in 2019 is
    a. Total taxes less 10 percent of AGI
    b. Limited to no more than $10,000
    c. Unlimited
    d. Only deductible if the taxes are business related
    e. Deductible if your home value is less than $750,000

LO 5.8

24. Which of the following is deductible as interest on Schedule A?
    a. Fees for having the home's value assessed by the bank for purposes of getting a mortgage
    b. Fees for having a new home inspected prior to purchase
    c. Interest of $32,000 on a mortgage of $967,000 for a primary residence that was purchased in 2016
    d. Interest on loans to finance tax-exempt bonds
    e. None of the above are deductible as interest

LO 5.8

25. Carrie, a single taxpayer, finished h3er undergraduate degree using money from a student loan. She earned $126,000 her first year and paid $2,600 in interest in 2019. She can take a deduction for student loan interest in the amount of:
    a. $2,600
    b. $2,500
    c. $1,500
    d. $0
    e. None of the above

LO 5.8

26. Which of the following interest expense amounts is *not* deductible in the current year?
    a. Education loan interest of $2,000, assuming the taxpayer has income of $30,000.
    b. Home equity loan interest of $6,000, on a loan of $90,000, the proceeds of which were used to add a new bedroom and bathroom to an existing primary residence.
    c. Investment interest expense of $10,000, assuming the taxpayer has no investment income.
    d. Qualified residence interest of $70,000 on a $730,000 loan used to purchase a luxury apartment in downtown San Diego.

LO 5.9

27. Which of the following donations are *not* deductible as a charitable contribution?
    a. A donation of clothing to Goodwill Industries
    b. A cash contribution to a church
    c. A contribution of stock to a public university
    d. A contribution of a taxpayer's time picking up trash on the beach
    e. A painting contributed to a museum

LO 5.9

28. Stanley donates a hotel to a university for use as a conference center. The building was purchased 3 years ago for $1,500,000 and has a fair market value of $1,900,000 on the date the contribution is made. If Stanley had sold the building, the $400,000 difference between the sales price and cost would have been a long-term capital gain. What is the amount of Stanley's deduction for this contribution, before considering any limitation based on adjusted gross income?
    a. $2,300,000
    b. $1,500,000
    c. $1,900,000
    d. $0
    e. The amount cannot be determined from the information given

LO 5.9

29. In March of 2019, Thomas makes a $5,000 cash contribution to a public university. In that month, he also donates $20,000 to an organization subject to the 30 percent limitation. Thomas has adjusted gross income for 2019 of $30,000. What is the amount of Thomas's 2019 charitable contribution deduction?
    a. $5,000
    b. $23,000
    c. $14,000
    d. $15,500
    e. None of the above

LO 5.9

30. Which of the following gifts is a deductible contribution?
    a. A gift of $100 to a homeless person
    b. A $500 gift to the Democratic National Committee
    c. $1,000 spent on church bingo games
    d. A $200 contribution to your child's public elementary school

LO 5.10

31. Which of the following would typically be deductible as a casualty loss in 2019?
    a. Long-term damage to a home from termites
    b. An automobile accident during the daily commute
    c. A theft of a big screen television
    d. Dropping your smartphone in the pool
    e. None of the above

LO 5.10

32. Which of the following is *not* a possible limitation on the deduction of a personal casualty loss?
    a. The lesser of the fair market value of the property or the adjusted basis at the time of the loss
    b. A $100 floor for each casualty event
    c. A 10 percent of AGI floor for all casualty losses during the year
    d. A personal casualty not associated with a federally declared disaster
    e. All of the above are possible limitations on a personal casualty loss

LO 5.10   33. Which of the following is deductible as a miscellaneous itemized deduction in 2019?
  a. Tax preparation fees
  b. Gambling losses in excess of gambling winnings
  c. Losses from Ponzi-type schemes
  d. Job-hunting expenses subject to the 2 percent of AGI floor
  e. None of the above are deductible as a miscellaneous itemized deduction.

LO 5.10   34. Which of the following items is deductible as a miscellaneous deduction on Schedule A?
  a. Investment expenses
  b. Gambling losses to the extent of gambling winnings
  c. Unreimbursed business expenses
  d. Subscriptions to professional publications
  e. Charitable contributions

GROUP 2:
PROBLEMS

LO 5.1   1. Evan participates in an HSA carrying family coverage for himself, his spouse, and two children. In 2019, Evan has $100 per month deducted from his paycheck and contributed to the HSA. In addition, Evan makes a one-time contribution of $2,000 on April 15, 2020 when he files his tax return. Evan also receives a 2019 Form 1099-SA that reports distributions to Evan of $3,200 which Evan used for medical expenses. Compute the effect of the HSA transactions on Evan's adjusted gross income.

LO 5.2   2. Serena is a 38-year-old single taxpayer. She operates a small business on the side as a sole proprietorship. Her 2019 Schedule C reports net profits of $15,624. Her employer does not offer health insurance. Serena pays health insurance premiums of $7,545 in 2019. Serena also pays long-term care insurance premiums of $600 in 2019. Calculate Serena's self-employed health care deduction.

LO 5.3   3. Karen, 28 years old and a single taxpayer, has a salary of $33,000 and rental income of $33,000 for the 2019 calendar tax year. Karen is covered by a pension through her employer.
  a. What is the maximum amount that Karen may deduct for contributions to her IRA for 2019?

  $_____

  b. If Karen is a calendar year taxpayer and files her tax return on August 15, what is the last date on which she can make her contribution to the IRA and deduct it for 2019?

  $_____

LO 5.3   4. Phil and Linda are 25-year-old newlyweds and file a joint tax return. Linda is covered by a retirement plan at work, but Phil is not.
  a. Assuming Phil's wages were $27,000 and Linda's wages were $18,500 for 2019 and they had no other income, what is the maximum amount of their deductible contributions to an IRA for 2019?

  Phil $_____
  Linda $_____

  b. Assuming Phil's wages were $55,000 and Linda's wages were $70,000 for 2019 and they had no other income, what is the maximum amount of their deductible contributions to an IRA for 2019?

  Phil $_____
  Linda $_____

LO 5.3   5. What is the maximum amount a 45-year-old taxpayer and 45-year-old spouse can put into a Traditional or Roth IRA for 2019 (assuming they have sufficient earned income, but do not have an income limitation and are not covered by another pension plan)? _____

LO 5.3   6. What is the maximum amount a 55-year-old taxpayer and 52-year-old spouse can put into a Traditional or Roth IRA for 2019, assuming they earn $70,000 in total and are not participants in pension plans? _____

LO 5.3   7. Barry is a single, 40-year-old software engineer earning $190,000 a year and is not covered by a pension plan at work. How much can he put into a Roth IRA in 2019? _____

LO 5.3   8. Bob is a single, 40-year-old doctor earning $190,000 a year and is not covered by a pension plan at work. What is the maximum deductible contribution into a Traditional IRA in 2019? _____

LO 5.3   9. Dori is 58 years old and retired in 2019. She receives a pension of $25,000 a year and no other income. She wishes to put the maximum allowed into an IRA. How much can she contribute to her IRA? _____

LO 5.4   10. During 2019, Jerry is a self-employed therapist, and his net earned income is $160,000 from his practice. Jerry's SEP Plan, a defined contribution plan, states that he will contribute the maximum amount allowable. Calculate Jerry's contribution.

$_____

LO 5.4   11. Tony is a 45-year-old psychiatrist who has net earned income of $300,000 in 2019. What is the maximum amount he can contribute to his SEP for the year? _____

LO 5.4   12. Anthony, a self-employed plumber, makes a maximum contribution to a SEP for his employee, Debra. Debra's compensation is $50,000 for the year. How much is he allowed to contribute to the plan for Debra?

$_____

LO 5.4   13. During 2019, Jill, age 39, participated in a Section 401(k) plan which provides for maximum employee contributions of 12 percent. Jill's salary was $80,000 for the year. Jill elects to make the maximum contribution. What is Jill's maximum tax-deferred contribution to the plan for the year?

$_____

LO 5.6   14. Linda installed a special pool for the hydrotherapeutic treatment of severe arthritis, as prescribed by her doctor. The cost of installing the pool was $20,000, and her insurance company paid $5,000 toward its cost. The pool increased the value of Linda's house by $7,000, and it has a useful life of 10 years. How much of a deduction is Linda entitled to in the year of installation of the pool?

$ _____

Explain _____
_____
_____

LO 5.6   15. In 2019, Margaret and John Murphy (both over age 65) are married taxpayers who file a joint tax return with AGI of $26,100. During the year they incurred the following expenses:

Medical insurance premiums	$1,300
Premiums on an insurance policy that pays $100 per day for each day Margaret is hospitalized	400
Medical care lodging (two people, one night)	65
Hospital bills	2,100
Doctor bills	850
Dentist bills	200
Prescription drugs and medicines	340
Psychiatric care	350

In addition, they drove 80 miles for medical transportation, and their insurance company reimbursed them $800 for the above expenses. On the following segment of Schedule A of Form 1040, calculate the Murphy's medical expense deduction.

Medical and Dental Expenses	Caution: Do not include expenses reimbursed or paid by others.		
	1 Medical and dental expenses (see instructions)	1	
	2 Enter amount from Form 1040 or 1040-SR, line 8b	2	
	3 Multiply line 2 by 10% (0.10)	3	
	4 Subtract line 3 from line 1. If line 3 is more than line 1, enter -0-		4

LO 5.6   16. Janet needs an elevator seat attached to her stairs since she has a medical condition that makes her unable to climb the stairs in her house. The $10,000 spent on the elevator seat does not increase the value of her house according to a local appraiser. How much of the capital asset is deductible in Janet's tax return as a medical expense?

_____

_____

_____

_____

LO 5.7   17. Lyndon's employer withheld $10,100 in state income taxes from Lyndon's wages in 2019. Lyndon obtained a refund of $1,700 this year for overpayment of state income taxes for 2018. State income taxes were an itemized deduction on his 2018 return. His 2019 liability for state income tax is $8,700. Indicate the amount of Lyndon's deduction for state income taxes on his federal tax return assuming he elects to deduct state income taxes for 2019.

$ _____

LO 5.7   18. Mike sells his home to Jane on April 2, 2019. Jane pays the property taxes covering the full calendar year in October, which amount to $2,500. How much may Mike and Jane each deduct for property taxes in 2019?

Mike's deduction $ _____

Jane's deduction $ _____

LO 5.7

19. Laura is a single taxpayer living in New Jersey with adjusted gross income for the 2019 tax year of $35,550. Laura's employer withheld $3,410 in state income tax from her salary. In April of 2019, she pays $550 in additional state taxes for her prior year's tax return. The real estate taxes on her home are $1,800 for 2019, and her personal property taxes, based on the value of the property, amount to $400. Also, she paid $80 for state gasoline taxes for the year. Complete the taxes section of Schedule A below to report Laura's 2019 deduction for taxes assuming she chooses to deduct state and local income taxes.

Taxes You Paid	5 State and local taxes.	
	a State and local income taxes or general sales taxes. You may include either income taxes or general sales taxes on line 5a, but not both. If you elect to include general sales taxes instead of income taxes, check this box . . . . ▶ ☐	5a
	b State and local real estate taxes (see instructions)	5b
	c State and local personal property taxes	5c
	d Add lines 5a through 5c	5d
	e Enter the smaller of line 5d or $10,000 ($5,000 if married filing separately)	5e
	6 Other taxes. List type and amount ▶ _____ _____	6
	7 Add lines 5e and 6	7

LO 5.7

20. Mary paid $2,000 of state income taxes in 2019. She paid $1,500 of state sales tax on the purchase of goods and she also purchased a car in 2019 and paid sales tax of $3,000. How should Mary treat the taxes paid on her 2019 tax return?

_____

_____

_____

_____

LO 5.8

21. Mary's mother defaults on a home loan and Mary pays $600 in loan payments, including $175 in interest. Mary is not legally obligated on the loan and has no ownership interest in her mother's home.
    a. What amount, if any, may Mary claim as an itemized deduction for the current tax year?

    $ _____

    b. Why? _____

    _____

LO 5.8

22. Matthew borrows $250,000 to invest in bonds. During the current year, his interest on the loan is $30,000. Matthew's taxable interest income from the bonds is $10,000. This is Matthew's only investment income.
    a. Calculate Matthew's itemized deduction for investment interest expense for this year.

    $ _____

    b. Is Matthew entitled to a deduction in future years?
       Explain _____

    _____

LO 5.8

23. Ken paid the following amounts for interest during 2019:

Qualified interest on home mortgage	$5,322
Auto loan interest	850
"Points" on the mortgage for acquisition of his personal residence	400
Service charges on his checking account	40
Mastercard interest	300

Calculate Ken's itemized deduction for interest on the following portion of Schedule A.

Interest You Paid			
Caution: Your mortgage interest deduction may be limited (see instructions).	8 Home mortgage interest and points. If you didn't use all of your home mortgage loan(s) to buy, build, or improve your home, see instructions and check this box . . . . ▶ ☐		
	a Home mortgage interest and points reported to you on Form 1098. See instructions if limited	8a	
	b Home mortgage interest not reported to you on Form 1098. If paid to the person from whom you bought the home, see instructions and show that person's name, identifying no., and address . . . . . ▶ _____ _____	8b	
	c Points not reported to you on Form 1098. See instructions for special rules	8c	
	d Reserved	8d	
	e Add lines 8a through 8c	8e	
	9 Investment interest. Attach Form 4952 if required. See instructions	9	
	10 Add lines 8e and 9		10

LO 5.8

24. Janet and James purchased their personal residence 15 years ago for $300,000. For the current year, they have an $80,000 first mortgage on their home, on which they paid $5,750 in interest. They also have a home equity loan to pay for the children's college tuition secured by their home with a balance throughout the year of $150,000. They paid interest on the home equity loan of $9,000 for the year. Calculate the amount of their deduction for interest paid on qualified residence acquisition debt and qualified home equity debt for the current year.

Qualified residence acquisition debt interest $ _____
Qualified home equity debt interest $ _____

LO 5.8

25. Helen paid the following amounts of interest during the 2019 tax year:

Mortgage interest on Dallas residence (loan balance $50,000)	$1,600
Automobile loan interest (personal use only)	440
Mortgage interest on Vail residence (loan balance $50,000)	3,100
Visa and Mastercard interest	165

Calculate the amount of Helen's itemized deduction for interest (after limitations) for 2019.

$ _____

LO 5.8

26. At the end of 2019, Mark owes $250,000 on the mortgage related to the 2016 purchase of his residence. When his daughter went to college in the fall of 2019, he borrowed $20,000 through a home equity loan on his house to help pay for her education. The interest expense on the main mortgage is $15,000, and the interest expense on the home equity loan is $1,500. How much of the interest is deductible as an itemized deduction and why?

_____
_____
_____
_____

LO 5.9

27. Barbara donates a painting that she purchased three years ago for $8,000, to a university for display in the president's office. The fair market value of the painting on the date of the gift is $14,000. If Barbara had sold the painting, the difference between the sales price and her cost would have been a long-term capital gain.

   a. How much is Barbara's charitable contribution deduction for this donation?

   $ _____

   b. Explain _____

   _____

   _____

LO 5.9

28. Jerry made the following contributions during 2019:

His synagogue (by check)	$1,100
The Republican Party (by check)	180
The American Red Cross (by check)	200
His fraternal organization for tickets to a holiday party	100

   In addition, Jerry donated used furniture to the Salvation Army that he purchased years ago for $400 with a fair market value of $200. Assuming Jerry has adjusted gross income of $45,000, has the necessary written acknowledgments, and itemizes deductions, complete the Gifts to Charity section of Schedule A below to show Jerry's deduction for 2019.

Gifts to Charity	11	Gifts by cash or check. If you made any gift of $250 or more, see instructions	11	
Caution: If you made a gift and got a benefit for it, see instructions.	12	Other than by cash or check. If you made any gift of $250 or more, see instructions. You **must** attach Form 8283 if over $500.	12	
	13	Carryover from prior year	13	
	14	Add lines 11 through 13	14	

LO 5.9

29. Richard donates publicly traded Gold Company stock with a basis of $1,000 and a fair market value of $15,000 to the college he attended, which is considered a public charity. Richard has owned the shares for 10 years. How is this contribution treated on Richard's tax return?

   _____

   _____

   _____

   _____

LO 5.10

30. In June of 2019, Maureen's house is vandalized during a long-term power failure after a hurricane hit the city. The president of the United States declares Maureen's city a disaster area as a result of the wide-scale vandalism. In which tax year may Maureen take her casualty loss deduction?

   _____

   Explain: _____

   _____

   _____

LO 5.10

31. On January 3, 2019, Carey discovers his diamond bracelet has been stolen. The bracelet had a fair market value and adjusted basis of $7,500. Assuming Carey had no insurance coverage on the bracelet and his adjusted gross income for 2019 is $45,000, calculate the amount of his theft loss deduction.

   $ _____

LO 5.10   32. Kerry's car is totaled in an auto accident. The car originally cost $18,000, but is worth $7,500 at the time of the accident. Kerry's insurance company gives her a check for $7,500. Kerry has $30,000 of adjusted gross income. How much can Kerry claim as a casualty loss on her tax return? Please explain.

_____

_____

_____

_____

LO 5.10   33. During the 2019 tax year, Irma incurred the following expenses:

Union dues	$244
Tax return preparation fee	150
Brokerage fees for the purchase of stocks	35
Uniform expenses not reimbursed by her employer	315

If Irma's adjusted gross income is $23,000, calculate her miscellaneous deductions.

GROUP 3:
WRITING ASSIGNMENT

ETHICS   1. While preparing Massie Miller's 2019 Schedule A, you review the following list of possible charitable deductions provided by Massie:

Cash contribution to a family whose house burned down	$1,000
Time while working as a volunteer at Food Bank	
(5 hours @ $50/hour)	250
Cash contribution to United Methodist Church (receipt provided)	800
Cash contribution to Salvation Army (*note from Massie: "I can't*	
remember exactly the amount that I gave and I can't find the receipt.	
I think it was around $500.")	500
Total	$2,550

What would you say to Massie regarding her listed deductions? How much of the deduction is allowed for charitable contributions?

RESEARCH   2. In 2019, Gale and Cathy Alexander hosted an exchange student, Axel Muller, for 9 months. Axel was part of International Student Exchange Programs (a qualified organization). Axel attended tenth grade at the local high school. Gale and Cathy did not claim Axel as a dependent but paid the following items for Axel's well-being:

Food and clothing	$1,500
Medical care	200
Fair market value of lodging	2,700
Entertainment	100
Total	$4,500

Gale and Cathy have asked for your help in determining if any of the $4,500 can be deducted as a charitable contribution.

Required: Go to the IRS website (**www.irs.gov**) and locate Publication 526. Write a letter to Gale and Cathy answering their question. If they can claim a deduction, be sure to include in your letter the amount that can be deducted and any substantiation requirements. (An example of a client letter is available at the website for this text located at **www.cengage.com.**)

1. John Williams (birthdate August 2, 1976) is a single taxpayer. John's earnings and withholdings as the manager of a local casino for 2019 are reported on his Form W-2:

a Employee's social security number		
555-94-9358		

Safe, accurate, FAST! Use IRS e-file   Visit the IRS website at www.irs.gov/efile

OMB No. 1545-0008

b Employer identification number (EIN)	1 Wages, tips, other compensation	2 Federal income tax withheld
31-1459656	196,000.00	25,000.00

c Employer's name, address, and ZIP code	3 Social security wages	4 Social security tax withheld
Lucky Ace Casino	132,900.00	8,239.80
700 N. Sierra Street	5 Medicare wages and tips	6 Medicare tax withheld
Reno, NV 89503	196,000.00	2,842.00
	7 Social security tips	8 Allocated tips

d Control number	9	10 Dependent care benefits

e Employee's first name and initial Last name Suff.	11 Nonqualified plans	12a See instructions for box 12
John Williams	13 Statutory employee Retirement plan Third-party sick pay	12b
1324 Skyewalker Drive	14 Other	12c
Reno, NV 89501		12d

f Employee's address and ZIP code

15 State Employer's state ID number	16 State wages, tips, etc.	17 State income tax	18 Local wages, tips, etc.	19 Local income tax	20 Locality name
NV					

Form **W-2** Wage and Tax Statement   **2019**   Department of the Treasury—Internal Revenue Service

Copy B—To Be Filed With Employee's FEDERAL Tax Return.
This information is being furnished to the Internal Revenue Service.

John's other income includes interest on a savings account at Nevada National Bank of $13,691.

John pays his ex-wife, Sarah McLoughlin, $3,900 per month in accordance with their February 12, 2013 divorce decree. When their 12-year-old child (in the ex-wife's custody) reaches the age of 18, the payments are reduced to $2,800 per month. His ex-wife's Social Security number is 554-44-5555.

In 2019, John purchased a new car and so he kept track of his sales tax receipts during the year. His actual sales tax paid is $3,700, which exceeds the estimated amount per the IRS tables.

John participates in a high-deductible health plan and is eligible to contribute to a health savings account. His HSA earned $75 in 2019.

During the year, John paid the following amounts (all of which can be substantiated):

Credit card interest	$1,760
Auto loan interest	4,300
Auto insurance	900
Contribution to IRA	6,000
Property taxes on personal residence	2,700
Contributions to HSA	2,850
Income tax preparation fee	900
Charitable contributions (all cash):	
Boy Scouts	1,350
St. Matthews Church	3,100
U. of Nevada (Reno) Medical School	27,000
Nevada Democratic Party	250
Fund-raising dinner for the Reno Auto Museum	100
(value of dinner is $25)	

John also received the following Form 1098:

☐ VOID	☐ CORRECTED	

RECIPIENT'S/LENDER'S name, street address, city or town, state or province, country, ZIP or foreign postal code, and telephone no. Reno Bank & Trust 49 Commerce Street Reno, NV 89501		OMB No. 1545-1380 20**19** Form **1098**	**Mortgage Interest Statement**
		1 Mortgage interest received from payer(s)/borrower(s) $ 19,003.41	**Copy C** **For Recipient/Lender**
RECIPIENT'S/LENDER'S TIN 33-1234569	PAYER'S/BORROWER'S TIN 555-94-9358	**2** Outstanding mortgage principal $ 591,786.32	**3** Mortgage origination date 3/01/2003
		4 Refund of overpaid interest $	**5** Mortgage insurance premiums $
PAYER'S/BORROWER'S name John Williams		**6** Points paid on purchase of principal residence $	For Privacy Act and Paperwork Reduction Act Notice, see the **2019 General Instructions for Certain Information Returns.**
Street address (including apt. no.) 1324 Skyewalker Drive		**7** ☒ If address of property securing mortgage is the same as PAYER'S/BORROWER'S address, check the box, or enter the address or description in box 8.	
City or town, state or province, country, and ZIP or foreign postal code Reno, NV 89501		**8** Address or description of property securing mortgage (see instructions)	
9 Number of properties securing the mortgage 1	**10** Other		**11** Mortgage acquisition date
Account number (see instructions)			

Form **1098**   www.irs.gov/Form1098   Department of the Treasury - Internal Revenue Service

Required: Complete John's federal tax return for 2019. Use Form 1040, Schedule 1, Schedule A, Schedule B, and Form 8889 to complete this tax return. Make realistic assumptions about any missing data.

2A. Bea Jones (birthdate March 27, 1984) moved from Texas to Florida in December 2018. She lives at 654 Ocean Way, Gulfport, FL 33707. Bea's Social Security number is 466-78-7359 and she is single. Her earnings and income tax withholding for 2019 for her job as a manager at a Florida shrimp-processing plant are:

Earnings from the Gulf Shrimp Co.	$44,000
Federal income tax withheld	4,600
State income tax withheld	0

Bea's other income includes interest on a savings account at Beach National Bank of $1,200 and $600 per month alimony from her ex-husband in accordance with their August 2011 divorce decree.

Bea's employer operates a 401(k) plan, and although she is eligible, Bea does not participate.

During 2019, Bea paid the following amounts (all of which can be substantiated):

Home mortgage interest (1098 not shown)	$8,800
Auto loan interest	2,300
State sales tax	820
Property taxes on personal residence	3,233
Unreimbursed hospital bills	3,275
Doctor bills	2,612
Other deductible medical expenses	720
Income tax preparation fee	600
Job-hunting expenses	925
Contribution to IRA	2,300

In September 2019, Tropical Storm Yuri struck Gulfport and a tree fell on Bea's home. Bea acquired the home in February 2012 for $110,000. The estimated loss in market value from damage was equal to her repair charge of $7,800. The damage caused by TS Yuri was declared a federal disaster (code EM-1212). Bea's deductible was quite high and her insurance company only reimbursed her $1,200.

Required: Complete Bea's federal tax return for 2019. Use Form 1040, Schedule A, and Form 4684 (if needed) to complete this tax return. Make realistic assumptions about any missing data.

2B. John Fuji (birthdate June 6, 1981) moved from California to Washington in December 2018. His earnings and income tax withholding for 2019 for his job as a manager at a Washington apple-processing plant are:

a Employee's social security number 571-78-5974		

OMB No. 1545-0008   Safe, accurate, FAST! Use IRS e-file   Visit the IRS website at www.irs.gov/efile

b Employer identification number (EIN) 34-7654321	1 Wages, tips, other compensation 77,300.00	2 Federal income tax withheld 8,100.00
c Employer's name, address, and ZIP code	3 Social security wages 77,300.00	4 Social security tax withheld 4,792.60
Granny Smith Apple Co. 200 Ahtanum Road Yakima, WA 98903	5 Medicare wages and tips 77,300.00	6 Medicare tax withheld 1,120.85
	7 Social security tips	8 Allocated tips
d Control number	9	10 Dependent care benefits
e Employee's first name and initial Last name Suff. John Fuji 468 Bonnie Doon Avenue Yakima, WA 98902	11 Nonqualified plans	12a See instructions for box 12
	13 Statutory employee ☐ Retirement plan ☒ Third-party sick pay ☐	12b
	14 Other	12c
		12d
f Employee's address and ZIP code		

15 State Employer's state ID number WA	16 State wages, tips, etc.	17 State income tax	18 Local wages, tips, etc.	19 Local income tax	20 Locality name

Form **W-2** Wage and Tax Statement   **2019**   Department of the Treasury—Internal Revenue Service

Copy B—To Be Filed With Employee's FEDERAL Tax Return.
This information is being furnished to the Internal Revenue Service.

John's other income includes interest on a Certificate of Deposit reported on a Form 1099-INT:

☐ CORRECTED (if checked)

PAYER'S name, street address, city or town, state or province, country, ZIP or foreign postal code, and telephone no.	Payer's RTN (optional)	OMB No. 1545-0112	**Interest Income**
Braeburn National Bank 1600 W. Nob Hill Blvd. Yakima, WA 98902	**1** Interest income $ 1,433.00	20**19** Form **1099-INT**	

PAYER'S TIN	RECIPIENT'S TIN	**2** Early withdrawal penalty $	**Copy B**
54-9019016	571-78-5974	**3** Interest on U.S. Savings Bonds and Treas. obligations $	**For Recipient**

RECIPIENT'S name	**4** Federal income tax withheld $ 0.00	**5** Investment expenses $	This is important tax information and is being furnished to the IRS. If you are required to file a return, a negligence penalty or other sanction may be imposed on you if this income is taxable and the IRS determines that it has not been reported.
John Fuji	**6** Foreign tax paid $	**7** Foreign country or U.S. possession	
Street address (including apt. no.) 468 Bonnie Doon Ave.	**8** Tax-exempt interest $	**9** Specified private activity bond interest $	
City or town, state or province, country, and ZIP or foreign postal code Yakima, WA 98902	**10** Market discount $	**11** Bond premium $	
FATCA filing requirement ☐	**12** Bond premium on Treasury obligations $	**13** Bond premium on tax-exempt bond $	
Account number (see instructions)	**14** Tax-exempt and tax credit bond CUSIP no.	**15** State | **16** State identification no.	**17** State tax withheld $ $

Form **1099-INT**   (keep for your records)   www.irs.gov/Form1099INT   Department of the Treasury - Internal Revenue Service

Also, in accordance with the January 2019 divorce decree he paid $500 per month alimony to his ex-wife (Dora Fuji, Social Security number 573-79-6075) starting with February 2019.

John received the following Form 1098 reporting mortgage interest and property taxes:

☐ VOID   ☐ CORRECTED

RECIPIENT'S/LENDER'S name, street address, city or town, state or province, country, ZIP or foreign postal code, and telephone no.		OMB No. 1545-1380	**Mortgage Interest Statement**
Braeburn National Bank 1600 W. Nob Hill Blvd. Yakima, WA 98902		20**19** Form **1098**	

		1 Mortgage interest received from payer(s)/borrower(s) $ 7,775.13	**Copy C** **For Recipient/Lender**
RECIPIENT'S/LENDER'S TIN	PAYER'S/BORROWER'S TIN	**2** Outstanding mortgage principal $ 255,321.78	**3** Mortgage origination date 12/1/2017	
54-9019016	571-78-5974	**4** Refund of overpaid interest $	**5** Mortgage insurance premiums $	
PAYER'S/BORROWER'S name John Fuji		**6** Points paid on purchase of principal residence $	For Privacy Act and Paperwork Reduction Act Notice, see the **2019 General Instructions for Certain Information Returns**.
Street address (including apt. no.) 468 Bonnie Doon Ave.		**7** ☒ If address of property securing mortgage is the same as PAYER'S/BORROWER'S address, check the box, or enter the address or description in box 8.	
City or town, state or province, country, and ZIP or foreign postal code Yakima, WA 98902		**8** Address or description of property securing mortgage (see instructions)	
9 Number of properties securing the mortgage 1	**10** Other Prop. Taxes $2,100		
Account number (see instructions)			**11** Mortgage acquisition date

Form **1098**   www.irs.gov/Form1098   Department of the Treasury - Internal Revenue Service

During 2019, John paid the following amounts (all of which can be substantiated):

Auto loan interest	1,575
Credit card interest	655
State sales tax	1,285
Assisted living charges for Gala	5,250
Doctor bills	2,550
Other deductible medical expenses	760
Income tax preparation fee	500
Job-hunting expenses	925
Cash charitable donation to the Jonagold Research Center	400

John's employer offers a retirement plan, but John does not participate. Instead, he made a $4,000 contribution to a Roth IRA.

John also provides 100 percent of the support for his mother, Gala Fuji (Social Security number 323-11-4455). Gala is chronically ill and lives in an assisted living facility in Yakima. Her only income is interest of about $400 on a modest savings account. John can claim the $500 other dependent credit for Gala.

Required: Complete John's federal tax return for 2019. Use Form 1040, Schedule 1, and Schedule A as needed to complete this tax return. Make realistic assumptions about any missing data.

GROUP 5:
CUMULATIVE SOFTWARE PROBLEM

1. The following information is available for the Albert and Allison Gaytor family in addition to that provided in Chapters 1–4.
   Albert and Allison received the following form:

☐ VOID   ☐ CORRECTED

RECIPIENT'S/LENDER'S name, street address, city or town, state or province, country, ZIP or foreign postal code, and telephone no.			OMB No. 1545-1380	Mortgage Interest Statement
Vizcaya National Bank 9871 Coral Way Miami, FL 33134			2019 Form **1098**	

		1 Mortgage interest received from payer(s)/borrower(s) $ 11,345.08		Copy C For Recipient/ Lender
RECIPIENT'S/LENDER'S TIN 60-7654321	PAYER'S/BORROWER'S TIN 266-51-1966	2 Outstanding mortgage principal $ 317,034.44	3 Mortgage origination date 03/01/2005	
PAYER'S/BORROWER'S name Albert and Allison Gaytor		4 Refund of overpaid interest $	5 Mortgage insurance premiums $	For Privacy Act and Paperwork Reduction Act Notice, see the **2019 General Instructions for Certain Information Returns.**
		6 Points paid on purchase of principal residence $		
Street address (including apt. no.) 12340 Cocoshell Road		7 ☒ If address of property securing mortgage is the same as PAYER'S/BORROWER'S address, check the box, or enter the address or description in box 8.		
City or town, state or province, country, and ZIP or foreign postal code Coral Gables, FL 33134		8 Address or description of property securing mortgage (see instructions)		
9 Number of properties securing the mortgage	10 Other			
Account number (see instructions)			11 Mortgage acquisition date	

Form **1098**   www.irs.gov/Form1098   Department of the Treasury - Internal Revenue Service

Albert and Allison paid the following in 2019 (all by check or can otherwise be substantiated):

Contributions to Perpetual Perpetuity Catholic Church	$ 510
Tuition to Perpetual Perpetuity Catholic School for Crocker	6,000
Clothes to Salvation Army (10 bags in good condition)	275
Contributions to George Kerry's Congressional campaign	250
Psychotherapy for Allison	2,298
Prescription eyeglasses for Crocker	413
Prescription medication and drugs	1,903
Credit card interest	1,345
Interest on Albert's college loans	3,125
Actual state sales tax (including sales tax on new auto of $2,000)	3,202
Investment interest expense on stock margin account	345
Auto loan interest reported on Form 1098 (not shown here; auto was paid for by a home equity loan on residence)	860
Auto insurance	1,600
Cosmetic surgery for Albert	4,500
Dave Deduction, CPA, for preparation of last year's tax return	765
Safe-deposit box for storage of stocks and tax data	100
Contribution to an educational savings account for Crocker	1,000
Home property taxes	4,888
Unreimbursed business expense (seminar on dealing with hijacking at sea)	700

In August 2019, Crocker was on an out-of-town field trip with the university band and his appendix burst. He required immediate surgery which was considered "out of network" for the Gaytor's health plan resulting in hospital and doctor's fees of $3,150 not covered by insurance. In addition, Allison drove 300 miles round trip to be with Crocker after the surgery and drive him home after he recovered. She spent two nights in a hotel at a cost of $140 per night.

In June, Albert purchased a new professional digital SLR camera for $7,950. While the Gaytors were on vacation in August, someone broke into their residence and stole the camera. Albert's homeowners' insurance did not reimburse him for any part of the loss since he declined the special premium add-on for high value items required by his policy.

For the 2019 tax year, on April 15, 2020, Albert contributes $6,000 to a traditional IRA for himself and $6,000 to a traditional IRA for his wife. He is not covered by a qualified retirement plan at work.

Albert managed to gather his gambling loss documentation and can substantiate gambling losses of $4,502 in 2019 (refer back to Chapter 2 for gambling winnings).

Required: Combine this new information about the Gaytor family with the information from Chapters 1–4 and complete a revised 2019 tax return for Albert and Allison. Be sure to save your data input files since this case will be expanded with more tax information in later chapters.

Form **1040**   Department of the Treasury—Internal Revenue Service   (99)   **2019**   OMB No. 1545-0074   IRS Use Only—Do not write or staple in this space.
U.S. Individual Income Tax Return

Filing Status
Check only one box.

☐ Single   ☐ Married filing jointly   ☐ Married filing separately (MFS)   ☐ Head of household (HOH)   ☐ Qualifying widow(er) (QW)

If you checked the MFS box, enter the name of spouse. If you checked the HOH or QW box, enter the child's name if the qualifying person is a child but not your dependent. ▶

Your first name and middle initial	Last name	Your social security number

If joint return, spouse's first name and middle initial	Last name	Spouse's social security number

Home address (number and street). If you have a P.O. box, see instructions.   Apt. no.

Presidential Election Campaign
Check here if you, or your spouse if filing jointly, want $3 to go to this fund. Checking a box below will not change your tax or refund.   ☐ You   ☐ Spouse

City, town or post office, state, and ZIP code. If you have a foreign address, also complete spaces below (see instructions).

Foreign country name	Foreign province/state/county	Foreign postal code

If more than four dependents, see instructions and ✓ here ▶ ☐

Standard Deduction

Someone can claim: ☐ You as a dependent   ☐ Your spouse as a dependent
☐ Spouse itemizes on a separate return or you were a dual-status alien

Age/Blindness   **You:** ☐ Were born before January 2, 1955   ☐ Are blind   **Spouse:** ☐ Was born before January 2, 1955   ☐ Is blind

Dependents (see instructions):

(1) First name Last name	(2) Social security number	(3) Relationship to you	(4) ✓ if qualifies for (see instructions):	
			Child tax credit	Credit for other dependents
			☐	☐
			☐	☐
			☐	☐
			☐	☐

Standard Deduction for—
- Single or Married filing separately, $12,200
- Married filing jointly or Qualifying widow(er), $24,400
- Head of household, $18,350
- If you checked any box under *Standard Deduction,* see instructions.

1	Wages, salaries, tips, etc. Attach Form(s) W-2		**1**	
2a	Tax-exempt interest	**2a**	**b** Taxable interest. Attach Sch. B if required	**2b**
3a	Qualified dividends	**3a**	**b** Ordinary dividends. Attach Sch. B if required	**3b**
4a	IRA distributions	**4a**	**b** Taxable amount	**4b**
c	Pensions and annuities	**4c**	**d** Taxable amount	**4d**
5a	Social security benefits	**5a**	**b** Taxable amount	**5b**
6	Capital gain or (loss). Attach Schedule D if required. If not required, check here ▶ ☐		**6**	
7a	Other income from Schedule 1, line 9		**7a**	
b	Add lines 1, 2b, 3b, 4b, 4d, 5b, 6, and 7a. This is your **total income** ▶		**7b**	
8a	Adjustments to income from Schedule 1, line 22		**8a**	
b	Subtract line 8a from line 7b. This is your **adjusted gross income** ▶		**8b**	
9	**Standard deduction or itemized deductions** (from Schedule A)	**9**		
10	Qualified business income deduction. Attach Form 8995 or Form 8995-A	**10**		
11a	Add lines 9 and 10		**11a**	
b	**Taxable income.** Subtract line 11a from line 8b		**11b**	

For Disclosure, Privacy Act, and Paperwork Reduction Act Notice, see separate instructions.   Cat. No. 11320B   Form **1040** (2019)

Form 1040 (2019) Page **2**

12a	**Tax** (see inst.) Check if any from Form(s): 1 ☐ 8814 2 ☐ 4972 3 ☐ _____	12a		
b	Add Schedule 2, line 3, and line 12a and enter the total . . . . ▶		12b	
13a	Child tax credit or credit for other dependents	13a		
b	Add Schedule 3, line 7, and line 13a and enter the total . . . . ▶		13b	
14	Subtract line 13b from line 12b. If zero or less, enter -0-		14	
15	Other taxes, including self-employment tax, from Schedule 2, line 10		15	
16	Add lines 14 and 15. This is your **total tax** . . . . ▶		16	
17	Federal income tax withheld from Forms W-2 and 1099		17	
18	Other payments and refundable credits:			
a	Earned income credit (EIC)	18a		
b	Additional child tax credit. Attach Schedule 8812	18b		
c	American opportunity credit from Form 8863, line 8	18c		
d	Schedule 3, line 14	18d		
e	Add lines 18a through 18d. These are your **total other payments and refundable credits** .		18e	
19	Add lines 17 and 18e. These are your **total payments** . . . . ▶		19	

• If you have a qualifying child, attach Sch. EIC.
• If you have nontaxable combat pay, see instructions.

Refund	20	If line 19 is more than line 16, subtract line 16 from line 19. This is the amount you **overpaid**		20	
	21a	Amount of line 20 you want **refunded to you.** If Form 8888 is attached, check here . . ▶ ☐		21a	
Direct deposit? See instructions.	▶ b	Routing number	▶ c Type: ☐ Checking ☐ Savings	
	▶ d	Account number		
	22	Amount of line 20 you want **applied to your 2020 estimated tax** . . . . ▶	22		
Amount You Owe	23	**Amount you owe.** Subtract line 19 from line 16. For details on how to pay, see instructions . . ▶		23	
	24	Estimated tax penalty (see instructions) . . . . ▶	24		

Third Party Designee (Other than paid preparer)	Do you want to allow another person (other than your paid preparer) to discuss this return with the IRS? See instructions.	☐ **Yes.** Complete below. ☐ **No**
	Designee's name ▶ Phone no. ▶ Personal identification number (PIN) ▶	

Sign Here

Joint return? See instructions. Keep a copy for your records.

Under penalties of perjury, I declare that I have examined this return and accompanying schedules and statements, and to the best of my knowledge and belief, they are true, correct, and complete. Declaration of preparer (other than taxpayer) is based on all information of which preparer has any knowledge.

Your signature	Date	Your occupation	If the IRS sent you an Identity Protection PIN, enter it here (see inst.)
Spouse's signature. If a joint return, **both** must sign.	Date	Spouse's occupation	If the IRS sent your spouse an Identity Protection PIN, enter it here (see inst.)

Phone no. Email address

Paid Preparer Use Only

Preparer's name	Preparer's signature	Date	PTIN	Check if: ☐ 3rd Party Designee ☐ Self-employed
Firm's name ▶		Phone no.		
Firm's address ▶			Firm's EIN ▶	

Go to *www.irs.gov/Form1040* for instructions and the latest information. Form **1040** (2019)

SCHEDULE 1
(Form 1040 or 1040-SR)

Department of the Treasury
Internal Revenue Service

Additional Income and Adjustments to Income

▶ Attach to Form 1040 or 1040-SR.
▶ Go to *www.irs.gov/Form1040* for instructions and the latest information.

OMB No. 1545-0074

2019

Attachment
Sequence No. **01**

Name(s) shown on Form 1040 or 1040-SR

Your social security number

Part I	Additional Income	
1	Taxable refunds, credits, or offsets of state and local income taxes	**1**
2a	Alimony received	**2a**
b	Date of original divorce or separation agreement (see instructions) ▶	
3	Business income or (loss). Attach Schedule C	**3**
4	Other gains or (losses). Attach Form 4797	**4**
5	Rental real estate, royalties, partnerships, S corporations, trusts, etc. Attach Schedule E	**5**
6	Farm income or (loss). Attach Schedule F	**6**
7	Unemployment compensation	**7**
8	Other income. List type and amount ▶	
		8
9	Combine lines 1 through 8. Enter here and on Form 1040 or 1040-SR, line 7a	**9**

Part II	Adjustments to Income	
10	Educator expenses	**10**
11	Certain business expenses of reservists, performing artists, and fee-basis government officials. Attach Form 2106	**11**
12	Health savings account deduction. Attach Form 8889	**12**
13	Moving expenses for members of the Armed Forces. Attach Form 3903	**13**
14	Deductible part of self-employment tax. Attach Schedule SE	**14**
15	Self-employed SEP, SIMPLE, and qualified plans	**15**
16	Self-employed health insurance deduction	**16**
17	Penalty on early withdrawal of savings	**17**
18a	Alimony paid	**18a**
b	Recipient's SSN . . . . ▶	
c	Date of original divorce or separation agreement (see instructions) ▶	
19	IRA deduction	**19**
20	Student loan interest deduction	**20**
21	Reserved for future use	**21**
22	Add lines 10 through 21. These are your **adjustments to income.** Enter here and on Form 1040 or 1040-SR, line 8a	**22**

For Paperwork Reduction Act Notice, see your tax return instructions.   Cat. No. 71479F   Schedule 1 (Form 1040 or 1040-SR) 2019

SCHEDULE A
(Form 1040 or 1040-SR)

Department of the Treasury
Internal Revenue Service (99)

Itemized Deductions

▶ Go to *www.irs.gov/ScheduleA* for instructions and the latest information.
▶ Attach to Form 1040 or 1040-SR.

Caution: If you are claiming a net qualified disaster loss on Form 4684, see the instructions for line 16.

OMB No. 1545-0074

2019

Attachment
Sequence No. **07**

Name(s) shown on Form 1040 or 1040-SR

Your social security number

Medical and Dental Expenses	**Caution:** Do not include expenses reimbursed or paid by others.	
	1 Medical and dental expenses (see instructions)	**1**
	2 Enter amount from Form 1040 or 1040-SR, line 8b **2**	
	3 Multiply line 2 by 10% (0.10)	**3**
	4 Subtract line 3 from line 1. If line 3 is more than line 1, enter -0-	**4**
Taxes You Paid	**5** State and local taxes.	
	a State and local income taxes or general sales taxes. You may include either income taxes or general sales taxes on line 5a, but not both. If you elect to include general sales taxes instead of income taxes, check this box . . . . ▶ ☐	**5a**
	b State and local real estate taxes (see instructions)	**5b**
	c State and local personal property taxes	**5c**
	d Add lines 5a through 5c	**5d**
	e Enter the smaller of line 5d or $10,000 ($5,000 if married filing separately)	**5e**
	6 Other taxes. List type and amount ▶ _____	**6**
	7 Add lines 5e and 6	**7**
Interest You Paid **Caution:** Your mortgage interest deduction may be limited (see instructions).	**8** Home mortgage interest and points. If you didn't use all of your home mortgage loan(s) to buy, build, or improve your home, see instructions and check this box . . . . ▶ ☐	
	a Home mortgage interest and points reported to you on Form 1098. See instructions if limited	**8a**
	b Home mortgage interest not reported to you on Form 1098. If paid to the person from whom you bought the home, see instructions and show that person's name, identifying no., and address . . . . . ▶ _____	**8b**
	c Points not reported to you on Form 1098. See instructions for special rules	**8c**
	d Reserved	**8d**
	e Add lines 8a through 8c	**8e**
	9 Investment interest. Attach Form 4952 if required. See instructions	**9**
	10 Add lines 8e and 9	**10**
Gifts to Charity **Caution:** If you made a gift and got a benefit for it, see instructions.	**11** Gifts by cash or check. If you made any gift of $250 or more, see instructions	**11**
	12 Other than by cash or check. If you made any gift of $250 or more, see instructions. You **must** attach Form 8283 if over $500. . . .	**12**
	13 Carryover from prior year	**13**
	14 Add lines 11 through 13	**14**
Casualty and Theft Losses	**15** Casualty and theft loss(es) from a federally declared disaster (other than net qualified disaster losses). Attach Form 4684 and enter the amount from line 18 of that form. See instructions	**15**
Other Itemized Deductions	**16** Other—from list in instructions. List type and amount ▶ _____	**16**
Total Itemized Deductions	**17** Add the amounts in the far right column for lines 4 through 16. Also, enter this amount on Form 1040 or 1040-SR, line 9	**17**
	18 If you elect to itemize deductions even though they are less than your standard deduction, check this box . . . . ▶ ☐	

For Paperwork Reduction Act Notice, see the Instructions for Forms 1040 and 1040-SR.   Cat. No. 17145C   **Schedule A (Form 1040 or 1040-SR) 2019**

SCHEDULE B
(Form 1040 or 1040-SR)

Department of the Treasury
Internal Revenue Service (99)

Interest and Ordinary Dividends

▶ Go to *www.irs.gov/ScheduleB* for instructions and the latest information.
▶ Attach to Form 1040 or 1040-SR.

OMB No. 1545-0074

2019

Attachment
Sequence No. **08**

Name(s) shown on return

Your social security number

Part I

Interest

(See instructions
and the
instructions for
Forms 1040 and
1040-SR, line 2b.)

Note: If you
received a Form
1099-INT, Form
1099-OID, or
substitute
statement from
a brokerage firm,
list the firm's
name as the
payer and enter
the total interest
shown on that
form.

1 List name of payer. If any interest is from a seller-financed mortgage and the buyer used the property as a personal residence, see the instructions and list this interest first. Also, show that buyer's social security number and address ▶

	Amount
	1

2 Add the amounts on line 1 . . . . | **2** |

3 Excludable interest on series EE and I U.S. savings bonds issued after 1989. Attach Form 8815 . . . . . . | **3** |

4 Subtract line 3 from line 2. Enter the result here and on Form 1040 or 1040-SR, line 2b . . . . ▶ | **4** |

Note: If line 4 is over $1,500, you must complete Part III.

Part II

Ordinary Dividends

(See instructions
and the
instructions for
Forms 1040 and
1040-SR, line 3b.)

Note: If you
received a Form
1099-DIV or
substitute
statement from
a brokerage firm,
list the firm's
name as the
payer and enter
the ordinary
dividends shown
on that form.

5 List name of payer ▶

	Amount
	5

6 Add the amounts on line 5. Enter the total here and on Form 1040 or 1040-SR, line 3b . . . . ▶ | **6** |

Note: If line 6 is over $1,500, you must complete Part III.

Part III

Foreign Accounts and Trusts

Caution: If
required, failure
to file FinCEN
Form 114 may
result in
substantial
penalties. See
instructions.

You must complete this part if you **(a)** had over $1,500 of taxable interest or ordinary dividends; **(b)** had a foreign account; or **(c)** received a distribution from, or were a grantor of, or a transferor to, a foreign trust.

	Yes	No

7a At any time during 2019, did you have a financial interest in or signature authority over a financial account (such as a bank account, securities account, or brokerage account) located in a foreign country? See instructions . . . .

If "Yes," are you required to file FinCEN Form 114, Report of Foreign Bank and Financial Accounts (FBAR), to report that financial interest or signature authority? See FinCEN Form 114 and its instructions for filing requirements and exceptions to those requirements . . . . . .

b If you are required to file FinCEN Form 114, enter the name of the foreign country where the financial account is located ▶

8 During 2019, did you receive a distribution from, or were you the grantor of, or transferor to, a foreign trust? If "Yes," you may have to file Form 3520. See instructions . . . .

For Paperwork Reduction Act Notice, see your tax return instructions.   Cat. No. 17146N   **Schedule B (Form 1040 or 1040-SR) 2019**

Form 4684

Department of the Treasury
Internal Revenue Service

Casualties and Thefts

▶ Go to *www.irs.gov/Form4684* for instructions and the latest information.
▶ Attach to your tax return.
▶ Use a separate Form 4684 for each casualty or theft.

OMB No. 1545-0177

2019

Attachment
Sequence No. **26**

Name(s) shown on tax return

Identifying number

SECTION A—Personal Use Property (Use this section to report casualties and thefts of property **not** used in a trade or business or for income-producing purposes. You must use a separate Form 4684 (through line 12) for each casualty or theft event involving personal use property. **If reporting a qualified disaster loss, see the instructions for special rules that apply before completing this section.**)

If the casualty or theft loss is attributable to a federally declared disaster, check here ☐ and enter the FEMA disaster declaration number. (See instructions.) _____

1   Description of properties (show type, location (city, state, and ZIP code), and date acquired for each property). Use a separate line for each property lost or damaged from the same casualty or theft. If you checked the box and entered the FEMA disaster declaration number above, enter the ZIP code for the property most affected on the line for Property **A**.

	Type of Property	City and State	ZIP Code	Date Acquired
Property **A**				
Property **B**				
Property **C**				
Property **D**				

		Properties			
		A	B	C	D
2	Cost or other basis of each property	2				
3	Insurance or other reimbursement (whether or not you filed a claim) (see instructions)	3				
	Note: If line 2 is **more** than line 3, skip line 4.					
4	Gain from casualty or theft. If line 3 is **more** than line 2, enter the difference here and skip lines 5 through 9 for that column. See instructions if line 3 includes insurance or other reimbursement you did not claim, or you received payment for your loss in a later tax year	4				
5	Fair market value **before** casualty or theft	5				
6	Fair market value **after** casualty or theft	6				
7	Subtract line 6 from line 5	7				
8	Enter the **smaller** of line 2 or line 7	8				
9	Subtract line 3 from line 8. If zero or less, enter -0-	9				

10   Casualty or theft loss. Add the amounts on line 9 in columns A through D . . . . **10** _____

11   Enter $100 ($500 if qualified disaster loss rules apply; see instructions) . . . . **11** _____

12   Subtract line 11 from line 10. If zero or less, enter -0- . . . . **12** _____

Caution: Use only one Form 4684 for lines 13 through 18.

13   Add the amounts on line 4 of all Forms 4684 . . . . **13** _____

14   Add the amounts on line 12 of all Forms 4684. If you have losses not attributable to a federally declared disaster, see the instructions . . . . **14** _____

Caution: See instructions before completing line 15.

15   • If line 13 is **more** than line 14, enter the difference here and on Schedule D. **Do not** complete the rest of this section.

• If line 13 is **equal** to line 14, enter -0- here. **Do not** complete the rest of this section.
• If line 13 is **less** than line 14, and you have no qualified disaster losses subject to the $500 reduction on line 11 on any Form(s) 4684, enter -0- here and go to line 16. If you have qualified disaster losses subject to the $500 reduction, subtract line 13 from line 14 and enter the smaller of this difference or the amount on line 12 of the Form(s) 4684 reporting those losses. Enter that result here and on Schedule A (Form 1040 or 1040-SR), line 16, or Form 1040-NR, Schedule A, line 7. If you claim the standard deduction, also include on Schedule A (Form 1040 or 1040-SR), line 16, the amount of your standard deduction (see the Instructions for Forms 1040 and 1040-SR). Do not complete the rest of this section if all of your casualty or theft losses are subject to the $500 reduction. . . . . **15** _____

16   Add lines 13 and 15. Subtract the result from line 14 . . . . **16** _____

17   Enter 10% of your adjusted gross income from Form 1040 or 1040-SR, line 8b, or Form 1040-NR, line 35. Estates and trusts, see instructions . . . . **17** _____

18   Subtract line 17 from line 16. If zero or less, enter -0-. Also, enter the result on Schedule A (Form 1040 or 1040-SR), line 15, or Form 1040-NR, Schedule A, line 6. Estates and trusts, enter the result on the "Other deductions" line of your tax return . . . . **18** _____

For Paperwork Reduction Act Notice, see instructions.   Cat. No. 12997O   Form **4684** (2019)

Form **8889**

Department of the Treasury
Internal Revenue Service

Health Savings Accounts (HSAs)

▶ **Attach to Form 1040, 1040-SR, or 1040-NR.**
▶ **Go to www.irs.gov/Form8889 for instructions and the latest information.**

OMB No. 1545-0074

2019

Attachment
Sequence No. **52**

Name(s) shown on Form 1040, 1040-SR, or 1040-NR

Social security number of HSA beneficiary. If both spouses have HSAs, see instructions ▶

Before you begin: Complete Form 8853, Archer MSAs and Long-Term Care Insurance Contracts, if required.

Part I	**HSA Contributions and Deduction.** See the instructions before completing this part. If you are filing jointly and both you and your spouse each have separate HSAs, complete a separate Part I for each spouse.

1	Check the box to indicate your coverage under a high-deductible health plan (HDHP) during 2019 (see instructions) . . . . ▶ ☐ Self-only ☐ Family	
2	HSA contributions you made for 2019 (or those made on your behalf), including those made from January 1, 2020, through April 15, 2020, that were for 2019. **Do not** include employer contributions, contributions through a cafeteria plan, or rollovers (see instructions)	**2**
3	If you were under age 55 at the end of 2019 and, on the first day of **every** month during 2019, you were, or were considered, an eligible individual with the **same** coverage, enter $3,500 ($7,000 for family coverage). **All others,** see the instructions for the amount to enter	**3**
4	Enter the amount you and your employer contributed to your Archer MSAs for 2019 from Form 8853, lines 1 and 2. If you or your spouse had family coverage under an HDHP at any time during 2019, also include any amount contributed to your spouse's Archer MSAs	**4**
5	Subtract line 4 from line 3. If zero or less, enter -0-	**5**
6	Enter the amount from line 5. But if you and your spouse each have separate HSAs and had family coverage under an HDHP at any time during 2019, see the instructions for the amount to enter . .	**6**
7	If you were age 55 or older at the end of 2019, married, and you or your spouse had family coverage under an HDHP at any time during 2019, enter your additional contribution amount (see instructions)	**7**
8	Add lines 6 and 7	**8**
9	Employer contributions made to your HSAs for 2019	**9**
10	Qualified HSA funding distributions	**10**
11	Add lines 9 and 10	**11**
12	Subtract line 11 from line 8. If zero or less, enter -0-	**12**
13	**HSA deduction.** Enter the **smaller** of line 2 or line 12 here and on Schedule 1 (Form 1040 or 1040-SR), line 12, or Form 1040-NR, line 25	**13**

Caution: If line 2 is more than line 13, you may have to pay an additional tax (see instructions).

Part II	**HSA Distributions.** If you are filing jointly and both you and your spouse each have separate HSAs, complete a separate Part II for each spouse.

14a	Total distributions you received in 2019 from all HSAs (see instructions)	**14a**
b	Distributions included on line 14a that you rolled over to another HSA. Also include any excess contributions (and the earnings on those excess contributions) included on line 14a that were withdrawn by the due date of your return (see instructions)	**14b**
c	Subtract line 14b from line 14a	**14c**
15	Qualified medical expenses paid using HSA distributions (see instructions)	**15**
16	**Taxable HSA distributions.** Subtract line 15 from line 14c. If zero or less, enter -0-. Also, include this amount in the total on Schedule 1 (Form 1040 or 1040-SR), line 8, or Form 1040-NR, line 21. Enter "HSA" and the amount on the line next to the box	**16**
17a	If any of the distributions included on line 16 meet any of the **Exceptions to the Additional 20% Tax** (see instructions), check here . . . . ▶ ☐	
b	**Additional 20% tax** (see instructions). Enter 20% (0.20) of the distributions included on line 16 that are subject to the additional 20% tax. Also include this amount in the total on Schedule 2 (Form 1040 or 1040-SR), line 8, or Form 1040-NR, line 60. Check box c on Schedule 2 (Form 1040 or 1040-SR), line 8, or box b on Form 1040-NR, line 60. Enter "HSA" and the amount on the line next to the box .	**17b**

For Paperwork Reduction Act Notice, see your tax return instructions.   Cat. No. 37621P   Form **8889** (2019)

Student Name _____

Class/Section _____

Date   _____

KEY NUMBER TAX RETURN SUMMARY

CHAPTER 5

Comprehensive Problem 1

Adjusted Gross Income (Line 8b) _____

Standard or Itemized Deductions (Line 9) _____

Taxable Income (Line 11b) _____

Total Tax (Line 16) _____

Amount Overpaid (Line 20) _____

Comprehensive Problem 2A

Adjusted Gross Income (Line 8b) _____

Standard or Itemized Deductions (Line 9) _____

Casualties and Thefts (Form 4684, Line 18) _____

Total Tax (Line 16) _____

Amount Overpaid (Line 20) _____

Comprehensive Problem 2B

Adjusted Gross Income (Line 8b) _____

Standard or Itemized Deductions (Line 9) _____

Child Tax Credit/Credit for Other Dependents (Line 13a) _____

Total Tax (Line 16) _____

Amount Overpaid (Line 20) _____

CHAPTER 6

Accounting Periods and Other Taxes

After completing this chapter, you should be able to:

LO 6.1   Determine the different accounting periods allowed for tax purposes.

LO 6.2   Determine the different accounting methods allowed for tax purposes.

LO 6.3   Determine whether parties are considered related for tax purposes, and classify the tax treatment of certain related-party transactions.

LO 6.4   Apply the rules for computing tax on the unearned income of minor children and certain students (the "kiddie tax").

LO 6.5   Calculate a basic alternative minimum tax.

LO 6.6   Calculate and report the self-employment tax (both Social Security and Medicare portions) for self-employed taxpayers.

LO 6.7   Apply the special tax and reporting requirements for household employees (the "nanny tax").

LO 6.8   Compute the special taxes for high-income taxpayers.

OVERVIEW

Taxpayers operating a business, whether professional, rental, manufacturing, or another activity, should have an understanding of the accounting periods (calendar, fiscal, or short-period tax years) and accounting methods (cash, accrual, or hybrid methods) allowed. Transactions involving related parties often have different rules for inclusion or exclusion of income and deductions. This chapter begins by addressing how and when individual, partnership, and corporate taxpayers should report taxable income.

In addition to the typical income tax, a number of other taxes are also reported through the individual income tax return. On the 2019 Form 1040, Schedule 2 is the primary reporting mechanism for additional taxes. This chapter covers the computation of taxes such as the "kiddie tax," the "nanny tax," alternative minimum tax, self-employment tax, the net investment income tax, and the additional Medicare tax.

Learning Objective 6.1

Determine the different accounting periods allowed for tax purposes.

6-1 ACCOUNTING PERIODS

6-1a Individual Tax Years

Almost all individuals file tax returns using a calendar-year accounting period. Individuals reporting for tax purposes on a fiscal year other than a calendar year are extremely rare since the tax system is set up to accommodate calendar-year taxpayers. However, there are no restrictions on an individual taking a tax year other than a calendar year. The choice to file on a fiscal year basis must be made with an initial tax return, and books and records must be kept on that basis. An individual may also request IRS approval to change to a fiscal year if certain conditions are met.

6-1b Partnership and Corporation Tax Years

Many individual tax returns include the pass-through of income from partnerships, limited liability companies, S corporations, and personal service corporations. The income or loss from partnerships and S corporations is passed through on Schedule K-1 to the owners and taxed on the owners' personal tax returns. Partnerships and S corporations are not taxable entities, only reporting entities. Similarly, wages are passed through to doctors, lawyers, accountants, actuaries, and other professionals from personal service corporations owned by them. Many individuals carry on businesses in partnerships which comprise a large part of the income shown on their tax returns. Other individuals make investments, including the operation of real estate rental activities, in these pass-through entities. Because the pass-through of income and loss from partnerships and S corporations plays a large role in the taxation of many individuals, it is important to understand the rules governing the allowed accounting periods for these entities.

Partnerships and corporations had a great deal of freedom in selecting a tax year in the past. However, Congress decided that this freedom often resulted in an inappropriate deferral of taxable income. For example, if an individual taxpayer has a calendar tax year and receives income from a partnership with a tax year ending September 30, the taxpayer is able to defer 3 months of partnership income for an indefinite period of time. Therefore, the tax law was changed to include provisions that specify the required tax year for many partnerships and certain corporations, reducing the opportunities for deferring income.

Corporations have much more flexibility and can generally choose any fiscal year-end for tax purposes. The primary restriction on choosing a fiscal year-end for a corporation is that its books and records must also be maintained on the same fiscal year-end. Fiscal year-ends must always occur on the last day of a month unless the taxpayer adopts a 52-53-week year, which permits the year-end to always fall on the same day of the week. That day of the week must be the one closest to the last day of the month.

Most partnerships, S corporations, and personal service corporations owned by individual taxpayers now conform to the same calendar-year reporting used by almost all individuals. These entities are allowed a September, October, or November year-end if the owners make an annual cash deposit on behalf of the entity or perform other required calculations to assure the IRS that they are not using the fiscal year to defer the payment of federal taxes. The details of the complex requirements which must be met by entities filing non-calendar tax years are beyond the scope of this textbook.

6-1c Short-Period Taxable Income

If taxpayers have a short year other than their first or last year of operations, they are required to annualize their taxable income to calculate the tax for the short period. The tax liability is calculated for the annualized period and allocated back to the short period. With the introduction of a flat 21 percent corporate tax rate, the annualization method is somewhat simplified.

EXAMPLE Omoto Corporation obtains permission to change from a calendar year to a tax year ending August 31. For the short period, January 1 through August 31, 2019, the corporation's taxable income was $40,000. Omoto Corporation's tax for the short period is calculated as follows:

Step 1: Annualize the income $40,000 \times 12/8 = \underline{\$60,000}$

Step 2: Tax on annualized income $21\% \times \$60,000 = \underline{\$12,600}$

Step 3: Short period tax $\$12,600 \times 8/12 = \underline{\$\ 8,400}$

With a flat rate, this is equivalent to $40,000 \times 21$ percent. ♦

Self-Study Problem 6.1 See Appendix E for Solutions to Self-Study Problems

For the following taxpayers, determine the choice of year-end and place an X in the correct column.

Taxpayer	Calendar year-end	Fiscal year-end	Fiscal year-end but some restrictions
1. Individual with no separate books and records	_____	_____	_____
2. Partnership for which all the partners are calendar year-end individuals	_____	_____	_____
3. A corporation that keeps in book and records on a fiscal year ending June 30	_____	_____	_____
4. An S corporation for which all shareholders are calendar year-end individuals	_____	_____	_____

6-2 ACCOUNTING METHODS

6.2 Learning Objective

Determine the different accounting methods allowed for tax purposes.

The tax law requires taxpayers to report taxable income using the method of accounting regularly used by the taxpayer in keeping his or her books, provided the method clearly reflects the taxpayer's income. The cash receipts and disbursements method, the accrual method, and the hybrid method are accounting methods specifically recognized in the tax law.

The cash receipts and disbursements method of accounting (commonly referred to as the cash method or cash basis) is used by most individuals for their overall method of accounting. Generally, wages, interest and dividend income, capital gains, and personal deductions are accounted for on the cash basis for individuals. Individuals may choose to account for a particular business, such as a sole proprietorship reported on Schedule C, using the accrual or hybrid method of accounting. If a taxpayer has two businesses, a different method of accounting may be used for each. The choice of a tax accounting method is a general rule which will be overridden by tax laws for some items of income and expense. For example, individuals reporting on a cash basis may deduct IRAs or pension contributions which are paid in cash in the year following the deduction, the income from savings bonds may be included in taxable income even though it is not received in cash, and prepaid interest may not be allowed as a deduction in the year paid.

The cash method generally results in the recognition of income when it is actually or constructively received; deductions are recognized in the year of payment. Taxpayers on the accrual basis generally recognize income when it is earned, regardless of when it is received, and generally recognize deductions when they are incurred, regardless of when they are paid. Cash basis taxpayers may not use the cash method for all expenses. Tax rules require cash basis taxpayers to always use the accrual basis for prepayments of interest. Other business expenses such as rent must also follow the accrual method if the prepayment extends substantially (generally 12 months) beyond the end of the tax year. Conversely, accrual basis taxpayers who receive certain types of prepaid income, such as rent in advance, must generally recognize the income on the cash basis.

EXAMPLE On December 1, 2019, Carol entered into a lease on a building for use in her business for $2,000 per month. Under the lease terms, Carol pays 18 months' rent ($36,000) in advance on December 1. Carol may deduct only 1 month's rent ($2,000) for the calendar year ended December 31, 2019 because the prepayment extends substantially beyond the end of the tax year, even though she is a cash basis taxpayer. The remainder of the prepaid rent is deducted at $2,000 per month in 2020 and 2021. The taxpayer receiving the rent must report all $36,000 as income even if he or she is an accrual basis taxpayer. ♦

The accrual method of accounting requires that income be recognized when (1) all events have occurred which fix the right to receive the income, and (2) the amount of income can be estimated with reasonable accuracy. An expense is deductible in the year in which all events have occurred that determine a liability exists and the amount can be estimated with reasonable accuracy. Also, "economic performance" must occur before an accrual basis deduction can be claimed. Economic performance means that all activities related to the incurrence of the liability have been performed. For example, economic performance occurs for the purchase of services when the taxpayer uses the services.

A hybrid method of accounting involves the use of both the cash and accrual methods of accounting. The tax law permits the use of a hybrid method, provided the taxpayer's income is clearly reflected by the method. An example of a hybrid method is the use of the accrual method for cost of products sold by the business and the use of the cash method for income and other expenses.

Taxpayers make an election to use an accounting method when they file an initial tax return and use that method. To change methods, taxpayers must obtain permission from the IRS.

TAX BREAK The cash method allows a certain amount of flexibility in tax planning. Payment of business expenses may be accelerated before year-end to generate additional deductions, if desired. In addition, billings for services may be postponed at year-end so payment will not be received and included in income until the following year. Some itemized deductions such as property taxes, state income taxes, and charitable contributions may also be paid before year-end for an immediate deduction.

Self-Study Problem 6.2A   *See Appendix E for Solutions to Self-Study Problems*

Melaleuca, Inc., is an accrual basis taxpayer with the following transactions during the calendar tax year:

Accrual business income (except rent and interest)	$63,000
Accrual business expenses (except rent)	42,000
Three months' rent received on a leased building on November 1 of this year	9,000
Prepaid interest for 1 year received on a note on July 1 of the current year	12,000
Six months' rent paid on December 1 for business property	7,200
Calculate Melaleuca, Inc.'s, net income for this year.	$_____

6-2a **Restrictions on the Use of the Cash Method**

The tax law contains certain restrictions on the use of the cash method of accounting. Regular corporations, partnerships that have a regular corporation as a partner, and tax-exempt trusts with unrelated business income are generally prohibited from using the cash method. However, this requirement does not apply to farming businesses, qualified personal service corporations, and entities with average annual gross receipts of $26 million or less in 2019.

EXAMPLE   Orange Associates is a manufacturer of light bulbs with gross receipts of $27 million. Orange would not be allowed to use the cash method of accounting for tax purposes. ◆

The IRS will pay informants cash rewards based on the value of the information they furnish and the amount recovered from the target of the investigation. In 2014, 2015, and 2016 the IRS paid 101, 99, and 418 whistleblowers $52 million, $103 million, and $61 million, respectively. Over the last three years, the amount of tax collected by the IRS as a result of whistleblowers was almost $1.2 billion.

Would You Believe?

Self-Study Problem 6.2B   *See Appendix E for Solutions to Self-Study Problems*

Indicate whether or not each of the following entities may use the cash method for tax purposes during 2019.

	Yes or No
1. A corporation engaged in orange farming.	_____
2. A dentist with a personal service corporation.	_____
3. A corporate car dealer with sales of $28 million per year.	_____
4. A corporation engaged in certified public accounting.	_____

6-3 **RELATED PARTIES (SECTION 267)**

> **6.3 Learning Objective**
>
> Determine whether parties are considered related for tax purposes, and classify the tax treatment of certain related-party transactions.

When taxpayers who are related to of each other engage in transactions, there is potential for abuse of the tax system. To prevent this abuse, the tax law contains provisions that govern related-party transactions. Under these rules, related parties who undertake certain types of transactions may find the timing of income or deduction recognition differs from typical rules.

There are two types of transactions between related parties restricted by Section 267 of the tax law. These transactions are:

1. Sales of property at a loss
2. Unpaid expenses and interest

6-3a **Losses**

Under the tax law "losses from sale or exchange of property . . . directly or indirectly" are disallowed between related parties. When the property is later sold to an unrelated party, any disallowed loss may be used to offset gain on that transaction.

EXAMPLE Mary sells IBM stock with a basis of $10,000 to her son, Steve, for $8,000, resulting in a disallowed loss of $2,000. Three years later, Steve sells the stock to Kim, an unrelated party, for $13,000. Steve has a gain on the sale of $5,000 ($13,000 − $8,000). However, only $3,000 ($5,000 − $2,000) of the gain is taxable to Steve since the previously disallowed loss can reduce his gain. ♦

EXAMPLE Assume the same facts as in the example above, except the IBM stock is sold for $9,500 (instead of $13,000). None of the gain of $1,500 ($9,500 − $8,000) would be taxable, because the disallowed loss would absorb it. $500 of Mary's disallowed loss is not available to her son. ♦

EXAMPLE Assume the same facts as in the example above, except Steve sells the IBM stock 3 years later for $7,000 (instead of $9,500). Steve now has a $1,000 realized loss, which can be deducted subject to any capital loss limitations. Because there is no gain on this transaction, the tax benefit of Mary's $2,000 disallowed loss is not available to her son. ♦

6-3b Unpaid Expenses and Interest

Under Section 267, related taxpayers are prevented from engaging in tax avoidance schemes in which one taxpayer uses the cash method of accounting and the other taxpayer uses the accrual method.

EXAMPLE Ficus Corporation, an accrual basis taxpayer, is owned by Bill, an individual who uses the cash method of accounting for tax purposes. On December 31, Ficus Corporation accrues interest expense of $10,000 on a loan from Bill, but the interest is not paid to him. Ficus Corporation may not deduct the $10,000 until the tax year in which it is actually paid to Bill. This rule also applies to other expenses such as salaries and bonuses. ♦

6-3c Relationships

Section 267 has a complex set of rules to define who is a related party for disallowance purposes. The common related parties under Section 267 include the following:

1. Family members. A taxpayer's family includes brothers and sisters (whole or half), a spouse, ancestors (parents, grandparents, etc.), and lineal descendants (children, grandchildren, etc.).
2. A corporation or an individual who directly or indirectly owns more than 50 percent of the corporation.
3. Two corporations that are members of the same controlled group.
4. Trusts, corporations, and certain charitable organizations. They are subject to a complex set of relationship rules.

EXAMPLE Kalmia Corporation is owned 70 percent by Jim and 30 percent by Kathy. Jim and Kathy are unrelated to each other. Since Jim owns over 50 percent of the corporation, he is deemed to be a related party to the corporation. As a result, if Jim sells property to the corporation at a loss, the loss will be disallowed. Since Kathy is not related to the corporation, the rules of Section 267 do not apply to Kathy. ♦

Related-party rules also consider constructive ownership in determining whether parties are related to each other. Under these rules, taxpayers are deemed to own stock owned by certain relatives and related entities. The common constructive ownership rules are as follows:

1. A taxpayer is deemed to own all the stock owned by his or her spouse, brothers and sisters (whole or half), ancestors, and lineal descendants.
2. A taxpayer is deemed to own his or her proportionate share of stock owned by any partnership, corporation, trust, or estate in which he or she is a partner, shareholder, or beneficiary.
3. A taxpayer is deemed to own any stock owned directly or indirectly by a partner.

EXAMPLE ABC Corporation is owned 40 percent by Andy, 30 percent by Betty, and 30 percent by Chee. Betty and Chee are married to each other. For purposes of related-party rules, Andy is not a related party to the corporation since he does not own more than 50 percent of the corporation. Betty is a related party because she is a 60 percent shareholder (30 percent directly and 30 percent from her husband, Chee). Using the same rule, Chee is also a related party since he also owns 60 percent (30 percent directly and 30 percent from his wife, Betty). ◆

EXAMPLE Robert owns 40 percent of R Corporation and 40 percent of T Corporation. T Corporation owns 60 percent of R Corporation. Since Robert is deemed to own 64 percent of R Corporation, he is a related party to R Corp. The 64 percent is calculated as 40 percent direct ownership and 24 percent (40% × 60%) constructive ownership. ◆

There are other sets of related-party and constructive ownership rules in the tax law, which differ from the related-party rules discussed in this section and should not be confused with the Section 267 related-party provisions.

Tax cuts and tax reform do not always represent the same change. Tax cuts often involve temporary provisions designed to stimulate the economy. The cuts are often paid for with the expiration of many of the favorable tax provisions toward the end of the budget window. Tax reform represents a long-term change in the method by which taxes are applied or calculated. Parts of the TCJA passed in 2017 are consistent with reform (permanent cut in corporate tax rates to 21percent) while other parts more closely resemble a temporary cut (the bevy of provisions expiring after 2025).

Self-Study Problem 6.3   *See Appendix E for Solutions to Self-Study Problems*

EFG Corporation is owned 40 percent by Ed, 20 percent by Frank, 20 percent by Gene, and 20 percent by X Corporation. X Corporation is owned 80 percent by Ed and 20 percent by an unrelated party. Frank and Gene are brothers. Answer each of the following questions about EFG under the constructive ownership rules of Section 267.

1. What is Ed's percentage ownership? _____ %
2. What is Frank's percentage ownership? _____ %
3. What is Gene's percentage ownership? _____ %
4. If EFG sells property to Ed for a $15,000 loss, what amount of that loss can be recognized for tax purposes?

$_____

6-4 UNEARNED INCOME OF MINOR CHILDREN AND CERTAIN STUDENTS

Many parents have found it beneficial from a tax-planning standpoint to give income earning assets, such as stocks, bonds, bank certificates of deposit, and mutual funds, to their minor children. Since the children are generally in a lower income tax bracket, the income earned from these assets such as interest, dividends, and capital gains on stock sales has traditionally been taxed at a lower rate than the parents' rate.

EXAMPLE   Don and Melanie are high-income taxpayers in the 37 percent income tax bracket. They would like to shift income to their 11-year old son Boris. Don and Melanie gift Boris some investments over a few years and Boris ends up with $100,000 of investments that generate taxable income of $5,000 during the year. Boris is in the 10 percent tax bracket. The tax savings from the income shift would be $1,350 [$5,000 pretax income × (37% − 10%)]. ◆

To prevent an income-shifting strategy such as that presented in the previous example, the child must compute tax on unearned income using the trust and estate tax rates. As shown in the following table, the 2019 trust and estate tax rates are extremely progressive:

Over	But not over	Tax is:		Of the excess over
$ 0	$ 2,600	–	+10%	$ 0
2,600	9,300	260.00	+24%	2,600
9,300	12,750	1,868.00	+35%	9,300
12,750		3,075.50	+37%	12,750

The tax on a child's unearned income (commonly referred to as the "kiddie tax") applies to dependent children who are ages 18 or younger and full-time students ages 19 through 23 at the end of the year, who have at least one living parent, and who have "net unearned income" of more than $2,200 for 2019. Although there is no statutory definition for a parent, the term is generally considered to mean a parent or step-parent of the child.

6-4a Computation of Tax on Child's Taxable Income

The computation of the tax on a child's unearned income remains a complex, multi-step process. Taxable income is bifurcated into earned income and unearned income. The kiddie tax is assessed using rates that apply to trusts and estate on the portion of taxable income that consists of net unearned income and that exceeds the unearned income threshold of $2,200 (in 2019).

Step 1: Compute taxable income

Taxable income is equal to the child's total (earned and unearned) income less the child's standard deduction. The standard deduction for an individual that can be claimed as a dependent is the greater of $1,100 or the sum of the individual's earned income and $350. The standard deduction cannot exceed the statutory standard deduction for that filing status (for example, single, $12,200).

EXAMPLE A   Alice is a single child under 18 with $3,200 of interest income and no earned income. Her standard deduction is $1,100 (the greater of $1,100 or earned income of $0 + $350). Alice's taxable income is $2,100 ($3,200 − $1,100). ◆

EXAMPLE B Boris is a single child under 18 with $3,200 of interest income and $5,000 of earned income. His standard deduction is $5,350 (the greater of $1,100 or $5,000 + $350). Boris' taxable income is $2,850 ($3,200 + $5,000 − $5,350). ♦

EXAMPLE C Carol is a single child under 18 with $12,500 of interest income and $12,400 of earned income. Her standard deduction is $12,200 ($12,400 + $350 exceeds the standard deduction for a single taxpayer). Carol's taxable income is $12,700 ($12,500 + $12,400 − $12,200). ♦

Step 2: Compute Net Unearned Income (NUI)

Net unearned income is generally defined as unearned income less $2,200 (a child with large itemized deductions associated with the unearned income may be different). Unearned income is income that is not derived from wages, salaries, or similar compensation or income from a trade or business. More generally, unearned income is thought of as investment income such as interest, dividends, and capital gains.

EXAMPLE A Alice is a single child under 18 with $3,200 of interest income and no earned income. Alice's NUI is $1,000 ($3,200 − $2,200). ♦

EXAMPLE B Boris is a single child under 18 with $3,200 of interest income and $5,000 of earned income. Boris' NUI is $1,000 ($3,200 − $2,200). ♦

EXAMPLE C Carol is a single child under 18 with $12,500 of interest income and $12,400 of earned income. Carol's NUI is $10,300 ($12,500 − $2,200). ♦

Step 3: Compute Earned Taxable Income (ETI)

Earned taxable income is the residual amount of taxable income after reduction by NUI (in other words, taxable income less NUI).

EXAMPLE A Alice is a single child under 18 with $3,200 of interest income and no earned income. Alice's ETI is $1,100 ($2,100 − $1,000). ♦

EXAMPLE B Boris is a single child under 18 with $3,200 of interest income and $5,000 of earned income. Boris' ETI is $1,850 ($2,850 − $1,000). ♦

EXAMPLE C Carol is a single child under 18 with $12,500 of interest income and $12,400 of earned income. Carol's ETI is $2,400 ($12,700 − $10,300). ♦

The above steps effectively bifurcate taxable income into two parts (NUI and ETI).

Step 4: Calculate the tax

The tax on the NUI is calculated at trust and estate rates and the tax on ETI is calculated at the rates applicable to the child's filing status. (In these examples, taxes are calculated using tax rate structures. For ETI below $100,000, the tax tables are required).

EXAMPLE A Alice is a single child under 18 with $3,200 of interest income and no earned income. Alice's tax is $210 [$1,000 × 10% (NUI taxed as a trust) + $1,100 × 10% (taxed as a single taxpayer)]. ♦

EXAMPLE B Boris is a single child under 18 with $3,200 of interest income and $5,000 of earned income. Boris' tax is $285 [$1,000 × 10% (NUI taxes as a trust) + $1,850 × 10% (taxed as a single taxpayer)]. ♦

EXAMPLE C   Carol is a single child under 18 with $12,500 of interest income and $12,400 of earned income. Carol's tax is $2,458 [($2,218 of trust tax on $10,300 [$1,868 + (($10,300 − $9,300) × 35%)] + $2,400 × 10% (taxed as a single taxpayer)]. ♦

The kiddie tax is reported on Form 8615 as presented on Page 6-11. Most of the complexity of the kiddie tax is revealed in the Line 7 tax computation worksheet in the instructions to Form 8615.

The taxation of a child's unearned income is made even more complex in situations where the child's earned income is unusually high (over approximately $70,000) or where the unearned income is subject to preferential rates such as qualified dividends or long-term capital gains. These situations are beyond the scope of this textbook.

TIP   Although the computation of the kiddie tax is complex, having ProConnect compute the kiddie tax requires no extra input on the part of the preparer. If the taxpayer is noted as being claimed as a dependent, fits the age requirements, and unearned income that exceeds the threshold is input (for example, form Forms 1099-INT or 1099-DIV), the software will automatically generate and populate the Form 8615 and calculate the kiddie tax.

6-4b   Election to Include a Child's Unearned Income on Parents' Return

If certain conditions are met, parents may elect to include a child's gross income on the parents' tax return. The election eliminates the child's return filing requirements and saves the parents from the trouble of filing the special calculation on Form 8615 for the "kiddie tax." To qualify for this election, the following conditions must be met:

1. The child's gross income is from interest and dividends only.
2. The gross income is more than $1,100 and less than $11,000 (or 10 times the lower amount).
3. No estimated tax has been paid in the name of the child and the child is not subject to backup withholding.

EXAMPLE   Sam Jackson is 12 years old and has $2,300 of interest from a savings account established for him by his grandparents. This is Sam's only income for the year. Instead of completing Form 8615 and paying the kiddie tax on his $2,300 in income, Sam's parents, Michael and Janet, may elect to include the $2,300 on their tax return, thereby eliminating Sam's filing requirement. The election to include the income of a minor child on the parents' return is made on Form 8814, as illustrated on Page 6-13. ♦

Self-Study Problem 6.4   *See Appendix E for Solutions to Self-Study Problems*

Bill and Janet are a married couple filing jointly in 2019 and have one child, Robert, who is 9 years old. Robert has interest income of $3,000 in 2019. Bill and Janet's taxable income in 2019 is $46,550 and they take the standard deduction as the only from AGI deduction. Calculate Robert's tax liability for 2019, assuming

a.   Bill and Janet do not make the election to include Robert's income on their tax return.

$_____

b.   Bill and Janet make the election to include Robert's income on their tax return.

$_____

Form **8615**

Department of the Treasury
Internal Revenue Service (99)

Tax for Certain Children Who Have Unearned Income

▶ Attach to your Form 1040 or Form 1040-NR.
▶ Go to *www.irs.gov/Form8615* for instructions and the latest information.

OMB No. 1545-0074

2019

Attachment
Sequence No. **33**

Name shown on return

Your social security number

Before you begin: If you must use the Schedule D Tax Worksheet or have income from farming or fishing, see the instructions. Also see **Pub. 929,** Tax Rules for Children and Dependents. It explains how to figure your tax using the **Schedule D Tax Worksheet** or **Schedule J** (Form 1040).

A Parent's name (first, initial, and last). **Caution:** See instructions before completing.

B Parent's social security number

Part I   Net Unearned Income

1	Enter your unearned income (see instructions)	1	
2	If you **did not** itemize deductions on **Schedule A** (Form 1040 or Form 1040-NR), enter $2,200. Otherwise, see instructions	2	
3	Subtract line 2 from line 1. If zero or less, **stop;** do not complete the rest of this form but **do** attach it to your return	3	
4	Enter your **taxable income** from Form 1040, line 11b, or Form 1040-NR, line 41. If you file Form 2555, see the instructions	4	
5	Enter the **smaller** of line 3 or line 4. If zero, **stop;** do not complete the rest of this form but **do** attach it to your return	5	

Part II   Tax

6	Subtract line 5 from line 4	6	
7	Enter the tax on the amount on line 4 (see instructions). If the Qualified Dividends and Capital Gain Tax Worksheet, Schedule D Tax Worksheet, or Schedule J (Form 1040) is used to figure the tax, check here. If applicable, include this amount on your Form 1040, line 12a, or Form 1040-NR, line 42 (see instructions). If you file Form 2555, see the instructions . . . . ▶ ☐	7	

For Paperwork Reduction Act Notice, see your tax return instructions.

Cat. No. 64113U

Form **8615** (2019)

Form **8814**	**Parents' Election To Report Child's Interest and Dividends**	OMB No. 1545-0074
Department of the Treasury Internal Revenue Service (99)	▶ Go to *www.irs.gov/Form8814* for the latest information. ▶ **Attach to parents' Form 1040, Form 1040-SR, or Form 1040-NR.**	**2019** Attachment Sequence No. **40**

Name(s) shown on your return	Your social security number
Michael and Janet Jackson	

Caution: The federal income tax on your child's income, including qualified dividends and capital gain distributions, may be less if you file a separate tax return for the child instead of making this election. This is because you cannot take certain tax benefits that your child could take on his or her own return. For details, see *Tax benefits you cannot take* in the instructions.

A Child's name (first, initial, and last)	**B** Child's social security number
Sam Jackson	

C If more than one Form 8814 is attached, check here . . . . ▶ ☐

Part I	**Child's Interest and Dividends To Report on Your Return**

1a	Enter your child's **taxable** interest. If this amount is different from the amounts shown on the child's Forms 1099-INT and 1099-OID, see the instructions	**1a**	2,300
b	Enter your child's **tax-exempt** interest. **Do not** include this amount on line 1a **1b**		
2a	Enter your child's ordinary dividends, including any Alaska Permanent Fund dividends. If your child received any ordinary dividends as a nominee, see the instructions	**2a**	
b	Enter your child's qualified dividends included on line 2a. See the instructions **2b**		
3	Enter your child's capital gain distributions. If your child received any capital gain distributions as a nominee, see the instructions	**3**	
4	Add lines 1a, 2a, and 3. If the total is $2,200 or less, skip lines 5 through 12 and go to line 13. If the total is $11,000 or more, **do not** file this form. Your child **must** file his or her own return to report the income	**4**	2,300
5	Base amount. Enter 2,200	**5**	2,200
6	Subtract line 5 from line 4	**6**	100
	If both lines 2b and 3 are zero or blank, skip lines 7 through 10, enter -0- on line 11, and go to line 12. Otherwise, go to line 7.		
7	Divide line 2b by line 4. Enter the result as a decimal (rounded to at least three places) **7**	.	
8	Divide line 3 by line 4. Enter the result as a decimal (rounded to at least three places) **8**	.	
9	Multiply line 6 by line 7. Enter the result here. See the instructions for where to report this amount on your return **9**		
10	Multiply line 6 by line 8. Enter the result here. See the instructions for where to report this amount on your return **10**		
11	Add lines 9 and 10	**11**	0
12	Subtract line 11 from line 6. Include this amount in the total on Schedule 1 (Form 1040 or 1040-SR), line 8, or Form 1040-NR, line 21. In the space next to that line, enter "Form 8814" and show the amount. If you checked the box on line C above, see the instructions. Go to line 13 below	**12**	100

Part II	**Tax on the First $2,200 of Child's Interest and Dividends**

13	Amount not taxed. Enter 1,100	**13**	1,100
14	Subtract line 13 from line 4. If the result is zero or less, enter -0-	**14**	1,200
15	**Tax.** Is the amount on line 14 less than $1,100? ☑ **No.** Enter $110 here and see the **Note** below. ☐ **Yes.** Multiply line 14 by 10% (0.10). Enter the result here and see the **Note** below.	**15**	110

Note: If you checked the box on line C above, see the instructions. Otherwise, include the amount from line 15 in the tax you enter on Form 1040 or Form 1040-SR, line 12a, or Form 1040-NR, line 42. Be sure to check box **1** on Form 1040 or Form 1040-SR, line 12a, or check box **a** on Form 1040-NR, line 42.

For Paperwork Reduction Act Notice, see your tax return instructions.   Cat. No. 10750J   Form **8814** (2019)

Calculate a basic
alternative minimum tax.

6-5 THE INDIVIDUAL ALTERNATIVE MINIMUM TAX (AMT)

A small number of individual taxpayers are subject to two parallel tax calculations, the regular tax and the alternative minimum tax (AMT). The AMT was designed in the 1960s to ensure that wealthy taxpayers could not take advantage of special tax write-offs (tax preferences and other adjustments) to avoid paying tax. In general, taxpayers must pay the alternative minimum tax if their AMT tax liability is larger than their regular tax liability.

The AMT is calculated on Form 6251, using the following formula simplified for purposes of this textbook:

> Regular taxable income (before exemptions (suspended in 2018) and standard deduction)
> ± Plus or minus AMT preferences and adjustments
> = Equals alternative minimum taxable income (AMTI)
> − Less AMT exemption (phased out to zero as AMTI increases)
> = Equals amount subject to AMT
> × Multiplied by the AMT tax rate(s)
> = Equals tentative minimum tax
> − Less regular tax
> = Equals amount of AMT due with tax return, if a positive amount

6-5a Common AMT Adjustments and Preferences

The terms "AMT adjustments" and "AMT preferences" are often used interchangeably, though they have slightly different meanings. In general, adjustments are *timing* differences that arise because of differences in the regular and AMT tax calculations (e.g., depreciation timing differences), while preferences are special provisions for the regular tax that are not allowed for the AMT (e.g., state income taxes). Both terms refer to items which adjust regular taxable income to arrive at income which is subject to alternative minimum tax. There are over twenty different types of adjustments and preferences used in the calculation of AMT on Form 6251. Some of the common adjustments and preferences are as follows:

- The standard deduction allowed for regular tax is not allowed for AMT.
- The deductions for property tax, state income tax, and other taxes allowed as itemized deductions for regular tax are not allowed for AMT.
- Depreciation is generally calculated over a longer life for AMT, sometimes using a different method.
- Net operating losses are calculated differently for AMT and often result in an adjustment when they are present.
- State income tax refunds are not considered income for AMT since the state income tax deduction is not allowed for AMT.
- Interest from specified private activity bonds is not taxed for regular tax purposes, but is taxable for AMT.
- Other less commonly seen AMT differences include such items as the calculations related to incentive stock options, oil and gas depletion, research and development expenses, gains on asset sales such as rental real estate, passive losses, and the gain exclusion for small business stock and other items.

The actual details of the calculation of several of the AMT tax preferences and adjustments are complex and infrequently seen in practice. For further information, please consult the IRS website, a tax service, or an advanced tax textbook.

6-5b AMT Exemption

To reduce the chances of subjecting a greater number of taxpayers to the AMT, an exemption amount is permitted as a deduction against AMT income. The 2019 AMT exemptions and thresholds are:

	Married filing jointly	Single and H of H	Married filing separately
Exemption amount	$ 111,700	$ 71,700	$ 55,850
Threshold	1,020,600	510,300	510,300

The exemption amount is phased out (reduced) 25 cents for each dollar by which the taxpayer's alternative minimum taxable income exceeds the threshold amounts.

EXAMPLE Abby, a single taxpayer, has AMTI of $126,000 in 2019. Her AMT exemption is $71,700 as she has not reached the threshold for phase-out. ◆

EXAMPLE Damon and Tiffany are married and file jointly. They have AMTI of $1,234,000 in 2019. Their AMT exemption is $58,350 [$111,700 − (($1,234,000 − $1,020,600) × 25%)]. ◆

The exemption amounts and phase-out thresholds are both indexed for inflation, but the amounts are scheduled to be reduced significantly after 2025.

6-5c Alternative Minimum Tax Rates

For 2019, the alternative minimum tax rates for calculating the tentative minimum tax are 26 percent of the first $194,800 ($97,400 for married taxpayers filing separately), plus 28 percent on amounts above $194,800 (amounts above $97,400 for married filing separately). These rates are applied to the taxpayer's alternative minimum tax base from the formula above. The alternative minimum tax rate for capital gains and dividends is limited to the rate paid for regular tax purposes (e.g., capital gain or qualified dividends taxed at 15 percent for regular tax purposes will also be taxed at a 15 percent alternative minimum tax rate).

EXAMPLE Teddy has alternative minimum taxable income after the exemption deduction of $270,000, none of which is from capital gains. His tentative minimum tax is $71,704, which is calculated as (26% × $194,800) + (28% × [$270,000 − $194,800]). ◆

The increase in the AMT exemption amount and exemption phase-out threshold in conjunction with the limitation on the itemized deduction for state and local taxes and the suspension of miscellaneous itemized deduction subject to the 2 percent floor results in many fewer taxpayers being subject to the AMT than prior to the enactment of the TCJA.

EXAMPLE   Gram and Sally are married taxpayers who file a joint tax return. Their taxable income and regular tax liability can be calculated as follows:

	2019
Adjusted gross income	$200,000
Itemized deductions:	
State income tax	10,000
Home mortgage interest	20,000
Contributions	1,906
Total itemized deductions	(31,906)
Taxable income	$168,094
Tax from rate schedule	$ 28,698

Gram and Sally have $30,000 of private activity bond interest which is taxable for AMT but not for regular tax. The AMT is calculated as follows (same format as the Form 6251 presented on Page 6-17):

	2019
Taxable income	$168,094
Interest on private activity bonds	30,000
Add back:	
Taxes	10,000
Alternative minimum	
taxable income	208,094
AMT exemption	(111,700)
AMT Base	96,394
Tentative minimum tax	25,062
AMT	$ 0

Because the regular tax exceeds the tentative minimum tax in 2019, no AMT is due. ◆

Self-Study Problem 6.5   *See Appendix E for Solutions to Self-Study Problems*

Harold Brown, a single taxpayer, has adjusted gross income of $600,000. He has a deduction for home mortgage interest of $23,000, cash contributions of $11,000, state income taxes of $10,000, and private activity bond interest income of $100,000. Assuming Harold's regular tax liability is $170,708, use Form 6251 on Page 6-17 to calculate the amount of Harold's net alternative minimum tax.

Self-Study Problem 6.5

Form **6251**	**Alternative Minimum Tax—Individuals**	OMB No. 1545-0074
Department of the Treasury Internal Revenue Service (99)	▶ Go to *www.irs.gov/Form6251* for instructions and the latest information. ▶ Attach to Form 1040, 1040-SR, or 1040-NR.	20**19** Attachment Sequence No. **32**

Name(s) shown on Form 1040, 1040-SR, or 1040-NR | Your social security number

Part I   **Alternative Minimum Taxable Income** (See instructions for how to complete each line.)

1	Enter the amount from Form 1040 or 1040-SR, line 11b, if more than zero. If Form 1040 or 1040-SR, line 11b, is zero, subtract lines 9 and 10 of Form 1040 or 1040-SR from line 8b of Form 1040 or 1040-SR and enter the result here. (If less than zero, enter as a negative amount.)	**1**
2a	If filing Schedule A (Form 1040 or 1040-SR), enter the taxes from Schedule A, line 7; otherwise, enter the amount from Form 1040 or 1040-SR, line 9.	**2a**
b	Tax refund from Schedule 1 (Form 1040 or 1040-SR), line 1 or line 8 .	**2b** ( )
c	Investment interest expense (difference between regular tax and AMT)	**2c**
d	Depletion (difference between regular tax and AMT)	**2d**
e	Net operating loss deduction from Schedule 1 (Form 1040 or 1040-SR), line 8. Enter as a positive amount	**2e**
f	Alternative tax net operating loss deduction	**2f** ( )
g	Interest from specified private activity bonds exempt from the regular tax	**2g**
h	Qualified small business stock, see instructions	**2h**
i	Exercise of incentive stock options (excess of AMT income over regular tax income)	**2i**
j	Estates and trusts (amount from Schedule K-1 (Form 1041), box 12, code A)	**2j**
k	Disposition of property (difference between AMT and regular tax gain or loss)	**2k**
l	Depreciation on assets placed in service after 1986 (difference between regular tax and AMT)	**2l**
m	Passive activities (difference between AMT and regular tax income or loss)	**2m**
n	Loss limitations (difference between AMT and regular tax income or loss)	**2n**
o	Circulation costs (difference between regular tax and AMT)	**2o**
p	Long-term contracts (difference between AMT and regular tax income)	**2p**
q	Mining costs (difference between regular tax and AMT)	**2q**
r	Research and experimental costs (difference between regular tax and AMT)	**2r**
s	Income from certain installment sales before January 1, 1987	**2s** ( )
t	Intangible drilling costs preference	**2t**
3	Other adjustments, including income-based related adjustments	**3**
4	**Alternative minimum taxable income.** Combine lines 1 through 3. (If married filing separately and line 4 is more than $733,700, see instructions.)	**4**

Part II   **Alternative Minimum Tax (AMT)**

5 Exemption. (If you were under age 24 at the end of 2019, see instructions.)

IF your filing status is . . .	AND line 4 is not over . . .	THEN enter on line 5 . . .	
Single or head of household	$ 510,300	$ 71,700	
Married filing jointly or qualifying widow(er)	1,020,600	111,700	
Married filing separately	510,300	55,850	**5**

If line 4 is **over** the amount shown above for your filing status, see instructions.

6	Subtract line 5 from line 4. If more than zero, go to line 7. If zero or less, enter -0- here and on lines 7, 9, and 11, and go to line 10 .	**6**
7	• If you are filing Form 2555, see instructions for the amount to enter. • If you reported capital gain distributions directly on Form 1040 or 1040-SR, line 6; you reported qualified dividends on Form 1040 or 1040-SR, line 3a; **or** you had a gain on both lines 15 and 16 of Schedule D (Form 1040 or 1040-SR) (as refigured for the AMT, if necessary), complete Part III on the back and enter the amount from line 40 here. • **All others:** If line 6 is $194,800 or less ($97,400 or less if married filing separately), multiply line 6 by 26% (0.26). Otherwise, multiply line 6 by 28% (0.28) and subtract $3,896 ($1,948 if married filing separately) from the result.	**7**
8	Alternative minimum tax foreign tax credit (see instructions)	**8**
9	Tentative minimum tax. Subtract line 8 from line 7	**9**
10	Add Form 1040 or 1040-SR, line 12a (minus any tax from Form 4972), and Schedule 2 (Form 1040 or 1040-SR), line 2. Subtract from the result any foreign tax credit from Schedule 3 (Form 1040 or 1040-SR), line 1. If you used Schedule J to figure your tax on Form 1040 or 1040-SR, line 12a, refigure that tax without using Schedule J before completing this line (see instructions)	**10**
11	**AMT.** Subtract line 10 from line 9. If zero or less, enter -0-. Enter here and on Schedule 2 (Form 1040 or 1040-SR), line 1	**11**

For Paperwork Reduction Act Notice, see your tax return instructions.   Cat. No. 13600G   Form **6251** (2019)

Sign Here	Under penalties of perjury, I declare that I have examined this return and accompanying schedules and statements, and to the best of my knowledge and belief, they are true, correct, and complete. Declaration of preparer (other than taxpayer) is based on all information of which preparer has any knowledge.			
	Your signature	Date	Your occupation	If the IRS sent you an Identity Protection PIN, enter it here (see inst.)
Joint return? See instructions. Keep a copy for your records.	Spouse's signature. If a joint return, **both** must sign.	Date	Spouse's occupation	If the IRS sent your spouse an Identity Protection PIN, enter it here (see inst.)
	Phone no.		Email address	
Paid Preparer Use Only	Preparer's name	Preparer's signature	Date	PTIN	Check if: ☐ 3rd Party Designee
	Firm's name ▶			Phone no.	☐ Self-employed
	Firm's address ▶			Firm's EIN ▶	

Would You Sign This Tax Return?

Your client, William Warrant, was hired for a management position at an Internet company planning to start a website called "indulgedanimals.com" for dogs, cats, and other pets. When he was hired, William was given an incentive stock option (ISO) worth $500,000, which he exercised during the year. Exercise of the ISO creates a tax preference item for alternative minimum tax (AMT) and causes him to have to pay substantial additional tax when combined with his other tax items for the year. He is livid about the extra tax and refuses to file the AMT Form 6251 with his tax return because the AMT tax is "unfair" and "un-American" according to him. Would you sign this tax return?

6-6 SELF-EMPLOYMENT TAX

6.6 Learning Objective

Calculate and report the self-employment tax (both Social Security and Medicare portions) for self-employed taxpayers.

The Federal Insurance Contributions Act (FICA) imposes Social Security (Old Age, Survivors, and Disability Insurance (OASDI)) and Medicare taxes. As discussed in Chapter 9, employees and their employers are both required to pay FICA taxes. Employers withhold a specified percentage of each employee's wages up to a maximum base amount, match the amount withheld with an equal amount, and pay the total to the Social Security Administration.

Self-employed individuals pay self-employment taxes instead of FICA taxes. Since these individuals have no employers, the entire tax is paid by self-employed individuals. Like the FICA taxes to which employees and their employers are subject, the self-employment tax also consists of two parts, Social Security and Medicare. The maximum base amount of earnings subject to the Social Security portion of the self-employment tax is $132,900 in 2019. All earnings are subject to the Medicare portion of the self-employment tax. The Social Security tax rate is 12.4 percent and the Medicare tax rate is 2.9 percent. The self-employment tax rates and the maximum base amounts for 5 years are illustrated in the following table:

Year	Maximum $ Base for 12.4%	Maximum $ Base for 2.90%*
2015	118,500	Unlimited
2016	118,500	Unlimited
2017	127,200	Unlimited
2018	128,400	Unlimited
2019	132,900	Unlimited

*A 0.9 percent additional Medicare tax on self-employment income over $200,000 single and head of household ($250,000 married filing jointly). See LO 6.8 for more information.

If a self-employed individual also receives wages subject to FICA taxes during a tax year, the Social Security tax maximum base amount for self-employment taxes is reduced by the amount of wages. Therefore, the total amount of earnings subject to the Social Security tax portion of both FICA and self-employment tax for 2019 cannot exceed $132,900.

The self-employment tax is imposed on net earnings of $400 or more from self-employment. Net earnings from self-employment include gross income from a trade or business less trade or business deductions, the distributive share of partnership income from a trade or business, and net income earned as an independent contractor. Gains and losses from property transactions, except inventory transactions, and other unearned income are not considered self-employment income. In arriving at net earnings for purposes of computing the self-employment tax, self-employed taxpayers are allowed a deduction for AGI of one-half of the otherwise applicable self-employment tax. A shortcut to arriving at the self-employment income subject to self-employment tax is to multiply the net earnings from self-employment by 92.35 percent. This shortcut is used on Schedule SE as illustrated below.

EXAMPLE   Norman is a self-employed accountant in 2019. From his practice, Norman earns $136,000, and has wages subject to FICA from a part-time job of $9,100. Norman's self-employment tax is calculated as follows:

Step 1:

Net earnings from self-employment, before the self-employment tax deduction	$136,000	
	× 92.35%	
Tentative net earnings from self-employment after deduction for self-employment tax	$125,596	

Step 2:

	Social Security	**Medicare**
Maximum base for 2019	$132,900	Unlimited
Less: FICA wages	(9,100)	Not Applicable
Maximum self-employment tax base	$123,800	Unlimited
Lesser of net earnings from self-employment after deduction for self-employment tax or maximum base	$123,800	$125,596
Self-employment tax rate	12.4%	2.9%
Self-employment tax for 2019	$ 15,351	$ 3,642

Norman's total self-employment tax for 2019 is $18,993 ($15,351 + $3,642). On his 2019 income tax return, Norman will report net earnings from self-employment of $136,000, a deduction for adjusted gross income of $9,497 (50% × $18,993), and a self-employment tax liability of $18,993. ♦

The calculation in this example is reported on page 2 of Schedule SE, Part I, and must be included with a taxpayer's Form 1040. See Page 6-22 which shows the same calculation on Schedule SE.

Self-Study Problem 6.6   *See Appendix E for Solutions to Self-Study Problems*

Joanne Plummer is self-employed in 2019. Her Schedule C net income is $36,600 for the year, and Joanne also had a part-time job and earned $4,400 that was subject to FICA tax. Joanne received taxable dividends of $1,110 during the year, and she had a capital gain on the sale of stock of $9,100. Calculate Joanne's self-employment tax using Schedule SE (page one only) of Form 1040 on Page 6-21.

Self-Study Problem 6.6

SCHEDULE SE (Form 1040 or 1040-SR) Department of the Treasury Internal Revenue Service (99)	**Self-Employment Tax** ▶ Go to *www.irs.gov/ScheduleSE* for instructions and the latest information. ▶ Attach to Form 1040, 1040-SR, or 1040-NR.	OMB No. 1545-0074 20**19** Attachment Sequence No. **17**

Name of person with self-employment income (as shown on Form 1040, 1040-SR, or 1040-NR)	Social security number of person with **self-employment** income ▶

Before you begin: To determine if you must file Schedule SE, see the instructions.

May I Use Short Schedule SE or Must I Use Long Schedule SE?

Note: Use this flowchart **only if** you must file Schedule SE. If unsure, see *Who Must File Schedule SE* in the instructions.

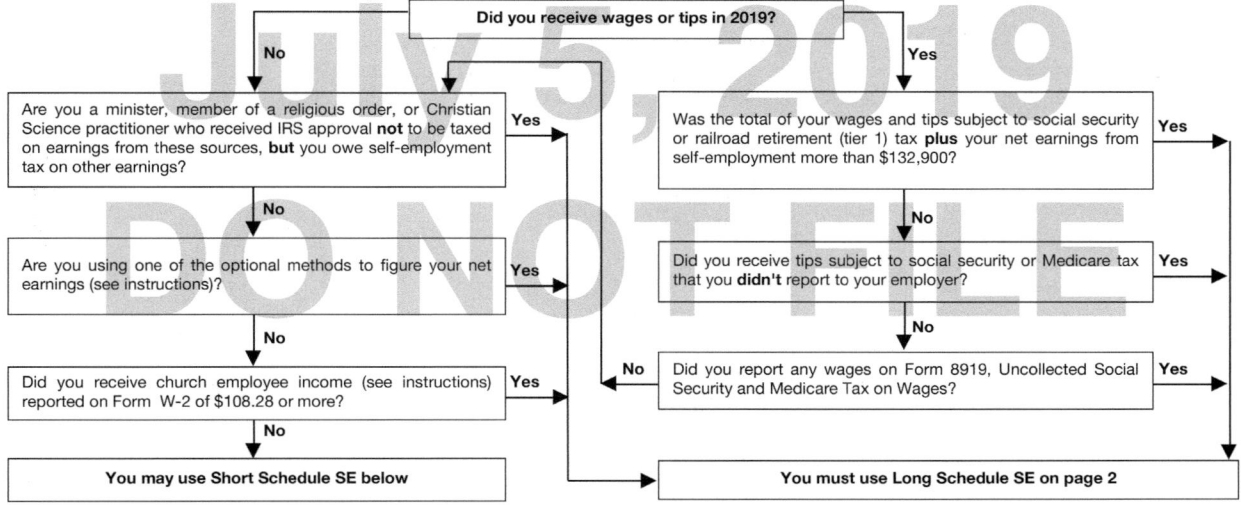

Section A—Short Schedule SE. Caution: Read above to see if you can use Short Schedule SE.

1a	Net farm profit or (loss) from Schedule F, line 34, and farm partnerships, Schedule K-1 (Form 1065), box 14, code A	**1a**
b	If you received social security retirement or disability benefits, enter the amount of Conservation Reserve Program payments included on Schedule F, line 4b, or listed on Schedule K-1 (Form 1065), box 20, code AH	**1b** ( )
2	Net profit or (loss) from Schedule C, line 31; and Schedule K-1 (Form 1065), box 14, code A (other than farming). Ministers and members of religious orders, see instructions for types of income to report on this line. See instructions for other income to report	**2**
3	Combine lines 1a, 1b, and 2	**3**
4	Multiply line 3 by 92.35% (0.9235). If less than $400, you don't owe self-employment tax; **don't** file this schedule unless you have an amount on line 1b . . . . ▶	**4**
	Note: If line 4 is less than $400 due to Conservation Reserve Program payments on line 1b, see instructions.	
5	**Self-employment tax.** If the amount on line 4 is: • $132,900 or less, multiply line 4 by 15.3% (0.153). Enter the result here and on **Schedule 2 (Form 1040 or 1040-SR), line 4,** or **Form 1040-NR, line 55.** • More than $132,900, multiply line 4 by 2.9% (0.029). Then, add $16,479.60 to the result. Enter the total here and on **Schedule 2 (Form 1040 or 1040-SR), line 4,** or **Form 1040-NR, line 55** .	**5**
6	**Deduction for one-half of self-employment tax.** Multiply line 5 by 50% (0.50). Enter the result here and on **Schedule 1 (Form 1040 or 1040-SR), line 14,** or **Form 1040-NR, line 27**	**6**

For Paperwork Reduction Act Notice, see your tax return instructions.   Cat. No. 11358Z   Schedule SE (Form 1040 or 1040-SR) 2019

Schedule SE (Form 1040 or 1040-SR) 2019   Attachment Sequence No. **17**   Page **2**

Name of person with self-employment income (as shown on Form 1040, 1040-SR, or 1040-NR)	Social security number of person with **self-employment** income ▶	
Norman		

Section B—Long Schedule SE

Part I   **Self-Employment Tax**

Note: If your only income subject to self-employment tax is **church employee income,** see instructions. Also see instructions for the definition of church employee income.

A	If you are a minister, member of a religious order, or Christian Science practitioner **and** you filed Form 4361, but you had $400 or more of **other** net earnings from self-employment, check here and continue with Part I . . . . . ▶ ☐		
1a	Net farm profit or (loss) from Schedule F, line 34, and farm partnerships, Schedule K-1 (Form 1065), box 14, code A. **Note:** Skip lines 1a and 1b if you use the farm optional method (see instructions)	**1a**	
b	If you received social security retirement or disability benefits, enter the amount of Conservation Reserve Program payments included on Schedule F, line 4b, or listed on Schedule K-1 (Form 1065), box 20, code AH	**1b**	( )
2	Net profit or (loss) from Schedule C, line 31; and Schedule K-1 (Form 1065), box 14, code A (other than farming). Ministers and members of religious orders, see instructions for types of income to report on this line. See instructions for other income to report. **Note:** Skip this line if you use the nonfarm optional method (see instructions)	**2**	136,000
3	Combine lines 1a, 1b, and 2	**3**	136,000
4a	If line 3 is more than zero, multiply line 3 by 92.35% (0.9235). Otherwise, enter amount from line 3 .	**4a**	125,596
	Note: If line 4a is less than $400 due to Conservation Reserve Program payments on line 1b, see instructions.		
b	If you elect one or both of the optional methods, enter the total of lines 15 and 17 here	**4b**	
c	Combine lines 4a and 4b. If less than $400, **stop;** you don't owe self-employment tax. **Exception:** If less than $400 and you had **church employee income,** enter -0- and continue . . . . . . ▶	**4c**	125,596
5a	Enter your **church employee income** from Form W-2. See instructions for definition of church employee income **5a**	**5b**	
b	Multiply line 5a by 92.35% (0.9235). If less than $100, enter -0-	**5b**	
6	Add lines 4c and 5b	**6**	125,596
7	Maximum amount of combined wages and self-employment earnings subject to social security tax or the 6.2% portion of the 7.65% railroad retirement (tier 1) tax for 2019	**7**	132,900
8a	Total social security wages and tips (total of boxes 3 and 7 on Form(s) W-2) and railroad retirement (tier 1) compensation. If $132,900 or more, skip lines 8b through 10, and go to line 11 . . . . **8a**	9,100	
b	Unreported tips subject to social security tax (from Form 4137, line 10) . . **8b**		
c	Wages subject to social security tax (from Form 8919, line 10) **8c**		
d	Add lines 8a, 8b, and 8c	**8d**	9,100
9	Subtract line 8d from line 7. If zero or less, enter -0- here and on line 10 and go to line 11 . . . ▶	**9**	123,800
10	Multiply the **smaller** of line 6 or line 9 by 12.4% (0.124)	**10**	15,351
11	Multiply line 6 by 2.9% (0.029)	**11**	3,642
12	**Self-employment tax.** Add lines 10 and 11. Enter here and on **Schedule 2 (Form 1040 or 1040-SR), line 4,** or **Form 1040-NR, line 55**	**12**	18,993
13	**Deduction for one-half of self-employment tax.** Multiply line 12 by 50% (0.50). Enter the result here and on **Schedule 1 (Form 1040 or 1040-SR), line 14,** or **Form 1040-NR, line 27** **13**	9,497	

Part II   **Optional Methods To Figure Net Earnings** (see instructions)

Farm Optional Method. You may use this method **only** if **(a)** your gross farm income[1] wasn't more than $8,160, **or (b)** your net farm profits[2] were less than $5,891.

14	Maximum income for optional methods	**14**	5,440
15	Enter the **smaller** of: two-thirds (2/3) of gross farm income[1] (not less than zero) or $5,440. Also include this amount on line 4b above	**15**	

Nonfarm Optional Method. You may use this method **only** if **(a)** your net nonfarm profits[3] were less than $5,891 and also less than 72.189% of your gross nonfarm income,[4] **and (b)** you had net earnings from self-employment of at least $400 in 2 of the prior 3 years. **Caution:** You may use this method no more than five times.

16	Subtract line 15 from line 14	**16**	
17	Enter the **smaller** of: two-thirds (2/3) of gross nonfarm income[4] (not less than zero) **or** the amount on line 16. Also include this amount on line 4b above	**17**	

[1] From Sch. F, line 9, and Sch. K-1 (Form 1065), box 14, code B.

[2] From Sch. F, line 34, and Sch. K-1 (Form 1065), box 14, code A—minus the amount you would have entered on line 1b had you not used the optional method.

[3] From Sch. C, line 31; and Sch. K-1 (Form 1065), box 14, code A.

[4] From Sch. C, line 7; and Sch. K-1 (Form 1065), box 14, code C.

Schedule SE (Form 1040 or 1040-SR) 2019

6-7 **THE NANNY TAX**

Apply the special tax and reporting requirements for household employees (the "nanny tax").

Over the years, the taxation and reporting of household employees' wages has caused many problems for taxpayers and the IRS. The threshold for filing was low ($50 per quarter of wages), and the tax forms to be completed were complex. As a result, many taxpayers ignored the reporting of household workers' wages and taxes. Congress addressed this problem by enacting what are commonly referred to as the "nanny tax" provisions. These provisions simplified the reporting process for employers of domestic household workers.

Household employers are not required to pay FICA taxes on cash payments of less than $2,100 paid to any household employee in a calendar year. If the cash payment to any household employee is $2,100 or more in a calendar year, all the cash payments (including the first $2,100) are subject to FICA taxes (see LO 9.3). The $2,100 threshold is adjusted for inflation each year. Household employers must also withhold income taxes if requested by the employee and are required to pay FUTA (Federal Unemployment Tax Act) tax (see LO 9.6) if more than $1,000 in cash wages are paid to household employees during any calendar quarter. The federal unemployment tax rate is 6 percent of an employee's wages up to $7,000.

A taxpayer is a household employer if he or she hires workers to perform household services, in or around the taxpayer's home, that are subject to the "will and control" of the taxpayer. Examples of household workers include:

- Babysitters
- Caretakers
- Cooks
- Drivers
- Gardeners
- Housekeepers
- Maids

If the household worker has an employee-employer relationship with the taxpayer, it does not matter if the worker is called something else, such as "independent contractor." Also, it does not matter if the worker is full-time or part-time. The household employer is responsible for the proper reporting, withholding, and payment of any taxes due.

The following workers are not subject to FICA taxes on wages paid for *work in the home*:

- The taxpayer's spouse
- The taxpayer's father or mother
- The taxpayer's children under 21 years of age
- Anyone who is under age 18 during the year, unless providing household services is his or her principal occupation (being a student is considered an occupation for purposes of this requirement)

EXAMPLE Allison is a 17-year-old high school student. During the year, she earns $2,200 by babysitting for a neighbor with four children. Any amount she earns is exempt from FICA requirements. However, if Allison is not a student and works full-time as a nanny, she will be subject to the general FICA withholding requirements under the nanny tax rules. ♦

Under the nanny tax provisions, household employers only have to report FICA, federal income tax withholding, and FUTA tax once a year. The taxpayer completes Schedule H and files it with his or her individual Form 1040. Taxpayers who have nonhousehold worker(s) in addition to household worker(s) can elect to report any FICA taxes and withholding on Forms 941 and 940 with their regular employees. Also, at the close of a tax year, taxpayers must file Form W-2 (Copy A) and Form W-3 with the Social Security Administration for each household employee who earned $2,100 or more in cash wages subject to FICA tax or had federal income taxes withheld from wages. For complete details on reporting the wages of household employees, see IRS Publication 926.

proconnect. TIP

Taxes for household employees are input in ProConnect under Taxes. There is a separate subheading for Household Employment Taxes (Schedule H).

Would You Believe?

In 1993, shortly after he was elected, President Bill Clinton nominated Zoë Baird as U.S. Attorney General. Her nomination was derailed in what would become known as "Nannygate" when it was discovered that Baird had hired household employees and not paid taxes. During that time, the level of scrutiny on this type of arrangement increased significantly and some Americans were being asked if they had a "Zoë Baird problem." Based on a 2006 study, some of the fear of Nannygate has subsided as filing rates for Schedule H have dropped on average across the United States. Interestingly, the filing rate for Schedule H was more than three times greater if you lived in or around Washington, DC.

Self-Study Problem 6.7   *See Appendix E for Solutions to Self-Study Problems*

Susan Green lives in Virginia and hires Helen in February 2019 to clean her house for $80 per week. Susan does not withhold income taxes from Helen's wages. Helen's quarterly wages are as follows:

1st quarter	$ 480	($80 × 6 weeks)
2nd quarter	1,040	($80 × 13 weeks)
3rd quarter	1,040	($80 × 13 weeks)
4th quarter	1,040	($80 × 13 weeks)
Total	$3,600	

Assume Susan pays her state unemployment of $194 to the state of Virginia during the year. Complete her 2019 Schedule H (Form 1040) on Pages 6-25 and 6-26, using the above information.

Learning Objective 6.8

Compute the special taxes for high-income taxpayers.

6-8 SPECIAL TAXES FOR HIGH-INCOME TAXPAYERS

There are two separate Medicare taxes for certain high-income taxpayers to help cover the cost of the Affordable Care Act (ACA). The first is the 3.8 percent Net Investment Income tax. The second is a 0.9 percent additional Medicare tax on wages and self-employment income.

6-8a The 3.8 Percent Medicare Tax on Net Investment Income

The ACA imposes a 3.8 percent Medicare tax on the net investment income of individuals with modified AGI over $250,000 for joint filers ($125,000 if married filing separate), and $200,000 for single filers (note that these amounts are not adjusted for inflation). Modified AGI is adjusted gross income increased by certain foreign earned income amounts not covered in this textbook. Investment income subject to the additional 3.8 percent tax includes the following:

- Interest and dividends
- Royalties
- Annuities
- Net rental income, with some exceptions
- Passive activities
- Most gains on the sale of capital and other assets

Self-Study Problem 6.7

SCHEDULE H **(Form 1040 or 1040-SR)** Department of the Treasury Internal Revenue Service (99)	**Household Employment Taxes** (For Social Security, Medicare, Withheld Income, and Federal Unemployment (FUTA) Taxes) ▶ **Attach to Form 1040, 1040-SR, 1040-NR, 1040-SS, or 1041.** ▶ **Go to** *www.irs.gov/ScheduleH* **for instructions and the latest information.**	OMB No. 1545-1971 **2019** Attachment Sequence No. **44**

Name of employer   Social security number

                                                                                          Employer identification number

Calendar year taxpayers having no household employees in 2019 don't have to complete this form for 2019.

A   Did you pay **any one** household employee cash wages of $2,100 or more in 2019? (If any household employee was your spouse, your child under age 21, your parent, or anyone under age 18, see the line A instructions before you answer this question.)

☐ **Yes.** Skip lines B and C and go to line 1.
☐ **No.**   Go to line B.

B   Did you withhold federal income tax during 2019 for any household employee?

☐ **Yes.** Skip line C and go to line 7.
☐ **No.**   Go to line C.

C   Did you pay **total** cash wages of $1,000 or more in **any** calendar **quarter** of 2018 or 2019 to **all** household employees? (**Don't** count cash wages paid in 2018 or 2019 to your spouse, your child under age 21, or your parent.)

☐ **No.**   **Stop.** Don't file this schedule.
☐ **Yes.** Skip lines 1–9 and go to line 10.

Part I	**Social Security, Medicare, and Federal Income Taxes**		
1	Total cash wages subject to social security tax	**1**	
2	Social security tax. Multiply line 1 by 12.4% (0.124)	**2**	
3	Total cash wages subject to Medicare tax	**3**	
4	Medicare tax. Multiply line 3 by 2.9% (0.029)	**4**	
5	Total cash wages subject to Additional Medicare Tax withholding	**5**	
6	Additional Medicare Tax withholding. Multiply line 5 by 0.9% (0.009)	**6**	
7	Federal income tax withheld, if any	**7**	
8	**Total social security, Medicare, and federal income taxes.** Add lines 2, 4, 6, and 7	**8**	

9   Did you pay **total** cash wages of $1,000 or more in **any** calendar **quarter** of 2018 or 2019 to **all** household employees? (**Don't** count cash wages paid in 2018 or 2019 to your spouse, your child under age 21, or your parent.)

☐ **No.**   **Stop.** Include the amount from line 8 above on Schedule 2 (Form 1040 or 1040-SR), line 7a. If you're not required to file Form 1040 or 1040-SR, see the line 9 instructions.

☐ **Yes.** Go to line 10.

For Privacy Act and Paperwork Reduction Act Notice, see the instructions.   Cat. No. 12187K   **Schedule H (Form 1040 or 1040-SR) 2019**

Schedule H (Form 1040 or 1040-SR) 2019   Page **2**

| Part II | Federal Unemployment (FUTA) Tax |

		Yes	No
10	Did you pay unemployment contributions to only one state? If you paid contributions to a credit reduction state, see instructions and check **"No."** · · · · · · · · · · · · · · · **10**		
11	Did you pay all state unemployment contributions for 2019 by April 15, 2020? Fiscal year filers, see instructions **11**		
12	Were all wages that are taxable for FUTA tax also taxable for your state's unemployment tax? · · · · · **12**		

Next: If you checked the **"Yes"** box on **all** the lines above, complete Section A.

If you checked the **"No"** box on **any** of the lines above, skip Section A and complete Section B.

Section A

| 13 | Name of the state where you paid unemployment contributions ▶ _____ |

14	Contributions paid to your state unemployment fund · · · · · · · ·	**14**	
15	Total cash wages subject to FUTA tax · · · · · · · · · · · ·	**15**	
16	**FUTA tax.** Multiply line 15 by 0.6% (0.006). Enter the result here, skip Section B, and go to line 25 · ·	**16**	

Section B

17 Complete all columns below that apply (if you need more space, see instructions):

(a) Name of state	(b) Taxable wages (as defined in state act)	(c) State experience rate period		(d) State experience rate	(e) Multiply col. (b) by 0.054	(f) Multiply col. (b) by col. (d)	(g) Subtract col. (f) from col. (e). If zero or less, enter -0-.	(h) Contributions paid to state unemployment fund
		From	To					

18	Totals · · · · · · · · · · · · · · · · · · ·	**18**	
19	Add columns (g) and (h) of line 18 · · · · · · · **19**		
20	Total cash wages subject to FUTA tax (see the line 15 instructions) · · · · ·	**20**	
21	Multiply line 20 by 6.0% (0.060) · · · · · · · · · · ·	**21**	
22	Multiply line 20 by 5.4% (0.054) · · · · · **22**		
23	Enter the **smaller** of line 19 or line 22 · · · · · · · ·		
	(If you paid state unemployment contributions late or you're in a credit reduction state, see instructions and check here) · · · · · · · · · · ☐	**23**	
24	**FUTA tax.** Subtract line 23 from line 21. Enter the result here and go to line 25 · · · · · · ·	**24**	

| Part III | Total Household Employment Taxes |

| 25 | Enter the amount from line 8. If you checked the **"Yes"** box on line C of page 1, enter -0- · · · · | **25** | |
| 26 | Add line 16 (or line 24) and line 25 · · · · · · · · · · · · | **26** | |

27 Are you required to file Form 1040 or 1040-SR?

☐ **Yes. Stop.** Include the amount from line 26 above on Schedule 2 (Form 1040 or 1040-SR), line 7a. **Don't** complete Part IV below.

☐ **No.** You may have to complete Part IV. See instructions for details.

| Part IV | Address and Signature — Complete this part **only** if required. See the line 27 instructions. |

Address (number and street) or P.O. box if mail isn't delivered to street address | Apt., room, or suite no. |

City, town or post office, state, and ZIP code

Under penalties of perjury, I declare that I have examined this schedule, including accompanying statements, and to the best of my knowledge and belief, it is true, correct, and complete. No part of any payment made to a state unemployment fund claimed as a credit was, or is to be, deducted from the payments to employees. Declaration of preparer (other than taxpayer) is based on all information of which preparer has any knowledge.

▶ _____   ▶ _____
   Employer's signature   Date

Paid Preparer Use Only	Print/Type preparer's name	Preparer's signature	Date	Check ☐ if self-employed	PTIN
	Firm's name ▶			Firm's EIN ▶	
	Firm's address ▶			Phone no.	

Schedule H (Form 1040 or 1040-SR) 2019

Income not subject to the 3.8 percent tax includes the following:

- Tax-exempt interest
- Excluded gain on the sale of a principal residence
- Distributions from retirement plans and individual retirement accounts
- Wages and self-employment income (earned income); however, this income may be subject to a 0.9 percent Medicare tax

Deductions allowed in arriving at net investment income subject to tax include:

- State income taxes reasonably allocated to the investment income
- Investment interest expense

The $3,000 net deduction allowed for capital losses in excess of capital gains for regular tax purposes and net operating losses are not allowed to reduce net investment income. Additional rules govern which income and deductions are included in calculating net investment income. The net investment income tax is reported on Form 8960 shown on Page 6-29.

EXAMPLE Consider each of the following single taxpayers:

Taxpayer	A	B	C
Investment Income	$ 50,000	$ 80,000	$ 80,000
Modified AGI	190,000	220,000	340,000

The 3.8 percent Net Investment Income tax would be calculated in each case as follows:

Taxpayer	A	B	C
Modified AGI	$190,000	$220,000	$340,000
Threshold	200,000	200,000	200,000
Excess over Threshold	n/a	20,000	140,000
Investment Income	50,000	80,000	80,000
Lesser of Excess or Investment Income	n/a	20,000	80,000
Tax Rate	3.8%	3.8%	3.8%
Net Investment Income Tax	$ 0	$ 760	$ 3,040

6-8b The 0.9 Percent Additional Medicare Tax on Earned Income

In addition to the 3.8 percent Medicare tax on net investment income, the ACA imposed a 0.9 percent Medicare tax on high-income taxpayers' earned income such as salaries, wages, and self-employment income. The 0.9 percent tax applies to high-income taxpayers defined as taxpayers with earned income from wages, compensation, and self-employment income over the following thresholds (which are not adjusted for inflation each year):

a. $250,000 for joint filers
b. $125,000 if married filing separately
c. $200,000 for single filers (including head of household and qualifying widow(er)s)

The ordinary Medicare tax is 2.9 percent of earned income with no upper limitation. Employees split the cost of this tax with employers, with the employee paying 1.45 percent through withholding, and the employer paying 1.45 percent directly. Self-employed individuals pay the full 2.9 percent as calculated on Schedule SE with their Form 1040 income tax return. There is no employer match for the 0.9 percent tax. The 0.9 percent Medicare tax is reported on Form 8959 (see Page 6-31).

6-8c Employees

The 0.9 percent Medicare tax must be withheld from each employee with a salary in excess of $200,000, whether single or married. Married couples must combine their earned income and compare the total with the $250,000 threshold for married taxpayers to determine if they owe the 0.9 percent Medicare tax. Depending on the income of each spouse, the couple may owe more 0.9 percent Medicare tax when computing the 0.9 percent Medicare tax on their Form 1040 to make up for amounts not fully withheld, or they may treat the excess amount withheld as an additional tax payment. The withholding is reported on each individual's Form W-2 along with other Medicare withholding.

EXAMPLE   Will and Karen are married. Will earns $225,000 in 2019 and Karen does not work. They have no other income in 2019. Will's employer must withhold $225 [0.9% × ($225,000 − $200,000)], from his wages. Because Will and Karen do not have earned income in their joint return in excess of the $250,000 threshold for joint filers, the $225 withholding will be treated as an additional payment when they file their Form 1040 income tax return for 2019. ♦

EXAMPLE   Fran and Steve are married and each has wages of $150,000. Because they each earn less than $200,000, their employers are not required to withhold the 0.9 percent Medicare tax. However, when they file their 2019 Form 1040, they will be required to pay $450 (0.9% × $50,000) with their tax return since their $300,000 in joint earnings exceeds the $250,000 threshold for married taxpayers filing jointly. ♦

EXAMPLE   Johnny is single and changes jobs during 2019. His wages are $175,000 from each job for a total of $350,000 of wage income. Johnny's employers are not required to withhold any 0.9 percent Medicare tax from his wages since he does not reach the $200,000 threshold in either job. Johnny must pay $1,350 (0.9% × $150,000, the excess of $350,000 over the $200,000 single threshold amount) with his tax return for 2019. ♦

6-8d Self-Employed Taxpayers

Self-employed taxpayers generally report earnings on Schedule C, Schedule F, and Schedule E in the case of earned royalty income and partnership income passed through on Schedule K-1. The 0.9 percent Medicare tax for self-employed taxpayers must be paid with Form 1040. The following additional rules apply to high-income, self-employed taxpayers:

a. The 0.9 percent Medicare tax is not allowed as part of the computation of the deductible self-employment tax adjustment for AGI shown on the front page of Form 1040.
b. A loss from self-employment may offset gains from another self-employment enterprise by the same individual. In the case of married individuals, a loss incurred by one spouse may offset the income earned by the other self-employed spouse for purposes of the 0.9 percent Medicare tax. This is not true for the 2.9 percent Medicare tax on self-employment income because the 2.9 percent Medicare tax of each spouse is required to be computed separately.
c. Losses from self-employment are not allowed to offset salary or wages for purposes of the 0.9 percent Medicare tax.

Self-Study Problem 6.8A.

Form 8960

Department of the Treasury
Internal Revenue Service (99)

Net Investment Income Tax—
Individuals, Estates, and Trusts

▶ Attach to your tax return.
▶ Go to *www.irs.gov/Form8960* for instructions and the latest information.

OMB No. 1545-2227

2019

Attachment
Sequence No. **72**

Name(s) shown on your tax return

Your social security number or EIN

Part I   Investment Income

☐ Section 6013(g) election (see instructions)
☐ Section 6013(h) election (see instructions)
☐ Regulations section 1.1411-10(g) election (see instructions)

1	Taxable interest (see instructions)	**1**
2	Ordinary dividends (see instructions)	**2**
3	Annuities (see instructions)	**3**
4a	Rental real estate, royalties, partnerships, S corporations, trusts, etc. (see instructions) **4a**	
b	Adjustment for net income or loss derived in the ordinary course of a non-section 1411 trade or business (see instructions) **4b**	
c	Combine lines 4a and 4b	**4c**
5a	Net gain or loss from disposition of property (see instructions) **5a**	
b	Net gain or loss from disposition of property that is not subject to net investment income tax (see instructions) **5b**	
c	Adjustment from disposition of partnership interest or S corporation stock (see instructions) **5c**	
d	Combine lines 5a through 5c	**5d**
6	Adjustments to investment income for certain CFCs and PFICs (see instructions)	**6**
7	Other modifications to investment income (see instructions)	**7**
8	Total investment income. Combine lines 1, 2, 3, 4c, 5d, 6, and 7	**8**

Part II   Investment Expenses Allocable to Investment Income and Modifications

9a	Investment interest expenses (see instructions) **9a**	
b	State, local, and foreign income tax (see instructions) **9b**	
c	Miscellaneous investment expenses (see instructions) **9c**	
d	Add lines 9a, 9b, and 9c	**9d**
10	Additional modifications (see instructions)	**10**
11	Total deductions and modifications. Add lines 9d and 10	**11**

Part III   Tax Computation

12	Net investment income. Subtract Part II, line 11, from Part I, line 8. Individuals, complete lines 13–17. Estates and trusts, complete lines 18a–21. If zero or less, enter -0-	**12**
	Individuals:	
13	Modified adjusted gross income (see instructions) **13**	
14	Threshold based on filing status (see instructions) **14**	
15	Subtract line 14 from line 13. If zero or less, enter -0- **15**	
16	Enter the smaller of line 12 or line 15	**16**
17	Net investment income tax for individuals. Multiply line 16 by 3.8% (0.038). **Enter here and include on your tax return** (see instructions)	**17**
	Estates and Trusts:	
18a	Net investment income (line 12 above) **18a**	
b	Deductions for distributions of net investment income and deductions under section 642(c) (see instructions) **18b**	
c	Undistributed net investment income. Subtract line 18b from 18a (see instructions). If zero or less, enter -0- **18c**	
19a	Adjusted gross income (see instructions) **19a**	
b	Highest tax bracket for estates and trusts for the year (see instructions) **19b**	
c	Subtract line 19b from line 19a. If zero or less, enter -0- **19c**	
20	Enter the smaller of line 18c or line 19c	**20**
21	Net investment income tax for estates and trusts. Multiply line 20 by 3.8% (0.038). **Enter here and include on your tax return** (see instructions)	**21**

For Paperwork Reduction Act Notice, see your tax return instructions.   Cat. No. 59474M   Form **8960** (2019)

Self-Study Problem 6.8B.

Form **8959**	**Additional Medicare Tax**	OMB No. 1545-0074

Department of the Treasury
Internal Revenue Service

► If any line does not apply to you, leave it blank. See separate instructions.
► Attach to Form 1040, 1040-SR, 1040-NR, 1040-PR, or 1040-SS.
► Go to *www.irs.gov/Form8959* for instructions and the latest information.

2019
Attachment Sequence No. **71**

Name(s) shown on return

Your social security number

DRAFT AS OF August 14, 2019 DO NOT FILE

Part I   Additional Medicare Tax on Medicare Wages

1	Medicare wages and tips from Form W-2, box 5. If you have more than one Form W-2, enter the total of the amounts from box 5	**1**
2	Unreported tips from Form 4137, line 6	**2**
3	Wages from Form 8919, line 6	**3**
4	Add lines 1 through 3	**4**
5	Enter the following amount for your filing status:	
	Married filing jointly $250,000	
	Married filing separately $125,000	
	Single, Head of household, or Qualifying widow(er) $200,000	**5**
6	Subtract line 5 from line 4. If zero or less, enter -0-	**6**
7	Additional Medicare Tax on Medicare wages. Multiply line 6 by 0.9% (0.009). Enter here and go to Part II	**7**

Part II   Additional Medicare Tax on Self-Employment Income

8	Self-employment income from Schedule SE (Form 1040 or 1040-SR), Section A, line 4, or Section B, line 6. If you had a loss, enter -0- (Form 1040-PR or 1040-SS filers, see instructions.)	**8**
9	Enter the following amount for your filing status:	
	Married filing jointly. $250,000	
	Married filing separately $125,000	
	Single, Head of household, or Qualifying widow(er) $200,000	**9**
10	Enter the amount from line 4	**10**
11	Subtract line 10 from line 9. If zero or less, enter -0-	**11**
12	Subtract line 11 from line 8. If zero or less, enter -0-	**12**
13	Additional Medicare Tax on self-employment income. Multiply line 12 by 0.9% (0.009). Enter here and go to Part III	**13**

Part III   Additional Medicare Tax on Railroad Retirement Tax Act (RRTA) Compensation

14	Railroad retirement (RRTA) compensation and tips from Form(s) W-2, box 14 (see instructions)	**14**
15	Enter the following amount for your filing status:	
	Married filing jointly $250,000	
	Married filing separately $125,000	
	Single, Head of household, or Qualifying widow(er) $200,000	**15**
16	Subtract line 15 from line 14. If zero or less, enter -0-	**16**
17	Additional Medicare Tax on railroad retirement (RRTA) compensation. Multiply line 16 by 0.9% (0.009). Enter here and go to Part IV	**17**

Part IV   Total Additional Medicare Tax

18	Add lines 7, 13, and 17. Also include this amount on Schedule 2 (Form 1040 or 1040-SR), line 8 (check box a) (Form 1040-NR, 1040-PR, or 1040-SS filers, see instructions), and go to Part V	**18**

Part V   Withholding Reconciliation

19	Medicare tax withheld from Form W-2, box 6. If you have more than one Form W-2, enter the total of the amounts from box 6	**19**
20	Enter the amount from line 1	**20**
21	Multiply line 20 by 1.45% (0.0145). This is your regular Medicare tax withholding on Medicare wages	**21**
22	Subtract line 21 from line 19. If zero or less, enter -0-. This is your Additional Medicare Tax withholding on Medicare wages	**22**
23	Additional Medicare Tax withholding on railroad retirement (RRTA) compensation from Form W-2, box 14 (see instructions)	**23**
24	**Total Additional Medicare Tax withholding.** Add lines 22 and 23. Also include this amount with federal income tax withholding on Form 1040 or 1040-SR, line 17 (Form 1040-NR, 1040-PR, or 1040-SS filers, see instructions)	**24**

For Paperwork Reduction Act Notice, see your tax return instructions.   Cat. No. 59475X   Form **8959** (2019)

EXAMPLE In 2019, Barry is single and earns $500,000 from his construction business, and has a loss of $100,000 from his commercial nursery business. Both businesses are reported on Schedule C in his income tax return. His net self-employment earnings of $400,000 exceed the single individual threshold by $200,000. He must pay $1,800 with his 2019 Form 1040 (0.9% × $200,000) to cover his 0.9 percent Medicare tax. None of the $1,800 is allowed as part of the computation of the self-employment tax adjustment included with his deductions for AGI. ♦

Self-Study Problem 6.8   *See Appendix E for Solutions to Self-Study Problems*

———— A. Ronald Trunk is single and independently wealthy. In 2019, Ronald's investment income is $110,000 (all interest) and his adjusted gross income is $380,000. He has no investment expenses associated with this income, no foreign earnings exclusion, and lives where there is no state income tax. Complete Form 8960 on Page 6-29 to calculate Ronald's 2019 net investment income tax.

———— B. Meng and Eang Ung are married. Meng is self-employed and generates self-employment income of $130,000. Eang is a physician at a local hospital and earns Social Security (Box 5) wages of $265,000. Her Medicare withholding (Box 6) is $4,427.50. Eang and Meng have no other earned or unearned income. Complete Form 8959 on Page 6-31 to determine how much 0.9 percent additional Medicare tax on earned income Meng and Eang must pay with their joint tax return in 2019 and what 0.9 percent additional Medicare tax withholding will they report?

The IRS recommends considering the following when getting married:

- Social Security numbers on the tax return need to match the Social Security Administration's (SSA) records. Be sure and report any name changes to the SSA.
- Taxpayers may want to consider changing their withholding, especially if both spouses work.
- Marriage is likely to trigger a "change in circumstance" if a taxpayer is receiving advance payments on the premium tax credit. The appropriate health insurance marketplace should be notified.
- Change of address with the U.S. Postal Service (online) and with the IRS (Form 8822).
- Change in filing status to married filing jointly or separately should be considered.

TAX BREAK

KEY TERMS

accounting periods, 6-2
fiscal year, 6-2
short-period taxable income, 6-2
annualized period, 6-2
accounting methods, 6-3
cash method, 6-3
accrual method, 6-4
economic performance, 6-4
hybrid method, 6-4

Section 267, 6-5
related parties, 6-6
constructive ownership, 6-6
"kiddie tax," 6-8
net unearned income (NUI), 6-9
earned taxable income (ETI), 6-9
alternative minimum tax (AMT), 6-14
AMT adjustments, 6-14
AMT preferences, 6-14

AMT exemption, 6-15
alternative minimum tax rates, 6-15
self-employment tax, 6-19
nanny tax, 6-23
household workers, 6-23
net investment income tax, 6-24
0.9 percent additional Medicare
    tax, 6-27

KEY POINTS

Learning Objectives	Key Points
LO 6.1: Determine the different accounting periods allowed for tax purposes.	• Almost all individuals file tax returns using a calendar-year accounting period. • Partnerships and corporations had a great deal of freedom in selecting a tax year in the past. However, Congress set limits on this freedom when it resulted in an inappropriate deferral of taxable income. • A personal service corporation is a corporation whose shareholder-employees provide personal services (e.g., medical, legal, accounting, actuarial, or consulting services) for the corporation's patients or clients. Personal service corporations generally must adopt a calendar year-end. • If taxpayers have a short year other than their first or last year of operations, they are required to annualize their taxable income to calculate the tax for the short period.
LO 6.2: Determine the different accounting methods allowed for tax purposes.	• The tax law requires taxpayers to report taxable income using the method of accounting regularly used by the taxpayer in keeping his or her books, provided the method clearly reflects the taxpayer's income. • The cash receipts and disbursements (cash) method, the accrual method, and the hybrid method are accounting methods specifically recognized in the tax law.
LO 6.3: Determine whether parties are considered related for tax purposes, and classify the tax treatment of certain related-party transactions.	• The two types of disallowed related-party transactions are (1) sales of property at a loss and (2) unpaid expenses and interest. • Any loss or deduction arising from transactions between related parties are disallowed by Section 267. • The common related parties under Section 267 include brothers and sisters (whole or half), a spouse, ancestors (parents, grandparents, etc.), lineal descendants (children, grandchildren, etc.), and a corporation or an individual shareholder who directly or constructively owns more than 50 percent of the corporation. • Related-party rules also consider constructive ownership in determining whether parties are related to each other (e.g., taxpayers are deemed to own stock owned by certain relatives and related entities).

LO 6.4:

Apply the rules for computing tax on the unearned income of minor children and certain students (the "kiddie tax").

- The tax law contains provisions that limit the benefit of shifting income to certain dependent children.
- The net unearned income of dependent children may be taxed using trust and estate rates.
- The trust tax rates apply to dependent children who are ages 18 or younger or are students ages 19 through 23 at the end of the year, who have at least one living parent, and who have "net unearned income" of more than $2,200 for 2019.
- If certain conditions are met, parents may elect to include a child's gross income on the parents' tax return. The election eliminates the child's return filing requirements including the special calculation on Form 8615 for the "kiddie tax."

LO 6.5:

Calculate a basic alternative minimum tax.

- The AMT was designed in the 1960s to ensure that wealthy taxpayers could not take advantage of special tax write-offs (tax preferences and other adjustments) to avoid paying tax. In general, taxpayers must pay the AMT if their AMT liability is greater than their regular tax liability.
- Adjustments are timing differences that arise because of differences in the regular and AMT tax calculations (e.g., depreciation timing differences), while preferences are special provisions for the regular tax that are not allowed for the AMT (e.g., state income taxes).
- For 2019, the AMT exemption allowance is $111,700 for married taxpayers filing joint returns, $71,700 for single and head of household taxpayers, and $55,850 for married taxpayers filing separate returns. The AMT exemption allowance amount is phased out for high-income taxpayers.
- For 2019, the alternative minimum tax rates for calculating the tentative minimum tax are 26 percent of the first $194,800 ($97,400 for married taxpayers filing separately), plus 28 percent on amounts above $194,800 applied to the taxpayer's alternative minimum tax base.
- The increases in the AMT exemptions and thresholds coupled with the limitations or suspension of certain itemized deduction are expected to reduce the number of taxpayers subject to the AMT.

LO 6.6:

Calculate and report the self-employment tax (both Social Security and Medicare portions) for self-employed taxpayers.

- Self-employed individuals pay self-employment (SE) taxes instead of FICA taxes and, since these individuals have no employers, the entire tax is paid by the self-employed individuals.
- For 2019, the Social Security (OASDI) tax rate is 12.4 percent and the Medicare tax rate is 2.9 percent with a maximum base amount of earnings subject to the Social Security portion of $132,900. All earnings are subject to the Medicare portion.
- If an individual, subject to self-employment taxes, also receives wages subject to FICA taxes during a tax year, the individual's maximum base amount for SE taxes is reduced by the amount of the wages when calculating the SE taxes.
- Net earnings from self-employment include gross income from a trade or business, less trade or business deductions, the distributive share of partnership income from a trade or business, and net income earned as an independent contractor.
- Self-employed taxpayers are allowed a deduction for AGI of one-half of the self-employment tax.

LO 6.7:

Apply the special tax and reporting requirements for household employees (the "nanny tax").

- The "nanny tax" provisions provide a simplified reporting process for employers of household workers.
- Household employers are not required to pay FICA taxes on cash payments of less than $2,100 paid to any household employee in a calendar year.
- If the cash payment to any household employee is $2,100 or more in a calendar year, all the cash payments (including the first $2,100) are subject to Social Security and Medicare taxes.
- If more than $1,000 in cash wages are paid to household employees during any calendar quarter, employers are required to pay FUTA taxes.
- A taxpayer is a household employer if he or she hires workers to perform household services, in or around the taxpayer's home, that are subject to the "will and control" of the taxpayer (e.g., babysitters, caretakers, cooks, drivers, gardeners, housekeepers, and maids).
- Certain workers are not subject to Social Security and Medicare taxes on wages paid for work in the home. These workers include the taxpayer's spouse, the taxpayer's father or mother, the taxpayer's children under 21 years of age, and anyone who is under age 18 during the year, unless providing household services is his or her principal occupation.
- Under the nanny tax provisions, a household employer must report Social Security and Medicare taxes, federal income tax withholding, and FUTA tax once a year by filing Schedule H with his or her individual Form 1040.
- At the close of the tax year, household employers must also file Form W-2 (copy A) and Form W-3 for each household employee whose income is reflected on Schedule H or had federal income tax withheld from wages.

LO 6.8

Compute the special taxes for high-income taxpayers.

- The Affordable Care Act (ACA) added a 3.8 percent Medicare tax on net investment income and a 0.9 percent additional Medicare tax on earned income for certain high-income taxpayers.
- The 3.8 percent Net Investment Income tax applies to the net investment income of individuals with modified AGI over $250,000 for joint filers ($125,000 if married filing separate), and $200,000 for single filers.
- The 0.9 percent Medicare tax is imposed on earned income from salaries, wages, and self-employment income of joint filers with earned income over $250,000 ($125,000 if married filing separate) and single taxpayers with earned income over $200,000.
- Employers are required to withhold the 0.9 percent Medicare tax when a taxpayer's salary exceeds $200,000.
- Self-employed taxpayers must pay the tax with their individual income tax returns.

QUESTIONS and PROBLEMS

GROUP 1:
MULTIPLE CHOICE QUESTIONS

LO 6.1

1. E Corporation is a subchapter S corporation owned by three individuals with calendar year-ends. The corporation sells a sports drink as its principal product and has similar sales each month. What options does E Corporation have in choosing a tax year?
   a. E Corporation may choose any month end as its tax year.
   b. Because the owners of E Corporation have tax years ending in December, E Corporation must also choose a December year-end.
   c. E Corporation may choose an October, November, or December tax year-end.
   d. E Corporation may choose a tax year ending in September, October, or November, but only if the corporation also makes an annual cash deposit and adjusts the amount every year depending on the income deferred.

LO 6.1

2. Income and loss from which of the following entities is passed through and taxed on the individual's personal tax returns?
   a. S corporation
   b. Partnership
   c. Sole proprietor
   d. All of the above

LO 6.1

3. Which of the following entities is likely to have the greatest flexibility in choosing a year-end other than a calendar year-end?
   a. Sole proprietor
   b. General partnership
   c. Corporation
   d. S corporation

LO 6.2

4. Which of the following is an acceptable method of accounting under the tax law?
   a. The accrual method
   b. The hybrid method
   c. The cash method
   d. All of the above are acceptable
   e. None of the above

LO 6.2

5. Which of the following entities is required to report on the accrual basis?
   a. An accounting firm operating as a Personal Service Corporation.
   b. A manufacturing business with $30 million of gross receipts operating as a regular C corporation.
   c. A corporation engaged in tropical fruit farming in Southern California.
   d. A partnership with gross receipts of $13 million and all of the partners are individuals with a December year-end.

LO 6.3

6. Pekoe sold stock to his sister Rose for $12,000, its fair market value. Pekoe bought the stock 5 years ago for $16,000. Also, Pekoe sold Earl (an unrelated party) stock for $6,500 that he bought 3 years ago for $9,500. What is Pekoe's recognized gain or loss?
   a. $7,500 loss
   b. $4,000 gain
   c. $3,000 loss
   d. $2,000 loss
   e. $1,000 gain

LO 6.3

7. B Corporation, a calendar year-end, accrual basis taxpayer, is owned 75 percent by Bonnie, a cash basis taxpayer. On December 31, 2019, the corporation accrues interest of $4,000 on a loan from Bonnie and also accrues a $15,000 bonus to Bonnie. The bonus is paid to Bonnie on February 1, 2020; the interest is not paid until 2021. How much can B Corporation deduct on its 2019 tax return for these two expenses?
   a. $0
   b. $4,000
   c. $15,000
   d. $19,000
   e. $12,000

LO 6.3

8. Using the same facts as in Question 7, how much can B Corporation deduct on its 2020 tax return?
   a. $0
   b. $4,000
   c. $15,000
   d. $19,000
   e. $12,000

LO 6.3

9. BJT Corporation is owned 40 percent by Bill, 30 percent by Jack, and 30 percent by the Trumpet Partnership. Bill and Jack are father and son. Jack has a 10 percent interest in Trumpet Partnership. What is Jack's total direct and constructive ownership of BJT Corporation under Section 267?
   a. 30 percent
   b. 70 percent
   c. 100 percent
   d. 73 percent
   e. 33 percent

LO 6.4

10. Which of the following is *not* required to subject a taxpayer to the tax on unearned income of minors (kiddie tax) in 2019?
    a. Must be claimed as a dependent
    b. 18 years of age or younger (full time student up to age 23)
    c. Both parents must be living
    d. Net unearned income must exceed $2,200
    e. All of the above are required

LO 6.4

11. Generally, the tax rate that applies to the unearned income of a minor under the kiddie tax in 2019 is:
    a. The same as the parents' tax rate
    b. The same as the single taxpayer rate
    c. The same as the head of household rate
    d. The same as the trust and estate rate
    e. The unearned income of a minor is not taxed

LO 6.5

12. The alternative minimum tax exemption:
    a. Is a direct reduction of the tentative minimum tax
    b. Is a reduction of alternative minimum taxable income for certain taxpayers
    c. Permits certain taxpayers to elect to treat AMT as a reduction of tax
    d. Is subject to carryback and carryforward provisions
    e. Increases the effects of tax preference items

LO 6.6

13. For 2019, Roberta is a self-employed truck driver with earnings of $47,000 from her business. During the year, Roberta received $2,500 in interest income and dividends of $500. She also sold investment property and recognized a $1,500 gain. What is the amount of Roberta's self-employment tax (Social Security and Medicare taxes) liability for 2019?
    a. $7,277
    b. $6,641
    c. $6,358
    d. $6,885
    e. $7,191

LO 6.6

14. Which of the following is *not* subject to self-employment tax?
    a. Gain on the sale of real estate held for investment
    b. Net earnings of a self-employed lawyer
    c. Distributive share of earnings of a partnership
    d. Net earnings of the owner of a shoe store
    e. Net earnings of the owner of a dry cleaner

LO 6.7

15. Bob employs a maid to clean his house. He pays her $1,040 during the current year. What is the proper tax treatment of the Social Security and Medicare tax for the maid?
    a. Bob is not required to pay or withhold Social Security and Medicare taxes on the $1,040.
    b. The $1,040 is subject to the Medicare tax, but not the Social Security tax.
    c. $500 is subject to the Social Security and Medicare tax.
    d. Bob is required to withhold Social Security and Medicare taxes on the entire $1,040.

LO 6.7

16. Which of the following employees would *not* be exempt from Social Security and Medicare taxes on wages paid for household work?
    a. The taxpayer's 16-year-old daughter
    b. The taxpayer's wife
    c. The taxpayer's 20-year-old sister
    d. The 14-year-old babysitter from down the street

LO 6.7

17. Individual taxpayers may pay withholding taxes due with their individual income tax returns using Schedule H for each of the following workers *except*:
    a. A nanny hired to watch their children
    b. A maid hired to clean house and cook every day
    c. An attorney with her own business, hired to handle a legal dispute with the taxpayers' neighbor
    d. An unlicensed caregiver for a disabled spouse

LO 6.8

18. The 3.8 percent Medicare tax on net investment income applies to:
    a. Tax-exempt interest income
    b. Interest and dividends
    c. IRA distributions
    d. Wages

LO 6.8

19. Skylar is single and earns $410,000 in salary during 2019. What is the amount of 0.9 percent Medicare tax for high-income taxpayers that his employer must withhold from his wages?
    a. $1,890
    b. $1,800
    c. $1,440
    d. $900

LO 6.8

20. Christine and Doug are married. In 2019, Christine earns a salary of $250,000 and Doug earns a salary of $50,000. They have no other income and work for the same employers for all of 2019. How much 0.9 percent Medicare tax for high-income taxpayers will Christine and Doug have to pay with their 2019 income tax return?
    a. $450
    b. $900
    c. $2,700
    d. None

GROUP 2:
PROBLEMS

LO 6.1

1. Explain why the tax law prefers flowthrough entities like partnerships and S corporation to have a year-end that matches the year-end of its owners.

_____

_____

_____

LO 6.2

2. Yolanda is a cash basis taxpayer with the following transactions during the year:

Cash received from sales of products	$70,000
Cash paid for expenses (except rent and interest)	40,000
Rent prepaid on a leased building for 18 months beginning December 1	48,600
Prepaid interest on a bank loan, paid on December 31 for the next 3 months	5,000

Calculate Yolanda's income from her business for this calendar year.

Sales income	$_____
Expenses:	
Other than rent and interest	$_____
Rent	$_____
Interest	$_____
Net income	$_____

LO 6.2

3. Geraldine is an accrual basis taxpayer who has the following transactions during the current calendar tax year:

Accrued business income (except rent)	$220,000
Accrued business expenses (except rent)	170,000
Rental income on a building lease for the next	
6 months, received on December 1	21,000
Prepaid rent expense for 6 months, paid on	
December 1	9,000

Calculate Geraldine's net income from her business for the current year.

Income:	
Other than rental	$_____
Rental	$_____
Expenses:	
Other than rental	$_____
Rental	$_____
Net income	$_____

LO 6.2

4. Amy is a calendar-year taxpayer reporting on the cash basis. Please indicate how she should treat the following items for 2019:

a. She makes a deductible contribution to an IRA on April 15, 2020.

_____

b. She has made an election to accrue the increase in value of savings bonds even though the increase is not received in cash.

_____

c. She prepays half a year of interest in advance on her mortgage on the last day of 2019. _____

d. She pays all of her outstanding invoices for standard business expenses in the last week of December. _____

e. She sends out a big bill to a customer on January 1, 2020, even though she did all of the work in December of 2019. _____

LO 6.3

5. JBC Corporation is owned 20 percent by John, 30 percent by Brian, 30 percent by Charlie, and 20 percent by Z Corporation. Z Corporation is owned 80 percent by John and 20 percent by an unrelated party. Brian and Charlie are brothers. Answer each of the following questions about JBC under the constructive ownership rules of Section 267:

a. What is John's percentage ownership?   _____%
b. What is Brian's percentage ownership?   _____%
c. What is Charlie's percentage ownership?   _____%
d. If Brian sells property to JBC for a $6,000 loss, what amount of that loss can be recognized for tax purposes (before any annual limitations)?

                                              $_____

LO 6.3

6. You have a problem and need a full-text copy of the Related Party Code Section 267. Go to the Office of the Law Revision Counsel of the United States House of Representatives website (**uscode.house.gov**) and enter Title 26 (the Internal Revenue Code) and Section 267 in the Jump To boxes. Print out a copy of Section 267(a).

LO 6.4

7. Explain the purpose of the provision in the tax law that taxes unearned income of certain minor children at their parents' tax rates.

_____

_____

_____

LO 6.4

8. Brian and Kim have a 12-year-old child, Stan. For 2019, Brian and Kim have taxable income of $52,000, and Stan has interest income of $4,500. No election is made to include Stan's income on Brian and Kim's return.
   a. For purposes of the tax on a child's unearned income, calculate Stan's taxable income. $_____
   b. Calculate Stan's net unearned income. $_____
   c. Calculate Stan's earned taxable income. $_____
   d. Calculate Stan's tax for 2019. $_____

LO 6.4

9. Refer to the previous problem 8. If Stan's parents elected to report Stan's income on his parents' return, what would the tax on Stan's income be?

LO 6.4

10. Explain the two different ways that the tax on unearned income of minor children, or "kiddie tax," can be reported.

_____

_____

_____

LO 6.4

11. Does the tax on unearned income of minor children, or "kiddie tax," apply to wages earned by minors in summer and other jobs?

_____

_____

_____

LO 6.5

12. Otto and Monica are married taxpayers who file a joint tax return. For the current tax year, they have AGI of $80,300. They have excess depreciation on real estate of $67,500, which must be added back to AGI to arrive at AMTI. The amount of their mortgage interest expense for the year was $25,000, and they made charitable contributions of $7,500. If Otto and Monica's taxable income for the current year is $47,800 determine the amount of their AMTI.

_____

LO 6.5

13. List two common deductions which are allowed for regular tax purposes but are not deductible for AMT purposes.

_____

_____

LO 6.5

14. What are the two tax rates which are used to calculate AMT, ignoring the special treatment of dividends and capital gains?

_____

LO 6.5

15. Show the simplified formula for calculating AMT. Do not show tax rates or an exemption amount.

_____

_____

_____

_____

_____

_____

_____

LO 6.6

16. Stewart Beauf is a self-employed surfboard maker in 2019. His Schedule C net income is $126,503 for the year. He also has a part-time job and earns $16,100 in wages subject to FICA taxes. Calculate Stewart's self-employment tax for 2019 using Schedule SE on Pages 6-43 and 6-44.

LO 6.7

17. Sally hires a maid to work in her home for $280 per month. The maid is 25 years old and not related to Sally. During 2019, the maid worked 9 months for Sally.
   a. What is the amount of Social Security tax Sally must pay as the maid's employer?

   $ _____

   b. What is the amount of Medicare tax Sally must pay as the maid's employer?

   $ _____

   c. What is the amount of Social Security and Medicare tax which must be withheld from the maid's wages?

   $ _____

LO 6.7

18. Ann hires a nanny to watch her two children while she works at a local hospital. She pays the 19-year-old nanny $170 per week for 42 weeks during the current year.
   a. What is the employer's portion of Social Security and Medicare tax for the nanny that Ann should pay when she files her Form 1040 for 2019?

   $ _____

   b. What is the nanny's portion of the Social Security and Medicare tax?

   $ _____

LO 6.8

19. Rachel is single and has wages of $150,000 and dividend income of $90,000. She has no investment expenses. Calculate the amount of the 3.8 percent net investment income tax she must pay.

_____

LO 6.8

20. Married taxpayers Otto and Ruth are both self-employed. Otto earns $352,000 of self-employment income and Ruth has a self-employment loss of $13,500. How much 0.9 percent Medicare tax for high-income taxpayers will Otto and Ruth have to pay with their 2018 income tax return?

   $ _____

GROUP 3:
WRITING ASSIGNMENT

ETHICS

Charlie's Green Lawn Care is a cash basis taxpayer. Charlie Adame, the sole proprietor, is considering delaying some of his December 2019 customer billings for lawn care into the next year. In addition, he is thinking about paying some of the bills in late December 2019, which he would ordinarily pay in January 2020. This way, Charlie claims, he will have "less income and more expenses, thereby paying less tax!" Is Charlie's way of thinking acceptable?

SCHEDULE SE
(Form 1040 or 1040-SR)

Department of the Treasury
Internal Revenue Service (99)

Self-Employment Tax

▶ Go to *www.irs.gov/ScheduleSE* for instructions and the latest information.
▶ **Attach to Form 1040, 1040-SR, or 1040-NR.**

OMB No. 1545-0074

2019

Attachment
Sequence No. **17**

Name of person with self-employment income (as shown on Form 1040, 1040-SR, or 1040-NR)

Social security number of person
with **self-employment** income ▶

Before you begin: To determine if you must file Schedule SE, see the instructions.

May I Use Short Schedule SE or Must I Use Long Schedule SE?

Note: Use this flowchart **only if** you must file Schedule SE. If unsure, see *Who Must File Schedule SE* in the instructions.

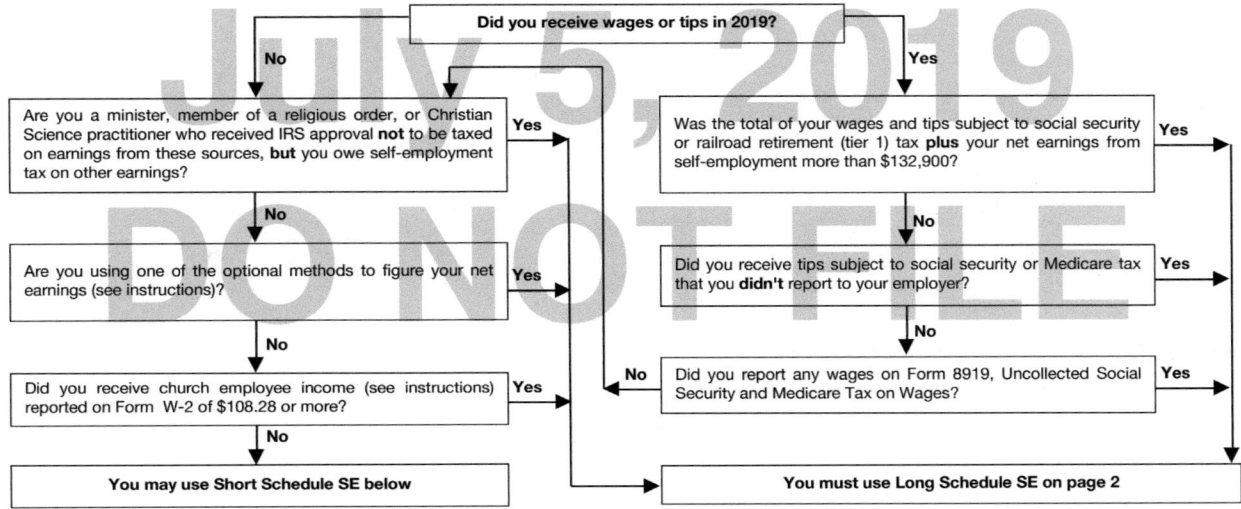

Section A—Short Schedule SE. Caution: Read above to see if you can use Short Schedule SE.

1a	Net farm profit or (loss) from Schedule F, line 34, and farm partnerships, Schedule K-1 (Form 1065), box 14, code A	**1a**
b	If you received social security retirement or disability benefits, enter the amount of Conservation Reserve Program payments included on Schedule F, line 4b, or listed on Schedule K-1 (Form 1065), box 20, code AH	**1b** ( )
2	Net profit or (loss) from Schedule C, line 31; and Schedule K-1 (Form 1065), box 14, code A (other than farming). Ministers and members of religious orders, see instructions for types of income to report on this line. See instructions for other income to report	**2**
3	Combine lines 1a, 1b, and 2	**3**
4	Multiply line 3 by 92.35% (0.9235). If less than $400, you don't owe self-employment tax; **don't** file this schedule unless you have an amount on line 1b . . . . ▶	**4**
	Note: If line 4 is less than $400 due to Conservation Reserve Program payments on line 1b, see instructions.	
5	**Self-employment tax.** If the amount on line 4 is:	
	• $132,900 or less, multiply line 4 by 15.3% (0.153). Enter the result here and on **Schedule 2 (Form 1040 or 1040-SR), line 4, or Form 1040-NR, line 55.**	
	• More than $132,900, multiply line 4 by 2.9% (0.029). Then, add $16,479.60 to the result.	
	Enter the total here and on **Schedule 2 (Form 1040 or 1040-SR), line 4, or Form 1040-NR, line 55** .	**5**
6	**Deduction for one-half of self-employment tax.**	
	Multiply line 5 by 50% (0.50). Enter the result here and on **Schedule 1 (Form 1040 or 1040-SR), line 14, or Form 1040-NR, line 27**	**6**

For Paperwork Reduction Act Notice, see your tax return instructions.   Cat. No. 11358Z   **Schedule SE (Form 1040 or 1040-SR) 2019**

Schedule SE (Form 1040 or 1040-SR) 2019   Attachment Sequence No. **17**   Page **2**

Name of person with self-employment income (as shown on Form 1040, 1040-SR, or 1040-NR)	Social security number of person with **self-employment** income ▶

Section B—Long Schedule SE

Part I   Self-Employment Tax

Note: If your only income subject to self-employment tax is **church employee income,** see instructions. Also see instructions for the definition of church employee income.

A	If you are a minister, member of a religious order, or Christian Science practitioner **and** you filed Form 4361, but you had $400 or more of **other** net earnings from self-employment, check here and continue with Part I . . . . ▶ ☐		
1a	Net farm profit or (loss) from Schedule F, line 34, and farm partnerships, Schedule K-1 (Form 1065), box 14, code A. **Note:** Skip lines 1a and 1b if you use the farm optional method (see instructions)	**1a**	
b	If you received social security retirement or disability benefits, enter the amount of Conservation Reserve Program payments included on Schedule F, line 4b, or listed on Schedule K-1 (Form 1065), box 20, code AH	**1b**	( )
2	Net profit or (loss) from Schedule C, line 31; and Schedule K-1 (Form 1065), box 14, code A (other than farming). Ministers and members of religious orders, see instructions for types of income to report on this line. See instructions for other income to report. **Note:** Skip this line if you use the nonfarm optional method (see instructions)	**2**	
3	Combine lines 1a, 1b, and 2	**3**	
4a	If line 3 is more than zero, multiply line 3 by 92.35% (0.9235). Otherwise, enter amount from line 3	**4a**	
	Note: If line 4a is less than $400 due to Conservation Reserve Program payments on line 1b, see instructions.		
b	If you elect one or both of the optional methods, enter the total of lines 15 and 17 here	**4b**	
c	Combine lines 4a and 4b. If less than $400, **stop;** you don't owe self-employment tax. **Exception:** If less than $400 and you had **church employee income,** enter -0- and continue . . . . . . ▶	**4c**	
5a	Enter your **church employee income** from Form W-2. See instructions for definition of church employee income **5a**	**5a**	
b	Multiply line 5a by 92.35% (0.9235). If less than $100, enter -0-	**5b**	
6	Add lines 4c and 5b	**6**	
7	Maximum amount of combined wages and self-employment earnings subject to social security tax or the 6.2% portion of the 7.65% railroad retirement (tier 1) tax for 2019	**7**	132,900
8a	Total social security wages and tips (total of boxes 3 and 7 on Form(s) W-2) and railroad retirement (tier 1) compensation. If $132,900 or more, skip lines 8b through 10, and go to line 11 . . . . **8a**		
b	Unreported tips subject to social security tax (from Form 4137, line 10) . . **8b**		
c	Wages subject to social security tax (from Form 8919, line 10) **8c**		
d	Add lines 8a, 8b, and 8c	**8d**	
9	Subtract line 8d from line 7. If zero or less, enter -0- here and on line 10 and go to line 11 . . . ▶	**9**	
10	Multiply the **smaller** of line 6 or line 9 by 12.4% (0.124)	**10**	
11	Multiply line 6 by 2.9% (0.029)	**11**	
12	**Self-employment tax.** Add lines 10 and 11. Enter here and on **Schedule 2 (Form 1040 or 1040-SR), line 4,** or **Form 1040-NR, line 55**	**12**	
13	**Deduction for one-half of self-employment tax.** Multiply line 12 by 50% (0.50). Enter the result here and on **Schedule 1 (Form 1040 or 1040-SR), line 14,** or **Form 1040-NR, line 27** **13**		

Part II   Optional Methods To Figure Net Earnings (see instructions)

Farm Optional Method. You may use this method **only** if **(a)** your gross farm income[1] wasn't more than $8,160, **or (b)** your net farm profits[2] were less than $5,891.

14	Maximum income for optional methods	**14**	5,440
15	Enter the **smaller** of: two-thirds (2/3) of gross farm income[1] (not less than zero) **or** $5,440. Also include this amount on line 4b above	**15**	

Nonfarm Optional Method. You may use this method **only** if **(a)** your net nonfarm profits[3] were less than $5,891 and also less than 72.189% of your gross nonfarm income,[4] **and (b)** you had net earnings from self-employment of at least $400 in 2 of the prior 3 years. **Caution:** You may use this method no more than five times.

16	Subtract line 15 from line 14	**16**	
17	Enter the **smaller** of: two-thirds (2/3) of gross nonfarm income[4] (not less than zero) **or** the amount on line 16. Also include this amount on line 4b above	**17**	

[1] From Sch. F, line 9, and Sch. K-1 (Form 1065), box 14, code B.
[2] From Sch. F, line 34, and Sch. K-1 (Form 1065), box 14, code A—minus the amount you would have entered on line 1b had you not used the optional method.

[3] From Sch. C, line 31; and Sch. K-1 (Form 1065), box 14, code A.
[4] From Sch. C, line 7; and Sch. K-1 (Form 1065), box 14, code C.

GROUP 4:
COMPREHENSIVE PROBLEMS

1. Richard and Christine McCarthy have a 19-year-old son (born 10/2/2000; Social Security number 555-55-1212), Jack, who is a full-time student at the University of Key West. Years ago, the McCarthys shifted a significant amount of investments into Jack's name. In 2019, Jack received Forms 1099-INT and 1099-DIV that reported the following:

Tandy Corporation Bonds interest	$11,300
Tandy Corporation ordinary dividends	3,400

The dividends are not qualified dividends. In addition, Jack works part-time as a waiter in an upscale seafood restaurant in Miami, FL. His 2019 Form W-2 reported:

Wages	$12,800
Federal withholding	1,080

In spite of his fairly large income, the McCarthys provide over 50 percent of his support and claim Jack as a dependent in 2019. Jack's mailing address is 100 Duval Street, Apt. #B12, Key West, FL 33040. Richard's Social Security number is 100-10-9090. Use Form 1040, Schedule B, Form 8615, and the Tax Computation Worksheet from the Form 8615 instructions to compute Jack's 2019 income tax.

2A. Richard McCarthy (born 2/14/1965; Social Security number 100-10-9090) and Christine McCarthy (born 6/1/1967; Social Security number 101-21-3434) have a 19-year-old son (born 10/2/2000 Social Security number 555-55-1212), Jack who is a full-time student at the University of Key West. The McCarthys also have a 12-year-old daughter (Social Security number 444-23-1212), Justine, that lives with them. The McCarthys can claim a $2,000 child tax credit for Justine and a $500 other dependent credit for Jack. Richard is the CEO at a paper company. His 2019 Form W-2:

a Employee's social security number 100-10-9090	OMB No. 1545-0008	Safe, accurate, FAST! Use	IRS e-file	Visit the IRS website at www.irs.gov/efile
b Employer identification number (EIN) 32-5656567		**1** Wages, tips, other compensation 230,500.00	**2** Federal income tax withheld 56,000.00	
c Employer's name, address, and ZIP code Mufflin-Dunder Paper 302 Lackawanna Ave. Scranton, PA 18503		**3** Social security wages 132,900.00	**4** Social security tax withheld 8,239.80	
		5 Medicare wages and tips 230,500.00	**6** Medicare tax withheld 3,616.75	
		7 Social security tips	**8** Allocated tips	
d Control number		**9**	**10** Dependent care benefits	
e Employee's first name and initial Last name Suff. Richard McCarthy 32 Sleepy Hollow Rd. Clarks Summit, PA 18411		**11** Nonqualified plans	**12a** See instructions for box 12	
		13 Statutory employee ☐ Retirement plan ☐ Third-party sick pay ☐	**12b**	
		14 Other	**12c**	
			12d	
f Employee's address and ZIP code				

15 State	Employer's state ID number	**16** State wages, tips, etc.	**17** State income tax	**18** Local wages, tips, etc.	**19** Local income tax	**20** Locality name
PA	1234824	230,500.00	13,800.00			

Form **W-2** Wage and Tax Statement   **2019**   Department of the Treasury—Internal Revenue Service

Copy B—To Be Filed With Employee's FEDERAL Tax Return.
This information is being furnished to the Internal Revenue Service.

Christine is an optometrist and operates her own practice ("The Eyes of March") in town as a sole proprietor. The shop address is 1030 Morgan Highway, Clarks Summit, PA 18411 and the business code is 621320. Christine keeps her books on the accrual basis and her bookkeeper provided the following information:

Gross sales		$270,541
Returns		8,994
Inventory:		
Beginning inventory	$ 24,000	
Purchases	120,000	
Ending inventory	30,000	
Rent		24,000
Insurance		11,019
Professional fees		2,998
Payroll		37,113
Payroll taxes		2,877
Utilities		3,961
Office expenses		1,995
Depreciation		5,000

The McCarthys have a nanny/housekeeper they paid $12,600 during 2019. They did not withhold income or FICA taxes. The McCarthys paid Pennsylvania state unemployment tax of $378 in 2019.

Christine received a 2019 Form 1099-INT from the National Bank of Scranton that listed interest income of $23,467. Note that McCarthys reasonably allocate $761 to state income tax expense for purposes of the Net Investment Income tax.

The McCarthys received a Form 1099-G from Pennsylvania that reported a $451 state income tax refund from 2018. The McCarthys itemized deductions in 2018 and had $14,223 of state income tax expense that was limited to $10,000.

The McCarthys paid the following in 2019:

Home mortgage interest	$15,661
Property taxes	5,436
Estimated state income tax payments	2,400
Estimated Federal income tax payments	10,500
Charitable contributions (all cash)	7,600

Required: Complete the McCarthys' federal tax return for 2019. Use Form 1040, Schedule 1, Schedule 2, Schedule 3, Schedule A, Schedule B, Schedule C, Schedule H, Schedule SE, Form 8959, and Form 8960 to complete this tax return. Make realistic assumptions about any missing data and ignore any alternative minimum tax. Do not complete Form 4952, which is used for depreciation.

2B. Warner and Augustine Robins, both 33 years old, have been married for 9 years and have no dependents. Warner is the president of Dragon Lady Corporation located in Macon. The Dragon Lady stock is owned 40 percent by Warner, 40 percent by Augustine, and 20 percent by Warner's father. Warner and Augustine received the following tax documents:

a Employee's social security number 798-09-8526	OMB No. 1545-0008	Safe, accurate, FAST! Use IRS e-file	Visit the IRS website at www.irs.gov/efile

b Employer identification number (EIN) 43-4321567	1 Wages, tips, other compensation 152,450.00	2 Federal income tax withheld 7,200.00

c Employer's name, address, and ZIP code Dragon Lady Corp. 1670 Eisenhower Pkwy. Macon, GA 31206	3 Social security wages 132,900.00	4 Social security tax withheld 8,239.80
	5 Medicare wages and tips 152,450.00	6 Medicare tax withheld 2,210.53
	7 Social security tips	8 Allocated tips

d Control number	9	10 Dependent care benefits

e Employee's first name and initial Last name Suff.	11 Nonqualified plans	12a See instructions for box 12
Warner Robins 638 Russell Parkway Macon, GA 31207	13 Statutory employee ☐ Retirement plan ☐ Third-party sick pay ☐	12b
	14 Other	12c
		12d

f Employee's address and ZIP code

15 State Employer's state ID number GA 5643E25	16 State wages, tips, etc. 152,450.00	17 State income tax 4,000.00	18 Local wages, tips, etc.	19 Local income tax	20 Locality name

Form **W-2** Wage and Tax Statement   **2019**   Department of the Treasury—Internal Revenue Service

Copy B—To Be Filed With Employee's FEDERAL Tax Return.
This information is being furnished to the Internal Revenue Service.

☐ CORRECTED (if checked)

PAYER'S name, street address, city or town, state or province, country, ZIP or foreign postal code, and telephone no. Georgia National Bank 520 Walnut Street Macon, GA 31201	Payer's RTN (optional)	OMB No. 1545-0112 20**19** Form **1099-INT**	**Interest Income**
	1 Interest income $ 532.12		
	2 Early withdrawal penalty $ 300.00		Copy B
PAYER'S TIN 23-8787878	RECIPIENT'S TIN 445-81-1423	3 Interest on U.S. Savings Bonds and Treas. obligations $	For Recipient
RECIPIENT'S name Augustine and Warner Robins	4 Federal income tax withheld $	5 Investment expenses $	This is important tax information and is being furnished to the IRS. If you are required to file a return, a negligence penalty or other sanction may be imposed on you if this income is taxable and the IRS determines that it has not been reported.
	6 Foreign tax paid $	7 Foreign country or U.S. possession	
Street address (including apt. no.) 638 Russell Parkway	8 Tax-exempt interest $	9 Specified private activity bond interest $	
City or town, state or province, country, and ZIP or foreign postal code Macon, GA 31207	10 Market discount $	11 Bond premium $	
FATCA filing requirement ☐	12 Bond premium on Treasury obligations $	13 Bond premium on tax-exempt bond $	
Account number (see instructions)	14 Tax-exempt and tax credit bond CUSIP no.	15 State 16 State identification no.	17 State tax withheld $ $

Form **1099-INT**   (keep for your records)   www.irs.gov/Form1099INT   Department of the Treasury - Internal Revenue Service

☐ VOID   ☐ CORRECTED

RECIPIENT'S/LENDER'S name, street address, city or town, state or province, country, ZIP or foreign postal code, and telephone no. Georgia National Bank 520 Walnut Street Macon, GA 31201		OMB No. 1545-1380 **2019** Form **1098**	**Mortgage Interest Statement**
		1 Mortgage interest received from payer(s)/borrower(s) $ 35,373.23	**Copy C** **For Recipient/ Lender**
RECIPIENT'S/LENDER'S TIN 23-8787878	PAYER'S/BORROWER'S TIN 798-09-8526	**2** Outstanding mortgage principal $ 870,000.00	**3** Mortgage origination date 10/13/2011	
		4 Refund of overpaid interest $	**5** Mortgage insurance premiums $	For Privacy Act and Paperwork Reduction Act Notice, see the **2019 General Instructions for Certain Information Returns.**
PAYER'S/BORROWER'S name Warner & Augustine Robins		**6** Points paid on purchase of principal residence $	
Street address (including apt. no.) 638 Russell Parkway		**7** ☒ If address of property securing mortgage is the same as PAYER'S/BORROWER'S address, check the box, or enter the address or description in box 8.	
City or town, state or province, country, and ZIP or foreign postal code Macon, GA 31207		**8** Address or description of property securing mortgage (see instructions)	
9 Number of properties securing the mortgage 1	**10** Other Prop Tax $6,650.00		**11** Mortgage acquisition date
Account number (see instructions)			

Form **1098**   www.irs.gov/Form1098   Department of the Treasury - Internal Revenue Service

Macon Museum of Arts
3231 Vineville Ave.
Macon, GA 31204

November 23, 2019

Mr. and Mrs. Warner and Augustine Robins
628 Russell Parkway
Macon, GA 31207

Dear Mr. and Mrs. Robins:

Thank you for your contribution of the original album cover art for the Almond Sisters Band to the Macon Museum of Arts.

This gift supports the Macon Museum's efforts to bring original and locally-sourced art work to Macon. This continuing support will guarantee our ability to display Almond Sister art work for many years to come.

We have attached a copy of the appraiser's market valuation. Her analysis estimates the value of the painting at $34,505.

Please keep this written acknowledgement of your donation for your tax records. As a token of our appreciation for your support, we have mailed you the Macon Museum tote bag. We estimate the value of the tote bag to be $5. We are required to inform you that your federal income tax deduction for your contribution is the amount of your contribution less the value of the tote bag. Thank you for your continuing support for our important work in this field!

Please retain this letter as proof of your charitable contribution.

Thank you for helping us to help veterans.

Sincerely,

Jack T. Mann

Jack T. Mann
Art Development Officer

Employer Identification Number **22-1234567**
Macon Museum of Arts is a registered 501(c)(3) corporation

The Robins paid the following amounts (all can be substantiated):

General state sales tax	2,120
Auto loan interest	4,800
Medical insurance	11,345
Income tax preparation fee	750
Charitable contributions in cash:	
Church	2,665
Tree Huggers Foundation (a qualified charity)	3,000
Central Georgia Technical University	5,000
Safe-deposit box	200

The tax basis for the donated painting is $25,000 and the painting has been owned by Warner and Augustine for 5 years.

Dragon Lady does not cover health insurance for its employees. In addition to Warner and Augustine's health insurance premiums shown above, Augustine required surgery which cost $6,654 for which only $3,002 was covered by insurance. Warner had to drive Augustine 150 miles each way to a surgical center.

On January 1, 2019, Warner sold land to Dragon Lady Corporation for $75,000. He acquired the land 5 years ago for $160,000. No Form 1099-B was filed for this transaction.

Dragon Lady Corporation does not have a qualified pension plan or Section 401(k) plan for its employees. Therefore, Warner deposited $12,000 ($6,000 each) into traditional IRA accounts for Augustine and himself (neither are covered by a qualified plan at work).

Required: Complete the Robins' federal tax return for 2019. Use Form 1040, Schedule 1, Schedule A, Schedule D, and Form 8949 to complete this tax return. Make realistic assumptions about any missing data and ignore any alternative minimum tax. Do not complete Form 8283, which is used when large noncash donations are made to charity.

GROUP 5:
CUMULATIVE SOFTWARE PROBLEM

1. The following information is available for the Albert and Allison Gaytor family in addition to that provided in Chapters 1–5.

Allison discovered a bookkeeping error in her business records. The revenues from Toge Pass should have been $85,100 (not the $64,050 originally recorded).

Albert owned 1,000 shares of Behemoth Airline stock with a basis of $30 per share. The stock was purchased 6 years ago on June 10. Albert sells 500 shares of Behemoth stock to his uncle Seth and 500 of the shares to his sister Sara for $5 per share on December 31, 2019.

Required: Combine this new information about the Gaytor family with the information from Chapters 1–5 and complete a revised 2019 tax return for Albert and Allison. Be sure to save your data input files since this case will be expanded with more tax information in the next chapter.

Form **1040** Department of the Treasury—Internal Revenue Service   (99)

U.S. Individual Income Tax Return |2019| OMB No. 1545-0074   IRS Use Only—Do not write or staple in this space.

Filing Status
Check only one box.

☐ Single   ☐ Married filing jointly   ☐ Married filing separately (MFS)   ☐ Head of household (HOH)   ☐ Qualifying widow(er) (QW)

If you checked the MFS box, enter the name of spouse. If you checked the HOH or QW box, enter the child's name if the qualifying person is a child but not your dependent. ▶

Your first name and middle initial	Last name	Your social security number
If joint return, spouse's first name and middle initial	Last name	Spouse's social security number

Home address (number and street). If you have a P.O. box, see instructions.	Apt. no.	**Presidential Election Campaign**

Check here if you, or your spouse if filing jointly, want $3 to go to this fund. Checking a box below will not change your tax or refund.   ☐ You   ☐ Spouse

City, town or post office, state, and ZIP code. If you have a foreign address, also complete spaces below (see instructions).

Foreign country name	Foreign province/state/county	Foreign postal code

If more than four dependents, see instructions and ✓ here ▶ ☐

Standard Deduction

Someone can claim: ☐ You as a dependent   ☐ Your spouse as a dependent

☐ Spouse itemizes on a separate return or you were a dual-status alien

Age/Blindness   **You:** ☐ Were born before January 2, 1955   ☐ Are blind   **Spouse:** ☐ Was born before January 2, 1955   ☐ Is blind

Dependents (see instructions):

(1) First name Last name	(2) Social security number	(3) Relationship to you	(4) ✓ if qualifies for (see instructions): Child tax credit	Credit for other dependents
			☐	☐
			☐	☐
			☐	☐
			☐	☐

Standard Deduction for—
- Single or Married filing separately, $12,200
- Married filing jointly or Qualifying widow(er), $24,400
- Head of household, $18,350
- If you checked any box under *Standard Deduction,* see instructions.

1	Wages, salaries, tips, etc. Attach Form(s) W-2		**1**	
2a	Tax-exempt interest	**2a**	**b** Taxable interest. Attach Sch. B if required	**2b**
3a	Qualified dividends	**3a**	**b** Ordinary dividends. Attach Sch. B if required	**3b**
4a	IRA distributions	**4a**	**b** Taxable amount	**4b**
c	Pensions and annuities . . .	**4c**	**d** Taxable amount	**4d**
5a	Social security benefits . . .	**5a**	**b** Taxable amount	**5b**
6	Capital gain or (loss). Attach Schedule D if required. If not required, check here . . . . . . ▶ ☐		**6**	
7a	Other income from Schedule 1, line 9		**7a**	
b	Add lines 1, 2b, 3b, 4b, 4d, 5b, 6, and 7a. This is your **total income** . . . . ▶		**7b**	
8a	Adjustments to income from Schedule 1, line 22		**8a**	
b	Subtract line 8a from line 7b. This is your **adjusted gross income** . . . . ▶		**8b**	
9	**Standard deduction or itemized deductions** (from Schedule A)	**9**		
10	Qualified business income deduction. Attach Form 8995 or Form 8995-A . . .	**10**		
11a	Add lines 9 and 10		**11a**	
b	**Taxable income.** Subtract line 11a from line 8b		**11b**	

For Disclosure, Privacy Act, and Paperwork Reduction Act Notice, see separate instructions.   Cat. No. 11320B   Form **1040** (2019)

Form 1040 (2019)   Page **2**

12a	**Tax** (see inst.) Check if any from Form(s): 1 ☐ 8814 2 ☐ 4972 3 ☐ _____	**12a**		
b	Add Schedule 2, line 3, and line 12a and enter the total . . . . ▶	**12b**		
13a	Child tax credit or credit for other dependents	**13a**		
b	Add Schedule 3, line 7, and line 13a and enter the total . . . . ▶	**13b**		
14	Subtract line 13b from line 12b. If zero or less, enter -0-	**14**		
15	Other taxes, including self-employment tax, from Schedule 2, line 10	**15**		
16	Add lines 14 and 15. This is your **total tax** . . . . ▶	**16**		
17	Federal income tax withheld from Forms W-2 and 1099	**17**		
18	Other payments and refundable credits:			
a	Earned income credit (EIC)	**18a**		
b	Additional child tax credit. Attach Schedule 8812	**18b**		
c	American opportunity credit from Form 8863, line 8	**18c**		
d	Schedule 3, line 14	**18d**		
e	Add lines 18a through 18d. These are your **total other payments and refundable credits** . . ▶	**18e**		
19	Add lines 17 and 18e. These are your **total payments** . . . . ▶	**19**		

- If you have a qualifying child, attach Sch. EIC.
- If you have nontaxable combat pay, see instructions.

Refund

Direct deposit?
See instructions.

20	If line 19 is more than line 16, subtract line 16 from line 19. This is the amount you **overpaid** . . .	**20**	
21a	Amount of line 20 you want **refunded to you.** If Form 8888 is attached, check here . . . . ▶ ☐	**21a**	
▶**b**	Routing number [ ] ▶ **c** Type: ☐ Checking ☐ Savings		
▶**d**	Account number [ ]		
22	Amount of line 20 you want **applied to your 2020 estimated tax** . . . . ▶	**22**	

Amount You Owe

23	**Amount you owe.** Subtract line 19 from line 16. For details on how to pay, see instructions . . . ▶	**23**	
24	Estimated tax penalty (see instructions) . . . . ▶	**24**	

Third Party Designee

(Other than paid preparer)

Do you want to allow another person (other than your paid preparer) to discuss this return with the IRS? See instructions. ☐ **Yes.** Complete below. ☐ **No**

Designee's name ▶   Phone no. ▶   Personal identification number (PIN) ▶ [   ]

Sign Here

Joint return?
See instructions.
Keep a copy for your records.

Under penalties of perjury, I declare that I have examined this return and accompanying schedules and statements, and to the best of my knowledge and belief, they are true, correct, and complete. Declaration of preparer (other than taxpayer) is based on all information of which preparer has any knowledge.

Your signature	Date	Your occupation	If the IRS sent you an Identity Protection PIN, enter it here (see inst.) [ ]
Spouse's signature. If a joint return, **both** must sign.	Date	Spouse's occupation	If the IRS sent your spouse an Identity Protection PIN, enter it here (see inst.) [ ]

Phone no.   Email address

Paid Preparer Use Only

Preparer's name	Preparer's signature		Date	PTIN	Check if:
					☐ 3rd Party Designee
Firm's name ▶			Phone no.		☐ Self-employed
Firm's address ▶				Firm's EIN ▶	

Go to *www.irs.gov/Form1040* for instructions and the latest information.   Form **1040** (2019)

SCHEDULE 1
(Form 1040 or 1040-SR)

Department of the Treasury
Internal Revenue Service

Additional Income and Adjustments to Income

▶ **Attach to Form 1040 or 1040-SR.**
▶ **Go to** *www.irs.gov/Form1040* **for instructions and the latest information.**

OMB No. 1545-0074

20**19**

Attachment
Sequence No. **01**

Name(s) shown on Form 1040 or 1040-SR

Your social security number

Part I	**Additional Income**		
1	Taxable refunds, credits, or offsets of state and local income taxes	**1**	
2a	Alimony received	**2a**	
b	Date of original divorce or separation agreement (see instructions) ▶		
3	Business income or (loss). Attach Schedule C	**3**	
4	Other gains or (losses). Attach Form 4797	**4**	
5	Rental real estate, royalties, partnerships, S corporations, trusts, etc. Attach Schedule E	**5**	
6	Farm income or (loss). Attach Schedule F	**6**	
7	Unemployment compensation	**7**	
8	Other income. List type and amount ▶		
		8	
9	Combine lines 1 through 8. Enter here and on Form 1040 or 1040-SR, line 7a	**9**	
Part II	**Adjustments to Income**		
10	Educator expenses	**10**	
11	Certain business expenses of reservists, performing artists, and fee-basis government officials. Attach Form 2106	**11**	
12	Health savings account deduction. Attach Form 8889	**12**	
13	Moving expenses for members of the Armed Forces. Attach Form 3903	**13**	
14	Deductible part of self-employment tax. Attach Schedule SE	**14**	
15	Self-employed SEP, SIMPLE, and qualified plans	**15**	
16	Self-employed health insurance deduction	**16**	
17	Penalty on early withdrawal of savings	**17**	
18a	Alimony paid	**18a**	
b	Recipient's SSN . . . . ▶		
c	Date of original divorce or separation agreement (see instructions) ▶		
19	IRA deduction	**19**	
20	Student loan interest deduction	**20**	
21	Reserved for future use	**21**	
22	Add lines 10 through 21. These are your **adjustments to income.** Enter here and on Form 1040 or 1040-SR, line 8a	**22**	

For Paperwork Reduction Act Notice, see your tax return instructions.   Cat. No. 71479F   Schedule 1 (Form 1040 or 1040-SR) 2019

SCHEDULE 2
(Form 1040 or 1040-SR)

Department of the Treasury
Internal Revenue Service

Additional Taxes

▶ Attach to Form 1040 or 1040-SR.
▶ Go to *www.irs.gov/Form1040* for instructions and the latest information.

OMB No. 1545-0074

2019

Attachment
Sequence No. **02**

Name(s) shown on Form 1040 or 1040-SR

Your social security number

Part I	**Tax**	
1	Alternative minimum tax. Attach Form 6251	**1**
2	Excess advance premium tax credit repayment. Attach Form 8962	**2**
3	Add lines 1 and 2. Enter here and include on Form 1040 or 1040-SR, line 12b	**3**

Part II	**Other Taxes**	
4	Self-employment tax. Attach Schedule SE	**4**
5	Unreported social security and Medicare tax from Form: **a** ☐ 4137 **b** ☐ 8919	**5**
6	Additional tax on IRAs, other qualified retirement plans, and other tax-favored accounts. Attach Form 5329 if required	**6**
7a	Household employment taxes. Attach Schedule H	**7a**
b	Repayment of first-time homebuyer credit from Form 5405. Attach Form 5405 if required . . .	**7b**
8	Taxes from: **a** ☐ Form 8959 **b** ☐ Form 8960 **c** ☐ Instructions; enter code(s) _____	**8**
9	Section 965 net tax liability installment from Form 965-A **9**	
10	Add lines 4 through 8. These are your **total other taxes.** Enter here and on Form 1040 or 1040-SR, line 15	**10**

For Paperwork Reduction Act Notice, see your tax return instructions.   Cat. No. 71478U   Schedule 2 (Form 1040 or 1040-SR) 2019

DRAFT AS OF JULY 11, 2019 DO NOT FILE

SCHEDULE 3
(Form 1040 or 1040-SR)

Department of the Treasury
Internal Revenue Service

Additional Credits and Payments

▶ Attach to Form 1040 or 1040-SR.
▶ Go to *www.irs.gov/Form1040* for instructions and the latest information.

OMB No. 1545-0074

2019

Attachment
Sequence No. **03**

Name(s) shown on Form 1040 or 1040-SR

Your social security number

Part I	Nonrefundable Credits		
1	Foreign tax credit. Attach Form 1116 if required	**1**	
2	Credit for child and dependent care expenses. Attach Form 2441	**2**	
3	Education credits from Form 8863, line 19	**3**	
4	Retirement savings contributions credit. Attach Form 8880	**4**	
5	Residential energy credit. Attach Form 5695	**5**	
6	Other credits from Form: **a** ☐ 3800 **b** ☐ 8801 **c** ☐ _____	**6**	
7	Add lines 1 through 6. Enter here and include on Form 1040 or 1040-SR, line 13b	**7**	

Part II	Other Payments and Refundable Credits		
8	2019 estimated tax payments and amount applied from 2018 return	**8**	
9	Net premium tax credit. Attach Form 8962	**9**	
10	Amount paid with request for extension to file (see instructions)	**10**	
11	Excess social security and tier 1 RRTA tax withheld	**11**	
12	Credit for federal tax on fuels. Attach Form 4136	**12**	
13	Credits from Form: **a** ☐ 2439 **b** ☐ Reserved **c** ☐ 8885 **d** ☐ _____	**13**	
14	Add lines 8 through 13. Enter here and on Form 1040 or 1040-SR, line 18d	**14**	

For Paperwork Reduction Act Notice, see your tax return instructions.   Cat. No. 71480G   Schedule 3 (Form 1040 or 1040-SR) 2019

SCHEDULE A
(Form 1040 or 1040-SR)

Department of the Treasury
Internal Revenue Service (99)

Itemized Deductions

▶ Go to *www.irs.gov/ScheduleA* for instructions and the latest information.
▶ Attach to Form 1040 or 1040-SR.

Caution: If you are claiming a net qualified disaster loss on Form 4684, see the instructions for line 16.

OMB No. 1545-0074

2019

Attachment
Sequence No. **07**

Name(s) shown on Form 1040 or 1040-SR

Your social security number

Medical and Dental Expenses	**Caution:** Do not include expenses reimbursed or paid by others.		
	1 Medical and dental expenses (see instructions)	**1**	
	2 Enter amount from Form 1040 or 1040-SR, line 8b **2**		
	3 Multiply line 2 by 10% (0.10)	**3**	
	4 Subtract line 3 from line 1. If line 3 is more than line 1, enter -0-		**4**
Taxes You Paid	**5** State and local taxes.		
	a State and local income taxes or general sales taxes. You may include either income taxes or general sales taxes on line 5a, but not both. If you elect to include general sales taxes instead of income taxes, check this box . . . . ▶ ☐	**5a**	
	b State and local real estate taxes (see instructions)	**5b**	
	c State and local personal property taxes	**5c**	
	d Add lines 5a through 5c	**5d**	
	e Enter the smaller of line 5d or $10,000 ($5,000 if married filing separately)	**5e**	
	6 Other taxes. List type and amount ▶ _____	**6**	
	7 Add lines 5e and 6		**7**
Interest You Paid **Caution:** Your mortgage interest deduction may be limited (see instructions).	**8** Home mortgage interest and points. If you didn't use all of your home mortgage loan(s) to buy, build, or improve your home, see instructions and check this box . . . . ▶ ☐		
	a Home mortgage interest and points reported to you on Form 1098. See instructions if limited	**8a**	
	b Home mortgage interest not reported to you on Form 1098. If paid to the person from whom you bought the home, see instructions and show that person's name, identifying no., and address . . . . . ▶ _____	**8b**	
	c Points not reported to you on Form 1098. See instructions for special rules	**8c**	
	d Reserved	**8d**	
	e Add lines 8a through 8c	**8e**	
	9 Investment interest. Attach Form 4952 if required. See instructions	**9**	
	10 Add lines 8e and 9		**10**
Gifts to Charity **Caution:** If you made a gift and got a benefit for it, see instructions.	**11** Gifts by cash or check. If you made any gift of $250 or more, see instructions	**11**	
	12 Other than by cash or check. If you made any gift of $250 or more, see instructions. You **must** attach Form 8283 if over $500. . . .	**12**	
	13 Carryover from prior year	**13**	
	14 Add lines 11 through 13		**14**
Casualty and Theft Losses	**15** Casualty and theft loss(es) from a federally declared disaster (other than net qualified disaster losses). Attach Form 4684 and enter the amount from line 18 of that form. See instructions		**15**
Other Itemized Deductions	**16** Other—from list in instructions. List type and amount ▶ _____		**16**
Total Itemized Deductions	**17** Add the amounts in the far right column for lines 4 through 16. Also, enter this amount on Form 1040 or 1040-SR, line 9		**17**
	18 If you elect to itemize deductions even though they are less than your standard deduction, check this box . . . . ▶ ☐		

For Paperwork Reduction Act Notice, see the Instructions for Forms 1040 and 1040-SR.   Cat. No. 17145C   **Schedule A (Form 1040 or 1040-SR) 2019**

SCHEDULE B
(Form 1040 or 1040-SR)

Department of the Treasury
Internal Revenue Service (99)

Interest and Ordinary Dividends

► Go to *www.irs.gov/ScheduleB* for instructions and the latest information.
► Attach to Form 1040 or 1040-SR.

OMB No. 1545-0074

2019

Attachment
Sequence No. **08**

Name(s) shown on return

Your social security number

Part I

Interest

(See instructions and the instructions for Forms 1040 and 1040-SR, line 2b.)

Note: If you received a Form 1099-INT, Form 1099-OID, or substitute statement from a brokerage firm, list the firm's name as the payer and enter the total interest shown on that form.

1 List name of payer. If any interest is from a seller-financed mortgage and the buyer used the property as a personal residence, see the instructions and list this interest first. Also, show that buyer's social security number and address ►

	Amount
1	

2 Add the amounts on line 1 . . . . | **2** | |

3 Excludable interest on series EE and I U.S. savings bonds issued after 1989. Attach Form 8815 . . . . | **3** | |

4 Subtract line 3 from line 2. Enter the result here and on Form 1040 or 1040-SR, line 2b . . . . ► | **4** | |

Note: If line 4 is over $1,500, you must complete Part III.

Part II

Ordinary Dividends

(See instructions and the instructions for Forms 1040 and 1040-SR, line 3b.)

Note: If you received a Form 1099-DIV or substitute statement from a brokerage firm, list the firm's name as the payer and enter the ordinary dividends shown on that form.

5 List name of payer ►

	Amount
5	

6 Add the amounts on line 5. Enter the total here and on Form 1040 or 1040-SR, line 3b . . . . ► | **6** | |

Note: If line 6 is over $1,500, you must complete Part III.

Part III

Foreign Accounts and Trusts

Caution: If required, failure to file FinCEN Form 114 may result in substantial penalties. See instructions.

You must complete this part if you **(a)** had over $1,500 of taxable interest or ordinary dividends; **(b)** had a foreign account; or **(c)** received a distribution from, or were a grantor of, or a transferor to, a foreign trust.

		Yes	No
7a	At any time during 2019, did you have a financial interest in or signature authority over a financial account (such as a bank account, securities account, or brokerage account) located in a foreign country? See instructions		
	If "Yes," are you required to file FinCEN Form 114, Report of Foreign Bank and Financial Accounts (FBAR), to report that financial interest or signature authority? See FinCEN Form 114 and its instructions for filing requirements and exceptions to those requirements		
b	If you are required to file FinCEN Form 114, enter the name of the foreign country where the financial account is located ►		
8	During 2019, did you receive a distribution from, or were you the grantor of, or transferor to, a foreign trust? If "Yes," you may have to file Form 3520. See instructions		

For Paperwork Reduction Act Notice, see your tax return instructions.   Cat. No. 17146N   **Schedule B (Form 1040 or 1040-SR) 2019**

SCHEDULE C
(Form 1040 or 1040-SR)

Department of the Treasury
Internal Revenue Service (99)

Profit or Loss From Business
(Sole Proprietorship)

▶ Go to *www.irs.gov/ScheduleC* for instructions and the latest information.
▶ **Attach to Form 1040, 1040-SR, 1040-NR, or 1041; partnerships generally must file Form 1065.**

OMB No. 1545-0074

2019

Attachment
Sequence No. **09**

Name of proprietor | Social security number (SSN)

A Principal business or profession, including product or service (see instructions) | **B Enter code from instructions** ▶

C Business name. If no separate business name, leave blank. | **D Employer ID number (EIN)** (see instr.)

E Business address (including suite or room no.) ▶
City, town or post office, state, and ZIP code

F Accounting method: **(1)** ☐ Cash **(2)** ☐ Accrual **(3)** ☐ Other (specify) ▶

G Did you "materially participate" in the operation of this business during 2019? If "No," see instructions for limit on losses . ☐ Yes ☐ No

H If you started or acquired this business during 2019, check here . . . . ▶ ☐

I Did you make any payments in 2019 that would require you to file Form(s) 1099? (see instructions) . . . ☐ Yes ☐ No

J If "Yes," did you or will you file required Forms 1099? . . . . ☐ Yes ☐ No

Part I   Income

1	Gross receipts or sales. See instructions for line 1 and check the box if this income was reported to you on Form W-2 and the "Statutory employee" box on that form was checked . . . . ▶ ☐	**1**
2	Returns and allowances	**2**
3	Subtract line 2 from line 1	**3**
4	Cost of goods sold (from line 42)	**4**
5	**Gross profit.** Subtract line 4 from line 3	**5**
6	Other income, including federal and state gasoline or fuel tax credit or refund (see instructions) . .	**6**
7	**Gross income.** Add lines 5 and 6 . . . . ▶	**7**

Part II   Expenses. Enter expenses for business use of your home **only** on line 30.

8	Advertising	**8**	18	Office expense (see instructions)	**18**
9	Car and truck expenses (see instructions)	**9**	19	Pension and profit-sharing plans .	**19**
10	Commissions and fees .	**10**	20	Rent or lease (see instructions):	
11	Contract labor (see instructions)	**11**	a	Vehicles, machinery, and equipment	**20a**
12	Depletion	**12**	b	Other business property . . .	**20b**
13	Depreciation and section 179 expense deduction (not included in Part III) (see instructions)	**13**	21	Repairs and maintenance . . .	**21**
			22	Supplies (not included in Part III) .	**22**
			23	Taxes and licenses	**23**
			24	Travel and meals:	
14	Employee benefit programs (other than on line 19) . .	**14**	a	Travel	**24a**
15	Insurance (other than health)	**15**	b	Deductible meals (see instructions)	**24b**
16	Interest (see instructions):		25	Utilities	**25**
a	Mortgage (paid to banks, etc.)	**16a**	26	Wages (less employment credits) .	**26**
b	Other	**16b**	27a	Other expenses (from line 48) . .	**27a**
17	Legal and professional services	**17**	b	**Reserved for future use** . . .	**27b**

28	**Total expenses** before expenses for business use of home. Add lines 8 through 27a . . . . . . ▶	**28**
29	Tentative profit or (loss). Subtract line 28 from line 7	**29**
30	Expenses for business use of your home. Do not report these expenses elsewhere. Attach Form 8829 unless using the simplified method (see instructions). **Simplified method filers only:** enter the total square footage of: (a) your home: _____ and (b) the part of your home used for business: _____ . Use the Simplified Method Worksheet in the instructions to figure the amount to enter on line 30	**30**
31	**Net profit or (loss).** Subtract line 30 from line 29. • If a profit, enter on both **Schedule 1 (Form 1040 or 1040-SR), line 3** (or **Form 1040-NR, line 13**) and on **Schedule SE, line 2.** (If you checked the box on line 1, see instructions). Estates and trusts, enter on **Form 1041, line 3.** • If a loss, you **must** go to line 32.	**31**
32	If you have a loss, check the box that describes your investment in this activity (see instructions). • If you checked 32a, enter the loss on both **Schedule 1 (Form 1040 or 1040-SR), line 3** (or **Form 1040-NR, line 13**) and on **Schedule SE, line 2.** (If you checked the box on line 1, see the line 31 instructions). Estates and trusts, enter on **Form 1041, line 3.** • If you checked 32b, you **must** attach **Form 6198.** Your loss may be limited.	32a ☐ All investment is at risk. 32b ☐ Some investment is not at risk.

For Paperwork Reduction Act Notice, see the separate instructions.   Cat. No. 11334P   Schedule C (Form 1040 or 1040-SR) 2019

DRAFT AS OF August 7, 2019 DO NOT FILE

Schedule C (Form 1040 or 1040-SR) 2019   Page **2**

Part III   Cost of Goods Sold (see instructions)

33   Method(s) used to
value closing inventory: **a** ☐ Cost   **b** ☐ Lower of cost or market   **c** ☐ Other (attach explanation)

34   Was there any change in determining quantities, costs, or valuations between opening and closing inventory?
If "Yes," attach explanation . . . .   ☐ Yes   ☐ No

35   Inventory at beginning of year. If different from last year's closing inventory, attach explanation . . . | **35** |

36   Purchases less cost of items withdrawn for personal use . . . . | **36** |

37   Cost of labor. Do not include any amounts paid to yourself . . . . | **37** |

38   Materials and supplies . . . . | **38** |

39   Other costs . . . . | **39** |

40   Add lines 35 through 39 . . . . | **40** |

41   Inventory at end of year . . . . | **41** |

42   **Cost of goods sold.** Subtract line 41 from line 40. Enter the result here and on line 4 . . . . . . | **42** |

Part IV   Information on Your Vehicle. Complete this part **only** if you are claiming car or truck expenses on line 9 and are not required to file Form 4562 for this business. See the instructions for line 13 to find out if you must file Form 4562.

43   When did you place your vehicle in service for business purposes? (month, day, year)   ▶ _____ / _____ / _____

44   Of the total number of miles you drove your vehicle during 2019, enter the number of miles you used your vehicle for:

   a   Business _____   **b** Commuting (see instructions) _____   **c** Other _____

45   Was your vehicle available for personal use during off-duty hours? . . . .   ☐ Yes   ☐ No

46   Do you (or your spouse) have another vehicle available for personal use?. . . . .   ☐ Yes   ☐ No

47a   Do you have evidence to support your deduction? . . . .   ☐ Yes   ☐ No

   b   If "Yes," is the evidence written? . . . .   ☐ Yes   ☐ No

Part V   Other Expenses. List below business expenses not included on lines 8–26 or line 30.

-- |

-- |

-- |

-- |

-- |

-- |

-- |

-- |

48   **Total other expenses.** Enter here and on line 27a . . . . | **48** |

Schedule C (Form 1040 or 1040-SR) 2019

SCHEDULE D
(Form 1040 or 1040-SR)

Department of the Treasury
Internal Revenue Service (99)

Capital Gains and Losses

▶ Attach to Form 1040, 1040-SR, or 1040-NR.
▶ Go to *www.irs.gov/ScheduleD* for instructions and the latest information.
▶ Use Form 8949 to list your transactions for lines 1b, 2, 3, 8b, 9, and 10.

OMB No. 1545-0074

2019

Attachment
Sequence No. **12**

Name(s) shown on return

Your social security number

Did you dispose of any investment(s) in a qualified opportunity fund during the tax year? ☐ **Yes** ☐ **No**
If "Yes," attach Form 8949 and see its instructions for additional requirements for reporting your gain or loss.

Part I Short-Term Capital Gains and Losses—Generally Assets Held One Year or Less (see instructions)

See instructions for how to figure the amounts to enter on the lines below. This form may be easier to complete if you round off cents to whole dollars.	(d) Proceeds (sales price)	(e) Cost (or other basis)	(g) Adjustments to gain or loss from Form(s) 8949, Part I, line 2, column (g)	(h) Gain or (loss) Subtract column (e) from column (d) and combine the result with column (g)
1a Totals for all short-term transactions reported on Form 1099-B for which basis was reported to the IRS and for which you have no adjustments (see instructions). However, if you choose to report all these transactions on Form 8949, leave this line blank and go to line 1b .				
1b Totals for all transactions reported on Form(s) 8949 with **Box A** checked				
2 Totals for all transactions reported on Form(s) 8949 with **Box B** checked				
3 Totals for all transactions reported on Form(s) 8949 with **Box C** checked				

4 Short-term gain from Form 6252 and short-term gain or (loss) from Forms 4684, 6781, and 8824 . .	**4**	
5 Net short-term gain or (loss) from partnerships, S corporations, estates, and trusts from Schedule(s) K-1	**5**	
6 Short-term capital loss carryover. Enter the amount, if any, from line 8 of your **Capital Loss Carryover Worksheet** in the instructions	**6** ( )	
7 **Net short-term capital gain or (loss).** Combine lines 1a through 6 in column (h). If you have any long-term capital gains or losses, go to Part II below. Otherwise, go to Part III on the back	**7**	

Part II Long-Term Capital Gains and Losses—Generally Assets Held More Than One Year (see instructions)

See instructions for how to figure the amounts to enter on the lines below. This form may be easier to complete if you round off cents to whole dollars.	(d) Proceeds (sales price)	(e) Cost (or other basis)	(g) Adjustments to gain or loss from Form(s) 8949, Part II, line 2, column (g)	(h) Gain or (loss) Subtract column (e) from column (d) and combine the result with column (g)
8a Totals for all long-term transactions reported on Form 1099-B for which basis was reported to the IRS and for which you have no adjustments (see instructions). However, if you choose to report all these transactions on Form 8949, leave this line blank and go to line 8b .				
8b Totals for all transactions reported on Form(s) 8949 with **Box D** checked				
9 Totals for all transactions reported on Form(s) 8949 with **Box E** checked				
10 Totals for all transactions reported on Form(s) 8949 with **Box F** checked.				

11 Gain from Form 4797, Part I; long-term gain from Forms 2439 and 6252; and long-term gain or (loss) from Forms 4684, 6781, and 8824	**11**	
12 Net long-term gain or (loss) from partnerships, S corporations, estates, and trusts from Schedule(s) K-1	**12**	
13 Capital gain distributions. See the instructions	**13**	
14 Long-term capital loss carryover. Enter the amount, if any, from line 13 of your **Capital Loss Carryover Worksheet** in the instructions	**14** ( )	
15 **Net long-term capital gain or (loss).** Combine lines 8a through 14 in column (h). Then go to Part III on the back	**15**	

For Paperwork Reduction Act Notice, see your tax return instructions.   Cat. No. 11338H   Schedule D (Form 1040 or 1040-SR) 2019

Schedule D (Form 1040 or 1040-SR) 2019   Page **2**

Part III	Summary

16 Combine lines 7 and 15 and enter the result **16**

- If line 16 is a **gain,** enter the amount from line 16 on Form 1040 or 1040-SR, line 6; or Form 1040-NR, line 14. Then go to line 17 below.
- If line 16 is a **loss,** skip lines 17 through 20 below. Then go to line 21. Also be sure to complete line 22.
- If line 16 is **zero,** skip lines 17 through 21 below and enter -0- on Form 1040 or 1040-SR, line 6; or Form 1040-NR, line 14. Then go to line 22.

17 Are lines 15 and 16 **both** gains?

☐ **Yes.** Go to line 18.

☐ **No.** Skip lines 18 through 21, and go to line 22.

18 If you are required to complete the **28% Rate Gain Worksheet** (see instructions), enter the amount, if any, from line 7 of that worksheet . . . . ▶   **18**

19 If you are required to complete the **Unrecaptured Section 1250 Gain Worksheet** (see instructions), enter the amount, if any, from line 18 of that worksheet . . . . ▶   **19**

20 Are lines 18 and 19 **both** zero or blank?

☐ **Yes.** Complete the **Qualified Dividends and Capital Gain Tax Worksheet** in the instructions for Forms 1040 and 1040-SR, line 12a (or in the instructions for Form 1040-NR, line 42). **Don't** complete lines 21 and 22 below.

☐ **No.** Complete the **Schedule D Tax Worksheet** in the instructions. **Don't** complete lines 21 and 22 below.

21 If line 16 is a loss, enter here and on Form 1040 or 1040-SR, line 6; or Form 1040-NR, line 14, the **smaller** of:

- The loss on line 16; or
- ($3,000), or if married filing separately, ($1,500)   }   . . . .   **21** (   )

Note: When figuring which amount is smaller, treat both amounts as positive numbers.

22 Do you have qualified dividends on Form 1040 or 1040-SR, line 3a; or Form 1040-NR, line 10b?

☐ **Yes.** Complete the **Qualified Dividends and Capital Gain Tax Worksheet** in the instructions for Forms 1040 and 1040-SR, line 12a (or in the instructions for Form 1040-NR, line 42).

☐ **No.** Complete the rest of Form 1040, 1040-SR, or 1040-NR.

Schedule D (Form 1040 or 1040-SR) 2019

SCHEDULE H
(Form 1040 or 1040-SR)

Department of the Treasury
Internal Revenue Service (99)

Household Employment Taxes

(For Social Security, Medicare, Withheld Income, and Federal Unemployment (FUTA) Taxes)

▶ **Attach to Form 1040, 1040-SR, 1040-NR, 1040-SS, or 1041.**
▶ **Go to www.irs.gov/ScheduleH for instructions and the latest information.**

OMB No. 1545-1971

2019

Attachment
Sequence No. **44**

Name of employer

Social security number

Employer identification number

Calendar year taxpayers having no household employees in 2019 don't have to complete this form for 2019.

A Did you pay **any one** household employee cash wages of $2,100 or more in 2019? (If any household employee was your spouse, your child under age 21, your parent, or anyone under age 18, see the line A instructions before you answer this question.)

☐ **Yes.** Skip lines B and C and go to line 1.
☐ **No.** Go to line B.

B Did you withhold federal income tax during 2019 for any household employee?

☐ **Yes.** Skip line C and go to line 7.
☐ **No.** Go to line C.

C Did you pay **total** cash wages of $1,000 or more in **any** calendar **quarter** of 2018 or 2019 to **all** household employees? (**Don't** count cash wages paid in 2018 or 2019 to your spouse, your child under age 21, or your parent.)

☐ **No.** **Stop.** Don't file this schedule.
☐ **Yes.** Skip lines 1–9 and go to line 10.

Part I	Social Security, Medicare, and Federal Income Taxes

1 Total cash wages subject to social security tax **1**

2 Social security tax. Multiply line 1 by 12.4% (0.124) **2**

3 Total cash wages subject to Medicare tax **3**

4 Medicare tax. Multiply line 3 by 2.9% (0.029) **4**

5 Total cash wages subject to Additional Medicare Tax withholding **5**

6 Additional Medicare Tax withholding. Multiply line 5 by 0.9% (0.009) **6**

7 Federal income tax withheld, if any **7**

8 **Total social security, Medicare, and federal income taxes.** Add lines 2, 4, 6, and 7 . . . . **8**

9 Did you pay **total** cash wages of $1,000 or more in **any** calendar **quarter** of 2018 or 2019 to **all** household employees? (**Don't** count cash wages paid in 2018 or 2019 to your spouse, your child under age 21, or your parent.)

☐ **No.** **Stop.** Include the amount from line 8 above on Schedule 2 (Form 1040 or 1040-SR), line 7a. If you're not required to file Form 1040 or 1040-SR, see the line 9 instructions.

☐ **Yes.** Go to line 10.

For Privacy Act and Paperwork Reduction Act Notice, see the instructions.   Cat. No. 12187K   **Schedule H (Form 1040 or 1040-SR) 2019**

Schedule H (Form 1040 or 1040-SR) 2019   Page **2**

Part II   **Federal Unemployment (FUTA) Tax**

		Yes	No
10	Did you pay unemployment contributions to only one state? If you paid contributions to a credit reduction state, see instructions and check **"No."** **10**		
11	Did you pay all state unemployment contributions for 2019 by April 15, 2020? Fiscal year filers, see instructions **11**		
12	Were all wages that are taxable for FUTA tax also taxable for your state's unemployment tax? **12**		

Next: If you checked the **"Yes"** box on **all** the lines above, complete Section A.
    If you checked the **"No"** box on **any** of the lines above, skip Section A and complete Section B.

Section A

13	Name of the state where you paid unemployment contributions ▶ _____	
14	Contributions paid to your state unemployment fund **14**	
15	Total cash wages subject to FUTA tax **15**	
16	**FUTA tax.** Multiply line 15 by 0.6% (0.006). Enter the result here, skip Section B, and go to line 25 . . **16**	

Section B

17   Complete all columns below that apply (if you need more space, see instructions):

(a) Name of state	(b) Taxable wages (as defined in state act)	(c) State experience rate period		(d) State experience rate	(e) Multiply col. (b) by 0.054	(f) Multiply col. (b) by col. (d)	(g) Subtract col. (f) from col. (e). If zero or less, enter -0-.	(h) Contributions paid to state unemployment fund
		From	To					

18	Totals **18**	
19	Add columns (g) and (h) of line 18 . . . . **19**	
20	Total cash wages subject to FUTA tax (see the line 15 instructions) **20**	
21	Multiply line 20 by 6.0% (0.060) **21**	
22	Multiply line 20 by 5.4% (0.054) **22**	
23	Enter the **smaller** of line 19 or line 22	
	(If you paid state unemployment contributions late or you're in a credit reduction state, see instructions and check here) . . . . ▶ ☐ **23**	
24	**FUTA tax.** Subtract line 23 from line 21. Enter the result here and go to line 25 . . . . **24**	

Part III   **Total Household Employment Taxes**

25	Enter the amount from line 8. If you checked the **"Yes"** box on line C of page 1, enter -0- **25**	
26	Add line 16 (or line 24) and line 25 . . . . **26**	
27	Are you required to file Form 1040 or 1040-SR?	

    ☐ **Yes. Stop.** Include the amount from line 26 above on Schedule 2 (Form 1040 or 1040-SR), line 7a. **Don't** complete Part IV below.

    ☐ **No.** You may have to complete Part IV. See instructions for details.

Part IV   **Address and Signature — Complete this part only if required. See the line 27 instructions.**

Address (number and street) or P.O. box if mail isn't delivered to street address	Apt., room, or suite no.
City, town or post office, state, and ZIP code	

Under penalties of perjury, I declare that I have examined this schedule, including accompanying statements, and to the best of my knowledge and belief, it is true, correct, and complete. No part of any payment made to a state unemployment fund claimed as a credit was, or is to be, deducted from the payments to employees. Declaration of preparer (other than taxpayer) is based on all information of which preparer has any knowledge.

▶ _____   ▶ _____
  Employer's signature   Date

Paid Preparer Use Only	Print/Type preparer's name	Preparer's signature	Date	Check ☐ if self-employed	PTIN
	Firm's name ▶			Firm's EIN ▶	
	Firm's address ▶			Phone no.	

SCHEDULE SE
(Form 1040 or
1040-SR)

Department of the Treasury
Internal Revenue Service (99)

Self-Employment Tax

▶ Go to *www.irs.gov/ScheduleSE* for instructions and the latest information.
▶ **Attach to Form 1040, 1040-SR, or 1040-NR.**

OMB No. 1545-0074

2019

Attachment
Sequence No. **17**

Name of person with self-employment income (as shown on Form 1040, 1040-SR, or 1040-NR)	Social security number of person with **self-employment** income ▶

Before you begin: To determine if you must file Schedule SE, see the instructions.

May I Use Short Schedule SE or Must I Use Long Schedule SE?

Note: Use this flowchart **only if** you must file Schedule SE. If unsure, see *Who Must File Schedule SE* in the instructions.

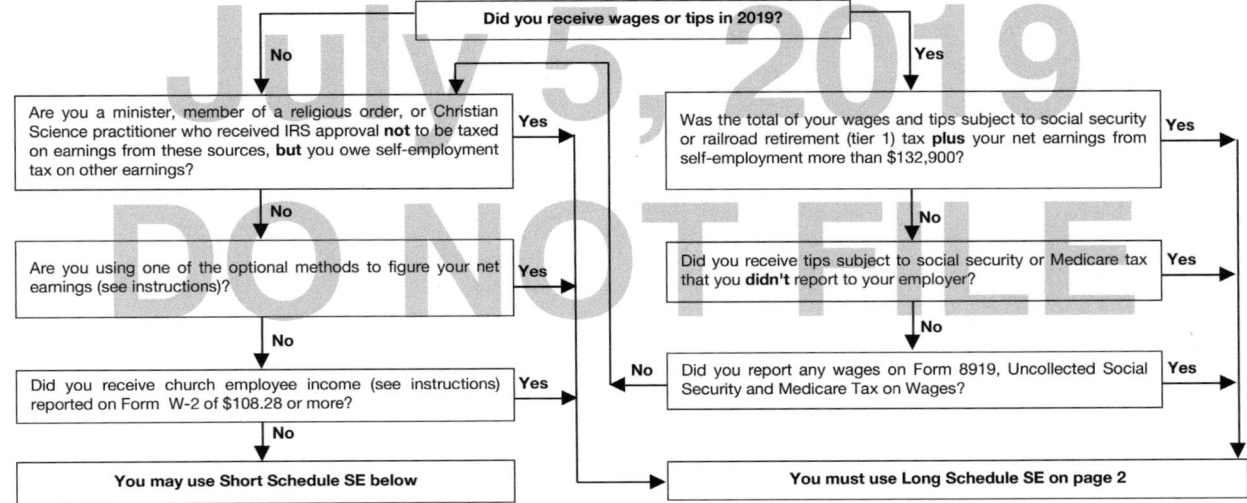

Section A—Short Schedule SE. Caution: Read above to see if you can use Short Schedule SE.

1a	Net farm profit or (loss) from Schedule F, line 34, and farm partnerships, Schedule K-1 (Form 1065), box 14, code A	**1a**	
b	If you received social security retirement or disability benefits, enter the amount of Conservation Reserve Program payments included on Schedule F, line 4b, or listed on Schedule K-1 (Form 1065), box 20, code AH	**1b**	( )
2	Net profit or (loss) from Schedule C, line 31; and Schedule K-1 (Form 1065), box 14, code A (other than farming). Ministers and members of religious orders, see instructions for types of income to report on this line. See instructions for other income to report	**2**	
3	Combine lines 1a, 1b, and 2	**3**	
4	Multiply line 3 by 92.35% (0.9235). If less than $400, you don't owe self-employment tax; **don't** file this schedule unless you have an amount on line 1b . . . . ▶	**4**	
	Note: If line 4 is less than $400 due to Conservation Reserve Program payments on line 1b, see instructions.		
5	**Self-employment tax.** If the amount on line 4 is:		
	• $132,900 or less, multiply line 4 by 15.3% (0.153). Enter the result here and on **Schedule 2 (Form 1040 or 1040-SR), line 4,** or **Form 1040-NR, line 55.**		
	• More than $132,900, multiply line 4 by 2.9% (0.029). Then, add $16,479.60 to the result. Enter the total here and on **Schedule 2 (Form 1040 or 1040-SR), line 4,** or **Form 1040-NR, line 55** .	**5**	
6	**Deduction for one-half of self-employment tax.** Multiply line 5 by 50% (0.50). Enter the result here and on **Schedule 1 (Form 1040 or 1040-SR), line 14,** or **Form 1040-NR, line 27**	**6**	

For Paperwork Reduction Act Notice, see your tax return instructions.   Cat. No. 11358Z   **Schedule SE (Form 1040 or 1040-SR) 2019**

Schedule SE (Form 1040 or 1040-SR) 2019   Attachment Sequence No. **17**   Page **2**

Name of person with self-employment income (as shown on Form 1040, 1040-SR, or 1040-NR)	Social security number of person with **self-employment** income ▶	

Section B—Long Schedule SE

Part I   Self-Employment Tax

Note: If your only income subject to self-employment tax is **church employee income,** see instructions. Also see instructions for the definition of church employee income.

A   If you are a minister, member of a religious order, or Christian Science practitioner **and** you filed Form 4361, but you had $400 or more of **other** net earnings from self-employment, check here and continue with Part I . . . . ▶ ☐

1a	Net farm profit or (loss) from Schedule F, line 34, and farm partnerships, Schedule K-1 (Form 1065), box 14, code A. **Note:** Skip lines 1a and 1b if you use the farm optional method (see instructions)	**1a**	
b	If you received social security retirement or disability benefits, enter the amount of Conservation Reserve Program payments included on Schedule F, line 4b, or listed on Schedule K-1 (Form 1065), box 20, code AH	**1b**	( )
2	Net profit or (loss) from Schedule C, line 31; and Schedule K-1 (Form 1065), box 14, code A (other than farming). Ministers and members of religious orders, see instructions for types of income to report on this line. See instructions for other income to report. **Note:** Skip this line if you use the nonfarm optional method (see instructions)	**2**	
3	Combine lines 1a, 1b, and 2	**3**	
4a	If line 3 is more than zero, multiply line 3 by 92.35% (0.9235). Otherwise, enter amount from line 3 .	**4a**	
	Note: If line 4a is less than $400 due to Conservation Reserve Program payments on line 1b, see instructions.		
b	If you elect one or both of the optional methods, enter the total of lines 15 and 17 here . . .	**4b**	
c	Combine lines 4a and 4b. If less than $400, **stop;** you don't owe self-employment tax. **Exception:** If less than $400 and you had **church employee income,** enter -0- and continue . . . . . . ▶	**4c**	
5a	Enter your **church employee income** from Form W-2. See instructions for definition of church employee income	**5a**	
b	Multiply line 5a by 92.35% (0.9235). If less than $100, enter -0-	**5b**	
6	Add lines 4c and 5b	**6**	
7	Maximum amount of combined wages and self-employment earnings subject to social security tax or the 6.2% portion of the 7.65% railroad retirement (tier 1) tax for 2019	**7**	132,900
8a	Total social security wages and tips (total of boxes 3 and 7 on Form(s) W-2) and railroad retirement (tier 1) compensation. If $132,900 or more, skip lines 8b through 10, and go to line 11	**8a**	
b	Unreported tips subject to social security tax (from Form 4137, line 10) . .	**8b**	
c	Wages subject to social security tax (from Form 8919, line 10)	**8c**	
d	Add lines 8a, 8b, and 8c	**8d**	
9	Subtract line 8d from line 7. If zero or less, enter -0- here and on line 10 and go to line 11 . . . ▶	**9**	
10	Multiply the **smaller** of line 6 or line 9 by 12.4% (0.124)	**10**	
11	Multiply line 6 by 2.9% (0.029)	**11**	
12	**Self-employment tax.** Add lines 10 and 11. Enter here and on **Schedule 2 (Form 1040 or 1040-SR), line 4,** or **Form 1040-NR, line 55**	**12**	
13	**Deduction for one-half of self-employment tax.** Multiply line 12 by 50% (0.50). Enter the result here and on **Schedule 1 (Form 1040 or 1040-SR), line 14,** or **Form 1040-NR, line 27**	**13**	

Part II   Optional Methods To Figure Net Earnings (see instructions)

Farm Optional Method. You may use this method **only** if **(a)** your gross farm income[1] wasn't more than $8,160, **or (b)** your net farm profits[2] were less than $5,891.

14	Maximum income for optional methods	**14**	5,440
15	Enter the **smaller** of: two-thirds (2/3) of gross farm income[1] (not less than zero) or $5,440. Also include this amount on line 4b above	**15**	

Nonfarm Optional Method. You may use this method **only** if **(a)** your net nonfarm profits[3] were less than $5,891 and also less than 72.189% of your gross nonfarm income,[4] **and (b)** you had net earnings from self-employment of at least $400 in 2 of the prior 3 years. **Caution:** You may use this method no more than five times.

16	Subtract line 15 from line 14	**16**	
17	Enter the **smaller** of: two-thirds (2/3) of gross nonfarm income[4] (not less than zero) **or** the amount on line 16. Also include this amount on line 4b above	**17**	

[1] From Sch. F, line 9, and Sch. K-1 (Form 1065), box 14, code B.
[2] From Sch. F, line 34, and Sch. K-1 (Form 1065), box 14, code A—minus the amount you would have entered on line 1b had you not used the optional method.

[3] From Sch. C, line 31; and Sch. K-1 (Form 1065), box 14, code A.
[4] From Sch. C, line 7; and Sch. K-1 (Form 1065), box 14, code C.

Schedule SE (Form 1040 or 1040-SR) 2019

Form **8615**

Department of the Treasury
Internal Revenue Service (99)

**Tax for Certain Children Who
Have Unearned Income**

► **Attach to your Form 1040 or Form 1040-NR.**
► **Go to *www.irs.gov/Form8615* for instructions and the latest information.**

OMB No. 1545-0074

20**19**

Attachment
Sequence No. **33**

Name shown on return

Your social security number

Before you begin: If you must use the Schedule D Tax Worksheet or have income from farming or fishing, see the instructions. Also see **Pub. 929,** Tax Rules for Children and Dependents. It explains how to figure your tax using the **Schedule D Tax Worksheet** or **Schedule J** (Form 1040).

A Parent's name (first, initial, and last). **Caution:** See instructions before completing.

B Parent's social security number

Part I   **Net Unearned Income**

1	Enter your unearned income (see instructions)	**1**
2	If you **did not** itemize deductions on **Schedule A** (Form 1040 or Form 1040-NR), enter $2,200. Otherwise, see instructions	**2**
3	Subtract line 2 from line 1. If zero or less, **stop;** do not complete the rest of this form but **do** attach it to your return	**3**
4	Enter your **taxable income** from Form 1040, line 11b, or Form 1040-NR, line 41. If you file Form 2555, see the instructions	**4**
5	Enter the **smaller** of line 3 or line 4. If zero, **stop;** do not complete the rest of this form but **do** attach it to your return	**5**

Part II   **Tax**

6	Subtract line 5 from line 4	**6**	
7	Enter the tax on the amount on line 4 (see instructions). If the Qualified Dividends and Capital Gain Tax Worksheet, Schedule D Tax Worksheet, or Schedule J (Form 1040) is used to figure the tax, check here. If applicable, include this amount on your Form 1040, line 12a, or Form 1040-NR, line 42 (see instructions). If you file Form 2555, see the instructions . . . . ► ☐	**7**	

For Paperwork Reduction Act Notice, see your tax return instructions.   Cat. No. 64113U   Form **8615** (2019)

2019 Line 7 Tax Computation Worksheet

1.	Add Form 8615, line 6, and $2,600	1.	_____
2.	Enter the **smaller** of Form 8615, line 4, or line 1	2.	_____
3.	Enter the **smaller** of line 2 or the amount listed below for your filing status. • Single or married filing separately—$9,700. • Head of household—$13,850	3.	_____
4.	Multiply line 3 by 10% (0.10)	4.	_____
5.	Enter the **smaller** of line 2 or the amount listed below for your filing status. • Single or married filing separately—$39,475. • Head of household—$52,850	5.	_____
6.	Subtract line 3 from line 5. If zero or less, enter -0-	6.	_____
7.	Multiply line 6 by 12% (0.12)	7.	_____
8.	Enter the **smaller** of line 2 or $84,200	8.	_____
9.	Subtract line 5 from line 8. If zero or less, enter -0-	9.	_____
10.	Multiply line 9 by 22% (0.22)	10.	_____
11.	Add Form 8615, line 6, and $9,300	11.	_____
12.	Enter the **smaller** of Form 8615, line 4, or line 11	12.	_____
13.	Enter the **smaller** of line 12 or the amount listed below for your filing status. • Single or married filing separately—$160,725. • Head of household—$160,700	13.	_____
14.	Subtract line 8 from line 13. If zero or less, enter -0-	14.	_____
15.	Multiply line 14 by 24% (0.24)	15.	_____
16.	Enter the **smaller** of line 12 or $204,100	16.	_____
17.	Subtract line 13 from line 16. If zero or less, enter -0-	17.	_____
18.	Multiply line 17 by 32% (0.32)	18.	_____
19.	Add Form 8615, line 6, and $12,750	19.	_____
20.	Enter the **smaller** of Form 8615, line 4, or line 19	20.	_____
21.	Enter the **smaller** of line 20 or the amount listed below for your filing status. • Single or head of household—$510,300. • Married filing separately—$306,175	21.	_____
22.	Subtract line 16 from line 21. If zero or less, enter -0-	22.	_____
23.	Multiply line 22 by 35% (0.35)	23.	_____
24.	Subtract line 21 from Form 8615, line 4. If zero or less, enter -0-	24.	_____
25.	Multiply line 24 by 37% (0.37)	25.	_____
26.	Add lines 4, 7, 10, 15, 18, 23, and 25. **Stop.** If the Qualified Dividends and Capital Gain Tax Worksheet, Schedule D Tax Worksheet, or Schedule J (Form 1040 or 1040-SR) is used to figure your tax, see the instructions, earlier. Otherwise, enter the result here and on Form 8615, line 7	26.	_____

Form **8949**

Department of the Treasury
Internal Revenue Service

Sales and Other Dispositions of Capital Assets

▶ Go to *www.irs.gov/Form8949* for instructions and the latest information.
▶ File with your Schedule D to list your transactions for lines 1b, 2, 3, 8b, 9, and 10 of Schedule D.

OMB No. 1545-0074

2019

Attachment
Sequence No. **12A**

Name(s) shown on return

Social security number or taxpayer identification number

Before you check Box A, B, or C below, see whether you received any Form(s) 1099-B or substitute statement(s) from your broker. A substitute statement will have the same information as Form 1099-B. Either will show whether your basis (usually your cost) was reported to the IRS by your broker and may even tell you which box to check.

Part I   **Short-Term.** Transactions involving capital assets you held 1 year or less are generally short-term (see instructions). For long-term transactions, see page 2.

Note: You may aggregate all short-term transactions reported on Form(s) 1099-B showing basis was reported to the IRS and for which no adjustments or codes are required. Enter the totals directly on Schedule D, line 1a; you aren't required to report these transactions on Form 8949 (see instructions).

You *must* check Box A, B, *or* C below. Check only one box. If more than one box applies for your short-term transactions, complete a separate Form 8949, page 1, for each applicable box. If you have more short-term transactions than will fit on this page for one or more of the boxes, complete as many forms with the same box checked as you need.

- ☐ **(A)** Short-term transactions reported on Form(s) 1099-B showing basis was reported to the IRS (see **Note** above)
- ☐ **(B)** Short-term transactions reported on Form(s) 1099-B showing basis **wasn't** reported to the IRS
- ☐ **(C)** Short-term transactions not reported to you on Form 1099-B

1	(a) Description of property (Example: 100 sh. XYZ Co.)	(b) Date acquired (Mo., day, yr.)	(c) Date sold or disposed of (Mo., day, yr.)	(d) Proceeds (sales price) (see instructions)	(e) Cost or other basis. See the **Note** below and see *Column (e)* in the separate instructions	Adjustment, if any, to gain or loss. If you enter an amount in column (g), enter a code in column (f). See the separate instructions.		(h) Gain or (loss). Subtract column (e) from column (d) and combine the result with column (g)
						(f) Code(s) from instructions	(g) Amount of adjustment	

2 Totals. Add the amounts in columns (d), (e), (g), and (h) (subtract negative amounts). Enter each total here and include on your Schedule D, **line 1b** (if **Box A** above is checked), **line 2** (if **Box B** above is checked), or **line 3** (if **Box C** above is checked) ▶

Note: If you checked Box A above but the basis reported to the IRS was incorrect, enter in column (e) the basis as reported to the IRS, and enter an adjustment in column (g) to correct the basis. See *Column (g)* in the separate instructions for how to figure the amount of the adjustment.

For Paperwork Reduction Act Notice, see your tax return instructions.   Cat. No. 37768Z   Form **8949** (2019)

Form 8949 (2019)   Attachment Sequence No. **12A**   Page **2**

Name(s) shown on return. Name and SSN or taxpayer identification no. not required if shown on other side	**Social security number or taxpayer identification number**

Before you check Box D, E, or F below, see whether you received any Form(s) 1099-B or substitute statement(s) from your broker. A substitute statement will have the same information as Form 1099-B. Either will show whether your basis (usually your cost) was reported to the IRS by your broker and may even tell you which box to check.

Part II **Long-Term.** Transactions involving capital assets you held more than 1 year are generally long-term (see instructions). For short-term transactions, see page 1.

    Note: You may aggregate all long-term transactions reported on Form(s) 1099-B showing basis was reported to the IRS and for which no adjustments or codes are required. Enter the totals directly on Schedule D, line 8a; you aren't required to report these transactions on Form 8949 (see instructions).

You *must* check Box D, E, *or* F below. Check only one box. If more than one box applies for your long-term transactions, complete a separate Form 8949, page 2, for each applicable box. If you have more long-term transactions than will fit on this page for one or more of the boxes, complete as many forms with the same box checked as you need.

- ☐ **(D)** Long-term transactions reported on Form(s) 1099-B showing basis was reported to the IRS (see **Note** above)
- ☐ **(E)** Long-term transactions reported on Form(s) 1099-B showing basis **wasn't** reported to the IRS
- ☐ **(F)** Long-term transactions not reported to you on Form 1099-B

1					Adjustment, if any, to gain or loss. If you enter an amount in column (g), enter a code in column (f). **See the separate instructions.**		
(a) Description of property (Example: 100 sh. XYZ Co.)	**(b)** Date acquired (Mo., day, yr.)	**(c)** Date sold or disposed of (Mo., day, yr.)	**(d)** Proceeds (sales price) (see instructions)	**(e)** Cost or other basis. See the **Note** below and see *Column (e)* in the separate instructions	**(f)** Code(s) from instructions	**(g)** Amount of adjustment	**(h)** Gain or (loss). Subtract column (e) from column (d) and combine the result with column (g)
2 Totals. Add the amounts in columns (d), (e), (g), and (h) (subtract negative amounts). Enter each total here and include on your Schedule D, **line 8b** (if **Box D** above is checked), **line 9** (if **Box E** above is checked), or **line 10** (if **Box F** above is checked) ▶							

Note: If you checked Box D above but the basis reported to the IRS was incorrect, enter in column (e) the basis as reported to the IRS, and enter an adjustment in column (g) to correct the basis. See *Column (g)* in the separate instructions for how to figure the amount of the adjustment.

Form **8949** (2019)

Form **8959**		
Department of the Treasury Internal Revenue Service		

Additional Medicare Tax

▶ **If any line does not apply to you, leave it blank. See separate instructions.**

▶ **Attach to Form 1040, 1040-SR, 1040-NR, 1040-PR, or 1040-SS.**

▶ Go to *www.irs.gov/Form8959* for instructions and the latest information.

OMB No. 1545-0074

2019

Attachment
Sequence No. **71**

Name(s) shown on return

Your social security number

Part I   Additional Medicare Tax on Medicare Wages

1	Medicare wages and tips from Form W-2, box 5. If you have more than one Form W-2, enter the total of the amounts from box 5	1	
2	Unreported tips from Form 4137, line 6	2	
3	Wages from Form 8919, line 6	3	
4	Add lines 1 through 3	4	
5	Enter the following amount for your filing status: Married filing jointly . . . . $250,000 Married filing separately . . . . $125,000 Single, Head of household, or Qualifying widow(er) $200,000	5	
6	Subtract line 5 from line 4. If zero or less, enter -0-	6	
7	Additional Medicare Tax on Medicare wages. Multiply line 6 by 0.9% (0.009). Enter here and go to Part II	7	

Part II   Additional Medicare Tax on Self-Employment Income

8	Self-employment income from Schedule SE (Form 1040 or 1040-SR), Section A, line 4, or Section B, line 6. If you had a loss, enter -0- (Form 1040-PR or 1040-SS filers, see instructions.)	8	
9	Enter the following amount for your filing status: Married filing jointly . . . . $250,000 Married filing separately . . . . $125,000 Single, Head of household, or Qualifying widow(er) $200,000	9	
10	Enter the amount from line 4	10	
11	Subtract line 10 from line 9. If zero or less, enter -0-	11	
12	Subtract line 11 from line 8. If zero or less, enter -0-	12	
13	Additional Medicare Tax on self-employment income. Multiply line 12 by 0.9% (0.009). Enter here and go to Part III	13	

Part III   Additional Medicare Tax on Railroad Retirement Tax Act (RRTA) Compensation

14	Railroad retirement (RRTA) compensation and tips from Form(s) W-2, box 14 (see instructions)	14	
15	Enter the following amount for your filing status: Married filing jointly . . . . $250,000 Married filing separately . . . . $125,000 Single, Head of household, or Qualifying widow(er) $200,000	15	
16	Subtract line 15 from line 14. If zero or less, enter -0-	16	
17	Additional Medicare Tax on railroad retirement (RRTA) compensation. Multiply line 16 by 0.9% (0.009). Enter here and go to Part IV	17	

Part IV   Total Additional Medicare Tax

18	Add lines 7, 13, and 17. Also include this amount on Schedule 2 (Form 1040 or 1040-SR), line 8 (check box a) (Form 1040-NR, 1040-PR, or 1040-SS filers, see instructions), and go to Part V	18	

Part V   Withholding Reconciliation

19	Medicare tax withheld from Form W-2, box 6. If you have more than one Form W-2, enter the total of the amounts from box 6	19	
20	Enter the amount from line 1	20	
21	Multiply line 20 by 1.45% (0.0145). This is your regular Medicare tax withholding on Medicare wages	21	
22	Subtract line 21 from line 19. If zero or less, enter -0-. This is your Additional Medicare Tax withholding on Medicare wages	22	
23	Additional Medicare Tax withholding on railroad retirement (RRTA) compensation from Form W-2, box 14 (see instructions)	23	
24	**Total Additional Medicare Tax withholding.** Add lines 22 and 23. Also include this amount with federal income tax withholding on Form 1040 or 1040-SR, line 17 (Form 1040-NR, 1040-PR, or 1040-SS filers, see instructions)	24	

For Paperwork Reduction Act Notice, see your tax return instructions.   Cat. No. 59475X   Form **8959** (2019)

DRAFT AS OF August 14, 2019 DO NOT FILE

Form **8960**

Department of the Treasury
Internal Revenue Service (99)

Net Investment Income Tax—
Individuals, Estates, and Trusts
▶ Attach to your tax return.
▶ **Go to** *www.irs.gov/Form8960* **for instructions and the latest information.**

OMB No. 1545-2227

2019

Attachment
Sequence No. **72**

Name(s) shown on your tax return

Your social security number or EIN

Part I	**Investment Income**	☐ Section 6013(g) election (see instructions)
		☐ Section 6013(h) election (see instructions)
		☐ Regulations section 1.1411-10(g) election (see instructions)

1	Taxable interest (see instructions)	**1**
2	Ordinary dividends (see instructions)	**2**
3	Annuities (see instructions)	**3**
4a	Rental real estate, royalties, partnerships, S corporations, trusts, etc. (see instructions) **4a**	
b	Adjustment for net income or loss derived in the ordinary course of a non-section 1411 trade or business (see instructions) **4b**	
c	Combine lines 4a and 4b	**4c**
5a	Net gain or loss from disposition of property (see instructions) **5a**	
b	Net gain or loss from disposition of property that is not subject to net investment income tax (see instructions) **5b**	
c	Adjustment from disposition of partnership interest or S corporation stock (see instructions) **5c**	
d	Combine lines 5a through 5c	**5d**
6	Adjustments to investment income for certain CFCs and PFICs (see instructions)	**6**
7	Other modifications to investment income (see instructions)	**7**
8	Total investment income. Combine lines 1, 2, 3, 4c, 5d, 6, and 7	**8**

Part II	**Investment Expenses Allocable to Investment Income and Modifications**

9a	Investment interest expenses (see instructions) **9a**	
b	State, local, and foreign income tax (see instructions) **9b**	
c	Miscellaneous investment expenses (see instructions) **9c**	
d	Add lines 9a, 9b, and 9c	**9d**
10	Additional modifications (see instructions)	**10**
11	Total deductions and modifications. Add lines 9d and 10	**11**

Part III	**Tax Computation**

12	Net investment income. Subtract Part II, line 11, from Part I, line 8. Individuals, complete lines 13–17. Estates and trusts, complete lines 18a–21. If zero or less, enter -0-	**12**
	Individuals:	
13	Modified adjusted gross income (see instructions) **13**	
14	Threshold based on filing status (see instructions) **14**	
15	Subtract line 14 from line 13. If zero or less, enter -0- **15**	
16	Enter the smaller of line 12 or line 15	**16**
17	Net investment income tax for individuals. Multiply line 16 by 3.8% (0.038). **Enter here and include on your tax return** (see instructions)	**17**
	Estates and Trusts:	
18a	Net investment income (line 12 above) **18a**	
b	Deductions for distributions of net investment income and deductions under section 642(c) (see instructions) **18b**	
c	Undistributed net investment income. Subtract line 18b from 18a (see instructions). If zero or less, enter -0- **18c**	
19a	Adjusted gross income (see instructions) **19a**	
b	Highest tax bracket for estates and trusts for the year (see instructions) . . **19b**	
c	Subtract line 19b from line 19a. If zero or less, enter -0- **19c**	
20	Enter the smaller of line 18c or line 19c	**20**
21	Net investment income tax for estates and trusts. Multiply line 20 by 3.8% (0.038). **Enter here and include on your tax return** (see instructions)	**21**

For Paperwork Reduction Act Notice, see your tax return instructions.   Cat. No. 59474M   Form **8960** (2019)

Student Name _____

Class/Section _____

Date _____

KEY NUMBER TAX RETURN SUMMARY

CHAPTER 6

Comprehensive Problem 1

Form 8615, Net Unearned Income (Line 3) _____

Form 8615, Taxable Earned Income (Line 6) _____

Form 8615, Tax (Line 7) _____

Form 1040, Taxable Income (Line 11b) _____

Form 1040, Amount You Owe (line 23) _____

Comprehensive Problem 2A

Schedule C, Net Profit or (Loss) (Line 31) _____

Schedule SE, Self-Employment Tax (Line 5) _____

Schedule H, Household Employment Taxes (Line 26) _____

Form 1040, Taxable Income (Line 11b) _____

Form 1040, Total Tax (Line 16) _____

Comprehensive Problem 2B

Total Income (Line 7b) _____

Adjusted Gross Income (Line 8b) _____

Itemized Deductions (Line 9) _____

Total Tax (Line 16) _____

Amount Overpaid (Line 20) _____

CHAPTER 7

Tax Credits

After completing this chapter, you should be able to:

LO 7.1 Calculate the child tax credit.

LO 7.2 Determine the earned income credit (EIC).

LO 7.3 Compute the child and dependent care credit for an individual taxpayer.

LO 7.4 Calculate the premium tax credit available under the Affordable Care Act.

LO 7.5 Apply the special rules applicable to the American Opportunity tax credit and lifetime learning credit.

LO 7.6 Compute the foreign income exclusion and tax credit.

LO 7.7 Determine the proper use and calculation of the adoption credit.

LO 7.8 Recognize the basic individual credits for energy efficiency.

LO 7.9 Calculate the low-income Retirement Plan Contribution Credit.

OVERVIEW

This chapter covers the most common tax credits. Credits differ from deductions. A credit is a direct reduction in tax liability instead of a deduction from income. Credits are used because they target tax relief to certain groups of taxpayers. Because of the progressive rate structure of the income tax, a deduction provides greater benefit to higher-income taxpayers, while a tax credit provides equal benefit, regardless of the taxpayer's income level. Many credits exist in the tax law that are not covered here, such as the credit for research and development, the Work Opportunity Tax Credit, and the credit for the elderly and disabled.

A deduction reduces taxable income by the amount of the deduction and thus results in a tax savings equal to the deduction multiplied by the tax rate. A credit is a dollar-for-dollar reduction of the taxpayer's tax liability. If a taxpayer has a choice between a credit or a deduction of equal amounts, generally the credit will result in greater tax savings.

EXAMPLE   Gordon is a single taxpayer. His 2019 taxable income is $60,000 placing him in the 22 percent tax bracket for ordinary income. His income tax liability is $9,064. Not included in the $60,000 of taxable income is a choice between a $1,000 deduction or a $1,000 credit.

	Deduction	Credit
Taxable income	$60,000	$60,000
Deduction	(1,000)	n/a
Revised taxable income	59,000	60,000
Tax on revised income	8,844	9,064
Tax credit	n/a	(1,000)
Tax after credits	8,844	8,064
Original tax	9,064	9,064
Tax savings	$ 220	$ 1,000

Gordon saves $1,000 (a dollar-for-dollar reduction in tax liability) with the credit. He saves on $220 ($1,000 × 22% tax rate) for the deduction. ◆

Learning Objective 7.1

7-1 CHILD TAX CREDIT

Calculate the child tax credit.

The child tax credit permits individual taxpayers to take a tax credit based on the number of their dependent children. The child tax credit comes in two parts, the nonrefundable child tax credit and the refundable additional child tax credit. Most tax credits are limited to the amount of total tax liability that a taxpayer has and thus are "nonrefundable." Certain credits allow taxpayers to claim the credit even when the amount of the credit exceeds their tax liability – these are known as refundable credits since they result in a "refund" of taxes that were never actually paid by the taxpayer.

EXAMPLE   Sandy is a taxpayer who files as head of household, with taxable income of $16,125 and a tax liability of $1,658 before any tax credits. Sandy has total tax payments (including withholding) of $2,200. Sandy has a daughter and is eligible for a child tax credit of $2,000. Sandy's refund is calculated as follows if the credit is refundable versus nonrefundable:

	Nonrefundable	Refundable
Total tax before credits	$1,658	$1,658
Tax credit	1,658	(2,000)
Tax after credits	0	(342)
Tax payments	(2,200)	(2,200)
Total refund	$(2,200)	$(2,542)

The refundable credit increases Sandy's refund to an amount in excess of her taxes paid. ◆

The TCJA made three significant, but temporary, changes to the child tax credit that apply in 2019: (1) increased the credit per child to $2,000, (2) increased the threshold for which the phase-out starts, and (3) increased the refundable amount of the credit for taxpayers whose credit is limited by their pre-credit tax liability. In addition, the TCJA added a new qualifying dependent credit of $500 for certain dependents.

To qualify for the child tax credit, the child must be under age 17, a U.S. citizen or U.S. resident alien, claimed as a dependent on the taxpayer's return, and meet the definition of "qualifying child" as discussed in Chapter 1. Thus the child must meet the six tests outlined in LO 1.6: (1) relationship test, (2) domicile test, (3) age test (except in the case of the child tax credit, the child must be under age 17), (4) joint return test, (5) citizenship test, and (6) self-support test. All qualifying children must have a Social Security number at the time of filing.

The maximum credit is $2,000 per qualifying child; however, the available credit begins phasing out when AGI reaches $400,000 for joint filers and $200,000 for all other taxpayers. The credit is phased out by $50 for each $1,000 (or part thereof) of AGI above the threshold amounts. Since the maximum credit available depends on the number of qualifying children, the income level at which the credit is fully phased out also depends on the number of children qualifying for the credit. The phase-out thresholds for the child tax credit are currently not adjusted for cost-of-living increases.

EXAMPLE Donna and Chris Howser are married and file a joint tax return. They have two children, ages 5 and 7, that are qualifying children under the dependency rules. All members of the family are U.S. citizens with Social Security numbers. In 2019, their AGI was $120,006. In 2019, both children qualify for the child tax credit of $2,000; thus, the maximum credit is $4,000. Because the phase-out for married filing jointly taxpayers in 2019 starts at $400,000, the Howsers are eligible for the maximum credit of $4,000. ◆

EXAMPLE Fiona and Kris Everest are married and file a joint return. They have one child aged 13. Each member of the Everest family has a Social Security number and their 2019 AGI is $409,800. The maximum child tax credit in 2019 is $2,000 per child; however, the Everest's AGI exceeds the $400,000 threshold. The phase-out amount is $500.

$409,100 − $400,000 = $9,100
$9,100/$1,000 = 9.1 rounded to 10
10 × $50 = $500

The Everest's child tax credit is $1,500 ($2,000 − $500). ◆

Since a portion of the child tax credit is nonrefundable, that portion is limited to the amount of tax liability before taking the child tax credit. Because taxpayers may be eligible for other tax credits that also reduce tax liability, the tax law prescribes a "pecking order" to prevent taxpayers from claiming more than one nonrefundable tax credit and creating a refundable credit.

EXAMPLE Eugene has a tax liability of $2,200 before any tax credits. Eugene has determined he is eligible for an education credit of $400 and a child tax credit of $2,000. Because his two nonrefundable credits exceed his tax liability, Eugene will take a $400 education credit and his nonrefundable child tax credit will be limited to $1,800 ($2,200 − $400). ◆

The refundable portion of the child tax credit is the amount of child tax credit that was limited by the taxpayer's tax liability.

EXAMPLE Eugene in the previous example, was eligible for a total child tax credit of $2,000; however, he could only take a credit of $1,800 due to the tax liability limitation. The $200 unclaimed child tax credit *may* be refundable.

If the taxpayer has fewer than three children that are eligible for the child tax credit, the refundable portion of the child tax credit is subject to two additional limitations. The first limitation is that the additional child tax credit cannot exceed $1,400 per child. The second limitation is that the refundable child tax credit cannot exceed 15 percent of the taxpayer's earned income less $2,500. The lower of these two amounts will apply.

EXAMPLE In 2019, Mike and Laura, married filing jointly taxpayers, have two qualifying children, AGI of $72,000 (all earned income) and tax liability before any credits of $1,043. As a result, their child tax credit of $4,000 is limited to $1,043. Mike and Laura can claim the refundable portion of child tax credit of $2,800; the lesser of the unclaimed child tax credit $2,957 ($4,000 − $1,043) or 15 percent of earned income less $2,500 [($72,000 − $2,500) × 15% = $10,425] limited to $2,800 ($1,400 per qualifying child). ◆

For taxpayers with three or more qualifying children, the child tax credit amount in excess of tax liability is subject to limitations. The same overall $1,400 limit per child applies. The refundable child tax credit is also limited by the greater of (1) 15 percent of earned income over $2,500 or (2) the amount of Social Security and Medicare taxes paid up to the unclaimed child tax credit. For purposes of the refundable child tax credit, Social Security and Medicare taxes are the amounts withheld for the employee and 50 percent of self-employment taxes.

EXAMPLE   Molly and Sam are married, file a joint tax return, have five qualifying children and earned income of $6,000. The children are qualifying children for purposes of the child tax credit, but do not qualify under the earned income tax credit. Molly and Sam had $459 of Social Security and Medicare taxes withheld by their employers. Their pre-credit tax liability is $0. Because their pre-credit tax liability is $0, Molly and Sam are not eligible for the $10,000 ($2,000 × 5 children) child tax credit. The refundable portion of the child tax credit is $525 which starts at $10,000 but is first limited to $7,000 ($1,400 × 5) and then further limited to the greater of $459 or $525 [($6,000 − $2,500) × 15%]. ♦

No form is required for the nonrefundable child tax credit. It is simply claimed on Line 13a of Form 1040. The child tax credit can be computed using the Child Tax Credit Worksheet included as part of Form 1040 Instructions and included on Pages 7-6 and 7-7. Fortunately, tax software is proficient at calculating the child tax credit. The refundable child tax credit is available to taxpayers whose child tax credit was limited by their tax liability and requires completion of Form 8812 (see Page 7-8). The amount from Form 8812 is carried over to Form 1040 Line 18b.

The $400,000 and $200,000 income thresholds are not adjusted for inflation while the $1,400 limit on the refundable portion is adjusted for inflation. Both of these provisions are scheduled to expire after 2025.

The child tax credit also includes a $500 "other dependent credit" for each qualifying dependent other than qualifying children under the child tax credit. For example, a dependent parent or dependent child age 17 or older can still be eligible dependents for the other dependent credit. The qualifying relative test for purposes of the other dependent credit requires the individual must be a U.S. citizen, a U.S. national, or a U.S. resident in order to be eligible for the credit. A Social Security number is not required for the other dependent credit and the credit is nonrefundable. The other dependent credit is reported in combination with the child tax credit on Line 13a of Form 1040.

EXAMPLE   Alex is a single taxpayer with a 15-year-old child. Alex also takes care of her elderly mother who qualifies as a dependent. Alex is eligible for a $2,000 child tax credit and an additional $500 other dependent credit for her mother. ♦

EXAMPLE   Marty is a single taxpayer with a dependent 21-year-old child who is a full-time student. Marty also takes care of his elderly mother who qualifies as a dependent. Marty is eligible for an additional $1,000 other dependent tax credit for her child and her mother. ♦

A taxpayer who erroneously claims the child tax credit due to reckless or intentional disregard of rules or regulations is ineligible to claim the credit for a period of two tax years. If the IRS determines the claim for the credit was fraudulent, the ineligibility window is extended to ten years.

If the IRS rejects a child tax credit for any reason other than a math or clerical error, the taxpayer must complete a Form 8862 in a year after a rejection. Form 8862 is also used for claiming an earned income credit or American Opportunities credit after rejection. Tax preparers that prepare returns on which the child tax credit is claimed will be required to complete Form 8867, a due diligence checklist that was previously used for only the earned income credit.

The IRS will not issue refunds for any tax returns that claim a child tax credit (or earned income credit) until February 15 of the year following the tax year. This tax provision is intended to provide the IRS with additional time to review refund claims that stem from refundable child tax credit claims.

The child tax credit is handled by ProConnect in an almost seamless fashion. By entering the dependent birthdate and status (e.g., full time student) the software will automatically compute the child tax credit, other dependent credit, and additional child credit. A number of dropdown boxes are available under the Dependent entry screen that permit overrides and other options for these credits. You will not find any child tax credit or related information under the Credits input.

intuit
proconnect.
TIP

Self-Study Problem 7.1   *See Appendix E for Solutions to Self-Study Problems*

a. Jose and Jane are married and file a joint tax return claiming their three children, ages 4, 5, and 18, as dependents. Their AGI for 2019 is $125,400 and their pre-credit tax liability is $13,937. They are not claiming any other tax credits in 2019. Complete the Child Tax Credit Worksheet Parts 1 and 2 on Pages 7-6 and 7-7 to determine Jose and Jane's child tax credit for 2019.

$_____

b. Herb and Carol are married and file a joint tax return claiming their three children, ages 4, 5, and 18, as dependents. Their AGI for 2019 is $405,600 and their pre-credit tax liability is about $84,000. What is Herb and Carol's child tax credit for 2019?

$_____

c. Marie and Pierre Curry are married and file a joint tax return claiming their three children, ages 4, 5, and 16, as dependents. Their AGI for 2019 is $36,400 (all wage income) and their pre-credit tax liability is $383. Marie and Pierre's employers withheld $2,785 in Social Security and Medicare taxes in 2019. They are not claiming any other tax credits. Complete the Child Tax Credit Worksheet Parts 1 and 2 on Pages 7-6 and 7-7 and Form 8812 on Page 7-8 to determine Marie and Pierre's child tax credit and additional child tax credit, if any, for 2019.

7-2 EARNED INCOME CREDIT

7.2 Learning Objective

Determine the earned income credit (EIC).

The earned income credit (EIC or sometimes EITC) is available to qualifying individuals with earned income and AGI below certain levels. The earned income credit is meant to assist the working poor by reducing their tax burden and to supplement wage income through a refundable credit when earnings are less than the taxpayer's maximum income for their filing status. Qualifying taxpayers can receive a refundable EIC even in situations when they have no filing requirement, owe no tax, and had no income tax withheld. Similar to the refundable child tax credit, the refundable EIC can in effect produce a "negative" income tax.

Proper calculation of the EIC requires a taxpayer to answer three important questions:

(1) Does the taxpayer qualify for the EIC?
(2) Does the taxpayer have a qualifying child?
(3) What is the amount of the EIC?

7-2a **Does the Taxpayer Qualify?**

There are seven rules that all taxpayers must meet in order to claim the EIC and the taxpayer must meet *all seven* rules. Failure to meet just one precludes the taxpayer from claiming the EIC. The seven rules fall into the following categories:

1. AGI limit–AGI limits are indexed for inflation and can change each year. In addition, the AGI limits vary based on filing status and number of qualifying children. The EIC phases out for taxpayers with income over the limits. For 2019, the limits are:

	Other than joint filers		Joint filers	
Qualifying Children	Phase-out Begins	Phase-out Ends	Phase-out Begins	Phase-out Ends
None	$ 8,650	$15,570	$14,450	$21,370
1	19,030	41,094	24,820	46,884
2	19,030	46,703	24,820	52,493
3 or more	19,030	50,162	24,820	55,952

   The phase-out percentages vary; however, only the IRS EIC Tables (Appendix B) may be used to calculate the EIC amount.
2. Social Security numbers – The taxpayer (and spouse, if filing jointly) plus any qualifying children, must all have valid Social Security numbers.
3. Married filing separate not allowed.
4. U.S. citizenship or resident alien status is required for the entire tax year.
5. Foreign income exclusion not allowed – tax law provides for certain taxpayers to exclude income earned overseas (reported on Form 2555 or Form 2555-EZ). The foreign income exclusion is beyond the scope of this textbook.
6. Investment income limit – generating a certain amount of "disqualified" income ($3,600 in 2019) precludes claiming the EIC. Disqualified income includes most typical forms of investment income such as interest, dividends, net income from rents and royalties and most forms of capital gains.
7. Earned income requirement – Since the design of the EIC is to assist the working poor, an obvious requirement is that the taxpayer (or spouse, if filing jointly) have earned income. For self-employed taxpayers, earned income includes income reported on Schedule SE. The earned income limits for 2019 are:

	Other than joint filers		Joint filers	
Qualifying Children	Minimum Earned Income	Maximum Earned Income	Minimum Earned Income	Maximum Earned Income
None	$1	$15,570	$1	$21,370
1	1	41,094	1	46,884
2	1	46,703	1	52,493
3 or more	1	50,162	1	55,952

EXAMPLE   Doug is married but files separately in 2019. Married filing separately taxpayers do not qualify for the EIC. ♦

EXAMPLE   In 2019, Jane has income of $7,000, is single, has a valid Social Security number, and is not a qualifying child of another taxpayer. Her income includes $4,500 of interest on a corporate bond. Jane is not eligible for the EIC because her investment income exceeds $3,600. ♦

Self-Study Problem 7.1, Parts a and c

2019 Child Tax Credit and Credit for Other Dependents
Worksheet—Line 13a

Keep for Your Records

1. To be a qualifying child for the child tax credit, the child must be your dependent, **under age 17** at the end of 2019, and meet all the conditions in Steps 1 through 3 under *Who Qualifies as Your Dependent*. Make sure you checked the "child tax credit" box in column (4) of the *Dependents* section on Form 1040 or 1040-SR for each qualifying child.

2. If you don't have a qualifying child, you can't claim the child tax credit; but you may be able to claim the credit for other dependents for that child. See Step 3 under *Who Qualifies as Your Dependent*.

3. To see if your qualifying relative qualifies you to take the credit for other dependents, see Step 5 under *Who Qualifies as Your Dependent*.

4. Be sure to see *Social security number* under *Who Qualifies as Your Dependent*.

5. Do **not** use this worksheet, but use Pub. 972 instead, if:

   a. You are claiming the adoption credit, mortgage interest credit, District of Columbia first-time homebuyer credit, or residential energy efficient property credit*;

   b. You are excluding income from Puerto Rico; or

   c. You are filing Form 2555 or 4563.

   * If applicable.

Part 1

1. Number of qualifying children under age 17 with the required social security number: _____ × $2,000. Enter the result. | **1** | |

2. Number of other dependents, including qualifying children without the required social security number: _____ × $500. Enter the result. | **2** | |

   Caution. Don't include yourself, your spouse, or anyone who is not a U.S. citizen, U.S. national, or U.S. resident alien. Also, don't include anyone you included on line 1.

3. Add lines 1 and 2. | **3** | |

4. Enter the amount from Form 1040 or 1040-SR, line 8b. | **4** | |

5. Enter the amount shown below for your filing status.

   • Married filing jointly — $400,000

   • All other filing statuses — $200,000 | **5** | |

6. Is the amount on line 4 more than the amount on line 5?

   ☐ **No.** Leave line 6 blank. Enter -0- on line 7, and go to line 8.

   ☐ **Yes.** Subtract line 5 from line 4.
   If the result isn't a multiple of $1,000, increase it to the next multiple of $1,000. For example, increase $425 to $1,000, increase $1,025 to $2,000, etc. | **6** | |

7. Multiply the amount on line 6 by 5% (0.05). Enter the result. | **7** | |

8. Is the amount on line 3 more than the amount on line 7?

   ☐ **No.** (STOP)
   You can't take the child tax credit on Form 1040 or 1040-SR, line 13a. You also can't take the additional child tax credit on Form 1040 or 1040-SR, line 18b. Complete the rest of your Form 1040 or 1040-SR.

   ☐ **Yes.** Subtract line 7 from line 3. Enter the result. *Go to Part 2.* | **8** | |

Self-Study Problem 7.1, Parts a and c

**2019 Child Tax Credit and Credit for Other Dependents
Worksheet**—*Continued*

Keep for Your Records

Before you begin Part 2: √ Figure the amount of any credits you are claiming on Schedule 3; Form 5695, Part II*;
Form 8910; Form 8936; or Schedule R.

Part 2

9. Enter the amount from Form 1040 or 1040-SR, line 12b. .... **9** _____

10. Add any amounts from:

   Schedule 3, line 1 _____

   Schedule 3, line 2 + _____

   Schedule 3, line 3 + _____

   Schedule 3, line 4 + _____

   Form 5695, line 30* + _____

   Form 8910, line 15* + _____

   Form 8936, line 23 + _____

   Schedule R, line 22 + _____

   Enter the total. **10** _____

11. Are the amounts on lines 9 and 10 the same?

   ☐ **Yes.** (STOP)
   You can't take this credit because there is no tax to reduce.
   However, you may be able to take the **additional child tax
   credit** if line 1 is more than zero. See the **TIP** below.

   ☐ **No.** Subtract line 10 from line 9. .... **11** _____

12. Is the amount on line 8 more than the amount on line 11?

   ☐ **Yes.** Enter the amount from line 11.
   Also, you may be able to take the
   additional child tax credit if line 1
   is more than zero. See the **TIP** below.

   ☐ **No.** Enter the amount from line 8.

   } **This is your child tax
   credit and credit for
   other dependents.**

   12 _____

   Enter this amount on
   Form 1040 or 1040-SR,
   line 13a.

TIP *You may be able to take the **additional child tax credit**
on Form 1040 or 1040-SR, line 18b, if you answered "Yes" on
line 11 **or** line 12 above.*

   ● *First, complete your Form 1040 or 1040-SR through line
   18a (also complete Schedule 3, line 11).*

   ● *Then, use Schedule 8812 to figure any additional child tax
   credit.*

CAUTION *If your child tax credit or additional child tax credit for a year after
2015 was reduced or disallowed, see Form 8862, who must file to
find out if you must file Form 8862 to take the credit for 2019.*

*If applicable.

Self-Study Problem 7.1, part c

SCHEDULE 8812
(Form 1040 or 1040-SR)

Department of the Treasury
Internal Revenue Service (99)

Additional Child Tax Credit

▶ Attach to Form 1040, 1040-SR, or 1040-NR.
▶ Go to *www.irs.gov/Schedule8812* for instructions and the latest information.

OMB No. 1545-0074

2019

Attachment
Sequence No. **47**

Name(s) shown on return

Your social security number

Part I	**All Filers**	

Caution: If you file Form 2555, **stop here;** you cannot claim the additional child tax credit.

1	If you are required to use the worksheet in Pub. 972, enter the amount from line 10 of the Child Tax Credit and Credit for Other Dependents Worksheet in the publication. Otherwise: **1040 and 1040-SR filers:** Enter the amount from line 8 of your Child Tax Credit and Credit for Other Dependents Worksheet (see the instructions for Forms 1040 and 1040-SR, line 13a). **1040-NR filers:** Enter the amount from line 8 of your Child Tax Credit and Credit for Other Dependents Worksheet (see the instructions for Form 1040-NR, line 49).	1	
2	Enter the amount from Form 1040, line 13a; Form 1040-SR, line 13a; or Form 1040-NR, line 49	2	
3	Subtract line 2 from line 1. If zero, **stop here;** you cannot claim this credit	3	
4	Number of qualifying children under 17 with the required social security number: _____ x $1,400. Enter the result. If zero, **stop here;** you cannot claim this credit **TIP:** The number of children you use for this line is the same as the number of children you used for line 1 of the Child Tax Credit and Credit for Other Dependents Worksheet.	4	
5	Enter the **smaller** of line 3 or line 4	5	
6a	Earned income (see instructions)	6a	
b	Nontaxable combat pay (see instructions) 6b		
7	Is the amount on line 6a more than $2,500? ☐ **No.** Leave line 7 blank and enter -0- on line 8. ☐ **Yes.** Subtract $2,500 from the amount on line 6a. Enter the result	7	
8	Multiply the amount on line 7 by 15% (0.15) and enter the result	8	

Next. On line 4, is the amount $4,200 or more?

☐ **No.** If line 8 is zero, **stop here;** you cannot claim this credit. Otherwise, skip Part II and enter the **smaller** of line 5 or line 8 on line 15.

☐ **Yes.** If line 8 is equal to or more than line 5, skip Part II and enter the amount from line 5 on line 15. Otherwise, go to line 9.

Part II	**Certain Filers Who Have Three or More Qualifying Children**	

9	Withheld social security, Medicare, and Additional Medicare taxes from Form(s) W-2, boxes 4 and 6. If married filing jointly, include your spouse's amounts with yours. If your employer withheld or you paid Additional Medicare Tax or tier 1 RRTA taxes, see instructions	9	
10	**1040 and 1040-SR filers:** Enter the total of the amounts from Schedule 1 (Form 1040 or 1040-SR), line 14, and Schedule 2 (Form 1040 or 1040-SR), line 5, plus any taxes that you identified using code "UT" and entered on Schedule 2 (Form 1040 or 1040-SR), line 8. **1040-NR filers:** Enter the total of the amounts from Form 1040-NR, lines 27 and 56, plus any taxes that you identified using code "UT" and entered on line 60.	10	
11	Add lines 9 and 10	11	
12	**1040 and 1040-SR filers:** Enter the total of the amounts from Form 1040 or 1040-SR, line 18a, and Schedule 3 (Form 1040 or 1040-SR), line 11. **1040-NR filers:** Enter the amount from Form 1040-NR, line 67.	12	
13	Subtract line 12 from line 11. If zero or less, enter -0-	13	
14	Enter the **larger** of line 8 or line 13	14	

Next, enter the **smaller** of line 5 or line 14 on line 15.

Part III	**Additional Child Tax Credit**	

15	This is your additional child tax credit	15	

Enter this amount on Form 1040, line 18b; Form 1040-SR, line 18b; or Form 1040-NR, line 64.

EXAMPLE In 2019, Eddie and Lindsey had a new baby. Their earned income and AGI in 2019 was $12,500, they filed jointly, lived in the United States, and had no investment income. Eddie and Lindsey have Social Security numbers but have not had the time to get a Social Security number for the baby yet. Eddie and Lindsey may claim an EIC in 2019 but only with no qualifying child since the baby does not have a valid Social Security number. They should consider applying for a Social Security number by the filing deadline. ◆

EXAMPLE In 2019, Jerry earns wages of $16,000 from his job and has no adjustments or other forms of income. He has no qualifying children and no investment income. Even if Jerry meets all the other requirements (Social Security number, U.S. residence, etc.), he will not be eligible for the EIC as his AGI exceeds the threshold amount for an unmarried taxpayer with no qualifying children ($15,570 in 2019). ◆

7-2b **Does the Taxpayer Have a Qualifying Child?**

Determining whether the taxpayer has a qualifying child is important because the eligibility rules differ based on whether a qualifying child is claimed or not. Because the rules defining a qualifying child for the EIC are similar to the rules for claiming a dependent, a review of the rules in Chapter 1 is suggested.

7-2c **Taxpayer with No Qualifying Child**

If the taxpayer does not have a qualifying child, the previous seven rules *must* be met along with four additional rules:

1. Taxpayer's age – the taxpayer or the spouse (but not both) must be at least 25 years of age by the end of the tax year but less than 65 years of age. For 2019, the taxpayer (or spouse) must have been born after December 31, 1954 but before January 2, 1995.
2. Dependency status – the taxpayer (or spouse, if filing jointly) must not be eligible to be claimed as a dependent on another taxpayer's return, whether they are claimed or not.
3. Cannot be a qualifying child – the taxpayer claiming the EIC may not be the qualifying child of another taxpayer. Note the qualifying child definition discussed in Chapter 1 applies here with two notable exceptions: (1) the child need not meet the support test, and (2) the child must live in a U.S. home for more than one-half of the year (a slight extension of the domicile test).
4. U.S. home – the taxpayer must have lived in the United States for more than one-half of the tax year.

EXAMPLE Marco and Llewelyn are married and file jointly with no qualifying children in 2019 and meet the general rules to claim the EIC. Marco turns 65 on December 14, 2019 and Llewelyn turns 64 on April 3, 2019. Marco and Llewelyn qualify to claim the EIC because Llewelyn is under age 65 at the end of the tax year. ◆

EXAMPLE Monica is a 23-year-old single taxpayer with no qualifying children in 2019. She is a full-time student at State College and generates enough income to live on from her nontaxable scholarships and a job on campus; however, she lets her father claim her as a dependent as the scholarship money is not included in her support test. Even if Monica meets the seven general rules, because she is claimed as a dependent by another taxpayer, she is not eligible to claim the EIC. ◆

7-2d **Taxpayer with a Qualifying Child**

To claim an EIC with a qualifying child, three additional rules must be considered:

1. Qualifying child tests – the child must meet the qualifying child tests. These are the same tests as discussed in Chapter 1 with two notable exceptions: (1) the child need not meet the support test, and (2) the child must live in a U.S. home for more than one-half of the year (a slight extension of the domicile test).

2. Qualifying child cannot be claimed by more than one person–only one taxpayer may claim a qualifying child for the EIC. If the child meets the definition of a qualifying child for more than one taxpayer, tiebreaker rules similar to those discussed in Chapter 1 must be applied.

3. Taxpayer cannot be a qualifying child of another taxpayer–see rule 3 under taxpayer with no qualifying child at Section 7-2c.

With so many qualification rules, it is no wonder that taxpayers and tax preparers have been known to make numerous errors when determining the EIC. Numerous checklists and aids have been prepared to assist taxpayers with preparing the EIC calculation. IRS Publication 596 contains an EIC Eligibility Checklist as shown on Page 7-15.

In addition to checklists, the IRS has implemented some additional procedural steps to ensure the EIC is not being abused by taxpayers. Similar to the child tax credit rules, taxpayers claiming an earned income credit must have a Social Security number for the taxpayer, spouse (if married), and each qualifying child by the due date (including extensions) of the return.

If the IRS rejects an earned income credit for any reason other than a math or clerical error, the taxpayer must complete a Form 8862 in order to claim the earned income credit in a future year.

In addition, a taxpayer who erroneously claims the earned income credit due to reckless or intentional disregard of rules or regulations is ineligible to claim the credit for a period of two tax years. If the IRS determines the claim for the credit was fraudulent, the ineligibility window is extended to ten years.

The IRS will not issue refunds for any tax returns that claim an earned income credit until February 15th of the following year to provide the IRS with additional time to review refund claims that stem from refundable earned income credit claims.

To assist tax preparers with the accurate completion of the EIC (and the child tax credit and American Opportunities tax credit), Form 8867 (see Pages 7-13 and 7-14) must be prepared and filed with the tax return and a copy retained by the tax preparer. If a taxpayer is claiming more than one of the credits covered by Form 8867, only one form is required to be filed. Failure to file Form 8867 could result in a $530 penalty.

7-2e **What Is the Amount of the EIC?**

Taxpayers are required to have some earned income to qualify for the EIC; however, too much earned income renders the taxpayer ineligible for the EIC (see Rule 7 under the general rules on Page 7-9). As stated previously, the EIC amount must be derived from the EIC Tables in Appendix B and should not be calculated using the statutory credit percentages to avoid rounding issues. To find the correct amount of EIC in the EIC Tables, the taxpayer must compare the EIC Table amount based on the taxpayer's earned income with the EIC Table amount associated with the taxpayer's AGI. The taxpayer is required to claim the smaller of the two EIC amounts.

Part of the complexity of the EIC is that a number of the thresholds, amounts, and limits change each year. As a result, new EIC tables must be used each year. The EIC is reported on Line 18a of Form 1040. Similar to the child tax credit, a specific form to support the EIC computation is not always required to be prepared and filed. Instead, a series of supporting worksheets found within the instructions to the Form 1040 are available to assist with preparation. Worksheet A is used for taxpayers with wage income only and Worksheet B is used by taxpayers with self-employment income. For taxpayers claiming a qualifying child for the EIC, Schedule EIC must also be filed.

Form **8867**

Department of the Treasury
Internal Revenue Service

Paid Preparer's Due Diligence Checklist

Earned Income Credit (EIC), American Opportunity Tax Credit (AOTC), Child Tax Credit (CTC) (including the Additional Child Tax Credit (ACTC) and Credit for Other Dependents (ODC)), and Head of Household (HOH) Filing Status

▶ **To be completed by preparer and filed with Form 1040, 1040-SR, 1040-NR, 1040-PR, or 1040-SS.**
▶ **Go to www.irs.gov/Form8867 for instructions and the latest information.**

OMB No. 1545-0074

2019

Attachment
Sequence No. **70**

Taxpayer name(s) shown on return

Taxpayer identification number

Enter preparer's name and PTIN

Part I	**Due Diligence Requirements**

Please check the appropriate box for the credit(s) and/or HOH filing status claimed on the return and complete the related Parts I–V for the benefit(s) claimed (check all that apply). ☐ EIC ☐ CTC/ACTC/ODC ☐ AOTC ☐ HOH

		Yes	No	N/A
1	Did you complete the return based on information for tax year 2019 provided by the taxpayer or reasonably obtained by you?	☐	☐	
2	If credits are claimed on the return, did you complete the applicable EIC and/or CTC/ACTC/ODC worksheets found in the Form 1040, 1040-SR, 1040-NR, 1040-PR, or 1040-SS instructions, and/or the AOTC worksheet in the Form 8863 instructions, or your own worksheet(s) that provides the same information, and all related forms and schedules for each credit claimed?	☐	☐	☐
3	Did you satisfy the knowledge requirement? To meet the knowledge requirement, you must do both of the following.			
	• Interview the taxpayer, ask questions, and contemporaneously document the taxpayer's responses to determine that the taxpayer is eligible to claim the credit(s) and/or HOH filing status.			
	• Review information to determine that the taxpayer is eligible to claim the credit(s) and/or HOH filing status and to compute the amount(s) of any credit(s)	☐	☐	
4	Did any information provided by the taxpayer or a third party for use in preparing the return, or information reasonably known to you, appear to be incorrect, incomplete, or inconsistent? (If "Yes," answer questions 4a and 4b. If "No," go to question 5.)	☐	☐	
a	Did you make reasonable inquiries to determine the correct, complete, and consistent information?	☐	☐	
b	Did you contemporaneously document your inquiries? (Documentation should include the questions you asked, whom you asked, when you asked, the information that was provided, and the impact the information had on your preparation of the return.)	☐	☐	
5	Did you satisfy the record retention requirement? To meet the record retention requirement, you must keep a copy of your documentation referenced in 4b, a copy of this Form 8867, a copy of any applicable worksheet(s), a record of how, when, and from whom the information used to prepare Form 8867 and any applicable worksheet(s) was obtained, and a copy of any document(s) provided by the taxpayer that you relied on to determine eligibility for the credit(s) and/or HOH filing status or to compute the amount(s) of the credit(s)	☐	☐	

List those documents, if any, that you relied on.

_____

_____

_____

		Yes	No	N/A
6	Did you ask the taxpayer whether he/she could provide documentation to substantiate eligibility for the credit(s) and/or HOH filing status and the amount(s) of any credit(s) claimed on the return if his/her return is selected for audit?	☐	☐	
7	Did you ask the taxpayer if any of these credits were disallowed or reduced in a previous year? (If credits were disallowed or reduced, go to question 7a; if not, go to question 8.)	☐	☐	☐
a	Did you complete the required recertification Form 8862?	☐	☐	☐
8	If the taxpayer is reporting self-employment income, did you ask questions to prepare a complete and correct Schedule C (Form 1040 or 1040-SR)?	☐	☐	☐

For Paperwork Reduction Act Notice, see separate instructions. Cat. No. 26142H Form **8867** (2019)

Form 8867 (2019)   Page **2**

Part II	**Due Diligence Questions for Returns Claiming EIC** (If the return does not claim EIC, go to Part III.)			
		Yes	**No**	**N/A**
9a	Have you determined that the taxpayer is, in fact, eligible to claim the EIC for the number of qualifying children claimed, or is eligible to claim the EIC without a qualifying child? (Skip 9b and 9c if the taxpayer is claiming the EIC and does not have a qualifying child.)	☐	☐	
b	Did you ask the taxpayer if the child lived with the taxpayer for over half of the year, even if the taxpayer has supported the child the entire year?	☐	☐	
c	Did you explain to the taxpayer the rules about claiming the EIC when a child is the qualifying child of more than one person (tiebreaker rules)?	☐	☐	☐

Part III	**Due Diligence Questions for Returns Claiming CTC/ACTC/ODC** (If the return does not claim CTC, ACTC, or ODC, go to Part IV.)			
		Yes	**No**	**N/A**
10	Have you determined that each qualifying person for the CTC/ACTC/ODC is the taxpayer's dependent who is a citizen, national, or resident of the United States?	☐	☐	
11	Did you explain to the taxpayer that he/she may not claim the CTC/ACTC if the taxpayer has not lived with the child for over half of the year, even if the taxpayer has supported the child, unless the child's custodial parent has released a claim to exemption for the child?	☐	☐	☐
12	Did you explain to the taxpayer the rules about claiming the CTC/ACTC/ODC for a child of divorced or separated parents (or parents who live apart), including any requirement to attach a Form 8332 or similar statement to the return?	☐	☐	☐

Part IV	**Due Diligence Questions for Returns Claiming AOTC** (If the return does not claim AOTC, go to Part V.)		
		Yes	**No**
13	Did the taxpayer provide substantiation for the credit, such as a Form 1098-T and/or receipts for the qualified tuition and related expenses for the claimed AOTC?	☐	☐

Part V	**Due Diligence Questions for Claiming HOH** (If the return does not claim HOH filing status, go to Part VI.)		
		Yes	**No**
14	Have you determined that the taxpayer was unmarried or considered unmarried on the last day of the tax year and provided more than half of the cost of keeping up a home for the year for a qualifying person? . . .	☐	☐

Part VI	**Eligibility Certification**

▶ **You will have complied with all due diligence requirements for claiming the applicable credit(s) and/or HOH filing status on the return of the taxpayer identified above if you:**

   A. Interview the taxpayer, ask adequate questions, contemporaneously document the taxpayer's responses on the return or in your notes, review adequate information to determine if the taxpayer is eligible to claim the credit(s) and/or HOH filing status and to compute the amount(s) of the credit(s);

   B. Complete this Form 8867 truthfully and accurately and complete the actions described in this checklist for any applicable credit(s) claimed and HOH filing status, if claimed;

   C. Submit Form 8867 in the manner required; **and**

   D. Keep all five of the following records for 3 years from the latest of the dates specified in the Form 8867 instructions under *Document Retention.*

      1. A copy of this Form 8867;

      2. The applicable worksheet(s) or your own worksheet(s) for any credit(s) claimed;

      3. Copies of any documents provided by the taxpayer on which you relied to determine the taxpayer's eligibility for the credit(s) and/or HOH filing status and to compute the amount(s) of the credit(s);

      4. A record of how, when, and from whom the information used to prepare this form and the applicable worksheet(s) was obtained; and

      5. A record of any additional information you relied upon, including questions you asked and the taxpayer's responses, to determine the taxpayer's eligibility for the credit(s) and/or, HOH filing status and to compute the amount(s) of the credit(s).

▶ **If you have not complied with all due diligence requirements, you may have to pay a $530 penalty for each failure to comply related to a claim of an applicable credit or HOH filing status.**

		Yes	**No**
15	Do you certify that all of the answers on this Form 8867 are, to the best of your knowledge, true, correct, and complete?	☐	☐

Form **8867** (2019)

EIC Eligibility Checklist

1. Is your AGI less than:	☐ Yes	☐ No

- $15,570 ($21,370 for married filing jointly) if you do not have a qualifying child,
- $41,094 ($46,884 for married filing jointly) if you have one qualifying child,
- $46,703 ($52,493 for married filing jointly) if you have two qualifying children, or
- $50,162 ($55,952 for married filing jointly) if you have more than two qualifying children?

2. Do you and your spouse each have a valid SSN (by the due date of your return including extensions)?	☐ Yes	☐ No
3. Is your filing status married filing jointly, head of household, qualifying widow(er), or single?	☐ Yes	☐ No
4. Answer "**Yes**" if you are not filing Form 2555 or Form 2555-EZ. Otherwise, answer "**No**."	☐ Yes	☐ No
5. Is your investment income $3,600 or less?	☐ Yes	☐ No
6. Is your total earned income at least $1 but less than:	☐ Yes	☐ No

- $15,570 ($21,370 for married filing jointly) if you do not have a qualifying child,
- $41,094 ($46,884 for married filing jointly) if you have one qualifying child,
- $46,703 ($52,493 for married filing jointly) if you have two qualifying children, or
- $50,162 ($55,952 for married filing jointly) if you have more than two qualifying children?

7. Answer "**Yes**" if (a) you are not a qualifying child of another taxpayer or (b) you are filing a joint return. Otherwise, answer "NO."	☐ Yes	☐ No
8. Does your child meet the relationship, age, residency, and joint return tests for a qualifying child and have a Social Security number received by the due date of the tax return (including extensions)?	☐ Yes	☐ No
9. Is your child a qualifying child only for you? Answer "**Yes**" if (a) your qualifying child does not meet the tests to be a qualifying child of any other person or (b) your qualifying child meets the tests to be a qualifying child of another person but you are the person entitled to treat the child as a qualifying child under the tiebreaker rules. Answer "**No**" if the other person is the one entitled to treat the child as a qualifying child under the tiebreaker rules.	☐ Yes	☐ No
10. Were you (or your spouse if filing a joint return) at least age 25 but under age 65 at the end of 2019?	☐ Yes	☐ No
11. Answer "**Yes**" if (a) you cannot be claimed as a dependent on anyone else's return or (b) you are filing a joint return. Otherwise, answer "**No**."	☐ Yes	☐ No
12. Was your main home (and your spouse's if filing a joint return) in the United States for more than half the year?	☐ Yes	☐ No

PERSONS WITH A QUALIFYING CHILD: If you answered "**Yes**" to questions 1 through 9, you can claim the EIC. Remember to fill out Schedule EIC and attach it to your Form 1040. If you answered "**Yes**" to questions 1 through 7 and "**No**" to question 8, answer questions 10 through 12 to see if you can claim the EIC without a qualifying child.

PERSONS WITHOUT A QUALIFYING CHILD: If you answered "**Yes**" to questions 1 through 7, and 10 through 12, you can claim the EIC.

If you answered "No" to any questions that applies to you: You cannot claim the EIC.

EXAMPLE   Ying and Michael are married filing jointly taxpayers with earned income and AGI of $23,200 in 2019. They have two children ages 3 and 5. All members of the family have Social Security numbers, are U.S. citizens, and lived together in the United States all year. Ying had $820 of tax withheld from her wages during the year. Michael did not work. Ying and Michael can claim the EIC as they meet all the tests for taxpayers with a qualifying child. Based on earned income of $23,200, filing jointly with two qualifying children, their EIC per the 2019 table (Appendix B) is $5,828. ♦

Self-Study Problem 7.2   *See Appendix E for Solutions to Self-Study Problems*

Dennis and Lynne have a 5-year-old child. Dennis has a salary of $16,200. Lynne is self-employed with a loss of $400 from her business. Dennis and Lynne receive $100 of taxable interest income during the year. Their earned income for the year is $15,800 and their adjusted gross income is $15,900 ($16,200 − $400 + $100).

Use the worksheet below and calculate their earned income credit from the EIC table in Appendix B.

$_____

ProConnect determines whether the earned income credit applies based on the information that the preparer inputs (most importantly income and dependent information). However, if the earned income credit is not computing and the preparer believes the taxpayer is eligible, the earned income credit worksheets can be produced by ProConnect to allow for the review the calculation. To produce the EIC worksheets, click on the Credits section and on EIC, Residential Energy, Other Credits screen, expand the Earned Income Credit section and scroll down to the bottom to select the box Force Earned Income Credit Worksheets.

7-3 CHILD AND DEPENDENT CARE CREDIT

7.3 Learning Objective

Compute the child and dependent care credit for an individual taxpayer.

Congress enacted tax laws to provide benefits to taxpayers with dependents who must be provided with care and supervision while the taxpayers work. Taxpayers are allowed a credit for expenses for the care of their children and certain other dependents. To be eligible for the child and dependent care credit, the dependent must either be under the age of 13 or be a dependent or spouse of any age who is incapable of self-care. If a child's parents are divorced, the child need not be the dependent of the taxpayer claiming the credit, but the child must live with that parent more than he or she lives with the other parent. For example, a divorced mother with custody of a child may be entitled to the credit even though the child is a dependent of the father.

7-3a Qualified Expenses

The expenses that qualify for the credit include amounts paid to enable both the taxpayer and his or her spouse to be employed. Qualified expenses include amounts paid for in-home care, such as a nanny, as well as out-of-home care, such as a day care center. Overnight camps do not qualify for the credit, nor do activities providing standard education such as kindergarten. Day camps such as soccer camps, music camps, math camps, and dinosaur camps do qualify for the credit since they are not considered standard education. Payments to relatives are eligible for the credit, unless the payments are to a dependent of the taxpayer or to the taxpayer's child who is under the age of 19 at the end of the tax year. To claim the credit, the taxpayer must include on his or her tax return, the name, address, and taxpayer identification number of the person or organization providing the care.

7-3b Allowable Credit

For taxpayers with AGI of less than $15,000, the child and dependent care credit is equal to 35 percent of the qualified expenses. For taxpayers with AGI of $15,000 or more, the amount of the percentage of qualified expenses is reduced as income increases. See Line 8 on Form 2441 on Page 7-19 for the applicable credit percentage (these amounts are not adjusted for inflation). In determining the credit, the maximum amount of qualified expenses to which the applicable percentage is applied is $3,000 for one dependent and $6,000 for two or more dependents. Form 2441 is used to calculate and report the credit for child and dependent care expenses.

Married taxpayers must file a joint return to claim the child and dependent care credit, and the qualifying dependent care expenses are limited to the lesser of either spouse's earned income. For example, if a taxpayer makes $22,000 and the spouse earns $1,500, and they spend $1,900 on child care, the maximum qualifying expenses are $1,500. A special rule applies when a taxpayer or spouse is a full-time student or disabled. Full-time students or disabled taxpayers with little or no income are deemed to have earned income of $250 per month for one dependent and $500 per month for two or more dependents for purposes of calculating this limitation. For example, if a taxpayer's spouse is a full-time student for 9 months of the year and has no income, the maximum amount of the qualifying expenses for the care of one dependent is $2,250 ($250 per month × 9 months).

EXAMPLE   Harry and Molly Grant are married and file a joint return. They have one child and pay $4,000 for child care expenses during the year. Harry earns $16,000 and Molly earns $8,500 during the year, resulting in adjusted gross income of $24,500. The Grant's child care credit is calculated as follows:

Qualified expenses	$4,000
Maximum for one dependent	3,000
Credit percentage from Form 2441	× 30%
Credit allowed	$ 900

♦

EXAMPLE   Assume the same facts as in the example above, except the qualified expenses are $2,100 (instead of $4,000). The credit is 30 percent of $2,100, or $630. ♦

Congress' choice to not adjust certain thresholds or amounts for inflation has over time, slowly reduced the advantage of a deduction or tax benefit. The last update to the deemed value placed on the earned income of a spouse that is a full-time student was in 2002 (for tax year 2003) and increased from $200 to $250 ($400 to $500 for two qualified dependents). Using inflation from the consumer price index, the value of $250 in 2003 would be $333 today. According to National Center for Education Statistics, the average cost of a university education in 2003 was $12,953 per year. In 2017 (the most current data available), the cost had increased to $23,091.

Self-Study Problem 7.3   *See Appendix E for Solutions to Self-Study Problems*

Julie Brown (Social Security number 456-23-6543) has been widowed for 5 years and has one dependent child, Chuck Brown (Social Security number 123-33-4444). Julie's adjusted gross income and her earned income are $90,000. Julie's employer withheld $2,000 in the dependent care flexible spending account (see Chapter 2). This amount was excluded from her wage income. Assume her taxable income is $45,500, and her regular tax is $5,186 (line 10 on Form 2441). Julie paid child care expenses of $1,500 to Ivy Childcare (1 Sunflower Street, Terre Haute, IN 47803, EIN 56-7654321) and expenses for the care of her disabled dependent mother, Devona Neuporte (Social Security number 214-55-6666), of $2,400 paid to De Anza Adult Care (13 Fort Harrison Rd., Dewey, IN 47805, EIN 43-1234567). Calculate Julie's child and dependent care credit for 2019 using Form 2441 on Pages 7-19 and 7-20. Make realistic assumptions about any missing data.

TIP   The child and dependent care credit is a function of two entry points in ProConnect. The first is the input in Dependents as discussed in Chapter 1 and in the other credits mentioned earlier in this chapter. The second important input occurs under Credits/Ind Qualifying for Dependant Care Cr. This screen and the Persons and Expenses Qualifying for the Dependant Care Credit are where you identify the dependant for which the expenses were incurred. The provider of the care is entered in the Provider of Dependent Care screen.

Self-Study Problem 7.3

Form **2441**	**Child and Dependent Care Expenses**		OMB No. 1545-0074

Form **2441**

Department of the Treasury
Internal Revenue Service (99)

Child and Dependent Care Expenses

▶ Attach to Form 1040, 1040-SR, or 1040-NR.

▶ Go to *www.irs.gov/Form2441* for instructions and the latest information.

1040
1040-SR
1040-NR
2441

OMB No. 1545-0074

2019

Attachment Sequence No. **21**

Name(s) shown on return | Your social security number

You cannot claim a credit for child and dependent care expenses if your filing status is married filing separately unless you meet the requirements listed in the instructions under "Married Persons Filing Separately." If you meet these requirements, check this box. ☐

Part I Persons or Organizations Who Provided the Care—You **must** complete this part.
(If you have more than two care providers, see the instructions.)

1	(a) Care provider's name	(b) Address (number, street, apt. no., city, state, and ZIP code)	(c) Identifying number (SSN or EIN)	(d) Amount paid (see instructions)

Did you receive **dependent care benefits?**

No ───▶ Complete only Part II below.

Yes ───▶ Complete Part III on the back next.

Caution: If the care was provided in your home, you may owe employment taxes. For details, see the instructions for Schedule 2 (Form 1040 or 1040-SR), line 7a; or Form 1040-NR, line 59a.

Part II Credit for Child and Dependent Care Expenses

2 Information about your **qualifying person(s)**. If you have more than two qualifying persons, see the instructions.

(a) Qualifying person's name		(b) Qualifying person's social security number	(c) **Qualified expenses** you incurred and paid in 2019 for the person listed in column (a)
First	Last		

3	Add the amounts in column (c) of line 2. **Don't** enter more than $3,000 for one qualifying person or $6,000 for two or more persons. If you completed Part III, enter the amount from line 31	**3**	
4	Enter your **earned income**. See instructions	**4**	
5	If married filing jointly, enter your spouse's earned income (if you or your spouse was a student or was disabled, see the instructions); **all others**, enter the amount from line 4	**5**	
6	Enter the **smallest** of line 3, 4, or 5	**6**	
7	Enter the amount from Form 1040 or 1040-SR, line 8b; or Form 1040-NR, line 35 ... **7**		
8	Enter on line 8 the decimal amount shown below that applies to the amount on line 7		

If line 7 is:			If line 7 is:		
Over	But not over	Decimal amount is	Over	But not over	Decimal amount is
$0—15,000		.35	$29,000—31,000		.27
15,000—17,000		.34	31,000—33,000		.26
17,000—19,000		.33	33,000—35,000		.25
19,000—21,000		.32	35,000—37,000		.24
21,000—23,000		.31	37,000—39,000		.23
23,000—25,000		.30	39,000—41,000		.22
25,000—27,000		.29	41,000—43,000		.21
27,000—29,000		.28	43,000—No limit		.20

8	X .

9	Multiply line 6 by the decimal amount on line 8. If you paid 2018 expenses in 2019, see the instructions	**9**	
10	Tax liability limit. Enter the amount from the Credit Limit Worksheet in the instructions ... **10**		
11	**Credit for child and dependent care expenses.** Enter the **smaller** of line 9 or line 10 here and on Schedule 3 (Form 1040 or 1040-SR), line 2; or Form 1040-NR, line 47	**11**	

For Paperwork Reduction Act Notice, see your tax return instructions. Cat. No. 11862M Form **2441** (2019)

Form 2441 (2019)   Page **2**

Part III	Dependent Care Benefits		

12 Enter the total amount of **dependent care benefits** you received in 2019. Amounts you received as an employee should be shown in box 10 of your Form(s) W-2. **Don't** include amounts reported as wages in box 1 of Form(s) W-2. If you were self-employed or a partner, include amounts you received under a dependent care assistance program from your sole proprietorship or partnership . | **12**

13 Enter the amount, if any, you carried over from 2018 and used in 2019 during the grace period. See instructions . . . . | **13**

14 Enter the amount, if any, you forfeited or carried forward to 2020. See instructions . . . . | **14** ( )

15 Combine lines 12 through 14. See instructions . . . . | **15**

16 Enter the total amount of **qualified expenses** incurred in 2019 for the care of the **qualifying person(s)** . . . . | **16**

17 Enter the **smaller** of line 15 or 16 . . . . | **17**

18 Enter your **earned income.** See instructions . . . . . | **18**

19 Enter the amount shown below that applies to you.

 • If married filing jointly, enter your spouse's earned income (if you or your spouse was a student or was disabled, see the instructions for line 5).

 • If married filing separately, see instructions.

 • All others, enter the amount from line 18. | **19**

20 Enter the **smallest** of line 17, 18, or 19 . . . . . . | **20**

21 Enter $5,000 ($2,500 if married filing separately **and** you were required to enter your spouse's earned income on line 19) . . . . . | **21**

22 Is any amount on line 12 from your sole proprietorship or partnership?

 ☐ **No.** Enter -0-.

 ☐ **Yes.** Enter the amount here . . . . | **22**

23 Subtract line 22 from line 15 . . . . | **23**

24 **Deductible benefits.** Enter the **smallest** of line 20, 21, or 22. Also, include this amount on the appropriate line(s) of your return. See instructions . . . . | **24**

25 **Excluded benefits.** If you checked "No" on line 22, enter the smaller of line 20 or 21. Otherwise, subtract line 24 from the smaller of line 20 or 21. If zero or less, enter -0- . . . . . . | **25**

26 **Taxable benefits.** Subtract line 25 from line 23. If zero or less, enter -0-. Also, include this amount on Form 1040 or 1040-SR, line 1; or Form 1040-NR, line 8. On the dotted line next to Form 1040 or 1040-SR, line 1; or Form 1040-NR, line 8, enter "DCB". . . . . | **26**

To claim the child and dependent care
credit, complete lines 27 through 31 below.

27 Enter $3,000 ($6,000 if two or more qualifying persons) . . . . | **27**

28 Add lines 24 and 25 . . . . | **28**

29 Subtract line 28 from line 27. If zero or less, **stop.** You can't take the credit. **Exception.** If you paid 2018 expenses in 2019, see the instructions for line 9 . . . . | **29**

30 Complete line 2 on the front of this form. **Don't** include in column (c) any benefits shown on line 28 above. Then, add the amounts in column (c) and enter the total here . . . . . | **30**

31 Enter the **smaller** of line 29 or 30. Also, enter this amount on line 3 on the front of this form and complete lines 4 through 11 . . . . | **31**

Form **2441** (2019)

7-4 THE AFFORDABLE CARE ACT

7.4 Learning Objective

Calculate the premium tax credit available under the Affordable Care Act.

The Affordable Care Act (also called the "ACA" or "Obamacare") contains a number of different provisions that affect a taxpayer's income tax liability and reporting. The Net Investment Income tax of 3.8 percent and 0.9 percent Medicare tax (both discussed in Chapter 6) are additional taxes for certain high income taxpayers.

Changes to the tax law now leave only one significant tax provision that relates to individuals from the ACA: health insurance premium tax credits. The other previous provision, the individual shared responsibility, was repealed starting in 2019.

7-4a Premium Tax Credit

Under the ACA, eligible taxpayers may receive a tax credit intended to lower the cost of health care. To be eligible, a taxpayer must meet all of the following requirements:

- Health insurance is purchased through one of the state exchanges or the federal exchange
- The taxpayer is not eligible for coverage through an employer or government plan
- The taxpayer's income falls below certain limits
- The taxpayer does not file Married Filing Separately except under very limited conditions
- The taxpayer cannot be claimed as a dependent by another

The income eligibility is based on household income where modified AGI requires the add-back of tax-exempt interest and any nontaxable Social Security benefits. The maximum household income is 400 percent of the federal poverty line for the taxpayer's family size. Taxpayers below the federal poverty line are eligible for Medicaid and thus not eligible for the credit.

Calculating the premium tax credit is similar to the EIC in that specific tables are required to compute the allowable credit. The credit is intended to take the form of the lesser of (1) actual health care premiums paid or (2) silver plan premiums less the amount the taxpayer is expected to contribute to health care. To calculate the premium tax credit, the following steps are required:

Step 1. Calculate modified AGI for all members of the household. This is AGI for all individuals claimed as a dependent (dependent's income is includable if they are required to file a tax return) adjusted for a number of items including tax-exempt interest and nontaxable Social Security benefits.

Step 2. Compare the household income to the previous year's federal poverty line (FPL). Under the ACA, the FPL is set in the *previous* year during open enrollment (around October). The FPL is defined in three ways: (a) the 48 contiguous states and the District of Columbia, (b) Alaska, or (c) Hawaii. The FPL selected is based on the household's state of residence (see FPL amounts below).

Persons in Family/Household	2019 FPL for 48 States and DC
1	$12,140
2	16,460
3	20,780
4	25,100
5	29,420
6	33,740
7	38,060
8	42,380
Each additional person	+$ 4,320

The household income is then expressed as a percentage of the FPL.

Step 3. The amount of income deemed appropriately spent on health care premiums is then identified on the 2019 Applicable Figure Table shown on Page 7-23. The applicable figure is designed to represent the maximum percentage of income a household will spend on health care premiums.

EXAMPLE   Ed and Milly are married with two children under the age of 21. Household income is $50,200. Ed and Milly's household income is at 200 percent of the FPL ($50,200 ÷ $25,100 = 2.0 or 200%). For household income of 200 percent of the FPL, the applicable figure is 0.0654; thus the intended or deemed to be paid for health care premiums is $50,200 × 6.54% or $3,283.08. ♦

Step 4. The amount of the credit is based on comparing the cost of premiums for a designated silver plan in the taxpayer's state with the deemed premium cost calculated above. For example, if the deemed premium to be paid is $3,283 and the cost of a silver plan for that household is $10,000 then the premium tax credit is $6,717 ($10,000 − $3,283). For households that did not have coverage for the entire year, the credit is prorated based on the number of months coverage was maintained.

Step 5. Lastly, the amount calculated in steps 1–4 is compared to the actual premiums paid and the lesser of the two is the premium tax credit (i.e., the credit cannot exceed the actual premiums paid).

The premium tax credit can be obtained at two different times: (1) in advance (i.e., as a direct reduction in the monthly health care premiums) or (2) at the end of the year when the tax return is filed. If the taxpayer elects to have the credit paid in advance, the exchange will automatically adjust the premiums to reflect an estimated credit based on estimated household income. Since the actual premium tax credit is not known until household income can be computed after the end of the tax year, Form 8962, shown on Page 7-25, provides a reconciliation of the estimated credit and the actual credit. If the actual credit is greater than the estimated credit, the difference between the two amounts is a refundable credit on the taxpayer's tax return. If the estimated credit taken throughout the year is greater than the actual credit, the difference is treated as additional tax due on the taxpayer's tax return. However, as long as the household income remains below 400 percent of the FPL, the repayment amount of the credit is limited:

	Single	Taxpayers Other Than Single
Less than 200%	$ 300	$ 600
At least 200% but less than 300%	800	1,600
At least 300% but less than 400%	1,325	2,650
At least 400%	No limit	No limit

2019 Applicable Figure Table

 If the amount on line 5 is less than 133, your applicable figure is 0.0208. If the amount on line 5 is between 300 through 400, your applicable figure is 0.0986.

IF Form 8962, line 5 is . . .	ENTER on Form 8962, line 7 . . .	IF Form 8962, line 5 is . . .	ENTER on Form 8962, line 7 . . .	IF Form 8962, line 5 is . . .	ENTER on Form 8962, line 7 . . .	IF Form 8962, line 5 is . . .	ENTER on Form 8962, line 7 . . .
less than 133	0.0208	175	0.0535	218	0.0720	261	0.0869
133	0.0311	176	0.0539	219	0.0723	262	0.0872
134	0.0317	177	0.0544	220	0.0727	263	0.0875
135	0.0323	178	0.0549	221	0.0730	264	0.0878
136	0.0329	179	0.0554	222	0.0734	265	0.0881
137	0.0335	180	0.0558	223	0.0738	266	0.0884
138	0.0342	181	0.0563	224	0.0741	267	0.0887
139	0.0348	182	0.0568	225	0.0745	268	0.0890
140	0.0354	183	0.0573	226	0.0749	269	0.0893
141	0.0360	184	0.0578	227	0.0752	270	0.0896
142	0.0366	185	0.0582	228	0.0756	271	0.0899
143	0.0372	186	0.0587	229	0.0760	272	0.0902
144	0.0378	187	0.0592	230	0.0763	273	0.0905
145	0.0384	188	0.0597	231	0.0767	274	0.0908
146	0.0391	189	0.0601	232	0.0770	275	0.0911
147	0.0397	190	0.0606	233	0.0774	276	0.0914
148	0.0403	191	0.0611	234	0.0778	277	0.0917
149	0.0409	192	0.0616	235	0.0781	278	0.0920
150	0.0415	193	0.0621	236	0.0785	279	0.0923
151	0.0420	194	0.0625	237	0.0789	280	0.0926
152	0.0425	195	0.0630	238	0.0792	281	0.0929
153	0.0429	196	0.0635	239	0.0796	282	0.0932
154	0.0434	197	0.0640	240	0.0800	283	0.0935
155	0.0439	198	0.0644	241	0.0803	284	0.0938
156	0.0444	199	0.0649	242	0.0807	285	0.0941
157	0.0448	200	0.0654	243	0.0811	286	0.0944
158	0.0453	201	0.0658	244	0.0814	287	0.0947
159	0.0458	202	0.0661	245	0.0818	288	0.0950
160	0.0463	203	0.0665	246	0.0821	289	0.0953
161	0.0468	204	0.0669	247	0.0825	290	0.0956
162	0.0472	205	0.0672	248	0.0829	291	0.0959
163	0.0477	206	0.0676	249	0.0832	292	0.0962
164	0.0482	207	0.0679	250	0.0836	293	0.0965
165	0.0487	208	0.0683	251	0.0839	294	0.0968
166	0.0491	209	0.0687	252	0.0842	295	0.0971
167	0.0496	210	0.0690	253	0.0845	296	0.0974
168	0.0501	211	0.0694	254	0.0848	297	0.0977
169	0.0506	212	0.0698	255	0.0851	298	0.0980
170	0.0511	213	0.0701	256	0.0854	299	0.0983
171	0.0515	214	0.0705	257	0.0857	300 thru 400	0.0986
172	0.0520	215	0.0709	258	0.0860		
173	0.0525	216	0.0712	259	0.0863		
174	0.0530	217	0.0716	260	0.0866		

Self-Study Problem 7.4

Form **8962**	**Premium Tax Credit (PTC)**	OMB No. 1545-0074
Department of the Treasury Internal Revenue Service	▶ Attach to Form 1040, 1040-SR, or 1040-NR ▶ Go to *www.irs.gov/Form8962* for instructions and the latest information.	**2019** Attachment Sequence No. **73**

Name shown on your return	Your social security number

You cannot take the PTC if your filing status is married filing separately unless you qualify for an exception (see instructions). If you qualify, check the box . . ▶ ☐

Part I　Annual and Monthly Contribution Amount

1	Tax family size. Enter your tax family size (see instructions)	**1**
2a	Modified AGI. Enter your modified AGI (see instructions) . . . . ┃ **2a** ┃	
b	Enter the total of your dependents' modified AGI (see instructions) . . . . . ┃ **2b** ┃	
3	Household income. Add the amounts on lines 2a and 2b (see instructions)	**3**
4	Federal poverty line. Enter the federal poverty line amount from Table 1-1, 1-2, or 1-3 (see instructions). Check the appropriate box for the federal poverty table used. **a** ☐ Alaska　**b** ☐ Hawaii　**c** ☐ Other 48 states and DC	**4**
5	Household income as a percentage of federal poverty line (see instructions)	**5**　%
6	Did you enter 401% on line 5? (See instructions if you entered less than 100%.) ☐ **No.** Continue to line 7. ☐ **Yes.** You are not eligible to take the PTC. If advance payment of the PTC was made, see the instructions for how to report your excess advance PTC repayment amount.	
7	Applicable Figure. Using your line 5 percentage, locate your "applicable figure" on the table in the instructions . .	**7**
8a	Annual contribution amount. Multiply line 3 by line 7. Round to nearest whole dollar amount　**8a**	**b** Monthly contribution amount. Divide line 8a by 12. Round to nearest whole dollar amount　**8b**

Part II　Premium Tax Credit Claim and Reconciliation of Advance Payment of Premium Tax Credit

9	Are you allocating policy amounts with another taxpayer or do you want to use the alternative calculation for year of marriage (see instructions)? ☐ **Yes.** Skip to Part IV, Allocation of Policy Amounts, or Part V, Alternative Calculation for Year of Marriage.　☐ **No.** Continue to line 10.
10	See the instructions to determine if you can use line 11 or must complete lines 12 through 23. ☐ **Yes.** Continue to line 11. Compute your annual PTC. Then skip lines 12–23 and continue to line 24.　　☐ **No.** Continue to lines 12–23. Compute your monthly PTC and continue to line 24.

Annual Calculation	(a) Annual enrollment premiums (Form(s) 1095-A, line 33A)	(b) Annual applicable SLCSP premium (Form(s) 1095-A, line 33B)	(c) Annual contribution amount (line 8a)	(d) Annual maximum premium assistance (subtract (c) from (b), if zero or less, enter -0-)	(e) Annual premium tax credit allowed (smaller of (a) or (d))	(f) Annual advance payment of PTC (Form(s) 1095-A, line 33C)
11 Annual Totals						

Monthly Calculation	(a) Monthly enrollment premiums (Form(s) 1095-A, lines 21–32, column A)	(b) Monthly applicable SLCSP premium (Form(s) 1095-A, lines 21–32, column B)	(c) Monthly contribution amount (amount from line 8b or alternative marriage monthly calculation)	(d) Monthly maximum premium assistance (subtract (c) from (b), if zero or less, enter -0-)	(e) Monthly premium tax credit allowed (smaller of (a) or (d))	(f) Monthly advance payment of PTC (Form(s) 1095-A, lines 21–32, column C)
12 January						
13 February						
14 March						
15 April						
16 May						
17 June						
18 July						
19 August						
20 September						
21 October						
22 November						
23 December						

24	Total premium tax credit. Enter the amount from line 11(e) or add lines 12(e) through 23(e) and enter the total here	**24**
25	Advance payment of PTC. Enter the amount from line 11(f) or add lines 12(f) through 23(f) and enter the total here	**25**
26	Net premium tax credit. If line 24 is greater than line 25, subtract line 25 from line 24. Enter the difference here and on Schedule 3 (Form 1040 or 1040-SR), line 9, or Form 1040-NR, line 65. If line 24 equals line 25, enter -0-. Stop here. If line 25 is greater than line 24, leave this line blank and continue to line 27	**26**

Part III　Repayment of Excess Advance Payment of the Premium Tax Credit

27	Excess advance payment of PTC. If line 25 is greater than line 24, subtract line 24 from line 25. Enter the difference here	**27**
28	Repayment limitation (see instructions)	**28**
29	Excess advance premium tax credit repayment. Enter the smaller of line 27 or line 28 here and on Schedule 2 (Form 1040 or 1040-SR), line 2, or Form 1040-NR, line 44	**29**

For Paperwork Reduction Act Notice, see your tax return instructions.　　Cat. No. 37784Z　　Form **8962** (2019)

Self-Study Problem 7.4

Form **1095-A**	**Health Insurance Marketplace Statement**	☐ VOID	OMB No. 1545-2232
Department of the Treasury Internal Revenue Service	▶ Do not attach to your tax return. Keep for your records. ▶ Go to *www.irs.gov/Form1095A* for instructions and the latest information.	☐ CORRECTED	2019

Part I   Recipient Information

1 Marketplace identifier 12-3456999	**2** Marketplace-assigned policy number XXX	**3** Policy issuer's name Covered California

4 Recipient's name Tracy Brigantine	**5** Recipient's SSN 123-44-5555	**6** Recipient's date of birth 07/01/1967
7 Recipient's spouse's name Marco Brigantine	**8** Recipient's spouse's SSN 124-55-6666	**9** Recipient's spouse's date of birth 09/22/1971
10 Policy start date 01/01/2019	**11** Policy termination date 12/31/2019	**12** Street address (including apartment no.) 317 Kendra Lane
13 City or town Poway	**14** State or province CA	**15** Country and ZIP or foreign postal code 92064

Part II   Covered Individuals

	A. Covered individual name	B. Covered individual SSN	C. Covered individual date of birth	D. Coverage start date	E. Coverage termination date
16	Tracy Brigantine	123-44-5555	07/01/1967	01/01/2019	12/31/2019
17	Marco Brigantine	124-55-6666	09/2/21971	01/01/2019	12/31/2019
18	Alex Brigantine	503-11-2222	04/28/2005	01/01/2019	12/31/2019
19	Bryan Brigantine	867-53-0922	01/28/2003	01/01/2019	12/31/2019
20					

Part III   Coverage Information

	Month	A. Monthly enrollment premiums	B. Monthly second lowest cost silver plan (SLCSP) premium	C. Monthly advance payment of premium tax credit
21	January	957.00	825.00	487.00
22	February	957.00	825.00	487.00
23	March	957.00	825.00	487.00
24	April	957.00	825.00	487.00
25	May	957.00	825.00	487.00
26	June	957.00	825.00	487.00
27	July	957.00	825.00	487.00
28	August	957.00	825.00	487.00
29	September	957.00	825.00	487.00
30	October	957.00	825.00	487.00
31	November	957.00	825.00	487.00
32	December	957.00	825.00	487.00
33	Annual Totals	11,484.00	9,900.00	5,844.00

For Privacy Act and Paperwork Reduction Act Notice, see separate instructions.   Cat. No. 60703Q   Form **1095-A** (2019)

Form 1095-A reports the taxpayer's actual premiums paid, the cost of the silver plan, and any advance credits received during the year from the exchange on which they purchased the insurance.

Self-Study Problem 7.4   *See Appendix E for Solutions to Self-Study Problems*

Marco and Tracy Brigantine live in California, are married filing jointly, under age 65, and have three children ages 14, 16, and 26. However, the oldest child is not claimed as a dependent and does not live at home. Tracy's adjusted gross income is $44,040 and Marco's is $22,000 and both are self-employed. They also have $2,000 in interest income from tax-exempt bonds. The Brigantines are enrolled in health insurance for all of 2019 through their state exchange and elected to have the credit paid in advance. Using the Brigantine's 2019 Form 1095-A on Page 7-26, complete the Form 8962 on Page 7-25 to determine the following:

1. The actual premium tax credit (Line 24).
2. The net premium tax credit to be claimed on the return, if any (Line 26) or the excess advance payment, if any (Line 27).
3. The repayment amount required, if any.

7-5 EDUCATION TAX CREDITS

The tax law contains a number of provisions that are intended to reduce the cost of education for taxpayers. Educational credits represent the last of these provisions covered in this textbook:

7.5 Learning Objective

Apply the special rules applicable to the American Opportunity tax credit and lifetime learning credit.

Educational Tax Benefit	Learning Objective
Exclusion from gross income for scholarships	2.12
Employer-provided education assistance plans	2.5
Tuition reduction for school employees	2.5
Deduction of business educational expenses	3.6
Student loan interest deduction	5.8
Qualified tuition programs (529 plans)	2.14
Coverdell educational savings accounts	2.14
Tuition deduction (currently expired)	2.14
American Opportunity tax credit	7.5
Lifetime learning credit	7.5

7-5a American Opportunity Tax Credit

The American Opportunity tax credit (AOTC) is an education credit available to help qualifying low-income and middle-income individuals defray the cost of higher education.

The AOTC is a credit for students in their first 4 years of postsecondary education. The AOTC may be claimed for the expenses of students pursuing bachelor's or associate's degrees or vocational training. To be eligible, the student must meet all of the following:

- Pursuing a degree or recognized credential,
- Enrolled at least half-time for one semester, quarter, trimester, etc. starting during the tax year,
- Received a Form 1098-T from the eligible education institution,
- Not have completed the first four years of higher education at the start of the tax year,
- The AOTC has not been claimed for more than four years, and
- Has not been convicted of a felony drug conviction.

Meeting either of the following criteria precludes claiming the AOTC:

- Married filing separate status, or
- Taxpayer is listed as a dependent on another's return.

EXAMPLE   Alice is a single parent filing as head of household. Alice has been taking nursing classes at night to help her improve her job performance at the hospital. Alice has a 19-year-old daughter, Melanie, who is a second year full-time student at Wake Tech Community College pursing her associate degree in accounting. She might go on to pursue a four-year degree at some later date. Alice claims Melanie as a dependent but Melanie files her own tax return to report the income she earns from her part-time job. Alice claimed the AOTC for Melanie last year. As Melanie is enrolled in school at least half-time, is pursuing a degree, and has not claimed the AOTC for more than 4 years, she is an eligible student for the AOTC. Although Alice's school expense does not qualify for the AOTC, since she is not pursuing a degree or certification, she may qualify for the lifetime learning credit (LLC) discussed below. ◆

Like many other education tax benefits, the AOTC depends on an accurate computation of "qualified higher education expenses." The table below shows how qualified educational expenses can differ across some of the common education benefits:

Qualifying expenses for the AOTC can be paid on behalf of the taxpayer, his or her spouse, or dependents. As noted previously, expenses paid for room and board, nonacademic fees or for expenses that are not related to the student's course of instruction, do not qualify. Also, expenses for courses that involve sports, games, and hobbies do not qualify for the credit unless the course is part of a degree program. Expenses paid from a gift or inheritance (which is tax-free) do qualify for credits.

Qualified Educational Expenses

Cost	Scholarship	AOTC	LLC	Student Loan Interest	Coverdell	QTP (529 Plan)	Employer Provided Education Assistance Plan	Business Deduction for Work-related Education
Tuition and enrollment fees	X	X	X	X	X	X	X	X
Course-related Books	X	X	X[a]	X	X	X	X	X
Course-related supplies and equipment	X	X	X[a]	X	X	X	X	X
Room and board				X	X	X		
Transportation				X				X
Certain K-12 education costs					X	X		
Other necessary expenses including special needs services				X	X	X		X

[a] Only if required to be paid to educational institution

EXAMPLE Trinity's grandmother paid her $4,000 tuition directly to the university. Assuming Trinity meets the qualifying requirements for the AOTC otherwise, Trinity's parents may include the $4,000 as a qualifying expense when calculating the AOTC. ♦

Qualifying expenses must be reduced by any tax-free scholarships, grants or other education assistance. Taxpayers claiming the AOTC must have received a Form 1098-T (shown below) and must report the employer identification number of the educational institution on the Form 8863.

☐ CORRECTED		
FILER'S name, street address, city or town, state or province, country, ZIP or foreign postal code, and telephone number	**1 Payments received for qualified tuition and related expenses** $	**OMB No. 1545-1574**
	2	**2019** Form **1098-T** — **Tuition Statement**
FILER'S employer identification no. / **STUDENT'S TIN**	**3**	**Copy B For Student**
STUDENT'S name	**4 Adjustments made for a prior year** $	**5 Scholarships or grants** $
Street address (including apt. no.)	**6 Adjustments to scholarships or grants for a prior year** $	**7 Checked if the amount in box 1 includes amounts for an academic period beginning January— March 2020** ☐
City or town, state or province, country, and ZIP or foreign postal code		
Service Provider/Acct. No. (see instr.)	**8 Check if at least half-time student** ☐	**9 Checked if a graduate student** ☐
		10 Ins. contract reimb./refund $

This is important tax information and is being furnished to the IRS. This form must be used to complete Form 8863 to claim education credits. Give it to the tax preparer or use it to prepare the tax return.

Form **1098-T** (keep for your records) www.irs.gov/Form1098T Department of the Treasury - Internal Revenue Service

EXAMPLE Alice's daughter Melanie is an eligible student for the AOTC. Melanie received a 2019 Form 1098-T from Wake Tech that reported $4,000 in Box 1 and $1,000 in Box 5. Additionally, Alice paid $400 for course-related books and materials related to Melanie's school in 2019. Qualified education expenses for the AOTC are $3,400 ($4,000 of tuition and fees less $1,000 of tax-free scholarships plus $400 for books). ♦

The AOTC is calculated as 100 percent of the first $2,000 of qualified expenses paid, and 25 percent of the next $2,000, for a maximum annual credit of $2,500 per student. For 2019, the AOTC is phased out ratably for joint return filers with income between $160,000 and $180,000 and for single, head of household, or qualifying widow(er) filers with income between $80,000 and $90,000 (these amounts are not adjusted for inflation). The AOTC is 40 percent refundable, so up to $1,000 (40 percent of $2,500) may be refunded to the taxpayer if the credit exceeds the taxpayer's tax liability.

Many college students earn income and provide some of their own support. As a result, many parents of college-age students start to consider the consequences of claiming a child as a dependent versus allowing the child to claim themselves as a dependent on the student's own tax return (of course, the support test and others discussed in Chapter 1 generally dictate whether a full-time college student can be claimed by their parents). In order to prevent abuse of the AOTC by students attempting to maximize the credit by filing their own tax return, there are special rules related to the refundable portion of the AOTC. If a student under the age of 24, with at least one parent still living and not filing a joint return, is filing his or her own tax return and any of the following apply, they may not claim the refundable portion of the AOTC:

- Under age 18 at end of 2019, or
- At age 18 and earned income is less than one-half of support, or
- Over age 18 and a full-time student and earned income is less than one-half of support

EXAMPLE Vance Wilder is a single, 20-year-old full-time student at Harrison College. Van earned $11,000 from his part-time accounting job and in 2019, provided over one-half of his own support. As a result, his parents no longer claim him as a dependent. Although Vance has a living parent and is not filing a joint return, because he is over age 18 and a full-time student whose earned income is over one-half of his support, he is eligible for the refundable portion of the AOTC. ♦

EXAMPLE Jenny graduates from high school in June 2019. In the fall, she enrolls for twelve units at Gwinett University. Gwinett University considers students who take twelve or more units to be full-time students. Jenny's father pays her tuition and fees of $2,300. The American Opportunity tax credit for Jenny is $2,075 [(100% × $2,000) + (25% × $300)]. ◆

EXAMPLE Jason, a single father, has AGI of $85,000 in 2019. In 2019, he pays $5,000 in qualified tuition for his son, who just started at Alamance University. Without any limitations, Jason would be entitled to a maximum American Opportunity tax credit of $2,500. However, after applying the AGI limitations, Jason's American Opportunity tax credit is reduced by $1,250 ($2,500 × ($90,000 − $85,000)/$10,000), resulting in a credit of $1,250. ◆

Qualifying expenses must be paid during the tax year for education during an academic year beginning within that tax year. If tuition expenses are paid during the tax year for an academic period beginning during the first 3 months of the following tax year, the expenses may be claimed during the payment year.

Similar to the child tax credit rules, a taxpayer identification number (Social Security number or individual tax identification number) is required for each AOTC qualifying student by the due date of the return (including extensions).

If the IRS rejects an AOTC for any reason other than a math or clerical error, the taxpayer must complete Form 8862 used for claiming an earned income credit in a year after a rejection.

In addition, a taxpayer who erroneously claims the AOTC due to reckless or intentional disregard of rules or regulations is ineligible to claim the credit for a period of two tax years. If the IRS determines the claim for the credit was fraudulent, the ineligibility window is extended to ten years.

Unlike the child tax credit and EIC, no time restriction was placed on the IRS issuing refunds for any tax returns that claim an AOTC.

Form 8867, a due diligence checklist for tax preparers previously required for only the earned income credit, has been expanded to include steps to be taken for returns that include a child tax credit or the AOTC. Failure to file Form 8867 could result in a $530 penalty.

7-5b Lifetime Learning Credit

Taxpayers can elect a nonrefundable tax credit of 20 percent of qualified expenses of up to $10,000 in 2019, for a maximum credit of $2,000. The lifetime learning credit is available for qualified expenses paid for education of the taxpayer, his or her spouse, and dependents. The credit is available for undergraduate, graduate, or professional courses at eligible educational institutions. The student can be enrolled in just one course and still get the credit. There is no limit on the number of years a taxpayer can claim the credit. The credit is not subject to felony drug offense restrictions. The purpose of this credit is to encourage taxpayers to take courses at eligible institutions to acquire or improve job skills.

EXAMPLE In September 2019, Scott pays $1,200 to take a course to improve his job skills to qualify for a new position at work. His lifetime learning credit for 2019 is $240 (20% × $1,200). ◆

The lifetime learning credit is phased out at different levels than the American Opportunity tax credit. Married taxpayers with income between $116,000 and $136,000, and single, head of household, or qualifying widow(er) taxpayers with income between $58,000 and $68,000, must phase the credit out evenly over the phase-out range for 2019.

EXAMPLE During 2019, Jason, a single father with AGI of $85,000, paid $2,500 of tuition for a master's degree program in fine arts which he has been attending with the hope of eventually becoming a writer. Without any limitations, Jason would be entitled to a maximum lifetime learning credit of

$500 (20% × $2,500). However, due to the income phase-out ranges for the lifetime learning credit, none of the credit may be claimed on his tax return. ◆

7-5c **Using Both Credits**

Taxpayers cannot take both the American Opportunity tax credit and the lifetime learning credit for the same student in the same tax year. An American Opportunity tax credit can be claimed for one or more students, and the lifetime learning credit can be claimed for other students in the same tax year. Also, the choice in one year does not bind the taxpayer for future years. For example, a taxpayer can claim the American Opportunity tax credit for a student in one tax year and take the lifetime learning credit for the same student the following year. Taxpayers should claim the credit or combination of credits that provides the best tax benefit. Both the AOTC and the lifetime learning credit are claimed using Form 8863 (see Pages 7-32 and 7-33).

Education credits are input under Credits/Education Tuition (1098-T). The typical starting point would be to enter the information on the student's 1098-T.

intuit
proconnect.
TIP

Self-Study Problem 7.5 *See Appendix E for Solutions to Self-Study Problems*

a. Judy Estudiante graduates from high school in June 2019. In the fall, she enrolls for twelve units in Southwest University and receives the following Form 1098-T.

☐ CORRECTED		
FILER'S name, street address, city or town, state or province, country, ZIP or foreign postal code, and telephone number Southwest University 1234 Cleveland Ave. El Paso, TX 79925	**1** Payments received for qualified tuition and related expenses $ 5,923.00 **2**	OMB No. 1545-1574 20**19** Form **1098-T**	Tuition Statement
FILER'S employer identification no. 12-7652311	STUDENT'S TIN 434-11-7812	**3**	Copy B For Student
STUDENT'S name Judy Estudiante	**4** Adjustments made for a prior year $	**5** Scholarships or grants $	This is important tax information and is being furnished to the IRS. This form must be used to complete Form 8863 to claim education credits. Give it to the tax preparer or use it to prepare the tax return.
Street address (including apt. no.) 12 Fannin Street	**6** Adjustments to scholarships or grants for a prior year	**7** Checked if the amount in box 1 includes amounts for an academic period beginning January–March 2020 ☐	
City or town, state or province, country, and ZIP or foreign postal code Van Horn, TX 79855	$		
Service Provider/Acct. No. (see instr.)	**8** Check if at least half-time student ☒	**9** Checked if a graduate student ☐	**10** Ins. contract reimb./refund $

Form **1098-T**   (keep for your records)   www.irs.gov/Form1098T   Department of the Treasury - Internal Revenue Service

Judy's parents, Santiago and Sophia Estudiante, pay her tuition and fees, have AGI of $170,000, have pre-credit tax liability of over $20,000, are claiming no other tax credits, and claim Judy as a dependent. Judy has never been arrested or convicted of any crimes. Complete Form 8863 on Pages 7-32 and 7-33 to determine what is the refundable and nonrefundable American Opportunity tax credit Judy's parents can claim for Judy if they file a joint return.

Refundable American Opportunity tax credit $_____

Nonrefundable American Opportunity tax credit $_____

b. In September 2019, Gene pays $5,200 to take a course to improve his job skills at work. Gene's AGI is $35,000 for 2019. What is Gene's lifetime learning credit for 2019?

$_____

Self-Study Problem 7.5 part a

Form **8863**	**Education Credits**	OMB No. 1545-0074
	(American Opportunity and Lifetime Learning Credits)	**2019**
Department of the Treasury Internal Revenue Service (99)	▶ Attach to Form 1040 or 1040-SR. ▶ Go to *www.irs.gov/Form8863* for instructions and the latest information.	Attachment Sequence No. **50**

Name(s) shown on return	Your social security number

⚠ **CAUTION** *Complete a separate Part III on page 2 for each student for whom you're claiming either credit before you complete Parts I and II.*

DRAFT AS OF September 16, 2019 DO NOT FILE

Part I   Refundable American Opportunity Credit

1	After completing Part III for each student, enter the total of all amounts from all Parts III, line 30 . .	**1**	
2	Enter: $180,000 if married filing jointly; $90,000 if single, head of household, or qualifying widow(er)	**2**	
3	Enter the amount from Form 1040 or 1040-SR, line 8b. If you're filing Form 2555 or 4563, or you're excluding income from Puerto Rico, see Pub. 970 for the amount to enter	**3**	
4	Subtract line 3 from line 2. If zero or less, **stop**; you can't take any education credit	**4**	
5	Enter: $20,000 if married filing jointly; $10,000 if single, head of household, or qualifying widow(er)	**5**	
6	If line 4 is: • Equal to or more than line 5, enter 1.000 on line 6 . . . . • Less than line 5, divide line 4 by line 5. Enter the result as a decimal (rounded to at least three places)	**6**	.
7	Multiply line 1 by line 6. **Caution:** If you were under age 24 at the end of the year **and** meet the conditions described in the instructions, you **can't** take the refundable American opportunity credit; skip line 8, enter the amount from line 7 on line 9, and check this box . . . . ▶ ☐	**7**	
8	**Refundable American opportunity credit.** Multiply line 7 by 40% (0.40). Enter the amount here and on Form 1040 or 1040-SR, line 18c. Then go to line 9 below	**8**	

Part II   Nonrefundable Education Credits

9	Subtract line 8 from line 7. Enter here and on line 2 of the Credit Limit Worksheet (see instructions) .	**9**	
10	After completing Part III for each student, enter the total of all amounts from all Parts III, line 31. If zero, skip lines 11 through 17, enter -0- on line 18, and go to line 19	**10**	
11	Enter the smaller of line 10 or $10,000	**11**	
12	Multiply line 11 by 20% (0.20)	**12**	
13	Enter: $136,000 if married filing jointly; $68,000 if single, head of household, or qualifying widow(er)	**13**	
14	Enter the amount from Form 1040 or 1040-SR, line 8b. If you're filing Form 2555 or 4563, or you're excluding income from Puerto Rico, see Pub. 970 for the amount to enter	**14**	
15	Subtract line 14 from line 13. If zero or less, skip lines 16 and 17, enter -0- on line 18, and go to line 19	**15**	
16	Enter: $20,000 if married filing jointly; $10,000 if single, head of household, or qualifying widow(er)	**16**	
17	If line 15 is: • Equal to or more than line 16, enter 1.000 on line 17 and go to line 18 • Less than line 16, divide line 15 by line 16. Enter the result as a decimal (rounded to at least three places)	**17**	.
18	Multiply line 12 by line 17. Enter here and on line 1 of the Credit Limit Worksheet (see instructions) ▶	**18**	
19	**Nonrefundable education credits.** Enter the amount from line 7 of the Credit Limit Worksheet (see instructions) here and on Schedule 3 (Form 1040 or 1040-SR), line 3	**19**	

For Paperwork Reduction Act Notice, see your tax return instructions.	Cat. No. 25379M	Form **8863** (2019)

Self-Study Problem 7.5 part a

Form 8863 (2019)   Page **2**

Name(s) shown on return	Your social security number

⚠ **CAUTION** **Complete Part III for each student for whom you're claiming either the American opportunity credit or lifetime learning credit. Use additional copies of page 2 as needed for each student.**

Part III **Student and Educational Institution Information.** See instructions.

20 Student name (as shown on page 1 of your tax return)	**21** Student social security number (as shown on page 1 of your tax return)

22 Educational institution information (see instructions)

a. Name of first educational institution	**b.** Name of second educational institution (if any)
(1) Address. Number and street (or P.O. box). City, town or post office, state, and ZIP code. If a foreign address, see instructions.	**(1)** Address. Number and street (or P.O. box). City, town or post office, state, and ZIP code. If a foreign address, see instructions.
(2) Did the student receive Form 1098-T from this institution for 2019? ☐ Yes ☐ No	**(2)** Did the student receive Form 1098-T from this institution for 2019? ☐ Yes ☐ No
(3) Did the student receive Form 1098-T from this institution for 2018 with box 2 filled in and box 7 checked? ☐ Yes ☐ No	**(3)** Did the student receive Form 1098-T from this institution for 2018 with box 2 filled in and box 7 checked? ☐ Yes ☐ No
(4) Enter the institution's employer identification number (EIN) if you're claiming the American opportunity credit or if you checked "Yes" in **(2)** or **(3)**. You can get the EIN from Form 1098-T or from the institution. __ __ – __ __ __ __ __ __ __	**(4)** Enter the institution's employer identification number (EIN) if you're claiming the American opportunity credit or if you checked "Yes" in **(2)** or **(3)**. You can get the EIN from Form 1098-T or from the institution. __ __ – __ __ __ __ __ __ __

23	Has the Hope Scholarship Credit or American opportunity credit been claimed for this student for any 4 tax years before 2019?	☐ Yes — **Stop!** Go to line 31 for this student.	☐ No — Go to line 24.
24	Was the student enrolled at least half-time for at least one academic period that began or is treated as having begun in 2019 at an eligible educational institution in a program leading towards a postsecondary degree, certificate, or other recognized postsecondary educational credential? See instructions.	☐ Yes — Go to line 25.	☐ No — **Stop!** Go to line 31 for this student.
25	Did the student complete the first 4 years of postsecondary education before 2019? See instructions.	☐ Yes — **Stop!** Go to line 31 for this student.	☐ No — Go to line 26.
26	Was the student convicted, before the end of 2019, of a felony for possession or distribution of a controlled substance?	☐ Yes — **Stop!** Go to line 31 for this student.	☐ No — Complete lines 27 through 30 for this student.

⚠ **CAUTION** You **can't** take the American opportunity credit and the lifetime learning credit for the **same student** in the same year. If you complete lines 27 through 30 for this student, don't complete line 31.

American Opportunity Credit

27	Adjusted qualified education expenses (see instructions). **Don't enter more than $4,000**	**27**	
28	Subtract $2,000 from line 27. If zero or less, enter -0-.	**28**	
29	Multiply line 28 by 25% (0.25)	**29**	
30	If line 28 is zero, enter the amount from line 27. Otherwise, add $2,000 to the amount on line 29 and enter the result. Skip line 31. Include the total of all amounts from all Parts III, line 30, on Part I, line 1 .	**30**	

Lifetime Learning Credit

31	Adjusted qualified education expenses (see instructions). Include the total of all amounts from all Parts III, line 31, on Part II, line 10	**31**	

Form **8863** (2019)

| Learning Objective 7.6 | # 7-6 FOREIGN EXCLUSION AND TAX CREDIT |

Compute the foreign income exclusion and tax credit.

Some of the most sweeping changes to the tax law under the TCJA are related to the taxation of international income but virtually all of these changes were directed at U.S. corporations; with little applying specifically to individuals. However, there are two main provisions related to U.S. taxation of international income that apply to individuals: (1) the foreign income exclusion and (2) the foreign tax credit.

7-6a Foreign Income Exclusion

Certain taxpayers working and living outside the U.S. are eligible to exclude a certain portion of their foreign income from taxable income under the foreign income exclusion. In addition, certain foreign housing can also be excluded or deducted. To qualify, the taxpayer must have a bona fide tax home outside the U.S. for a certain number of days. The exclusion limit in 2019 is $105,900.

EXAMPLE   John Adams, a single U.S. citizen, is an employee of a large multinational corporation and works at the company's Mexican subsidiary. He has established a bona fide tax home in Mexico. During the year, John spent 355 days in Mexico and 10 days vacationing in Hawaii. His employer paid him wages of $107,000 in 2019. John excludes $105,900 of his wages from U.S. taxable income. John will not be eligible to claim a foreign tax credit (see below) on the wages excluded. ♦

The foreign income exclusion is claimed on Form 2555. Form 2555-EZ has been discontinued by the IRS after 2018. Use of the foreign income exclusion precludes the use of certain credits or deductions (for example, the EITC). In addition, a number of provisions that require the computation of modified taxable income require the foreign income exclusion to be added back (for example, the limits for a deduction for contributions to an IRA).

Employees and self-employed taxpayers that qualify for the foreign income exclusion are also eligible for a housing exclusion or deduction. The foreign housing exclusion is an additional exclusion designed to represent the incremental cost of housing in a foreign country above a base amount. The details are beyond the scope of this textbook.

7-6b Foreign Tax Credit

An individual will typically incur foreign taxes under two possible scenarios: (1) they have engaged in work outside the United States as either an employee or as self-employed individual (expats) or (2) as a result of foreign investments either directly or through an investment portfolio such as a mutual fund or exchange-traded fund. Although the tax treatment of expats is beyond the scope of this textbook, aside from the benefit available for many expats under the foreign income exclusions described above, an expat may use a foreign tax credit for foreign taxes paid to reduce their U.S. income tax liability. The same is true of an investor whose income is subject to foreign taxes. In both cases, the amount of the credit is limited to the U.S. tax that applies to that income.

EXAMPLE   Thomas Jefferson, a single U.S. citizen, works for his employer in France and he is not eligible to use the foreign income exclusion. In 2019, Thomas paid income taxes in France of $3,500 on his income of $50,000. This was his only income during the year (U.S. or otherwise). Thomas claims the standard deduction. Thomas' foreign-sourced income is $37,800 ($50,000 less standard deduction of $12,200). His U.S. income for purposes of the foreign tax credit limitation is also $37,800. Thomas calculates his U.S.

income tax liability before any credits as $4,345. His foreign tax credit limit in this case is:

$$\frac{\text{Net foreign income } \$37,800}{\text{U.S. taxable income } \$37,800} \times \text{U.S. tax liability } \$4,345 = \$4,345$$

Thomas' actual foreign taxes paid are $3,500; thus, his foreign tax credit is not limited and he is eligible for a $3,500 foreign tax credit. ◆

EXAMPLE Alexander Hamilton held shares in the Federalist International Stock Fund, a mutual fund with extensive foreign holdings. Alexander's earnings of $2,300 from the fund and foreign taxes paid of $632 were reported to him on a Form 1099-DIV. This was Alexander's only portfolio income during the year. Alexander's taxable income was $75,950 and his tax liability before the credit was $12,573 including Alexander's U.S. tax liability associated with dividend income of $345. Alexander's limitation is calculated as

$$\frac{\text{Net foreign income } \$2,300}{\text{U.S. taxable income } \$75,950} \times \text{U.S. tax liability } \$12,573 = \$381$$

As a result, Alexander's foreign tax credit is limited to $381. The unused credit of $251 ($632 foreign taxes paid less $381 limitation) can be carried back one year or forward for up to 10 years. ◆

A number of simplifications were used in the above examples and the actual computation of the limit can be considerably more complex. Different rules apply to income earned in a U.S. possession. The foreign tax credit is typically claimed on Form 1116 and the rules are explained in the instructions to Form 1116.

A simplified foreign tax credit that does not require the completion of Form 1116 is available if you meet all of the following requirements:

1. All of the foreign-sourced gross income was "passive category income" (which includes most interest and dividends).
2. All the income and any foreign taxes paid on it were reported on a qualified payee statement such as a Form 1099-DIV, Form 1099-INT, Schedule K-1, or similar substitute statements.
3. Total creditable foreign taxes aren't more than $300 ($600 if married filing a joint return).

If the Form 1116 is not used, the foreign tax credit is entered directly on Schedule 3 of Form 1040, Line 1. The foreign tax credit is nonrefundable and thus limited to the pre-credit tax amount. Use of the simplified method precludes a carryback of any limited foreign tax credit but the unused credit can be carried forward up to 10 years.

As a reminder, this is just an overview of these areas which are, in most instances, extremely complex. Useful publications are IRS Publication 54, Form 1116 and instructions, and Form 2555 and instructions.

One of the most common ways to pay foreign taxes is through an investment in a mutual fund that happens to hold some international investments and pays foreign taxes at the fund level. The foreign tax payments are generally reported on the taxpayer's Form 1099-DIV and are entered into ProConnect as part of recording the dividend income.

TIP

Self-Study Problem 7.6 *See Appendix E for Solutions to Self-Study Problems*

Benny Franklin receives a Form 1099-DIV from his investment manager that lists foreign taxes paid of $432 and Benny's foreign investment earnings of $1,500. Benny had no other investment earnings and his total taxable income for the year is $58,000. Benny's tax liability before any foreign taxes is $8,624. Calculate the amount of the foreign tax credit.

$_____

Learning Objective 7.7

Determine the proper use and calculation of the adoption credit.

7-7 ADOPTION EXPENSES

Taxpayers are allowed two tax breaks for adoption expenses. A tax credit is allowed for qualified adoption expenses paid by taxpayers, and an exclusion from W-2 income is allowed for qualified adoption expenses paid by taxpayers' employers.

7-7a Adoption Credit

Individuals are allowed a nonrefundable income tax credit for qualified adoption expenses (defined below). Form 8839 is used to calculate and report the adoption credit. The total expense that can be taken as a credit for all tax years with respect to an adoption of a child is $14,080 for 2019. The credit is the total amount for each adoption and is not an annual amount (i.e., there is only one $14,080 credit per adopted child). The amount of the credit allowable for any tax year is reduced for taxpayers with AGI over $211,160 and is fully phased out when AGI reaches $251,160. The amount of the credit is reduced (but not below zero) by a factor equal to the excess of the taxpayer's AGI over $211,160 divided by $40,000. In some cases, beyond the scope of this textbook, AGI must be modified prior to calculating the adoption credit phase-out. For additional information on calculating modified adjusted gross income (MAGI) with respect to the adoption credit, see the IRS website at **www.irs.gov.**

EXAMPLE   Ben and Beverly pay $5,000 of qualified adoption expenses in 2019 to adopt a qualified child. Their AGI is $214,160 for 2019, which causes an adoption credit reduction for 2019 of $375 [$5,000 × ($214,160 − $211,160)/$40,000)]. Thus, Ben and Beverly's allowable adoption credit for 2019 is $4,625 ($5,000 − $375). ◆

The credit is not refundable; however, the unused portion may be carried forward for 5 years. To claim the credit, married individuals must file jointly, and the taxpayer must include (if known) the name, age, and taxpayer identification number (TIN) of the child on the return.

7-7b Domestic Multiyear Adoptions

In the case of the adoption of an eligible child who is a U.S. citizen or resident of the United States at the time the adoption commenced, the credit for qualified adoption expenses is allowed for the tax year that follows the year during which the expenses are paid or incurred, unless the expenses are paid or incurred in the tax year the adoption becomes final. If the expenses are paid or incurred during the tax year in which the adoption becomes final, the credit is allowed for that year. The full $14,080 credit is allowed in special-needs adoptions regardless of the amount of qualified adoption expenses paid.

EXAMPLE In connection with the adoption of an eligible child who is a U.S. citizen and is not a child with special needs, a taxpayer pays $6,000 of qualified adoption expenses in 2018 and $8,600 of qualified adoption expenses in 2019. The adoption is not finalized until 2020. The $6,000 of expenses paid or incurred in 2018 would be allowed in 2019, and $8,080 of the $8,600 paid or incurred in 2019 would be allowed in 2020. On the other hand, if the adoption were finalized in 2019, then $14,080 of qualified expenses would be allowed in 2019 (the maximum credit permitted as of 2019). ♦

7-7c **Foreign Multiyear Adoptions**

In the case of the adoption of a child who is *not* a U.S. citizen or resident of the United States, the credit for qualified adoption expenses is not available unless the adoption becomes final. Qualified adoption expenses paid or incurred before the tax year in which the adoption becomes final are taken into account for the credit as if the expenses were paid or incurred in the tax year in which the adoption becomes final. Therefore, the credit for qualified adoption expenses paid or incurred in the tax year in which the adoption becomes final, or in any earlier tax year, is allowed only in the tax year the adoption becomes final.

EXAMPLE In 2017 and 2018, a taxpayer pays $3,000 and $6,000, respectively, of qualified adoption expenses in connection with the adoption of an eligible child who is not a U.S. citizen or resident of the United States. In 2019, the year the adoption becomes final, the taxpayer pays an additional $3,000 of qualified expenses. The taxpayer may claim a credit of $12,000 on his or her income tax return for 2019 (the year the adoption becomes final). Note: If a foreign adoption does not become final, no credit is allowed. ♦

7-7d **Employer-Provided Adoption Assistance**

An employee may exclude from W-2 earnings amounts paid or expenses incurred by his or her employer for qualified adoption expenses connected with the adoption of a child by the employee, if the amounts are furnished under an adoption assistance program. The total amount excludable per child is the same as the adoption credit amount ($14,080). The phase-out is calculated in the same manner as the phase-out for the adoption credit. An individual may claim both a credit and an exclusion in connection with the adoption of an eligible child, but may not claim both a credit and an exclusion for the same expense.

The following quotation is often attributed to Albert Einstein: "The hardest thing in the world to understand is the income tax."

Self-Study Problem 7.7 *See Appendix E for Solutions to Self-Study Problems*

James and Michael Bass finalized the adoption of their daughter Allison in October 2019, one month after her birth. Allison is a U.S. citizen and is not a child with special needs. Her Social Security number is 466-47-3311. In 2019, James and Michael paid $17,000 in qualified adoption expenses. In addition, Michael's employer paid $4,000 directly to an adoption agency as an employer-provided adoption benefit. The Bass' AGI for 2019 is $219,160 (assume adjusted gross income and modified adjusted gross income are the same for purposes of this problem). The Bass' tax liability is $22,332 and they are not using tax credits except the adoption credit. Use Form 8839 on Pages 7-39 and 7-40 to calculate the Bass' adoption credit and the amount of any employee adoption exclusion.

Learning Objective 7.8

Recognize the basic individual credits for energy efficiency.

7-8 ENERGY CREDITS

Over the past decade, the tax law has included a number of personal tax credits associated with energy-efficient products. These credits have been slowly expiring. By design, many tax credits are temporary additions to the tax law and are designed to create short-term or limited changes in taxpayer behavior as mentioned in Chapter 1. The current status of many of these credits is presented below:

Credit	IRC Section	Status
Electric vehicle credit	30D	Active
Nonbusiness energy property credit	25C	Expired 2017
Residential energy efficient property (REEP) credit	25D	Active
Qualified fuel cell motor vehicle credit	30B	Expired 2017
Qualified alternative fuel vehicle refueling property	30C	Expired 2017

Because credits are often retroactively extended, be sure and check **www.irs.gov** for any changes that may have occurred after we went to print.

Two of the remaining credits are discussed here.

7-8a Plug-In Electric Vehicle Credits

Taxpayers are allowed a credit for the purchase of plug-in electric drive vehicles used for either business or personal purposes. The credit, which ranges between $2,500 and $7,500 for light-duty vehicles, varies depending on the weight of the vehicle and the kilowatt hour of battery capacity. The Hyundai Kona, Nissan Leaf, Honda Clarity, and numerous other new electric vehicles qualify for the full $7,500 credit. The credit phases out for each car manufacturer when they reach a total of 200,000 electric cars sold for use in the United States (e.g., the Toyota Prius Plug-In). More information on federal and state electric vehicle tax incentives may be found at **www.fueleconomy.gov.**

7-8b Credits for Residential Energy-Efficient Property (REEP Credit)

Taxpayers may claim a credit of 30 percent of the amount paid for qualified solar electric property (property which uses solar power to generate electricity in a home), qualified solar water-heating property, qualified fuel cell property, qualified small wind energy property, and qualified geothermal heat pump property. The REEP credit for all property types

Self-Study Problem 7.7

Form **8839**

Department of the Treasury
Internal Revenue Service (99)

Qualified Adoption Expenses

▶ Attach to Form 1040, 1040-SR, or 1040-NR.
▶ Go to *www.irs.gov/Form8839* for instructions and the latest information.

OMB No. 1545-0074

20**19**

Attachment
Sequence No. **38**

Name(s) shown on return

Your social security number

Part I **Information About Your Eligible Child or Children—**You **must** complete this part. See instructions for details, including what to do if you need more space.

1	(a) Child's name		(b) Child's year of birth	Check if child was—			(f) Child's identifying number	(g) Check if adoption became final in 2019 or earlier
	First	Last		(c) born **before 2002** and disabled	(d) a child with special needs	(e) a foreign child		
Child 1				☐	☐	☐		☐
Child 2				☐	☐	☐		☐
Child 3				☐	☐	☐		☐

Caution: If the child was a foreign child, see **Special rules** in the instructions for line 1, column (e), before you complete Part II or Part III. If you received **employer-provided adoption benefits,** complete Part III on the back next.

Part II **Adoption Credit**

			Child 1	Child 2	Child 3
2	Maximum adoption credit per child. Enter $14,080 (see instructions)	**2**			
3	Did you file Form 8839 for a prior year for the same child? ☐ **No.** Enter -0-. ☐ **Yes.** See instructions for the amount to enter.	**3**			
4	Subtract line 3 from line 2	**4**			
5	**Qualified adoption expenses** (see instructions) . . **Caution:** Your qualified adoption expenses may not be equal to the adoption expenses you paid in 2019.	**5**			
6	Enter the **smaller** of line 4 or line 5	**6**			
7	Enter modified adjusted gross income (see instructions)	**7**			
8	Is line 7 more than $211,160? ☐ **No.** Skip lines 8 and 9, and enter -0- on line 10. ☐ **Yes.** Subtract $211,160 from line 7	**8**			
9	Divide line 8 by $40,000. Enter the result as a decimal (rounded to at least three places). Do not enter more than 1.000	**9**	× .
10	Multiply each amount on line 6 by line 9	**10**			
11	Subtract line 10 from line 6	**11**			
12	Add the amounts on line 11	**12**	
13	Credit carryforward, if any, from prior years. See your Adoption Credit Carryforward Worksheet in the 2018 Form 8839 instructions	**13**	
14	Add lines 12 and 13	**14**	
15	Enter the amount from line 5 of the Credit Limit Worksheet in the instructions	**15**	
16	**Adoption Credit.** Enter the smaller of line 14 or line 15 here and on Schedule 3 (Form 1040 or 1040-SR), line 6, or Form 1040-NR, line 51. Check box **c** on that line and enter "**8839**" in the space next to box **c.** If line 15 is smaller than line 14, you may have a credit carryforward (see instructions) . . .	**16**	

For Paperwork Reduction Act Notice, see your tax return instructions.   Cat. No. 22843L   Form **8839** (2019)

Form 8839 (2019)   Page **2**

Part III	**Employer-Provided Adoption Benefits**			
		Child 1	Child 2	Child 3

17 Maximum exclusion per child. Enter $14,080 (see instructions) **17**

18 Did you receive employer-provided adoption benefits for a prior year for the same child?
☐ **No.** Enter -0-.
☐ **Yes.** See instructions for the amount to enter.   **18**

19 Subtract line 18 from line 17 . . . . **19**

20 Employer-provided adoption benefits you received in 2019. This amount should be shown in box 12 of your 2019 Form(s) W-2 with code **T** **20**

21 Add the amounts on line 20 . . . . **21**

22 Enter the **smaller** of line 19 or line 20. But if the child was a child with special needs and the adoption became final in 2019, enter the amount from line 19 . **22**

23 Enter modified adjusted gross income (from the worksheet in the instructions) **23**

24 Is line 23 more than $211,160?
☐ **No.** Skip lines 24 and 25, and enter -0- on line 26.
☐ **Yes.** Subtract $211,160 from line 23 . . . . . . **24**

25 Divide line 24 by $40,000. Enter the result as a decimal (rounded to at least three places). Do not enter more than 1.000 . . . . **25** × .

26 Multiply each amount on line 22 by line 25 . . . . **26**

27 **Excluded benefits.** Subtract line 26 from line 22 . . **27**

28 Add the amounts on line 27 . . . . **28**

29 **Taxable benefits.** Is line 28 more than line 21?
☐ **No.** Subtract line 28 from line 21. Also, include this amount, if more than zero, on line 1 of Form 1040 or 1040-SR or line 8 of Form 1040-NR. On the dotted line next to line 1 of Form 1040 or 1040-SR or line 8 of Form 1040-NR, enter "AB."
☐ **Yes.** Subtract line 21 from line 28. Enter the result as a negative number. Reduce the total you would enter on line 1 of Form 1040 or 1040-SR or line 8 of Form 1040-NR by the amount on Form 8839, line 29. Enter the result on line 1 of Form 1040 or 1040-SR or line 8 of Form 1040-NR. Enter "SNE" on the dotted line next to the entry line. **29**

You may be able to claim the adoption credit in Part II on the front of this form if any of the following apply.

TIP

• You paid adoption expenses in 2018, those expenses were not fully reimbursed by your employer or otherwise, and the adoption was not final by the end of 2018.

• The total adoption expenses you paid in 2019 were not fully reimbursed by your employer or otherwise, and the adoption became final in 2019 or earlier.

• You adopted a child with special needs and the adoption became final in 2019.

Form **8839** (2019)

except for qualified solar electric and water heating had expired at the end of 2017 but was extended through 2022. The credit percentage is reduced to 26 percent for property placed in service starting in 2020 and then further reduced to 22 percent in 2021.

The REEP credits described in the paragraph above may be claimed for both principal residences and vacation homes. No credit is allowed for installations used to heat swimming pools or hot tubs. The REEP credit is reported on Form 5695.

EXAMPLE   In 2019, Mary buys $30,000 of solar electric property for her second (vacation) home. The equipment is not used to heat her swimming pool or hot tub. She may claim a credit of $9,000 ($30,000 × 30%) for 2019. ♦

Self-Study Problem 7.8   *See Appendix E for Solutions to Self-Study Problems*

Calculate the energy credit allowed for the following purchases:

a. Geoffrey purchases a Nissan Leaf in May of 2019.

Credit Allowed $_____

b. Betty purchases a solar system to heat her hot tub for $2,000 and a second, certified, energy-efficient solar system to heat her home for $10,000 in 2019.

Credit Allowed $_____

7-9 LOW-INCOME RETIREMENT PLAN CONTRIBUTION CREDIT

7.9 Learning Objective

Calculate the low-income Retirement Plan Contribution Credit.

Certain low-income taxpayers may claim a nonrefundable "Low-Income Retirement Plan Contribution Credit," also called the "Saver's Credit," to encourage them to participate in tax-saving retirement plans, including IRAs. The credit rate is 50 percent, 20 percent, or 10 percent depending on the taxpayer's filing status and adjusted gross income. The credit is a direct deduction from income taxes otherwise payable, and the cash saved may be used to make part of the contribution to the plan. Taxpayers receive up to a 50 percent credit for contribution amounts up to $2,000 ($4,000 married filing jointly) or a maximum credit of $1,000 ($2,000 for married filing jointly). The credit phases out for adjusted gross income over certain income limits, as shown below.

Filing Status/Adjusted Gross Income for 2019—Saver's Credit			
Amount of Credit	*Joint*	*Head of Household*	*Single/Others*
50% of first $2,000 ($4,000) deferred	$0 to $38,500	$0 to $28,875	$0 to $19,250
20% of first $2,000 ($4,000) deferred	$38,501 to $41,500	$28,876 to $31,125	$19,251 to $20,750
10% of first $2,000 ($4,000) deferred	$41,501 to $64,000	$31,126 to $48,000	$20,751 to $32,000

EXAMPLE   In 2019, Teddy and Abby file a joint tax return with AGI of $29,000. Teddy contributes $1,500 to a Section 401(k) plan at work. Teddy and Abby are entitled to a $750 (50% × $1,500) Retirement Plan Contribution Credit. The credit is in addition to any deduction or exclusion allowed for the contribution. ♦

The Saver's Credit is claimed on Form 8880. Because the Saver's Credit is nonrefundable, the amount of the credit is limited to the income tax liability after reflecting any foreign tax credit, child and dependent care expense credit, educations credits, or credit for the elderly and disabled.

EXAMPLE In 2019, Whitney and Melissa file a joint tax return that reflects AGI of $37,100, income tax liability before any credits of $1,270, and a lifetime learning credit of $240. If Whitney and Melissa contribute $2,100 to an IRA, their Saver's Credit is $1,030 calculated as the credit amount of $1,050 ($2,100 × 50%) limited to tax liability before the credit of $1,030 ($1,270 − $240). ♦

Self-Study Problem 7.9 *See Appendix E for Solutions to Self-Study Problems*

Steve and Robin Harrington are married filing jointly taxpayers, both 61 years of age and semi-retired. Robin earns wages of $32,000 as a part-time school librarian and Steve sharpens knives as a hobby and their 2019 AGI is $39,500. Their tax liability before any credit is $1,510. The Harringtons are not eligible for any other tax credits. Neither Harrington is active in any other income deferral plans. Because the Harringtons have limited financial needs, they also made an IRA contribution of $12,000 ($6,000 each) trying to get ready for retirement. Use the Form 8880 on Pages 7-43 and 7-44 to determine the Harrington's Saver's Credit.

TAX BREAK

Numerous tax credits may be claimed by taxpayers in addition to the tax credits discussed in this textbook. Several of the more common credits not covered here include:

- **The Elderly or Disabled Credit** provides relief for low-income taxpayers who are not receiving substantial tax-free retirement benefits.
- **The Disabled Access Credit** is 50 percent of eligible access expenditures up to a maximum credit of $5,000, and is meant to encourage small businesses to become more accessible to disabled individuals.
- **The General Business Credit** is made up of a number of credits which are bundled into one credit for carryback and carryforward purposes, including the credit for **rehabilitation expenditures**, the **low-income housing credit**, and the credit for **employer-provided child care.**
- **The Small Employer Health Insurance Credit** provides small employers a credit for health insurance paid on behalf of workers who are not owners and who meet certain criteria.
- **The Research Activities Credit** is an incremental credit of 20 percent of expenditures in excess of a base amount, and is intended to encourage high-tech and energy research.
- **The Work Opportunity Credit** is limited to 40 percent of the first $6,000 of wages paid to each eligible employee. The purpose is to encourage employment of individuals in certain specified disadvantaged groups and has been extended through December 31, 2019.

Credits have a greater tendency to expire after a few years than do other tax code provisions. Be sure and check on the latest status of available individual and business credits at **www.irs.gov/credits-deductions**.

Self-Study Problem 7.9

Form **8880**	**Credit for Qualified Retirement Savings Contributions**	OMB No. 1545-0074

Form **8880**

Department of the Treasury
Internal Revenue Service

Credit for Qualified Retirement Savings Contributions

▶ Attach to Form 1040, 1040-SR, or 1040-NR.
▶ Go to *www.irs.gov/Form8880* for the latest information.

OMB No. 1545-0074

20**19**

Attachment
Sequence No. **54**

Name(s) shown on return

Your social security number

CAUTION

*You **cannot** take this credit if **either** of the following applies.*

- *The amount on Form 1040 or 1040-SR, line 8b; or Form 1040-NR, line 35, is more than $32,000 ($48,000 if head of household; $64,000 if married filing jointly).*
- *The person(s) who made the qualified contribution or elective deferral **(a)** was born after January 1, 2002; **(b)** is claimed as a dependent on someone else's 2019 tax return; or **(c)** was a **student** (see instructions).*

		(a) You	**(b) Your spouse**
1	Traditional and Roth IRA contributions, and ABLE account contributions by the designated beneficiary for 2019. **Do not** include rollover contributions **1**		
2	Elective deferrals to a 401(k) or other qualified employer plan, voluntary employee contributions, and 501(c)(18)(D) plan contributions for 2019 (see instructions) . . **2**		
3	Add lines 1 and 2 . . . . **3**		
4	Certain distributions received **after** 2016 and **before** the due date (including extensions) of your 2019 tax return (see instructions). If married filing jointly, include **both** spouses' amounts in **both** columns. See instructions for an exception . . . **4**		
5	Subtract line 4 from line 3. If zero or less, enter -0- **5**		
6	In each column, enter the **smaller** of line 5 or $2,000 . . . . . . **6**		
7	Add the amounts on line 6. If zero, **stop;** you can't take this credit **7**		
8	Enter the amount from Form 1040 or 1040-SR, line 8b;* or Form 1040-NR, line 35 . . . . **8**		
9	Enter the applicable decimal amount from the table below.		

If line 8 is—		And your filing status is—		
Over—	But not over—	Married filing jointly	Head of household	Single, Married filing separately, or Qualifying widow(er)
		Enter on line 9—		
---	$19,250	0.5	0.5	0.5
$19,250	$20,750	0.5	0.5	0.2
$20,750	$28,875	0.5	0.5	0.1
$28,875	$31,125	0.5	0.2	0.1
$31,125	$32,000	0.5	0.1	0.1
$32,000	$38,500	0.5	0.1	0.0
$38,500	$41,500	0.2	0.1	0.0
$41,500	$48,000	0.1	0.1	0.0
$48,000	$64,000	0.1	0.0	0.0
$64,000	---	0.0	0.0	0.0

9 x 0.

Note: If line 9 is zero, **stop;** you can't take this credit.

10	Multiply line 7 by line 9 . . . . **10**	
11	Limitation based on tax liability. Enter the amount from the Credit Limit Worksheet in the instructions **11**	
12	**Credit for qualified retirement savings contributions.** Enter the **smaller** of line 10 or line 11 here and on Schedule 3 (Form 1040 or 1040-SR), line 4; or Form 1040-NR, line 48 . . . . **12**	

* See Pub. 590-A for the amount to enter if you claim any exclusion or deduction for foreign earned income, foreign housing, or income from Puerto Rico or for bona fide residents of American Samoa.

For Paperwork Reduction Act Notice, see your tax return instructions.   Cat. No. 33394D   Form **8880** (2019)

Form 8880 (2019)   Page **2**

General Instructions

Section references are to the Internal Revenue Code.

Reminder

Contributions by a designated beneficiary to an Achieving a Better Life Experience (ABLE) account. A retirement savings contribution credit may be claimed for the amount of contributions you, as the designated beneficiary of an ABLE account, make before January 1, 2026, to the ABLE account. See Pub. 907, Tax Highlights for Persons With Disabilities, for more information.

Future Developments

For the latest information about developments related to Form 8880 and its instructions, such as legislation enacted after they were published, go to *www.irs.gov/Form8880.*

Purpose of Form

Use Form 8880 to figure the amount, if any, of your retirement savings contributions credit (also known as the saver's credit).

This credit can be claimed in addition to any IRA deduction claimed on Schedule 1 (Form 1040 or 1040-SR), line 19; or Form 1040-NR, line 32.

Who Can Take This Credit

You may be able to take this credit if you, or your spouse if filing jointly, made (a) contributions (other than rollover contributions) to a traditional or Roth IRA; (b) elective deferrals to a 401(k), 403(b), governmental 457(b), SEP, or SIMPLE plan; (c) voluntary employee contributions to a qualified retirement plan, as defined in section 4974(c) (including the federal Thrift Savings Plan); (d) contributions to a 501(c)(18)(D) plan; or (e) contributions, as a designated beneficiary of an ABLE account, to the ABLE account, as defined in section 529A.

However, you can't take the credit if either of the following applies.

• The amount on Form 1040 or 1040-SR, line 8b; or Form 1040-NR, line 35, is more than $32,000 ($48,000 if head of household; $64,000 if married filing jointly).

• The person(s) who made the qualified contribution or elective deferral (a) was born after January 1, 2002; (b) is claimed as a dependent on someone else's 2019 tax return; or (c) was a student.

You'll need to refigure the amount on Form 1040 or 1040-SR, line 8b, if you're filing Form 2555 or Form 4563 or you're excluding income from Puerto Rico. See Pub. 590-A at www.irs.gov/Pub590A for details.

You were a student if during any part of 5 calendar months of 2019 you:

• Were enrolled as a full-time student at a school; or

• Took a full-time, on-farm training course given by a school or a state, county, or local government agency.

A school includes technical, trade, and mechanical schools. It doesn't include on-the-job training courses, correspondence schools, or schools offering courses only through the Internet.

Specific Instructions

Column (b)

Complete column (b) only if you're filing a joint return.

Line 2

Include on line 2 any of the following amounts.

• Elective deferrals to a 401(k) or 403(b) plan (including designated Roth contributions under section 402A), or to a governmental 457(b), SEP, or SIMPLE plan.

• Voluntary employee contributions to a qualified retirement plan, as defined in section 4974(c) (including the federal Thrift Savings Plan).

• Contributions to a 501(c)(18)(D) plan.

These amounts may be shown in box 12 of your Form(s) W-2 for 2019.

Note: Contributions designated under section 414(h)(2) are treated as employer contributions and, as such, they aren't voluntary contributions made by the employee. They don't qualify for the credit and shouldn't be included on line 2.

Line 4

Enter the total amount of distributions you, and your spouse if filing jointly, received after 2016 and before the due date of your 2019 return (including extensions) from any of the following types of plans.

• Traditional or Roth IRAs (including *my*RAs), or ABLE accounts.

• 401(k), 403(b), governmental 457(b), 501(c)(18)(D), SEP, or SIMPLE plans.

• Qualified retirement plans, as defined in section 4974(c) (including the federal Thrift Savings Plan).

Don't include any of the following.

• Distributions not taxable as the result of a rollover or a trustee-to-trustee transfer.

• Distributions that are taxable as the result of an in-plan rollover to your designated Roth account.

• Distributions from your eligible retirement plan (other than a Roth IRA) rolled over or converted to your Roth IRA.

• Loans from a qualified employer plan treated as a distribution.

• Distributions of excess contributions or deferrals (and income allocable to such contributions or deferrals).

• Distributions of contributions made to an IRA during a tax year and returned (with any income allocable to such contributions) on or before the due date (including extensions) for that tax year.

• Distributions of dividends paid on stock held by an employee stock ownership plan under section 404(k).

• Distributions from a military retirement plan (other than the federal Thrift Savings Plan).

• Distributions from an inherited IRA by a nonspousal beneficiary.

If you're filing a joint return, include both spouses' amounts in both columns.

Exception. Don't include your spouse's distributions with yours when entering an amount on line 4 if you and your spouse didn't file a joint return for the year the distribution was received.

Example. You received a distribution of $5,000 from a qualified retirement plan in 2019. Your spouse received a distribution of $2,000 from a Roth IRA in 2017. You and your spouse file a joint return in 2019, but didn't file a joint return in 2017. You would include $5,000 in column (a) and $7,000 in column (b).

Line 7

Add the amounts from line 6, columns (a) and (b), and enter the total.

Line 11

Before you complete the following worksheet, figure the amount of any credit for the elderly or the disabled you're claiming on Schedule 3 (Form 1040 or 1040-SR), line 6. See Schedule R (Form 1040 or 1040-SR) to figure the credit.

Credit Limit Worksheet

Complete this worksheet to figure the amount to enter on line 11.

1. Enter the amount from Form 1040 or 1040-SR, line 12b; or Form 1040-NR, line 45 . . . . .   **1.** _____

2. Form 1040 or 1040-SR filers: Enter the total of your credits from Schedule 3, lines 1 through 3, and Schedule R, line 22.

   Form 1040-NR filers: Enter the total of your credits from lines 46 and 47 . . . .   **2.** _____

3. Subtract line 2 from line 1. Also enter this amount on Form 8880, line 11. But if zero or less, **stop;** you can't take the credit—don't file this form .   **3.** _____

KEY TERMS

child tax credit, 7-2
nonrefundable tax credit, 7-2
refundable tax credit, 7-2
qualifying dependent credit, 7-2
additional child tax credit, 7-3
earned income credit (EIC), 7-5
"negative" income tax, 7-5
child and dependent care credit, 7-17

Affordable Care Act (ACA), 7-21
premium tax credit, 7-21
federal poverty line (FPL), 7-21
American Opportunity tax
    credit, 7-27
qualified higher education
    expenses, 7-28
lifetime learning credit, 7-30

foreign income exclusion, 7-34
foreign tax credit, 7-34
adoption credit, 7-36
energy credit, 7-38
low-income Retirement Plan
    Contribution Credit, 7-41
Saver's Credit, 7-41

KEY POINTS

Learning Objectives	Key Points
LO 7.1: Calculate the child tax credit.	• Credits are a direct reduction in tax liability instead of a deduction from income. • The child tax credit is $2,000 per qualifying child. • All qualifying children must have a Social Security number at the time of filing. • The child tax credit begins phasing out when AGI reaches $400,000 for joint filers and $200,000 for all others. • The additional child tax credit is available to certain taxpayers whose child tax credit was limited by their tax liability. • The child tax credit also includes an "other dependent credit" of $500 for taxpayers with dependents that do not qualify for the child tax credit.
LO 7.2: Determine the earned income credit (EIC).	• The earned income credit (EIC) is available to qualifying individuals with earned income and AGI below certain levels and is meant to assist the working poor. • The EIC formula for calculating the credit is based on the AGI of the taxpayer and the number of qualifying children of the taxpayer. • To compute the credit, the taxpayer must fill out a worksheet calculating the credit from the tables based on earned income from wages, salaries, and self-employment income. • To be eligible for the credit with no qualifying children, a worker must be over 25 and under 65 years old and not be claimed as a dependent by another taxpayer.
LO 7.3: Compute the child and dependent care credit for an individual taxpayer.	• To be eligible for the child and dependent care credit, the dependent must either be under the age of 13 or be a dependent or spouse of any age who is incapable of self-care. • If a child's parents are divorced, the child need not be the dependent of the taxpayer claiming the credit, but the child must live with that parent more than he or she lives with the other parent. • The expenses that qualify for the credit include amounts paid to enable both the taxpayer and his or her spouse to be employed. • For taxpayers with AGI of less than $15,000, the child and dependent care credit is equal to 35 percent of the qualified expenses. For taxpayers with AGI of $15,000 or more, the credit gradually decreases from 35 percent to 20 percent. • In determining the credit, the maximum amount of qualified expenses to which the applicable percentage is applied is $3,000 for one dependent and $6,000 for two or more dependents. • Full-time students with little or no income are deemed to have earned income of $250 per month for one dependent and $500 per month for two or more dependents for purposes of calculating this limitation.

LO 7.4: Calculate the premium tax credit available under the Affordable Care Act.	• Certain lower income taxpayers may be eligible for a premium tax credit to offset some or all of the cost of health care purchased through an exchange. • The premium tax credit can be paid in advance or at the time the tax return is filed. • The advanced premium tax credit and the actual premium tax credit are reconciled at the time the tax return is prepared. Repayments may be limited.
LO 7.5: Apply the special rules applicable to the American Opportunity tax credit and lifetime learning credit.	• The partially refundable American Opportunity tax credit is 100 percent of the first $2,000 of tuition, fees, books, and course materials paid and 25 percent of the next $2,000, for a total maximum annual credit of $2,500 per student. • The American Opportunity tax credit is available for the first 4 years of postsecondary education. • Taxpayers can elect a nonrefundable lifetime learning credit of 20 percent of the first $10,000 in qualified expenses for education. • The American Opportunity tax credit is phased out for joint filers with income between $160,000 and $180,000 and for single and head of household filers with income between $80,000 and $90,000. The lifetime learning credit is phased out between $116,000 and $136,000 for joint filers, and between $58,000 and $68,000 for those single or head of household taxpayers. • Taxpayers cannot take both the American Opportunity tax credit and the lifetime learning credit for the same student in the same tax year.
LO 7.6: Compute the foreign income exclusion and tax credit.	• The foreign income exclusion amount for 2019 is $105,900. • U.S. taxpayers are allowed to claim a foreign tax credit on income earned in a foreign country and subject to income taxes in that country. • Generally, the foreign tax credit is equal to the amount of the taxes paid to foreign governments; however, there is an "overall" limitation on the amount of the credit, which is calculated as the ratio of net foreign income to U.S. taxable income multiplied by the U.S. tax liability. • Unused foreign tax credits may be carried back 1 year and forward 10 years to reduce any tax liability in those years.
LO 7.7: Determine the proper use and calculation of the adoption credit.	• Individuals are allowed an income tax credit for qualified adoption expenses. The maximum total expense that can be taken as a credit for all tax years with respect to an adoption of a child is $14,080 for 2019. • The maximum exclusion from income for benefits under an employer's adoption assistance program is $14,080. • These amounts are phased out if modified AGI is between $211,160 and $251,160.
LO 7.8: Recognize the basic individual credits for energy efficiency.	• A tax credit of up to $7,500 for the purchase of new plug-in electric drive vehicles is available. • Taxpayers may claim a 30 percent credit of the amount paid for qualified property such as solar electric property and solar water-heating property.
LO 7.9: Calculate the low-income Retirement Plan Contribution Credit.	• Certain low-income taxpayers may claim a nonrefundable low-income Retirement Plan Contribution. • Credit, also called the "Saver's Credit," to encourage them to participate in tax-saving retirement plans.

QUESTIONS and PROBLEMS

GROUP 1:
MULTIPLE CHOICE QUESTIONS

LO 7.1
1. Russ and Linda are married and file a joint tax return claiming their three children, ages 4, 7, and 18, as dependents. Their adjusted gross income for 2019 is $415,300. What is Russ and Linda's total child and other dependent credit for 2019?
   a. $500
   b. $2,500
   c. $3,700
   d. $4,500
   e. $4,700

LO 7.1
2. Jennifer is divorced and files a head of household tax return claiming her children, ages 4, 7, and 17, as dependents. Her adjusted gross income for 2019 is $81,200. What is Jennifer's total child and other dependent credit for 2019?
   a. $500
   b. $2,500
   c. $3,700
   d. $4,500
   e. $4,700

LO 7.2
3. Assuming they all meet the income requirements, which of the following taxpayers qualify for the earned income credit in 2019?
   a. A married taxpayer who files a separate tax return and has a dependent child
   b. A single taxpayer who waited on tables for 3 months of the tax year and is claimed as a dependent by her mother
   c. A single taxpayer who is self-employed and has a dependent child
   d. a and c above
   e. None of the above qualify for the earned income credit

LO 7.3
4. Which of the following payments does *not* qualify as a child care expense for purposes of the child and dependent care credit?
   a. Payments to a day care center
   b. Payments to the taxpayer's sister (21 years old) for daytime babysitting
   c. Payments to a housekeeper who also babysits the child
   d. Payments to the taxpayer's dependent brother (16 years old) for daytime babysitting
   e. All of the above qualify for the child and dependent care credit

LO 7.4
5. Which of the following is *not* a requirement to receive the premium tax credit for health care?
   a. Health care through the employer is not available
   b. Health insurance is purchased through the state or federal exchange
   c. Income must be no greater than 200 percent of the federal poverty line
   d. The taxpayer cannot be claimed as a dependent

LO 7.4
6. For purposes of determining income eligibility for the premium tax credit, household AGI is
   a. AGI for the taxpayer and spouse
   b. AGI for the taxpayer, spouse, and any other household members required to file a tax return
   c. AGI for the taxpayer, spouse, and any other household members required to file a tax return plus any tax-exempt income
   d. AGI for the taxpayer, spouse, and any other household members required to file a tax return plus any tax-exempt income and untaxed Social Security benefits

LO 7.5

7. The American Opportunity tax credit is 100 percent of the first _____ of tuition and fees paid and 25 percent of the next _____.
   a. $600; $1,200
   b. $1,100; $550
   c. $2,000; $2,000
   d. $1,100; $5,500
   e. None of the above

LO 7.5

8. Jane graduates from high school in June 2019. In the fall, she enrolls for twelve units at Big State University. Big State University considers students who take twelve or more units to be full-time. Jane's father pays her tuition and fees of $2,500 for the fall semester and in December 2019 prepays $2,500 for the spring semester. In 2019, the American Opportunity tax credit for Jane's tuition and fees before any AGI limitation is:
   a. $5,000
   b. $2,500
   c. $2,200
   d. $1,800
   e. Some other amount

LO 7.5

9. Which of the following costs is *not* a qualified education expense for the American Opportunity tax credit?
   a. tuition
   b. room and board
   c. course-related books
   d. lab supplies required by the course

LO 7.5

10. In September 2019, Sam pays $6,200 to take a course to improve his job skills to qualify for a new position at work. Assuming there is no phase-out of the credit, his lifetime learning credit for 2019 is:
    a. $220
    b. $1,240
    c. $2,500
    d. $6,200
    e. None of the above

LO 7.5

11. In November 2019, Simon pays $1,000 to take a course to improve his job skills to qualify for a new position at work. Simon's employer reimbursed him for the cost of the course. For 2019, Simon's lifetime learning credit is:
    a. $200
    b. $500
    c. $1,000
    d. $2,500
    e. None of the above

LO 7.5

12. John, a single father, has AGI of $81,000 in 2019. During the year, he pays $4,000 in qualified tuition for his dependent son, who just started attending Small University. What is John's American Opportunity tax credit for 2019?
    a. $0
    b. $2,000
    c. $2,250
    d. $2,500
    e. Some other amount

LO 7.5

13. Joan, a single mother, has AGI of $61,500 in 2019. In September 2019, she pays $5,000 in qualified tuition for her dependent son who just started at Big University. What is Joan's American Opportunity credit for 2019?
   a. $0
   b. $1,250
   c. $2,125
   d. $2,500
   e. Some other amount

LO 7.5

14. Becky, a college freshman, works part-time and pays $1,650 of her college tuition expenses. Although Becky files her own tax return, her parents claim her as a dependent on their tax return. Becky's parents file jointly and have AGI of $50,000. What is the amount of American Opportunity tax credit her parents can claim on their tax return for the tuition Becky paid?
   a. $0
   b. $495
   c. $1,600
   d. $1,650
   e. Some other amount

LO 7.6

15. Lucas, a single U.S. citizen, works in Denmark for MNC Corp during all of 2019. His MNC salary is $87,000. Lucas may exclude from his gross income wages of:
   a. $0
   b. $40,000
   c. $87,000
   d. $105,900

LO 7.6

16. Taxpayer L has income of $55,000 from Norway, which imposes a 40 percent income tax, and income of $45,000 from France, which imposes a 30 percent income tax. L has additional taxable income from U.S. sources of $200,000 and U.S. tax liability before credits of $105,000. What is the amount of the foreign tax credit?
   a. $16,500
   b. $35,000
   c. $35,500
   d. $100,000
   e. $45,000

LO 7.7

17. John and Joan pay $16,500 of qualified adoption expenses in 2019 to finalize the adoption of a qualified child. Their AGI is $197,000 for 2019. What is their adoption credit for 2019?
   a. $0
   b. $16,500
   c. $14,080
   d. $13,810

LO 7.7

18. In connection with the adoption of an eligible child who is a U.S. citizen and who is not a child with special needs, Sean pays $4,000 of qualified adoption expenses in 2018 and $3,000 of qualified adoption expenses in 2019. The adoption is finalized in 2019. There is no phase-out of the adoption credit. What are the adoption credits for both 2018 and 2019, respectively?
   a. $0; $7,000
   b. $4,000; $1,000
   c. $4,000; $3,000
   d. $7,000; $0

LO 7.7

19. If a taxpayer does not have enough tax liability to use all the available adoption credit, the unused portion may be carried forward for how many years?
    a. Two
    b. Three
    c. Five
    d. There is no carryforward

LO 7.8

20. Barbara purchased a new Honda Clarity electric vehicle in 2019 for $36,000. Her federal tax credit will be:
    a. $0
    b. $2,500
    c. $5,000
    d. $7,500
    e. $10,000

LO 7.9

21. Virginia and Richard are married taxpayers with adjusted gross income of $28,000 in 2019. If Virginia is able to make a $1,500 contribution to her IRA and Richard makes a $1,500 contribution to his IRA, what is the Saver's Credit Virginia and Richard will be eligible for?
    a. $0
    b. $1,500
    c. $2,000
    d. $3,000
    e. $4,000

GROUP 2:
PROBLEMS

LO 7.1

1. Calculate the total child and other dependent credit for the following taxpayers. Please show your work.
   a. Jeremy is a single (head of household) father with $80,100 of AGI and has a dependent 8-year-old son:

   _____

   b. Jerry and Ann have $100,000 of AGI, file jointly, and claim two dependent preschool children:

   _____

   c. James and Apple have AGI of $417,100, file jointly, and claim three dependent children (ages 7, 10, and 19):

   _____

LO 7.2

2. How does the earned income credit produce a "negative" income tax?

   _____

   _____

   _____

LO 7.2

3. List the 7 rules that all taxpayers must meet in order to claim the EIC.

   _____

   _____

   _____

LO 7.2

4. List the rules that apply to taxpayers without a qualifying child in order to claim the EIC.

   _____

   _____

LO 7.2

5. List the rules that apply to taxpayers with a qualifying child in order to claim the EIC.

   _____

   _____

LO 7.2

6. Diane is a single taxpayer who qualifies for the earned income credit. Diane has two qualifying children who are 3 and 5 years old. During 2019, Diane's wages are $18,900 and she receives dividend income of $900. Calculate Diane's earned income credit using the EIC table in Appendix B.

$_____

LO 7.2

7. Margaret and David Simmons are married and file a joint income tax return. They have two dependent children, Margo, 5 years old (Social Security number 316-31-4890), and Daniel, who was born during the year (Social Security number 316-31-7894). Margaret's wages are $3,000, and David has wages of $14,000. In addition, they receive interest income of $200 during the year. Margaret and David do not have any other items of income and do not have any deductions for adjusted gross income. Assuming the Simmons file Form 1040 for 2019, complete Schedule EIC and the Earned Income Credit Worksheet A, on Pages 7-55 and 7-56. (The EIC table is in Appendix B.)

LO 7.2

8. What is the maximum investment income a taxpayer is allowed to have and still be allowed to claim the earned income credit? Please speculate as to why there is an investment income limit in the tax law.

_____

_____

_____

LO 7.3

9. Calculate the amount of the child and dependent care credit allowed before any tax liability limitations or other credits for 2019 in each of the following cases, assuming the taxpayers had no income other than the stated amounts.
   a. William and Carla file a joint tax return. Carla earned $27,500 during the year, while William attended law school full-time for 9 months and earned no income. They paid $3,500 for the care of their 3-year-old child, Carl.

   $_____

   b. Raymond and Michele file a joint tax return. Raymond earned $32,500 during the year, while Michele earned $9,000 for the year from a part-time job. They paid $7,000 for the care of their two children under age 13.

   $_____

   c. Beth is a single taxpayer who has two dependent children under age 5. Beth earned $25,500 in wages during the year and paid $6,700 for the care of her children.

   $_____

LO 7.3

10. Clarita is a single taxpayer with two dependent children, ages 10 and 12. Clarita pays $3,000 in qualified child care expenses during the year. If her adjusted gross income (all from wages) for the year is $19,600 and she takes the standard deduction, calculate Clarita's earned income credit and child and dependent care credit for 2019.

$_____

LO 7.3

11. Go to the IRS website (**www.irs.gov**) and redo Problem 10 above using the most recent Form 2441, Child and Dependent Care Expenses. Print out the *completed Form 2441*. Do not calculate the earned income credit here.

LO 7.3

12. Mary and John are married and have AGI of $100,000 and two young children. John doesn't work, and they pay $6,000 a year to day care providers so he can shop, clean, and read a little bit in peace. How much child and dependent care credit can Mary and John claim? Why?

LO 7.3

13. Martha has a 3-year-old child and pays $10,000 a year in day care costs. Her salary is $45,000. How much is her child and dependent care credit?

LO 7.3

14. Marty and Jean are married and have 4-year-old twins. Jean is going to school full-time for 9 months of the year, and Marty earns $45,000. The twins are in day care so Jean can go to school while Marty is at work. The cost of day care is $10,000. What is their child and dependent care credit? Please explain your calculation.

_____

_____

_____

LO 7.4

15. Susan and Stan Collins live in Iowa, are married and have two children ages 6 and 10. In 2019, Susan's income is $41,214 and Stan's is $12,000 and both are self-employed. They also have $500 in interest income from tax-exempt bonds. The Collins enrolled in health insurance for all of 2019 through their state exchange but did not elect to have the credit paid in advance. The 2019 Form 1095-A that the Collins received from the exchange lists the following information:

Annual premiums	$9,800
Annual premium for the designated silver plan in the state	$10,800

Compute the Collins' premium tax credit for 2019.

LO 7.4

16. Using the information in the previous question, assume that the Collins' Form 1095-A also indicated that the total advance payment of the premium tax credit was $9,200. Calculate the excess advance premium tax credit and the repayment amount for 2019.

LO 7.5

17. What is the reason there are education tax credits in the tax law?

_____

_____

_____

LO 7.5

18. Please explain the difference between the types of education covered by the American Opportunity tax credit and the lifetime learning credit.

_____

_____

_____

LO 7.5

19. Janie graduates from high school in 2019 and enrolls in college in the fall. Her parents pay $4,000 for her tuition and fees.
    a. Assuming Janie's parents have AGI of $170,000, what is the American Opportunity tax credit they can claim for Janie?

    _____

    _____

    _____

    b. Assuming Janie's parents have AGI of $75,000, what is the American Opportunity tax credit they can claim for Janie?

LO 7.5

20. Jasper is single and is a computer software consultant with a college degree. He feels that one of the reasons for his success is that he continually updates his knowledge by taking classes at the local college in various areas related to software design and information technology. This year he spent $2,000 on course tuition and fees.

   a. Assuming Jasper has AGI of $92,000, how much lifetime learning credit can Jasper claim on his tax return? Would the answer be different if Jasper were married and supporting a wife who was not working?

   _____

   _____

   _____

   b. Assuming Jasper has AGI of $45,000, how much lifetime learning credit can Jasper claim on his tax return?

   _____

   _____

   _____

LO 7.6

21. Martha and Lew are married taxpayers with $400 of foreign tax withholding from dividends in a mutual fund. They have enough foreign income from the mutual fund to claim the full $400 as a foreign tax credit. Their tax bracket is 24 percent and they itemize deductions. Should they claim the foreign tax credit or a deduction for foreign taxes on their Schedule A? Why?

   _____

   _____

   _____

LO 7.7

22. Carl and Jenny adopt a Korean orphan. The adoption takes 2 years and two trips to Korea and is finalized in 2019. They pay $7,000 in 2018 and $7,500 in 2019 for qualified adoption expenses. In 2019, Carl and Jenny have AGI of $150,000.

   a. What is the adoption credit Carl and Jenny can claim in 2019?

   $_____

   b. How much credit could they claim if the adoption falls through and is never finalized?

   _____

   c. How much credit could they claim if their AGI was $217,160?

   _____

LO 7.8

23. Mike bought a solar electric pump to heat his pool at a cost of $2,500 in 2019. What is Mike's credit?

   $_____

LO 7.8

24. In 2019, Jeff spends $6,000 on solar panels to heat water for his main home. What is Jeff's credit for his 2019 purchases?

   $_____

LO 7.9

25. George and Amal file a joint return in 2019 and have AGI of $39,800. They each make a $1,600 contribution to their respective IRAs. Assuming that they are not eligible for any other credits, what is the amount of their Saver's Credit?

   $_____

SCHEDULE EIC
(Form 1040 or 1040-SR)

Department of the Treasury
Internal Revenue Service (99)

Earned Income Credit

Qualifying Child Information

▶ Complete and attach to Form 1040 or 1040-SR only if you have a
qualifying child.
▶ Go to *www.irs.gov/ScheduleEIC* for the latest information.

OMB No. 1545-0074

2019

Attachment
Sequence No. **43**

Name(s) shown on return

Your social security number

Before you begin:
- See the instructions for Form 1040 or 1040-SR, line 18a, to make sure that **(a)** you can take the EIC, and **(b)** you have a qualifying child.
- Be sure the child's name on line 1 and social security number (SSN) on line 2 agree with the child's social security card. Otherwise, at the time we process your return, we may reduce or disallow your EIC. If the name or SSN on the child's social security card is not correct, call the Social Security Administration at 1-800-772-1213.

CAUTION
- *You can't claim the EIC for a child who didn't live with you for more than half of the year.*
- *If you take the EIC even though you are not eligible, you may not be allowed to take the credit for up to 10 years. See the instructions for details.*
- *It will take us longer to process your return and issue your refund if you do not fill in all lines that apply for each qualifying child.*

Qualifying Child Information

	Child 1		Child 2		Child 3	
1 Child's name If you have more than three qualifying children, you have to list only three to get the maximum credit.	First name	Last name	First name	Last name	First name	Last name
2 Child's SSN The child must have an SSN as defined in the instructions for Form 1040 or 1040-SR, line 18a, unless the child was born and died in 2019. If your child was born and died in 2019 and did not have an SSN, enter "Died" on this line and attach a copy of the child's birth certificate, death certificate, or hospital medical records showing a live birth.						
3 Child's year of birth	Year ___ ___ ___ ___ *If born after 2000 and the child is younger than you (or your spouse, if filing jointly), skip lines 4a and 4b; go to line 5.*		Year ___ ___ ___ ___ *If born after 2000 and the child is younger than you (or your spouse, if filing jointly), skip lines 4a and 4b; go to line 5.*		Year ___ ___ ___ ___ *If born after 2000 and the child is younger than you (or your spouse, if filing jointly), skip lines 4a and 4b; go to line 5.*	
4 a Was the child under age 24 at the end of 2019, a student, and younger than you (or your spouse, if filing jointly)?	☐ **Yes.** *Go to line 5.*	☐ **No.** *Go to line 4b.*	☐ **Yes.** *Go to line 5.*	☐ **No.** *Go to line 4b.*	☐ **Yes.** *Go to line 5.*	☐ **No.** *Go to line 4b.*
b Was the child permanently and totally disabled during any part of 2019?	☐ **Yes.** *Go to line 5.*	☐ **No.** The child is not a qualifying child.	☐ **Yes.** *Go to line 5.*	☐ **No.** The child is not a qualifying child.	☐ **Yes.** *Go to line 5.*	☐ **No.** The child is not a qualifying child.
5 Child's relationship to you (for example, son, daughter, grandchild, niece, nephew, eligible foster child, etc.)						
6 Number of months child lived with you in the United States during 2019 • If the child lived with you for more than half of 2019 but less than 7 months, enter "7." • If the child was born or died in 2019 and your home was the child's home for more than half the time he or she was alive during 2019, enter "12."	_____ months *Do not enter more than 12 months.*		_____ months *Do not enter more than 12 months.*		_____ months *Do not enter more than 12 months.*	

For Paperwork Reduction Act Notice, see your tax return instructions.   Cat. No. 13339M   **Schedule EIC (Form 1040 or 1040-SR) 2019**

Worksheet A—2019 EIC—Line 18a

Before you begin: √ Be sure you are using the correct worksheet. Use this worksheet only if you answered "No" to Step 5, question 2. Otherwise, use Worksheet B.

Part 1
 	
All Filers Using Worksheet A
	1. Enter your earned income from Step 5. \[1\] _____
	            Wages, salaries
	
	2. Look up the amount on line 1 above in the EIC Table (right after Worksheet B) to find the credit. Be sure you use the correct column for your filing status and the number of children you have. Enter the credit here. \[2\] _____
	
	    If line 2 is zero, (STOP) You can't take the credit.
	    Enter "No" on the dotted line next to Form 1040 or 1040-SR, line 18a.
	
	3. Enter the amount from Form 1040 or 1040-SR, line 8b. \[3\] _____
	            Adjusted gross income
	
	4. Are the amounts on lines 3 and 1 the same?
	
	    ☐ **Yes.** Skip line 5; enter the amount from line 2 on line 6.
	
	    ☐ **No.** Go to line 5.

Part 2
 	
Filers Who Answered "No" on Line 4
	5. If you have:
	    ● No qualifying children, is the amount on line 3 less than $8,650 ($14,450 if married filing jointly)?
	    ● 1 or more qualifying children, is the amount on line 3 less than $19,050 ($24,850 if married filing jointly)?
	
	    ☐ **Yes.** Leave line 5 blank; enter the amount from line 2 on line 6.
	
	    ☐ **No.** Look up the amount on line 3 in the EIC Table to find the credit. Be sure you use the correct column for your filing status and the number of children you have. Enter the credit here. \[5\] _____
	            Look at the amounts on lines 5 and 2.
	            Then, enter the **smaller** amount on line 6.

Part 3
 	
Your Earned Income Credit
	6. **This is your earned income credit.** \[6\] _____
	
	    Enter this amount on Form 1040 or 1040-SR, line 18a.
	
	    Reminder—
	    √ If you have a qualifying child, complete and attach Schedule EIC.
	
	    ⚠ **CAUTION** *If your EIC for a year after 1996 was reduced or disallowed, see Form 8862, who must file, earlier, to find out if you must file Form 8862 to take the credit for 2019.*

WRITING ASSIGNMENT

RESEARCH Your supervisor has asked you to research the following situation concerning Scott and Heather Moore. Scott and Heather are married and file a joint return. Scott works full-time as a wildlife biologist, and Heather is a full-time student enrolled at Online University. Scott's earned income for the year is $36,000. Heather does not have a job and concentrates solely on her schoolwork. The university she is enrolled in offers courses only through the Internet. Scott and Heather have one child, Elizabeth (age 8), and pay $3,000 for child care expenses during the year.

Required: Go to the IRS website **(www.irs.gov)**. Locate and review Publication 503. Write a file memorandum stating the amount of child and dependent care credit that Scott and Heather Moore can claim. (An example of a file memorandum is available at the website for this textbook located at **www.cengagebrain.com.)**

COMPREHENSIVE PROBLEMS

1. David and Darlene Jasper have one child, Sam, who is 6 years old (birthdate July 1, 2013). The Jaspers reside at 4639 Honeysuckle Lane, Los Angeles, CA 90248. David's Social Security number is 577-11-3311, Darlene's is 477-98-4731, and Sam's is 589-22-1142. David's birthdate is May 29, 1986 and Darlene's birthday is January 31, 1988. David and Darlene's earnings and withholdings for 2019 are:

David:	Earnings from Apple Company (office manager)	$26,600
	Federal income tax withheld	800
	State income tax withheld	1,050
Darlene:	Earnings from Rose Company (perfume tester)	$25,500
	Federal income tax withheld	1,050
	State income tax withheld	1,000

Their other income includes interest from Pine Tree Savings and Loan of $1,900. Other information and expenditures for 2019 are as follows:

Interest:	On home acquisition mortgage	$11,312
	Credit card	925
Taxes:	Property taxes on personal residence	1,300
	State income taxes paid in 2019 (for 2018)	315
Contribution (with written acknowledgement) to church		1,045
Medical insurance		675
Medical and dental expenses		6,175
Income tax return preparation fee paid in 2019		200
Actual general state sales tax for 2019		1,016
Payment of union dues		225
Contribution to David's IRA		1,000

David and Darlene received the following letter from Sam's daycare provider:

KIDDIECARE INC.

10250 Santa Monica Blvd.
Los Angeles, CA 90067
EIN: 13-3345678

January 14, 2020

David and Darlene Jasper
4639 Honeysuckle Lane
Los Angeles, CA 90248

Dear David and Darlene,

Thank you for your patronage of our day care center with your child, Sam Jasper, in 2019. This statement serves as a record of the cost of daycare services we provided during calendar year 2019:

Child	Amount	Dates of Service
Sam Jasper	$3,429.00	1/1/2019 – 08/25/2019

Sincerely,

/s/ Marcia Clarke

Marcia Clarke
Director, KiddieCare Inc.

Required: Complete the Jaspers' federal tax return for 2019. Use Form 1040, Schedule 1, Schedule 3, Schedule A, Schedule B, Form 2441, and Form 8880, as needed. Make realistic assumptions about any missing data.

2A. Steve Jackson (birthdate December 13, 1966) is a single taxpayer living at 3215 Pacific Dr., Apt. B, Pacific Beach, CA 92109. His Social Security number is 465-88-9415. In 2019, Steve's earnings and income tax withholding as laundry attendant of a local hotel are:

Earnings from the Ocean View Hotel	$21,900
Federal income tax withheld	219
State income tax withheld	100

Steve has a daughter, Janet, from a previous marriage. Janet is 11 years old (Social Security number 654-12-6543). Steve provides all Janet's support. Also living with Steve is his younger brother, Michael (Social Security number 667-21-8998). Michael, age 47, is unable to care for himself due to a disability. On a reasonably regular basis, Steve has a care giver come to the house to help with Michael. He uses a company called HomeAid, 456 La Jolla Dr., San Diego, CA 92182 (EIN 17-9876543). Steve made payments of $1,000 to HomeAid in 2019. Janet receives free after-school care provided by the local school district.

Required: Complete Steve's federal tax return for 2019. Use Form 1040, Schedule 3, Form 2441, Child Tax Credit Worksheet, Form 8812, EITC Worksheet A, and Schedule EIC.

2B. David Fleming is a single taxpayer living at 169 Trendie Street, Apartment 6B, La Jolla, CA 92037. His Social Security number is 865-68-9635 and his birthdate is September 18, 1974.

David was employed as a delivery person for a local pizza restaurant. David's W-2 showed the following:

a Employee's social security number 865-68-9635	OMB No. 1545-0008	Safe, accurate, FAST! Use IRS e~file Visit the IRS website at www.irs.gov/efile

b Employer identification number (EIN) 23-4567321	**1** Wages, tips, other compensation 23,654.00	**2** Federal income tax withheld 1,279.00
c Employer's name, address, and ZIP code California Pizza Cafe 231 Foodie Street La Jolla, CA 92037	**3** Social security wages 23,654.00	**4** Social security tax withheld 1,446.55
	5 Medicare wages and tips 23,654.00	**6** Medicare tax withheld 342.98
	7 Social security tips	**8** Allocated tips
d Control number	**9**	**10** Dependent care benefits
e Employee's first name and initial Last name Suff.	**11** Nonqualified plans	**12a** See instructions for box 12
David Fleming 169 Trendie Street, Apt 6B La Jolla, CA 92037	**13** Statutory employee ☐ Retirement plan ☐ Third-party sick pay ☐	**12b**
	14 Other	**12c**
		12d
f Employee's address and ZIP code		

15 State	Employer's state ID number	16 State wages, tips, etc.	17 State income tax	18 Local wages, tips, etc.	19 Local income tax	20 Locality name
CA	D4567221	23,654.00	367.77			

Form **W-2** Wage and Tax Statement   **2019**   Department of the Treasury—Internal Revenue Service

Copy B—To Be Filed With Employee's FEDERAL Tax Return.
This information is being furnished to the Internal Revenue Service.

David's only other source of income during the year was a prize he won appearing on a game show. The game show sent David home with a Form 1099-MISC:

☐ CORRECTED (if checked)

PAYER'S name, street address, city or town, state or province, country, ZIP or foreign postal code, and telephone no. Price is Accurate Studios, Inc. Studio 44 Studio City, CA 91604	**1** Rents $	OMB No. 1545-0115 **2019**	**Miscellaneous Income**
	2 Royalties $	Form **1099-MISC**	
	3 Other income $ 10,000.00	**4** Federal income tax withheld $ 2,400.00	**Copy B** For Recipient
PAYER'S TIN RECIPIENT'S TIN 21-8675309 865-68-9635	**5** Fishing boat proceeds $	**6** Medical and health care payments $	
RECIPIENT'S name David Fleming	**7** Nonemployee compensation $	**8** Substitute payments in lieu of dividends or interest $	This is important tax information and is being furnished to the IRS. If you are required to file a return, a negligence penalty or other sanction may be imposed on you if this income is taxable and the IRS determines that it has not been reported.
Street address (including apt. no.) 169 Trendie Street, Apt 6B	**9** Payer made direct sales of $5,000 or more of consumer products to a buyer (recipient) for resale ▶ ☐	**10** Crop insurance proceeds $	
City or town, state or province, country, and ZIP or foreign postal code La Jolla, CA 92037	**11**	**12**	
Account number (see instructions) FATCA filing requirement ☐	**13** Excess golden parachute payments $	**14** Gross proceeds paid to an attorney $	
15a Section 409A deferrals 15b Section 409A income $ $	**16** State tax withheld $ 200.00	**17** State/Payer's state no.	**18** State income $ 10,000.00

Form **1099-MISC**   (keep for your records)   www.irs.gov/Form1099MISC   Department of the Treasury - Internal Revenue Service

He has no other adjustments to income or deductible expenses. Unfortunately, David's employer did not provide health care to its employees but David signed up for coverage through his state's health care exchange. The exchange sent him a Form 1095-A as shown on Page 7-61.

Required: Complete David's federal tax return for 2019. Use Form 1040, Schedule 1, Schedule 2, and Form 8962. Make realistic assumptions about any missing data.

GROUP 5:
CUMULATIVE SOFTWARE PROBLEM

1. The following information is available for the Albert and Allison Gaytor family in addition to that provided in Chapters 1–6.

The Gaytors paid tuition and fees for both Crocker and Cayman to attend college. Recall that Crocker is a freshman at Brickell State and Cayman is a part-time student in community college. Crocker received a $995 scholarship from Brickell State. Crocker's Form 1098-T is shown below. The Gaytors paid tuition and fees of $1,400 for Cayman in 2019.

☐ CORRECTED

FILER'S name, street address, city or town, state or province, country, ZIP or foreign postal code, and telephone number	1 Payments received for qualified tuition and related expenses	OMB No. 1545-1574	Tuition Statement
Brickell State University 605 Crandon Blvd. Key Biscayne, FL 33149	$ 2 4,750.00	2019 Form 1098-T	
FILER'S employer identification no. 44-3421456	STUDENT'S TIN 261-55-1212	3	Copy B For Student
STUDENT'S name Crocker Gaytor	4 Adjustments made for a prior year $	5 Scholarships or grants $ 995.00	This is important tax information and is being furnished to the IRS. This form must be used to complete Form 8863 to claim education credits. Give it to the tax preparer or use it to prepare the tax return.
Street address (including apt. no.) 12340 Cocoshell Rd	6 Adjustments to scholarships or grants for a prior year $	7 Checked if the amount in box 1 includes amounts for an academic period beginning January— March 2020 ☐	
City or town, state or province, country, and ZIP or foreign postal code Coral Gables, FL 33134			
Service Provider/Acct. No. (see instr.)	8 Check if at least half-time student ☒	9 Checked if a graduate student ☐	10 Ins. contract reimb./refund $

Form **1098-T**   (keep for your records)   www.irs.gov/Form1098T   Department of the Treasury - Internal Revenue Service

In December 2018, Albert's 82 year-old aunt, Virginia Everglades (Social Security number 699-19-9000), was unable to support herself and moved in with the Gaytors. She lived with them for all of 2019. The Gaytors provided more than one-half of Aunt Virginia's support. Virginia's only source of income is a small annuity that paid her $3,100 in 2019. While Albert and Allison were working, the Gaytors hired a nanny service from time to time to take care of Aunt Virginia. The Gaytors paid $3,400 to Nannys R Us in 2019. Nannys R Us (EIN 34-1234123) is located at 80 SW 22nd Avenue, Miami, FL 33133.

Required: Combine this new information about the Gaytor family with the information from Chapters 1–6 and complete a revised 2019 tax return for Albert and Allison. Be sure to save your data input files since this case will be expanded and completed with more tax information in Chapter 8.

Form **1095-A**

Department of the Treasury
Internal Revenue Service

Health Insurance Marketplace Statement

▶ Do not attach to your tax return. Keep for your records.
▶ Go to *www.irs.gov/Form1095A* for instructions and the latest information.

☐ VOID

☐ CORRECTED

OMB No. 1545-2232

2019

Part I   Recipient Information

| **1** Marketplace identifier
31-9876543 | **2** Marketplace-assigned policy number
B1234TH | **3** Policy issuer's name
Covered California | |
|---|---|---|---|
| **4** Recipient's name
David Fleming | | **5** Recipient's SSN
865-68-9635 | **6** Recipient's date of birth
09/18/1974 |
| **7** Recipient's spouse's name | | **8** Recipient's spouse's SSN | **9** Recipient's spouse's date of birth |
| **10** Policy start date
01/01/2019 | **11** Policy termination date
12/31/2019 | **12** Street address (including apartment no.)
169 Trendie St. Apt 6B | |
| **13** City or town
La Jolla | **14** State or province
CA | **15** Country and ZIP or foreign postal code
92037 | |

Part II   Covered Individuals

	A. Covered individual name	**B.** Covered individual SSN	**C.** Covered individual date of birth	**D.** Coverage start date	**E.** Coverage termination date
16	David Fleming	865-68-9635	09/18/1974	01/01/2019	12/31/2019
17					
18					
19					
20					

Part III   Coverage Information

Month	**A.** Monthly enrollment premiums	**B.** Monthly second lowest cost silver plan (SLCSP) premium	**C.** Monthly advance payment of premium tax credit
21 January	308.00	339.00	145.00
22 February	308.00	339.00	145.00
23 March	308.00	339.00	145.00
24 April	308.00	339.00	145.00
25 May	308.00	339.00	145.00
26 June	308.00	339.00	145.00
27 July	308.00	339.00	145.00
28 August	308.00	339.00	145.00
29 September	308.00	339.00	145.00
30 October	308.00	339.00	145.00
31 November	308.00	339.00	145.00
32 December	308.00	339.00	145.00
33 Annual Totals	3,696.00	4,068.00	1,740.00

For Privacy Act and Paperwork Reduction Act Notice, see separate instructions.   Cat. No. 60703Q   Form **1095-A** (2019)

Form **1040** Department of the Treasury—Internal Revenue Service   (99) **2019** OMB No. 1545-0074 IRS Use Only—Do not write or staple in this space.
U.S. Individual Income Tax Return

Filing Status	☐ Single ☐ Married filing jointly ☐ Married filing separately (MFS) ☐ Head of household (HOH) ☐ Qualifying widow(er) (QW)

Check only one box.   If you checked the MFS box, enter the name of spouse. If you checked the HOH or QW box, enter the child's name if the qualifying person is a child but not your dependent. ▶

Your first name and middle initial	Last name	Your social security number

If joint return, spouse's first name and middle initial	Last name	Spouse's social security number

Home address (number and street). If you have a P.O. box, see instructions.   Apt. no.

Presidential Election Campaign
Check here if you, or your spouse if filing jointly, want $3 to go to this fund. Checking a box below will not change your tax or refund.   ☐ You   ☐ Spouse

City, town or post office, state, and ZIP code. If you have a foreign address, also complete spaces below (see instructions).

Foreign country name	Foreign province/state/county	Foreign postal code

If more than four dependents, see instructions and ✓ here ▶ ☐

Standard Deduction   Someone can claim: ☐ You as a dependent   ☐ Your spouse as a dependent
☐ Spouse itemizes on a separate return or you were a dual-status alien

Age/Blindness   **You:** ☐ Were born before January 2, 1955   ☐ Are blind   **Spouse:** ☐ Was born before January 2, 1955   ☐ Is blind

Dependents (see instructions):

(1) First name Last name	(2) Social security number	(3) Relationship to you	(4) ✓ if qualifies for (see instructions):	
			Child tax credit	Credit for other dependents
			☐	☐
			☐	☐
			☐	☐
			☐	☐

Standard Deduction for—
- Single or Married filing separately, $12,200
- Married filing jointly or Qualifying widow(er), $24,400
- Head of household, $18,350
- If you checked any box under *Standard Deduction,* see instructions.

1	Wages, salaries, tips, etc. Attach Form(s) W-2			1	
2a	Tax-exempt interest . . .	2a	b Taxable interest. Attach Sch. B if required	2b	
3a	Qualified dividends	3a	b Ordinary dividends. Attach Sch. B if required	3b	
4a	IRA distributions	4a	b Taxable amount	4b	
c	Pensions and annuities . . .	4c	d Taxable amount	4d	
5a	Social security benefits . . .	5a	b Taxable amount	5b	
6	Capital gain or (loss). Attach Schedule D if required. If not required, check here . . . . ▶ ☐			6	
7a	Other income from Schedule 1, line 9			7a	
b	Add lines 1, 2b, 3b, 4b, 4d, 5b, 6, and 7a. This is your **total income** . . . . . ▶			7b	
8a	Adjustments to income from Schedule 1, line 22			8a	
b	Subtract line 8a from line 7b. This is your **adjusted gross income** . . . . . ▶			8b	
9	**Standard deduction or itemized deductions** (from Schedule A)	9			
10	Qualified business income deduction. Attach Form 8995 or Form 8995-A . . .	10			
11a	Add lines 9 and 10			11a	
b	**Taxable income.** Subtract line 11a from line 8b			11b	

For Disclosure, Privacy Act, and Paperwork Reduction Act Notice, see separate instructions.   Cat. No. 11320B   Form **1040** (2019)

Form 1040 (2019)   Page **2**

12a	**Tax** (see inst.) Check if any from Form(s): 1 ☐ 8814 2 ☐ 4972 3 ☐ _____	**12a**		
b	Add Schedule 2, line 3, and line 12a and enter the total . . . . ▶	**12b**	
13a	Child tax credit or credit for other dependents	**13a**		
b	Add Schedule 3, line 7, and line 13a and enter the total . . . . ▶	**13b**	
14	Subtract line 13b from line 12b. If zero or less, enter -0-	**14**	
15	Other taxes, including self-employment tax, from Schedule 2, line 10 . . .	**15**	
16	Add lines 14 and 15. This is your **total tax** . . . . ▶	**16**	
17	Federal income tax withheld from Forms W-2 and 1099	**17**	
18	Other payments and refundable credits:		
a	Earned income credit (EIC)	**18a**		
b	Additional child tax credit. Attach Schedule 8812	**18b**		
c	American opportunity credit from Form 8863, line 8	**18c**		
d	Schedule 3, line 14	**18d**		
e	Add lines 18a through 18d. These are your **total other payments and refundable credits** ▶	**18e**	
19	Add lines 17 and 18e. These are your **total payments** . . . . ▶	**19**	

If you have a qualifying child, attach Sch. EIC.
If you have nontaxable combat pay, see instructions.

Refund

Direct deposit?
See instructions.

20	If line 19 is more than line 16, subtract line 16 from line 19. This is the amount you **overpaid**	**20**	
21a	Amount of line 20 you want **refunded to you.** If Form 8888 is attached, check here . . ▶ ☐	**21a**	
▶**b**	Routing number [ ][ ][ ][ ][ ][ ][ ][ ][ ] ▶ **c** Type: ☐ Checking ☐ Savings		
▶**d**	Account number [ ][ ][ ][ ][ ][ ][ ][ ][ ][ ][ ][ ][ ][ ][ ][ ][ ]		
22	Amount of line 20 you want **applied to your 2020 estimated tax** . . . . ▶	**22**	

Amount You Owe

23	**Amount you owe.** Subtract line 19 from line 16. For details on how to pay, see instructions . . . . ▶	**23**	
24	Estimated tax penalty (see instructions) . . . . ▶	**24**	

Third Party Designee

(Other than paid preparer)

Do you want to allow another person (other than your paid preparer) to discuss this return with the IRS? See instructions. ☐ **Yes.** Complete below. ☐ **No**

Designee's name ▶	Phone no. ▶	Personal identification number (PIN) ▶ [ ][ ][ ][ ][ ][ ]

Sign Here

Joint return?
See instructions.
Keep a copy for your records.

Under penalties of perjury, I declare that I have examined this return and accompanying schedules and statements, and to the best of my knowledge and belief, they are true, correct, and complete. Declaration of preparer (other than taxpayer) is based on all information of which preparer has any knowledge.

Your signature	Date	Your occupation	If the IRS sent you an Identity Protection PIN, enter it here (see inst.) [ ][ ][ ][ ][ ][ ]
Spouse's signature. If a joint return, **both** must sign.	Date	Spouse's occupation	If the IRS sent your spouse an Identity Protection PIN, enter it here (see inst.) [ ][ ][ ][ ][ ][ ]
Phone no.		Email address	

Paid Preparer Use Only

Preparer's name	Preparer's signature	Date	PTIN	Check if: ☐ 3rd Party Designee
Firm's name ▶		Phone no.		☐ Self-employed
Firm's address ▶			Firm's EIN ▶	

Go to *www.irs.gov/Form1040* for instructions and the latest information.   Form **1040** (2019)

SCHEDULE 1
(Form 1040 or 1040-SR)

Department of the Treasury
Internal Revenue Service

Additional Income and Adjustments to Income

▶ Attach to Form 1040 or 1040-SR.
▶ Go to *www.irs.gov/Form1040* for instructions and the latest information.

OMB No. 1545-0074

2019

Attachment
Sequence No. **01**

Name(s) shown on Form 1040 or 1040-SR

Your social security number

Part I	**Additional Income**		
1	Taxable refunds, credits, or offsets of state and local income taxes	**1**	
2a	Alimony received	**2a**	
b	Date of original divorce or separation agreement (see instructions) ▶		
3	Business income or (loss). Attach Schedule C	**3**	
4	Other gains or (losses). Attach Form 4797	**4**	
5	Rental real estate, royalties, partnerships, S corporations, trusts, etc. Attach Schedule E	**5**	
6	Farm income or (loss). Attach Schedule F	**6**	
7	Unemployment compensation	**7**	
8	Other income. List type and amount ▶		
		8	
9	Combine lines 1 through 8. Enter here and on Form 1040 or 1040-SR, line 7a	**9**	
Part II	**Adjustments to Income**		
10	Educator expenses	**10**	
11	Certain business expenses of reservists, performing artists, and fee-basis government officials. Attach Form 2106	**11**	
12	Health savings account deduction. Attach Form 8889	**12**	
13	Moving expenses for members of the Armed Forces. Attach Form 3903	**13**	
14	Deductible part of self-employment tax. Attach Schedule SE	**14**	
15	Self-employed SEP, SIMPLE, and qualified plans	**15**	
16	Self-employed health insurance deduction	**16**	
17	Penalty on early withdrawal of savings	**17**	
18a	Alimony paid	**18a**	
b	Recipient's SSN . . . . ▶		
c	Date of original divorce or separation agreement (see instructions) ▶		
19	IRA deduction	**19**	
20	Student loan interest deduction	**20**	
21	Reserved for future use	**21**	
22	Add lines 10 through 21. These are your **adjustments to income.** Enter here and on Form 1040 or 1040-SR, line 8a	**22**	

For Paperwork Reduction Act Notice, see your tax return instructions.   Cat. No. 71479F   Schedule 1 (Form 1040 or 1040-SR) 2019

SCHEDULE 2
(Form 1040 or 1040-SR)

Department of the Treasury
Internal Revenue Service

Additional Taxes

▶ Attach to Form 1040 or 1040-SR.
▶ Go to *www.irs.gov/Form1040* for instructions and the latest information.

OMB No. 1545-0074

2019

Attachment
Sequence No. **02**

Name(s) shown on Form 1040 or 1040-SR

Your social security number

Part I	Tax		
1	Alternative minimum tax. Attach Form 6251	1	
2	Excess advance premium tax credit repayment. Attach Form 8962	2	
3	Add lines 1 and 2. Enter here and include on Form 1040 or 1040-SR, line 12b . .	3	

Part II	Other Taxes		
4	Self-employment tax. Attach Schedule SE	4	
5	Unreported social security and Medicare tax from Form: **a** ☐ 4137 **b** ☐ 8919	5	
6	Additional tax on IRAs, other qualified retirement plans, and other tax-favored accounts. Attach Form 5329 if required	6	
7a	Household employment taxes. Attach Schedule H	7a	
b	Repayment of first-time homebuyer credit from Form 5405. Attach Form 5405 if required . . .	7b	
8	Taxes from: **a** ☐ Form 8959 **b** ☐ Form 8960		
	c ☐ Instructions; enter code(s)	8	
9	Section 965 net tax liability installment from Form 965-A	9	
10	Add lines 4 through 8. These are your **total other taxes.** Enter here and on Form 1040 or 1040-SR, line 15	10	

For Paperwork Reduction Act Notice, see your tax return instructions.   Cat. No. 71478U   Schedule 2 (Form 1040 or 1040-SR) 2019

SCHEDULE 3
(Form 1040 or 1040-SR)

Department of the Treasury
Internal Revenue Service

Additional Credits and Payments

▶ **Attach to Form 1040 or 1040-SR.**
▶ **Go to** *www.irs.gov/Form1040* **for instructions and the latest information.**

OMB No. 1545-0074

2019

Attachment
Sequence No. **03**

Name(s) shown on Form 1040 or 1040-SR

Your social security number

Part I	**Nonrefundable Credits**	
1	Foreign tax credit. Attach Form 1116 if required	1
2	Credit for child and dependent care expenses. Attach Form 2441	2
3	Education credits from Form 8863, line 19	3
4	Retirement savings contributions credit. Attach Form 8880	4
5	Residential energy credit. Attach Form 5695	5
6	Other credits from Form: **a** ☐ 3800 **b** ☐ 8801 **c** ☐ _____	6
7	Add lines 1 through 6. Enter here and include on Form 1040 or 1040-SR, line 13b	7

Part II	**Other Payments and Refundable Credits**	
8	2019 estimated tax payments and amount applied from 2018 return	8
9	Net premium tax credit. Attach Form 8962	9
10	Amount paid with request for extension to file (see instructions)	10
11	Excess social security and tier 1 RRTA tax withheld	11
12	Credit for federal tax on fuels. Attach Form 4136	12
13	Credits from Form: **a** ☐ 2439 **b** ☐ Reserved **c** ☐ 8885 **d** ☐	13
14	Add lines 8 through 13. Enter here and on Form 1040 or 1040-SR, line 18d	14

For Paperwork Reduction Act Notice, see your tax return instructions.   Cat. No. 71480G   Schedule 3 (Form 1040 or 1040-SR) 2019

DRAFT AS OF July 11, 2019 DO NOT FILE

SCHEDULE A
(Form 1040 or 1040-SR)

Department of the Treasury
Internal Revenue Service (99)

Itemized Deductions

▶ Go to *www.irs.gov/ScheduleA* for instructions and the latest information.
▶ Attach to Form 1040 or 1040-SR.

Caution: If you are claiming a net qualified disaster loss on Form 4684, see the instructions for line 16.

OMB No. 1545-0074

2019

Attachment
Sequence No. **07**

Name(s) shown on Form 1040 or 1040-SR

Your social security number

Medical and Dental Expenses	**Caution:** Do not include expenses reimbursed or paid by others.		
	1 Medical and dental expenses (see instructions)	**1**	
	2 Enter amount from Form 1040 or 1040-SR, line 8b	**2**	
	3 Multiply line 2 by 10% (0.10)	**3**	
	4 Subtract line 3 from line 1. If line 3 is more than line 1, enter -0-		**4**
Taxes You Paid	5 State and local taxes.		
	a State and local income taxes or general sales taxes. You may include either income taxes or general sales taxes on line 5a, but not both. If you elect to include general sales taxes instead of income taxes, check this box ▶ ☐	**5a**	
	b State and local real estate taxes (see instructions)	**5b**	
	c State and local personal property taxes	**5c**	
	d Add lines 5a through 5c	**5d**	
	e Enter the smaller of line 5d or $10,000 ($5,000 if married filing separately)	**5e**	
	6 Other taxes. List type and amount ▶ _____	**6**	
	7 Add lines 5e and 6		**7**
Interest You Paid **Caution:** Your mortgage interest deduction may be limited (see instructions).	8 Home mortgage interest and points. If you didn't use all of your home mortgage loan(s) to buy, build, or improve your home, see instructions and check this box ▶ ☐		
	a Home mortgage interest and points reported to you on Form 1098. See instructions if limited	**8a**	
	b Home mortgage interest not reported to you on Form 1098. If paid to the person from whom you bought the home, see instructions and show that person's name, identifying no., and address ▶ _____	**8b**	
	c Points not reported to you on Form 1098. See instructions for special rules	**8c**	
	d Reserved	**8d**	
	e Add lines 8a through 8c	**8e**	
	9 Investment interest. Attach Form 4952 if required. See instructions	**9**	
	10 Add lines 8e and 9		**10**
Gifts to Charity **Caution:** If you made a gift and got a benefit for it, see instructions.	11 Gifts by cash or check. If you made any gift of $250 or more, see instructions	**11**	
	12 Other than by cash or check. If you made any gift of $250 or more, see instructions. You **must** attach Form 8283 if over $500.	**12**	
	13 Carryover from prior year	**13**	
	14 Add lines 11 through 13		**14**
Casualty and Theft Losses	15 Casualty and theft loss(es) from a federally declared disaster (other than net qualified disaster losses). Attach Form 4684 and enter the amount from line 18 of that form. See instructions		**15**
Other Itemized Deductions	16 Other—from list in instructions. List type and amount ▶ _____		**16**
Total Itemized Deductions	17 Add the amounts in the far right column for lines 4 through 16. Also, enter this amount on Form 1040 or 1040-SR, line 9		**17**
	18 If you elect to itemize deductions even though they are less than your standard deduction, check this box ▶ ☐		

For Paperwork Reduction Act Notice, see the Instructions for Forms 1040 and 1040-SR.   Cat. No. 17145C   **Schedule A (Form 1040 or 1040-SR) 2019**

SCHEDULE B
(Form 1040 or 1040-SR)

Department of the Treasury
Internal Revenue Service (99)

Interest and Ordinary Dividends

▶ Go to *www.irs.gov/ScheduleB* for instructions and the latest information.
▶ Attach to Form 1040 or 1040-SR.

OMB No. 1545-0074

2019

Attachment
Sequence No. **08**

Name(s) shown on return

Your social security number

Part I **Interest** (See instructions and the instructions for Forms 1040 and 1040-SR, line 2b.) **Note:** If you received a Form 1099-INT, Form 1099-OID, or substitute statement from a brokerage firm, list the firm's name as the payer and enter the total interest shown on that form.	**1**	List name of payer. If any interest is from a seller-financed mortgage and the buyer used the property as a personal residence, see the instructions and list this interest first. Also, show that buyer's social security number and address ▶		**Amount**
			1	
	2	Add the amounts on line 1	**2**	
	3	Excludable interest on series EE and I U.S. savings bonds issued after 1989. Attach Form 8815	**3**	
	4	Subtract line 3 from line 2. Enter the result here and on Form 1040 or 1040-SR, line 2b . . . . ▶	**4**	

Note: If line 4 is over $1,500, you must complete Part III.

Part II **Ordinary Dividends** (See instructions and the instructions for Forms 1040 and 1040-SR, line 3b.) **Note:** If you received a Form 1099-DIV or substitute statement from a brokerage firm, list the firm's name as the payer and enter the ordinary dividends shown on that form.	**5**	List name of payer ▶		**Amount**
			5	
	6	Add the amounts on line 5. Enter the total here and on Form 1040 or 1040-SR, line 3b . . . . ▶	**6**	

Note: If line 6 is over $1,500, you must complete Part III.

Part III **Foreign Accounts and Trusts** **Caution:** If required, failure to file FinCEN Form 114 may result in substantial penalties. See instructions.		You must complete this part if you **(a)** had over $1,500 of taxable interest or ordinary dividends; **(b)** had a foreign account; or **(c)** received a distribution from, or were a grantor of, or a transferor to, a foreign trust.	**Yes**	**No**
	7a	At any time during 2019, did you have a financial interest in or signature authority over a financial account (such as a bank account, securities account, or brokerage account) located in a foreign country? See instructions		
		If "Yes," are you required to file FinCEN Form 114, Report of Foreign Bank and Financial Accounts (FBAR), to report that financial interest or signature authority? See FinCEN Form 114 and its instructions for filing requirements and exceptions to those requirements		
	b	If you are required to file FinCEN Form 114, enter the name of the foreign country where the financial account is located ▶		
	8	During 2019, did you receive a distribution from, or were you the grantor of, or transferor to, a foreign trust? If "Yes," you may have to file Form 3520. See instructions		

For Paperwork Reduction Act Notice, see your tax return instructions.   Cat. No. 17146N   **Schedule B (Form 1040 or 1040-SR) 2019**

Form **2441**

Child and Dependent Care Expenses

▶ Attach to Form 1040, 1040-SR, or 1040-NR.

▶ Go to *www.irs.gov/Form2441* for instructions and the latest information.

Department of the Treasury
Internal Revenue Service (99)

OMB No. 1545-0074

2019

Attachment Sequence No. **21**

Name(s) shown on return | Your social security number

You cannot claim a credit for child and dependent care expenses if your filing status is married filing separately unless you meet the requirements listed in the instructions under "Married Persons Filing Separately." If you meet these requirements, check this box. ☐

Part I   Persons or Organizations Who Provided the Care—You **must** complete this part.
(If you have more than two care providers, see the instructions.)

1	(a) Care provider's name	(b) Address (number, street, apt. no., city, state, and ZIP code)	(c) Identifying number (SSN or EIN)	(d) Amount paid (see instructions)

Did you receive **dependent care benefits?**
No ▶ Complete only Part II below.
Yes ▶ Complete Part III on the back next.

Caution: If the care was provided in your home, you may owe employment taxes. For details, see the instructions for Schedule 2 (Form 1040 or 1040-SR), line 7a; or Form 1040-NR, line 59a.

Part II   Credit for Child and Dependent Care Expenses

2   Information about your **qualifying person(s).** If you have more than two qualifying persons, see the instructions.

(a) Qualifying person's name		(b) Qualifying person's social security number	(c) Qualified expenses you incurred and paid in 2019 for the person listed in column (a)
First	Last		

3	Add the amounts in column (c) of line 2. **Don't** enter more than $3,000 for one qualifying person or $6,000 for two or more persons. If you completed Part III, enter the amount from line 31 . .	3	
4	Enter your **earned income.** See instructions	4	
5	If married filing jointly, enter your spouse's earned income (if you or your spouse was a student or was disabled, see the instructions); **all others,** enter the amount from line 4	5	
6	Enter the **smallest** of line 3, 4, or 5	6	

7   Enter the amount from Form 1040 or 1040-SR, line 8b; or Form 1040-NR, line 35 . . . . **7**

8   Enter on line 8 the decimal amount shown below that applies to the amount on line 7

If line 7 is:			If line 7 is:		
Over	But not over	Decimal amount is	Over	But not over	Decimal amount is
$0—15,000		.35	$29,000—31,000		.27
15,000—17,000		.34	31,000—33,000		.26
17,000—19,000		.33	33,000—35,000		.25
19,000—21,000		.32	35,000—37,000		.24
21,000—23,000		.31	37,000—39,000		.23
23,000—25,000		.30	39,000—41,000		.22
25,000—27,000		.29	41,000—43,000		.21
27,000—29,000		.28	43,000—No limit		.20

8	X.

9	Multiply line 6 by the decimal amount on line 8. If you paid 2018 expenses in 2019, see the instructions	9	

10   Tax liability limit. Enter the amount from the Credit Limit Worksheet in the instructions **10**

11	**Credit for child and dependent care expenses.** Enter the **smaller** of line 9 or line 10 here and on Schedule 3 (Form 1040 or 1040-SR), line 2; or Form 1040-NR, line 47	11	

For Paperwork Reduction Act Notice, see your tax return instructions.   Cat. No. 11862M   Form **2441** (2019)

Form 2441 (2019)   Page **2**

Part III	**Dependent Care Benefits**

12 Enter the total amount of **dependent care benefits** you received in 2019. Amounts you received as an employee should be shown in box 10 of your Form(s) W-2. **Don't** include amounts reported as wages in box 1 of Form(s) W-2. If you were self-employed or a partner, include amounts you received under a dependent care assistance program from your sole proprietorship or partnership . **12**

13 Enter the amount, if any, you carried over from 2018 and used in 2019 during the grace period. See instructions **13**

14 Enter the amount, if any, you forfeited or carried forward to 2020. See instructions . . **14** ( )

15 Combine lines 12 through 14. See instructions **15**

16 Enter the total amount of **qualified expenses** incurred in 2019 for the care of the **qualifying person(s)** **16**

17 Enter the **smaller** of line 15 or 16 . . . . **17**

18 Enter your **earned income.** See instructions **18**

19 Enter the amount shown below that applies to you.

- If married filing jointly, enter your spouse's earned income (if you or your spouse was a student or was disabled, see the instructions for line 5).
- If married filing separately, see instructions.
- All others, enter the amount from line 18. **19**

20 Enter the **smallest** of line 17, 18, or 19 . . . . **20**

21 Enter $5,000 ($2,500 if married filing separately **and** you were required to enter your spouse's earned income on line 19) **21**

22 Is any amount on line 12 from your sole proprietorship or partnership?
☐ **No.** Enter -0-.
☐ **Yes.** Enter the amount here **22**

23 Subtract line 22 from line 15 . . . . **23**

24 Deductible benefits. Enter the **smallest** of line 20, 21, or 22. Also, include this amount on the appropriate line(s) of your return. See instructions **24**

25 Excluded benefits. If you checked "No" on line 22, enter the smaller of line 20 or 21. Otherwise, subtract line 24 from the smaller of line 20 or line 21. If zero or less, enter -0- **25**

26 Taxable benefits. Subtract line 25 from line 23. If zero or less, enter -0-. Also, include this amount on Form 1040 or 1040-SR, line 1; or Form 1040-NR, line 8. On the dotted line next to Form 1040 or 1040-SR, line 1; or Form 1040-NR, line 8, enter "DCB" **26**

To claim the child and dependent care
credit, complete lines 27 through 31 below.

27 Enter $3,000 ($6,000 if two or more qualifying persons) **27**

28 Add lines 24 and 25 . . . . **28**

29 Subtract line 28 from line 27. If zero or less, **stop.** You can't take the credit. **Exception.** If you paid 2018 expenses in 2019, see the instructions for line 9 . . . . **29**

30 Complete line 2 on the front of this form. **Don't** include in column (c) any benefits shown on line 28 above. Then, add the amounts in column (c) and enter the total here **30**

31 Enter the **smaller** of line 29 or 30. Also, enter this amount on line 3 on the front of this form and complete lines 4 through 11 . . . . **31**

Form **2441** (2019)

Form **8880**

Department of the Treasury
Internal Revenue Service

Credit for Qualified Retirement Savings Contributions

▶ Attach to Form 1040, 1040-SR, or 1040-NR.

▶ Go to *www.irs.gov/Form8880* for the latest information.

OMB No. 1545-0074

2019

Attachment
Sequence No. **54**

Name(s) shown on return

Your social security number

 CAUTION

*You **cannot** take this credit if **either** of the following applies.*

• *The amount on Form 1040 or 1040-SR, line 8b; or Form 1040-NR, line 35, is more than $32,000 ($48,000 if head of household; $64,000 if married filing jointly).*

• *The person(s) who made the qualified contribution or elective deferral **(a)** was born after January 1, 2002; **(b)** is claimed as a dependent on someone else's 2019 tax return; or **(c)** was a **student** (see instructions).*

		(a) You	(b) Your spouse
1	Traditional and Roth IRA contributions, and ABLE account contributions by the designated beneficiary for 2019. **Do not** include rollover contributions **1**		
2	Elective deferrals to a 401(k) or other qualified employer plan, voluntary employee contributions, and 501(c)(18)(D) plan contributions for 2019 (see instructions) **2**		
3	Add lines 1 and 2 . . . . **3**		
4	Certain distributions received **after** 2016 and **before** the due date (including extensions) of your 2019 tax return (see instructions). If married filing jointly, include **both** spouses' amounts in **both** columns. See instructions for an exception . . . **4**		
5	Subtract line 4 from line 3. If zero or less, enter -0- **5**		
6	In each column, enter the **smaller** of line 5 or $2,000 . . . . . . **6**		

7	Add the amounts on line 6. If zero, **stop;** you can't take this credit	**7**	
8	Enter the amount from Form 1040 or 1040-SR, line 8b;* or Form 1040-NR, line 35 . . . . **8**		
9	Enter the applicable decimal amount from the table below.		

If line 8 is—		And your filing status is—		
Over—	But not over—	Married filing jointly	Head of household	Single, Married filing separately, or Qualifying widow(er)
		Enter on line 9—		
---	$19,250	0.5	0.5	0.5
$19,250	$20,750	0.5	0.5	0.2
$20,750	$28,875	0.5	0.5	0.1
$28,875	$31,125	0.5	0.2	0.1
$31,125	$32,000	0.5	0.1	0.1
$32,000	$38,500	0.5	0.1	0.0
$38,500	$41,500	0.2	0.1	0.0
$41,500	$48,000	0.1	0.1	0.0
$48,000	$64,000	0.1	0.0	0.0
$64,000	---	0.0	0.0	0.0

9 x 0.

Note: If line 9 is zero, **stop;** you can't take this credit.

10	Multiply line 7 by line 9	**10**	
11	Limitation based on tax liability. Enter the amount from the Credit Limit Worksheet in the instructions	**11**	
12	**Credit for qualified retirement savings contributions.** Enter the **smaller** of line 10 or line 11 here and on Schedule 3 (Form 1040 or 1040-SR), line 4; or Form 1040-NR, line 48	**12**	

* See Pub. 590-A for the amount to enter if you claim any exclusion or deduction for foreign earned income, foreign housing, or income from Puerto Rico or for bona fide residents of American Samoa.

For Paperwork Reduction Act Notice, see your tax return instructions.   Cat. No. 33394D   Form **8880** (2019)

Form 8880 (2019)   Page **2**

General Instructions

Section references are to the Internal Revenue Code.

Reminder

Contributions by a designated beneficiary to an Achieving a Better Life Experience (ABLE) account. A retirement savings contribution credit may be claimed for the amount of contributions you, as the designated beneficiary of an ABLE account, make before January 1, 2026, to the ABLE account. See Pub. 907, Tax Highlights for Persons With Disabilities, for more information.

Future Developments

For the latest information about developments related to Form 8880 and its instructions, such as legislation enacted after they were published, go to www.irs.gov/Form8880.

Purpose of Form

Use Form 8880 to figure the amount, if any, of your retirement savings contributions credit (also known as the saver's credit).

 This credit can be claimed in addition to any IRA deduction claimed on Schedule 1 (Form 1040 or 1040-SR), line 19; or Form 1040-NR, line 32.

Who Can Take This Credit

You may be able to take this credit if you, or your spouse if filing jointly, made (a) contributions (other than rollover contributions) to a traditional or Roth IRA; (b) elective deferrals to a 401(k), 403(b), governmental 457(b), SEP, or SIMPLE plan; (c) voluntary employee contributions to a qualified retirement plan, as defined in section 4974(c) (including the federal Thrift Savings Plan); (d) contributions to a 501(c)(18)(D) plan; or (e) contributions, as a designated beneficiary of an ABLE account, to the ABLE account, as defined in section 529A.

However, you can't take the credit if either of the following applies.

• The amount on Form 1040 or 1040-SR, line 8b; or Form 1040-NR, line 35, is more than $32,000 ($48,000 if head of household; $64,000 if married filing jointly).

• The person(s) who made the qualified contribution or elective deferral (a) was born after January 1, 2002; (b) is claimed as a dependent on someone else's 2019 tax return; or (c) was a student.

 You'll need to refigure the amount on Form 1040 or 1040-SR, line 8b, if you're filing Form 2555 or Form 4563 or you're excluding income from Puerto Rico. See Pub. 590-A at www.irs.gov/Pub590A for details.

You were a student if during any part of 5 calendar months of 2019 you:

• Were enrolled as a full-time student at a school; or

• Took a full-time, on-farm training course given by a school or a state, county, or local government agency.

A school includes technical, trade, and mechanical schools. It doesn't include on-the-job training courses, correspondence schools, or schools offering courses only through the Internet.

Specific Instructions

Column (b)

Complete column (b) only if you're filing a joint return.

Line 2

Include on line 2 any of the following amounts.

• Elective deferrals to a 401(k) or 403(b) plan (including designated Roth contributions under section 402A), or to a governmental 457(b), SEP, or SIMPLE plan.

• Voluntary employee contributions to a qualified retirement plan, as defined in section 4974(c) (including the federal Thrift Savings Plan).

• Contributions to a 501(c)(18)(D) plan.

These amounts may be shown in box 12 of your Form(s) W-2 for 2019.

Note: Contributions designated under section 414(h)(2) are treated as employer contributions and, as such, they aren't voluntary contributions made by the employee. They don't qualify for the credit and shouldn't be included on line 2.

Line 4

Enter the total amount of distributions you, and your spouse if filing jointly, received after 2016 and before the due date of your 2019 return (including extensions) from any of the following types of plans.

• Traditional or Roth IRAs (including *my*RAs), or ABLE accounts.

• 401(k), 403(b), governmental 457(b), 501(c)(18)(D), SEP, or SIMPLE plans.

• Qualified retirement plans, as defined in section 4974(c) (including the federal Thrift Savings Plan).

Don't include any of the following.

• Distributions not taxable as the result of a rollover or a trustee-to-trustee transfer.

• Distributions that are taxable as the result of an in-plan rollover to your designated Roth account.

• Distributions from your eligible retirement plan (other than a Roth IRA) rolled over or converted to your Roth IRA.

• Loans from a qualified employer plan treated as a distribution.

• Distributions of excess contributions or deferrals (and income allocable to such contributions or deferrals).

• Distributions of contributions made to an IRA during a tax year and returned (with any income allocable to such contributions) on or before the due date (including extensions) for that tax year.

• Distributions of dividends paid on stock held by an employee stock ownership plan under section 404(k).

• Distributions from a military retirement plan (other than the federal Thrift Savings Plan).

• Distributions from an inherited IRA by a nonspousal beneficiary.

If you're filing a joint return, include both spouses' amounts in both columns.

Exception. Don't include your spouse's distributions with yours when entering an amount on line 4 if you and your spouse didn't file a joint return for the year the distribution was received.

Example. You received a distribution of $5,000 from a qualified retirement plan in 2019. Your spouse received a distribution of $2,000 from a Roth IRA in 2017. You and your spouse file a joint return in 2019, but didn't file a joint return in 2017. You would include $5,000 in column (a) and $7,000 in column (b).

Line 7

Add the amounts from line 6, columns (a) and (b), and enter the total.

Line 11

Before you complete the following worksheet, figure the amount of any credit for the elderly or the disabled you're claiming on Schedule 3 (Form 1040 or 1040-SR), line 6. See Schedule R (Form 1040 or 1040-SR) to figure the credit.

Credit Limit Worksheet

Complete this worksheet to figure the amount to enter on line 11.

1. Enter the amount from Form 1040 or 1040-SR, line 12b; or Form 1040-NR, line 45 . . . . .   **1.** _____

2. Form 1040 or 1040-SR filers: Enter the total of your credits from Schedule 3, lines 1 through 3, and Schedule R, line 22.

   Form 1040-NR filers: Enter the total of your credits from lines 46 and 47 . . . .   **2.** _____

3. Subtract line 2 from line 1. Also enter this amount on Form 8880, line 11. But if zero or less, **stop;** you can't take the credit—don't file this form .   **3.** _____

2019 Child Tax Credit and Credit for Other Dependents
Worksheet—Line 13a

Keep for Your Records

CAUTION

1. To be a qualifying child for the child tax credit, the child must be your dependent, **under age 17** at the end of 2019, and meet all the conditions in Steps 1 through 3 under *Who Qualifies as Your Dependent*. Make sure you checked the "child tax credit" box in column (4) of the *Dependents* section on Form 1040 or 1040-SR for each qualifying child.

2. If you don't have a qualifying child, you can't claim the child tax credit; but you may be able to claim the credit for other dependents for that child. See Step 3 under *Who Qualifies as Your Dependent*.

3. To see if your qualifying relative qualifies you to take the credit for other dependents, see Step 5 under *Who Qualifies as Your Dependent*.

4. Be sure to see *Social security number* under *Who Qualifies as Your Dependent*.

5. Do **not** use this worksheet, but use Pub. 972 instead, if:

   a. You are claiming the adoption credit, mortgage interest credit, District of Columbia first-time homebuyer credit, or residential energy efficient property credit*;

   b. You are excluding income from Puerto Rico; or

   c. You are filing Form 2555 or 4563.
   * If applicable.

Part 1

1. Number of qualifying children under age 17 with the required social security number: _____ × $2,000. Enter the result. **1** ☐

2. Number of other dependents, including qualifying children without the required social security number: _____ × $500. Enter the result. **2** ☐

   Caution. Don't include yourself, your spouse, or anyone who is not a U.S. citizen, U.S. national, or U.S. resident alien. Also, don't include anyone you included on line 1.

3. Add lines 1 and 2. **3** ☐

4. Enter the amount from Form 1040 or 1040-SR, line 8b. **4** ☐

5. Enter the amount shown below for your filing status.

   • Married filing jointly — $400,000

   • All other filing statuses — $200,000

   5 ☐

6. Is the amount on line 4 more than the amount on line 5?

   ☐ **No.** Leave line 6 blank. Enter -0- on line 7, and go to line 8.

   ☐ **Yes.** Subtract line 5 from line 4.

   If the result isn't a multiple of $1,000, increase it to the next multiple of $1,000. For example, increase $425 to $1,000, increase $1,025 to $2,000, etc.

   6 ☐

7. Multiply the amount on line 6 by 5% (0.05). Enter the result. **7** ☐

8. Is the amount on line 3 more than the amount on line 7?

   ☐ **No.** (STOP)

   You can't take the child tax credit on Form 1040 or 1040-SR, line 13a. You also can't take the additional child tax credit on Form 1040 or 1040-SR, line 18b. Complete the rest of your Form 1040 or 1040-SR.

   ☐ **Yes.** Subtract line 7 from line 3. Enter the result. *Go to Part 2.* **8** ☐

2019 Child Tax Credit and Credit for Other Dependents
Worksheet—*Continued*

Keep for Your Records

Before you begin Part 2: √ Figure the amount of any credits you are claiming on Schedule 3; Form 5695, Part II*; Form 8910; Form 8936; or Schedule R.

Part 2

9. Enter the amount from Form 1040 or 1040-SR, line 12b.   **9** _____

10. Add any amounts from:

    Schedule 3, line 1   _____

    Schedule 3, line 2 + _____

    Schedule 3, line 3 + _____

    Schedule 3, line 4 + _____

    Form 5695, line 30* + _____

    Form 8910, line 15* + _____

    Form 8936, line 23 + _____

    Schedule R, line 22 + _____

    Enter the total. **10** _____

11. Are the amounts on lines 9 and 10 the same?

    ☐ **Yes.** (STOP)
    You can't take this credit because there is no tax to reduce.
    However, you may be able to take the **additional child tax
    credit** if line 1 is more than zero. See the **TIP** below.

    ☐ **No.** Subtract line 10 from line 9.   **11** _____

12. Is the amount on line 8 more than the amount on line 11?

    ☐ **Yes.** Enter the amount from line 11.
    Also, you may be able to take the
    additional child tax credit if line 1
    is more than zero. See the **TIP** below.   } **This is your child tax credit and credit for other dependents.**

    ☐ **No.** Enter the amount from line 8.   **12** _____

    Enter this amount on
    Form 1040 or 1040-SR,
    line 13a.

TIP *You may be able to take the **additional child tax credit**
on Form 1040 or 1040-SR, line 18b, if you answered "Yes" on
line 11 **or** line 12 above.*

- *First, complete your Form 1040 or 1040-SR through line
  18a (also complete Schedule 3, line 11).*
- *Then, use Schedule 8812 to figure any additional child tax
  credit.*

CAUTION *If your child tax credit or additional child tax credit for a year after
2015 was reduced or disallowed, see Form 8862, who must file to
find out if you must file Form 8862 to take the credit for 2019.*

*If applicable.

SCHEDULE 8812
(Form 1040 or 1040-SR)

Department of the Treasury
Internal Revenue Service (99)

Additional Child Tax Credit

▶ Attach to Form 1040, 1040-SR, or 1040-NR.
▶ Go to *www.irs.gov/Schedule8812* for instructions and the latest information.

OMB No. 1545-0074

2019

Attachment
Sequence No. **47**

Name(s) shown on return

Your social security number

DRAFT AS OF JULY 17, 2019 DO NOT FILE

Part I	All Filers

Caution: If you file Form 2555, **stop here;** you cannot claim the additional child tax credit.

1   If you are required to use the worksheet in Pub. 972, enter the amount from line 10 of the Child Tax Credit and Credit for Other Dependents Worksheet in the publication. Otherwise:

1040 and Enter the amount from line 8 of your Child Tax Credit and Credit for Other Dependents
1040-SR filers: Worksheet (see the instructions for Forms 1040 and 1040-SR, line 13a).

1040-NR filers: Enter the amount from line 8 of your Child Tax Credit and Credit for Other Dependents Worksheet (see the instructions for Form 1040-NR, line 49).   **1**

2   Enter the amount from Form 1040, line 13a; Form 1040-SR, line 13a; or Form 1040-NR, line 49   **2**

3   Subtract line 2 from line 1. If zero, **stop here;** you cannot claim this credit.   **3**

4   Number of qualifying children under 17 with the required social security number: _____ x $1,400.
Enter the result. If zero, **stop here;** you cannot claim this credit   **4**

TIP: The number of children you use for this line is the same as the number of children you used for line 1 of the Child Tax Credit and Credit for Other Dependents Worksheet.

5   Enter the **smaller** of line 3 or line 4   **5**

6a   Earned income (see instructions)   **6a**

b   Nontaxable combat pay (see instructions)   **6b**

7   Is the amount on line 6a more than $2,500?
☐ **No.** Leave line 7 blank and enter -0- on line 8.
☐ **Yes.** Subtract $2,500 from the amount on line 6a. Enter the result   **7**

8   Multiply the amount on line 7 by 15% (0.15) and enter the result   **8**

Next. On line 4, is the amount $4,200 or more?

☐ **No.** If line 8 is zero, **stop here;** you cannot claim this credit. Otherwise, skip Part II and enter the **smaller** of line 5 or line 8 on line 15.

☐ **Yes.** If line 8 is equal to or more than line 5, skip Part II and enter the amount from line 5 on line 15. Otherwise, go to line 9.

Part II	Certain Filers Who Have Three or More Qualifying Children

9   Withheld social security, Medicare, and Additional Medicare taxes from Form(s) W-2, boxes 4 and 6. If married filing jointly, include your spouse's amounts with yours. If your employer withheld or you paid Additional Medicare Tax or tier 1 RRTA taxes, see instructions   **9**

10   **1040 and** Enter the total of the amounts from Schedule 1 (Form 1040 or 1040-SR),
1040-SR filers: line 14, and Schedule 2 (Form 1040 or 1040-SR), line 5, plus any taxes that you identified using code "UT" and entered on Schedule 2 (Form 1040 or 1040-SR), line 8.

1040-NR filers: Enter the total of the amounts from Form 1040-NR, lines 27 and 56, plus any taxes that you identified using code "UT" and entered on line 60.   **10**

11   Add lines 9 and 10   **11**

12   **1040 and** Enter the total of the amounts from Form 1040 or 1040-SR, line
1040-SR filers: 18a, and Schedule 3 (Form 1040 or 1040-SR), line 11.
1040-NR filers: Enter the amount from Form 1040-NR, line 67.   **12**

13   Subtract line 12 from line 11. If zero or less, enter -0-   **13**

14   Enter the **larger** of line 8 or line 13   **14**

Next, enter the **smaller** of line 5 or line 14 on line 15.

Part III	Additional Child Tax Credit

15   **This is your additional child tax credit**   **15**

Enter this amount on
Form 1040, line 18b;
Form 1040-SR, line 18b; or
Form 1040-NR, line 64.

For Paperwork Reduction Act Notice, see your tax return instructions.   Cat. No. 59761M   Schedule 8812 (Form 1040 or 1040-SR) 2019

Worksheet A—2019 EIC—Line 18a

Before you begin: √ Be sure you are using the correct worksheet. Use this worksheet only if you answered "No" to Step 5, question 2. Otherwise, use Worksheet B.

Part 1
 	
All Filers Using Worksheet A
	1. Enter your earned income from Step 5.
	    Wages, salaries
	
	2. Look up the amount on line 1 above in the EIC Table (right after Worksheet B) to find the credit. Be sure you use the correct column for your filing status and the number of children you have. Enter the credit here.
	    If line 2 is zero, (STOP) You can't take the credit.
	    Enter "No" on the dotted line next to Form 1040 or 1040-SR, line 18a.
	
	3. Enter the amount from Form 1040 or 1040-SR, line 8b.
	    Adjusted gross income
	
	4. Are the amounts on lines 3 and 1 the same?
	    ☐ **Yes.** Skip line 5; enter the amount from line 2 on line 6.
	    ☐ **No.** Go to line 5.
		1
		
		2
		
		3

Part 2
 	
Filers Who Answered "No" on Line 4
	5. If you have:
	  ● No qualifying children, is the amount on line 3 less than $8,650 ($14,450 if married filing jointly)?
	  ● 1 or more qualifying children, is the amount on line 3 less than $19,050 ($24,850 if married filing jointly)?
	    ☐ **Yes.** Leave line 5 blank; enter the amount from line 2 on line 6.
	    ☐ **No.** Look up the amount on line 3 in the EIC Table to find the credit. Be sure you use the correct column for your filing status and the number of children you have. Enter the credit here.
	    Look at the amounts on lines 5 and 2.
	    Then, enter the **smaller** amount on line 6.
		5

Part 3 **Your Earned Income Credit**	**6.** **This is your earned income credit.** Enter this amount on Form 1040 or 1040-SR, line 18a. **Reminder—** √ If you have a qualifying child, complete and attach Schedule EIC. ⚠ **CAUTION** *If your EIC for a year after 1996 was reduced or disallowed, see Form 8862, who must file, earlier, to find out if you must file Form 8862 to take the credit for 2019.*	**6**

SCHEDULE EIC
(Form 1040 or 1040-SR)

Department of the Treasury
Internal Revenue Service (99)

Earned Income Credit

Qualifying Child Information

► Complete and attach to Form 1040 or 1040-SR only if you have a qualifying child.
► Go to *www.irs.gov/ScheduleEIC* for the latest information.

OMB No. 1545-0074

2019

Attachment
Sequence No. **43**

Name(s) shown on return

Your social security number

Before you begin:
- See the instructions for Form 1040 or 1040-SR, line 18a, to make sure that **(a)** you can take the EIC, and **(b)** you have a qualifying child.
- Be sure the child's name on line 1 and social security number (SSN) on line 2 agree with the child's social security card. Otherwise, at the time we process your return, we may reduce or disallow your EIC. If the name or SSN on the child's social security card is not correct, call the Social Security Administration at 1-800-772-1213.

⚠️ **CAUTION**
- *You can't claim the EIC for a child who didn't live with you for more than half of the year.*
- *If you take the EIC even though you are not eligible, you may not be allowed to take the credit for up to 10 years. See the instructions for details.*
- *It will take us longer to process your return and issue your refund if you do not fill in all lines that apply for each qualifying child.*

Qualifying Child Information	Child 1		Child 2		Child 3	
1 Child's name If you have more than three qualifying children, you have to list only three to get the maximum credit.	First name	Last name	First name	Last name	First name	Last name
2 Child's SSN The child must have an SSN as defined in the instructions for Form 1040 or 1040-SR, line 18a, unless the child was born and died in 2019. If your child was born and died in 2019 and did not have an SSN, enter "Died" on this line and attach a copy of the child's birth certificate, death certificate, or hospital medical records showing a live birth.						
3 Child's year of birth	Year _ _ _ _ *If born after 2000 and the child is younger than you (or your spouse, if filing jointly), skip lines 4a and 4b; go to line 5.*		Year _ _ _ _ *If born after 2000 and the child is younger than you (or your spouse, if filing jointly), skip lines 4a and 4b; go to line 5.*		Year _ _ _ _ *If born after 2000 and the child is younger than you (or your spouse, if filing jointly), skip lines 4a and 4b; go to line 5.*	
4 a Was the child under age 24 at the end of 2019, a student, and younger than you (or your spouse, if filing jointly)?	☐ **Yes.** *Go to line 5.*	☐ **No.** *Go to line 4b.*	☐ **Yes.** *Go to line 5.*	☐ **No.** *Go to line 4b.*	☐ **Yes.** *Go to line 5.*	☐ **No.** *Go to line 4b.*
b Was the child permanently and totally disabled during any part of 2019?	☐ **Yes.** *Go to line 5.*	☐ **No.** The child is not a qualifying child.	☐ **Yes.** *Go to line 5.*	☐ **No.** The child is not a qualifying child.	☐ **Yes.** *Go to line 5.*	☐ **No.** The child is not a qualifying child.
5 Child's relationship to you (for example, son, daughter, grandchild, niece, nephew, eligible foster child, etc.)						
6 Number of months child lived with you in the United States during 2019 • If the child lived with you for more than half of 2019 but less than 7 months, enter "7." • If the child was born or died in 2019 and your home was the child's home for more than half the time he or she was alive during 2019, enter "12."	_____ months *Do not enter more than 12 months.*		_____ months *Do not enter more than 12 months.*		_____ months *Do not enter more than 12 months.*	

For Paperwork Reduction Act Notice, see your tax return instructions.   Cat. No. 13339M   **Schedule EIC (Form 1040 or 1040-SR) 2019**

Form **8962**

Department of the Treasury
Internal Revenue Service

Premium Tax Credit (PTC)

▶ Attach to Form 1040, 1040-SR, or 1040-NR
▶ Go to *www.irs.gov/Form8962* for instructions and the latest information.

OMB No. 1545-0074

2019
Attachment
Sequence No. **73**

Name shown on your return

Your social security number

You cannot take the PTC if your filing status is married filing separately unless you qualify for an exception (see instructions). If you qualify, check the box . . ▶ ☐

Part I Annual and Monthly Contribution Amount

1	Tax family size. Enter your tax family size (see instructions)	**1**
2a	Modified AGI. Enter your modified AGI (see instructions) **2a**	
b	Enter the total of your dependents' modified AGI (see instructions) **2b**	
3	Household income. Add the amounts on lines 2a and 2b (see instructions)	**3**
4	Federal poverty line. Enter the federal poverty line amount from Table 1-1, 1-2, or 1-3 (see instructions). Check the appropriate box for the federal poverty table used. **a** ☐ Alaska **b** ☐ Hawaii **c** ☐ Other 48 states and DC	**4**
5	Household income as a percentage of federal poverty line (see instructions)	**5** %
6	Did you enter 401% on line 5? (See instructions if you entered less than 100%.)	

☐ **No.** Continue to line 7.

☐ **Yes.** You are not eligible to take the PTC. If advance payment of the PTC was made, see the instructions for how to report your excess advance PTC repayment amount.

7	Applicable Figure. Using your line 5 percentage, locate your "applicable figure" on the table in the instructions . .	**7**
8a	Annual contribution amount. Multiply line 3 by line 7. Round to nearest whole dollar amount **8a**	**b** Monthly contribution amount. Divide line 8a by 12. Round to nearest whole dollar amount **8b**

Part II Premium Tax Credit Claim and Reconciliation of Advance Payment of Premium Tax Credit

9 Are you allocating policy amounts with another taxpayer or do you want to use the alternative calculation for year of marriage (see instructions)?

☐ **Yes.** Skip to Part IV, Allocation of Policy Amounts, or Part V, Alternative Calculation for Year of Marriage. ☐ **No.** Continue to line 10.

10 See the instructions to determine if you can use line 11 or must complete lines 12 through 23.

☐ **Yes.** Continue to line 11. Compute your annual PTC. Then skip lines 12–23 and continue to line 24. ☐ **No.** Continue to lines 12–23. Compute your monthly PTC and continue to line 24.

Annual Calculation	(a) Annual enrollment premiums (Form(s) 1095-A, line 33A)	(b) Annual applicable SLCSP premium (Form(s) 1095-A, line 33B)	(c) Annual contribution amount (line 8a)	(d) Annual maximum premium assistance (subtract (c) from (b), if zero or less, enter -0-)	(e) Annual premium tax credit allowed (smaller of (a) or (d))	(f) Annual advance payment of PTC (Form(s) 1095-A, line 33C)
11 Annual Totals						

Monthly Calculation	(a) Monthly enrollment premiums (Form(s) 1095-A, lines 21–32, column A)	(b) Monthly applicable SLCSP premium (Form(s) 1095-A, lines 21–32, column B)	(c) Monthly contribution amount (amount from line 8b or alternative marriage monthly calculation)	(d) Monthly maximum premium assistance (subtract (c) from (b), if zero or less, enter -0-)	(e) Monthly premium tax credit allowed (smaller of (a) or (d))	(f) Monthly advance payment of PTC (Form(s) 1095-A, lines 21–32, column C)
12 January						
13 February						
14 March						
15 April						
16 May						
17 June						
18 July						
19 August						
20 September						
21 October						
22 November						
23 December						

24	Total premium tax credit. Enter the amount from line 11(e) or add lines 12(e) through 23(e) and enter the total here	**24**
25	Advance payment of PTC. Enter the amount from line 11(f) or add lines 12(f) through 23(f) and enter the total here	**25**
26	Net premium tax credit. If line 24 is greater than line 25, subtract line 25 from line 24. Enter the difference here and on Schedule 3 (Form 1040 or 1040-SR), line 9, or Form 1040-NR, line 65. If line 24 equals line 25, enter -0-. Stop here. If line 25 is greater than line 24, leave this line blank and continue to line 27	**26**

Part III Repayment of Excess Advance Payment of the Premium Tax Credit

27	Excess advance payment of PTC. If line 25 is greater than line 24, subtract line 24 from line 25. Enter the difference here	**27**
28	Repayment limitation (see instructions)	**28**
29	Excess advance premium tax credit repayment. Enter the smaller of line 27 or line 28 here and on Schedule 2 (Form 1040 or 1040-SR), line 2, or Form 1040-NR, line 44	**29**

For Paperwork Reduction Act Notice, see your tax return instructions. Cat. No. 37784Z Form **8962** (2019)

Student Name _____

Class/Section _____

Date _____

KEY NUMBER TAX RETURN SUMMARY

CHAPTER 7

Comprehensive Problem 1

Adjusted Gross Income (Line 8b) _____

Taxable Income (Line 11b) _____

Total Nonrefundable Credits (Schedule 3, Line 7) _____

Child Tax Credit (Line 13a) _____

Amount Overpaid (Line 20) _____

Comprehensive Problem 2A

Adjusted Gross Income (Line 8b) _____

Taxable Income (Line 11b) _____

Credit for Child and Dependent Care Expenses (Schedule 3, Line 2) _____

Earned Income Credit (line 18a) _____

Amount Overpaid (Line 20) _____

Comprehensive Problem 2B

Adjusted Gross Income (Line 8b) _____

Taxable Income (Line 11b) _____

Excess Advance Premium Tax Credit Repayment (Schedule 2, Line 2) _____

Total Tax (Line 16) _____

Amount Overpaid (Line 20) _____

Depreciation and Sale of Business Property

LEARNING OBJECTIVES

After completing this chapter, you should be able to:

LO 8.1   Explain the concept of depreciation.

LO 8.2   Calculate depreciation expense using the MACRS tables.

LO 8.3   Identify when a Section 179 election to expense the cost of property may be used.

LO 8.4   Apply the limitations placed on depreciation of "listed property."

LO 8.5   Apply the limitations on depreciation of "luxury automobiles."

LO 8.6   Calculate the amortization of goodwill and certain other intangibles.

LO 8.7   Classify gains and losses from Section 1231 assets.

LO 8.8   Apply the depreciation recapture rules.

LO 8.9   Apply the general treatment of casualty gains and losses for business purposes.

LO 8.10   Compute the gain on installment sales.

LO 8.11   Calculate recognized and deferred gains on like-kind exchanges.

LO 8.12   Calculate recognized and deferred gains on involuntary conversions.

OVERVIEW

The calculation of depreciation of business assets is an important issue for most businesses. The Modified Accelerated Cost Recovery System (MACRS) is the tax depreciation method currently in use under U.S. tax law. Many special depreciation provisions which are discussed in this chapter including bonus depreciation and the election to expense (Section 179) were updated by the TCJA starting in 2018.

The chapter covers the tax treatment of goodwill, going-concern value, covenants not to compete, franchises, trademarks, and other intangibles. Also covered is the limitation on the deduction of losses realized in certain related-party transactions.

As discussed in Chapter 4, realized gains and losses are generally recognized for tax purposes unless there is a tax provision that specifically allows for a different treatment. This chapter focuses on business-related gains and losses. Transactions covered in this chapter include:

1. Section 1231 (business) gains and losses
2. Depreciation recapture on business assets
3. Installment sales
4. Like-kind exchanges
5. Involuntary conversions

Unlike capital gains and losses which are generally reported on Schedule D, many business asset sale transactions are reported on Form 4797, and installment sales are reported on Form 6252.

| **Learning Objective 8.1** | **8-1 DEPRECIATION** |

Explain the concept of depreciation.

Since many assets are used in the production of income over a number of years, accrual-based income is not properly measured if the entire cost of these assets is deducted in the year the assets are purchased. Depreciation is the accounting process of allocating and deducting the cost of an asset over a period of years. The term *depreciation* does not necessarily mean physical deterioration or loss of value of the asset. In fact, in some cases the value of the asset may increase while it is being depreciated. Certain assets, such as land, cannot be depreciated for tax purposes. Under U.S. tax law, land is considered an asset that is not subject to obsolescence. These assets remain on the taxpayer's records at original cost.

It is important to distinguish maintenance expenses from depreciation. Depreciation expense is the deduction of a portion of the original cost of the asset, whereas maintenance expenses are those expenditures incurred to keep the asset in good operating condition. For example, a taxpayer who purchases a truck for use in his business depreciates the cost of the truck over a period of years. Maintenance costs such as tires and repairs are deducted in the year they are incurred.

The simplest method of depreciation is the straight-line method. Use of the straight-line method results in an equal portion of the cost being deducted in each period of the asset's life. Straight-line depreciation expense is calculated by dividing the cost by the asset's estimated useful life. The formula is:

$$\frac{\text{Cost}}{\text{Estimated useful life}} = \text{Depreciation for the period}$$

EXAMPLE   Wilson purchases an asset for use in his business. The asset cost $14,400 on October 1, 20X1, and has a 3-year (36-month) useful life. Depreciation is calculated as follows:

$$\frac{\$14,400}{36 \text{ months}} = \$400 \text{ per month}$$

The depreciation for each year is displayed in the following table:

Year	Months	Rate	Depreciation Deduction
20X1	3	$400	$ 1,200
20X2	12	400	4,800
20X3	12	400	4,800
20X4	9	400	3,600
Total depreciation deduction			$14,400

At the end of 36 months, the asset has a basis of $0. ◆

The calculation of depreciation expense for tax purposes involves certain conventions and limitations which are not reflected in the previous example. The example is intended to illustrate the *concept* of depreciation expense as an allocation of the cost of an asset over the asset's estimated useful life. If more information is needed about depreciation, see any standard financial accounting textbook.

The regular straight-line depreciation method described above may be used for financial accounting purposes and for calculating tax depreciation expense on assets acquired before 1981. The tax depreciation rules for assets acquired after 1980 are described in the following sections of this chapter.

Self-Study Problem 8.1   *See Appendix E for Solutions to Self-Study Problems*

On March 1, 20X1, Jack purchases office equipment for use in his business. The equipment cost $3,500 and has a 5-year (60-month) estimated useful life. Calculate the depreciation expense for the following years, assuming the regular straight-line depreciation method (used for financial accounting purposes or for pre-1981 assets) is used.

Year	Depreciation Deduction
20X1	$_____
20X2	$_____
20X3	$_____
20X4	$_____
20X5	$_____
20X6	$_____
Total	$_____

8-2 MODIFIED ACCELERATED COST RECOVERY SYSTEM (MACRS) AND BONUS DEPRECIATION

8.2 Learning Objective

Calculate depreciation expense using the MACRS tables.

For tax years after 1980, modifications in the tax law were made to encourage capital investment. As a major part of this tax law change, the Accelerated Cost Recovery System (ACRS) was enacted and later modified in 1986 to become the current tax depreciation system referred to as the Modified Accelerated Cost Recovery System (MACRS). The current MACRS allows taxpayers who invest in capital assets to write off an asset's cost over a period designated in the tax law and to use an accelerated method for depreciation of assets other than real estate. The minimum number of years over which the cost of an asset may be deducted (the recovery period) depends on the type of the property and the year in which the property was acquired. The recovery periods are based on asset depreciation ranges (ADRs) as published by the IRS. A schedule of the recovery periods for assets acquired after 1986 is presented in Table 8.1.

TABLE 8.1   RECOVERY PERIODS FOR ASSETS PLACED IN SERVICE AFTER 1986

Recovery Period	Recovery Method	Assets
3-year	200% declining balance	ADR midpoint life of 4 years or less, excluding cars and light trucks.
5-year	200% declining balance	ADR midpoint life of more than 4 years but less than 10 years, cars and light trucks, office machinery, certain energy property, R&D property, computers, and certain equipment.
7-year	200% declining balance	ADR midpoint life of 10 years or more but less than 16 years and property without an ADR life (e.g., most business furniture and certain equipment).
10-year	200% declining balance	ADR midpoint life of 16 years or more but less than 20 years, including trees and vines.
15-year	150% declining balance	ADR midpoint life of 20 years or more but less than 25 years, including treatment plants and land improvements (sidewalks, roads, fences, and landscaping).
20-year	150% declining balance	ADR midpoint life of 25 years or more, other than real property with an ADR life of 27.5 years or longer and municipal sewers.
27.5-year	Straight-line	Residential rental real estate, elevators, and escalators.
39-year	Straight-line	Other real property purchased generally on or after May 13, 1993 (previously 31.5-year straight-line).

The recovery period classification for assets acquired after 1980, but before 1987, differs from the recovery period classification presented in Table 8.1.

Under MACRS, taxpayers calculate the depreciation of an asset using a table which contains a percentage rate for each year of the property's recovery period. The yearly rate is applied to the cost of the asset. The cost of the property to which the rate is applied is not reduced for prior years' depreciation. For personal property (all property except real estate) the percentages in Table 8.2 apply.

EXAMPLE Assume a taxpayer acquires an asset (5-year class property) in 2019 with a cost basis of $15,000 and uses accelerated depreciation under MACRS. The depreciation expense deduction for each year of the asset's life is calculated (using the percentages in Table 8.2) as follows:

Year	Percent		Cost		Deduction
2019	20.00	×	$15,000	=	$ 3,000
2020	32.00	×	15,000	=	4,800
2021	19.20	×	15,000	=	2,880
2022	11.52	×	15,000	=	1,728
2023	11.52	×	15,000	=	1,728
2024	5.76	×	15,000	=	864
Total	100.00%				$15,000

In the above example, note that even though the asset is a 5-year class property, the cost is written off over a period of 6 tax years. This is due to the convention under MACRS which provides for 6 months of depreciation during the year the asset is first acquired and 6 months of depreciation during the year the asset is fully depreciated, sold, or disposed. This convention is referred to as the *half-year convention* since only one-half of the year of depreciation is allowed in both the year of acquisition and the year of disposition, regardless of the actual acquisition and disposition dates. The half-year convention is built into the rates in Table 8.2.

TABLE 8.2

Accelerated Depreciation for Personal Property Assuming Half-Year Convention (For Property Placed in Service after December 31, 1986)

Recovery Year	3-Year (200% DB)	5-Year (200% DB)	7-Year (200% DB)	10-Year (200% DB)	15-Year (150% DB)	20-Year (150% DB)
1	33.33	20.00	14.29	10.00	5.00	3.750
2	44.45	32.00	24.49	18.00	9.50	7.219
3	14.81*	19.20	17.49	14.40	8.55	6.677
4	7.41	11.52*	12.49	11.52	7.70	6.177
5		11.52	8.93*	9.22	6.93	5.713
6		5.76	8.92	7.37	6.23	5.285
7			8.93	6.55*	5.90*	4.888
8			4.46	6.55	5.90	4.522
9				6.56	5.91	4.462*
10				6.55	5.90	4.461
11				3.28	5.91	4.462
12					5.90	4.461
13					5.91	4.462
14					5.90	4.461
15					5.91	4.462
16					2.95	4.461
17						4.462
18						4.461
19						4.462
20						4.461
21						2.231

*Switch to straight-line depreciation.

TABLE 8.3

Straight-Line Depreciation for Personal Property, Assuming Half-Year Convention* (For Property Placed in Service after December 31, 1986)

Recovery Period	% First Recovery Year	Other Recovery Years		Last Recovery Years	
		Years	%	Year	%
3-year	16.67	2–3	33.33	4	16.67
5-year	10.00	2–5	20.00	6	10.00
7-year	7.14	2–7	14.29	8	7.14
10-year	5.00	2–10	10.00	11	5.00
15-year	3.33	2–15	6.67	16	3.33
20-year	2.50	2–20	5.00	21	2.50

*The official table contains a separate row for each year. For ease of presentation, certain years are grouped together in this table. In some instances, this will cause a difference of 0.01 percent for the last digit when compared with the official table.

For property (other than real estate), a taxpayer may elect to use straight-line depreciation instead of the accelerated depreciation rates under MACRS. The taxpayer must use the straight-line MACRS tables for assets for which a straight-line election has been made. The annual percentage rates to be applied to the cost of an asset for which a straight-line election under MACRS has been made are presented in Table 8.3.

EXAMPLE On April 1, 2019, Lori purchased and placed in service a specialized computer for use in her business. The computer cost $18,000 and Lori elects to use straight-line depreciation over 5 years instead of accelerated depreciation under MACRS. The annual deduction for depreciation over the life of the computer is calculated below (the percentages are taken from Table 8.3).

Year	Percent		Cost		Deduction
2019	10.00	×	$18,000	=	$ 1,800
2020	20.00	×	18,000	=	3,600
2021	20.00	×	18,000	=	3,600
2022	20.00	×	18,000	=	3,600
2023	20.00	×	18,000	=	3,600
2024	10.00	×	18,000	=	1,800
Total	100.00%				$18,000

Note that Lori receives a deduction based on 6 months in the year of purchase (half-year convention), even though the asset was put into service on April 1. If the asset had been placed into service on September 1, Lori still would have received a deduction for 6 months of depreciation. ◆

Under MACRS, the same method of depreciation (accelerated or straight-line) must be used for all property in a given class placed in service during that year.

8-2a Mid-Quarter Convention

When a taxpayer acquires a significant amount of assets during the last quarter of the tax year, the half-year convention, referred to in the above examples, is replaced by the *mid-quarter convention*. The mid-quarter convention must be applied if more than 40 percent of the total cost of a taxpayer's property acquired during the year, other than real property, is placed in service during the last 3 months of the tax year. The mid-quarter

TABLE 8.4

Accelerated Depreciation for Personal Property Assuming Mid-Quarter Convention* (For Property Placed in Service after December 31, 1986)

Recovery Year	3-Year (200% DB)	5-Year (200% DB)	7-Year (200% DB)
First Quarter			
1	58.33	35.00	25.00
2	27.78	26.00	21.43
3	12.35	15.60	15.31
4	1.54	11.01	10.93
5		11.01	8.75
Second Quarter			
1	41.67	25.00	17.85
2	38.89	30.00	23.47
3	14.14	18.00	16.76
4	5.30	11.37	11.97
5		11.37	8.87
Third Quarter			
1	25.00	15.00	10.71
2	50.00	34.00	25.51
3	16.67	20.40	18.22
4	8.33	12.24	13.02
5		11.30	9.30
Fourth Quarter			
1	8.33	5.00	3.57
2	61.11	38.00	27.55
3	20.37	22.80	19.68
4	10.19	13.68	14.06
5		10.94	10.04

*For ease of presentation, only 3-year, 5-year, and 7-year property and only depreciation rates for the first 5 years are provided. The official table also includes 10-, 15-, and 20-year property. See IRS Publication 946 for the complete table.

convention treats all property placed in service during any quarter of the tax year as being placed in service on the midpoint of the quarter. The mid-quarter convention, if applied in the year the asset is acquired, also applies upon the disposition of the asset. Assets placed in service and disposed of during the same tax year are not considered in determining whether the taxpayer meets the 40-percent test. An excerpt from the mid-quarter tables can be found in Table 8.4. Complete mid-quarter tables may be found at any of the major tax services (such as CCH IntelliConnect or Thomson Reuters Checkpoint).

EXAMPLE Jane, a calendar-year taxpayer, purchases the following property during 2019 for use in her business:

Placed in Service	Property	Original Cost	Recovery Period
March 2	Office furniture	$ 3,000	7 years
July 31	Apartment building	200,000	27.5 years
November 1	Automobile	18,000	5 years

Jane does not elect Section 179 and elects out of bonus depreciation. The cost of the automobile acquired during the last 3 months of the year represents 86 percent of the total cost of assets, other than real property, acquired during the tax year. Since more than 40 percent of Jane's purchases, other than real property, were made during the last 3 months of the tax year, the mid-quarter convention would apply. Depreciation for 2019 on the furniture is $750 ($3,000 × 25%) and on the auto is $900 ($18,000 × 5%). ♦

8-2b Bonus Depreciation

Because the cost recovery of long-lived assets occurs over many years, one way to lower the after-tax cost of capital expenditures is through accelerated depreciation. At times, the tax law has provided for "bonus depreciation," which is the immediate deduction of all or some of the cost of otherwise slowly depreciated property. The TCJA increased the bonus depreciation percentage to 100 percent for qualified property acquired and placed in service after September 27, 2017 and through December 31, 2022 (certain long-lived assets have an additional year), but the 100 percent bonus depreciation phases out starting in 2023 as follows:

Year	Bonus Percentage
2023	80
2024	60
2025	40
2026	20
2027	0

The bonus depreciation rules allow taxpayers purchasing property with a MACRS recovery period of 20 years or less (see Table 8.1), computer software, and certain leasehold improvements to directly write off up to 100 percent of the cost of the assets in the year placed in service. Bonus depreciation is presumed to apply unless the taxpayer elects out of the provision. The taxable income limits and thresholds associated with Section 179 (see LO 8.3) do not apply to bonus depreciation.

Both new and used property are generally eligible for bonus depreciation.

EXAMPLE Mary places a new 5-year MACRS-class machine costing $20,000 into service on March 1, 2019. She does not elect out of bonus depreciation on the machine. The bonus depreciation on the machine for 2019 is $20,000. The basis is reduced to $0 and no additional MACRS depreciation on the machine is deducted. ♦

Between bonus depreciation and the expanded immediate expensing under Section 179, small businesses are not likely to capitalize the cost of any non-real property unless they have a net operating loss or anticipate using larger depreciation deductions during higher tax bracket years in the future.

8-2c Real Estate

For real estate acquired after 1986, MACRS requires the property to be depreciated using the straight-line method. The straight-line MACRS realty tables for residential realty (e.g., an apartment building) provide for depreciation over 27.5 years. Nonresidential realty (e.g., an office building) is depreciated over 39 years (31.5 years for realty acquired generally before May 13, 1993). The annual depreciation percentages for real estate under MACRS are shown in Table 8.5.

TABLE 8.5

Straight-Line Depreciation for Real Property Assuming Mid-Month Convention*

27.5-Year Residential Real Property

The applicable annual percentage is (use the column for the month in the first year the property is placed in service):

Recovery Year(s)	1	2	3	4	5	6	7	8	9	10	11	12
1	3.485	3.182	2.879	2.576	2.273	1.970	1.667	1.364	1.061	0.758	0.455	0.152
2–18	3.636	3.636	3.636	3.636	3.636	3.636	3.636	3.636	3.636	3.636	3.636	3.636
19–27	3.637	3.637	3.637	3.637	3.637	3.637	3.637	3.637	3.637	3.637	3.637	3.637
28	1.970	2.273	2.576	2.879	3.182	3.485	3.636	3.636	3.636	3.636	3.636	3.636
29	0.000	0.000	0.000	0.000	0.000	0.000	0.152	0.455	0.758	1.061	1.364	1.667

39-Year Nonresidential Real Property

The applicable annual percentage is (use the column for the month in the first year the property is placed in service):

Recovery Year(s)	1	2	3	4	5	6	7	8	9	10	11	12
1	2.461	2.247	2.033	1.819	1.605	1.391	1.177	0.963	0.749	0.535	0.321	0.107
2–39	2.564	2.564	2.564	2.564	2.564	2.564	2.564	2.564	2.564	2.564	2.564	2.564
40	0.107	0.321	0.535	0.749	0.963	1.177	1.391	1.605	1.819	2.033	2.247	2.461

*The official tables contain a separate row for each year. For ease of presentation, certain years are grouped together in these two tables. In some instances, this will produce a difference of .001 percent when compared with the official tables.

EXAMPLE Carlos purchases a rental house on September 3, 2019, for $90,000 (the land is accounted for separately). The house is already rented to a tenant. The annual depreciation expense deduction under MACRS for each of the first 4 years is illustrated below (the percentages are taken from Table 8.5, 27.5-Year Residential Real Property).

Year	Percent		Cost		Deduction
2019	1.061	×	$90,000	=	$ 955
2020	3.636	×	90,000	=	3,272
2021	3.636	×	90,000	=	3,272
2022	3.636	×	90,000	=	3,272

Note that the percentages are taken from Table 8.5 under column 9, because the month of acquisition (September) is the ninth month of the year. ♦

Since 2018, most real property is not eligible for bonus depreciation or Section 179 immediate expensing (LO 8.3).

8-2d Mid-Month Convention

For the depreciation of real property under MACRS, a *mid-month convention* replaces the half-year convention. Real estate is treated as placed in service in the middle of the month the property is placed in service. Likewise, a disposition during a month is treated as occurring on the midpoint of such month. For example, under the mid-month convention, an asset purchased and placed in service on April 2 is treated as being placed in service on April 15. The mid-month convention is built into the first year's rates in Table 8.5.

8-2e Reporting Depreciation Expense

Depreciation expense is reported on Form 4562, Depreciation and Amortization. Individual taxpayers who have no current year asset additions and who are not reporting depreciation on listed property (see LO 8.4) are not required to file Form 4562 with their return.

Intuit ProConnect includes a powerful depreciation calculator included as part of the software. There are two ways to report depreciation. The first method is to enter the property details into the software. Property can be entered through either a quick entry or detail input screen. Both are located under Deductions. The first subheading in the left-hand margin is depreciation. The property is linked to a business (for example, Schedule C or Schedule E). Based on the type and cost of property placed in service, the software will automatically apply bonus depreciation ("SDA") unless overridden in the detail screen. Section 179 immediate expensing can be input directly. The second method is to compute depreciation outside the ProConnect software and input the deduction as an override. There are screens for direct input located under the normal depreciation screens in the left-hand margin.

Self-Study Problem 8.2   *See Appendix E for Solutions to Self-Study Problems*

During 2019, Mary Moser purchases the following items for use in her business:

Manufacturing equipment	$ 12,000
(7-year property, placed in service August 1)	
Office furniture	4,000
(7-year property, placed in service December 15)	
Office building, land is accounted for separately	175,000
(placed in service March 30)	

Assume that Mary uses the accelerated depreciation method under MACRS.

a. Use Form 4562 on Pages 8-11 and 8-12 to report Mary's depreciation deduction for 2019 including bonus depreciation.

b. Calculate Mary's depreciation (but do not complete Form 4562) assuming she elects out of bonus depreciation.

7-year property $_____

Office building $_____

c. Calculate Mary's depreciation deduction on the assets for 2020 (Year 2). Compute amounts assuming bonus depreciation was taken in 2019.

Year 2 *Depreciation*
Deduction

7-year property $_____

Office building $_____

8-3 ELECTION TO EXPENSE (SECTION 179)

Identify when a Section 179 election to expense the cost of property may be used.

As part of the landmark Tax Reform Act of 1986, Internal Revenue Code Section 179 was implemented to decrease the cost of investments in business property by permitting small businesses to expense the costs of certain property that would otherwise be capitalized and depreciated over time.

Under Section 179, taxpayers may elect to expense the acquisition cost of certain property, subject to certain limitations. This cost would otherwise have been deducted over a period of time using the regular cost recovery depreciation rules. Similar to bonus depreciation, the Section 179 deduction applies to both new and used property. To qualify for this limited expensing election, the property must be personal property (property other than real estate or assets used in residential real estate rental activities except for certain qualified improvement property, the treatment of which is beyond the scope of this textbook) placed in service during the year and used in a trade or business.

Section 179 places three limitations on the expensing election: (1) a maximum on the annual amount expensed, (2) a phase-out of the annual amount limit, and (3) the taxable income limit.

Originally, the maximum annual expensing amount was a modest $10,000. Over the years the amount was adjusted for inflation and also increased with economic stimulus in mind. As a result of the financial crisis, the annual maximum was increased to $250,000 in 2008 and then increased again to $500,000 in 2010. Although subject to repeated expiration and extension, the limit had remained at $500,000 until 2015 when it was made permanent and subject to inflation adjustment each year. The maximum annual amount that can be expensed under Section 179 is $1,020,000 in 2019.

The annual maximum expense amount is reduced dollar-for-dollar by the amount of Section 179 property acquired during the year in excess of a threshold amount. Similar to the annual limit, the Section 179 phase-out threshold amount has fluctuated over time. In 2019, the threshold is $2,550,000. As a result, a taxpayer that acquires $3,570,000 or more of Section 179 property during 2019 may not immediately expense under Section 179.

Lastly, the amount of acquired qualified property that may be expensed annually is limited to the taxpayer's taxable income, before considering any amount expensed under the Section 179 election, from any trade or business of the taxpayer. Any amount which is limited due to the taxable income limitation may be carried over to succeeding tax years.

EXAMPLE During 2019, Bob buys used equipment that cost $1,520,000 for his factory. Bob's business generates taxable income of well over $3,000,000 and he elects out of bonus depreciation. Bob's Section 179 property placed in service is below $2,550,000 and thus is not subject to phase-out. With $3 million in taxable income, Bob's Section 179 deduction is not subject to the income limitation. Bob may immediately expense $1,020,000 of his equipment. The remaining $500,000 of equipment cost will be depreciated over the recovery period under MACRS. ♦

EXAMPLE During 2019, Joe places in service used manufacturing equipment for use in his business. The machinery cost $1,030,000. Joe has taxable income (after considering any MACRS depreciation) from his business of $200,000. Under the annual maximum limitation, Joe can immediately expense up to $1,020,000 and would depreciate the remaining $10,000 under MACRS. However, the maximum amount under the taxable income limitation is only $200,000. The remaining $820,000 ($1,020,000 annual maximum less $200,000 permitted under the income limit) is carried forward to succeeding tax years. ♦

Self-Study Problem 8.2

Form **4562**

Department of the Treasury
Internal Revenue Service   (99)

Depreciation and Amortization
(Including Information on Listed Property)
▶ Attach to your tax return.
▶ Go to *www.irs.gov/Form4562* for instructions and the latest information.

OMB No. 1545-0172

2019

Attachment
Sequence No. **179**

Name(s) shown on return

Business or activity to which this form relates

Identifying number

Part I **Election To Expense Certain Property Under Section 179**
Note: If you have any listed property, complete Part V before you complete Part I.

1	Maximum amount (see instructions)	**1**
2	Total cost of section 179 property placed in service (see instructions)	**2**
3	Threshold cost of section 179 property before reduction in limitation (see instructions)	**3**
4	Reduction in limitation. Subtract line 3 from line 2. If zero or less, enter -0-	**4**
5	Dollar limitation for tax year. Subtract line 4 from line 1. If zero or less, enter -0-. If married filing separately, see instructions	**5**

6	**(a)** Description of property	**(b)** Cost (business use only)	**(c)** Elected cost

7	Listed property. Enter the amount from line 29	**7**	
8	Total elected cost of section 179 property. Add amounts in column (c), lines 6 and 7	**8**
9	Tentative deduction. Enter the **smaller** of line 5 or line 8	**9**
10	Carryover of disallowed deduction from line 13 of your 2018 Form 4562	**10**
11	Business income limitation. Enter the smaller of business income (not less than zero) or line 5. See instructions	**11**
12	Section 179 expense deduction. Add lines 9 and 10, but don't enter more than line 11 . . .	**12**
13	Carryover of disallowed deduction to 2020. Add lines 9 and 10, less line 12 ▶	**13**	

Note: Don't use Part II or Part III below for listed property. Instead, use Part V.

Part II **Special Depreciation Allowance and Other Depreciation (Don't** include listed property. See instructions.**)**

14	Special depreciation allowance for qualified property (other than listed property) placed in service during the tax year. See instructions	**14**
15	Property subject to section 168(f)(1) election	**15**
16	Other depreciation (including ACRS)	**16**

Part III **MACRS Depreciation (Don't** include listed property. See instructions.**)**

Section A

17	MACRS deductions for assets placed in service in tax years beginning before 2019	**17**
18	If you are electing to group any assets placed in service during the tax year into one or more general asset accounts, check here . . . . ▶ ☐	

Section B—Assets Placed in Service During 2019 Tax Year Using the General Depreciation System

(a) Classification of property	**(b)** Month and year placed in service	**(c)** Basis for depreciation (business/investment use only—see instructions)	**(d)** Recovery period	**(e)** Convention	**(f)** Method	**(g)** Depreciation deduction
19a 3-year property						
b 5-year property						
c 7-year property						
d 10-year property						
e 15-year property						
f 20-year property						
g 25-year property			25 yrs.		S/L	
h Residential rental			27.5 yrs.	MM	S/L	
property			27.5 yrs.	MM	S/L	
i Nonresidential real			39 yrs.	MM	S/L	
property				MM	S/L	

Section C—Assets Placed in Service During 2019 Tax Year Using the Alternative Depreciation System

20a Class life					S/L	
b 12-year			12 yrs.		S/L	
c 30-year			30 yrs.	MM	S/L	
d 40-year			40 yrs.	MM	S/L	

Part IV **Summary** (See instructions.)

21	Listed property. Enter amount from line 28	**21**
22	**Total.** Add amounts from line 12, lines 14 through 17, lines 19 and 20 in column (g), and line 21. Enter here and on the appropriate lines of your return. Partnerships and S corporations—see instructions .	**22**
23	For assets shown above and placed in service during the current year, enter the portion of the basis attributable to section 263A costs	**23**	

For Paperwork Reduction Act Notice, see separate instructions.   Cat. No. 12906N   Form **4562** (2019)

Form 4562 (2019)   Page **2**

Part V **Listed Property** (Include automobiles, certain other vehicles, certain aircraft, and property used for entertainment, recreation, or amusement.)

Note: For any vehicle for which you are using the standard mileage rate or deducting lease expense, complete **only** 24a, 24b, columns (a) through (c) of Section A, all of Section B, and Section C if applicable.

Section A—Depreciation and Other Information (Caution: See the instructions for limits for passenger automobiles.**)**

24a Do you have evidence to support the business/investment use claimed? ☐ **Yes** ☐ **No**   24b If "Yes," is the evidence written? ☐ **Yes** ☐ **No**

(a) Type of property (list vehicles first)	(b) Date placed in service	(c) Business/ investment use percentage	(d) Cost or other basis	(e) Basis for depreciation (business/investment use only)	(f) Recovery period	(g) Method/ Convention	(h) Depreciation deduction	(i) Elected section 179 cost
25 Special depreciation allowance for qualified listed property placed in service during the tax year and used more than 50% in a qualified business use. See instructions . **25**								
26 Property used more than 50% in a qualified business use:								
		%						
		%						
		%						
27 Property used 50% or less in a qualified business use:								
		%				S/L –		
		%				S/L –		
		%				S/L –		

28 Add amounts in column (h), lines 25 through 27. Enter here and on line 21, page 1 . **28**

29 Add amounts in column (i), line 26. Enter here and on line 7, page 1 . . . . **29**

Section B—Information on Use of Vehicles

Complete this section for vehicles used by a sole proprietor, partner, or other "more than 5% owner," or related person. If you provided vehicles to your employees, first answer the questions in Section C to see if you meet an exception to completing this section for those vehicles.

	(a) Vehicle 1		(b) Vehicle 2		(c) Vehicle 3		(d) Vehicle 4		(e) Vehicle 5		(f) Vehicle 6	
30 Total business/investment miles driven during the year (**don't** include commuting miles) .												
31 Total commuting miles driven during the year												
32 Total other personal (noncommuting) miles driven												
33 Total miles driven during the year. Add lines 30 through 32												
34 Was the vehicle available for personal use during off-duty hours?	**Yes**	**No**	**Yes**	**No**	**Yes**	**No**	**Yes**	**No**	**Yes**	**No**	**Yes**	**No**
35 Was the vehicle used primarily by a more than 5% owner or related person? . .												
36 Is another vehicle available for personal use?												

Section C—Questions for Employers Who Provide Vehicles for Use by Their Employees

Answer these questions to determine if you meet an exception to completing Section B for vehicles used by employees who **aren't** more than 5% owners or related persons. See instructions.

		Yes	No
37	Do you maintain a written policy statement that prohibits all personal use of vehicles, including commuting, by your employees?		
38	Do you maintain a written policy statement that prohibits personal use of vehicles, except commuting, by your employees? See the instructions for vehicles used by corporate officers, directors, or 1% or more owners . .		
39	Do you treat all use of vehicles by employees as personal use?		
40	Do you provide more than five vehicles to your employees, obtain information from your employees about the use of the vehicles, and retain the information received?		
41	Do you meet the requirements concerning qualified automobile demonstration use? See instructions.		

Note: If your answer to 37, 38, 39, 40, or 41 is "Yes," don't complete Section B for the covered vehicles.

Part VI **Amortization**

(a) Description of costs	(b) Date amortization begins	(c) Amortizable amount	(d) Code section	(e) Amortization period or percentage	(f) Amortization for this year
42 Amortization of costs that begins during your 2019 tax year (see instructions):					

43 Amortization of costs that began before your 2019 tax year **43**

44 **Total.** Add amounts in column (f). See the instructions for where to report **44**

Form **4562** (2019)

EXAMPLE During 2019, Portia purchased $2,760,000 of new equipment for use in her business. Portia's taxable income before considering immediate expensing is over $4 million. Because the amount of Section 179 property placed in service during the year exceeds the phase-out threshold of $2,550,000, Portia's annual Section 179 expensing limit of $1,020,000 is reduced by the $210,000 phase-out ($2,760,000 − $2,550,000) resulting in a maximum allowable expensing amount of only $810,000. ♦

A taxpayer who has made the Section 179 election to expense must reduce the basis of the asset by the amount expensed before calculating regular MACRS depreciation on the remaining cost of the asset. Even if the taxpayer is not able to deduct the full amount expensed in the current year due to the *taxable income limitation*, the basis must be reduced by the full amount of the Section 179 expense election.

When calculating depreciation on an asset, if an election to expense only part of the asset has been made, the amount of the Section 179 election to expense must be decided first. When a taxpayer decides to take only a portion of the cost of the asset as a Section 179 deduction, the rest of the cost of the asset must be depreciated. The depreciation must be deducted from taxable income to determine the income limitation for the Section 179 deduction.

EXAMPLE On August 1, 2019, Joan purchases a machine for use in her business. It is her only purchase of business property in 2019. The machine cost $1,050,000 and qualifies as 5-year MACRS property. Her business income before any cost recovery is $1,008,000. Joan elects to immediately expense the entire $1,020,000. She elects out of bonus depreciation, thus $30,000 of remaining basis is subject to MACRS depreciation of $6,000 ($30,000 × 0.20 depreciation factor). As a result of deducting MACRS depreciation of $6,000, Joan's taxable income before Section 179 is reduced to $1,002,000. Joan may only immediately expense $1,002,000 due to the income limit. The excess $18,000 of Section 179 deduction will be carried forward to 2020. ♦

The effects of bonus depreciation, Section 179 and MACRS depreciation can combine to create substantially accelerated cost recovery. If a taxpayer elects Section 179 immediate expensing and uses bonus depreciation, the cost basis of the property is first reduced by the Section 179 deduction, then by bonus depreciation then lastly, by typical MACRS depreciation. With 100 percent bonus depreciation, the need to deduct Section 179 and then bonus depreciation is an unlikely occurrence since the entire cost of many types of property can be recovered under bonus depreciation without annual or income limits.

Self-Study Problem 8.3   *See Appendix E for Solutions to Self-Study Problems*

On June 15, 2019, Chang purchases $2,837,000 of equipment (7-year property) for use in her business. It is her only purchase of business property in 2019. Chang has taxable income from her business of $2.5 million before any cost recovery.

a. Assuming Chang does not elect Section 179 and elects out of bonus depreciation, what is her total 2019 cost recovery?

b. Assuming Chang elects the maximum Section 179 deduction allowable and elects out of bonus depreciation, what is her total 2019 cost recovery?

c. Assuming Chang does not elect Section 179 deduction allowable and does not elect out of bonus depreciation, what is her total cost recovery?

Learning Objective 8.4

8-4 LISTED PROPERTY

Apply the limitations placed on depreciation of "listed property."

Congress felt some taxpayers were using the favorable tax incentives of the accelerated cost recovery system and the limited expensing election to claim depreciation deductions on assets used for personal purposes. To curtail this perceived abuse of the tax system, Congress enacted special rules which apply to the depreciation of "listed property." Listed property includes those types of assets which lend themselves to personal use, including the following:

1. Passenger automobiles, defined to include any four-wheeled vehicle manufactured primarily for use on public streets, roads, and highways, rated at 6,000 pounds or less unloaded gross vehicle weight. Specifically excluded from the definition of passenger automobiles are vehicles used directly in the trade or business of transporting persons or property, ambulances and hearses used in a trade or business, and certain trucks and vans not likely to be used more than a de minimis amount for personal purposes, including vehicles which display the company name or advertising.

2. Other property used as a means of transportation (trucks, buses, boats, airplanes, and motorcycles), except vehicles which are not likely to be used for personal purposes, such as marked police cars, school buses, and tractors, or vehicles used for transporting persons or cargo for compensation.

3. Property generally used for entertainment, recreation, or amusement (video recording equipment, communication equipment, etc.).

If listed property is used 50 percent or less in a qualified business use, any depreciation deduction must be calculated using the straight-line method of depreciation over an alternate recovery period, and the special election to expense under Section 179 and bonus depreciation are not allowed.

Qualified business use does not include investment use or the use of property owned by an employee in performing services as an employee, unless the use meets the convenience-of-employer and condition-of-employment tests. In addition, the excess depreciation allowed by reason of the property meeting the more-than-50-percent-use test must be included in income if property which meets the test in one year subsequently fails to meet the more-than-50-percent-use test in a succeeding year.

EXAMPLE   Oscar has an automobile he uses 45 percent of the time for personal use and 55 percent of the time in his accounting business. Since Oscar's business-use percentage of 55 percent exceeds 50 percent, Oscar is not required to use the straight-line method in calculating depreciation. The accelerated depreciation method and the election to expense may be used by Oscar. ♦

Self-Study Problem 8.4   *See Appendix E for Solutions to Self-Study Problems*

For each of the following independent situations, indicate with a Y (yes) or an N (no) whether or not the taxpayer is required to depreciate the property using the straight-line method over the alternate recovery period:

Straight Line Required?

1. Alvarez uses an automobile 80 percent for his business and 20 percent for personal reasons.   _____

2. Laura has a truck she uses in her business 55 percent of the time, 15 percent for her real estate investment, and 30 percent for personal use.   _____

8-5 LIMITATION ON DEPRECIATION OF LUXURY AUTOMOBILES

In addition to the limitations on the depreciation of passenger automobiles imposed by the listed property rules discussed in the preceding section, the depreciation of passenger automobiles is subject to an additional limitation, commonly referred to as the "luxury automobile" limitation. Regardless of the method of depreciation used by the taxpayer, accelerated or straight-line, the election to expense, or bonus depreciation, the amount of depreciation expense that may be claimed on a passenger automobile is subject to an annual dollar limitation. The annual dollar limitations that apply to passenger automobiles acquired in 2019 are listed below. Any automobile which would have actual MACRS depreciation exceeding the limits is considered a "luxury automobile" by the IRS for purposes of the depreciation limitation rules.

ANNUAL AUTOMOBILE DEPRECIATION LIMITATIONS

Year of Use	2019 Limits	2018 Limits
Year 1	$18,100*	$18,000*
Year 2	16,100	16,000
Year 3	9,700	9,600
Year 4 (and subsequent years until fully depreciated)	5,760	5,760

*Additional bonus depreciation of $8,000 is included in this amount.

Separate higher depreciation limits apply for certain trucks and vans and also for electric automobiles.

Some sport utility vehicles fall outside of the definition of passenger automobiles and can be depreciated or expensed under Section 179 or the bonus depreciation rules without regard to the automobile depreciation limits. To qualify for the exception, the sport utility vehicle must have a gross vehicle weight rating above 6,000 pounds. Vehicles that meet the large sport utility vehicle exception are limited to $25,000 in Section 179 expensing but may depreciate using the 5-year MACRS percentages without the typical auto depreciation limitations.

The annual limitations must be reduced to reflect the actual business-use percentage where business use is less than 100 percent.

EXAMPLE Sally purchased a new car for $60,000 in September 2019 which she uses 75 percent for business. Sally elects out of bonus depreciation. Depreciation on the automobile is calculated as follows:

Total cost	$60,000
	× 0.75
Limited to business use	$45,000
MACRS depreciation (half-year convention)	$45,000 × 20% = $ 9,000
Maximum luxury automobile depreciation allowed	$10,100 × 75% = $ 7,575

Because the luxury automobile limitation is less than the actual depreciation calculated, Sally's depreciation deduction is limited to $7,575. ♦

EXAMPLE In September 2019, Joan purchased a passenger automobile which cost $60,000. The automobile is used 100 percent for business purposes and

Joan elects out of bonus depreciation. A comparison of MACRS, with and without the limitation, is as follows:

	Five-Year MACRS	Annual Limit
Year 1	$12,000	$10,100
Year 2	19,200	16,100
Year 3	11,520	9,700
Year 4	6,912	5,760
Year 5	6,912	5,760
Year 6	3,456	5,760
Year 7		5,760
Year 8		1,060

Note that, although the automobile is a 5-year property, it will take 8 years to recover the entire cost of the asset because of the annual dollar limits, assuming no election to expense under Section 179 or bonus depreciation. ♦

TAX BREAK   Taxpayers hoping to get around the luxury auto depreciation limits by leasing an auto should be aware that there is a rule designed to put them in the same economic position as if they had purchased the auto. The IRS issued tables for computation of an "income inclusion" which must be used to reduce the lease expense deduction for leased autos.

Bonus depreciation on autos is subject to annual depreciation limits also. For years after the first year, the unrecovered basis of the auto is subject to MACRS depreciation but remains limited by the auto limits.

EXAMPLE   Sally purchased a new automobile for $60,000 in September 2019 which she uses 100 percent for business during the life of the auto. Assuming half-year convention, bonus depreciation and no Section 179 depreciation, Sally's 2019 cost recovery is computed as follows:

Cost basis	$60,000
Depreciation limit for autos, Year 1	18,100
Basis unrecovered at end of 2019	$41,900

In 2020, MACRS depreciation is $13,408 (unrecovered basis of $41,900 × 32%, which is the depreciation factor for the second year of 5-year property). The second year limit of $16,100 exceeds the deduction and thus does not apply. ♦

Self-Study Problem 8.5   *See Appendix E for Solutions to Self-Study Problems*

On June 17, 2019, Donald purchased a passenger automobile at a cost of $56,000. The automobile is used 90 percent for qualified business use and 10 percent for personal purposes. Calculate the depreciation expense (without bonus depreciation) for the automobile for 2019, 2020, and 2021, assuming half-year convention and no Section 179 immediate expensing.

$ _____

$ _____

$ _____

Sign Here	Under penalties of perjury, I declare that I have examined this return and accompanying schedules and statements, and to the best of my knowledge and belief, they are true, correct, and complete. Declaration of preparer (other than taxpayer) is based on all information of which preparer has any knowledge.			
	Your signature	Date	Your occupation	If the IRS sent you an Identity Protection PIN, enter it here (see inst.)
Joint return? See instructions. Keep a copy for your records.	Spouse's signature. If a joint return, **both** must sign.	Date	Spouse's occupation	If the IRS sent your spouse an Identity Protection PIN, enter it here (see inst.)
	Phone no.	Email address		
Paid Preparer Use Only	Preparer's name	Preparer's signature	Date	PTIN	Check if: ☐ 3rd Party Designee
	Firm's name ▶		Phone no.		☐ Self-employed
	Firm's address ▶			Firm's EIN ▶

Duncan Devious (age 52) is a self-employed attorney. Duncan loves to be noticed in public and, therefore, he drives a 7,000-pound, military-type, SUV, the only vehicle he owns. When you are preparing his tax return, you notice that he claims 90 percent of his total auto expenses as a business deduction on his Schedule C and 10 percent as personal use, with total miles driven in 2019 as 10,000. You note from his home and office addresses on his tax return that he lives approximately 15 miles from his office. The total of the expenses (i.e., gas, oil, maintenance, depreciation) he claims is $31,200. He does not have a mileage log to substantiate the business use of the SUV. Would you sign the Paid Preparer's declaration (see example above) on this return? Why or why not?

Would You Sign This Tax Return?

8-6 INTANGIBLES

8.6 Learning Objective

Calculate the amortization of goodwill and certain other intangibles.

The current tax guidance provides for two main categories of intangibles: (1) Section 197 intangibles and (2) non-Section 197 intangibles. Section 197 intangibles are those acquired by a taxpayer as part of the acquisition of a trade or business. Section 197 intangibles are amortized over a 15-year period, beginning with the month of acquisition. Amortization is a cost recovery method similar to depreciation in that it spreads the cost recovery over a fixed period of years. It differs from depreciation in that it is applied to intangible assets rather than tangible personal or real property and does not include the half-year or mid-quarter conventions. The 15-year life applies regardless of the actual useful life of the intangible asset. No other amortization or depreciation method may be claimed on Section 197 assets. When acquired as part of a trade or business, the following are defined as qualified Section 197 intangibles:

- Goodwill
- Going-concern value
- Workforce in place
- Information bases including business books and records and operating systems
- Know-how
- Customer-based intangibles
- License, permit, or right granted by a governmental unit
- Covenant not to compete
- Franchise, trademark, or trade name

EXAMPLE In March 2019, Mary purchases a business from Bill for $250,000. Section 197 goodwill of $36,000 is included in the $250,000 purchase price. Mary amortizes the goodwill over a 15-year period at the rate of $200 per month, starting with the month of purchase. ♦

8-6a Exclusions

Many intangible assets are specifically excluded from the definition of Section 197 intangibles. Examples of these Section 197 exclusions include items which are not generally amortizable:

- Interests in a corporation, partnership, trust, or estate
- Interests in land

Section 197 exclusions that are generally amortizable:

- Computer software readily available for purchase by the general public
- Interests in films, sound recordings, video recordings, and similar property
- Self-created intangible assets

Non-Section 197 intangibles that are separately acquired are generally amortized over their remaining useful life using the straight-line method. For example, a patent could be acquired as part of the purchase of a business (Section 197 intangible) or a patent could be acquired separately (non-Section 197 intangible). A franchise, trademark, or tradename is treated as a Section 197 intangible whether acquired as part of a business or not.

EXAMPLE   Sam purchases computer software sold to the general public for $20,000. The $20,000 is not a Section 197 intangible and therefore the amount would be amortized under regular amortization rules (typically 3 years). ♦

---

intuit proconnect TIP   Amortization is entered into the software in the Depreciation section. Select Non-recovery/Straight-line as the depreciation method. The recovery period (e.g., 15 years for Section 197 intangibles) must be input. An amortization code is available in the detailed input screen.

Self-Study Problem 8.6   *See Appendix E for Solutions to Self-Study Problems*

Indicate by check marks whether the following items are generally amortizable over 15 years, amortized over their useful life, or not amortized.

	15-Year Amortization	Useful Life	Not Amortizable
1. Patent acquired as part of a business	_____	_____	_____
2. Separately acquired film rights	_____	_____	_____
3. Computer software sold at an office supply store	_____	_____	_____
4. Goodwill	_____	_____	_____
5. Franchise	_____	_____	_____
6. Land	_____	_____	_____
7. Trademark	_____	_____	_____
8. Interest in a corporation	_____	_____	_____

Learning Objective 8.7

Classify gains and losses from Section 1231 assets.

8-7 SECTION 1231 GAINS AND LOSSES

The first part of this chapter has dealt with the acquisition and cost recovery of business property. The remaining sections deal with the sale, exchange, or disposal of business property. The tax rules on capital gains and losses covered in Chapter 4 continue to apply here, but the tax law has been crafted in a way to provide capital treatment for certain business gains and losses and ordinary treatment for others. Unlike much of the tax law covered elsewhere in this textbook, these tax concepts often refer to the Internal Revenue Code section number as the identifying name. For example, Section 1231 is used to describe property used in a trade or business and held for more than one year. Depreciation recapture is commonly referred to as Section 1245 or Section 1250 recapture.

Section 1231 assets are not capital assets (see Chapter 4), but they are given special tax treatment. Gains on Section 1231 assets may be treated as long-term capital gains, while losses in some cases may be deducted as ordinary losses. Section 1231 assets include:

1. Depreciable or real property used in a trade or business;
2. Timber, coal, or domestic iron ore;
3. Livestock (not including poultry) held for draft, breeding, dairy, or sporting purposes; and
4. Unharvested crops on land used in a trade or business.

Any property held 1 year or less, inventory and property held for sale to customers, and copyrights, paintings, government publications, etc., are not Section 1231 property.

The calculation of net Section 1231 gains and losses is summarized as follows:

Combine *all* Section 1231 gains and losses to compute *net* Section 1231 gains or losses. If the gains exceed the losses, the excess is a long-term capital gain. When the losses exceed the gains, all gains are treated as ordinary income, and all losses are fully deductible as ordinary losses.

EXAMPLE   Frank Harper had the following business gains and (losses) on the sale of business property during August of 2019:

Sale of land held for 4 years	$ 9,500
Sale of truck held for 3 years	(2,100)
Sale of inventory	6,000

Frank's Section 1231 gains and losses would be calculated as follows:

Gain on land	$ 9,500
Loss on truck	(2,100)
Net Section 1231 gain	$ 7,400

The $7,400 net Section 1231 gain would be treated as a long-term capital gain and would be reported on Form 4797 and transferred to Line 11 of Schedule D of Form 1040. Inventory is not Section 1231 property and thus results in an ordinary gain. ◆

Self-Study Problem 8.7   *See Appendix E for Solutions to Self-Study Problems*

Gary Farmer had the following sales of business property during the 2019 tax year:

1. Sold land acquired on December 3, 2008, at a cost of $24,000, for $37,000 on January 5, 2019. The cost of selling the land was $500, and there was no depreciation allowable or capital improvements made to the asset over the life of the asset.

2. Sold a business computer with an adjusted basis of $20,700 that was acquired on April 5, 2016. The original cost was $25,875, and accumulated depreciation was $5,175. The computer was sold on May 2, 2019, for $14,000, resulting in a $6,700 loss.

3. Sold equipment on July 22, 2019 for gross proceeds of $16,000. The equipment was acquired on October 21, 2018 at a cost of $25,000 and accumulated depreciation was $4,300 at the time of the sale. Gary used an equipment broker on this sale and paid a sales commission of $1,600.

Calculate Gary's net gain or loss and determine the character as either capital or ordinary (ignore any depreciation recapture).

8-8 DEPRECIATION RECAPTURE

Apply the depreciation recapture rules.

Since long-term capital gains traditionally have been taxed at a lower rate than ordinary income, taxpayers have attempted to maximize the amount of income treated as capital gain. Congress enacted depreciation recapture provisions to prevent taxpayers from converting ordinary income into capital gains by claiming maximum depreciation deductions over the life of the asset and then selling the asset and receiving capital gain treatment on the resulting gain at the time of the sale. There are three major depreciation recapture provisions: (1) Section 1245, which generally applies to personal property, (2) Section 1250, which applies to real estate, and (3) "unrecaptured depreciation" previously taken on real estate. The depreciation recapture provisions are extremely complex. Only a brief overview of the general provisions contained in the tax law is presented here.

8-8a Section 1245 Recapture

Under the provisions of Section 1245, any gain recognized on the disposition of a Section 1245 asset will be classified as ordinary income up to an amount equal to the depreciation claimed. Any gain in excess of depreciation taken is classified as a Section 1231 gain. Section 1245 property is:

- Depreciable tangible personal property such as furniture, machines, computers, and automobiles
- Amortizable intangible personal property such as patents, copyrights, leaseholds, and professional sports contracts
- Other tangible property (except buildings) used as an integral part of manufacturing, production or extraction
- Single purpose agricultural or horticultural structures

Section 1245 recapture potential is defined as the total depreciation claimed on Section 1245 property. The amount of ordinary income recognized upon the sale of an asset under Section 1245 is equal to the lesser of (1) the recomputed basis less the adjusted basis, or (2) the amount realized less the adjusted basis. The recomputed basis of an asset is the adjusted basis of the property plus Section 1245 recapture potential. Any gain recognized in excess of the amount of ordinary income is a Section 1231 gain.

EXAMPLE On March 1 of the current year, Melvin sells Section 1245 property, which was purchased four years ago for $6,000. Melvin had claimed depreciation on the property of $2,500, and sold the property for $5,000. The recapture under Section 1245 is calculated below:

Section 1245 recapture potential	$2,500
Adjusted basis ($6,000 − $2,500)	3,500
Recomputed basis ($3,500 + $2,500)	6,000
Gain realized ($5,000 − $3,500)	1,500

The ordinary income is equal to the lesser of (1) $2,500, the recomputed basis ($6,000) less the adjusted basis ($3,500), or (2) $1,500, the amount realized ($5,000) less the adjusted basis ($3,500). The entire gain of $1,500 is subject to Section 1245 recapture and is taxed as ordinary income. ♦

EXAMPLE Assume the same facts as in the previous example, except that the property is sold for $7,800. The recapture under Section 1245 is calculated below:

Section 1245 recapture potential	$2,500
Adjusted basis ($6,000 − $2,500)	3,500
Recomputed basis ($3,500 + $2,500)	6,000
Gain realized ($7,800 − $3,500)	4,300

The portion classified as ordinary income is equal to the lesser of (1) $2,500, the recomputed basis ($6,000) less the adjusted basis ($3,500), or (2) $4,300, the amount realized ($7,800) less the adjusted basis ($3,500). Of the $4,300 total gain, $2,500 is classified as ordinary income and the remaining $1,800 ($4,300 − $2,500) is a Section 1231 gain. ◆

8-8b Section 1250 Recapture

Section 1250 applies to the gain on the sale of depreciable real property, other than real property included in the definition of Section 1245 property. The amount of Section 1250 recapture potential is equal to the excess of depreciation expense claimed over the life of the asset under an *accelerated* method of depreciation over the amount of depreciation that would have been allowed if the straight-line method of depreciation had been used. If property is depreciated using the straight-line method, there is no Section 1250 recapture potential. Since the use of the straight-line method is required for real property acquired after 1986, there will be no Section 1250 recapture on the disposition of such property. In practice, Section 1250 recapture is rarely seen.

8-8c "Unrecaptured Depreciation" on Real Estate—25 Percent Rate

A special 25 percent tax rate applies to real property gains attributable to depreciation previously taken and not already recaptured under the Section 1245 or Section 1250 rules discussed above. Any remaining gain attributable to "unrecaptured depreciation" previously taken, including straight-line depreciation, is taxed at 25 percent rather than the long-term capital gain rate of 15 percent. When the taxpayer's ordinary tax rate is below 25 percent, the depreciation recapture will be taxed at the lower ordinary tax rate to the extent of the remaining amount in the less than 25 percent bracket and then at 25 percent. The application of the 25 percent rate for "unrecaptured depreciation" is frequently seen in practice because it applies to every rental property which is depreciated and then sold at a gain. If the 3.8 percent Net Investment Income tax discussed in Chapter 6 applies, the 25 percent rate will be increased to 28.8 percent and the 15 percent rate will be increased to 18.8 percent.

EXAMPLE Lew, an individual taxpayer, acquires an apartment building in 2009 for $300,000, and he sells it in October 2019 for $500,000. The accumulated straight-line depreciation on the building at the time of the sale is $45,000. Lew is in the 35 percent tax bracket for ordinary income. Lew's gain on the sale of the property is $245,000 ($500,000 less adjusted basis of $255,000). $45,000 of the gain is attributable to unrecaptured depreciation and is taxed at 25 percent, while the remaining $200,000 gain is taxed at the 15 percent long-term capital gains rate. Lew may also be subject to the 3.8 percent Net Investment Income tax which is discussed in Chapter 6. If this is the case, his tax rates will increase to 28.8 percent and 18.8 percent, respectively. ◆

The reporting of unrecaptured depreciation on 1250 property gains subject to the 25 percent rate is considerably complex. The amounts from the Form 4797 are reported on Schedule D and the use of the Unrecaptured Section 1250 Gain Worksheet from the Schedule D instructions is also suggested. Amounts from this worksheet are transferred to the Schedule D Tax worksheet (also part of the Schedule D instructions) which is similar to the Qualified Dividends and Capital Gain Tax Worksheet used in earlier chapters of this textbook.

Self-Study Problem 8.8   *See Appendix E for Solutions to Self-Study Problems*

The following information is from Self-Study Problem 8.7:

Gary Farmer, an individual taxpayer, had the following sales of business property during the 2019 tax year:

1. Sold land acquired on December 3, 2008, at a cost of $24,000, for $37,000 on January 5, 2019. The cost of selling the land was $500, and there was no depreciation allowable or capital improvements made to the asset over the life of the asset.

2. Sold a business computer with an adjusted basis of $20,700 that was acquired on April 5, 2016. The original cost was $25,875, and accumulated depreciation was $5,175. The computer was sold on May 2, 2019, for $14,000, resulting in a $6,700 loss.

3. Sold equipment on July 22, 2019 for gross proceeds of $16,000. The equipment was acquired on October 21, 2018 at a cost of $25,000 and accumulated depreciation was $4,300 at the time of the sale. Gary used an equipment broker on this sale and paid a sales commission of $1,600.

Add this new information:

4. Sold a building on October 7, 2019 for $340,000, net of sales commissions of $15,000. Gary acquired the building on December 3, 2008 at a cost of $320,000. Accumulated depreciation has been computed using the straight-line method since acquisition and totaled $126,050 at the time of the sale.

5. Sold furniture on October 7, 2019 for $7,600. The furniture was acquired on December 3, 2008 for $15,000 and accumulated depreciation was $15,000 at the time of the sale.

Gary's employer identification number is 74-8976432. Use Form 4797 on Pages 8-23 and 8-24 to report the above gains and losses (hint: do **not** ignore depreciation recapture and complete Part III first).

TIP

The sale of business property is entered on the Sale of Asset 4797/6252 screens under deductions.

Self-Study Problem 8.8

Form **4797**	**Sales of Business Property** (Also Involuntary Conversions and Recapture Amounts Under Sections 179 and 280F(b)(2)) ▶ Attach to your tax return. ▶ Go to *www.irs.gov/Form4797* for instructions and the latest information.	OMB No. 1545-0184 **2019**
Department of the Treasury Internal Revenue Service		Attachment Sequence No. **27**

Name(s) shown on return | **Identifying number**

1 Enter the gross proceeds from sales or exchanges reported to you for 2019 on Form(s) 1099-B or 1099-S (or substitute statement) that you are including on line 2, 10, or 20. See instructions . . . . | **1**

Part I Sales or Exchanges of Property Used in a Trade or Business and Involuntary Conversions From Other Than Casualty or Theft—Most Property Held More Than 1 Year (see instructions)

2	(a) Description of property	(b) Date acquired (mo., day, yr.)	(c) Date sold (mo., day, yr.)	(d) Gross sales price	(e) Depreciation allowed or allowable since acquisition	(f) Cost or other basis, plus improvements and expense of sale	(g) Gain or (loss) Subtract (f) from the sum of (d) and (e)

3 Gain, if any, from Form 4684, line 39 . . . . | **3**
4 Section 1231 gain from installment sales from Form 6252, line 26 or 37 . . . . | **4**
5 Section 1231 gain or (loss) from like-kind exchanges from Form 8824 . . . . | **5**
6 Gain, if any, from line 32, from other than casualty or theft . . . . | **6**
7 Combine lines 2 through 6. Enter the gain or (loss) here and on the appropriate line as follows . . . . | **7**

Partnerships and S corporations. Report the gain or (loss) following the instructions for Form 1065, Schedule K, line 10, or Form 1120-S, Schedule K, line 9. Skip lines 8, 9, 11, and 12 below.

Individuals, partners, S corporation shareholders, and all others. If line 7 is zero or a loss, enter the amount from line 7 on line 11 below and skip lines 8 and 9. If line 7 is a gain and you didn't have any prior year section 1231 losses, or they were recaptured in an earlier year, enter the gain from line 7 as a long-term capital gain on the Schedule D filed with your return and skip lines 8, 9, 11, and 12 below.

8 Nonrecaptured net section 1231 losses from prior years. See instructions . . . . | **8**
9 Subtract line 8 from line 7. If zero or less, enter -0-. If line 9 is zero, enter the gain from line 7 on line 12 below. If line 9 is more than zero, enter the amount from line 8 on line 12 below and enter the gain from line 9 as a long-term capital gain on the Schedule D filed with your return. See instructions . . . . | **9**

Part II Ordinary Gains and Losses (see instructions)

10 Ordinary gains and losses not included on lines 11 through 16 (include property held 1 year or less):

11 Loss, if any, from line 7 . . . . | **11** ( )
12 Gain, if any, from line 7 or amount from line 8, if applicable . . . . | **12**
13 Gain, if any, from line 31 . . . . | **13**
14 Net gain or (loss) from Form 4684, lines 31 and 38a . . . . | **14**
15 Ordinary gain from installment sales from Form 6252, line 25 or 36 . . . . . . | **15**
16 Ordinary gain or (loss) from like-kind exchanges from Form 8824 . . . . | **16**
17 Combine lines 10 through 16 . . . . | **17**

18 For all except individual returns, enter the amount from line 17 on the appropriate line of your return and skip lines a and b below. For individual returns, complete lines a and b below.

a If the loss on line 11 includes a loss from Form 4684, line 35, column (b)(ii), enter that part of the loss here. Enter the loss from income-producing property on Schedule A (Form 1040 or Form 1040-SR), line 16. (Do not include any loss on property used as an employee.) Identify as from "Form 4797, line 18a." See instructions . . . . | **18a**

b Redetermine the gain or (loss) on line 17 excluding the loss, if any, on line 18a. Enter here and on Schedule 1 (Form 1040 or Form 1040-SR), Part I, line 4 . . . . | **18b**

For Paperwork Reduction Act Notice, see separate instructions.   Cat. No. 13086I   Form **4797** (2019)

Form 4797 (2019)   Page **2**

Part III	**Gain From Disposition of Property Under Sections 1245, 1250, 1252, 1254, and 1255** (see instructions)

19	**(a)** Description of section 1245, 1250, 1252, 1254, or 1255 property:	**(b)** Date acquired (mo., day, yr.)	**(c)** Date sold (mo., day, yr.)
A			
B			
C			
D			

	These columns relate to the properties on lines 19A through 19D. ▶		Property A	Property B	Property C	Property D
20	Gross sales price (**Note:** *See line 1 before completing.*)	20				
21	Cost or other basis plus expense of sale	21				
22	Depreciation (or depletion) allowed or allowable	22				
23	Adjusted basis. Subtract line 22 from line 21	23				
24	Total gain. Subtract line 23 from line 20	24				
25	**If section 1245 property:**					
a	Depreciation allowed or allowable from line 22	25a				
b	Enter the **smaller** of line 24 or 25a	25b				
26	**If section 1250 property:** If straight line depreciation was used, enter -0- on line 26g, except for a corporation subject to section 291.					
a	Additional depreciation after 1975. See instructions	26a				
b	Applicable percentage multiplied by the **smaller** of line 24 or line 26a. See instructions.	26b				
c	Subtract line 26a from line 24. If residential rental property **or** line 24 isn't more than line 26a, skip lines 26d and 26e	26c				
d	Additional depreciation after 1969 and before 1976.	26d				
e	Enter the **smaller** of line 26c or 26d	26e				
f	Section 291 amount (corporations only)	26f				
g	Add lines 26b, 26e, and 26f	26g				
27	**If section 1252 property:** Skip this section if you didn't dispose of farmland or if this form is being completed for a partnership.					
a	Soil, water, and land clearing expenses	27a				
b	Line 27a multiplied by applicable percentage. See instructions	27b				
c	Enter the **smaller** of line 24 or 27b	27c				
28	**If section 1254 property:**					
a	Intangible drilling and development costs, expenditures for development of mines and other natural deposits, mining exploration costs, and depletion. See instructions	28a				
b	Enter the **smaller** of line 24 or 28a.	28b				
29	**If section 1255 property:**					
a	Applicable percentage of payments excluded from income under section 126. See instructions	29a				
b	Enter the **smaller** of line 24 or 29a. See instructions	29b				

Summary of Part III Gains. Complete property columns A through D through line 29b before going to line 30.

30	Total gains for all properties. Add property columns A through D, line 24	30	
31	Add property columns A through D, lines 25b, 26g, 27c, 28b, and 29b. Enter here and on line 13	31	
32	Subtract line 31 from line 30. Enter the portion from casualty or theft on Form 4684, line 33. Enter the portion from other than casualty or theft on Form 4797, line 6	32	

Part IV	**Recapture Amounts Under Sections 179 and 280F(b)(2) When Business Use Drops to 50% or Less** (see instructions)

			(a) Section 179	**(b)** Section 280F(b)(2)
33	Section 179 expense deduction or depreciation allowable in prior years.	33		
34	Recomputed depreciation. See instructions	34		
35	Recapture amount. Subtract line 34 from line 33. See the instructions for where to report	35		

Form **4797** (2019)

8-9 BUSINESS CASUALTY GAINS AND LOSSES

Apply the general treatment of casualty gains and losses for business purposes.

The treatment of casualty gains and losses differs depending on whether the property involved is held for personal-use or held for business or investment purposes. Therefore, a taxpayer's business and investment casualty gains and losses are computed separately from personal casualty gains and losses. Deductions for personal casualty losses are restricted to those associated with a federally-declared disaster area. Since the casualty loss is an itemized deduction, the rules for personal casualties are discussed in Chapter 5.

Would You Believe?

The Ninth Circuit Court decided that a man's payment to a woman to keep her from revealing their extramarital affair was not a deductible casualty loss.

The amount of a business casualty or loss depends on whether the property was completely or partially destroyed. If business property is completely destroyed, the loss is the adjusted basis of the property less any insurance reimbursement. If business property is partially destroyed, the loss is insurance proceeds less the lesser of the adjusted basis at the time of the casualty or the decrease in the property's fair market value associated with the casualty.

EXAMPLE   Joan's business suffered two casualties in the current year. Theft 1: One of Joan's employees stole a business vehicle and ended up abandoning the vehicle. The car was vandalized and damaged. The adjusted basis of the car was $14,000 at the time of the theft and the car was repairable but decreased in value $7,000 because of the damage. Theft 2: A car owned by Joan's business was stolen. The thief was involved in a traffic accident and the car was totally destroyed. The basis of the car was $7,600 at the time of the theft and had fair market value of $5,000 before the crash. Joan's insurance company reimbursed her $6,000 for the first theft and $4,000 for the second. Theft 1 is a partial destruction and the lesser of the decrease in market value or the adjusted basis is used to compute the loss. Theft 2 is a complete destruction and so the adjusted basis is used to compute the loss.

	Theft 1 Partial Destruction	Theft 2 Complete Destruction
Insurance proceeds	$ 6,000	$ 4,000
Adjusted basis	14,000	**7,600**
Decrease in FMV	**7,000**	n/a
Loss	$(1,000)	$(3,600)

Business and investment property must be identified as a capital asset, trade or business property subject to an allowance for depreciation, or ordinary income property. The following rules apply to the treatment of business or investment property:

1. Property held for 1 year or less—gains from trade or business property (including property used in the production of rental or royalty income) and gains from investment property are netted against losses from trade or business property, and the resulting net gain or loss is treated as ordinary income or loss. Losses from investment property are considered separately.

2. Property held over 1 year—gains and losses from trade or business property and investment property are netted.

    a. Net gain—if the result is a net gain, the net gain is included in the calculation of the net Section 1231 gain or loss (the gains and losses are treated as Section 1231 gains and losses).

    b. Net loss—if the result is a net loss, the gains and losses from business and investment property are excluded from Section 1231 treatment. The tax treatment of the gains and losses depends on whether the property was used in the taxpayer's trade or business or held for investment. Gains and losses from business-use assets are treated as ordinary income and ordinary losses, respectively.

If the taxpayer recognizes a gain as a result of a casualty, and the property involved is depreciable property, the depreciation recapture provisions may cause all or a part of the gain to be treated as ordinary income. A casualty involving business property is included in the definition of an involuntary conversion, so that gain realized may be eligible for deferral under the special involuntary conversion provisions discussed in LO 8.12 of this chapter. The interaction of Section 1231 and casualty gains and losses from business or investment property is complex. Taxpayers should follow the instructions included with Form 4684 and Form 4797. See the IRS website (**www.irs.gov**) for samples of these forms and instructions.

EXAMPLE   Two pieces of manufacturing equipment used by Robert in his business are completely destroyed by fire. One of the pieces of equipment had an adjusted basis of $5,000 ($11,000 original basis less $6,000 accumulated depreciation) and a fair market value of $3,000 on the date of the fire. The other piece of equipment had an adjusted basis of $7,000 ($18,000 original basis less $11,000 of accumulated depreciation) and a fair market value of $10,000. Robert receives $3,000 from his insurance company to compensate him for the loss of the first piece of equipment, and he receives $8,000 for the second piece of equipment. As a result of the casualty, Robert's casualty gain or loss is calculated as follows:

	Item 1	Item 2
Insurance proceeds	$ 3,000	$ 8,000
Basis of property	(5,000)	(7,000)
(Loss) gain	$(2,000)	$ 1,000

The netting of the business casualty gains and losses results in a net loss of $1,000; thus, the gains and losses are excluded from Section 1231 treatment. Since the loss on Item 1 represents a loss arising from an asset used in the taxpayer's business (not an asset held for investment), the loss is considered an ordinary loss. The $1,000 gain from Item 2 is treated as ordinary income under Section 1245 recapture. ♦

Self-Study Problem 8.9   *See Appendix E for Solutions to Self-Study Problems*

Jonathan has the following separate casualties during the year:

	Decrease in Fair Market Value	Adjusted Basis	Insurance Reimbursement	Holding Period
Business furniture	$ 4,000	$ 5,000	$ 0	3 years
Business machinery	15,000	14,000	10,000	3 years

The furniture was completely destroyed while the machinery was partially destroyed. Jonathan also sold business land for a Section 1231 gain of $10,000. Calculate the amount and nature of Jonathan's gains and losses as a result of these casualties.

8-10 INSTALLMENT SALES

Some taxpayers sell property and do not receive payment immediately. Instead, they take a note from the purchaser and receive payments over an extended period of time. It would be a financial hardship to require those taxpayers to pay tax on all of the gain on the sale of the property in the year of sale when they may not have received enough cash to cover the taxes. To provide equity in such situations, Congress passed the installment sale provision. The installment sale provision allows taxpayers to spread the gain (but not a loss) over the tax years in which payments are received. On an installment sale, the taxable gain reported each year is determined as follows:

$$\text{Taxable gain} = \frac{\text{Total gain realized on the sale}}{\text{Contract price}} \times \text{Cash collections during the year}$$

Taxpayers who receive payments over a period of time automatically report gain on the installment method, unless they elect to report all the gain in the year of the sale. An election to report all the gain in the year of sale is made by including all the gain in income for the year of the sale. Taxpayers use Form 6252, Installment Sale Income, to report the installment sale gain on their income tax returns.

EXAMPLE Howard Scripp sells land with an adjusted basis of $20,000 for $50,000. He receives $10,000 in the year of sale, and the balance is payable at $8,000 per year for 5 years, plus a reasonable amount of interest. If Howard elects not to report under the installment method, the gain in the year of sale would be calculated in the following manner:

Cash	$ 10,000
Note at fair market value	40,000
Amount realized	50,000
Less: the land's basis	(20,000)
Taxable gain	$ 30,000

◆

EXAMPLE If, instead, Howard reports the gain on the installment method, the amount of the taxable gain in the year of sale is $6,000, which is calculated below.

$$\text{Taxable gain} = \frac{\text{Total gain}}{\text{Contract price}} \times \text{Cash collections}$$

$$\text{Taxable gain} = \frac{\$30,000}{\$50,000} \times \$10,000 = \$6,000$$

Howard must complete Form 6252 as illustrated on Page 8-29.

If $8,000 is collected in the first year after the year of sale, the gain in that year would be $4,800, as illustrated below.

$$\text{Taxable gain} = \frac{\$30,000}{\$50,000} \times \$8,000 = \$4,800$$

Of course, any interest income received on the note is also included in income as portfolio income. ◆

Complex installment sale rules apply to taxpayers who regularly sell real or personal property and to taxpayers who sell certain business or rental real property. For example, any recapture under Section 1245 or Section 1250 must be reported in full in the year of sale, regardless of the taxpayer's use of the installment method. Any remaining gain may be reported under the installment method. In addition, certain limitations apply where there is an installment sale between related parties.

8-10a **The Contract Price**

The contract price used in calculating the taxable gain is the amount the seller will ultimately collect from the purchaser (other than interest). This amount is usually the sale price of the property. However, the purchaser will occasionally assume the seller's liability on the property, in which case the contract price is computed by subtracting from the selling price any mortgage or notes assumed by the buyer. If the mortgage or notes assumed by the buyer exceed the adjusted basis of the property, the excess is treated as a cash payment received in the year of sale and must be included in the contract price.

EXAMPLE   Roger receives the following for an installment sale of real estate:

Cash	$ 3,000
Roger's mortgage assumed by the purchaser	9,000
Note payable to Roger from the purchaser	39,000
Selling price	$ 51,000

Roger's total gain is computed as follows:

Selling price	$ 51,000
Less: selling expenses	(1,500)
Amount realized	49,500
Less: Roger's basis in the property	(30,000)
Total gain	$ 19,500

The contract price is $42,000 ($51,000 − $9,000), and assuming the $3,000 is the only cash received in the year of sale, the taxable gain in the year of sale is $1,393 as shown below:

$$\text{Taxable gain} = \frac{\$19,500}{\$42,000} \times \$3,000 = \$1,393 \; \blacklozenge$$

Self-Study Problem 8.10   *See Appendix E for Solutions to Self-Study Problems*

Brian acquired a rental house in 2003 for a cost of $80,000. Straight-line depreciation on the property of $26,000 has been claimed by Brian. In January 2019, he sells the property for $120,000, receiving $20,000 cash on March 1 and the buyer's note for $100,000 at 10 percent interest. The note is payable at $10,000 per year for 10 years, with the first payment to be received 1 year after the date of sale. Calculate his taxable gain under the installment method for the year of sale of the rental house.

Gain reportable in 2019 $ _____

TAX BREAK   Taxpayers may wish to elect out of the installment treatment for a sale which could qualify, and instead recognize all of the gain in the year of sale when they have low income and expect that the gain would be taxed at a higher rate if deferred to later years.

Form **6252**

Department of the Treasury
Internal Revenue Service

Installment Sale Income

▶ **Attach to your tax return.**
▶ **Use a separate form for each sale or other disposition of property on the installment method.**
▶ **Go to** *www.irs.gov/Form6252* **for the latest information.**

OMB No. 1545-0228

20**19**

Attachment
Sequence No. **79**

Name(s) shown on return
Howard Scripp

Identifying number

1	Description of property ▶ Land			
2a	Date acquired (mm/dd/yyyy) ▶		**b** Date sold (mm/dd/yyyy) ▶	
3	Was the property sold to a related party (see instructions) after May 14, 1980? If "No," skip line 4			☐ Yes ☑ No
4	Was the property you sold to a related party a marketable security? If "As," complete Part III. If "No," complete Part III for the year of sale and the 2 years after the year of sale			☐ Yes ☐ No

Part I Gross Profit and Contract Price. Complete this part for all years of the installment agreement.

5	Selling price including mortgages and other debts. **Don't** include interest, whether stated or unstated		**5**	50,000
6	Mortgages, debts, and other liabilities the buyer assumed or took the property subject to (see instructions)	**6**	0	
7	Subtract line 6 from line 5	**7**	50,000	
8	Cost or other basis of property sold	**8**	20,000	
9	Depreciation allowed or allowable	**9**	0	
10	Adjusted basis. Subtract line 9 from line 8	**10**	20,000	
11	Commissions and other expenses of sale	**11**		
12	Income recapture from Form 4797, Part III (see instructions) . . .	**12**		
13	Add lines 10, 11, and 12		**13**	20,000
14	Subtract line 13 from line 5. If zero or less, **don't** complete the rest of this form (see instructions) . .		**14**	30,000
15	If the property described on line 1 above was your main home, enter the amount of your excluded gain (see instructions). Otherwise, enter -0-		**15**	
16	**Gross profit.** Subtract line 15 from line 14		**16**	30,000
17	Subtract line 13 from line 6. If zero or less, enter -0-		**17**	0
18	**Contract price.** Add line 7 and line 17		**18**	50,000

Part II Installment Sale Income. Complete this part for all years of the installment agreement.

19	Gross profit percentage (expressed as a decimal amount). Divide line 16 by line 18. (For years after the year of sale, see instructions)		**19**	.60
20	If this is the year of sale, enter the amount from line 17. Otherwise, enter -0-		**20**	0
21	Payments received during year (see instructions). **Don't** include interest, whether stated or unstated .		**21**	10,000
22	Add lines 20 and 21		**22**	10,000
23	Payments received in prior years (see instructions). **Don't** include interest, whether stated or unstated	**23**		
24	**Installment sale income.** Multiply line 22 by line 19		**24**	6,000
25	Enter the part of line 24 that is ordinary income under the recapture rules (see instructions) . . .		**25**	
26	Subtract line 25 from line 24. Enter here and on Schedule D or Form 4797 (see instructions) . . .		**26**	6,000

Part III Related Party Installment Sale Income. **Don't** complete if you received the final payment this tax year.

27	Name, address, and taxpayer identifying number of related party			

28	Did the related party resell or dispose of the property ("second disposition") during this tax year?		☐ Yes ☐ No
29	**If the answer to question 28 is "Yes," complete lines 30 through 37 below unless one of the following conditions is met. Check the box that applies.**		
a	☐ The second disposition was more than 2 years after the first disposition (other than dispositions of marketable securities). If this box is checked, enter the date of disposition (mm/dd/yyyy) . . . . ▶ _____		
b	☐ The first disposition was a sale or exchange of stock to the issuing corporation.		
c	☐ The second disposition was an involuntary conversion and the threat of conversion occurred after the first disposition.		
d	☐ The second disposition occurred after the death of the original seller or buyer.		
e	☐ It can be established to the satisfaction of the IRS that tax avoidance wasn't a principal purpose for either of the dispositions. If this box is checked, attach an explanation (see instructions).		

30	Selling price of property sold by related party (see instructions)	**30**	
31	Enter contract price from line 18 for year of first sale	**31**	
32	Enter the **smaller** of line 30 or line 31	**32**	
33	Total payments received by the end of your 2019 tax year (see instructions)	**33**	
34	Subtract line 33 from line 32. If zero or less, enter -0-	**34**	
35	Multiply line 34 by the gross profit percentage on line 19 for year of first sale	**35**	
36	Enter the part of line 35 that is ordinary income under the recapture rules (see instructions)	**36**	
37	Subtract line 36 from line 35. Enter here and on Schedule D or Form 4797 (see instructions) . . .	**37**	

For Paperwork Reduction Act Notice, see page 4.   Cat. No. 13601R   Form **6252** (2019)

8-11 LIKE-KIND EXCHANGES

Although a taxpayer realizes a gain or loss on the sale or exchange of property, the recognition of the gain or loss may be deferred for tax purposes. One example of such a situation arises when a taxpayer exchanges real property for other real property of a like kind. Under certain circumstances, the transaction may be nontaxable. To qualify as a nontaxable exchange, the property exchanged must be real property held for productive use in a trade or business or for investment. Exchanges of personal or intangible property used in a business or for investment such as machines, cars, trucks, patents, furniture, etc. do not qualify as like-kind. Property held for personal purposes, such as a taxpayer's residence, also does not qualify for a like-kind exchange.

When the exchange involves only qualified like-kind property, no gain or loss is recognized. However, some exchanges include cash or other property in addition to the like-kind property. Even when the exchange is not solely for like-kind assets, the nontaxable treatment usually is not completely lost. Gain is recognized in an amount equal to the lesser of (1) the gain realized or (2) the "boot" received. Boot is money or the fair market value of other property received in addition to the like-kind property. Relief from a liability is the same as receiving cash and is treated as boot.

The basis of other property received as boot in an exchange is its fair market value on the date of the exchange. The basis of the like-kind property received is:

> The basis of the like-kind property given up
> + Any boot paid
> − Any boot received
> + Any gain recognized
> Basis of property received

The holding period for property acquired in a like-kind exchange includes the holding period of the property exchanged. For example, if long-term capital gain property is exchanged today, the new property may be sold immediately, and the gain recognized would be long-term capital gain.

Taxpayers must file Form 8824, Like-Kind Exchanges, to report the exchange of property. This form must be completed even if no gain is recognized.

EXAMPLE Janis and Kevin exchange real estate held as an investment. Janis gives up property with an adjusted basis of $350,000 and a fair market value of $560,000. The property is subject to a mortgage of $105,000 which is assumed by Kevin. In return for this property, Janis receives from Kevin land with a fair market value of $420,000 and cash of $35,000. Kevin's adjusted basis in the property he exchanges is $280,000.

1. Janis recognizes a gain of $140,000, equal to the lesser of the gain realized or the boot received as calculated below.

Calculation of gain realized:	
Fair market value of property received	$ 420,000
Cash received	35,000
Liability assumed by Kevin	105,000
Total amount realized	$ 560,000
Less: the adjusted basis of the property given up	(350,000)
Gain realized	$ 210,000
Calculation of boot received:	
Cash received	$ 35,000
Liability assumed by Kevin	105,000
Total boot received	$ 140,000
Gain recognized: Lesser of gain realized or boot received	$ 140,000

2. The basis of Janis's property is calculated below.

Basis of the property given up	$ 350,000
+ Boot paid	0
− Boot received	(140,000)
+ Gain recognized	140,000
Basis of the like-kind property received	$ 350,000

3. Kevin's recognized gain is equal to the lesser of the gain realized or the boot received. Since he received no boot, the recognized gain is zero.

Calculation of gain realized:	
Fair market value of the property received	$ 560,000
Less: boot paid ($105,000 + $35,000)	(140,000)
Less: adjusted basis of property given up	(280,000)
Gain realized	$ 140,000
Boot received	$ 0

4. The basis of Kevin's new property is calculated below.

Basis of the property given up	$ 280,000
+ Boot paid	140,000
− Boot received	0
+ Gain recognized	0
Basis of the property received	$ 420,000

◆

8-11a Like-Kind Property

The term "like-kind property" does not include inventory, stocks, bonds, or other securities or any personal property such as inventory, equipment, cars, trucks, machines, and furniture. Real property is more or less considered to be like-kind with any other real property so long as the original property and the new property are both used in a trade or business or held for investment.

Although the repeal of like-kind treatment for personal property does not permit the deferral of gains on that type of property, this may result in some favorable outcomes as well. The deferral on a like-kind exchange is not elective, it is required. One of the most common forms of exchange for a small business is the trade-in of a business auto. Because the market value of a used auto is almost always below its adjusted basis, the losses were not deductible under the previous like-kind exchange rules. Now that personal property is not eligible for like-kind treatment, these losses may be deductible.

TAX BREAK

Self-Study Problem 8.11   *See Appendix E for Solutions to Self-Study Problems*

During the current year, Daniel James exchanges land used in his business for a new parcel of land. Daniel's basis in the land is $18,000, and the land is subject to a mortgage of $8,000, which is assumed by the other party to the exchange. Daniel receives new land worth $22,000. Calculate Daniel's recognized gain on the exchange and his basis in the new land.

Recognized gain $_____
Basis in the new land $_____

Calculate recognized
and deferred gains on
involuntary conversions.

8-12 INVOLUNTARY CONVERSIONS

Occasionally, taxpayers are forced to dispose of property as a result of circumstances beyond their control. At the election of the taxpayer, and provided certain conditions are met, the gain on an involuntary conversion of property may be deferred. The provisions require that the property must be replaced and the basis of the replacement property reduced by the amount of the gain deferred. An involuntary conversion is defined as the destruction of the taxpayer's property in whole or in part, or loss of the property by theft, seizure, requisition, or condemnation. Also, property sold pursuant to reclamation laws, and livestock destroyed by disease or drought, are subject to the involuntary conversion rules. To qualify for nonrecognition of gain, the taxpayer must obtain qualified replacement property. The replacement property must be "similar or related in service or use." This definition is narrower than the like-kind rule; the property must be very similar to the property converted. Generally, a taxpayer has 2 years after the close of the tax year in which a gain was realized to obtain replacement property.

A realized gain on the involuntary conversion of property occurs when the taxpayer receives insurance proceeds or other payments in excess of his or her adjusted basis in the converted property. Taxpayers need not recognize any gain if they completely reinvest the proceeds or payments in qualified replacement property within the required time period. If they do not reinvest the total amount of the payments received, they must recognize a gain equal to the amount of the payment not reinvested (but limited to the gain realized). The basis of the replacement property is equal to the cost of the replacement property reduced by any gain not recognized on the transaction. The holding period of the replacement property includes the period the original property was held.

EXAMPLE   Tammy's office building, which has an adjusted basis of $600,000, is destroyed by fire in 2019. In the same year, Tammy receives $700,000 of insurance proceeds for the loss. She has until December 31, 2021 (2 years after the end of the taxable year in which the gain is realized), to acquire a replacement building. In 2020, Tammy replaces the building with a new building costing $680,000. Her realized gain on the involuntary conversion is $100,000 ($700,000 − $600,000), and the gain recognized is $20,000, which is the $700,000 of cash received less the amount reinvested ($680,000). The basis of the new building is $600,000 ($680,000 − $80,000), the cost of the new building less the portion of the gain not recognized. ♦

The involuntary conversion provision applies only to gains, not to losses. The provision must be elected by the taxpayer. In contrast, the like-kind exchange provision discussed previously applies to both gains and losses and is not elective.

Self-Study Problem 8.12   *See Appendix E for Solutions to Self-Study Problems*

Sam's store is destroyed in 2019 as a result of a flood. The store has an adjusted basis of $70,000, and Sam receives insurance proceeds of $150,000 on the loss. Sam invests $135,000 in a replacement store in 2020.

1. Calculate Sam's recognized gain, assuming an election under the involuntary conversion provision is made. $_____

2. Calculate Sam's basis in the replacement store. $_____

KEY TERMS

depreciation, 8-2
straight-line depreciation, 8-2
Modified Accelerated Cost Recovery
    System (MACRS), 8-3
recovery period, 8-3
asset depreciation ranges
    (ADRs), 8-3
accelerated depreciation, 8-4
half-year convention, 8-4
mid-quarter convention, 8-5

bonus depreciation, 8-7
mid-month convention, 8-8
Section 179, 8-10
election to expense, 8-10
listed property, 8-14
intangibles, 8-17
Section 197 intangibles, 8-17
amortization, 8-17
goodwill and going-concern
    values, 8-17

Section 1231 assets, 8-19
depreciation recapture, 8-20
Section 1245 recapture, 8-20
Section 1250 recapture, 8-21
installment sales, 8-27
like-kind exchange, 8-30
boot, 8-30
like-kind property, 8-31
involuntary conversion, 8-32
qualified replacement property, 8-32

KEY POINTS

Learning Objectives	Key Points
LO 8.1: Explain the concept of depreciation.	• Depreciation is the accounting process of allocating and deducting the cost of an asset over a period of years and does not necessarily mean physical deterioration or loss of value of the asset. • The simplest method of depreciation is the straight-line method, which results in an equal portion of the cost of an asset being deducted in each period of the asset's life.
LO 8.2: Calculate depreciation expense using the MACRS tables.	• The Modified Accelerated Cost Recovery System (MACRS) allows taxpayers who invest in capital assets to write off an asset's cost over a period designated in the tax law and to use an accelerated method of depreciation for assets other than real estate. • The minimum number of years over which the cost of an asset may be deducted (the recovery period) depends on the type of property and the year in which the property was acquired. • Under MACRS, taxpayers calculate the depreciation of an asset using a table, which contains a percentage rate for each year of the property's recovery period and includes the half-year convention for personal property and mid-month convention for real property. • The mid-quarter convention must be applied if more than 40 percent of the total cost of a taxpayer's tangible property acquired during the year, other than real property, is placed in service during the last quarter of the tax year. • The bonus depreciation rules allow taxpayers purchasing property with a MACRS recovery period of 20 years or less (see Table 8.1), computer software, and certain leasehold improvements to directly write off 100 percent of the cost of the assets in the year placed in service. • There are no taxable income limits or thresholds associated with bonus depreciation. • For post-1986 acquired real estate, MACRS uses the straight-line method over 27.5 years for residential realty and 39 years for nonresidential realty (31.5 years for realty acquired generally before May 13, 1993).

LO 8.3: Identify when a Section 179 election to expense the cost of property may be used.	• Qualified Section 179 property is personal property (property other than real estate or assets used in residential real estate rental activities) placed in service during the year and used in a trade or business. • The maximum cost that may be expensed in the year of acquisition under Section 179 is $1,020,000 for 2019. The property may be new or used. • The $1,020,000 maximum is reduced dollar for dollar by the cost of qualifying property placed in service during the year in excess of $2,550,000. • The amount that may be expensed is limited to the taxpayer's taxable income, before considering any amount expensed under this election, from any trade or business of the taxpayer. • Section 179 expensed amounts reduce the basis of the asset before calculating any regular MACRS depreciation on the remaining cost of the asset.
LO 8.4: Apply the limitations placed on depreciation of "listed property."	• Special rules apply to the depreciation of listed property. • Listed property includes those types of assets which lend themselves to personal use. • Listed property includes automobiles, certain other vehicles, and property used for entertainment, recreation, or amusement. • If listed property is used 50 percent or less in a qualified business use, any depreciation deduction must be calculated using the straight-line method of depreciation over an alternate recovery period, and the special election to expense under Section 179 and bonus depreciation are not allowed.
LO 8.5: Apply the limitations on depreciation of "luxury automobiles."	• The depreciation of passenger automobiles is subject to a limitation, commonly referred to as the luxury automobile limitation. • For automobiles acquired in 2019, the maximum depreciation is $18,100 (Year 1), $16,100 (Year 2), $9,700 (Year 3), and $5,760 (Year 4 and subsequent years until fully depreciated). Bonus depreciation of $8,000 is included in the first year limit of $18,100.
LO 8.6: Calculate the amortization of goodwill and certain other intangibles.	• Section 197 intangibles are amortized over a 15-year period, beginning with the month of acquisition. • Qualified Section 197 intangibles include goodwill, going-concern value, workforce in place, information bases, know-how, customer-based intangibles, licenses, permits, rights granted by a governmental unit, covenants not to compete, franchises, trademarks, and trade names. • Examples of Section 197 exclusions are interests in a corporation, partnership, trust, or estate; interests in land; computer software readily available for purchase by the general public; interests in films, sound recordings, and video recordings; and self-created intangible assets.
LO 8.7: Classify gains and losses from Section 1231 assets.	• Section 1231 assets include (1) depreciable or real property used in a trade or business, (2) timber, coal, or domestic iron ore, (3) livestock (not including poultry) held for draft, breeding, dairy, or sporting purposes, and (4) unharvested crops on land used in a trade or business. • If net Section 1231 gains exceed the losses, the excess is a long-term capital gain. When the net Section 1231 losses exceed the gains, all gains are treated as ordinary income, and all losses are fully deductible as ordinary losses.

LO 8.8: Apply the depreciation recapture rules.	• Depreciation recapture provisions are meant to prevent taxpayers from converting ordinary income into capital gain by claiming maximum depreciation deductions over the life of the asset and then selling the asset and receiving capital gain treatment on the resulting gain at sale. • Under Section 1245, any gain recognized on the disposition of a Section 1245 asset (generally personal property) will be classified as ordinary income up to an amount equal to the accumulated depreciation. Any gain in excess of depreciation taken is classified as a Section 1231 gain. • Section 1250 real property recapture is the excess of depreciation expense claimed, using an accelerated method of depreciation, over what would have been allowed if the straight-line method were used. • Since the straight-line method is required for real property acquired after 1986, there will be no Section 1250 recapture on the disposition of real property. • A special 25 or 28.8 percent tax rate applies to real property gains attributable to depreciation previously taken and not already recaptured under Section 1245 or Section 1250.
LO 8.9: Apply the general treatment of casualty gains and losses for business purposes.	• The amount of a partial casualty loss from business property is insurance proceeds less the decrease in the value of the property or the adjusted basis, whichever is smaller. • The amount of a casualty loss from a complete destruction of business property is the insurance proceeds less the adjusted basis of the property.
LO 8.10: Compute the gain on installment sales.	• On an installment sale, the taxable gain reported each year is determined as follows: taxable gain equals total gain realized on the sale, divided by the contract price, and multiplied by the payment received during the year.
LO 8.11: Calculate recognized and deferred gains on like-kind exchanges.	• To qualify as a nontaxable like-kind exchange, the property exchanged must be real property held for use in a trade or business or for investment, and exchanged for property of a like kind. • Personal property no longer qualifies for like-kind exchange treatment. • Like-kind gain is recognized in an amount equal to the lesser of (1) the gain realized or (2) the "boot" received. Boot is money or the fair market value of other property received in addition to the like-kind property. • If a transaction qualifies as a like-kind exchange, the like-kind exchange provisions must be followed.
LO 8.12: Calculate recognized and deferred gains on involuntary conversions.	• A realized gain on the involuntary conversion of property occurs when the taxpayer receives proceeds in excess of his or her adjusted basis. • Involuntary conversion gain is not recognized if the proceeds or payments are reinvested in qualified replacement property within the required time period and the taxpayer makes the proper election.

QUESTIONS and PROBLEMS

GROUP 1:
MULTIPLE CHOICE QUESTIONS

LO 8.2

1. Alice purchases a rental house on August 22, 2019, for a cost of $174,000. Of this amount, $100,000 is considered to be allocable to the cost of the home, with the remaining $74,000 allocable to the cost of the land. What is Alice's maximum depreciation deduction for 2019 using MACRS?
   a. $2,373
   b. $1,970
   c. $1,364
   d. $1,061
   e. $1,009

LO 8.2

2. An asset (not an automobile) put in service in June 2019 has a depreciable basis of $30,000 and a recovery period of 5 years. Assuming half-year convention, no bonus depreciation, and no election to expense is made, what is the maximum amount of cost that can be deducted in 2019?
   a. $2,500
   b. $5,000
   c. $6,000
   d. $30,000
   e. None of the above

LO 8.2

3. An asset (not an automobile) put in service in June 2019 has a depreciable basis of $40,000 and a recovery period of 5 years. Assuming bonus depreciation is used, half-year convention and no election to expense is made, what is the maximum amount of cost that can be deducted in 2019?
   a. $4,000
   b. $20,000
   c. $24,000
   d. $28,000
   e. $40,000

LO 8.2

4. James purchased office equipment for his business. The equipment has a depreciable basis of $7,000 and was put in service on June 1, 2019. James decides to elect straight-line depreciation under MACRS for the asset over the minimum number of years (7 years), and does not use bonus depreciation or make the election to expense. What is the amount of his depreciation deduction for the equipment for the 2019 tax year?
   a. $2,000
   b. $1,000
   c. $500
   d. $0
   e. None of the above

LO 8.2

5. Which of the following statements with respect to the depreciation of property under MACRS is *incorrect*?
   a. Under the half-year convention, one-half year of depreciation is allowed in the year the property is placed in service.
   b. If a taxpayer elects to use the straight-line method of depreciation for property in the 5-year class, all other 5-year class property acquired during the year must also be depreciated using the straight-line method.

c. In some cases, when a taxpayer places a significant amount of property in service during the last quarter of the year, real property must be depreciated using a mid-quarter convention.

d. Real property acquired after 1986 must be depreciated using the straight-line method.

e. The cost of property to which the MACRS rate is applied is not reduced for estimated salvage value.

LO 8.2

6. Which of the following is *not* true about the MACRS depreciation system:

a. A salvage value must be determined before depreciation percentages are applied to depreciable real estate.

b. Residential rental buildings are depreciated over 27.5 years straight-line.

c. Commercial real estate buildings are depreciated over 39 years straight-line.

d. No matter when during the month depreciable real estate is purchased, it is considered to have been placed in service at mid-month for MACRS depreciation purposes.

LO 8.3

7. On July 20, 2019, Kelli purchases office equipment at a cost of $12,000. Kelli elects out of bonus depreciation but makes the election to expense for 2019. She is self-employed as an attorney, and, in 2019, her business has a net income of $6,000 before considering this election to expense. Kelli has no other income or expenses for the year. What is the maximum amount that Kelli may deduct for 2019 under the election to expense, assuming she elects to expense the entire $12,000 purchase?

a. $24,000
b. $12,000
c. $6,000
d. $3,000
e. $1,000

LO 8.3

8. Which of the following is *not* considered a limit on the immediate expensing election of Section 179?

a. Fifty percent of qualified improvement property
b. Total Section 179-eligible property acquired in excess of $3,570,000
c. The taxable income of the taxpayer considering all income and deductions except for Section 179 immediate expensing
d. An annual limit of $1,020,000
e. None of the above

LO 8.5

9. In 2019, Ben purchases and places in service a new auto for his business. The auto costs $57,000 and will be used 60 percent for business. Assuming the half-year convention applies and Ben elects out of bonus depreciation and Section 179, what will depreciation on the auto be in 2019?

a. $11,400
b. $6,840
c. $6,060
d. $6,000
e. None of the above

LO 8.5

10. In 2019, Ben purchases and places in service a new auto for his business. The auto costs $57,000 and will be used 100 percent for business. Assuming the half-year convention applies and Ben does not elect out of bonus depreciation, what will depreciation on the auto be in 2018?

a. $57,000
b. $18,000
c. $18,100
d. $10,000
e. None of the above

LO 8.6 11. The amortization period for Section 197 intangibles is:
  a. 5 years
  b. 7 years
  c. 10 years
  d. 15 years
  e. 40 years

LO 8.6 12. Which of the following intangibles is defined as a Section 197 intangible asset?
  a. An interest in land
  b. A partnership interest
  c. An interest in a corporation
  d. A covenant not to compete acquired as part of a business
  e. A separately acquired sound recording

LO 8.7 13. Which of the following is Section 1231 property?
  a. Land held for investment purposes
  b. A machine used in a business
  c. Accounts receivable
  d. Inventory
  e. Paintings owned by the artist

LO 8.7
LO 8.8 14. In 2019, Mary sells for $24,000 a machine used in her business. The machine was purchased on May 1, 2017, at a cost of $22,000. Mary has deducted depreciation on the machine of $6,000. What is the amount and nature of Mary's gain as a result of the sale of the machine?
  a. $2,000 Section 1231 gain
  b. $8,000 ordinary income under Section 1245
  c. $6,000 ordinary income and $2,000 Section 1231 gain
  d. $6,000 Section 1231 gain and $2,000 ordinary income under Section 1245
  e. None of the above

LO 8.7
LO 8.8 15. During 2019, Paul sells residential rental property for $240,000, which he acquired in 1998 for $160,000. Paul has claimed straight-line depreciation on the building of $60,000. What is the amount and nature of Paul's gain on the sale of the rental property?
  a. $140,000 ordinary income
  b. $80,000 "unrecaptured depreciation" and $60,000 ordinary gain
  c. $140,000 Section 1231 gain
  d. $80,000 Section 1231 gain, $60,000 "unrecaptured depreciation"
  e. None of the above

LO 8.8 16. Jeanie acquires an apartment building in 2008 for $280,000 and sells it for $480,000 in 2019. At the time of sale there is $60,000 of accumulated straight-line depreciation on the apartment building. Assuming Jeanie is in the highest tax bracket for ordinary income and the Medicare tax on net investment income applies, how much of her gain is taxed at 28.8 percent?
  a. None
  b. $60,000
  c. $200,000
  d. $280,000
  e. $260,000

LO 8.9 17. Virginia has business property that is stolen and partially destroyed by the time it was recovered. She receives an insurance reimbursement of $6,000 on property that had a $14,000 basis and a decrease in market value of $10,000 due to damage caused by the theft. What is the amount of Virginia's casualty loss?
  a. $14,000
  b. $8,000
  c. $10,000
  d. $4,000
  e. None of the above

LO 8.10

18. Pat sells land for $25,000 cash and a $75,000 5-year note. If her basis in the property is $30,000 and she receives only the $25,000 down payment in the year of sale, how much is Pat's taxable gain in the year of sale using the installment sales method?
    a. $0
    b. $5,000
    c. $17,500
    d. $25,000
    e. $75,000

LO 8.11

19. Fred and Sarajane exchanged land in a qualifying like-kind exchange. Fred gives up land with an adjusted basis of $11,000 (fair market value of $16,000) in exchange for Sarajane's land with a fair market value of $12,000 plus $4,000 cash. How much gain should Fred recognize on the exchange?
    a. $5,000
    b. $4,000
    c. $1,000
    d. $0
    e. None of the above

LO 8.11

20. What is Sarajane's basis in the equipment received in the exchange described in Question 19, assuming her basis in the equipment given up was $12,000?
    a. $0
    b. $12,000
    c. $14,000
    d. $16,000
    e. None of the above

LO 8.12

21. Oscar owns a building that is destroyed in a hurricane. His adjusted basis in the building before the hurricane is $130,000. His insurance company pays him $140,000 and he immediately invests in a new building at a cost of $142,000. What is the amount of recognized gain or loss on the destruction of Oscar's building?
    a. $0
    b. $10,000 gain
    c. $8,000 gain
    d. $12,000 gain
    e. $2,000 loss

LO 8.12

22. Using the information from Question 21, what is Oscar's basis on his new building?
    a. $130,000
    b. $132,000
    c. $140,000
    d. $142,000

GROUP 2:
PROBLEMS

LO 8.2

1. Is land allowed to be depreciated? Why or why not?

_____

_____

_____

LO 8.2

2. Is it possible to depreciate a residential rental building when it is actually increasing in value? Why?

_____

_____

LO 8.2
LO 8.3

3. Mike purchases a new heavy-duty truck (5-year class recovery property) for his delivery service on March 30, 2019. No other assets were purchased during the year. The truck is not considered a passenger automobile for purposes of the listed property and luxury automobile limitations. The truck has a depreciable basis of $42,000 and an estimated useful life of 5 years. Assume half-year convention for tax.

   a. Calculate the amount of depreciation for 2019 using financial accounting straight-line depreciation (not the straight-line MACRS election) over the truck's estimated useful life.

   $_____

   b. Calculate the amount of depreciation for 2019 using the straight-line depreciation election, using MACRS tables over the minimum number of years with no bonus depreciation or election to expense.

   $_____

   c. Calculate the amount of depreciation for 2019, including bonus depreciation but no election to expense, that Mike could deduct using the MACRS tables.

   $_____

   d. Calculate the amount of depreciation for 2019 including the election to expense but no bonus depreciation that Mike could deduct. Assume no income limit on the expense election.

   $_____

LO 8.2

4. On March 8, 2019, Holly purchased a residential apartment building. The cost basis assigned to the building is $700,000. Holly also owns another residential apartment building that she purchased on October 15, 2019, with a cost basis of $400,000.

   a. Calculate Holly's total depreciation deduction for the apartments for 2019 using MACRS.

   $_____

   b. Calculate Holly's total depreciation deduction for the apartments for 2020 using MACRS.

   $_____

LO 8.2

5. Give the MACRS depreciation life of the following assets:
   a. An automobile _____
   b. Business furniture _____
   c. A computer _____
   d. Residential real estate _____
   e. Commercial real estate _____
   f. Land _____

LO 8.2

6. Explain the use of the mid-quarter convention for MACRS depreciation:

   _____
   _____
   _____
   _____

LO 8.2

7. Calculate the following:
   a. The first year of depreciation on a residential rental building costing $250,000 purchased June 2, 2019.

   $_____

   b. The second year (2020) of depreciation on a computer costing $5,000 purchased in May 2019, using the half-year convention and accelerated depreciation considering any bonus depreciation taken.

   $_____

c. The first year of depreciation on a computer costing $2,800 purchased in May 2019, using the half-year convention and straight-line depreciation with no bonus depreciation.

$_____

d. The third year of depreciation on business furniture costing $10,000 purchased in March 2017, using the half-year convention and accelerated depreciation but no bonus depreciation.

$_____

LO 8.2
LO 8.3
LO 8.4
LO 8.5

8. During 2019, William purchases the following capital assets for use in his catering business:

New passenger automobile (September 30)	$54,000
Baking equipment (June 30)	7,000

Assume that William decides to use the election to expense on the baking equipment (and has adequate taxable income to cover the deduction) but not on the automobile, and he also uses the MACRS accelerated method to calculate depreciation but elects out of bonus depreciation. Calculate William's maximum depreciation deduction for 2019, assuming he uses the automobile 100 percent in his business.

$_____

LO 8.2
LO 8.4

9. On February 2, 2019, Alexandra purchases a personal computer. The computer cost $1,800. Alexandra uses the computer 85 percent of the time in her accounting business, and the remaining 15 percent of the time for various personal uses. Calculate Alexandra's maximum depreciation deduction for 2019 for the computer, assuming half-year convention and she does not use bonus depreciation or make the election to expense.

$_____

LO 8.2
LO 8.4
LO 8.5

10. On September 14, 2019, Jay purchased a passenger automobile that is used 75 percent in his accounting business. The automobile has a basis for depreciation purposes of $40,000, and Jay uses the accelerated method under MACRS. Jay does not elect to expense. Calculate Jay's depreciation deduction for 2019 assuming bonus depreciation.

$_____

LO 8.2
LO 8.4
LO 8.5

11. During 2019, Pepe Guardio purchases the following property for use in his calendar year-end manufacturing business:

Item	Date Acquired	Cost
Manufacturing equipment (7 year)	June 2	$ 40,000
Office furniture	September 15	6,000
Office computer	November 18	2,000
Passenger automobile (used		
90 percent for business)	May 31	54,000
Warehouse	June 23	
Building		165,000
Land		135,000

Pepe uses the accelerated depreciation method under MACRS, if available, and does not make the election to expense or take bonus depreciation. Use Form 4562 on Pages 8-43 and 8-44 to report Pepe's depreciation expense for 2019.

LO 8.2
LO 8.4
LO 8.5

12. Go to the IRS website (**www.irs.gov**) and assuming bonus depreciation is used, redo Problem 11, using the most recent interactive Form 4562, Depreciation and Amortization. Print out the *completed Form 4562*.

LO 8.2
LO 8.3

13. Tom has a successful business with $100,000 of taxable income before the election to expense in 2019. He purchases one new asset in 2019, a new machine which is 7-year MACRS property and costs $25,000. If you are Tom's tax advisor, how would you advise Tom to treat the purchase for tax purposes in 2019? Why?

_____

_____

LO 8.6

14. Derek purchases a small business from Art on June 30, 2019. He paid the following amounts for the business:

Fixed assets	$180,000
Goodwill	40,000
Covenant not to compete	30,000
Total	$250,000

a. How much of the $250,000 purchase price is for Section 197 intangible assets?

$_____

b. What amount can Derek deduct on his 2019 tax return as Section 197 intangible amortization?

$_____

LO 8.6

15. Annie develops a successful tax practice. She sells the practice to her friend Carol for $54,000 and moves to Florida to retire. The tax practice has no assets except intangible benefits such as the goodwill and going-concern value Annie has developed over the years. How should Carol treat the $54,000 cost of the tax practice she has purchased?

LO 8.7
LO 8.8

16. Nadia Shalom has the following transactions during the year:

Sale of office equipment on March 15 that cost $20,000 when purchased on July 1, 2017. Nadia has claimed $3,100 in depreciation and sells the asset for $13,500 with no selling costs.

Sale of land on April 19 for $125,000. The land cost $132,500 when purchased on February 1, 2008. Nadia's selling costs are $6,500.

Assume there were no capital improvements on either business asset sold. Nadia's Social Security number is 924-56-5783. Complete Form 4797 on Pages 8-45 and 8-46 to report the above gains or losses.

LO 8.8
LO 8.10

17. Steve Drake sells a rental house on January 1, 2019, and receives $100,000 cash and a note for $50,000 at 7 percent interest. The purchaser also assumes the mortgage on the property of $25,000. Steve's original cost for the house was $170,000 on January 1, 2011 and accumulated depreciation was $27,000 on the date of sale. He collects only the $100,000 down payment in the year of sale.

a. If Steve elects to recognize the total gain on the property in the year of sale, calculate the taxable gain.

$_____

b. Assuming Steve uses the installment sale method, complete Form 6252 on Page 8-47 for the year of the sale.

c. Assuming Steve collects $5,000 (not including interest) of the note principal in the year following the year of sale, calculate the amount of income recognized in that year under the installment sale method.

$_____

GROUP 2:

PROBLEM 11

Form **4562**	**Depreciation and Amortization**	OMB No. 1545-0172
	(Including Information on Listed Property)	**2019**
Department of the Treasury Internal Revenue Service (99)	▶ Attach to your tax return. ▶ Go to *www.irs.gov/Form4562* for instructions and the latest information.	Attachment Sequence No. **179**

Name(s) shown on return	Business or activity to which this form relates	Identifying number

Part I   Election To Expense Certain Property Under Section 179
Note: If you have any listed property, complete Part V before you complete Part I.

1	Maximum amount (see instructions)	**1**
2	Total cost of section 179 property placed in service (see instructions)	**2**
3	Threshold cost of section 179 property before reduction in limitation (see instructions)	**3**
4	Reduction in limitation. Subtract line 3 from line 2. If zero or less, enter -0-	**4**
5	Dollar limitation for tax year. Subtract line 4 from line 1. If zero or less, enter -0-. If married filing separately, see instructions	**5**

6	(a) Description of property	(b) Cost (business use only)	(c) Elected cost	

7	Listed property. Enter the amount from line 29 . . . . **7**	
8	Total elected cost of section 179 property. Add amounts in column (c), lines 6 and 7	**8**
9	Tentative deduction. Enter the **smaller** of line 5 or line 8	**9**
10	Carryover of disallowed deduction from line 13 of your 2018 Form 4562	**10**
11	Business income limitation. Enter the smaller of business income (not less than zero) or line 5. See instructions	**11**
12	Section 179 expense deduction. Add lines 9 and 10, but don't enter more than line 11	**12**
13	Carryover of disallowed deduction to 2020. Add lines 9 and 10, less line 12 ▶ **13**	

Note: Don't use Part II or Part III below for listed property. Instead, use Part V.

Part II   Special Depreciation Allowance and Other Depreciation (Don't include listed property. See instructions.**)**

14	Special depreciation allowance for qualified property (other than listed property) placed in service during the tax year. See instructions	**14**
15	Property subject to section 168(f)(1) election	**15**
16	Other depreciation (including ACRS)	**16**

Part III   MACRS Depreciation (Don't include listed property. See instructions.**)**

Section A

17	MACRS deductions for assets placed in service in tax years beginning before 2019	**17**
18	If you are electing to group any assets placed in service during the tax year into one or more general asset accounts, check here . . . . ▶ ☐	

Section B—Assets Placed in Service During 2019 Tax Year Using the General Depreciation System

(a) Classification of property	(b) Month and year placed in service	(c) Basis for depreciation (business/investment use only—see instructions)	(d) Recovery period	(e) Convention	(f) Method	(g) Depreciation deduction
19a 3-year property						
b 5-year property						
c 7-year property						
d 10-year property						
e 15-year property						
f 20-year property						
g 25-year property			25 yrs.		S/L	
h Residential rental property			27.5 yrs.	MM	S/L	
			27.5 yrs.	MM	S/L	
i Nonresidential real property			39 yrs.	MM	S/L	
				MM	S/L	

Section C—Assets Placed in Service During 2019 Tax Year Using the Alternative Depreciation System

20a Class life					S/L	
b 12-year			12 yrs.		S/L	
c 30-year			30 yrs.	MM	S/L	
d 40-year			40 yrs.	MM	S/L	

Part IV   Summary (See instructions.)

21	Listed property. Enter amount from line 28	**21**
22	**Total.** Add amounts from line 12, lines 14 through 17, lines 19 and 20 in column (g), and line 21. Enter here and on the appropriate lines of your return. Partnerships and S corporations—see instructions	**22**
23	For assets shown above and placed in service during the current year, enter the portion of the basis attributable to section 263A costs **23**	

For Paperwork Reduction Act Notice, see separate instructions.	Cat. No. 12906N	Form **4562** (2019)

Form 4562 (2019)   Page **2**

Part V **Listed Property** (Include automobiles, certain other vehicles, certain aircraft, and property used for entertainment, recreation, or amusement.)

Note: For any vehicle for which you are using the standard mileage rate or deducting lease expense, complete **only** 24a, 24b, columns (a) through (c) of Section A, all of Section B, and Section C if applicable.

Section A—Depreciation and Other Information (Caution: See the instructions for limits for passenger automobiles.)

24a Do you have evidence to support the business/investment use claimed? ☐ **Yes** ☐ **No** | 24b If "Yes," is the evidence written? ☐ **Yes** ☐ **No**

(a) Type of property (list vehicles first)	(b) Date placed in service	(c) Business/ investment use percentage	(d) Cost or other basis	(e) Basis for depreciation (business/investment use only)	(f) Recovery period	(g) Method/ Convention	(h) Depreciation deduction	(i) Elected section 179 cost
25 Special depreciation allowance for qualified listed property placed in service during the tax year and used more than 50% in a qualified business use. See instructions . **25**								
26 Property used more than 50% in a qualified business use:								
		%						
		%						
		%						
27 Property used 50% or less in a qualified business use:								
		%			S/L –			
		%			S/L –			
		%			S/L –			

28 Add amounts in column (h), lines 25 through 27. Enter here and on line 21, page 1 . **28**

29 Add amounts in column (i), line 26. Enter here and on line 7, page 1 . . . . **29**

Section B—Information on Use of Vehicles

Complete this section for vehicles used by a sole proprietor, partner, or other "more than 5% owner," or related person. If you provided vehicles to your employees, first answer the questions in Section C to see if you meet an exception to completing this section for those vehicles.

	(a) Vehicle 1		(b) Vehicle 2		(c) Vehicle 3		(d) Vehicle 4		(e) Vehicle 5		(f) Vehicle 6	
30 Total business/investment miles driven during the year (**don't** include commuting miles) .												
31 Total commuting miles driven during the year												
32 Total other personal (noncommuting) miles driven												
33 Total miles driven during the year. Add lines 30 through 32												
34 Was the vehicle available for personal use during off-duty hours?	Yes	No	Yes	No	Yes	No	Yes	No	Yes	No	Yes	No
35 Was the vehicle used primarily by a more than 5% owner or related person? . .												
36 Is another vehicle available for personal use?												

Section C—Questions for Employers Who Provide Vehicles for Use by Their Employees

Answer these questions to determine if you meet an exception to completing Section B for vehicles used by employees who **aren't** more than 5% owners or related persons. See instructions.

	Yes	No
37 Do you maintain a written policy statement that prohibits all personal use of vehicles, including commuting, by your employees?		
38 Do you maintain a written policy statement that prohibits personal use of vehicles, except commuting, by your employees? See the instructions for vehicles used by corporate officers, directors, or 1% or more owners . .		
39 Do you treat all use of vehicles by employees as personal use?		
40 Do you provide more than five vehicles to your employees, obtain information from your employees about the use of the vehicles, and retain the information received?		
41 Do you meet the requirements concerning qualified automobile demonstration use? See instructions.		

Note: If your answer to 37, 38, 39, 40, or 41 is "Yes," don't complete Section B for the covered vehicles.

Part VI **Amortization**

(a) Description of costs	(b) Date amortization begins	(c) Amortizable amount	(d) Code section	(e) Amortization period or percentage	(f) Amortization for this year
42 Amortization of costs that begins during your 2019 tax year (see instructions):					
43 Amortization of costs that began before your 2019 tax year **43**					
44 **Total.** Add amounts in column (f). See the instructions for where to report **44**					

Form **4562** (2019)

GROUP 2:

PROBLEM 16

Form **4797** Department of the Treasury Internal Revenue Service	**Sales of Business Property** (Also Involuntary Conversions and Recapture Amounts Under Sections 179 and 280F(b)(2)) ▶ **Attach to your tax return.** ▶ Go to *www.irs.gov/Form4797* for instructions and the latest information.	OMB No. 1545-0184 2019 Attachment Sequence No. **27**

Name(s) shown on return | Identifying number

1 Enter the gross proceeds from sales or exchanges reported to you for 2019 on Form(s) 1099-B or 1099-S (or substitute statement) that you are including on line 2, 10, or 20. See instructions . . . . | **1**

Part I **Sales or Exchanges of Property Used in a Trade or Business and Involuntary Conversions From Other Than Casualty or Theft—Most Property Held More Than 1 Year** (see instructions)

2	(a) Description of property	(b) Date acquired (mo., day, yr.)	(c) Date sold (mo., day, yr.)	(d) Gross sales price	(e) Depreciation allowed or allowable since acquisition	(f) Cost or other basis, plus improvements and expense of sale	(g) Gain or (loss) Subtract (f) from the sum of (d) and (e)

3 Gain, if any, from Form 4684, line 39 . . . . | **3**

4 Section 1231 gain from installment sales from Form 6252, line 26 or 37 . . . . | **4**

5 Section 1231 gain or (loss) from like-kind exchanges from Form 8824 . . . . | **5**

6 Gain, if any, from line 32, from other than casualty or theft . . . . | **6**

7 Combine lines 2 through 6. Enter the gain or (loss) here and on the appropriate line as follows . . . . . . | **7**

Partnerships and S corporations. Report the gain or (loss) following the instructions for Form 1065, Schedule K, line 10, or Form 1120-S, Schedule K, line 9. Skip lines 8, 9, 11, and 12 below.

Individuals, partners, S corporation shareholders, and all others. If line 7 is zero or a loss, enter the amount from line 7 on line 11 below and skip lines 8 and 9. If line 7 is a gain and you didn't have any prior year section 1231 losses, or they were recaptured in an earlier year, enter the gain from line 7 as a long-term capital gain on the Schedule D filed with your return and skip lines 8, 9, 11, and 12 below.

8 Nonrecaptured net section 1231 losses from prior years. See instructions . . . . | **8**

9 Subtract line 8 from line 7. If zero or less, enter -0-. If line 9 is zero, enter the gain from line 7 on line 12 below. If line 9 is more than zero, enter the amount from line 8 on line 12 below and enter the gain from line 9 as a long-term capital gain on the Schedule D filed with your return. See instructions . . . . | **9**

Part II **Ordinary Gains and Losses** (see instructions)

10 Ordinary gains and losses not included on lines 11 through 16 (include property held 1 year or less):

11 Loss, if any, from line 7 . . . . | **11** ( )

12 Gain, if any, from line 7 or amount from line 8, if applicable . . . . | **12**

13 Gain, if any, from line 31 . . . . | **13**

14 Net gain or (loss) from Form 4684, lines 31 and 38a . . . . | **14**

15 Ordinary gain from installment sales from Form 6252, line 25 or 36 . . . . | **15**

16 Ordinary gain or (loss) from like-kind exchanges from Form 8824 . . . . | **16**

17 Combine lines 10 through 16 . . . . | **17**

18 For all except individual returns, enter the amount from line 17 on the appropriate line of your return and skip lines a and b below. For individual returns, complete lines a and b below.

a If the loss on line 11 includes a loss from Form 4684, line 35, column (b)(ii), enter that part of the loss here. Enter the loss from income-producing property on Schedule A (Form 1040 or Form 1040-SR), line 16. (Do not include any loss on property used as an employee.) Identify as from "Form 4797, line 18a." See instructions . . . . | **18a**

b Redetermine the gain or (loss) on line 17 excluding the loss, if any, on line 18a. Enter here and on Schedule 1 (Form 1040 or Form 1040-SR), Part I, line 4 . . . . | **18b**

For Paperwork Reduction Act Notice, see separate instructions. | Cat. No. 13086I | Form **4797** (2019)

Form 4797 (2019)   Page **2**

Part III   **Gain From Disposition of Property Under Sections 1245, 1250, 1252, 1254, and 1255** (see instructions)

19	(a) Description of section 1245, 1250, 1252, 1254, or 1255 property:	(b) Date acquired (mo., day, yr.)	(c) Date sold (mo., day, yr.)
A			
B			
C			
D			

	These columns relate to the properties on lines 19A through 19D. ▶		Property A	Property B	Property C	Property D
20	Gross sales price (**Note:** See line 1 before completing.)	20				
21	Cost or other basis plus expense of sale	21				
22	Depreciation (or depletion) allowed or allowable	22				
23	Adjusted basis. Subtract line 22 from line 21	23				
24	Total gain. Subtract line 23 from line 20	24				
25	**If section 1245 property:**					
a	Depreciation allowed or allowable from line 22	25a				
b	Enter the **smaller** of line 24 or 25a	25b				
26	**If section 1250 property:** If straight line depreciation was used, enter -0- on line 26g, except for a corporation subject to section 291.					
a	Additional depreciation after 1975. See instructions	26a				
b	Applicable percentage multiplied by the **smaller** of line 24 or line 26a. See instructions.	26b				
c	Subtract line 26a from line 24. If residential rental property **or** line 24 isn't more than line 26a, skip lines 26d and 26e	26c				
d	Additional depreciation after 1969 and before 1976.	26d				
e	Enter the **smaller** of line 26c or 26d	26e				
f	Section 291 amount (corporations only)	26f				
g	Add lines 26b, 26e, and 26f	26g				
27	**If section 1252 property:** Skip this section if you didn't dispose of farmland or if this form is being completed for a partnership.					
a	Soil, water, and land clearing expenses	27a				
b	Line 27a multiplied by applicable percentage. See instructions	27b				
c	Enter the **smaller** of line 24 or 27b	27c				
28	**If section 1254 property:**					
a	Intangible drilling and development costs, expenditures for development of mines and other natural deposits, mining exploration costs, and depletion. See instructions	28a				
b	Enter the **smaller** of line 24 or 28a.	28b				
29	**If section 1255 property:**					
a	Applicable percentage of payments excluded from income under section 126. See instructions	29a				
b	Enter the **smaller** of line 24 or 29a. See instructions	29b				

Summary of Part III Gains. Complete property columns A through D through line 29b before going to line 30.

30	Total gains for all properties. Add property columns A through D, line 24	30	
31	Add property columns A through D, lines 25b, 26g, 27c, 28b, and 29b. Enter here and on line 13	31	
32	Subtract line 31 from line 30. Enter the portion from casualty or theft on Form 4684, line 33. Enter the portion from other than casualty or theft on Form 4797, line 6	32	

Part IV   **Recapture Amounts Under Sections 179 and 280F(b)(2) When Business Use Drops to 50% or Less** (see instructions)

			(a) Section 179	(b) Section 280F(b)(2)
33	Section 179 expense deduction or depreciation allowable in prior years.	33		
34	Recomputed depreciation. See instructions	34		
35	Recapture amount. Subtract line 34 from line 33. See the instructions for where to report	35		

Form **4797** (2019)

Form **6252**	**Installment Sale Income**	OMB No. 1545-0228
Department of the Treasury Internal Revenue Service	▶ **Attach to your tax return.** ▶ **Use a separate form for each sale or other disposition of property on the installment method.** ▶ Go to *www.irs.gov/Form6252* for the latest information.	20**19** Attachment Sequence No. **79**

Name(s) shown on return

Identifying number

1	Description of property ▶				
2a	Date acquired (mm/dd/yyyy) ▶		**b** Date sold (mm/dd/yyyy) ▶		
3	Was the property sold to a related party (see instructions) after May 14, 1980? If "No," skip line 4			☐ Yes	☐ No
4	Was the property you sold to a related party a marketable security? If "Yes," complete Part III. If "No," complete Part III for the year of sale and the 2 years after the year of sale			☐ Yes	☐ No

Part I **Gross Profit and Contract Price.** Complete this part for all years of the installment agreement.

5	Selling price including mortgages and other debts. **Don't** include interest, whether stated or unstated	**5**	
6	Mortgages, debts, and other liabilities the buyer assumed or took the property subject to (see instructions)	**6**	
7	Subtract line 6 from line 5	**7**	
8	Cost or other basis of property sold	**8**	
9	Depreciation allowed or allowable	**9**	
10	Adjusted basis. Subtract line 9 from line 8	**10**	
11	Commissions and other expenses of sale	**11**	
12	Income recapture from Form 4797, Part III (see instructions)	**12**	
13	Add lines 10, 11, and 12	**13**	
14	Subtract line 13 from line 5. If zero or less, **don't** complete the rest of this form (see instructions) . .	**14**	
15	If the property described on line 1 above was your main home, enter the amount of your excluded gain (see instructions). Otherwise, enter -0-	**15**	
16	**Gross profit.** Subtract line 15 from line 14	**16**	
17	Subtract line 13 from line 6. If zero or less, enter -0-	**17**	
18	**Contract price.** Add line 7 and line 17	**18**	

Part II **Installment Sale Income.** Complete this part for all years of the installment agreement.

19	Gross profit percentage (expressed as a decimal amount). Divide line 16 by line 18. (For years after the year of sale, see instructions)	**19**	
20	If this is the year of sale, enter the amount from line 17. Otherwise, enter -0-	**20**	
21	Payments received during year (see instructions). **Don't** include interest, whether stated or unstated .	**21**	
22	Add lines 20 and 21	**22**	
23	Payments received in prior years (see instructions). **Don't** include interest, whether stated or unstated	**23**	
24	**Installment sale income.** Multiply line 22 by line 19	**24**	
25	Enter the part of line 24 that is ordinary income under the recapture rules (see instructions)	**25**	
26	Subtract line 25 from line 24. Enter here and on Schedule D or Form 4797 (see instructions) . . .	**26**	

Part III **Related Party Installment Sale Income. Don't** complete if you received the final payment this tax year.

27	Name, address, and taxpayer identifying number of related party

28	Did the related party resell or dispose of the property ("second disposition") during this tax year?	☐ Yes ☐ No
29	If the answer to question 28 is "Yes," complete lines 30 through 37 below unless one of the following conditions is met. **Check the box that applies.**	
a	☐ The second disposition was more than 2 years after the first disposition (other than dispositions of marketable securities). If this box is checked, enter the date of disposition (mm/dd/yyyy) . . . . ▶	
b	☐ The first disposition was a sale or exchange of stock to the issuing corporation.	
c	☐ The second disposition was an involuntary conversion and the threat of conversion occurred after the first disposition.	
d	☐ The second disposition occurred after the death of the original seller or buyer.	
e	☐ It can be established to the satisfaction of the IRS that tax avoidance wasn't a principal purpose for either of the dispositions. If this box is checked, attach an explanation (see instructions).	

30	Selling price of property sold by related party (see instructions)	**30**	
31	Enter contract price from line 18 for year of first sale	**31**	
32	Enter the **smaller** of line 30 or line 31	**32**	
33	Total payments received by the end of your 2019 tax year (see instructions)	**33**	
34	Subtract line 33 from line 32. If zero or less, enter -0-	**34**	
35	Multiply line 34 by the gross profit percentage on line 19 for year of first sale	**35**	
36	Enter the part of line 35 that is ordinary income under the recapture rules (see instructions)	**36**	
37	Subtract line 36 from line 35. Enter here and on Schedule D or Form 4797 (see instructions) . . .	**37**	

For Paperwork Reduction Act Notice, see page 4.   Cat. No. 13601R   Form **6252** (2019)

DRAFT AS OF JULY 2, 2019 DO NOT FILE

LO 8.7
LO 8.8

18. William sold Section 1245 property for $25,000 in 2019. The property cost $38,500 when it was purchased 5 years ago. The depreciation claimed on the property was $19,200.

a. Calculate the adjusted basis of the property. $_____

b. Calculate the recomputed basis of the property. $_____

c. Calculate the amount of ordinary income under Section 1245. $_____

d. Calculate the Section 1231 gain. $_____

LO 8.9

19. An office machine used by Josie in her accounting business was completely destroyed by fire. The adjusted basis of the machine was $8,000 (original basis of $14,000 less accumulated depreciation of $6,000). The machine was not insured. Calculate the amount and nature of Josie's gain or loss as a result of this casualty.

Amount of gain or loss $_____

Nature   _____

LO 8.11

20. Carey exchanges land for other land in a qualifying like-kind exchange. Carey's basis in the land given up is $115,000, and the property has a fair market value of $150,000. In exchange for her property, Carey receives land with a fair market value of $100,000 and cash of $10,000. In addition, the other party to the exchange assumes a mortgage loan on Carey's property of $40,000.

a. Calculate Carey's recognized gain, if any, on the exchange. $_____

b. Calculate Carey's basis in the property received. $_____

LO 8.12

21. Teresa's manufacturing plant is destroyed by fire. The plant has an adjusted basis of $270,000, and Teresa receives insurance proceeds of $410,000 for the loss. Teresa reinvests $420,000 in a replacement plant within 2 years of receiving the insurance proceeds.

a. Calculate Teresa's recognized gain if she elects to utilize the involuntary conversion provision. $_____

b. Calculate Teresa's basis in the new plant. $_____

GROUP 3:
WRITING ASSIGNMENT

RESEARCH

1. Your supervisor has asked you to research the following situation concerning Owen and Lisa Cordoncillo. Owen and Lisa are brother and sister. In May 2019, Owen and Lisa exchange land they both held separately for investment. Lisa gives up a 2 acre property in Texas with an adjusted basis of $2,000 and a fair market value of $6,000. In return for this property, Lisa receives from Owen a 1 acre property in Arkansas with a fair market value of $5,500 and cash of $500. Owen's adjusted basis in the land he exchanges is $2,500. In March 2020, Owen sells the Texas land to a third party for $5,800.

Required: Go to the IRS website (**www.irs.gov**). Locate and review Publication 544, Chapter 1, Nontaxable Exchanges. Write a file memorandum stating the amount of Owen and Lisa's gain recognition for 2019. Also determine the effect, if any, of the subsequent sale in 2020. (An example of a file memorandum is available at the website for this textbook located at **www.cengage.com.**)

GROUP 4:
COMPREHENSIVE PROBLEMS

1. Trish Himple owns a retail family clothing store. Her store is located at 4321 Heather Drive, Henderson, NV 89002. Her employer identification number is 95-1234321 and her Social Security number is 123-45-6789. Trish keeps her books on an accrual basis. The income and expenses for the year are:

Gross sales		$352,000
Returns and allowances		4,000
Expenses:		
Beginning inventory (at cost)	$ 85,000	
Add: purchases	101,000	
Cost of goods available for sale	186,000	
Less: ending inventory (at cost)	75,000	
Cost of goods sold		$111,000
Rent		24,200
Insurance		1,800
Legal and accounting fees		5,600
Payroll		56,430
Payroll taxes		4,400
Utilities		2,100
Office supplies		750
Advertising		6,200

Trish's bookkeeper has provided the following *book-basis* fixed asset rollforward:

Himple Retail
Fixed Asset Rollforward
12/31/2019
(book basis)

ASSET	IN SERVICE	DEPR METHOD	LIFE	COST BASIS	2017 DEPR	2018 DEPR	2019 DEPR	ACCUM DEPR	NET BOOK VALUE
CASH REGISTER	2/15/2017	SL	5	9,900.00	1,815.00	1,980.00	1,980.00	5,775.00	4,125.00
2017 TOTAL ADDITIONS				9,900.00	1,815.00	1,980.00	1,980.00	5,775.00	4,125.00
RETAIL FIXTURES	10/12/2018	SL	7	4,750.00		169.64	678.57	848.21	3,901.79
FURNITURE	10/12/2018	SL	7	3,900.00		139.29	557.14	696.43	3,203.57
2018 TOTAL ADDITIONS				8,650.00	-	308.93	1,235.71	1,544.64	7,105.36
TOTAL				18,550.00	1,815.00	2,288.93	3,215.71	7,319.64	11,230.36
DELIVERY TRUCK	6/1/2019	SL	5	37,500.00			4,375.00	4,375.00	33,125.00
DESK AND CABINETRY	6/1/2019	SL	7	11,900.00			991.67	991.67	10,908.33
COMPUTER	6/1/2019	SL	5	2,800.00			326.67	326.67	2,473.33
2019 TOTAL ADDITIONS				52,200.00	-	-	5,693.34	5,693.34	46,506.66
TOTAL				70,750.00	1,815.00	2,288.93	8,909.05	13,012.98	57,737.02

The truck is not considered a passenger automobile for purposes of the luxury automobile limitations.

Trish also has a qualified home office of 250 sq. ft. Her home is 2,500 sq. ft. Her 2014 purchase price and basis in the home, not including land, is $100,000 (the home's market value is $150,000). She incurred the following costs in 2019 related to the entire home:

Utilities	$2,800
Cleaning	900
Insurance	1,100
Property taxes	2,000

Required: For tax purposes, Trish elected out of bonus depreciation in all years except 2019. She did not elect immediate expensing in any year. The tax lives of the assets are the same as the book lives shown in the fixed asset schedule above. Complete Trish's Schedule C, Form 8829, and Form 4562 (as necessary). Make realistic assumptions about any missing data.

2. Lisa Kohl (birthdate 02/14/1953) is an unmarried high school principal. Lisa received the following tax documents:

a Employee's social security number 467-98-9784	OMB No. 1545-0008	Safe, accurate, FAST! Use	IRS e-file	Visit the IRS website at www.irs.gov/efile

b Employer identification number (EIN) 56-1357924	1 Wages, tips, other compensation 56,640.00	2 Federal income tax withheld 6,100.00

c Employer's name, address, and ZIP code Shawnee Mission School District 8200 W. 71st Street Shawnee Mission, KS 66204	3 Social security wages 59,000.00	4 Social security tax withheld 3,658.00
	5 Medicare wages and tips 59,000.00	6 Medicare tax withheld 855.50
	7 Social security tips	8 Allocated tips

d Control number	9	10 Dependent care benefits

e Employee's first name and initial Last name Suff. Lisa Kohl 212 Quivira Road Overland Park, KS 66210	11 Nonqualified plans	12a See instructions for box 12 E 2,360.00
	13 Statutory employee ☐ Retirement plan ☒ Third-party sick pay ☐	12b DD 9,800.00
	14 Other	12c
		12d

f Employee's address and ZIP code						
15 State Employer's state ID number KS	16 State wages, tips, etc. 56,640.00	17 State income tax 1,150.00	18 Local wages, tips, etc.	19 Local income tax	20 Locality name

Form **W-2** Wage and Tax Statement   **2019**   Department of the Treasury—Internal Revenue Service

Copy B—To Be Filed With Employee's **FEDERAL** Tax Return.
This information is being furnished to the Internal Revenue Service.

☐ CORRECTED (if checked)

PAYER'S name, street address, city or town, state or province, country, ZIP or foreign postal code, and telephone no. Olanthe National Bank 1240 E. Sante Fe Street Olanthe, KS 66061	Payer's RTN (optional)	OMB No. 1545-0112	**Interest Income**
	1 Interest income $ 203.88	20**19** Form **1099-INT**	

	2 Early withdrawal penalty $	Copy B

PAYER'S TIN 44-1352469	RECIPIENT'S TIN 467-98-9784	3 Interest on U.S. Savings Bonds and Treas. obligations $	For Recipient

RECIPIENT'S name Lisa Kohl	4 Federal income tax withheld $	5 Investment expenses $	This is important tax information and is being furnished to the IRS. If you are required to file a return, a negligence penalty or other sanction may be imposed on you if this income is taxable and the IRS determines that it has not been reported.
	6 Foreign tax paid $	7 Foreign country or U.S. possession	
Street address (including apt. no.) 212 Quivira Rd.	8 Tax-exempt interest $	9 Specified private activity bond interest $	
City or town, state or province, country, and ZIP or foreign postal code Overland Park, KS 66210	10 Market discount $	11 Bond premium $	
	FATCA filing requirement ☐	12 Bond premium on Treasury obligations $	13 Bond premium on tax-exempt bond $	
Account number (see instructions)	14 Tax-exempt and tax credit bond CUSIP no.	15 State	16 State identification no.	17 State tax withheld $ $

Form **1099-INT**   (keep for your records)   www.irs.gov/Form1099INT   Department of the Treasury - Internal Revenue Service

☐ CORRECTED (if checked)

PAYER'S name, street address, city or town, state or province, country, ZIP or foreign postal code, and telephone no. Johnson Corporation 100 E. 49th Street New York, NY 10017	**1a** Total ordinary dividends $ 4,122.40	OMB No. 1545-0110 2019 Form **1099-DIV**	**Dividends and Distributions**
	1b Qualified dividends $ 4,122.40		

PAYER'S TIN 17-2468135	RECIPIENT'S TIN 467-98-9784	**2a** Total capital gain distr. $	**2b** Unrecap. Sec. 1250 gain $	**Copy B** **For Recipient**
		2c Section 1202 gain $	**2d** Collectibles (28%) gain $	

RECIPIENT'S name Lisa Kohl	**3** Nondividend distributions $	**4** Federal income tax withheld $ 0.00	This is important tax information and is being furnished to the IRS. If you are required to file a return, a negligence penalty or other sanction may be imposed on you if this income is taxable and the IRS determines that it has not been reported.
Street address (including apt. no.) 212 Quivira Road	**5** Section 199A dividends $	**6** Investment expenses $	
	7 Foreign tax paid $	**8** Foreign country or U.S. possession	
City or town, state or province, country, and ZIP or foreign postal code Overland Park, KS 66210	**9** Cash liquidation distributions $	**10** Noncash liquidation distributions $	
FATCA filing requirement ☐	**11** Exempt-interest dividends $	**12** Specified private activity bond interest dividends $	
Account number (see instructions)	**13** State **14** State identification no.	**15** State tax withheld $ $	

Form **1099-DIV**   (keep for your records)   www.irs.gov/Form1099DIV   Department of the Treasury - Internal Revenue Service

During the year, Lisa paid the following amounts (all of which can be substantiated):

Home mortgage interest reported on Form 1098 (not shown)	$9,540
KS state income tax payment for 2018	$475
MasterCard interest	550
Life insurance (whole life policy)	750
Property taxes on personal residence	1,525
Blue Cross medical insurance premiums	250
Other medical expenses	780
Income tax preparation fee	300
Charitable contributions (in cash)	750

Lisa's sole stock transaction was reported to her on a Form 1099-B:

☐ CORRECTED (if checked)

PAYER'S name, street address, city or town, state or province, country, ZIP or foreign postal code, and telephone no. Big Brokerage Company 123 Wall Street New York, NY 10014	Applicable checkbox on Form 8949	OMB No. 1545-0715 2019 Form **1099-B**	**Proceeds From Broker and Barter Exchange Transactions**
	1a Description of property (Example: 100 sh. XYZ Co.) 100 shs. Johnson Corp.		

PAYER'S TIN 11-0010011	RECIPIENT'S TIN 467-98-9784	**1b** Date acquired 12/13/2018	**1c** Date sold or disposed 11/05/2019	**Copy B** **For Recipient**
		1d Proceeds $ 17,200.00	**1e** Cost or other basis $ 35,600.00	
		1f Accrued market discount $	**1g** Wash sale loss disallowed $	

RECIPIENT'S name Lisa Kohl	**2** Short-term gain or loss ☐ Long-term gain or loss ☐ Ordinary ☐	**3** If checked, proceeds from: Collectibles ☐ QOF ☐	This is important tax information and is being furnished to the IRS. If you are required to file a return, a negligence penalty or other sanction may be imposed on you if this income is taxable and the IRS determines that it has not been reported.
Street address (including apt. no.) 212 Quivira Rd.	**4** Federal income tax withheld $	**5** If checked, noncovered security ☐	
	6 Reported to IRS: Gross proceeds ☐ Net proceeds ☒	**7** If checked, loss is not allowed based on amount in 1d ☐	
City or town, state or province, country, and ZIP or foreign postal code Overland Park, KS 66210	**8** Profit or (loss) realized in 2019 on closed contracts $	**9** Unrealized profit or (loss) on open contracts—12/31/2018 $	
Account number (see instructions)			
CUSIP number	FATCA filing requirement ☐	**10** Unrealized profit or (loss) on open contracts—12/31/2019 $	**11** Aggregate profit or (loss) on contracts $	
14 State name	**15** State identification no. **16** State tax withheld $ $	**12** If checked, basis reported to IRS ☒	**13** Bartering $	

Form **1099-B**   (Keep for your records)   www.irs.gov/Form1099B   Department of the Treasury - Internal Revenue Service

On January 28, 2019, Lisa sold land for $175,000 (basis to Lisa of $130,000). The land was purchased 6 years ago as an investment. She received $25,000 as a down payment and the buyer's 10-year note for $150,000. The note is payable at the rate of $15,000 per year plus 8 percent interest. On January 28, 2020, the first of the ten principal and interest payments is due.

Lisa also helps support her father, Jay Hawke, who lives in a nearby senior facility. Jay's Social Security number is 433-33-2121. Lisa provides over one-half of Jay's support but Jay also has a pension that paid him income of $14,000 in 2019. His Social Security benefits were $3,200 in 2019.

Required: Complete Lisa's federal tax return for 2019. Use Form 1040-SR, Schedule A, Schedule B, Schedule D, Form 8949, the Qualified Dividends and Capital Gain Tax Worksheet, and Form 6252 as needed to complete this tax return. Make realistic assumptions about any missing data.

GROUP 5:
CUMULATIVE SOFTWARE PROBLEM

1. The following information is available for the Albert and Allison Gaytor family in addition to that provided in Chapters 1–7.

On August 14, 2019, Allison purchased the building where her store is located. She paid $335,000 for the building (including $100,000 for the land it is located on). Allison's store is the only business in the building. The depreciation on the store needs to be reflected on Schedule C of the business.

Required: Combine this new information about the Gaytor family with the information from Chapters 1 to 7 and complete a revised 2019 tax return for Albert and Allison. This completes the Group 5 multichapter case.

SCHEDULE C
(Form 1040 or 1040-SR)

Department of the Treasury
Internal Revenue Service (99)

Profit or Loss From Business
(Sole Proprietorship)

► Go to *www.irs.gov/ScheduleC* for instructions and the latest information.
► **Attach to Form 1040, 1040-SR, 1040-NR, or 1041; partnerships generally must file Form 1065.**

OMB No. 1545-0074

2019

Attachment
Sequence No. **09**

Name of proprietor

Social security number (SSN)

A	Principal business or profession, including product or service (see instructions)	**B Enter code from instructions** ►
C	Business name. If no separate business name, leave blank.	**D Employer ID number (EIN)** (see instr.)
E	Business address (including suite or room no.) ►	
	City, town or post office, state, and ZIP code	

F Accounting method: **(1)** ☐ Cash **(2)** ☐ Accrual **(3)** ☐ Other (specify) ►

G Did you "materially participate" in the operation of this business during 2019? If "No," see instructions for limit on losses . ☐ **Yes** ☐ No

H If you started or acquired this business during 2019, check here . . . . ► ☐

I Did you make any payments in 2019 that would require you to file Form(s) 1099? (see instructions) . . . . ☐ **Yes** ☐ No

J If "Yes," did you or will you file required Forms 1099? . . . . ☐ **Yes** ☐ No

Part I Income

1	Gross receipts or sales. See instructions for line 1 and check the box if this income was reported to you on Form W-2 and the "Statutory employee" box on that form was checked . . . . ► ☐	**1**	
2	Returns and allowances	**2**	
3	Subtract line 2 from line 1	**3**	
4	Cost of goods sold (from line 42)	**4**	
5	**Gross profit.** Subtract line 4 from line 3	**5**	
6	Other income, including federal and state gasoline or fuel tax credit or refund (see instructions) . . .	**6**	
7	**Gross income.** Add lines 5 and 6 . . . . ►	**7**	

Part II Expenses. Enter expenses for business use of your home **only** on line 30.

8	Advertising	**8**		**18**	Office expense (see instructions)	**18**	
9	Car and truck expenses (see instructions)	**9**		**19**	Pension and profit-sharing plans .	**19**	
				20	Rent or lease (see instructions):		
10	Commissions and fees .	**10**		**a**	Vehicles, machinery, and equipment	**20a**	
11	Contract labor (see instructions)	**11**		**b**	Other business property . . .	**20b**	
12	Depletion	**12**		**21**	Repairs and maintenance . . .	**21**	
13	Depreciation and section 179 expense deduction (not included in Part III) (see instructions)	**13**		**22**	Supplies (not included in Part III) .	**22**	
				23	Taxes and licenses	**23**	
				24	Travel and meals:		
14	Employee benefit programs (other than on line 19) . .	**14**		**a**	Travel	**24a**	
15	Insurance (other than health)	**15**		**b**	Deductible meals (see instructions)	**24b**	
16	Interest (see instructions):			**25**	Utilities	**25**	
a	Mortgage (paid to banks, etc.)	**16a**		**26**	Wages (less employment credits) .	**26**	
b	Other	**16b**		**27a**	Other expenses (from line 48) . .	**27a**	
17	Legal and professional services	**17**		**b**	**Reserved for future use** . . .	**27b**	

28	**Total expenses** before expenses for business use of home. Add lines 8 through 27a . . . . . . ►	**28**	
29	Tentative profit or (loss). Subtract line 28 from line 7	**29**	
30	Expenses for business use of your home. Do not report these expenses elsewhere. Attach Form 8829 unless using the simplified method (see instructions). **Simplified method filers only:** enter the total square footage of: (a) your home: _____ and (b) the part of your home used for business: _____ . Use the Simplified Method Worksheet in the instructions to figure the amount to enter on line 30	**30**	
31	**Net profit or (loss).** Subtract line 30 from line 29. • If a profit, enter on both **Schedule 1 (Form 1040 or 1040-SR), line 3** (or **Form 1040-NR, line 13**) and on **Schedule SE, line 2**. (If you checked the box on line 1, see instructions). Estates and trusts, enter on **Form 1041, line 3.** • If a loss, you **must** go to line 32.	**31**	
32	If you have a loss, check the box that describes your investment in this activity (see instructions). • If you checked 32a, enter the loss on both **Schedule 1 (Form 1040 or 1040-SR), line 3** (or **Form 1040-NR, line 13**) and on **Schedule SE, line 2.** (If you checked the box on line 1, see the line 31 instructions). Estates and trusts, enter on **Form 1041, line 3.** • If you checked 32b, you **must** attach **Form 6198.** Your loss may be limited.	**32a** ☐ All investment is at risk. **32b** ☐ Some investment is not at risk.	

For Paperwork Reduction Act Notice, see the separate instructions. Cat. No. 11334P Schedule C (Form 1040 or 1040-SR) 2019

Schedule C (Form 1040 or 1040-SR) 2019   Page **2**

Part III   **Cost of Goods Sold** (see instructions)

33 Method(s) used to
    value closing inventory: **a** ☐ Cost   **b** ☐ Lower of cost or market   **c** ☐ Other (attach explanation)

34 Was there any change in determining quantities, costs, or valuations between opening and closing inventory?
    If "Yes," attach explanation . . . . ☐ Yes   ☐ No

35 Inventory at beginning of year. If different from last year's closing inventory, attach explanation . . . | 35 |

36 Purchases less cost of items withdrawn for personal use . . . . | 36 |

37 Cost of labor. Do not include any amounts paid to yourself . . . . | 37 |

38 Materials and supplies . . . . | 38 |

39 Other costs . . . . | 39 |

40 Add lines 35 through 39 . . . . | 40 |

41 Inventory at end of year . . . . | 41 |

42 **Cost of goods sold.** Subtract line 41 from line 40. Enter the result here and on line 4 . . . . . . | 42 |

Part IV   **Information on Your Vehicle.** Complete this part **only** if you are claiming car or truck expenses on line 9 and are not required to file Form 4562 for this business. See the instructions for line 13 to find out if you must file Form 4562.

43 When did you place your vehicle in service for business purposes? (month, day, year) ▶ _____ / _____ / _____

44 Of the total number of miles you drove your vehicle during 2019, enter the number of miles you used your vehicle for:

    a Business _____ **b** Commuting (see instructions) _____ **c** Other _____

45 Was your vehicle available for personal use during off-duty hours? . . . . ☐ Yes   ☐ No

46 Do you (or your spouse) have another vehicle available for personal use?. . . . . ☐ Yes   ☐ No

47a Do you have evidence to support your deduction? . . . . ☐ Yes   ☐ No

  b If "Yes," is the evidence written? . . . . ☐ Yes   ☐ No

Part V   **Other Expenses.** List below business expenses not included on lines 8–26 or line 30.

----

48 **Total other expenses.** Enter here and on line 27a . . . . | 48 |

Schedule C (Form 1040 or 1040-SR) 2019

Form **4562**	**Depreciation and Amortization** **(Including Information on Listed Property)** ▶ Attach to your tax return. ▶ Go to *www.irs.gov/Form4562* for instructions and the latest information.	OMB No. 1545-0172 **2019** Attachment Sequence No. **179**
Department of the Treasury Internal Revenue Service (99)		

Name(s) shown on return	Business or activity to which this form relates	Identifying number

Part I **Election To Expense Certain Property Under Section 179**
Note: If you have any listed property, complete Part V before you complete Part I.

1	Maximum amount (see instructions)	**1**
2	Total cost of section 179 property placed in service (see instructions)	**2**
3	Threshold cost of section 179 property before reduction in limitation (see instructions)	**3**
4	Reduction in limitation. Subtract line 3 from line 2. If zero or less, enter -0-	**4**
5	Dollar limitation for tax year. Subtract line 4 from line 1. If zero or less, enter -0-. If married filing separately, see instructions	**5**

6	(a) Description of property	(b) Cost (business use only)	(c) Elected cost

7	Listed property. Enter the amount from line 29	**7**	
8	Total elected cost of section 179 property. Add amounts in column (c), lines 6 and 7	**8**
9	Tentative deduction. Enter the **smaller** of line 5 or line 8	**9**
10	Carryover of disallowed deduction from line 13 of your 2018 Form 4562	**10**
11	Business income limitation. Enter the smaller of business income (not less than zero) or line 5. See instructions	**11**
12	Section 179 expense deduction. Add lines 9 and 10, but don't enter more than line 11	**12**
13	Carryover of disallowed deduction to 2020. Add lines 9 and 10, less line 12 ▶	**13**	

Note: Don't use Part II or Part III below for listed property. Instead, use Part V.

Part II **Special Depreciation Allowance and Other Depreciation (Don't** include listed property. See instructions.)

14	Special depreciation allowance for qualified property (other than listed property) placed in service during the tax year. See instructions	**14**
15	Property subject to section 168(f)(1) election	**15**
16	Other depreciation (including ACRS)	**16**

Part III **MACRS Depreciation (Don't** include listed property. See instructions.)

Section A

17	MACRS deductions for assets placed in service in tax years beginning before 2019	**17**
18	If you are electing to group any assets placed in service during the tax year into one or more general asset accounts, check here . . . . ▶ ☐	

Section B—Assets Placed in Service During 2019 Tax Year Using the General Depreciation System

(a) Classification of property	(b) Month and year placed in service	(c) Basis for depreciation (business/investment use only—see instructions)	(d) Recovery period	(e) Convention	(f) Method	(g) Depreciation deduction
19a 3-year property						
b 5-year property						
c 7-year property						
d 10-year property						
e 15-year property						
f 20-year property						
g 25-year property			25 yrs.		S/L	
h Residential rental property			27.5 yrs.	MM	S/L	
			27.5 yrs.	MM	S/L	
i Nonresidential real property			39 yrs.	MM	S/L	
				MM	S/L	

Section C—Assets Placed in Service During 2019 Tax Year Using the Alternative Depreciation System

20a Class life					S/L	
b 12-year			12 yrs.		S/L	
c 30-year			30 yrs.	MM	S/L	
d 40-year			40 yrs.	MM	S/L	

Part IV **Summary** (See instructions.)

21	Listed property. Enter amount from line 28	**21**
22	**Total.** Add amounts from line 12, lines 14 through 17, lines 19 and 20 in column (g), and line 21. Enter here and on the appropriate lines of your return. Partnerships and S corporations—see instructions .	**22**
23	For assets shown above and placed in service during the current year, enter the portion of the basis attributable to section 263A costs	**23**	

For Paperwork Reduction Act Notice, see separate instructions. Cat. No. 12906N Form **4562** (2019)

Form 4562 (2019)   Page **2**

Part V **Listed Property** (Include automobiles, certain other vehicles, certain aircraft, and property used for entertainment, recreation, or amusement.)

Note: For any vehicle for which you are using the standard mileage rate or deducting lease expense, complete **only** 24a, 24b, columns (a) through (c) of Section A, all of Section B, and Section C if applicable.

Section A—Depreciation and Other Information (Caution: See the instructions for limits for passenger automobiles.**)**

24a Do you have evidence to support the business/investment use claimed? ☐ **Yes** ☐ **No**   **24b** If "Yes," is the evidence written? ☐ **Yes** ☐ **No**

(a) Type of property (list vehicles first)	(b) Date placed in service	(c) Business/investment use percentage	(d) Cost or other basis	(e) Basis for depreciation (business/investment use only)	(f) Recovery period	(g) Method/Convention	(h) Depreciation deduction	(i) Elected section 179 cost
25 Special depreciation allowance for qualified listed property placed in service during the tax year and used more than 50% in a qualified business use. See instructions .				**25**				
26 Property used more than 50% in a qualified business use:								
		%						
		%						
		%						
27 Property used 50% or less in a qualified business use:								
		%				S/L –		
		%				S/L –		
		%				S/L –		
28 Add amounts in column (h), lines 25 through 27. Enter here and on line 21, page 1 .						**28**		
29 Add amounts in column (i), line 26. Enter here and on line 7, page 1								**29**

Section B—Information on Use of Vehicles

Complete this section for vehicles used by a sole proprietor, partner, or other "more than 5% owner," or related person. If you provided vehicles to your employees, first answer the questions in Section C to see if you meet an exception to completing this section for those vehicles.

		(a) Vehicle 1		(b) Vehicle 2		(c) Vehicle 3		(d) Vehicle 4		(e) Vehicle 5		(f) Vehicle 6	
30	Total business/investment miles driven during the year (**don't** include commuting miles) .												
31	Total commuting miles driven during the year												
32	Total other personal (noncommuting) miles driven												
33	Total miles driven during the year. Add lines 30 through 32												
34	Was the vehicle available for personal use during off-duty hours?	Yes	No	Yes	No	Yes	No	Yes	No	Yes	No	Yes	No
35	Was the vehicle used primarily by a more than 5% owner or related person? . .												
36	Is another vehicle available for personal use?												

Section C—Questions for Employers Who Provide Vehicles for Use by Their Employees

Answer these questions to determine if you meet an exception to completing Section B for vehicles used by employees who **aren't** more than 5% owners or related persons. See instructions.

		Yes	No
37	Do you maintain a written policy statement that prohibits all personal use of vehicles, including commuting, by your employees?		
38	Do you maintain a written policy statement that prohibits personal use of vehicles, except commuting, by your employees? See the instructions for vehicles used by corporate officers, directors, or 1% or more owners . .		
39	Do you treat all use of vehicles by employees as personal use?		
40	Do you provide more than five vehicles to your employees, obtain information from your employees about the use of the vehicles, and retain the information received?		
41	Do you meet the requirements concerning qualified automobile demonstration use? See instructions.		

Note: If your answer to 37, 38, 39, 40, or 41 is "Yes," don't complete Section B for the covered vehicles.

Part VI **Amortization**

(a) Description of costs	(b) Date amortization begins	(c) Amortizable amount	(d) Code section	(e) Amortization period or percentage	(f) Amortization for this year
42 Amortization of costs that begins during your 2019 tax year (see instructions):					
43 Amortization of costs that began before your 2019 tax year			**43**		
44 **Total.** Add amounts in column (f). See the instructions for where to report			**44**		

Form **4562** (2019)

Form 8829

Department of the Treasury
Internal Revenue Service (99)

Expenses for Business Use of Your Home

▶ **File only with Schedule C (Form 1040 or 1040-SR). Use a separate Form 8829 for each home you used for business during the year.**
▶ Go to *www.irs.gov/Form8829* for instructions and the latest information.

OMB No. 1545-0074

2019

Attachment
Sequence No. **176**

Name(s) of proprietor(s)

Your social security number

Part I — Part of Your Home Used for Business

1	Area used regularly and exclusively for business, regularly for daycare, or for storage of inventory or product samples (see instructions)	1	
2	Total area of home	2	
3	Divide line 1 by line 2. Enter the result as a percentage	3	%

For daycare facilities not used exclusively for business, go to line 4. All others, go to line 7.

4	Multiply days used for daycare during year by hours used per day	4		hr.
5	If you started or stopped using your home for daycare during the year, see instructions; otherwise, enter 8,760	5		hr.
6	Divide line 4 by line 5. Enter the result as a decimal amount	6		
7	Business percentage. For daycare facilities not used exclusively for business, multiply line 6 by line 3 (enter the result as a percentage). All others, enter the amount from line 3 ▶	7		%

Part II — Figure Your Allowable Deduction

8	Enter the amount from Schedule C, line 29, **plus** any gain derived from the business use of your home, **minus** any loss from the trade or business not derived from the business use of your home (see instructions)	8	

See instructions for columns (a) and (b) before completing lines 9–22.

		(a) Direct expenses	(b) Indirect expenses	
9	Casualty losses (see instructions)	9		
10	Deductible mortgage interest (see instructions)	10		
11	Real estate taxes (see instructions)	11		
12	Add lines 9, 10, and 11	12		
13	Multiply line 12, column (b), by line 7	13		
14	Add line 12, column (a), and line 13			14
15	Subtract line 14 from line 8. If zero or less, enter -0-			15
16	Excess mortgage interest (see instructions)	16		
17	Excess real estate taxes (see instructions)	17		
18	Insurance	18		
19	Rent	19		
20	Repairs and maintenance	20		
21	Utilities	21		
22	Other expenses (see instructions)	22		
23	Add lines 16 through 22	23		
24	Multiply line 23, column (b), by line 7	24		
25	Carryover of prior year operating expenses (see instructions)	25		
26	Add line 23, column (a), line 24, and line 25			26
27	Allowable operating expenses. Enter the **smaller** of line 15 or line 26			27
28	Limit on excess casualty losses and depreciation. Subtract line 27 from line 15			28
29	Excess casualty losses (see instructions)	29		
30	Depreciation of your home from line 42 below	30		
31	Carryover of prior year excess casualty losses and depreciation (see instructions)	31		
32	Add lines 29 through 31			32
33	Allowable excess casualty losses and depreciation. Enter the **smaller** of line 28 or line 32			33
34	Add lines 14, 27, and 33			34
35	Casualty loss portion, if any, from lines 14 and 33. Carry amount to **Form 4684** (see instructions)			35
36	**Allowable expenses for business use of your home.** Subtract line 35 from line 34. Enter here and on Schedule C, line 30. If your home was used for more than one business, see instructions ▶			36

Part III — Depreciation of Your Home

37	Enter the **smaller** of your home's adjusted basis or its fair market value (see instructions)	37	
38	Value of land included on line 37	38	
39	Basis of building. Subtract line 38 from line 37	39	
40	Business basis of building. Multiply line 39 by line 7	40	
41	Depreciation percentage (see instructions)	41	%
42	Depreciation allowable (see instructions). Multiply line 40 by line 41. Enter here and on line 30 above	42	

Part IV — Carryover of Unallowed Expenses to 2020

43	Operating expenses. Subtract line 27 from line 26. If less than zero, enter -0-	43	
44	Excess casualty losses and depreciation. Subtract line 33 from line 32. If less than zero, enter -0-	44	

For Paperwork Reduction Act Notice, see your tax return instructions.   Cat. No. 13232M   Form **8829** (2019)

Form **1040-SR** Department of the Treasury—Internal Revenue Service (99) | **2019** | OMB No. 1545-0074 | IRS Use Only—Do not write or staple in this space.
U.S. Tax Return for Seniors

Filing Status
Check only one box.

☐ Single   ☐ Married filing jointly   ☐ Married filing separately (MFS)
☐ Head of household (HOH)   ☐ Qualifying widow(er) (QW)

If you checked the MFS box, enter the name of spouse. If you checked the HOH or QW box, enter the child's name if the qualifying person is a child but not your dependent. ▶

Your first name and middle initial | Last name | Your social security number

If joint return, spouse's first name and middle initial | Last name | Spouse's social security number

Home address (number and street). If you have a P.O. box, see instructions. | Apt. no. | **Presidential Election Campaign**
Check here if you, or your spouse if filing jointly, want $3 to go to this fund. Checking a box below will not change your tax or refund. ☐ You ☐ Spouse

City, town or post office, state, and ZIP code. If you have a foreign address, also complete spaces below (see instructions).

Foreign country name | Foreign province/state/county | Foreign postal code | If more than four dependents, see inst. and ✓ here ▶ ☐

Standard Deduction
Someone can claim: ☐ You as a dependent ☐ Your spouse as a dependent
☐ Spouse itemizes on a separate return or you were a dual-status alien

Age/Blindness
You: ☐ Were born before January 2, 1955 ☐ Are blind
Spouse: ☐ Was born before January 2, 1955 ☐ Is blind

Dependents (see instructions):

(1) First name Last name	(2) Social security number	(3) Relationship to you	(4) ✓ if qualifies for (see inst.):	
			Child tax credit	Credit for other dependents
			☐	☐
			☐	☐
			☐	☐
			☐	☐

Attach Schedule B if required.

1	Wages, salaries, tips, etc. Attach Form(s) W-2			**1**	
2a	Tax-exempt interest . .	**2a**	**b** Taxable interest . . .	**2b**	
3a	Qualified dividends . . .	**3a**	**b** Ordinary dividends . .	**3b**	
4a	IRA distributions	**4a**	**b** Taxable amount . . .	**4b**	
c	Pensions and annuities .	**4c**	**d** Taxable amount . . .	**4d**	
5a	Social security benefits . .	**5a**	**b** Taxable amount . . .	**5b**	
6	Capital gain or (loss). Attach Schedule D if required. If not required, check here . ▶ ☐			**6**	
7a	Other income from Schedule 1, line 9			**7a**	
b	Add lines 1, 2b, 3b, 4b, 4d, 5b, 6, and 7a. This is your **total income** . . . . ▶			**7b**	
8a	Adjustments to income from Schedule 1, line 22			**8a**	
b	Subtract line 8a from line 7b. This is your **adjusted gross income** . . . . ▶			**8b**	

Standard Deduction
See *Standard Deduction Chart* below.

9	**Standard deduction or itemized deductions** (from Schedule A)	**9**		
10	Qualified business income deduction. Attach Form 8995 or Form 8995-A	**10**		
11a	Add lines 9 and 10			**11a**
b	**Taxable income.** Subtract line 11a from line 8b			**11b**

Standard Deduction Chart

Don't use this chart if someone can claim you (or your spouse if filing jointly) as a dependent, your spouse itemizes on a separate return, or you were a dual-status alien. Instead, see instructions.

Add the number of boxes checked in the "Age/Blindness" section of *Standard Deduction* . . . . ▶

IF your filing status is. . .	AND the number of boxes checked is. . .	THEN your standard deduction is. . .	IF your filing status is. . .	AND the number of boxes checked is. . .	THEN your standard deduction is. . .
Single	0	$12,200	Head of household	0	$18,350
	1	13,850		1	20,000
	2	15,500		2	21,650
Married filing jointly or Qualifying widow(er)	0	24,400	Married filing separately	0	12,200
	1	25,700		1	13,500
	2	27,000		2	14,800
	3	28,300		3	16,100
	4	29,600		4	17,400

For Disclosure, Privacy Act, and Paperwork Reduction Act Notice, see separate instructions. | Cat. No. 71930F | Form **1040-SR** (2019)

DRAFT AS OF July 11, 2019 DO NOT FILE

Form 1040-SR (2019)   Page **2**

12a	**Tax** (see instructions). Check if any from:			
	1 ☐ Form(s) 8814 2 ☐ Form 4972 3 ☐ _____	**12a**		
b	Add Schedule 2, line 3, and line 12a and enter the total . . . . ▶		**12b**	
13a	Child tax credit or credit for other dependents	**13a**		
b	Add Schedule 3, line 7, and line 13a and enter the total . . . . ▶		**13b**	
14	Subtract line 13b from line 12b. If zero or less, enter -0-		**14**	
15	Other taxes, including self-employment tax, from Schedule 2, line 10 . .		**15**	
16	Add lines 14 and 15. This is your **total tax** . . . . ▶		**16**	
17	Federal income tax withheld from Forms W-2 and 1099		**17**	
18	Other payments and refundable credits:			
a	Earned income credit (EIC)	**18a**		
b	Additional child tax credit. Attach Schedule 8812 . . .	**18b**		
c	American opportunity credit from Form 8863, line 8 . . .	**18c**		
d	Schedule 3, line 14	**18d**		
e	Add lines 18a through 18d. These are your **total other payments and refundable credits** ▶		**18e**	
19	Add lines 17 and 18e. These are your **total payments** . . . . ▶		**19**	

• If you have a qualifying child, attach Sch. EIC.
• If you have nontaxable combat pay, see instructions.

Refund	**20**	If line 19 is more than line 16, subtract line 16 from line 19. This is the amount you **overpaid**	**20**
	21a	Amount of line 20 you want **refunded to you.** If Form 8888 is attached, check here ▶ ☐	**21a**
Direct deposit? ▶ See instructions. ▶	**b**	Routing number ⎥⎥⎥⎥⎥⎥⎥⎥⎥ ▶ **c** Type: ☐ Checking ☐ Savings	
	d	Account number ⎥⎥⎥⎥⎥⎥⎥⎥⎥⎥⎥⎥⎥⎥⎥⎥	
	22	Amount of line 20 you want **applied to your 2020 estimated tax** ▶	**22**
Amount You Owe	**23**	**Amount you owe.** Subtract line 19 from line 16. For details on how to pay, see instructions ▶	**23**
	24	Estimated tax penalty (see instructions) . . . . . ▶	**24**

Third Party Designee (Other than paid preparer)	Do you want to allow another person (other than your paid preparer) to discuss this return with the IRS? See instructions.		☐ **Yes.** Complete below. ☐ **No**
	Designee's name ▶	Phone no. ▶	Personal identification number (PIN) ▶ ⎥⎥⎥⎥⎥⎥

Sign Here

Under penalties of perjury, I declare that I have examined this return and accompanying schedules and statements, and to the best of my knowledge and belief, they are true, correct, and complete. Declaration of preparer (other than taxpayer) is based on all information of which preparer has any knowledge.

Joint return? See instructions. Keep a copy for your records.

Your signature	Date	Your occupation	If the IRS sent you an Identity Protection PIN, enter it here (see inst.) ⎥⎥⎥⎥⎥⎥
Spouse's signature. If a joint return, **both** must sign.	Date	Spouse's occupation	If the IRS sent your spouse an Identity Protection PIN, enter it here (see inst.) ⎥⎥⎥⎥⎥⎥
Phone no.		Email address	

Paid Preparer Use Only	Preparer's name	Preparer's signature	Date	PTIN	Check if: ☐ 3rd Party Designee ☐ Self-employed
	Firm's name ▶				Phone no.
	Firm's address ▶				Firm's EIN ▶

Go to *www.irs.gov/Form1040SR* for instructions and the latest information.   Form **1040-SR** (2019)

SCHEDULE A
(Form 1040 or 1040-SR)

Department of the Treasury
Internal Revenue Service (99)

Itemized Deductions

▶ Go to *www.irs.gov/ScheduleA* for instructions and the latest information.
▶ Attach to Form 1040 or 1040-SR.
Caution: If you are claiming a net qualified disaster loss on Form 4684, see the instructions for line 16.

OMB No. 1545-0074

2019

Attachment
Sequence No. **07**

Name(s) shown on Form 1040 or 1040-SR

Your social security number

DRAFT AS OF JULY 19, 2019 DO NOT FILE

Medical and Dental Expenses	**Caution:** Do not include expenses reimbursed or paid by others.	
	1 Medical and dental expenses (see instructions)	**1**
	2 Enter amount from Form 1040 or 1040-SR, line 8b **2**	
	3 Multiply line 2 by 10% (0.10) **3**	
	4 Subtract line 3 from line 1. If line 3 is more than line 1, enter -0-	**4**
Taxes You Paid	**5** State and local taxes.	
	a State and local income taxes or general sales taxes. You may include either income taxes or general sales taxes on line 5a, but not both. If you elect to include general sales taxes instead of income taxes, check this box . . . . ▶ ☐	**5a**
	b State and local real estate taxes (see instructions)	**5b**
	c State and local personal property taxes	**5c**
	d Add lines 5a through 5c	**5d**
	e Enter the smaller of line 5d or $10,000 ($5,000 if married filing separately)	**5e**
	6 Other taxes. List type and amount ▶ _____ _____	**6**
	7 Add lines 5e and 6	**7**
Interest You Paid **Caution:** Your mortgage interest deduction may be limited (see instructions).	**8** Home mortgage interest and points. If you didn't use all of your home mortgage loan(s) to buy, build, or improve your home, see instructions and check this box . . . . ▶ ☐	
	a Home mortgage interest and points reported to you on Form 1098. See instructions if limited	**8a**
	b Home mortgage interest not reported to you on Form 1098. If paid to the person from whom you bought the home, see instructions and show that person's name, identifying no., and address . . . . . ▶ _____ _____	**8b**
	c Points not reported to you on Form 1098. See instructions for special rules	**8c**
	d Reserved	**8d**
	e Add lines 8a through 8c	**8e**
	9 Investment interest. Attach Form 4952 if required. See instructions	**9**
	10 Add lines 8e and 9	**10**
Gifts to Charity **Caution:** If you made a gift and got a benefit for it, see instructions.	**11** Gifts by cash or check. If you made any gift of $250 or more, see instructions	**11**
	12 Other than by cash or check. If you made any gift of $250 or more, see instructions. You **must** attach Form 8283 if over $500 . . .	**12**
	13 Carryover from prior year	**13**
	14 Add lines 11 through 13	**14**
Casualty and Theft Losses	**15** Casualty and theft loss(es) from a federally declared disaster (other than net qualified disaster losses). Attach Form 4684 and enter the amount from line 18 of that form. See instructions	**15**
Other Itemized Deductions	**16** Other—from list in instructions. List type and amount ▶ _____ _____	**16**
Total Itemized Deductions	**17** Add the amounts in the far right column for lines 4 through 16. Also, enter this amount on Form 1040 or 1040-SR, line 9	**17**
	18 If you elect to itemize deductions even though they are less than your standard deduction, check this box . . . . ▶ ☐	

For Paperwork Reduction Act Notice, see the Instructions for Forms 1040 and 1040-SR.   Cat. No. 17145C   **Schedule A (Form 1040 or 1040-SR) 2019**

SCHEDULE B	Interest and Ordinary Dividends	OMB No. 1545-0074
(Form 1040 or 1040-SR)		**2019**

SCHEDULE B
(Form 1040 or 1040-SR)

Department of the Treasury
Internal Revenue Service (99)

Interest and Ordinary Dividends

► Go to *www.irs.gov/ScheduleB* for instructions and the latest information.
► Attach to Form 1040 or 1040-SR.

OMB No. 1545-0074

2019

Attachment
Sequence No. **08**

Name(s) shown on return

Your social security number

Part I

Interest

(See instructions and the instructions for Forms 1040 and 1040-SR, line 2b.)

Note: If you received a Form 1099-INT, Form 1099-OID, or substitute statement from a brokerage firm, list the firm's name as the payer and enter the total interest shown on that form.

1 List name of payer. If any interest is from a seller-financed mortgage and the buyer used the property as a personal residence, see the instructions and list this interest first. Also, show that buyer's social security number and address ►

Amount

1

2 Add the amounts on line 1 . . . . **2**

3 Excludable interest on series EE and I U.S. savings bonds issued after 1989. Attach Form 8815 . . . . **3**

4 Subtract line 3 from line 2. Enter the result here and on Form 1040 or 1040-SR, line 2b . . . . ► **4**

Note: If line 4 is over $1,500, you must complete Part III.

Part II

Ordinary Dividends

(See instructions and the instructions for Forms 1040 and 1040-SR, line 3b.)

Note: If you received a Form 1099-DIV or substitute statement from a brokerage firm, list the firm's name as the payer and enter the ordinary dividends shown on that form.

5 List name of payer ►

Amount

5

6 Add the amounts on line 5. Enter the total here and on Form 1040 or 1040-SR, line 3b . . . . ► **6**

Note: If line 6 is over $1,500, you must complete Part III.

Part III

Foreign Accounts and Trusts

Caution: If required, failure to file FinCEN Form 114 may result in substantial penalties. See instructions.

You must complete this part if you **(a)** had over $1,500 of taxable interest or ordinary dividends; **(b)** had a foreign account; or **(c)** received a distribution from, or were a grantor of, or a transferor to, a foreign trust.

	Yes	No

7a At any time during 2019, did you have a financial interest in or signature authority over a financial account (such as a bank account, securities account, or brokerage account) located in a foreign country? See instructions . . . .

If "Yes," are you required to file FinCEN Form 114, Report of Foreign Bank and Financial Accounts (FBAR), to report that financial interest or signature authority? See FinCEN Form 114 and its instructions for filing requirements and exceptions to those requirements . . . . . .

b If you are required to file FinCEN Form 114, enter the name of the foreign country where the financial account is located ►

8 During 2019, did you receive a distribution from, or were you the grantor of, or transferor to, a foreign trust? If "Yes," you may have to file Form 3520. See instructions . . . .

For Paperwork Reduction Act Notice, see your tax return instructions.   Cat. No. 17146N   **Schedule B (Form 1040 or 1040-SR) 2019**

SCHEDULE D	**Capital Gains and Losses**	OMB No. 1545-0074
(Form 1040 or 1040-SR)		**2019**
Department of the Treasury Internal Revenue Service (99)	▶ Attach to Form 1040, 1040-SR, or 1040-NR. ▶ Go to *www.irs.gov/ScheduleD* for instructions and the latest information. ▶ Use Form 8949 to list your transactions for lines 1b, 2, 3, 8b, 9, and 10.	Attachment Sequence No. **12**

Name(s) shown on return	Your social security number

Did you dispose of any investment(s) in a qualified opportunity fund during the tax year? ☐ **Yes** ☐ **No**
If "Yes," attach Form 8949 and see its instructions for additional requirements for reporting your gain or loss.

Part I   **Short-Term Capital Gains and Losses—Generally Assets Held One Year or Less** (see instructions)

See instructions for how to figure the amounts to enter on the lines below. This form may be easier to complete if you round off cents to whole dollars.	**(d)** Proceeds (sales price)	**(e)** Cost (or other basis)	**(g)** Adjustments to gain or loss from Form(s) 8949, Part I, line 2, column (g)	**(h) Gain or (loss)** Subtract column (e) from column (d) and combine the result with column (g)
1a Totals for all short-term transactions reported on Form 1099-B for which basis was reported to the IRS and for which you have no adjustments (see instructions). However, if you choose to report all these transactions on Form 8949, leave this line blank and go to line 1b .				
1b Totals for all transactions reported on Form(s) 8949 with **Box A** checked				
2 Totals for all transactions reported on Form(s) 8949 with **Box B** checked				
3 Totals for all transactions reported on Form(s) 8949 with **Box C** checked				

4 Short-term gain from Form 6252 and short-term gain or (loss) from Forms 4684, 6781, and 8824 . .	**4**	
5 Net short-term gain or (loss) from partnerships, S corporations, estates, and trusts from Schedule(s) K-1	**5**	
6 Short-term capital loss carryover. Enter the amount, if any, from line 8 of your **Capital Loss Carryover Worksheet** in the instructions	**6**	( )
7 **Net short-term capital gain or (loss).** Combine lines 1a through 6 in column (h). If you have any long-term capital gains or losses, go to Part II below. Otherwise, go to Part III on the back	**7**	

Part II   **Long-Term Capital Gains and Losses—Generally Assets Held More Than One Year** (see instructions)

See instructions for how to figure the amounts to enter on the lines below. This form may be easier to complete if you round off cents to whole dollars.	**(d)** Proceeds (sales price)	**(e)** Cost (or other basis)	**(g)** Adjustments to gain or loss from Form(s) 8949, Part II, line 2, column (g)	**(h) Gain or (loss)** Subtract column (e) from column (d) and combine the result with column (g)
8a Totals for all long-term transactions reported on Form 1099-B for which basis was reported to the IRS and for which you have no adjustments (see instructions). However, if you choose to report all these transactions on Form 8949, leave this line blank and go to line 8b .				
8b Totals for all transactions reported on Form(s) 8949 with **Box D** checked				
9 Totals for all transactions reported on Form(s) 8949 with **Box E** checked				
10 Totals for all transactions reported on Form(s) 8949 with **Box F** checked.				

11 Gain from Form 4797, Part I; long-term gain from Forms 2439 and 6252; and long-term gain or (loss) from Forms 4684, 6781, and 8824	**11**	
12 Net long-term gain or (loss) from partnerships, S corporations, estates, and trusts from Schedule(s) K-1	**12**	
13 Capital gain distributions. See the instructions	**13**	
14 Long-term capital loss carryover. Enter the amount, if any, from line 13 of your **Capital Loss Carryover Worksheet** in the instructions	**14**	( )
15 **Net long-term capital gain or (loss).** Combine lines 8a through 14 in column (h). Then go to Part III on the back	**15**	

For Paperwork Reduction Act Notice, see your tax return instructions.	Cat. No. 11338H	**Schedule D (Form 1040 or 1040-SR) 2019**

Schedule D (Form 1040 or 1040-SR) 2019   Page **2**

Part III   **Summary**

16   Combine lines 7 and 15 and enter the result **16**

     • If line 16 is a **gain,** enter the amount from line 16 on Form 1040 or 1040-SR, line 6; or Form 1040-NR, line 14. Then go to line 17 below.

     • If line 16 is a **loss,** skip lines 17 through 20 below. Then go to line 21. Also be sure to complete line 22.

     • If line 16 is **zero,** skip lines 17 through 21 below and enter -0- on Form 1040 or 1040-SR, line 6; or Form 1040-NR, line 14. Then go to line 22.

17   Are lines 15 and 16 **both** gains?
     ☐ **Yes.** Go to line 18.
     ☐ **No.** Skip lines 18 through 21, and go to line 22.

18   If you are required to complete the **28% Rate Gain Worksheet** (see instructions), enter the amount, if any, from line 7 of that worksheet   . . . . ▶   **18**

19   If you are required to complete the **Unrecaptured Section 1250 Gain Worksheet** (see instructions), enter the amount, if any, from line 18 of that worksheet   . . . . ▶   **19**

20   Are lines 18 and 19 **both** zero or blank?
     ☐ **Yes.** Complete the **Qualified Dividends and Capital Gain Tax Worksheet** in the instructions for Forms 1040 and 1040-SR, line 12a (or in the instructions for Form 1040-NR, line 42). **Don't** complete lines 21 and 22 below.

     ☐ **No.** Complete the **Schedule D Tax Worksheet** in the instructions. **Don't** complete lines 21 and 22 below.

21   If line 16 is a loss, enter here and on Form 1040 or 1040-SR, line 6; or Form 1040-NR, line 14, the **smaller** of:

     • The loss on line 16; or
     • ($3,000), or if married filing separately, ($1,500)   } . . . .   **21** (   )

     Note: When figuring which amount is smaller, treat both amounts as positive numbers.

22   Do you have qualified dividends on Form 1040 or 1040-SR, line 3a; or Form 1040-NR, line 10b?

     ☐ **Yes.** Complete the **Qualified Dividends and Capital Gain Tax Worksheet** in the instructions for Forms 1040 and 1040-SR, line 12a (or in the instructions for Form 1040-NR, line 42).

     ☐ **No.** Complete the rest of Form 1040, 1040-SR, or 1040-NR.

Schedule D (Form 1040 or 1040-SR) 2019

Form **6252**

Department of the Treasury
Internal Revenue Service

Installment Sale Income

► Attach to your tax return.
► Use a separate form for each sale or other disposition of property on the installment method.
► Go to *www.irs.gov/Form6252* for the latest information.

OMB No. 1545-0228

2019

Attachment
Sequence No. **79**

Name(s) shown on return

Identifying number

1	Description of property ►

2a Date acquired (mm/dd/yyyy) ► _____ **b** Date sold (mm/dd/yyyy) ► _____

3 Was the property sold to a related party (see instructions) after May 14, 1980? If "No," skip line 4 . . . . . ☐ Yes ☐ No

4 Was the property you sold to a related party a marketable security? If "Yes," complete Part III. If "No," complete Part III for the year of sale and the 2 years the year of sale . . . . ☐ Yes ☐ No

Part I **Gross Profit and Contract Price.** Complete this part for all years of the installment agreement.

5	Selling price including mortgages and other debts. **Don't** include interest, whether stated or unstated	**5**	
6	Mortgages, debts, and other liabilities the buyer assumed or took the property subject to (see instructions)	**6**	
7	Subtract line 6 from line 5	**7**	
8	Cost or other basis of property sold	**8**	
9	Depreciation allowed or allowable	**9**	
10	Adjusted basis. Subtract line 9 from line 8	**10**	
11	Commissions and other expenses of sale	**11**	
12	Income recapture from Form 4797, Part III (see instructions) . . .	**12**	
13	Add lines 10, 11, and 12	**13**	
14	Subtract line 13 from line 5. If zero or less, **don't** complete the rest of this form (see instructions) . .	**14**	
15	If the property described on line 1 above was your main home, enter the amount of your excluded gain (see instructions). Otherwise, enter -0-	**15**	
16	**Gross profit.** Subtract line 15 from line 14	**16**	
17	Subtract line 13 from line 6. If zero or less, enter -0-	**17**	
18	**Contract price.** Add line 7 and line 17	**18**	

Part II **Installment Sale Income.** Complete this part for all years of the installment agreement.

19	Gross profit percentage (expressed as a decimal amount). Divide line 16 by line 18. (For years after the year of sale, see instructions)	**19**	
20	If this is the year of sale, enter the amount from line 17. Otherwise, enter -0-	**20**	
21	Payments received during year (see instructions). **Don't** include interest, whether stated or unstated .	**21**	
22	Add lines 20 and 21	**22**	
23	Payments received in prior years (see instructions). **Don't** include interest, whether stated or unstated	**23**	
24	**Installment sale income.** Multiply line 22 by line 19	**24**	
25	Enter the part of line 24 that is ordinary income under the recapture rules (see instructions)	**25**	
26	Subtract line 25 from line 24. Enter here and on Schedule D or Form 4797 (see instructions) . . .	**26**	

Part III **Related Party Installment Sale Income. Don't** complete if you received the final payment this tax year.

27 Name, address, and taxpayer identifying number of related party _____

28 Did the related party resell or dispose of the property ("second disposition") during this tax year? . . . . . ☐ Yes ☐ No

29 **If the answer to question 28 is "Yes," complete lines 30 through 37 below unless one of the following conditions is met. Check the box that applies.**

a ☐ The second disposition was more than 2 years after the first disposition (other than dispositions of marketable securities). If this box is checked, enter the date of disposition (mm/dd/yyyy) . . . . ► _____

b ☐ The first disposition was a sale or exchange of stock to the issuing corporation.

c ☐ The second disposition was an involuntary conversion and the threat of conversion occurred after the first disposition.

d ☐ The second disposition occurred after the death of the original seller or buyer.

e ☐ It can be established to the satisfaction of the IRS that tax avoidance wasn't a principal purpose for either of the dispositions. If this box is checked, attach an explanation (see instructions).

30	Selling price of property sold by related party (see instructions)	**30**	
31	Enter contract price from line 18 for year of first sale	**31**	
32	Enter the **smaller** of line 30 or line 31	**32**	
33	Total payments received by the end of your 2019 tax year (see instructions)	**33**	
34	Subtract line 33 from line 32. If zero or less, enter -0-	**34**	
35	Multiply line 34 by the gross profit percentage on line 19 for year of first sale	**35**	
36	Enter the part of line 35 that is ordinary income under the recapture rules (see instructions)	**36**	
37	Subtract line 36 from line 35. Enter here and on Schedule D or Form 4797 (see instructions) . . .	**37**	

For Paperwork Reduction Act Notice, see page 4. Cat. No. 13601R Form **6252** (2019)

Form **8949**

Department of the Treasury
Internal Revenue Service

Sales and Other Dispositions of Capital Assets

▶ Go to *www.irs.gov/Form8949* for instructions and the latest information.

▶ File with your Schedule D to list your transactions for lines 1b, 2, 3, 8b, 9, and 10 of Schedule D.

OMB No. 1545-0074

2019

Attachment
Sequence No. **12A**

Name(s) shown on return

Social security number or taxpayer identification number

Before you check Box A, B, or C below, see whether you received any Form(s) 1099-B or substitute statement(s) from your broker. A substitute statement will have the same information as Form 1099-B. Either will show whether your basis (usually your cost) was reported to the IRS by your broker and may even tell you which box to check.

Part I   **Short-Term.** Transactions involving capital assets you held 1 year or less are generally short-term (see instructions). For long-term transactions, see page 2.

Note: You may aggregate all short-term transactions reported on Form(s) 1099-B showing basis was reported to the IRS and for which no adjustments or codes are required. Enter the totals directly on Schedule D, line 1a; you aren't required to report these transactions on Form 8949 (see instructions).

You *must* check Box A, B, *or* C below. Check only one box. If more than one box applies for your short-term transactions, complete a separate Form 8949, page 1, for each applicable box. If you have more short-term transactions than will fit on this page for one or more of the boxes, complete as many forms with the same box checked as you need.

☐ **(A)** Short-term transactions reported on Form(s) 1099-B showing basis was reported to the IRS (see **Note** above)

☐ **(B)** Short-term transactions reported on Form(s) 1099-B showing basis **wasn't** reported to the IRS

☐ **(C)** Short-term transactions not reported to you on Form 1099-B

1 **(a)** Description of property (Example: 100 sh. XYZ Co.)	**(b)** Date acquired (Mo., day, yr.)	**(c)** Date sold or disposed of (Mo., day, yr.)	**(d)** Proceeds (sales price) (see instructions)	**(e)** Cost or other basis. See the **Note** below and see *Column (e)* in the separate instructions	Adjustment, if any, to gain or loss. If you enter an amount in column (g), enter a code in column (f). See the separate instructions.		**(h)** Gain or (loss). Subtract column (e) from column (d) and combine the result with column (g)
					(f) Code(s) from instructions	**(g)** Amount of adjustment	

2 Totals. Add the amounts in columns (d), (e), (g), and (h) (subtract negative amounts). Enter each total here and include on your Schedule D, **line 1b** (if **Box A** above is checked), **line 2** (if **Box B** above is checked), or **line 3** (if **Box C** above is checked) ▶

Note: If you checked Box A above but the basis reported to the IRS was incorrect, enter in column (e) the basis as reported to the IRS, and enter an adjustment in column (g) to correct the basis. See *Column (g)* in the separate instructions for how to figure the amount of the adjustment.

For Paperwork Reduction Act Notice, see your tax return instructions.   Cat. No. 37768Z   Form **8949** (2019)

Form 8949 (2019)   Attachment Sequence No. **12A**   Page **2**

Name(s) shown on return. Name and SSN or taxpayer identification no. not required if shown on other side	Social security number or taxpayer identification number

Before you check Box D, E, or F below, see whether you received any Form(s) 1099-B or substitute statement(s) from your broker. A substitute statement will have the same information as Form 1099-B. Either will show whether your basis (usually your cost) was reported to the IRS by your broker and may even tell you which box to check.

Part II   **Long-Term.** Transactions involving capital assets you held more than 1 year are generally long-term (see instructions). For short-term transactions, see page 1.

Note: You may aggregate all long-term transactions reported on Form(s) 1099-B showing basis was reported to the IRS and for which no adjustments or codes are required. Enter the totals directly on Schedule D, line 8a; you aren't required to report these transactions on Form 8949 (see instructions).

You *must* check Box D, E, *or* F below. Check only one box. If more than one box applies for your long-term transactions, complete a separate Form 8949, page 2, for each applicable box. If you have more long-term transactions than will fit on this page for one or more of the boxes, complete as many forms with the same box checked as you need.

☐ **(D)** Long-term transactions reported on Form(s) 1099-B showing basis was reported to the IRS (see **Note** above)

☐ **(E)** Long-term transactions reported on Form(s) 1099-B showing basis **wasn't** reported to the IRS

☐ **(F)** Long-term transactions not reported to you on Form 1099-B

1 (a) Description of property (Example: 100 sh. XYZ Co.)	(b) Date acquired (Mo., day, yr.)	(c) Date sold or disposed of (Mo., day, yr.)	(d) Proceeds (sales price) (see instructions)	(e) Cost or other basis. See the **Note** below and see *Column (e)* in the separate instructions	Adjustment, if any, to gain or loss. If you enter an amount in column (g), enter a code in column (f). See the separate instructions.		(h) Gain or (loss). Subtract column (e) from column (d) and combine the result with column (g)
					(f) Code(s) from instructions	(g) Amount of adjustment	

2 Totals. Add the amounts in columns (d), (e), (g), and (h) (subtract negative amounts). Enter each total here and include on your Schedule D, **line 8b** (if **Box D** above is checked), **line 9** (if **Box E** above is checked), or **line 10** (if **Box F** above is checked) ▶

Note: If you checked Box D above but the basis reported to the IRS was incorrect, enter in column (e) the basis as reported to the IRS, and enter an adjustment in column (g) to correct the basis. See *Column (g)* in the separate instructions for how to figure the amount of the adjustment.

Form **8949** (2019)

Qualified Dividends and Capital Gain Tax Worksheet—Line 12a

Before you begin:	✓ See the earlier instructions for line 12a to see if you can use this worksheet to figure your tax.
	✓ Before completing this worksheet, complete Form 1040 or 1040-SR through line 11b.
	✓ If you don't have to file Schedule D and you received capital gain distributions, be sure you checked the box on Form 1040 or 1040-SR, line 6.

1. Enter the amount from Form 1040 or 1040-SR, line 11b. However, if you are filing Form 2555 (relating to foreign earned income), enter the amount from line 3 of the Foreign Earned Income Tax Worksheet .... **1.** _____

2. Enter the amount from Form 1040 or 1040-SR, line 3a* .... **2.** _____

3. Are you filing Schedule D?*

☐ **Yes.** Enter the **smaller** of line 15 or 16 of Schedule D. If either line 15 or 16 is blank or a loss, enter -0-.

☐ **No.** Enter the amount from Form 1040 or 1040-SR, line 6. } **3.** _____

4. Add lines 2 and 3 .... **4.** _____

5. If filing Form 4952 (used to figure investment interest expense deduction), enter any amount from line 4g of that form. Otherwise, enter -0- .... **5.** _____

6. Subtract line 5 from line 4. If zero or less, enter -0- .... **6.** _____

7. Subtract line 6 from line 1. If zero or less, enter -0- .... **7.** _____

8. Enter:

$39,375 if single or married filing separately,
$78,750 if married filing jointly or qualifying widow(er),
$52,750 if head of household. } .... **8.** _____

9. Enter the smaller of line 1 or line 8 .... **9.** _____

10. Enter the smaller of line 7 or line 9 .... **10.** _____

11. Subtract line 10 from line 9. This amount is taxed at 0% .... **11.** _____

12. Enter the smaller of line 1 or line 6 .... **12.** _____

13. Enter the amount from line 11 .... **13.** _____

14. Subtract line 13 from line 12 .... **14.** _____

15. Enter:

$434,550 if single,
$244,425 if married filing separately,
$488,850 if married filing jointly or qualifying widow(er),
$461,700 if head of household. } .... **15.** _____

16. Enter the smaller of line 1 or line 15 .... **16.** _____

17. Add lines 7 and 11 .... **17.** _____

18. Subtract line 17 from line 16. If zero or less, enter -0- .... **18.** _____

19. Enter the smaller of line 14 or line 18 .... **19.** _____

20. Multiply line 19 by 15% (0.15) .... **20.** _____

21. Add lines 11 and 19 .... **21.** _____

22. Subtract line 21 from line 12 .... **22.** _____

23. Multiply line 22 by 20% (0.20) .... **23.** _____

24. Figure the tax on the amount on line 7. If the amount on line 7 is less than $100,000, use the Tax Table to figure the tax. If the amount on line 7 is $100,000 or more, use the Tax Computation Worksheet .... **24.** _____

25. Add lines 20, 23, and 24 .... **25.** _____

26. Figure the tax on the amount on line 1. If the amount on line 1 is less than $100,000, use the Tax Table to figure the tax. If the amount on line 1 is $100,000 or more, use the Tax Computation Worksheet .... **26.** _____

27. **Tax on all taxable income.** Enter the **smaller** of line 25 or 26. Also include this amount on the entry space on Form 1040 or 1040-SR, line 12a. If you are filing Form 2555, don't enter this amount on the entry space on Form 1040 or 1040-SR, line 12a. Instead, enter it on line 4 of the Foreign Earned Income Tax Worksheet .... **27.** _____

* If you are filing Form 2555, see the footnote in the Foreign Earned Income Tax Worksheet before completing this line.

Student Name _____

Class/Section _____

Date _____

KEY NUMBER TAX RETURN SUMMARY

CHAPTER 8

Comprehensive Problem 1

Form 4562, Special Depreciation Allowance (Line 14) _____

Form 4562, MACRS Deduction for Assets Placed in
Service Before 2019 (Line 17) _____

Schedule C, Depreciation (Line 13) _____

Schedule C, Total Expenses (Line 28) _____

Schedule C, Net Profit or Loss (Line 31) _____

Comprehensive Problem 2

Capital Gain or (Loss) (Line 6) _____

Adjusted Gross Income (Line 8b) _____

Standard Deduction or Itemized Deductions (Line 9) _____

Total Tax (Line 16) _____

Amount Overpaid (Line 20) _____

CHAPTER 9

Payroll, Estimated Payments, and Retirement Plans

After completing this chapter, you should be able to:

LO 9.1   Compute the income tax withholding from employee wages.

LO 9.2   Determine taxpayers' quarterly estimated payments.

LO 9.3   Compute the FICA tax.

LO 9.4   Apply the federal deposit system to payroll withholding.

LO 9.5   Prepare employer payroll reporting.

LO 9.6   Compute the amount of FUTA tax for an employer.

LO 9.7   Describe the general rules for qualified retirement plans.

LO 9.8   Explain the pension plan rollover rules.

OVERVIEW

This chapter focuses on the payment and reporting of income and other taxes by employers, employees, and self-employed taxpayers. Payroll and other tax topics covered include withholding methods for employees, estimated payments, the FICA tax (Social Security and Medicare taxes), the federal tax deposit system, and employer reporting requirements. In addition, other payroll-related topics such as retirement plans and pensions are covered.

The FICA tax is a combined Social Security (6.2 percent up to the annual wage limit, $132,900 in 2019) and Medicare tax (1.45 percent with no limit) that is paid by both employees and employers. The FICA tax is withheld from each employee's paycheck, the tax is then matched by the employer, and the total amount is remitted to the IRS.

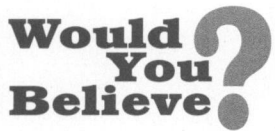

In 1938, a wallet manufacturer used Hilda Schrader Whitcher's Social Security number for a specimen card to show how nicely the card fit inside the wallet. At the time Hilda was an employee of the company. Although the fake card was not the correct size or color and had "specimen" reflected across the front, by 1943 over 5,000 people were using Hilda's Social Security number and 10 were still doing so as late as 1970. Eventually, the Social Security Administration voided Hilda's number and gave her a new one.

The Federal Unemployment Tax Act (FUTA) tax is unemployment insurance with a joint state and federal payment plan to provide benefits for taxpayers when they become unemployed. The FUTA tax is paid only by employers, not employees.

Learning Objective 9.1

Compute the income tax withholding from employee wages.

9-1 WITHHOLDING METHODS

Employers are required to withhold taxes from amounts paid to employees for wages, including salaries, fees, bonuses, commissions, vacation and retirement pay. Employees complete Form W-4 to provide the information necessary for the employer to withhold income taxes at the prescribed amount. Although most taxpayers' withholding should be adequate to result in an income tax refund at filing time, calculating withholding is more of an art than a science and is subject to the accurate estimation of income and deductions that are ultimately reported for the tax year.

Form W-4 was redesigned for 2019 but retains the typical elements of filing status and the number of withholding allowances an employee is claiming. Form W-4 is the key to the amount of the employee's withholding for federal income taxes. As illustrated in the next part of this section, employers use the number of allowances to compute the amount of income tax withheld from each period's pay.

The allowances are designed to be fairly straightforward for most taxpayers and are generally based on completion of the Personal Allowances Worksheet included as part of the Form W-4. Employees with less typical adjustments to income or additional deductions such as a second job, deductible alimony payments, a large amount of itemized deductions, or tax credits, may claim additional withholding allowances by completing one of the two additional worksheets included with Form W-4: (1) the Deductions, Adjustments, and Additional Income Worksheet and (2) the Two-Earners/Multiple Jobs Worksheet. The instructions are designed to allow employees to determine when either of these worksheets are required. Employees can authorize a set amount of additional income tax withheld from their wages each pay period using Line 6 of Form W-4. Also, exemption from withholding may be claimed on Form W-4 by employees who anticipate no federal tax liability for the current year. To be exempt from withholding, the employee must also have had no tax liability for the prior year. If an employee does not complete Form W-4, the employer is required to withhold as if the employee is single with no allowances.

EXAMPLE   Tom Berry (Social Security number 555-12-1212) expects to earn $90,000 of wages from his new job. Tom's spouse, Alicia, is a stay-at-home mom who operates a catering business on the side. Her business is expected to generate $10,000 of qualified business income (and a $2,000 QBI deduction) but they do not wish to make estimated payments and instead adjust Tom's withholding. They live at 123 Main Street, Paris, TX 75460. The Berrys also expect interest income of $5,000 and qualified dividend income of $4,000. They have three kids ages 5, 15, and 17 at the end of 2019. Their 2019 itemized deductions are estimated at $27,000. Tom should claim four allowances as illustrated on Form W-4 on Pages 9-3 through 9-6. ♦

Form W-4 (2019)

Future developments. For the latest information about any future developments related to Form W-4, such as legislation enacted after it was published, go to *www.irs.gov/FormW4*.

Purpose. Complete Form W-4 so that your employer can withhold the correct federal income tax from your pay. Consider completing a new Form W-4 each year and when your personal or financial situation changes.

Exemption from withholding. You may claim exemption from withholding for 2019 if **both** of the following apply.

• For 2018 you had a right to a refund of **all** federal income tax withheld because you had **no** tax liability, **and**

• For 2019 you expect a refund of **all** federal income tax withheld because you expect to have **no** tax liability.

If you're exempt, complete **only** lines 1, 2, 3, 4, and 7 and sign the form to validate it. Your exemption for 2019 expires February 17, 2020. See Pub. 505, Tax Withholding and Estimated Tax, to learn more about whether you qualify for exemption from withholding.

General Instructions

If you aren't exempt, follow the rest of these instructions to determine the number of withholding allowances you should claim for withholding for 2019 and any additional amount of tax to have withheld. For regular wages, withholding must be based on allowances you claimed and may not be a flat amount or percentage of wages.

You can also use the calculator at *www.irs.gov/W4App* to determine your tax withholding more accurately. Consider using this calculator if you have a more complicated tax situation, such as if you have a working spouse, more than one job, or a large amount of nonwage income not subject to withholding outside of your job. After your Form W-4 takes effect, you can also use this calculator to see how the amount of tax you're having withheld compares to your projected total tax for 2019. If you use the calculator, you don't need to complete any of the worksheets for Form W-4.

Note that if you have too much tax withheld, you will receive a refund when you file your tax return. If you have too little tax withheld, you will owe tax when you file your tax return, and you might owe a penalty.

Filers with multiple jobs or working spouses. If you have more than one job at a time, or if you're married filing jointly and your spouse is also working, read all of the instructions including the instructions for the Two-Earners/Multiple Jobs Worksheet before beginning.

Nonwage income. If you have a large amount of nonwage income not subject to withholding, such as interest or dividends, consider making estimated tax payments using Form 1040-ES, Estimated Tax for Individuals. Otherwise, you might owe additional tax. Or, you can use the Deductions, Adjustments, and Additional Income Worksheet on page 3 or the calculator at *www.irs.gov/W4App* to make sure you have enough tax withheld from your paycheck. If you have pension or annuity income, see Pub. 505 or use the calculator at *www.irs.gov/W4App* to find out if you should adjust your withholding on Form W-4 or W-4P.

Nonresident alien. If you're a nonresident alien, see Notice 1392, Supplemental Form W-4 Instructions for Nonresident Aliens, before completing this form.

Specific Instructions
Personal Allowances Worksheet

Complete this worksheet on page 3 first to determine the number of withholding allowances to claim.

Line C. *Head of household please note:* Generally, you may claim head of household filing status on your tax return only if you're unmarried and pay more than 50% of the costs of keeping up a home for yourself and a qualifying individual. See Pub. 501 for more information about filing status.

Line E. Child tax credit. When you file your tax return, you may be eligible to claim a child tax credit for each of your eligible children. To qualify, the child must be under age 17 as of December 31, must be your dependent who lives with you for more than half the year, and must have a valid social security number. To learn more about this credit, see Pub. 972, Child Tax Credit. To reduce the tax withheld from your pay by taking this credit into account, follow the instructions on line E of the worksheet. On the worksheet you will be asked about your total income. For this purpose, total income includes all of your wages and other income, including income earned by a spouse if you are filing a joint return.

Line F. Credit for other dependents. When you file your tax return, you may be eligible to claim a credit for other dependents for whom a child tax credit can't be claimed, such as a qualifying child who doesn't meet the age or social security number requirement for the child tax credit, or a qualifying relative. To learn more about this credit, see Pub. 972. To reduce the tax withheld from your pay by taking this credit into account, follow the instructions on line F of the worksheet. On the worksheet, you will be asked about your total income. For this purpose, total

---

Separate here and give Form W-4 to your employer. Keep the worksheet(s) for your records.

Form W-4
Department of the Treasury
Internal Revenue Service

Employee's Withholding Allowance Certificate

▶ Whether you're entitled to claim a certain number of allowances or exemption from withholding is subject to review by the IRS. Your employer may be required to send a copy of this form to the IRS.

OMB No. 1545-0074

2019

1 Your first name and middle initial	Last name	2 Your social security number
Tom	Berry	555-12-1212

Home address (number and street or rural route)
123 Main Street

3 ☐ Single ☑ Married ☐ Married, but withhold at higher Single rate.
Note: If married filing separately, check "Married, but withhold at higher Single rate."

City or town, state, and ZIP code
Paris, TX 75460

4 If your last name differs from that shown on your social security card, check here. You must call 800-772-1213 for a replacement card. ▶ ☐

5	Total number of allowances you're claiming (from the applicable worksheet on the following pages)	5	4
6	Additional amount, if any, you want withheld from each paycheck	6	$

7 I claim exemption from withholding for 2019, and I certify that I meet **both** of the following conditions for exemption.
• Last year I had a right to a refund of **all** federal income tax withheld because I had **no** tax liability, **and**
• This year I expect a refund of **all** federal income tax withheld because I expect to have **no** tax liability.
If you meet both conditions, write "Exempt" here ▶ | 7 |

Under penalties of perjury, I declare that I have examined this certificate and, to the best of my knowledge and belief, it is true, correct, and complete.

Employee's signature
(This form is not valid unless you sign it.) ▶   Date ▶

8 Employer's name and address (**Employer:** Complete boxes 8 and 10 if sending to IRS and complete boxes 8, 9, and 10 if sending to State Directory of New Hires.)	9 First date of employment	10 Employer identification number (EIN)

For Privacy Act and Paperwork Reduction Act Notice, see page 4.   Cat. No. 10220Q   Form **W-4** (2019)

income includes all of your wages and other income, including income earned by a spouse if you are filing a joint return.

Line G. Other credits. You may be able to reduce the tax withheld from your paycheck if you expect to claim other tax credits, such as tax credits for education (see Pub. 970). If you do so, your paycheck will be larger, but the amount of any refund that you receive when you file your tax return will be smaller. Follow the instructions for Worksheet 1-6 in Pub. 505 if you want to reduce your withholding to take these credits into account. Enter "-0-" on lines E and F if you use Worksheet 1-6.

Deductions, Adjustments, and Additional Income Worksheet

Complete this worksheet to determine if you're able to reduce the tax withheld from your paycheck to account for your itemized deductions and other adjustments to income, such as IRA contributions. If you do so, your refund at the end of the year will be smaller, but your paycheck will be larger. You're not required to complete this worksheet or reduce your withholding if you don't wish to do so.

You can also use this worksheet to figure out how much to increase the tax withheld from your paycheck if you have a large amount of nonwage income not subject to withholding, such as interest or dividends.

Another option is to take these items into account and make your withholding more accurate by using the calculator at *www.irs.gov/W4App*. If you use the calculator, you don't need to complete any of the worksheets for Form W-4.

Two-Earners/Multiple Jobs Worksheet

Complete this worksheet if you have more than one job at a time or are married filing jointly and have a working spouse. If you don't complete this worksheet, you might have too little tax withheld. If so, you will owe tax when you file your tax return and might be subject to a penalty.

Figure the total number of allowances you're entitled to claim and any additional amount of tax to withhold on all jobs using worksheets from only one Form W-4. Claim all allowances on the W-4 that you or your spouse file for the highest paying job in your family and claim zero allowances on Forms W-4 filed for all other jobs. For example, if you earn $60,000 per year and your spouse earns $20,000, you should complete the worksheets to determine what to enter on lines 5 and 6 of your Form W-4, and your spouse should enter zero ("-0-") on lines 5 and 6 of his or her Form W-4. See Pub. 505 for details.

Another option is to use the calculator at *www.irs.gov/W4App* to make your withholding more accurate.

Tip: If you have a working spouse and your incomes are similar, you can check the "Married, but withhold at higher Single rate" box instead of using this worksheet. If you choose this option, then each spouse should fill out the Personal Allowances Worksheet and check the "Married, but withhold at higher Single rate" box on Form W-4, but only one spouse should claim any allowances for credits or fill out the Deductions, Adjustments, and Additional Income Worksheet.

Instructions for Employer

Employees, do not complete box 8, 9, or 10. Your employer will complete these boxes if necessary.

New hire reporting. Employers are required by law to report new employees to a designated State Directory of New Hires. Employers may use Form W-4, boxes 8, 9, and 10 to comply with the new hire reporting requirement for a newly hired employee. A newly hired employee is an employee who hasn't previously been employed by the employer, or who was previously employed by the employer but has been separated from such prior employment for at least 60 consecutive days. Employers should contact the appropriate State Directory of New Hires to find out how to submit a copy of the completed Form W-4. For information and links to each designated State Directory of New Hires (including for U.S. territories), go to *www.acf.hhs.gov/css/employers.*

If an employer is sending a copy of Form W-4 to a designated State Directory of New Hires to comply with the new hire reporting requirement for a newly hired employee, complete boxes 8, 9, and 10 as follows.

Box 8. Enter the employer's name and address. If the employer is sending a copy of this form to a State Directory of New Hires, enter the address where child support agencies should send income withholding orders.

Box 9. If the employer is sending a copy of this form to a State Directory of New Hires, enter the employee's first date of employment, which is the date services for payment were first performed by the employee. If the employer rehired the employee after the employee had been separated from the employer's service for at least 60 days, enter the rehire date.

Box 10. Enter the employer's employer identification number (EIN).

Form W-4 (2019)   Page **3**

Personal Allowances Worksheet (Keep for your records.)

A	Enter "1" for yourself	A	1
B	Enter "1" if you will file as married filing jointly	B	1
C	Enter "1" if you will file as head of household	C	

D   Enter "1" if: { • You're single, or married filing separately, and have only one job; or
• You're married filing jointly, have only one job, and your spouse doesn't work; or
• Your wages from a second job or your spouse's wages (or the total of both) are $1,500 or less. }   D ____

E   **Child tax credit.** See Pub. 972, Child Tax Credit, for more information.
- If your total income will be less than $71,201 ($103,351 if married filing jointly), enter "4" for each eligible child.
- If your total income will be from $71,201 to $179,050 ($103,351 to $345,850 if married filing jointly), enter "2" for each eligible child.
- If your total income will be from $179,051 to $200,000 ($345,851 to $400,000 if married filing jointly), enter "1" for each eligible child.
- If your total income will be higher than $200,000 ($400,000 if married filing jointly), enter "-0-" . . . .   **E**   4 (a)

F   **Credit for other dependents.** See Pub. 972, Child Tax Credit, for more information.
- If your total income will be less than $71,201 ($103,351 if married filing jointly), enter "1" for each eligible dependent.
- If your total income will be from $71,201 to $179,050 ($103,351 to $345,850 if married filing jointly), enter "1" for every two dependents (for example, "-0-" for one dependent, "1" if you have two or three dependents, and "2" if you have four dependents).
- If your total income will be higher than $179,050 ($345,850 if married filing jointly), enter "-0-" . . . .   **F**   1 (b)

G   **Other credits.** If you have other credits, see Worksheet 1-6 of Pub. 505 and enter the amount from that worksheet here. If you use Worksheet 1-6, enter "-0-" on lines E and F . . . .   **G**   ____

H   Add lines A through G and enter the total here . . . . ▶   **H**   7

For accuracy, **complete all worksheets that apply.**   { • If you plan to **itemize** or **claim adjustments to income** and want to reduce your withholding, or if you have a large amount of nonwage income not subject to withholding and want to increase your withholding, see the **Deductions, Adjustments, and Additional Income Worksheet** below.
• If you **have more than one job at a time** or are **married filing jointly and you and your spouse both work,** and the combined earnings from all jobs exceed $53,000 ($24,450 if married filing jointly), see the **Two-Earners/Multiple Jobs Worksheet** on page 4 to avoid having too little tax withheld.
• If **neither** of the above situations applies, **stop here** and enter the number from line H on line 5 of Form W-4 above. }

Deductions, Adjustments, and Additional Income Worksheet

Note: Use this worksheet *only* if you plan to itemize deductions, claim certain adjustments to income, or have a large amount of nonwage income not subject to withholding.

1	Enter an estimate of your 2019 itemized deductions. These include qualifying home mortgage interest, charitable contributions, state and local taxes (up to $10,000), and medical expenses in excess of 10% of your income. See Pub. 505 for details	1	$	27,000
2	Enter: { $24,400 if you're married filing jointly or qualifying widow(er) $18,350 if you're head of household $12,200 if you're single or married filing separately }	2	$	24,400
3	**Subtract** line 2 from line 1. If zero or less, enter "-0-"	3	$	2,600
4	Enter an estimate of your 2019 adjustments to income, qualified business income deduction, and any additional standard deduction for age or blindness (see Pub. 505 for information about these items) . .	4	$	2,000
5	**Add** lines 3 and 4 and enter the total	5	$	4,600
6	Enter an estimate of your 2019 nonwage income not subject to withholding (such as dividends or interest) .	6	$	9,000 (c)
7	**Subtract** line 6 from line 5. If zero, enter "-0-". If less than zero, enter the amount in parentheses . . .	7	$	(4,400)
8	**Divide** the amount on line 7 by $4,200 and enter the result here. If a negative amount, enter in parentheses. Drop any fraction	8		(1)
9	Enter the number from the **Personal Allowances Worksheet,** line H, above	9		7
10	**Add** lines 8 and 9 and enter the total here. If zero or less, enter "-0-". If you plan to use the **Two-Earners/ Multiple Jobs Worksheet,** also enter this total on line 1 of that worksheet on page 4. Otherwise, **stop here** and enter this total on Form W-4, line 5, page 1	10		6

(a) - The Berrys have two children that qualify for the child tax credit and based on the information provided, will have total income between $103,351 and $345,850.

(b) - The Berrys have one child that is too old for the child tax credit.

(c) - Interest and dividends total $9,000.

Form W-4 (2019)   Page **4**

Two-Earners/Multiple Jobs Worksheet

Note: Use this worksheet *only* if the instructions under line H from the **Personal Allowances Worksheet** direct you here.

1	Enter the number from the **Personal Allowances Worksheet,** line H, page 3 (or, if you used the **Deductions, Adjustments, and Additional Income Worksheet** on page 3, the number from line 10 of that worksheet)	**1**	6
2	Find the number in **Table 1** below that applies to the **LOWEST** paying job and enter it here. **However,** if you're married filing jointly and wages from the highest paying job are $75,000 or less and the combined wages for you and your spouse are $107,000 or less, don't enter more than "3"	**2**	2
3	If line 1 is **more than or equal to** line 2, subtract line 2 from line 1. Enter the result here (if zero, enter "-0-") and on Form W-4, line 5, page 1. **Do not** use the rest of this worksheet	**3**	4

Note: If line 1 is **less than** line 2, enter "-0-" on Form W-4, line 5, page 1. Complete lines 4 through 9 below to figure the additional withholding amount necessary to avoid a year-end tax bill.

4	Enter the number from line 2 of this worksheet	**4**	
5	Enter the number from line 1 of this worksheet	**5**	
6	**Subtract** line 5 from line 4	**6**	
7	Find the amount in **Table 2** below that applies to the **HIGHEST** paying job and enter it here	**7** $	
8	**Multiply** line 7 by line 6 and enter the result here. This is the additional annual withholding needed . . .	**8** $	
9	**Divide** line 8 by the number of pay periods remaining in 2019. For example, divide by 18 if you're paid every 2 weeks and you complete this form on a date in late April when there are 18 pay periods remaining in 2019. Enter the result here and on Form W-4, line 6, page 1. This is the additional amount to be withheld from each paycheck	**9** $	

Table 1				Table 2			
Married Filing Jointly		**All Others**		**Married Filing Jointly**		**All Others**	
If wages from **LOWEST** paying job are—	Enter on line 2 above	If wages from **LOWEST** paying job are—	Enter on line 2 above	If wages from **HIGHEST** paying job are—	Enter on line 7 above	If wages from **HIGHEST** paying job are—	Enter on line 7 above
$0 - $5,000	0	$0 - $7,000	0	$0 - $24,900	$420	$0 - $7,200	$420
5,001 - 9,500	1	7,001 - 13,000	1	24,901 - 84,450	500	7,201 - 36,975	500
9,501 - 19,500	2	13,001 - 27,500	2	84,451 - 173,900	910	36,976 - 81,700	910
19,501 - 35,000	3	27,501 - 32,000	3	173,901 - 326,950	1,000	81,701 - 158,225	1,000
35,001 - 40,000	4	32,001 - 40,000	4	326,951 - 413,700	1,330	158,226 - 201,600	1,330
40,001 - 46,000	5	40,001 - 60,000	5	413,701 - 617,850	1,450	201,601 - 507,800	1,450
46,001 - 55,000	6	60,001 - 75,000	6	617,851 and over	1,540	507,801 and over	1,540
55,001 - 60,000	7	75,001 - 85,000	7				
60,001 - 70,000	8	85,001 - 95,000	8				
70,001 - 75,000	9	95,001 - 100,000	9				
75,001 - 85,000	10	100,001 - 110,000	10				
85,001 - 95,000	11	110,001 - 115,000	11				
95,001 - 125,000	12	115,001 - 125,000	12				
125,001 - 155,000	13	125,001 - 135,000	13				
155,001 - 165,000	14	135,001 - 145,000	14				
165,001 - 175,000	15	145,001 - 160,000	15				
175,001 - 180,000	16	160,001 - 180,000	16				
180,001 - 195,000	17	180,001 and over	17				
195,001 - 205,000	18						
205,001 and over	19						

In 2020, the IRS has eliminated the "allowances" method of withholding reported on Form W-4 and used by employers for years. A new Form W-4, which replaces the allowance method with a standard withholding based on income and filing status only, is in draft as we go to print. The Form W-4 then provides dollar adjustments to reflect married filing jointly taxpayers that both work, a credit for dependents, multiple jobs, other forms of income, and itemized deductions. To assist taxpayers, an online withholding calculator will be available on the **www.irs.gov** website by the start of 2020.

New Tax Law!

Single employees with only one job may claim one "special withholding allowance." Married employees may also claim a "special withholding allowance" if one of the following conditions exists:

1. The employee has only one job and his or her spouse does not work, or
2. Annual wages earned from the employee's second job, or wages earned by his or her spouse, or the total of both are $1,500 or less.

The guidance on how an employer handles an unusual Form W-4 is somewhat contradictory. If an employer receives a W-4 from an employee that is known to be false based on oral or written statements made by the employee, the employer should notify the employee to file a corrected W-4. If the employee does not file a corrected W-4, the employer should withhold based on single with no allowances. However, employees do not have to provide proof to their employers that they are entitled to the number of allowances claimed on their Forms W-4. If an employee claims "exempt" and therefore requests no withholding, the employer is required to verify (1) that the employee was entitled to a full refund of all income taxes withheld because there was no income tax liability for the prior year, and (2) that the taxpayer expects a full refund during the current year because the taxpayer expects to have no tax liability. Employers are also instructed to carefully consider a large increase in withholding allowances, especially if the employee has otherwise had regular withholdings during the rest of the year.

An employee who claims withholding allowances on Form W-4 with no reasonable basis can be subject to fines of up to $500 plus underpayment of tax penalties. Willfully filing a fraudulent Form W-4 or failing to supply information that would increase the amount withheld can result in a fine of up to $1,000 or imprisonment for up to 1 year, or both. Employers must submit copies of Forms W-4 to the IRS only when directed to do so by written notice. Where there is significant underwithholding for a particular employee, the IRS may require the employer to withhold income tax at a higher rate and will notify the employer in writing (known as a "lock-in" letter). Employees are given the right to contest the IRS determination.

EXAMPLE Brianne is the payroll manager at her company and receives a Form W-4 from her employee, Mike. Mike has indicated that he is a married employee with two children and claims 10 allowances on his Form W-4. Brianne also noted that Mike did not list his "spouse" or children on his application or retirement plan paperwork and earlier mentioned that he was single. Based on both written and oral statements made by Mike, Brianne should ask Mike to prepare a corrected W-4. If he is unwilling to do so, she should withhold as if Mike is a single taxpayer with no allowances. ♦

EXAMPLE George works in the payroll department and receives a W-4 from a new employee, Beatrice. Beatrice indicates married status and two children and claims 10 allowances on her W-4. George notes that her married status is consistent with her other paperwork and Beatrice has provided no oral or written statements that would indicate she is not married and has two children. George is not required to verify the existence of Beatrice's spouse and children. ♦

Although employers are not required to submit Forms W-4 to the Internal Revenue Service, that does not mean that new hires are not reported. In large part designed to assist with the enforcement of child support payments, the Personal Responsibility and Work Opportunity Reconciliation Act of 1996 (PRWORA) was passed requiring states to maintain a database of all new hires. Although many states use a specific form for reporting new hires, they will often also accept a completed Form W-4.

9-1a Computing Income Tax Withholding

The amount of income tax to be withheld by the employer is based on gross taxable wages before deducting FICA taxes, pension payments, union dues, insurance, and other deductions. An employer may elect to use any of several methods to determine the amount of the income tax withholding for each individual employee. Most commonly, withholding amounts are determined by use of the percentage method or by use of wage bracket tables. To compute the withholding amount under the percentage method, the employer should:

1. Multiply the number of allowances claimed by the employee (from Form W-4) by the allowance amount;
2. Subtract that amount from the employee's gross taxable wages for the pay period; and
3. Apply the result in Step 2 to the applicable withholding table in Appendix C for the appropriate marital status.

The allowance amounts used in Step 1 for 2019 for various pay periods are from IRS Publication 15, "(Circular E), Employer's Tax Guide." Although exemptions were repealed by the TCJA, allowance amounts remain based on what would have been the 2019 exemption amount of $4,200.

Pay Period	2019 Allowance Amount
Weekly	$ 80.80
Biweekly	161.50
Semimonthly	175.00
Monthly	350.00
Quarterly	1,050.00
Semiannually	2,100.00
Annually	4,200.00

EXAMPLE   Sharon is married, and her pay is $2,300 per month. On her Form W-4, Sharon claims married with a total of two allowances. Using the percentage method, the amount of withholding for Sharon is calculated as follows:

1. Allowances amount (monthly) $ 350.00
   Number of allowances claimed   × 2
   Total $ 700.00

2. Gross wages $2,300.00
   Less: amount from above   (700.00)
   Withholding income $1,600.00

3. Withholding from percentage tables in Appendix C:
   ($1,600.00 − $983.00) × 10% = $61.70 ♦

Under the wage bracket method of determining withholding, wage bracket tables are provided for weekly, biweekly, semimonthly, monthly, and daily payroll periods for both married and single taxpayers. The amount of withholding is obtained from the table for the appropriate payroll period and marital status, and is based on the total wages and the number of withholding allowances claimed. The monthly tables for single and married taxpayers are reproduced in Appendix C.

EXAMPLE Sharon's withholding from the previous example may also be obtained from the wage bracket tables in Appendix C. For a wage payment of $2,300 with two allowances, using the married person's monthly payroll period table, the amount of the withholding is found to be $62. ♦

The income tax withholding tables are constructed so that taxpayers that have completed their W-4 properly, will receive an income tax refund during tax filing season. Many taxpayers are satisfied with the resulting refund even though a tax refund represents an interest-free loan to the government. The overpayment of taxes serves as a "forced" savings account which provides the opportunity to purchase a big ticket item in late spring when the refund is received. Taxpayers should also be aware that interest is not charged symmetrically: underpayments of tax may result in penalties and interest (see LO 9.2), while overpayments are not usually credited with interest. Given the changes to the individual tax structure by the TCJA and the pending 2020 changes to the Form W-4, taxpayers should consider using the withholding calculator at **www.irs.gov**, complete an accurate Form W-4, and consider a mid-year review to ensure that the withholding amounts are proper given current income and other circumstances.

TAX BREAK

9-1b Pension and Deferred Income

Income tax withholding is also required on pension and other deferred income payments based on Form W-4P, Withholding Certificate for Pension or Annuity Payments, as completed and signed by the taxpayer. Financial institutions and corporations must withhold on the taxable part of pension, profit sharing, stock bonus, and individual retirement account payments. The rates used for withholding vary depending on the nature of the payment, as described below:

1. Periodic payments (such as annuities): Rates are based on the taxpayer's Form W-4P or if no W-4P is filed, tax will be withheld as if the taxpayer were married and claiming three withholding allowances.
2. Nonperiodic payments: Withholding is deducted at a flat 10 percent rate, except for certain distributions from qualified retirement plans, which have a required 20 percent withholding tax rate. See LO 9.8 for a discussion of withholding on rollover distributions.

EXAMPLE Adam is a retired college professor and receives a pension of $775 per month. The payor should withhold on the pension, based on Adam's signed W-4P, in the same manner as if it were Adam's salary. ♦

9-1c Tip Reporting

Tips are a significant part of the compensation received by employees in many types of jobs such as the following:

- Barber
- Hairdresser
- Parking attendant
- Porter
- Food and beverage servers
- Busser and others who share restaurant tip pools

- Delivery driver
- Airport skycap
- Bartenders
- Hotel housekeepers
- Manicurists
- Taxi, Uber and Lyft drivers

Tips are generally not paid directly by the employer to the employee and as a result, create a unique challenge for tax reporting for both the employee and employer. Additionally, tips are often paid in cash and thus capturing tips as income presents a challenge to the IRS.

To reduce the underreporting of tip income, the IRS requires employees to report tip income to their employers on Form 4070.

Form **4070** (Rev. August 2005) Department of the Treasury Internal Revenue Service	**Employee's Report of Tips to Employer**	OMB No. 1545-0074
Employee's name and address		**Social security number**
Employer's name and address (include establishment name, if different)		**1** Cash tips received
		2 Credit and debit card tips received
		3 Tips paid out
Month or shorter period in which tips were received from , , to ,		**4** Net tips (lines **1** + **2** - **3**)
Signature		Date

For Paperwork Reduction Act Notice, see the instructions on the back of this form.   Cat. No. 41320P   Form **4070** (Rev. 8-2005)

The employer uses the information from Form 4070 to properly withhold employment and income taxes on tip income. To provide some assurance that accurate tip income is being reported by employees in large food or beverage establishments, the employer must compare employee-reported tips to 8 percent of the employer's sales. If the reported tips are less than 8 percent of sales, the employer must allocate the difference to each employee and report this amount on each employee's Form W-2 in Box 8 (Allocated Tips). The allocation of tip income can be accomplished in one of three ways. The employer may allocate the amount based on (1) gross receipts per employee, (2) hours worked by each employee (available only to employers having fewer than the equivalent of twenty-five full-time employees), or (3) a good faith agreement as explained on Form 8027, Employer's Annual Information Return of Tip Income and Allocated Tips. For a detailed explanation of the allocation process, see the instructions for Form 8027. With the diversity of businesses and tipping customs, the IRS also permits employers to enter into the Tip Rate Determination Education Program, in which the employer and the IRS work out a tip rate and reporting system. For more information on tip reporting in general, see the IRS website (**www.irs.gov**) or a tax research service.

TAX BREAK The IRS has created two programs to help employers in businesses in which employees are compensated with tips: Tip Rate Determination Agreement (TRDA) and Tip Reporting Alternative Commitment (TRAC). These two programs are designed to help employers and employees more accurately report tip income and simplify the process for reporting tips by employees and employers.

9-1d Backup Withholding

In some situations, individuals may be subject to backup withholding on payments such as interest and dividends. The purpose of backup withholding is to ensure that income tax is paid on income reported on Form 1099. If backup withholding applies, the payor (e.g., bank or insurance company) must withhold 24 percent of the amount paid to the taxpayer. Payors are required to use backup withholding in the following cases:

1. The taxpayer does not give the payor his or her taxpayer identification number (e.g., Social Security number),
2. The taxpayer fails to certify that he or she is not subject to backup withholding,
3. The IRS informs the payor that the taxpayer gave an incorrect identification number, or

4. The IRS informs the payor to start withholding because the taxpayer has not reported the income on his or her tax return.

EXAMPLE   Kamili earned $2,000 in interest income from Cactus Savings Bank. Kamili failed to certify that she was not subject to backup withholding. As a result, the bank must withhold taxes of $480 (24 percent of $2,000) from the interest payments to Kamili. ◆

Taxpayers who give false information to avoid backup withholding are subject to a $500 civil penalty and criminal penalties, including fines and/or imprisonment.

Self-Study Problem 9.1   *See Appendix E for Solutions to Self-Study Problems*

For 2019, John earns $2,500 per month and has two dependent children. He is divorced and claims three allowances on his Form W-4. Calculate John's withholding using:

1. The percentage method $_____
2. The wage bracket method $_____

9-2 ESTIMATED PAYMENTS

9.2 Learning Objective

Determine taxpayers' quarterly estimated payments.

Self-employed taxpayers are not subject to withholding; however, they must make quarterly estimated tax payments. Taxpayers with large amounts of interest, dividends, and other income not subject to withholding are also generally required to make estimated payments. Payments are made in four installments on April 15, June 15, and September 15 of the tax year, and January 15 of the following year (or the first business day after if the dates fall on a weekend or holiday), based on the taxpayer's estimate of the amount of the tax liability for the year. A taxpayer with self-employment income must begin making the payments when he or she first meets the filing requirements.

Never write out a check to the "IRS." The IRS issues this warning every year, because "IRS" may be easily changed to "MRS" plus an individual's name if the check falls into the wrong hands. Checks must be made payable to the U.S. Treasury, as a reminder that the IRS is merely the collector of revenue for the federal government. Alternatively, individual taxpayers can draft their bank account using Direct Pay or, for a fee, pay using a debit or credit card. Both methods are available on the IRS website.

Any individual taxpayer who has estimated tax for the year of $1,000 or more, after subtracting withholding, and whose withholding does not equal or exceed the "required annual payment," must make quarterly estimated payments. The required annual payment is the smallest of the following amounts:

1. Ninety percent of the tax shown on the current year's return,
2. One hundred percent of the tax shown on the preceding year's return (such return must cover a full 12 months), or
3. Ninety percent of the current-year tax determined by placing taxable income, alternative minimum taxable income, and adjusted self-employment income on an annualized basis for each quarter.

A special rule applies to individuals with adjusted gross income in excess of $150,000 for the previous year. These high-income taxpayers must pay 110 percent of the amount of tax shown on the prior year tax return for the current year estimated payments, instead of 100 percent, to meet the requirements in the second option on the previous page.

Estimated payments need not be paid if the estimated tax, after subtracting withholding, can reasonably be expected to be less than $1,000. Therefore, employees who also have self-employment income may avoid making estimated payments by filing a new Form W-4 and increasing the amount of their withholding on their regular salary.

The IRS imposes a nondeductible penalty on the amounts of any underpayments of estimated tax. The penalty applies when any installment is less than the required annual payment divided by the number of installments that should have been made, which is usually four. Form 2210, Underpayment of Estimated Tax by Individuals, Estates, and Trusts, is used for the calculation of the penalty associated with the underpayment of estimated tax.

Good tax planning dictates that a taxpayer postpone payment of taxes as long as no penalty is imposed. Unpaid taxes are equivalent to an interest-free loan from the government. Therefore, taxpayers should base their estimated payments on the method which results in the lowest amount of required quarterly or annual payment. For example, a taxpayer who expects his tax liability to increase might base his or her estimated payments this year on the amount of the tax liability for the prior year.

Self-Study Problem 9.2   *See Appendix E for Solutions to Self-Study Problems*

Ray Adams (Social Security number 466-47-1131) estimates his required annual payment for 2019 to be $8,140. He has a $365 overpayment of last year's taxes that he wishes to apply to the first quarter estimated tax payment for 2019. Complete the first quarter voucher below for Ray for 2019 by assuming any additional information, such as Ray's address.

Form **1040-ES** Department of the Treasury Internal Revenue Service	20**19 Estimated Tax**	Payment **1** Voucher	OMB No. 1545-0074

File only if you are making a payment of estimated tax by check or money order. Mail this voucher with your check or money order payable to "**United States Treasury.**" Write your social security number and "2019 Form 1040-ES" on your check or money order. Do not send cash. Enclose, but do not staple or attach, your payment with this voucher.	**Calendar year—Due April 15, 2019**
	Amount of estimated tax you are paying by check or money order.
	Dollars / Cents

Pay online at www.irs.gov/etpay

Simple.
Fast.
Secure.

Print or type

Your first name and initial	Your last name	Your social security number
If joint payment, complete for spouse		
Spouse's first name and initial	Spouse's last name	Spouse's social security number
Address (number, street, and apt. no.)		
City, state, and ZIP code. (If a foreign address, enter city, also complete spaces below.)		
Foreign country name	Foreign province/county	Foreign postal code

For Privacy Act and Paperwork Reduction Act Notice, see instructions.   Form 1040-ES (2019)

9-3 THE FICA TAX

Compute the FICA tax.

The Federal Insurance Contributions Act (FICA) imposes Social Security and Medicare taxes. It was passed by Congress in 1935 to provide benefits for qualified retired and disabled workers. If a worker should die, it would also provide the family of the worker with benefits. The Medicare program for the elderly is also funded by FICA taxes.

FICA taxes have two parts, Social Security (Old Age, Survivors, and Disability Insurance [OASDI]) and Medicare. Employees and their employers are both required to pay FICA taxes. Employers withhold a specified percentage of each employee's wages up to a maximum base amount, match the amount withheld with an equal amount, and pay the total to the Social Security Administration.

The Social Security (OASDI) tax rate is 6.2 percent and the Medicare tax rate is 1.45 percent each for employees and employers in 2019. The original FICA tax in 1935 was 1 percent of the first $3,000 in earnings. The maximum wage subject to the Social Security portion of the FICA tax is $132,900 in 2019, and all wages are subject to the Medicare portion of the FICA tax. The maximum wages to which the rates apply have increased over the years as presented in the following table.

Year	Maximum $ Base for 6.2% (employee and employer)	Maximum $ Base for 1.45% (employee and employer)*
2015	118,500	Unlimited
2016	118,500	Unlimited
2017	127,200	Unlimited
2018	128,400	Unlimited
2019	132,900	Unlimited

*Employees pay a 0.9 percent Medicare tax on wages over $200,000 single and head of household ($250,000 married filing jointly). See Chapter 6 for more information.

Taxpayers age 18 and older may request an online statement of Social Security benefits including estimates of projected retirement, survivors', and disability benefits. The statement also shows the taxpayer's Social Security earnings history, giving the taxpayer an opportunity to correct any errors or omissions. The personalized online statement is available at **www.ssa.gov/myaccount**. In some cases, the Social Security Administration will provide a paper version of this statement by mail.

EXAMPLE Katherine earns $21,500 for 2019. The FICA tax on her wages is calculated as follows:

Katherine:	Soc. Sec. − 6.2% × $21,500	$1,333.00
	Medicare − 1.45% × $21,500	311.75
	Total employee FICA tax	$1,644.75
Katherine's employer:	Soc. Sec. − 6.2% × $21,500	$1,333.00
	Medicare − 1.45% × $21,500	311.75
	Total employer FICA tax	$1,644.75
Total FICA tax		$3,289.50

♦

EXAMPLE Nora is an employee of Serissa Company. Her salary for 2019 is $138,000. Nora's portion of the FICA tax is calculated as follows:

Soc. Sec. − 6.2% × $132,900	$8,239.80
Medicare − 1.45% × $138,000	2,001.00
Total employee FICA tax	$10,240.80

The total combined FICA tax (employee's and employer's share) is $20,481.60. ♦

FICA taxes are paid one-half by employees through withholding and one-half by employers. Since the employer portion of the tax increases the cost of employees, many economists believe that even the employer's share of FICA tax is passed on to employees in the form of lower compensation. Thus, employees, like self-employed individuals, effectively bear both halves of FICA taxes.

9-3a Overpayment of Social Security Taxes

Taxpayers who work for more than one employer during the same tax year may pay more than the maximum amount of Social Security taxes. This occurs when the taxpayer's total wages are more than the maximum base amount for the year. When this happens, the taxpayer should compute the excess taxes paid, and report the excess on Line 11 of Schedule 3 of Form 1040 as an additional payment against his or her tax liability. This way, the taxpayer is refunded the excess Social Security tax. Note that the employer is not entitled to a similar refund for the overpaid matching Social Security tax.

EXAMPLE   Jerry worked for two employers during 2019. The first employer withheld and paid Social Security taxes on $80,000 of salary paid to Jerry, and the second employer withheld and paid Social Security taxes on $60,000 of salary paid to Jerry. The amount of Jerry's excess Social Security taxes paid for 2019 is computed as follows: 6.2% (Social Security rate) × [$80,000 + $60,000 − $132,900 (maximum for Social Security portion of FICA tax)] = $440.20. Jerry receives credit against his 2019 income tax liability equal to the excess Social Security taxes of $440. No excess Medicare tax has been paid, as there is no upper limit on Medicare wages. ♦

Self-Study Problem 9.3	**See Appendix E for Solutions to Self-Study Problems**

Debbie earns $137,000 in 2019. Calculate the total FICA tax that must be paid by:

Debbie:	Soc. Sec.	$_____
	Medicare	$_____
Debbie's employer:	Soc. Sec.	$_____
	Medicare	$_____
Total FICA tax		$_____

<table>
<tr><td>**Learning Objective 9.4**</td><td>## 9-4 FEDERAL TAX DEPOSIT SYSTEM</td></tr>
<tr><td>Apply the federal deposit system to payroll withholding.</td><td>Employers must make periodic deposits of the taxes that are withheld from employees' wages. The frequency of the deposits depends on the total income tax withheld and the total FICA taxes for all employees. Employers are either monthly depositors or semiweekly depositors. Prior to the beginning of each calendar year, taxpayers are required to determine which of the two deposit schedules they are required to use. If income tax withholding and FICA taxes of $100,000 or more are accumulated at any time during the year, the depositor is subject to a special one-day deposit rule.</td></tr>
</table>

Monthly or semiweekly deposit status is determined by using a lookback period, consisting of the four quarters beginning July 1 of the second preceding year and ending June 30 of the prior year. If the total income tax withheld from wages and FICA taxes attributable to wages for the four quarters in the lookback period is $50,000 or less, employers are monthly depositors for the current year. Monthly depositors must make deposits of employment taxes and taxes withheld by the fifteenth day of the month following the month of withholding. New employers are automatically monthly depositors.

If the total income tax withheld from wages and FICA attributable to wages for the four quarters in the lookback period is more than $50,000, the employer is a semiweekly depositor for the current year. Taxes on payments made on Wednesday, Thursday, or Friday must be deposited by the following Wednesday; taxes on payments made on the other days of the week must be deposited by the following Friday. If a deposit is scheduled for a day that is not a banking day, the deposit is considered to be made timely if it is made by the close of the next banking day.

EXAMPLE Tom runs a small business with ten employees. During the lookback period for the current year, the total withholding and FICA taxes amounted to $40,000. Since this is less than $50,000, Tom is a monthly depositor. His payroll tax deposits must be made by the fifteenth day of the month following the month of withholding. ◆

Tax payments (monthly, semiweekly, or daily for large depositors) must be made by Electronic Federal Tax Payment System (EFTPS), or by another electronic transfer method. Generally, employers must file Form 941, Employer's Quarterly Federal Tax Return, which reports the federal income taxes withheld from wages and the total FICA taxes attributable to wages paid during each quarter. Form 941 must be accompanied by any payroll taxes not yet deposited for the quarter. A special deposit rule allows small employers who accumulate less than $2,500 tax liability during a quarter to skip monthly payments and pay the entire amount of their payroll taxes with their quarterly Form 941. Form 941 must be filed by the last day of the month following the end of the quarter. For example, the first quarter Form 941, covering the months of January through March, must be filed by April 30. The Form 941 e-file program allows a taxpayer to electronically file Form 941 or Form 944.

Nearly a million very small employers with employment tax liability of $1,000 or less per year are allowed to file employment tax returns just once a year, instead of quarterly; for example, by January 31 of 2019 for 2018 employment taxes. Qualifying small employers receive written notification from the IRS that they should file using a Form 944 instead of the standard Form 941 used by most employers. The Form 944 is due annually, at the end of the month, following the taxpayer's year end.

IRS Publication 15, "(Circular E), Employers Tax Guide," covers the rules regarding the calculation and deposit of payroll taxes in detail and is an indispensable resource for those working in this complex area.

Self-Study Problem 9.4 *See Appendix E for Solutions to Self-Study Problems*

For the first quarter of 2019, Charlotte York has two employees. The payroll information for these two employees for the first quarter is as follows:

	Mary			Chris		
	January	**February**	**March**	**January**	**February**	**March**
Gross wages	$2,000	$2,000	$2,100	$1,000	$1,000	$1,500
Federal income tax withheld	230	230	235	60	60	180
FICA tax withheld	153	153	161	77	77	115

Charlotte deposited $750 on February 15, $750 on March 15, and $967 on April 15. Using this information, complete only page 1 of Charlotte's Form 941, on Page 9-17, for the first quarter of 2019.

Self-Study Problem 9.4

Form 941 for 2019: Employer's QUARTERLY Federal Tax Return

(Rev. January 2019)   Department of the Treasury — Internal Revenue Service

950117

OMB No. 1545-0029

Employer identification number (EIN) ☐☐ – ☐☐☐☐☐☐☐

Name *(not your trade name)*

Trade name *(if any)*

Address
Number   Street   Suite or room number

City   State   ZIP code

Foreign country name   Foreign province/county   Foreign postal code

Report for this Quarter of 2019
(Check one.)

☐ **1:** January, February, March

☐ **2:** April, May, June

☐ **3:** July, August, September

☐ **4:** October, November, December

Go to *www.irs.gov/Form941* for instructions and the latest information.

Read the separate instructions before you complete Form 941. Type or print within the boxes.

Part 1:   Answer these questions for this quarter.

1   Number of employees who received wages, tips, or other compensation for the pay period including: *Mar. 12* (Quarter 1), *June 12* (Quarter 2), *Sept. 12* (Quarter 3), or *Dec. 12* (Quarter 4) ... **1** ☐

2   Wages, tips, and other compensation ... **2** ☐

3   Federal income tax withheld from wages, tips, and other compensation ... **3** ☐

4   If no wages, tips, and other compensation are subject to social security or Medicare tax ☐ Check and go to line 6.

	Column 1		Column 2
5a Taxable social security wages . .	☐	× 0.124 =	☐
5b Taxable social security tips . . .	☐	× 0.124 =	☐
5c Taxable Medicare wages & tips. .	☐	× 0.029 =	☐
5d Taxable wages & tips subject to Additional Medicare Tax withholding	☐	× 0.009 =	☐

5e   Add Column 2 from lines 5a, 5b, 5c, and 5d ... **5e** ☐

5f   Section 3121(q) Notice and Demand—Tax due on unreported tips (see instructions) ... **5f** ☐

6   Total taxes before adjustments. Add lines 3, 5e, and 5f ... **6** ☐

7   Current quarter's adjustment for fractions of cents ... **7** ☐

8   Current quarter's adjustment for sick pay ... **8** ☐

9   Current quarter's adjustments for tips and group-term life insurance ... **9** ☐

10   Total taxes after adjustments. Combine lines 6 through 9 ... **10** ☐

11   Qualified small business payroll tax credit for increasing research activities. Attach Form 8974 ... **11** ☐

12   Total taxes after adjustments and credits. Subtract line 11 from line 10 ... **12** ☐

13   Total deposits for this quarter, including overpayment applied from a prior quarter and overpayments applied from Form 941-X, 941-X (PR), 944-X, or 944-X (SP) filed in the current quarter ... **13** ☐

14   Balance due. If line 12 is more than line 13, enter the difference and see instructions ... **14** ☐

15   Overpayment. If line 13 is more than line 12, enter the difference ☐ Check one: ☐ Apply to next return. ☐ Send a refund.

▶ You MUST complete both pages of Form 941 and SIGN it.

Next ▶

For Privacy Act and Paperwork Reduction Act Notice, see the back of the Payment Voucher.   Cat. No. 17001Z   Form **941** (Rev. 1-2019)

950217

Name *(not your trade name)*	Employer identification number (EIN)

Part 2: **Tell us about your deposit schedule and tax liability for this quarter.**

If you are unsure about whether you are a monthly schedule depositor or a semiweekly schedule depositor, see section 11 of Pub. 15.

16   Check one: ☐   **Line 12 on this return is less than $2,500 or line 12 on the return for the prior quarter was less than $2,500, and you didn't incur a $100,000 next-day deposit obligation during the current quarter.** If line 12 for the prior quarter was less than $2,500 but line 12 on this return is $100,000 or more, you must provide a record of your federal tax liability. If you are a monthly schedule depositor, complete the deposit schedule below; if you are a semiweekly schedule depositor, attach Schedule B (Form 941). Go to Part 3.

☐   **You were a monthly schedule depositor for the entire quarter.** Enter your tax liability for each month and total liability for the quarter, then go to Part 3.

Tax liability: Month 1   [_____ . ___]

Month 2   [_____ . ___]

Month 3   [_____ . ___]

Total liability for quarter   [_____ . ___]   **Total must equal line 12.**

☐   **You were a semiweekly schedule depositor for any part of this quarter.** Complete Schedule B (Form 941), Report of Tax Liability for Semiweekly Schedule Depositors, and attach it to Form 941.

Part 3: **Tell us about your business. If a question does NOT apply to your business, leave it blank.**

17   If your business has closed or you stopped paying wages . . . . ☐ Check here, and

enter the final date you paid wages   [___/___/___] .

18   If you are a seasonal employer and you don't have to file a return for every quarter of the year   . . ☐ Check here.

Part 4: **May we speak with your third-party designee?**

Do you want to allow an employee, a paid tax preparer, or another person to discuss this return with the IRS? See the instructions for details.

☐ Yes.   Designee's name and phone number   [_____]   [_____]

Select a 5-digit Personal Identification Number (PIN) to use when talking to the IRS.   ☐ ☐ ☐ ☐ ☐

☐ No.

Part 5: **Sign here. You MUST complete both pages of Form 941 and SIGN it.**

Under penalties of perjury, I declare that I have examined this return, including accompanying schedules and statements, and to the best of my knowledge and belief, it is true, correct, and complete. Declaration of preparer (other than taxpayer) is based on all information of which preparer has any knowledge.

✗	Sign your name here	[_____]	Print your name here	[_____]
			Print your title here	[_____]
	Date	[___/___/___]	Best daytime phone	[_____]

Paid Preparer Use Only   Check if you are self-employed . . . ☐

Preparer's name	[_____]	PTIN	[_____]
Preparer's signature	[_____]	Date	[___/___/___]
Firm's name (or yours if self-employed)	[_____]	EIN	[_____]
Address	[_____]	Phone	[_____]
City	[_____]	State [_____]	ZIP code	[_____]

Form **941** (Rev. 1-2019)

9-5 **EMPLOYER REPORTING REQUIREMENTS**

Prepare employer payroll reporting.

On or before January 31 of the year following the calendar year of payment, an employer must furnish to each employee two copies of the employee's Wage and Tax Statement, Form W-2, for the previous calendar year. If employment is terminated before the end of the year and the employee requests a Form W-2, the employer must furnish the Form W-2 within 30 days after the last wage payment is made or after the employee request, whichever is later. Otherwise, the general rule requiring the W-2 to be furnished to the employee by January 31 applies. The original copy (Copy A) of all Forms W-2 and Form W-3 (Transmittal of Wage and Tax Statements) must be filed by the employer with the Social Security Administration by January 31 of the year following the calendar year of payment. Copy B of Form W-2 is filed with the employee's federal tax return. Employers retain Copy D of Form W-2 for their records. Extra copies of Form W-2 are prepared for the employee to use when filing state and local tax returns.

Form W-2 is used to report wages, tips, and other compensation paid to an employee. Form W-2 also provides the employee with additional supplemental information. Among the items which must be reported on the employee's Form W-2 are the cost of employer-sponsored health coverage, employer contributions to a health savings account (HSA), excess group-term life insurance premiums, Roth contributions to an employer plan, and certain reimbursements of travel and other ordinary and necessary expenses.

Special rules apply to the reimbursement of travel and other ordinary and necessary employee business expenses. If an employee is reimbursed for travel and other ordinary and necessary business expenses, income and employment tax withholding may be required. If a reimbursement payment is considered to have been made under an accountable plan, the amount is excluded from the employee's gross income and consequently is not required to be included on Form W-2, and no withholding is required. Alternatively, reimbursements of travel and other employee business expenses made under a nonaccountable plan must be included as wages on Form W-2, and the amounts are subject to withholding. Payments are considered made under a nonaccountable plan in the following circumstances: (1) the employee receives a reimbursement for expenses under an arrangement which does not require the employee to account adequately to the employer, or the employee receives advances under an arrangement which does not require the employee to return amounts in excess of substantiated expenses; or (2) the employee receives amounts under an arrangement that requires the employee to substantiate reimbursed expenses, but the amounts are not substantiated within a reasonable period of time, or the employee receives amounts under a plan which requires excess reimbursements to be returned to the employer, but the employee does not return such excess amounts within a reasonable period of time. In the first case, the entire amount paid under the expense account plan is considered wages subject to withholding, whereas under the circumstances described in the second situation, only the amounts in excess of the substantiated expenses are subject to withholding.

The Social Security Administration permits employers to prepare and file up to 50 Forms W-2 using their online business services. Employers should go to **www.ssa.gov** to register for the service.

TAX BREAK

9-5a **Form W-2G**

Gambling winnings are reported by gambling establishments on Form W-2G. Amounts that must be reported include certain winnings from horse and dog racing, jai alai, lotteries, state-conducted lotteries, sweepstakes, wagering pools, bingo, keno, and slot machines. In certain cases, withholding of income taxes is required. Forms W-2G must be transmitted to the taxpayer no later than January 31 of the year following the calendar year of payment, and to the IRS along with Form 1096 by the last day of February of the year following the calendar year of payment. Requirements to file Form W-2G can differ between the type of wagering or gaming. The due date is March 31 if transmitting electronically to the IRS. More information can be found in the instructions for Form W-2G.

9-5b   Information Returns

Taxpayers engaged in a trade or business are required to file Form 1099 for each recipient of certain payments made in the course of their trade or business. Where applicable, federal income tax withheld with respect to the payment is also reported on Form 1099. The common types of payments and the related Form 1099 are summarized in Table 9.1.

TABLE 9.1	1099 FORMS
Form	**Used For**
1099-B	Payments of proceeds from brokers
1099-DIV	Dividend payments
1099-G	Certain government payments (state income tax refund)
1099-INT	Interest payments
1099-K	Merchant card and third-party network transactions
1099-MISC	Miscellaneous payments
1099-R	Payments of pension, annuity, profit sharing, retirement plan, IRA, insurance contracts, etc.
1099-S	Payments from real estate transactions

Forms 1099 must be mailed to the recipients by January 31 of the year following the calendar year of payment. However, payors are allowed until February 15 of the year following the calendar year of payment to provide Forms 1099-B, 1099-S, and certain 1099-MISC forms. A separate Form 1096 must be used to transmit each type of 1099 to the appropriate IRS Campus Processing Site by the last day of February (or by January 31 if payments are reported in Box 7) of the year following the calendar year of payment. The due date is March 31 if transmitting electronically to the IRS.

New Tax Law

Typically, nonemployee compensation has been reported in Box 7 on Form 1099-MISC. Nonemployee compensation is generally when an individual who does not qualify as an employee is paid for services provided. The IRS has released a draft Form 1099-NEC to begin reporting nonemployee compensation starting in 2020.

9-5c   Form 1099-K Reporting Merchant Card and Third-Party Payments

Banks and online payment networks ("payment settlement entities"), such as PayPal, Venmo, VISA, and MasterCard, are required to use Form 1099-K to report credit card sales and other reportable sales transactions to the IRS and to the businesses making reportable sales. The reporting requirement is triggered for an entity when the total dollar amount of transactions for a particular merchant exceeds $20,000 and the total number of transactions exceeds 200.

TAX BREAK

If a taxpayer receives a Form 1099, the income reported on that form should be included on the tax return. The IRS is going to match the identification number on the Form 1099 to the taxpayer's tax return and will likely notice if that income is missing. Form 1099s are not usually required to be attached to the taxpayer's return; however, if tax was withheld on the payment reported, the Form 1099 should be attached as necessary.

Self-Study Problem 9.5   *See Appendix E for Solutions to Self-Study Problems*

Big Bank (P.O. Box 12344, San Diego, CA 92101; E.I.N. 95-1234567; California ID 800 4039250 092; and telephone number 800-555-1212) paid an employee, Mary Jones (6431 Gary Street, San Diego, CA 92115), wages of $16,150 for 2019. The federal income tax withholding for the year amounted to $2,422, and FICA withheld was $1,235.48 ($1,001.30 for Social Security tax and $234.18 for Medicare tax). State income tax withheld was $969.00. Mary's FICA wages were the same as her total wages, and her Social Security number is 464-74-1132.

a.   Complete the following Form W-2 for Mary Jones from Big Bank.

a Employee's social security number	OMB No. 1545-0008	Safe, accurate, FAST! Use	IRS e~file	Visit the IRS website at www.irs.gov/efile

b Employer identification number (EIN)	**1** Wages, tips, other compensation | **2** Federal income tax withheld
c Employer's name, address, and ZIP code	**3** Social security wages | **4** Social security tax withheld
	5 Medicare wages and tips | **6** Medicare tax withheld
	7 Social security tips | **8** Allocated tips
d Control number	**9** | **10** Dependent care benefits
e Employee's first name and initial Last name Suff.	**11** Nonqualified plans | **12a** See instructions for box 12
	13 Statutory employee Retirement plan Third-party sick pay | **12b**
	14 Other | **12c**
	| **12d**
f Employee's address and ZIP code	

15 State	Employer's state ID number	16 State wages, tips, etc.	17 State income tax	18 Local wages, tips, etc.	19 Local income tax	20 Locality name

Form **W-2** Wage and Tax Statement   **2019**   Department of the Treasury—Internal Revenue Service

Copy B—To Be Filed With Employee's FEDERAL Tax Return.
This information is being furnished to the Internal Revenue Service.

b.   Mary also has a savings account at Big Bank, which paid her interest for 2019 of $461. Complete the following Form 1099-INT for Mary's interest income.

☐ CORRECTED (if checked)

PAYER'S name, street address, city or town, state or province, country, ZIP or foreign postal code, and telephone no.	Payer's RTN (optional)	OMB No. 1545-0112 20**19** Form **1099-INT**	**Interest Income**
	1 Interest income $		
PAYER'S TIN RECIPIENT'S TIN	**2** Early withdrawal penalty $		**Copy B**
	3 Interest on U.S. Savings Bonds and Treas. obligations $		**For Recipient**
RECIPIENT'S name	**4** Federal income tax withheld $	**5** Investment expenses $	This is important tax information and is being furnished to the IRS. If you are required to file a return, a negligence penalty or other sanction may be imposed on you if this income is taxable and the IRS determines that it has not been reported.
	6 Foreign tax paid $	**7** Foreign country or U.S. possession	
Street address (including apt. no.)	**8** Tax-exempt interest $	**9** Specified private activity bond interest $	
City or town, state or province, country, and ZIP or foreign postal code	**10** Market discount $	**11** Bond premium $	
FATCA filing requirement ☐	**12** Bond premium on Treasury obligations $	**13** Bond premium on tax-exempt bond $	
Account number (see instructions)	**14** Tax-exempt and tax credit bond CUSIP no.	**15** State **16** State identification no. **17** State tax withheld $ $	

Form **1099-INT**   (keep for your records)   www.irs.gov/Form1099INT   Department of the Treasury - Internal Revenue Service

<table>
<tr><td>

Learning Objective 9.6

Compute the amount of FUTA tax for an employer.

</td><td>

9-6 THE FUTA TAX

Please note: Employers in jurisdictions that have not repaid money borrowed from the federal government for unemployment benefits will have a higher FUTA tax than the 0.6 percent illustrated below. At the time we go to print, only the U.S. Virgin Islands may have a credit reduction in 2019. For purposes of the problems and examples in this textbook, assume that the employer does not reside in one of the jurisdictions where a higher FUTA tax applies.

The Federal Unemployment Tax Act (FUTA) instituted a tax that is not withheld from employees' wages, but instead is paid in full by employers. The federal unemployment tax rate is 6 percent of an employee's wages up to $7,000. A credit is allowed for state unemployment taxes of 5.4 percent. Therefore, the effective federal unemployment tax rate is only 0.6 percent if the state also assesses an unemployment tax.

</td></tr>
</table>

EXAMPLE   Karen has two employees in 2019, John, who earned $12,500 this year, and Sue, who earned $15,000. The FUTA tax is calculated as follows:

John's wages, $12,500	
(maximum $7,000)	$ 7,000
Sue's wages, $15,000	
(maximum $7,000)	7,000
Total FUTA wages	14,000
FUTA tax at 0.6%	$ 84

        ◆

Employers report their FUTA liability for the year on Form 940, Employer's Annual Federal Unemployment (FUTA) Tax Return. Like federal income tax withholding and FICA taxes, federal unemployment taxes must be deposited by electronic funds transfer (EFTPS). A deposit is required when the FUTA taxes for the quarter, plus any amount not yet deposited for the prior quarter(s), exceed $500. If required, the deposit must be made by the last day of the month after the end of each quarter.

EXAMPLE   Ti Corporation's federal unemployment tax liability for the first quarter of 2019, after reduction by the credit for state unemployment taxes, is $255; for the second quarter, $200; for the third quarter, $75; and for the fourth quarter, $25. Ti Corporation must deposit $530, the sum of the first, second, and third quarters' liability, by October 31, 2019. The remaining $25 may be either deposited or paid with Form 940. ◆

Because states administer federal-state unemployment programs, most of the unemployment tax is paid to the state. Employers must pay all state unemployment taxes for the year by the due date of the federal Form 940 to get full credit for the state taxes against FUTA.

Self-Study Problem 9.6	*See Appendix E for Solutions to Self-Study Problems*

The Rhus Company's payroll information for 2019 is summarized as follows:

	Quarter 1	*Quarter 2*	*Quarter 3*	*Quarter 4*
Gross earnings of employees	$25,000	$30,000	$26,000	$32,000
Individual employee earnings in excess of $7,000	None	$ 4,000	$10,000	$ 8,000

Rhus Company (E.I.N. 94-0001112), located at 400 8th Street N., La Crosse, WI 54601, pays Wisconsin state unemployment tax. The company makes the *required* deposits of both federal and state unemployment taxes on a timely basis and had no overpayment in 2018. Complete Parts 1–5 of the Rhus Company's 2019 Form 940 on Pages 9-23 and 9-24, using the above information.

Self-Study Problem 9.6

Form **940** for 2019: **Employer's Annual Federal Unemployment (FUTA) Tax Return**

Department of the Treasury — Internal Revenue Service

850113

OMB No. 1545-0028

Employer identification number (EIN) ☐☐ – ☐☐☐☐☐☐☐

Name *(not your trade name)*

Trade name *(if any)*

Address

Number   Street   Suite or room number

City   State   ZIP code

Foreign country name   Foreign province/county   Foreign postal code

DRAFT AS July 17, 2019 DO NOT FILE

Type of Return
(Check all that apply.)

☐ **a.** Amended

☐ **b.** Successor employer

☐ **c.** No payments to employees in 2019

☐ **d.** Final: Business closed or stopped paying wages

Go to *www.irs.gov/Form940* for instructions and the latest information.

Read the separate instructions before you complete this form. Please type or print within the boxes.

Part 1: Tell us about your return. If any line does NOT apply, leave it blank. See instructions before completing Part 1.

1a If you had to pay state unemployment tax in one state only, enter the state abbreviation . **1a** ☐☐

1b If you had to pay state unemployment tax in more than one state, you are a multi-state employer . . . . **1b** ☐ Check here. Complete Schedule A (Form 940).

2 If you paid wages in a state that is subject to **CREDIT REDUCTION** . . . . **2** ☐ Check here. Complete Schedule A (Form 940).

Part 2: Determine your FUTA tax before adjustments. If any line does NOT apply, leave it blank.

3 Total payments to all employees . . . . **3** _____ .

4 Payments exempt from FUTA tax . . . . **4** _____ .

Check all that apply: **4a** ☐ Fringe benefits   **4c** ☐ Retirement/Pension   **4e** ☐ Other
4b ☐ Group-term life insurance   **4d** ☐ Dependent care

5 Total of payments made to each employee in excess of $7,000 . . . . **5** _____ .

6 **Subtotal** (line 4 + line 5 = line 6) . . . . **6** _____ .

7 Total taxable FUTA wages (line 3 – line 6 = line 7). See instructions . . . . **7** _____ .

8 FUTA tax before adjustments (line 7 × 0.006 = line 8) . . . . **8** _____ .

Part 3: Determine your adjustments. If any line does NOT apply, leave it blank.

9 If ALL of the taxable FUTA wages you paid were excluded from state unemployment tax, multiply line 7 by 0.054 (line 7 × 0.054 = line 9). Go to line 12 . . . . **9** _____ .

10 If SOME of the taxable FUTA wages you paid were excluded from state unemployment tax, OR you paid ANY state unemployment tax late (after the due date for filing Form 940), complete the worksheet in the instructions. Enter the amount from line 7 of the worksheet . . **10** _____ .

11 If credit reduction applies, enter the total from Schedule A (Form 940) . . . . **11** _____ .

Part 4: Determine your FUTA tax and balance due or overpayment. If any line does NOT apply, leave it blank.

12 Total FUTA tax after adjustments (lines 8 + 9 + 10 + 11 = line 12) . . . . **12** _____ .

13 FUTA tax deposited for the year, including any overpayment applied from a prior year . **13** _____ .

14 Balance due. If line 12 is more than line 13, enter the excess on line 14.
• If line 14 is more than $500, you must deposit your tax.
• If line 14 is $500 or less, you may pay with this return. See instructions . . . . **14** _____ .

15 Overpayment. If line 13 is more than line 12, enter the excess on line 15 and check a box below **15** _____ .

▶ You **MUST** complete both pages of this form and **SIGN** it.   Check one: ☐ Apply to next return. ☐ Send a refund.

Next ▶

For Privacy Act and Paperwork Reduction Act Notice, see the back of the Payment Voucher.   Cat. No. 11234O   Form **940** (2019)

850212

Name (not your trade name)	Employer identification number (EIN)

Part 5:   Report your FUTA tax liability by quarter only if line 12 is more than $500. If not, go to Part 6.

16 Report the amount of your FUTA tax liability for each quarter; do NOT enter the amount you deposited. If you had no liability for a quarter, leave the line blank.

16a **1st quarter** (January 1 – March 31) . . . . **16a** ☐ .

16b **2nd quarter** (April 1 – June 30) . . . . **16b** ☐ .

16c **3rd quarter** (July 1 – September 30) . . . . **16c** ☐ .

16d **4th quarter** (October 1 – December 31) . . . . . . **16d** ☐ .

17 **Total tax liability for the year** (lines 16a + 16b + 16c + 16d = line 17) **17** ☐ .   **Total must equal line 12.**

Part 6:   May we speak with your third-party designee?

Do you want to allow an employee, a paid tax preparer, or another person to discuss this return with the IRS? See the instructions for details.

☐ **Yes.**   Designee's name and phone number

Select a 5-digit Personal Identification Number (PIN) to use when talking to IRS

☐ **No.**

Part 7:   Sign here. You MUST complete both pages of this form and SIGN it.

Under penalties of perjury, I declare that I have examined this return, including accompanying schedules and statements, and to the best of my knowledge and belief, it is true, correct, and complete, and that no part of any payment made to a state unemployment fund claimed as a credit was, or is to be, deducted from the payments made to employees. Declaration of preparer (other than taxpayer) is based on all information of which preparer has any knowledge.

✗ Sign your name here

| Print your name here | |
| Print your title here | |

Date   /   /

Best daytime phone

Paid Preparer Use Only   Check if you are self-employed ☐

Preparer's name		PTIN	
Preparer's signature		Date / /	
Firm's name (or yours if self-employed)		EIN	
Address		Phone	
City	State	ZIP code	

DRAFT AS OF JULY 17, 2019 DO NOT FILE

9-7 QUALIFIED RETIREMENT PLANS

9-7a Qualified Plans

For a retirement plan to be a qualified plan for income tax purposes, it must meet the following general requirements:

1. A plan must be created by an employer for the *exclusive benefit* of employees or their beneficiaries.
2. The contributions and benefits under a plan must *not discriminate in* favor of highly compensated employees.
3. A plan must meet certain *participation and coverage requirements*. The plan must provide that all employees who are 21 years old and who have completed at least 1 year of service with the employer are eligible to participate. If the plan provides for 100 percent vesting of accrued benefits upon commencement of participation in the plan, the 1 year of service requirement may be replaced with a requirement that the employee has completed at least 2 years of service.
4. *Minimum vesting* requirements must be met with respect to both employee and employer contributions.
5. *Uniform minimum distribution* rules must be met.

9-7b Types of Qualified Plans

The tax law provides for several types of qualified plans: pension plans, profit-sharing plans, stock bonus plans, and Employee Stock Ownership Plans (ESOPs). The pension plan can take one of two forms: the defined contribution plan or the defined benefit plan. Under a defined contribution plan, the amount of contribution for the employee is determined by reference to a formula based on the employee's current compensation. The employee's retirement benefits will be dependent upon the accumulated contributions and earnings in the account at the time of retirement. Under a defined benefit plan, the future retirement benefits of the employee are specified, and a formula is used to determine the contributions necessary to provide for the defined benefit. Defined benefit plans are being used more sparingly by employers over the last three decades. Profit-sharing plans are structured to allow the employee to share in company profits through employer contributions from such profits. Under a stock bonus plan, employer contributions on behalf of the employee consist of stock of the employer company.

EXAMPLE Heather is an employee who earned $30,000 during the current year. Her employer contributed $1,200 (4 percent of Heather's salary) to a qualified retirement plan. This plan is a defined contribution plan. ◆

EXAMPLE Alan works for an employer whose qualified retirement plan states that Alan will receive a retirement benefit at age 65 equal to 40 percent of his last year's salary. The employer must make adequate contributions to the plan to enable the stated retirement benefit to be paid (a sufficient amount of money must be in the plan upon Alan's retirement to pay for Alan's defined retirement benefit). This plan is a defined benefit plan. ◆

9-7c Limitations on Contributions to and Benefits from Qualified Plans

Employee and employer contributions to qualified plans are subject to certain dollar or percentage limitations. Under a defined contribution plan (including profit sharing plans), the annual addition to an employee's account is generally not allowed to exceed the lesser of $56,000 (in 2019) or 25 percent of the employee's compensation. Under a defined benefit plan, the annual benefit payable to an employee upon retirement is limited to the lesser of $225,000 (for 2019) or 100 percent of the employee's average compensation for the highest three consecutive years of employment. The operational rules for qualified pension plans and the other types of qualified plans are complex.

Self-Study Problem 9.7 *See Appendix E for Solutions to Self-Study Problems*

Jeannie is employed by a business that operates a qualified profit-sharing plan.

a. In 2019, when her compensation is $50,000, what is the maximum contribution the business can make for her?

$_____

b. If Jeannie's salary was $250,000, what is the maximum contribution?

$_____

Learning Objective 9.8

Explain the pension plan rollover rules.

9-8 ROLLOVERS

In many situations, taxpayers need to transfer assets from one retirement plan to another plan of the same or different type. For example, the taxpayer may change jobs, take early retirement, or simply seek a better retirement fund manager. There are two ways this transfer can be accomplished: (1) direct transfer, also known as a trustee-to-trustee transfer, and (2) rollover of the distribution, in whole or in part, to an IRA or other qualified plan. There are potentially different tax treatments for the two types of transfers.

9-8a Direct Transfers

In direct transfers, the taxpayer instructs the trustee of the retirement plan to transfer assets to the trustee of another plan. There are no current-year tax consequences for this transaction. Also, there is no limit to the dollar amount of the transfer or the number of times a taxpayer can do this in a single tax year.

EXAMPLE Juan has $90,000 in a Section 401(k) plan with his employer. He also has two IRAs, one with ABC Bank ($20,000) and one with XYZ Mutual Fund ($30,000). In March of 20XX, Juan instructs ABC Bank to make a direct transfer to XYZ Mutual Fund of all of his funds ($20,000). In August of 20XX, Juan quits his job and instructs the trustee of the Section 401(k) plan to transfer his $90,000 directly to XYZ Mutual Fund. On December 31, 20XX, Juan has $140,000 in his XYZ Mutual Fund IRA. Since the two transactions were direct transfers, there are no tax consequences to Juan in the current year. ◆

9-8b Distribution Rollovers

In a distribution rollover, the taxpayer receives a distribution of funds from a retirement plan and then transfers part or all of the funds to the new retirement plan trustee. The taxpayer has a maximum of 60 days in which to transfer funds to the new plan and avoid taxes and penalties. The 60-day rollover period may be waived in cases of casualty, disaster, and other events beyond the reasonable control of the taxpayer such as death, disability, incarceration, and postal error. The 60-day time limit is extended to 120 days for first-time home buyers.

The major drawback to distribution rollovers is that the trustee must withhold 20 percent of the amount distributed for federal income taxes, giving the taxpayer only 80 percent of the amount in his or her plan. However, the taxpayer must contribute 100 percent of the amount in the old plan to the new trustee within the required 60-day period to avoid tax on the distribution. Amounts that are not placed in a new plan within the required period are taxable as ordinary income in the current year. Also, if the taxpayer is under 59½ years old, the portion of the retirement plan distribution not transferred will be subject to a 10 percent penalty tax.

The exception to mandatory withholding is a distribution from an IRA; such distributions are not subject to the 20 percent withholding tax. Also, taxpayers are allowed only one distribution rollover each year for transfers from one IRA to another IRA. There are many other complex rules concerning retirement plan rollovers.

EXAMPLE Bea is 50 years old, has worked for Gold Company for 25 years, and has $200,000 in her retirement plan. This year, Gold Company is purchased by Green Company. As a result of the takeover, Bea was laid off. Bea requests a distribution of her $200,000 from Gold Company's retirement plan. The trustee of Gold's retirement plan must withhold $40,000 (20% of $200,000) from the distribution. Bea only receives $160,000 from her retirement plan distribution. If Bea wants to roll her funds into an IRA and avoid taxes, she must contribute $200,000, even though she only received $160,000. If Bea has no other resources and cannot make up the $40,000, the amount not contributed to the IRA will be taxable income to her and subject to a 10 percent penalty. If Bea makes the total rollover contribution of $200,000 within the 60-day timeframe, then the distribution will be nontaxable. The $40,000 will be reported as taxes withheld on her tax return. ◆

Self-Study Problem 9.8   *See Appendix E for Solutions to Self-Study Problems*

Carol, age 40, has an IRA with Blue Mutual Fund. Her balance in the fund is $150,000. She has heard good things about the management of Red Mutual Fund, so she opens a Red Fund IRA. Carol requests her balance from the Blue Fund be distributed to her on July 1, 20XX. She opted to have no withholding on the distribution.

a. How much will Carol receive from the Blue Fund IRA?

$_____

b. If the funds were distributed from a qualified retirement plan (not an IRA), how much would Carol receive?

$_____

c. When is the last day Carol can roll over the amount received into the Red Fund IRA and avoid taxation in the current year?

$_____

d. Assuming the funds were distributed from a qualified retirement plan, not from an IRA, how much will Carol have to contribute to the Red Fund IRA to avoid taxable income and any penalties?

$_____

KEY TERMS

KEY POINTS

Learning Objectives	Key Points
LO 9.1: Compute the income tax withholding from employee wages.	• Employers are required to withhold taxes from amounts paid to employees for wages, including salaries, fees, bonuses, commissions, vacation and retirement pay. • Form W-4, showing the filing status and the number of withholding allowances an employee is claiming, is furnished to the employer by the employee. • When using the percentage method of withholding, an employer (1) multiplies the number of allowances by a specified allowance amount, (2) subtracts that amount from the employee's gross wages for the pay period, and (3) applies the result to the percentage method withholding tables. • Under the wage bracket method, the amount of withholding is obtained from the wage bracket method witholding tables based on the total wages and the number of withholding allowances claimed for the appropriate payroll period and marital status. • Tip income must be reported using one of several methods.
LO 9.2: Determine taxpayers' quarterly estimated payments.	• Self-employed taxpayers are not subject to withholding; however, they must make quarterly estimated tax payments. • Estimated payments are made in four installments on April 15, June 15, and September 15 of the tax year, and January 15 of the following year. • Any individual taxpayer who has estimated tax for the year of $1,000 or more, after subtracting withholding, and whose withholding does not equal or exceed the "required annual payment," must make quarterly estimated payments. • The required annual payment is the smallest of three amounts: (1) 90 percent of the tax shown on the current year's return, (2) 100 percent (or 110 percent at higher income levels) of the tax shown on the preceding year's return, or (3) 90 percent of the current-year tax determined each quarter on an annualized basis.
LO 9.3: Compute the FICA tax.	• For 2019, the Social Security (OASDI) tax rate is 6.2 percent and the Medicare tax rate is 1.45 percent for employers and employees. The maximum wage subject to the Social Security portion of the FICA tax is $132,900 for 2019, and all wages are subject to the Medicare portion of the FICA tax. • Taxpayers working for more than one employer during the same tax year may pay more than the maximum amount of Social Security taxes. If this happens, the taxpayer should compute the excess taxes paid, and report the excess on Schedule 3 of Form 1040 as a payment against his or her income tax liability.

LO 9.4: Apply the federal deposit system to payroll withholding.	• Employers must make periodic deposits of the taxes that are withheld from employees' wages. Deposits must be made electronically. • Employers are either monthly depositors or semiweekly depositors, depending on the total income taxes withheld from wages and FICA taxes attributable to wages. However, if withholding and FICA taxes of $100,000 or more are accumulated at any time during the year, the depositor is subject to a special one-day deposit rule.
LO 9.5: Prepare employer payroll reporting.	• On or before January 31 of the year following the calendar year of payment, an employer must furnish to each employee two copies of the employee's Wage and Tax Statement, Form W-2, for the previous calendar year. • The original copy (Copy A) of all Forms W-2 and Form W-3 (Transmittal of Wage and Tax Statements) must be filed with the Social Security Administration by January 31 of the year following the calendar year of payment. • Forms 1099 must be mailed to the recipients by January 31 of the year following the calendar year of payment.
LO 9.6: Compute the amount of FUTA tax for an employer.	• The FUTA (Federal Unemployment Tax Act) tax is not withheld from employees' wages, but instead is paid in full by employers. • The federal unemployment tax rate is 6.0 percent of an employee's wages up to $7,000. A credit of up to 5.4 percent is allowed if state unemployment taxes are paid, resulting in an effective federal unemployment tax rate of 0.6 percent.
LO 9.7: Describe the general rules for qualified retirement plans.	• In order to be qualified, retirement plans must meet certain requirements related to non-discrimination of lower compensated employees, participation eligibility, vesting requirements, and distribution rules.
LO 9.8: Explain the pension plan rollover rules.	• There are two ways to transfer assets from one retirement plan to another of the same or different type: (1) a direct transfer, also known as a trustee-to-trustee transfer, and (2) a rollover of an actual cash distribution, in whole or in part, to an IRA or other qualified plan. • There are no current-year tax consequences for a direct trustee-to-trustee transfer. • Distribution rollovers are subject to a 60-day time limit for completion and may also be subject to income tax withholding and tax penalties.

QUESTIONS and PROBLEMS

GROUP 1:
MULTIPLE CHOICE QUESTIONS

LO 9.1

1. Which of the following amounts paid by an employer to an employee is *not* subject to withholding?
   a. Salary
   b. Bonus
   c. Commissions
   d. Reimbursement of expenses under a non-accountable plan
   e. All of the above are subject to withholding

LO 9.1

2. Abbe, age 56, is married and has two dependent children, one age 14, and the other a 21-year-old full-time student. Abbe has one job, and her husband, age 58, is not employed. If she expects to earn wages of $50,000, file jointly, and take the standard deduction, how many allowances should Abbe claim on her Form W-4?
   a. 4
   b. 5
   c. 7
   d. 8
   e. 9

LO 9.1

3. Michele is single with no dependents and earns $23,000 this year. Michele claims sixteen allowances on her Form W-4. Which of the following is correct concerning her Form W-4?
   a. Michele may not under any circumstances claim sixteen allowances.
   b. Michele's employer will require her to verify her right to claim sixteen allowances.
   c. Michele's employer should ask her to prepare a corrected Form W-4. If Michele is unwilling to update her Form W-4, then her employer should disregard her Form W-4 and withhold at the single taxpayer rate with no allowances.
   d. Michele's employer will submit a copy of her W-4 to the IRS if directed to do so by written notice.
   e. None of the above is correct.

LO 9.1

4. Flo is a server at a diner in Phoenix and earns a significant portion of her pay through tips from customers. Some of these tips are paid via credit card and others are paid in cash. Flo's employer will:
   a. withhold employment taxes but no income taxes on the tips
   b. withhold both employment and income taxes on the cash tips but only employment taxes on the tips paid by credit card
   c. withhold both employment and income taxes on all tips
   d. not withhold any taxes on cash tips but will withhold both employment and income taxes on credit card tips

LO 9.1

5. The process for employee withholding involves:
   a. the employee computes the number of allowances on Form W-4 and the employer uses the W-4 information to calculate income tax withholding
   b. the employee provides wage information and the employer completes Form W-4 and withholds based on employee instruction
   c. the employee provides filing status and the employer completes the Form W-4 and submits to the IRS for proper withholding
   d. the employee completes most of the Form W-4 and the employer submits the form to the IRS and awaits withholding instructions

LO 9.2

6. Estimated payments for individual taxpayers are due on the following dates:
   a. Twice a year on April 15 and September 15
   b. Four installments on April 15, June 15, September 15, and January 15 of the next year
   c. Four times a year on April 15, July 15, September 15, and December 15
   d. Twice a year on June 15 and December 15

LO 9.2

7. Amy is a single taxpayer. Her income tax liability in the prior year was $5,178. Amy earns $50,000 of income ratably during the current year and her tax liability is $4,342. In order to avoid penalty, Amy's smallest amount of required annual withholding and estimated payments is:
   a. $4,372
   b. $3,935
   c. $3,908
   d. $4,660
   e. $4,342

LO 9.2

8. Jane is a single taxpayer with a current year AGI of $181,000 and current year income tax liability of $39,610. Her AGI in the prior year was $150,400 and prior year tax liability was $32,182. Jane earns her income ratably during the year. In order to avoid penalty, the smallest amount of required annual withholding and estimated payments is:
    a. $39,610
    b. $32,182
    c. $35,649
    d. $35,400
    e. $43,571

LO 9.3

9. Which of the following is *not* true about FICA taxes?
    a. The FICA tax has two parts, Social Security (Old Age, Survivors, and Disability Insurance) and Medicare.
    b. In 2019, the maximum wage base for Social Security tax withholding is $128,400.
    c. In 2019, there is no maximum wage base for Medicare tax withholding.
    d. When employees work for more than one employer and exceed the maximum wage base for Social Security tax withholding in total, they are allowed a refund of excess tax withheld.

LO 9.3

10. Terry worked for two employers during 2019. The amount of wages paid to Terry by both employers totaled $168,400 and the employers properly withheld both income and employment taxes. As a result of Terry's two jobs:
    a. Terry will receive a credit against his employment taxes in 2020 from his employer
    b. Terry will request a refund of overpaid employment taxes from his second employer
    c. Terry will claim a credit for excess Social Security taxes paid on his 2019 income tax return
    d. Terry will claim a credit for excess Social Security and Medicare taxes on his 2019 income tax return
    e. Terry will file a Form 843 with the Social Security Administration to claim back excess withheld employment taxes

LO 9.3

11. Ran's wage income is $47,350 in 2019. The combined employer and employee FICA tax rates that apply to Ran's wages are:
    a. 15.3% for Social Security and Medicare
    b. 6.2% for Social Security and Medicare
    c. 1.45% for Medicare
    d. 7.65 for Social Security
    e. None of the above

LO 9.4

12. Employers generally must file a quarterly tax return showing the amount of wages paid and the amount of income tax and FICA tax withholding due. This tax return is filed on:
    a. Form 944 or Form 945
    b. Schedule H
    c. Schedule SE
    d. Form 941

LO 9.4

13. Yamin operates a small business with a few part-time employees. Her annual employment tax withholding in 2019 is $467.80. Yamin should file which employment tax reporting form?
    a. Form 944
    b. Form 940
    c. Form 941
    d. Form 9000
    e. Form 409

LO 9.5

14. Which of the following forms is used to report wages, tips and other compensation paid to employees?
    a. Form W-4
    b. Form W-2G
    c. Form W-2
    d. Form 1099-R
    e. Form 1099-MISC

LO 9.5

15. Which of the following forms is used to report government payments such as a state income tax refund?
    a. Form W-2G
    b. Form 1099-Casino
    c. Form 1099-G
    d. Form 1099-Lottery
    e. Form 1099-C

LO 9.6

16. The FUTA tax is:
    a. An unemployment tax with a rate of 2.9 percent up to $132,900 of salary per employee.
    b. A disability tax with a rate of 2.9 percent up to $7,000 of salary per employee.
    c. An unemployment tax with a rate as low as 0.6 percent on up to $7,000 of salary per employee.
    d. A disability tax with a rate of 0.6 percent up to $132,900 of salary per employee.

LO 9.6

17. Wei has four employees: Anna, Kenny, Stan, and Seth, who were paid $12,000, $5,000, $8,000, and $3,000, respectively. Assuming a full state credit, Wei's FUTA taxable wages for the year are:
    a. $28,000
    b. $21,000
    c. $22,000
    d. $186

LO 9.7

18. Gail's employer contributes $2,000 (5% of her $40,000 salary) to a qualified retirement plan for Gail. This pension plan is what kind of plan?
    a. Defined benefit plan
    b. Defined contribution plan
    c. Employee Stock Ownership Plan
    d. Profit-sharing plan
    e. None of the above

LO 9.8

19. When taxpayers receive distributions from qualified retirement plans, how much time is allowed to roll over the amount received into a new plan to avoid paying taxes on the distribution in the current year, assuming there are no unusual events?
    a. 60 days
    b. 90 days
    c. 180 days
    d. 1 year
    e. There is no time limit

LO 9.8

20. Tom quits his job with $150,000 in his employer's qualified retirement plan. Since he is broke, Tom instructs the plan trustee to pay him the balance in his retirement account. How much will Tom receive when he gets his check from the retirement plan?
    a. $120,000
    b. $100,000
    c. $96,000
    d. $24,000
    e. Some other amount

LO 9.8   21. Betty owns three separate IRA accounts with different banks. She wishes to consolidate her three IRAs into one IRA in 2019. How many distribution rollovers may Betty make in 2019?
   a. One
   b. Two
   c. Four
   d. Ten
   e. There is no limit

LO 9.8   22. Bonnie is getting close to retirement and realizes she has three different IRA accounts at three different financial institutions. To make life simpler, Bonnie wishes to consolidate her three IRAs into a single account in 2019 using trustee-to-trustee direct rollovers. How many rollovers of this type can Bonnie make in 2019?
   a. One
   b. Two
   c. Four
   d. Ten
   e. There is no limit

GROUP 2:
PROBLEMS

LO 9.1   1. Phan Mai is single with two dependent children under age 17. Phan estimates her wages for the year will be $42,000 and her itemized deductions will be $14,000. In the previous year, Phan had a small tax liability. Assuming Phan files as head of household, use Form W-4 on Pages 9-35 and 9-36 to determine the number of withholding allowances Phan should claim.

LO 9.1   2. Ralph and Kathy Gump are married with one 20-year-old dependent child. Ralph earns a total of $98,000 and estimates their itemized deductions to be $29,500 for the year. Kathy is not employed. Use Form W-4 on Pages 9-35 and 9-36 to determine the number of withholding allowances that Ralph should claim.

LO 9.1   3. Sophie is a single taxpayer. For the first payroll period in July 2019, she is paid wages of $2,200 monthly. Sophie claims one allowance on her Form W-4.
   a. Use the percentage method to calculate the amount of Sophie's withholding for a monthly pay period.

   $ _____

   b. Use the wage bracket method to determine the amount of Sophie's withholding for the same period.

   $ _____

LO 9.1   4. Cassie works at Capital Bank and is in charge of issuing Form 1099s to bank customers. Please describe for Cassie the 4 possible situations that require the bank to implement backup withholding on a customer.

   _____

   _____

   _____

   _____

   _____

   _____

   _____

   _____

LO 9.2

5. Sherina Smith (Social Security number 785-23-9873) lives at 536 West Lapham Street, Milwaukee, WI 53204, and is self-employed for 2019. She estimates her required annual estimated tax payment for 2019 to be $8,468. She had a $417 overpayment of last year's taxes, which she will apply against her first quarter estimated payment. Complete the first quarter voucher below for Sherina for 2019.

Form **1040-ES** Department of the Treasury Internal Revenue Service	**20̲19 Estimated Tax**	**Payment Voucher 1** OMB No. 1545-0074

File only if you are making a payment of estimated tax by check or money order. Mail this voucher with your check or money order payable to **"United States Treasury."** Write your social security number and "2019 Form 1040-ES" on your check or money order. Do not send cash. Enclose, but do not staple or attach, your payment with this voucher.

Calendar year—Due April 15, 2019

Amount of estimated tax you are paying by check or money order.

	Dollars	Cents

Pay online at www.irs.gov/etpay

Simple. Fast. Secure.

Print or type

Your first name and initial	Your last name	Your social security number
If joint payment, complete for spouse		
Spouse's first name and initial	Spouse's last name	Spouse's social security number
Address (number, street, and apt. no.)		
City, state, and ZIP code. (If a foreign address, enter city, also complete spaces below.)		
Foreign country name	Foreign province/county	Foreign postal code

For Privacy Act and Paperwork Reduction Act Notice, see instructions.   **Form 1040-ES (2019)**

Form W-4 (2019)

Future developments. For the latest information about any future developments related to Form W-4, such as legislation enacted after it was published, go to *www.irs.gov/FormW4*.

Purpose. Complete Form W-4 so that your employer can withhold the correct federal income tax from your pay. Consider completing a new Form W-4 each year and when your personal or financial situation changes.

Exemption from withholding. You may claim exemption from withholding for 2019 if **both** of the following apply.

• For 2018 you had a right to a refund of **all** federal income tax withheld because you had **no** tax liability, **and**

• For 2019 you expect a refund of **all** federal income tax withheld because you expect to have **no** tax liability.

If you're exempt, complete **only** lines 1, 2, 3, 4, and 7 and sign the form to validate it. Your exemption for 2019 expires February 17, 2020. See Pub. 505, Tax Withholding and Estimated Tax, to learn more about whether you qualify for exemption from withholding.

General Instructions

If you aren't exempt, follow the rest of these instructions to determine the number of withholding allowances you should claim for withholding for 2019 and any additional amount of tax to have withheld. For regular wages, withholding must be based on allowances you claimed and may not be a flat amount or percentage of wages.

You can also use the calculator at *www.irs.gov/W4App* to determine your tax withholding more accurately. Consider using this calculator if you have a more complicated tax situation, such as if you have a working spouse, more than one job, or a large amount of nonwage income not subject to withholding outside of your job. After your Form W-4 takes effect, you can also use this calculator to see how the amount of tax you're having withheld compares to your projected total tax for 2019. If you use the calculator, you don't need to complete any of the worksheets for Form W-4.

Note that if you have too much tax withheld, you will receive a refund when you file your tax return. If you have too little tax withheld, you will owe tax when you file your tax return, and you might owe a penalty.

Filers with multiple jobs or working spouses. If you have more than one job at a time, or if you're married filing jointly and your spouse is also working, read all of the instructions including the instructions for the Two-Earners/Multiple Jobs Worksheet before beginning.

Nonwage income. If you have a large amount of nonwage income not subject to withholding, such as interest or dividends, consider making estimated tax payments using Form 1040-ES, Estimated Tax for Individuals. Otherwise, you might owe additional tax. Or, you can use the Deductions, Adjustments, and Additional Income Worksheet on page 3 or the calculator at *www.irs.gov/W4App* to make sure you have enough tax withheld from your paycheck. If you have pension or annuity income, see Pub. 505 or use the calculator at *www.irs.gov/W4App* to find out if you should adjust your withholding on Form W-4 or W-4P.

Nonresident alien. If you're a nonresident alien, see Notice 1392, Supplemental Form W-4 Instructions for Nonresident Aliens, before completing this form.

Specific Instructions
Personal Allowances Worksheet

Complete this worksheet on page 3 first to determine the number of withholding allowances to claim.

Line C. *Head of household please note:* Generally, you may claim head of household filing status on your tax return only if you're unmarried and pay more than 50% of the costs of keeping up a home for yourself and a qualifying individual. See Pub. 501 for more information about filing status.

Line E. Child tax credit. When you file your tax return, you may be eligible to claim a child tax credit for each of your eligible children. To qualify, the child must be under age 17 as of December 31, must be your dependent who lives with you for more than half the year, and must have a valid social security number. To learn more about this credit, see Pub. 972, Child Tax Credit. To reduce the tax withheld from your pay by taking this credit into account, follow the instructions on line E of the worksheet. On the worksheet you will be asked about your total income. For this purpose, total income includes all of your wages and other income, including income earned by a spouse if you are filing a joint return.

Line F. Credit for other dependents. When you file your tax return, you may be eligible to claim a credit for other dependents for whom a child tax credit can't be claimed, such as a qualifying child who doesn't meet the age or social security number requirement for the child tax credit, or a qualifying relative. To learn more about this credit, see Pub. 505. To reduce the tax withheld from your pay by taking this credit into account, follow the instructions on line F of the worksheet. On the worksheet, you will be asked about your total income. For this purpose, total

---

------------------------ **Separate here and give Form W-4 to your employer. Keep the worksheet(s) for your records.** ------------------------

Form W-4
Department of the Treasury
Internal Revenue Service

Employee's Withholding Allowance Certificate

▶ Whether you're entitled to claim a certain number of allowances or exemption from withholding is subject to review by the IRS. Your employer may be required to send a copy of this form to the IRS.

OMB No. 1545-0074

2019

1 Your first name and middle initial	Last name		2 Your social security number

Home address (number and street or rural route)	**3** ☐ Single ☐ Married ☐ Married, but withhold at higher Single rate.
	Note: If married filing separately, check "Married, but withhold at higher Single rate."
City or town, state, and ZIP code	**4** If your last name differs from that shown on your social security card, check here. You must call 800-772-1213 for a replacement card. ▶ ☐

5	Total number of allowances you're claiming (from the applicable worksheet on the following pages)	**5**	
6	Additional amount, if any, you want withheld from each paycheck	**6** $	
7	I claim exemption from withholding for 2019, and I certify that I meet **both** of the following conditions for exemption.		
	• Last year I had a right to a refund of **all** federal income tax withheld because I had **no** tax liability, **and**		
	• This year I expect a refund of **all** federal income tax withheld because I expect to have **no** tax liability.		
	If you meet both conditions, write "Exempt" here . . . . ▶	**7**	

Under penalties of perjury, I declare that I have examined this certificate and, to the best of my knowledge and belief, it is true, correct, and complete.

Employee's signature
(This form is not valid unless you sign it.) ▶ _____   Date ▶ _____

8 Employer's name and address (**Employer:** Complete boxes 8 and 10 if sending to IRS and complete boxes 8, 9, and 10 if sending to State Directory of New Hires.)	9 First date of employment	10 Employer identification number (EIN)

For Privacy Act and Paperwork Reduction Act Notice, see page 4.   Cat. No. 10220Q   Form **W-4** (2019)

Personal Allowances Worksheet (Keep for your records.)

A	Enter "1" for yourself	A	_____
B	Enter "1" if you will file as married filing jointly	B	_____
C	Enter "1" if you will file as head of household	C	_____

D Enter "1" if: { • You're single, or married filing separately, and have only one job; or
• You're married filing jointly, have only one job, and your spouse doesn't work; or
• Your wages from a second job or your spouse's wages (or the total of both) are $1,500 or less. }   D _____

E **Child tax credit.** See Pub. 972, Child Tax Credit, for more information.
- If your total income will be less than $71,201 ($103,351 if married filing jointly), enter "4" for each eligible child.
- If your total income will be from $71,201 to $179,050 ($103,351 to $345,850 if married filing jointly), enter "2" for each eligible child.
- If your total income will be from $179,051 to $200,000 ($345,851 to $400,000 if married filing jointly), enter "1" for each eligible child.
- If your total income will be higher than $200,000 ($400,000 if married filing jointly), enter "-0-" . . . .   **E** _____

F **Credit for other dependents.** See Pub. 972, Child Tax Credit, for more information.
- If your total income will be less than $71,201 ($103,351 if married filing jointly), enter "1" for each eligible dependent.
- If your total income will be from $71,201 to $179,050 ($103,351 to $345,850 if married filing jointly), enter "1" for every two dependents (for example, "-0-" for one dependent, "1" if you have two or three dependents, and "2" if you have four dependents).
- If your total income will be higher than $179,050 ($345,850 if married filing jointly), enter "-0-" . . . .   **F** _____

G **Other credits.** If you have other credits, see Worksheet 1-6 of Pub. 505 and enter the amount from that worksheet here. If you use Worksheet 1-6, enter "-0-" on lines E and F . . . .   **G** _____

H Add lines A through G and enter the total here . . . . ▶ **H** _____

For accuracy, complete all worksheets that apply.	{ • If you plan to **itemize** or **claim adjustments to income** and want to reduce your withholding, or if you have a large amount of nonwage income not subject to withholding and want to increase your withholding, see the **Deductions, Adjustments, and Additional Income Worksheet** below. • If you **have more than one job at a time** or are **married filing jointly and you and your spouse both work,** and the combined earnings from all jobs exceed $53,000 ($24,450 if married filing jointly), see the **Two-Earners/Multiple Jobs Worksheet** on page 4 to avoid having too little tax withheld. • If **neither** of the above situations applies, **stop here** and enter the number from line H on line 5 of Form W-4 above.

Deductions, Adjustments, and Additional Income Worksheet

Note: Use this worksheet *only* if you plan to itemize deductions, claim certain adjustments to income, or have a large amount of nonwage income not subject to withholding.

1	Enter an estimate of your 2019 itemized deductions. These include qualifying home mortgage interest, charitable contributions, state and local taxes (up to $10,000), and medical expenses in excess of 10% of your income. See Pub. 505 for details	1	$ _____
2	Enter: { $24,400 if you're married filing jointly or qualifying widow(er) $18,350 if you're head of household $12,200 if you're single or married filing separately }	2	$ _____
3	**Subtract** line 2 from line 1. If zero or less, enter "-0-"	3	$ _____
4	Enter an estimate of your 2019 adjustments to income, qualified business income deduction, and any additional standard deduction for age or blindness (see Pub. 505 for information about these items) . .	4	$ _____
5	**Add** lines 3 and 4 and enter the total	5	$ _____
6	Enter an estimate of your 2019 nonwage income not subject to withholding (such as dividends or interest) .	6	$ _____
7	**Subtract** line 6 from line 5. If zero, enter "-0-". If less than zero, enter the amount in parentheses . . .	7	$ _____
8	**Divide** the amount on line 7 by $4,200 and enter the result here. If a negative amount, enter in parentheses. Drop any fraction	8	_____
9	Enter the number from the **Personal Allowances Worksheet,** line H, above	9	_____
10	**Add** lines 8 and 9 and enter the total here. If zero or less, enter "-0-". If you plan to use the **Two-Earners/Multiple Jobs Worksheet,** also enter this total on line 1 of that worksheet on page 4. Otherwise, **stop here** and enter this total on Form W-4, line 5, page 1	10	_____

LO 9.2

6. Kana is a single wage earner with no dependents and taxable income of $205,000 in 2019. Her 2018 taxable income was $155,000 and tax liability was $31,490. Calculate the following (note: this question requires the use of the tax tables in Appendix A):

Kana's 2019 income tax liability $_____

Kana's minimum required 2019 annual payment necessary to avoid penalty $_____

LO 9.3

7. Lamden Company paid its employee, Trudy, wages of $52,000 in 2019. Calculate the FICA tax:

Withheld from		
Trudy's wages:	Social Security	$_____
	Medicare	$_____
Paid by Lamden:	Social Security	$_____
	Medicare	$_____
Total FICA Tax		$_____

LO 9.3

8. Fiduciary Investments paid its employee, Yolanda, wages of $139,000 in 2019. Calculate the FICA tax:

Withheld from		
Yolanda's wages:	Social Security	$_____
	Medicare	$_____
Paid by Fiduciary:	Social Security	$_____
	Medicare	$_____
Total FICA Tax		$_____

LO 9.3

9. Thuy worked as the assistant manager at Burger Crown through August 2019 and received wages of $79,000. Thuy then worked at Up and Down Burger starting in September of 2019 and received wages of $61,500. Calculate the amount of Thuy's overpayment of Social Security taxes that she should report on her 2019 Form 1040.

$ _____

LO 9.4

10. Drew Freeman operates a small business and his payroll records for the first quarter of 2019 reflect the following:

Employee	Matt D.	Jack F.	Avery F.	Tiffany Y.
Gross wages	$2,870.00	$1,400.00	$1,750.00	$4,200.00
Federal income tax withheld	37.00	18.00	24.00	191.00
FICA taxes	439.11	214.20	267.75	642.60

Drew's employee identification number is 34-4321321 and his business is located at 732 Nob Hill Blvd. in Yakima, WA 98902. Drew is eligible to pay his withholding at the time he files his quarterly Form 941. Complete Form 941 located on Pages 9-39 and 9-40 for Drew for the first quarter of 2019.

LO 9.5

11. For each of the following payments, indicate the form that should be used to report the payment:
a. Interest of $400 paid by a bank _____
b. Payment of $400 in dividends by a corporation to a shareholder _____
c. Periodic payments from a retirement plan _____
d. Salary as president of the company _____
e. Las Vegas keno winnings of $25,000 _____

Form **941 for 2019:** Employer's QUARTERLY Federal Tax Return

(Rev. January 2019)

Department of the Treasury — Internal Revenue Service

950117

OMB No. 1545-0029

Employer identification number (EIN)   [ ][ ] – [ ][ ][ ][ ][ ][ ][ ]

Name *(not your trade name)*

Trade name *(if any)*

Address

Number   Street   Suite or room number

City   State   ZIP code

Foreign country name   Foreign province/county   Foreign postal code

Report for this Quarter of 2019
(Check one.)

[ ] **1:** January, February, March

[ ] **2:** April, May, June

[ ] **3:** July, August, September

[ ] **4:** October, November, December

Go to *www.irs.gov/Form941* for instructions and the latest information.

Read the separate instructions before you complete Form 941. Type or print within the boxes.

Part 1:   **Answer these questions for this quarter.**

1   Number of employees who received wages, tips, or other compensation for the pay period including: *Mar. 12* (Quarter 1), *June 12* (Quarter 2), *Sept. 12* (Quarter 3), or *Dec. 12* (Quarter 4)   **1** [   ]

2   Wages, tips, and other compensation   **2** [   ]

3   Federal income tax withheld from wages, tips, and other compensation   **3** [   ]

4   If no wages, tips, and other compensation are subject to social security or Medicare tax   [ ] Check and go to line 6.

	Column 1		Column 2
5a Taxable social security wages	[ ]	× 0.124 =	[ ]
5b Taxable social security tips	[ ]	× 0.124 =	[ ]
5c Taxable Medicare wages & tips.	[ ]	× 0.029 =	[ ]
5d Taxable wages & tips subject to Additional Medicare Tax withholding	[ ]	× 0.009 =	[ ]

5e   Add Column 2 from lines 5a, 5b, 5c, and 5d   **5e** [   ]

5f   Section 3121(q) Notice and Demand—Tax due on unreported tips (see instructions)   **5f** [   ]

6   Total taxes before adjustments. Add lines 3, 5e, and 5f   **6** [   ]

7   Current quarter's adjustment for fractions of cents   **7** [   ]

8   Current quarter's adjustment for sick pay   **8** [   ]

9   Current quarter's adjustments for tips and group-term life insurance   **9** [   ]

10   Total taxes after adjustments. Combine lines 6 through 9   **10** [   ]

11   Qualified small business payroll tax credit for increasing research activities. Attach Form 8974   **11** [   ]

12   Total taxes after adjustments and credits. Subtract line 11 from line 10   **12** [   ]

13   Total deposits for this quarter, including overpayment applied from a prior quarter and overpayments applied from Form 941-X, 941-X (PR), 944-X, or 944-X (SP) filed in the current quarter   **13** [   ]

14   Balance due. If line 12 is more than line 13, enter the difference and see instructions   **14** [   ]

15   Overpayment. If line 13 is more than line 12, enter the difference   [   ]   Check one: [ ] Apply to next return.   [ ] Send a refund.

▶ **You MUST complete both pages of Form 941 and SIGN it.**

Next ▶

For Privacy Act and Paperwork Reduction Act Notice, see the back of the Payment Voucher.   Cat. No. 17001Z   Form **941** (Rev. 1-2019)

950217

Name *(not your trade name)*	Employer identification number (EIN)

Part 2: **Tell us about your deposit schedule and tax liability for this quarter.**

If you are unsure about whether you are a monthly schedule depositor or a semiweekly schedule depositor, see section 11 of Pub. 15.

16 Check one: ☐ **Line 12 on this return is less than $2,500 or line 12 on the return for the prior quarter was less than $2,500, and you didn't incur a $100,000 next-day deposit obligation during the current quarter.** If line 12 for the prior quarter was less than $2,500 but line 12 on this return is $100,000 or more, you must provide a record of your federal tax liability. If you are a monthly schedule depositor, complete the deposit schedule below; if you are a semiweekly schedule depositor, attach Schedule B (Form 941). Go to Part 3.

☐ **You were a monthly schedule depositor for the entire quarter.** Enter your tax liability for each month and total liability for the quarter, then go to Part 3.

Tax liability: Month 1   ⬚ .

Month 2   ⬚ .

Month 3   ⬚ .

Total liability for quarter   ⬚ .   **Total must equal line 12.**

☐ **You were a semiweekly schedule depositor for any part of this quarter.** Complete Schedule B (Form 941), Report of Tax Liability for Semiweekly Schedule Depositors, and attach it to Form 941.

Part 3: **Tell us about your business. If a question does NOT apply to your business, leave it blank.**

17 If your business has closed or you stopped paying wages . . . . ☐ Check here, and

enter the final date you paid wages   ⬚ / / .

18 If you are a seasonal employer and you don't have to file a return for every quarter of the year . . ☐ Check here.

Part 4: **May we speak with your third-party designee?**

Do you want to allow an employee, a paid tax preparer, or another person to discuss this return with the IRS? See the instructions for details.

☐ Yes. Designee's name and phone number

Select a 5-digit Personal Identification Number (PIN) to use when talking to the IRS. ☐ ☐ ☐ ☐ ☐

☐ No.

Part 5: **Sign here. You MUST complete both pages of Form 941 and SIGN it.**

Under penalties of perjury, I declare that I have examined this return, including accompanying schedules and statements, and to the best of my knowledge and belief, it is true, correct, and complete. Declaration of preparer (other than taxpayer) is based on all information of which preparer has any knowledge.

X **Sign your name here**

Print your name here

Print your title here

Date   / /

Best daytime phone

Paid Preparer Use Only   Check if you are self-employed . . . ☐

Preparer's name		PTIN	
Preparer's signature		Date	/ /
Firm's name (or yours if self-employed)		EIN	
Address		Phone	
City		State	ZIP code	

Form **941** (Rev. 1-2019)

LO 9.5

12. Philcon Corporation created the following 2019 employee payroll report for one of its employees.

Philcon Corporation   **Employee Payroll Report**

EIN: 12-3456789   **2019**

PO Box 4563

Anchorage, AK 99508

Emp ID	Name	Wage Type	Date	Period Gross Pay	YTD Gross Pay	W-4 Allow	FIT w/h	SS Tax w/h	Med Tax w/h	Total Tax	Net Pay
A1246G	Louise Chugach	Monthly	1/31/2019	11,100.00	11,100.00	4	1,766.54	688.20	160.95	2,615.69	8,484.31
A1246G	Louise Chugach	Monthly	2/28/2019	11,100.00	22,200.00	4	1,766.54	688.20	160.95	2,615.69	8,484.31
A1246G	Louise Chugach	Bonus	3/15/2019	6,400.00	28,600.00		1,408.00	396.80	92.80	1,897.60	4,502.40
A1246G	Louise Chugach	Monthly	3/31/2019	11,100.00	39,700.00	4	1,766.54	688.20	160.95	2,615.69	8,484.31
A1246G	Louise Chugach	Monthly	4/30/2019	11,100.00	50,800.00	4	1,766.54	688.20	160.95	2,615.69	8,484.31
A1246G	Louise Chugach	Monthly	5/31/2019	11,100.00	61,900.00	4	1,766.54	688.20	160.95	2,615.69	8,484.31
A1246G	Louise Chugach	Monthly	6/30/2019	11,100.00	73,000.00	4	1,766.54	688.20	160.95	2,615.69	8,484.31
A1246G	Louise Chugach	Monthly	7/31/2019	11,100.00	84,100.00	4	1,766.54	688.20	160.95	2,615.69	8,484.31
A1246G	Louise Chugach	Monthly	8/31/2019	11,100.00	95,200.00	4	1,766.54	688.20	160.95	2,615.69	8,484.31
A1246G	Louise Chugach	Monthly	9/30/2019	11,100.00	106,300.00	4	1,766.54	688.20	160.95	2,615.69	8,484.31
A1246G	Louise Chugach	Monthly	10/31/2019	11,100.00	117,400.00	4	1,766.54	688.20	160.95	2,615.69	8,484.31
A1246G	Louise Chugach	Monthly	11/30/2019	11,100.00	128,500.00	4	1,766.54	688.20	160.95	2,615.69	8,484.31
A1246G	Louise Chugach	Monthly	12/31/2019	11,100.00	139,600.00	4	1,766.54	272.80	160.95	2,200.29	8,899.71
A1246G	Louise Chugach	YTD Total		139,600.00			22,606.48	8,239.80	2,024.20	32,870.48	106,729.52

Employee Mailing Address:

Louise Chugach

5471 East Tudor Road

Anchorage, AK 99508

SSN: 545-64-7745

a. Complete the following Form W-2 for Louise Chugach from Philcon Corporation.

a Employee's social security number			Safe, accurate, FAST! Use ins·e~file	Visit the IRS website at www.irs.gov/efile
		OMB No. 1545-0008		
b Employer identification number (EIN)			**1** Wages, tips, other compensation	**2** Federal income tax withheld
c Employer's name, address, and ZIP code			**3** Social security wages	**4** Social security tax withheld
			5 Medicare wages and tips	**6** Medicare tax withheld
			7 Social security tips	**8** Allocated tips
d Control number			**9**	**10** Dependent care benefits
e Employee's first name and initial Last name		Suff.	**11** Nonqualified plans	**12a** See instructions for box 12
			13 Statutory employee / Retirement plan / Third-party sick pay	**12b**
			14 Other	**12c**
				12d
f Employee's address and ZIP code				
15 State Employer's state ID number	**16** State wages, tips, etc.	**17** State income tax	**18** Local wages, tips, etc.	**19** Local income tax	**20** Locality name

Form **W-2** **Wage and Tax Statement**   **2019**   Department of the Treasury—Internal Revenue Service

Copy B—To Be Filed With Employee's FEDERAL Tax Return.

This information is being furnished to the Internal Revenue Service.

b. Philcon Corporation also paid $1,100 to Ralph Kincaid for presenting a management seminar. Ralph lives at 1455 Raspberry Road, Anchorage, AK 99508, and his Social Security number is 475-45-3226. Complete the Form 1099-MISC located on Page 9-42 for the payment to Ralph from Philcon Corporation.

☐ CORRECTED (if checked)

PAYER'S name, street address, city or town, state or province, country, ZIP or foreign postal code, and telephone no.	**1 Rents** $	OMB No. 1545-0115 20**19** Form **1099-MISC**	**Miscellaneous Income**
	2 Royalties $		
	3 Other income $	**4 Federal income tax withheld** $	**Copy B** **For Recipient**
PAYER'S TIN	RECIPIENT'S TIN	**5 Fishing boat proceeds** $	**6 Medical and health care payments** $	
RECIPIENT'S name		**7 Nonemployee compensation** $	**8 Substitute payments in lieu of dividends or interest** $	This is important tax information and is being furnished to the IRS. If you are required to file a return, a negligence penalty or other sanction may be imposed on you if this income is taxable and the IRS determines that it has not been reported.
Street address (including apt. no.)				
City or town, state or province, country, and ZIP or foreign postal code		**9 Payer made direct sales of $5,000 or more of consumer products to a buyer (recipient) for resale ▶** ☐	**10 Crop insurance proceeds** $	
		11	**12**	
Account number (see instructions)	FATCA filing requirement ☐	**13 Excess golden parachute payments** $	**14 Gross proceeds paid to an attorney** $	
15a Section 409A deferrals $	**15b** Section 409A income $	**16 State tax withheld** $ $	**17 State/Payer's state no.**	**18 State income** $ $

Form **1099-MISC**   (keep for your records)   www.irs.gov/Form1099MISC   Department of the Treasury - Internal Revenue Service

LO 9.6

13. Thomas is an employer with two employees, Patty and Selma. Patty's wages are $12,450 and Selma's wages are $1,310. The state unemployment tax rate is 5.4 percent. Calculate the following amounts for Thomas:

    a. FUTA tax before the state tax credit $_____

    b. State unemployment tax $_____

    c. FUTA tax after the state tax credit $_____

LO 9.8

14. Telly, age 38, has a $140,000 IRA with Blue Mutual Fund. He has read good things about the management of Green Mutual Fund, so he opens a Green Fund IRA. Telly asked for a distribution rollover and received his balance from the Blue Fund on May 1, 2019. Telly opted to have no withholding on the distribution.

    a. What amount will Telly receive from the Blue Fund IRA?

                                                       $_____

    b. What amount must Telly contribute to the Green Fund IRA to avoid having taxable income and penalties for early withdrawal?

                                                       $_____

    c. When is the last day Telly can roll over the amount received into the Green Fund IRA and avoid taxation in the current year, assuming no unusual circumstances?

                                                       $_____

    d. What amount would Telly receive if the distribution were from his employer's qualified retirement plan?

                                                       $_____

LO 9.8

15. Allen (age 32) takes a distribution of $20,000 from his traditional IRA account which he plans to deposit into an IRA with a different bank. During the 60-day rollover period, he gambles and loses the entire IRA balance. What income and/or penalties must he show on his tax return related to the failed rollover?

    _____

    _____

    _____

    _____

GROUP 3:
WRITING ASSIGNMENT

ETHICS

Eric, your friend, received his Form W-2 from his employer (below) and has asked for your help. Eric's 2019 salary was $145,200 and he does not understand why the amounts in Boxes 1, 3 and 5 are not $145,200? His final paycheck for the year included the following information:

– Eric contributed 5 percent of his salary to the company 401(k) plan on a pre-tax basis.
– Eric is married with two children. He had $5,000 deducted from his wages for a Dependent Care Flexible Spending Account.
– Eric is enrolled in the company-sponsored life insurance program. He has a policy that provides a benefit of $145,200.
– Eric contributed $2,650 to the Health Care Flexible Spending Account (he keeps forgetting that the maximum deferral has increased over the years).

Using the information and Eric's Form W-2, prepare an email to Eric reconciling his salary of $145,200 to the amounts in Boxes 1, 3, and 5.

a Employee's social security number 791-51-4335	OMB No. 1545-0008	Safe, accurate, FAST! Use	IRS e-file	Visit the IRS website at www.irs.gov/efile

	1 Wages, tips, other compensation	2 Federal income tax withheld
b Employer identification number (EIN) 12-3456789	130,417.00	15,184.00

c Employer's name, address, and ZIP code	3 Social security wages	4 Social security tax withheld
Ivy Technologies, Inc.	132,900.00	8,239.80
436 E. 35 Avenue	5 Medicare wages and tips	6 Medicare tax withheld
Gary, IN 46409	137,677.00	1,996.32
	7 Social security tips	8 Allocated tips

d Control number	9	10 Dependent care benefits 5,000.00

e Employee's first name and initial Last name Suff.	11 Nonqualified plans	12a See instructions for box 12 C	127.00
Eric Hayes	13 Statutory employee ☐ Retirement plan ☒ Third-party sick pay ☐	12b D	7,260.00
555 E. 81st Street	14 Other	12c DD	12,345.00
Merrillville, IN 46410		12d

f Employee's address and ZIP code					

15 State Employer's state ID number	16 State wages, tips, etc.	17 State income tax	18 Local wages, tips, etc.	19 Local income tax	20 Locality name
IN	00122231001	130,417.00	4,956.00	130,417.00	987.00	LAKE

Form **W-2** Wage and Tax Statement   **2019**   Department of the Treasury—Internal Revenue Service

Copy B—To Be Filed With Employee's FEDERAL Tax Return.
This information is being furnished to the Internal Revenue Service.

Partnership Taxation

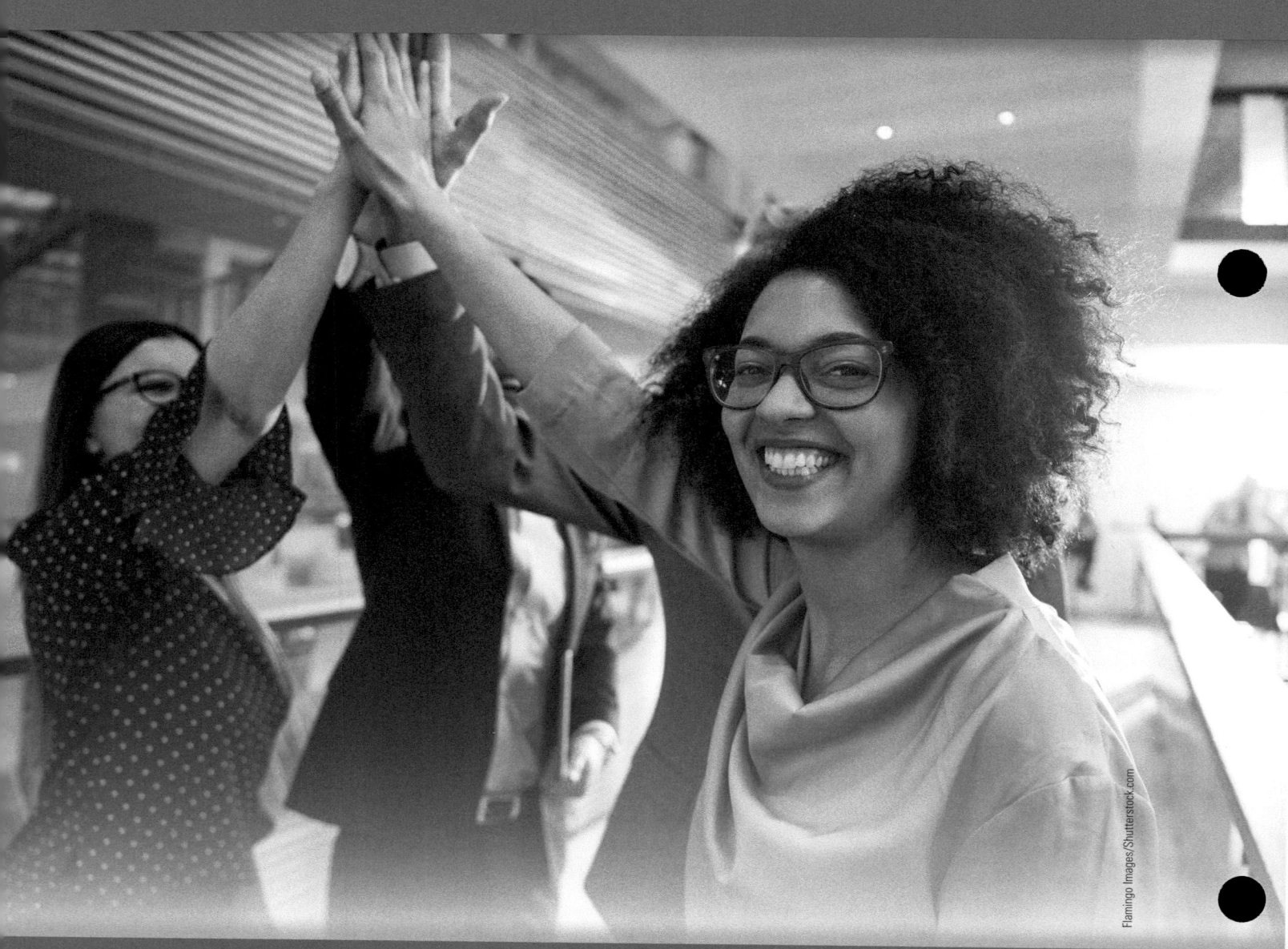

LEARNING OBJECTIVES

After completing this chapter, you should be able to:

LO 10.1   Define a partnership for tax purposes.

LO 10.2   Describe the basic tax rules for partnership formation and operation.

LO 10.3   Summarize the rules for partnership income reporting.

LO 10.4   Describe the tax treatment of partnership distributions.

LO 10.5   Determine partnership tax years.

LO 10.6   Describe the tax treatment of transactions between partners and their partnerships.

LO 10.7   Apply the qualified business income deduction to partners.

LO 10.8   Apply the at-risk rule to partnerships.

LO 10.9   Describe the tax treatment of limited liability companies (LLCs).

OVERVIEW

The partnership form allows taxpayers considerable flexibility in terms of contributions, income and loss allocations, and distributions. One of the primary benefits of the partnership is that partnership income is only taxed at the partner level. Corporate taxpayers (other than S corporations) pay tax at the corporate level and often again at the shareholder level (see Chapter 11), which results in corporate double taxation. Since a partnership's income passes through to the partners, there is no federal income tax at the entity level, only at the partner level. Currently, the tax law permits an additional qualified business income deduction for pass-through entities like partnerships.

One of the disadvantages of partnerships over corporations has been the lack of limited liability for partners whereas corporate shareholders enjoy protection from liability to third parties (e.g., creditors of the corporation). The advent of the limited liability company (LLC) and the limited liability partnership (LLP) has provided partners this important legal benefit. Because LLCs and LLPs are taxed like partnerships, they are included in this chapter on partnership taxation.

This chapter will provide an understanding of the tax treatment of partnerships and the tax forms (Form 1065 and Schedule K-1) related to reporting partnership income or loss.

Learning Objective 10.1

Define a partnership for tax purposes.

10-1 NATURE OF PARTNERSHIP TAXATION

Partnership federal income tax returns are information returns only. Returns show the amount of income by type and the allocation of the income to the partners. Partnership income and other items are passed through to the partners, and each partner is taxed on the individual's distributive share of partnership income. Partnership income is taxable to the partner even if he or she does not actually receive the income in cash.

Even though the partnership tax return is only informational, partnerships do have to make various elections and select accounting methods and periods. For example, partnerships must select depreciation and inventory methods. In addition, partnerships are legal entities under civil law, and in most states have rights under the Uniform Partnership Act.

10-1a What Is a Partnership?

The tax law defines a partnership as a syndicate, group, pool, joint venture, or other unincorporated organization through or by means of which any business, financial operation, or venture is carried on, and which is not classified as a corporation, trust, or estate. The mere co-ownership of property does not constitute a partnership; the partners must engage in some type of business or financial activity.

Ordinary partnerships, or general partnerships as they are often called, may be formed by a simple verbal agreement or "handshake" between partners. In contrast, the formation of corporations, limited partnerships, limited liability companies (LLCs), and limited liability partnerships (LLPs) must be documented in writing and the entity must be legally registered in the state in which it is formed. Even though general partnerships may be formed by verbal agreement between partners, partners usually document their agreement in writing with the help of attorneys in the event disagreements arise during the course of operations.

General partners usually take on the risk of legal liability for certain actions of the partnership or debts of the partnership, as specified under state law. To limit some of the liability exposure of operating a joint business, many partnerships are created formally as limited partnerships, LLCs, or LLPs. LLPs are used for licensed professionals such as attorneys and accountants.

Entities generally treated as partnerships for tax law purposes include limited partnerships, LLCs, and LLPs. Limited partnerships have one or more general partners and one or more limited partners. General partners participate in management and have unlimited liability for partnership obligations. Limited partners may not participate in management and have no liability for partnership obligations beyond their capital contributions. Many partnerships are formed as limited partnerships because the limited liability helps to attract passive investors. LLCs and LLPs are legal entities which combine the limited liability of corporations with the tax treatment of partnerships. LLCs and LLPs are discussed later in this chapter.

EXAMPLE Avery and Roberta buy a rental house which they hold jointly. The house is rented and they share the income and expenses for the year. Avery and Roberta have not formed a partnership. However, if they had bought and operated a store together, a partnership would have been formed. Although the ownership of real estate may not rise to the level of a business requiring a partnership return, co-owners of real estate frequently do choose to operate in a partnership, limited partnership, LLP, or LLC form. ♦

For federal tax purposes, an unincorporated business operated by spouses is considered a partnership. As a result, a business co-run by spouses is generally required to comply with filing and record-keeping requirements for partnerships and partners. Married co-owners wishing to avoid the burden of partnership documentation can form a qualified joint venture. The election to do so is made by simply reporting each spouse's share of income, losses, gains, and deductions on a Schedule C (along with other related forms) in respect of each spouse's interest in the joint venture.

TAX BREAK

Self-Study Problem 10.1   *See Appendix E for Solutions to Self-Study Problems*

Indicate, by placing a check in the appropriate blank, whether each of the following is or is not required to file a partnership return.

	Yes	No
1. Duncan and Clyde purchase and operate a plumbing business together.	_____	_____
2. Ellen and Walter form a corporation to operate a plumbing business.	_____	_____
3. George and Marty buy a duplex to hold as rental property, which is not considered an active business.	_____	_____
4. Howard and Sally (both single taxpayers) form a joint venture to drill for and sell oil.	_____	_____
5. Ted and Joyce, a married couple, purchase and operate a candy store.	_____	_____

10-2 PARTNERSHIP FORMATION

10.2 Learning Objective

Describe the basic tax rules for partnership formation and operation.

Generally, there is no gain or loss recognized by a partnership or any of its partners when property is contributed to a partnership in exchange for an interest in the partnership. This rule applies to the formation of a partnership as well as any subsequent contributions to the partnership. However, there are exceptions to the nonrecognition rule. Income may be recognized when a partnership interest is received in exchange for services performed by the partner for the partnership or when a partner transfers to a partnership, property subject to a liability exceeding that partner's basis in the property transferred. In this situation, gain is recognized to the extent that the portion of the liability allocable to the other partners exceeds the basis of the property contributed. If a partner receives money or other property from the partnership, in addition to an interest in the partnership, the transaction may be considered in part a sale or exchange, and a gain or loss may be recognized.

EXAMPLE Dunn and Church form the Dunn & Church Partnership. Dunn contributes a building with a fair market value of $90,000 and an adjusted basis of $55,000 for a 50 percent interest in the partnership. Dunn does not recognize a gain on the transfer of the building to the partnership. Church performs services for the partnership for his 50 percent interest which is worth $90,000. Church must report $90,000 in ordinary income for the receipt of an interest in the partnership in exchange for services provided to the partnership. ◆

EXAMPLE   Ann and Keith form the A&K Partnership. Ann contributes a building with a fair market value of $200,000 and an adjusted basis of $45,000 for a 50 percent interest in the partnership. The building is subject to a liability of $130,000. Keith contributes cash of $70,000 for a 50 percent interest in the partnership. Ann must recognize a gain on the transfer of the building to the partnership equal to $20,000, the amount by which the liability allocable to Keith, $65,000 (50% × $130,000), exceeds the basis of the building, $45,000. Keith does not recognize a gain on the contribution of cash to the partnership. ◆

A partner's initial basis in a partnership interest is equal to the basis of the property transferred plus cash contributed to the partnership. If gain is recognized on the transfer, the partner's basis in the partnership interest is increased by the gain recognized. The basis is reduced by any liabilities of the contributing partner assumed by the other partners through the partnership. For example, if a one-third partner is relieved of a $90,000 liability by the partnership, they would reduce by $60,000 ($\frac{2}{3}$ of $90,000) their partnership interest basis. After the initial basis in the partnership interest is established, the basis is adjusted for future earnings, losses, contributions to the partnership, and distributions from the partnership.

EXAMPLE   Prentice contributes cash of $50,000 and property with a fair market value of $110,000 (adjusted basis of $30,000) to the P&H Partnership. Prentice's basis in the partnership interest is $80,000 ($50,000 + $30,000). ◆

EXAMPLE   Assume that Prentice, in the example above, also received a partnership interest worth $15,000 for services provided to the partnership. She must recognize $15,000 as ordinary income, and her basis in the partnership interest is $95,000 ($80,000 + $15,000). ◆

EXAMPLE   Darnell contributes property with a fair market value of $110,000 and an adjusted basis of $30,000, subject to a liability of $20,000, to a partnership in exchange for a 25 percent interest in the partnership. Darnell's basis in his partnership interest is $15,000 [$30,000 − ($20,000 × 75%)]. ◆

The basis of a partner's interest in a partnership changes due to partnership activities. A partner's basis in their partnership interest is increased by the partner's share of (1) additional contributions to the partnership, (2) net ordinary taxable income of the partnership, and (3) capital gains and other income of the partnership. Alternatively, a partner's basis is reduced (but not below zero) by the partner's share of (1) distributions of partnership property, (2) losses from operations of the partnership, and (3) capital losses and other deductions of the partnership. In addition, changes in the partner's share of partnership liabilities affects the basis of a partner's partnership interest.

EXAMPLE   Reid has a 50 percent interest in the Reid Partnership. Her basis in her partnership interest at the beginning of the tax year is $12,000. For the current tax year, the partnership reports ordinary income of $15,000, a capital gain of $3,000, and charitable contributions of $700. The basis of Reid's partnership interest, after considering the above items, would be $20,650 ($12,000 beginning basis + $7,500 share of partnership ordinary income + $1,500 share of partnership capital gain − $350 share of partnership charitable contributions). ◆

The partnership's basis in property contributed by a partner is equal to the partner's adjusted basis in the property at the time of the contribution plus any gain recognized by the partner. The transfer of liabilities to the partnership by the partner does not impact the basis of the property to the partnership. The partnership's holding period for the property contributed to the partnership includes the partner's holding period. For example, long-term capital gain property may be transferred to a partnership by a partner and sold immediately, and any gain would be long-term, assuming the property is a capital asset to the partnership.

EXAMPLE Clark contributes property to the Rose Partnership in exchange for a partnership interest. The property contributed has an adjusted basis to Clark of $45,000 and a fair market value of $75,000 on the date of the contribution. The partnership's basis in the property is $45,000. ♦

Self-Study Problem 10.2   *See Appendix E for Solutions to Self-Study Problems*

John and Linda form the J&L Partnership. John contributes cash of $36,000 for a 40 percent interest in the partnership. Linda contributes equipment worth $54,000 with an adjusted basis of $17,500 for a 60 percent partnership interest.

1. What is John's recognized gain or loss on the contribution? $_____

2. What is John's basis in his partnership interest? $_____

3. What is Linda's recognized gain or loss on the contribution? $_____

4. What is Linda's basis in her partnership interest? $_____

5. What is J&L Partnership's basis in the equipment received from Linda? $_____

10-3 PARTNERSHIP INCOME REPORTING

10.3 Learning Objective

Summarize the rules for partnership income reporting.

A partnership is required to report its income and other items on Form 1065, U.S. Return of Partnership Income, even though the partnership entity does not pay federal income tax. The tax return is due on the fifteenth day of the third month following the close of the partnership's tax year. When reporting partnership taxable income, certain transactions must be separated rather than being reported as part of ordinary income. The primary items that must be reported separately are capital gains and losses, Section 1231 gains and losses, dividends, interest income, tax-exempt income, retirement contributions, charitable contributions, and most credits. These items are listed as separate income or expenses, since they are often subject to special calculations or limitations on the tax returns of the partners.

After the special items are separated, the partnership reports the remainder of its ordinary income or loss. The ordinary income or loss of a partnership is calculated in the same manner as that of an individual, except the partnership is not allowed to deduct the standard deduction, foreign taxes paid, charitable contributions, net operating losses, or personal itemized deductions. Schedule K-1 of Form 1065 presents the allocation of ordinary income or loss, special income and deductions, and gains and losses to each partner. The partners report the amounts from their Schedules K-1 on their own tax returns.

A partner's deductible loss from a partnership is limited to the basis of the partner's partnership interest at the end of the year in which the loss was incurred. The partner's basis is not affected by the qualified business income deduction. The partner's partnership basis cannot be reduced below zero. Any unused losses may be carried forward and reported in a future year when there is partnership basis available to be reduced by the loss.

Self-Study Problem 10.3   *See Appendix E for Solutions to Self-Study Problems*

Robert Conrad and Jan Springs are equal partners in the newly formed Malus Valley Partnership. During 2019, the partnership began operations and had the following income and expenses:

Gross income from operations	$255,600
Deductions:	
Salaries to employees	$168,000
Rent	12,000
Payroll taxes	6,100
Depreciation	9,250
Charitable contributions (to 50 percent organizations)	1,500
Cash withdrawals ($25,000 for each partner)	50,000

The partnership's balance sheet is as follows:

Malus Valley Balance Sheet as of December 31, 2019

Assets:		
Cash		$ 27,000
Accounts receivable		10,000
Land		115,000
Building	$115,000	
Less: accumulated depreciation	(9,250)	105,750
Total Assets		$257,750
Liabilities and Partners' Capital:		
Accounts payable		$ 29,750
Mortgage payable		187,750
Partners' capital (includes $31,500 originally contributed, $15,750 by each partner)		40,250
Total Liabilities and Partners' Capital		$257,750

Complete Form 1065, Page 1, and Schedules K, L, M-1, and M-2 on Pages 10-7 to 10-11 for Malus Valley. Also, complete Schedule K-1 on Pages 10-13 and 10-14 for Robert.

Self-Study Problem 10.3

Form **1065**	**U.S. Return of Partnership Income**	OMB No. 1545-0123

Department of the Treasury
Internal Revenue Service

For calendar year 2019, or tax year beginning _____ , 2019, ending _____ , 20 _____ .

▶ Go to *www.irs.gov/Form1065* for instructions and the latest information.

2019

A Principal business activity	Name of partnership		**D** Employer identification number
B Principal product or service	**Type or Print** Number, street, and room or suite no. If a P.O. box, see instructions.		**E** Date business started
C Business code number	City or town, state or province, country, and ZIP or foreign postal code		**F** Total assets (see instructions) $

G Check applicable boxes: **(1)** ☐ Initial return **(2)** ☐ Final return **(3)** ☐ Name change **(4)** ☐ Address change **(5)** ☐ Amended return

H Check accounting method: **(1)** ☐ Cash **(2)** ☐ Accrual **(3)** ☐ Other (specify) ▶ _____

I Number of Schedules K-1. Attach one for each person who was a partner at any time during the tax year ▶ _____

J Check if Schedules C and M-3 are attached . . . . ▶ ☐

K Check if partnership: **(1)** ☐ Aggregated activities for section 465 at-risk purposes **(2)** ☐ Grouped activities for section 469 passive activity purposes

Caution: Include **only** trade or business income and expenses on lines 1a through 22 below. See instructions for more information.

Income	**1a** Gross receipts or sales	**1a**	
	b Returns and allowances	**1b**	
	c Balance. Subtract line 1b from line 1a	**1c**	
	2 Cost of goods sold (attach Form 1125-A)	**2**	
	3 Gross profit. Subtract line 2 from line 1c	**3**	
	4 Ordinary income (loss) from other partnerships, estates, and trusts (attach statement) .	**4**	
	5 Net farm profit (loss) (attach Schedule F (Form 1040 or 1040-SR))	**5**	
	6 Net gain (loss) from Form 4797, Part II, line 17 (attach Form 4797)	**6**	
	7 Other income (loss) (attach statement)	**7**	
	8 **Total income (loss).** Combine lines 3 through 7	**8**	
Deductions (see instructions for limitations)	**9** Salaries and wages (other than to partners) (less employment credits)	**9**	
	10 Guaranteed payments to partners	**10**	
	11 Repairs and maintenance	**11**	
	12 Bad debts	**12**	
	13 Rent	**13**	
	14 Taxes and licenses	**14**	
	15 Interest (see instructions)	**15**	
	16a Depreciation (if required, attach Form 4562) . **16a**		
	b Less depreciation reported on Form 1125-A and elsewhere on return . **16b**	**16c**	
	17 Depletion (**Do not deduct oil and gas depletion.**)	**17**	
	18 Retirement plans, etc.	**18**	
	19 Employee benefit programs	**19**	
	20 Other deductions (attach statement)	**20**	
	21 **Total deductions.** Add the amounts shown in the far right column for lines 9 through 20 . . .	**21**	
	22 **Ordinary business income (loss).** Subtract line 21 from line 8	**22**	
Tax and Payment	**23** Interest due under the look-back method—completed long-term contracts (attach Form 8697) .	**23**	
	24 Interest due under the look-back method—income forecast method (attach Form 8866) . . .	**24**	
	25 BBA AAR imputed underpayment (see instructions)	**25**	
	26 Other taxes (see instructions)	**26**	
	27 **Total balance due.** Add lines 23 through 26	**27**	
	28 Payment (see instructions)	**28**	
	29 **Amount owed.** If line 28 is smaller than line 27, enter amount owed	**29**	
	30 **Overpayment.** If line 28 is larger than line 27, enter overpayment	**30**	

Sign Here

Under penalties of perjury, I declare that I have examined this return, including accompanying schedules and statements, and to the best of my knowledge and belief, it is true, correct, and complete. Declaration of preparer (other than partner or limited liability company member) is based on all information of which preparer has any knowledge.

▶ _____   ▶ _____
Signature of partner or limited liability company member   Date

May the IRS discuss this return with the preparer shown below? See instructions. ☐ Yes ☐ No

Paid Preparer Use Only

Print/Type preparer's name	Preparer's signature	Date	Check ☐ if self-employed	PTIN
Firm's name ▶			Firm's EIN ▶	
Firm's address ▶			Phone no.	

For Paperwork Reduction Act Notice, see separate instructions.   Cat. No. 11390Z   Form **1065** (2019)

Form 1065 (2019)   Page **2**

Schedule B	**Other Information**		

		Yes	**No**
1	What type of entity is filing this return? Check the applicable box:		

a ☐ Domestic general partnership   **b** ☐ Domestic limited partnership

c ☐ Domestic limited liability company   **d** ☐ Domestic limited liability partnership

e ☐ Foreign partnership   **f** ☐ Other ▶

2 At the end of the tax year:

a Did any foreign or domestic corporation, partnership (including any entity treated as a partnership), trust, or tax-exempt organization, or any foreign government own, directly or indirectly, an interest of 50% or more in the profit, loss, or capital of the partnership? For rules of constructive ownership, see instructions. If "Yes," attach Schedule B-1, Information on Partners Owning 50% or More of the Partnership

b Did any individual or estate own, directly or indirectly, an interest of 50% or more in the profit, loss, or capital of the partnership? For rules of constructive ownership, see instructions. If "Yes," attach Schedule B-1, Information on Partners Owning 50% or More of the Partnership . . . .

3 At the end of the tax year, did the partnership:

a Own directly 20% or more, or own, directly or indirectly, 50% or more of the total voting power of all classes of stock entitled to vote of any foreign or domestic corporation? For rules of constructive ownership, see instructions. If "Yes," complete (i) through (iv) below . . . .

(i) Name of Corporation	**(ii)** Employer Identification Number (if any)	**(iii)** Country of Incorporation	**(iv)** Percentage Owned in Voting Stock

b Own directly an interest of 20% or more, or own, directly or indirectly, an interest of 50% or more in the profit, loss, or capital in any foreign or domestic partnership (including an entity treated as a partnership) or in the beneficial interest of a trust? For rules of constructive ownership, see instructions. If "Yes," complete (i) through (v) below .

(i) Name of Entity	**(ii)** Employer Identification Number (if any)	**(iii)** Type of Entity	**(iv)** Country of Organization	**(v)** Maximum Percentage Owned in Profit, Loss, or Capital

		Yes	**No**
4	Does the partnership satisfy **all four** of the following conditions?		

a The partnership's total receipts for the tax year were less than $250,000.

b The partnership's total assets at the end of the tax year were less than $1 million.

c Schedules K-1 are filed with the return and furnished to the partners on or before the due date (including extensions) for the partnership return.

d The partnership is not filing and is not required to file Schedule M-3 . . . .

If "Yes," the partnership is not required to complete Schedules L, M-1, and M-2; item F on page 1 of Form 1065; or item L on Schedule K-1.

5 Is this partnership a publicly traded partnership, as defined in section 469(k)(2)? . . . .

6 During the tax year, did the partnership have any debt that was canceled, was forgiven, or had the terms modified so as to reduce the principal amount of the debt? . . . .

7 Has this partnership filed, or is it required to file, Form 8918, Material Advisor Disclosure Statement, to provide information on any reportable transaction?

8 At any time during calendar year 2019, did the partnership have an interest in or a signature or other authority over a financial account in a foreign country (such as a bank account, securities account, or other financial account)? See instructions for exceptions and filing requirements for FinCEN Form 114, Report of Foreign Bank and Financial Accounts (FBAR). If "Yes," enter the name of the foreign country ▶

9 At any time during the tax year, did the partnership receive a distribution from, or was it the grantor of, or transferor to, a foreign trust? If "Yes," the partnership may have to file Form 3520, Annual Return To Report Transactions With Foreign Trusts and Receipt of Certain Foreign Gifts. See instructions . . . .

10a Is the partnership making, or had it previously made (and not revoked), a section 754 election? . . . . . . See instructions for details regarding a section 754 election.

b Did the partnership make for this tax year an optional basis adjustment under section 743(b) or 734(b)? If "Yes," attach a statement showing the computation and allocation of the basis adjustment. See instructions . . . .

Form **1065** (2019)

Form 1065 (2019)   Page **3**

Schedule B	Other Information *(continued)*	Yes	No

c Is the partnership required to adjust the basis of partnership assets under section 743(b) or 734(b) because of a substantial built-in loss (as defined under section 743(d)) or substantial basis reduction (as defined under section 734(d))? If "Yes," attach a statement showing the computation and allocation of the basis adjustment. See instructions . . . .

11 Check this box if, during the current or prior tax year, the partnership distributed any property received in a like-kind exchange or contributed such property to another entity (other than disregarded entities wholly owned by the partnership throughout the tax year) . . . . ▶ ☐

12 At any time during the tax year, did the partnership distribute to any partner a tenancy-in-common or other undivided interest in partnership property? . . . .

13 If the partnership is required to file Form 8858, Information Return of U.S. Persons With Respect To Foreign Disregarded Entities (FDEs) and Foreign Branches (FBs), enter the number of Forms 8858 attached. See instructions . . . . ▶

14 Does the partnership have any foreign partners? If "Yes," enter the number of Forms 8805, Foreign Partner's Information Statement of Section 1446 Withholding Tax, filed for this partnership . . . ▶

15 Enter the number of Forms 8865, Return of U.S. Persons With Respect to Certain Foreign Partnerships, attached to this return . . . . ▶

16a Did you make any payments in 2019 that would require you to file Form(s) 1099? See instructions . . . . .
b If "Yes," did you or will you file required Form(s) 1099? . . . .

17 Enter the number of Forms 5471, Information Return of U.S. Persons With Respect To Certain Foreign Corporations, attached to this return . . . . ▶

18 Enter the number of partners that are foreign governments under section 892 . . . . ▶

19 During the partnership's tax year, did the partnership make any payments that would require it to file Form 1042 and 1042-S under chapter 3 (sections 1441 through 1464) or chapter 4 (sections 1471 through 1474)? . . . . .

20 Was the partnership a specified domestic entity required to file Form 8938 for the tax year? See the Instructions for Form 8938 . . . .

21 Is the partnership a section 721(c) partnership, as defined in Regulations section 1.721(c)-1T(b)(14)? . . . . .

22 During the tax year, did the partnership pay or accrue any interest or royalty for which the deduction is not allowed under section 267A? See instructions . . . .
If "Yes," enter the total amount of the disallowed deductions . . . . ▶ $

23 Did the partnership have an election under section 163(j) for any real property trade or business or any farming business in effect during the tax year? See instructions . . . .

24 Does the partnership satisfy one or more of the following? See instructions . . . .
a The partnership owns a pass-through entity with current, or prior year carryover, excess business interest expense.
b The partnership's aggregate average annual gross receipts (determined under section 448(c)) for the 3 tax years preceding the current tax year are more than $26 million and the partnership has business interest.
c The partnership is a tax shelter (see instructions) and the partnership has business interest expense.
If "Yes" to any, complete and attach Form 8990.

25 Is the partnership electing out of the centralized partnership audit regime under section 6221(b)? See instructions.
If "Yes," the partnership must complete Schedule B-2 (Form 1065). Enter the total from Schedule B-2, Part III, line 3 . . . . ▶ _____
If "No," complete Designation of Partnership Representative below.

Designation of Partnership Representative (see instructions)
Enter below the information for the partnership representative (PR) for the tax year covered by this return.

Name of PR ▶

U.S. address of PR ▶	U.S. phone number of PR ▶

If the PR is an entity, name of the designated individual for the PR ▶

U.S. address of designated individual ▶	U.S. phone number of designated individual ▶

26 Is the partnership attaching Form 8996 to certify as a Qualified Opportunity Fund? . . . .
If "Yes," enter the amount from Form 8996, line 14 . . . . ▶ $

27 Enter the number of foreign partners subject to section 864(c)(8) as a result of transferring all or a portion of an interest in the partnership or of receiving a distribution from the partnership . . . . . ▶

28 At any time during the tax year, were there any transfers between the partnership and its partners subject to the disclosure requirements of Regulations section 1.707-8? . . . .

Form **1065** (2019)

Self-Study Problem 10.3

Form 1065 (2019)   Page **4**

Schedule K		Partners' Distributive Share Items		Total amount

Income (Loss)

	1	Ordinary business income (loss) (page 1, line 22)	**1**	
	2	Net rental real estate income (loss) (attach Form 8825)	**2**	
	3a	Other gross rental income (loss) **3a**		
	b	Expenses from other rental activities (attach statement) **3b**		
	c	Other net rental income (loss). Subtract line 3b from line 3a	**3c**	
	4	Guaranteed payments: **a** Services **4a** **b** Capital **4b**		
		c Total. Add lines 4a and 4b	**4c**	
	5	Interest income	**5**	
	6	Dividends and dividend equivalents: **a** Ordinary dividends	**6a**	
		b Qualified dividends **6b** **c** Dividend equivalents **6c**		
	7	Royalties	**7**	
	8	Net short-term capital gain (loss) (attach Schedule D (Form 1065))	**8**	
	9a	Net long-term capital gain (loss) (attach Schedule D (Form 1065))	**9a**	
	b	Collectibles (28%) gain (loss) **9b**		
	c	Unrecaptured section 1250 gain (attach statement) **9c**		
	10	Net section 1231 gain (loss) (attach Form 4797)	**10**	
	11	Other income (loss) (see instructions) Type ▶	**11**	

Deductions

	12	Section 179 deduction (attach Form 4562)	**12**	
	13a	Contributions	**13a**	
	b	Investment interest expense	**13b**	
	c	Section 59(e)(2) expenditures: **(1)** Type ▶____ **(2)** Amount ▶	**13c(2)**	
	d	Other deductions (see instructions) Type ▶	**13d**	

Self-Employ-ment

	14a	Net earnings (loss) from self-employment	**14a**	
	b	Gross farming or fishing income	**14b**	
	c	Gross nonfarm income	**14c**	

Credits

	15a	Low-income housing credit (section 42(j)(5))	**15a**	
	b	Low-income housing credit (other)	**15b**	
	c	Qualified rehabilitation expenditures (rental real estate) (attach Form 3468, if applicable)	**15c**	
	d	Other rental real estate credits (see instructions) Type ▶	**15d**	
	e	Other rental credits (see instructions) Type ▶	**15e**	
	f	Other credits (see instructions) Type ▶	**15f**	

Foreign Transactions

	16a	Name of country or U.S. possession ▶		
	b	Gross income from all sources	**16b**	
	c	Gross income sourced at partner level	**16c**	
		Foreign gross income sourced at partnership level		
	d	Reserved for future use ▶ **e** Foreign branch category . . . . . ▶	**16e**	
	f	Passive category ▶____ **g** General category ▶____ **h** Other (attach statement) ▶	**16h**	
		Deductions allocated and apportioned at partner level		
	i	Interest expense ▶____ **j** Other ▶	**16j**	
		Deductions allocated and apportioned at partnership level to foreign source income		
	k	Reserved for future use ▶ **l** Foreign branch category . . . . . ▶	**16l**	
	m	Passive category ▶____ **n** General category ▶____ **o** Other (attach statement) ▶	**16o**	
	p	Total foreign taxes (check one): ▶ Paid ☐ Accrued ☐	**16p**	
	q	Reduction in taxes available for credit (attach statement)	**16q**	
	r	Other foreign tax information (attach statement)		

Alternative Minimum Tax (AMT) Items

	17a	Post-1986 depreciation adjustment	**17a**	
	b	Adjusted gain or loss	**17b**	
	c	Depletion (other than oil and gas)	**17c**	
	d	Oil, gas, and geothermal properties—gross income	**17d**	
	e	Oil, gas, and geothermal properties—deductions	**17e**	
	f	Other AMT items (attach statement)	**17f**	

Other Information

	18a	Tax-exempt interest income	**18a**	
	b	Other tax-exempt income	**18b**	
	c	Nondeductible expenses	**18c**	
	19a	Distributions of cash and marketable securities	**19a**	
	b	Distributions of other property	**19b**	
	20a	Investment income	**20a**	
	b	Investment expenses	**20b**	
	c	Other items and amounts (attach statement)		

Form **1065** (2019)

Form 1065 (2019)   Page **5**

Analysis of Net Income (Loss)

1	Net income (loss). Combine Schedule K, lines 1 through 11. From the result, subtract the sum of Schedule K, lines 12 through 13d, and 16p				**1**		

2	Analysis by partner type:	**(i)** Corporate	**(ii)** Individual (active)	**(iii)** Individual (passive)	**(iv)** Partnership	**(v)** Exempt Organization	**(vi)** Nominee/Other
a	General partners						
b	Limited partners						

Schedule L — Balance Sheets per Books

	Assets	Beginning of tax year (a)	(b)	End of tax year (c)	(d)
1	Cash				
2a	Trade notes and accounts receivable				
b	Less allowance for bad debts				
3	Inventories				
4	U.S. government obligations				
5	Tax-exempt securities				
6	Other current assets (attach statement)				
7a	Loans to partners (or persons related to partners) .				
b	Mortgage and real estate loans				
8	Other investments (attach statement)				
9a	Buildings and other depreciable assets				
b	Less accumulated depreciation				
10a	Depletable assets				
b	Less accumulated depletion				
11	Land (net of any amortization)				
12a	Intangible assets (amortizable only)				
b	Less accumulated amortization				
13	Other assets (attach statement)				
14	Total assets				
	Liabilities and Capital				
15	Accounts payable				
16	Mortgages, notes, bonds payable in less than 1 year				
17	Other current liabilities (attach statement)				
18	All nonrecourse loans				
19a	Loans from partners (or persons related to partners) .				
b	Mortgages, notes, bonds payable in 1 year or more .				
20	Other liabilities (attach statement)				
21	Partners' capital accounts				
22	Total liabilities and capital				

Schedule M-1 — Reconciliation of Income (Loss) per Books With Income (Loss) per Return

Note: The partnership may be required to file Schedule M-3. See instructions.

1	Net income (loss) per books		6	Income recorded on books this year not included on Schedule K, lines 1 through 11 (itemize):	
2	Income included on Schedule K, lines 1, 2, 3c, 5, 6a, 7, 8, 9a, 10, and 11, not recorded on books this year (itemize): _____		a	Tax-exempt interest $_____	
3	Guaranteed payments (other than health insurance)		7	Deductions included on Schedule K, lines 1 through 13d, and 16p, not charged against book income this year (itemize):	
4	Expenses recorded on books this year not included on Schedule K, lines 1 through 13d, and 16p (itemize):		a	Depreciation $_____	
a	Depreciation $_____		8	Add lines 6 and 7	
b	Travel and entertainment $_____		9	Income (loss) (Analysis of Net Income (Loss), line 1). Subtract line 8 from line 5	
5	Add lines 1 through 4				

Schedule M-2 — Analysis of Partners' Capital Accounts

1	Balance at beginning of year . . .		6	Distributions: **a** Cash	
2	Capital contributed: **a** Cash . . .			**b** Property	
	b Property . .		7	Other decreases (itemize): _____	
3	Net income (loss) per books				
4	Other increases (itemize): _____		8	Add lines 6 and 7	
5	Add lines 1 through 4		9	Balance at end of year. Subtract line 8 from line 5	

Form **1065** (2019)

Self-Study Problem 10.3

651119

☐ Final K-1 ☐ Amended K-1	OMB No. 1545-0123

Schedule K-1
(Form 1065)

2019

Department of the Treasury
Internal Revenue Service

For calendar year 2019, or tax year

beginning ___ / ___ / 2019   ending ___ / ___ / ___

Partner's Share of Income, Deductions, Credits, etc. ▶ See back of form and separate instructions.

Part III   Partner's Share of Current Year Income, Deductions, Credits, and Other Items

1	Ordinary business income (loss)	**15**	Credits
2	Net rental real estate income (loss)		
3	Other net rental income (loss)	**16**	Foreign transactions
4a	Guaranteed payments for services		
4b	Guaranteed payments for capital		
4c	Total guaranteed payments		
5	Interest income		
6a	Ordinary dividends		
6b	Qualified dividends		
6c	Dividend equivalents	**17**	Alternative minimum tax (AMT) items
7	Royalties		
8	Net short-term capital gain (loss)		
9a	Net long-term capital gain (loss)	**18**	Tax-exempt income and nondeductible expenses
9b	Collectibles (28%) gain (loss)		
9c	Unrecaptured section 1250 gain		
10	Net section 1231 gain (loss)		
11	Other income (loss)	**19**	Distributions
12	Section 179 deduction	**20**	Other information
13	Other deductions		
14	Self-employment earnings (loss)		

Part I   Information About the Partnership

A Partnership's employer identification number

B Partnership's name, address, city, state, and ZIP code

C IRS Center where partnership filed return ▶

D ☐ Check if this is a publicly traded partnership (PTP)

Part II   Information About the Partner

E Partner's identifying number (Do not use TIN of a disregarded entity. See instructions.)

F Partner's name, address, city, state, and ZIP code

G ☐ General partner or LLC member-manager   ☐ Limited partner or other LLC member

H ☐ Domestic partner   ☐ Foreign partner
☐ Disregarded entity:
Name of beneficial owner _____

I1 What type of entity is this partner? _____

I2 If this partner is a retirement plan (IRA/SEP/Keogh/etc.), check here ☐

J Partner's share of profit, loss, and capital (see instructions):

	Beginning	Ending
Profit	_____ %	_____ %
Loss	_____ %	_____ %
Capital	_____ %	_____ %

Check if decrease is due to sale or exchange of partnership interest . . ☐

K Partner's share of liabilities:

	Beginning	Ending
Nonrecourse . . .	$	$
Qualified nonrecourse financing . . .	$	$
Recourse . . .	$	$

☐ Check this box if Item K includes liability amounts from lower tier partnerships.

L   **Partner's Capital Account Analysis**

Tax Basis Capital

Beginning capital account . . .	$ _____
Capital contributed during the year . .	$ _____
Current year net income (loss) . . .	$ _____
Other increase (decrease) (attach explanation)	$ _____
Withdrawals & distributions . . .	$ (_____)
Ending capital account	$ _____

M Did the partner contribute property with a built-in gain or loss?
☐ Yes   ☐ No   If "Yes," attach statement. See instructions.

N Partner's Share of Net Unrecognized Section 704(c) Gain or (Loss)
Beginning . . . . $ _____
Ending . . . . $ _____

21 ☐ More than one activity for at-risk purposes*
22 ☐ More than one activity for passive activity purposes*
*See attached statement for additional information.

For IRS Use Only

For Paperwork Reduction Act Notice, see Instructions for Form 1065.   www.irs.gov/Form1065   Cat. No. 11394R   **Schedule K-1 (Form 1065) 2019**

Schedule K-1 (Form 1065) 2019   Page **2**

This list identifies the codes used on Schedule K-1 for all partners and provides summarized reporting information for partners who file Form 1040 or 1040-SR.
For detailed reporting and filing information, see the separate Partner's Instructions for Schedule K-1 and the instructions for your income tax return.

1. Ordinary business income (loss). Determine whether the income (loss) is passive or nonpassive and enter on your return as follows.

	Report on
Passive loss	See the Partner's Instructions
Passive income	Schedule E, line 28, column (h)
Nonpassive loss	See the Partner's Instructions
Nonpassive income	Schedule E, line 28, column (k)

2. Net rental real estate income (loss) — See the Partner's Instructions

3. Other net rental income (loss)
Net income	Schedule E, line 28, column (h)
Net loss	See the Partner's Instructions

4a. Guaranteed payment Services	See the Partner's Instructions
4b. Guaranteed payment Capital	See the Partner's Instructions
4c. Guaranteed payment Total	See the Partner's Instructions
5. Interest income	Form 1040 or 1040-SR, line 2b
6a. Ordinary dividends	Form 1040 or 1040-SR, line 3b
6b. Qualified dividends	Form 1040 or 1040-SR, line 3a
6c. Dividend equivalents	See the Partner's Instructions
7. Royalties	Schedule E, line 4
8. Net short-term capital gain (loss)	Schedule D, line 5
9a. Net long-term capital gain (loss)	Schedule D, line 12
9b. Collectibles (28%) gain (loss)	28% Rate Gain Worksheet, line 4 (Schedule D instructions)
9c. Unrecaptured section 1250 gain	See the Partner's Instructions
10. Net section 1231 gain (loss)	See the Partner's Instructions

11. Other income (loss)
Code		
A	Other portfolio income (loss)	See the Partner's Instructions
B	Involuntary conversions	See the Partner's Instructions
C	Sec. 1256 contracts & straddles	Form 6781, line 1
D	Mining exploration costs recapture	See Pub. 535
E	Cancellation of debt	
F	Section 743(b) positive adjustments	
G	Section 965(a) inclusion	
H	Income under subpart F (other than inclusions under sections 951A and 965)	See the Partner's Instructions
I	Other income (loss)	

12. Section 179 deduction — See the Partner's Instructions

13. Other deductions
A	Cash contributions (60%)	
B	Cash contributions (30%)	
C	Noncash contributions (50%)	
D	Noncash contributions (30%)	See the Partner's Instructions
E	Capital gain property to a 50% organization (30%)	
F	Capital gain property (20%)	
G	Contributions (100%)	
H	Investment interest expense	Form 4952, line 1
I	Deductions—royalty income	Schedule E, line 19
J	Section 59(e)(2) expenditures	See the Partner's Instructions
K	Excess business interest expense	See the Partner's Instructions
L	Deductions—portfolio (other)	Schedule A, line 16
M	Amounts paid for medical insurance	Schedule A, line 1, or Schedule 1 (Form 1040 or 1040-SR), line 16
N	Educational assistance benefits	See the Partner's Instructions
O	Dependent care benefits	Form 2441, line 12
P	Preproductive period expenses	See the Partner's Instructions
Q	Commercial revitalization deduction from rental real estate activities	See Form 8582 instructions
R	Pensions and IRAs	See the Partner's Instructions
S	Reforestation expense deduction	See the Partner's Instructions
T	through **U**	Reserved for future use
V	Section 743(b) negative adjustments	
W	Other deductions	See the Partner's Instructions
X	Section 965(c) deduction	

14. Self-employment earnings (loss)
Note: If you have a section 179 deduction or any partner-level deductions, see the Partner's Instructions before completing Schedule SE.
A	Net earnings (loss) from self-employment	Schedule SE, Section A or B
B	Gross farming or fishing income	See the Partner's Instructions
C	Gross non-farm income	See the Partner's Instructions

15. Credits
A	Low-income housing credit (section 42(j)(5)) from pre-2008 buildings	
B	Low-income housing credit (other) from pre-2008 buildings	
C	Low-income housing credit (section 42(j)(5)) from post-2007 buildings	See the Partner's Instructions
D	Low-income housing credit (other) from post-2007 buildings	
E	Qualified rehabilitation expenditures (rental real estate)	
F	Other rental real estate credits	
G	Other rental credits	

Code		*Report on*
H	Undistributed capital gains credit	Schedule 3 (Form 1040 or 1040-SR), line 13, box a
I	Biofuel producer credit	See the Partner's Instructions
J	Work opportunity credit	
K	Disabled access credit	
L	Empowerment zone employment credit	
M	Credit for increasing research activities	See the Partner's Instructions
N	Credit for employer social security and Medicare taxes	
O	Backup withholding	
P	Other credits	

16. Foreign transactions
A	Name of country or U.S. possession	
B	Gross income from all sources	Form 1116, Part I
C	Gross income sourced at partner level	

Foreign gross income sourced at partnership level
D	Reserved for future use	
E	Foreign branch category	
F	Passive category	Form 1116, Part I
G	General category	
H	Other	

Deductions allocated and apportioned at partner level
I	Interest expense	Form 1116, Part I
J	Other	Form 1116, Part I

Deductions allocated and apportioned at partnership level to foreign source income
K	Reserved for future use	
L	Foreign branch category	
M	Passive category	Form 1116, Part I
N	General category	
O	Other	

Other information
P	Total foreign taxes paid	Form 1116, Part II
Q	Total foreign taxes accrued	Form 1116, Part II
R	Reduction in taxes available for credit	Form 1116, line 12
S	Foreign trading gross receipts	Form 8873
T	Extraterritorial income exclusion	Form 8873
U	through **V**	Reserved for future use
W	Section 965 information	See the Partner's Instructions
X	Other foreign transactions	

17. Alternative minimum tax (AMT) items
A	Post-1986 depreciation adjustment	
B	Adjusted gain or loss	See the Partner's Instructions and the Instructions for Form 6251
C	Depletion (other than oil & gas)	
D	Oil, gas, & geothermal—gross income	
E	Oil, gas, & geothermal—deductions	
F	Other AMT items	

18. Tax-exempt income and nondeductible expenses
A	Tax-exempt interest income	Form 1040 or 1040-SR, line 2a
B	Other tax-exempt income	See the Partner's Instructions
C	Nondeductible expenses	See the Partner's Instructions

19. Distributions
A	Cash and marketable securities	
B	Distribution subject to section 737	See the Partner's Instructions
C	Other property	

20. Other information
A	Investment income	Form 4952, line 4a
B	Investment expenses	Form 4952, line 5
C	Fuel tax credit information	Form 4136
D	Qualified rehabilitation expenditures (other than rental real estate)	
E	Basis of energy property	See the Partner's Instructions
F	through **G**	
H	Recapture of investment credit	See Form 4255
I	Recapture of other credits	See the Partner's Instructions
J	Look-back interest—completed long-term contracts	See Form 8697
K	Look-back interest—income forecast method	See Form 8866
L	Dispositions of property with section 179 deductions	
M	Recapture of section 179 deduction	
N	Interest expense for corporate partners	
O	through **Y**	
Z	Section 199A information	
AA	Section 704(c) information	
AB	Section 751 gain (loss)	See the Partner's Instructions
AC	Section 1(h)(5) gain (loss)	
AD	Section 1250 unrecaptured gain	
AE	Excess taxable income	
AF	Excess business interest income	
AG	Gross receipts for section 59A(e)	
AH	Other information	

10-4 CURRENT DISTRIBUTIONS AND GUARANTEED PAYMENTS

10.4 Learning Objective

Describe the tax treatment of partnership distributions.

A partnership may make distributions of money or other property to the partners. A current distribution is defined as one which does not result in the complete termination of the partner's interest in the partnership.

In a current distribution, no gain is recognized by the partner receiving the distribution unless the partner's basis in the partnership has reached zero. In such a case, gain is recognized only to the extent that a distribution of money exceeds the partner's basis in their partnership interest.

The distribution of money or other property reduces the partner's basis in their partnership interest, but not below zero.

EXAMPLE Calvin is a partner in K&G Interests, and his basis in his partnership interest is $75,000. In the current tax year, Calvin receives a $45,000 cash distribution from the partnership. He does not recognize a gain or loss on the distribution, but his basis in his partnership interest is reduced to $30,000 ($75,000 − $45,000). If the distribution of cash were $80,000 instead of $45,000, Calvin would have a taxable gain of $5,000 ($80,000 − $75,000), and his basis in the partnership interest would be reduced to zero ($75,000 − $80,000 + $5,000). ◆

The basis of property received by a partner in a current distribution will generally be the same as the basis of the property to the partnership immediately prior to the distribution. An overall limitation is imposed which states that the basis of the assets distributed cannot exceed the partner's basis in his partnership interest, reduced by any money distributed. In some cases, this overall limitation may require that the partner's basis in the partnership interest be allocated among the assets received in the distribution.

10-4a Guaranteed Payments

Payments made to a partner for services rendered or for use of the partner's capital that are made without regard to the income of the partnership are termed *guaranteed payments*. Such payments are treated by the partnership in the same manner as payments made to a person who is not a partner. The payments are ordinary income to the partner and deductible by the partnership. Guaranteed payments are separately reported on Line 4 of Schedule K-1.

EXAMPLE Alexander and Bryant operate the A&B Partnership. Alexander, a 50 percent partner, receives guaranteed payments of $15,000 for the year. If A&B has net ordinary income (after guaranteed payments) of $53,000, Alexander's total income from A&B is $41,500 ($15,000 + 50% of $53,000). Alexander's Schedule K-1 would report $26,500 on Line 1 (ordinary business income) and $15,000 on Line 4 (guaranteed payments). ◆

A partnership may show a loss after deducting guaranteed payments. In that case, the partner reports the guaranteed payments as income and reports their share of the partnership loss.

Self-Study Problem 10.4 | *See Appendix E for Solutions to Self-Study Problems*

Jim and Jack are equal partners in J&J Interests, which has ordinary income for the year of $32,000 before guaranteed payments. Jim receives guaranteed payments of $36,000 during the year. Calculate the total amount of income or loss from the partnership that should be reported by Jim and by Jack.

1. Jim should report total income (loss) of $_____

2. Jack should report total income (loss) of $_____

Determine partnership
tax years.

10-5 TAX YEARS

The tax law requires that each partner include in gross income for a particular tax year the individual's distributive share of income, including guaranteed payments, from a partnership whose tax year ends with or within that partner's tax year. For example, a calendar-year individual partner should report their income from a partnership with a tax year ending June 30, 2019, on his or her 2019 tax return. Since a partner reports only income reported by a partnership whose year ends with or within their tax year, it is possible to delay the reporting of partnership income and guaranteed payments for almost an entire year. This would happen, for example, if the partnership's year-end is January 31, and the partner's tax year is a calendar year. To prevent this deferral of income, rigid rules have been established regarding partnership tax years. Under these rules, unless a partnership can establish a business purpose for a fiscal year-end or meet certain tests, it must adopt the same taxable year as that of the majority partners. If such partners do not have the same tax year, then the partnership is required to adopt the tax year of all its principal partners. If neither of these rules can be met, the partnership must adopt a tax year based on the least aggregate deferral method (see IRS Publication 538 for more information).

Once established, a partnership will not close its tax year early unless the partnership is terminated. The tax year does not generally close upon the entry of a new partner, or the liquidation, sale, or exchange of an existing partnership interest. A partnership is terminated, and will close its tax year, if business activity by the partnership ceases.

Self-Study Problem 10.5 *See Appendix E for Solutions to Self-Study Problems*

R&S Associates is a partnership with a tax year that ends on August 31, 2019. During the partnership's tax year, Robert, a partner, received $1,000 per month as a guaranteed payment, and his share of partnership income after guaranteed payments was $21,000. For September through December of 2019, Robert's guaranteed payment was increased to $1,500 per month. Calculate the amount of income from the partnership that Robert should report for his 2019 calendar tax year.

$_____

Describe the tax
treatment of transactions
between partners and
their partnerships.

10-6 TRANSACTIONS BETWEEN PARTNERS AND THE PARTNERSHIP

When engaging in a transaction with a partnership, a partner is generally regarded as an outside party, and the transaction is reported as it would be if the two parties were unrelated. However, it is recognized that occasionally transactions may lack substance because one party to the transaction exercises significant influence over the other party. Therefore, losses are disallowed for (1) transactions between a partnership and a partner who has a direct or indirect capital or profit interest in the partnership of more than 50 percent, and (2) transactions between two partnerships owned more than 50 percent by the same partners. When a loss is disallowed, the purchaser may reduce a future gain on the disposition of the property by the amount of the disallowed loss.

EXAMPLE   Kyle owns 55 percent of Willow Interests, a partnership. During the current year, Kyle sells property to the partnership for $60,000. Kyle's adjusted basis in the property is $75,000. The $15,000 loss is disallowed, since Kyle is a more than 50 percent partner. If later the partnership sells the property for $80,000, realizing a $20,000 gain ($80,000 − $60,000), only $5,000 of the gain is recognized, since the partnership can use Kyle's disallowed loss to offset $15,000 of the gain. ♦

In a transaction between a partner and a partnership, a gain will be taxed as ordinary income if the partner has more than a 50 percent interest in the partnership and the property sold or transferred is not a capital asset to the transferee. The interest may be owned directly or indirectly. For example, a taxpayer indirectly owns the interests owned by their spouse, brothers, sisters, ancestors, and lineal descendants.

EXAMPLE   Amy is a 50 percent partner in the A&B Partnership, and her brother, Ben, is the other 50 percent partner. Amy sells for $65,000 a building (with a basis of $50,000) to the partnership for use in its business. The property qualifies as a long-term capital asset to Amy. The gain of $15,000 ($65,000 − $50,000), however, is ordinary income, since Amy is considered a 100 percent partner (50 percent directly and 50 percent indirectly) and the building is a Section 1231 asset to the partnership. ♦

Self-Study Problem 10.6   *See Appendix E for Solutions to Self-Study Problems*

Maxwell is a 50 percent partner in M&P Associates. Pam, Maxwell's daughter, owns the other 50 percent interest in the partnership. During the current tax year, Maxwell sells ordinary income property to M&P Associates for $70,000. The property's basis to Maxwell is $75,000. Also, Pam sells her personal Mercedes-Benz, with a basis of $25,000, for $40,000 to M&P Associates for use in the partnership's business.

1. What is the amount of Maxwell's recognized gain or loss on his transaction, and what is the nature of the gain or loss?

   $_____

2. What is the amount and nature of Pam's gain or loss on her transaction with the partnership?

   $_____

10-7   QUALIFIED BUSINESS INCOME DEDUCTION FOR PARTNERS

10.7 Learning Objective

Apply the qualified business income deduction to partners.

The TCJA introduced a new qualified business income deduction available to individual owners of pass-through businesses such as partnerships and LLCs. The deduction in general is covered in Chapter 4. This section covers some of the items applicable specifically to partnerships.

Qualified business income (QBI) generally includes all items of ordinary business income; however, the tax law specifically excludes certain items including guaranteed payments to partners and payments made to partners by the partnership in situations in which the partner is not acting in their capacity as a partner.

EXAMPLE   Rigby is a 30 percent partner in Regular Partnership. In 2019, Regular has $50,000 of ordinary business income and no other separately stated items. In 2019, Rigby receives guaranteed payments of $10,000. Rigby also enters into a loan between himself and Regular and receives interest income from the partnership of $1,000. Rigby also receives a cash distribution from Regular of $5,000 and maintains a positive basis at year-end. The loan is treated as a transaction in which Rigby is not acting in his capacity as a partner and thus the guaranteed payment and the interest are both not included in Rigby's QBI and thus Rigby's QBI is $15,000 ($50,000 × 30%). ♦

Although guaranteed payments and payments to partners not acting as partners are not included in QBI, they are deductible by the partnership in computing ordinary business income (to the extent the items would be deductible otherwise).

TAX BREAK   Partners may want to reconsider a characterization away from guaranteed payments as part of a revision to the partnership agreement. Guaranteed payments and the allocation of business income to an individual partner are both generally subject to self-employment taxes; however, guaranteed payments are a deduction from ordinary business income while cash distributions from basis are not. In addition, guaranteed payments are not part of QBI. By treating former guaranteed payments instead as cash distributions, the partnership (and thus the partner) will have greater QBI eligible for the 20 percent QBI deduction. Of course, the "guarantee" of guaranteed payments will also be eliminated by the recharacterization.

For high income taxpayers, the QBI deduction is limited by W-2 wages or a combination of W-2 wages and qualified property. A partner must be allocated their share of these items in order to properly apply the limitations when applicable.

EXAMPLE   Mordecai is a 50 percent partner in Park Partnership. In 2019, Mordecai's taxable income is high enough to subject his QBI deduction to the wage limitation. Park pays W-2 wages of $70,000 and has qualified property of $300,000 in 2019. If these items are allocated in accordance with the partnership interest, Mordecai will be allocated $35,000 of W-2 wages ($70,000 × 50%) and $150,000 of qualified property ($300,000 × 50%) to compute his wage limitation. ♦

Self-Study Problem 10.7   *See Appendix E for Solutions to Self-Study Problems*

a. Dr. Marla Cratchitt is a single taxpayer and works as cardiologist. Marla is an investor in Salem Healthcare LLC, a business that manufactures stents for a variety of cardiovascular issues. Marla's member's interest in Salem is 20 percent and the LLC agreement calls for guaranteed payments to Marla of $75,000 per year. In 2019, Marla's ordinary business income allocation from Salem is $200,000. Salem also allocated $5,000 of long-term capital gains to Marla. Salem paid wages to employees of $230,000 and has qualified property of $1,200,000. Marla has taxable income of $776,000 for purposes of the QBI limit. Compute Marla's QBI deduction.

$_____

b. Assume that same facts as part a. except that Salem is a service business. Compute Marla's QBI deduction.

$_____

10-8 **THE AT-RISK RULE**

The at-risk rule is designed to prevent taxpayers from deducting losses from activities in excess of their investment in those activities. Although the at-risk rule applies to most taxpayers, it is discussed here because the rule is a common problem related to investments in partnerships. In general, the at-risk rule limits the losses from a taxpayer's business activities to "amounts at risk" (AAR) in the activity.

To understand the at-risk rule, it is necessary to understand two related terms, "nonrecourse liabilities" and "encumbered property." A nonrecourse liability is a debt for which the borrower is not personally liable. If the debt is not paid, the lender generally can only repossess the property pledged as collateral on the loan. Encumbered property (also referred to as "collateral") is property pledged for the liability. The property is said to be encumbered in the amount of the liability. Taxpayers are at risk in amounts equal to their cash and property contributions to the activities, borrowed amounts to the extent of the property pledged, liabilities for which the taxpayers are personally liable, and retained profits of the activity. For contributions of unencumbered property, the amount considered at risk is the adjusted basis of the property contributed to the activity. For encumbered property, the amount at risk is also the adjusted basis of the property to the taxpayer if he or she is personally liable for repayment of the debt. If there is no personal liability for the debt, the amount at risk is the difference between the adjusted basis of the property and the amount of the nonrecourse debt on the property.

EXAMPLE   A taxpayer contributes property with an adjusted basis of $100,000, subject to a recourse liability of $25,000 and a nonrecourse liability of $40,000. The taxpayer's AAR is the basis of the property less the amount of the nonrecourse liability, or $60,000 ($100,000 − $40,000). ♦

Under the at-risk rule, taxpayers are allowed a deduction for losses allocable to a business activity to the extent of (1) income received or accrued from the activity without regard to the amount at risk, or (2) the taxpayer's amount at risk at the end of the tax year. Any losses not allowed in the current year may be treated as deductions in succeeding years, with no limit on the number of years the losses may be carried forward. Remember that passive loss rules (discussed in Chapter 4) may also limit the taxpayer's ability to deduct certain losses.

EXAMPLE   A taxpayer contributes $100,000 to an activity. Her amount at risk is $100,000. In the current year, the activity incurs losses of $250,000. For the current year, the taxpayer is allowed a loss of $100,000, the amount at risk. ♦

While real estate acquired before 1987 is not subject to the at-risk rules, the at-risk rules do apply to real estate acquired after 1986. For real estate acquired after 1986, "qualified nonrecourse financing" on real estate is still considered to be an amount at risk. Qualified nonrecourse financing is debt that is secured by the real estate and loaned or guaranteed by a governmental agency or borrowed from any person who actively and regularly engages in the lending of money, such as a bank, savings and loan, or insurance company. A taxpayer is not considered at risk for financing obtained from sellers or promoters, including loans from parties related to the sellers or promoters.

EXAMPLE   In the current tax year, Donna buys a real estate investment for a $20,000 cash down payment and she borrows $80,000 from a savings and loan company secured by a mortgage on the property. Donna has $100,000 at risk in this investment. If the mortgage were obtained from the seller, her amount at risk would be limited to her down payment of $20,000. ♦

Self-Study Problem 10.8   *See Appendix E for Solutions to Self-Study Problems*

During the current tax year, Joe is a partner in a plumbing business. His amount at risk at the beginning of the year is $45,000. During the year, Joe's share of loss is $60,000.

1. What is the amount of the loss that Joe may deduct for the current tax year? $_____

2. If Joe has a profit of $31,000 in the following tax year, how much is taxable? $_____

Learning Objective 10.9

Describe the tax treatment of limited liability companies (LLCs).

10-9 LIMITED LIABILITY COMPANIES

A limited liability company (LLC) is a hybrid form of business organization having some attributes of a partnership and other attributes of a corporation. Each owner, referred to as a member, of an LLC has limited liability, which may be similar to a stockholder in a corporation. However, an LLC is generally treated as a partnership for tax purposes. Because of this tax treatment, members of LLCs can have the tax advantages of a partnership and still have limited liability similar to a corporation. The benefits of LLCs have made them very popular as an entity choice for small business and LLCs are recognized legal entities in all 50 states and the District of Columbia. Many states prohibit certain licensed professionals such as attorneys, architects, and accountants from forming LLCs but allow the formation of limited liability partnerships (LLPs) if they wish to operate in a partnership form with legal liability protection similar to LLCs.

For the most part, LLCs follow partnership taxation rules. For example, taxable income and losses pass through to members, thereby either avoiding the corporate tax or allowing the member to use the losses. An LLC may elect to be taxed like a corporation rather than a partnership, but very few do. Like partnerships, LLCs' items of income and expense retain their tax attributes (e.g., capital gains and charitable contributions). However, LLCs are not required to have a general partner, unlike a limited partnership in which there has to be at least one general partner who does not have limited liability. Also, LLC members can participate in the management of the business. Because of the limited liability associated with LLCs, the debt of the LLC is generally treated as non-recourse. Lastly, LLCs may have a single member, whereas a partnership must have at least two partners. A single-member LLC is treated as a disregarded entity for tax purposes (i.e., the taxable income of the single-member LLC is reported directly on the tax return of its member, not on a separate Form 1065).

Self-Study Problem 10.9   *See Appendix E for Solutions to Self-Study Problems*

Indicate whether the following statements are true or false by circling the appropriate letter.

T F 1. A limited liability company is generally treated like a corporation for federal income tax purposes.

T F 2. A general partner is required for a limited liability company.

T F 3. Tax attributes of an LLC transaction pass through to the owners of an LLC.

T F 4. Owners of an LLC can participate in the management of the LLC business.

T F 5. Limited liability debt is generally treated as recourse debt and thus included in a member's basis computations.

KEY TERMS

partnership, 10-2
general (ordinary) partnerships,
    10-2
general partners, 10-2
limited partnerships, 10-2
limited partners, 10-2
initial basis, 10-4
basis, 10-4

Form 1065, 10-5
Schedule K-1, 10-5
current distribution, 10-15
guaranteed payments, 10-15
qualified business income deduction,
    10-17
at-risk rule, 10-19
nonrecourse liabilities, 10-19

encumbered property ("collateral"),
    10-19
qualified nonrecourse financing,
    10-19
limited liability companies ("LLCs"),
    10-20
limited liability partnerships
    ("LLPs"), 10-20

KEY POINTS

Learning Objectives	Key Points
LO 10.1: Define a partnership for tax purposes.	• A partnership is a syndicate, group, pool, joint venture, or other unincorporated organization through or by means of which any business, financial operation, or venture is carried on, and which is not classified as a corporation, trust, or estate. • Partnership tax returns are information returns only, which show the amount of income by type and the allocation of the income to the partners. • Partnership income is taxable to the partner even if that individual does not actually receive it in cash. • Co-ownership of property does not constitute a partnership (e.g., owning investment property); the partners must engage in some type of business or financial activity. • Limited partnerships, limited liability partnerships (LLPs), and limited liability companies (LLCs) are generally treated as partnerships for tax law purposes.
LO 10.2: Describe the basic tax rules for partnership formation and operation.	• Generally, there is no gain or loss recognized by a partnership or any of its partners when property is contributed to a partnership in exchange for an interest in the partnership. • When a partner receives a partnership interest in exchange for providing services to the partnership, income is recognized by the partner. • When a partner transfers property to a partnership in exchange for a partnership interest and that property is subject to a liability exceeding the partner's basis, income may be recognized by the partner. • A partner's basis is increased by the partner's contributions to the partnership, income and gains of the partnership, and increases in the partner's share of partnership liabilities. • A partner's basis is decreased by distributions by the partnership, losses of the partnership, and decreases in the partner's share of partnership liabilities.
LO 10.3: Summarize the rules for partnership income reporting.	• A partnership is required to report its income and other items on Form 1065, U.S. Return of Partnership Income, even though the partnership does not pay federal income tax. • When reporting partnership taxable income, certain transactions must be separated rather than being reported as part of ordinary income. Separately reported items include capital gains and losses, Section 1231 gains and losses, dividends, interest income, tax-exempt income, retirement contributions, charitable contributions, and most credits. • Schedule K-1 of Form 1065 presents the allocation of ordinary income or loss, special income and deductions, and gains and losses to each partner. The partners report the K-1 amounts on their own individual tax returns.

LO 10.4: Describe the tax treatment of partnership distributions.	• No gain is recognized by the partner receiving a current distribution unless the partner's basis in the partnership has reached zero, in which case, gain is recognized to the extent that a distribution of money exceeds the partner's basis in their partnership interest. • Payments made to a partner for services rendered or for use of the partner's capital that are made without regard to the income of the partnership are termed *guaranteed payments*. • Guaranteed payments are treated by the partnership in the same manner as payments made to a person who is not a partner. • Guaranteed payments are ordinary income to the partner and deductible by the partnership. • A partnership may show a loss after deducting guaranteed payments, in which case, the partner reports the guaranteed payments as income and reports their share of the partnership loss.
LO 10.5: Determine partnership tax years.	• Each partner includes in gross income for a particular tax year their individual distributive share of income, including guaranteed payments, from a partnership whose tax year ends with or within that tax year. • Unless a partnership can establish a business purpose for a fiscal year-end or meet certain tests, it must adopt the same taxable year as that of the majority partners. • If the majority partners do not have the same tax year, then the partnership is required to adopt the tax year of all its principal partners; otherwise, the partnership must adopt a tax year based on the least aggregate deferral method. • The tax year does not generally close upon the entry of a new partner, or upon the liquidation, sale, or exchange of an existing partnership interest. • A partnership will not close its tax year early unless the partnership is terminated, which occurs when business activity by the partnership ceases.
LO 10.6: Describe the tax treatment of transactions between partners and their partnerships.	• Generally, in a transaction with a partnership, a partner is regarded as an outside party, and the transaction is reported as it would be if the two parties were unrelated. • Losses, however, are disallowed for (1) transactions between a partnership and a partner who has a direct or indirect capital or profit interest in the partnership of more than 50 percent, and (2) transactions between two partnerships owned more than 50 percent by the same partners. • When a loss is disallowed, the purchaser may reduce a future gain on the disposition of the property by the amount of the disallowed loss. • A gain in a transaction between a partner and a partnership will be taxed as ordinary income if the partner has more than a 50 percent interest in the partnership and the property sold or transferred is not a capital asset to the transferee.
LO 10.7: Apply the qualified business income deduction to partners.	• Qualified business income does not include guaranteed payments or payments made to partners by the partnership in situations in which the partner is not acting in their capacity as a partner. • Partners are allocated only their share of wages paid and qualified property of the partnership when computing the QBI deduction.

LO 10.8: Apply the at-risk rule to partnerships.	• In general, the at-risk rule limits the losses from a taxpayer's business activities to "amounts at risk" in the activity. • Taxpayers are at risk in amounts equal to their cash and property contributions to the activities, borrowed amounts to the extent of the property pledged, liabilities for which the taxpayers are personally liable, and retained profits of the activity. • Under the at-risk rule, taxpayers are allowed a deduction for losses allocable to a business activity to the extent of (1) income received or accrued from the activity without regard to the amount at risk, or (2) the taxpayer's amount at risk at the end of the tax year. • Any losses not allowed in the current year may be treated as deductions in succeeding years, with no limit on the number of years the losses may be carried forward.
LO 10.9: Describe the tax treatment of limited liability companies (LLCs).	• A limited liability company (LLC) is a hybrid form of business organization having some attributes of a partnership and other attributes of a corporation. • Each member of an LLC has limited liability similar to that of a stockholder in a corporation and at the same time has the tax advantages of a partnership (e.g., no tax at the entity level, loss pass-through, etc.). • Licensed professionals, such as attorneys, architects, and accountants, must often use limited liability partnerships (LLPs), which are similar in many respects to LLCs.

QUESTIONS and PROBLEMS

GROUP 1:
MULTIPLE CHOICE QUESTIONS

LO 10.1

1. Which of the following may *not* be treated as a partnership for tax purposes?
   a. Arnold and Willis operate a restaurant.
   b. Thelma and Louise establish an LLP to operate an accounting practice.
   c. Lucy and Desi purchase real estate together as a business.
   d. Jennifer and Ben form a corporation to purchase and operate a hardware store.
   e. All of the above are partnerships.

LO 10.1

2. Which of the following is a partnership for tax purposes?
   a. Monica and Chandler form a corporation to acquire a trucking business.
   b. Jimmy and Stephen both purchase a small stock interest in a manufacturing corporation as an investment.
   c. Emeril and Rachel purchase a food truck and sell prepared food dishes at various spots around the city.
   d. Melissa purchases a shoe store and hires her sister, Whitney, to manage the store.
   e. None of the above.

LO 10.2

3. A partner's interest in a partnership is increased by:
   a. Capital losses of the partnership
   b. Tax-exempt interest earned by the partnership
   c. Losses of the partnership
   d. Distributions by the partnership
   e. None of the above

LO 10.2
4. Abigail contributes land with an adjusted basis of $56,000 and a fair market value of $58,000 to Blair and Partners, a partnership. Abigail receives a 50 percent interest in Blair. What is Blair's basis in the land?
   a. $0
   b. $28,000
   c. $29,000
   d. $56,000
   e. $58,000

LO 10.2
5. Abigail contributes land with an adjusted basis of $56,000 and a fair market value of $58,000 to Blair and Partners, a partnership. Abigail receives a 50 percent interest in Blair. What is Abigail's basis in her partnership interest?
   a. $0
   b. $28,000
   c. $29,000
   d. $56,000
   e. $58,000

LO 10.2
6. Abigail contributes land with an adjusted basis of $56,000 and a fair market value of $58,000 to Blair and Partners, a partnership. Abigail receives a 50 percent interest in Blair. What is Abigail's recognized gain or loss on the contribution?
   a. $0
   b. $2,000 gain
   c. $2,000 loss
   d. $1,000 gain
   e. $1,000 loss

LO 10.2
7. Abigail contributes land with an adjusted basis of $56,000 and a fair market value of $58,000 to Blair and Partners, a partnership. Abigail receives a 50 percent interest in Blair. What is Blair's recognized gain or loss on the contribution?
   a. $0
   b. $2,000 gain
   c. $2,000 loss
   d. $1,000 gain
   e. $1,000 loss

LO 10.2
8. Blake and Ryan form the Poole Partnership. Blake contributes cash of $15,000. Ryan contributes land with an adjusted basis of $10,000 and a fair market value of $21,000. The land is subject to a $6,000 mortgage that Poole assumes. Blake and Ryan both receive a 50 percent interest in Poole. What is Ryan's recognized gain or loss on the contribution?
   a. $4,000
   b. $5,000
   c. $11,000
   d. $16,000
   e. None of the above

LO 10.3
9. Which of the following items do *not* have to be reported separately on a partnership return?
   a. Tax-exempt income
   b. Dividend income
   c. Interest expense on business loans
   d. Capital gains and losses
   e. Charitable contributions

LO 10.3 10. Which of the following items is generally reported separately on a partnership return?
  a. Ordinary income from the operations of the partnership business
  b. Bonus depreciation
  c. Interest expense on business debts
  d. Net rental income
  e. Factory rent expense

LO 10.3 11. When calculating ordinary income, partnerships are *not* allowed which of the following deductions?
  a. Miscellaneous expenses
  b. Qualified business income deduction
  c. Depreciation
  d. Cost of goods sold
  e. Employee wages

LO 10.4 12. Feela is a one-third partner in Alchemy LLC, which is taxed as a partnership. Her basis prior to Alchemy paying Feela an $11,000 cash distribution is $27,000. How much income does Feela recognize from the distribution and what is her basis in her interest in Alchemy after the distribution?
  a. $11,000 income and $27,000 basis
  b. $0 income and $16,000 basis
  c. $11,000 income and $16,000 basis
  d. $0 income and $27,000 basis
  e. None of these choices

LO 10.4 13. Which of the following items is generally reported separately on a partnership return?
  a. Ordinary income from the operations of the partnership business
  b. Typical MACRS depreciation
  c. Employee salaries expense
  d. Insurance expense
  e. Guaranteed payments to a partner

LO 10.4 14. Khushboo's basis in her 30 percent interest in the Rishi Partnership is $46,000 at the start of the current year. During the current year, Rishi reports ordinary business income of $70,000. Rishi also makes a $16,000 guaranteed payment and $10,000 cash distribution, both to Khushboo. What will Khushboo's basis be at the end of the current year and how much income will Khushboo recognize from these transactions?
  a. Basis of $57,000 and income of $37,000
  b. Basis of $41,000 and income of $47,000
  c. Basis of $90,000 and income of $96,000
  d. Basis of $57,000 and income of $21,000
  e. Basis of $41,000 and income of $37,000

LO 10.5 15. Which of the following circumstances will *not* cause a partnership to close its tax year early?
  a. The partnership terminates by agreement of the partners.
  b. The business activity of the partnership permanently ceases.
  c. All the partners decide to retire, permanently close their stores and stop conducting business.
  d. A new partner enters the partnership.

LO 10.5 16. Joe, Ben, and Melissa are partners in Collins Partnership. All three use a calendar year-end for their individual taxes. Collins Partnership's year-end is likely to be:
  a. October 31 since that is only three months prior to calendar year-end
  b. The end of any month during the year
  c. January 31 but only if Collins Partnership's accounting year-end is January 31
  d. December 31
  e. None of the above

LO 10.6   17. Kendra is an attorney and owns 60 percent of a law partnership. Kendra sells land to the partnership for $50,000 in the current tax year. She bought the land for $100,000 eight years ago when real estate prices were at their peak. How much gain or loss must Kendra recognize on the land sale to the partnership?
   a. No gain or loss
   b. $30,000 loss
   c. $50,000 loss
   d. $50,000 short-term capital loss, limited to $3,000 allowed per year

LO 10.6   18. A loss from the sale or exchange of property will be disallowed in which of the following situations?
   a. A transaction between a partnership and a partner who owns 40 percent of the partnership capital
   b. A transaction between a partnership and a partner who has a 40 percent profit interest in the partnership
   c. A transaction between two partnerships owned 40 percent by the same partners
   d. A transaction between two partners with investments in the same partnership
   e. None of the above

LO 10.7   19. In 2019, Gloria, a single taxpayer, receives a Schedule K-1 from a partnership she is invested in. The K-1 reports ordinary business income of $40,000, dividend income of $500, tax-exempt interest of $300, and a guaranteed payment to Gloria of $10,000. Gloria's taxable income before the QBI deduction is $87,000. What is Gloria's QBI deduction?
   a. $17,400
   b. $10,160
   c. $10,000
   d. $8,160
   e. $8,000

LO 10.7   20. Jay is a 30 percent partner in the Closet Partnership. In 2019, Closet paid W-2 wages of $24,000 and held qualified property of $600,000. In 2019, Jay's QBI deduction is subject to the wage limitation due to his income. If Closet allocates wages and qualified property in the same manner as income (based on percentage ownership), what is Jay's wage and qualified property limit on the QBI deduction?
   a. $12,000
   b. $3,600
   c. $6,300
   d. $4,500

LO 10.8   21. Mike purchases a rental property for $200,000 and takes out a loan from a lending institution to finance half of the purchase, or $100,000. The loan is considered to be qualified nonrecourse financing. What is Mike's at-risk amount?
   a. $300,000
   b. $200,000
   c. $100,000
   d. $0

LO 10.8   22. Gloria is a 30 percent general partner in the VH Partnership. During the year, VH borrows $40,000 from a bank to fund operations and is able to pay back $10,000 before year-end. VH also borrows $100,000 from Gloria's wealthy retired uncle on a nonrecourse basis using land held by the partnership as the collateral. How much does Gloria's at-risk amount increase or decrease as a result of these transactions?
   a. $9,000 increase
   b. $30,000 decrease
   c. $12,000 increase
   d. $42,000 increase
   e. $42,000 decrease

LO 10.9

23. Which of the following properly describes a difference between a partnership and an LLC?
   a. Partnerships pass income and losses through to the partners while LLCs generally pay an entity level tax and owners pay tax on distributions.
   b. Partners are often personally responsible for the debts of the partnership while LLC members are not liable for LLC debt.
   c. Partnerships may have only one partner but LLCs must have more than one member.
   d. The tax attributes of income in a partnership are retained when included in the partner's income but LLC income is treated as capital income in all cases.

GROUP 2:
PROBLEMS

LO 10.1

1. Debbie and Alan open a web-based bookstore together. They have been friends for so long that they start their business on a handshake after discussing how they will share both work and profits or losses from the business. Explain whether Debbie and Alan formed a partnership given that they have signed no written partnership agreement?

_____

_____

LO 10.2

2. Martha, Steve, and Lew form a partnership to operate a grocery store. For each of the following contributions by the partners, indicate (1) the amount of income or gain recognized, if any, by the partner, and (2) the partner's basis in the partnership interest immediately after the contribution including the allocation of liabilities.
   a. Martha contributes property with a basis of $45,000 and subject to a $75,000 liability to the partnership for a one-third partnership interest worth $105,000. The partnership assumes the liability.

Income or gain recognized	$ _____
Her basis in the partnership interest	$ _____

   b. Steve contributes property with a basis of $25,000 and a fair market value of $105,000 to the partnership for a one-third partnership interest.

Income or gain recognized	$ _____
His basis in the partnership interest	$ _____

   c. Lew performs services valued at $105,000 for the partnership for his one-third interest in the partnership.

Income or gain recognized	$ _____
His basis in the partnership interest	$ _____

LO 10.2

3. Nan contributes property with an adjusted basis of $60,000 to a partnership. The property has a fair market value of $75,000 on the date of the contribution. What is the partnership's basis in the property contributed by Nan?

$ _____

LO 10.2

4. Elaine's original basis in the Hornbeam Partnership was $30,000. Her share of the taxable income from the partnership since she purchased the interest has been $90,000, and Elaine has received $80,000 in cash distributions from the partnership. Elaine did not recognize any gains as a result of the distributions. Calculate Elaine's current basis in her partnership interest.

$ _____

LO 10.2

5. Larry and Jessica form the L&J Partnership. Larry contributes property with an adjusted basis of $70,000, a fair market value of $200,000, and subject to a liability of $80,000 in exchange for a 40 percent interest in the partnership. Jessica receives a 60 percent interest in the partnership in exchange for services performed for the partnership, valued at $10,000, and cash of $170,000.

    a. What amount of gain or loss must Larry recognize as a result of his transfer of the property to the partnership?

        $ _____

    b. What is Larry's basis in his partnership interest immediately after the formation of the partnership including allocation of partnership liabilities?

        $ _____

    c. What is the partnership's basis in the property contributed by Larry?

        $ _____

    d. What is Jessica's basis in her partnership interest immediately after the formation of the partnership including allocation of partnership liabilities?

        $ _____

    e. How much income does Jessica recognize on the exchange?

        $ _____

LO 10.2

6. Jay contributes property with a fair market value of $16,000 and an adjusted basis of $5,000 to a partnership in exchange for an 8 percent partnership interest.

    a. Calculate the amount of gain recognized by Jay as a result of the transfer of the property to the partnership.

        $ _____

    b. Calculate Jay's basis in his partnership interest immediately following the contribution to the partnership.

        $ _____

LO 10.2
LO 10.4

7. Wilson has a 40 percent interest in the assets and income of the CC&W Partnership, and the basis in his partnership interest is $45,000 at the beginning of 2019. During 2019, the partnership's net loss is $60,000 and Wilson's share of the loss is $24,000. Also, Wilson receives a cash distribution from the partnership of $12,000 on June 30, 2019.

    a. Indicate the amount of income or loss from the partnership that should be reported by Wilson on his 2019 individual income tax return.

        $ _____

    b. Calculate Wilson's basis in his partnership interest at the end of 2019.

        $ _____

LO 10.3

8. Go to the IRS website (**www.irs.gov**) and print pages 1 and 2 of Schedule K-1 (Form 1065), Partner's Share of Income, Deductions, Credits, etc. Review the different elements of income which must be passed through to each partner and be reported as separately stated items. Review the numerous codes on page 2 of Schedule K-1 which identify additional items that are required to be separately stated.

LO 10.4

9. L&J Interests is a partnership with two equal partners, Linda and Joanne. The partnership has income of $75,000 for the year before guaranteed payments. Guaranteed payments of $45,000 are paid to Linda during the year. Calculate the amount of income that should be reported by Linda and Joanne from the partnership for the year.

    Linda should report income of $ _____

    Joanne should report income of $ _____

LO 10.4 10. Walter receives cash of $18,000 and land with a fair market value of $75,000 (adjusted basis of $50,000) in a current distribution. His basis in his partnership interest is $16,000 before the distribution.

a. What amount of gain must Walter recognize as a result of the current distribution?

$ _____

b. What amount of gain must the partnership recognize as a result of the distribution?

$ _____

c. What is Walter's basis in his partnership interest immediately after the distribution?

$ _____

LO 10.5 11. Quince Interests is a partnership with a tax year that ends on September 30, 2019. During that year, Potter, a partner, received $3,000 per month as a guaranteed payment, and his share of partnership income after guaranteed payments was $23,000. For October through December of 2019, Potter received guaranteed payments of $4,000 per month. Calculate the amount of income from the partnership that Potter should report for his tax year ending December 31, 2019.

$ _____

LO 10.6 12. Louise owns 45 percent of a partnership, and her brother owns the remaining 55 percent interest. During the current tax year, Louise sold a building to the partnership for $160,000 to be used for the partnership's office. She had held the building for 3 years, and it had an adjusted basis of $120,000 at the time of the sale. What is the amount and nature of Louise's gain on this transaction?

$ _____

LO 10.7 13. Janie owns a 40 percent interest in Chang Partnership. Chang has W-2 wages of $50,000 and qualified property of $450,000 in 2019.

a. When computing the W-2 wages limitation, what is the amount of wages that will be allocated to Janie?

$ _____

b. What is the amount of qualified property that will be allocated to Janie?

$ _____

LO 10.8 14. Van makes an investment in a partnership in 2019. Van's capital contributions to the partnership consist of $30,000 cash and a building with an adjusted basis of $70,000, subject to a nonrecourse liability (seller financing) of $20,000.

a. Calculate the amount that Van has at risk in the partnership immediately after making the capital contributions.

$ _____

b. If Van's share of the loss from the partnership is $100,000 in 2019, and assuming that Van has sufficient amounts of passive income, how much of the loss may he deduct in 2019?

$ _____

c. What may be done with the nondeductible part of the loss in Part b?

_____

_____

LO 10.9 15. Van makes an investment in an LLC in 2019. Van's capital contributions to the LLC consist of $30,000 cash and a building with an adjusted basis of $70,000, subject to a nonrecourse liability (seller financing) of $20,000. Calculate the amount that Van has at risk in the LLC immediately after making the capital contributions.

$ _____

LO 10.9 16. Describe ways in which LLCs might differ from partnerships.

GROUP 3:
COMPREHENSIVE PROBLEM

Emily Jackson (Social Security number 765-12-4326) and James Stewart (Social Security number 466-74-9932) are partners in a partnership that owns and operates a barber shop. The partnership's first year of operation is 2019. Emily and James divide income and expenses equally. The partnership name is J&S Barbers, it is located at 1023 Broadway, New York, NY 10004, and its Federal ID number is 95-6767676. The 2019 financial statements for the partnership are presented below.

J&S Barbers Income Statement
for the Year Ending December 31, 2019

Gross income from operations	$372,300
Deductions:	
Salaries to employees	94,600
Payroll taxes	14,500
Supplies	9,000
Rent	41,000
Depreciation	5,100
Short-term capital loss	2,000
Charitable contributions	500
Net income	$205,600
Partners' withdrawals (each partner)	$ 80,000

J&S Barbers Balance Sheet
as of December 31, 2019

Assets:		
Cash		$100,450
Accounts receivable		10,000
Equipment	$32,000	
Accum. depreciation	(5,100)	26,900
		$137,350
Liabilities and Capital:		
Accounts payable		$ 29,750
Notes payable		22,000
Partners' capital ($20,000		
contributed by each partner)		85,600
		$137,350

Emily lives at 456 E. 70th Street, New York, NY 10006, and James lives at 436 E. 63rd Street, New York, NY 10012.

Required: Complete J&S Barbers' Form 1065 and Emily and James' Schedule K-1s. Do not fill in Schedule D for the capital loss, Form 4562 for depreciation, or Schedule B-1 related to ownership of the partnership. Make realistic assumptions about any missing data.

Form **1065**		**U.S. Return of Partnership Income**		OMB No. 1545-0123

Form **1065**

Department of the Treasury
Internal Revenue Service

U.S. Return of Partnership Income

For calendar year 2019, or tax year beginning _____, 2019, ending _____, 20_____.

▶ Go to *www.irs.gov/Form1065* for instructions and the latest information.

OMB No. 1545-0123

2019

			D Employer identification number
A Principal business activity	**Type or Print**	Name of partnership	
B Principal product or service		Number, street, and room or suite no. If a P.O. box, see instructions.	**E** Date business started
C Business code number		City or town, state or province, country, and ZIP or foreign postal code	**F** Total assets (see instructions) $

G Check applicable boxes: **(1)** ☐ Initial return **(2)** ☐ Final return **(3)** ☐ Name change **(4)** ☐ Address change **(5)** ☐ Amended return

H Check accounting method: **(1)** ☐ Cash **(2)** ☐ Accrual **(3)** ☐ Other (specify) ▶ _____

I Number of Schedules K-1. Attach one for each person who was a partner at any time during the tax year ▶ _____

J Check if Schedules C and M-3 are attached . . . . ▶ ☐

K Check if partnership: **(1)** ☐ Aggregated activities for section 465 at-risk purposes **(2)** ☐ Grouped activities for section 469 passive activity purposes

Caution: Include **only** trade or business income and expenses on lines 1a through 22 below. See instructions for more information.

Income (see instructions for limitations)

1a	Gross receipts or sales	1a	
b	Returns and allowances	1b	
c	Balance. Subtract line 1b from line 1a	1c	
2	Cost of goods sold (attach Form 1125-A)	2	
3	Gross profit. Subtract line 2 from line 1c	3	
4	Ordinary income (loss) from other partnerships, estates, and trusts (attach statement) . .	4	
5	Net farm profit (loss) (attach Schedule F (Form 1040 or 1040-SR))	5	
6	Net gain (loss) from Form 4797, Part II, line 17 (attach Form 4797)	6	
7	Other income (loss) (attach statement)	7	
8	**Total income (loss).** Combine lines 3 through 7	8	

Deductions (see instructions for limitations)

9	Salaries and wages (other than to partners) (less employment credits)	9	
10	Guaranteed payments to partners	10	
11	Repairs and maintenance	11	
12	Bad debts	12	
13	Rent	13	
14	Taxes and licenses	14	
15	Interest (see instructions)	15	
16a	Depreciation (if required, attach Form 4562)	16a	
b	Less depreciation reported on Form 1125-A and elsewhere on return .	16b	16c
17	Depletion **(Do not deduct oil and gas depletion.)**	17	
18	Retirement plans, etc.	18	
19	Employee benefit programs	19	
20	Other deductions (attach statement)	20	
21	**Total deductions.** Add the amounts shown in the far right column for lines 9 through 20 . . .	21	
22	**Ordinary business income (loss).** Subtract line 21 from line 8	22	

Tax and Payment

23	Interest due under the look-back method—completed long-term contracts (attach Form 8697) . .	23	
24	Interest due under the look-back method—income forecast method (attach Form 8866) . .	24	
25	BBA AAR imputed underpayment (see instructions)	25	
26	Other taxes (see instructions)	26	
27	**Total balance due.** Add lines 23 through 26	27	
28	Payment (see instructions)	28	
29	**Amount owed.** If line 28 is smaller than line 27, enter amount owed	29	
30	**Overpayment.** If line 28 is larger than line 27, enter overpayment	30	

Sign Here

Under penalties of perjury, I declare that I have examined this return, including accompanying schedules and statements, and to the best of my knowledge and belief, it is true, correct, and complete. Declaration of preparer (other than partner or limited liability company member) is based on all information of which preparer has any knowledge.

▶ _____
Signature of partner or limited liability company member

▶ _____
Date

May the IRS discuss this return with the preparer shown below? See instructions. ☐ Yes ☐ No

Paid Preparer Use Only

Print/Type preparer's name	Preparer's signature	Date	Check ☐ if self-employed	PTIN
Firm's name ▶			Firm's EIN ▶	
Firm's address ▶			Phone no.	

For Paperwork Reduction Act Notice, see separate instructions.   Cat. No. 11390Z   Form **1065** (2019)

Form 1065 (2019)   Page **2**

Schedule B   Other Information

		Yes	No
1	What type of entity is filing this return? Check the applicable box:		

a ☐ Domestic general partnership   **b** ☐ Domestic limited partnership
c ☐ Domestic limited liability company   **d** ☐ Domestic limited liability partnership
e ☐ Foreign partnership   **f** ☐ Other ▶

2   At the end of the tax year:

a   Did any foreign or domestic corporation, partnership (including any entity treated as a partnership), trust, or tax-exempt organization, or any foreign government own, directly or indirectly, an interest of 50% or more in the profit, loss, or capital of the partnership? For rules of constructive ownership, see instructions. If "Yes," attach Schedule B-1, Information on Partners Owning 50% or More of the Partnership . . . .

b   Did any individual or estate own, directly or indirectly, an interest of 50% or more in the profit, loss, or capital of the partnership? For rules of constructive ownership, see instructions. If "Yes," attach Schedule B-1, Information on Partners Owning 50% or More of the Partnership . . . .

3   At the end of the tax year, did the partnership:

a   Own directly 20% or more, or own, directly or indirectly, 50% or more of the total voting power of all classes of stock entitled to vote of any foreign or domestic corporation? For rules of constructive ownership, see instructions. If "Yes," complete (i) through (iv) below . . . .

(i) Name of Corporation	**(ii)** Employer Identification Number (if any)	**(iii)** Country of Incorporation	**(iv)** Percentage Owned in Voting Stock

b   Own directly an interest of 20% or more, or own, directly or indirectly, an interest of 50% or more in the profit, loss, or capital in any foreign or domestic partnership (including an entity treated as a partnership) or in the beneficial interest of a trust? For rules of constructive ownership, see instructions. If "Yes," complete (i) through (v) below . .

(i) Name of Entity	**(ii)** Employer Identification Number (if any)	**(iii)** Type of Entity	**(iv)** Country of Organization	**(v)** Maximum Percentage Owned in Profit, Loss, or Capital

		Yes	No
4	Does the partnership satisfy **all four** of the following conditions?		
a	The partnership's total receipts for the tax year were less than $250,000.		
b	The partnership's total assets at the end of the tax year were less than $1 million.		
c	Schedules K-1 are filed with the return and furnished to the partners on or before the due date (including extensions) for the partnership return.		
d	The partnership is not filing and is not required to file Schedule M-3		

If "Yes," the partnership is not required to complete Schedules L, M-1, and M-2; item F on page 1 of Form 1065; or item L on Schedule K-1.

		Yes	No
5	Is this partnership a publicly traded partnership, as defined in section 469(k)(2)?		
6	During the tax year, did the partnership have any debt that was canceled, was forgiven, or had the terms modified so as to reduce the principal amount of the debt?		
7	Has this partnership filed, or is it required to file, Form 8918, Material Advisor Disclosure Statement, to provide information on any reportable transaction?		
8	At any time during calendar year 2019, did the partnership have an interest in or a signature or other authority over a financial account in a foreign country (such as a bank account, securities account, or other financial account)? See instructions for exceptions and filing requirements for FinCEN Form 114, Report of Foreign Bank and Financial Accounts (FBAR). If "Yes," enter the name of the foreign country ▶		
9	At any time during the tax year, did the partnership receive a distribution from, or was it the grantor of, or transferor to, a foreign trust? If "Yes," the partnership may have to file Form 3520, Annual Return To Report Transactions With Foreign Trusts and Receipt of Certain Foreign Gifts. See instructions		
10a	Is the partnership making, or had it previously made (and not revoked), a section 754 election?		
	See instructions for details regarding a section 754 election.		
b	Did the partnership make for this tax year an optional basis adjustment under section 743(b) or 734(b)? If "Yes," attach a statement showing the computation and allocation of the basis adjustment. See instructions		

                                                          Form **1065** (2019)

Schedule B | **Other Information** *(continued)*

		Yes	No
c	Is the partnership required to adjust the basis of partnership assets under section 743(b) or 734(b) because of a substantial built-in loss (as defined under section 743(d)) or substantial basis reduction (as defined under section 734(d))? If "Yes," attach a statement showing the computation and allocation of the basis adjustment. See instructions		
11	Check this box if, during the current or prior tax year, the partnership distributed any property received in a like-kind exchange or contributed such property to another entity (other than disregarded entities wholly owned by the partnership throughout the tax year) . . . . ▶ ☐		
12	At any time during the tax year, did the partnership distribute to any partner a tenancy-in-common or other undivided interest in partnership property?		
13	If the partnership is required to file Form 8858, Information Return of U.S. Persons With Respect To Foreign Disregarded Entities (FDEs) and Foreign Branches (FBs), enter the number of Forms 8858 attached. See instructions . . . . ▶		
14	Does the partnership have any foreign partners? If "Yes," enter the number of Forms 8805, Foreign Partner's Information Statement of Section 1446 Withholding Tax, filed for this partnership . . . . ▶		
15	Enter the number of Forms 8865, Return of U.S. Persons With Respect to Certain Foreign Partnerships, attached to this return . . . . ▶		
16a	Did you make any payments in 2019 that would require you to file Form(s) 1099? See instructions		
b	If "Yes," did you or will you file required Form(s) 1099?		
17	Enter the number of Forms 5471, Information Return of U.S. Persons With Respect To Certain Foreign Corporations, attached to this return . . . . ▶		
18	Enter the number of partners that are foreign governments under section 892 . . . . ▶		
19	During the partnership's tax year, did the partnership make any payments that would require it to file Form 1042 and 1042-S under chapter 3 (sections 1441 through 1464) or chapter 4 (sections 1471 through 1474)?		
20	Was the partnership a specified domestic entity required to file Form 8938 for the tax year? See the Instructions for Form 8938		
21	Is the partnership a section 721(c) partnership, as defined in Regulations section 1.721(c)-1T(b)(14)?		
22	During the tax year, did the partnership pay or accrue any interest or royalty for which the deduction is not allowed under section 267A? See instructions . . . . If "Yes," enter the total amount of the disallowed deductions . . . . ▶ $		
23	Did the partnership have an election under section 163(j) for any real property trade or business or any farming business in effect during the tax year? See instructions		
24	Does the partnership satisfy one or more of the following? See instructions		
a	The partnership owns a pass-through entity with current, or prior year carryover, excess business interest expense.		
b	The partnership's aggregate average annual gross receipts (determined under section 448(c)) for the 3 tax years preceding the current tax year are more than $26 million and the partnership has business interest.		
c	The partnership is a tax shelter (see instructions) and the partnership has business interest expense. If "Yes" to any, complete and attach Form 8990.		
25	Is the partnership electing out of the centralized partnership audit regime under section 6221(b)? See instructions. If "Yes," the partnership must complete Schedule B-2 (Form 1065). Enter the total from Schedule B-2, Part III, line 3 . . . . ▶ _____ If "No," complete Designation of Partnership Representative below.		

Designation of Partnership Representative (see instructions)

Enter below the information for the partnership representative (PR) for the tax year covered by this return.

Name of PR ▶

U.S. address of PR ▶ _____	U.S. phone number of ▶ PR

If the PR is an entity, name of the designated individual for the PR ▶

U.S. address of ▶ _____ designated individual	U.S. phone number of ▶ designated individual

26	Is the partnership attaching Form 8996 to certify as a Qualified Opportunity Fund? . . . . If "Yes," enter the amount from Form 8996, line 14 . . . . ▶ $		
27	Enter the number of foreign partners subject to section 864(c)(8) as a result of transferring all or a portion of an interest in the partnership or of receiving a distribution from the partnership . . . . . ▶		
28	At any time during the tax year, were there any transfers between the partnership and its partners subject to the disclosure requirements of Regulations section 1.707-8?		

Form **1065** (2019)

Form 1065 (2019)   Page **4**

Schedule K	Partners' Distributive Share Items	Total amount

Income (Loss)

1	Ordinary business income (loss) (page 1, line 22)	**1**	
2	Net rental real estate income (loss) (attach Form 8825)	**2**	
3a	Other gross rental income (loss) **3a**		
b	Expenses from other rental activities (attach statement) **3b**		
c	Other net rental income (loss). Subtract line 3b from line 3a	**3c**	
4	Guaranteed payments: a Services **4a** b Capital **4b**		
c	Total. Add lines 4a and 4b	**4c**	
5	Interest income	**5**	
6	Dividends and dividend equivalents: a Ordinary dividends	**6a**	
b	Qualified dividends **6b** c Dividend equivalents **6c**		
7	Royalties	**7**	
8	Net short-term capital gain (loss) (attach Schedule D (Form 1065))	**8**	
9a	Net long-term capital gain (loss) (attach Schedule D (Form 1065))	**9a**	
b	Collectibles (28%) gain (loss) **9b**		
c	Unrecaptured section 1250 gain (attach statement) **9c**		
10	Net section 1231 gain (loss) (attach Form 4797)	**10**	
11	Other income (loss) (see instructions) Type ▶	**11**	

Deductions

12	Section 179 deduction (attach Form 4562)	**12**	
13a	Contributions	**13a**	
b	Investment interest expense	**13b**	
c	Section 59(e)(2) expenditures: (1) Type ▶ _____ (2) Amount ▶	**13c(2)**	
d	Other deductions (see instructions) Type ▶	**13d**	

Self-Employ-ment

14a	Net earnings (loss) from self-employment	**14a**	
b	Gross farming or fishing income	**14b**	
c	Gross nonfarm income	**14c**	

Credits

15a	Low-income housing credit (section 42(j)(5))	**15a**	
b	Low-income housing credit (other)	**15b**	
c	Qualified rehabilitation expenditures (rental real estate) (attach Form 3468, if applicable) . .	**15c**	
d	Other rental real estate credits (see instructions) Type ▶ _____	**15d**	
e	Other rental credits (see instructions) Type ▶ _____	**15e**	
f	Other credits (see instructions) Type ▶	**15f**	

Foreign Transactions

16a	Name of country or U.S. possession ▶ _____		
b	Gross income from all sources	**16b**	
c	Gross income sourced at partner level	**16c**	
	Foreign gross income sourced at partnership level		
d	Reserved for future use ▶ ▓▓▓▓ e Foreign branch category . . . . . ▶	**16e**	
f	Passive category ▶ _____ g General category ▶ _____ h Other (attach statement) ▶	**16h**	
	Deductions allocated and apportioned at partner level		
i	Interest expense ▶ _____ j Other . . . . ▶	**16j**	
	Deductions allocated and apportioned at partnership level to foreign source income		
k	Reserved for future use ▶ ▓▓▓▓ l Foreign branch category . . . . . ▶	**16l**	
m	Passive category ▶ _____ n General category ▶ _____ o Other (attach statement) ▶	**16o**	
p	Total foreign taxes (check one): ▶ Paid ☐ Accrued ☐	**16p**	
q	Reduction in taxes available for credit (attach statement)	**16q**	
r	Other foreign tax information (attach statement)		

Alternative Minimum Tax (AMT) Items

17a	Post-1986 depreciation adjustment	**17a**	
b	Adjusted gain or loss	**17b**	
c	Depletion (other than oil and gas)	**17c**	
d	Oil, gas, and geothermal properties—gross income	**17d**	
e	Oil, gas, and geothermal properties—deductions	**17e**	
f	Other AMT items (attach statement)	**17f**	

Other Information

18a	Tax-exempt interest income	**18a**	
b	Other tax-exempt income	**18b**	
c	Nondeductible expenses	**18c**	
19a	Distributions of cash and marketable securities	**19a**	
b	Distributions of other property	**19b**	
20a	Investment income	**20a**	
b	Investment expenses	**20b**	
c	Other items and amounts (attach statement)		

Form **1065** (2019)

Form 1065 (2019)   Page **5**

Analysis of Net Income (Loss)

1 Net income (loss). Combine Schedule K, lines 1 through 11. From the result, subtract the sum of Schedule K, lines 12 through 13d, and 16p **1**

2	Analysis by partner type:	(i) Corporate	(ii) Individual (active)	(iii) Individual (passive)	(iv) Partnership	(v) Exempt Organization	(vi) Nominee/Other
a	General partners						
b	Limited partners						

Schedule L   Balance Sheets per Books

	Assets	Beginning of tax year (a)	(b)	End of tax year (c)	(d)
1	Cash				
2a	Trade notes and accounts receivable				
b	Less allowance for bad debts				
3	Inventories				
4	U.S. government obligations				
5	Tax-exempt securities				
6	Other current assets (attach statement) . .				
7a	Loans to partners (or persons related to partners) .				
b	Mortgage and real estate loans				
8	Other investments (attach statement) . . .				
9a	Buildings and other depreciable assets . . .				
b	Less accumulated depreciation				
10a	Depletable assets				
b	Less accumulated depletion				
11	Land (net of any amortization)				
12a	Intangible assets (amortizable only)				
b	Less accumulated amortization				
13	Other assets (attach statement)				
14	Total assets				
	Liabilities and Capital				
15	Accounts payable				
16	Mortgages, notes, bonds payable in less than 1 year				
17	Other current liabilities (attach statement)				
18	All nonrecourse loans				
19a	Loans from partners (or persons related to partners) .				
b	Mortgages, notes, bonds payable in 1 year or more .				
20	Other liabilities (attach statement)				
21	Partners' capital accounts				
22	Total liabilities and capital				

Schedule M-1   Reconciliation of Income (Loss) per Books With Income (Loss) per Return

Note: The partnership may be required to file Schedule M-3. See instructions.

1	Net income (loss) per books . . .		6	Income recorded on books this year not included on Schedule K, lines 1 through 11 (itemize):	
2	Income included on Schedule K, lines 1, 2, 3c, 5, 6a, 7, 8, 9a, 10, and 11, not recorded on books this year (itemize): _____		a	Tax-exempt interest $_____	
3	Guaranteed payments (other than health insurance)		7	Deductions included on Schedule K, lines 1 through 13d, and 16p, not charged against book income this year (itemize):	
4	Expenses recorded on books this year not included on Schedule K, lines 1 through 13d, and 16p (itemize):		a	Depreciation $_____	
a	Depreciation $_____		8	Add lines 6 and 7	
b	Travel and entertainment $_____		9	Income (loss) (Analysis of Net Income (Loss), line 1). Subtract line 8 from line 5	
5	Add lines 1 through 4				

Schedule M-2   Analysis of Partners' Capital Accounts

1	Balance at beginning of year . . .		6	Distributions: **a** Cash	
2	Capital contributed: **a** Cash . . .			**b** Property	
	b Property . .		7	Other decreases (itemize): _____	
3	Net income (loss) per books				
4	Other increases (itemize): _____		8	Add lines 6 and 7	
5	Add lines 1 through 4		9	Balance at end of year. Subtract line 8 from line 5	

Form **1065** (2019)

651119

□ Final K-1   □ Amended K-1   OMB No. 1545-0123

Schedule K-1
(Form 1065)   20**19**
Department of the Treasury
Internal Revenue Service   For calendar year 2019, or tax year

beginning [/ / 2019] ending [/ /]

Partner's Share of Income, Deductions,
Credits, etc.   ► See back of form and separate instructions.

Part I	**Information About the Partnership**

A   Partnership's employer identification number

B   Partnership's name, address, city, state, and ZIP code

C   IRS Center where partnership filed return ►

D   □ Check if this is a publicly traded partnership (PTP)

Part II	**Information About the Partner**

E   Partner's identifying number (Do not use TIN of a disregarded entity. See instructions.)

F   Partner's name, address, city, state, and ZIP code

G   □ General partner or LLC member-manager   □ Limited partner or other LLC member

H   □ Domestic partner   □ Foreign partner
    □ Disregarded entity: Name of beneficial owner

I1 What type of entity is this partner? _____

I2 If this partner is a retirement plan (IRA/SEP/Keogh/etc.), check here □

J   Partner's share of profit, loss, and capital (see instructions):

	Beginning	**Ending**
Profit	%	%
Loss	%	%
Capital	%	%

Check if decrease is due to sale or exchange of partnership interest . . □

K   Partner's share of liabilities:

	Beginning	**Ending**
Nonrecourse . .	$	$
Qualified nonrecourse financing . .	$	$
Recourse . . .	$	$

□ Check this box if Item K includes liability amounts from lower tier partnerships.

L	**Partner's Capital Account Analysis**

Tax Basis Capital

Beginning capital account . . . $ _____
Capital contributed during the year . . $ _____
Current year net income (loss) . . . $ _____
Other increase (decrease) (attach explanation) $ _____
Withdrawals & distributions . . . $ (_____)
Ending capital account . . . . $ _____

M   Did the partner contribute property with a built-in gain or loss?
    □ Yes □ No   If "Yes," attach statement. See instructions.

N   **Partner's Share of Net Unrecognized Section 704(c) Gain or (Loss)**
    Beginning . . . . $ _____
    Ending . . . . $ _____

Part III	**Partner's Share of Current Year Income, Deductions, Credits, and Other Items**

1	Ordinary business income (loss)	15	Credits
2	Net rental real estate income (loss)		
3	Other net rental income (loss)	16	Foreign transactions
4a	Guaranteed payments for services		
4b	Guaranteed payments for capital		
4c	Total guaranteed payments		
5	Interest income		
6a	Ordinary dividends		
6b	Qualified dividends		
6c	Dividend equivalents	17	Alternative minimum tax (AMT) items
7	Royalties		
8	Net short-term capital gain (loss)		
9a	Net long-term capital gain (loss)	18	Tax-exempt income and nondeductible expenses
9b	Collectibles (28%) gain (loss)		
9c	Unrecaptured section 1250 gain		
10	Net section 1231 gain (loss)		
		19	Distributions
11	Other income (loss)		
		20	Other information
12	Section 179 deduction		
13	Other deductions		
14	Self-employment earnings (loss)		

21 □ More than one activity for at-risk purposes*
22 □ More than one activity for passive activity purposes*
*See attached statement for additional information.

For IRS Use Only

For Paperwork Reduction Act Notice, see Instructions for Form 1065.   www.irs.gov/Form1065   Cat. No. 11394R   **Schedule K-1 (Form 1065) 2019**

DRAFT AS OF September 26, 2019 DO NOT FILE

Schedule K-1 (Form 1065) 2019   Page **2**

This list identifies the codes used on Schedule K-1 for all partners and provides summarized reporting information for partners who file Form 1040 or 1040-SR. For detailed reporting and filing information, see the separate Partner's Instructions for Schedule K-1 and the instructions for your income tax return.

1. Ordinary business income (loss). Determine whether the income (loss) is passive or nonpassive and enter on your return as follows.

	Report on
Passive loss	See the Partner's Instructions
Passive income	Schedule E, line 28, column (h)
Nonpassive loss	See the Partner's Instructions
Nonpassive income	Schedule E, line 28, column (k)

2. Net rental real estate income (loss) — See the Partner's Instructions
3. Other net rental income (loss)
- Net income — Schedule E, line 28, column (h)
- Net loss — See the Partner's Instructions

4a. Guaranteed payment Services — See the Partner's Instructions
4b. Guaranteed payment Capital — See the Partner's Instructions
4c. Guaranteed payment Total — See the Partner's Instructions
5. Interest income — Form 1040 or 1040-SR, line 2b
6a. Ordinary dividends — Form 1040 or 1040-SR, line 3b
6b. Qualified dividends — Form 1040 or 1040-SR, line 3a
6c. Dividend equivalents — See the Partner's Instructions
7. Royalties — Schedule E, line 4
8. Net short-term capital gain (loss) — Schedule D, line 5
9a. Net long-term capital gain (loss) — Schedule D, line 12
9b. Collectibles (28%) gain (loss) — 28% Rate Gain Worksheet, line 4 (Schedule D instructions)
9c. Unrecaptured section 1250 gain — See the Partner's Instructions
10. Net section 1231 gain (loss) — See the Partner's Instructions
11. Other income (loss)

Code		Report on
A	Other portfolio income (loss)	See the Partner's Instructions
B	Involuntary conversions	See the Partner's Instructions
C	Sec. 1256 contracts & straddles	Form 6781, line 1
D	Mining exploration costs recapture	See Pub. 535
E	Cancellation of debt	
F	Section 743(b) positive adjustments	
G	Section 965(a) inclusion	
H	Income under subpart F (other than inclusions under sections 951A and 965)	See the Partner's Instructions
I	Other income (loss)	

12. Section 179 deduction — See the Partner's Instructions
13. Other deductions

A	Cash contributions (60%)	
B	Cash contributions (30%)	
C	Noncash contributions (50%)	
D	Noncash contributions (30%)	See the Partner's Instructions
E	Capital gain property to a 50% organization (30%)	
F	Capital gain property (20%)	
G	Contributions (100%)	
H	Investment interest expense	Form 4952, line 1
I	Deductions—royalty income	Schedule E, line 19
J	Section 59(e)(2) expenditures	See the Partner's Instructions
K	Excess business interest expense	See the Partner's Instructions
L	Deductions—portfolio (other)	Schedule A, line 16
M	Amounts paid for medical insurance	Schedule A, line 1, or Schedule 1 (Form 1040 or 1040-SR), line 16
N	Educational assistance benefits	See the Partner's Instructions
O	Dependent care benefits	Form 2441, line 12
P	Preproductive period expenses	See the Partner's Instructions
Q	Commercial revitalization deduction from rental real estate activities	See Form 8582 instructions
R	Pensions and IRAs	See the Partner's Instructions
S	Reforestation expense deduction	See the Partner's Instructions
T	through U	Reserved for future use
V	Section 743(b) negative adjustments	
W	Other deductions	See the Partner's Instructions
X	Section 965(c) deduction	

14. Self-employment earnings (loss)

Note: If you have a section 179 deduction or any partner-level deductions, see the Partner's Instructions before completing Schedule SE.

A	Net earnings (loss) from self-employment	Schedule SE, Section A or B
B	Gross farming or fishing income	See the Partner's Instructions
C	Gross non-farm income	See the Partner's Instructions

15. Credits

A	Low-income housing credit (section 42(j)(5)) from pre-2008 buildings	
B	Low-income housing credit (other) from pre-2008 buildings	
C	Low-income housing credit (section 42(j)(5)) from post-2007 buildings	See the Partner's Instructions
D	Low-income housing credit (other) from post-2007 buildings	
E	Qualified rehabilitation expenditures (rental real estate)	
F	Other rental real estate credits	
G	Other rental credits	

Code		Report on
H	Undistributed capital gains credit	Schedule 3 (Form 1040 or 1040-SR), line 13, box a
I	Biofuel producer credit	See the Partner's Instructions
J	Work opportunity credit	
K	Disabled access credit	
L	Empowerment zone employment credit	
M	Credit for increasing research activities	See the Partner's Instructions
N	Credit for employer social security and Medicare taxes	
O	Backup withholding	
P	Other credits	

16. Foreign transactions

A	Name of country or U.S. possession	
B	Gross income from all sources	Form 1116, Part I
C	Gross income sourced at partner level	

Foreign gross income sourced at partnership level

D	Reserved for future use	
E	Foreign branch category	
F	Passive category	Form 1116, Part I
G	General category	
H	Other	

Deductions allocated and apportioned at partner level

I	Interest expense	Form 1116, Part I
J	Other	Form 1116, Part I

Deductions allocated and apportioned at partnership level to foreign source income

K	Reserved for future use	
L	Foreign branch category	
M	Passive category	Form 1116, Part I
N	General category	
O	Other	

Other information

P	Total foreign taxes paid	Form 1116, Part II
Q	Total foreign taxes accrued	Form 1116, Part II
R	Reduction in taxes available for credit	Form 1116, line 12
S	Foreign trading gross receipts	Form 8873
T	Extraterritorial income exclusion	Form 8873
U	through V	Reserved for future use
W	Section 965 information	See the Partner's Instructions
X	Other foreign transactions	

17. Alternative minimum tax (AMT) items

A	Post-1986 depreciation adjustment	
B	Adjusted gain or loss	See the Partner's Instructions and the Instructions for Form 6251
C	Depletion (other than oil & gas)	
D	Oil, gas, & geothermal—gross income	
E	Oil, gas, & geothermal—deductions	
F	Other AMT items	

18. Tax-exempt income and nondeductible expenses

A	Tax-exempt interest income	Form 1040 or 1040-SR, line 2a
B	Other tax-exempt income	See the Partner's Instructions
C	Nondeductible expenses	See the Partner's Instructions

19. Distributions

A	Cash and marketable securities	
B	Distribution subject to section 737	See the Partner's Instructions
C	Other property	

20. Other information

A	Investment income	Form 4952, line 4a
B	Investment expenses	Form 4952, line 5
C	Fuel tax credit information	Form 4136
D	Qualified rehabilitation expenditures (other than rental real estate)	
E	Basis of energy property	See the Partner's Instructions
F	through G	
H	Recapture of investment credit	See Form 4255
I	Recapture of other credits	See the Partner's Instructions
J	Look-back interest—completed long-term contracts	See Form 8697
K	Look-back interest—income forecast method	See Form 8866
L	Dispositions of property with section 179 deductions	
M	Recapture of section 179 deduction	
N	Interest expense for corporate partners	
O	through Y	
Z	Section 199A information	
AA	Section 704(c) information	See the Partner's Instructions
AB	Section 751 gain (loss)	
AC	Section 1(h)(5) gain (loss)	
AD	Section 1250 unrecaptured gain	
AE	Excess taxable income	
AF	Excess business interest income	
AG	Gross receipts for section 59A(e)	
AH	Other information	

651119

☐ Final K-1   ☐ Amended K-1   OMB No. 1545-0123

Schedule K-1
(Form 1065)

20**19**

Department of the Treasury
Internal Revenue Service

For calendar year 2019, or tax year

beginning [/ / 2019] ending [/ /]

Partner's Share of Income, Deductions, Credits, etc.   ▶ See back of form and separate instructions.

Part I	Information About the Partnership

A Partnership's employer identification number

B Partnership's name, address, city, state, and ZIP code

C IRS Center where partnership filed return ▶

D ☐ Check if this is a publicly traded partnership (PTP)

Part II	Information About the Partner

E Partner's identifying number (Do not use TIN of a disregarded entity. See instructions.)

F Partner's name, address, city, state, and ZIP code

G ☐ General partner or LLC member-manager   ☐ Limited partner or other LLC member

H ☐ Domestic partner   ☐ Foreign partner
☐ Disregarded entity: Name of beneficial owner _____

I1 What type of entity is this partner? _____

I2 If this partner is a retirement plan (IRA/SEP/Keogh/etc.), check here ☐

J Partner's share of profit, loss, and capital (see instructions):

	Beginning	Ending
Profit	%	%
Loss	%	%
Capital	%	%

Check if decrease is due to sale or exchange of partnership interest . . ☐

K Partner's share of liabilities:

	Beginning	Ending
Nonrecourse . . $		$
Qualified nonrecourse financing . . . $		$
Recourse . . . $		$

☐ Check this box if Item K includes liability amounts from lower tier partnerships.

L   **Partner's Capital Account Analysis**

Tax Basis Capital

Beginning capital account . . . $ _____
Capital contributed during the year . . $ _____
Current year net income (loss) . . $ _____
Other increase (decrease) (attach explanation) $ _____
Withdrawals & distributions . . . $ (_____)
Ending capital account . . . $ _____

M Did the partner contribute property with a built-in gain or loss?
☐ Yes   ☐ No   If "Yes," attach statement. See instructions.

N   **Partner's Share of Net Unrecognized Section 704(c) Gain or (Loss)**
Beginning . . . . $ _____
Ending . . . . $ _____

Part III	Partner's Share of Current Year Income, Deductions, Credits, and Other Items

1 Ordinary business income (loss)		**15** Credits	
2 Net rental real estate income (loss)			
3 Other net rental income (loss)		**16** Foreign transactions	
4a Guaranteed payments for services			
4b Guaranteed payments for capital			
4c Total guaranteed payments			
5 Interest income			
6a Ordinary dividends			
6b Qualified dividends			
6c Dividend equivalents		**17** Alternative minimum tax (AMT) items	
7 Royalties			
8 Net short-term capital gain (loss)			
9a Net long-term capital gain (loss)		**18** Tax-exempt income and nondeductible expenses	
9b Collectibles (28%) gain (loss)			
9c Unrecaptured section 1250 gain			
10 Net section 1231 gain (loss)			
		19 Distributions	
11 Other income (loss)			
12 Section 179 deduction		**20** Other information	
13 Other deductions			
14 Self-employment earnings (loss)			
		21 ☐ More than one activity for at-risk purposes*	
		22 ☐ More than one activity for passive activity purposes*	

*See attached statement for additional information.

For IRS Use Only

For Paperwork Reduction Act Notice, see Instructions for Form 1065.   www.irs.gov/Form1065   Cat. No. 11394R   **Schedule K-1 (Form 1065) 2019**

Schedule K-1 (Form 1065) 2019   Page **2**

This list identifies the codes used on Schedule K-1 for all partners and provides summarized reporting information for partners who file Form 1040 or 1040-SR. For detailed reporting and filing information, see the separate Partner's Instructions for Schedule K-1 and the instructions for your income tax return.

1. Ordinary business income (loss). Determine whether the income (loss) is passive or nonpassive and enter on your return as follows.

	Report on
Passive loss	See the Partner's Instructions
Passive income	Schedule E, line 28, column (h)
Nonpassive loss	See the Partner's Instructions
Nonpassive income	Schedule E, line 28, column (k)

2. Net rental real estate income (loss) — See the Partner's Instructions

3. Other net rental income (loss)
Net income	Schedule E, line 28, column (h)
Net loss	See the Partner's Instructions

4a. Guaranteed payment Services — See the Partner's Instructions
4b. Guaranteed payment Capital — See the Partner's Instructions
4c. Guaranteed payment Total — See the Partner's Instructions
5. Interest income — Form 1040 or 1040-SR, line 2b
6a. Ordinary dividends — Form 1040 or 1040-SR, line 3b
6b. Qualified dividends — Form 1040 or 1040-SR, line 3a
6c. Dividend equivalents — See the Partner's Instructions
7. Royalties — Schedule E, line 4
8. Net short-term capital gain (loss) — Schedule D, line 5
9a. Net long-term capital gain (loss) — Schedule D, line 12
9b. Collectibles (28%) gain (loss) — 28% Rate Gain Worksheet, line 4 (Schedule D instructions)
9c. Unrecaptured section 1250 gain — See the Partner's Instructions
10. Net section 1231 gain (loss) — See the Partner's Instructions

11. Other income (loss)
Code
A	Other portfolio income (loss)	See the Partner's Instructions
B	Involuntary conversions	See the Partner's Instructions
C	Sec. 1256 contracts & straddles	Form 6781, line 1
D	Mining exploration costs recapture	See Pub. 535
E	Cancellation of debt	
F	Section 743(b) positive adjustments	
G	Section 965(a) inclusion	
H	Income under subpart F (other than inclusions under sections 951A and 965)	See the Partner's Instructions
I	Other income (loss)	

12. Section 179 deduction — See the Partner's Instructions

13. Other deductions
A	Cash contributions (60%)	
B	Cash contributions (30%)	
C	Noncash contributions (50%)	
D	Noncash contributions (30%)	See the Partner's Instructions
E	Capital gain property to a 50% organization (30%)	
F	Capital gain property (20%)	
G	Contributions (100%)	
H	Investment interest expense	Form 4952, line 1
I	Deductions—royalty income	Schedule E, line 19
J	Section 59(e)(2) expenditures	See the Partner's Instructions
K	Excess business interest expense	See the Partner's Instructions
L	Deductions—portfolio (other)	Schedule A, line 16
M	Amounts paid for medical insurance	Schedule A, line 1, or Schedule 1 (Form 1040 or 1040-SR), line 16
N	Educational assistance benefits	See the Partner's Instructions
O	Dependent care benefits	Form 2441, line 12
P	Preproductive period expenses	See the Partner's Instructions
Q	Commercial revitalization deduction from rental real estate activities	See Form 8582 instructions
R	Pensions and IRAs	See the Partner's Instructions
S	Reforestation expense deduction	See the Partner's Instructions
T	through **U**	Reserved for future use
V	Section 743(b) negative adjustments	
W	Other deductions	See the Partner's Instructions
X	Section 965(c) deduction	

14. Self-employment earnings (loss)
Note: If you have a section 179 deduction or any partner-level deductions, see the Partner's Instructions before completing Schedule SE.
A	Net earnings (loss) from self-employment	Schedule SE, Section A or B
B	Gross farming or fishing income	See the Partner's Instructions
C	Gross non-farm income	See the Partner's Instructions

15. Credits
A	Low-income housing credit (section 42(j)(5)) from pre-2008 buildings	
B	Low-income housing credit (other) from pre-2008 buildings	
C	Low-income housing credit (section 42(j)(5)) from post-2007 buildings	See the Partner's Instructions
D	Low-income housing credit (other) from post-2007 buildings	
E	Qualified rehabilitation expenditures (rental real estate)	
F	Other rental real estate credits	
G	Other rental credits	

		Report on
H	Undistributed capital gains credit	Schedule 3 (Form 1040 or 1040-SR), line 13, box a
I	Biofuel producer credit	See the Partner's Instructions
J	Work opportunity credit	
K	Disabled access credit	
L	Empowerment zone employment credit	
M	Credit for increasing research activities	See the Partner's Instructions
N	Credit for employer social security and Medicare taxes	
O	Backup withholding	
P	Other credits	

16. Foreign transactions
A	Name of country or U.S. possession	
B	Gross income from all sources	Form 1116, Part I
C	Gross income sourced at partner level	

Foreign gross income sourced at partnership level
D	Reserved for future use	
E	Foreign branch category	
F	Passive category	Form 1116, Part I
G	General category	
H	Other	

Deductions allocated and apportioned at partner level
I	Interest expense	Form 1116, Part I
J	Other	Form 1116, Part I

Deductions allocated and apportioned at partnership level to foreign source income
K	Reserved for future use	
L	Foreign branch category	
M	Passive category	Form 1116, Part I
N	General category	
O	Other	

Other information
P	Total foreign taxes paid	Form 1116, Part II
Q	Total foreign taxes accrued	Form 1116, Part II
R	Reduction in taxes available for credit	Form 1116, line 12
S	Foreign trading gross receipts	Form 8873
T	Extraterritorial income exclusion	Form 8873
U	through **V**	Reserved for future use
W	Section 965 information	
X	Other foreign transactions	See the Partner's Instructions

17. Alternative minimum tax (AMT) items
A	Post-1986 depreciation adjustment	
B	Adjusted gain or loss	See the Partner's Instructions and the Instructions for Form 6251
C	Depletion (other than oil & gas)	
D	Oil, gas, & geothermal—gross income	
E	Oil, gas, & geothermal—deductions	
F	Other AMT items	

18. Tax-exempt income and nondeductible expenses
A	Tax-exempt interest income	Form 1040 or 1040-SR, line 2a
B	Other tax-exempt income	See the Partner's Instructions
C	Nondeductible expenses	See the Partner's Instructions

19. Distributions
A	Cash and marketable securities	
B	Distribution subject to section 737	See the Partner's Instructions
C	Other property	

20. Other information
A	Investment income	Form 4952, line 4a
B	Investment expenses	Form 4952, line 5
C	Fuel tax credit information	Form 4136
D	Qualified rehabilitation expenditures (other than rental real estate)	
E	Basis of energy property	See the Partner's Instructions
F	through **G**	
H	Recapture of investment credit	See Form 4255
I	Recapture of other credits	See the Partner's Instructions
J	Look-back interest—completed long-term contracts	See Form 8697
K	Look-back interest—income forecast method	See Form 8866
L	Dispositions of property with section 179 deductions	
M	Recapture of section 179 deduction	
N	Interest expense for corporate partners	
O	through **Y**	
Z	Section 199A information	
AA	Section 704(c) information	
AB	Section 751 gain (loss)	See the Partner's Instructions
AC	Section 1(h)(5) gain (loss)	
AD	Section 1250 unrecaptured gain	
AE	Excess taxable income	
AF	Excess business interest income	
AG	Gross receipts for section 59A(e)	
AH	Other information	

Student Name _____

Class/Section _____

Date   _____

KEY NUMBER TAX RETURN SUMMARY

CHAPTER 10

Comprehensive Problem

Ordinary Business Income (Loss) (Page 1, Line 22)   _____

Net Income (Loss) (Page 5, Line 1)   _____

Net Short-Term Capital Gain (Loss) (Page 4, Line 8)   _____

Contributions (Page 4, Line 13a)   _____

Net Income (Loss) per Books (Schedule M-2, Line 3)   _____

The Corporate Income Tax

Cash Flow

Profit & Loss

LEARNING OBJECTIVES

After completing this chapter, you should be able to:

LO 11.1   Employ the corporate tax rates to calculate corporate tax liability.

LO 11.2   Compute basic gains and losses for corporations.

LO 11.3   Apply special corporate deductions to corporate taxable income.

LO 11.4   Identify the components of Schedule M-1 and how they are reported to the IRS.

LO 11.5   Describe the corporate tax return filing and estimated tax payment requirements.

LO 11.6   Explain how an S corporation operates and is taxed.

LO 11.7   Describe the basic tax rules for the formation of a corporation.

LO 11.8   Describe the rules for the accumulated earnings tax and the personal holding company tax.

LO 11.9   Describe tax issues associated with the repeal of the alternative minimum tax.

OVERVIEW

There are many forms of organization which may be used by taxpayers to operate a business. These include the sole proprietorship (Form 1040, Schedule C, covered in Chapter 3); the partnership, LLC, and LLP (Form 1065 covered in Chapter 10); and the regular C corporation and S corporation (covered in this chapter). Regular C corporations are taxed as separate legal taxpaying entities, and S corporations are taxed as flow-through entities similar to partnerships.

This chapter covers corporate tax rates, capital gains and losses, special deductions, the Schedule M-1, filing requirements, corporate formations, and corporate earnings accumulations. Additionally, basic coverage of the S corporation election and operating requirements are presented in this chapter.

This chapter provides a summary of corporate taxation and the tax forms (Form 1120, Form 1120S, and related schedules) associated with reporting C or S corporation income or loss.

11-1 CORPORATE TAX RATES

Prior to 2018, the U.S. corporate tax rate structure had eight tax brackets with progressive marginal tax rates ranging from 15 percent to 39 percent. Starting in 2018, corporations are subject to a flat income tax rate of 21 percent.

EXAMPLE   Jasmine Corporation has taxable income of $175,000 for 2019. The corporation's tax liability for the year is calculated as follows:

Taxable income	$ 175,000
Corporate tax rate	21%
Tax liability	$ 36,750

◆

Personal service corporations are taxed at the same 21 percent tax rate on all taxable income. A personal service corporation is substantially employee-owned and engages in one of the following activities:

- Health
- Law
- Engineering
- Architecture
- Accounting
- Actuarial science
- Performing arts
- Consulting

EXAMPLE   Elm & Ash, Inc., is a professional service corporation of CPAs. For the current tax year, the corporation has taxable income of $175,000. Elm & Ash will have a 21 percent tax rate like any other corporation and thus a tax liability of $36,750 (21% × $175,000). ◆

Self-Study Problem 11.1 **See Appendix E for Solutions to Self-Study Problems**

Maple Corporation has taxable income of $275,000 for the current tax year. Calculate the corporation's tax liability, before tax credits.

Tax liability $_____

11-2 CORPORATE GAINS AND LOSSES

If a corporation generates a net capital gain, the net gain is included in ordinary income and the tax is computed at the regular rate except under very rare circumstances. The tax law provides for a maximum rate of 21 percent on corporate capital gains. Thus, Congress intends the ordinary income and capital gains rates to be the same for corporations, so there is no tax rate benefit to having long-term capital gains in a corporation. Net short-term capital gains of a corporation are taxed as ordinary income.

11-2a Capital Losses

Corporations are not allowed to deduct capital losses against ordinary income. Capital losses may be used only to offset capital gains. If capital losses cannot be used in the year they occur, they may be carried back 3 years and forward 5 years to offset capital gains in those years. When a long-term capital loss is carried to another year, it is treated as a short-term capital loss, and may be offset against either long-term or short-term capital gains.

EXAMPLE In 2019, Eucalyptus Corporation incurs a long-term capital loss of $8,000, none of which may be deducted in that year. The loss is carried back to tax years 2016, 2017, and 2018, in that order. If the loss is not entirely used to offset capital gains in those years, it may be carried forward to 2020, 2021, 2022, 2023, and 2024, in that order. When the long-term loss is carried to another year, it is considered to be short-term, and may offset against either long-term or short-term capital gains. ♦

11-2b Net Operating Losses

As discussed in Chapter 3, similar to individuals, corporations may also carryforward net operating losses (NOLs) to offset future taxable income. The TCJA made significant changes to carryback and carryforward of NOLs after 2017. The use of an NOL generated after December 31, 2017 is limited to 80 percent of the current year's taxable income (without regard to the NOL deduction) when used. NOLs generated prior to January 1, 2018 continue to be used 100 percent necessitating tracking of different NOL periods. In addition, for NOLs generated after December 31, 2017, the carryback provisions are repealed and NOLs may only be carried forward; however, the carryforward period is now indefinite. The previous 2-year carryback and 20-year carryforward rules continue to apply to NOLs generated prior to January 1, 2018. For a corporation with NOLs from both the pre-2018 period and the post-2017 period—although the tax law is not entirely settled—the pre-2018 loss can be used to offset up to 100 percent of the current year income and then any income remaining is subject to the 80 percent limitation.

EXAMPLE In 2017, Dez Corp has a net operating loss of $10,000. Dez elects to forego any carryback and instead carries the NOL forward to 2018. In 2018, Dez generates taxable income of $12,000 eligible to be offset by the 2017 NOL without regard to the new 80 percent of taxable income limitation. Dez's 2018 taxable income is $2,000. ♦

EXAMPLE In 2017, Rusk Corporation has a net operating loss of $10,000 that Rusk may only carry forward. In 2018, Rusk has a net operating loss of $12,000. In 2019, Rusk generates taxable income of $15,000. Rusk must first use the $10,000 2017 NOL leaving taxable income of $5,000. Rusk may use $4,000 ($5,000 × 80% limit) of the 2018 NOL and will report taxable income of $1,000 for 2019. The remaining 2018 NOL of $11,000 may be carried forward indefinitely, subject to the 80% income limitation each year. ♦

Self-Study Problem 11.2 *See Appendix E for Solutions to Self-Study Problems*

a. During the current tax year, Taxus Corporation has ordinary income of $110,000, a long-term capital loss of $20,000, and a short-term capital loss of $5,000. Calculate Taxus Corporation's tax liability.

$_____

b. In 2018, Maxus Corporation generates a net operating loss of $40,000. In 2019, Maxus generates taxable income of $45,000. What is the NOL carryforward to 2020, if any?

$_____

11-3 SPECIAL DEDUCTIONS AND LIMITATIONS

Apply special corporate deductions to corporate taxable income.

Corporations are allowed certain "special deductions," including the dividends received deduction and the deduction for organizational expenditures and start-up costs. In addition, corporations are subject to limitations on the deduction of charitable contributions.

11-3a Dividends Received Deduction

When a corporation owns stock in another corporation, income earned by the first corporation could be taxed at least three times in the absence of a special provision. The income would be taxed to the first corporation when earned by the first corporation. Then it would be taxed to the corporation owning the stock in the first corporation when the income is distributed as dividend income. Finally, the income would be taxed to the shareholders of the second corporation when that corporation in turn distributes the earnings to its stockholders as dividends. To mitigate this potential for triple taxation of corporate earnings, corporations are allowed a deduction for all or a portion of dividends received from domestic corporations. Corporations are entitled to a dividends received deduction based on their percentage of ownership in the corporation paying the dividend. The 2019 deduction percentages are described below:

Percent Ownership	2019 Dividends Received Percentage
Less than 20 percent	50%
20 percent or more, but less than 80 percent	65%
80 percent or more	100%

The dividends received deduction is limited to the applicable deduction percentage times the corporation's taxable income calculated before the dividends received deduction, the net operating loss deduction, and capital loss carrybacks. This taxable income limitation, however, does not apply if the receiving corporation has a net operating loss after reducing taxable income by the dividends received deduction. In other words, there is no taxable income limit if the dividends received deduction creates or increases a net operating loss.

EXAMPLE During 2019, Hackberry Corporation has the following income and expenses:

Gross income from operations	$240,000
Expenses from operations	200,000
Dividend received from a 30 percent-owned domestic corporation	100,000

The dividends received deduction is equal to the lesser of $65,000 (65% × $100,000) or 65 percent of taxable income before the dividends received deduction. Since taxable income (for computing this limitation) is $140,000 ($240,000 − $200,000 + $100,000) and 65 percent of $140,000 is $91,000, the full $65,000 is allowed as a deduction. ◆

EXAMPLE Assume the same facts as in the previous example, except Hackberry Corporation's gross income from operations is $190,000 (instead of $240,000). The dividends received deduction is equal to the lesser of $65,000 or 65 percent of $90,000 ($190,000 − $200,000 + $100,000), $58,500. Therefore, the dividends received deduction is limited to $58,500. Note that deducting the potential $65,000 dividends received deduction from taxable income does not generate a net operating loss. Accordingly, the taxable income limit is not avoided. ◆

11-3b Organizational Expenditures and Start-Up Costs

New businesses may incur organizational expenditures or start-up costs, or both, prior to starting a business. Organizational expenditures are incurred by partnerships, LLCs, and corporations in the process of forming an entity in which to operate a business. Start-up costs may be incurred by any business, including sole proprietorships reported on Schedule C, as well as the entities listed above.

Corporations amortize qualifying *organizational* costs over 180 months, and there is no upper limit to the amount of qualifying costs that can be amortized. Corporations can elect to deduct up to $5,000 of organizational costs in the year they begin business. The $5,000 amount is reduced by each dollar of organizational expenses exceeding $50,000. Costs not expensed as part of the first-year election to expense are amortized ratably over the 180-month period beginning with the month the corporation begins business. Generally, organizational expenditures that qualify for amortization include legal and accounting services incident to organization, expenses of temporary directors and organizational meetings, and fees paid to the state for incorporation. Expenses such as the cost of transferring assets to the corporation and expenses connected with selling the corporation's stock are not organizational expenditures and, therefore, are not subject to amortization.

EXAMPLE In 2019, Coco Bola Corporation, an accrual-basis, calendar-year taxpayer, incurred $500 in fees to the state for incorporation, legal and accounting fees incident to the incorporation of $1,000, and temporary directors' expenses of $300. Assuming the corporation does not make an election to expense in the first year, the total $1,800 ($500 + $1,000 + $300) may be amortized over 15 years at a rate of $10 per month ($1,800/180 months). If the corporation began operations on June 1, 2019, $70 ($10 per month × 7 months) may be deducted for organizational expenditures for 2019. Alternatively, the corporation could elect to deduct the full $1,800 of organization costs in the first year of business. ♦

The *start-up costs* of a new business are given the same tax treatment as organizational costs, as illustrated in the previous paragraph and example. Start-up costs include both investigatory expenses and preopening costs. Investigatory expenses are expenses to investigate the potential success of a new business before the decision is made to actually pursue the business. Preopening costs are incurred after the taxpayer decides to start a new business but prior to the date the business actually begins. These expenses may include the training of new employees, advertising, and fees paid to consultants and professionals for advisory services.

11-3c Charitable Contributions

Corporations are allowed a deduction for contributions to qualified charitable organizations. Generally, a deduction is allowed in the year in which a payment is made. If, however, the directors of a corporation which maintains its books on the accrual basis make a pledge before year-end and the payment is made on or before the fifteenth day of the third month after the close of the tax year, the deduction may be claimed in the year of the pledge.

A corporation's charitable contribution deduction is limited to 10 percent of taxable income, computed before the deduction for charitable contributions, net operating loss carrybacks, capital loss carrybacks, and the dividends received deduction. Any excess contributions may be carried forward to the 5 succeeding tax years, but carryforward amounts are subject to the 10 percent annual limitation in the carryover years, with the current year's contributions deducted first.

EXAMPLE Zircote Corporation had net operating income of $40,000 for the current tax year and made a charitable contribution of $6,000 (not included in the operating income amount). Also not included in the operating income were dividends received of $10,000. The corporation's charitable contribution deduction is limited to 10 percent of $50,000 ($40,000 + $10,000), or $5,000. Note that the dividends received deduction is not used in calculating taxable income for purposes of determining the limitation on the charitable contribution deduction. The $1,000 ($6,000 − $5,000) of the charitable contribution that is disallowed is carried forward for up to 5 years. ◆

Self-Study Problem 11.3   *See Appendix E for Solutions to Self-Study Problems*

a. During 2019, Fraxinia Corporation has the following income and expenses:

Gross income from operations, excluding dividends	$ 90,000
Expenses from operations	100,000
Dividends received from a 25 percent-owned domestic corporation	70,000

Calculate the amount of Fraxinia Corporation's dividends received deduction.

$_____

b. Boyce Inc., a calendar year corporation, incurred organizational costs of $13,000 and start-up costs of $52,000 in 2019. Boyce started business on August 3, 2019. What is the maximum deduction for organizational and start-up costs for Boyce in 2019 and what is Boyce's 2020 deduction for the same costs?

c. Gant Corporation has income in 2019 of $95,000 before a dividends received deduction of $15,000 and a charitable contribution of $10,000. What is the deductible amount of the charitable contribution?

11-4 SCHEDULE M-1

Learning Objective 11.4

Identify the components of Schedule M-1 and how they are reported to the IRS.

A corporation is required to report its income and other items on Form 1120, U.S. Corporation Income Tax Return. Because of various provisions in the tax law, a corporation's taxable income seldom is the same as its accounting income (commonly referred to as "book income"). The purpose of Schedule M-1 of the Form 1120 corporate tax return is to reconcile a corporation's book income to its taxable income, computed before the net operating loss and special deductions such as the dividends received deduction. On the left side of Schedule M-1 are adjustments that must be added to book income, and on the right side of the schedule are adjustments that must be subtracted from book income to arrive at the amount of taxable income. The amounts that must be added to book income include the amount of federal income tax expense, net capital losses deducted for book purposes, income recorded on the tax return but not on the books, and expenses recorded on the books but not deducted on the tax return. Alternatively, the amounts that must be deducted from book income are income recorded on the books but not included on the tax return, and deductions on the return not deducted on the books.

EXAMPLE For the current tax year, Wisteria Corporation, an accrual-basis taxpayer, has net income reported on its books of $44,975. Included in this figure are the following items:

Net capital loss	$ 5,000
Interest income on tax-exempt bonds	9,000
Federal income tax expense	11,025
Depreciation deducted on the tax return, not deducted on the books	3,500
Interest deducted on the books, not deductible for tax purposes	4,000

Wisteria Corporation's Schedule M-1, Form 1120, is illustrated below.

Schedule M-1	Reconciliation of Income (Loss) per Books With Income per Return				
	Note: The corporation may be required to file Schedule M-3. See instructions.				
1	Net income (loss) per books	44,975	7	Income recorded on books this year not included on this return (itemize):	
2	Federal income tax per books	11,025			
3	Excess of capital losses over capital gains .	5,000		Tax-exempt interest $ 9,000	
4	Income subject to tax not recorded on books this year (itemize): _____			_____	
	_____			_____	9,000
			8	Deductions on this return not charged against book income this year (itemize):	
5	Expenses recorded on books this year not deducted on this return (itemize):		a	Depreciation . . $ 3,500	
a	Depreciation . . . . $ _____		b	Charitable contributions $ _____	
b	Charitable contributions . $ _____			_____	
c	Travel and entertainment . $ _____			_____	3,500
	interest	4,000	9	Add lines 7 and 8	12,500
6	Add lines 1 through 5	65,000	10	Income (page 1, line 28)—line 6 less line 9	52,500

◆

Self-Study Problem 11.4 *See Appendix E for Solutions to Self-Study Problems*

Redwood Corporation has net income reported on its books of $115,600. For the current year, the corporation had federal income tax expense of $29,400, a net capital loss of $9,100, and tax-exempt interest income of $4,700. The company deducted depreciation of $17,000 on its tax return and $13,000 on its books. Using Schedule M-1 below, calculate Redwood Corporation's taxable income, before any net operating loss or special deductions, for the current year.

Schedule M-1	Reconciliation of Income (Loss) per Books With Income per Return				
	Note: The corporation may be required to file Schedule M-3. See instructions.				
1	Net income (loss) per books		7	Income recorded on books this year not included on this return (itemize):	
2	Federal income tax per books				
3	Excess of capital losses over capital gains .			Tax-exempt interest $ _____	
4	Income subject to tax not recorded on books this year (itemize): _____			_____	
	_____			_____	
			8	Deductions on this return not charged against book income this year (itemize):	
5	Expenses recorded on books this year not deducted on this return (itemize):		a	Depreciation . . $ _____	
a	Depreciation . . . . $ _____		b	Charitable contributions $ _____	
b	Charitable contributions . $ _____			_____	
c	Travel and entertainment . $ _____			_____	
			9	Add lines 7 and 8	
6	Add lines 1 through 5		10	Income (page 1, line 28)—line 6 less line 9	

11-5 **FILING REQUIREMENTS AND ESTIMATED TAX**

11.5 Learning Objective

Describe the corporate tax return filing and estimated tax payment requirements.

For all tax year-ends except for June 30, the due date for filing a corporate tax return is the fifteenth day of the fourth month after year-end. For June 30 year-end corporations, the filing due date is September 15 (fifteenth day of the third month). An extension provides an additional 6 months; thus, a calendar year-end corporation has an initial filing deadline of April 15 and an extended deadline of October 15 (6 month extension). However, corporations with tax years ending on June 30 will have an extended filing deadline of April 15 (7 month extension). When the due date falls on a weekend or holiday, the due date is the next business day. To avoid penalties, a corporation must pay any tax liability by the original due date of the return.

Corporations must make estimated tax payments in a manner similar to those made by self-employed individual taxpayers. The payments are made in four installments due on the fifteenth day of the fourth, sixth, ninth, and twelfth months of the corporation's tax year.

Small corporations with less than $250,000 in gross receipts and less than $250,000 in assets do not have to complete Schedule L (Balance Sheet) or Schedules M-1 and M-2. The rule applies to both S and C corporations, and allows small businesses to keep records based on their checkbook or cash receipts and disbursements journal. This makes the reporting requirements for a small corporation similar to the reporting requirements for a Schedule C sole proprietorship.

TAX BREAK

Self-Study Problem 11.5 — *See Appendix E for Solutions to Self-Study Problems*

Aspen Corporation was formed and began operations on January 1, 2019.

Aspen Corporation
Income Statement
for the Year Ended December 31, 2019

Gross income from operations	$ 285,000
Qualified dividends received from a 10 percent-owned domestic corporation	10,000
Total gross income	295,000
Cost of goods sold	(80,000)
Total income	215,000
Other expenses:	
Compensation of officers $90,000	
Salaries and wages 82,000	
Repairs 8,000	
Depreciation expense for book and tax purposes 5,000	
Payroll taxes 11,000	
Total other expenses	(196,000)
Net income (before federal income tax expense)	$ 19,000

Aspen Corporation
Balance Sheet
as of December 31, 2019

Assets:		
Cash	$ 35,000	
Accounts receivable	10,000	
Land	18,000	
Building	125,000	
Less: accumulated depreciation	(5,000)	
Total assets		$ 183,000
Liabilities and owners' equity:		
Accounts payable	$ 26,940	
Common stock	140,000	
Retained earnings	16,060	
Total liabilities and owners' equity		$ 183,000

Aspen Corporation made estimated tax payments of $3,000.

Based on the above information, complete Form 1120 on Pages 11-9 through 11-14. Assume the corporation's book federal income tax expense is equal to its 2019 federal income tax liability and that any tax overpayment is to be applied to the next year's estimated tax. Schedule UTP, Form 4562, Form 1125-A, and Form 1125-E are not required. Make reasonable assumptions for any missing data.

Self-Study Problem 11.5

Form **1120**		**U.S. Corporation Income Tax Return**			OMB No. 1545-0123
Department of the Treasury Internal Revenue Service		For calendar year 2019 or tax year beginning _____, 2019, ending _____, 20 ____ ▶ Go to *www.irs.gov/Form1120* for instructions and the latest information.			**2019**

A Check if:
1a Consolidated return (attach Form 851) . ☐
  b Life/nonlife consoli-dated return . . . ☐
2 Personal holding co. (attach Sch. PH) . ☐
3 Personal service corp. (see instructions) . ☐
4 Schedule M-3 attached ☐

TYPE OR PRINT	Name	B **Employer identification number**
	Number, street, and room or suite no. If a P.O. box, see instructions.	C Date incorporated
	City or town, state or province, country, and ZIP or foreign postal code	D Total assets (see instructions) $

E Check if: **(1)** ☐ Initial return   **(2)** ☐ Final return   **(3)** ☐ Name change   **(4)** ☐ Address change

Income

1a	Gross receipts or sales	1a		
b	Returns and allowances	1b		
c	Balance. Subtract line 1b from line 1a		1c	
2	Cost of goods sold (attach Form 1125-A)		2	
3	Gross profit. Subtract line 2 from line 1c		3	
4	Dividends and inclusions (Schedule C, line 23)		4	
5	Interest		5	
6	Gross rents		6	
7	Gross royalties		7	
8	Capital gain net income (attach Schedule D (Form 1120))		8	
9	Net gain or (loss) from Form 4797, Part II, line 17 (attach Form 4797)		9	
10	Other income (see instructions—attach statement)		10	
11	**Total income.** Add lines 3 through 10 ▶		11	

Deductions (See instructions for limitations on deductions.)

12	Compensation of officers (see instructions—attach Form 1125-E) ▶		12	
13	Salaries and wages (less employment credits)		13	
14	Repairs and maintenance		14	
15	Bad debts		15	
16	Rents		16	
17	Taxes and licenses		17	
18	Interest (see instructions)		18	
19	Charitable contributions		19	
20	Depreciation from Form 4562 not claimed on Form 1125-A or elsewhere on return (attach Form 4562)		20	
21	Depletion		21	
22	Advertising		22	
23	Pension, profit-sharing, etc., plans		23	
24	Employee benefit programs		24	
25	Reserved for future use		25	
26	Other deductions (attach statement)		26	
27	**Total deductions.** Add lines 12 through 26 ▶		27	
28	Taxable income before net operating loss deduction and special deductions. Subtract line 27 from line 11.		28	
29a	Net operating loss deduction (see instructions)	29a		
b	Special deductions (Schedule C, line 24)	29b		
c	Add lines 29a and 29b		29c	

Tax, Refundable Credits, and Payments

30	**Taxable income.** Subtract line 29c from line 28. See instructions		30	
31	Total tax (Schedule J, Part I, line 11)		31	
32	2019 net 965 tax liability paid (Schedule J, Part II, line 12)		32	
33	Total payments, credits, and section 965 net tax liability (Schedule J, Part III, line 23)		33	
34	Estimated tax penalty. See instructions. Check if Form 2220 is attached ▶ ☐		34	
35	**Amount owed.** If line 33 is smaller than the total of lines 31, 32, and 34, enter amount owed		35	
36	**Overpayment.** If line 33 is larger than the total of lines 31, 32, and 34, enter amount overpaid		36	
37	Enter amount from line 36 you want: **Credited to 2020 estimated tax ▶** _____ Refunded ▶		37	

Sign Here ▶

Under penalties of perjury, I declare that I have examined this return, including accompanying schedules and statements, and to the best of my knowledge and belief, it is true, correct, and complete. Declaration of preparer (other than taxpayer) is based on all information of which preparer has any knowledge.

_____   _____   ▶ _____
Signature of officer   Date   Title

May the IRS discuss this return with the preparer shown below? See instructions. ☐ **Yes** ☐ **No**

Paid Preparer Use Only

Print/Type preparer's name	Preparer's signature	Date	Check ☐ if self-employed	PTIN
Firm's name ▶			Firm's EIN ▶	
Firm's address ▶			Phone no.	

For Paperwork Reduction Act Notice, see separate instructions.   Cat. No. 11450Q   Form **1120** (2019)

Form 1120 (2019)   Page **2**

Schedule C Dividends, Inclusions, and Special Deductions (see instructions)	(a) Dividends and inclusions	(b) %	(c) Special deductions (a) × (b)
1 Dividends from less-than-20%-owned domestic corporations (other than debt-financed stock)		50	
2 Dividends from 20%-or-more-owned domestic corporations (other than debt-financed stock)		65	
3 Dividends on certain debt-financed stock of domestic and foreign corporations		see instructions	
4 Dividends on certain preferred stock of less-than-20%-owned public utilities . . .		23.3	
5 Dividends on certain preferred stock of 20%-or-more-owned public utilities		26.7	
6 Dividends from less-than-20%-owned foreign corporations and certain FSCs . . .		50	
7 Dividends from 20%-or-more-owned foreign corporations and certain FSCs		65	
8 Dividends from wholly owned foreign subsidiaries		100	
9 **Subtotal.** Add lines 1 through 8. See instructions for limitations		see instructions	
10 Dividends from domestic corporations received by a small business investment company operating under the Small Business Investment Act of 1958		100	
11 Dividends from affiliated group members		100	
12 Dividends from certain FSCs		100	
13 Foreign-source portion of dividends received from a specified 10%-owned foreign corporation (excluding hybrid dividends) (see instructions)		100	
14 Dividends from foreign corporations not included on line 3, 6, 7, 8, 11, 12, or 13 (including any hybrid dividends)			
15 Section 965(a) inclusion		see instructions	
16a Subpart F inclusions derived from the sale by a controlled foreign corporation (CFC) of the stock of a lower-tier foreign corporation treated as a dividend (attach Form(s) 5471) (see instructions)		100	
b Subpart F inclusions derived from hybrid dividends of tiered corporations (attach Form(s) 5471) (see instructions)			
c Other inclusions from CFCs under subpart F not included on line 15, 16a, 16b, or 17 (attach Form(s) 5471) (see instructions).			
17 Global Intangible Low-Taxed Income (GILTI) (attach Form(s) 5471 and Form 8992) . .			
18 Gross-up for foreign taxes deemed paid			
19 IC-DISC and former DISC dividends not included on line 1, 2, or 3			
20 Other dividends			
21 Deduction for dividends paid on certain preferred stock of public utilities			
22 Section 250 deduction (attach Form 8993)			
23 **Total dividends and inclusions.** Add column (a), lines 9 through 20. Enter here and on page 1, line 4			
24 **Total special deductions.** Add column (c), lines 9 through 22. Enter here and on page 1, line 29b			

Form **1120** (2019)

Form 1120 (2019)   Page **3**

Schedule J	Tax Computation and Payment (see instructions)

Part I—Tax Computation

1	Check if the corporation is a member of a controlled group (attach Schedule O (Form 1120)). See instructions ▶ ☐		
2	Income tax. See instructions	**2**	
3	Base erosion minimum tax amount (attach Form 8991)	**3**	
4	Add lines 2 and 3	**4**	
5a	Foreign tax credit (attach Form 1118)	**5a**	
b	Credit from Form 8834 (see instructions)	**5b**	
c	General business credit (attach Form 3800)	**5c**	
d	Credit for prior year minimum tax (attach Form 8827)	**5d**	
e	Bond credits from Form 8912	**5e**	
6	**Total credits.** Add lines 5a through 5e	**6**	
7	Subtract line 6 from line 4	**7**	
8	Personal holding company tax (attach Schedule PH (Form 1120))	**8**	
9a	Recapture of investment credit (attach Form 4255)	**9a**	
b	Recapture of low-income housing credit (attach Form 8611)	**9b**	
c	Interest due under the look-back method—completed long-term contracts (attach Form 8697)	**9c**	
d	Interest due under the look-back method—income forecast method (attach Form 8866)	**9d**	
e	Alternative tax on qualifying shipping activities (attach Form 8902)	**9e**	
f	Other (see instructions—attach statement)	**9f**	
10	**Total.** Add lines 9a through 9f	**10**	
11	**Total tax.** Add lines 7, 8, and 10. Enter here and on page 1, line 31	**11**	

Part II—Section 965 Payments (see instructions)

12	2019 net 965 tax liability paid from Form 965-B, Part II, column (k), line 3. Enter here and on page 1, line 32	**12**	

Part III—Payments, Refundable Credits, and Section 965 Net Tax Liability

13	2018 overpayment credited to 2019	**13**	
14	2019 estimated tax payments	**14**	
15	2019 refund applied for on Form 4466	**15**	( )
16	Combine lines 13, 14, and 15	**16**	
17	Tax deposited with Form 7004	**17**	
18	Withholding (see instructions)	**18**	
19	**Total payments.** Add lines 16, 17, and 18	**19**	
20	Refundable credits from:		
a	Form 2439	**20a**	
b	Form 4136	**20b**	
c	Form 8827, line 5c	**20c**	
d	Other (attach statement—see instructions)	**20d**	
21	**Total credits.** Add lines 20a through 20d	**21**	
22	2019 net 965 tax liability from Form 965-B, Part I, column (d), line 3. See instructions	**22**	
23	**Total payments, credits, and section 965 net tax liability.** Add lines 19, 21, and 22. Enter here and on page 1, line 33	**23**	

Form **1120** (2019)

Form 1120 (2019)   Page **4**

Schedule K	**Other Information** (see instructions)				Yes	No

1 Check accounting method: **a** ☐ Cash   **b** ☐ Accrual   **c** ☐ Other (specify) ▶ _____

2 See the instructions and enter the:

a Business activity code no. ▶ _____

b Business activity ▶ _____

c Product or service ▶ _____

3 Is the corporation a subsidiary in an affiliated group or a parent–subsidiary controlled group? . . . .

If "Yes," enter name and EIN of the parent corporation ▶ _____

4 At the end of the tax year:

a Did any foreign or domestic corporation, partnership (including any entity treated as a partnership), trust, or tax-exempt organization own directly 20% or more, or own, directly or indirectly, 50% or more of the total voting power of all classes of the corporation's stock entitled to vote? If "Yes," complete Part I of Schedule G (Form 1120) (attach Schedule G) . . . . . .

b Did any individual or estate own directly 20% or more, or own, directly or indirectly, 50% or more of the total voting power of all classes of the corporation's stock entitled to vote? If "Yes," complete Part II of Schedule G (Form 1120) (attach Schedule G) .

5 At the end of the tax year, did the corporation:

a Own directly 20% or more, or own, directly or indirectly, 50% or more of the total voting power of all classes of stock entitled to vote of any foreign or domestic corporation not included on **Form 851,** Affiliations Schedule? For rules of constructive ownership, see instructions.

If "Yes," complete (i) through (iv) below.

(i) Name of Corporation	**(ii)** Employer Identification Number (if any)	**(iii)** Country of Incorporation	**(iv)** Percentage Owned in Voting Stock

b Own directly an interest of 20% or more, or own, directly or indirectly, an interest of 50% or more in any foreign or domestic partnership (including an entity treated as a partnership) or in the beneficial interest of a trust? For rules of constructive ownership, see instructions.

If "Yes," complete (i) through (iv) below.

(i) Name of Entity	**(ii)** Employer Identification Number (if any)	**(iii)** Country of Organization	**(iv)** Maximum Percentage Owned in Profit, Loss, or Capital

6 During this tax year, did the corporation pay dividends (other than stock dividends and distributions in exchange for stock) in excess of the corporation's current and accumulated earnings and profits? See sections 301 and 316 . . . .

If "Yes," file **Form 5452,** Corporate Report of Nondividend Distributions. See the instructions for Form 5452.

If this is a consolidated return, answer here for the parent corporation and on Form 851 for each subsidiary.

7 At any time during the tax year, did one foreign person own, directly or indirectly, at least 25% of the total voting power of all classes of the corporation's stock entitled to vote or at least 25% of the total value of all classes of the corporation's stock? .

For rules of attribution, see section 318. If "Yes," enter:

(a) Percentage owned ▶ _____ and **(b)** Owner's country ▶ _____

(c) The corporation may have to file **Form 5472,** Information Return of a 25% Foreign-Owned U.S. Corporation or a Foreign Corporation Engaged in a U.S. Trade or Business. Enter the number of Forms 5472 attached ▶ _____

8 Check this box if the corporation issued publicly offered debt instruments with original issue discount . . . . ▶ ☐

If checked, the corporation may have to file **Form 8281,** Information Return for Publicly Offered Original Issue Discount Instruments.

9 Enter the amount of tax-exempt interest received or accrued during the tax year ▶ $ _____

10 Enter the number of shareholders at the end of the tax year (if 100 or fewer) ▶ _____

11 If the corporation has an NOL for the tax year and is electing to forego the carryback period, check here (see instructions) ▶ ☐

If the corporation is filing a consolidated return, the statement required by Regulations section 1.1502-21(b)(3) must be attached or the election will not be valid.

12 Enter the available NOL carryover from prior tax years (do not reduce it by any deduction reported on page 1, line 29a.) . . . . ▶ $ _____

Form **1120** (2019)

Form 1120 (2019)   Page **5**

Schedule K	**Other Information** *(continued from page 4)*	Yes	No

13 Are the corporation's total receipts (page 1, line 1a, plus lines 4 through 10) for the tax year **and** its total assets at the end of the tax year less than $250,000? . . . .

If "Yes," the corporation is not required to complete Schedules L, M-1, and M-2. Instead, enter the total amount of cash distributions and the book value of property distributions (other than cash) made during the tax year ▶ $ _____

14 Is the corporation required to file Schedule UTP (Form 1120), Uncertain Tax Position Statement? See instructions . . . .

If "Yes," complete and attach Schedule UTP.

15a Did the corporation make any payments in 2019 that would require it to file Form(s) 1099? . . . .

b If "Yes," did or will the corporation file required Form(s) 1099? . . . .

16 During this tax year, did the corporation have an 80%-or-more change in ownership, including a change due to redemption of its own stock? . . . .

17 During or subsequent to this tax year, but before the filing of this return, did the corporation dispose of more than 65% (by value) of its assets in a taxable, non-taxable, or tax deferred transaction? . . . .

18 Did the corporation receive assets in a section 351 transfer in which any of the transferred assets had a fair market basis or fair market value of more than $1 million? . . . .

19 During the corporation's tax year, did the corporation make any payments that would require it to file Forms 1042 and 1042-S under chapter 3 (sections 1441 through 1464) or chapter 4 (sections 1471 through 1474) of the Code? . . . .

20 Is the corporation operating on a cooperative basis? . . . .

21 During the tax year, did the corporation pay or accrue any interest or royalty for which the deduction is not allowed under section 267A? See instructions . . . .

If "Yes," enter the total amount of the disallowed deductions ▶ $ _____

22 Does the corporation have gross receipts of at least $500 million in any of the 3 preceding tax years? (See sections 59A(e)(2) and (3)) . . . .

If "Yes," complete and attach Form 8991.

23 Did the corporation have an election under section 163(j) for any real property trade or business or any farming business in effect during the tax year? See instructions . . . .

24 Does the corporation satisfy one or more of the following? See instructions . . . .

a The corporation owns a pass-through entity with current, or prior year carryover, excess business interest expense.

b The corporation's aggregate average annual gross receipts (determined under section 448(c)) for the 3 tax years preceding the current tax year are more than $26 million and the corporation has business interest expense.

c The corporation is a tax shelter and the corporation has business interest expense.

If "Yes," to any, complete and attach Form 8990.

25 Is the corporation attaching Form 8996 to certify as a Qualified Opportunity Fund? . . . .

If "Yes," enter amount from Form 8996, line 14 . . . . . ▶ $ _____

Form **1120** (2019)

Form 1120 (2019)   Page **6**

Schedule L	**Balance Sheets per Books**	Beginning of tax year		End of tax year	
	Assets	(a)	(b)	(c)	(d)
1	Cash				
2a	Trade notes and accounts receivable				
b	Less allowance for bad debts	( )		( )	
3	Inventories				
4	U.S. government obligations				
5	Tax-exempt securities (see instructions)				
6	Other current assets (attach statement)				
7	Loans to shareholders				
8	Mortgage and real estate loans				
9	Other investments (attach statement)				
10a	Buildings and other depreciable assets				
b	Less accumulated depreciation	( )		( )	
11a	Depletable assets				
b	Less accumulated depletion	( )		( )	
12	Land (net of any amortization)				
13a	Intangible assets (amortizable only)				
b	Less accumulated amortization	( )		( )	
14	Other assets (attach statement)				
15	Total assets				
	Liabilities and Shareholders' Equity				
16	Accounts payable				
17	Mortgages, notes, bonds payable in less than 1 year				
18	Other current liabilities (attach statement)				
19	Loans from shareholders				
20	Mortgages, notes, bonds payable in 1 year or more				
21	Other liabilities (attach statement)				
22	Capital stock: **a** Preferred stock				
	b Common stock				
23	Additional paid-in capital				
24	Retained earnings—Appropriated (attach statement)				
25	Retained earnings—Unappropriated				
26	Adjustments to shareholders' equity (attach statement)				
27	Less cost of treasury stock		( )		( )
28	Total liabilities and shareholders' equity				

Schedule M-1	**Reconciliation of Income (Loss) per Books With Income per Return**

Note: The corporation may be required to file Schedule M-3. See instructions.

1	Net income (loss) per books		**7**	Income recorded on books this year not included on this return (itemize):	
2	Federal income tax per books			Tax-exempt interest $_____	
3	Excess of capital losses over capital gains			_____	
4	Income subject to tax not recorded on books this year (itemize):_____		**8**	Deductions on this return not charged against book income this year (itemize):	
	_____		**a**	Depreciation . . $_____	
5	Expenses recorded on books this year not deducted on this return (itemize):		**b**	Charitable contributions $_____	
a	Depreciation . . . . $_____			_____	
b	Charitable contributions . $_____				
c	Travel and entertainment . $_____		**9**	Add lines 7 and 8	
	_____		**10**	Income (page 1, line 28)—line 6 less line 9	
6	Add lines 1 through 5				

Schedule M-2	**Analysis of Unappropriated Retained Earnings per Books (Line 25, Schedule L)**

1	Balance at beginning of year		**5**	Distributions: **a** Cash	
2	Net income (loss) per books			**b** Stock	
3	Other increases (itemize): _____			**c** Property	
	_____		**6**	Other decreases (itemize): _____	
	_____		**7**	Add lines 5 and 6	
4	Add lines 1, 2, and 3		**8**	Balance at end of year (line 4 less line 7)	

Form **1120** (2019)

11-6 S CORPORATIONS

Qualified corporations may elect to be taxed under Subchapter S of the Internal Revenue Code in a manner similar to partnerships. An S corporation does not generally pay tax, and each shareholder reports his or her share of corporate income. The S corporation election is designed to relieve corporations of certain corporate tax disadvantages, such as the double taxation of income.

To elect S corporation status, a corporation must have the following characteristics:

1. The corporation must be a domestic corporation;
2. The corporation must have 100 or fewer shareholders who are either individuals, estates, certain trusts, certain financial institutions, or certain exempt organizations;
3. The corporation must have only one class of stock; and
4. All shareholders must be U.S. citizens or resident aliens.

The S corporation election must be made during the prior year or the first two months and 15 days of the current tax year to obtain the status for the current year. Relief provisions may apply for elections that are filed late.

EXAMPLE Laurel Corporation is a calendar-year corporation that makes an S corporation election on November 2, 2019. The corporation does not qualify for any of the relief provisions for late S corporation elections for the 2019 tax year. The corporation is not an S corporation until the 2020 tax year; it is a regular C corporation for 2019. ♦

After electing S corporation status, the corporation retains the status until the election is voluntarily revoked or statutorily terminated. If the corporation ceases to qualify as an S corporation (e.g., it has 102 shareholders during the year), the election is statutorily terminated. Also, the election is terminated when a corporation receives 25 percent or more of its gross income from passive investments for 3 consecutive tax years and the corporation has accumulated earnings and profits at the end of each of those years. If a corporation experiences an involuntary termination of S corporation status, the election is terminated on the day the status changes. For example, the loss of S corporation status on June 1 causes the corporation to be a regular C corporation from that day on.

Upon consent of shareholders owning a majority of the voting stock, an S corporation election can be voluntarily revoked. If the consent to revoke the election is made during the first two months and 15 days of the tax year, the S corporation status will be considered voluntarily terminated effective at the beginning of that year. Shareholders may specify a date on or after the date of the revocation as the effective date for the voluntary termination of the S corporation election. If a prospective revocation date is not specified, and the consent to revoke the election is made after two months and 15 days of the tax year, the earliest that the S corporation status can be terminated is the first day of the following tax year.

EXAMPLE On January 20, 2019, Juniper Corporation, a calendar-year corporation, files a consent to revoke its S corporation election. No date is specified in the consent as the effective date of the revocation. The corporation is no longer an S corporation effective January 1, 2019. If the election were made after March 15, the corporation would not become a regular C corporation until the 2020 tax year. ♦

11-6a Reporting Income

An S corporation is required to report its income and other items on Form 1120S, U.S. Income Tax Return for an S Corporation, even though the corporate entity does not pay federal income tax. The tax return is due on the fifteenth day of the third month following the close of the corporation's tax year. S corporations may request a 6-month extension for filing its tax return. Each shareholder of an S corporation reports his or her share of corporate income based on his or her stock ownership during the year. The taxable income of an S corporation is computed in the same manner as a partnership.

Each shareholder of an S corporation takes into account separately his or her share of items of income, deductions, and credits on a per share per day basis. Schedule K-1 of Form 1120S is used to report the allocation of ordinary income or loss, plus all separately stated items of income or loss, to each of the shareholders. Each shareholder's share of these items is included in the shareholder's computation of taxable income for the tax year during which the corporation's year ends. In the case of the death of a shareholder, the shareholder's portion of S corporation items will be taken into account on the shareholder's final tax return.

EXAMPLE   Freda is the sole shareholder of the Freda Corporation, which has an S corporation election in effect. During calendar year 2019, the corporation has ordinary taxable income of $100,000. Freda must report $100,000 on her individual income tax return for 2019 as income from the Freda Corporation. ◆

11-6b S Corporation Losses

Losses from an S corporation also pass through to the shareholders. However, the amount of loss from an S corporation that a shareholder may report is limited to his or her adjusted basis in the corporation's stock plus the amount of any loans from the shareholder to the corporation. Any loss in excess of the shareholder's basis in the stock of the corporation plus loans is disallowed and becomes a carryforward loss. If a shareholder was not a shareholder for the entire tax year, losses must be allocated to the shareholder on a daily basis (the seller gets credit for the date of sale). This prevents a shareholder from selling losses late in the year to another taxpayer by selling the stock of an S corporation.

EXAMPLE   Lawson and Mary are equal shareholders in L&M Corporation, an S corporation. On December 1, 2019, Mary sells her interest to Connley for $15,000. Lawson's basis in his L&M Corporation stock is $10,000. For the 2019 tax year, the corporation has a loss of $24,000. Lawson can deduct only $10,000 of his half of the loss ($12,000), since that is the amount of his stock basis. Even though she is not a shareholder at year-end, Mary may deduct $11,014 of the loss, which is 335/365 of $12,000, assuming her basis was at least that amount. Connley may deduct $986, 30/365 of $12,000. In leap years, the amounts would be $11,016 (336/366 × $12,000) and $984 (30/366 × $12,000) for Mary and Connley, respectively. ◆

11-6c Pass-Through Items

Certain items pass through from an S corporation to the shareholders and retain their tax attributes on the shareholders' tax returns. The following are examples of pass-through items that are separately stated on the shareholders' Schedule K-1:

- Capital gains and losses
- Section 1231 gains and losses
- Dividend income
- Charitable contributions
- Tax-exempt interest
- Most credits

11-6d Qualified Business Income Deduction

Similar to partnerships, S corporations are flow-through entities that may generate qualified business income (QBI) and thus individual shareholders may be eligible for the QBI deduction. The same wage and service business limits apply as with other flow-through entities.

S corporations have a unique interaction between wages and qualified business income. The wages paid to an S corporation shareholder are not considered part of qualified business income; however, the wages count toward the wage limit, to the extent one applies to the taxpayer:

EXAMPLE Hogarth is a single taxpayer and the sole shareholder of Giant Corporation, which is an S corporation for tax purposes. Giant pays reasonable wages to Hogarth, the only employee, of $80,000 and allocates $100,000 of income. Hogarth's taxable income is above the threshold for a single taxpayer and he is required to apply the wage limitation to his QBI deduction. Hogarth can include $40,000 ($80,000 × 50%) of wages in computing the wage limit for the QBI deduction but may not consider the $80,000 of wages as QBI, only the $100,000 of income allocated. ♦

11-6e **Special Taxes**

S corporations are not subject to the corporate income tax on their regular taxable income. Under certain circumstances, an S corporation may be liable for tax at the corporate level. An S corporation may be subject to a tax on gains attributable to appreciation in the value of assets held by the corporation prior to the S corporation election, the built-in gains tax. In addition, a tax may be imposed on certain S corporations that have large amounts of passive investment income, such as income from dividends and interest. The rules for the application of these taxes are complex.

Self-Study Problem 11.6 *See Appendix E for Solutions to Self-Study Problems*

Assume that Aspen Corporation in Self-Study Problem 11.5 is owned by Janet Nall, who is a 100 percent shareholder. Also, assume that the corporation has a valid S corporation election in effect for 2019 and is not subject to any special taxes. Assume no wages are included in Aspen's cost of goods sold. Using the relevant information given in Self-Study Problem 11.5 and assuming the corporation's retained earnings are $19,000, instead of $16,060, accounts payable are $24,000, rather than $26,940, and no estimated tax payments are made, complete Form 1120S on Pages 11–19 through 11–23 for Aspen Corporation, and complete Schedule K-1 on Pages 11–25 and 11–26 for Janet. Assume there were no cash distributions to Janet during the year.

11-7 **CORPORATE FORMATION**

11.7 Learning Objective

Describe the basic tax rules for the formation of a corporation.

When a taxpayer incorporates a business and transfers high-value, low-basis property to the corporation in exchange for corporate stock, a substantial gain is realized. This gain is measured at the value of the shares received less the basis of the property transferred. Favorable tax treatment is available in certain cases, which allows many taxpayers to defer the recognition of the gain in the year of formation. To defer the gain, the taxpayer must meet certain requirements, including:

1. The taxpayer must transfer property or money to the corporation,
2. The transfer must be solely in exchange for stock of the corporation, and
3. The shareholder(s) qualifying for nonrecognition must own at least 80 percent of the corporation's stock after the transfer.

When the above requirements are met, gains and losses are not recognized on the formation of the corporation.

The shareholder must transfer property or cash to the corporation; performing services for corporate stock does not qualify for nonrecognition treatment. The shareholder performing services must recognize income in an amount equal to the value of the stock received. If the shareholder receives other property (boot) in addition to stock of the corporation in exchange for the transfer of cash or other property, the transaction may still qualify for partial nonrecognition treatment, provided the control requirement is met. However, realized gain must be recognized to the extent of the boot received.

11-7a Liabilities

As a general rule, the assumption of shareholder liabilities by the corporation is not considered boot. For example, if a shareholder transfers land to the corporation for stock and the land is subject to a liability that is assumed by the corporation, no gain would normally be recognized on the transfer. However, if there is no business purpose for transfer of the liability, or tax avoidance appears to be involved, the recognition of any realized gain is required. Also, when the total liabilities transferred to the corporation by a shareholder exceed the total basis of the property transferred by the shareholder, the excess amount is a gain that must be recognized without regard to whether gain is realized.

EXAMPLE Robusta Corporation is formed by Max, who contributes property with a basis of $12,000 in exchange for 100 percent of the company's stock. On the date of the contribution, the property contributed has a fair market value of $120,000 and is subject to a liability of $20,000. Max must recognize a gain of $8,000 on the transfer of the property to the corporation since the liability transferred to the corporation exceeds his basis in the property transferred. ♦

11-7b Shareholder's Stock Basis

After the transfer, the shareholder's basis in his or her stock is determined by the following formula:

Basis of the property transferred	$ xxxx
Less: boot received	(xxxx)
Plus: gain recognized	xxxx
Less: liabilities transferred	(xxxx)
Basis in the stock	$ xxxx

11-7c Corporation's Basis in Property Contributed

The corporation's basis in the property received from a shareholder in a transaction to which nonrecognition treatment applies is the same as the basis of the property to the shareholder, increased by any gain recognized by the shareholder on the transfer.

EXAMPLE A, B, and C form Hornbeam Corporation. A contributes property with a basis of $25,000 in exchange for 40 shares of stock worth $40,000. B performs services for the corporation in exchange for 10 shares of stock worth $10,000. C contributes property with a basis of $10,000 in exchange for 45 shares of stock worth $45,000 and $5,000 cash. The stock described above is all of the outstanding stock of the corporation. A and C qualify for complete or partial nonrecognition treatment, since together they own

Self-Study Problem 11.6

Form **1120-S**	**U.S. Income Tax Return for an S Corporation**	OMB No. 1545-0123
Department of the Treasury Internal Revenue Service	▶ Do not file this form unless the corporation has filed or is attaching Form 2553 to elect to be an S corporation. ▶ Go to *www.irs.gov/Form1120S* for instructions and the latest information.	20**19**

For calendar year 2019 or tax year beginning _____ , 2019, ending _____ , 20____

A S election effective date		**TYPE OR PRINT**	Name	**D** Employer identification number
B Business activity code number (see instructions)			Number, street, and room or suite no. If a P.O. box, see instructions.	**E** Date incorporated
			City or town, state or province, country, and ZIP or foreign postal code	**F** Total assets (see instructions) $
C Check if Sch. M-3 attached ☐				

G Is the corporation electing to be an S corporation beginning with this tax year? ☐ Yes ☐ No If "Yes," attach Form 2553 if not already filed

H Check if: **(1)** ☐ Final return **(2)** ☐ Name change **(3)** ☐ Address change **(4)** ☐ Amended return **(5)** ☐ S election termination or revocation

I Enter the number of shareholders who were shareholders during any part of the tax year . . . . ▶ _____

J Check if corporation: **(1)** ☐ Aggregated activities for section 465 at-risk purposes **(2)** ☐ Grouped activities for section 469 passive activity purposes

Caution: Include **only** trade or business income and expenses on lines 1a through 21. See the instructions for more information.

Income	**1a**	Gross receipts or sales	**1a**		
	b	Returns and allowances	**1b**		
	c	Balance. Subtract line 1b from line 1a		**1c**	
	2	Cost of goods sold (attach Form 1125-A)		**2**	
	3	Gross profit. Subtract line 2 from line 1c		**3**	
	4	Net gain (loss) from Form 4797, line 17 (attach Form 4797) . .		**4**	
	5	Other income (loss) (see instructions—attach statement) . . .		**5**	
	6	**Total income (loss).** Add lines 3 through 5 . . . . . . ▶		**6**	
Deductions (see instructions for limitations)	**7**	Compensation of officers (see instructions—attach Form 1125-E) .		**7**	
	8	Salaries and wages (less employment credits)		**8**	
	9	Repairs and maintenance		**9**	
	10	Bad debts		**10**	
	11	Rents		**11**	
	12	Taxes and licenses		**12**	
	13	Interest (see instructions)		**13**	
	14	Depreciation not claimed on Form 1125-A or elsewhere on return (attach Form 4562)		**14**	
	15	Depletion **(Do not deduct oil and gas depletion.)**		**15**	
	16	Advertising		**16**	
	17	Pension, profit-sharing, etc., plans		**17**	
	18	Employee benefit programs		**18**	
	19	Other deductions (attach statement)		**19**	
	20	**Total deductions.** Add lines 7 through 19 . . . . . . ▶		**20**	
	21	**Ordinary business income (loss).** Subtract line 20 from line 6 .		**21**	
Tax and Payments	**22a**	Excess net passive income or LIFO recapture tax (see instructions) . . .	**22a**		
	b	Tax from Schedule D (Form 1120-S)	**22b**		
	c	Add lines 22a and 22b (see instructions for additional taxes) . .		**22c**	
	23a	2019 estimated tax payments and 2018 overpayment credited to 2019 .	**23a**		
	b	Tax deposited with Form 7004	**23b**		
	c	Credit for federal tax paid on fuels (attach Form 4136) . . .	**23c**		
	d	Refundable credit from Form 8827, line 5c	**23d**		
	e	Add lines 23a through 23d		**23e**	
	24	Estimated tax penalty (see instructions). Check if Form 2220 is attached . . . . ▶ ☐		**24**	
	25	**Amount owed.** If line 23e is smaller than the total of lines 22c and 24, enter amount owed . .		**25**	
	26	**Overpayment.** If line 23e is larger than the total of lines 22c and 24, enter amount overpaid .		**26**	
	27	Enter amount from line 26: **Credited to 2020 estimated tax ▶** _____ **Refunded ▶**		**27**	

Sign Here	Under penalties of perjury, I declare that I have examined this return, including accompanying schedules and statements, and to the best of my knowledge and belief, it is true, correct, and complete. Declaration of preparer (other than taxpayer) is based on all information of which preparer has any knowledge.	May the IRS discuss this return with the preparer shown below? See instructions. ☐ Yes ☐ No
	▶ _____ Signature of officer Date ▶ _____ Title	

Paid Preparer Use Only	Print/Type preparer's name	Preparer's signature	Date	Check ☐ if self-employed	PTIN
	Firm's name ▶			Firm's EIN ▶	
	Firm's address ▶			Phone no.	

For Paperwork Reduction Act Notice, see separate instructions.   Cat. No. 11510H   Form **1120-S** (2019)

Form 1120-S (2019)   Page **2**

Schedule B	**Other Information** (see instructions)				Yes	No

1 Check accounting method: **a** ☐ Cash **b** ☐ Accrual
  c ☐ Other (specify) ▶ _____

2 See the instructions and enter the:
  a Business activity ▶ _____ **b** Product or service ▶ _____

3 At any time during the tax year, was any shareholder of the corporation a disregarded entity, a trust, an estate, or a nominee or similar person? If "Yes," attach Schedule B-1, Information on Certain Shareholders of an S Corporation .

4 At the end of the tax year, did the corporation:

a Own directly 20% or more, or own, directly or indirectly, 50% or more of the total stock issued and outstanding of any foreign or domestic corporation? For rules of constructive ownership, see instructions. If "Yes," complete (i) through (v) below . . . .

(i) Name of Corporation	**(ii)** Employer Identification Number (if any)	**(iii)** Country of Incorporation	**(iv)** Percentage of Stock Owned	**(v)** If Percentage in (iv) Is 100%, Enter the Date (if any) a Qualified Subchapter S Subsidiary Election Was Made

b Own directly an interest of 20% or more, or own, directly or indirectly, an interest of 50% or more in the profit, loss, or capital in any foreign or domestic partnership (including an entity treated as a partnership) or in the beneficial interest of a trust? For rules of constructive ownership, see instructions. If "Yes," complete (i) through (v) below

(i) Name of Entity	**(ii)** Employer Identification Number (if any)	**(iii)** Type of Entity	**(iv)** Country of Organization	**(v)** Maximum Percentage Owned in Profit, Loss, or Capital

5a At the end of the tax year, did the corporation have any outstanding shares of restricted stock? . . . .
  If "Yes," complete lines (i) and (ii) below.
  (i) Total shares of restricted stock . . . . ▶ _____
  (ii) Total shares of non-restricted stock . . . . ▶ _____

b At the end of the tax year, did the corporation have any outstanding stock options, warrants, or similar instruments? .
  If "Yes," complete lines (i) and (ii) below.
  (i) Total shares of stock outstanding at the end of the tax year . ▶ _____
  (ii) Total shares of stock outstanding if all instruments were executed ▶ _____

6 Has this corporation filed, or is it required to file, **Form 8918,** Material Advisor Disclosure Statement, to provide information on any reportable transaction? . . . .

7 Check this box if the corporation issued publicly offered debt instruments with original issue discount . . . . ▶ ☐
  If checked, the corporation may have to file **Form 8281,** Information Return for Publicly Offered Original Issue Discount Instruments.

8 If the corporation **(a)** was a C corporation before it elected to be an S corporation **or** the corporation acquired an asset with a basis determined by reference to the basis of the asset (or the basis of any other property) in the hands of a C corporation **and (b)** has net unrealized built-in gain in excess of the net recognized built-in gain from prior years, enter the net unrealized built-in gain reduced by net recognized built-in gain from prior years. See instructions . . . . . . ▶ $ _____

9 Did the corporation have an election under section 163(j) for any real property trade or business or any farming business in effect during the tax year? See instructions . . . .

10 Does the corporation satisfy one or more of the following? See instructions . . . .

a The corporation owns a pass-through entity with current, or prior year carryover, excess business interest expense.

b The corporation's aggregate average annual gross receipts (determined under section 448(c)) for the 3 tax years preceding the current tax year are more than $26 million and the corporation has business interest expense.

c The corporation is a tax shelter and the corporation has business interest expense.
  If "Yes," complete and attach Form 8990.

11 Does the corporation satisfy **both** of the following conditions? . . . .

a The corporation's total receipts (see instructions) for the tax year were less than $250,000.

b The corporation's total assets at the end of the tax year were less than $250,000.
  If "Yes," the corporation is not required to complete Schedules L and M-1.

Form **1120-S** (2019)

Form 1120-S (2019) Page **3**

Schedule B	Other Information (see instructions) *(continued)*	Yes	No
12	During the tax year, did the corporation have any non-shareholder debt that was canceled, was forgiven, or had the terms modified so as to reduce the principal amount of the debt?		
	If "Yes," enter the amount of principal reduction . . . . ▶ $_____		
13	During the tax year, was a qualified subchapter S subsidiary election terminated or revoked? If "Yes," see instructions .		
14a	Did the corporation make any payments in 2019 that would require it to file Form(s) 1099?		
b	If "Yes," did the corporation file or will it file required Form(s) 1099?		
15	Is the corporation attaching Form 8996 to certify as a Qualified Opportunity Fund?		
	If "Yes," enter the amount from Form 8996, line 14 . . . . ▶ $_____		

Schedule K		Shareholders' Pro Rata Share Items			Total amount
Income (Loss)	1	Ordinary business income (loss) (page 1, line 21)		**1**	
	2	Net rental real estate income (loss) (attach Form 8825)		**2**	
	3a	Other gross rental income (loss)	**3a**		
	b	Expenses from other rental activities (attach statement) . . .	**3b**		
	c	Other net rental income (loss). Subtract line 3b from line 3a		**3c**	
	4	Interest income		**4**	
	5	Dividends: **a** Ordinary dividends		**5a**	
		b Qualified dividends	**5b**		
	6	Royalties		**6**	
	7	Net short-term capital gain (loss) (attach Schedule D (Form 1120-S)) . .		**7**	
	8a	Net long-term capital gain (loss) (attach Schedule D (Form 1120-S)) . .		**8a**	
	b	Collectibles (28%) gain (loss)	**8b**		
	c	Unrecaptured section 1250 gain (attach statement) . . .	**8c**		
	9	Net section 1231 gain (loss) (attach Form 4797)		**9**	
	10	Other income (loss) (see instructions) . . . Type ▶		**10**	
Deductions	11	Section 179 deduction (attach Form 4562)		**11**	
	12a	Charitable contributions		**12a**	
	b	Investment interest expense . . . . b		**12b**	
	c	Section 59(e)(2) expenditures **(1)** Type ▶ _____ **(2)** Amount ▶		**12c(2)**	
	d	Other deductions (see instructions) . . . . Type ▶		**12d**	
Credits	13a	Low-income housing credit (section 42(j)(5))		**13a**	
	b	Low-income housing credit (other)		**13b**	
	c	Qualified rehabilitation expenditures (rental real estate) (attach Form 3468, if applicable) . .		**13c**	
	d	Other rental real estate credits (see instructions) Type ▶		**13d**	
	e	Other rental credits (see instructions) . . . Type ▶		**13e**	
	f	Biofuel producer credit (attach Form 6478)		**13f**	
	g	Other credits (see instructions) . . . . . Type ▶		**13g**	
Foreign Transactions	14a	Name of country or U.S. possession ▶ _____			
	b	Gross income from all sources		**14b**	
	c	Gross income sourced at shareholder level		**14c**	
		Foreign gross income sourced at corporate level			
	d	Reserved for future use		**14d**	
	e	Foreign branch category		**14e**	
	f	Passive category		**14f**	
	g	General category		**14g**	
	h	Other (attach statement)		**14h**	
		Deductions allocated and apportioned at shareholder level			
	i	Interest expense		**14i**	
	j	Other		**14j**	
		Deductions allocated and apportioned at corporate level to foreign source income			
	k	Reserved for future use		**14k**	
	l	Foreign branch category		**14l**	
	m	Passive category		**14m**	
	n	General category		**14n**	
	o	Other (attach statement)		**14o**	
		Other information			
	p	Total foreign taxes (check one): ☐ Paid ☐ Accrued . . . . ▶		**14p**	
	q	Reduction in taxes available for credit (attach statement)		**14q**	
	r	Other foreign tax information (attach statement)			

Form **1120-S** (2019)

Form 1120-S (2019)   Page **4**

Schedule K		Shareholders' Pro Rata Share Items *(continued)*		Total amount

Alternative Minimum Tax (AMT) Items

	15a	Post-1986 depreciation adjustment	15a	
	b	Adjusted gain or loss	15b	
	c	Depletion (other than oil and gas)	15c	
	d	Oil, gas, and geothermal properties—gross income	15d	
	e	Oil, gas, and geothermal properties—deductions	15e	
	f	Other AMT items (attach statement)	15f	

Items Affecting Shareholder Basis

	16a	Tax-exempt interest income	16a	
	b	Other tax-exempt income	16b	
	c	Nondeductible expenses	16c	
	d	Distributions (attach statement if required) (see instructions)	16d	
	e	Repayment of loans from shareholders	16e	

Other Information

	17a	Investment income	17a	
	b	Investment expenses	17b	
	c	Dividend distributions paid from accumulated earnings and profits . . .	17c	
	d	Other items and amounts (attach statement)		

Reconciliation

	18	**Income (loss) reconciliation.** Combine the amounts on lines 1 through 10 in the far right column. From the result, subtract the sum of the amounts on lines 11 through 12d and 14p .	18	

Schedule L		Balance Sheets per Books	Beginning of tax year		End of tax year	
		Assets	(a)	(b)	(c)	(d)
1		Cash				
2a		Trade notes and accounts receivable . .				
b		Less allowance for bad debts	( )		( )	
3		Inventories				
4		U.S. government obligations				
5		Tax-exempt securities (see instructions) . .				
6		Other current assets (attach statement) . . .				
7		Loans to shareholders				
8		Mortgage and real estate loans				
9		Other investments (attach statement) . . .				
10a		Buildings and other depreciable assets . . .				
b		Less accumulated depreciation	( )		( )	
11a		Depletable assets				
b		Less accumulated depletion	( )		( )	
12		Land (net of any amortization)				
13a		Intangible assets (amortizable only) . . .				
b		Less accumulated amortization	( )		( )	
14		Other assets (attach statement)				
15		Total assets				
		Liabilities and Shareholders' Equity				
16		Accounts payable				
17		Mortgages, notes, bonds payable in less than 1 year				
18		Other current liabilities (attach statement) . .				
19		Loans from shareholders				
20		Mortgages, notes, bonds payable in 1 year or more				
21		Other liabilities (attach statement)				
22		Capital stock				
23		Additional paid-in capital				
24		Retained earnings				
25		Adjustments to shareholders' equity (attach statement)				
26		Less cost of treasury stock		( )		( )
27		Total liabilities and shareholders' equity . .				

Form **1120-S** (2019)

Form 1120-S (2019)   Page **5**

Schedule M-1   Reconciliation of Income (Loss) per Books With Income (Loss) per Return

Note: The corporation may be required to file Schedule M-3. See instructions.

1	Net income (loss) per books	
2	Income included on Schedule K, lines 1, 2, 3c, 4, 5a, 6, 7, 8a, 9, and 10, not recorded on books this year (itemize) _____	
3	Expenses recorded on books this year not included on Schedule K, lines 1 through 12 and 14p (itemize):	
a	Depreciation $ _____	
b	Travel and entertainment $ _____	
4	Add lines 1 through 3	

5	Income recorded on books this year not included on Schedule K, lines 1 through 10 (itemize):	
a	Tax-exempt interest $ _____	
6	Deductions included on Schedule K, lines 1 through 12 and 14p, not charged against book income this year (itemize):	
a	Depreciation $ _____	
7	Add lines 5 and 6	
8	Income (loss) (Schedule K, line 18). Subtract line 7 from line 4	

Schedule M-2   Analysis of Accumulated Adjustments Account, Shareholders' Undistributed Taxable Income Previously Taxed, Accumulated Earnings and Profits, and Other Adjustments Account

(see instructions)

		(a) Accumulated adjustments account	**(b)** Shareholders' undistributed taxable income previously taxed	**(c)** Accumulated earnings and profits	**(d)** Other adjustments account
1	Balance at beginning of tax year				
2	Ordinary income from page 1, line 21 . .				
3	Other additions				
4	Loss from page 1, line 21	( )			
5	Other reductions	( )			( )
6	Combine lines 1 through 5				
7	Distributions				
8	Balance at end of tax year. Subtract line 7 from line 6				

Form **1120-S** (2019)

Self-Study Problem 11.6

671119

☐ Final K-1   ☐ Amended K-1   OMB No. 1545-0123

Schedule K-1
(Form 1120-S)
Department of the Treasury
Internal Revenue Service

20**19**

For calendar year 2019, or tax year

beginning / / 2019 ending / /

Shareholder's Share of Income, Deductions, Credits, etc.   ► See back of form and separate instructions.

Part III	Shareholder's Share of Current Year Income, Deductions, Credits, and Other Items

Part I **Information About the Corporation**			
A Corporation's employer identification number	**1** Ordinary business income (loss)	**13** Credits	
	2 Net rental real estate income (loss)		
B Corporation's name, address, city, state, and ZIP code	**3** Other net rental income (loss)		
	4 Interest income		
	5a Ordinary dividends		
	5b Qualified dividends	**14** Foreign transactions	
	6 Royalties		
	7 Net short-term capital gain (loss)		
C IRS Center where corporation filed return	**8a** Net long-term capital gain (loss)		
	8b Collectibles (28%) gain (loss)		
Part II **Information About the Shareholder**	**8c** Unrecaptured section 1250 gain		
D Shareholder's identifying number	**9** Net section 1231 gain (loss)		
E Shareholder's name, address, city, state, and ZIP code	**10** Other income (loss)	**15** Alternative minimum tax (AMT) items	
F Shareholder's percentage of stock ownership for tax year . . . . _____ %	**11** Section 179 deduction	**16** Items affecting shareholder basis	
	12 Other deductions		
		17 Other information	
	18 ☐ More than one activity for at-risk purposes*		
	19 ☐ More than one activity for passive activity purposes*		

For IRS Use Only

* See attached statement for additional information.

For Paperwork Reduction Act Notice, see the Instructions for Form 1120-S.   www.irs.gov/Form1120S   Cat. No. 11520D   **Schedule K-1 (Form 1120-S) 2019**

Schedule K-1 (Form 1120-S) 2019   Page **2**

This list identifies the codes used on Schedule K-1 for all shareholders and provides summarized reporting information for shareholders who file Form 1040 or 1040-SR. For detailed reporting and filing information, see the separate Shareholder's Instructions for Schedule K-1 and the instructions for your income tax return.

1. **Ordinary business income (loss).** Determine whether the income (loss) is passive or nonpassive and enter on your return as follows:

	Report on
Passive loss	See the Shareholder's Instructions
Passive income	Schedule E, line 28, column (h)
Nonpassive loss	See the Shareholder's Instructions
Nonpassive income	Schedule E, line 28, column (k)

2. **Net rental real estate income (loss)**   See the Shareholder's Instructions
3. **Other net rental income (loss)**
   - Net income   Schedule E, line 28, column (h)
   - Net loss   See the Shareholder's Instructions
4. **Interest income**   Form 1040 or 1040-SR, line 2b
5a. **Ordinary dividends**   Form 1040 or 1040-SR, line 3b
5b. **Qualified dividends**   Form 1040 or 1040-SR, line 3a
6. **Royalties**   Schedule E, line 4
7. **Net short-term capital gain (loss)**   Schedule D, line 5
8a. **Net long-term capital gain (loss)**   Schedule D, line 12
8b. **Collectibles (28%) gain (loss)**   28% Rate Gain Worksheet, line 4 (Schedule D instructions)
8c. **Unrecaptured section 1250 gain**   See the Shareholder's Instructions
9. **Net section 1231 gain (loss)**   See the Shareholder's Instructions
10. **Other income (loss)**
   Code
   - A   Other portfolio income (loss)   See the Shareholder's Instructions
   - B   Involuntary conversions   See the Shareholder's Instructions
   - C   Sec. 1256 contracts & straddles   Form 6781, line 1
   - D   Mining exploration costs recapture   See Pub. 535
   - E   Reserved for future use
   - F   Section 965(a) inclusion
   - G   Income under subpart F (other than inclusions under sections 951A and 965)   } See the Shareholder's Instructions
   - H   Other income (loss)
11. **Section 179 deduction**   See the Shareholder's Instructions
12. **Other deductions**
   - A   Cash contributions (60%)
   - B   Cash contributions (30%)
   - C   Noncash contributions (50%)
   - D   Noncash contributions (30%)
   - E   Capital gain property to a 50% organization (30%)   } See the Shareholder's Instructions
   - F   Capital gain property (20%)
   - G   Contributions (100%)
   - H   Investment interest expense   Form 4952, line 1
   - I   Deductions—royalty income   Schedule E, line 19
   - J   Section 59(e)(2) expenditures   See the Shareholder's Instructions
   - K   Section 965(c) deduction   See the Shareholder's Instructions
   - L   Deductions—portfolio (other)   Schedule A, line 16
   - M   Preproductive period expenses   See the Shareholder's Instructions
   - N   Commercial revitalization deduction from rental real estate activities   See Form 8582 instructions
   - O   Reforestation expense deduction   See the Shareholder's Instructions
   - P   through **R**   Reserved for future use
   - S   Other deductions   See the Shareholder's Instructions
13. **Credits**
   - A   Low-income housing credit (section 42(j)(5)) from pre-2008 buildings
   - B   Low-income housing credit (other) from pre-2008 buildings
   - C   Low-income housing credit (section 42(j)(5)) from post-2007 buildings
   - D   Low-income housing credit (other) from post-2007 buildings   } See the Shareholder's Instructions
   - E   Qualified rehabilitation expenditures (rental real estate)
   - F   Other rental real estate credits
   - G   Other rental credits
   - H   Undistributed capital gains credit   Schedule 3 (Form 1040 or 1040-SR), line 13, box a
   - I   Biofuel producer credit
   - J   Work opportunity credit
   - K   Disabled access credit   } See the Shareholder's Instructions
   - L   Empowerment zone employment credit
   - M   Credit for increasing research activities

	Code		Report on
	N	Credit for employer social security and Medicare taxes	} See the Shareholder's Instructions
	O	Backup withholding	
	P	Other credits	

14. **Foreign transactions**
   - A   Name of country or U.S. possession
   - B   Gross income from all sources   } Form 1116, Part I
   - C   Gross income sourced at shareholder level

   Foreign gross income sourced at corporate level
   - D   Reserved for future use
   - E   Foreign branch category
   - F   Passive category   } Form 1116, Part I
   - G   General category
   - H   Other

   Deductions allocated and apportioned at shareholder level
   - I   Interest expense   Form 1116, Part I
   - J   Other   Form 1116, Part I

   Deductions allocated and apportioned at corporate level to foreign source income
   - K   Reserved for future use
   - L   Foreign branch category
   - M   Passive category   } Form 1116, Part I
   - N   General category
   - O   Other

   Other information
   - P   Total foreign taxes paid   Form 1116, Part II
   - Q   Total foreign taxes accrued   Form 1116, Part II
   - R   Reduction in taxes available for credit   Form 1116, line 12
   - S   Foreign trading gross receipts   Form 8873
   - T   Extraterritorial income exclusion   Form 8873
   - U   Section 965 information   See the Shareholder's Instructions
   - V   Other foreign transactions   See the Shareholder's Instructions
15. **Alternative minimum tax (AMT) items**
   - A   Post-1986 depreciation adjustment
   - B   Adjusted gain or loss
   - C   Depletion (other than oil & gas)   See the Shareholder's Instructions and the Instructions for Form 6251
   - D   Oil, gas, & geothermal—gross income
   - E   Oil, gas, & geothermal—deductions
   - F   Other AMT items
16. **Items affecting shareholder basis**
   - A   Tax-exempt interest income   Form 1040 or 1040-SR, line 2a
   - B   Other tax-exempt income
   - C   Nondeductible expenses
   - D   Distributions   } See the Shareholder's Instructions
   - E   Repayment of loans from shareholders
17. **Other information**
   - A   Investment income   Form 4952, line 4a
   - B   Investment expenses   Form 4952, line 5
   - C   Qualified rehabilitation expenditures (other than rental real estate)   See the Shareholder's Instructions
   - D   Basis of energy property   See the Shareholder's Instructions
   - E   Recapture of low-income housing credit (section 42(j)(5))   Form 8611, line 8
   - F   Recapture of low-income housing credit (other)   Form 8611, line 8
   - G   Recapture of investment credit   See Form 4255
   - H   Recapture of other credits   See the Shareholder's Instructions
   - I   Look-back interest—completed long-term contracts   See Form 8697
   - J   Look-back interest—income forecast method   See Form 8866
   - K   Dispositions of property with section 179 deductions
   - L   Recapture of section 179 deduction   See the Shareholder's Instructions
   - M   through **U**
   - V   Section 199A information
   - W   through **Z**   Reserved for future use
   - AA   Excess taxable income
   - AB   Excess business interest income   } See the Shareholder's Instructions
   - AC   Other information

89 percent (85 of 95 shares) of the stock after the transfer. B's stock is not considered because it was received in exchange for services.

1. A has a realized gain of $15,000 ($40,000 − $25,000), but no recognized gain since no boot was received.
2. B's recognized income is $10,000, since she performed services in exchange for the stock, and stock received for services does not fall within the nonrecognition provisions.
3. C's realized gain is $40,000 ($45,000 + $5,000 − $10,000), but only $5,000 of the gain is recognized, the amount of boot received.
4. A's basis in the stock is $25,000 ($25,000 − $0 + $0 − $0), B's basis in the stock is $10,000 ($0 − $0 + $10,000 − $0), and C's basis in the stock is $10,000 ($10,000 − $5,000 + $5,000 − $0).
5. Hornbeam Corporation's basis in the property contributed by A is $25,000 ($25,000 + $0). The corporation's basis in the property contributed by C is $15,000 ($10,000 + $5,000 gain recognized). ◆

Self-Study Problem 11.7 *See Appendix E for Solutions to Self-Study Problems*

Tammy has a business which she decides to incorporate. She transfers to the new corporation, real estate with a basis of $75,000 and subject to a $34,000 mortgage in exchange for all of its stock. The stock is worth $125,000.

What is Tammy's realized gain?	$_____
What is Tammy's recognized gain?	$_____
What is Tammy's basis in her stock?	$_____
What is the corporation's basis in the real estate?	$_____

11-8 CORPORATE ACCUMULATIONS

In many cases, taxpayers have established corporations to avoid paying income taxes at the shareholder level by allowing earnings to be accumulated by the corporations, rather than paid out as taxable dividends. To prevent that practice, Congress has enacted two special taxes which may be applied to certain corporations: the accumulated earnings tax and the personal holding company tax.

The TCJA made no direct changes to the accumulated earnings tax or the personal holding company tax; however, the significant decrease in the corporate tax rate makes deferring income without distributing the earnings and profits of a corporation considerably more attractive from a tax planning perspective. Undoubtedly, this will increase both the use of this strategy and the IRS' sensitivity to this matter.

New Tax! Law

11-8a Accumulated Earnings Tax

The accumulated earnings tax is designed to prevent the shareholders of a corporation from avoiding tax at the shareholder level by retaining earnings in the corporation. The tax is a penalty tax imposed in addition to the regular corporate income tax. The tax is imposed at a rate of 20 percent on amounts that are deemed to be unreasonable accumulations of earnings. For all corporations except service corporations, such as accounting, law, and health care corporations, the first $250,000 in accumulated earnings is exempt from tax. Service corporations will not be taxed on their first $150,000 of accumulated earnings. Even if the accumulated earnings of a corporation exceed the exemption amount, the tax will not be imposed on accumulations that can be shown to be necessary to meet the reasonable needs of the business.

EXAMPLE   Alder Corporation is a manufacturing corporation that has accumulated earnings of $625,000. The corporation can establish reasonable needs for $450,000 of this accumulation. Alder Corporation would be subject to the accumulated earnings tax on $175,000 ($625,000 − $450,000). The amount of the accumulated earnings tax is $35,000 (20% of $175,000). ♦

11-8b **Personal Holding Company Tax**

Personal holding companies, which are corporations with few shareholders and with income primarily from investments, are subject to a 20 percent tax on their undistributed earnings. The tax is imposed in addition to the regular corporate income tax; however, a corporation cannot be subject to both the accumulated earnings tax and the personal holding company tax in the same year. If both taxes are imposed, the taxpayer pays only the personal holding company tax. The rules for the personal holding company tax are very complex.

Self-Study Problem 11.8   *See Appendix E for Solutions to Self-Study Problems*

Sugarbush Corporation, an accounting corporation, has accumulated earnings of $340,000, and the corporation cannot establish a reasonable need for any of that amount. Calculate the amount of accumulated earnings tax (if any) that will be imposed on Sugarbush Corporation.

$_____

Learning Objective 11.9

11-9 **THE CORPORATE ALTERNATIVE MINIMUM TAX**

Describe tax issues associated with the repeal of the alternative minimum tax.

Unlike the individual alternative minimum tax (AMT), which remains in force, the corporate AMT was repealed for tax years after 2017 by the TCJA. Under the prior corporate AMT regime, a corporation subject to AMT may have had unused AMT credits that can be carried over indefinitely to offset regular tax. Although beyond the scope of this textbook, under the TCJA, AMT credits may offset regular tax liability for any future tax year. Additionally, the AMT credit is a refundable credit for any tax year beginning after 2017 and before 2022 in an amount equal to 50 percent (100 percent for tax years beginning in 2021) of the excess AMT credits for the tax year, over the amount of the credit allowable for the year against regular tax liability.

EXAMPLE   Lloyd Corporation, a calendar year C corporation, has unused AMT credits of $10,000 at the end 2017. In 2018, Lloyd has corporate income tax liability as $2,000 before any AMT credits. Lloyd may apply $2,000 of its AMT credit carryforward to reduce the 2018 income tax to $0. In addition, Lloyd is permitted to apply a refundable AMT credit of $4,000 (($10,000 − $2,000) × 50%). ♦

Self-Study Problem 11.9   *See Appendix E for Solutions to Self-Study Problems*

In 2019, Plum Corporation has regular income tax liability of $12,500. Plum has AMT credit carryforwards of $20,000 from prior years. What is Plum Corporation's remaining AMT credit carryforward after applying the maximum credit against 2019?

$_____

KEY TERMS

corporate tax rates, 11-2
personal service corporation, 11-2
corporate capital gains and
    losses, 11-2
net operating losses, 11-3
special deductions, 11-4
dividends received deduction, 11-4
organizational expenditures, 11-5
start-up costs, 11-5
corporate charitable contributions
    deduction, 11-5

Form 1120, 11-6
Schedule M-1, 11-6
book income, 11-6
Schedule L (Balance Sheet), 11-7
S Corporation, 11-15
statutorily terminated, 11-15
Form 1120S, 11-15
Schedule K-1, 11-16
pass-through items, 11-16
built-in gains tax, 11-17
nonrecognition treatment, 11-18

boot, 11-18
stock basis, 11-18
corporation's basis, 11-18
accumulated earnings tax, 11-27
personal holding company
    tax, 11-28
corporate alternative minimum
    tax, 11-28

KEY POINTS

Learning Objectives	Key Points
LO 11.1: Employ the corporate tax rates to calculate corporate tax liability.	• The U.S. corporate tax rate is now a flat 21 percent regardless of income level. • Qualified personal service corporations (health, law, engineering, architecture, accounting, actuarial science, performing arts, and consulting) are taxed at a flat 21 percent tax rate on all taxable income.
LO 11.2: Compute basic gains and losses for corporations.	• Corporate ordinary income and capital gains tax rates are the same, so there is no tax rate benefit to having long-term capital gains in a corporation. • Net short-term capital gains of a corporation are taxed as ordinary income. • Capital losses may be used only to offset capital gains. • If capital losses cannot be used in the year they occur, they may be carried back 3 years and forward 5 years to offset capital gains in those years. • When a long-term capital loss is carried to another year, it is treated as a short-term capital loss and may be offset against either long-term or short-term capital gains. • Net operating losses generated after 2017 may only be carried forward to offset no more than 80 percent of the taxable income of the future year.
LO 11.3: Apply special corporate deductions to corporate taxable income.	• Corporations are allowed a dividends received deduction based on their percentage of ownership in the corporation paying the dividend. • The dividends received deduction percentage is 50 percent (for ownership less than 20 percent), 65 percent (for ownership of 20 percent or more, but less than 80 percent), or 100 percent (for ownership of 80 percent or more). • Corporations amortize qualifying organizational costs over 180 months, and there is no upper limit to the amount of qualifying costs that can be amortized.

- Corporations can elect to deduct up to $5,000 of organizational costs and $5,000 of start-up costs in the year they begin business. The $5,000 amounts are reduced by each dollar of organizational expenses and start-up costs exceeding $50,000.
- A corporation's charitable contribution deduction is limited to 10 percent of taxable income, computed before the deduction for charitable contributions, net operating loss carrybacks, capital loss carrybacks, and the dividends received deduction.
- Excess charitable contributions are carried forward to the 5 succeeding tax years, subject to the 10 percent annual limitation in the carryover years, with the current year's contributions deducted first.

LO 11.4:

Identify the components of Schedule M-1 and how they are reported to the IRS.

- The purpose of Schedule M-1 of the corporate tax return is to reconcile a corporation's accounting "book" income to its taxable income.
- On the left side of Schedule M-1 are adjustments that must be added to book income, and on the right side of the schedule are adjustments that must be subtracted from book income to arrive at the amount of taxable income.
- The additions to book income include the amount of federal income tax expense, net capital losses deducted for book purposes, income recorded on the tax return but not on the books, and expenses recorded on the books but not deducted on the tax return.
- The amounts that must be deducted from book income include income recorded on the books but not included on the tax return, and deductions included on the return but not deducted on the books.

LO 11.5:

Describe the corporate tax return filing and estimated tax payment requirements.

- The due date for filing a corporate tax return is the fifteenth day of the fourth month after year-end. An extension provides an additional 6 months; thus a calendar year-end corporation has an initial deadline of April 15 and an extended deadline of October 15.
- A corporation must pay any tax liability by the original due date of the return.
- Corporations must make estimated tax payments similar to those made by self-employed individual taxpayers. The payments are due on the fifteenth day of the fourth, sixth, ninth, and twelfth months of the corporation's tax year.

LO 11.6:

Explain how an S corporation operates and is taxed.

- Certain qualified corporations may elect to be taxed under Subchapter S of the Internal Revenue Code in a manner similar to partnerships.
- To elect S corporation status, a corporation *must* have the following characteristics: (1) be a domestic corporation; (2) have 100 or fewer shareholders who are either individuals, estates, certain trusts, certain financial institutions, or certain exempt organizations; (3) have only one class of stock; and (4) all shareholders must be U.S. citizens or resident aliens.
- Each shareholder of an S corporation reports his or her share of corporate income based on his or her stock ownership during the year.
- Schedule K-1 of Form 1120S is used to report the allocation of ordinary income or loss, and all separately stated items of income or loss, to each of the shareholders.
- Losses from an S corporation pass through to the shareholders, but the loss deduction is limited to the shareholders' adjusted basis in the corporation's stock plus the amount of any loans from the shareholder to the corporation.
- S corporation shareholders are eligible for the qualified business income deduction.

LO 11.7:

Describe the basic tax rules for the formation of a corporation.

- If property is exchanged for stock in a corporation, the shareholders are in "control" of the corporation after the transfer, and the shareholders receive no boot, gain on the transfer is not recognized.
- Realized gain is recognized to the extent that the shareholder receives boot.
- The basis of the stock received by the shareholder is equal to the basis of the property transferred plus any gain recognized by the shareholder, less the fair market value of any boot received by the shareholder, less liabilities assumed by the corporation.
- The basis of property received by the corporation is equal to the basis in the hands of the transferor plus any gain recognized by the transferor.

LO 11.8:

Describe the rules for the accumulated earnings tax and the personal holding company tax.

- The accumulated earnings tax is a penalty tax, imposed in addition to the regular corporate income tax, at a rate of 20 percent on amounts that are deemed to be unreasonable accumulations of earnings.
- For all corporations, except personal service corporations such as accounting, law, and health care corporations, the first $250,000 in accumulated earnings is exempt from tax. The first $150,000 in accumulated earnings is exempt for personal service corporations.
- Personal holding companies, which are corporations with few shareholders and income primarily from investments, are subject to a 20 percent tax on undistributed earnings.

LO 11.9:

Describe tax issues associated with the repeal of the alternative minimum tax.

- The corporate AMT was repealed for tax years after 2017.
- Any AMT credit carryforwards may be used to offset regular tax liability and are refundable up to 50 percent (100 percent for tax years beginning in 2021) of the remaining unused AMT credit carryforward amount.

QUESTIONS and PROBLEMS

GROUP 1:
MULTIPLE CHOICE QUESTIONS

LO 11.1

1. Ironwood Corporation has ordinary taxable income of $65,000 in 2019, and a short-term capital loss of $15,000. What is the corporation's tax liability for 2019?
   a. $7,500
   b. $5,250
   c. $10,500
   d. $13,650
   e. None of the above

LO 11.1

2. Tayla Corporation generated $400,000 of taxable income in the 2019. What is Tayla's corporate tax liability?
   a. $71,400
   b. $84,000
   c. $115,600
   d. $0
   e. None of the above

LO 11.2

3. Which of the following statements is *false* regarding corporate capital losses?
   a. Corporations may deduct $3,000 of net capital loss each year until the loss is used up.
   b. Corporations may carry capital losses back 3 years and forward 5 years to offset capital gains in those years.
   c. Corporations are not allowed to deduct capital losses against ordinary income.
   d. A long-term capital loss carried to another year is treated as a short-term capital loss.

LO 11.2

4. Harrison Corporation generates capital gains/(losses) of $30,000, $2,000, ($40,000) in 2017, 2018, and 2019, respectively. Harrison started operating in 2017. What is Harrison's capital loss carryforward into 2020?
   a. $0
   b. $8,000
   c. $10,000
   d. $38,000
   e. None of the above

LO 11.2

5. Mask Corporation generated a net operating loss of $24,000 in 2019 and taxable income of $10,000 in 2020. How much NOL can Mask use in 2020 to reduce taxable income?
   a. $8,000
   b. $10,000
   c. $19,200
   d. $24,000

LO 11.3

6. Walnut Corporation owns 6 percent of Teak Corporation, a domestic corporation. During the current year, Walnut Corporation received $20,000 in dividends from Teak Corporation. Assuming that Walnut's taxable income for the current year before the dividends received deduction is $500,000, what is the amount of Walnut's dividends received deduction for the current year?
   a. $10,000
   b. $13,000
   c. $16,000
   d. $20,000
   e. None of the above

LO 11.3

7. Which of the following is *not* a corporate organizational expenditure that may be amortized?
   a. The cost of organizational meetings
   b. Fees paid to the state for incorporation
   c. Accounting fees incident to organization
   d. Legal fees incident to organization
   e. All of the above are organizational expenditures

LO 11.4

8. The purpose of Schedule M-1 on the corporate tax return is to:
   a. Reconcile accounting (book) income to taxable income.
   b. Summarize the dividends received deduction calculation.
   c. List the officers of the corporation and their compensation.
   d. Calculate the net operating loss deduction.

LO 11.4

9. Which of the following would not generally appear on the M-1 reconciliation?
   a. Federal income tax expense per books
   b. Tax-exempt interest income
   c. Excess tax over book depreciation
   d. Dividends received deduction

LO 11.5

10. Which of the following statements is *false* regarding corporate tax return due dates?
    a. Corporate tax returns for 2019 calendar-year corporations are due April 15, 2020.
    b. Corporate tax returns may receive an automatic 6-month extension.
    c. Corporate taxes due must be paid no later than the extended due date of the tax return.
    d. When an IRS due date falls on a weekend or holiday, the due date is the next business day.

LO 11.5

11. Mansfield Incorporated, a calendar year corporation, is expecting to have a current year tax liability of $100,000. Which best describes the tax payments Mansfield should make to avoid penalty?
    a. Make payments at the end of June and December of $40,000 each and $20,000 when filing the return on the original due date.
    b. Make no payments during the year but pay the entire balance on the extended due date.
    c. Make no payments during the year but pay the entire balance on the original due date.
    d. Make quarterly payments totaling $100,000, all during the current year.
    e. None of these will avoid penalty.

LO 11.6 12. Which of the following is *not* required for a corporation to be eligible to make an S corporation election?
   a. The corporation must have 100 or fewer shareholders.
   b. The corporation must be a domestic corporation.
   c. The corporation must have both common and preferred stock.
   d. The shareholders of the corporation must not be nonresident aliens.
   e. All shareholders must be either individuals, estates, certain trusts, or financial institutions.

LO 11.6 13. Which of the following items are passed through and separately stated on Schedule K-1 to shareholders of an S corporation?
   a. Wages paid
   b. Typical MACRS depreciation
   c. Net long-term capital gains
   d. Advertising expense
   e. All of the above retain their character when passed through

LO 11.6 14. Which of the following is *true* about S corporations?
   a. S corporations pay corporate taxes like other corporations.
   b. S corporations pay the alternative minimum tax for all income.
   c. S corporations cannot issue corporate stock.
   d. The S corporation status may be elected by stockholders only for corporations that meet certain qualifications.
   e. None of the above.

LO 11.7 15. Travis transfers land with a fair market value of $125,000 and basis of $25,000, to a corporation in exchange for 100 percent of the corporation's stock. What amount of gain must Travis recognize as a result of this transaction?
   a. $0   d. $125,000
   b. $25,000   e. None of the above
   c. $100,000

LO 11.7 16. Carl transfers land with a fair market value of $120,000 and basis of $30,000, to a new corporation in exchange for 85 percent of the corporation's stock. The land is subject to a $45,000 liability, which the corporation assumes. What amount of gain must Carl recognize as a result of this transaction?
   a. $0
   b. $15,000
   c. $30,000
   d. $45,000
   e. None of the above

LO 11.7 17. What is the shareholder's basis in stock of a corporation received as a result of the transfer of property to the corporation and as a result of which gain was recognized by the stockholder?
   a. The shareholder's basis is equal to the basis of the property transferred less the gain.
   b. The shareholder's basis is equal to the fair market value of the stock received, less any liabilities transferred by the stockholder.
   c. The shareholder's basis is equal to the basis of the property transferred to the corporation, minus any liabilities transferred by the shareholder, plus the gain.
   d. The shareholder's basis is equal to the basis of the property transferred to the corporation, plus any liabilities transferred by the shareholder.
   e. None of the above.

LO 11.8 18. Which of the following statements regarding personal holding companies is *false*?
   a. A personal holding company is one which has few shareholders.
   b. A personal holding company has income primarily from investments.
   c. A personal holding company operates a business which is a hobby for its owners.
   d. Personal holding companies are subject to a 20 percent tax on income that is left undistributed.

LO 11.8

19. Boyce Industries, a manufacturing corporation, has accumulated earnings of $325,000 and cannot show any reasonable need for the accumulated earnings. What is Boyce's accumulated earnings tax?
    a. $15,000
    b. $0
    c. $13,750
    d. $75,000

LO 11.9

20. Which of the following statements is *true* about the 2019 corporate alternative minimum tax?
    a. The corporate alternative minimum tax only applies to small corporations.
    b. The corporate alternative minimum tax preferences and adjustments are exactly the same as those for individuals.
    c. The corporate alternative minimum tax was repealed for tax years after 2017.
    d. Corporations with alternative minimum taxable income greater than $310,000 receive no exemption.

LO 11.9

21. Any corporate AMT credit carryovers that existed at the end of 2017:
    a. can be used to offset tax liability generated in 2018 and thereafter
    b. do not expire
    c. can generate a refundable credit of 50 percent of any unused AMT credits in 2019
    d. all of the above

GROUP 2:
PROBLEMS

LO 11.1

1. Quince Corporation has taxable income of $485,000 for its calendar tax year. Calculate the corporation's income tax liability for 2019 before tax credits.

    $ _____

LO 11.1

2. Ulmus Corporation is an engineering consulting firm and has $1,120,000 in taxable income for 2019. Calculate the corporation's income tax liability for 2019.

    $ _____

LO 11.1
LO 11.2

3. For its current tax year, Ilex Corporation has ordinary income of $260,000, a short-term capital loss of $60,000, and a long-term capital gain of $20,000. Calculate Ilex Corporation's tax liability for 2019.

    $ _____

LO 11.2

4. DeMaria Corporation, a calendar year corporation, generates the following taxable income (net operating losses) since its inception in 2016:

Year	Taxable result
2016	40,000
2017	(15,000)
2018	(5,000)
2019	6,000

    Assuming Demaria makes no special elections with regard to NOLs, what is DeMaria's net operating loss carryforward into 2020?

LO 11.3

5. Fisafolia Corporation has gross income from operations of $210,000 and operating expenses of $160,000 for 2019. The corporation also has $30,000 in dividends from publicly traded domestic corporations in which the ownership percentage was 45 percent.
    a. Calculate the corporation's dividends received deduction for 2019.

    $ _____

b. Assume that instead of $210,000, Fisafolia Corporation has gross income from operations of $135,000. Calculate the corporation's dividends received deduction for 2019.

$ _____

c. Assume that instead of $210,000, Fisafolia Corporation has gross income from operations of $158,000. Calculate the corporation's dividends received deduction for 2019.

$_____

LO 11.3

6. Beech Corporation, an accrual basis calendar year taxpayer, was organized and began business on July of the current calendar tax year. During the current year, the corporation incurred the following expenses:

State fees for incorporation	$ 500
Legal and accounting fees incident to organization	4,150
Expenses for the sale of stock	2,100
Organizational meeting expenses	750

Assuming that Beech Corporation does not elect to expense but chooses to amortize organizational expenditures over 15 years, calculate the corporation's deduction for its current calendar tax year.

$ _____

LO 11.3

7. In Year 1, Citradoria Corporation is a regular corporation that contributes $35,000 cash to qualified charitable organizations during the current tax year. The corporation has net operating income of $145,000, before deducting the contributions, and dividends received from domestic corporations (ownership in all corporations is less than 20 percent) in the amount of $25,000.

a. What is the amount of Citradoria Corporation's allowable deduction for charitable contributions for Year 1?

$ _____

b. In Year 2, Citradoria contributes $5,000 to charitable organizations. The corporation has net operating income of $150,000 before deducting the contributions, and no dividend income. What is the amount of Citradoria's allowable deduction for charitable contributions for Year 2?

$ _____

c. If there is any carryover of the charitable contribution deduction from Year 2, what year will it expire (e.g., Year 3)?

$ _____

LO 11.4

8. The Loquat Corporation has book net income of $50,000 for the current year. Included in this figure are the following items, which are reported on the corporation's Schedule M-1, Reconciliation of Income (Loss) per Books with Income per Return.

Federal income tax expense	$ 7,500
Depreciation deducted on the books which is not deductible for tax purposes	10,000
Deduction for 50 percent of meals expense which is not allowed for tax purposes	5,500
Deduction for a tax penalty not allowed for tax purposes	2,000
Tax-exempt interest income included in book income but not in tax income	4,200

Calculate Loquat Corporation's taxable income for the current year based on the information given. Show your calculations.

$ _____

LO 11.4

9. Caloundra Corporation has book income of $40,000. Included in the book income is $3,000 of tax-exempt interest, $7,000 of book income tax expense, and a $2,000 non-deductible fine. Also included in book income are $10,000 of dividends Caloundra received from a 30 percent owned corporation. Using this information and Form 1120, provide the amounts that go on each line on the form.
   a. Form 1120, Schedule M-1 Line 1 $ _____
   b. Form 1120, Schedule M-1, Line 10 $ _____
   c. Form 1120, Page 1, Line 28 $ _____
   d. Form 1120, Schedule C, Line 2(a) $ _____ and 2(c) $ _____
   e. Form 1120, Schedule C, Line 24 $ _____
   f. Form 1120, Page 1, Line 29b $ _____
   g. Form 1120, Page 1, Line 30 $ _____

LO 11.5

10. Mallory Corporation has a calendar year-end. The corporation has paid estimated taxes of $10,000 during 2019 but still owes an additional $5,000 for its 2019 tax year.
   a. When is the 2019 tax return due?

   _____

   b. If an automatic extension of time to file is requested, when is the 2019 tax return due?

   _____

   c. If an extension of time to file is requested, when is the additional $5,000 of tax for 2019 due?

   _____

LO 11.6

11. Cedar Corporation has an S corporation election in effect. During the 2019 calendar tax year, the corporation had ordinary taxable income of $200,000, and on January 15, 2019, the corporation paid dividends to shareholders in the amount of $120,000. How much taxable income, in total, must the shareholders of the corporation report on their 2019 tax returns?

   $ _____

   Explain your answer _____

   _____

LO 11.6

12. Bill and Guilda each own 50 percent of the stock of Radiata Corporation, an S corporation. Guilda's basis in her stock is $21,000. On May 26, 2019, Bill sells his stock, with a basis of $40,000, to Loraine for $50,000. For the 2019 tax year, Radiata Corporation has a loss of $104,000.
   a. Calculate the amount of the corporation's loss that may be deducted by Bill on his 2019 tax return.

   $ _____

   b. Calculate the amount of the corporation's loss that may be deducted by Guilda on her 2019 tax return.

   $ _____

   c. Calculate the amount of the corporation's loss that may be deducted by Loraine on her 2019 tax return.

   $ _____

LO 11.7

13. Karen, in forming a new corporation, transfers land to the corporation in exchange for 100 percent of the stock of the corporation. Karen's basis in the land is $275,000, and the corporation assumes a liability on the property in the amount of $300,000. The stock received by Karen has a fair market value of $550,000.
   a. What is the amount of gain or loss that must be recognized by Karen on this transfer?

   $ _____

b. What is the amount of Karen's basis in the corporation's stock?

$ _____

c. What is the amount of the corporation's basis in the land?

$ _____

LO 11.8   14. Grevilla Corporation is a manufacturing company. The corporation has accumulated earnings of $950,000, and it can establish reasonable needs for $400,000 of that amount. Calculate the amount of the accumulated earnings tax (if any) that Grevilla Corporation is subject to for this year.

$ _____

LO 11.9   15. Cypress Corporation, a calendar year end corporation, has an AMT credit carryforward from 2018 (the credit arose in 2017) in the amount of $43,000. In 2019, Cypress has $170,000 of taxable income. Assuming Cypress is not a personal service corporation, what is the amount of refund Cypress can expect to receive from its 2019 tax return filing?

$ _____

LO 11.9   16. Go to the IRS website (**www.irs.gov**) and determine which IRS publication addresses the topic of corporate taxation. Print out the page with the *Table of Contents* of this IRS publication.

GROUP 3:
COMPREHENSIVE PROBLEMS

1. Olive Corporation was formed and began operations on January 1, 2019. The corporation's income statement for the year and the balance sheet at year-end are presented below.

The Olive Corporation Income Statement
for the Year Ended December 31, 2019

Gross income from operations		$ 270,000
Qualified dividends received from a 35 percent-		
owned domestic corporation		20,000
Total gross income		290,000
Cost of goods sold		(110,000)
Total income		180,000
Other expenses:		
Compensation of officers	$77,000	
Salaries and wages	30,000	
Bad debts (direct charge-offs)	9,000	
Repairs	3,000	
Depreciation for book and tax purposes	10,000	
Advertising	2,000	
Payroll taxes	16,000	
Total other expenses		(147,000)
Net income (before federal income tax expense)		$ 33,000

The Olive Corporation Balance Sheet
as of December 31, 2019

Assets:

Cash	$ 30,000	
Accounts receivable	20,000	
Inventory (at cost)	70,000	
Equipment	90,000	
Less: accumulated depreciation	(10,000)	
Total assets		$200,000

Liabilities and owners' equity:

Accounts payable	$ 6,200	
Note payable (due in 10 years)	85,000	
Common stock	80,000	
Retained earnings	28,800	
Total liabilities and owners' equity		$200,000

The corporation made estimated tax payments of $5,000 and the corporation's book federal income tax expense is equal to the federal tax liability. Complete Form 1120 for Olive Corporation on Pages 11-39 through 11-44.

2. Assume that Olive Corporation, in Comprehensive Problem 1, is an S corporation owned 50 percent by Linda Holiday and 50 percent by Ralph Winston. The corporation is not subject to any special taxes and no wages are included in cost of goods sold. Using the relevant information given in Comprehensive Problem 1 and assuming the corporation's retained earnings are $33,000 instead of $28,800, accounts payable are $2,000 instead of $6,200, and no estimated tax payments are made, complete Form 1120S for Olive Corporation and Schedule K-1 for Linda on Pages 11-45 through 11-52. Assume there were no cash distributions during the year.

Form **1120**
Department of the Treasury
Internal Revenue Service

U.S. Corporation Income Tax Return

For calendar year 2019 or tax year beginning _____ , 2019, ending _____ , 20 _____
▶ **Go to www.irs.gov/Form1120 for instructions and the latest information.**

OMB No. 1545-0123

2019

A Check if:

1a Consolidated return (attach Form 851) ☐
  b Life/nonlife consoli-dated return . ☐
2 Personal holding co. (attach Sch. PH) . ☐
3 Personal service corp. (see instructions) . ☐
4 Schedule M-3 attached ☐

TYPE OR PRINT

Name

Number, street, and room or suite no. If a P.O. box, see instructions.

City or town, state or province, country, and ZIP or foreign postal code

B Employer identification number

C Date incorporated

D Total assets (see instructions)
$

E Check if: **(1)** ☐ Initial return **(2)** ☐ Final return **(3)** ☐ Name change **(4)** ☐ Address change

Income	1a	Gross receipts or sales	1a	
	b	Returns and allowances	1b	
	c	Balance. Subtract line 1b from line 1a	1c	
	2	Cost of goods sold (attach Form 1125-A)	2	
	3	Gross profit. Subtract line 2 from line 1c	3	
	4	Dividends and inclusions (Schedule C, line 23)	4	
	5	Interest	5	
	6	Gross rents	6	
	7	Gross royalties	7	
	8	Capital gain net income (attach Schedule D (Form 1120))	8	
	9	Net gain or (loss) from Form 4797, Part II, line 17 (attach Form 4797)	9	
	10	Other income (see instructions—attach statement)	10	
	11	**Total income.** Add lines 3 through 10 . . . . ▶	11	
Deductions (See instructions for limitations on deductions.)	12	Compensation of officers (see instructions—attach Form 1125-E) . . . . ▶	12	
	13	Salaries and wages (less employment credits)	13	
	14	Repairs and maintenance	14	
	15	Bad debts	15	
	16	Rents	16	
	17	Taxes and licenses	17	
	18	Interest (see instructions)	18	
	19	Charitable contributions	19	
	20	Depreciation from Form 4562 not claimed on Form 1125-A or elsewhere on return (attach Form 4562) . . .	20	
	21	Depletion	21	
	22	Advertising	22	
	23	Pension, profit-sharing, etc., plans	23	
	24	Employee benefit programs	24	
	25	Reserved for future use	25	
	26	Other deductions (attach statement)	26	
	27	**Total deductions.** Add lines 12 through 26 . . . . ▶	27	
	28	Taxable income before net operating loss deduction and special deductions. Subtract line 27 from line 11. .	28	
	29a	Net operating loss deduction (see instructions)	29a	
	b	Special deductions (Schedule C, line 24)	29b	
	c	Add lines 29a and 29b	29c	
Tax, Refundable Credits, and Payments	30	**Taxable income.** Subtract line 29c from line 28. See instructions	30	
	31	Total tax (Schedule J, Part I, line 11)	31	
	32	2019 net 965 tax liability paid (Schedule J, Part II, line 12)	32	
	33	Total payments, credits, and section 965 net tax liability (Schedule J, Part III, line 23)	33	
	34	Estimated tax penalty. See instructions. Check if Form 2220 is attached . . . . ▶ ☐	34	
	35	**Amount owed.** If line 33 is smaller than the total of lines 31, 32, and 34, enter amount owed	35	
	36	**Overpayment.** If line 33 is larger than the total of lines 31, 32, and 34, enter amount overpaid	36	
	37	Enter amount from line 36 you want: **Credited to 2020 estimated tax** ▶ _____ Refunded ▶	37	

Sign Here

Under penalties of perjury, I declare that I have examined this return, including accompanying schedules and statements, and to the best of my knowledge and belief, it is true, correct, and complete. Declaration of preparer (other than taxpayer) is based on all information of which preparer has any knowledge.

▶ _____ _____ ▶ _____
Signature of officer   Date   Title

May the IRS discuss this return with the preparer shown below? See instructions. ☐ **Yes** ☐ **No**

Paid Preparer Use Only

Print/Type preparer's name	Preparer's signature	Date	Check ☐ if self-employed	PTIN
Firm's name ▶			Firm's EIN ▶	
Firm's address ▶			Phone no.	

For Paperwork Reduction Act Notice, see separate instructions.   Cat. No. 11450Q   Form **1120** (2019)

DRAFT AS OF August 21, 2019 DO NOT FILE

Form 1120 (2019)   Page **2**

Schedule C	Dividends, Inclusions, and Special Deductions (see instructions)	(a) Dividends and inclusions	(b) %	(c) Special deductions (a) × (b)
1	Dividends from less-than-20%-owned domestic corporations (other than debt-financed stock)		50	
2	Dividends from 20%-or-more-owned domestic corporations (other than debt-financed stock)		65	
3	Dividends on certain debt-financed stock of domestic and foreign corporations . .		*see instructions*	
4	Dividends on certain preferred stock of less-than-20%-owned public utilities . . .		23.3	
5	Dividends on certain preferred stock of 20%-or-more-owned public utilities		26.7	
6	Dividends from less-than-20%-owned foreign corporations and certain FSCs . .		50	
7	Dividends from 20%-or-more-owned foreign corporations and certain FSCs . .		65	
8	Dividends from wholly owned foreign subsidiaries		100	
9	**Subtotal.** Add lines 1 through 8. See instructions for limitations		*see instructions*	
10	Dividends from domestic corporations received by a small business investment company operating under the Small Business Investment Act of 1958		100	
11	Dividends from affiliated group members		100	
12	Dividends from certain FSCs		100	
13	Foreign-source portion of dividends received from a specified 10%-owned foreign corporation (excluding hybrid dividends) (see instructions)		100	
14	Dividends from foreign corporations not included on line 3, 6, 7, 8, 11, 12, or 13 (including any hybrid dividends)			
15	Section 965(a) inclusion		*see instructions*	
16a	Subpart F inclusions derived from the sale by a controlled foreign corporation (CFC) of the stock of a lower-tier foreign corporation treated as a dividend (attach Form(s) 5471) (see instructions)		100	
b	Subpart F inclusions derived from hybrid dividends of tiered corporations (attach Form(s) 5471) (see instructions)			
c	Other inclusions from CFCs under subpart F not included on line 15, 16a, 16b, or 17 (attach Form(s) 5471) (see instructions).			
17	Global Intangible Low-Taxed Income (GILTI) (attach Form(s) 5471 and Form 8992) . .			
18	Gross-up for foreign taxes deemed paid			
19	IC-DISC and former DISC dividends not included on line 1, 2, or 3			
20	Other dividends			
21	Deduction for dividends paid on certain preferred stock of public utilities			
22	Section 250 deduction (attach Form 8993)			
23	**Total dividends and inclusions.** Add column (a), lines 9 through 20. Enter here and on page 1, line 4			
24	**Total special deductions.** Add column (c), lines 9 through 22. Enter here and on page 1, line 29b			

Form **1120** (2019)

Form 1120 (2019) Page **3**

Schedule J   Tax Computation and Payment (see instructions)

Part I–Tax Computation

1	Check if the corporation is a member of a controlled group (attach Schedule O (Form 1120)). See instructions ▶ ☐		
2	Income tax. See instructions	**2**	
3	Base erosion minimum tax amount (attach Form 8991)	**3**	
4	Add lines 2 and 3	**4**	
5a	Foreign tax credit (attach Form 1118)	**5a**	
b	Credit from Form 8834 (see instructions)	**5b**	
c	General business credit (attach Form 3800)	**5c**	
d	Credit for prior year minimum tax (attach Form 8827)	**5d**	
e	Bond credits from Form 8912	**5e**	
6	**Total credits.** Add lines 5a through 5e	**6**	
7	Subtract line 6 from line 4	**7**	
8	Personal holding company tax (attach Schedule PH (Form 1120))	**8**	
9a	Recapture of investment credit (attach Form 4255)	**9a**	
b	Recapture of low-income housing credit (attach Form 8611)	**9b**	
c	Interest due under the look-back method—completed long-term contracts (attach Form 8697)	**9c**	
d	Interest due under the look-back method—income forecast method (attach Form 8866)	**9d**	
e	Alternative tax on qualifying shipping activities (attach Form 8902)	**9e**	
f	Other (see instructions—attach statement)	**9f**	
10	**Total.** Add lines 9a through 9f	**10**	
11	**Total tax.** Add lines 7, 8, and 10. Enter here and on page 1, line 31	**11**	

Part II–Section 965 Payments (see instructions)

12	2019 net 965 tax liability paid from Form 965-B, Part II, column (k), line 3. Enter here and on page 1, line 32	**12**	

Part III–Payments, Refundable Credits, and Section 965 Net Tax Liability

13	2018 overpayment credited to 2019	**13**	
14	2019 estimated tax payments	**14**	
15	2019 refund applied for on Form 4466	**15**	( )
16	Combine lines 13, 14, and 15	**16**	
17	Tax deposited with Form 7004	**17**	
18	Withholding (see instructions)	**18**	
19	**Total payments.** Add lines 16, 17, and 18	**19**	
20	Refundable credits from:		
a	Form 2439	**20a**	
b	Form 4136	**20b**	
c	Form 8827, line 5c	**20c**	
d	Other (attach statement—see instructions)	**20d**	
21	**Total credits.** Add lines 20a through 20d	**21**	
22	2019 net 965 tax liability from Form 965-B, Part I, column (d), line 3. See instructions	**22**	
23	**Total payments, credits, and section 965 net tax liability.** Add lines 19, 21, and 22. Enter here and on page 1, line 33	**23**	

Form **1120** (2019)

Form 1120 (2019)   Page **4**

Schedule K	**Other Information** (see instructions)				Yes	No

1 Check accounting method: **a** ☐ Cash   **b** ☐ Accrual   **c** ☐ Other (specify) ▶ _____

2 See the instructions and enter the:

a Business activity code no. ▶ _____

b Business activity ▶ _____

c Product or service ▶ _____

3 Is the corporation a subsidiary in an affiliated group or a parent–subsidiary controlled group? . . . .

 If "Yes," enter name and EIN of the parent corporation ▶ _____

4 At the end of the tax year:

a Did any foreign or domestic corporation, partnership (including any entity treated as a partnership), trust, or tax-exempt organization own directly 20% or more, or own, directly or indirectly, 50% or more of the total voting power of all classes of the corporation's stock entitled to vote? If "Yes," complete Part I of Schedule G (Form 1120) (attach Schedule G) . . . . .

b Did any individual or estate own directly 20% or more, or own, directly or indirectly, 50% or more of the total voting power of all classes of the corporation's stock entitled to vote? If "Yes," complete Part II of Schedule G (Form 1120) (attach Schedule G) .

5 At the end of the tax year, did the corporation:

a Own directly 20% or more, or own, directly or indirectly, 50% or more of the total voting power of all classes of stock entitled to vote of any foreign or domestic corporation not included on **Form 851**, Affiliations Schedule? For rules of constructive ownership, see instructions.

 If "Yes," complete (i) through (iv) below.

(i) Name of Corporation	**(ii)** Employer Identification Number (if any)	**(iii)** Country of Incorporation	**(iv)** Percentage Owned in Voting Stock

b Own directly an interest of 20% or more, or own, directly or indirectly, an interest of 50% or more in any foreign or domestic partnership (including an entity treated as a partnership) or in the beneficial interest of a trust? For rules of constructive ownership, see instructions.

 If "Yes," complete (i) through (iv) below.

(i) Name of Entity	**(ii)** Employer Identification Number (if any)	**(iii)** Country of Organization	**(iv)** Maximum Percentage Owned in Profit, Loss, or Capital

6 During this tax year, did the corporation pay dividends (other than stock dividends and distributions in exchange for stock) in excess of the corporation's current and accumulated earnings and profits? See sections 301 and 316 . . . .

 If "Yes," file **Form 5452**, Corporate Report of Nondividend Distributions. See the instructions for Form 5452.

 If this is a consolidated return, answer here for the parent corporation and on Form 851 for each subsidiary.

7 At any time during the tax year, did one foreign person own, directly or indirectly, at least 25% of the total voting power of all classes of the corporation's stock entitled to vote or at least 25% of the total value of all classes of the corporation's stock?   .

 For rules of attribution, see section 318. If "Yes," enter:

 (a) Percentage owned ▶ _____ and **(b)** Owner's country ▶ _____

 (c) The corporation may have to file **Form 5472**, Information Return of a 25% Foreign-Owned U.S. Corporation or a Foreign Corporation Engaged in a U.S. Trade or Business. Enter the number of Forms 5472 attached ▶ _____

8 Check this box if the corporation issued publicly offered debt instruments with original issue discount . . . . ▶ ☐

 If checked, the corporation may have to file **Form 8281**, Information Return for Publicly Offered Original Issue Discount Instruments.

9 Enter the amount of tax-exempt interest received or accrued during the tax year ▶ $ _____

10 Enter the number of shareholders at the end of the tax year (if 100 or fewer) ▶ _____

11 If the corporation has an NOL for the tax year and is electing to forego the carryback period, check here (see instructions) ▶ ☐

 If the corporation is filing a consolidated return, the statement required by Regulations section 1.1502-21(b)(3) must be attached or the election will not be valid.

12 Enter the available NOL carryover from prior tax years (do not reduce it by any deduction reported on page 1, line 29a.) . . . . ▶ $ _____

Form **1120** (2019)

Form 1120 (2019)   Page **5**

Schedule K	Other Information *(continued from page 4)*

		Yes	No
13	Are the corporation's total receipts (page 1, line 1a, plus lines 4 through 10) for the tax year **and** its total assets at the end of the tax year less than $250,000?		
	If "Yes," the corporation is not required to complete Schedules L, M-1, and M-2. Instead, enter the total amount of cash distributions and the book value of property distributions (other than cash) made during the tax year ▶ $ _____		
14	Is the corporation required to file Schedule UTP (Form 1120), Uncertain Tax Position Statement? See instructions		
	If "Yes," complete and attach Schedule UTP.		
15a	Did the corporation make any payments in 2019 that would require it to file Form(s) 1099?		
b	If "Yes," did or will the corporation file required Form(s) 1099?		
16	During this tax year, did the corporation have an 80%-or-more change in ownership, including a change due to redemption of its own stock?		
17	During or subsequent to this tax year, but before the filing of this return, did the corporation dispose of more than 65% (by value) of its assets in a taxable, non-taxable, or tax deferred transaction?		
18	Did the corporation receive assets in a section 351 transfer in which any of the transferred assets had a fair market basis or fair market value of more than $1 million?		
19	During the corporation's tax year, did the corporation make any payments that would require it to file Forms 1042 and 1042-S under chapter 3 (sections 1441 through 1464) or chapter 4 (sections 1471 through 1474) of the Code?		
20	Is the corporation operating on a cooperative basis?		
21	During the tax year, did the corporation pay or accrue any interest or royalty for which the deduction is not allowed under section 267A? See instructions		
	If "Yes," enter the total amount of the disallowed deductions ▶ $ _____		
22	Does the corporation have gross receipts of at least $500 million in any of the 3 preceding tax years? (See sections 59A(e)(2) and (3))		
	If "Yes," complete and attach Form 8991.		
23	Did the corporation have an election under section 163(j) for any real property trade or business or any farming business in effect during the tax year? See instructions		
24	Does the corporation satisfy one or more of the following? See instructions		
a	The corporation owns a pass-through entity with current, or prior year carryover, excess business interest expense.		
b	The corporation's aggregate average annual gross receipts (determined under section 448(c)) for the 3 tax years preceding the current tax year are more than $26 million and the corporation has business interest expense.		
c	The corporation is a tax shelter and the corporation has business interest expense.		
	If "Yes," to any, complete and attach Form 8990.		
25	Is the corporation attaching Form 8996 to certify as a Qualified Opportunity Fund?		
	If "Yes," enter amount from Form 8996, line 14 . . . . . ▶ $		

Form **1120** (2019)

Form 1120 (2019) Page **6**

Schedule L	Balance Sheets per Books	Beginning of tax year		End of tax year	
	Assets	(a)	(b)	(c)	(d)
1	Cash				
2a	Trade notes and accounts receivable . . .				
b	Less allowance for bad debts	( )		( )	
3	Inventories				
4	U.S. government obligations				
5	Tax-exempt securities (see instructions) .				
6	Other current assets (attach statement) .				
7	Loans to shareholders				
8	Mortgage and real estate loans . . .				
9	Other investments (attach statement) .				
10a	Buildings and other depreciable assets . .				
b	Less accumulated depreciation	( )		( )	
11a	Depletable assets				
b	Less accumulated depletion	( )		( )	
12	Land (net of any amortization)				
13a	Intangible assets (amortizable only) . . .				
b	Less accumulated amortization	( )		( )	
14	Other assets (attach statement)				
15	Total assets				
	Liabilities and Shareholders' Equity				
16	Accounts payable				
17	Mortgages, notes, bonds payable in less than 1 year				
18	Other current liabilities (attach statement) . .				
19	Loans from shareholders				
20	Mortgages, notes, bonds payable in 1 year or more				
21	Other liabilities (attach statement)				
22	Capital stock: **a** Preferred stock				
	b Common stock				
23	Additional paid-in capital				
24	Retained earnings—Appropriated (attach statement)				
25	Retained earnings—Unappropriated . . .				
26	Adjustments to shareholders' equity (attach statement)				
27	Less cost of treasury stock		( )		( )
28	Total liabilities and shareholders' equity . .				

Schedule M-1	Reconciliation of Income (Loss) per Books With Income per Return

Note: The corporation may be required to file Schedule M-3. See instructions.

1	Net income (loss) per books		7	Income recorded on books this year not included on this return (itemize):	
2	Federal income tax per books			Tax-exempt interest $_____	
3	Excess of capital losses over capital gains .			_____	
4	Income subject to tax not recorded on books this year (itemize): _____		8	Deductions on this return not charged against book income this year (itemize):	
	_____		a	Depreciation . . $_____	
5	Expenses recorded on books this year not deducted on this return (itemize):		b	Charitable contributions $_____	
	_____			_____	
a	Depreciation . . . . $_____				
b	Charitable contributions . $_____				
c	Travel and entertainment . $_____			_____	
	_____		9	Add lines 7 and 8	
6	Add lines 1 through 5		10	Income (page 1, line 28)—line 6 less line 9	

Schedule M-2	Analysis of Unappropriated Retained Earnings per Books (Line 25, Schedule L)

1	Balance at beginning of year		5	Distributions: **a** Cash	
2	Net income (loss) per books			**b** Stock	
3	Other increases (itemize): _____			**c** Property	
	_____		6	Other decreases (itemize): _____	
	_____		7	Add lines 5 and 6	
4	Add lines 1, 2, and 3		8	Balance at end of year (line 4 less line 7)	

Form **1120** (2019)

Form **1120-S**

Department of the Treasury
Internal Revenue Service

U.S. Income Tax Return for an S Corporation

▶ Do not file this form unless the corporation has filed or
is attaching Form 2553 to elect to be an S corporation.
▶ Go to *www.irs.gov/Form1120S* for instructions and the latest information.

OMB No. 1545-0123

20**19**

For calendar year 2019 or tax year beginning _____ , 2019, ending _____ , 20 ____

A S election effective date	TYPE OR PRINT	Name	**D** Employer identification number
B Business activity code number (see instructions)		Number, street, and room or suite no. If a P.O. box, see instructions.	**E** Date incorporated
C Check if Sch. M-3 attached ☐		City or town, state or province, country, and ZIP or foreign postal code	**F** Total assets (see instructions) $

G Is the corporation electing to be an S corporation beginning with this tax year? ☐ Yes ☐ No   If "Yes," attach Form 2553 if not already filed

H Check if: **(1)** ☐ Final return **(2)** ☐ Name change **(3)** ☐ Address change **(4)** ☐ Amended return **(5)** ☐ S election termination or revocation

I Enter the number of shareholders who were shareholders during any part of the tax year . . . . ▶

J Check if corporation: **(1)** ☐ Aggregated activities for section 465 at-risk purposes **(2)** ☐ Grouped activities for section 469 passive activity purposes

Caution: Include **only** trade or business income and expenses on lines 1a through 21. See the instructions for more information.

Income					
	1a	Gross receipts or sales	**1a**		
	b	Returns and allowances	**1b**		
	c	Balance. Subtract line 1b from line 1a		**1c**	
	2	Cost of goods sold (attach Form 1125-A)		**2**	
	3	Gross profit. Subtract line 2 from line 1c		**3**	
	4	Net gain (loss) from Form 4797, line 17 (attach Form 4797)		**4**	
	5	Other income (loss) (see instructions—attach statement)		**5**	
	6	**Total income (loss).** Add lines 3 through 5 . . . . ▶		**6**	

Deductions (see instructions for limitations)				
	7	Compensation of officers (see instructions—attach Form 1125-E)	**7**	
	8	Salaries and wages (less employment credits)	**8**	
	9	Repairs and maintenance	**9**	
	10	Bad debts	**10**	
	11	Rents	**11**	
	12	Taxes and licenses	**12**	
	13	Interest (see instructions)	**13**	
	14	Depreciation not claimed on Form 1125-A or elsewhere on return (attach Form 4562)	**14**	
	15	Depletion **(Do not deduct oil and gas depletion.)**	**15**	
	16	Advertising	**16**	
	17	Pension, profit-sharing, etc., plans	**17**	
	18	Employee benefit programs	**18**	
	19	Other deductions (attach statement)	**19**	
	20	**Total deductions.** Add lines 7 through 19 . . . . ▶	**20**	
	21	**Ordinary business income (loss).** Subtract line 20 from line 6	**21**	

Tax and Payments					
	22a	Excess net passive income or LIFO recapture tax (see instructions) . . .	**22a**		
	b	Tax from Schedule D (Form 1120-S)	**22b**		
	c	Add lines 22a and 22b (see instructions for additional taxes)		**22c**	
	23a	2019 estimated tax payments and 2018 overpayment credited to 2019	**23a**		
	b	Tax deposited with Form 7004	**23b**		
	c	Credit for federal tax paid on fuels (attach Form 4136)	**23c**		
	d	Refundable credit from Form 8827, line 5c	**23d**		
	e	Add lines 23a through 23d		**23e**	
	24	Estimated tax penalty (see instructions). Check if Form 2220 is attached . . . . . ▶ ☐		**24**	
	25	**Amount owed.** If line 23e is smaller than the total of lines 22c and 24, enter amount owed . . .		**25**	
	26	**Overpayment.** If line 23e is larger than the total of lines 22c and 24, enter amount overpaid . . .		**26**	
	27	Enter amount from line 26: **Credited to 2020 estimated tax** ▶ _____ **Refunded** ▶		**27**	

Sign Here

Under penalties of perjury, I declare that I have examined this return, including accompanying schedules and statements, and to the best of my knowledge and belief, it is true, correct, and complete. Declaration of preparer (other than taxpayer) is based on all information of which preparer has any knowledge.

▶ _____   ▶ _____
Signature of officer   Date   Title

May the IRS discuss this return with the preparer shown below? See instructions. ☐ Yes ☐ No

Paid Preparer Use Only

Print/Type preparer's name	Preparer's signature	Date	Check ☐ if self-employed	PTIN
Firm's name ▶			Firm's EIN ▶	
Firm's address ▶			Phone no.	

For Paperwork Reduction Act Notice, see separate instructions.   Cat. No. 11510H   Form **1120-S** (2019)

DRAFT AS OF September 26, 2019 DO NOT FILE

Form 1120-S (2019)   Page **2**

Schedule B	**Other Information** (see instructions)		Yes	No

1 Check accounting method: **a** ☐ Cash   **b** ☐ Accrual

   c ☐ Other (specify) ▶ _____

2 See the instructions and enter the:

   a Business activity ▶ _____   **b** Product or service ▶ _____

3 At any time during the tax year, was any shareholder of the corporation a disregarded entity, a trust, an estate, or a nominee or similar person? If "Yes," attach Schedule B-1, Information on Certain Shareholders of an S Corporation   .   .

4 At the end of the tax year, did the corporation:

a Own directly 20% or more, or own, directly or indirectly, 50% or more of the total stock issued and outstanding of any foreign or domestic corporation? For rules of constructive ownership, see instructions. If "Yes," complete (i) through (v) below   .   .   .   .

(i) Name of Corporation	**(ii)** Employer Identification Number (if any)	**(iii)** Country of Incorporation	**(iv)** Percentage of Stock Owned	**(v)** If Percentage in (iv) Is 100%, Enter the Date (if any) a Qualified Subchapter S Subsidiary Election Was Made

b Own directly an interest of 20% or more, or own, directly or indirectly, an interest of 50% or more in the profit, loss, or capital in any foreign or domestic partnership (including an entity treated as a partnership) or in the beneficial interest of a trust? For rules of constructive ownership, see instructions. If "Yes," complete (i) through (v) below   .   .   .   .   .   .

(i) Name of Entity	**(ii)** Employer Identification Number (if any)	**(iii)** Type of Entity	**(iv)** Country of Organization	**(v)** Maximum Percentage Owned in Profit, Loss, or Capital

5a At the end of the tax year, did the corporation have any outstanding shares of restricted stock?   .   .   .   .

   If "Yes," complete lines (i) and (ii) below.

   (i)   Total shares of restricted stock   .   .   .   .   ▶ _____

   (ii)   Total shares of non-restricted stock   .   .   .   .   ▶ _____

b At the end of the tax year, did the corporation have any outstanding stock options, warrants, or similar instruments?   .

   If "Yes," complete lines (i) and (ii) below.

   (i)   Total shares of stock outstanding at the end of the tax year   .   ▶ _____

   (ii)   Total shares of stock outstanding if all instruments were executed ▶ _____

6 Has this corporation filed, or is it required to file, **Form 8918,** Material Advisor Disclosure Statement, to provide information on any reportable transaction?   .   .   .   .

7 Check this box if the corporation issued publicly offered debt instruments with original issue discount   .   .   .   .   ▶ ☐

   If checked, the corporation may have to file **Form 8281,** Information Return for Publicly Offered Original Issue Discount Instruments.

8 If the corporation **(a)** was a C corporation before it elected to be an S corporation **or** the corporation acquired an asset with a basis determined by reference to the basis of the asset (or the basis of any other property) in the hands of a C corporation **and (b)** has net unrealized built-in gain in excess of the net recognized built-in gain from prior years, enter the net unrealized built-in gain reduced by net recognized built-in gain from prior years. See instructions   .   .   .   .   .   ▶ $ _____

9 Did the corporation have an election under section 163(j) for any real property trade or business or any farming business in effect during the tax year? See instructions   .   .   .   .

10 Does the corporation satisfy one or more of the following? See instructions   .   .   .   .

a The corporation owns a pass-through entity with current, or prior year carryover, excess business interest expense.

b The corporation's aggregate average annual gross receipts (determined under section 448(c)) for the 3 tax years preceding the current tax year are more than $26 million and the corporation has business interest expense.

c The corporation is a tax shelter and the corporation has business interest expense.

   If "Yes," complete and attach Form 8990.

11 Does the corporation satisfy **both** of the following conditions?   .   .   .   .

a The corporation's total receipts (see instructions) for the tax year were less than $250,000.

b The corporation's total assets at the end of the tax year were less than $250,000.

   If "Yes," the corporation is not required to complete Schedules L and M-1.

Form **1120-S** (2019)

Form 1120-S (2019)   Page **3**

Schedule B	**Other Information** (see instructions) *(continued)*	Yes	No
12	During the tax year, did the corporation have any non-shareholder debt that was canceled, was forgiven, or had the terms modified so as to reduce the principal amount of the debt?		
	If "Yes," enter the amount of principal reduction ▶ $ _____		
13	During the tax year, was a qualified subchapter S subsidiary election terminated or revoked? If "Yes," see instructions .		
14a	Did the corporation make any payments in 2019 that would require it to file Form(s) 1099?		
b	If "Yes," did the corporation file or will it file required Form(s) 1099?		
15	Is the corporation attaching Form 8996 to certify as a Qualified Opportunity Fund?		
	If "Yes," enter the amount from Form 8996, line 14 ▶ $ _____		

	Schedule K	**Shareholders' Pro Rata Share Items**			**Total amount**
Income (Loss)	1	Ordinary business income (loss) (page 1, line 21)		**1**	
	2	Net rental real estate income (loss) (attach Form 8825)		**2**	
	3a	Other gross rental income (loss)	**3a**		
	b	Expenses from other rental activities (attach statement)	**3b**		
	c	Other net rental income (loss). Subtract line 3b from line 3a		**3c**	
	4	Interest income		**4**	
	5	Dividends: **a** Ordinary dividends		**5a**	
		b Qualified dividends	**5b**		
	6	Royalties		**6**	
	7	Net short-term capital gain (loss) (attach Schedule D (Form 1120-S))		**7**	
	8a	Net long-term capital gain (loss) (attach Schedule D (Form 1120-S))		**8a**	
	b	Collectibles (28%) gain (loss)	**8b**		
	c	Unrecaptured section 1250 gain (attach statement)	**8c**		
	9	Net section 1231 gain (loss) (attach Form 4797)		**9**	
	10	Other income (loss) (see instructions) Type ▶		**10**	
Deductions	11	Section 179 deduction (attach Form 4562)		**11**	
	12a	Charitable contributions		**12a**	
	b	Investment interest expense		**12b**	
	c	Section 59(e)(2) expenditures **(1)** Type ▶ _____ **(2)** Amount ▶		**12c(2)**	
	d	Other deductions (see instructions) Type ▶		**12d**	
Credits	13a	Low-income housing credit (section 42(j)(5))		**13a**	
	b	Low-income housing credit (other)		**13b**	
	c	Qualified rehabilitation expenditures (rental real estate) (attach Form 3468, if applicable)		**13c**	
	d	Other rental real estate credits (see instructions) Type ▶ _____		**13d**	
	e	Other rental credits (see instructions) Type ▶ _____		**13e**	
	f	Biofuel producer credit (attach Form 6478)		**13f**	
	g	Other credits (see instructions) Type ▶		**13g**	
Foreign Transactions	14a	Name of country or U.S. possession ▶ _____			
	b	Gross income from all sources		**14b**	
	c	Gross income sourced at shareholder level		**14c**	
		Foreign gross income sourced at corporate level			
	d	Reserved for future use		**14d**	
	e	Foreign branch category		**14e**	
	f	Passive category		**14f**	
	g	General category		**14g**	
	h	Other (attach statement)		**14h**	
		Deductions allocated and apportioned at shareholder level			
	i	Interest expense		**14i**	
	j	Other		**14j**	
		Deductions allocated and apportioned at corporate level to foreign source income			
	k	Reserved for future use		**14k**	
	l	Foreign branch category		**14l**	
	m	Passive category		**14m**	
	n	General category		**14n**	
	o	Other (attach statement)		**14o**	
		Other information			
	p	Total foreign taxes (check one): ☐ Paid ☐ Accrued ▶		**14p**	
	q	Reduction in taxes available for credit (attach statement)		**14q**	
	r	Other foreign tax information (attach statement)			

Form **1120-S** (2019)

Form 1120-S (2019)   Page **4**

Schedule K		Shareholders' Pro Rata Share Items *(continued)*		Total amount

Alternative Minimum Tax (AMT) Items	**15a**	Post-1986 depreciation adjustment	**15a**	
	b	Adjusted gain or loss	**15b**	
	c	Depletion (other than oil and gas)	**15c**	
	d	Oil, gas, and geothermal properties—gross income	**15d**	
	e	Oil, gas, and geothermal properties—deductions	**15e**	
	f	Other AMT items (attach statement)	**15f**	
Items Affecting Shareholder Basis	**16a**	Tax-exempt interest income	**16a**	
	b	Other tax-exempt income	**16b**	
	c	Nondeductible expenses	**16c**	
	d	Distributions (attach statement if required) (see instructions)	**16d**	
	e	Repayment of loans from shareholders	**16e**	
Other Information	**17a**	Investment income	**17a**	
	b	Investment expenses	**17b**	
	c	Dividend distributions paid from accumulated earnings and profits	**17c**	
	d	Other items and amounts (attach statement)		
Reconciliation	**18**	**Income (loss) reconciliation.** Combine the amounts on lines 1 through 10 in the far right column. From the result, subtract the sum of the amounts on lines 11 through 12d and 14p	**18**	

Schedule L		Balance Sheets per Books	Beginning of tax year		End of tax year	
		Assets	**(a)**	**(b)**	**(c)**	**(d)**
1		Cash				
2a		Trade notes and accounts receivable				
b		Less allowance for bad debts	(	)	(	)
3		Inventories				
4		U.S. government obligations				
5		Tax-exempt securities (see instructions)				
6		Other current assets (attach statement)				
7		Loans to shareholders				
8		Mortgage and real estate loans				
9		Other investments (attach statement)				
10a		Buildings and other depreciable assets				
b		Less accumulated depreciation	(	)	(	)
11a		Depletable assets				
b		Less accumulated depletion	(	)	(	)
12		Land (net of any amortization)				
13a		Intangible assets (amortizable only)				
b		Less accumulated amortization	(	)	(	)
14		Other assets (attach statement)				
15		Total assets				
		Liabilities and Shareholders' Equity				
16		Accounts payable				
17		Mortgages, notes, bonds payable in less than 1 year				
18		Other current liabilities (attach statement)				
19		Loans from shareholders				
20		Mortgages, notes, bonds payable in 1 year or more				
21		Other liabilities (attach statement)				
22		Capital stock				
23		Additional paid-in capital				
24		Retained earnings				
25		Adjustments to shareholders' equity (attach statement)				
26		Less cost of treasury stock		(	)	(	)
27		Total liabilities and shareholders' equity				

Form **1120-S** (2019)

Form 1120-S (2019)
Page **5**

Schedule M-1   Reconciliation of Income (Loss) per Books With Income (Loss) per Return

Note: The corporation may be required to file Schedule M-3. See instructions.

1	Net income (loss) per books		5	Income recorded on books this year not included on Schedule K, lines 1 through 10 (itemize):	
2	Income included on Schedule K, lines 1, 2, 3c, 4, 5a, 6, 7, 8a, 9, and 10, not recorded on books this year (itemize) _____		a	Tax-exempt interest $ _____	
3	Expenses recorded on books this year not included on Schedule K, lines 1 through 12 and 14p (itemize):		6	Deductions included on Schedule K, lines 1 through 12 and 14p, not charged against book income this year (itemize):	
a	Depreciation $ _____		a	Depreciation $ _____	
b	Travel and entertainment $ _____		7	Add lines 5 and 6	
4	Add lines 1 through 3		8	Income (loss) (Schedule K, line 18). Subtract line 7 from line 4	

Schedule M-2   Analysis of Accumulated Adjustments Account, Shareholders' Undistributed Taxable Income Previously Taxed, Accumulated Earnings and Profits, and Other Adjustments Account

(see instructions)

		(a) Accumulated adjustments account	(b) Shareholders' undistributed taxable income previously taxed	(c) Accumulated earnings and profits	(d) Other adjustments account
1	Balance at beginning of tax year				
2	Ordinary income from page 1, line 21 . . .				
3	Other additions				
4	Loss from page 1, line 21	( )			
5	Other reductions	( )			( )
6	Combine lines 1 through 5				
7	Distributions				
8	Balance at end of tax year. Subtract line 7 from line 6				

Form **1120-S** (2019)

Schedule K-1
(Form 1120-S)

Department of the Treasury
Internal Revenue Service

2019

For calendar year 2019, or tax year

beginning / / 2019 ending / /

Shareholder's Share of Income, Deductions, Credits, etc. ▶ See back of form and separate instructions.

Part I Information About the Corporation

A Corporation's employer identification number

B Corporation's name, address, city, state, and ZIP code

C IRS Center where corporation filed return

Part II Information About the Shareholder

D Shareholder's identifying number

E Shareholder's name, address, city, state, and ZIP code

F Shareholder's percentage of stock
ownership for tax year . . . . _____ %

For IRS Use Only

671119

☐ Final K-1   ☐ Amended K-1   OMB No. 1545-0123

Part III Shareholder's Share of Current Year Income, Deductions, Credits, and Other Items

1	Ordinary business income (loss)	13	Credits
2	Net rental real estate income (loss)		
3	Other net rental income (loss)		
4	Interest income		
5a	Ordinary dividends		
5b	Qualified dividends	14	Foreign transactions
6	Royalties		
7	Net short-term capital gain (loss)		
8a	Net long-term capital gain (loss)		
8b	Collectibles (28%) gain (loss)		
8c	Unrecaptured section 1250 gain		
9	Net section 1231 gain (loss)		
10	Other income (loss)	15	Alternative minimum tax (AMT) items
11	Section 179 deduction	16	Items affecting shareholder basis
12	Other deductions		
		17	Other information

18 ☐ More than one activity for at-risk purposes*
19 ☐ More than one activity for passive activity purposes*

* See attached statement for additional information.

For Paperwork Reduction Act Notice, see the Instructions for Form 1120-S.   www.irs.gov/Form1120S   Cat. No. 11520D   **Schedule K-1 (Form 1120-S) 2019**

This list identifies the codes used on Schedule K-1 for all shareholders and provides summarized reporting information for shareholders who file Form 1040 or 1040-SR. For detailed reporting and filing information, see the separate Shareholder's Instructions for Schedule K-1 and the instructions for your income tax return.

1. Ordinary business income (loss). Determine whether the income (loss) is passive or nonpassive and enter on your return as follows:

	Report on
Passive loss	See the Shareholder's Instructions
Passive income	Schedule E, line 28, column (h)
Nonpassive loss	See the Shareholder's Instructions
Nonpassive income	Schedule E, line 28, column (k)

2. Net rental real estate income (loss) See the Shareholder's Instructions

3. Other net rental income (loss)
Net income	Schedule E, line 28, column (h)
Net loss	See the Shareholder's Instructions

4. Interest income Form 1040 or 1040-SR, line 2b
5a. Ordinary dividends Form 1040 or 1040-SR, line 3b
5b. Qualified dividends Form 1040 or 1040-SR, line 3a
6. Royalties Schedule E, line 4
7. Net short-term capital gain (loss) Schedule D, line 5
8a. Net long-term capital gain (loss) Schedule D, line 12
8b. Collectibles (28%) gain (loss) 28% Rate Gain Worksheet, line 4 (Schedule D instructions)
8c. Unrecaptured section 1250 gain See the Shareholder's Instructions
9. Net section 1231 gain (loss) See the Shareholder's Instructions
10. Other income (loss)
Code
A	Other portfolio income (loss)	See the Shareholder's Instructions
B	Involuntary conversions	See the Shareholder's Instructions
C	Sec. 1256 contracts & straddles	Form 6781, line 1
D	Mining exploration costs recapture	See Pub. 535
E	Reserved for future use	
F	Section 965(a) inclusion	}
G	Income under subpart F (other than inclusions under sections 951A and 965)	See the Shareholder's Instructions
H	Other income (loss)	}

11. Section 179 deduction See the Shareholder's Instructions

12. Other deductions
A	Cash contributions (60%)	}
B	Cash contributions (30%)	
C	Noncash contributions (50%)	
D	Noncash contributions (30%)	
E	Capital gain property to a 50% organization (30%)	See the Shareholder's Instructions
F	Capital gain property (20%)	
G	Contributions (100%)	
H	Investment interest expense	Form 4952, line 1
I	Deductions—royalty income	Schedule E, line 19
J	Section 59(e)(2) expenditures	See the Shareholder's Instructions
K	Section 965(c) deduction	See the Shareholder's Instructions
L	Deductions—portfolio (other)	Schedule A, line 16
M	Preproductive period expenses	See the Shareholder's Instructions
N	Commercial revitalization deduction from rental real estate activities	See Form 8582 instructions
O	Reforestation expense deduction	See the Shareholder's Instructions
P	through R	Reserved for future use
S	Other deductions	See the Shareholder's Instructions

13. Credits
A	Low-income housing credit (section 42(j)(5)) from pre-2008 buildings	}
B	Low-income housing credit (other) from pre-2008 buildings	
C	Low-income housing credit (section 42(j)(5)) from post-2007 buildings	See the Shareholder's Instructions
D	Low-income housing credit (other) from post-2007 buildings	
E	Qualified rehabilitation expenditures (rental real estate)	
F	Other rental real estate credits	
G	Other rental credits	
H	Undistributed capital gains credit	Schedule 3 (Form 1040 or 1040-SR), line 13, box a
I	Biofuel producer credit	}
J	Work opportunity credit	
K	Disabled access credit	See the Shareholder's Instructions
L	Empowerment zone employment credit	
M	Credit for increasing research activities	

Code		Report on
N	Credit for employer social security and Medicare taxes	}
O	Backup withholding	See the Shareholder's Instructions
P	Other credits	

14. Foreign transactions
A	Name of country or U.S. possession	}
B	Gross income from all sources	Form 1116, Part I
C	Gross income sourced at shareholder level	

Foreign gross income sourced at corporate level
D	Reserved for future use	
E	Foreign branch category	}
F	Passive category	Form 1116, Part I
G	General category	
H	Other	

Deductions allocated and apportioned at shareholder level
I	Interest expense	Form 1116, Part I
J	Other	Form 1116, Part I

Deductions allocated and apportioned at corporate level to foreign source income
K	Reserved for future use	
L	Foreign branch category	}
M	Passive category	
N	General category	Form 1116, Part I
O	Other	

Other information
P	Total foreign taxes paid	Form 1116, Part II
Q	Total foreign taxes accrued	Form 1116, Part II
R	Reduction in taxes available for credit	Form 1116, line 12
S	Foreign trading gross receipts	Form 8873
T	Extraterritorial income exclusion	Form 8873
U	Section 965 information	See the Shareholder's Instructions
V	Other foreign transactions	See the Shareholder's Instructions

15. Alternative minimum tax (AMT) items
A	Post-1986 depreciation adjustment	}
B	Adjusted gain or loss	
C	Depletion (other than oil & gas)	See the Shareholder's Instructions
D	Oil, gas, & geothermal—gross income	and the Instructions for Form 6251
E	Oil, gas, & geothermal—deductions	
F	Other AMT items	

16. Items affecting shareholder basis
A	Tax-exempt interest income	Form 1040 or 1040-SR, line 2a
B	Other tax-exempt income	}
C	Nondeductible expenses	
D	Distributions	See the Shareholder's Instructions
E	Repayment of loans from shareholders	

17. Other information
A	Investment income	Form 4952, line 4a
B	Investment expenses	Form 4952, line 5
C	Qualified rehabilitation expenditures (other than rental real estate)	See the Shareholder's Instructions
D	Basis of energy property	See the Shareholder's Instructions
E	Recapture of low-income housing credit (section 42(j)(5))	Form 8611, line 8
F	Recapture of low-income housing credit (other)	Form 8611, line 8
G	Recapture of investment credit	See Form 4255
H	Recapture of other credits	See the Shareholder's Instructions
I	Look-back interest—completed long-term contracts	See Form 8697
J	Look-back interest—income forecast method	See Form 8866
K	Dispositions of property with section 179 deductions	}
L	Recapture of section 179 deduction	See the Shareholder's Instructions
M	through U	
V	Section 199A information	
W	through Z	Reserved for future use
AA	Excess taxable income	}
AB	Excess business interest income	See the Shareholder's Instructions
AC	Other information	

Student Name _____

Class/Section _____

Date _____

KEY NUMBER TAX RETURN SUMMARY

CHAPTER 11

Comprehensive Problem 1

Total Income (Line 11)   _____

Dividends Received Deduction (Line 29b)   _____

Taxable Income (Line 30)   _____

Total Tax (Line 31)   _____

Overpayment (Line 36)   _____

Comprehensive Problem 2

Cost of Goods Sold (Line 2)   _____

Total Income (Loss) (Line 6)   _____

Ordinary Business Income (Loss) (Line 21)   _____

Amount Owed (Line 25)   _____

Qualified Dividends (Schedule K-1, Line 5b)   _____

Tax Administration and Tax Planning

LEARNING OBJECTIVES

After completing this chapter, you should be able to:

LO 12.1   Identify the organizational structure of the Internal Revenue Service (IRS).

LO 12.2   Describe the IRS audit process.

LO 12.3   Define the common penalties for taxpayers and be able to apply them to specific situations.

LO 12.4   Apply the general rule for the statute of limitations on tax returns and the important exceptions to the general rule.

LO 12.5   Describe the rules and penalties that apply to tax practitioners.

LO 12.6   Describe the Taxpayer Bill of Rights.

LO 12.7   Explain the basic concepts of tax planning.

OVERVIEW

Knowing how the Internal Revenue Service (IRS) operates, and how and why the IRS audits certain tax returns, is extremely important to tax practitioners. This chapter covers these topics as well as tax penalties that apply to taxpayers and tax preparers, the statute of limitations on tax liabilities and refund claims, and rules applicable to tax practitioners (i.e., Circular 230). The Taxpayer Bill of Rights, also covered in this chapter, provides taxpayers with significant rights when dealing with the IRS, such as the ability to record an IRS interview.

Arranging one's financial affairs in order to maximize after-tax cash flows is referred to as tax planning. This chapter includes a discussion of basic tax-planning techniques that may be used by individual taxpayers. This final chapter is intended to give an appreciation for the process of dealing with the IRS and several of the many issues involved in conducting a tax practice.

12-1 THE INTERNAL REVENUE SERVICE

The tax laws of the United States are administered by the IRS. In administering the tax law, the IRS has the responsibility for determining, assessing, and collecting internal revenue taxes and enforcing other provisions of the tax law. The IRS is a bureau of the Treasury Department. The mission of the IRS is to provide America's taxpayers quality service by helping them understand and meet their tax responsibilities and enforce the law with integrity and fairness. Congress passes tax laws and requires taxpayers to comply. A taxpayer is expected to understand and meet his or her tax obligations. The role of the IRS is to help the majority of compliant taxpayers with the tax law, while ensuring that the minority who are unwilling to comply pay their fair share.

The IRS organization currently consists of a national office in Washington, D.C., IRS Campus Processing Sites, and various operational offices throughout the United States. The national office is the headquarters of the commissioner of internal revenue and various deputy and associate commissioners. The commissioner of internal revenue is appointed by the president of the United States with the advice and consent of the Senate. The responsibilities of the commissioner are to establish policy, to supervise the activities of the organization, and to act in an advisory capacity to the Treasury Department on legislative matters. In addition, the commissioner is responsible for the collection of income tax, auditing of tax returns, intelligence operations, and appellate procedures.

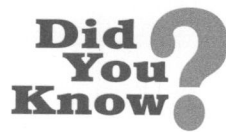

When the Form 1040 was introduced in 1914, it was 3 pages including the instructions. Today, the Form 1040 instructions are over 100 pages.

12-1a IRS Campus Processing Sites

In addition to the various operational offices discussed below, the IRS currently maintains IRS Campus Processing Sites. At these processing sites, the IRS computers process the information from tax documents such as tax returns, payroll tax forms, Form 1099s, and withholding forms.

Paper returns for individuals are processed at the Austin, Fresno, Kansas City, and Ogden offices while e-filings are processed at many sites. The IRS also maintains a national computer center in Martinsburg, West Virginia, where information from various processing sites is matched with records from other processing sites. This cross-matching of records helps to assure that taxpayers report all their income and do not file multiple refund claims.

"Tax day is the day that ordinary Americans send their money to Washington, D.C., and wealthy Americans send their money to the Cayman Islands." – Jimmy Kimmel

12-1b **The IRS Organizational Structure**

The Internal Revenue Service was completely reorganized under the 1998 IRS Restructuring Act (RRA 98), which provided the foundation for the current structure as shown in Figure 12.1.

FIGURE 12.1

Note: In addition to Figure 12.1 above, more extensive information about the IRS organizational structure is available to the public at **www.irs.gov.**

The Services and Enforcement arm of the IRS, as shown in Figure 12.1, is now responsible for the collection of taxes and the auditing of tax returns, which is done through the following offices:

INTERNAL REVENUE SERVICE DIVISIONS AND PRINCIPAL OFFICES

Division	Responsibility
Small Business/Self-Employed (SB/SE)	Small business taxpayers including individuals who file business forms with their tax returns
Wage and Investment (W&I)	Taxpayers whose primary income is derived from wages and investments and who do not file business forms with their tax returns
Large Business and International (LB&I)	Taxpayers with assets of $10 million or more and the International Program
Tax Exempt & Government Entities (TE/GE)	Tax exempt and government entities

Office	Responsibility
Criminal Investigation	Law enforcement activities
Office of Professional Responsibility (OPR)	Regulating enrolled agents, attorneys, and CPAs who practice before the Service
Whistleblower Office (WO)	Handling information that helps uncover tax cheating and providing appropriate rewards to whistleblowers
Return Preparer Office	Registers and promotes a qualified tax professional community
Office of Online Services	Develops and executes strategies to update and integrate IRS Web services

---

Of these IRS divisions, the most significant to individual and small business taxpayers are the Small Business/Self-Employed (SB/SE) and the Wage and Investment (W&I) offices.

12-1c Small Business/Self-Employed (SB/SE) Division

The SB/SE headquarters are located in Lanham, Maryland, with a mission to serve SB/SE customers by educating and informing them of their tax obligations. The division develops educational products and services and helps the public to understand and comply with applicable laws. The SB/SE Division serves the following taxpayers:

- Individuals filing Forms 1040 and 1040-SR (U.S. Individual Income Tax Return), Schedules C, E, or F, and
- All other businesses with assets under $10 million.

The SB/SE Division serves this taxpayer segment through three organizations:
- Collection (specializing in delinquent taxes and tax returns)
- Examination (specializing in correspondence, office and field audits)
- Operations Support (provides support to other segments to ensure they are properly equipped)

12-1d **Wage and Investment (W&I) Division**

The mission of the W&I Division is to help taxpayers understand and comply with applicable tax laws and to protect the public interest by applying the tax law with integrity and fairness. The headquarters of the W&I office is in Atlanta, Georgia. The taxpayer profile of W&I is as follows:

- Most pay taxes through withholdings,
- More than half prepare their own returns,
- Most interact with the IRS once a year, and
- Most receive refunds.

Organizationally, the W&I Division is broken down into several operational administrative centers (offices). The key functional operations of the W&I offices include:

- Customer Assistance, Relationships, and Education (CARE)
- Customer Account Services (CAS)
- Return Integrity and Compliance Services (RICS)

12-1e **Examination of Records**

Federal tax law gives the IRS authority to examine a taxpayer's books and records to determine the correct amount of tax due. The IRS also has the right to summon taxpayers and to make them appear before the IRS and produce necessary accounting records. Taxpayers are required by law to maintain accounting records to facilitate an IRS audit.

The IRS may also issue a summons for taxpayer records from third parties such as banks, brokers, and CPAs. Effective August 2019, the IRS must notify the taxpayer 45 days in advance of serving a third-party summons to allow the taxpayer to intervene in any proceeding involving the summons. If a taxpayer receives notice that the IRS is summoning records from a third party, he or she should seek immediate professional tax advice.

In July 2019, the Taxpayer First Act (P.L. 116-25) was signed into law. This law contains a number of potential changes to the operations of the IRS that are expected to come to fruition over the next few years. For example, the law calls for changes to the management and oversight of IRS to improve customer service and calls for a new process for assisting taxpayers with appeals. The act also makes minor modifications to the IRS's organization and provides some new safeguards to protect taxpayers and their private information when dealing with the IRS.

New Tax Law

12-1f **Collections**

Taxpayers have several options when they are unable to pay the money they owe to the IRS as outlined in Publication 594. The IRS wants to help taxpayers move their issues toward resolution, and it has tools to help delinquent taxpayers pay the taxes they owe. Taxpayers may ask the IRS for a short-term administrative extension of time and then borrow money or sell assets to pay their tax debt. They may also enter into an installment agreement with the IRS, if their debt is below certain limits, and pay the debt within a 2-year or 3-year time frame. Another option for certain taxpayers is an *offer in compromise* where the IRS accepts a settlement less than the total amount of tax due. Generally, taxpayers who qualify for an offer in compromise are unlikely to ever be able to pay the amount they owe. Alternatively, sometimes the IRS will accept an offer in compromise when the tax liability is disputed, or to avert a costly and time-consuming legal battle.

If a taxpayer does not pay taxes that are due, ignores notices and demands for payment, and fails to make arrangements to pay the amount owed, the IRS will generally start a collection process. This process may include a tax levy that allows the IRS to take a portion of a taxpayer's wages or to seize property such as the taxpayer's house, car, bank account, or other financial accounts. The IRS may also put a tax lien on the taxpayer's property, which is a legal claim to the property. Liens will not be filed unless a taxpayer owes more than $10,000 in taxes. The IRS also has the power to assess significant penalties, some of which are covered later in this chapter.

Self-Study Problem 12.1   *See Appendix E for Solutions to Self-Study Problems*

Indicate whether the following statements are true or false in the current year by circling the appropriate letter.

T F   1. The Wage and Investment Division deals with individuals filing a Form 1040.

T F   2. Tax returns are processed at IRS Campus Processing Sites.

T F   3. The commissioner of internal revenue is an elected position.

T F   4. The IRS is part of the Justice Department.

T F   5. The IRS has the right to summon a taxpayer's tax records.

Learning Objective 12.2

Describe the IRS audit process.

12-2 THE AUDIT PROCESS

A primary function of the IRS is to audit taxpayers' tax returns. After the service centers have checked the returns for accuracy, some returns are selected for audit. When a return is selected for examination, it may be subject to an "office audit" or a "field audit." An audit may also be conducted through the mail in what is called a "correspondence audit."

Correspondence audits now account for about 75 percent of the IRS examinations of individual returns each year. Correspondence audits are generally handled entirely by mail. The audit begins when the IRS sends a letter to a taxpayer requesting specific information about their tax return. Usually, the areas covered in correspondence audits relate to questions about Forms W-2 and 1099 that do not agree with the tax return, requests for information supporting charitable contributions, and information related to eligibility for claimed earned income credits.

The office audit is conducted in an IRS office and is typically used for individual taxpayers with little or no business activities. In an office audit, the taxpayer takes his or her records to the IRS office where they are reviewed by a revenue agent. The taxpayer is simply required to substantiate deductions, credits, or income items that appear on his or her tax return.

In a field audit, the IRS agent reviews a taxpayer's books and records at the taxpayer's place of business or at the office of the taxpayer's accountant. This type of audit is generally used when the accounting records are too extensive to take to the IRS office. Field audits are usually used for taxpayers with substantial trade or business activities. If a taxpayer can present a valid reason, he or she may have an office audit changed to a field audit.

12-2a **Selection of Returns for Audits**

The IRS selects returns for audit through a number of different methods:

- Identification of participants in abusive tax avoidance transactions
- Computer scoring (DIF)
- Large corporations
- Information matching
- Related examinations
- Other means

In 2017, only 0.6 percent of individual income tax returns were selected for audit, the lowest level in over a decade. However, the higher the income, the more likely the audit. The IRS audited 3.4 percent of returns that reported more than $1 million in income. Recent audit rates continue to be lower than historical levels.

The IRS uses information gleaned from other sources to identify taxpayers involved in abusive tax avoidance transactions. For example, the IRS may identify a promoter of abusive transactions and then use the promoter's records to identify taxpayers that may have engaged in the abusive planning. The IRS also may select a tax return for audit through a related examination. For example, if the IRS selects an entity or taxpayer for examination, they may also select business partners or other investors.

Most large corporations are involved with an IRS audit on a continuous basis and many have set aside permanent office space to house the IRS agents.

For computer scoring, the IRS uses the DIF (Discriminant Function System) and UIDIF (Unreported Income DIF) to select taxpayers for audit. Under the DIF system, the IRS uses mathematical formulas to assign a DIF score to each return. The DIF score represents the potential for discovery of improper treatment of items on the tax return. The higher the DIF score, the more likely the tax return is to be audited. The DIF score is designed to identify tax returns likely to contain errors because they contain amounts of income, deductions, or tax credits that fall outside "normal" ranges. For example, a tax return that contains unusually large charitable contribution claimed as a deduction will be assigned a high DIF score, and the chances of it being selected for audit are greater. The UIDIF scores returns for the likelihood of unreported income.

The IRS has operated a random audit selection process for many years under different program names such as the Taxpayer Compliance Measurement Program (TCMP) or, as currently more benignly named, the National Research Program (NRP). These programs are used to assist the IRS in determining which types of taxpayers should be audited and gather data to update the DIF system. These programs have not been without controversy and remain a sensitive issue for the IRS. The National Taxpayer Advocate has suggested providing compensation to taxpayers that are subjected to an NRP audit that results in no change to tax liability.

The old TCMP audits were sometimes so time-consuming and intrusive that one taxpayer referred to them as "an autopsy without the benefit of dying," according to a *Wall Street Journal*'s "Tax Report" column.

Other tax returns that are audited are selected due to matching problems between the information forms such as Forms W-2 and 1099 and the related taxpayer's return. From time to time, the IRS will also target special projects at a local or industry segment. For example, a "random" audit might reveal a tax issue with small auto repair shops. After required approvals from higher positions within the IRS, a number of small auto repair shops may be selected for audit to see if the issue is pervasive within the industry segment.

Lastly, the IRS can also select returns based on information obtained from other taxing jurisdictions, news sources, or whistleblowers. For example, the IRS and many state departments of revenue share tax information to assist in identification of returns for examination. Although the IRS has procedures in place to ensure that audits are not targeted at certain groups for political or other motivations, the history of such reported behavior continues to haunt the organization.

TAX BREAK

Taxpayers selected for audit should consider hiring professionals to represent them. Lawyers say taxpayers confronted by IRS agents often tend to get nervous and talk too much, blurting out unnecessary details or becoming overly emotional and arousing needless suspicions.

12-2b **The Appeals Process**

After a return is selected for examination, an agent is assigned to perform the audit. There are three possible results arising from the agent's audit. First, the tax return may be found to require no adjustment, in which case the findings are reviewed and the tax return is sent to storage. A second possible outcome of the audit is an agreement between the agent and the taxpayer on a needed change in the tax liability on the tax return. Then, the tax is collected or the refund is paid, and after a review, the return is stored.

The final possible outcome of the audit is a disagreement between the agent and the taxpayer on the amount of the required adjustment to the tax return. In this situation, the appeals procedure begins with the IRS inviting the taxpayer to an informal conference with an appellate agent. If an agreement cannot be reached at the appeals level, then the matter is taken into the federal court system. The Federal Tax Court is open to the public. For tax professionals and tax students, watching the Tax Court in action can be an educational experience. Any group planning a court visit should contact the judge's chambers in advance since the courts are often small and cannot accommodate many spectators. Figures 12.2 and 12.3 on Pages 12-9 and 12-10, respectively, illustrate the audit process, beginning with the selection of a tax return for audit and ending with a decision of the federal courts.

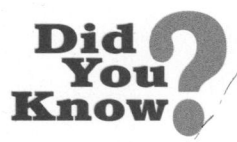
Did You Know?

The IRS considers the Appeals function to be highly successful, negotiating and settling 85 to 90 percent of the cases with taxpayers. If this high rate of settlement were not achieved, the number of unagreed cases would soon overwhelm the courts hearing tax cases.

FIGURE 12.2

INCOME TAX AUDIT PROCEDURE
OF THE INTERNAL REVENUE SERVICE

Returns are selected for examination on the basis of:

1. Apparent reporting errors on face of return.
2. Sampling to test and encourage correct reporting.
3. Information from various sources indicating incorrect reporting.
4. Taxpayer-initiated action, such as claim for refund.

Audit Division

Returns scrutinized

Selected for examination

Not selected for examination

Examined

Agreed as to tax or refund due

Findings may be reviewed

Tax collected or refund paid

No adjustment necessary

Disagreed as to tax or refund due

Findings reviewed

Appeals procedure beginning with an opportunity to meet with an appellate agent

Returns stored (Processing Site)

FIGURE 12.3

INCOME TAX APPEAL PROCEDURE OF THE INTERNAL REVENUE SERVICE

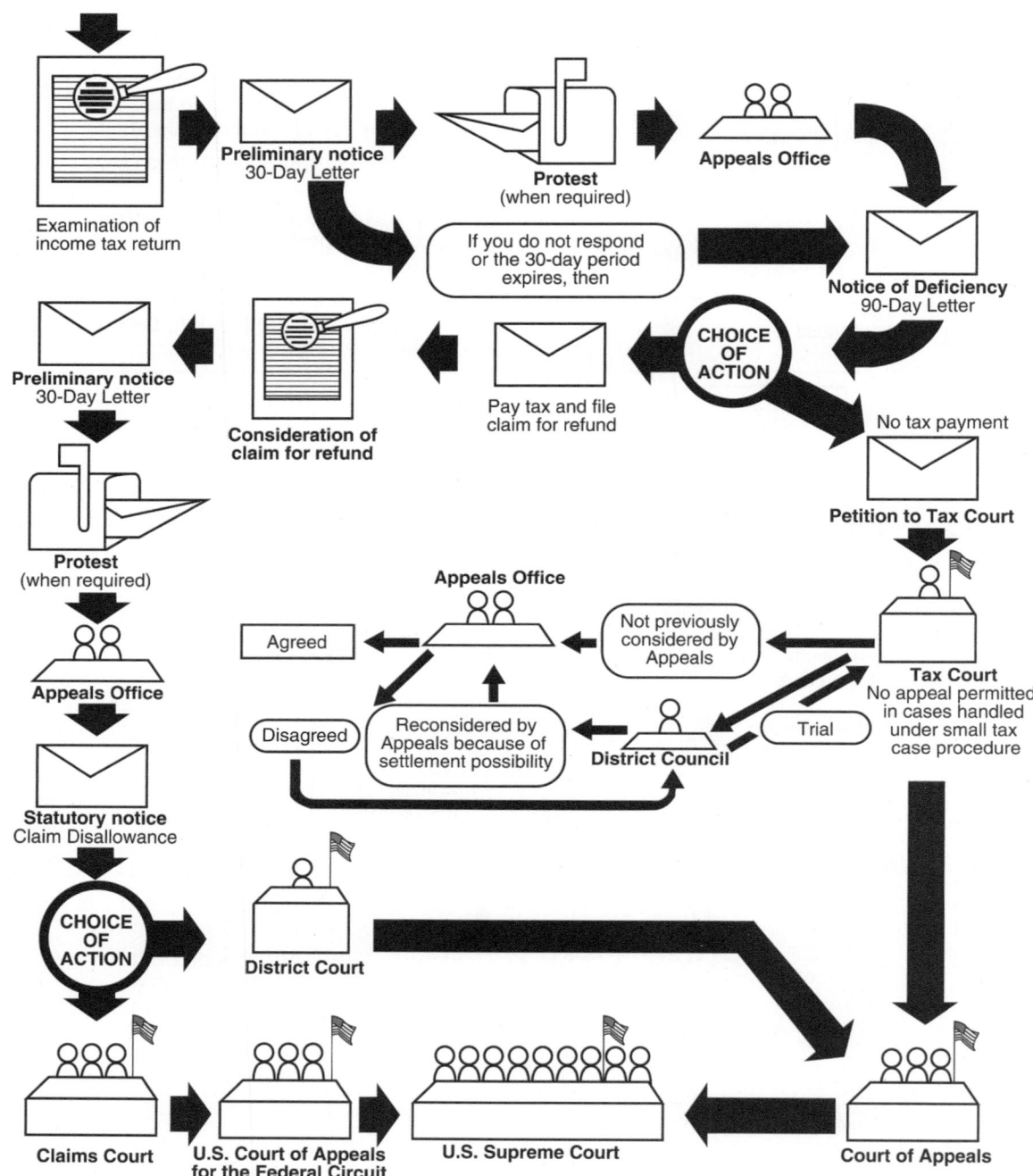

At any stage of procedure:
- You can agree and arrange to pay.
- You can ask the IRS to issue you a notice of deficiency so you can file a petition with the Tax Court.
- You can pay the tax and file a claim for a refund.

Self-Study Problem 12.2 *See Appendix E for Solutions to Self-Study Problems*

Indicate whether the following statements are true or false by circling the appropriate letter.

T F 1. The IRS uses computers to select tax returns for most audits.

T F 2. An office audit is done at the taxpayer's office.

T F 3. NRP audits are selected randomly.

T F 4. An audit may result in a refund.

T F 5. A taxpayer cannot appeal the results of an IRS audit.

12-3 INTEREST AND PENALTIES

12.3 Learning Objective

Define the common penalties for taxpayers and be able to apply them to specific situations.

Taxpayers are charged interest on underpayments of taxes, and in some cases the IRS pays interest to taxpayers when they overpay their taxes. Usually, these interest charges or payments result from the settlement of a tax liability for a prior year's tax return. For example, when an IRS audit results in the taxpayer paying additional taxes for a prior tax year, the IRS will charge the taxpayer interest on the amount of additional taxes from the original due date to the date of payment of the tax. If the audit results in a refund, interest will be paid to the taxpayer based on the amount of the refund. The IRS also imposes a nondeductible penalty based on amounts of underpayments of estimated taxes for the current tax year (see Chapter 9), but a taxpayer is not paid interest on a refund arising from an overpayment of estimated taxes during the current tax year.

The interest rate applicable to underpayments and overpayments of taxes is adjusted each quarter based on the short-term federal rate. The rate is equal to the federal short-term rate plus 3 percentage points. Interest is compounded daily except when calculating the penalty for underpayment of estimated taxes by individuals and corporations. In calculating the penalty for underpayment of estimated taxes, the penalty is calculated as simple interest.

The rate of interest for selected recent periods is as follows:

2019	Rate
1st quarter	6%
2nd quarter	6%
3rd quarter	5%
4th quarter	5%

Tables are available from the IRS for performing the actual calculation of interest owed from or due to taxpayers. Interest paid on an underpayment of tax is considered consumer interest and, therefore, no deduction is allowed (see Chapter 5). The penalty for underpayment of estimated tax is calculated as interest but is a nondeductible penalty. Interest received on an overpayment is income in the year the payment is received. No interest is paid on a current year overpayment, unless the IRS takes more than 45 days to process the return.

EXAMPLE James pays $2,000 of interest in 2019 for an underpayment of taxes on his 2016 tax return. The $2,000 is not deductible since no deduction is allowed for consumer interest. ◆

EXAMPLE John receives $700 of interest income on the overpayment of his taxes resulting from an IRS audit on his 2016 tax return. The $700 interest is income in the year it is received by John. ◆

The tax law contains various penalties to ensure taxpayers accurately report and pay their taxes. Penalty payments are considered an addition to the amount of the taxes and, therefore, are not deductible. Several of the major taxpayer penalties are described in the following paragraphs.

12-3a The Failure-to-Pay and Failure-to-File Penalties

Taxpayers are subject to a penalty for failure to pay the amount of the taxes due on the due date of their tax return. The penalty for failure to pay is ½ of 1 percent of the amount of taxes due for every month or portion of a month that the payment is late, up to a maximum of 25 percent of the amount of taxes due. The penalty increases to 1 percent per month beginning 10 days after a notice of levy has been given to the taxpayer.

If a taxpayer does not file a tax return on the due date (including extensions), he or she is subject to a penalty equal to 5 percent of the tax due with the return for every month or portion of a month the return is late. The amount of the penalty for failure to file, however, is limited to a maximum of 25 percent of the amount of taxes due with the tax return. In the event the failure to file is fraudulent, the penalty is increased from 5 percent for each month or portion thereof to 15 percent, and the maximum penalty is increased from 25 percent to 75 percent. Also, if the taxpayer fails to file their tax return within 60 days of its due date, the minimum failure-to-file penalty is the lesser of $210 or the total amount of the taxes due with the tax return.

Starting with tax year 2020, the Taxpayer First Act of 2019 increases the failure-to-file penalty to the lesser of the total amount of taxes due or $330.

If both the failure-to-file and the failure-to-pay penalties apply, the failure-to-file penalty (5 percent) is reduced by the amount of the failure-to-pay penalty (½ of 1 percent) to 4.5 percent so the total combined penalty stays at 5 percent. The maximum combined penalty is 25 percent for the first 5 months. After 5 months, the failure-to-pay penalty continues at ½ of 1 percent per month for up to an additional 45 months. Thus, the maximum combined penalty could reach 47.5 percent.

Both the failure-to-file and the failure-to-pay penalties are zero if there is no tax due or if a refund is due from the IRS on the late tax return. The failure-to-file and the failure-to-pay penalty will not be assessed if the taxpayer can demonstrate that he or she had "reasonable cause" for failing to pay or file the tax return on time.

EXAMPLE Nancy filed her 2019 tax return 3½ months after the due date, and she had not requested an extension of time to file. The failure to file was not due to fraud. She included with her late return a check for $2,000, which was the balance of the tax she owed. Disregarding interest, her penalties are calculated as follows:

Failure-to-pay penalty		$ 40
(0.5% × $2,000) × 4 months		
Plus:		
Failure-to-file penalty	$400	
(5% × $2,000) × 4 months		
Less: Failure-to-pay penalty	(40)	
Net failure-to-file penalty		360
Total penalties		$400 ♦

The IRS has a first-time penalty abatement program which was meant to allow taxpayers who were assessed penalties for the first time to request a one-time penalty amnesty. The program applies to the failure-to-file and failure-to-pay penalties as well as several others, and can save taxpayers significant amounts of money in certain cases. The penalty abatement waiver must be requested by the taxpayer, but few taxpayers who qualify for the waiver request it or even know the program exists.

12-3b **Accuracy-Related Penalty**

The tax law imposes a penalty of 20 percent of the applicable underpayment due to (1) negligence of or disregard for rules or regulations, (2) a substantial understatement of income tax, or (3) a substantial valuation overstatement, as well as certain other understatements of income tax. Negligence includes the failure to make a reasonable attempt to comply with the tax law. For example, the penalty could be imposed on a taxpayer who deducts a personal expenditure as a business expense. A substantial understatement of income tax occurs where the required amount of tax exceeds the tax shown on the taxpayer's return by the greater of 10 percent (5 percent if claiming a qualified business income deduction) of the amount of tax that should be shown on the return or $5,000 ($10,000 for corporate taxpayers other than S corporations). A substantial valuation overstatement occurs when the value of property is 150 percent or more of the correct valuation. For example, a taxpayer who inflates the value of depreciable property to generate additional depreciation deductions may be subject to this penalty. The accuracy-related penalty applies only if the taxpayer has filed a return. In addition, if the taxpayer can demonstrate that he or she has reasonable cause for the understatement of tax and that he or she acted in good faith, the penalty will not be assessed.

EXAMPLE Kim underpaid her taxes for the current year by $15,000 due to negligence. Kim's penalty for negligence under the accuracy-related penalty is calculated as follows:

Accuracy-related penalty (20% × $15,000)	$3,000 ♦

12-3c **Fraud Penalty**

The tax law also contains provisions for penalties for filing fraudulent tax returns. The fraud penalty is equal to 75 percent of the amount of underpayment of taxes attributable to fraud.

For the IRS to impose the fraud penalty, it must be shown by a "preponderance of evidence" that the taxpayer had an intent to evade taxes; however, once the IRS establishes that any portion of an underpayment of taxes is due to fraud, the entire underpayment is assumed to be attributable to fraud unless the taxpayer establishes otherwise. The tax law does not provide clear rules for what constitutes fraud; however, what is clearly mere negligence by a taxpayer will not cause this penalty to be imposed. When the fraud penalty is applicable, the accuracy-related penalty cannot be imposed. The fraud penalty will be applied only where the taxpayer has actually filed a return. Like the accuracy-related penalty, the fraud penalty will not be assessed if the taxpayer can demonstrate reasonable cause for the underpayment of tax and the taxpayer acted in good faith.

EXAMPLE Jeff has a $20,000 tax deficiency because of civil fraud. Interest on this underpayment amounts to $8,000. Jeff's total amount due on this underpayment is calculated as follows:

Tax deficiency	$20,000
Fraud penalty (75% × $20,000)	15,000
Interest	8,000
Total due	$43,000

The interest is not deductible due to the disallowance of deductions for consumer interest. The fraud penalty is also not deductible. ♦

According to IRS data, 11 to 16 percent of Americans feel cheating on taxes is acceptable. Experts agree that tax cheating is a significant problem for the IRS, which must enforce the laws, and for honest taxpayers who pay more in taxes than they would otherwise have to. It is generally believed that tax evasion and noncompliance are costing the government more than $300 billion dollars in lost revenue each year.

Sign Here	Under penalties of perjury, I declare that I have examined this return and accompanying schedules and statements, and to the best of my knowledge and belief, they are true, correct, and complete. Declaration of preparer (other than taxpayer) is based on all information of which preparer has any knowledge.			
	Your signature	Date	Your occupation	If the IRS sent you an Identity Protection PIN, enter it here (see inst.)
Joint return? See instructions. Keep a copy for your records.	Spouse's signature. If a joint return, **both** must sign.	Date	Spouse's occupation	If the IRS sent your spouse an Identity Protection PIN, enter it here (see inst.)
	Phone no.		Email address	
Paid Preparer Use Only	Preparer's name	Preparer's signature	Date	PTIN	Check if: ☐ 3rd Party Designee
	Firm's name ▶		Phone no.		☐ Self-employed
	Firm's address ▶			Firm's EIN ▶

Would You Sign This Tax Return?

Tim Trying, who is single, purchased a house on the beach in sunny Southern California 35 years ago. He is now retiring and moving to Hawaii for his golden years. Tim sold his house for $1,200,000 this year. Tim has been a client of yours for the past decade. He became a client when he was referred to you by your parents, who lived two houses away from Tim. When asked what his tax basis is in the house, Tim says it is $975,000. Your parents bought their house at about the same time, and you know they paid $100,000 for it. You have seen Tim's house many times and, although the house is well-maintained, you know it does not have any major improvements or betterments. You are reasonably certain that Tim is overstating his tax basis by hundreds of thousands of dollars in order to avoid reporting a taxable gain on the sale. Would you sign the Paid Preparer's declaration (see example above) on this return? Why or why not?

12-3d Miscellaneous Penalties

The tax law contains many other penalties applicable to taxpayers. The following are examples of such penalties:

- A civil penalty of $500 and a criminal penalty of $1,000 are imposed for filing false withholding information.
- An immediate $5,000 penalty can be assessed against a taxpayer who files a "frivolous" tax return (or document) as a tax protest.
- A tiered penalty system dependent on the timeliness of correction and filing of information returns (including payee information returns) is imposed for failing to file correct information returns. The penalties for tax returns filed in 2020 are up to $270 per return, $3,339,000 ($1,113,000 for small business) annual maximum. If the failure to file is corrected or the information returns are filed closer to the due date, the penalties may be reduced. Exceptions to the information return penalties may be made for reasonable cause.
- Employers are subject to a penalty of 2, 5, or 10 percent of the amount of payroll taxes not deposited on time, depending on the number of days the taxes remain undeposited. A 15 percent penalty may apply where taxes remain undeposited after a delinquency notice has been presented to the taxpayer.
- Taxpayers are subject to a penalty for failure to pay estimated taxes. The penalty is calculated using the interest rates for the period of underpayment (but it is not deductible as interest).
- Taxpayers are subject to a penalty for issuing a "bad" check, unless the taxpayer can demonstrate that the check was issued in good faith. The penalty is equal to 2 percent of the amount of the check. If the check is less than $1,250, then the penalty is the lesser of $25 or the amount of the check.

Would You Believe?

In 2016, the European Commission levied taxes and interest due from Apple of €14.4 billion. Although Apple contests the charge, the US $20 billion tax has been paid and is sitting in an escrow account awaiting appeal. Apple's pretax income in 2018 was almost $73 billion.

Self-Study Problem 12.3   *See Appendix E for Solutions to Self-Study Problems*

Part a

Linda filed her tax return 2 months late. The tax paid with the return amounts to $3,000. What is Linda's total penalty for failure to file and failure to pay, assuming the failure to file is not fraudulent?

$_____

Part b

Kim underpaid her taxes by $10,000 due to negligence. What is Kim's penalty for negligence?

$_____

Part c

Using the same information as in Part b, what is the amount of the penalty if the underpayment were determined to be due to civil fraud?

$_____

12-4 STATUTE OF LIMITATIONS

12.4 Learning Objective

Apply the general rule for the statute of limitations on tax returns and the important exceptions to the general rule.

The statute of limitations is the time period within which an action may be taken by the IRS and the taxpayer on a tax return. After the statute of limitations has run out on a given tax return, the government cannot assess additional taxes and the taxpayer cannot amend the return to request a refund. In general, the statute of limitations for a tax return runs for 3 years from the date the tax return was filed or the return due date (without extensions), whichever is later. For taxpayers seeking a refund, the statute of limitations is the later of 3 years from the time of filing or 2 years from the date that the taxes were actually paid.

EXAMPLE   Norm files his 2019 tax return on March 19, 2020. Unless an exception discussed below applies, the IRS has until April 15, 2023, to assess any additional taxes. ♦

12-4a Exceptions

The tax law contains several exceptions to the general rule of a 3-year statute of limitations. Several of these special rules are summarized below:

- If a fraudulent tax return is filed or no return is filed, there is no statute of limitations. The IRS may assess a tax deficiency at any time in the future.
- If a taxpayer omits an amount of gross income in excess of 25 percent of the gross income shown on the return, then the statute of limitations is increased to 6 years. For example, if a tax return with gross income of $40,000 contains an omission of over $10,000 (25 percent of $40,000) of gross income, the statute of limitations is increased to 6 years.
- The statute of limitations for the deduction of a bad debt or worthless securities is 7 years. This limitation applies only to the bad debt deduction or the worthless security deduction; all other items on the tax return would normally close out after 3 years.

Besides these exceptions, the statute of limitations may be extended by mutual consent of the IRS and the taxpayer. This extension is for a specific time period and is made by signing the appropriate form in the Form 872 series. An extension is generally used when the statute of limitations is about to lapse and an audit has not been completed.

If a tax deficiency has been assessed by the IRS within the period of the statute of limitations, then the government has 10 years from the date of assessment to collect the tax due.

An IRS study shows that many taxpayers lose refunds because they fail to file their returns within the statute of limitations for claiming a refund, which can be either 2 or 3 years depending on the circumstances. The IRS denies millions of dollars in refunds each year which were claimed in delinquent returns.

Self-Study Problem 12.4   *See Appendix E for Solutions to Self-Study Problems*

Indicate whether the following statements are true or false by circling the appropriate letter.

T   F   1.   The general statute of limitations for a tax return is 3 years.

T   F   2.   The statute of limitations for a bad debt deduction on a tax return is 6 years.

T   F   3.   The statute of limitations for a fraudulent tax return is 7 years.

T   F   4.   The special statute of limitations for a tax return that omits income greater than 25 percent of gross income is 6 years.

T   F   5.   For the deduction of worthless securities, the statute of limitations is 7 years.

Learning Objective 12.5

Describe the rules and penalties that apply to tax practitioners.

12-5 PREPARERS, PROOF, AND PRIVILEGE

12-5a Tax Practitioners

Many taxpayers find it desirable or necessary to have their tax returns prepared by a tax practitioner. Tax practitioners include commercial preparers, enrolled agents, attorneys, and certified public accountants (CPAs). Commercial preparers generally prepare non-complex returns of individuals, small corporations, and partnerships. Enrolled agents are individuals who have passed an IRS exam and are allowed to represent clients at IRS proceedings, as well as prepare tax returns. Attorneys and CPAs are individuals who have met education, examination, and experience requirements and are licensed to practice in their respective professions. CPAs and attorneys normally work with complex tax returns of individuals, corporations, partnerships, estates, and trusts. They also provide tax-planning advice to aid their clients in minimizing the amount of their taxes. Preparers that are enrolled agents, CPAs, and attorneys are sometimes referred to as enrolled preparers while other non-credentialed preparers are known as unenrolled preparers.

The IRS operated a program for taxpayers who failed to report offshore income known as the offshore voluntary disclosure program (OVDP). The Taxpayer Advocate's Office examined taxpayers who participated in the OVDP and found that those with the largest offshore accounts ($4.2 million or more) paid penalties of about three times the unpaid taxes. However, those with the smallest accounts (about $87,000 of less) paid nearly six times the unpaid tax. The OVDP closed in September 2018.

12-5b Annual Filing Season Program

In 2011, the IRS attempted to regulate the national tax preparation industry by implementing the Registered Tax Return Preparer (RTRP) system which required all unenrolled tax preparers to obtain a preparer tax identification number (PTIN), pass a background check, and pass a competency exam. In 2013, the RTRP program was put on hold as a result of a court decision and finally the program was disbanded after the IRS exhausted its appeals of the case. Unless Congress takes legislative action, the RTRP program is dead. One important part of the RTRP program that did remain is the PTIN requirement. All paid tax return preparers must sign up with the IRS and obtain a PTIN. Every year, paid tax preparers must sign up or renew their PTIN online. There is no charge to obtain or renew a PTIN.

In lieu of the RTRP program, the IRS now operates the Annual Filing Season Program (AFSP), a voluntary tax return preparer program designed to encourage preparers to participate in continuing education courses to help stay abreast of changes in tax law and help reduce the risk of using a preparer without professional credentials. The AFSP requires unenrolled preparers to obtain 18 hours of continuing education from an approved provider including at least 6 hours of an Annual Federal Tax Refresher (AFTR) course focused on filing season issues and tax updates and two hours of ethics. The AFTR must include a knowledge-based exam administered at the end of the course by the course provider.

In addition to being better prepared for the upcoming filing season, a list of tax preparers meeting the AFSP requirements is published at **www.irs.gov** to permit taxpayers to search for qualified tax return preparers. For additional information on the Annual Filing Season Program requirements, see the IRS website **(www.irs.gov)**.

12-5c Preparer Penalties

Under the tax law, any person who prepares a tax return, including nonincome tax returns (e.g., excise tax returns), for compensation is a "tax return preparer." The tax law has various penalty provisions applicable to tax return preparers. These penalties are designed to help the IRS regulate the preparation of tax returns. The more significant penalties are described below:

- $50 for failing to sign a tax return or failing to furnish the preparer's identifying number, $26,500 annual maximum
- $50 for each failure to keep a copy of the prepared return or include the return on a list of taxpayers for whom returns have been prepared, $26,500 annual maximum
- $50 for failing to provide a taxpayer a copy of the tax return prepared, $26,500 annual maximum
- $530 for endorsing or cashing a refund check issued to a taxpayer, or failing in due diligence for a taxpayer claiming the earned income credit
- Greater of $1,000 or 50 percent of the income derived (or to be derived) by the tax return preparer for an undisclosed unrealistic position on a return which does not meet a "substantial authority" standard, and which the preparer knew or reasonably should have known about

- Greater of $5,000 or 75 percent of the income derived (or to be derived) by the tax return preparer for each return in which the preparer willfully attempts to understate the amount of the taxpayer's tax liability, or each return in which an understatement is due to the preparer's reckless or intentional disregard of rules or regulations, reduced by the amount of the $1,000 (or 50 percent) penalty for unrealistic positions (discussed above)
- $1,000 ($10,000 for corporate returns) for each return or document filed in aiding or abetting a taxpayer in understating a tax liability
- For each separate activity (sale of an interest, organization of an entity, etc.), the lesser of $1,000 or 100 percent of the gross income derived by the promoter from promoting an "abusive tax shelter"

12-5d Burden of Proof

In most litigation, the party initiating the case has the burden of convincing the court that he or she is correct with respect to the issue. Historically, however, in most civil tax cases, the Internal Revenue Code (the Code) placed the burden of proof on the taxpayer, whether or not he or she initiated the case, except in cases involving such items as hobby losses, fraud with intent to evade tax, and the accumulated earnings tax.

In the IRS Restructuring and Reform Act of 1998, the tax law was changed to shift the burden of proof to the IRS in many situations. The IRS now has the burden of proof in any court proceeding on an income, gift, estate, or generation-skipping tax liability with respect to factual issues, provided the taxpayer (1) introduces credible evidence of the factual issue, (2) maintains records and substantiates items as presently required under the Code and Regulations, and (3) cooperates with reasonable IRS requests for meetings, interviews, witnesses, information, and documents. For corporations, trusts, and partnerships with net worth exceeding $7 million, the burden of proof remains on the taxpayer.

The burden of proof also automatically shifts to the IRS in two situations:

1. If the IRS uses statistics to reconstruct an individual's income, or
2. If the court proceeding against an individual taxpayer involves a penalty or addition to tax.

12-5e Tax Confidentiality Privilege

The 1998 Act also extended the existing attorney-client privilege of confidentiality in tax matters to nonattorneys authorized to practice before the IRS (e.g., CPAs and enrolled agents). The nonattorney-client privilege may be asserted only in a *noncriminal tax* proceeding before the IRS or federal courts. Also, the nonattorney-client privilege does not extend to written communications between a tax practitioner and a corporation in connection with the promotion of any tax shelter.

CPAs and enrolled agents need to understand the rules regarding tax confidentiality as they have been applied to lawyers to be aware of the tax privilege limits. For example, tax privileged communication usually does not apply to the preparation of tax returns, the giving of accounting or business advice, or to tax accrual workpapers. Also, unlike the general attorney-client privilege, the nonattorney-client privilege does not automatically apply to state tax situations.

Self-Study Problem 12.5 *See Appendix E for Solutions to Self-Study Problems*

Indicate whether the following statements are true or false by circling the appropriate letter.

T F 1. Only certified public accountants may represent taxpayers before the IRS.

T F 2. A college degree is required to prepare tax returns for compensation.

T F 3. Only attorneys may prepare corporate tax returns.

T F 4. The tax preparer penalty for filing a document aiding and abetting an individual taxpayer in the understatement of a tax liability is $1,000.

T F 5. The tax preparer penalty for endorsing a taxpayer's refund check is $520.

T F 6. The tax preparer penalty for failing to provide a copy of a tax return to a taxpayer is $50.

T F 7. For audits after 1998, if the IRS uses statistics to reconstruct an individual taxpayer's income, the burden of proof is on the taxpayer.

T F 8. For corporations, trusts, and partnerships with net worth over $7 million, the burden of proof is on the IRS in civil tax matters.

T F 9. CPAs and enrolled agents have tax privileged communication only in noncriminal proceedings before the IRS or federal courts.

T F 10. If an individual taxpayer does not cooperate with reasonable IRS requests for meetings, interviews, witnesses, information, and documents, the burden of proof in a tax matter is on the taxpayer.

T F 11. Commercial tax preparers must have a PTIN.

12-6 THE TAXPAYER BILL OF RIGHTS

12.6 Learning Objective

Describe the Taxpayer Bill of Rights.

Over the years, the news media carried many horror stories about taxpayers who claimed they had been abused by the IRS. As a result of this publicity, in 1988 Congress passed a set of provisions referred to as the Taxpayer Bill of Rights. The Taxpayer Bill of Rights has been amended several times since it was originally passed by Congress. This set of provisions requires the IRS to inform taxpayers of their rights in dealing with the IRS, and expands taxpayers' rights and remedies when they are involved in disputes with the IRS. The provisions of the Taxpayer Bill of Rights are summarized in IRS Publication 1, which is reproduced on Pages 12-20 and 12-21. Also note, Publication 1 directs taxpayers to other IRS publications with more details on specific taxpayer rights.

The first part of this publication explains some of the most important rights as a taxpayer. The second part explains the examination, appeal, collection, and refund processes.

Your Rights as a Taxpayer

Publication 1

This publication explains your rights as a taxpayer and the processes for examination, appeal, collection, and refunds. Also available in Spanish.

The Taxpayer Bill of Rights

1. The Right to Be Informed

Taxpayers have the right to know what they need to do to comply with the tax laws. They are entitled to clear explanations of the laws and IRS procedures in all tax forms, instructions, publications, notices, and correspondence. They have the right to be informed of IRS decisions about their tax accounts and to receive clear explanations of the outcomes.

2. The Right to Quality Service

Taxpayers have the right to receive prompt, courteous, and professional assistance in their dealings with the IRS, to be spoken to in a way they can easily understand, to receive clear and easily understandable communications from the IRS, and to speak to a supervisor about inadequate service.

3. The Right to Pay No More than the Correct Amount of Tax

Taxpayers have the right to pay only the amount of tax legally due, including interest and penalties, and to have the IRS apply all tax payments properly.

4. The Right to Challenge the IRS's Position and Be Heard

Taxpayers have the right to raise objections and provide additional documentation in response to formal IRS actions or proposed actions, to expect that the IRS will consider their timely objections and documentation promptly and fairly, and to receive a response if the IRS does not agree with their position.

5. The Right to Appeal an IRS Decision in an Independent Forum

Taxpayers are entitled to a fair and impartial administrative appeal of most IRS decisions, including many penalties, and have the right to receive a written response regarding the Office of Appeals' decision. Taxpayers generally have the right to take their cases to court.

6. The Right to Finality

Taxpayers have the right to know the maximum amount of time they have to challenge the IRS's position as well as the maximum amount of time the IRS has to audit a particular tax year or collect a tax debt. Taxpayers have the right to know when the IRS has finished an audit.

7. The Right to Privacy

Taxpayers have the right to expect that any IRS inquiry, examination, or enforcement action will comply with the law and be no more intrusive than necessary, and will respect all due process rights, including search and seizure protections, and will provide, where applicable, a collection due process hearing.

8. The Right to Confidentiality

Taxpayers have the right to expect that any information they provide to the IRS will not be disclosed unless authorized by the taxpayer or by law. Taxpayers have the right to expect appropriate action will be taken against employees, return preparers, and others who wrongfully use or disclose taxpayer return information.

9. The Right to Retain Representation

Taxpayers have the right to retain an authorized representative of their choice to represent them in their dealings with the IRS. Taxpayers have the right to seek assistance from a Low Income Taxpayer Clinic if they cannot afford representation.

10. The Right to a Fair and Just Tax System

Taxpayers have the right to expect the tax system to consider facts and circumstances that might affect their underlying liabilities, ability to pay, or ability to provide information timely. Taxpayers have the right to receive assistance from the Taxpayer Advocate Service if they are experiencing financial difficulty or if the IRS has not resolved their tax issues properly and timely through its normal channels.

The IRS Mission | Provide America's taxpayers top-quality service by helping them understand and meet their tax responsibilities and enforce the law with integrity and fairness to all.

Publication 1 (Rev. 9-2017) Catalog Number 64731W Department of the Treasury **Internal Revenue Service** www.irs.gov

Examinations, Appeals, Collections, and Refunds

Examinations (Audits)

We accept most taxpayers' returns as filed. If we inquire about your return or select it for examination, it does not suggest that you are dishonest. The inquiry or examination may or may not result in more tax. We may close your case without change; or, you may receive a refund.

The process of selecting a return for examination usually begins in one of two ways. First, we use computer programs to identify returns that may have incorrect amounts. These programs may be based on information returns, such as Forms 1099 and W-2, on studies of past examinations, or on certain issues identified by compliance projects. Second, we use information from outside sources that indicates that a return may have incorrect amounts. These sources may include newspapers, public records, and individuals. If we determine that the information is accurate and reliable, we may use it to select a return for examination.

Publication 556, Examination of Returns, Appeal Rights, and Claims for Refund, explains the rules and procedures that we follow in examinations. The following sections give an overview of how we conduct examinations.

By Mail

We handle many examinations and inquiries by mail. We will send you a letter with either a request for more information or a reason why we believe a change to your return may be needed. You can respond by mail or you can request a personal interview with an examiner. If you mail us the requested information or provide an explanation, we may or may not agree with you, and we will explain the reasons for any changes. Please do not hesitate to write to us about anything you do not understand.

By Interview

If we notify you that we will conduct your examination through a personal interview, or you request such an interview, you have the right to ask that the examination take place at a reasonable time and place that is convenient for both you and the IRS. If our examiner proposes any changes to your return, he or she will explain the reasons for the changes. If you do not agree with these changes, you can meet with the examiner's supervisor.

Repeat Examinations

If we examined your return for the same items in either of the 2 previous years and proposed no change to your tax liability, please contact us as soon as possible so we can see if we should discontinue the examination.

Appeals

If you do not agree with the examiner's proposed changes, you can appeal them to the Appeals Office of the IRS. Most differences can be settled without expensive and time-consuming court trials. Your appeal rights are explained in detail in both Publication 5, Your Appeal Rights and How To Prepare a Protest If You Don't Agree, and Publication 556, Examination of Returns, Appeal Rights, and Claims for Refund.

If you do not wish to use the Appeals Office or disagree with its findings, you may be able to take your case to the U.S. Tax Court, U.S. Court of Federal Claims, or the U.S. District Court where you live. If you take your case to court, the IRS will have the burden of proving certain facts if you kept adequate records to show your tax liability, cooperated with the IRS, and meet certain other conditions. If the court agrees with you on most issues in your case and finds that our position was largely unjustified, you may be able to recover some of your administrative and litigation costs. You will not be eligible to recover these costs unless you tried to resolve your case administratively, including going through the appeals system, and you gave us the information necessary to resolve the case.

Collections

Publication 594, The IRS Collection Process, explains your rights and responsibilities regarding payment of federal taxes. It describes:

- What to do when you owe taxes. It describes what to do if you get a tax bill and what to do if you think your bill is wrong. It also covers making installment payments, delaying collection action, and submitting an offer in compromise.

- IRS collection actions. It covers liens, releasing a lien, levies, releasing a levy, seizures and sales, and release of property.

- IRS certification to the State Department of a seriously delinquent tax debt, which will generally result in denial of a passport application and may lead to revocation of a passport.

Your collection appeal rights are explained in detail in Publication 1660, Collection Appeal Rights.

Innocent Spouse Relief

Generally, both you and your spouse are each responsible for paying the full amount of tax, interest, and penalties due on your joint return. However, if you qualify for innocent spouse relief, you may be relieved of part or all of the joint liability. To request relief, you must file Form 8857, Request for Innocent Spouse Relief. For more information on innocent spouse relief, see Publication 971, Innocent Spouse Relief, and Form 8857.

Potential Third Party Contacts

Generally, the IRS will deal directly with you or your duly authorized representative. However, we sometimes talk with other persons if we need information that you have been unable to provide, or to verify information we have received. If we do contact other persons, such as a neighbor, bank, employer, or employees, we will generally need to tell them limited information, such as your name. The law prohibits us from disclosing any more information than is necessary to obtain or verify the information we are seeking. Our need to contact other persons may continue as long as there is activity in your case. If we do contact other persons, you have a right to request a list of those contacted. Your request can be made by telephone, in writing, or during a personal interview.

Refunds

You may file a claim for refund if you think you paid too much tax. You must generally file the claim within 3 years from the date you filed your original return or 2 years from the date you paid the tax, whichever is later. The law generally provides for interest on your refund if it is not paid within 45 days of the date you filed your return or claim for refund. Publication 556, Examination of Returns, Appeal Rights, and Claims for Refund, has more information on refunds.

If you were due a refund but you did not file a return, you generally must file your return within 3 years from the date the return was due (including extensions) to get that refund.

Taxpayer Advocate Service

TAS is an *independent* organization within the IRS that can help protect your taxpayer rights. We can offer you help if your tax problem is causing a hardship, or you've tried but haven't been able to resolve your problem with the IRS. If you qualify for our assistance, which is always free, we will do everything possible to help you. Visit *www.taxpayeradvocate.irs.gov* or call 1-877-777-4778.

Tax Information

The IRS provides the following sources for forms, publications, and additional information.

- *Tax Questions:* 1-800-829-1040 (1-800-829-4059 for TTY/TDD)
- *Forms and Publications:* 1-800-829-3676 (1-800-829-4059 for TTY/TDD)
- *Internet: www.irs.gov*
- *Small Business Ombudsman:* A small business entity can participate in the regulatory process and comment on enforcement actions of the IRS by calling 1-888-REG-FAIR.
- *Treasury Inspector General for Tax Administration:* You can confidentially report misconduct, waste, fraud, or abuse by an IRS employee by calling 1-800-366-4484 (1-800-877-8339 for TTY/TDD). You can remain anonymous.

Internal Revenue Service (IRS)

Self-Study Problem 12.6   *See Appendix E for Solutions to Self-Study Problems*

Indicate whether the following statements are true or false by circling the appropriate letter.

T   F   1. Taxpayers have the right to represent themselves or, with proper written authorization, have someone else represent them.

T   F   2. The IRS may contact a taxpayer's neighbor or employer to verify information.

T   F   3. IRS Publication 594 explains a taxpayer's rights and responsibilities regarding payment of federal taxes.

T   F   4. If a taxpayer is audited in the current year for an item that was audited in either of the 2 previous years and the IRS proposed no change to the tax liability, the taxpayer should contact the IRS as soon as possible to attempt to stop the repeat audit.

T   F   5. Generally, both a taxpayer and his or her spouse are responsible, jointly and individually, for the tax and any interest or penalty due on a joint return.

T   F   6. Taxpayers must file a claim for refund within 3 years of the date they filed their return or 2 years from the date they paid the tax if they think they paid too much tax.

Learning Objective 12.7

Explain the basic concepts of tax planning.

12-7 TAX PLANNING

The process of arranging one's financial affairs to maximize one's after-tax wealth is often referred to as tax planning. There is nothing wrong with tax planning to avoid tax, provided legal methods are used. Judge Learned Hand best stated the doctrine of tax planning in 1947 when he wrote:

"Over and over again, courts have said there is nothing sinister in so arranging one's affairs as to keep taxes as low as possible. Everybody does so, rich or poor, and all do right, for nobody owes any public duty to pay more than the law demands: taxes are enforced extractions, not voluntary contributions." *Commissioner v. Newman*, 159 F.2d 848 (CA-2, 1947).

When illegal methods are used to reduce tax liability, the process can no longer be considered tax planning, but instead becomes tax evasion. Tax evasion can subject the taxpayer and tax practitioner to fines, penalties, and incarceration. Illegal acts are outside the realm of tax-planning services offered by a professional tax practitioner.

Tax planning covers two basic categories of transactions, the "open transaction" and the "closed transaction." In an open transaction, all the events have not yet been completed; therefore, the taxpayer has some degree of control over the tax consequences. In a closed transaction, all material parts of the transaction have been completed. As a result, tax planning involving a closed transaction is limited to presentation of the facts to the IRS in the most favorable, legally acceptable manner possible.

EXAMPLE   Annie enters into an agreement with Erik to exchange real estate held as an investment. Escrow has not closed and the title of the property has not passed between the parties. Since all significant events (title passing) are not complete, the transaction is considered an open transaction. Once the title to the real estate passes, the tax planning involves a closed transaction. ♦

Tax planning cannot be considered in a void. Any tax-planning advice must consider the business goals of the taxpayer. Tax planning for a transaction should not override sound business judgment.

12-7a Tax Rate Terminology

Important to any tax-planning situation is an evaluation of the tax savings arising from increasing deductions or the tax cost of generating additional income. The tax consequences are dependent on the taxpayer's tax rate. The taxpayer's tax rate may be defined in several ways. For tax-planning purposes, the taxpayer needs to understand the difference between the "average" tax rate and the "marginal" tax rate. The average tax rate merely represents the average rate of tax applicable to the taxpayer's income and is calculated as the total tax paid divided by the total income of the taxpayer. The marginal tax rate represents the rate at which tax is imposed on the "next" dollar of income.

EXAMPLE   Becky, a single taxpayer, has income of $40,000 during the current year on which she pays tax of $4,740. Her average tax rate is 11.85 percent ($4,740 ÷ $40,000). If Becky's income increases to $50,000, her tax liability will be $6,940. Thus, Becky's marginal rate is 22 percent [($6,940 − $4,740) ÷ ($50,000 − $40,000)]. ♦

When making tax-planning decisions, the taxpayer's marginal tax rate is the most important tax rate. For example, Jason has a 30 percent marginal tax rate and a 20 percent average tax rate and is considering making a tax-deductible expenditure of $2,000. His after-tax cost of the expenditure is calculated using his marginal tax rate, not his average tax rate. Jason's after-tax cost of the expenditure would be $1,400, calculated as follows: [$2,000 − ($2,000 × 30 percent)]. On the other hand, if Jason is to receive any additional income, he knows that he will pay tax at a rate of 30 percent on the next dollar of income.

12-7b Examples of Tax Planning

Tax planning opportunities can be classified into four categories: (1) timing, (2) jurisdiction, (3) entity, and (4) character. Most tax-planning techniques employ at least one of these characteristics in an attempt to save taxpayers money.

12-7c Timing

In its simplest form, timing implies deferring the payment of taxes to a future year and is generally achieved by either deferring income recognition or accelerating expense deduction.

EXAMPLE   Karen operates a small cash basis, calendar year-end business. In order to lower her current year's income, Karen may prepay January's rent in December. She could also delay invoicing her customers in an attempt to defer the recognition of income. ♦

Most simple timing techniques work best when tax rates are not expected to change. If tax rates are expected to change across the periods in which the timing is being changed, a more thorough analysis is going to be required.

EXAMPLE   If in the previous example Karen expects her tax rate to increase from 24 percent in the current year to 37 percent next year, she may want to consider accelerating the recognition of income into the current year at the lower rate and deferring the deduction of expenses until next year increasing the value of the deduction. ♦

One disadvantage of using the timing technique is that tax recognition frequently occurs simultaneously with cash transactions. For example, one way to defer income recognition might be to earn no income; however, that generally spells the end of the business as well.

12-7d Jurisdiction

Using jurisdiction for tax planning involves exploiting differences in tax rates or tax systems to lower tax liabilities.

EXAMPLE Mark worked for the Lake Tahoe office of the state of California Department of Motor Vehicles for 35 years. In the current year, he starts his well-deserved retirement. Realizing that the individual tax rate in California can be over 10 percent, he moves to nearby Reno, Nevada, knowing that Nevada has no state income tax on individuals. He continues to collect his pension without paying state income tax. ♦

Jurisdiction, although simple in concept, can be difficult to implement for many taxpayers. Most individuals do not have the luxury to simply move to a new state to lower the state income tax rate. Larger businesses may have more flexibility than individuals or small businesses to implement a jurisdictional tax plan.

12-7e Entity

Entity-based tax planning involves making a choice about the type of entity a taxpayer chooses to operate as.

EXAMPLE Raquel is starting a new small business and expects to operate at a loss for the first few years. In an attempt to take advantage of using the losses to offset her other forms of income, she establishes her new business as a flow-through entity such as an LLC in hopes of passing those losses through to her individual tax return. ♦

12-7f Character

Using character for tax planning often requires a deeper understanding of tax law than the other tax-planning techniques. Using character means the transaction will be designed to take advantage of the tax law or a taxpayer's current situation.

EXAMPLE Axel owns stock purchased 11 months ago and has now doubled in value. Although Axel thinks the stock's value has peaked, he wishes to wait one additional month before selling to convert the short-term capital gain taxed at ordinary tax rates into a long-term capital gain taxed at preferential rates. Although this might also feel like a timing-based plan, the one month deferral of taxes is not likely to be significant. ♦

EXAMPLE Beck is a single taxpayer with a 24 percent marginal tax rate. Beck is debating between an investment in a taxable bond that pays 5 percent or a tax-exempt bond that pays 4.5 percent. Although the pre-tax return on the taxable bond of 5 percent is higher than the 4.5 percent exempt bond, the after-tax return of the taxable bond is only 3.8 percent [5% $\times$ (1 − 0.24 tax rate)]. ♦

Self-Study Problem 12.7   *See Appendix E for Solutions to Self-Study Problems*

During the current year, K's taxable income is $89,000 and he pays income tax of $15,541.00. K is single, has no dependents, and does not itemize his deductions. J, who files in *exactly* the same manner as K, has taxable income of $90,000 and pays income tax of $15,781.00.

1. What is K's average tax rate?   _____

2. What is J's average tax rate?   _____

3. If K's income increased to the same amount as J,
   what would K's marginal tax rate be?   _____

KEY TERMS

Internal Revenue Service (IRS), 12-2
commissioner of internal revenue, 12-2
IRS Campus Processing Sites, 12-2
IRS organizational structure, 12-3
Small Business/Self-Employed
    (SB/SE) Division, 12-4
Wage and Investment (W&I)
    Division, 12-5
offer in compromise, 12-5
office audit, 12-6
field audit, 12-6
correspondence audit, 12-6
Discriminant Function System
    (DIF), 12-7
appeals process of IRS, 12-8
Federal Tax Court, 12-8

audit procedure of IRS, 12-9
appeal procedure of IRS, 12-10
interest, 12-11
nondeductible penalty, 12-11
interest rate, 12-11
failure-to-pay penalty, 12-12
failure-to-file penalty, 12-12
accuracy-related penalty, 12-13
fraud penalty, 12-13
statute of limitations, 12-15
tax practitioners, 12-16
registered tax return preparer
    (RTRP), 12-17
preparer tax identification number
    (PTIN), 12-17

annual filing season program
    (AFSP), 12-17
annual federal tax refresher (AFTR),
    12-17
tax return preparer, 12-17
burden of proof, 12-18
nonattorney-client privilege, 12-18
Taxpayer Bill of Rights, 12-19
tax planning, 12-22
tax evasion, 12-22
open transaction, 12-22
closed transaction, 12-22
average tax rate, 12-23
marginal tax rate, 12-23

KEY POINTS

Learning Objectives	Key Points
LO 12.1: Identify the organizational structure of the Internal Revenue Service (IRS).	• The IRS is a bureau of the Treasury Department, tasked with administering the tax laws of the United States. • The national IRS office is the headquarters of the commissioner of internal revenue. The commissioner of internal revenue is appointed by the president of the United States with the advice and consent of the Senate. • The IRS maintains Campus Processing Sites where the IRS computers process the information from tax documents such as tax returns, payroll tax forms, Form 1099s, and withholding forms. • The IRS maintains a national computer center in Martinsburg, West Virginia, where information from various processing sites is matched with records from other processing sites. • The IRS has the authority to examine a taxpayer's books and records to determine the correct amount of tax due. The IRS also has the right to summon taxpayers to appear before the IRS and produce necessary accounting records.

LO 12.2:

Describe the IRS audit process.

- A primary function of the IRS is to audit taxpayers' tax returns.
- Correspondence audits are generally handled entirely by mail and account for the majority of the individual tax returns examined each year.
- The office audit is conducted in an IRS office and is typically used for individual taxpayers with little or no business activities.
- In a field audit, the IRS agent reviews a taxpayer's books and records at the taxpayer's place of business or at the office of the taxpayer's accountant.
- The IRS uses a computerized statistical sampling technique called the Discriminant Function System (DIF) to select tax returns for most audits of individuals.
- Under the DIF system, the IRS uses mathematical formulas to assign a DIF score to each return, which represents the potential for discovery of improper treatment of items on the tax return.
- The IRS also selects returns for audit using information from other sources such as informants, other governmental agencies, news items, and associated tax returns.
- If an audit results in a disagreement between the agent and the taxpayer, the appeals procedure begins with the IRS inviting the taxpayer to an informal conference with an appellate agent.

LO 12.3:

Define the common penalties for taxpayers and be able to apply them to specific situations.

- Taxpayers are charged interest on underpayments of taxes, and in some cases, the IRS pays interest to taxpayers when they overpay their taxes.
- The interest rate applicable to underpayments and overpayments of taxes is adjusted each quarter and is equal to the federal short-term rate plus 3 percentage points.
- The failure to file a tax return is subject to a penalty equal to 5 percent of the tax due with the return, for every month or portion of a month the return is late (up to a maximum of 25 percent).
- The penalty for failure to pay is ½ of 1 percent of the amount of taxes due for every month or portion of a month that the payment is late (up to a maximum of 25 percent of the total taxes due).
- The accuracy-related penalty is 20 percent of the applicable underpayment due to (1) negligence of or disregard for rules or regulations, (2) a substantial understatement of income tax, or (3) a substantial valuation overstatement, as well as certain other understatements of income tax.
- When a taxpayer files a fraudulent tax return, there is a fraud penalty equal to 75 percent of the amount of underpayment of taxes attributable to fraud.
- The tax law contains many other penalties applicable to taxpayers, including but not limited to a civil penalty of $500 and a criminal penalty of $1,000 imposed for filing false withholding information, and there is an immediate $5,000 penalty for filing a "frivolous" tax return (or document) as a tax protest.

LO 12.4:

Apply the general rule for the statute of limitations on tax returns and the important exceptions to the general rule.

- In general, the statute of limitations for a tax return runs for 3 years from the date the tax return was filed or the return due date, whichever is later.
- If a fraudulent tax return is filed or no return is filed, there is no statute of limitations.
- If a taxpayer omits an amount of gross income in excess of 25 percent of the gross income shown on the return, then the statute of limitations is increased to 6 years.
- The statute of limitations for the deduction of a bad debt or worthless securities is 7 years (all other items on the tax return would normally be considered closed out after 3 years).
- The statute of limitations may be extended by mutual consent of the IRS and the taxpayer.

LO 12.5: Describe the rules and penalties that apply to tax practitioners.	• Tax practitioners include commercial preparers, enrolled agents, attorneys, and certified public accountants (CPAs). • Unenrolled preparers can currently participate in the Annual Filing Season Program, a voluntary program created to encourage preparers to participate in continuing education. • Tax return preparer penalties include, but are not limited to, (1) $50 for failing to sign a tax return or failing to furnish the preparer's identifying number, (2) $50 for each failure to keep a copy of the prepared return or include the return on a list of taxpayers for whom returns have been prepared, or (3) $50 for failing to provide a taxpayer with a copy of the tax return prepared. • The IRS has the burden of proof in any court proceeding with respect to factual issues, provided the taxpayer (1) introduces credible evidence of the factual issue, (2) maintains records and substantiates items, and (3) cooperates with reasonable IRS requests for meetings, interviews, witnesses, information, and documents. • The tax law extends the attorney-client privilege of confidentiality in noncriminal tax matters to nonattorneys authorized to practice before the IRS (e.g., CPAs and enrolled agents).
LO 12.6: Describe the Taxpayer Bill of Rights.	• The Taxpayer Bill of Rights (IRS Publication 1) requires the IRS to inform taxpayers of their rights in dealing with the IRS, and expands taxpayers' rights and remedies when they are involved in disputes with the IRS.
LO 12.7: Explain the basic concepts of tax planning.	• Tax planning is the process of arranging one's financial affairs to minimize one's overall tax liability. • When illegal methods are used to reduce tax liability, the process can no longer be considered tax planning, but instead becomes tax evasion. • For making tax-planning decisions, the taxpayer's marginal tax rate is the most important tax rate to consider.

QUESTIONS and PROBLEMS

GROUP 1:
MULTIPLE CHOICE QUESTIONS

LO 12.1
1. Which of the following is a responsibility of a local office of the IRS?
   a. Advising the Treasury Department on legislation
   b. Intelligence operations
   c. Appellate procedures
   d. Developing IRS rules and regulations
   e. None of the above

LO 12.1
2. The IRS does *not* have the authority to:
   a. Examine a taxpayer's books and records
   b. Summon taxpayers to make them appear before the IRS
   c. Summon third parties for taxpayer records
   d. Place a lien on taxpayer property
   e. None of the above—the IRS has the authority to do all these

LO 12.2
3. Which of the following is the most common type of audit for an individual taxpayer?
   a. Office audit
   b. Correspondence audit
   c. Telephone audit
   d. Field audit
   e. Service center audit

LO 12.2

4. In which of the following ways are tax returns selected for audits?
   a. Through the Discriminant Function System
   b. Through informants
   c. Through news sources
   d. Through information matching
   e. All of the above

LO 12.3

5. Which of the following is *not* a penalty that may be imposed by the IRS?
   a. Failure-to-file penalty
   b. Failure-to-pay penalty
   c. Penalty for negligence
   d. Early filing penalty
   e. All of the above may be imposed by the IRS

LO 12.3

6. Martha inadvertently failed to file her tax return for 11 months. Her failure to file penalty will be:
   a. 55% of the tax due
   b. 25% of the tax due
   c. 5.5% of the tax due
   d. $5,000

LO 12.4

7. If a taxpayer's 2019 individual income tax return was filed on March 3, 2020, the statute of limitations would normally run out on:
   a. April 15, 2022
   b. March 3, 2021
   c. April 15, 2023
   d. March 3, 2023
   e. None of the above

LO 12.4

8. Which of the following has a 6-year statute of limitations?
   a. Depreciation
   b. Salaries
   c. Travel and entertainment
   d. A return in which the taxpayer omitted gross income in excess of 25 percent of the gross income shown on the return
   e. Worthless securities

LO 12.5

9. Which of the following tax preparers may *not* represent their clients in all IRS proceedings?
   a. An enrolled agent
   b. A certified public accountant
   c. An attorney
   d. All of the above may represent their clients in IRS proceedings

LO 12.5

10. Which of the following is *not* required to participate in the Annual Filing Season Program?
    a. 18 total hours of continuing education from an approved provider
    b. An annual federal tax refresher course lasting at least 6 hours
    c. A comprehensive oral exam administered by the IRS that tests preparer knowledge
    d. A PTIN if the preparer wishes to prepare and file tax returns
    e. All of the above are required

LO 12.5

11. Which of the following does *not* result in a minimum $50 fine for an income tax preparer?
    a. Failure to provide a tax preparer identification number
    b. Cashing a refund check for a customer
    c. Failing to keep any record of the returns prepared
    d. Failing to provide a copy of their prepared return to a customer

LO 12.5

12. In which of the following situations does the burden of proof in a tax matter *not* automatically shift to the IRS?
    a. The IRS uses statistics to reconstruct an individual's income.
    b. A court proceeding against an individual taxpayer involves a penalty or addition to tax.
    c. A taxpayer who did not maintain records.
    d. a and b are correct.
    e. a, b, and c are correct.

LO 12.5 13. Which of the following have privileged communication with a client in a noncriminal tax matter?
a. CPAs
b. Enrolled agents
c. Attorneys
d. a and c
e. a, b, and c

LO 12.5 14. The burden of proof remains on the taxpayer for corporations, trusts, and partnerships with net worth exceeding:
a. $1 million
b. $3 million
c. $5 million
d. $7 million
e. Some other amount

LO 12.6 15. The IRS does *not* have to furnish the taxpayer with information concerning which of the following items?
a. The way the taxpayer's return was selected for audit
b. The procedures for appealing an IRS ruling
c. The refund claims process
d. The IRS collection process
e. All of the above must be provided to the taxpayer

LO 12.6 16. Both spouses are responsible, jointly and individually, for paying the full amount of any tax, interest, or penalties due on a joint return.
a. This does not apply to spouses who have divorced after the return was filed.
b. Spouses are responsible jointly but not individually.
c. Spouses are responsible individually but not jointly.
d. Innocent spouses may be relieved of the liability for tax, interest, and penalties.
e. None of the above.

LO 12.6 17. A taxpayer's rights are explained in:
a. Publication 5
b. Publication 17
c. Publication 556
d. Publication 1
e. None of the above

LO 12.6 18. Taxpayers have the right to have an IRS examination take place at:
a. The IRS office
b. Any city of the taxpayer's choosing
c. A neutral site
d. A reasonable time and place
e. None of the above

LO 12.6 19. If a U.S. Tax Court agrees with the taxpayer on appeal that the IRS position was largely unjustified, which of the following is correct?
a. The taxpayer must still pay administrative and litigation costs.
b. The taxpayer may recover administrative but not litigation costs.
c. The taxpayer may recover litigation but not administrative costs.
d. To be eligible to recover some of the administrative and litigation costs, the taxpayer must have tried to resolve the case administratively, including going through the appeals process, and must have given the IRS the information necessary to resolve the case.
e. None of the above.

LO 12.6 20. If the IRS owes a taxpayer a refund, the law generally provides that the IRS must pay interest on the refund if it is not paid within _____ days of the date the taxpayer filed his or her tax return or claim for refund.
a. 30
b. 45

c. 60

d. 90

e. None of the above

LO 12.7

21. Glen's taxable income is $50,000 and he pays income tax of $6,864. If his income were $60,000, he would pay taxes of $9,064. What is Glen's marginal tax rate?

a. 18.23%

b. 22.00%

c. 12.00%

d. 25.00%

e. Some other amount

LO 12.7

22. Melodie's taxable income is $39,000 and she pays income tax of $4,489. If Melodie's taxable income increases to $41,000, she would pay income taxes of $4,884. What is Melodie's marginal tax rate?

a. 19.75%

b. 22.00%

c. 18.50%

d. 12.00%

e. Some other amount

LO 12.7

23. Jim has a house payment of $2,000 per month of which $1,700 is deductible interest and real estate taxes with the remaining $300 representing a repayment of the principal balance of the note. Jim's marginal tax rate is 30 percent. What is Jim's after-tax cost of his house payment?

a. $600

b. $540

c. $1,490

d. $1,460

e. Some other amount

GROUP 2:
PROBLEMS

LO 12.1
LO 12.2

1. Indicate which of the following statements are true or false:

   _____ The IRS is a division of the Treasury Department.

   _____ The IRS has four major divisions.

   _____ The IRS local offices process most individual tax returns.

   _____ IRS Campus Processing Sites are the locations that taxpayers should call to obtain tax information.

   _____ Taxpayers should have their CPAs keep their tax records to prevent the IRS from being able to summon their records.

   _____ Most IRS audits are conducted through the mail.

LO 12.2
LO 12.3

2. Indicate whether the following statements are true or false:

   _____ A field audit by the IRS is an audit conducted at the IRS field office.

   _____ A low Discriminant Function System score for a tax return increases the possibility that the return will be selected for audit.

   _____ The IRS charges interest on underpayments of taxes, but never pays interest on amounts of overpayments of taxes.

   _____ If a taxpayer fails to file a tax return on its due date, he or she may be subject to a failure-to-file penalty.

   _____ The tax law includes a penalty for preparing a tax return in a negligent manner.

   _____ If a taxpayer fails to file a tax return, the IRS may impose both the failure-to-file penalty and the fraud penalty.

LO 12.3

3. a. Wilson filed his individual tax return on the original due date, but failed to pay $700 in taxes that were due with the return. If Wilson pays the taxes exactly 2 months late, calculate the amount of his failure-to-pay penalty.

$ _____

b. Joan filed her individual income tax return 4½ months after it was due. She did not request an extension of time for filing. Along with her return, Joan remitted a check for $750, which was the balance of the taxes she owed with her return. Disregarding interest, calculate the total penalty that Joan will be required to pay, assuming the failure to file was not fraudulent.

$ _____

c. Jack filed his tax return 2 months and 3 days late and did not request an extension of time for filing. Jack's return indicated that he is to receive a $50 refund in taxes. Calculate the amount of Jack's penalty for failure to file his tax return on time, assuming the failure to file was not fraudulent.

$ _____

LO 12.3 4. In the 2019 tax year, Michelle paid the following amounts relating to her 2017 tax return:

Tax deficiency	$5,000
Negligence penalty	1,000
Interest	500
Underpayment of estimated tax penalty	350

Which of the above items may be deducted on Michelle's 2019 individual income tax return?

$ _____

Explain _____
_____

LO 12.3 5. Linda underpaid her taxes for the current year by $4,000 due to negligence.
a. Calculate Linda's accuracy-related penalty for negligence.

$ _____

b. Assume that the underpayment of taxes by Linda was determined to be fraudulent, and calculate the total amount of Linda's fraud penalty.

$ _____

LO 12.3 6. For each of the following situations, indicate the nature and amount of the penalty that could be imposed.

	Description of the Penalty	Penalty Amount
a. Larry is a tax protester and files his tax return in the name of "Mickey Mouse."	_____	$ _____
b. Anne writes a check for $900 in payment of her taxes that she knows will not clear the bank due to insufficient funds in her account.	_____	$ _____
c. Gerald understated his tax liability by $10,000. The total amount of tax that should have been shown on his return was $70,000.	_____	$ _____

LO 12.3
LO 12.4
LO 12.5
LO 12.6
7. Indicate whether the following statements are true or false:

_____ The tax law includes a penalty for writing a "bad" check in payment of the taxpayer's tax liability.
_____ The statute of limitations for a tax return is normally 4 years.
_____ If a fraudulent tax return is filed, the IRS may assess a deficiency at any time in the future.
_____ Enrolled agents work for the IRS.

_____ A commercial tax preparer may represent tax clients in any proceeding with the IRS.

_____ The IRS is entitled to choose a place and time for an audit, without regard to the inconvenience to the taxpayer or the reasonableness of the request.

LO 12.4

8. Indicate the date that the statute of limitations would run out on each of the following 2018 individual tax returns:

   a. A fraudulent tax return that was filed April 15, 2020   _____
   b. A tax return that was filed May 19, 2020   _____
   c. A tax return that was filed February 12, 2020   _____
   d. A tax return that was filed March 1, 2020, and   _____
      omitted $15,000 in income. The total gross income
      shown on the tax return was $50,000

LO 12.5

9. For each of the following situations, indicate the amount of the penalty that could be imposed on the tax return preparer:

   a. A tax return preparer understates the taxpayer's tax $ _____
      liability with a frivolous position and does not disclose
      the position.
   b. A tax return preparer fails to furnish his identifying $ _____
      number.
   c. A tax return preparer aids a taxpayer in understating a $ _____
      tax liability.
   d. A tax return preparer endorses and cashes a client's tax $ _____
      refund check.

LO 12.5

10. Classify each of the following as an enrolled or unenrolled preparer:
    a. Certified public accountant
    b. Enrolled agent
    c. A preparer that has completed the annual filing season program
    d. An attorney

LO 12.6

11. The Taxpayer Bill of Rights lists 10 different rights. Name four of those rights.

    _____
    _____
    _____
    _____

LO 12.7

12. Indicate whether the following statements are true or false:

    _____ Decreasing one's tax liability through legal methods is called tax planning, while illegally reducing taxes is called tax evasion.
    _____ In a "closed" transaction, all tax-significant events have been completed.
    _____ The marginal tax rate is computed as the total tax paid divided by the total income of the taxpayer.
    _____ The marginal tax rate is the most important rate for decision making in tax planning situations.
    _____ The timing tax planning technique usually takes advantage of deferring the payment of tax until a later year.

Tax Rate Schedules and Tax Table

CONTENTS

2019 Tax Rate Schedules

Schedule X—If your filing status is **Single**

If your taxable income is: Over—	But not over—	The tax is:	of the amount over—
$0	$9,700	.... 10%	$0
9,700	39,475	$970.00 + 12%	9,700
39,475	84,200	4,543.00 + 22%	39,475
84,200	160,725	14,382.50 + 24%	84,200
160,725	204,100	32,748.50 + 32%	160,725
204,100	510,300	46,628.50 + 35%	204,100
510,300	....	153,798.50 + 37%	510,300

Schedule Y-1—If your filing status is **Married filing jointly** or **Qualifying widow(er)**

If your taxable income is: Over—	But not over—	The tax is:	of the amount over—
$0	$19,400	.... 10%	$0
19,400	78,950	$1,940.00 + 12%	19,400
78,950	168,400	9,086.00 + 22%	78,950
168,400	321,450	28,765.00 + 24%	168,400
321,450	408,200	65,497.00 + 32%	321,450
408,200	612,350	93,257.00 + 35%	408,200
612,350	....	164,709.50 + 37%	612,350

Schedule Y-2—If your filing status is **Married filing separately**

If your taxable income is: Over—	But not over—	The tax is:	of the amount over—
$0	$9,700	.... 10%	$0
9,700	39,475	$970.00 + 12%	9,700
39,475	84,200	4,543.00 + 22%	39,475
84,200	160,725	14,382.50 + 24%	84,200
160,725	204,100	32,748.50 + 32%	160,725
204,100	306,175	46,628.50 + 35%	204,100
306,175	....	82,354.75 + 37%	306,175

Schedule Z—If your filing status is **Head of household**

If your taxable income is: Over—	But not over—	The tax is:	of the amount over—
$0	$13,850	.... 10%	$0
13,850	52,850	$1,385.00 + 12%	13,850
52,850	84,200	6,065.00 + 22%	52,850
84,200	160,700	12,962.00 + 24%	84,200
160,700	204,100	31,322.00 + 32%	160,700
204,100	510,300	45,210.00 + 35%	204,100
510,300	....	152,380.00 + 37%	510,300

Note: The tax rate schedules for income of at least $100,000 are presented in the traditional "additive" format on this page and in the somewhat lesser used "deductive" style on Page A-3. Both formats will compute the same tax amounts for taxable income of at least $100,000.

2019 Tax Computation Worksheet—Line 12a

Section A—Use if your filing status is **Single.** Complete the row below that applies to you.

Taxable income. If line 11b is—	(a) Enter the amount from line 11b	(b) Multiplication amount	(c) Multiply (a) by (b)	(d) Subtraction amount	Tax. Subtract (d) from (c). Enter the result here and on the entry space on line 12a.
At least $100,000 but not over $160,725	$	× 24% (0.24)	$	$ 5,825.50	$
Over $160,725 but not over $204,100	$	× 32% (0.32)	$	$ 18,683.50	$
Over $204,100 but not over $510,300	$	× 35% (0.35)	$	$ 24,806.50	$
Over $510,300	$	× 37% (0.37)	$	$ 35,012.50	$

Section B—Use if your filing status is **Married filing jointly** or **Qualifying widow(er).** Complete the row below that applies to you.

Taxable income. If line 11b is—	(a) Enter the amount from line 11b	(b) Multiplication amount	(c) Multiply (a) by (b)	(d) Subtraction amount	Tax. Subtract (d) from (c). Enter the result here and on the entry space on line 12a.
At least $100,000 but not over $168,400	$	× 22% (0.22)	$	$ 8,283.00	$
Over $168,400 but not over $321,450	$	× 24% (0.24)	$	$ 11,651.00	$
Over $321,450 but not over $408,200	$	× 32% (0.32)	$	$ 37,367.00	$
Over $408,200 but not over $612,350	$	× 35% (0.35)	$	$ 49,613.00	$
Over $612,350	$	× 37% (0.37)	$	$ 61,860.00	$

Section C—Use if your filing status is **Married filing separately.** Complete the row below that applies to you.

Taxable income. If line 11b is—	(a) Enter the amount from line 11b	(b) Multiplication amount	(c) Multiply (a) by (b)	(d) Subtraction amount	Tax. Subtract (d) from (c). Enter the result here and on the entry space on line 12a.
At least $100,000 but not over $160,725	$	× 24% (0.24)	$	$ 5,825.50	$
Over $160,725 but not over $204,100	$	× 32% (0.32)	$	$ 18,683.50	$
Over $204,100 but not over $306,175	$	× 35% (0.35)	$	$ 24,806.50	$
Over $306,175	$	× 37% (0.37)	$	$ 30,930.00	$

Section D—Use if your filing status is **Head of household.** Complete the row below that applies to you.

Taxable income. If line 11b is—	(a) Enter the amount from line 11b	(b) Multiplication amount	(c) Multiply (a) by (b)	(d) Subtraction amount	Tax. Subtract (d) from (c). Enter the result here and on the entry space on line 12a.
At least $100,000 but not over $160,700	$	× 24% (0.24)	$	$ 7,246.00	$
Over $160,700 but not over $204,100	$	× 32% (0.32)	$	$ 20,102.00	$
Over $204,100 but not over $510,300	$	× 35% (0.35)	$	$ 26,225.00	$
Over $510,300	$	× 37% (0.37)	$	$ 36,431.00	$

2019 Tax Table

See the instructions for line 12a to see if you must use the Tax Table below to figure your tax.

Example. Mr. and Mrs. Brown are filing a joint return. Their taxable income on Form 1040, line 11b, is $25,300. First, they find the $25,300–25,350 taxable income line. Next, they find the column for married filing jointly and read down the column. The amount shown where the taxable income line and filing status column meet is $2,651. This is the tax amount they should enter in the entry space on Form 1040, line 12a.

Sample Table

At Least	But Less Than	Single	Married filing jointly*	Married filing separately	Head of a household
			Your tax is—		
25,200	25,250	2,833	2,639	2,833	2,750
25,250	25,300	2,839	2,645	2,839	2,756
25,300	25,350	2,845	(2,651)	2,845	2,762
25,350	25,400	2,851	2,657	2,851	2,768

If line 11b (taxable income) is—		And you are—			
At least	But less than	Single	Married filing jointly *	Married filing separately	Head of a household
			Your tax is—		
0	5	0	0	0	0
5	15	1	1	1	1
15	25	2	2	2	2
25	50	4	4	4	4
50	75	6	6	6	6
75	100	9	9	9	9
100	125	11	11	11	11
125	150	14	14	14	14
150	175	16	16	16	16
175	200	19	19	19	19
200	225	21	21	21	21
225	250	24	24	24	24
250	275	26	26	26	26
275	300	29	29	29	29
300	325	31	31	31	31
325	350	34	34	34	34
350	375	36	36	36	36
375	400	39	39	39	39
400	425	41	41	41	41
425	450	44	44	44	44
450	475	46	46	46	46
475	500	49	49	49	49
500	525	51	51	51	51
525	550	54	54	54	54
550	575	56	56	56	56
575	600	59	59	59	59
600	625	61	61	61	61
625	650	64	64	64	64
650	675	66	66	66	66
675	700	69	69	69	69
700	725	71	71	71	71
725	750	74	74	74	74
750	775	76	76	76	76
775	800	79	79	79	79
800	825	81	81	81	81
825	850	84	84	84	84
850	875	86	86	86	86
875	900	89	89	89	89
900	925	91	91	91	91
925	950	94	94	94	94
950	975	96	96	96	96
975	1,000	99	99	99	99

1,000

If line 11b (taxable income) is—		And you are—			
At least	But less than	Single	Married filing jointly *	Married filing separately	Head of a household
			Your tax is—		
1,000	1,025	101	101	101	101
1,025	1,050	104	104	104	104
1,050	1,075	106	106	106	106
1,075	1,100	109	109	109	109
1,100	1,125	111	111	111	111
1,125	1,150	114	114	114	114
1,150	1,175	116	116	116	116
1,175	1,200	119	119	119	119
1,200	1,225	121	121	121	121
1,225	1,250	124	124	124	124
1,250	1,275	126	126	126	126
1,275	1,300	129	129	129	129
1,300	1,325	131	131	131	131
1,325	1,350	134	134	134	134
1,350	1,375	136	136	136	136
1,375	1,400	139	139	139	139
1,400	1,425	141	141	141	141
1,425	1,450	144	144	144	144
1,450	1,475	146	146	146	146
1,475	1,500	149	149	149	149
1,500	1,525	151	151	151	151
1,525	1,550	154	154	154	154
1,550	1,575	156	156	156	156
1,575	1,600	159	159	159	159
1,600	1,625	161	161	161	161
1,625	1,650	164	164	164	164
1,650	1,675	166	166	166	166
1,675	1,700	169	169	169	169
1,700	1,725	171	171	171	171
1,725	1,750	174	174	174	174
1,750	1,775	176	176	176	176
1,775	1,800	179	179	179	179
1,800	1,825	181	181	181	181
1,825	1,850	184	184	184	184
1,850	1,875	186	186	186	186
1,875	1,900	189	189	189	189
1,900	1,925	191	191	191	191
1,925	1,950	194	194	194	194
1,950	1,975	196	196	196	196
1,975	2,000	199	199	199	199

2,000

If line 11b (taxable income) is—		And you are—			
At least	But less than	Single	Married filing jointly *	Married filing separately	Head of a household
			Your tax is—		
2,000	2,025	201	201	201	201
2,025	2,050	204	204	204	204
2,050	2,075	206	206	206	206
2,075	2,100	209	209	209	209
2,100	2,125	211	211	211	211
2,125	2,150	214	214	214	214
2,150	2,175	216	216	216	216
2,175	2,200	219	219	219	219
2,200	2,225	221	221	221	221
2,225	2,250	224	224	224	224
2,250	2,275	226	226	226	226
2,275	2,300	229	229	229	229
2,300	2,325	231	231	231	231
2,325	2,350	234	234	234	234
2,350	2,375	236	236	236	236
2,375	2,400	239	239	239	239
2,400	2,425	241	241	241	241
2,425	2,450	244	244	244	244
2,450	2,475	246	246	246	246
2,475	2,500	249	249	249	249
2,500	2,525	251	251	251	251
2,525	2,550	254	254	254	254
2,550	2,575	256	256	256	256
2,575	2,600	259	259	259	259
2,600	2,625	261	261	261	261
2,625	2,650	264	264	264	264
2,650	2,675	266	266	266	266
2,675	2,700	269	269	269	269
2,700	2,725	271	271	271	271
2,725	2,750	274	274	274	274
2,750	2,775	276	276	276	276
2,775	2,800	279	279	279	279
2,800	2,825	281	281	281	281
2,825	2,850	284	284	284	284
2,850	2,875	286	286	286	286
2,875	2,900	289	289	289	289
2,900	2,925	291	291	291	291
2,925	2,950	294	294	294	294
2,950	2,975	296	296	296	296
2,975	3,000	299	299	299	299

(Continued)

* This column must also be used by a qualifying widow(er).

2019 Tax Table — *Continued*

DRAFT AS OF September 2019

3,000 / 4,000 / 5,000

If line 11b (taxable income) is—		And you are—			
At least	But less than	Single	Married filing jointly *	Married filing separately	Head of a household
		Your tax is—			
3,000					
3,000	3,050	303	303	303	303
3,050	3,100	308	308	308	308
3,100	3,150	313	313	313	313
3,150	3,200	318	318	318	318
3,200	3,250	323	323	323	323
3,250	3,300	328	328	328	328
3,300	3,350	333	333	333	333
3,350	3,400	338	338	338	338
3,400	3,450	343	343	343	343
3,450	3,500	348	348	348	348
3,500	3,550	353	353	353	353
3,550	3,600	358	358	358	358
3,600	3,650	363	363	363	363
3,650	3,700	368	368	368	368
3,700	3,750	373	373	373	373
3,750	3,800	378	378	378	378
3,800	3,850	383	383	383	383
3,850	3,900	388	388	388	388
3,900	3,950	393	393	393	393
3,950	4,000	398	398	398	398
4,000					
4,000	4,050	403	403	403	403
4,050	4,100	408	408	408	408
4,100	4,150	413	413	413	413
4,150	4,200	418	418	418	418
4,200	4,250	423	423	423	423
4,250	4,300	428	428	428	428
4,300	4,350	433	433	433	433
4,350	4,400	438	438	438	438
4,400	4,450	443	443	443	443
4,450	4,500	448	448	448	448
4,500	4,550	453	453	453	453
4,550	4,600	458	458	458	458
4,600	4,650	463	463	463	463
4,650	4,700	468	468	468	468
4,700	4,750	473	473	473	473
4,750	4,800	478	478	478	478
4,800	4,850	483	483	483	483
4,850	4,900	488	488	488	488
4,900	4,950	493	493	493	493
4,950	5,000	498	498	498	498
5,000					
5,000	5,050	503	503	503	503
5,050	5,100	508	508	508	508
5,100	5,150	513	513	513	513
5,150	5,200	518	518	518	518
5,200	5,250	523	523	523	523
5,250	5,300	528	528	528	528
5,300	5,350	533	533	533	533
5,350	5,400	538	538	538	538
5,400	5,450	543	543	543	543
5,450	5,500	548	548	548	548
5,500	5,550	553	553	553	553
5,550	5,600	558	558	558	558
5,600	5,650	563	563	563	563
5,650	5,700	568	568	568	568
5,700	5,750	573	573	573	573
5,750	5,800	578	578	578	578
5,800	5,850	583	583	583	583
5,850	5,900	588	588	588	588
5,900	5,950	593	593	593	593
5,950	6,000	598	598	598	598

6,000 / 7,000 / 8,000

If line 11b (taxable income) is—		And you are—			
At least	But less than	Single	Married filing jointly *	Married filing separately	Head of a household
		Your tax is—			
6,000					
6,000	6,050	603	603	603	603
6,050	6,100	608	608	608	608
6,100	6,150	613	613	613	613
6,150	6,200	618	618	618	618
6,200	6,250	623	623	623	623
6,250	6,300	628	628	628	628
6,300	6,350	633	633	633	633
6,350	6,400	638	638	638	638
6,400	6,450	643	643	643	643
6,450	6,500	648	648	648	648
6,500	6,550	653	653	653	653
6,550	6,600	658	658	658	658
6,600	6,650	663	663	663	663
6,650	6,700	668	668	668	668
6,700	6,750	673	673	673	673
6,750	6,800	678	678	678	678
6,800	6,850	683	683	683	683
6,850	6,900	688	688	688	688
6,900	6,950	693	693	693	693
6,950	7,000	698	698	698	698
7,000					
7,000	7,050	703	703	703	703
7,050	7,100	708	708	708	708
7,100	7,150	713	713	713	713
7,150	7,200	718	718	718	718
7,200	7,250	723	723	723	723
7,250	7,300	728	728	728	728
7,300	7,350	733	733	733	733
7,350	7,400	738	738	738	738
7,400	7,450	743	743	743	743
7,450	7,500	748	748	748	748
7,500	7,550	753	753	753	753
7,550	7,600	758	758	758	758
7,600	7,650	763	763	763	763
7,650	7,700	768	768	768	768
7,700	7,750	773	773	773	773
7,750	7,800	778	778	778	778
7,800	7,850	783	783	783	783
7,850	7,900	788	788	788	788
7,900	7,950	793	793	793	793
7,950	8,000	798	798	798	798
8,000					
8,000	8,050	803	803	803	803
8,050	8,100	808	808	808	808
8,100	8,150	813	813	813	813
8,150	8,200	818	818	818	818
8,200	8,250	823	823	823	823
8,250	8,300	828	828	828	828
8,300	8,350	833	833	833	833
8,350	8,400	838	838	838	838
8,400	8,450	843	843	843	843
8,450	8,500	848	848	848	848
8,500	8,550	853	853	853	853
8,550	8,600	858	858	858	858
8,600	8,650	863	863	863	863
8,650	8,700	868	868	868	868
8,700	8,750	873	873	873	873
8,750	8,800	878	878	878	878
8,800	8,850	883	883	883	883
8,850	8,900	888	888	888	888
8,900	8,950	893	893	893	893
8,950	9,000	898	898	898	898

9,000 / 10,000 / 11,000

If line 11b (taxable income) is—		And you are—			
At least	But less than	Single	Married filing jointly *	Married filing separately	Head of a household
		Your tax is—			
9,000					
9,000	9,050	903	903	903	903
9,050	9,100	908	908	908	908
9,100	9,150	913	913	913	913
9,150	9,200	918	918	918	918
9,200	9,250	923	923	923	923
9,250	9,300	928	928	928	928
9,300	9,350	933	933	933	933
9,350	9,400	938	938	938	938
9,400	9,450	943	943	943	943
9,450	9,500	948	948	948	948
9,500	9,550	953	953	953	953
9,550	9,600	958	958	958	958
9,600	9,650	963	963	963	963
9,650	9,700	968	968	968	968
9,700	9,750	973	973	973	973
9,750	9,800	979	978	979	978
9,800	9,850	985	983	985	983
9,850	9,900	991	988	991	988
9,900	9,950	997	993	997	993
9,950	10,000	1,003	998	1,003	998
10,000					
10,000	10,050	1,009	1,003	1,009	1,003
10,050	10,100	1,015	1,008	1,015	1,008
10,100	10,150	1,021	1,013	1,021	1,013
10,150	10,200	1,027	1,018	1,027	1,018
10,200	10,250	1,033	1,023	1,033	1,023
10,250	10,300	1,039	1,028	1,039	1,028
10,300	10,350	1,045	1,033	1,045	1,033
10,350	10,400	1,051	1,038	1,051	1,038
10,400	10,450	1,057	1,043	1,057	1,043
10,450	10,500	1,063	1,048	1,063	1,048
10,500	10,550	1,069	1,053	1,069	1,053
10,550	10,600	1,075	1,058	1,075	1,058
10,600	10,650	1,081	1,063	1,081	1,063
10,650	10,700	1,087	1,068	1,087	1,068
10,700	10,750	1,093	1,073	1,093	1,073
10,750	10,800	1,099	1,078	1,099	1,078
10,800	10,850	1,105	1,083	1,105	1,083
10,850	10,900	1,111	1,088	1,111	1,088
10,900	10,950	1,117	1,093	1,117	1,093
10,950	11,000	1,123	1,098	1,123	1,098
11,000					
11,000	11,050	1,129	1,103	1,129	1,103
11,050	11,100	1,135	1,108	1,135	1,108
11,100	11,150	1,141	1,113	1,141	1,113
11,150	11,200	1,147	1,118	1,147	1,118
11,200	11,250	1,153	1,123	1,153	1,123
11,250	11,300	1,159	1,128	1,159	1,128
11,300	11,350	1,165	1,133	1,165	1,133
11,350	11,400	1,171	1,138	1,171	1,138
11,400	11,450	1,177	1,143	1,177	1,143
11,450	11,500	1,183	1,148	1,183	1,148
11,500	11,550	1,189	1,153	1,189	1,153
11,550	11,600	1,195	1,158	1,195	1,158
11,600	11,650	1,201	1,163	1,201	1,163
11,650	11,700	1,207	1,168	1,207	1,168
11,700	11,750	1,213	1,173	1,213	1,173
11,750	11,800	1,219	1,178	1,219	1,178
11,800	11,850	1,225	1,183	1,225	1,183
11,850	11,900	1,231	1,188	1,231	1,188
11,900	11,950	1,237	1,193	1,237	1,193
11,950	12,000	1,243	1,198	1,243	1,198

(Continued)

* This column must also be used by a qualifying widow(er).

2019 Tax Table — *Continued*

12,000

If line 11b (taxable income) is—		And you are—			
At least	But less than	Single	Married filing jointly *	Married filing separately	Head of a household
		Your tax is—			
12,000	12,050	1,249	1,203	1,249	1,203
12,050	12,100	1,255	1,208	1,255	1,208
12,100	12,150	1,261	1,213	1,261	1,213
12,150	12,200	1,267	1,218	1,267	1,218
12,200	12,250	1,273	1,223	1,273	1,223
12,250	12,300	1,279	1,228	1,279	1,228
12,300	12,350	1,285	1,233	1,285	1,233
12,350	12,400	1,291	1,238	1,291	1,238
12,400	12,450	1,297	1,243	1,297	1,243
12,450	12,500	1,303	1,248	1,303	1,248
12,500	12,550	1,309	1,253	1,309	1,253
12,550	12,600	1,315	1,258	1,315	1,258
12,600	12,650	1,321	1,263	1,321	1,263
12,650	12,700	1,327	1,268	1,327	1,268
12,700	12,750	1,333	1,273	1,333	1,273
12,750	12,800	1,339	1,278	1,339	1,278
12,800	12,850	1,345	1,283	1,345	1,283
12,850	12,900	1,351	1,288	1,351	1,288
12,900	12,950	1,357	1,293	1,357	1,293
12,950	13,000	1,363	1,298	1,363	1,298

13,000

At least	But less than	Single	MFJ *	MFS	HoH
13,000	13,050	1,369	1,303	1,369	1,303
13,050	13,100	1,375	1,308	1,375	1,308
13,100	13,150	1,381	1,313	1,381	1,313
13,150	13,200	1,387	1,318	1,387	1,318
13,200	13,250	1,393	1,323	1,393	1,323
13,250	13,300	1,399	1,328	1,399	1,328
13,300	13,350	1,405	1,333	1,405	1,333
13,350	13,400	1,411	1,338	1,411	1,338
13,400	13,450	1,417	1,343	1,417	1,343
13,450	13,500	1,423	1,348	1,423	1,348
13,500	13,550	1,429	1,353	1,429	1,353
13,550	13,600	1,435	1,358	1,435	1,358
13,600	13,650	1,441	1,363	1,441	1,363
13,650	13,700	1,447	1,368	1,447	1,368
13,700	13,750	1,453	1,373	1,453	1,373
13,750	13,800	1,459	1,378	1,459	1,378
13,800	13,850	1,465	1,383	1,465	1,383
13,850	13,900	1,471	1,388	1,471	1,388
13,900	13,950	1,477	1,393	1,477	1,394
13,950	14,000	1,483	1,398	1,483	1,400

14,000

At least	But less than	Single	MFJ *	MFS	HoH
14,000	14,050	1,489	1,403	1,489	1,406
14,050	14,100	1,495	1,408	1,495	1,412
14,100	14,150	1,501	1,413	1,501	1,418
14,150	14,200	1,507	1,418	1,507	1,424
14,200	14,250	1,513	1,423	1,513	1,430
14,250	14,300	1,519	1,428	1,519	1,436
14,300	14,350	1,525	1,433	1,525	1,442
14,350	14,400	1,531	1,438	1,531	1,448
14,400	14,450	1,537	1,443	1,537	1,454
14,450	14,500	1,543	1,448	1,543	1,460
14,500	14,550	1,549	1,453	1,549	1,466
14,550	14,600	1,555	1,458	1,555	1,472
14,600	14,650	1,561	1,463	1,561	1,478
14,650	14,700	1,567	1,468	1,567	1,484
14,700	14,750	1,573	1,473	1,573	1,490
14,750	14,800	1,579	1,478	1,579	1,496
14,800	14,850	1,585	1,483	1,585	1,502
14,850	14,900	1,591	1,488	1,591	1,508
14,900	14,950	1,597	1,493	1,597	1,514
14,950	15,000	1,603	1,498	1,603	1,520

15,000

At least	But less than	Single	MFJ *	MFS	HoH
15,000	15,050	1,609	1,503	1,609	1,526
15,050	15,100	1,615	1,508	1,615	1,532
15,100	15,150	1,621	1,513	1,621	1,538
15,150	15,200	1,627	1,518	1,627	1,544
15,200	15,250	1,633	1,523	1,633	1,550
15,250	15,300	1,639	1,528	1,639	1,556
15,300	15,350	1,645	1,533	1,645	1,562
15,350	15,400	1,651	1,538	1,651	1,568
15,400	15,450	1,657	1,543	1,657	1,574
15,450	15,500	1,663	1,548	1,663	1,580
15,500	15,550	1,669	1,553	1,669	1,586
15,550	15,600	1,675	1,558	1,675	1,592
15,600	15,650	1,681	1,563	1,681	1,598
15,650	15,700	1,687	1,568	1,687	1,604
15,700	15,750	1,693	1,573	1,693	1,610
15,750	15,800	1,699	1,578	1,699	1,616
15,800	15,850	1,705	1,583	1,705	1,622
15,850	15,900	1,711	1,588	1,711	1,628
15,900	15,950	1,717	1,593	1,717	1,634
15,950	16,000	1,723	1,598	1,723	1,640

16,000

At least	But less than	Single	MFJ *	MFS	HoH
16,000	16,050	1,729	1,603	1,729	1,646
16,050	16,100	1,735	1,608	1,735	1,652
16,100	16,150	1,741	1,613	1,741	1,658
16,150	16,200	1,747	1,618	1,747	1,664
16,200	16,250	1,753	1,623	1,753	1,670
16,250	16,300	1,759	1,628	1,759	1,676
16,300	16,350	1,765	1,633	1,765	1,682
16,350	16,400	1,771	1,638	1,771	1,688
16,400	16,450	1,777	1,643	1,777	1,694
16,450	16,500	1,783	1,648	1,783	1,700
16,500	16,550	1,789	1,653	1,789	1,706
16,550	16,600	1,795	1,658	1,795	1,712
16,600	16,650	1,801	1,663	1,801	1,718
16,650	16,700	1,807	1,668	1,807	1,724
16,700	16,750	1,813	1,673	1,813	1,730
16,750	16,800	1,819	1,678	1,819	1,736
16,800	16,850	1,825	1,683	1,825	1,742
16,850	16,900	1,831	1,688	1,831	1,748
16,900	16,950	1,837	1,693	1,837	1,754
16,950	17,000	1,843	1,698	1,843	1,760

17,000

At least	But less than	Single	MFJ *	MFS	HoH
17,000	17,050	1,849	1,703	1,849	1,766
17,050	17,100	1,855	1,708	1,855	1,772
17,100	17,150	1,861	1,713	1,861	1,778
17,150	17,200	1,867	1,718	1,867	1,784
17,200	17,250	1,873	1,723	1,873	1,790
17,250	17,300	1,879	1,728	1,879	1,796
17,300	17,350	1,885	1,733	1,885	1,802
17,350	17,400	1,891	1,738	1,891	1,808
17,400	17,450	1,897	1,743	1,897	1,814
17,450	17,500	1,903	1,748	1,903	1,820
17,500	17,550	1,909	1,753	1,909	1,826
17,550	17,600	1,915	1,758	1,915	1,832
17,600	17,650	1,921	1,763	1,921	1,838
17,650	17,700	1,927	1,768	1,927	1,844
17,700	17,750	1,933	1,773	1,933	1,850
17,750	17,800	1,939	1,778	1,939	1,856
17,800	17,850	1,945	1,783	1,945	1,862
17,850	17,900	1,951	1,788	1,951	1,868
17,900	17,950	1,957	1,793	1,957	1,874
17,950	18,000	1,963	1,798	1,963	1,880

18,000

At least	But less than	Single	MFJ *	MFS	HoH
18,000	18,050	1,969	1,803	1,969	1,886
18,050	18,100	1,975	1,808	1,975	1,892
18,100	18,150	1,981	1,813	1,981	1,898
18,150	18,200	1,987	1,818	1,987	1,904
18,200	18,250	1,993	1,823	1,993	1,910
18,250	18,300	1,999	1,828	1,999	1,916
18,300	18,350	2,005	1,833	2,005	1,922
18,350	18,400	2,011	1,838	2,011	1,928
18,400	18,450	2,017	1,843	2,017	1,934
18,450	18,500	2,023	1,848	2,023	1,940
18,500	18,550	2,029	1,853	2,029	1,946
18,550	18,600	2,035	1,858	2,035	1,952
18,600	18,650	2,041	1,863	2,041	1,958
18,650	18,700	2,047	1,868	2,047	1,964
18,700	18,750	2,053	1,873	2,053	1,970
18,750	18,800	2,059	1,878	2,059	1,976
18,800	18,850	2,065	1,883	2,065	1,982
18,850	18,900	2,071	1,888	2,071	1,988
18,900	18,950	2,077	1,893	2,077	1,994
18,950	19,000	2,083	1,898	2,083	2,000

19,000

At least	But less than	Single	MFJ *	MFS	HoH
19,000	19,050	2,089	1,903	2,089	2,006
19,050	19,100	2,095	1,908	2,095	2,012
19,100	19,150	2,101	1,913	2,101	2,018
19,150	19,200	2,107	1,918	2,107	2,024
19,200	19,250	2,113	1,923	2,113	2,030
19,250	19,300	2,119	1,928	2,119	2,036
19,300	19,350	2,125	1,933	2,125	2,042
19,350	19,400	2,131	1,938	2,131	2,048
19,400	19,450	2,137	1,943	2,137	2,054
19,450	19,500	2,143	1,949	2,143	2,060
19,500	19,550	2,149	1,955	2,149	2,066
19,550	19,600	2,155	1,961	2,155	2,072
19,600	19,650	2,161	1,967	2,161	2,078
19,650	19,700	2,167	1,973	2,167	2,084
19,700	19,750	2,173	1,979	2,173	2,090
19,750	19,800	2,179	1,985	2,179	2,096
19,800	19,850	2,185	1,991	2,185	2,102
19,850	19,900	2,191	1,997	2,191	2,108
19,900	19,950	2,197	2,003	2,197	2,114
19,950	20,000	2,203	2,009	2,203	2,120

20,000

At least	But less than	Single	MFJ *	MFS	HoH
20,000	20,050	2,209	2,015	2,209	2,126
20,050	20,100	2,215	2,021	2,215	2,132
20,100	20,150	2,221	2,027	2,221	2,138
20,150	20,200	2,227	2,033	2,227	2,144
20,200	20,250	2,233	2,039	2,233	2,150
20,250	20,300	2,239	2,045	2,239	2,156
20,300	20,350	2,245	2,051	2,245	2,162
20,350	20,400	2,251	2,057	2,251	2,168
20,400	20,450	2,257	2,063	2,257	2,174
20,450	20,500	2,263	2,069	2,263	2,180
20,500	20,550	2,269	2,075	2,269	2,186
20,550	20,600	2,275	2,081	2,275	2,192
20,600	20,650	2,281	2,087	2,281	2,198
20,650	20,700	2,287	2,093	2,287	2,204
20,700	20,750	2,293	2,099	2,293	2,210
20,750	20,800	2,299	2,105	2,299	2,216
20,800	20,850	2,305	2,111	2,305	2,222
20,850	20,900	2,311	2,117	2,311	2,228
20,900	20,950	2,317	2,123	2,317	2,234
20,950	21,000	2,323	2,129	2,323	2,240

(Continued)

* This column must also be used by a qualifying widow(er).

2019 Tax Table — *Continued*

DRAFT AS OF September 11, 2019

At least	But less than	Single	Married filing jointly *	Married filing separately	Head of a household

Your tax is—

21,000

At least	But less than	Single	Married filing jointly *	Married filing separately	Head of a household
21,000	21,050	2,329	2,135	2,329	2,246
21,050	21,100	2,335	2,141	2,335	2,252
21,100	21,150	2,341	2,147	2,341	2,258
21,150	21,200	2,347	2,153	2,347	2,264
21,200	21,250	2,353	2,159	2,353	2,270
21,250	21,300	2,359	2,165	2,359	2,276
21,300	21,350	2,365	2,171	2,365	2,282
21,350	21,400	2,371	2,177	2,371	2,288
21,400	21,450	2,377	2,183	2,377	2,294
21,450	21,500	2,383	2,189	2,383	2,300
21,500	21,550	2,389	2,195	2,389	2,306
21,550	21,600	2,395	2,201	2,395	2,312
21,600	21,650	2,401	2,207	2,401	2,318
21,650	21,700	2,407	2,213	2,407	2,324
21,700	21,750	2,413	2,219	2,413	2,330
21,750	21,800	2,419	2,225	2,419	2,336
21,800	21,850	2,425	2,231	2,425	2,342
21,850	21,900	2,431	2,237	2,431	2,348
21,900	21,950	2,437	2,243	2,437	2,354
21,950	22,000	2,443	2,249	2,443	2,360

22,000

At least	But less than	Single	Married filing jointly *	Married filing separately	Head of a household
22,000	22,050	2,449	2,255	2,449	2,366
22,050	22,100	2,455	2,261	2,455	2,372
22,100	22,150	2,461	2,267	2,461	2,378
22,150	22,200	2,467	2,273	2,467	2,384
22,200	22,250	2,473	2,279	2,473	2,390
22,250	22,300	2,479	2,285	2,479	2,396
22,300	22,350	2,485	2,291	2,485	2,402
22,350	22,400	2,491	2,297	2,491	2,408
22,400	22,450	2,497	2,303	2,497	2,414
22,450	22,500	2,503	2,309	2,503	2,420
22,500	22,550	2,509	2,315	2,509	2,426
22,550	22,600	2,515	2,321	2,515	2,432
22,600	22,650	2,521	2,327	2,521	2,438
22,650	22,700	2,527	2,333	2,527	2,444
22,700	22,750	2,533	2,339	2,533	2,450
22,750	22,800	2,539	2,345	2,539	2,456
22,800	22,850	2,545	2,351	2,545	2,462
22,850	22,900	2,551	2,357	2,551	2,468
22,900	22,950	2,557	2,363	2,557	2,474
22,950	23,000	2,563	2,369	2,563	2,480

23,000

At least	But less than	Single	Married filing jointly *	Married filing separately	Head of a household
23,000	23,050	2,569	2,375	2,569	2,486
23,050	23,100	2,575	2,381	2,575	2,492
23,100	23,150	2,581	2,387	2,581	2,498
23,150	23,200	2,587	2,393	2,587	2,504
23,200	23,250	2,593	2,399	2,593	2,510
23,250	23,300	2,599	2,405	2,599	2,516
23,300	23,350	2,605	2,411	2,605	2,522
23,350	23,400	2,611	2,417	2,611	2,528
23,400	23,450	2,617	2,423	2,617	2,534
23,450	23,500	2,623	2,429	2,623	2,540
23,500	23,550	2,629	2,435	2,629	2,546
23,550	23,600	2,635	2,441	2,635	2,552
23,600	23,650	2,641	2,447	2,641	2,558
23,650	23,700	2,647	2,453	2,647	2,564
23,700	23,750	2,653	2,459	2,653	2,570
23,750	23,800	2,659	2,465	2,659	2,576
23,800	23,850	2,665	2,471	2,665	2,582
23,850	23,900	2,671	2,477	2,671	2,588
23,900	23,950	2,677	2,483	2,677	2,594
23,950	24,000	2,683	2,489	2,683	2,600

24,000

At least	But less than	Single	Married filing jointly *	Married filing separately	Head of a household
24,000	24,050	2,689	2,495	2,689	2,606
24,050	24,100	2,695	2,501	2,695	2,612
24,100	24,150	2,701	2,507	2,701	2,618
24,150	24,200	2,707	2,513	2,707	2,624
24,200	24,250	2,713	2,519	2,713	2,630
24,250	24,300	2,719	2,525	2,719	2,636
24,300	24,350	2,725	2,531	2,725	2,642
24,350	24,400	2,731	2,537	2,731	2,648
24,400	24,450	2,737	2,543	2,737	2,654
24,450	24,500	2,743	2,549	2,743	2,660
24,500	24,550	2,749	2,555	2,749	2,666
24,550	24,600	2,755	2,561	2,755	2,672
24,600	24,650	2,761	2,567	2,761	2,678
24,650	24,700	2,767	2,573	2,767	2,684
24,700	24,750	2,773	2,579	2,773	2,690
24,750	24,800	2,779	2,585	2,779	2,696
24,800	24,850	2,785	2,591	2,785	2,702
24,850	24,900	2,791	2,597	2,791	2,708
24,900	24,950	2,797	2,603	2,797	2,714
24,950	25,000	2,803	2,609	2,803	2,720

25,000

At least	But less than	Single	Married filing jointly *	Married filing separately	Head of a household
25,000	25,050	2,809	2,615	2,809	2,726
25,050	25,100	2,815	2,621	2,815	2,732
25,100	25,150	2,821	2,627	2,821	2,738
25,150	25,200	2,827	2,633	2,827	2,744
25,200	25,250	2,833	2,639	2,833	2,750
25,250	25,300	2,839	2,645	2,839	2,756
25,300	25,350	2,845	2,651	2,845	2,762
25,350	25,400	2,851	2,657	2,851	2,768
25,400	25,450	2,857	2,663	2,857	2,774
25,450	25,500	2,863	2,669	2,863	2,780
25,500	25,550	2,869	2,675	2,869	2,786
25,550	25,600	2,875	2,681	2,875	2,792
25,600	25,650	2,881	2,687	2,881	2,798
25,650	25,700	2,887	2,693	2,887	2,804
25,700	25,750	2,893	2,699	2,893	2,810
25,750	25,800	2,899	2,705	2,899	2,816
25,800	25,850	2,905	2,711	2,905	2,822
25,850	25,900	2,911	2,717	2,911	2,828
25,900	25,950	2,917	2,723	2,917	2,834
25,950	26,000	2,923	2,729	2,923	2,840

26,000

At least	But less than	Single	Married filing jointly *	Married filing separately	Head of a household
26,000	26,050	2,929	2,735	2,929	2,846
26,050	26,100	2,935	2,741	2,935	2,852
26,100	26,150	2,941	2,747	2,941	2,858
26,150	26,200	2,947	2,753	2,947	2,864
26,200	26,250	2,953	2,759	2,953	2,870
26,250	26,300	2,959	2,765	2,959	2,876
26,300	26,350	2,965	2,771	2,965	2,882
26,350	26,400	2,971	2,777	2,971	2,888
26,400	26,450	2,977	2,783	2,977	2,894
26,450	26,500	2,983	2,789	2,983	2,900
26,500	26,550	2,989	2,795	2,989	2,906
26,550	26,600	2,995	2,801	2,995	2,912
26,600	26,650	3,001	2,807	3,001	2,918
26,650	26,700	3,007	2,813	3,007	2,924
26,700	26,750	3,013	2,819	3,013	2,930
26,750	26,800	3,019	2,825	3,019	2,936
26,800	26,850	3,025	2,831	3,025	2,942
26,850	26,900	3,031	2,837	3,031	2,948
26,900	26,950	3,037	2,843	3,037	2,954
26,950	27,000	3,043	2,849	3,043	2,960

27,000

At least	But less than	Single	Married filing jointly *	Married filing separately	Head of a household
27,000	27,050	3,049	2,855	3,049	2,966
27,050	27,100	3,055	2,861	3,055	2,972
27,100	27,150	3,061	2,867	3,061	2,978
27,150	27,200	3,067	2,873	3,067	2,984
27,200	27,250	3,073	2,879	3,073	2,990
27,250	27,300	3,079	2,885	3,079	2,996
27,300	27,350	3,085	2,891	3,085	3,002
27,350	27,400	3,091	2,897	3,091	3,008
27,400	27,450	3,097	2,903	3,097	3,014
27,450	27,500	3,103	2,909	3,103	3,020
27,500	27,550	3,109	2,915	3,109	3,026
27,550	27,600	3,115	2,921	3,115	3,032
27,600	27,650	3,121	2,927	3,121	3,038
27,650	27,700	3,127	2,933	3,127	3,044
27,700	27,750	3,133	2,939	3,133	3,050
27,750	27,800	3,139	2,945	3,139	3,056
27,800	27,850	3,145	2,951	3,145	3,062
27,850	27,900	3,151	2,957	3,151	3,068
27,900	27,950	3,157	2,963	3,157	3,074
27,950	28,000	3,163	2,969	3,163	3,080

28,000

At least	But less than	Single	Married filing jointly *	Married filing separately	Head of a household
28,000	28,050	3,169	2,975	3,169	3,086
28,050	28,100	3,175	2,981	3,175	3,092
28,100	28,150	3,181	2,987	3,181	3,098
28,150	28,200	3,187	2,993	3,187	3,104
28,200	28,250	3,193	2,999	3,193	3,110
28,250	28,300	3,199	3,005	3,199	3,116
28,300	28,350	3,205	3,011	3,205	3,122
28,350	28,400	3,211	3,017	3,211	3,128
28,400	28,450	3,217	3,023	3,217	3,134
28,450	28,500	3,223	3,029	3,223	3,140
28,500	28,550	3,229	3,035	3,229	3,146
28,550	28,600	3,235	3,041	3,235	3,152
28,600	28,650	3,241	3,047	3,241	3,158
28,650	28,700	3,247	3,053	3,247	3,164
28,700	28,750	3,253	3,059	3,253	3,170
28,750	28,800	3,259	3,065	3,259	3,176
28,800	28,850	3,265	3,071	3,265	3,182
28,850	28,900	3,271	3,077	3,271	3,188
28,900	28,950	3,277	3,083	3,277	3,194
28,950	29,000	3,283	3,089	3,283	3,200

29,000

At least	But less than	Single	Married filing jointly *	Married filing separately	Head of a household
29,000	29,050	3,289	3,095	3,289	3,206
29,050	29,100	3,295	3,101	3,295	3,212
29,100	29,150	3,301	3,107	3,301	3,218
29,150	29,200	3,307	3,113	3,307	3,224
29,200	29,250	3,313	3,119	3,313	3,230
29,250	29,300	3,319	3,125	3,319	3,236
29,300	29,350	3,325	3,131	3,325	3,242
29,350	29,400	3,331	3,137	3,331	3,248
29,400	29,450	3,337	3,143	3,337	3,254
29,450	29,500	3,343	3,149	3,343	3,260
29,500	29,550	3,349	3,155	3,349	3,266
29,550	29,600	3,355	3,161	3,355	3,272
29,600	29,650	3,361	3,167	3,361	3,278
29,650	29,700	3,367	3,173	3,367	3,284
29,700	29,750	3,373	3,179	3,373	3,290
29,750	29,800	3,379	3,185	3,379	3,296
29,800	29,850	3,385	3,191	3,385	3,302
29,850	29,900	3,391	3,197	3,391	3,308
29,900	29,950	3,397	3,203	3,397	3,314
29,950	30,000	3,403	3,209	3,403	3,320

(Continued)

* This column must also be used by a qualifying widow(er).

2019 Tax Table — *Continued*

30,000 / 31,000 / 32,000

At least	But less than	Single	Married filing jointly *	Married filing separately	Head of a household
30,000					
30,000	30,050	3,409	3,215	3,409	3,326
30,050	30,100	3,415	3,221	3,415	3,332
30,100	30,150	3,421	3,227	3,421	3,338
30,150	30,200	3,427	3,233	3,427	3,344
30,200	30,250	3,433	3,239	3,433	3,350
30,250	30,300	3,439	3,245	3,439	3,356
30,300	30,350	3,445	3,251	3,445	3,362
30,350	30,400	3,451	3,257	3,451	3,368
30,400	30,450	3,457	3,263	3,457	3,374
30,450	30,500	3,463	3,269	3,463	3,380
30,500	30,550	3,469	3,275	3,469	3,386
30,550	30,600	3,475	3,281	3,475	3,392
30,600	30,650	3,481	3,287	3,481	3,398
30,650	30,700	3,487	3,293	3,487	3,404
30,700	30,750	3,493	3,299	3,493	3,410
30,750	30,800	3,499	3,305	3,499	3,416
30,800	30,850	3,505	3,311	3,505	3,422
30,850	30,900	3,511	3,317	3,511	3,428
30,900	30,950	3,517	3,323	3,517	3,434
30,950	31,000	3,523	3,329	3,523	3,440
31,000					
31,000	31,050	3,529	3,335	3,529	3,446
31,050	31,100	3,535	3,341	3,535	3,452
31,100	31,150	3,541	3,347	3,541	3,458
31,150	31,200	3,547	3,353	3,547	3,464
31,200	31,250	3,553	3,359	3,553	3,470
31,250	31,300	3,559	3,365	3,559	3,476
31,300	31,350	3,565	3,371	3,565	3,482
31,350	31,400	3,571	3,377	3,571	3,488
31,400	31,450	3,577	3,383	3,577	3,494
31,450	31,500	3,583	3,389	3,583	3,500
31,500	31,550	3,589	3,395	3,589	3,506
31,550	31,600	3,595	3,401	3,595	3,512
31,600	31,650	3,601	3,407	3,601	3,518
31,650	31,700	3,607	3,413	3,607	3,524
31,700	31,750	3,613	3,419	3,613	3,530
31,750	31,800	3,619	3,425	3,619	3,536
31,800	31,850	3,625	3,431	3,625	3,542
31,850	31,900	3,631	3,437	3,631	3,548
31,900	31,950	3,637	3,443	3,637	3,554
31,950	32,000	3,643	3,449	3,643	3,560
32,000					
32,000	32,050	3,649	3,455	3,649	3,566
32,050	32,100	3,655	3,461	3,655	3,572
32,100	32,150	3,661	3,467	3,661	3,578
32,150	32,200	3,667	3,473	3,667	3,584
32,200	32,250	3,673	3,479	3,673	3,590
32,250	32,300	3,679	3,485	3,679	3,596
32,300	32,350	3,685	3,491	3,685	3,602
32,350	32,400	3,691	3,497	3,691	3,608
32,400	32,450	3,697	3,503	3,697	3,614
32,450	32,500	3,703	3,509	3,703	3,620
32,500	32,550	3,709	3,515	3,709	3,626
32,550	32,600	3,715	3,521	3,715	3,632
32,600	32,650	3,721	3,527	3,721	3,638
32,650	32,700	3,727	3,533	3,727	3,644
32,700	32,750	3,733	3,539	3,733	3,650
32,750	32,800	3,739	3,545	3,739	3,656
32,800	32,850	3,745	3,551	3,745	3,662
32,850	32,900	3,751	3,557	3,751	3,668
32,900	32,950	3,757	3,563	3,757	3,674
32,950	33,000	3,763	3,569	3,763	3,680

33,000 / 34,000 / 35,000

At least	But less than	Single	Married filing jointly *	Married filing separately	Head of a household
33,000					
33,000	33,050	3,769	3,575	3,769	3,686
33,050	33,100	3,775	3,581	3,775	3,692
33,100	33,150	3,781	3,587	3,781	3,698
33,150	33,200	3,787	3,593	3,787	3,704
33,200	33,250	3,793	3,599	3,793	3,710
33,250	33,300	3,799	3,605	3,799	3,716
33,300	33,350	3,805	3,611	3,805	3,722
33,350	33,400	3,811	3,617	3,811	3,728
33,400	33,450	3,817	3,623	3,817	3,734
33,450	33,500	3,823	3,629	3,823	3,740
33,500	33,550	3,829	3,635	3,829	3,746
33,550	33,600	3,835	3,641	3,835	3,752
33,600	33,650	3,841	3,647	3,841	3,758
33,650	33,700	3,847	3,653	3,847	3,764
33,700	33,750	3,853	3,659	3,853	3,770
33,750	33,800	3,859	3,665	3,859	3,776
33,800	33,850	3,865	3,671	3,865	3,782
33,850	33,900	3,871	3,677	3,871	3,788
33,900	33,950	3,877	3,683	3,877	3,794
33,950	34,000	3,883	3,689	3,883	3,800
34,000					
34,000	34,050	3,889	3,695	3,889	3,806
34,050	34,100	3,895	3,701	3,895	3,812
34,100	34,150	3,901	3,707	3,901	3,818
34,150	34,200	3,907	3,713	3,907	3,824
34,200	34,250	3,913	3,719	3,913	3,830
34,250	34,300	3,919	3,725	3,919	3,836
34,300	34,350	3,925	3,731	3,925	3,842
34,350	34,400	3,931	3,737	3,931	3,848
34,400	34,450	3,937	3,743	3,937	3,854
34,450	34,500	3,943	3,749	3,943	3,860
34,500	34,550	3,949	3,755	3,949	3,866
34,550	34,600	3,955	3,761	3,955	3,872
34,600	34,650	3,961	3,767	3,961	3,878
34,650	34,700	3,967	3,773	3,967	3,884
34,700	34,750	3,973	3,779	3,973	3,890
34,750	34,800	3,979	3,785	3,979	3,896
34,800	34,850	3,985	3,791	3,985	3,902
34,850	34,900	3,991	3,797	3,991	3,908
34,900	34,950	3,997	3,803	3,997	3,914
34,950	35,000	4,003	3,809	4,003	3,920
35,000					
35,000	35,050	4,009	3,815	4,009	3,926
35,050	35,100	4,015	3,821	4,015	3,932
35,100	35,150	4,021	3,827	4,021	3,938
35,150	35,200	4,027	3,833	4,027	3,944
35,200	35,250	4,033	3,839	4,033	3,950
35,250	35,300	4,039	3,845	4,039	3,956
35,300	35,350	4,045	3,851	4,045	3,962
35,350	35,400	4,051	3,857	4,051	3,968
35,400	35,450	4,057	3,863	4,057	3,974
35,450	35,500	4,063	3,869	4,063	3,980
35,500	35,550	4,069	3,875	4,069	3,986
35,550	35,600	4,075	3,881	4,075	3,992
35,600	35,650	4,081	3,887	4,081	3,998
35,650	35,700	4,087	3,893	4,087	4,004
35,700	35,750	4,093	3,899	4,093	4,010
35,750	35,800	4,099	3,905	4,099	4,016
35,800	35,850	4,105	3,911	4,105	4,022
35,850	35,900	4,111	3,917	4,111	4,028
35,900	35,950	4,117	3,923	4,117	4,034
35,950	36,000	4,123	3,929	4,123	4,040

36,000 / 37,000 / 38,000

At least	But less than	Single	Married filing jointly *	Married filing separately	Head of a household
36,000					
36,000	36,050	4,129	3,935	4,129	4,046
36,050	36,100	4,135	3,941	4,135	4,052
36,100	36,150	4,141	3,947	4,141	4,058
36,150	36,200	4,147	3,953	4,147	4,064
36,200	36,250	4,153	3,959	4,153	4,070
36,250	36,300	4,159	3,965	4,159	4,076
36,300	36,350	4,165	3,971	4,165	4,082
36,350	36,400	4,171	3,977	4,171	4,088
36,400	36,450	4,177	3,983	4,177	4,094
36,450	36,500	4,183	3,989	4,183	4,100
36,500	36,550	4,189	3,995	4,189	4,106
36,550	36,600	4,195	4,001	4,195	4,112
36,600	36,650	4,201	4,007	4,201	4,118
36,650	36,700	4,207	4,013	4,207	4,124
36,700	36,750	4,213	4,019	4,213	4,130
36,750	36,800	4,219	4,025	4,219	4,136
36,800	36,850	4,225	4,031	4,225	4,142
36,850	36,900	4,231	4,037	4,231	4,148
36,900	36,950	4,237	4,043	4,237	4,154
36,950	37,000	4,243	4,049	4,243	4,160
37,000					
37,000	37,050	4,249	4,055	4,249	4,166
37,050	37,100	4,255	4,061	4,255	4,172
37,100	37,150	4,261	4,067	4,261	4,178
37,150	37,200	4,267	4,073	4,267	4,184
37,200	37,250	4,273	4,079	4,273	4,190
37,250	37,300	4,279	4,085	4,279	4,196
37,300	37,350	4,285	4,091	4,285	4,202
37,350	37,400	4,291	4,097	4,291	4,208
37,400	37,450	4,297	4,103	4,297	4,214
37,450	37,500	4,303	4,109	4,303	4,220
37,500	37,550	4,309	4,115	4,309	4,226
37,550	37,600	4,315	4,121	4,315	4,232
37,600	37,650	4,321	4,127	4,321	4,238
37,650	37,700	4,327	4,133	4,327	4,244
37,700	37,750	4,333	4,139	4,333	4,250
37,750	37,800	4,339	4,145	4,339	4,256
37,800	37,850	4,345	4,151	4,345	4,262
37,850	37,900	4,351	4,157	4,351	4,268
37,900	37,950	4,357	4,163	4,357	4,274
37,950	38,000	4,363	4,169	4,363	4,280
38,000					
38,000	38,050	4,369	4,175	4,369	4,286
38,050	38,100	4,375	4,181	4,375	4,292
38,100	38,150	4,381	4,187	4,381	4,298
38,150	38,200	4,387	4,193	4,387	4,304
38,200	38,250	4,393	4,199	4,393	4,310
38,250	38,300	4,399	4,205	4,399	4,316
38,300	38,350	4,405	4,211	4,405	4,322
38,350	38,400	4,411	4,217	4,411	4,328
38,400	38,450	4,417	4,223	4,417	4,334
38,450	38,500	4,423	4,229	4,423	4,340
38,500	38,550	4,429	4,235	4,429	4,346
38,550	38,600	4,435	4,241	4,435	4,352
38,600	38,650	4,441	4,247	4,441	4,358
38,650	38,700	4,447	4,253	4,447	4,364
38,700	38,750	4,453	4,259	4,453	4,370
38,750	38,800	4,459	4,265	4,459	4,376
38,800	38,850	4,465	4,271	4,465	4,382
38,850	38,900	4,471	4,277	4,471	4,388
38,900	38,950	4,477	4,283	4,477	4,394
38,950	39,000	4,483	4,289	4,483	4,400

* This column must also be used by a qualifying widow(er).

(Continued)

2019 Tax Table — *Continued*

If line 11b (taxable income) is—		And you are—				If line 11b (taxable income) is—		And you are—				If line 11b (taxable income) is—		And you are—			
At least	But less than	Single	Married filing jointly *	Married filing separately	Head of a household	At least	But less than	Single	Married filing jointly *	Married filing separately	Head of a household	At least	But less than	Single	Married filing jointly *	Married filing separately	Head of a household
		Your tax is—						Your tax is—						Your tax is—			

39,000 — 42,000 — 45,000

At least	But less than	Single	MFJ	MFS	HoH	At least	But less than	Single	MFJ	MFS	HoH	At least	But less than	Single	MFJ	MFS	HoH
39,000	39,050	4,489	4,295	4,489	4,406	42,000	42,050	5,104	4,655	5,104	4,766	45,000	45,050	5,764	5,015	5,764	5,126
39,050	39,100	4,495	4,301	4,495	4,412	42,050	42,100	5,115	4,661	5,115	4,772	45,050	45,100	5,775	5,021	5,775	5,132
39,100	39,150	4,501	4,307	4,501	4,418	42,100	42,150	5,126	4,667	5,126	4,778	45,100	45,150	5,786	5,027	5,786	5,138
39,150	39,200	4,507	4,313	4,507	4,424	42,150	42,200	5,137	4,673	5,137	4,784	45,150	45,200	5,797	5,033	5,797	5,144
39,200	39,250	4,513	4,319	4,513	4,430	42,200	42,250	5,148	4,679	5,148	4,790	45,200	45,250	5,808	5,039	5,808	5,150
39,250	39,300	4,519	4,325	4,519	4,436	42,250	42,300	5,159	4,685	5,159	4,796	45,250	45,300	5,819	5,045	5,819	5,156
39,300	39,350	4,525	4,331	4,525	4,442	42,300	42,350	5,170	4,691	5,170	4,802	45,300	45,350	5,830	5,051	5,830	5,162
39,350	39,400	4,531	4,337	4,531	4,448	42,350	42,400	5,181	4,697	5,181	4,808	45,350	45,400	5,841	5,057	5,841	5,168
39,400	39,450	4,537	4,343	4,537	4,454	42,400	42,450	5,192	4,703	5,192	4,814	45,400	45,450	5,852	5,063	5,852	5,174
39,450	39,500	4,543	4,349	4,543	4,460	42,450	42,500	5,203	4,709	5,203	4,820	45,450	45,500	5,863	5,069	5,863	5,180
39,500	39,550	4,554	4,355	4,554	4,466	42,500	42,550	5,214	4,715	5,214	4,826	45,500	45,550	5,874	5,075	5,874	5,186
39,550	39,600	4,565	4,361	4,565	4,472	42,550	42,600	5,225	4,721	5,225	4,832	45,550	45,600	5,885	5,081	5,885	5,192
39,600	39,650	4,576	4,367	4,576	4,478	42,600	42,650	5,236	4,727	5,236	4,838	45,600	45,650	5,896	5,087	5,896	5,198
39,650	39,700	4,587	4,373	4,587	4,484	42,650	42,700	5,247	4,733	5,247	4,844	45,650	45,700	5,907	5,093	5,907	5,204
39,700	39,750	4,598	4,379	4,598	4,490	42,700	42,750	5,258	4,739	5,258	4,850	45,700	45,750	5,918	5,099	5,918	5,210
39,750	39,800	4,609	4,385	4,609	4,496	42,750	42,800	5,269	4,745	5,269	4,856	45,750	45,800	5,929	5,105	5,929	5,216
39,800	39,850	4,620	4,391	4,620	4,502	42,800	42,850	5,280	4,751	5,280	4,862	45,800	45,850	5,940	5,111	5,940	5,222
39,850	39,900	4,631	4,397	4,631	4,508	42,850	42,900	5,291	4,757	5,291	4,868	45,850	45,900	5,951	5,117	5,951	5,228
39,900	39,950	4,642	4,403	4,642	4,514	42,900	42,950	5,302	4,763	5,302	4,874	45,900	45,950	5,962	5,123	5,962	5,234
39,950	40,000	4,653	4,409	4,653	4,520	42,950	43,000	5,313	4,769	5,313	4,880	45,950	46,000	5,973	5,129	5,973	5,240

40,000 — 43,000 — 46,000

At least	But less than	Single	MFJ	MFS	HoH	At least	But less than	Single	MFJ	MFS	HoH	At least	But less than	Single	MFJ	MFS	HoH
40,000	40,050	4,664	4,415	4,664	4,526	43,000	43,050	5,324	4,775	5,324	4,886	46,000	46,050	5,984	5,135	5,984	5,246
40,050	40,100	4,675	4,421	4,675	4,532	43,050	43,100	5,335	4,781	5,335	4,892	46,050	46,100	5,995	5,141	5,995	5,252
40,100	40,150	4,686	4,427	4,686	4,538	43,100	43,150	5,346	4,787	5,346	4,898	46,100	46,150	6,006	5,147	6,006	5,258
40,150	40,200	4,697	4,433	4,697	4,544	43,150	43,200	5,357	4,793	5,357	4,904	46,150	46,200	6,017	5,153	6,017	5,264
40,200	40,250	4,708	4,439	4,708	4,550	43,200	43,250	5,368	4,799	5,368	4,910	46,200	46,250	6,028	5,159	6,028	5,270
40,250	40,300	4,719	4,445	4,719	4,556	43,250	43,300	5,379	4,805	5,379	4,916	46,250	46,300	6,039	5,165	6,039	5,276
40,300	40,350	4,730	4,451	4,730	4,562	43,300	43,350	5,390	4,811	5,390	4,922	46,300	46,350	6,050	5,171	6,050	5,282
40,350	40,400	4,741	4,457	4,741	4,568	43,350	43,400	5,401	4,817	5,401	4,928	46,350	46,400	6,061	5,177	6,061	5,288
40,400	40,450	4,752	4,463	4,752	4,574	43,400	43,450	5,412	4,823	5,412	4,934	46,400	46,450	6,072	5,183	6,072	5,294
40,450	40,500	4,763	4,469	4,763	4,580	43,450	43,500	5,423	4,829	5,423	4,940	46,450	46,500	6,083	5,189	6,083	5,300
40,500	40,550	4,774	4,475	4,774	4,586	43,500	43,550	5,434	4,835	5,434	4,946	46,500	46,550	6,094	5,195	6,094	5,306
40,550	40,600	4,785	4,481	4,785	4,592	43,550	43,600	5,445	4,841	5,445	4,952	46,550	46,600	6,105	5,201	6,105	5,312
40,600	40,650	4,796	4,487	4,796	4,598	43,600	43,650	5,456	4,847	5,456	4,958	46,600	46,650	6,116	5,207	6,116	5,318
40,650	40,700	4,807	4,493	4,807	4,604	43,650	43,700	5,467	4,853	5,467	4,964	46,650	46,700	6,127	5,213	6,127	5,324
40,700	40,750	4,818	4,499	4,818	4,610	43,700	43,750	5,478	4,859	5,478	4,970	46,700	46,750	6,138	5,219	6,138	5,330
40,750	40,800	4,829	4,505	4,829	4,616	43,750	43,800	5,489	4,865	5,489	4,976	46,750	46,800	6,149	5,225	6,149	5,336
40,800	40,850	4,840	4,511	4,840	4,622	43,800	43,850	5,500	4,871	5,500	4,982	46,800	46,850	6,160	5,231	6,160	5,342
40,850	40,900	4,851	4,517	4,851	4,628	43,850	43,900	5,511	4,877	5,511	4,988	46,850	46,900	6,171	5,237	6,171	5,348
40,900	40,950	4,862	4,523	4,862	4,634	43,900	43,950	5,522	4,883	5,522	4,994	46,900	46,950	6,182	5,243	6,182	5,354
40,950	41,000	4,873	4,529	4,873	4,640	43,950	44,000	5,533	4,889	5,533	5,000	46,950	47,000	6,193	5,249	6,193	5,360

41,000 — 44,000 — 47,000

At least	But less than	Single	MFJ	MFS	HoH	At least	But less than	Single	MFJ	MFS	HoH	At least	But less than	Single	MFJ	MFS	HoH
41,000	41,050	4,884	4,535	4,884	4,646	44,000	44,050	5,544	4,895	5,544	5,006	47,000	47,050	6,204	5,255	6,204	5,366
41,050	41,100	4,895	4,541	4,895	4,652	44,050	44,100	5,555	4,901	5,555	5,012	47,050	47,100	6,215	5,261	6,215	5,372
41,100	41,150	4,906	4,547	4,906	4,658	44,100	44,150	5,566	4,907	5,566	5,018	47,100	47,150	6,226	5,267	6,226	5,378
41,150	41,200	4,917	4,553	4,917	4,664	44,150	44,200	5,577	4,913	5,577	5,024	47,150	47,200	6,237	5,273	6,237	5,384
41,200	41,250	4,928	4,559	4,928	4,670	44,200	44,250	5,588	4,919	5,588	5,030	47,200	47,250	6,248	5,279	6,248	5,390
41,250	41,300	4,939	4,565	4,939	4,676	44,250	44,300	5,599	4,925	5,599	5,036	47,250	47,300	6,259	5,285	6,259	5,396
41,300	41,350	4,950	4,571	4,950	4,682	44,300	44,350	5,610	4,931	5,610	5,042	47,300	47,350	6,270	5,291	6,270	5,402
41,350	41,400	4,961	4,577	4,961	4,688	44,350	44,400	5,621	4,937	5,621	5,048	47,350	47,400	6,281	5,297	6,281	5,408
41,400	41,450	4,972	4,583	4,972	4,694	44,400	44,450	5,632	4,943	5,632	5,054	47,400	47,450	6,292	5,303	6,292	5,414
41,450	41,500	4,983	4,589	4,983	4,700	44,450	44,500	5,643	4,949	5,643	5,060	47,450	47,500	6,303	5,309	6,303	5,420
41,500	41,550	4,994	4,595	4,994	4,706	44,500	44,550	5,654	4,955	5,654	5,066	47,500	47,550	6,314	5,315	6,314	5,426
41,550	41,600	5,005	4,601	5,005	4,712	44,550	44,600	5,665	4,961	5,665	5,072	47,550	47,600	6,325	5,321	6,325	5,432
41,600	41,650	5,016	4,607	5,016	4,718	44,600	44,650	5,676	4,967	5,676	5,078	47,600	47,650	6,336	5,327	6,336	5,438
41,650	41,700	5,027	4,613	5,027	4,724	44,650	44,700	5,687	4,973	5,687	5,084	47,650	47,700	6,347	5,333	6,347	5,444
41,700	41,750	5,038	4,619	5,038	4,730	44,700	44,750	5,698	4,979	5,698	5,090	47,700	47,750	6,358	5,339	6,358	5,450
41,750	41,800	5,049	4,625	5,049	4,736	44,750	44,800	5,709	4,985	5,709	5,096	47,750	47,800	6,369	5,345	6,369	5,456
41,800	41,850	5,060	4,631	5,060	4,742	44,800	44,850	5,720	4,991	5,720	5,102	47,800	47,850	6,380	5,351	6,380	5,462
41,850	41,900	5,071	4,637	5,071	4,748	44,850	44,900	5,731	4,997	5,731	5,108	47,850	47,900	6,391	5,357	6,391	5,468
41,900	41,950	5,082	4,643	5,082	4,754	44,900	44,950	5,742	5,003	5,742	5,114	47,900	47,950	6,402	5,363	6,402	5,474
41,950	42,000	5,093	4,649	5,093	4,760	44,950	45,000	5,753	5,009	5,753	5,120	47,950	48,000	6,413	5,369	6,413	5,480

(Continued)

* This column must also be used by a qualifying widow(er).

2019 Tax Table — *Continued*

48,000

At least	But less than	Single	Married filing jointly *	Married filing separately	Head of a household
			Your tax is—		
48,000	48,050	6,424	5,375	6,424	5,486
48,050	48,100	6,435	5,381	6,435	5,492
48,100	48,150	6,446	5,387	6,446	5,498
48,150	48,200	6,457	5,393	6,457	5,504
48,200	48,250	6,468	5,399	6,468	5,510
48,250	48,300	6,479	5,405	6,479	5,516
48,300	48,350	6,490	5,411	6,490	5,522
48,350	48,400	6,501	5,417	6,501	5,528
48,400	48,450	6,512	5,423	6,512	5,534
48,450	48,500	6,523	5,429	6,523	5,540
48,500	48,550	6,534	5,435	6,534	5,546
48,550	48,600	6,545	5,441	6,545	5,552
48,600	48,650	6,556	5,447	6,556	5,558
48,650	48,700	6,567	5,453	6,567	5,564
48,700	48,750	6,578	5,459	6,578	5,570
48,750	48,800	6,589	5,465	6,589	5,576
48,800	48,850	6,600	5,471	6,600	5,582
48,850	48,900	6,611	5,477	6,611	5,588
48,900	48,950	6,622	5,483	6,622	5,594
48,950	49,000	6,633	5,489	6,633	5,600

49,000

At least	But less than	Single	Married filing jointly *	Married filing separately	Head of a household
49,000	49,050	6,644	5,495	6,644	5,606
49,050	49,100	6,655	5,501	6,655	5,612
49,100	49,150	6,666	5,507	6,666	5,618
49,150	49,200	6,677	5,513	6,677	5,624
49,200	49,250	6,688	5,519	6,688	5,630
49,250	49,300	6,699	5,525	6,699	5,636
49,300	49,350	6,710	5,531	6,710	5,642
49,350	49,400	6,721	5,537	6,721	5,648
49,400	49,450	6,732	5,543	6,732	5,654
49,450	49,500	6,743	5,549	6,743	5,660
49,500	49,550	6,754	5,555	6,754	5,666
49,550	49,600	6,765	5,561	6,765	5,672
49,600	49,650	6,776	5,567	6,776	5,678
49,650	49,700	6,787	5,573	6,787	5,684
49,700	49,750	6,798	5,579	6,798	5,690
49,750	49,800	6,809	5,585	6,809	5,696
49,800	49,850	6,820	5,591	6,820	5,702
49,850	49,900	6,831	5,597	6,831	5,708
49,900	49,950	6,842	5,603	6,842	5,714
49,950	50,000	6,853	5,609	6,853	5,720

50,000

At least	But less than	Single	Married filing jointly *	Married filing separately	Head of a household
50,000	50,050	6,864	5,615	6,864	5,726
50,050	50,100	6,875	5,621	6,875	5,732
50,100	50,150	6,886	5,627	6,886	5,738
50,150	50,200	6,897	5,633	6,897	5,744
50,200	50,250	6,908	5,639	6,908	5,750
50,250	50,300	6,919	5,645	6,919	5,756
50,300	50,350	6,930	5,651	6,930	5,762
50,350	50,400	6,941	5,657	6,941	5,768
50,400	50,450	6,952	5,663	6,952	5,774
50,450	50,500	6,963	5,669	6,963	5,780
50,500	50,550	6,974	5,675	6,974	5,786
50,550	50,600	6,985	5,681	6,985	5,792
50,600	50,650	6,996	5,687	6,996	5,798
50,650	50,700	7,007	5,693	7,007	5,804
50,700	50,750	7,018	5,699	7,018	5,810
50,750	50,800	7,029	5,705	7,029	5,816
50,800	50,850	7,040	5,711	7,040	5,822
50,850	50,900	7,051	5,717	7,051	5,828
50,900	50,950	7,062	5,723	7,062	5,834
50,950	51,000	7,073	5,729	7,073	5,840

51,000

At least	But less than	Single	Married filing jointly *	Married filing separately	Head of a household
51,000	51,050	7,084	5,735	7,084	5,846
51,050	51,100	7,095	5,741	7,095	5,852
51,100	51,150	7,106	5,747	7,106	5,858
51,150	51,200	7,117	5,753	7,117	5,864
51,200	51,250	7,128	5,759	7,128	5,870
51,250	51,300	7,139	5,765	7,139	5,876
51,300	51,350	7,150	5,771	7,150	5,882
51,350	51,400	7,161	5,777	7,161	5,888
51,400	51,450	7,172	5,783	7,172	5,894
51,450	51,500	7,183	5,789	7,183	5,900
51,500	51,550	7,194	5,795	7,194	5,906
51,550	51,600	7,205	5,801	7,205	5,912
51,600	51,650	7,216	5,807	7,216	5,918
51,650	51,700	7,227	5,813	7,227	5,924
51,700	51,750	7,238	5,819	7,238	5,930
51,750	51,800	7,249	5,825	7,249	5,936
51,800	51,850	7,260	5,831	7,260	5,942
51,850	51,900	7,271	5,837	7,271	5,948
51,900	51,950	7,282	5,843	7,282	5,954
51,950	52,000	7,293	5,849	7,293	5,960

52,000

At least	But less than	Single	Married filing jointly *	Married filing separately	Head of a household
52,000	52,050	7,304	5,855	7,304	5,966
52,050	52,100	7,315	5,861	7,315	5,972
52,100	52,150	7,326	5,867	7,326	5,978
52,150	52,200	7,337	5,873	7,337	5,984
52,200	52,250	7,348	5,879	7,348	5,990
52,250	52,300	7,359	5,885	7,359	5,996
52,300	52,350	7,370	5,891	7,370	6,002
52,350	52,400	7,381	5,897	7,381	6,008
52,400	52,450	7,392	5,903	7,392	6,014
52,450	52,500	7,403	5,909	7,403	6,020
52,500	52,550	7,414	5,915	7,414	6,026
52,550	52,600	7,425	5,921	7,425	6,032
52,600	52,650	7,436	5,927	7,436	6,038
52,650	52,700	7,447	5,933	7,447	6,044
52,700	52,750	7,458	5,939	7,458	6,050
52,750	52,800	7,469	5,945	7,469	6,056
52,800	52,850	7,480	5,951	7,480	6,062
52,850	52,900	7,491	5,957	7,491	6,071
52,900	52,950	7,502	5,963	7,502	6,082
52,950	53,000	7,513	5,969	7,513	6,093

53,000

At least	But less than	Single	Married filing jointly *	Married filing separately	Head of a household
53,000	53,050	7,524	5,975	7,524	6,104
53,050	53,100	7,535	5,981	7,535	6,115
53,100	53,150	7,546	5,987	7,546	6,126
53,150	53,200	7,557	5,993	7,557	6,137
53,200	53,250	7,568	5,999	7,568	6,148
53,250	53,300	7,579	6,005	7,579	6,159
53,300	53,350	7,590	6,011	7,590	6,170
53,350	53,400	7,601	6,017	7,601	6,181
53,400	53,450	7,612	6,023	7,612	6,192
53,450	53,500	7,623	6,029	7,623	6,203
53,500	53,550	7,634	6,035	7,634	6,214
53,550	53,600	7,645	6,041	7,645	6,225
53,600	53,650	7,656	6,047	7,656	6,236
53,650	53,700	7,667	6,053	7,667	6,247
53,700	53,750	7,678	6,059	7,678	6,258
53,750	53,800	7,689	6,065	7,689	6,269
53,800	53,850	7,700	6,071	7,700	6,280
53,850	53,900	7,711	6,077	7,711	6,291
53,900	53,950	7,722	6,083	7,722	6,302
53,950	54,000	7,733	6,089	7,733	6,313

54,000

At least	But less than	Single	Married filing jointly *	Married filing separately	Head of a household
54,000	54,050	7,744	6,095	7,744	6,324
54,050	54,100	7,755	6,101	7,755	6,335
54,100	54,150	7,766	6,107	7,766	6,346
54,150	54,200	7,777	6,113	7,777	6,357
54,200	54,250	7,788	6,119	7,788	6,368
54,250	54,300	7,799	6,125	7,799	6,379
54,300	54,350	7,810	6,131	7,810	6,390
54,350	54,400	7,821	6,137	7,821	6,401
54,400	54,450	7,832	6,143	7,832	6,412
54,450	54,500	7,843	6,149	7,843	6,423
54,500	54,550	7,854	6,155	7,854	6,434
54,550	54,600	7,865	6,161	7,865	6,445
54,600	54,650	7,876	6,167	7,876	6,456
54,650	54,700	7,887	6,173	7,887	6,467
54,700	54,750	7,898	6,179	7,898	6,478
54,750	54,800	7,909	6,185	7,909	6,489
54,800	54,850	7,920	6,191	7,920	6,500
54,850	54,900	7,931	6,197	7,931	6,511
54,900	54,950	7,942	6,203	7,942	6,522
54,950	55,000	7,953	6,209	7,953	6,533

55,000

At least	But less than	Single	Married filing jointly *	Married filing separately	Head of a household
55,000	55,050	7,964	6,215	7,964	6,544
55,050	55,100	7,975	6,221	7,975	6,555
55,100	55,150	7,986	6,227	7,986	6,566
55,150	55,200	7,997	6,233	7,997	6,577
55,200	55,250	8,008	6,239	8,008	6,588
55,250	55,300	8,019	6,245	8,019	6,599
55,300	55,350	8,030	6,251	8,030	6,610
55,350	55,400	8,041	6,257	8,041	6,621
55,400	55,450	8,052	6,263	8,052	6,632
55,450	55,500	8,063	6,269	8,063	6,643
55,500	55,550	8,074	6,275	8,074	6,654
55,550	55,600	8,085	6,281	8,085	6,665
55,600	55,650	8,096	6,287	8,096	6,676
55,650	55,700	8,107	6,293	8,107	6,687
55,700	55,750	8,118	6,299	8,118	6,698
55,750	55,800	8,129	6,305	8,129	6,709
55,800	55,850	8,140	6,311	8,140	6,720
55,850	55,900	8,151	6,317	8,151	6,731
55,900	55,950	8,162	6,323	8,162	6,742
55,950	56,000	8,173	6,329	8,173	6,753

56,000

At least	But less than	Single	Married filing jointly *	Married filing separately	Head of a household
56,000	56,050	8,184	6,335	8,184	6,764
56,050	56,100	8,195	6,341	8,195	6,775
56,100	56,150	8,206	6,347	8,206	6,786
56,150	56,200	8,217	6,353	8,217	6,797
56,200	56,250	8,228	6,359	8,228	6,808
56,250	56,300	8,239	6,365	8,239	6,819
56,300	56,350	8,250	6,371	8,250	6,830
56,350	56,400	8,261	6,377	8,261	6,841
56,400	56,450	8,272	6,383	8,272	6,852
56,450	56,500	8,283	6,389	8,283	6,863
56,500	56,550	8,294	6,395	8,294	6,874
56,550	56,600	8,305	6,401	8,305	6,885
56,600	56,650	8,316	6,407	8,316	6,896
56,650	56,700	8,327	6,413	8,327	6,907
56,700	56,750	8,338	6,419	8,338	6,918
56,750	56,800	8,349	6,425	8,349	6,929
56,800	56,850	8,360	6,431	8,360	6,940
56,850	56,900	8,371	6,437	8,371	6,951
56,900	56,950	8,382	6,443	8,382	6,962
56,950	57,000	8,393	6,449	8,393	6,973

(Continued)

* This column must also be used by a qualifying widow(er).

2019 Tax Table — *Continued*

DRAFT AS OF September 13, 2019

57,000

If line 11b (taxable income) is— At least	But less than	Single	Married filing jointly *	Married filing separately	Head of a household
57,000	57,050	8,404	6,455	8,404	6,984
57,050	57,100	8,415	6,461	8,415	6,995
57,100	57,150	8,426	6,467	8,426	7,006
57,150	57,200	8,437	6,473	8,437	7,017
57,200	57,250	8,448	6,479	8,448	7,028
57,250	57,300	8,459	6,485	8,459	7,039
57,300	57,350	8,470	6,491	8,470	7,050
57,350	57,400	8,481	6,497	8,481	7,061
57,400	57,450	8,492	6,503	8,492	7,072
57,450	57,500	8,503	6,509	8,503	7,083
57,500	57,550	8,514	6,515	8,514	7,094
57,550	57,600	8,525	6,521	8,525	7,105
57,600	57,650	8,536	6,527	8,536	7,116
57,650	57,700	8,547	6,533	8,547	7,127
57,700	57,750	8,558	6,539	8,558	7,138
57,750	57,800	8,569	6,545	8,569	7,149
57,800	57,850	8,580	6,551	8,580	7,160
57,850	57,900	8,591	6,557	8,591	7,171
57,900	57,950	8,602	6,563	8,602	7,182
57,950	58,000	8,613	6,569	8,613	7,193

58,000

At least	But less than	Single	Married filing jointly *	Married filing separately	Head of a household
58,000	58,050	8,624	6,575	8,624	7,204
58,050	58,100	8,635	6,581	8,635	7,215
58,100	58,150	8,646	6,587	8,646	7,226
58,150	58,200	8,657	6,593	8,657	7,237
58,200	58,250	8,668	6,599	8,668	7,248
58,250	58,300	8,679	6,605	8,679	7,259
58,300	58,350	8,690	6,611	8,690	7,270
58,350	58,400	8,701	6,617	8,701	7,281
58,400	58,450	8,712	6,623	8,712	7,292
58,450	58,500	8,723	6,629	8,723	7,303
58,500	58,550	8,734	6,635	8,734	7,314
58,550	58,600	8,745	6,641	8,745	7,325
58,600	58,650	8,756	6,647	8,756	7,336
58,650	58,700	8,767	6,653	8,767	7,347
58,700	58,750	8,778	6,659	8,778	7,358
58,750	58,800	8,789	6,665	8,789	7,369
58,800	58,850	8,800	6,671	8,800	7,380
58,850	58,900	8,811	6,677	8,811	7,391
58,900	58,950	8,822	6,683	8,822	7,402
58,950	59,000	8,833	6,689	8,833	7,413

59,000

At least	But less than	Single	Married filing jointly *	Married filing separately	Head of a household
59,000	59,050	8,844	6,695	8,844	7,424
59,050	59,100	8,855	6,701	8,855	7,435
59,100	59,150	8,866	6,707	8,866	7,446
59,150	59,200	8,877	6,713	8,877	7,457
59,200	59,250	8,888	6,719	8,888	7,468
59,250	59,300	8,899	6,725	8,899	7,479
59,300	59,350	8,910	6,731	8,910	7,490
59,350	59,400	8,921	6,737	8,921	7,501
59,400	59,450	8,932	6,743	8,932	7,512
59,450	59,500	8,943	6,749	8,943	7,523
59,500	59,550	8,954	6,755	8,954	7,534
59,550	59,600	8,965	6,761	8,965	7,545
59,600	59,650	8,976	6,767	8,976	7,556
59,650	59,700	8,987	6,773	8,987	7,567
59,700	59,750	8,998	6,779	8,998	7,578
59,750	59,800	9,009	6,785	9,009	7,589
59,800	59,850	9,020	6,791	9,020	7,600
59,850	59,900	9,031	6,797	9,031	7,611
59,900	59,950	9,042	6,803	9,042	7,622
59,950	60,000	9,053	6,809	9,053	7,633

60,000

If line 11b (taxable income) is— At least	But less than	Single	Married filing jointly *	Married filing separately	Head of a household
60,000	60,050	9,064	6,815	9,064	7,644
60,050	60,100	9,075	6,821	9,075	7,655
60,100	60,150	9,086	6,827	9,086	7,666
60,150	60,200	9,097	6,833	9,097	7,677
60,200	60,250	9,108	6,839	9,108	7,688
60,250	60,300	9,119	6,845	9,119	7,699
60,300	60,350	9,130	6,851	9,130	7,710
60,350	60,400	9,141	6,857	9,141	7,721
60,400	60,450	9,152	6,863	9,152	7,732
60,450	60,500	9,163	6,869	9,163	7,743
60,500	60,550	9,174	6,875	9,174	7,754
60,550	60,600	9,185	6,881	9,185	7,765
60,600	60,650	9,196	6,887	9,196	7,776
60,650	60,700	9,207	6,893	9,207	7,787
60,700	60,750	9,218	6,899	9,218	7,798
60,750	60,800	9,229	6,905	9,229	7,809
60,800	60,850	9,240	6,911	9,240	7,820
60,850	60,900	9,251	6,917	9,251	7,831
60,900	60,950	9,262	6,923	9,262	7,842
60,950	61,000	9,273	6,929	9,273	7,853

61,000

At least	But less than	Single	Married filing jointly *	Married filing separately	Head of a household
61,000	61,050	9,284	6,935	9,284	7,864
61,050	61,100	9,295	6,941	9,295	7,875
61,100	61,150	9,306	6,947	9,306	7,886
61,150	61,200	9,317	6,953	9,317	7,897
61,200	61,250	9,328	6,959	9,328	7,908
61,250	61,300	9,339	6,965	9,339	7,919
61,300	61,350	9,350	6,971	9,350	7,930
61,350	61,400	9,361	6,977	9,361	7,941
61,400	61,450	9,372	6,983	9,372	7,952
61,450	61,500	9,383	6,989	9,383	7,963
61,500	61,550	9,394	6,995	9,394	7,974
61,550	61,600	9,405	7,001	9,405	7,985
61,600	61,650	9,416	7,007	9,416	7,996
61,650	61,700	9,427	7,013	9,427	8,007
61,700	61,750	9,438	7,019	9,438	8,018
61,750	61,800	9,449	7,025	9,449	8,029
61,800	61,850	9,460	7,031	9,460	8,040
61,850	61,900	9,471	7,037	9,471	8,051
61,900	61,950	9,482	7,043	9,482	8,062
61,950	62,000	9,493	7,049	9,493	8,073

62,000

At least	But less than	Single	Married filing jointly *	Married filing separately	Head of a household
62,000	62,050	9,504	7,055	9,504	8,084
62,050	62,100	9,515	7,061	9,515	8,095
62,100	62,150	9,526	7,067	9,526	8,106
62,150	62,200	9,537	7,073	9,537	8,117
62,200	62,250	9,548	7,079	9,548	8,128
62,250	62,300	9,559	7,085	9,559	8,139
62,300	62,350	9,570	7,091	9,570	8,150
62,350	62,400	9,581	7,097	9,581	8,161
62,400	62,450	9,592	7,103	9,592	8,172
62,450	62,500	9,603	7,109	9,603	8,183
62,500	62,550	9,614	7,115	9,614	8,194
62,550	62,600	9,625	7,121	9,625	8,205
62,600	62,650	9,636	7,127	9,636	8,216
62,650	62,700	9,647	7,133	9,647	8,227
62,700	62,750	9,658	7,139	9,658	8,238
62,750	62,800	9,669	7,145	9,669	8,249
62,800	62,850	9,680	7,151	9,680	8,260
62,850	62,900	9,691	7,157	9,691	8,271
62,900	62,950	9,702	7,163	9,702	8,282
62,950	63,000	9,713	7,169	9,713	8,293

63,000

If line 11b (taxable income) is— At least	But less than	Single	Married filing jointly *	Married filing separately	Head of a household
63,000	63,050	9,724	7,175	9,724	8,304
63,050	63,100	9,735	7,181	9,735	8,315
63,100	63,150	9,746	7,187	9,746	8,326
63,150	63,200	9,757	7,193	9,757	8,337
63,200	63,250	9,768	7,199	9,768	8,348
63,250	63,300	9,779	7,205	9,779	8,359
63,300	63,350	9,790	7,211	9,790	8,370
63,350	63,400	9,801	7,217	9,801	8,381
63,400	63,450	9,812	7,223	9,812	8,392
63,450	63,500	9,823	7,229	9,823	8,403
63,500	63,550	9,834	7,235	9,834	8,414
63,550	63,600	9,845	7,241	9,845	8,425
63,600	63,650	9,856	7,247	9,856	8,436
63,650	63,700	9,867	7,253	9,867	8,447
63,700	63,750	9,878	7,259	9,878	8,458
63,750	63,800	9,889	7,265	9,889	8,469
63,800	63,850	9,900	7,271	9,900	8,480
63,850	63,900	9,911	7,277	9,911	8,491
63,900	63,950	9,922	7,283	9,922	8,502
63,950	64,000	9,933	7,289	9,933	8,513

64,000

At least	But less than	Single	Married filing jointly *	Married filing separately	Head of a household
64,000	64,050	9,944	7,295	9,944	8,524
64,050	64,100	9,955	7,301	9,955	8,535
64,100	64,150	9,966	7,307	9,966	8,546
64,150	64,200	9,977	7,313	9,977	8,557
64,200	64,250	9,988	7,319	9,988	8,568
64,250	64,300	9,999	7,325	9,999	8,579
64,300	64,350	10,010	7,331	10,010	8,590
64,350	64,400	10,021	7,337	10,021	8,601
64,400	64,450	10,032	7,343	10,032	8,612
64,450	64,500	10,043	7,349	10,043	8,623
64,500	64,550	10,054	7,355	10,054	8,634
64,550	64,600	10,065	7,361	10,065	8,645
64,600	64,650	10,076	7,367	10,076	8,656
64,650	64,700	10,087	7,373	10,087	8,667
64,700	64,750	10,098	7,379	10,098	8,678
64,750	64,800	10,109	7,385	10,109	8,689
64,800	64,850	10,120	7,391	10,120	8,700
64,850	64,900	10,131	7,397	10,131	8,711
64,900	64,950	10,142	7,403	10,142	8,722
64,950	65,000	10,153	7,409	10,153	8,733

65,000

At least	But less than	Single	Married filing jointly *	Married filing separately	Head of a household
65,000	65,050	10,164	7,415	10,164	8,744
65,050	65,100	10,175	7,421	10,175	8,755
65,100	65,150	10,186	7,427	10,186	8,766
65,150	65,200	10,197	7,433	10,197	8,777
65,200	65,250	10,208	7,439	10,208	8,788
65,250	65,300	10,219	7,445	10,219	8,799
65,300	65,350	10,230	7,451	10,230	8,810
65,350	65,400	10,241	7,457	10,241	8,821
65,400	65,450	10,252	7,463	10,252	8,832
65,450	65,500	10,263	7,469	10,263	8,843
65,500	65,550	10,274	7,475	10,274	8,854
65,550	65,600	10,285	7,481	10,285	8,865
65,600	65,650	10,296	7,487	10,296	8,876
65,650	65,700	10,307	7,493	10,307	8,887
65,700	65,750	10,318	7,499	10,318	8,898
65,750	65,800	10,329	7,505	10,329	8,909
65,800	65,850	10,340	7,511	10,340	8,920
65,850	65,900	10,351	7,517	10,351	8,931
65,900	65,950	10,362	7,523	10,362	8,942
65,950	66,000	10,373	7,529	10,373	8,953

(Continued)

* This column must also be used by a qualifying widow(er).

2019 Tax Table — Continued

DRAFT AS OF September 11, 2019

If line 11b (taxable income) is—		And you are—				If line 11b (taxable income) is—		And you are—				If line 11b (taxable income) is—		And you are—			
At least	But less than	Single	Married filing jointly *	Married filing sepa-rately	Head of a house-hold	At least	But less than	Single	Married filing jointly *	Married filing sepa-rately	Head of a house-hold	At least	But less than	Single	Married filing jointly *	Married filing sepa-rately	Head of a house-hold
		Your tax is—						Your tax is—						Your tax is—			
66,000						**69,000**						**72,000**					
66,000	66,050	10,384	7,535	10,384	8,964	69,000	69,050	11,044	7,895	11,044	9,624	72,000	72,050	11,704	8,255	11,704	10,284
66,050	66,100	10,395	7,541	10,395	8,975	69,050	69,100	11,055	7,901	11,055	9,635	72,050	72,100	11,715	8,261	11,715	10,295
66,100	66,150	10,406	7,547	10,406	8,986	69,100	69,150	11,066	7,907	11,066	9,646	72,100	72,150	11,726	8,267	11,726	10,306
66,150	66,200	10,417	7,553	10,417	8,997	69,150	69,200	11,077	7,913	11,077	9,657	72,150	72,200	11,737	8,273	11,737	10,317
66,200	66,250	10,428	7,559	10,428	9,008	69,200	69,250	11,088	7,919	11,088	9,668	72,200	72,250	11,748	8,279	11,748	10,328
66,250	66,300	10,439	7,565	10,439	9,019	69,250	69,300	11,099	7,925	11,099	9,679	72,250	72,300	11,759	8,285	11,759	10,339
66,300	66,350	10,450	7,571	10,450	9,030	69,300	69,350	11,110	7,931	11,110	9,690	72,300	72,350	11,770	8,291	11,770	10,350
66,350	66,400	10,461	7,577	10,461	9,041	69,350	69,400	11,121	7,937	11,121	9,701	72,350	72,400	11,781	8,297	11,781	10,361
66,400	66,450	10,472	7,583	10,472	9,052	69,400	69,450	11,132	7,943	11,132	9,712	72,400	72,450	11,792	8,303	11,792	10,372
66,450	66,500	10,483	7,589	10,483	9,063	69,450	69,500	11,143	7,949	11,143	9,723	72,450	72,500	11,803	8,309	11,803	10,383
66,500	66,550	10,494	7,595	10,494	9,074	69,500	69,550	11,154	7,955	11,154	9,734	72,500	72,550	11,814	8,315	11,814	10,394
66,550	66,600	10,505	7,601	10,505	9,085	69,550	69,600	11,165	7,961	11,165	9,745	72,550	72,600	11,825	8,321	11,825	10,405
66,600	66,650	10,516	7,607	10,516	9,096	69,600	69,650	11,176	7,967	11,176	9,756	72,600	72,650	11,836	8,327	11,836	10,416
66,650	66,700	10,527	7,613	10,527	9,107	69,650	69,700	11,187	7,973	11,187	9,767	72,650	72,700	11,847	8,333	11,847	10,427
66,700	66,750	10,538	7,619	10,538	9,118	69,700	69,750	11,198	7,979	11,198	9,778	72,700	72,750	11,858	8,339	11,858	10,438
66,750	66,800	10,549	7,625	10,549	9,129	69,750	69,800	11,209	7,985	11,209	9,789	72,750	72,800	11,869	8,345	11,869	10,449
66,800	66,850	10,560	7,631	10,560	9,140	69,800	69,850	11,220	7,991	11,220	9,800	72,800	72,850	11,880	8,351	11,880	10,460
66,850	66,900	10,571	7,637	10,571	9,151	69,850	69,900	11,231	7,997	11,231	9,811	72,850	72,900	11,891	8,357	11,891	10,471
66,900	66,950	10,582	7,643	10,582	9,162	69,900	69,950	11,242	8,003	11,242	9,822	72,900	72,950	11,902	8,363	11,902	10,482
66,950	67,000	10,593	7,649	10,593	9,173	69,950	70,000	11,253	8,009	11,253	9,833	72,950	73,000	11,913	8,369	11,913	10,493
67,000						**70,000**						**73,000**					
67,000	67,050	10,604	7,655	10,604	9,184	70,000	70,050	11,264	8,015	11,264	9,844	73,000	73,050	11,924	8,375	11,924	10,504
67,050	67,100	10,615	7,661	10,615	9,195	70,050	70,100	11,275	8,021	11,275	9,855	73,050	73,100	11,935	8,381	11,935	10,515
67,100	67,150	10,626	7,667	10,626	9,206	70,100	70,150	11,286	8,027	11,286	9,866	73,100	73,150	11,946	8,387	11,946	10,526
67,150	67,200	10,637	7,673	10,637	9,217	70,150	70,200	11,297	8,033	11,297	9,877	73,150	73,200	11,957	8,393	11,957	10,537
67,200	67,250	10,648	7,679	10,648	9,228	70,200	70,250	11,308	8,039	11,308	9,888	73,200	73,250	11,968	8,399	11,968	10,548
67,250	67,300	10,659	7,685	10,659	9,239	70,250	70,300	11,319	8,045	11,319	9,899	73,250	73,300	11,979	8,405	11,979	10,559
67,300	67,350	10,670	7,691	10,670	9,250	70,300	70,350	11,330	8,051	11,330	9,910	73,300	73,350	11,990	8,411	11,990	10,570
67,350	67,400	10,681	7,697	10,681	9,261	70,350	70,400	11,341	8,057	11,341	9,921	73,350	73,400	12,001	8,417	12,001	10,581
67,400	67,450	10,692	7,703	10,692	9,272	70,400	70,450	11,352	8,063	11,352	9,932	73,400	73,450	12,012	8,423	12,012	10,592
67,450	67,500	10,703	7,709	10,703	9,283	70,450	70,500	11,363	8,069	11,363	9,943	73,450	73,500	12,023	8,429	12,023	10,603
67,500	67,550	10,714	7,715	10,714	9,294	70,500	70,550	11,374	8,075	11,374	9,954	73,500	73,550	12,034	8,435	12,034	10,614
67,550	67,600	10,725	7,721	10,725	9,305	70,550	70,600	11,385	8,081	11,385	9,965	73,550	73,600	12,045	8,441	12,045	10,625
67,600	67,650	10,736	7,727	10,736	9,316	70,600	70,650	11,396	8,087	11,396	9,976	73,600	73,650	12,056	8,447	12,056	10,636
67,650	67,700	10,747	7,733	10,747	9,327	70,650	70,700	11,407	8,093	11,407	9,987	73,650	73,700	12,067	8,453	12,067	10,647
67,700	67,750	10,758	7,739	10,758	9,338	70,700	70,750	11,418	8,099	11,418	9,998	73,700	73,750	12,078	8,459	12,078	10,658
67,750	67,800	10,769	7,745	10,769	9,349	70,750	70,800	11,429	8,105	11,429	10,009	73,750	73,800	12,089	8,465	12,089	10,669
67,800	67,850	10,780	7,751	10,780	9,360	70,800	70,850	11,440	8,111	11,440	10,020	73,800	73,850	12,100	8,471	12,100	10,680
67,850	67,900	10,791	7,757	10,791	9,371	70,850	70,900	11,451	8,117	11,451	10,031	73,850	73,900	12,111	8,477	12,111	10,691
67,900	67,950	10,802	7,763	10,802	9,382	70,900	70,950	11,462	8,123	11,462	10,042	73,900	73,950	12,122	8,483	12,122	10,702
67,950	68,000	10,813	7,769	10,813	9,393	70,950	71,000	11,473	8,129	11,473	10,053	73,950	74,000	12,133	8,489	12,133	10,713
68,000						**71,000**						**74,000**					
68,000	68,050	10,824	7,775	10,824	9,404	71,000	71,050	11,484	8,135	11,484	10,064	74,000	74,050	12,144	8,495	12,144	10,724
68,050	68,100	10,835	7,781	10,835	9,415	71,050	71,100	11,495	8,141	11,495	10,075	74,050	74,100	12,155	8,501	12,155	10,735
68,100	68,150	10,846	7,787	10,846	9,426	71,100	71,150	11,506	8,147	11,506	10,086	74,100	74,150	12,166	8,507	12,166	10,746
68,150	68,200	10,857	7,793	10,857	9,437	71,150	71,200	11,517	8,153	11,517	10,097	74,150	74,200	12,177	8,513	12,177	10,757
68,200	68,250	10,868	7,799	10,868	9,448	71,200	71,250	11,528	8,159	11,528	10,108	74,200	74,250	12,188	8,519	12,188	10,768
68,250	68,300	10,879	7,805	10,879	9,459	71,250	71,300	11,539	8,165	11,539	10,119	74,250	74,300	12,199	8,525	12,199	10,779
68,300	68,350	10,890	7,811	10,890	9,470	71,300	71,350	11,550	8,171	11,550	10,130	74,300	74,350	12,210	8,531	12,210	10,790
68,350	68,400	10,901	7,817	10,901	9,481	71,350	71,400	11,561	8,177	11,561	10,141	74,350	74,400	12,221	8,537	12,221	10,801
68,400	68,450	10,912	7,823	10,912	9,492	71,400	71,450	11,572	8,183	11,572	10,152	74,400	74,450	12,232	8,543	12,232	10,812
68,450	68,500	10,923	7,829	10,923	9,503	71,450	71,500	11,583	8,189	11,583	10,163	74,450	74,500	12,243	8,549	12,243	10,823
68,500	68,550	10,934	7,835	10,934	9,514	71,500	71,550	11,594	8,195	11,594	10,174	74,500	74,550	12,254	8,555	12,254	10,834
68,550	68,600	10,945	7,841	10,945	9,525	71,550	71,600	11,605	8,201	11,605	10,185	74,550	74,600	12,265	8,561	12,265	10,845
68,600	68,650	10,956	7,847	10,956	9,536	71,600	71,650	11,616	8,207	11,616	10,196	74,600	74,650	12,276	8,567	12,276	10,856
68,650	68,700	10,967	7,853	10,967	9,547	71,650	71,700	11,627	8,213	11,627	10,207	74,650	74,700	12,287	8,573	12,287	10,867
68,700	68,750	10,978	7,859	10,978	9,558	71,700	71,750	11,638	8,219	11,638	10,218	74,700	74,750	12,298	8,579	12,298	10,878
68,750	68,800	10,989	7,865	10,989	9,569	71,750	71,800	11,649	8,225	11,649	10,229	74,750	74,800	12,309	8,585	12,309	10,889
68,800	68,850	11,000	7,871	11,000	9,580	71,800	71,850	11,660	8,231	11,660	10,240	74,800	74,850	12,320	8,591	12,320	10,900
68,850	68,900	11,011	7,877	11,011	9,591	71,850	71,900	11,671	8,237	11,671	10,251	74,850	74,900	12,331	8,597	12,331	10,911
68,900	68,950	11,022	7,883	11,022	9,602	71,900	71,950	11,682	8,243	11,682	10,262	74,900	74,950	12,342	8,603	12,342	10,922
68,950	69,000	11,033	7,889	11,033	9,613	71,950	72,000	11,693	8,249	11,693	10,273	74,950	75,000	12,353	8,609	12,353	10,933

(Continued)

* This column must also be used by a qualifying widow(er).

2019 Tax Table — Continued

DRAFT AS OF September 11, 2019

* This column must also be used by a qualifying widow(er).

(Continued)

75,000

At least	But less than	Single	Married filing jointly *	Married filing separately	Head of a household
			Your tax is—		
75,000	75,050	12,364	8,615	12,364	10,944
75,050	75,100	12,375	8,621	12,375	10,955
75,100	75,150	12,386	8,627	12,386	10,966
75,150	75,200	12,397	8,633	12,397	10,977
75,200	75,250	12,408	8,639	12,408	10,988
75,250	75,300	12,419	8,645	12,419	10,999
75,300	75,350	12,430	8,651	12,430	11,010
75,350	75,400	12,441	8,657	12,441	11,021
75,400	75,450	12,452	8,663	12,452	11,032
75,450	75,500	12,463	8,669	12,463	11,043
75,500	75,550	12,474	8,675	12,474	11,054
75,550	75,600	12,485	8,681	12,485	11,065
75,600	75,650	12,496	8,687	12,496	11,076
75,650	75,700	12,507	8,693	12,507	11,087
75,700	75,750	12,518	8,699	12,518	11,098
75,750	75,800	12,529	8,705	12,529	11,109
75,800	75,850	12,540	8,711	12,540	11,120
75,850	75,900	12,551	8,717	12,551	11,131
75,900	75,950	12,562	8,723	12,562	11,142
75,950	76,000	12,573	8,729	12,573	11,153

76,000

At least	But less than	Single	Married filing jointly *	Married filing separately	Head of a household
76,000	76,050	12,584	8,735	12,584	11,164
76,050	76,100	12,595	8,741	12,595	11,175
76,100	76,150	12,606	8,747	12,606	11,186
76,150	76,200	12,617	8,753	12,617	11,197
76,200	76,250	12,628	8,759	12,628	11,208
76,250	76,300	12,639	8,765	12,639	11,219
76,300	76,350	12,650	8,771	12,650	11,230
76,350	76,400	12,661	8,777	12,661	11,241
76,400	76,450	12,672	8,783	12,672	11,252
76,450	76,500	12,683	8,789	12,683	11,263
76,500	76,550	12,694	8,795	12,694	11,274
76,550	76,600	12,705	8,801	12,705	11,285
76,600	76,650	12,716	8,807	12,716	11,296
76,650	76,700	12,727	8,813	12,727	11,307
76,700	76,750	12,738	8,819	12,738	11,318
76,750	76,800	12,749	8,825	12,749	11,329
76,800	76,850	12,760	8,831	12,760	11,340
76,850	76,900	12,771	8,837	12,771	11,351
76,900	76,950	12,782	8,843	12,782	11,362
76,950	77,000	12,793	8,849	12,793	11,373

77,000

At least	But less than	Single	Married filing jointly *	Married filing separately	Head of a household
77,000	77,050	12,804	8,855	12,804	11,384
77,050	77,100	12,815	8,861	12,815	11,395
77,100	77,150	12,826	8,867	12,826	11,406
77,150	77,200	12,837	8,873	12,837	11,417
77,200	77,250	12,848	8,879	12,848	11,428
77,250	77,300	12,859	8,885	12,859	11,439
77,300	77,350	12,870	8,891	12,870	11,450
77,350	77,400	12,881	8,897	12,881	11,461
77,400	77,450	12,892	8,903	12,892	11,472
77,450	77,500	12,903	8,909	12,903	11,483
77,500	77,550	12,914	8,915	12,914	11,494
77,550	77,600	12,925	8,921	12,925	11,505
77,600	77,650	12,936	8,927	12,936	11,516
77,650	77,700	12,947	8,933	12,947	11,527
77,700	77,750	12,958	8,939	12,958	11,538
77,750	77,800	12,969	8,945	12,969	11,549
77,800	77,850	12,980	8,951	12,980	11,560
77,850	77,900	12,991	8,957	12,991	11,571
77,900	77,950	13,002	8,963	13,002	11,582
77,950	78,000	13,013	8,969	13,013	11,593

78,000

At least	But less than	Single	Married filing jointly *	Married filing separately	Head of a household
78,000	78,050	13,024	8,975	13,024	11,604
78,050	78,100	13,035	8,981	13,035	11,615
78,100	78,150	13,046	8,987	13,046	11,626
78,150	78,200	13,057	8,993	13,057	11,637
78,200	78,250	13,068	8,999	13,068	11,648
78,250	78,300	13,079	9,005	13,079	11,659
78,300	78,350	13,090	9,011	13,090	11,670
78,350	78,400	13,101	9,017	13,101	11,681
78,400	78,450	13,112	9,023	13,112	11,692
78,450	78,500	13,123	9,029	13,123	11,703
78,500	78,550	13,134	9,035	13,134	11,714
78,550	78,600	13,145	9,041	13,145	11,725
78,600	78,650	13,156	9,047	13,156	11,736
78,650	78,700	13,167	9,053	13,167	11,747
78,700	78,750	13,178	9,059	13,178	11,758
78,750	78,800	13,189	9,065	13,189	11,769
78,800	78,850	13,200	9,071	13,200	11,780
78,850	78,900	13,211	9,077	13,211	11,791
78,900	78,950	13,222	9,083	13,222	11,802
78,950	79,000	13,233	9,092	13,233	11,813

79,000

At least	But less than	Single	Married filing jointly *	Married filing separately	Head of a household
79,000	79,050	13,244	9,103	13,244	11,824
79,050	79,100	13,255	9,114	13,255	11,835
79,100	79,150	13,266	9,125	13,266	11,846
79,150	79,200	13,277	9,136	13,277	11,857
79,200	79,250	13,288	9,147	13,288	11,868
79,250	79,300	13,299	9,158	13,299	11,879
79,300	79,350	13,310	9,169	13,310	11,890
79,350	79,400	13,321	9,180	13,321	11,901
79,400	79,450	13,332	9,191	13,332	11,912
79,450	79,500	13,343	9,202	13,343	11,923
79,500	79,550	13,354	9,213	13,354	11,934
79,550	79,600	13,365	9,224	13,365	11,945
79,600	79,650	13,376	9,235	13,376	11,956
79,650	79,700	13,387	9,246	13,387	11,967
79,700	79,750	13,398	9,257	13,398	11,978
79,750	79,800	13,409	9,268	13,409	11,989
79,800	79,850	13,420	9,279	13,420	12,000
79,850	79,900	13,431	9,290	13,431	12,011
79,900	79,950	13,442	9,301	13,442	12,022
79,950	80,000	13,453	9,312	13,453	12,033

80,000

At least	But less than	Single	Married filing jointly *	Married filing separately	Head of a household
80,000	80,050	13,464	9,323	13,464	12,044
80,050	80,100	13,475	9,334	13,475	12,055
80,100	80,150	13,486	9,345	13,486	12,066
80,150	80,200	13,497	9,356	13,497	12,077
80,200	80,250	13,508	9,367	13,508	12,088
80,250	80,300	13,519	9,378	13,519	12,099
80,300	80,350	13,530	9,389	13,530	12,110
80,350	80,400	13,541	9,400	13,541	12,121
80,400	80,450	13,552	9,411	13,552	12,132
80,450	80,500	13,563	9,422	13,563	12,143
80,500	80,550	13,574	9,433	13,574	12,154
80,550	80,600	13,585	9,444	13,585	12,165
80,600	80,650	13,596	9,455	13,596	12,176
80,650	80,700	13,607	9,466	13,607	12,187
80,700	80,750	13,618	9,477	13,618	12,198
80,750	80,800	13,629	9,488	13,629	12,209
80,800	80,850	13,640	9,499	13,640	12,220
80,850	80,900	13,651	9,510	13,651	12,231
80,900	80,950	13,662	9,521	13,662	12,242
80,950	81,000	13,673	9,532	13,673	12,253

81,000

At least	But less than	Single	Married filing jointly *	Married filing separately	Head of a household
81,000	81,050	13,684	9,543	13,684	12,264
81,050	81,100	13,695	9,554	13,695	12,275
81,100	81,150	13,706	9,565	13,706	12,286
81,150	81,200	13,717	9,576	13,717	12,297
81,200	81,250	13,728	9,587	13,728	12,308
81,250	81,300	13,739	9,598	13,739	12,319
81,300	81,350	13,750	9,609	13,750	12,330
81,350	81,400	13,761	9,620	13,761	12,341
81,400	81,450	13,772	9,631	13,772	12,352
81,450	81,500	13,783	9,642	13,783	12,363
81,500	81,550	13,794	9,653	13,794	12,374
81,550	81,600	13,805	9,664	13,805	12,385
81,600	81,650	13,816	9,675	13,816	12,396
81,650	81,700	13,827	9,686	13,827	12,407
81,700	81,750	13,838	9,697	13,838	12,418
81,750	81,800	13,849	9,708	13,849	12,429
81,800	81,850	13,860	9,719	13,860	12,440
81,850	81,900	13,871	9,730	13,871	12,451
81,900	81,950	13,882	9,741	13,882	12,462
81,950	82,000	13,893	9,752	13,893	12,473

82,000

At least	But less than	Single	Married filing jointly *	Married filing separately	Head of a household
82,000	82,050	13,904	9,763	13,904	12,484
82,050	82,100	13,915	9,774	13,915	12,495
82,100	82,150	13,926	9,785	13,926	12,506
82,150	82,200	13,937	9,796	13,937	12,517
82,200	82,250	13,948	9,807	13,948	12,528
82,250	82,300	13,959	9,818	13,959	12,539
82,300	82,350	13,970	9,829	13,970	12,550
82,350	82,400	13,981	9,840	13,981	12,561
82,400	82,450	13,992	9,851	13,992	12,572
82,450	82,500	14,003	9,862	14,003	12,583
82,500	82,550	14,014	9,873	14,014	12,594
82,550	82,600	14,025	9,884	14,025	12,605
82,600	82,650	14,036	9,895	14,036	12,616
82,650	82,700	14,047	9,906	14,047	12,627
82,700	82,750	14,058	9,917	14,058	12,638
82,750	82,800	14,069	9,928	14,069	12,649
82,800	82,850	14,080	9,939	14,080	12,660
82,850	82,900	14,091	9,950	14,091	12,671
82,900	82,950	14,102	9,961	14,102	12,682
82,950	83,000	14,113	9,972	14,113	12,693

83,000

At least	But less than	Single	Married filing jointly *	Married filing separately	Head of a household
83,000	83,050	14,124	9,983	14,124	12,704
83,050	83,100	14,135	9,994	14,135	12,715
83,100	83,150	14,146	10,005	14,146	12,726
83,150	83,200	14,157	10,016	14,157	12,737
83,200	83,250	14,168	10,027	14,168	12,748
83,250	83,300	14,179	10,038	14,179	12,759
83,300	83,350	14,190	10,049	14,190	12,770
83,350	83,400	14,201	10,060	14,201	12,781
83,400	83,450	14,212	10,071	14,212	12,792
83,450	83,500	14,223	10,082	14,223	12,803
83,500	83,550	14,234	10,093	14,234	12,814
83,550	83,600	14,245	10,104	14,245	12,825
83,600	83,650	14,256	10,115	14,256	12,836
83,650	83,700	14,267	10,126	14,267	12,847
83,700	83,750	14,278	10,137	14,278	12,858
83,750	83,800	14,289	10,148	14,289	12,869
83,800	83,850	14,300	10,159	14,300	12,880
83,850	83,900	14,311	10,170	14,311	12,891
83,900	83,950	14,322	10,181	14,322	12,902
83,950	84,000	14,333	10,192	14,333	12,913

2019 Tax Table — *Continued*

If line 11b (taxable income) is—		And you are—			
At least	But less than	Single	Married filing jointly *	Married filing separately	Head of a house-hold
		Your tax is—			

84,000

At least	But less than	Single	Married jointly *	Married separately	Head of household
84,000	84,050	14,344	10,203	14,344	12,924
84,050	84,100	14,355	10,214	14,355	12,935
84,100	84,150	14,366	10,225	14,366	12,946
84,150	84,200	14,377	10,236	14,377	12,957
84,200	84,250	14,389	10,247	14,389	12,968
84,250	84,300	14,401	10,258	14,401	12,980
84,300	84,350	14,413	10,269	14,413	12,992
84,350	84,400	14,425	10,280	14,425	13,004
84,400	84,450	14,437	10,291	14,437	13,016
84,450	84,500	14,449	10,302	14,449	13,028
84,500	84,550	14,461	10,313	14,461	13,040
84,550	84,600	14,473	10,324	14,473	13,052
84,600	84,650	14,485	10,335	14,485	13,064
84,650	84,700	14,497	10,346	14,497	13,076
84,700	84,750	14,509	10,357	14,509	13,088
84,750	84,800	14,521	10,368	14,521	13,100
84,800	84,850	14,533	10,379	14,533	13,112
84,850	84,900	14,545	10,390	14,545	13,124
84,900	84,950	14,557	10,401	14,557	13,136
84,950	85,000	14,569	10,412	14,569	13,148

85,000

At least	But less than	Single	Married jointly *	Married separately	Head of household
85,000	85,050	14,581	10,423	14,581	13,160
85,050	85,100	14,593	10,434	14,593	13,172
85,100	85,150	14,605	10,445	14,605	13,184
85,150	85,200	14,617	10,456	14,617	13,196
85,200	85,250	14,629	10,467	14,629	13,208
85,250	85,300	14,641	10,478	14,641	13,220
85,300	85,350	14,653	10,489	14,653	13,232
85,350	85,400	14,665	10,500	14,665	13,244
85,400	85,450	14,677	10,511	14,677	13,256
85,450	85,500	14,689	10,522	14,689	13,268
85,500	85,550	14,701	10,533	14,701	13,280
85,550	85,600	14,713	10,544	14,713	13,292
85,600	85,650	14,725	10,555	14,725	13,304
85,650	85,700	14,737	10,566	14,737	13,316
85,700	85,750	14,749	10,577	14,749	13,328
85,750	85,800	14,761	10,588	14,761	13,340
85,800	85,850	14,773	10,599	14,773	13,352
85,850	85,900	14,785	10,610	14,785	13,364
85,900	85,950	14,797	10,621	14,797	13,376
85,950	86,000	14,809	10,632	14,809	13,388

86,000

At least	But less than	Single	Married jointly *	Married separately	Head of household
86,000	86,050	14,821	10,643	14,821	13,400
86,050	86,100	14,833	10,654	14,833	13,412
86,100	86,150	14,845	10,665	14,845	13,424
86,150	86,200	14,857	10,676	14,857	13,436
86,200	86,250	14,869	10,687	14,869	13,448
86,250	86,300	14,881	10,698	14,881	13,460
86,300	86,350	14,893	10,709	14,893	13,472
86,350	86,400	14,905	10,720	14,905	13,484
86,400	86,450	14,917	10,731	14,917	13,496
86,450	86,500	14,929	10,742	14,929	13,508
86,500	86,550	14,941	10,753	14,941	13,520
86,550	86,600	14,953	10,764	14,953	13,532
86,600	86,650	14,965	10,775	14,965	13,544
86,650	86,700	14,977	10,786	14,977	13,556
86,700	86,750	14,989	10,797	14,989	13,568
86,750	86,800	15,001	10,808	15,001	13,580
86,800	86,850	15,013	10,819	15,013	13,592
86,850	86,900	15,025	10,830	15,025	13,604
86,900	86,950	15,037	10,841	15,037	13,616
86,950	87,000	15,049	10,852	15,049	13,628

87,000

At least	But less than	Single	Married jointly *	Married separately	Head of household
87,000	87,050	15,061	10,863	15,061	13,640
87,050	87,100	15,073	10,874	15,073	13,652
87,100	87,150	15,085	10,885	15,085	13,664
87,150	87,200	15,097	10,896	15,097	13,676
87,200	87,250	15,109	10,907	15,109	13,688
87,250	87,300	15,121	10,918	15,121	13,700
87,300	87,350	15,133	10,929	15,133	13,712
87,350	87,400	15,145	10,940	15,145	13,724
87,400	87,450	15,157	10,951	15,157	13,736
87,450	87,500	15,169	10,962	15,169	13,748
87,500	87,550	15,181	10,973	15,181	13,760
87,550	87,600	15,193	10,984	15,193	13,772
87,600	87,650	15,205	10,995	15,205	13,784
87,650	87,700	15,217	11,006	15,217	13,796
87,700	87,750	15,229	11,017	15,229	13,808
87,750	87,800	15,241	11,028	15,241	13,820
87,800	87,850	15,253	11,039	15,253	13,832
87,850	87,900	15,265	11,050	15,265	13,844
87,900	87,950	15,277	11,061	15,277	13,856
87,950	88,000	15,289	11,072	15,289	13,868

88,000

At least	But less than	Single	Married jointly *	Married separately	Head of household
88,000	88,050	15,301	11,083	15,301	13,880
88,050	88,100	15,313	11,094	15,313	13,892
88,100	88,150	15,325	11,105	15,325	13,904
88,150	88,200	15,337	11,116	15,337	13,916
88,200	88,250	15,349	11,127	15,349	13,928
88,250	88,300	15,361	11,138	15,361	13,940
88,300	88,350	15,373	11,149	15,373	13,952
88,350	88,400	15,385	11,160	15,385	13,964
88,400	88,450	15,397	11,171	15,397	13,976
88,450	88,500	15,409	11,182	15,409	13,988
88,500	88,550	15,421	11,193	15,421	14,000
88,550	88,600	15,433	11,204	15,433	14,012
88,600	88,650	15,445	11,215	15,445	14,024
88,650	88,700	15,457	11,226	15,457	14,036
88,700	88,750	15,469	11,237	15,469	14,048
88,750	88,800	15,481	11,248	15,481	14,060
88,800	88,850	15,493	11,259	15,493	14,072
88,850	88,900	15,505	11,270	15,505	14,084
88,900	88,950	15,517	11,281	15,517	14,096
88,950	89,000	15,529	11,292	15,529	14,108

89,000

At least	But less than	Single	Married jointly *	Married separately	Head of household
89,000	89,050	15,541	11,303	15,541	14,120
89,050	89,100	15,553	11,314	15,553	14,132
89,100	89,150	15,565	11,325	15,565	14,144
89,150	89,200	15,577	11,336	15,577	14,156
89,200	89,250	15,589	11,347	15,589	14,168
89,250	89,300	15,601	11,358	15,601	14,180
89,300	89,350	15,613	11,369	15,613	14,192
89,350	89,400	15,625	11,380	15,625	14,204
89,400	89,450	15,637	11,391	15,637	14,216
89,450	89,500	15,649	11,402	15,649	14,228
89,500	89,550	15,661	11,413	15,661	14,240
89,550	89,600	15,673	11,424	15,673	14,252
89,600	89,650	15,685	11,435	15,685	14,264
89,650	89,700	15,697	11,446	15,697	14,276
89,700	89,750	15,709	11,457	15,709	14,288
89,750	89,800	15,721	11,468	15,721	14,300
89,800	89,850	15,733	11,479	15,733	14,312
89,850	89,900	15,745	11,490	15,745	14,324
89,900	89,950	15,757	11,501	15,757	14,336
89,950	90,000	15,769	11,512	15,769	14,348

90,000

At least	But less than	Single	Married jointly *	Married separately	Head of household
90,000	90,050	15,781	11,523	15,781	14,360
90,050	90,100	15,793	11,534	15,793	14,372
90,100	90,150	15,805	11,545	15,805	14,384
90,150	90,200	15,817	11,556	15,817	14,396
90,200	90,250	15,829	11,567	15,829	14,408
90,250	90,300	15,841	11,578	15,841	14,420
90,300	90,350	15,853	11,589	15,853	14,432
90,350	90,400	15,865	11,600	15,865	14,444
90,400	90,450	15,877	11,611	15,877	14,456
90,450	90,500	15,889	11,622	15,889	14,468
90,500	90,550	15,901	11,633	15,901	14,480
90,550	90,600	15,913	11,644	15,913	14,492
90,600	90,650	15,925	11,655	15,925	14,504
90,650	90,700	15,937	11,666	15,937	14,516
90,700	90,750	15,949	11,677	15,949	14,528
90,750	90,800	15,961	11,688	15,961	14,540
90,800	90,850	15,973	11,699	15,973	14,552
90,850	90,900	15,985	11,710	15,985	14,564
90,900	90,950	15,997	11,721	15,997	14,576
90,950	91,000	16,009	11,732	16,009	14,588

91,000

At least	But less than	Single	Married jointly *	Married separately	Head of household
91,000	91,050	16,021	11,743	16,021	14,600
91,050	91,100	16,033	11,754	16,033	14,612
91,100	91,150	16,045	11,765	16,045	14,624
91,150	91,200	16,057	11,776	16,057	14,636
91,200	91,250	16,069	11,787	16,069	14,648
91,250	91,300	16,081	11,798	16,081	14,660
91,300	91,350	16,093	11,809	16,093	14,672
91,350	91,400	16,105	11,820	16,105	14,684
91,400	91,450	16,117	11,831	16,117	14,696
91,450	91,500	16,129	11,842	16,129	14,708
91,500	91,550	16,141	11,853	16,141	14,720
91,550	91,600	16,153	11,864	16,153	14,732
91,600	91,650	16,165	11,875	16,165	14,744
91,650	91,700	16,177	11,886	16,177	14,756
91,700	91,750	16,189	11,897	16,189	14,768
91,750	91,800	16,201	11,908	16,201	14,780
91,800	91,850	16,213	11,919	16,213	14,792
91,850	91,900	16,225	11,930	16,225	14,804
91,900	91,950	16,237	11,941	16,237	14,816
91,950	92,000	16,249	11,952	16,249	14,828

92,000

At least	But less than	Single	Married jointly *	Married separately	Head of household
92,000	92,050	16,261	11,963	16,261	14,840
92,050	92,100	16,273	11,974	16,273	14,852
92,100	92,150	16,285	11,985	16,285	14,864
92,150	92,200	16,297	11,996	16,297	14,876
92,200	92,250	16,309	12,007	16,309	14,888
92,250	92,300	16,321	12,018	16,321	14,900
92,300	92,350	16,333	12,029	16,333	14,912
92,350	92,400	16,345	12,040	16,345	14,924
92,400	92,450	16,357	12,051	16,357	14,936
92,450	92,500	16,369	12,062	16,369	14,948
92,500	92,550	16,381	12,073	16,381	14,960
92,550	92,600	16,393	12,084	16,393	14,972
92,600	92,650	16,405	12,095	16,405	14,984
92,650	92,700	16,417	12,106	16,417	14,996
92,700	92,750	16,429	12,117	16,429	15,008
92,750	92,800	16,441	12,128	16,441	15,020
92,800	92,850	16,453	12,139	16,453	15,032
92,850	92,900	16,465	12,150	16,465	15,044
92,900	92,950	16,477	12,161	16,477	15,056
92,950	93,000	16,489	12,172	16,489	15,068

(Continued)

* This column must also be used by a qualifying widow(er).

2019 Tax Table — *Continued*

DRAFT AS OF September 11, 2019

If line 11b (taxable income) is—		And you are—			
At least	But less than	Single	Married filing jointly *	Married filing separately	Head of a household
		Your tax is—			

93,000

At least	But less than	Single	Married filing jointly *	Married filing separately	Head of a household
93,000	93,050	16,501	12,183	16,501	15,080
93,050	93,100	16,513	12,194	16,513	15,092
93,100	93,150	16,525	12,205	16,525	15,104
93,150	93,200	16,537	12,216	16,537	15,116
93,200	93,250	16,549	12,227	16,549	15,128
93,250	93,300	16,561	12,238	16,561	15,140
93,300	93,350	16,573	12,249	16,573	15,152
93,350	93,400	16,585	12,260	16,585	15,164
93,400	93,450	16,597	12,271	16,597	15,176
93,450	93,500	16,609	12,282	16,609	15,188
93,500	93,550	16,621	12,293	16,621	15,200
93,550	93,600	16,633	12,304	16,633	15,212
93,600	93,650	16,645	12,315	16,645	15,224
93,650	93,700	16,657	12,326	16,657	15,236
93,700	93,750	16,669	12,337	16,669	15,248
93,750	93,800	16,681	12,348	16,681	15,260
93,800	93,850	16,693	12,359	16,693	15,272
93,850	93,900	16,705	12,370	16,705	15,284
93,900	93,950	16,717	12,381	16,717	15,296
93,950	94,000	16,729	12,392	16,729	15,308

94,000

At least	But less than	Single	Married filing jointly *	Married filing separately	Head of a household
94,000	94,050	16,741	12,403	16,741	15,320
94,050	94,100	16,753	12,414	16,753	15,332
94,100	94,150	16,765	12,425	16,765	15,344
94,150	94,200	16,777	12,436	16,777	15,356
94,200	94,250	16,789	12,447	16,789	15,368
94,250	94,300	16,801	12,458	16,801	15,380
94,300	94,350	16,813	12,469	16,813	15,392
94,350	94,400	16,825	12,480	16,825	15,404
94,400	94,450	16,837	12,491	16,837	15,416
94,450	94,500	16,849	12,502	16,849	15,428
94,500	94,550	16,861	12,513	16,861	15,440
94,550	94,600	16,873	12,524	16,873	15,452
94,600	94,650	16,885	12,535	16,885	15,464
94,650	94,700	16,897	12,546	16,897	15,476
94,700	94,750	16,909	12,557	16,909	15,488
94,750	94,800	16,921	12,568	16,921	15,500
94,800	94,850	16,933	12,579	16,933	15,512
94,850	94,900	16,945	12,590	16,945	15,524
94,900	94,950	16,957	12,601	16,957	15,536
94,950	95,000	16,969	12,612	16,969	15,548

95,000

At least	But less than	Single	Married filing jointly *	Married filing separately	Head of a household
95,000	95,050	16,981	12,623	16,981	15,560
95,050	95,100	16,993	12,634	16,993	15,572
95,100	95,150	17,005	12,645	17,005	15,584
95,150	95,200	17,017	12,656	17,017	15,596
95,200	95,250	17,029	12,667	17,029	15,608
95,250	95,300	17,041	12,678	17,041	15,620
95,300	95,350	17,053	12,689	17,053	15,632
95,350	95,400	17,065	12,700	17,065	15,644
95,400	95,450	17,077	12,711	17,077	15,656
95,450	95,500	17,089	12,722	17,089	15,668
95,500	95,550	17,101	12,733	17,101	15,680
95,550	95,600	17,113	12,744	17,113	15,692
95,600	95,650	17,125	12,755	17,125	15,704
95,650	95,700	17,137	12,766	17,137	15,716
95,700	95,750	17,149	12,777	17,149	15,728
95,750	95,800	17,161	12,788	17,161	15,740
95,800	95,850	17,173	12,799	17,173	15,752
95,850	95,900	17,185	12,810	17,185	15,764
95,900	95,950	17,197	12,821	17,197	15,776
95,950	96,000	17,209	12,832	17,209	15,788

96,000

At least	But less than	Single	Married filing jointly *	Married filing separately	Head of a household
96,000	96,050	17,221	12,843	17,221	15,800
96,050	96,100	17,233	12,854	17,233	15,812
96,100	96,150	17,245	12,865	17,245	15,824
96,150	96,200	17,257	12,876	17,257	15,836
96,200	96,250	17,269	12,887	17,269	15,848
96,250	96,300	17,281	12,898	17,281	15,860
96,300	96,350	17,293	12,909	17,293	15,872
96,350	96,400	17,305	12,920	17,305	15,884
96,400	96,450	17,317	12,931	17,317	15,896
96,450	96,500	17,329	12,942	17,329	15,908
96,500	96,550	17,341	12,953	17,341	15,920
96,550	96,600	17,353	12,964	17,353	15,932
96,600	96,650	17,365	12,975	17,365	15,944
96,650	96,700	17,377	12,986	17,377	15,956
96,700	96,750	17,389	12,997	17,389	15,968
96,750	96,800	17,401	13,008	17,401	15,980
96,800	96,850	17,413	13,019	17,413	15,992
96,850	96,900	17,425	13,030	17,425	16,004
96,900	96,950	17,437	13,041	17,437	16,016
96,950	97,000	17,449	13,052	17,449	16,028

97,000

At least	But less than	Single	Married filing jointly *	Married filing separately	Head of a household
97,000	97,050	17,461	13,063	17,461	16,040
97,050	97,100	17,473	13,074	17,473	16,052
97,100	97,150	17,485	13,085	17,485	16,064
97,150	97,200	17,497	13,096	17,497	16,076
97,200	97,250	17,509	13,107	17,509	16,088
97,250	97,300	17,521	13,118	17,521	16,100
97,300	97,350	17,533	13,129	17,533	16,112
97,350	97,400	17,545	13,140	17,545	16,124
97,400	97,450	17,557	13,151	17,557	16,136
97,450	97,500	17,569	13,162	17,569	16,148
97,500	97,550	17,581	13,173	17,581	16,160
97,550	97,600	17,593	13,184	17,593	16,172
97,600	97,650	17,605	13,195	17,605	16,184
97,650	97,700	17,617	13,206	17,617	16,196
97,700	97,750	17,629	13,217	17,629	16,208
97,750	97,800	17,641	13,228	17,641	16,220
97,800	97,850	17,653	13,239	17,653	16,232
97,850	97,900	17,665	13,250	17,665	16,244
97,900	97,950	17,677	13,261	17,677	16,256
97,950	98,000	17,689	13,272	17,689	16,268

98,000

At least	But less than	Single	Married filing jointly *	Married filing separately	Head of a household
98,000	98,050	17,701	13,283	17,701	16,280
98,050	98,100	17,713	13,294	17,713	16,292
98,100	98,150	17,725	13,305	17,725	16,304
98,150	98,200	17,737	13,316	17,737	16,316
98,200	98,250	17,749	13,327	17,749	16,328
98,250	98,300	17,761	13,338	17,761	16,340
98,300	98,350	17,773	13,349	17,773	16,352
98,350	98,400	17,785	13,360	17,785	16,364
98,400	98,450	17,797	13,371	17,797	16,376
98,450	98,500	17,809	13,382	17,809	16,388
98,500	98,550	17,821	13,393	17,821	16,400
98,550	98,600	17,833	13,404	17,833	16,412
98,600	98,650	17,845	13,415	17,845	16,424
98,650	98,700	17,857	13,426	17,857	16,436
98,700	98,750	17,869	13,437	17,869	16,448
98,750	98,800	17,881	13,448	17,881	16,460
98,800	98,850	17,893	13,459	17,893	16,472
98,850	98,900	17,905	13,470	17,905	16,484
98,900	98,950	17,917	13,481	17,917	16,496
98,950	99,000	17,929	13,492	17,929	16,508

99,000

At least	But less than	Single	Married filing jointly *	Married filing separately	Head of a household
99,000	99,050	17,941	13,503	17,941	16,520
99,050	99,100	17,953	13,514	17,953	16,532
99,100	99,150	17,965	13,525	17,965	16,544
99,150	99,200	17,977	13,536	17,977	16,556
99,200	99,250	17,989	13,547	17,989	16,568
99,250	99,300	18,001	13,558	18,001	16,580
99,300	99,350	18,013	13,569	18,013	16,592
99,350	99,400	18,025	13,580	18,025	16,604
99,400	99,450	18,037	13,591	18,037	16,616
99,450	99,500	18,049	13,602	18,049	16,628
99,500	99,550	18,061	13,613	18,061	16,640
99,550	99,600	18,073	13,624	18,073	16,652
99,600	99,650	18,085	13,635	18,085	16,664
99,650	99,700	18,097	13,646	18,097	16,676
99,700	99,750	18,109	13,657	18,109	16,688
99,750	99,800	18,121	13,668	18,121	16,700
99,800	99,850	18,133	13,679	18,133	16,712
99,850	99,900	18,145	13,690	18,145	16,724
99,900	99,950	18,157	13,701	18,157	16,736
99,950	100,000	18,169	13,712	18,169	16,748

$100,000 or over use the Tax Computation Worksheet

* This column must also be used by a qualifying widow(er).

Earned Income Credit Table

CONTENTS

Worksheet A—2019 EIC—Line 18a

Before you begin: √ Be sure you are using the correct worksheet. Use this worksheet only if you answered "No" to Step 5, question 2. Otherwise, use Worksheet B.

Part 1

All Filers Using Worksheet A

1. Enter your earned income from Step 5.   `1`
    Wages, salaries

2. Look up the amount on line 1 above in the EIC Table (right after Worksheet B) to find the credit. Be sure you use the correct column for your filing status and the number of children you have. Enter the credit here.   `2`

    If line 2 is zero, **STOP** You can't take the credit.
    Enter "No" on the dotted line next to Form 1040 or 1040-SR, line 18a.

3. Enter the amount from Form 1040 or 1040-SR, line 8b.   `3`
    Adjusted gross income

4. Are the amounts on lines 3 and 1 the same?

    ☐ **Yes.** Skip line 5; enter the amount from line 2 on line 6.

    ☐ **No.** Go to line 5.

Part 2

Filers Who Answered "No" on Line 4

5. If you have:
    • No qualifying children, is the amount on line 3 less than $8,650 ($14,450 if married filing jointly)?
    • 1 or more qualifying children, is the amount on line 3 less than $19,050 ($24,850 if married filing jointly)?

    ☐ **Yes.** Leave line 5 blank; enter the amount from line 2 on line 6.

    ☐ **No.** Look up the amount on line 3 in the EIC Table to find the credit. Be sure you use the correct column for your filing status and the number of children you have. Enter the credit here.
    Look at the amounts on lines 5 and 2.
    Then, enter the *smaller* amount on line 6.   `5`

Part 3

Your Earned Income Credit

6. This is your earned income credit.   `6`

    Enter this amount on Form 1040 or 1040-SR, line 18a.

    Reminder—

    √ If you have a qualifying child, complete and attach Schedule EIC.

    1040 or 1040-SR   EIC   →   1040 or 1040-SR ◄

    ⚠ CAUTION *If your EIC for a year after 1996 was reduced or disallowed, see Form 8862, who must file, earlier, to find out if you must file Form 8862 to take the credit for 2019.*

2019 Earned Income Credit (EIC) Table
Caution. This is **not** a tax table.

1. To find your credit, read down the "At least - But less than" columns and find the line that includes the amount you were told to look up from your EIC Worksheet.

2. Then, go to the column that includes your filing status and the number of qualifying children you have. Enter the credit from that column on your EIC Worksheet.

Example. If your filing status is single, you have one qualifying child, and the amount you are looking up from your EIC Worksheet is $2,455, you would enter $842.

If the amount you are looking up from the worksheet is—		And your filing status is—			
		Single, head of household, or qualifying widow(er) and the number of children you have is—			
		0	1	2	3
At least	But less than	Your credit is—			
2,400	2,450	186	825	970	1,091
2,450	2,500	189	842	990	1,114

If the amount you are looking up from the worksheet is—		And your filing status is—							
		Single, head of household, or qualifying widow(er) and you have—				Married filing jointly and you have—			
		0	1	2	3	0	1	2	3
At least	But less than	Your credit is—				Your credit is—			
$1	$50	$2	$9	$10	$11	$2	$9	$10	$11
50	100	6	26	30	34	6	26	30	34
100	150	10	43	50	56	10	43	50	56
150	200	13	60	70	79	13	60	70	79
200	250	17	77	90	101	17	77	90	101
250	300	21	94	110	124	21	94	110	124
300	350	25	111	130	146	25	111	130	146
350	400	29	128	150	169	29	128	150	169
400	450	33	145	170	191	33	145	170	191
450	500	36	162	190	214	36	162	190	214
500	550	40	179	210	236	40	179	210	236
550	600	44	196	230	259	44	196	230	259
600	650	48	213	250	281	48	213	250	281
650	700	52	230	270	304	52	230	270	304
700	750	55	247	290	326	55	247	290	326
750	800	59	264	310	349	59	264	310	349
800	850	63	281	330	371	63	281	330	371
850	900	67	298	350	394	67	298	350	394
900	950	71	315	370	416	71	315	370	416
950	1,000	75	332	390	439	75	332	390	439
1,000	1,050	78	349	410	461	78	349	410	461
1,050	1,100	82	366	430	484	82	366	430	484
1,100	1,150	86	383	450	506	86	383	450	506
1,150	1,200	90	400	470	529	90	400	470	529
1,200	1,250	94	417	490	551	94	417	490	551
1,250	1,300	98	434	510	574	98	434	510	574
1,300	1,350	101	451	530	596	101	451	530	596
1,350	1,400	105	468	550	619	105	468	550	619
1,400	1,450	109	485	570	641	109	485	570	641
1,450	1,500	113	502	590	664	113	502	590	664
1,500	1,550	117	519	610	686	117	519	610	686
1,550	1,600	120	536	630	709	120	536	630	709
1,600	1,650	124	553	650	731	124	553	650	731
1,650	1,700	128	570	670	754	128	570	670	754
1,700	1,750	132	587	690	776	132	587	690	776
1,750	1,800	136	604	710	799	136	604	710	799
1,800	1,850	140	621	730	821	140	621	730	821
1,850	1,900	143	638	750	844	143	638	750	844
1,900	1,950	147	655	770	866	147	655	770	866
1,950	2,000	151	672	790	889	151	672	790	889
2,000	2,050	155	689	810	911	155	689	810	911
2,050	2,100	159	706	830	934	159	706	830	934
2,100	2,150	163	723	850	956	163	723	850	956
2,150	2,200	166	740	870	979	166	740	870	979
2,200	2,250	170	757	890	1,001	170	757	890	1,001
2,250	2,300	174	774	910	1,024	174	774	910	1,024
2,300	2,350	178	791	930	1,046	178	791	930	1,046
2,350	2,400	182	808	950	1,069	182	808	950	1,069
2,400	2,450	186	825	970	1,091	186	825	970	1,091
2,450	2,500	189	842	990	1,114	189	842	990	1,114
2,500	2,550	193	859	1,010	1,136	193	859	1,010	1,136
2,550	2,600	197	876	1,030	1,159	197	876	1,030	1,159
2,600	2,650	201	893	1,050	1,181	201	893	1,050	1,181
2,650	2,700	205	910	1,070	1,204	205	910	1,070	1,204
2,700	2,750	208	927	1,090	1,226	208	927	1,090	1,226
2,750	2,800	212	944	1,110	1,249	212	944	1,110	1,249

If the amount you are looking up from the worksheet is—		And your filing status is—							
		Single, head of household, or qualifying widow(er) and you have—				Married filing jointly and you have—			
		0	1	2	3	0	1	2	3
At least	But less than	Your credit is—				Your credit is—			
2,800	2,850	216	961	1,130	1,271	216	961	1,130	1,271
2,850	2,900	220	978	1,150	1,294	220	978	1,150	1,294
2,900	2,950	224	995	1,170	1,316	224	995	1,170	1,316
2,950	3,000	228	1,012	1,190	1,339	228	1,012	1,190	1,339
3,000	3,050	231	1,029	1,210	1,361	231	1,029	1,210	1,361
3,050	3,100	235	1,046	1,230	1,384	235	1,046	1,230	1,384
3,100	3,150	239	1,063	1,250	1,406	239	1,063	1,250	1,406
3,150	3,200	243	1,080	1,270	1,429	243	1,080	1,270	1,429
3,200	3,250	247	1,097	1,290	1,451	247	1,097	1,290	1,451
3,250	3,300	251	1,114	1,310	1,474	251	1,114	1,310	1,474
3,300	3,350	254	1,131	1,330	1,496	254	1,131	1,330	1,496
3,350	3,400	258	1,148	1,350	1,519	258	1,148	1,350	1,519
3,400	3,450	262	1,165	1,370	1,541	262	1,165	1,370	1,541
3,450	3,500	266	1,182	1,390	1,564	266	1,182	1,390	1,564
3,500	3,550	270	1,199	1,410	1,586	270	1,199	1,410	1,586
3,550	3,600	273	1,216	1,430	1,609	273	1,216	1,430	1,609
3,600	3,650	277	1,233	1,450	1,631	277	1,233	1,450	1,631
3,650	3,700	281	1,250	1,470	1,654	281	1,250	1,470	1,654
3,700	3,750	285	1,267	1,490	1,676	285	1,267	1,490	1,676
3,750	3,800	289	1,284	1,510	1,699	289	1,284	1,510	1,699
3,800	3,850	293	1,301	1,530	1,721	293	1,301	1,530	1,721
3,850	3,900	296	1,318	1,550	1,744	296	1,318	1,550	1,744
3,900	3,950	300	1,335	1,570	1,766	300	1,335	1,570	1,766
3,950	4,000	304	1,352	1,590	1,789	304	1,352	1,590	1,789
4,000	4,050	308	1,369	1,610	1,811	308	1,369	1,610	1,811
4,050	4,100	312	1,386	1,630	1,834	312	1,386	1,630	1,834
4,100	4,150	316	1,403	1,650	1,856	316	1,403	1,650	1,856
4,150	4,200	319	1,420	1,670	1,879	319	1,420	1,670	1,879
4,200	4,250	323	1,437	1,690	1,901	323	1,437	1,690	1,901
4,250	4,300	327	1,454	1,710	1,924	327	1,454	1,710	1,924
4,300	4,350	331	1,471	1,730	1,946	331	1,471	1,730	1,946
4,350	4,400	335	1,488	1,750	1,969	335	1,488	1,750	1,969
4,400	4,450	339	1,505	1,770	1,991	339	1,505	1,770	1,991
4,450	4,500	342	1,522	1,790	2,014	342	1,522	1,790	2,014
4,500	4,550	346	1,539	1,810	2,036	346	1,539	1,810	2,036
4,550	4,600	350	1,556	1,830	2,059	350	1,556	1,830	2,059
4,600	4,650	354	1,573	1,850	2,081	354	1,573	1,850	2,081
4,650	4,700	358	1,590	1,870	2,104	358	1,590	1,870	2,104
4,700	4,750	361	1,607	1,890	2,126	361	1,607	1,890	2,126
4,750	4,800	365	1,624	1,910	2,149	365	1,624	1,910	2,149
4,800	4,850	369	1,641	1,930	2,171	369	1,641	1,930	2,171
4,850	4,900	373	1,658	1,950	2,194	373	1,658	1,950	2,194
4,900	4,950	377	1,675	1,970	2,216	377	1,675	1,970	2,216
4,950	5,000	381	1,692	1,990	2,239	381	1,692	1,990	2,239
5,000	5,050	384	1,709	2,010	2,261	384	1,709	2,010	2,261
5,050	5,100	388	1,726	2,030	2,284	388	1,726	2,030	2,284
5,100	5,150	392	1,743	2,050	2,306	392	1,743	2,050	2,306
5,150	5,200	396	1,760	2,070	2,329	396	1,760	2,070	2,329
5,200	5,250	400	1,777	2,090	2,351	400	1,777	2,090	2,351
5,250	5,300	404	1,794	2,110	2,374	404	1,794	2,110	2,374
5,300	5,350	407	1,811	2,130	2,396	407	1,811	2,130	2,396
5,350	5,400	411	1,828	2,150	2,419	411	1,828	2,150	2,419
5,400	5,450	415	1,845	2,170	2,441	415	1,845	2,170	2,441
5,450	5,500	419	1,862	2,190	2,464	419	1,862	2,190	2,464
5,500	5,550	423	1,879	2,210	2,486	423	1,879	2,210	2,486
5,550	5,600	426	1,896	2,230	2,509	426	1,896	2,230	2,509

(Continued)

Earned Income Credit (EIC) Table - Continued

(**Caution.** This is **not** a tax table.)

If the amount you are looking up from the worksheet is— At least	But less than	Single, head of household, or qualifying widow(er) and you have— 0	1	2	3	Married filing jointly and you have— 0	1	2	3
5,600	5,650	430	1,913	2,250	2,531	430	1,913	2,250	2,531
5,650	5,700	434	1,930	2,270	2,554	434	1,930	2,270	2,554
5,700	5,750	438	1,947	2,290	2,576	438	1,947	2,290	2,576
5,750	5,800	442	1,964	2,310	2,599	442	1,964	2,310	2,599
5,800	5,850	446	1,981	2,330	2,621	446	1,981	2,330	2,621
5,850	5,900	449	1,998	2,350	2,644	449	1,998	2,350	2,644
5,900	5,950	453	2,015	2,370	2,666	453	2,015	2,370	2,666
5,950	6,000	457	2,032	2,390	2,689	457	2,032	2,390	2,689
6,000	6,050	461	2,049	2,410	2,711	461	2,049	2,410	2,711
6,050	6,100	465	2,066	2,430	2,734	465	2,066	2,430	2,734
6,100	6,150	469	2,083	2,450	2,756	469	2,083	2,450	2,756
6,150	6,200	472	2,100	2,470	2,779	472	2,100	2,470	2,779
6,200	6,250	476	2,117	2,490	2,801	476	2,117	2,490	2,801
6,250	6,300	480	2,134	2,510	2,824	480	2,134	2,510	2,824
6,300	6,350	484	2,151	2,530	2,846	484	2,151	2,530	2,846
6,350	6,400	488	2,168	2,550	2,869	488	2,168	2,550	2,869
6,400	6,450	492	2,185	2,570	2,891	492	2,185	2,570	2,891
6,450	6,500	495	2,202	2,590	2,914	495	2,202	2,590	2,914
6,500	6,550	499	2,219	2,610	2,936	499	2,219	2,610	2,936
6,550	6,600	503	2,236	2,630	2,959	503	2,236	2,630	2,959
6,600	6,650	507	2,253	2,650	2,981	507	2,253	2,650	2,981
6,650	6,700	511	2,270	2,670	3,004	511	2,270	2,670	3,004
6,700	6,750	514	2,287	2,690	3,026	514	2,287	2,690	3,026
6,750	6,800	518	2,304	2,710	3,049	518	2,304	2,710	3,049
6,800	6,850	522	2,321	2,730	3,071	522	2,321	2,730	3,071
6,850	6,900	526	2,338	2,750	3,094	526	2,338	2,750	3,094
6,900	6,950	529	2,355	2,770	3,116	529	2,355	2,770	3,116
6,950	7,000	529	2,372	2,790	3,139	529	2,372	2,790	3,139
7,000	7,050	529	2,389	2,810	3,161	529	2,389	2,810	3,161
7,050	7,100	529	2,406	2,830	3,184	529	2,406	2,830	3,184
7,100	7,150	529	2,423	2,850	3,206	529	2,423	2,850	3,206
7,150	7,200	529	2,440	2,870	3,229	529	2,440	2,870	3,229
7,200	7,250	529	2,457	2,890	3,251	529	2,457	2,890	3,251
7,250	7,300	529	2,474	2,910	3,274	529	2,474	2,910	3,274
7,300	7,350	529	2,491	2,930	3,296	529	2,491	2,930	3,296
7,350	7,400	529	2,508	2,950	3,319	529	2,508	2,950	3,319
7,400	7,450	529	2,525	2,970	3,341	529	2,525	2,970	3,341
7,450	7,500	529	2,542	2,990	3,364	529	2,542	2,990	3,364
7,500	7,550	529	2,559	3,010	3,386	529	2,559	3,010	3,386
7,550	7,600	529	2,576	3,030	3,409	529	2,576	3,030	3,409
7,600	7,650	529	2,593	3,050	3,431	529	2,593	3,050	3,431
7,650	7,700	529	2,610	3,070	3,454	529	2,610	3,070	3,454
7,700	7,750	529	2,627	3,090	3,476	529	2,627	3,090	3,476
7,750	7,800	529	2,644	3,110	3,499	529	2,644	3,110	3,499
7,800	7,850	529	2,661	3,130	3,521	529	2,661	3,130	3,521
7,850	7,900	529	2,678	3,150	3,544	529	2,678	3,150	3,544
7,900	7,950	529	2,695	3,170	3,566	529	2,695	3,170	3,566
7,950	8,000	529	2,712	3,190	3,589	529	2,712	3,190	3,589
8,000	8,050	529	2,729	3,210	3,611	529	2,729	3,210	3,611
8,050	8,100	529	2,746	3,230	3,634	529	2,746	3,230	3,634
8,100	8,150	529	2,763	3,250	3,656	529	2,763	3,250	3,656
8,150	8,200	529	2,780	3,270	3,679	529	2,780	3,270	3,679
8,200	8,250	529	2,797	3,290	3,701	529	2,797	3,290	3,701
8,250	8,300	529	2,814	3,310	3,724	529	2,814	3,310	3,724
8,300	8,350	529	2,831	3,330	3,746	529	2,831	3,330	3,746
8,350	8,400	529	2,848	3,350	3,769	529	2,848	3,350	3,769
8,400	8,450	529	2,865	3,370	3,791	529	2,865	3,370	3,791
8,450	8,500	529	2,882	3,390	3,814	529	2,882	3,390	3,814
8,500	8,550	529	2,899	3,410	3,836	529	2,899	3,410	3,836
8,550	8,600	529	2,916	3,430	3,859	529	2,916	3,430	3,859
8,600	8,650	529	2,933	3,450	3,881	529	2,933	3,450	3,881
8,650	8,700	527	2,950	3,470	3,904	529	2,950	3,470	3,904
8,700	8,750	524	2,967	3,490	3,926	529	2,967	3,490	3,926
8,750	8,800	520	2,984	3,510	3,949	529	2,984	3,510	3,949
8,800	8,850	516	3,001	3,530	3,971	529	3,001	3,530	3,971
8,850	8,900	512	3,018	3,550	3,994	529	3,018	3,550	3,994
8,900	8,950	508	3,035	3,570	4,016	529	3,035	3,570	4,016
8,950	9,000	505	3,052	3,590	4,039	529	3,052	3,590	4,039
9,000	9,050	501	3,069	3,610	4,061	529	3,069	3,610	4,061
9,050	9,100	497	3,086	3,630	4,084	529	3,086	3,630	4,084
9,100	9,150	493	3,103	3,650	4,106	529	3,103	3,650	4,106
9,150	9,200	489	3,120	3,670	4,129	529	3,120	3,670	4,129

If the amount you are looking up from the worksheet is— At least	But less than	Single, head of household, or qualifying widow(er) and you have— 0	1	2	3	Married filing jointly and you have— 0	1	2	3
9,200	9,250	485	3,137	3,690	4,151	529	3,137	3,690	4,151
9,250	9,300	482	3,154	3,710	4,174	529	3,154	3,710	4,174
9,300	9,350	478	3,171	3,730	4,196	529	3,171	3,730	4,196
9,350	9,400	474	3,188	3,750	4,219	529	3,188	3,750	4,219
9,400	9,450	470	3,205	3,770	4,241	529	3,205	3,770	4,241
9,450	9,500	466	3,222	3,790	4,264	529	3,222	3,790	4,264
9,500	9,550	462	3,239	3,810	4,286	529	3,239	3,810	4,286
9,550	9,600	459	3,256	3,830	4,309	529	3,256	3,830	4,309
9,600	9,650	455	3,273	3,850	4,331	529	3,273	3,850	4,331
9,650	9,700	451	3,290	3,870	4,354	529	3,290	3,870	4,354
9,700	9,750	447	3,307	3,890	4,376	529	3,307	3,890	4,376
9,750	9,800	443	3,324	3,910	4,399	529	3,324	3,910	4,399
9,800	9,850	439	3,341	3,930	4,421	529	3,341	3,930	4,421
9,850	9,900	436	3,358	3,950	4,444	529	3,358	3,950	4,444
9,900	9,950	432	3,375	3,970	4,466	529	3,375	3,970	4,466
9,950	10,000	428	3,392	3,990	4,489	529	3,392	3,990	4,489
10,000	10,050	424	3,409	4,010	4,511	529	3,409	4,010	4,511
10,050	10,100	420	3,426	4,030	4,534	529	3,426	4,030	4,534
10,100	10,150	417	3,443	4,050	4,556	529	3,443	4,050	4,556
10,150	10,200	413	3,460	4,070	4,579	529	3,460	4,070	4,579
10,200	10,250	409	3,477	4,090	4,601	529	3,477	4,090	4,601
10,250	10,300	405	3,494	4,110	4,624	529	3,494	4,110	4,624
10,300	10,350	401	3,511	4,130	4,646	529	3,511	4,130	4,646
10,350	10,400	397	3,526	4,150	4,669	529	3,526	4,150	4,669
10,400	10,450	394	3,526	4,170	4,691	529	3,526	4,170	4,691
10,450	10,500	390	3,526	4,190	4,714	529	3,526	4,190	4,714
10,500	10,550	386	3,526	4,210	4,736	529	3,526	4,210	4,736
10,550	10,600	382	3,526	4,230	4,759	529	3,526	4,230	4,759
10,600	10,650	378	3,526	4,250	4,781	529	3,526	4,250	4,781
10,650	10,700	374	3,526	4,270	4,804	529	3,526	4,270	4,804
10,700	10,750	371	3,526	4,290	4,826	529	3,526	4,290	4,826
10,750	10,800	367	3,526	4,310	4,849	529	3,526	4,310	4,849
10,800	10,850	363	3,526	4,330	4,871	529	3,526	4,330	4,871
10,850	10,900	359	3,526	4,350	4,894	529	3,526	4,350	4,894
10,900	10,950	355	3,526	4,370	4,916	529	3,526	4,370	4,916
10,950	11,000	352	3,526	4,390	4,939	529	3,526	4,390	4,939
11,000	11,050	348	3,526	4,410	4,961	529	3,526	4,410	4,961
11,050	11,100	344	3,526	4,430	4,984	529	3,526	4,430	4,984
11,100	11,150	340	3,526	4,450	5,006	529	3,526	4,450	5,006
11,150	11,200	336	3,526	4,470	5,029	529	3,526	4,470	5,029
11,200	11,250	332	3,526	4,490	5,051	529	3,526	4,490	5,051
11,250	11,300	329	3,526	4,510	5,074	529	3,526	4,510	5,074
11,300	11,350	325	3,526	4,530	5,096	529	3,526	4,530	5,096
11,350	11,400	321	3,526	4,550	5,119	529	3,526	4,550	5,119
11,400	11,450	317	3,526	4,570	5,141	529	3,526	4,570	5,141
11,450	11,500	313	3,526	4,590	5,164	529	3,526	4,590	5,164
11,500	11,550	309	3,526	4,610	5,186	529	3,526	4,610	5,186
11,550	11,600	306	3,526	4,630	5,209	529	3,526	4,630	5,209
11,600	11,650	302	3,526	4,650	5,231	529	3,526	4,650	5,231
11,650	11,700	298	3,526	4,670	5,254	529	3,526	4,670	5,254
11,700	11,750	294	3,526	4,690	5,276	529	3,526	4,690	5,276
11,750	11,800	290	3,526	4,710	5,299	529	3,526	4,710	5,299
11,800	11,850	286	3,526	4,730	5,321	529	3,526	4,730	5,321
11,850	11,900	283	3,526	4,750	5,344	529	3,526	4,750	5,344
11,900	11,950	279	3,526	4,770	5,366	529	3,526	4,770	5,366
11,950	12,000	275	3,526	4,790	5,389	529	3,526	4,790	5,389
12,000	12,050	271	3,526	4,810	5,411	529	3,526	4,810	5,411
12,050	12,100	267	3,526	4,830	5,434	529	3,526	4,830	5,434
12,100	12,150	264	3,526	4,850	5,456	529	3,526	4,850	5,456
12,150	12,200	260	3,526	4,870	5,479	529	3,526	4,870	5,479
12,200	12,250	256	3,526	4,890	5,501	529	3,526	4,890	5,501
12,250	12,300	252	3,526	4,910	5,524	529	3,526	4,910	5,524
12,300	12,350	248	3,526	4,930	5,546	529	3,526	4,930	5,546
12,350	12,400	244	3,526	4,950	5,569	529	3,526	4,950	5,569
12,400	12,450	241	3,526	4,970	5,591	529	3,526	4,970	5,591
12,450	12,500	237	3,526	4,990	5,614	529	3,526	4,990	5,614
12,500	12,550	233	3,526	5,010	5,636	529	3,526	5,010	5,636
12,550	12,600	229	3,526	5,030	5,659	529	3,526	5,030	5,659
12,600	12,650	225	3,526	5,050	5,681	529	3,526	5,050	5,681
12,650	12,700	221	3,526	5,070	5,704	529	3,526	5,070	5,704
12,700	12,750	218	3,526	5,090	5,726	529	3,526	5,090	5,726
12,750	12,800	214	3,526	5,110	5,749	529	3,526	5,110	5,749

(Continued)

Earned Income Credit (EIC) Table - *Continued*   (**Caution.** This is **not** a tax table.)

If the amount you are looking up from the worksheet is—		Single, head of household, or qualifying widow(er) and you have—				Married filing jointly and you have—			
At least	But less than	0	1	2	3	0	1	2	3
		Your credit is—				Your credit is—			
12,800	12,850	210	3,526	5,130	5,771	529	3,526	5,130	5,771
12,850	12,900	206	3,526	5,150	5,794	529	3,526	5,150	5,794
12,900	12,950	202	3,526	5,170	5,816	529	3,526	5,170	5,816
12,950	13,000	199	3,526	5,190	5,839	529	3,526	5,190	5,839
13,000	13,050	195	3,526	5,210	5,861	529	3,526	5,210	5,861
13,050	13,100	191	3,526	5,230	5,884	529	3,526	5,230	5,884
13,100	13,150	187	3,526	5,250	5,906	529	3,526	5,250	5,906
13,150	13,200	183	3,526	5,270	5,929	529	3,526	5,270	5,929
13,200	13,250	179	3,526	5,290	5,951	529	3,526	5,290	5,951
13,250	13,300	176	3,526	5,310	5,974	529	3,526	5,310	5,974
13,300	13,350	172	3,526	5,330	5,996	529	3,526	5,330	5,996
13,350	13,400	168	3,526	5,350	6,019	529	3,526	5,350	6,019
13,400	13,450	164	3,526	5,370	6,041	529	3,526	5,370	6,041
13,450	13,500	160	3,526	5,390	6,064	529	3,526	5,390	6,064
13,500	13,550	156	3,526	5,410	6,086	529	3,526	5,410	6,086
13,550	13,600	153	3,526	5,430	6,109	529	3,526	5,430	6,109
13,600	13,650	149	3,526	5,450	6,131	529	3,526	5,450	6,131
13,650	13,700	145	3,526	5,470	6,154	529	3,526	5,470	6,154
13,700	13,750	141	3,526	5,490	6,176	529	3,526	5,490	6,176
13,750	13,800	137	3,526	5,510	6,199	529	3,526	5,510	6,199
13,800	13,850	133	3,526	5,530	6,221	529	3,526	5,530	6,221
13,850	13,900	130	3,526	5,550	6,244	529	3,526	5,550	6,244
13,900	13,950	126	3,526	5,570	6,266	529	3,526	5,570	6,266
13,950	14,000	122	3,526	5,590	6,289	529	3,526	5,590	6,289
14,000	14,050	118	3,526	5,610	6,311	529	3,526	5,610	6,311
14,050	14,100	114	3,526	5,630	6,334	529	3,526	5,630	6,334
14,100	14,150	111	3,526	5,650	6,356	529	3,526	5,650	6,356
14,150	14,200	107	3,526	5,670	6,379	529	3,526	5,670	6,379
14,200	14,250	103	3,526	5,690	6,401	529	3,526	5,690	6,401
14,250	14,300	99	3,526	5,710	6,424	529	3,526	5,710	6,424
14,300	14,350	95	3,526	5,730	6,446	529	3,526	5,730	6,446
14,350	14,400	91	3,526	5,750	6,469	529	3,526	5,750	6,469
14,400	14,450	88	3,526	5,770	6,491	529	3,526	5,770	6,491
14,450	14,500	84	3,526	5,790	6,514	527	3,526	5,790	6,514
14,500	14,550	80	3,526	5,810	6,536	524	3,526	5,810	6,536
14,550	14,600	76	3,526	5,828	6,557	520	3,526	5,828	6,557
14,600	14,650	72	3,526	5,828	6,557	516	3,526	5,828	6,557
14,650	14,700	68	3,526	5,828	6,557	512	3,526	5,828	6,557
14,700	14,750	65	3,526	5,828	6,557	508	3,526	5,828	6,557
14,750	14,800	61	3,526	5,828	6,557	505	3,526	5,828	6,557
14,800	14,850	57	3,526	5,828	6,557	501	3,526	5,828	6,557
14,850	14,900	53	3,526	5,828	6,557	497	3,526	5,828	6,557
14,900	14,950	49	3,526	5,828	6,557	493	3,526	5,828	6,557
14,950	15,000	46	3,526	5,828	6,557	489	3,526	5,828	6,557
15,000	15,050	42	3,526	5,828	6,557	485	3,526	5,828	6,557
15,050	15,100	38	3,526	5,828	6,557	482	3,526	5,828	6,557
15,100	15,150	34	3,526	5,828	6,557	478	3,526	5,828	6,557
15,150	15,200	30	3,526	5,828	6,557	474	3,526	5,828	6,557
15,200	15,250	26	3,526	5,828	6,557	470	3,526	5,828	6,557
15,250	15,300	23	3,526	5,828	6,557	466	3,526	5,828	6,557
15,300	15,350	19	3,526	5,828	6,557	462	3,526	5,828	6,557
15,350	15,400	15	3,526	5,828	6,557	459	3,526	5,828	6,557
15,400	15,450	11	3,526	5,828	6,557	455	3,526	5,828	6,557
15,450	15,500	7	3,526	5,828	6,557	451	3,526	5,828	6,557
15,500	15,550	3	3,526	5,828	6,557	447	3,526	5,828	6,557
15,550	15,600	*	3,526	5,828	6,557	443	3,526	5,828	6,557
15,600	15,650	0	3,526	5,828	6,557	439	3,526	5,828	6,557
15,650	15,700	0	3,526	5,828	6,557	436	3,526	5,828	6,557
15,700	15,750	0	3,526	5,828	6,557	432	3,526	5,828	6,557
15,750	15,800	0	3,526	5,828	6,557	428	3,526	5,828	6,557
15,800	15,850	0	3,526	5,828	6,557	424	3,526	5,828	6,557
15,850	15,900	0	3,526	5,828	6,557	420	3,526	5,828	6,557
15,900	15,950	0	3,526	5,828	6,557	417	3,526	5,828	6,557
15,950	16,000	0	3,526	5,828	6,557	413	3,526	5,828	6,557
16,000	16,050	0	3,526	5,828	6,557	409	3,526	5,828	6,557
16,050	16,100	0	3,526	5,828	6,557	405	3,526	5,828	6,557
16,100	16,150	0	3,526	5,828	6,557	401	3,526	5,828	6,557
16,150	16,200	0	3,526	5,828	6,557	397	3,526	5,828	6,557
16,200	16,250	0	3,526	5,828	6,557	394	3,526	5,828	6,557
16,250	16,300	0	3,526	5,828	6,557	390	3,526	5,828	6,557
16,300	16,350	0	3,526	5,828	6,557	386	3,526	5,828	6,557
16,350	16,400	0	3,526	5,828	6,557	382	3,526	5,828	6,557
16,400	16,450	0	3,526	5,828	6,557	378	3,526	5,828	6,557
16,450	16,500	0	3,526	5,828	6,557	374	3,526	5,828	6,557
16,500	16,550	0	3,526	5,828	6,557	371	3,526	5,828	6,557
16,550	16,600	0	3,526	5,828	6,557	367	3,526	5,828	6,557
16,600	16,650	0	3,526	5,828	6,557	363	3,526	5,828	6,557
16,650	16,700	0	3,526	5,828	6,557	359	3,526	5,828	6,557
16,700	16,750	0	3,526	5,828	6,557	355	3,526	5,828	6,557
16,750	16,800	0	3,526	5,828	6,557	352	3,526	5,828	6,557
16,800	16,850	0	3,526	5,828	6,557	348	3,526	5,828	6,557
16,850	16,900	0	3,526	5,828	6,557	344	3,526	5,828	6,557
16,900	16,950	0	3,526	5,828	6,557	340	3,526	5,828	6,557
16,950	17,000	0	3,526	5,828	6,557	336	3,526	5,828	6,557
17,000	17,050	0	3,526	5,828	6,557	332	3,526	5,828	6,557
17,050	17,100	0	3,526	5,828	6,557	329	3,526	5,828	6,557
17,100	17,150	0	3,526	5,828	6,557	325	3,526	5,828	6,557
17,150	17,200	0	3,526	5,828	6,557	321	3,526	5,828	6,557
17,200	17,250	0	3,526	5,828	6,557	317	3,526	5,828	6,557
17,250	17,300	0	3,526	5,828	6,557	313	3,526	5,828	6,557
17,300	17,350	0	3,526	5,828	6,557	309	3,526	5,828	6,557
17,350	17,400	0	3,526	5,828	6,557	306	3,526	5,828	6,557
17,400	17,450	0	3,526	5,828	6,557	302	3,526	5,828	6,557
17,450	17,500	0	3,526	5,828	6,557	298	3,526	5,828	6,557
17,500	17,550	0	3,526	5,828	6,557	294	3,526	5,828	6,557
17,550	17,600	0	3,526	5,828	6,557	290	3,526	5,828	6,557
17,600	17,650	0	3,526	5,828	6,557	286	3,526	5,828	6,557
17,650	17,700	0	3,526	5,828	6,557	283	3,526	5,828	6,557
17,700	17,750	0	3,526	5,828	6,557	279	3,526	5,828	6,557
17,750	17,800	0	3,526	5,828	6,557	275	3,526	5,828	6,557
17,800	17,850	0	3,526	5,828	6,557	271	3,526	5,828	6,557
17,850	17,900	0	3,526	5,828	6,557	267	3,526	5,828	6,557
17,900	17,950	0	3,526	5,828	6,557	264	3,526	5,828	6,557
17,950	18,000	0	3,526	5,828	6,557	260	3,526	5,828	6,557
18,000	18,050	0	3,526	5,828	6,557	256	3,526	5,828	6,557
18,050	18,100	0	3,526	5,828	6,557	252	3,526	5,828	6,557
18,100	18,150	0	3,526	5,828	6,557	248	3,526	5,828	6,557
18,150	18,200	0	3,526	5,828	6,557	244	3,526	5,828	6,557
18,200	18,250	0	3,526	5,828	6,557	241	3,526	5,828	6,557
18,250	18,300	0	3,526	5,828	6,557	237	3,526	5,828	6,557
18,300	18,350	0	3,526	5,828	6,557	233	3,526	5,828	6,557
18,350	18,400	0	3,526	5,828	6,557	229	3,526	5,828	6,557
18,400	18,450	0	3,526	5,828	6,557	225	3,526	5,828	6,557
18,450	18,500	0	3,526	5,828	6,557	221	3,526	5,828	6,557
18,500	18,550	0	3,526	5,828	6,557	218	3,526	5,828	6,557
18,550	18,600	0	3,526	5,828	6,557	214	3,526	5,828	6,557
18,600	18,650	0	3,526	5,828	6,557	210	3,526	5,828	6,557
18,650	18,700	0	3,526	5,828	6,557	206	3,526	5,828	6,557
18,700	18,750	0	3,526	5,828	6,557	202	3,526	5,828	6,557
18,750	18,800	0	3,526	5,828	6,557	199	3,526	5,828	6,557
18,800	18,850	0	3,526	5,828	6,557	195	3,526	5,828	6,557
18,850	18,900	0	3,526	5,828	6,557	191	3,526	5,828	6,557
18,900	18,950	0	3,526	5,828	6,557	187	3,526	5,828	6,557
18,950	19,000	0	3,526	5,828	6,557	183	3,526	5,828	6,557
19,000	19,050	0	3,526	5,828	6,557	179	3,526	5,828	6,557
19,050	19,100	0	3,519	5,819	6,547	176	3,526	5,828	6,557
19,100	19,150	0	3,511	5,808	6,536	172	3,526	5,828	6,557
19,150	19,200	0	3,503	5,797	6,526	168	3,526	5,828	6,557

* If the amount you are looking up from the worksheet is at least $15,550 but less than $15,570, and you have no qualifying children, your credit is $1.
If the amount you are looking up from the worksheet is $15,570 or more, and you have no qualifying children, you can't take the credit.

(Continued)

Earned Income Credit (EIC) Table - *Continued*   (**Caution.** This is **not** a tax table.)

If the amount you are looking up from the worksheet is—		And your filing status is—							
		Single, head of household, or qualifying widow(er) and you have—				Married filing jointly and you have—			
At least	But less than	0	1	2	3	0	1	2	3
		Your credit is—				Your credit is—			
19,200	19,250	0	3,495	5,787	6,515	164	3,526	5,828	6,557
19,250	19,300	0	3,487	5,776	6,505	160	3,526	5,828	6,557
19,300	19,350	0	3,479	5,766	6,494	156	3,526	5,828	6,557
19,350	19,400	0	3,471	5,755	6,484	153	3,526	5,828	6,557
19,400	19,450	0	3,463	5,745	6,473	149	3,526	5,828	6,557
19,450	19,500	0	3,455	5,734	6,463	145	3,526	5,828	6,557
19,500	19,550	0	3,447	5,724	6,452	141	3,526	5,828	6,557
19,550	19,600	0	3,439	5,713	6,442	137	3,526	5,828	6,557
19,600	19,650	0	3,431	5,703	6,431	133	3,526	5,828	6,557
19,650	19,700	0	3,423	5,692	6,421	130	3,526	5,828	6,557
19,700	19,750	0	3,415	5,682	6,410	126	3,526	5,828	6,557
19,750	19,800	0	3,407	5,671	6,400	122	3,526	5,828	6,557
19,800	19,850	0	3,399	5,661	6,389	118	3,526	5,828	6,557
19,850	19,900	0	3,391	5,650	6,379	114	3,526	5,828	6,557
19,900	19,950	0	3,383	5,640	6,368	111	3,526	5,828	6,557
19,950	20,000	0	3,375	5,629	6,357	107	3,526	5,828	6,557
20,000	20,050	0	3,367	5,618	6,347	103	3,526	5,828	6,557
20,050	20,100	0	3,359	5,608	6,336	99	3,526	5,828	6,557
20,100	20,150	0	3,351	5,597	6,326	95	3,526	5,828	6,557
20,150	20,200	0	3,343	5,587	6,315	91	3,526	5,828	6,557
20,200	20,250	0	3,335	5,576	6,305	88	3,526	5,828	6,557
20,250	20,300	0	3,327	5,566	6,294	84	3,526	5,828	6,557
20,300	20,350	0	3,319	5,555	6,284	80	3,526	5,828	6,557
20,350	20,400	0	3,311	5,545	6,273	76	3,526	5,828	6,557
20,400	20,450	0	3,303	5,534	6,263	72	3,526	5,828	6,557
20,450	20,500	0	3,295	5,524	6,252	68	3,526	5,828	6,557
20,500	20,550	0	3,287	5,513	6,242	65	3,526	5,828	6,557
20,550	20,600	0	3,279	5,503	6,231	61	3,526	5,828	6,557
20,600	20,650	0	3,271	5,492	6,221	57	3,526	5,828	6,557
20,650	20,700	0	3,263	5,482	6,210	53	3,526	5,828	6,557
20,700	20,750	0	3,255	5,471	6,200	49	3,526	5,828	6,557
20,750	20,800	0	3,247	5,461	6,189	46	3,526	5,828	6,557
20,800	20,850	0	3,239	5,450	6,178	42	3,526	5,828	6,557
20,850	20,900	0	3,231	5,439	6,168	38	3,526	5,828	6,557
20,900	20,950	0	3,223	5,429	6,157	34	3,526	5,828	6,557
20,950	21,000	0	3,215	5,418	6,147	30	3,526	5,828	6,557
21,000	21,050	0	3,207	5,408	6,136	26	3,526	5,828	6,557
21,050	21,100	0	3,199	5,397	6,126	23	3,526	5,828	6,557
21,100	21,150	0	3,191	5,387	6,115	19	3,526	5,828	6,557
21,150	21,200	0	3,183	5,376	6,105	15	3,526	5,828	6,557
21,200	21,250	0	3,175	5,366	6,094	11	3,526	5,828	6,557
21,250	21,300	0	3,167	5,355	6,084	7	3,526	5,828	6,557
21,300	21,350	0	3,159	5,345	6,073	3	3,526	5,828	6,557
21,350	21,400	0	3,151	5,334	6,063	*	3,526	5,828	6,557
21,400	21,450	0	3,143	5,324	6,052	0	3,526	5,828	6,557
21,450	21,500	0	3,135	5,313	6,042	0	3,526	5,828	6,557
21,500	21,550	0	3,127	5,303	6,031	0	3,526	5,828	6,557
21,550	21,600	0	3,119	5,292	6,021	0	3,526	5,828	6,557
21,600	21,650	0	3,111	5,281	6,010	0	3,526	5,828	6,557
21,650	21,700	0	3,103	5,271	5,999	0	3,526	5,828	6,557
21,700	21,750	0	3,095	5,260	5,989	0	3,526	5,828	6,557
21,750	21,800	0	3,087	5,250	5,978	0	3,526	5,828	6,557
21,800	21,850	0	3,079	5,239	5,968	0	3,526	5,828	6,557
21,850	21,900	0	3,071	5,229	5,957	0	3,526	5,828	6,557
21,900	21,950	0	3,063	5,218	5,947	0	3,526	5,828	6,557
21,950	22,000	0	3,055	5,208	5,936	0	3,526	5,828	6,557
22,000	22,050	0	3,047	5,197	5,926	0	3,526	5,828	6,557
22,050	22,100	0	3,039	5,187	5,915	0	3,526	5,828	6,557
22,100	22,150	0	3,031	5,176	5,905	0	3,526	5,828	6,557
22,150	22,200	0	3,023	5,166	5,894	0	3,526	5,828	6,557
22,200	22,250	0	3,015	5,155	5,884	0	3,526	5,828	6,557
22,250	22,300	0	3,007	5,145	5,873	0	3,526	5,828	6,557
22,300	22,350	0	2,999	5,134	5,863	0	3,526	5,828	6,557
22,350	22,400	0	2,991	5,124	5,852	0	3,526	5,828	6,557

If the amount you are looking up from the worksheet is—		And your filing status is—							
		Single, head of household, or qualifying widow(er) and you have—				Married filing jointly and you have—			
At least	But less than	0	1	2	3	0	1	2	3
		Your credit is—				Your credit is—			
22,400	22,450	0	2,983	5,113	5,842	0	3,526	5,828	6,557
22,450	22,500	0	2,975	5,102	5,831	0	3,526	5,828	6,557
22,500	22,550	0	2,967	5,092	5,820	0	3,526	5,828	6,557
22,550	22,600	0	2,959	5,081	5,810	0	3,526	5,828	6,557
22,600	22,650	0	2,951	5,071	5,799	0	3,526	5,828	6,557
22,650	22,700	0	2,943	5,060	5,789	0	3,526	5,828	6,557
22,700	22,750	0	2,935	5,050	5,778	0	3,526	5,828	6,557
22,750	22,800	0	2,927	5,039	5,768	0	3,526	5,828	6,557
22,800	22,850	0	2,919	5,029	5,757	0	3,526	5,828	6,557
22,850	22,900	0	2,911	5,018	5,747	0	3,526	5,828	6,557
22,900	22,950	0	2,903	5,008	5,736	0	3,526	5,828	6,557
22,950	23,000	0	2,895	4,997	5,726	0	3,526	5,828	6,557
23,000	23,050	0	2,887	4,987	5,715	0	3,526	5,828	6,557
23,050	23,100	0	2,879	4,976	5,705	0	3,526	5,828	6,557
23,100	23,150	0	2,871	4,966	5,694	0	3,526	5,828	6,557
23,150	23,200	0	2,863	4,955	5,684	0	3,526	5,828	6,557
23,200	23,250	0	2,855	4,945	5,673	0	3,526	5,828	6,557
23,250	23,300	0	2,847	4,934	5,663	0	3,526	5,828	6,557
23,300	23,350	0	2,839	4,923	5,652	0	3,526	5,828	6,557
23,350	23,400	0	2,831	4,913	5,641	0	3,526	5,828	6,557
23,400	23,450	0	2,823	4,902	5,631	0	3,526	5,828	6,557
23,450	23,500	0	2,815	4,892	5,620	0	3,526	5,828	6,557
23,500	23,550	0	2,807	4,881	5,610	0	3,526	5,828	6,557
23,550	23,600	0	2,800	4,871	5,599	0	3,526	5,828	6,557
23,600	23,650	0	2,792	4,860	5,589	0	3,526	5,828	6,557
23,650	23,700	0	2,784	4,850	5,578	0	3,526	5,828	6,557
23,700	23,750	0	2,776	4,839	5,568	0	3,526	5,828	6,557
23,750	23,800	0	2,768	4,829	5,557	0	3,526	5,828	6,557
23,800	23,850	0	2,760	4,818	5,547	0	3,526	5,828	6,557
23,850	23,900	0	2,752	4,808	5,536	0	3,526	5,828	6,557
23,900	23,950	0	2,744	4,797	5,526	0	3,526	5,828	6,557
23,950	24,000	0	2,736	4,787	5,515	0	3,526	5,828	6,557
24,000	24,050	0	2,728	4,776	5,505	0	3,526	5,828	6,557
24,050	24,100	0	2,720	4,766	5,494	0	3,526	5,828	6,557
24,100	24,150	0	2,712	4,755	5,483	0	3,526	5,828	6,557
24,150	24,200	0	2,704	4,744	5,473	0	3,526	5,828	6,557
24,200	24,250	0	2,696	4,734	5,462	0	3,526	5,828	6,557
24,250	24,300	0	2,688	4,723	5,452	0	3,526	5,828	6,557
24,300	24,350	0	2,680	4,713	5,441	0	3,526	5,828	6,557
24,350	24,400	0	2,672	4,702	5,431	0	3,526	5,828	6,557
24,400	24,450	0	2,664	4,692	5,420	0	3,526	5,828	6,557
24,450	24,500	0	2,656	4,681	5,410	0	3,526	5,828	6,557
24,500	24,550	0	2,648	4,671	5,399	0	3,526	5,828	6,557
24,550	24,600	0	2,640	4,660	5,389	0	3,526	5,828	6,557
24,600	24,650	0	2,632	4,650	5,378	0	3,526	5,828	6,557
24,650	24,700	0	2,624	4,639	5,368	0	3,526	5,828	6,557
24,700	24,750	0	2,616	4,629	5,357	0	3,526	5,828	6,557
24,750	24,800	0	2,608	4,618	5,347	0	3,526	5,828	6,557
24,800	24,850	0	2,600	4,608	5,336	0	3,526	5,828	6,557
24,850	24,900	0	2,592	4,597	5,326	0	3,517	5,816	6,545
24,900	24,950	0	2,584	4,587	5,315	0	3,509	5,806	6,534
24,950	25,000	0	2,576	4,576	5,304	0	3,501	5,795	6,524
25,000	25,050	0	2,568	4,565	5,294	0	3,493	5,785	6,513
25,050	25,100	0	2,560	4,555	5,283	0	3,485	5,774	6,503
25,100	25,150	0	2,552	4,544	5,273	0	3,477	5,764	6,492
25,150	25,200	0	2,544	4,534	5,262	0	3,469	5,753	6,482
25,200	25,250	0	2,536	4,523	5,252	0	3,461	5,743	6,471
25,250	25,300	0	2,528	4,513	5,241	0	3,453	5,732	6,461
25,300	25,350	0	2,520	4,502	5,231	0	3,445	5,722	6,450
25,350	25,400	0	2,512	4,492	5,220	0	3,437	5,711	6,440
25,400	25,450	0	2,504	4,481	5,210	0	3,429	5,701	6,429
25,450	25,500	0	2,496	4,471	5,199	0	3,421	5,690	6,419
25,500	25,550	0	2,488	4,460	5,189	0	3,413	5,680	6,408
25,550	25,600	0	2,480	4,450	5,178	0	3,405	5,669	6,397

*   If the amount you are looking up from the worksheet is at least $21,350 but less than $21,370, and you have no qualifying children, your credit is $1.
If the amount you are looking up from the worksheet is $21,370 or more, and you have no qualifying children, you can't take the credit.

(Continued)

Earned Income Credit (EIC) Table - *Continued*   (**Caution.** This is **not** a tax table.)

If the amount you are looking up from the worksheet is—		And your filing status is—							
		Single, head of household, or qualifying widow(er) and you have—				Married filing jointly and you have—			
At least	But less than	0	1	2	3	0	1	2	3
		Your credit is—				Your credit is—			
25,600	25,650	0	2,472	4,439	5,168	0	3,397	5,658	6,387
25,650	25,700	0	2,464	4,429	5,157	0	3,389	5,648	6,376
25,700	25,750	0	2,456	4,418	5,147	0	3,381	5,637	6,366
25,750	25,800	0	2,448	4,408	5,136	0	3,373	5,627	6,355
25,800	25,850	0	2,440	4,397	5,125	0	3,365	5,616	6,345
25,850	25,900	0	2,432	4,386	5,115	0	3,357	5,606	6,334
25,900	25,950	0	2,424	4,376	5,104	0	3,349	5,595	6,324
25,950	26,000	0	2,416	4,365	5,094	0	3,341	5,585	6,313
26,000	26,050	0	2,408	4,355	5,083	0	3,333	5,574	6,303
26,050	26,100	0	2,400	4,344	5,073	0	3,325	5,564	6,292
26,100	26,150	0	2,392	4,334	5,062	0	3,317	5,553	6,282
26,150	26,200	0	2,384	4,323	5,052	0	3,309	5,543	6,271
26,200	26,250	0	2,376	4,313	5,041	0	3,301	5,532	6,261
26,250	26,300	0	2,368	4,302	5,031	0	3,293	5,522	6,250
26,300	26,350	0	2,360	4,292	5,020	0	3,285	5,511	6,240
26,350	26,400	0	2,352	4,281	5,010	0	3,277	5,501	6,229
26,400	26,450	0	2,344	4,271	4,999	0	3,269	5,490	6,218
26,450	26,500	0	2,336	4,260	4,989	0	3,261	5,479	6,208
26,500	26,550	0	2,328	4,250	4,978	0	3,253	5,469	6,197
26,550	26,600	0	2,320	4,239	4,968	0	3,245	5,458	6,187
26,600	26,650	0	2,312	4,228	4,957	0	3,237	5,448	6,176
26,650	26,700	0	2,304	4,218	4,946	0	3,229	5,437	6,166
26,700	26,750	0	2,296	4,207	4,936	0	3,221	5,427	6,155
26,750	26,800	0	2,288	4,197	4,925	0	3,213	5,416	6,145
26,800	26,850	0	2,280	4,186	4,915	0	3,205	5,406	6,134
26,850	26,900	0	2,272	4,176	4,904	0	3,197	5,395	6,124
26,900	26,950	0	2,264	4,165	4,894	0	3,189	5,385	6,113
26,950	27,000	0	2,256	4,155	4,883	0	3,181	5,374	6,103
27,000	27,050	0	2,248	4,144	4,873	0	3,173	5,364	6,092
27,050	27,100	0	2,240	4,134	4,862	0	3,165	5,353	6,082
27,100	27,150	0	2,232	4,123	4,852	0	3,157	5,343	6,071
27,150	27,200	0	2,224	4,113	4,841	0	3,149	5,332	6,061
27,200	27,250	0	2,216	4,102	4,831	0	3,141	5,322	6,050
27,250	27,300	0	2,208	4,092	4,820	0	3,133	5,311	6,039
27,300	27,350	0	2,200	4,081	4,810	0	3,126	5,300	6,029
27,350	27,400	0	2,192	4,071	4,799	0	3,118	5,290	6,018
27,400	27,450	0	2,184	4,060	4,789	0	3,110	5,279	6,008
27,450	27,500	0	2,176	4,049	4,778	0	3,102	5,269	5,997
27,500	27,550	0	2,168	4,039	4,767	0	3,094	5,258	5,987
27,550	27,600	0	2,160	4,028	4,757	0	3,086	5,248	5,976
27,600	27,650	0	2,152	4,018	4,746	0	3,078	5,237	5,966
27,650	27,700	0	2,144	4,007	4,736	0	3,070	5,227	5,955
27,700	27,750	0	2,136	3,997	4,725	0	3,062	5,216	5,945
27,750	27,800	0	2,128	3,986	4,715	0	3,054	5,206	5,934
27,800	27,850	0	2,120	3,976	4,704	0	3,046	5,195	5,924
27,850	27,900	0	2,112	3,965	4,694	0	3,038	5,185	5,913
27,900	27,950	0	2,104	3,955	4,683	0	3,030	5,174	5,903
27,950	28,000	0	2,096	3,944	4,673	0	3,022	5,164	5,892
28,000	28,050	0	2,088	3,934	4,662	0	3,014	5,153	5,882
28,050	28,100	0	2,080	3,923	4,652	0	3,006	5,142	5,871
28,100	28,150	0	2,072	3,913	4,641	0	2,998	5,132	5,860
28,150	28,200	0	2,064	3,902	4,631	0	2,990	5,121	5,850
28,200	28,250	0	2,056	3,892	4,620	0	2,982	5,111	5,839
28,250	28,300	0	2,048	3,881	4,610	0	2,974	5,100	5,829
28,300	28,350	0	2,040	3,870	4,599	0	2,966	5,090	5,818
28,350	28,400	0	2,032	3,860	4,588	0	2,958	5,079	5,808
28,400	28,450	0	2,024	3,849	4,578	0	2,950	5,069	5,797
28,450	28,500	0	2,016	3,839	4,567	0	2,942	5,058	5,787
28,500	28,550	0	2,008	3,828	4,557	0	2,934	5,048	5,776
28,550	28,600	0	2,001	3,818	4,546	0	2,926	5,037	5,766
28,600	28,650	0	1,993	3,807	4,536	0	2,918	5,027	5,755
28,650	28,700	0	1,985	3,797	4,525	0	2,910	5,016	5,745
28,700	28,750	0	1,977	3,786	4,515	0	2,902	5,006	5,734
28,750	28,800	0	1,969	3,776	4,504	0	2,894	4,995	5,724
28,800	28,850	0	1,961	3,765	4,494	0	2,886	4,985	5,713
28,850	28,900	0	1,953	3,755	4,483	0	2,878	4,974	5,703
28,900	28,950	0	1,945	3,744	4,473	0	2,870	4,963	5,692
28,950	29,000	0	1,937	3,734	4,462	0	2,862	4,953	5,681
29,000	29,050	0	1,929	3,723	4,452	0	2,854	4,942	5,671
29,050	29,100	0	1,921	3,713	4,441	0	2,846	4,932	5,660
29,100	29,150	0	1,913	3,702	4,430	0	2,838	4,921	5,650
29,150	29,200	0	1,905	3,691	4,420	0	2,830	4,911	5,639
29,200	29,250	0	1,897	3,681	4,409	0	2,822	4,900	5,629
29,250	29,300	0	1,889	3,670	4,399	0	2,814	4,890	5,618
29,300	29,350	0	1,881	3,660	4,388	0	2,806	4,879	5,608
29,350	29,400	0	1,873	3,649	4,378	0	2,798	4,869	5,597
29,400	29,450	0	1,865	3,639	4,367	0	2,790	4,858	5,587
29,450	29,500	0	1,857	3,628	4,357	0	2,782	4,848	5,576
29,500	29,550	0	1,849	3,618	4,346	0	2,774	4,837	5,566
29,550	29,600	0	1,841	3,607	4,336	0	2,766	4,827	5,555
29,600	29,650	0	1,833	3,597	4,325	0	2,758	4,816	5,545
29,650	29,700	0	1,825	3,586	4,315	0	2,750	4,806	5,534
29,700	29,750	0	1,817	3,576	4,304	0	2,742	4,795	5,524
29,750	29,800	0	1,809	3,565	4,294	0	2,734	4,784	5,513
29,800	29,850	0	1,801	3,555	4,283	0	2,726	4,774	5,502
29,850	29,900	0	1,793	3,544	4,273	0	2,718	4,763	5,492
29,900	29,950	0	1,785	3,534	4,262	0	2,710	4,753	5,481
29,950	30,000	0	1,777	3,523	4,251	0	2,702	4,742	5,471
30,000	30,050	0	1,769	3,512	4,241	0	2,694	4,732	5,460
30,050	30,100	0	1,761	3,502	4,230	0	2,686	4,721	5,450
30,100	30,150	0	1,753	3,491	4,220	0	2,678	4,711	5,439
30,150	30,200	0	1,745	3,481	4,209	0	2,670	4,700	5,429
30,200	30,250	0	1,737	3,470	4,199	0	2,662	4,690	5,418
30,250	30,300	0	1,729	3,460	4,188	0	2,654	4,679	5,408
30,300	30,350	0	1,721	3,449	4,178	0	2,646	4,669	5,397
30,350	30,400	0	1,713	3,439	4,167	0	2,638	4,658	5,387
30,400	30,450	0	1,705	3,428	4,157	0	2,630	4,648	5,376
30,450	30,500	0	1,697	3,418	4,146	0	2,622	4,637	5,366
30,500	30,550	0	1,689	3,407	4,136	0	2,614	4,627	5,355
30,550	30,600	0	1,681	3,397	4,125	0	2,606	4,616	5,344
30,600	30,650	0	1,673	3,386	4,115	0	2,598	4,605	5,334
30,650	30,700	0	1,665	3,376	4,104	0	2,590	4,595	5,323
30,700	30,750	0	1,657	3,365	4,094	0	2,582	4,584	5,313
30,750	30,800	0	1,649	3,355	4,083	0	2,574	4,574	5,302
30,800	30,850	0	1,641	3,344	4,072	0	2,566	4,563	5,292
30,850	30,900	0	1,633	3,333	4,062	0	2,558	4,553	5,281
30,900	30,950	0	1,625	3,323	4,051	0	2,550	4,542	5,271
30,950	31,000	0	1,617	3,312	4,041	0	2,542	4,532	5,260
31,000	31,050	0	1,609	3,302	4,030	0	2,534	4,521	5,250
31,050	31,100	0	1,601	3,291	4,020	0	2,526	4,511	5,239
31,100	31,150	0	1,593	3,281	4,009	0	2,518	4,500	5,229
31,150	31,200	0	1,585	3,270	3,999	0	2,510	4,490	5,218
31,200	31,250	0	1,577	3,260	3,988	0	2,502	4,479	5,208
31,250	31,300	0	1,569	3,249	3,978	0	2,494	4,469	5,197
31,300	31,350	0	1,561	3,239	3,967	0	2,486	4,458	5,187
31,350	31,400	0	1,553	3,228	3,957	0	2,478	4,448	5,176
31,400	31,450	0	1,545	3,218	3,946	0	2,470	4,437	5,165
31,450	31,500	0	1,537	3,207	3,936	0	2,462	4,426	5,155
31,500	31,550	0	1,529	3,197	3,925	0	2,454	4,416	5,144
31,550	31,600	0	1,521	3,186	3,915	0	2,446	4,405	5,134
31,600	31,650	0	1,513	3,175	3,904	0	2,438	4,395	5,123
31,650	31,700	0	1,505	3,165	3,893	0	2,430	4,384	5,113
31,700	31,750	0	1,497	3,154	3,883	0	2,422	4,374	5,102
31,750	31,800	0	1,489	3,144	3,872	0	2,414	4,363	5,092
31,800	31,850	0	1,481	3,133	3,862	0	2,406	4,353	5,081
31,850	31,900	0	1,473	3,123	3,851	0	2,398	4,342	5,071
31,900	31,950	0	1,465	3,112	3,841	0	2,390	4,332	5,060
31,950	32,000	0	1,457	3,102	3,830	0	2,382	4,321	5,050
32,000	32,050	0	1,449	3,091	3,820	0	2,374	4,311	5,039
32,050	32,100	0	1,441	3,081	3,809	0	2,366	4,300	5,029
32,100	32,150	0	1,433	3,070	3,799	0	2,358	4,290	5,018
32,150	32,200	0	1,425	3,060	3,788	0	2,350	4,279	5,008
32,200	32,250	0	1,417	3,049	3,778	0	2,342	4,269	4,997
32,250	32,300	0	1,409	3,039	3,767	0	2,334	4,258	4,986
32,300	32,350	0	1,401	3,028	3,757	0	2,327	4,247	4,976
32,350	32,400	0	1,393	3,018	3,746	0	2,319	4,237	4,965
32,400	32,450	0	1,385	3,007	3,736	0	2,311	4,226	4,955
32,450	32,500	0	1,377	2,996	3,725	0	2,303	4,216	4,944
32,500	32,550	0	1,369	2,986	3,714	0	2,295	4,205	4,934
32,550	32,600	0	1,361	2,975	3,704	0	2,287	4,195	4,923
32,600	32,650	0	1,353	2,965	3,693	0	2,279	4,184	4,913
32,650	32,700	0	1,345	2,954	3,683	0	2,271	4,174	4,902
32,700	32,750	0	1,337	2,944	3,672	0	2,263	4,163	4,892
32,750	32,800	0	1,329	2,933	3,662	0	2,255	4,153	4,881

(Continued)

Earned Income Credit (EIC) Table - *Continued*

(Caution. This is not a tax table.)

At least	But less than	Single, head of household, or qualifying widow(er) and you have— 0	1	2	3	Married filing jointly and you have— 0	1	2	3
32,800	32,850	0	1,321	2,923	3,651	0	2,247	4,142	4,871
32,850	32,900	0	1,313	2,912	3,641	0	2,239	4,132	4,860
32,900	32,950	0	1,305	2,902	3,630	0	2,231	4,121	4,850
32,950	33,000	0	1,297	2,891	3,620	0	2,223	4,111	4,839
33,000	33,050	0	1,289	2,881	3,609	0	2,215	4,100	4,829
33,050	33,100	0	1,281	2,870	3,599	0	2,207	4,089	4,818
33,100	33,150	0	1,273	2,860	3,588	0	2,199	4,079	4,807
33,150	33,200	0	1,265	2,849	3,578	0	2,191	4,068	4,797
33,200	33,250	0	1,257	2,839	3,567	0	2,183	4,058	4,786
33,250	33,300	0	1,249	2,828	3,557	0	2,175	4,047	4,776
33,300	33,350	0	1,241	2,817	3,546	0	2,167	4,037	4,765
33,350	33,400	0	1,233	2,807	3,535	0	2,159	4,026	4,755
33,400	33,450	0	1,225	2,796	3,525	0	2,151	4,016	4,744
33,450	33,500	0	1,217	2,786	3,514	0	2,143	4,005	4,734
33,500	33,550	0	1,209	2,775	3,504	0	2,135	3,995	4,723
33,550	33,600	0	1,202	2,765	3,493	0	2,127	3,984	4,713
33,600	33,650	0	1,194	2,754	3,483	0	2,119	3,974	4,702
33,650	33,700	0	1,186	2,744	3,472	0	2,111	3,963	4,692
33,700	33,750	0	1,178	2,733	3,462	0	2,103	3,953	4,681
33,750	33,800	0	1,170	2,723	3,451	0	2,095	3,942	4,671
33,800	33,850	0	1,162	2,712	3,441	0	2,087	3,932	4,660
33,850	33,900	0	1,154	2,702	3,430	0	2,079	3,921	4,650
33,900	33,950	0	1,146	2,691	3,420	0	2,071	3,910	4,639
33,950	34,000	0	1,138	2,681	3,409	0	2,063	3,900	4,628
34,000	34,050	0	1,130	2,670	3,399	0	2,055	3,889	4,618
34,050	34,100	0	1,122	2,660	3,388	0	2,047	3,879	4,607
34,100	34,150	0	1,114	2,649	3,377	0	2,039	3,868	4,597
34,150	34,200	0	1,106	2,638	3,367	0	2,031	3,858	4,586
34,200	34,250	0	1,098	2,628	3,356	0	2,023	3,847	4,576
34,250	34,300	0	1,090	2,617	3,346	0	2,015	3,837	4,565
34,300	34,350	0	1,082	2,607	3,335	0	2,007	3,826	4,555
34,350	34,400	0	1,074	2,596	3,325	0	1,999	3,816	4,544
34,400	34,450	0	1,066	2,586	3,314	0	1,991	3,805	4,534
34,450	34,500	0	1,058	2,575	3,304	0	1,983	3,795	4,523
34,500	34,550	0	1,050	2,565	3,293	0	1,975	3,784	4,513
34,550	34,600	0	1,042	2,554	3,283	0	1,967	3,774	4,502
34,600	34,650	0	1,034	2,544	3,272	0	1,959	3,763	4,492
34,650	34,700	0	1,026	2,533	3,262	0	1,951	3,753	4,481
34,700	34,750	0	1,018	2,523	3,251	0	1,943	3,742	4,471
34,750	34,800	0	1,010	2,512	3,241	0	1,935	3,731	4,460
34,800	34,850	0	1,002	2,502	3,230	0	1,927	3,721	4,449
34,850	34,900	0	994	2,491	3,220	0	1,919	3,710	4,439
34,900	34,950	0	986	2,481	3,209	0	1,911	3,700	4,428
34,950	35,000	0	978	2,470	3,198	0	1,903	3,689	4,418
35,000	35,050	0	970	2,459	3,188	0	1,895	3,679	4,407
35,050	35,100	0	962	2,449	3,177	0	1,887	3,668	4,397
35,100	35,150	0	954	2,438	3,167	0	1,879	3,658	4,386
35,150	35,200	0	946	2,428	3,156	0	1,871	3,647	4,376
35,200	35,250	0	938	2,417	3,146	0	1,863	3,637	4,365
35,250	35,300	0	930	2,407	3,135	0	1,855	3,626	4,355
35,300	35,350	0	922	2,396	3,125	0	1,847	3,616	4,344
35,350	35,400	0	914	2,386	3,114	0	1,839	3,605	4,334
35,400	35,450	0	906	2,375	3,104	0	1,831	3,595	4,323
35,450	35,500	0	898	2,365	3,093	0	1,823	3,584	4,313
35,500	35,550	0	890	2,354	3,083	0	1,815	3,574	4,302
35,550	35,600	0	882	2,344	3,072	0	1,807	3,563	4,291
35,600	35,650	0	874	2,333	3,062	0	1,799	3,552	4,281
35,650	35,700	0	866	2,323	3,051	0	1,791	3,542	4,270
35,700	35,750	0	858	2,312	3,041	0	1,783	3,531	4,260
35,750	35,800	0	850	2,302	3,030	0	1,775	3,521	4,249
35,800	35,850	0	842	2,291	3,019	0	1,767	3,510	4,239
35,850	35,900	0	834	2,280	3,009	0	1,759	3,500	4,228
35,900	35,950	0	826	2,270	2,998	0	1,751	3,489	4,218
35,950	36,000	0	818	2,259	2,988	0	1,743	3,479	4,207
36,000	36,050	0	810	2,249	2,977	0	1,735	3,468	4,197
36,050	36,100	0	802	2,238	2,967	0	1,727	3,458	4,186
36,100	36,150	0	794	2,228	2,956	0	1,719	3,447	4,176
36,150	36,200	0	786	2,217	2,946	0	1,711	3,437	4,165
36,200	36,250	0	778	2,207	2,935	0	1,703	3,426	4,155
36,250	36,300	0	770	2,196	2,925	0	1,695	3,416	4,144
36,300	36,350	0	762	2,186	2,914	0	1,687	3,405	4,134
36,350	36,400	0	754	2,175	2,904	0	1,679	3,395	4,123
36,400	36,450	0	746	2,165	2,893	0	1,671	3,384	4,112
36,450	36,500	0	738	2,154	2,883	0	1,663	3,373	4,102
36,500	36,550	0	730	2,144	2,872	0	1,655	3,363	4,091
36,550	36,600	0	722	2,133	2,862	0	1,647	3,352	4,081
36,600	36,650	0	714	2,122	2,851	0	1,639	3,342	4,070
36,650	36,700	0	706	2,112	2,840	0	1,631	3,331	4,060
36,700	36,750	0	698	2,101	2,830	0	1,623	3,321	4,049
36,750	36,800	0	690	2,091	2,819	0	1,615	3,310	4,039
36,800	36,850	0	682	2,080	2,809	0	1,607	3,300	4,028
36,850	36,900	0	674	2,070	2,798	0	1,599	3,289	4,018
36,900	36,950	0	666	2,059	2,788	0	1,591	3,279	4,007
36,950	37,000	0	658	2,049	2,777	0	1,583	3,268	3,997
37,000	37,050	0	650	2,038	2,767	0	1,575	3,258	3,986
37,050	37,100	0	642	2,028	2,756	0	1,567	3,247	3,976
37,100	37,150	0	634	2,017	2,746	0	1,559	3,237	3,965
37,150	37,200	0	626	2,007	2,735	0	1,551	3,226	3,955
37,200	37,250	0	618	1,996	2,725	0	1,543	3,216	3,944
37,250	37,300	0	610	1,986	2,714	0	1,535	3,205	3,933
37,300	37,350	0	602	1,975	2,704	0	1,528	3,194	3,923
37,350	37,400	0	594	1,965	2,693	0	1,520	3,184	3,912
37,400	37,450	0	586	1,954	2,683	0	1,512	3,173	3,902
37,450	37,500	0	578	1,943	2,672	0	1,504	3,163	3,891
37,500	37,550	0	570	1,933	2,661	0	1,496	3,152	3,881
37,550	37,600	0	562	1,922	2,651	0	1,488	3,142	3,870
37,600	37,650	0	554	1,912	2,640	0	1,480	3,131	3,860
37,650	37,700	0	546	1,901	2,630	0	1,472	3,121	3,849
37,700	37,750	0	538	1,891	2,619	0	1,464	3,110	3,839
37,750	37,800	0	530	1,880	2,609	0	1,456	3,100	3,828
37,800	37,850	0	522	1,870	2,598	0	1,448	3,089	3,818
37,850	37,900	0	514	1,859	2,588	0	1,440	3,079	3,807
37,900	37,950	0	506	1,849	2,577	0	1,432	3,068	3,797
37,950	38,000	0	498	1,838	2,567	0	1,424	3,058	3,786
38,000	38,050	0	490	1,828	2,556	0	1,416	3,047	3,776
38,050	38,100	0	482	1,817	2,546	0	1,408	3,036	3,765
38,100	38,150	0	474	1,807	2,535	0	1,400	3,026	3,754
38,150	38,200	0	466	1,796	2,525	0	1,392	3,015	3,744
38,200	38,250	0	458	1,786	2,514	0	1,384	3,005	3,733
38,250	38,300	0	450	1,775	2,504	0	1,376	2,994	3,723
38,300	38,350	0	442	1,764	2,493	0	1,368	2,984	3,712
38,350	38,400	0	434	1,754	2,482	0	1,360	2,973	3,702
38,400	38,450	0	426	1,743	2,472	0	1,352	2,963	3,691
38,450	38,500	0	418	1,733	2,461	0	1,344	2,952	3,681
38,500	38,550	0	410	1,722	2,451	0	1,336	2,942	3,670
38,550	38,600	0	403	1,712	2,440	0	1,328	2,931	3,660
38,600	38,650	0	395	1,701	2,430	0	1,320	2,921	3,649
38,650	38,700	0	387	1,691	2,419	0	1,312	2,910	3,639
38,700	38,750	0	379	1,680	2,409	0	1,304	2,900	3,628
38,750	38,800	0	371	1,670	2,398	0	1,296	2,889	3,618
38,800	38,850	0	363	1,659	2,388	0	1,288	2,879	3,607
38,850	38,900	0	355	1,649	2,377	0	1,280	2,868	3,597
38,900	38,950	0	347	1,638	2,367	0	1,272	2,857	3,586
38,950	39,000	0	339	1,628	2,356	0	1,264	2,847	3,575
39,000	39,050	0	331	1,617	2,346	0	1,256	2,836	3,565
39,050	39,100	0	323	1,607	2,335	0	1,248	2,826	3,554
39,100	39,150	0	315	1,596	2,324	0	1,240	2,815	3,544
39,150	39,200	0	307	1,585	2,314	0	1,232	2,805	3,533
39,200	39,250	0	299	1,575	2,303	0	1,224	2,794	3,523
39,250	39,300	0	291	1,564	2,293	0	1,216	2,784	3,512
39,300	39,350	0	283	1,554	2,282	0	1,208	2,773	3,502
39,350	39,400	0	275	1,543	2,272	0	1,200	2,763	3,491
39,400	39,450	0	267	1,533	2,261	0	1,192	2,752	3,481
39,450	39,500	0	259	1,522	2,251	0	1,184	2,742	3,470
39,500	39,550	0	251	1,512	2,240	0	1,176	2,731	3,460
39,550	39,600	0	243	1,501	2,230	0	1,168	2,721	3,449
39,600	39,650	0	235	1,491	2,219	0	1,160	2,710	3,439
39,650	39,700	0	227	1,480	2,209	0	1,152	2,700	3,428
39,700	39,750	0	219	1,470	2,198	0	1,144	2,689	3,418
39,750	39,800	0	211	1,459	2,188	0	1,136	2,678	3,407
39,800	39,850	0	203	1,449	2,177	0	1,128	2,668	3,396
39,850	39,900	0	195	1,438	2,167	0	1,120	2,657	3,386
39,900	39,950	0	187	1,428	2,156	0	1,112	2,647	3,375
39,950	40,000	0	179	1,417	2,145	0	1,104	2,636	3,365

(Continued)

Earned Income Credit (EIC) Table - *Continued* (**Caution.** This is **not** a tax table.)

If the amount you are looking up from the worksheet is—		Single, head of household, or qualifying widow(er) and you have—				Married filing jointly and you have—			
At least	But less than	0	1	2	3	0	1	2	3
		Your credit is—				Your credit is—			
40,000	40,050	0	171	1,406	2,135	0	1,096	2,626	3,354
40,050	40,100	0	163	1,396	2,124	0	1,088	2,615	3,344
40,100	40,150	0	155	1,385	2,114	0	1,080	2,605	3,333
40,150	40,200	0	147	1,375	2,103	0	1,072	2,594	3,323
40,200	40,250	0	139	1,364	2,093	0	1,064	2,584	3,312
40,250	40,300	0	131	1,354	2,082	0	1,056	2,573	3,302
40,300	40,350	0	123	1,343	2,072	0	1,048	2,563	3,291
40,350	40,400	0	115	1,333	2,061	0	1,040	2,552	3,281
40,400	40,450	0	107	1,322	2,051	0	1,032	2,542	3,270
40,450	40,500	0	99	1,312	2,040	0	1,024	2,531	3,260
40,500	40,550	0	91	1,301	2,030	0	1,016	2,521	3,249
40,550	40,600	0	83	1,291	2,019	0	1,008	2,510	3,238
40,600	40,650	0	75	1,280	2,009	0	1,000	2,499	3,228
40,650	40,700	0	67	1,270	1,998	0	992	2,489	3,217
40,700	40,750	0	59	1,259	1,988	0	984	2,478	3,207
40,750	40,800	0	51	1,249	1,977	0	976	2,468	3,196
40,800	40,850	0	43	1,238	1,966	0	968	2,457	3,186
40,850	40,900	0	35	1,227	1,956	0	960	2,447	3,175
40,900	40,950	0	27	1,217	1,945	0	952	2,436	3,165
40,950	41,000	0	19	1,206	1,935	0	944	2,426	3,154
41,000	41,050	0	11	1,196	1,924	0	936	2,415	3,144
41,050	41,100	0	*	1,185	1,914	0	928	2,405	3,133
41,100	41,150	0	0	1,175	1,903	0	920	2,394	3,123
41,150	41,200	0	0	1,164	1,893	0	912	2,384	3,112
41,200	41,250	0	0	1,154	1,882	0	904	2,373	3,102
41,250	41,300	0	0	1,143	1,872	0	896	2,363	3,091
41,300	41,350	0	0	1,133	1,861	0	888	2,352	3,081
41,350	41,400	0	0	1,122	1,851	0	880	2,342	3,070
41,400	41,450	0	0	1,112	1,840	0	872	2,331	3,059
41,450	41,500	0	0	1,101	1,830	0	864	2,320	3,049
41,500	41,550	0	0	1,091	1,819	0	856	2,310	3,038
41,550	41,600	0	0	1,080	1,809	0	848	2,299	3,028
41,600	41,650	0	0	1,069	1,798	0	840	2,289	3,017
41,650	41,700	0	0	1,059	1,787	0	832	2,278	3,007
41,700	41,750	0	0	1,048	1,777	0	824	2,268	2,996
41,750	41,800	0	0	1,038	1,766	0	816	2,257	2,986
41,800	41,850	0	0	1,027	1,756	0	808	2,247	2,975
41,850	41,900	0	0	1,017	1,745	0	800	2,236	2,965
41,900	41,950	0	0	1,006	1,735	0	792	2,226	2,954
41,950	42,000	0	0	996	1,724	0	784	2,215	2,944
42,000	42,050	0	0	985	1,714	0	776	2,205	2,933
42,050	42,100	0	0	975	1,703	0	768	2,194	2,923
42,100	42,150	0	0	964	1,693	0	760	2,184	2,912
42,150	42,200	0	0	954	1,682	0	752	2,173	2,902
42,200	42,250	0	0	943	1,672	0	744	2,163	2,891
42,250	42,300	0	0	933	1,661	0	736	2,152	2,880
42,300	42,350	0	0	922	1,651	0	729	2,141	2,870
42,350	42,400	0	0	912	1,640	0	721	2,131	2,859
42,400	42,450	0	0	901	1,630	0	713	2,120	2,849
42,450	42,500	0	0	890	1,619	0	705	2,110	2,838
42,500	42,550	0	0	880	1,608	0	697	2,099	2,828
42,550	42,600	0	0	869	1,598	0	689	2,089	2,817
42,600	42,650	0	0	859	1,587	0	681	2,078	2,807
42,650	42,700	0	0	848	1,577	0	673	2,068	2,796
42,700	42,750	0	0	838	1,566	0	665	2,057	2,786
42,750	42,800	0	0	827	1,556	0	657	2,047	2,775
42,800	42,850	0	0	817	1,545	0	649	2,036	2,765
42,850	42,900	0	0	806	1,535	0	641	2,026	2,754
42,900	42,950	0	0	796	1,524	0	633	2,015	2,744
42,950	43,000	0	0	785	1,514	0	625	2,005	2,733
43,000	43,050	0	0	775	1,503	0	617	1,994	2,723
43,050	43,100	0	0	764	1,493	0	609	1,983	2,712
43,100	43,150	0	0	754	1,482	0	601	1,973	2,701
43,150	43,200	0	0	743	1,472	0	593	1,962	2,691

If the amount you are looking up from the worksheet is—		Single, head of household, or qualifying widow(er) and you have—				Married filing jointly and you have—			
At least	But less than	0	1	2	3	0	1	2	3
		Your credit is—				Your credit is—			
43,200	43,250	0	0	733	1,461	0	585	1,952	2,680
43,250	43,300	0	0	722	1,451	0	577	1,941	2,670
43,300	43,350	0	0	711	1,440	0	569	1,931	2,659
43,350	43,400	0	0	701	1,429	0	561	1,920	2,649
43,400	43,450	0	0	690	1,419	0	553	1,910	2,638
43,450	43,500	0	0	680	1,408	0	545	1,899	2,628
43,500	43,550	0	0	669	1,398	0	537	1,889	2,617
43,550	43,600	0	0	659	1,387	0	529	1,878	2,607
43,600	43,650	0	0	648	1,377	0	521	1,868	2,596
43,650	43,700	0	0	638	1,366	0	513	1,857	2,586
43,700	43,750	0	0	627	1,356	0	505	1,847	2,575
43,750	43,800	0	0	617	1,345	0	497	1,836	2,565
43,800	43,850	0	0	606	1,335	0	489	1,826	2,554
43,850	43,900	0	0	596	1,324	0	481	1,815	2,544
43,900	43,950	0	0	585	1,314	0	473	1,804	2,533
43,950	44,000	0	0	575	1,303	0	465	1,794	2,522
44,000	44,050	0	0	564	1,293	0	457	1,783	2,512
44,050	44,100	0	0	554	1,282	0	449	1,773	2,501
44,100	44,150	0	0	543	1,271	0	441	1,762	2,491
44,150	44,200	0	0	532	1,261	0	433	1,752	2,480
44,200	44,250	0	0	522	1,250	0	425	1,741	2,470
44,250	44,300	0	0	511	1,240	0	417	1,731	2,459
44,300	44,350	0	0	501	1,229	0	409	1,720	2,449
44,350	44,400	0	0	490	1,219	0	401	1,710	2,438
44,400	44,450	0	0	480	1,208	0	393	1,699	2,428
44,450	44,500	0	0	469	1,198	0	385	1,689	2,417
44,500	44,550	0	0	459	1,187	0	377	1,678	2,407
44,550	44,600	0	0	448	1,177	0	369	1,668	2,396
44,600	44,650	0	0	438	1,166	0	361	1,657	2,386
44,650	44,700	0	0	427	1,156	0	353	1,647	2,375
44,700	44,750	0	0	417	1,145	0	345	1,636	2,365
44,750	44,800	0	0	406	1,135	0	337	1,625	2,354
44,800	44,850	0	0	396	1,124	0	329	1,615	2,343
44,850	44,900	0	0	385	1,114	0	321	1,604	2,333
44,900	44,950	0	0	375	1,103	0	313	1,594	2,322
44,950	45,000	0	0	364	1,092	0	305	1,583	2,312
45,000	45,050	0	0	353	1,082	0	297	1,573	2,301
45,050	45,100	0	0	343	1,071	0	289	1,562	2,291
45,100	45,150	0	0	332	1,061	0	281	1,552	2,280
45,150	45,200	0	0	322	1,050	0	273	1,541	2,270
45,200	45,250	0	0	311	1,040	0	265	1,531	2,259
45,250	45,300	0	0	301	1,029	0	257	1,520	2,249
45,300	45,350	0	0	290	1,019	0	249	1,510	2,238
45,350	45,400	0	0	280	1,008	0	241	1,499	2,228
45,400	45,450	0	0	269	998	0	233	1,489	2,217
45,450	45,500	0	0	259	987	0	225	1,478	2,207
45,500	45,550	0	0	248	977	0	217	1,468	2,196
45,550	45,600	0	0	238	966	0	209	1,457	2,185
45,600	45,650	0	0	227	956	0	201	1,446	2,175
45,650	45,700	0	0	217	945	0	193	1,436	2,164
45,700	45,750	0	0	206	935	0	185	1,425	2,154
45,750	45,800	0	0	196	924	0	177	1,415	2,143
45,800	45,850	0	0	185	913	0	169	1,404	2,133
45,850	45,900	0	0	174	903	0	161	1,394	2,122
45,900	45,950	0	0	164	892	0	153	1,383	2,112
45,950	46,000	0	0	153	882	0	145	1,373	2,101
46,000	46,050	0	0	143	871	0	137	1,362	2,091
46,050	46,100	0	0	132	861	0	129	1,352	2,080
46,100	46,150	0	0	122	850	0	121	1,341	2,070
46,150	46,200	0	0	111	840	0	113	1,331	2,059
46,200	46,250	0	0	101	829	0	105	1,320	2,049
46,250	46,300	0	0	90	819	0	97	1,310	2,038
46,300	46,350	0	0	80	808	0	89	1,299	2,028
46,350	46,400	0	0	69	798	0	81	1,289	2,017

* If the amount you are looking up from the worksheet is at least $41,050 but less than $41,094, and you have one qualifying child, your credit is $3.
If the amount you are looking up from the worksheet is $41,094 or more, and you have one qualifying child, you can't take the credit.

(Continued)

Earned Income Credit (EIC) Table - *Continued*

(**Caution.** This is **not** a tax table.)

If the amount you are looking up from the worksheet is–		Single, head of household, or qualifying widow(er) and you have–				Married filing jointly and you have–			
At least	But less than	0	1	2	3	0	1	2	3
		Your credit is–				Your credit is–			
46,400	46,450	0	0	59	787	0	73	1,278	2,006
46,450	46,500	0	0	48	777	0	65	1,267	1,996
46,500	46,550	0	0	38	766	0	57	1,257	1,985
46,550	46,600	0	0	27	756	0	49	1,246	1,975
46,600	46,650	0	0	16	745	0	41	1,236	1,964
46,650	46,700	0	0	6	734	0	33	1,225	1,954
46,700	46,750	0	0	0	724	0	25	1,215	1,943
46,750	46,800	0	0	0	713	0	17	1,204	1,933
46,800	46,850	0	0	0	703	0	9	1,194	1,922
46,850	46,900	0	0	0	692	0	*	1,183	1,912
46,900	46,950	0	0	0	682	0	0	1,173	1,901
46,950	47,000	0	0	0	671	0	0	1,162	1,891
47,000	47,050	0	0	0	661	0	0	1,152	1,880
47,050	47,100	0	0	0	650	0	0	1,141	1,870
47,100	47,150	0	0	0	640	0	0	1,131	1,859
47,150	47,200	0	0	0	629	0	0	1,120	1,849
47,200	47,250	0	0	0	619	0	0	1,110	1,838
47,250	47,300	0	0	0	608	0	0	1,099	1,827
47,300	47,350	0	0	0	598	0	0	1,088	1,817
47,350	47,400	0	0	0	587	0	0	1,078	1,806
47,400	47,450	0	0	0	577	0	0	1,067	1,796
47,450	47,500	0	0	0	566	0	0	1,057	1,785
47,500	47,550	0	0	0	555	0	0	1,046	1,775
47,550	47,600	0	0	0	545	0	0	1,036	1,764
47,600	47,650	0	0	0	534	0	0	1,025	1,754
47,650	47,700	0	0	0	524	0	0	1,015	1,743
47,700	47,750	0	0	0	513	0	0	1,004	1,733
47,750	47,800	0	0	0	503	0	0	994	1,722
47,800	47,850	0	0	0	492	0	0	983	1,712
47,850	47,900	0	0	0	482	0	0	973	1,701
47,900	47,950	0	0	0	471	0	0	962	1,691
47,950	48,000	0	0	0	461	0	0	952	1,680
48,000	48,050	0	0	0	450	0	0	941	1,670
48,050	48,100	0	0	0	440	0	0	930	1,659
48,100	48,150	0	0	0	429	0	0	920	1,648
48,150	48,200	0	0	0	419	0	0	909	1,638
48,200	48,250	0	0	0	408	0	0	899	1,627
48,250	48,300	0	0	0	398	0	0	888	1,617
48,300	48,350	0	0	0	387	0	0	878	1,606
48,350	48,400	0	0	0	376	0	0	867	1,596
48,400	48,450	0	0	0	366	0	0	857	1,585
48,450	48,500	0	0	0	355	0	0	846	1,575
48,500	48,550	0	0	0	345	0	0	836	1,564
48,550	48,600	0	0	0	334	0	0	825	1,554
48,600	48,650	0	0	0	324	0	0	815	1,543
48,650	48,700	0	0	0	313	0	0	804	1,533
48,700	48,750	0	0	0	303	0	0	794	1,522
48,750	48,800	0	0	0	292	0	0	783	1,512
48,800	48,850	0	0	0	282	0	0	773	1,501
48,850	48,900	0	0	0	271	0	0	762	1,491
48,900	48,950	0	0	0	261	0	0	751	1,480
48,950	49,000	0	0	0	250	0	0	741	1,469
49,000	49,050	0	0	0	240	0	0	730	1,459
49,050	49,100	0	0	0	229	0	0	720	1,448
49,100	49,150	0	0	0	218	0	0	709	1,438
49,150	49,200	0	0	0	208	0	0	699	1,427

If the amount you are looking up from the worksheet is–		Single, head of household, or qualifying widow(er) and you have–				Married filing jointly and you have–			
At least	But less than	0	1	2	3	0	1	2	3
		Your credit is–				Your credit is–			
49,200	49,250	0	0	0	197	0	0	688	1,417
49,250	49,300	0	0	0	187	0	0	678	1,406
49,300	49,350	0	0	0	176	0	0	667	1,396
49,350	49,400	0	0	0	166	0	0	657	1,385
49,400	49,450	0	0	0	155	0	0	646	1,375
49,450	49,500	0	0	0	145	0	0	636	1,364
49,500	49,550	0	0	0	134	0	0	625	1,354
49,550	49,600	0	0	0	124	0	0	615	1,343
49,600	49,650	0	0	0	113	0	0	604	1,333
49,650	49,700	0	0	0	103	0	0	594	1,322
49,700	49,750	0	0	0	92	0	0	583	1,312
49,750	49,800	0	0	0	82	0	0	572	1,301
49,800	49,850	0	0	0	71	0	0	562	1,290
49,850	49,900	0	0	0	61	0	0	551	1,280
49,900	49,950	0	0	0	50	0	0	541	1,269
49,950	50,000	0	0	0	39	0	0	530	1,259
50,000	50,050	0	0	0	29	0	0	520	1,248
50,050	50,100	0	0	0	18	0	0	509	1,238
50,100	50,150	0	0	0	8	0	0	499	1,227
50,150	50,200	0	0	0	**	0	0	488	1,217
50,200	50,250	0	0	0	0	0	0	478	1,206
50,250	50,300	0	0	0	0	0	0	467	1,196
50,300	50,350	0	0	0	0	0	0	457	1,185
50,350	50,400	0	0	0	0	0	0	446	1,175
50,400	50,450	0	0	0	0	0	0	436	1,164
50,450	50,500	0	0	0	0	0	0	425	1,154
50,500	50,550	0	0	0	0	0	0	415	1,143
50,550	50,600	0	0	0	0	0	0	404	1,132
50,600	50,650	0	0	0	0	0	0	393	1,122
50,650	50,700	0	0	0	0	0	0	383	1,111
50,700	50,750	0	0	0	0	0	0	372	1,101
50,750	50,800	0	0	0	0	0	0	362	1,090
50,800	50,850	0	0	0	0	0	0	351	1,080
50,850	50,900	0	0	0	0	0	0	341	1,069
50,900	50,950	0	0	0	0	0	0	330	1,059
50,950	51,000	0	0	0	0	0	0	320	1,048
51,000	51,050	0	0	0	0	0	0	309	1,038
51,050	51,100	0	0	0	0	0	0	299	1,027
51,100	51,150	0	0	0	0	0	0	288	1,017
51,150	51,200	0	0	0	0	0	0	278	1,006
51,200	51,250	0	0	0	0	0	0	267	996
51,250	51,300	0	0	0	0	0	0	257	985
51,300	51,350	0	0	0	0	0	0	246	975
51,350	51,400	0	0	0	0	0	0	236	964
51,400	51,450	0	0	0	0	0	0	225	953
51,450	51,500	0	0	0	0	0	0	214	943
51,500	51,550	0	0	0	0	0	0	204	932
51,550	51,600	0	0	0	0	0	0	193	922
51,600	51,650	0	0	0	0	0	0	183	911
51,650	51,700	0	0	0	0	0	0	172	901
51,700	51,750	0	0	0	0	0	0	162	890
51,750	51,800	0	0	0	0	0	0	151	880
51,800	51,850	0	0	0	0	0	0	141	869
51,850	51,900	0	0	0	0	0	0	130	859
51,900	51,950	0	0	0	0	0	0	120	848
51,950	52,000	0	0	0	0	0	0	109	838

* If the amount you are looking up from the worksheet is at least $46,850 but less than $46,884, and you have one qualifying child, your credit is $3.
If the amount you are looking up from the worksheet is $46,884 or more, and you have one qualifying child, you can't take the credit.

** If the amount you are looking up from the worksheet is at least $50,150 but less than $50,162, and you have three qualifying children, your credit is $1.
If the amount you are looking up from the worksheet is $51,162 or more, and you have three qualifying children, you can't take the credit

(Continued)

Earned Income Credit (EIC) Table - *Continued*   (**Caution.** This is **not** a tax table.)

If the amount you are looking up from the worksheet is—		And your filing status is—								If the amount you are looking up from the worksheet is—		And your filing status is—							
		Single, head of household, or qualifying widow(er) and you have—				Married filing jointly and you have—						Single, head of household, or qualifying widow(er) and you have—				Married filing jointly and you have—			
At least	But less than	0	1	2	3	0	1	2	3	At least	But less than	0	1	2	3	0	1	2	3
		Your credit is—				Your credit is—						Your credit is—				Your credit is—			
52,000	52,050	0	0	0	0	0	0	99	827	54,000	54,050	0	0	0	0	0	0	0	406
52,050	52,100	0	0	0	0	0	0	88	817	54,050	54,100	0	0	0	0	0	0	0	395
52,100	52,150	0	0	0	0	0	0	78	806	54,100	54,150	0	0	0	0	0	0	0	385
52,150	52,200	0	0	0	0	0	0	67	796	54,150	54,200	0	0	0	0	0	0	0	374
52,200	52,250	0	0	0	0	0	0	57	785	54,200	54,250	0	0	0	0	0	0	0	364
52,250	52,300	0	0	0	0	0	0	46	774	54,250	54,300	0	0	0	0	0	0	0	353
52,300	52,350	0	0	0	0	0	0	35	764	54,300	54,350	0	0	0	0	0	0	0	343
52,350	52,400	0	0	0	0	0	0	25	753	54,350	54,400	0	0	0	0	0	0	0	332
52,400	52,450	0	0	0	0	0	0	14	743	54,400	54,450	0	0	0	0	0	0	0	322
52,450	52,500	0	0	0	0	0	0	*	732	54,450	54,500	0	0	0	0	0	0	0	311
52,500	52,550	0	0	0	0	0	0	0	722	54,500	54,550	0	0	0	0	0	0	0	301
52,550	52,600	0	0	0	0	0	0	0	711	54,550	54,600	0	0	0	0	0	0	0	290
52,600	52,650	0	0	0	0	0	0	0	701	54,600	54,650	0	0	0	0	0	0	0	280
52,650	52,700	0	0	0	0	0	0	0	690	54,650	54,700	0	0	0	0	0	0	0	269
52,700	52,750	0	0	0	0	0	0	0	680	54,700	54,750	0	0	0	0	0	0	0	259
52,750	52,800	0	0	0	0	0	0	0	669	54,750	54,800	0	0	0	0	0	0	0	248
52,800	52,850	0	0	0	0	0	0	0	659	54,800	54,850	0	0	0	0	0	0	0	237
52,850	52,900	0	0	0	0	0	0	0	648	54,850	54,900	0	0	0	0	0	0	0	227
52,900	52,950	0	0	0	0	0	0	0	638	54,900	54,950	0	0	0	0	0	0	0	216
52,950	53,000	0	0	0	0	0	0	0	627	54,950	55,000	0	0	0	0	0	0	0	206
53,000	53,050	0	0	0	0	0	0	0	617	55,000	55,050	0	0	0	0	0	0	0	195
53,050	53,100	0	0	0	0	0	0	0	606	55,050	55,100	0	0	0	0	0	0	0	185
53,100	53,150	0	0	0	0	0	0	0	595	55,100	55,150	0	0	0	0	0	0	0	174
53,150	53,200	0	0	0	0	0	0	0	585	55,150	55,200	0	0	0	0	0	0	0	164
53,200	53,250	0	0	0	0	0	0	0	574	55,200	55,250	0	0	0	0	0	0	0	153
53,250	53,300	0	0	0	0	0	0	0	564	55,250	55,300	0	0	0	0	0	0	0	143
53,300	53,350	0	0	0	0	0	0	0	553	55,300	55,350	0	0	0	0	0	0	0	132
53,350	53,400	0	0	0	0	0	0	0	543	55,350	55,400	0	0	0	0	0	0	0	122
53,400	53,450	0	0	0	0	0	0	0	532	55,400	55,450	0	0	0	0	0	0	0	111
53,450	53,500	0	0	0	0	0	0	0	522	55,450	55,500	0	0	0	0	0	0	0	101
53,500	53,550	0	0	0	0	0	0	0	511	55,500	55,550	0	0	0	0	0	0	0	90
53,550	53,600	0	0	0	0	0	0	0	501	55,550	55,600	0	0	0	0	0	0	0	79
53,600	53,650	0	0	0	0	0	0	0	490	55,600	55,650	0	0	0	0	0	0	0	69
53,650	53,700	0	0	0	0	0	0	0	480	55,650	55,700	0	0	0	0	0	0	0	58
53,700	53,750	0	0	0	0	0	0	0	469	55,700	55,750	0	0	0	0	0	0	0	48
53,750	53,800	0	0	0	0	0	0	0	459	55,750	55,800	0	0	0	0	0	0	0	37
53,800	53,850	0	0	0	0	0	0	0	448	55,800	55,850	0	0	0	0	0	0	0	27
53,850	53,900	0	0	0	0	0	0	0	438	55,850	55,900	0	0	0	0	0	0	0	16
53,900	53,950	0	0	0	0	0	0	0	427	55,900	55,950	0	0	0	0	0	0	0	6
53,950	54,000	0	0	0	0	0	0	0	416	55,950	55,952	0	0	0	0	0	0	0	0

* If the amount you are looking up from the worksheet is at least $52,450 but less than $52,493, and you have two qualifying children, your credit is $5.
If the amount you are looking up from the worksheet is $52,493 or more, and you have two qualifying children, you can't take the credit.

Withholding Tables

CONTENTS

Percentage Method Tables for Income Tax Withholding

(For Wages Paid in 2019)

TABLE 1—WEEKLY Payroll Period

(a) SINGLE person (including head of household)—

If the amount of wages (after subtracting withholding allowances) is: The amount of income tax to withhold is:

Not over $73 . . . . $0

Over—	But not over—		of excess over—
$73	—$260 . .	$0.00 plus 10%	—$73
$260	—$832 . .	$18.70 plus 12%	—$260
$832	—$1,692 . .	$87.34 plus 22%	—$832
$1,692	—$3,164 . .	$276.54 plus 24%	—$1,692
$3,164	—$3,998 . .	$629.82 plus 32%	—$3,164
$3,998	—$9,887 . .	$896.70 plus 35%	—$3,998
$9,887	. . . .	$2,957.85 plus 37%	—$9,887

(b) MARRIED person—

If the amount of wages (after subtracting withholding allowances) is: The amount of income tax to withhold is:

Not over $227 . . . . $0

Over—	But not over—		of excess over—
$227	—$600 . .	$0.00 plus 10%	—$227
$600	—$1,745 . .	$37.30 plus 12%	—$600
$1,745	—$3,465 . .	$174.70 plus 22%	—$1,745
$3,465	—$6,409 . .	$553.10 plus 24%	—$3,465
$6,409	—$8,077 . .	$1,259.66 plus 32%	—$6,409
$8,077	—$12,003 . .	$1,793.42 plus 35%	—$8,077
$12,003	. . . .	$3,167.52 plus 37%	—$12,003

TABLE 2—BIWEEKLY Payroll Period

(a) SINGLE person (including head of household)—

If the amount of wages (after subtracting withholding allowances) is: The amount of income tax to withhold is:

Not over $146 . . . . $0

Over—	But not over—		of excess over—
$146	—$519 . .	$0.00 plus 10%	—$146
$519	—$1,664 . .	$37.30 plus 12%	—$519
$1,664	—$3,385 . .	$174.70 plus 22%	—$1,664
$3,385	—$6,328 . .	$553.32 plus 24%	—$3,385
$6,328	—$7,996 . .	$1,259.64 plus 32%	—$6,328
$7,996	—$19,773 . .	$1,793.40 plus 35%	—$7,996
$19,773	. . . .	$5,915.35 plus 37%	—$19,773

(b) MARRIED person—

If the amount of wages (after subtracting withholding allowances) is: The amount of income tax to withhold is:

Not over $454 . . . . $0

Over—	But not over—		of excess over—
$454	—$1,200 . .	$0.00 plus 10%	—$454
$1,200	—$3,490 . .	$74.60 plus 12%	—$1,200
$3,490	—$6,931 . .	$349.40 plus 22%	—$3,490
$6,931	—$12,817 . .	$1,106.42 plus 24%	—$6,931
$12,817	—$16,154 . .	$2,519.06 plus 32%	—$12,817
$16,154	—$24,006 . .	$3,586.90 plus 35%	—$16,154
$24,006	. . . .	$6,335.10 plus 37%	—$24,006

TABLE 3—SEMIMONTHLY Payroll Period

(a) SINGLE person (including head of household)—

If the amount of wages (after subtracting withholding allowances) is: The amount of income tax to withhold is:

Not over $158 . . . . $0

Over—	But not over—		of excess over—
$158	—$563 . .	$0.00 plus 10%	—$158
$563	—$1,803 . .	$40.50 plus 12%	—$563
$1,803	—$3,667 . .	$189.30 plus 22%	—$1,803
$3,667	—$6,855 . .	$599.38 plus 24%	—$3,667
$6,855	—$8,663 . .	$1,364.50 plus 32%	—$6,855
$8,663	—$21,421 . .	$1,943.06 plus 35%	—$8,663
$21,421	. . . .	$6,408.36 plus 37%	—$21,421

(b) MARRIED person—

If the amount of wages (after subtracting withholding allowances) is: The amount of income tax to withhold is:

Not over $492 . . . . $0

Over—	But not over—		of excess over—
$492	—$1,300 . .	$0.00 plus 10%	—$492
$1,300	—$3,781 . .	$80.80 plus 12%	—$1,300
$3,781	—$7,508 . .	$378.52 plus 22%	—$3,781
$7,508	—$13,885 . .	$1,198.46 plus 24%	—$7,508
$13,885	—$17,500 . .	$2,728.94 plus 32%	—$13,885
$17,500	—$26,006 . .	$3,885.74 plus 35%	—$17,500
$26,006	. . . .	$6,862.84 plus 37%	—$26,006

TABLE 4—MONTHLY Payroll Period

(a) SINGLE person (including head of household)—

If the amount of wages (after subtracting withholding allowances) is: The amount of income tax to withhold is:

Not over $317 . . . . $0

Over—	But not over—		of excess over—
$317	—$1,125 . .	$0.00 plus 10%	—$317
$1,125	—$3,606 . .	$80.80 plus 12%	—$1,125
$3,606	—$7,333 . .	$378.52 plus 22%	—$3,606
$7,333	—$13,710 . .	$1,198.46 plus 24%	—$7,333
$13,710	—$17,325 . .	$2,728.94 plus 32%	—$13,710
$17,325	—$42,842 . .	$3,885.74 plus 35%	—$17,325
$42,842	. . . .	$12,816.69 plus 37%	—$42,842

(b) MARRIED person—

If the amount of wages (after subtracting withholding allowances) is: The amount of income tax to withhold is:

Not over $983 . . . . $0

Over—	But not over—		of excess over—
$983	—$2,600 . .	$0.00 plus 10%	—$983
$2,600	—$7,563 . .	$161.70 plus 12%	—$2,600
$7,563	—$15,017 . .	$757.26 plus 22%	—$7,563
$15,017	—$27,771 . .	$2,397.14 plus 24%	—$15,017
$27,771	—$35,000 . .	$5,458.10 plus 32%	—$27,771
$35,000	—$52,013 . .	$7,771.38 plus 35%	—$35,000
$52,013	. . . .	$13,725.93 plus 37%	—$52,013

Percentage Method Tables for Income Tax Withholding (continued)

(For Wages Paid in 2019)

TABLE 5—QUARTERLY Payroll Period

(a) SINGLE person (including head of household)—

If the amount of wages (after subtracting withholding allowances) is:		The amount of income tax to withhold is:	of excess over—
Not over $950		$0	
Over—	**But not over—**		
$950	—$3,375 . .	$0.00 plus 10%	—$950
$3,375	—$10,819 . .	$242.50 plus 12%	—$3,375
$10,819	—$22,000 . .	$1,135.78 plus 22%	—$10,819
$22,000	—$41,131 . .	$3,595.60 plus 24%	—$22,000
$41,131	—$51,975 . .	$8,187.04 plus 32%	—$41,131
$51,975	—$128,525 . .	$11,657.12 plus 35%	—$51,975
$128,525	. . . .	$38,449.62 plus 37%	—$128,525

(b) MARRIED person—

If the amount of wages (after subtracting withholding allowances) is:		The amount of income tax to withhold is:	of excess over—
Not over $2,950		$0	
Over—	**But not over—**		
$2,950	—$7,800 . .	$0.00 plus 10%	—$2,950
$7,800	—$22,688 . .	$485.00 plus 12%	—$7,800
$22,688	—$45,050 . .	$2,271.56 plus 22%	—$22,688
$45,050	—$83,313 . .	$7,191.20 plus 24%	—$45,050
$83,313	—$105,000 . .	$16,374.32 plus 32%	—$83,313
$105,000	—$156,038 . .	$23,314.16 plus 35%	—$105,000
$156,038	. . . .	$41,177.46 plus 37%	—$156,038

TABLE 6—SEMIANNUAL Payroll Period

(a) SINGLE person (including head of household)—

If the amount of wages (after subtracting withholding allowances) is:		The amount of income tax to withhold is:	of excess over—
Not over $1,900		$0	
Over—	**But not over—**		
$1,900	—$6,750 . .	$0.00 plus 10%	—$1,900
$6,750	—$21,638 . .	$485.00 plus 12%	—$6,750
$21,638	—$44,000 . .	$2,271.56 plus 22%	—$21,638
$44,000	—$82,263 . .	$7,191.20 plus 24%	—$44,000
$82,263	—$103,950 . .	$16,374.32 plus 32%	—$82,263
$103,950	—$257,050 . .	$23,314.16 plus 35%	—$103,950
$257,050	. . . .	$76,899.16 plus 37%	—$257,050

(b) MARRIED person—

If the amount of wages (after subtracting withholding allowances) is:		The amount of income tax to withhold is:	of excess over—
Not over $5,900		$0	
Over—	**But not over—**		
$5,900	—$15,600 . .	$0.00 plus 10%	—$5,900
$15,600	—$45,375 . .	$970.00 plus 12%	—$15,600
$45,375	—$90,100 . .	$4,543.00 plus 22%	—$45,375
$90,100	—$166,625 . .	$14,382.50 plus 24%	—$90,100
$166,625	—$210,000 . .	$32,748.50 plus 32%	—$166,625
$210,000	—$312,075 . .	$46,628.50 plus 35%	—$210,000
$312,075	. . . .	$82,354.75 plus 37%	—$312,075

TABLE 7—ANNUAL Payroll Period

(a) SINGLE person (including head of household)—

If the amount of wages (after subtracting withholding allowances) is:		The amount of income tax to withhold is:	of excess over—
Not over $3,800		$0	
Over—	**But not over—**		
$3,800	—$13,500 . .	$0.00 plus 10%	—$3,800
$13,500	—$43,275 . .	$970.00 plus 12%	—$13,500
$43,275	—$88,000 . .	$4,543.00 plus 22%	—$43,275
$88,000	—$164,525 . .	$14,382.50 plus 24%	—$88,000
$164,525	—$207,900 . .	$32,748.50 plus 32%	—$164,525
$207,900	—$514,100 . .	$46,628.50 plus 35%	—$207,900
$514,100	. . . .	$153,798.50 plus 37%	—$514,100

(b) MARRIED person—

If the amount of wages (after subtracting withholding allowances) is:		The amount of income tax to withhold is:	of excess over—
Not over $11,800		$0	
Over—	**But not over—**		
$11,800	—$31,200 . .	$0.00 plus 10%	—$11,800
$31,200	—$90,750 . .	$1,940.00 plus 12%	—$31,200
$90,750	—$180,200 . .	$9,086.00 plus 22%	—$90,750
$180,200	—$333,250 . .	$28,765.00 plus 24%	—$180,200
$333,250	—$420,000 . .	$65,497.00 plus 32%	—$333,250
$420,000	—$624,150 . .	$93,257.00 plus 35%	—$420,000
$624,150	. . . .	$164,709.50 plus 37%	—$624,150

TABLE 8—DAILY or MISCELLANEOUS Payroll Period

(a) SINGLE person (including head of household)—

If the amount of wages (after subtracting withholding allowances) divided by the number of days in the payroll period is:		The amount of income tax to withhold per day is:	of excess over—
Not over $14.60		$0	
Over—	**But not over—**		
$14.60	—$51.90 . .	$0.00 plus 10%	—$14.60
$51.90	—$166.40 . .	$3.73 plus 12%	—$51.90
$166.40	—$338.50 . .	$17.47 plus 22%	—$166.40
$338.50	—$632.80 . .	$55.33 plus 24%	—$338.50
$632.80	—$799.60 . .	$125.96 plus 32%	—$632.80
$799.60	—$1,977.30 . .	$179.34 plus 35%	—$799.60
$1,977.30	. . . .	$591.54 plus 37%	—$1,977.30

(b) MARRIED person—

If the amount of wages (after subtracting withholding allowances) divided by the number of days in the payroll period is:		The amount of income tax to withhold per day is:	of excess over—
Not over $45.40		$0	
Over—	**But not over—**		
$45.40	—$120.00 . .	$0.00 plus 10%	—$45.40
$120.00	—$349.00 . .	$7.46 plus 12%	—$120.00
$349.00	—$693.10 . .	$34.94 plus 22%	—$349.00
$693.10	—$1,281.70 . .	$110.64 plus 24%	—$693.10
$1,281.70	—$1,615.40 . .	$251.90 plus 32%	—$1,281.70
$1,615.40	—$2,400.60 . .	$358.68 plus 35%	—$1,615.40
$2,400.60	. . . .	$633.50 plus 37%	—$2,400.60

Wage Bracket Method Tables for Income Tax Withholding

SINGLE Persons—**MONTHLY** Payroll Period

(For Wages Paid through December 2019)

And the wages are–		And the number of withholding allowances claimed is—										
At least	But less than	0	1	2	3	4	5	6	7	8	9	10
		The amount of income tax to be withheld is—										
$ 0	$317	$0	$0	$0	$0	$0	$0	$0	$0	$0	$0	$0
317	327	1	0	0	0	0	0	0	0	0	0	0
327	337	2	0	0	0	0	0	0	0	0	0	0
337	347	3	0	0	0	0	0	0	0	0	0	0
347	357	4	0	0	0	0	0	0	0	0	0	0
357	367	5	0	0	0	0	0	0	0	0	0	0
367	377	6	0	0	0	0	0	0	0	0	0	0
377	387	7	0	0	0	0	0	0	0	0	0	0
387	397	8	0	0	0	0	0	0	0	0	0	0
397	407	9	0	0	0	0	0	0	0	0	0	0
407	417	10	0	0	0	0	0	0	0	0	0	0
417	427	11	0	0	0	0	0	0	0	0	0	0
427	437	12	0	0	0	0	0	0	0	0	0	0
437	447	13	0	0	0	0	0	0	0	0	0	0
447	457	14	0	0	0	0	0	0	0	0	0	0
457	467	15	0	0	0	0	0	0	0	0	0	0
467	477	16	0	0	0	0	0	0	0	0	0	0
477	487	17	0	0	0	0	0	0	0	0	0	0
487	497	18	0	0	0	0	0	0	0	0	0	0
497	507	19	0	0	0	0	0	0	0	0	0	0
507	517	20	0	0	0	0	0	0	0	0	0	0
517	527	21	0	0	0	0	0	0	0	0	0	0
527	537	22	0	0	0	0	0	0	0	0	0	0
537	547	23	0	0	0	0	0	0	0	0	0	0
547	557	24	0	0	0	0	0	0	0	0	0	0
557	567	25	0	0	0	0	0	0	0	0	0	0
567	577	26	0	0	0	0	0	0	0	0	0	0
577	587	27	0	0	0	0	0	0	0	0	0	0
587	597	28	0	0	0	0	0	0	0	0	0	0
597	607	29	0	0	0	0	0	0	0	0	0	0
607	617	30	0	0	0	0	0	0	0	0	0	0
617	627	31	0	0	0	0	0	0	0	0	0	0
627	637	32	0	0	0	0	0	0	0	0	0	0
637	647	33	0	0	0	0	0	0	0	0	0	0
647	657	34	0	0	0	0	0	0	0	0	0	0
657	667	35	0	0	0	0	0	0	0	0	0	0
667	677	36	1	0	0	0	0	0	0	0	0	0
677	687	37	2	0	0	0	0	0	0	0	0	0
687	697	38	3	0	0	0	0	0	0	0	0	0
697	707	39	4	0	0	0	0	0	0	0	0	0
707	717	40	5	0	0	0	0	0	0	0	0	0
717	727	41	6	0	0	0	0	0	0	0	0	0
727	737	42	7	0	0	0	0	0	0	0	0	0
737	747	43	8	0	0	0	0	0	0	0	0	0
747	757	44	9	0	0	0	0	0	0	0	0	0
757	767	45	10	0	0	0	0	0	0	0	0	0
767	777	46	11	0	0	0	0	0	0	0	0	0
777	787	47	12	0	0	0	0	0	0	0	0	0
787	797	48	13	0	0	0	0	0	0	0	0	0
797	807	49	14	0	0	0	0	0	0	0	0	0
807	817	50	15	0	0	0	0	0	0	0	0	0
817	827	51	16	0	0	0	0	0	0	0	0	0
827	837	52	17	0	0	0	0	0	0	0	0	0
837	847	53	18	0	0	0	0	0	0	0	0	0
847	857	54	19	0	0	0	0	0	0	0	0	0
857	867	55	20	0	0	0	0	0	0	0	0	0
867	877	56	21	0	0	0	0	0	0	0	0	0
877	887	57	22	0	0	0	0	0	0	0	0	0
887	897	58	23	0	0	0	0	0	0	0	0	0
897	907	59	24	0	0	0	0	0	0	0	0	0
907	917	60	25	0	0	0	0	0	0	0	0	0
917	927	61	26	0	0	0	0	0	0	0	0	0
927	937	62	27	0	0	0	0	0	0	0	0	0
937	947	63	28	0	0	0	0	0	0	0	0	0
947	957	64	29	0	0	0	0	0	0	0	0	0
957	967	65	30	0	0	0	0	0	0	0	0	0
967	977	66	31	0	0	0	0	0	0	0	0	0
977	987	67	32	0	0	0	0	0	0	0	0	0
987	997	68	33	0	0	0	0	0	0	0	0	0
997	1,007	69	34	0	0	0	0	0	0	0	0	0

Wage Bracket Method Tables for Income Tax Withholding

SINGLE Persons—MONTHLY Payroll Period

(For Wages Paid through December 2019)

And the wages are–		And the number of withholding allowances claimed is—										
At least	But less than	0	1	2	3	4	5	6	7	8	9	10
		The amount of income tax to be withheld is—										
1,007	1,027	70	35	0	0	0	0	0	0	0	0	0
1,027	1,047	72	37	2	0	0	0	0	0	0	0	0
1,047	1,067	74	39	4	0	0	0	0	0	0	0	0
1,067	1,087	76	41	6	0	0	0	0	0	0	0	0
1,087	1,107	78	43	8	0	0	0	0	0	0	0	0
1,107	1,127	80	45	10	0	0	0	0	0	0	0	0
1,127	1,147	82	47	12	0	0	0	0	0	0	0	0
1,147	1,167	85	49	14	0	0	0	0	0	0	0	0
1,167	1,187	87	51	16	0	0	0	0	0	0	0	0
1,187	1,207	89	53	18	0	0	0	0	0	0	0	0
1,207	1,227	92	55	20	0	0	0	0	0	0	0	0
1,227	1,247	94	57	22	0	0	0	0	0	0	0	0
1,247	1,267	97	59	24	0	0	0	0	0	0	0	0
1,267	1,287	99	61	26	0	0	0	0	0	0	0	0
1,287	1,307	101	63	28	0	0	0	0	0	0	0	0
1,307	1,327	104	65	30	0	0	0	0	0	0	0	0
1,327	1,347	106	67	32	0	0	0	0	0	0	0	0
1,347	1,367	109	69	34	0	0	0	0	0	0	0	0
1,367	1,387	111	71	36	1	0	0	0	0	0	0	0
1,387	1,407	113	73	38	3	0	0	0	0	0	0	0
1,407	1,427	116	75	40	5	0	0	0	0	0	0	0
1,427	1,447	118	77	42	7	0	0	0	0	0	0	0
1,447	1,467	121	79	44	9	0	0	0	0	0	0	0
1,467	1,487	123	81	46	11	0	0	0	0	0	0	0
1,487	1,507	125	83	48	13	0	0	0	0	0	0	0
1,507	1,527	128	86	50	15	0	0	0	0	0	0	0
1,527	1,547	130	88	52	17	0	0	0	0	0	0	0
1,547	1,567	133	91	54	19	0	0	0	0	0	0	0
1,567	1,587	135	93	56	21	0	0	0	0	0	0	0
1,587	1,607	137	95	58	23	0	0	0	0	0	0	0
1,607	1,627	140	98	60	25	0	0	0	0	0	0	0
1,627	1,647	142	100	62	27	0	0	0	0	0	0	0
1,647	1,667	145	103	64	29	0	0	0	0	0	0	0
1,667	1,687	147	105	66	31	0	0	0	0	0	0	0
1,687	1,707	149	107	68	33	0	0	0	0	0	0	0
1,707	1,727	152	110	70	35	0	0	0	0	0	0	0
1,727	1,747	154	112	72	37	2	0	0	0	0	0	0
1,747	1,767	157	115	74	39	4	0	0	0	0	0	0
1,767	1,787	159	117	76	41	6	0	0	0	0	0	0
1,787	1,807	161	119	78	43	8	0	0	0	0	0	0
1,807	1,827	164	122	80	45	10	0	0	0	0	0	0
1,827	1,847	166	124	82	47	12	0	0	0	0	0	0
1,847	1,867	169	127	85	49	14	0	0	0	0	0	0
1,867	1,887	171	129	87	51	16	0	0	0	0	0	0
1,887	1,907	173	131	89	53	18	0	0	0	0	0	0
1,907	1,927	176	134	92	55	20	0	0	0	0	0	0
1,927	1,947	178	136	94	57	22	0	0	0	0	0	0
1,947	1,967	181	139	97	59	24	0	0	0	0	0	0
1,967	1,987	183	141	99	61	26	0	0	0	0	0	0
1,987	2,007	185	143	101	63	28	0	0	0	0	0	0
2,007	2,047	189	147	105	66	31	0	0	0	0	0	0
2,047	2,087	194	152	110	70	35	0	0	0	0	0	0
2,087	2,127	199	157	115	74	39	4	0	0	0	0	0
2,127	2,167	203	161	119	78	43	8	0	0	0	0	0
2,167	2,207	208	166	124	82	47	12	0	0	0	0	0
2,207	2,247	213	171	129	87	51	16	0	0	0	0	0
2,247	2,287	218	176	134	92	55	20	0	0	0	0	0
2,287	2,327	223	181	139	97	59	24	0	0	0	0	0
2,327	2,367	227	185	143	101	63	28	0	0	0	0	0
2,367	2,407	232	190	148	106	67	32	0	0	0	0	0
2,407	2,447	237	195	153	111	71	36	1	0	0	0	0
2,447	2,487	242	200	158	116	75	40	5	0	0	0	0
2,487	2,527	247	205	163	121	79	44	9	0	0	0	0
2,527	2,567	251	209	167	125	83	48	13	0	0	0	0
2,567	2,607	256	214	172	130	88	52	17	0	0	0	0
2,607	2,647	261	219	177	135	93	56	21	0	0	0	0

2,647 and over   Use Table 4(a) for a SINGLE person on page 46. Also see the instructions on page 44.

Wage Bracket Method Tables for Income Tax Withholding

MARRIED Persons—MONTHLY Payroll Period

(For Wages Paid through December 2019)

And the wages are–		And the number of withholding allowances claimed is—										
At least	But less than	0	1	2	3	4	5	6	7	8	9	10
		The amount of income tax to be withheld is—										
$ 0	$983	$0	$0	$0	$0	$0	$0	$0	$0	$0	$0	$0
983	994	1	0	0	0	0	0	0	0	0	0	0
994	1,005	2	0	0	0	0	0	0	0	0	0	0
1,005	1,016	3	0	0	0	0	0	0	0	0	0	0
1,016	1,027	4	0	0	0	0	0	0	0	0	0	0
1,027	1,038	5	0	0	0	0	0	0	0	0	0	0
1,038	1,049	6	0	0	0	0	0	0	0	0	0	0
1,049	1,060	7	0	0	0	0	0	0	0	0	0	0
1,060	1,071	8	0	0	0	0	0	0	0	0	0	0
1,071	1,082	9	0	0	0	0	0	0	0	0	0	0
1,082	1,093	10	0	0	0	0	0	0	0	0	0	0
1,093	1,104	12	0	0	0	0	0	0	0	0	0	0
1,104	1,115	13	0	0	0	0	0	0	0	0	0	0
1,115	1,126	14	0	0	0	0	0	0	0	0	0	0
1,126	1,137	15	0	0	0	0	0	0	0	0	0	0
1,137	1,148	16	0	0	0	0	0	0	0	0	0	0
1,148	1,159	17	0	0	0	0	0	0	0	0	0	0
1,159	1,170	18	0	0	0	0	0	0	0	0	0	0
1,170	1,181	19	0	0	0	0	0	0	0	0	0	0
1,181	1,192	20	0	0	0	0	0	0	0	0	0	0
1,192	1,203	21	0	0	0	0	0	0	0	0	0	0
1,203	1,214	23	0	0	0	0	0	0	0	0	0	0
1,214	1,225	24	0	0	0	0	0	0	0	0	0	0
1,225	1,236	25	0	0	0	0	0	0	0	0	0	0
1,236	1,247	26	0	0	0	0	0	0	0	0	0	0
1,247	1,258	27	0	0	0	0	0	0	0	0	0	0
1,258	1,269	28	0	0	0	0	0	0	0	0	0	0
1,269	1,280	29	0	0	0	0	0	0	0	0	0	0
1,280	1,291	30	0	0	0	0	0	0	0	0	0	0
1,291	1,302	31	0	0	0	0	0	0	0	0	0	0
1,302	1,313	32	0	0	0	0	0	0	0	0	0	0
1,313	1,324	34	0	0	0	0	0	0	0	0	0	0
1,324	1,335	35	0	0	0	0	0	0	0	0	0	0
1,335	1,346	36	1	0	0	0	0	0	0	0	0	0
1,346	1,357	37	2	0	0	0	0	0	0	0	0	0
1,357	1,368	38	3	0	0	0	0	0	0	0	0	0
1,368	1,379	39	4	0	0	0	0	0	0	0	0	0
1,379	1,390	40	5	0	0	0	0	0	0	0	0	0
1,390	1,401	41	6	0	0	0	0	0	0	0	0	0
1,401	1,412	42	7	0	0	0	0	0	0	0	0	0
1,412	1,423	43	8	0	0	0	0	0	0	0	0	0
1,423	1,434	45	10	0	0	0	0	0	0	0	0	0
1,434	1,445	46	11	0	0	0	0	0	0	0	0	0
1,445	1,456	47	12	0	0	0	0	0	0	0	0	0
1,456	1,467	48	13	0	0	0	0	0	0	0	0	0
1,467	1,478	49	14	0	0	0	0	0	0	0	0	0
1,478	1,489	50	15	0	0	0	0	0	0	0	0	0
1,489	1,500	51	16	0	0	0	0	0	0	0	0	0
1,500	1,511	52	17	0	0	0	0	0	0	0	0	0
1,511	1,522	53	18	0	0	0	0	0	0	0	0	0
1,522	1,533	54	19	0	0	0	0	0	0	0	0	0
1,533	1,544	56	21	0	0	0	0	0	0	0	0	0
1,544	1,555	57	22	0	0	0	0	0	0	0	0	0
1,555	1,566	58	23	0	0	0	0	0	0	0	0	0
1,566	1,577	59	24	0	0	0	0	0	0	0	0	0
1,577	1,588	60	25	0	0	0	0	0	0	0	0	0
1,588	1,599	61	26	0	0	0	0	0	0	0	0	0
1,599	1,610	62	27	0	0	0	0	0	0	0	0	0
1,610	1,621	63	28	0	0	0	0	0	0	0	0	0
1,621	1,632	64	29	0	0	0	0	0	0	0	0	0
1,632	1,643	65	30	0	0	0	0	0	0	0	0	0
1,643	1,654	67	32	0	0	0	0	0	0	0	0	0
1,654	1,665	68	33	0	0	0	0	0	0	0	0	0
1,665	1,676	69	34	0	0	0	0	0	0	0	0	0
1,676	1,687	70	35	0	0	0	0	0	0	0	0	0
1,687	1,698	71	36	1	0	0	0	0	0	0	0	0
1,698	1,709	72	37	2	0	0	0	0	0	0	0	0
1,709	1,720	73	38	3	0	0	0	0	0	0	0	0
1,720	1,731	74	39	4	0	0	0	0	0	0	0	0
1,731	1,742	75	40	5	0	0	0	0	0	0	0	0

Wage Bracket Method Tables for Income Tax Withholding

MARRIED Persons—MONTHLY Payroll Period

(For Wages Paid through December 2019)

And the wages are–		And the number of withholding allowances claimed is—										
At least	But less than	0	1	2	3	4	5	6	7	8	9	10
		The amount of income tax to be withheld is—										
1,742	1,753	76	41	6	0	0	0	0	0	0	0	0
1,753	1,773	78	43	8	0	0	0	0	0	0	0	0
1,773	1,793	80	45	10	0	0	0	0	0	0	0	0
1,793	1,813	82	47	12	0	0	0	0	0	0	0	0
1,813	1,833	84	49	14	0	0	0	0	0	0	0	0
1,833	1,853	86	51	16	0	0	0	0	0	0	0	0
1,853	1,873	88	53	18	0	0	0	0	0	0	0	0
1,873	1,893	90	55	20	0	0	0	0	0	0	0	0
1,893	1,913	92	57	22	0	0	0	0	0	0	0	0
1,913	1,933	94	59	24	0	0	0	0	0	0	0	0
1,933	1,953	96	61	26	0	0	0	0	0	0	0	0
1,953	1,973	98	63	28	0	0	0	0	0	0	0	0
1,973	1,993	100	65	30	0	0	0	0	0	0	0	0
1,993	2,013	102	67	32	0	0	0	0	0	0	0	0
2,013	2,033	104	69	34	0	0	0	0	0	0	0	0
2,033	2,053	106	71	36	1	0	0	0	0	0	0	0
2,053	2,073	108	73	38	3	0	0	0	0	0	0	0
2,073	2,093	110	75	40	5	0	0	0	0	0	0	0
2,093	2,113	112	77	42	7	0	0	0	0	0	0	0
2,113	2,133	114	79	44	9	0	0	0	0	0	0	0
2,133	2,153	116	81	46	11	0	0	0	0	0	0	0
2,153	2,173	118	83	48	13	0	0	0	0	0	0	0
2,173	2,193	120	85	50	15	0	0	0	0	0	0	0
2,193	2,213	122	87	52	17	0	0	0	0	0	0	0
2,213	2,233	124	89	54	19	0	0	0	0	0	0	0
2,233	2,253	126	91	56	21	0	0	0	0	0	0	0
2,253	2,273	128	93	58	23	0	0	0	0	0	0	0
2,273	2,293	130	95	60	25	0	0	0	0	0	0	0
2,293	2,313	132	97	62	27	0	0	0	0	0	0	0
2,313	2,333	134	99	64	29	0	0	0	0	0	0	0
2,333	2,353	136	101	66	31	0	0	0	0	0	0	0
2,353	2,373	138	103	68	33	0	0	0	0	0	0	0
2,373	2,393	140	105	70	35	0	0	0	0	0	0	0
2,393	2,413	142	107	72	37	2	0	0	0	0	0	0
2,413	2,433	144	109	74	39	4	0	0	0	0	0	0
2,433	2,453	146	111	76	41	6	0	0	0	0	0	0
2,453	2,473	148	113	78	43	8	0	0	0	0	0	0
2,473	2,493	150	115	80	45	10	0	0	0	0	0	0
2,493	2,513	152	117	82	47	12	0	0	0	0	0	0
2,513	2,553	155	120	85	50	15	0	0	0	0	0	0
2,553	2,593	159	124	89	54	19	0	0	0	0	0	0
2,593	2,633	163	128	93	58	23	0	0	0	0	0	0
2,633	2,673	168	132	97	62	27	0	0	0	0	0	0
2,673	2,713	173	136	101	66	31	0	0	0	0	0	0
2,713	2,753	178	140	105	70	35	0	0	0	0	0	0
2,753	2,793	182	144	109	74	39	4	0	0	0	0	0
2,793	2,833	187	148	113	78	43	8	0	0	0	0	0
2,833	2,873	192	152	117	82	47	12	0	0	0	0	0
2,873	2,913	197	156	121	86	51	16	0	0	0	0	0
2,913	2,953	202	160	125	90	55	20	0	0	0	0	0
2,953	2,993	206	164	129	94	59	24	0	0	0	0	0
2,993	3,033	211	169	133	98	63	28	0	0	0	0	0
3,033	3,073	216	174	137	102	67	32	0	0	0	0	0
3,073	3,113	221	179	141	106	71	36	1	0	0	0	0
3,113	3,153	226	184	145	110	75	40	5	0	0	0	0
3,153	3,193	230	188	149	114	79	44	9	0	0	0	0
3,193	3,233	235	193	153	118	83	48	13	0	0	0	0
3,233	3,273	240	198	157	122	87	52	17	0	0	0	0
3,273	3,313	245	203	161	126	91	56	21	0	0	0	0
3,313	3,353	250	208	166	130	95	60	25	0	0	0	0
3,353	3,393	254	212	170	134	99	64	29	0	0	0	0
3,393	3,433	259	217	175	138	103	68	33	0	0	0	0
3,433	3,473	264	222	180	142	107	72	37	2	0	0	0
3,473	3,513	269	227	185	146	111	76	41	6	0	0	0
3,513	3,553	274	232	190	150	115	80	45	10	0	0	0
3,553	3,593	278	236	194	154	119	84	49	14	0	0	0

3,593 and over   Use Table 4(b) for a MARRIED person on page 46. Also see the instructions on page 44.

Additional Comprehensive Tax Return Problems

CONTENTS

*Please note: Additional tax forms can be printed by going to the IRS website at **www.irs.gov**.

Comprehensive Problem One

Noah and Joan Arc's Tax Return

Noah and Joan Arc live with their family in Dayton, OH. Noah's Social Security number is 434-11-3311. Noah was born on February 22, 1984 and Joan was born on July 1, 1985. Both enjoy good health and eyesight. Noah owns and operates a pet store and Joan is a firefighter for the city of Dayton.

1. The Arcs have two children, a son named Billie Bob (Social Security number 598-01-2345), born on March 21, 2012, and a daughter named Mary Sue (Social Security number 554-33-2411), born on December 3, 2015.
2. Joan and Noah brought a folder of tax documents located on Pages D-3 to D-5.
3. Noah's pet store is located at 1415 S. Patterson Blvd, Dayton, OH 45409. The name of the store is "The Arc," and its taxpayer identification number is 95-9876556. Since you handle Noah's bookkeeping, you have printed the income statement from your Quickbooks software, shown on Page D-5.
4. Detail of The Arc's meals and entertainment:

$ 400	Meals associated with business travel
60	Overtime meals for employees
878	Sports tickets for entertaining large customers
$ 1,338	

5. Travel costs are business related and do not include meals.

6. Noah and Joan paid the following amounts during the year (all by check):

Political contributions	$ 250
Church donations (for which a written acknowledgment was received)	5,025
Real estate taxes on their home	2,375
Medical co-pays for doctor visits	700
Mortgage interest for purchase of home	See Form 1098 (Page D-4)
Tax return preparation fees	350
Credit card interest	220
Automobile insurance premiums	600
Uniforms for Joan	125
Contribution to Noah's individual retirement account (made on April 1, 2020)	6,000

7. Noah has a long-term capital loss carryover from last year of $2,400.
8. Noah and Joan own a condo and use it as a rental property. The condo is located at 16 Oakwood Ave, Unit A, Dayton, OH 45409. Noah provides the management services for the rental including selection of tenants, maintenance, repairs, rent collection, and other services as needed. On average, Noah spends about 2 hours per week on the rental activity. The revenue and expenses for the year are as follows:

Rental income	$13,800
Insurance	575
Interest expense	6,870
Property taxes	1,016
Miscellaneous expenses	700

The home was acquired for $85,000 in 2003. No improvements have been made to the property.

9. The Arcs paid Ohio general sales tax of $976 during the year.

Required: You are to prepare the Arc's federal income tax return in good form, signing the return as the preparer. Do not complete an Ohio state income tax return. Make realistic assumptions about any missing data (addresses, etc.) that you may need. The following forms and schedules are required:

Form 1040	Schedule SE
Schedule 1	Form 2441
Schedule 2	Form 4562
Schedule 3	Form 8812
Schedule A	Form 8949
Schedule B	Form 8995
Schedule C	Child Tax Credit Worksheet
Schedule D	Qualified Dividends and Capital Gain Tax Worksheet
Schedule E	

Note: The forms included in Appendix D are provided for the student to work on only one of the two additional comprehensive problems. If desired, additional tax forms may be obtained from the IRS website at **www.irs.gov**.

a Employee's social security number 456-87-5432	OMB No. 1545-0008 — Safe, accurate, FAST! Use — IRS e~file — Visit the IRS website at www.irs.gov/efile

b Employer identification number (EIN) 33-4382966	**1** Wages, tips, other compensation 30,240.00	**2** Federal income tax withheld 5,120.00
c Employer's name, address, and ZIP code	**3** Social security wages 30,240.00	**4** Social security tax withheld 1,874.88
City of Dayton Fire and Rescue	**5** Medicare wages and tips 30,240.00	**6** Medicare tax withheld 438.48
123 Warren Street Dayton, OH 45402	**7** Social security tips	**8** Allocated tips
d Control number	**9**	**10** Dependent care benefits
e Employee's first name and initial Last name Suff.	**11** Nonqualified plans	**12a** See instructions for box 12 DD | 12,200.00
Joan Arc 1265 W. Riverview Ave. Dayton, OH 45402	**13** Statutory employee ☐ Retirement plan ☒ Third-party sick pay ☐	**12b**
	14 Other	**12c**
		12d
f Employee's address and ZIP code		

15 State Employer's state ID number	**16** State wages, tips, etc.	**17** State income tax	**18** Local wages, tips, etc.	**19** Local income tax	**20** Locality name
OH | 1126-87021	30,240.00	1,850.00			

Form **W-2** Wage and Tax Statement   **2019**   Department of the Treasury—Internal Revenue Service

Copy B—To Be Filed With Employee's **FEDERAL** Tax Return.
This information is being furnished to the Internal Revenue Service.

Substitute 1099 Statement

Charlotte Squab Financial Services

123 Wall Street
New York, NY 10005

Joan and Noah Arc
1265 W. Riverview Avenue
Dayton, OH 45402
SSN: 456-87-5432

Date

December 31, 2019

Dividends						
Payor	Box 1a Ordinary Dividends	Box 1b Qualified Dividends	Box 2a Cap Gain Distrib	Box 4 Federal Income Tax withheld	Box 6 Foreign Tax Paid	Box 10-Tax exempt Dividends
ExxonMobil	312.00	312.00	0.00	0.00	0.00	0.00
Texas Util.	1,188.00	1,188.00	0.00	0.00	0.00	0.00
CS Growth Fund	418.00	418.00	245.00	0.00	19.00	0.00

Stock Transactions				
Description	Date Acq.	Date Sold	Proceeds	Basis (reported to IRS)
100 shs. Blue Corp.	02/11/2009	08/15/2019	4,537.00	2,576.00
50 shs. Yellow Corp.	01/13/2019	06/05/2019	6,090.00	5,345.00
25 shs. Red Co.	10/02/2010	10/07/2019	12,212.00	1,655.00

☐ VOID   ☐ CORRECTED

RECIPIENT'S/LENDER'S name, street address, city or town, state or province, country, ZIP or foreign postal code, and telephone no. Chase Mortgage 100 Park Avenue New York, NY 10017	OMB No. 1545-1380 20**19** Form **1098**	Mortgage Interest Statement
	1 Mortgage interest received from payer(s)/borrower(s) $ 11,100.00	Copy C **For Recipient/ Lender**
RECIPIENT'S/LENDER'S TIN PAYER'S/BORROWER'S TIN 13-4296127 434-11-3311	**2** Outstanding mortgage principal $ 274,200.00	**3** Mortgage origination date 03/13/2010	
	4 Refund of overpaid interest $	**5** Mortgage insurance premiums $	For Privacy Act and Paperwork Reduction Act Notice, see the **2019 General Instructions for Certain Information Returns.**
PAYER'S/BORROWER'S name Noah and Joan Arc	**6** Points paid on purchase of principal residence $	
Street address (including apt. no.) 1265 W. Riverview Avenue	**7** ☒ If address of property securing mortgage is the same as PAYER'S/BORROWER'S address, check the box, or enter the address or description in box 8.	
City or town, state or province, country, and ZIP or foreign postal code Dayton, OH 45402	**8** Address or description of property securing mortgage (see instructions)	
9 Number of properties securing the mortgage **10** Other 1		**11** Mortgage acquisition date
Account number (see instructions)		

Form **1098**   www.irs.gov/Form1098   Department of the Treasury - Internal Revenue Service

ROUNDUP DAY CARE CENTER
245 N. WILKINSON STREET
DAYTON, OH 45402

January 12, 2020

Joan and Noah Arc
1265 W. Riverview Avenue
Dayton, OH 45402

Dear Joan and Noah,

Thank you for a great 2019 at Roundup! We appreciate your patronage during the year and hope to continue to provide excellent service for Mary Sue in 2020. We have provided the tax information for calendar year 2019 below. Please let us know if you need any additional information.

Sincerely,

Charles F. Burgundian

Charles F. Burgundian
Executive Director, Roundup Day Care
EIN 54-0983456

Date of service	Amount Paid	Child
January 1, 2019 – December 31, 2019	$3,000.00	Mary Sue Arc

The Arc
95-9876556
Income Statement
For the Year Ended December 31, 2019

Revenue:		
Gross Sales		$143,245.00
Less: Sales Returns and Allowances		$0.00
Net Sales		$143,245.00
Cost of Goods Sold:		
Beginning Inventory	$10,204.00	
Add: Purchases	$62,111.00	
	$72,315.00	
Less: Ending Inventory	$9,987.00	
Cost of Goods Sold		$62,328.00
Gross Profit (Loss)		$80,917.00
Expenses:		
Dues and Subscriptions	$0.00	
Estimated Federal Tax Payments	$8,000.00	
Estimated State Tax Payments	$4,000.00	
Insurance	$780.00	
Meals and Entertainment	$1,338.00	
Miscellaneous	$0.00	
Payroll Taxes	$3,840.00	
Professional Fees	$1,700.00	
Rent	$8,400.00	
Travel	$1,231.00	
Utilities	$1,254.00	
Vehicle Expenses	$0.00	
Wages	$25,113.00	
Total Expenses		$55,656.00
Net Operating Income		$25,261.00

Comprehensive Problem Two

Gregory and Lulu Clifden's Tax Return

Gregory R. and Lulu B. Clifden live with their family at the Rock Glen House Bed & Breakfast, which Gregory operates. The Bed & Breakfast (B&B) is located at 33333 Fume Blanc Way, Temecula, CA 92591. Gregory (born May 4, 1976) and Lulu (born June 12, 1977) enjoy good health and eyesight.

1. The Clifdens have three sons. Gerald was born April 16, 2002, Gary was born December 2, 2007, and Glenn was born January 13, 2009. All three boys live at home and the Clifdens provide more than 50% of their support.

2. The Rock Glen House B&B is operated as a sole proprietorship and had the following income and expenses for the year:

Room rental income	$137,896
Vending machine income	2,100
Advertising expense	4,810
Depreciation for book and tax purposes	18,100
Mortgage interest on the B&B	22,987
Wages of cleaning people	17,540
Taxes and licenses	6,420
Supplies consumed	18,870
Business insurance	6,300
Laundry expenses	4,289
Accounting fees	1,850
Office expenses	2,400
Utilities	6,350

All of the above amounts relate to the business portion of the Bed & Breakfast; the personal portion is accounted for separately. The Rock Glen House B&B uses the cash method of accounting and has no inventory. The employer tax ID number is 95-1234567.

3. The Clifdens made estimated federal income tax payments of $2,000 and estimated state income tax payments of $6,000 (all made during 2019).

4. Lulu worked about 1,000 hours as a substitute schoolteacher with the local school district. She also spent $276 out-of-pocket for various supplies for her classroom. For the current year, Lulu's Form W-2 from the school district showed the following:

a Employee's social security number 256-43-8819	OMB No. 1545-0008	Safe, accurate, FAST! Use	IRS e~file	Visit the IRS website at www.irs.gov/efile
b Employer identification number (EIN) 43-7654321		**1** Wages, tips, other compensation 13,700.00		**2** Federal income tax withheld 1,694.00
c Employer's name, address, and ZIP code Temecula Valley Unified School Dist. 31350 Rancho Vista Rd. Temecula, CA 92592		**3** Social security wages 13,700.00		**4** Social security tax withheld 849.40
		5 Medicare wages and tips 13,700.00		**6** Medicare tax withheld 198.65
		7 Social security tips		**8** Allocated tips
d Control number		**9**		**10** Dependent care benefits
e Employee's first name and initial Last name Suff. Lulu B. Clifden 33333 Fume Blanc Way Temecula, CA 92591		**11** Nonqualified plans		**12a** See instructions for box 12
		13 Statutory employee ☐ Retirement plan ☐ Third-party sick pay ☐		**12b**
		14 Other		**12c**
				12d
f Employee's address and ZIP code				
15 State Employer's state ID number CA	**16** State wages, tips, etc. 13,700.00	**17** State income tax 400.00	**18** Local wages, tips, etc. **19** Local income tax	**20** Locality name

Form **W-2** Wage and Tax Statement   **2019**   Department of the Treasury—Internal Revenue Service

Copy B—To Be Filed With Employee's FEDERAL Tax Return.
This information is being furnished to the Internal Revenue Service.

5. Gregory is retired from the U.S. Navy. His annual statement from the Navy, Form 1099-R, is on Page D-12.

6. Gregory and Lulu paid (and can substantiate) the following amounts during the year:

Mastercard interest	$1,480
Dental expenses (orthodontics for Gary)	5,457
California state income tax (for 2018)	2,130
Charitable contributions	4,875
Deductible interest on home (personal portion)	9,631
Real estate taxes (personal portion)	3,830
Life insurance premiums	845
Automobile registration fees (deductible portion)	45
Tax return preparation fee	475
Contributions to Donald Trump's re-election campaign	1,000

7. During the year, Gregory and Lulu received the following qualifying dividends and interest:

Interest:

Bob's Big Bank	$ 381
Bank of Ireland	271
City of Temecula Tax Exempt Bonds	1,490
Vintage Bank	See 1099-INT (Page D-12)

Qualified dividends:

Southwest Airlines	$ 250
Heinz Foods	550

Also, Lulu owns Series EE U.S. savings bonds. During the year, the bond redemption value increased by $1,300. Lulu has not elected the accrual method for these bonds. There were no Irish taxes paid on the interest from the Bank of Ireland. All the above stocks, bonds, and bank accounts are community property.

8. Lulu has a stock portfolio. During the year, she sold the following stock, shown on her Forms 1099-B as follows (basis was provided to the IRS in all cases):

	Orange Co.	Gold Co.	Green Co.
Sales price	$8,114	See	$1,449
Basis	3,803	Form	2,578
Date acquired	02/11/19	1099-B	10/31/14
Date sold	06/19/19	(Page D-12)	10/23/19

9. Lulu paid her ex-husband $4,800 alimony in the current year, as required under the 2002 divorce decree. Her ex-husband's name is Hector Leach and his Social Security number is 566-23-5431.

10. Gregory does all the significant work in the Bed & Breakfast and therefore he pays self-employment tax on 100 percent of the earnings from the B&B.

11. During the year, Gregory's uncle Martin died. Martin had a $50,000 life insurance policy that named Gregory as the beneficiary. Gregory received the check for the benefits payable under the policy on November 30 of the current year. Martin also left Gregory a parcel of land with an appraised value of $120,000.

12. Gary is a general partner in a partnership that owns a boutique hotel in northern California and leases the property to a hotel management company. Gary does not materially participate in the partnership activity but the partnership activity does rise to the level of a trade or business. The Schedule K-1 from the partnership is shown on Page D-9.

13. Lulu was not eligible for health care benefits due to the part-time nature of her job, thus health insurance for the Clifden household was purchased by Gregory. The Clifdens purchased health insurance through the Covered California program and received the Form 1095-A shown on Page D-11. They had no other health insurance during 2019. Assume that the self-employed health insurance deduction is $1,424. The Clifdens did not claim an advance premium credit.

Required: Gregory and Lulu have come to you to prepare their 2019 federal income tax return. Do not complete a California state income tax return. Gregory and Lulu have given you several IRS forms (see Pages D-11 and D-12). Make realistic assumptions about any missing data (addresses, etc.) that you need. Do not file a federal Form 4952. The following is a list of the forms and schedules that you will need to complete the tax return:

Form 1040	Schedule E
Schedule 1	Schedule SE
Schedule 2	Form 8812
Schedule 3	Form 8949
Schedule A	Form 8962
Schedule B	Form 8995
Schedule C	Child Tax Credit Worksheet
Schedule D	Qualified Dividends and Capital Gain Tax Worksheet

Note: The forms included in Appendix D are provided for the student to work on only one of the two additional comprehensive problems. If desired, additional tax forms may be obtained from the IRS website at **www.irs.gov**.

651119

| Schedule K-1 | | Final K-1 | Amended K-1 | OMB No. 1545-0123 |

Schedule K-1 (Form 1065)
Department of the Treasury
Internal Revenue Service

2019

For calendar year 2019, or tax year

beginning ___/___/2019   ending ___/___/___

Partner's Share of Income, Deductions, Credits, etc.   ▶ See back of form and separate instructions.

Part III	Partner's Share of Current Year Income, Deductions, Credits, and Other Items

1	Ordinary business income (loss)	**15**	Credits
2	Net rental real estate income (loss) 1,578		
3	Other net rental income (loss)	**16**	Foreign transactions
4a	Guaranteed payments for services		
4b	Guaranteed payments for capital		
4c	Total guaranteed payments		
5	Interest income		
6a	Ordinary dividends 12		
6b	Qualified dividends 12		
6c	Dividend equivalents	**17**	Alternative minimum tax (AMT) items
7	Royalties		
8	Net short-term capital gain (loss)		
9a	Net long-term capital gain (loss) (900)	**18**	Tax-exempt income and nondeductible expenses
9b	Collectibles (28%) gain (loss)		
9c	Unrecaptured section 1250 gain		
10	Net section 1231 gain (loss)		
11	Other income (loss)	**19**	Distributions
		A	400
12	Section 179 deduction	**20**	Other information
		Z	1,578
13	Other deductions		
14	Self-employment earnings (loss)		
A	1,578		
21 ☐ More than one activity for at-risk purposes*			
22 ☐ More than one activity for passive activity purposes*			
*See attached statement for additional information.			

Part I   Information About the Partnership

A Partnership's employer identification number
11-2343212

B Partnership's name, address, city, state, and ZIP code
Wine Acres Partners
581 Coombs Street, Napa, CA 94559

C IRS Center where partnership filed return ▶ Ogden, UT

D ☐ Check if this is a publicly traded partnership (PTP)

Part II   Information About the Partner

E Partner's identifying number (Do not use TIN of a disregarded entity. See instructions.)
543-88-9756

F Partner's name, address, city, state, and ZIP code
Gregory R. Clifden
33333 Fume Blanc Way, Temecula, CA 92591

G ☒ General partner or LLC member-manager   ☐ Limited partner or other LLC member

H ☒ Domestic partner   ☐ Foreign partner
☐ Disregarded entity: Name of beneficial owner ___

I1 What type of entity is this partner?   Individual

I2 If this partner is a retirement plan (IRA/SEP/Keogh/etc.), check here ☐

J Partner's share of profit, loss, and capital (see instructions):

	Beginning	Ending
Profit	2 %	2 %
Loss	2 %	2 %
Capital	2 %	2 %

Check if decrease is due to sale or exchange of partnership interest . . ☐

K Partner's share of liabilities:

	Beginning	Ending
Nonrecourse $	4,679	$ 4,679
Qualified nonrecourse financing $		$
Recourse $		$

☐ Check this box if Item K includes liability amounts from lower tier partnerships.

L   **Partner's Capital Account Analysis**

Tax Basis Capital

Beginning capital account . . . $	13,256
Capital contributed during the year . . $	0
Current year net income (loss) . . . $	690
Other increase (decrease) (attach explanation) $	
Withdrawals & distributions . . . $ (	400)
Ending capital account . . . . $	13,546

M Did the partner contribute property with a built-in gain or loss?
☐ Yes   ☒ No   If "Yes," attach statement. See instructions.

N Partner's Share of Net Unrecognized Section 704(c) Gain or (Loss)
Beginning . . . . $ ___
Ending . . . . $ ___

For IRS Use Only

For Paperwork Reduction Act Notice, see Instructions for Form 1065.   www.irs.gov/Form1065   Cat. No. 11394R   **Schedule K-1 (Form 1065) 2019**

Schedule K-1 (Form 1065) 2019   Page **2**

This list identifies the codes used on Schedule K-1 for all partners and provides summarized reporting information for partners who file Form 1040 or 1040-SR. For detailed reporting and filing information, see the separate Partner's Instructions for Schedule K-1 and the instructions for your income tax return.

1. Ordinary business income (loss). Determine whether the income (loss) is passive or nonpassive and enter on your return as follows.

	Report on
Passive loss	See the Partner's Instructions
Passive income	Schedule E, line 28, column (h)
Nonpassive loss	See the Partner's Instructions
Nonpassive income	Schedule E, line 28, column (k)

2. Net rental real estate income (loss) — See the Partner's Instructions
3. Other net rental income (loss)
Net income	Schedule E, line 28, column (h)
Net loss	See the Partner's Instructions

4a. Guaranteed payment Services — See the Partner's Instructions
4b. Guaranteed payment Capital — See the Partner's Instructions
4c. Guaranteed payment Total — See the Partner's Instructions
5. Interest income — Form 1040 or 1040-SR, line 2b
6a. Ordinary dividends — Form 1040 or 1040-SR, line 3b
6b. Qualified dividends — Form 1040 or 1040-SR, line 3a
6c. Dividend equivalents — See the Partner's Instructions
7. Royalties — Schedule E, line 4
8. Net short-term capital gain (loss) — Schedule D, line 5
9a. Net long-term capital gain (loss) — Schedule D, line 12
9b. Collectibles (28%) gain (loss) — 28% Rate Gain Worksheet, line 4 (Schedule D instructions)
9c. Unrecaptured section 1250 gain — See the Partner's Instructions
10. Net section 1231 gain (loss) — See the Partner's Instructions
11. Other income (loss)

Code		
A	Other portfolio income (loss)	See the Partner's Instructions
B	Involuntary conversions	See the Partner's Instructions
C	Sec. 1256 contracts & straddles	Form 6781, line 1
D	Mining exploration costs recapture	See Pub. 535
E	Cancellation of debt	
F	Section 743(b) positive adjustments	
G	Section 965(a) inclusion	
H	Income under subpart F (other than inclusions under sections 951A and 965)	See the Partner's Instructions
I	Other income (loss)	

12. Section 179 deduction — See the Partner's Instructions
13. Other deductions

A	Cash contributions (60%)	
B	Cash contributions (30%)	
C	Noncash contributions (50%)	
D	Noncash contributions (30%)	
E	Capital gain property to a 50% organization (30%)	See the Partner's Instructions
F	Capital gain property (20%)	
G	Contributions (100%)	
H	Investment interest expense	Form 4952, line 1
I	Deductions—royalty income	Schedule E, line 19
J	Section 59(e)(2) expenditures	See the Partner's Instructions
K	Excess business interest expense	See the Partner's Instructions
L	Deductions—portfolio (other)	Schedule A, line 16
M	Amounts paid for medical insurance	Schedule A, line 1, or Schedule 1 (Form 1040 or 1040-SR), line 16
N	Educational assistance benefits	See the Partner's Instructions
O	Dependent care benefits	Form 2441, line 12
P	Preproductive period expenses	See the Partner's Instructions
Q	Commercial revitalization deduction from rental real estate activities	See Form 8582 instructions
R	Pensions and IRAs	See the Partner's Instructions
S	Reforestation expense deduction	See the Partner's Instructions
T	through **U**	Reserved for future use
V	Section 743(b) negative adjustments	
W	Other deductions	See the Partner's Instructions
X	Section 965(c) deduction	

14. Self-employment earnings (loss)
Note: If you have a section 179 deduction or any partner-level deductions, see the Partner's Instructions before completing Schedule SE.

A	Net earnings (loss) from self-employment	Schedule SE, Section A or B
B	Gross farming or fishing income	See the Partner's Instructions
C	Gross non-farm income	See the Partner's Instructions

15. Credits

A	Low-income housing credit (section 42(j)(5)) from pre-2008 buildings	
B	Low-income housing credit (other) from pre-2008 buildings	
C	Low-income housing credit (section 42(j)(5)) from post-2007 buildings	See the Partner's Instructions
D	Low-income housing credit (other) from post-2007 buildings	
E	Qualified rehabilitation expenditures (rental real estate)	
F	Other rental real estate credits	
G	Other rental credits	

Code		*Report on*
H	Undistributed capital gains credit	Schedule 3 (Form 1040 or 1040-SR), line 13, box a
I	Biofuel producer credit	See the Partner's Instructions
J	Work opportunity credit	
K	Disabled access credit	
L	Empowerment zone employment credit	
M	Credit for increasing research activities	See the Partner's Instructions
N	Credit for employer social security and Medicare taxes	
O	Backup withholding	
P	Other credits	

16. Foreign transactions

A	Name of country or U.S. possession	
B	Gross income from all sources	Form 1116, Part I
C	Gross income sourced at partner level	

Foreign gross income sourced at partnership level

D	Reserved for future use	
E	Foreign branch category	
F	Passive category	Form 1116, Part I
G	General category	
H	Other	

Deductions allocated and apportioned at partner level

I	Interest expense	Form 1116, Part I
J	Other	Form 1116, Part I

Deductions allocated and apportioned at partnership level to foreign source income

K	Reserved for future use	
L	Foreign branch category	
M	Passive category	Form 1116, Part I
N	General category	
O	Other	

Other information

P	Total foreign taxes paid	Form 1116, Part II
Q	Total foreign taxes accrued	Form 1116, Part II
R	Reduction in taxes available for credit	Form 1116, line 12
S	Foreign trading gross receipts	Form 8873
T	Extraterritorial income exclusion	Form 8873
U	through **V**	Reserved for future use
W	Section 965 information	See the Partner's Instructions
X	Other foreign transactions	See the Partner's Instructions

17. Alternative minimum tax (AMT) items

A	Post-1986 depreciation adjustment	
B	Adjusted gain or loss	See the Partner's Instructions and the Instructions for Form 6251
C	Depletion (other than oil & gas)	
D	Oil, gas, & geothermal—gross income	
E	Oil, gas, & geothermal—deductions	
F	Other AMT items	

18. Tax-exempt income and nondeductible expenses

A	Tax-exempt interest income	Form 1040 or 1040-SR, line 2a
B	Other tax-exempt income	See the Partner's Instructions
C	Nondeductible expenses	See the Partner's Instructions

19. Distributions

A	Cash and marketable securities	
B	Distribution subject to section 737	See the Partner's Instructions
C	Other property	

20. Other information

A	Investment income	Form 4952, line 4a
B	Investment expenses	Form 4952, line 5
C	Fuel tax credit information	Form 4136
D	Qualified rehabilitation expenditures (other than rental real estate)	
E	Basis of energy property	See the Partner's Instructions
F	through **G**	
H	Recapture of investment credit	See Form 4255
I	Recapture of other credits	See the Partner's Instructions
J	Look-back interest—completed long-term contracts	See Form 8697
K	Look-back interest—income forecast method	See Form 8866
L	Dispositions of property with section 179 deductions	
M	Recapture of section 179 deduction	
N	Interest expense for corporate partners	
O	through **Y**	
Z	Section 199A information	
AA	Section 704(c) information	
AB	Section 751 gain (loss)	See the Partner's Instructions
AC	Section 1(h)(5) gain (loss)	
AD	Section 1250 unrecaptured gain	
AE	Excess taxable income	
AF	Excess business interest income	
AG	Gross receipts for section 59A(e)	
AH	Other information	

Form **1095-A**

Department of the Treasury
Internal Revenue Service

Health Insurance Marketplace Statement

☐ VOID

► **Do not attach to your tax return. Keep for your records.**
► **Go to www.irs.gov/Form1095A for instructions and the latest information.**

☐ CORRECTED

OMB No. 1545-2232

2019

Part I   Recipient Information

1 Marketplace identifier 31-1234567	2 Marketplace-assigned policy number A1000HT	3 Policy issuer's name Covered California	
4 Recipient's name Gregory R. Clifden		5 Recipient's SSN 543-88-9756	6 Recipient's date of birth 05/04/1976
7 Recipient's spouse's name Lulu B. Clifden		8 Recipient's spouse's SSN 256-43-8819	9 Recipient's spouse's date of birth 06/12/1977
10 Policy start date 05/01/2019	11 Policy termination date 12/31/2019	12 Street address (including apartment no.) 33333 Fume Blanc Way	
13 City or town Temecula	14 State or province CA	15 Country and ZIP or foreign postal code 92591	

Part II   Covered Individuals

	A. Covered individual name	B. Covered individual SSN	C. Covered individual date of birth	D. Coverage start date	E. Coverage termination date
16	Gregory R. Clifden	543-88-9756	05/04/1976	05/01/2019	12/31/2019
17	Lulu B. Clifden	256-43-8819	06/12/1977	05/01/2019	12/31/2019
18	Gerald Clifden	466-74-1131	04/16/2002	05/01/2019	12/31/2019
19	Gary Clifden	465-76-8375	12/02/2007	05/01/2019	12/31/2019
20	Glenn Clifden	475-23-1426	01/13/2009	05/01/2019	12/31/2019

Part III   Coverage Information

Month	A. Monthly enrollment premiums	B. Monthly second lowest cost silver plan (SLCSP) premium	C. Monthly advance payment of premium tax credit
21 January			
22 February			
23 March			
24 April			
25 May	1,533	1,621	0
26 June	1,533	1,621	0
27 July	1,533	1,621	0
28 August	1,533	1,621	0
29 September	1,533	1,621	0
30 October	1,533	1,621	0
31 November	1,533	1,621	0
32 December	1,533	1,621	0
33 **Annual Totals**	12,264	12,968	0

For Privacy Act and Paperwork Reduction Act Notice, see separate instructions.   Cat. No. 60703Q   Form **1095-A** (2019)

☐ CORRECTED (if checked)

PAYER'S name, street address, city or town, state or province, country, ZIP or foreign postal code, and phone no.	**1** Gross distribution $ 14,545.00	OMB No. 1545-0119 **20**19 Form **1099-R**	Distributions From Pensions, Annuities, Retirement or Profit-Sharing Plans, IRAs, Insurance Contracts, etc.
United States Navy Retired Benefits Center Cleveland, OH 43267	**2a** Taxable amount $ 14,545.00		
	2b Taxable amount not determined ☐ Total distribution ☐		**Copy B** **Report this income on your federal tax return.** If this form shows federal income tax withheld in box 4, attach this copy to your return.
PAYER'S TIN 11-4662891	RECIPIENT'S TIN 543-88-9765	**3** Capital gain (included in box 2a) $	**4** Federal income tax withheld $ 1,487.12	
RECIPIENT'S name Gregory R. Clifden	**5** Employee contributions/Designated Roth contributions or insurance premiums $	**6** Net unrealized appreciation in employer's securities $	
Street address (including apt. no.) 33333 Fume Blanc Way	**7** Distribution code(s) IRA/SEP/SIMPLE ☐	**8** Other $ %	This information is being furnished to the IRS.
City or town, state or province, country, and ZIP or foreign postal code Temecula, CA 92591	**9a** Your percentage of total distribution %	**9b** Total employee contributions $	
10 Amount allocable to IRR within 5 years $	**11** 1st year of desig. Roth contrib.	FATCA filing requirement ☐	**12** State tax withheld $ 350.00	**13** State/Payer's state no. CA	**14** State distribution $ 14,545.00
Account number (see instructions)	Date of payment	**15** Local tax withheld $	**16** Name of locality	**17** Local distribution $

Form **1099-R**   www.irs.gov/Form1099R   Department of the Treasury - Internal Revenue Service

☐ CORRECTED (if checked)

PAYER'S name, street address, city or town, state or province, country, ZIP or foreign postal code, and telephone no.	Applicable checkbox on Form 8949 A	OMB No. 1545-0715 **20**19 Form **1099-B**	Proceeds From Broker and Barter Exchange Transactions
Bear Stearns 269 Wall Street New York, NY 10001	**1a** Description of property (Example: 100 sh. XYZ Co.) Gold Company Common		
	1b Date acquired 03/27/2019	**1c** Date sold or disposed 09/18/2019	**Copy B** **For Recipient**
PAYER'S TIN 11-4396782	RECIPIENT'S TIN 256-43-8819	**1d** Proceeds $ 12,100.00	**1e** Cost or other basis $ 14,188.00	
	1f Accrued market discount $	**1g** Wash sale loss disallowed $	
RECIPIENT'S name Lulu B. Clifden	**2** Short-term gain or loss ☒ Long-term gain or loss ☐ Ordinary ☐	**3** If checked, proceeds from: Collectibles ☐ QOF ☐	This is important tax information and is being furnished to the IRS. If you are required to file a return, a negligence penalty or other sanction may be imposed on you if this income is taxable and the IRS determines that it has not been reported.
Street address (including apt. no.) 33333 Fume Blanc Way	**4** Federal income tax withheld $	**5** If checked, noncovered security ☐	
City or town, state or province, country, and ZIP or foreign postal code Temecula, CA 92591	**6** Reported to IRS: Gross proceeds ☐ Net proceeds ☒	**7** If checked, loss is not allowed based on amount in 1d ☐	
Account number (see instructions)	**8** Profit or (loss) realized in 2019 on closed contracts $	**9** Unrealized profit or (loss) on open contracts—12/31/2018 $	
CUSIP number	FATCA filing requirement ☐	**10** Unrealized profit or (loss) on open contracts—12/31/2019 $	**11** Aggregate profit or (loss) on contracts $	
14 State name	**15** State identification no.	**16** State tax withheld $ $	**12** If checked, basis reported to IRS ☒	**13** Bartering $

Form **1099-B**   (Keep for your records)   www.irs.gov/Form1099B   Department of the Treasury - Internal Revenue Service

☐ CORRECTED (if checked)

PAYER'S name, street address, city or town, state or province, country, ZIP or foreign postal code, and telephone no.	Payer's RTN (optional)	OMB No. 1545-0112 **20**19 Form **1099-INT**	**Interest Income**
Vintage Bank 6792 Main Street Temecula, CA 92591	**1** Interest income $ 1,403.80		
	2 Early withdrawal penalty $		**Copy B**
PAYER'S TIN 96-8724390	RECIPIENT'S TIN 543-88-9756	**3** Interest on U.S. Savings Bonds and Treas. obligations $	**For Recipient**
RECIPIENT'S name Gregory R. Clifden	**4** Federal income tax withheld $	**5** Investment expenses $	This is important tax information and is being furnished to the IRS. If you are required to file a return, a negligence penalty or other sanction may be imposed on you if this income is taxable and the IRS determines that it has not been reported.
	6 Foreign tax paid $	**7** Foreign country or U.S. possession	
Street address (including apt. no.) 33333 Fume Blanc Way	**8** Tax-exempt interest $	**9** Specified private activity bond interest $	
City or town, state or province, country, and ZIP or foreign postal code Temecula, CA 92591	**10** Market discount $	**11** Bond premium $	
	FATCA filing requirement ☐	**12** Bond premium on Treasury obligations $	**13** Bond premium on tax-exempt bond $	
Account number (see instructions)	**14** Tax-exempt and tax credit bond CUSIP no.	**15** State **16** State identification no.	**17** State tax withheld $ $

Form **1099-INT**   (keep for your records)   www.irs.gov/Form1099INT   Department of the Treasury - Internal Revenue Service

| Form **1040** | Department of the Treasury—Internal Revenue Service (99) **U.S. Individual Income Tax Return** | **2019** | OMB No. 1545-0074 | IRS Use Only—Do not write or staple in this space. |

Filing Status
Check only one box.

☐ Single   ☐ Married filing jointly   ☐ Married filing separately (MFS)   ☐ Head of household (HOH)   ☐ Qualifying widow(er) (QW)

If you checked the MFS box, enter the name of spouse. If you checked the HOH or QW box, enter the child's name if the qualifying person is a child but not your dependent. ▶

| Your first name and middle initial | Last name | Your social security number |

| If joint return, spouse's first name and middle initial | Last name | Spouse's social security number |

| Home address (number and street). If you have a P.O. box, see instructions. | Apt. no. | **Presidential Election Campaign** Check here if you, or your spouse if filing jointly, want $3 to go to this fund. Checking a box below will not change your tax or refund.   ☐ You   ☐ Spouse |

City, town or post office, state, and ZIP code. If you have a foreign address, also complete spaces below (see instructions).

| Foreign country name | Foreign province/state/county | Foreign postal code | If more than four dependents, see instructions and ✓ here ▶ ☐ |

Standard Deduction   Someone can claim: ☐ You as a dependent   ☐ Your spouse as a dependent

☐ Spouse itemizes on a separate return or you were a dual-status alien

Age/Blindness   **You:** ☐ Were born before January 2, 1955   ☐ Are blind   **Spouse:** ☐ Was born before January 2, 1955   ☐ Is blind

Dependents (see instructions):

(1) First name Last name	(2) Social security number	(3) Relationship to you	(4) ✓ if qualifies for (see instructions):	
			Child tax credit	Credit for other dependents
			☐	☐
			☐	☐
			☐	☐
			☐	☐

Standard Deduction for—
- Single or Married filing separately, $12,200
- Married filing jointly or Qualifying widow(er), $24,400
- Head of household, $18,350
- If you checked any box under *Standard Deduction,* see instructions.

1	Wages, salaries, tips, etc. Attach Form(s) W-2			1	
2a	Tax-exempt interest	2a	**b** Taxable interest. Attach Sch. B if required	2b	
3a	Qualified dividends	3a	**b** Ordinary dividends. Attach Sch. B if required	3b	
4a	IRA distributions	4a	**b** Taxable amount	4b	
c	Pensions and annuities	4c	**d** Taxable amount	4d	
5a	Social security benefits	5a	**b** Taxable amount	5b	
6	Capital gain or (loss). Attach Schedule D if required. If not required, check here ▶ ☐			6	
7a	Other income from Schedule 1, line 9			7a	
b	Add lines 1, 2b, 3b, 4b, 4d, 5b, 6, and 7a. This is your **total income** ▶			7b	
8a	Adjustments to income from Schedule 1, line 22			8a	
b	Subtract line 8a from line 7b. This is your **adjusted gross income** ▶			8b	
9	**Standard deduction or itemized deductions** (from Schedule A)	9			
10	Qualified business income deduction. Attach Form 8995 or Form 8995-A	10			
11a	Add lines 9 and 10			11a	
b	**Taxable income.** Subtract line 11a from line 8b			11b	

For Disclosure, Privacy Act, and Paperwork Reduction Act Notice, see separate instructions.   Cat. No. 11320B   Form **1040** (2019)

Form 1040 (2019)   Page **2**

12a	**Tax** (see inst.) Check if any from Form(s): **1** ☐ 8814 **2** ☐ 4972 **3** ☐ _____		**12a**			
b	Add Schedule 2, line 3, and line 12a and enter the total . . . . ▶				**12b**	
13a	Child tax credit or credit for other dependents		**13a**			
b	Add Schedule 3, line 7, and line 13a and enter the total . . . . ▶				**13b**	
14	Subtract line 13b from line 12b. If zero or less, enter -0-				**14**	
15	Other taxes, including self-employment tax, from Schedule 2, line 10				**15**	
16	Add lines 14 and 15. This is your **total tax** . . . . ▶				**16**	
17	Federal income tax withheld from Forms W-2 and 1099				**17**	
18	Other payments and refundable credits:					
a	Earned income credit (EIC)		**18a**			
b	Additional child tax credit. Attach Schedule 8812		**18b**			
c	American opportunity credit from Form 8863, line 8		**18c**			
d	Schedule 3, line 14		**18d**			
e	Add lines 18a through 18d. These are your **total other payments and refundable credits** . . . ▶				**18e**	
19	Add lines 17 and 18e. These are your **total payments** . . . . ▶				**19**	

• If you have a qualifying child, attach Sch. EIC.
• If you have nontaxable combat pay, see instructions.

Refund	**20**	If line 19 is more than line 16, subtract line 16 from line 19. This is the amount you **overpaid**				**20**	
	21a	Amount of line 20 you want **refunded to you.** If Form 8888 is attached, check here . . . . . ▶ ☐				**21a**	
Direct deposit? See instructions.	▶ **b**	Routing number		▶ **c** Type: ☐ Checking ☐ Savings			
	▶ **d**	Account number					
	22	Amount of line 20 you want **applied to your 2020 estimated tax** . . . . . ▶		**22**			
Amount You Owe	**23**	**Amount you owe.** Subtract line 19 from line 16. For details on how to pay, see instructions . . . . ▶				**23**	
	24	Estimated tax penalty (see instructions) . . . . ▶		**24**			

Third Party Designee	Do you want to allow another person (other than your paid preparer) to discuss this return with the IRS? See instructions.		☐ **Yes.** Complete below. ☐ **No**
(Other than paid preparer)	Designee's name ▶	Phone no. ▶	Personal identification number (PIN) ▶ ☐☐☐☐☐

Sign Here

Under penalties of perjury, I declare that I have examined this return and accompanying schedules and statements, and to the best of my knowledge and belief, they are true, correct, and complete. Declaration of preparer (other than taxpayer) is based on all information of which preparer has any knowledge.

Joint return? See instructions. Keep a copy for your records.

Your signature	Date	Your occupation	If the IRS sent you an Identity Protection PIN, enter it here (see inst.)
Spouse's signature. If a joint return, **both** must sign.	Date	Spouse's occupation	If the IRS sent your spouse an Identity Protection PIN, enter it here (see inst.)
Phone no.	Email address		

Paid Preparer Use Only	Preparer's name	Preparer's signature	Date	PTIN	Check if: ☐ 3rd Party Designee ☐ Self-employed
	Firm's name ▶			Phone no.	
	Firm's address ▶			Firm's EIN ▶	

Go to *www.irs.gov/Form1040* for instructions and the latest information.   Form **1040** (2019)

SCHEDULE 1
(Form 1040 or 1040-SR)

Department of the Treasury
Internal Revenue Service

Additional Income and Adjustments to Income

▶ Attach to Form 1040 or 1040-SR.
▶ Go to *www.irs.gov/Form1040* for instructions and the latest information.

OMB No. 1545-0074

2019

Attachment
Sequence No. **01**

Name(s) shown on Form 1040 or 1040-SR

Your social security number

Part I   Additional Income

1	Taxable refunds, credits, or offsets of state and local income taxes	1	
2a	Alimony received	2a	
b	Date of original divorce or separation agreement (see instructions) ▶		
3	Business income or (loss). Attach Schedule C	3	
4	Other gains or (losses). Attach Form 4797	4	
5	Rental real estate, royalties, partnerships, S corporations, trusts, etc. Attach Schedule E	5	
6	Farm income or (loss). Attach Schedule F	6	
7	Unemployment compensation	7	
8	Other income. List type and amount ▶		
		8	
9	Combine lines 1 through 8. Enter here and on Form 1040 or 1040-SR, line 7a	9	

Part II   Adjustments to Income

10	Educator expenses	10	
11	Certain business expenses of reservists, performing artists, and fee-basis government officials. Attach Form 2106	11	
12	Health savings account deduction. Attach Form 8889	12	
13	Moving expenses for members of the Armed Forces. Attach Form 3903	13	
14	Deductible part of self-employment tax. Attach Schedule SE	14	
15	Self-employed SEP, SIMPLE, and qualified plans	15	
16	Self-employed health insurance deduction	16	
17	Penalty on early withdrawal of savings	17	
18a	Alimony paid	18a	
b	Recipient's SSN ▶		
c	Date of original divorce or separation agreement (see instructions) ▶		
19	IRA deduction	19	
20	Student loan interest deduction	20	
21	Reserved for future use	21	
22	Add lines 10 through 21. These are your **adjustments to income.** Enter here and on Form 1040 or 1040-SR, line 8a	22	

For Paperwork Reduction Act Notice, see your tax return instructions.   Cat. No. 71479F   **Schedule 1 (Form 1040 or 1040-SR) 2019**

DRAFT AS OF July 11, 2019 DO NOT FILE

SCHEDULE 2
(Form 1040 or 1040-SR)

Department of the Treasury
Internal Revenue Service

Additional Taxes

▶ Attach to Form 1040 or 1040-SR.
▶ Go to *www.irs.gov/Form1040* for instructions and the latest information.

OMB No. 1545-0074

2019

Attachment
Sequence No. **02**

Name(s) shown on Form 1040 or 1040-SR

Your social security number

Part I	Tax		
1	Alternative minimum tax. Attach Form 6251	1	
2	Excess advance premium tax credit repayment. Attach Form 8962	2	
3	Add lines 1 and 2. Enter here and include on Form 1040 or 1040-SR, line 12b	3	

Part II	Other Taxes		
4	Self-employment tax. Attach Schedule SE	4	
5	Unreported social security and Medicare tax from Form: **a** ☐ 4137 **b** ☐ 8919	5	
6	Additional tax on IRAs, other qualified retirement plans, and other tax-favored accounts. Attach Form 5329 if required	6	
7a	Household employment taxes. Attach Schedule H	7a	
b	Repayment of first-time homebuyer credit from Form 5405. Attach Form 5405 if required . . .	7b	
8	Taxes from: **a** ☐ Form 8959 **b** ☐ Form 8960		
	c ☐ Instructions; enter code(s)	8	
9	Section 965 net tax liability installment from Form 965-A	9		
10	Add lines 4 through 8. These are your **total other taxes.** Enter here and on Form 1040 or 1040-SR, line 15	10	

For Paperwork Reduction Act Notice, see your tax return instructions.   Cat. No. 71478U   Schedule 2 (Form 1040 or 1040-SR) 2019

SCHEDULE 3
(Form 1040 or 1040-SR)

Department of the Treasury
Internal Revenue Service

Additional Credits and Payments

▶ Attach to Form 1040 or 1040-SR.
▶ Go to *www.irs.gov/Form1040* for instructions and the latest information.

OMB No. 1545-0074

2019

Attachment
Sequence No. **03**

Name(s) shown on Form 1040 or 1040-SR

Your social security number

Part I	Nonrefundable Credits	
1	Foreign tax credit. Attach Form 1116 if required	1
2	Credit for child and dependent care expenses. Attach Form 2441	2
3	Education credits from Form 8863, line 19	3
4	Retirement savings contributions credit. Attach Form 8880	4
5	Residential energy credit. Attach Form 5695	5
6	Other credits from Form: **a** ☐ 3800 **b** ☐ 8801 **c** ☐	6
7	Add lines 1 through 6. Enter here and include on Form 1040 or 1040-SR, line 13b	7

Part II	Other Payments and Refundable Credits	
8	2019 estimated tax payments and amount applied from 2018 return	8
9	Net premium tax credit. Attach Form 8962	9
10	Amount paid with request for extension to file (see instructions)	10
11	Excess social security and tier 1 RRTA tax withheld	11
12	Credit for federal tax on fuels. Attach Form 4136	12
13	Credits from Form: **a** ☐ 2439 **b** ☐ Reserved **c** ☐ 8885 **d** ☐	13
14	Add lines 8 through 13. Enter here and on Form 1040 or 1040-SR, line 18d	14

For Paperwork Reduction Act Notice, see your tax return instructions.   Cat. No. 71480G   Schedule 3 (Form 1040 or 1040-SR) 2019

SCHEDULE A
(Form 1040 or 1040-SR)

Department of the Treasury
Internal Revenue Service (99)

Itemized Deductions

▶ Go to *www.irs.gov/ScheduleA* for instructions and the latest information.
▶ **Attach to Form 1040 or 1040-SR.**

Caution: If you are claiming a net qualified disaster loss on Form 4684, see the instructions for line 16.

OMB No. 1545-0074

2019

Attachment
Sequence No. **07**

Name(s) shown on Form 1040 or 1040-SR

Your social security number

Medical and Dental Expenses	**Caution:** Do not include expenses reimbursed or paid by others.		
	1 Medical and dental expenses (see instructions)	**1**	
	2 Enter amount from Form 1040 or 1040-SR, line 8b **2**		
	3 Multiply line 2 by 10% (0.10)	**3**	
	4 Subtract line 3 from line 1. If line 3 is more than line 1, enter -0-		**4**
Taxes You Paid	5 State and local taxes.		
	a State and local income taxes or general sales taxes. You may include either income taxes or general sales taxes on line 5a, but not both. If you elect to include general sales taxes instead of income taxes, check this box . . . . ▶ ☐	**5a**	
	b State and local real estate taxes (see instructions)	**5b**	
	c State and local personal property taxes	**5c**	
	d Add lines 5a through 5c	**5d**	
	e Enter the smaller of line 5d or $10,000 ($5,000 if married filing separately)	**5e**	
	6 Other taxes. List type and amount ▶ _____	**6**	
	7 Add lines 5e and 6		**7**
Interest You Paid	8 Home mortgage interest and points. If you didn't use all of your home mortgage loan(s) to buy, build, or improve your home, see instructions and check this box . . . . ▶ ☐		
Caution: Your mortgage interest deduction may be limited (see instructions).	**a** Home mortgage interest and points reported to you on Form 1098. See instructions if limited	**8a**	
	b Home mortgage interest not reported to you on Form 1098. If paid to the person from whom you bought the home, see instructions and show that person's name, identifying no., and address . . . . . ▶ _____ _____	**8b**	
	c Points not reported to you on Form 1098. See instructions for special rules	**8c**	
	d Reserved	**8d**	
	e Add lines 8a through 8c	**8e**	
	9 Investment interest. Attach Form 4952 if required. See instructions	**9**	
	10 Add lines 8e and 9		**10**
Gifts to Charity	11 Gifts by cash or check. If you made any gift of $250 or more, see instructions	**11**	
Caution: If you made a gift and got a benefit for it, see instructions.	12 Other than by cash or check. If you made any gift of $250 or more, see instructions. You **must** attach Form 8283 if over $500. . . .	**12**	
	13 Carryover from prior year	**13**	
	14 Add lines 11 through 13		**14**
Casualty and Theft Losses	15 Casualty and theft loss(es) from a federally declared disaster (other than net qualified disaster losses). Attach Form 4684 and enter the amount from line 18 of that form. See instructions		**15**
Other Itemized Deductions	16 Other—from list in instructions. List type and amount ▶ _____ _____		**16**
Total Itemized Deductions	17 Add the amounts in the far right column for lines 4 through 16. Also, enter this amount on Form 1040 or 1040-SR, line 9		**17**
	18 If you elect to itemize deductions even though they are less than your standard deduction, check this box . . . . ▶ ☐		

For Paperwork Reduction Act Notice, see the Instructions for Forms 1040 and 1040-SR.   Cat. No. 17145C   **Schedule A (Form 1040 or 1040-SR) 2019**

DRAFT AS OF JULY 19, 2019 DO NOT FILE

SCHEDULE B
(Form 1040 or 1040-SR)

Department of the Treasury
Internal Revenue Service (99)

Interest and Ordinary Dividends

▶ Go to *www.irs.gov/ScheduleB* for instructions and the latest information.
▶ Attach to Form 1040 or 1040-SR.

OMB No. 1545-0074

2019

Attachment
Sequence No. **08**

Name(s) shown on return

Your social security number

DRAFT AS OF July 24, 2019 DO NOT FILE

Part I **Interest** (See instructions and the instructions for Forms 1040 and 1040-SR, line 2b.) **Note:** If you received a Form 1099-INT, Form 1099-OID, or substitute statement from a brokerage firm, list the firm's name as the payer and enter the total interest shown on that form.	**1**	List name of payer. If any interest is from a seller-financed mortgage and the buyer used the property as a personal residence, see the instructions and list this interest first. Also, show that buyer's social security number and address ▶		**Amount**
			1	
	2	Add the amounts on line 1	**2**	
	3	Excludable interest on series EE and I U.S. savings bonds issued after 1989. Attach Form 8815	**3**	
	4	Subtract line 3 from line 2. Enter the result here and on Form 1040 or 1040-SR, line 2b . . . . ▶	**4**	

Note: If line 4 is over $1,500, you must complete Part III.

Part II **Ordinary Dividends** (See instructions and the instructions for Forms 1040 and 1040-SR, line 3b.) **Note:** If you received a Form 1099-DIV or substitute statement from a brokerage firm, list the firm's name as the payer and enter the ordinary dividends shown on that form.	**5**	List name of payer ▶		**Amount**
			5	
	6	Add the amounts on line 5. Enter the total here and on Form 1040 or 1040-SR, line 3b . . . . ▶	**6**	

Note: If line 6 is over $1,500, you must complete Part III.

Part III **Foreign Accounts and Trusts** **Caution:** If required, failure to file FinCEN Form 114 may result in substantial penalties. See instructions.	You must complete this part if you **(a)** had over $1,500 of taxable interest or ordinary dividends; **(b)** had a foreign account; or **(c)** received a distribution from, or were a grantor of, or a transferor to, a foreign trust.	**Yes**	**No**
	7a At any time during 2019, did you have a financial interest in or signature authority over a financial account (such as a bank account, securities account, or brokerage account) located in a foreign country? See instructions		
	If "Yes," are you required to file FinCEN Form 114, Report of Foreign Bank and Financial Accounts (FBAR), to report that financial interest or signature authority? See FinCEN Form 114 and its instructions for filing requirements and exceptions to those requirements		
	b If you are required to file FinCEN Form 114, enter the name of the foreign country where the financial account is located ▶		
	8 During 2019, did you receive a distribution from, or were you the grantor of, or transferor to, a foreign trust? If "Yes," you may have to file Form 3520. See instructions		

For Paperwork Reduction Act Notice, see your tax return instructions.   Cat. No. 17146N   **Schedule B (Form 1040 or 1040-SR) 2019**

SCHEDULE C
(Form 1040 or 1040-SR)

Department of the Treasury
Internal Revenue Service (99)

Profit or Loss From Business
(Sole Proprietorship)

▶ Go to *www.irs.gov/ScheduleC* for instructions and the latest information.
▶ **Attach to Form 1040, 1040-SR, 1040-NR, or 1041; partnerships generally must file Form 1065.**

OMB No. 1545-0074

2019

Attachment
Sequence No. **09**

Name of proprietor

Social security number (SSN)

A Principal business or profession, including product or service (see instructions)	**B** Enter code from instructions ▶
C Business name. If no separate business name, leave blank.	**D** Employer ID number (EIN) (see instr.)

E Business address (including suite or room no.) ▶
City, town or post office, state, and ZIP code

F Accounting method: **(1)** ☐ Cash **(2)** ☐ Accrual **(3)** ☐ Other (specify) ▶

G Did you "materially participate" in the operation of this business during 2019? If "No," see instructions for limit on losses . ☐ Yes ☐ No

H If you started or acquired this business during 2019, check here . . . . ▶ ☐

I Did you make any payments in 2019 that would require you to file Form(s) 1099? (see instructions) . . . . . ☐ Yes ☐ No

J If "Yes," did you or will you file required Forms 1099? . . . . ☐ Yes ☐ No

Part I   Income

1	Gross receipts or sales. See instructions for line 1 and check the box if this income was reported to you on Form W-2 and the "Statutory employee" box on that form was checked . . . . ▶ ☐	**1**
2	Returns and allowances	**2**
3	Subtract line 2 from line 1	**3**
4	Cost of goods sold (from line 42)	**4**
5	**Gross profit.** Subtract line 4 from line 3	**5**
6	Other income, including federal and state gasoline or fuel tax credit or refund (see instructions) . .	**6**
7	**Gross income.** Add lines 5 and 6 . . . . ▶	**7**

Part II   Expenses. Enter expenses for business use of your home **only** on line 30.

8	Advertising	**8**	**18** Office expense (see instructions)	**18**	
9	Car and truck expenses (see instructions)	**9**	**19** Pension and profit-sharing plans .	**19**	
			20 Rent or lease (see instructions):		
10	Commissions and fees .	**10**	**a** Vehicles, machinery, and equipment	**20a**	
11	Contract labor (see instructions)	**11**	**b** Other business property . . .	**20b**	
12	Depletion	**12**	**21** Repairs and maintenance . . .	**21**	
13	Depreciation and section 179 expense deduction (not included in Part III) (see instructions)	**13**	**22** Supplies (not included in Part III) .	**22**	
			23 Taxes and licenses	**23**	
			24 Travel and meals:		
14	Employee benefit programs (other than on line 19) . .	**14**	**a** Travel	**24a**	
15	Insurance (other than health)	**15**	**b** Deductible meals (see instructions)	**24b**	
16	Interest (see instructions):		**25** Utilities	**25**	
a	Mortgage (paid to banks, etc.)	**16a**	**26** Wages (less employment credits) .	**26**	
b	Other	**16b**	**27a** Other expenses (from line 48) . .	**27a**	
17	Legal and professional services	**17**	**b** **Reserved for future use** . . .	**27b**	

28	**Total expenses** before expenses for business use of home. Add lines 8 through 27a . . . . . . ▶	**28**
29	Tentative profit or (loss). Subtract line 28 from line 7	**29**
30	Expenses for business use of your home. Do not report these expenses elsewhere. Attach Form 8829 unless using the simplified method (see instructions). **Simplified method filers only:** enter the total square footage of: (a) your home: _____ and (b) the part of your home used for business: _____ . Use the Simplified Method Worksheet in the instructions to figure the amount to enter on line 30	**30**
31	**Net profit or (loss).** Subtract line 30 from line 29. • If a profit, enter on both **Schedule 1 (Form 1040 or 1040-SR), line 3** (or **Form 1040-NR, line 13**) and on **Schedule SE, line 2.** (If you checked the box on line 1, see instructions). Estates and trusts, enter on **Form 1041, line 3.** • If a loss, you **must** go to line 32.	**31**
32	If you have a loss, check the box that describes your investment in this activity (see instructions). • If you checked 32a, enter the loss on both **Schedule 1 (Form 1040 or 1040-SR), line 3** (or **Form 1040-NR, line 13**) and on **Schedule SE, line 2.** (If you checked the box on line 1, see the line 31 instructions). Estates and trusts, enter on **Form 1041, line 3.** • If you checked 32b, you **must** attach **Form 6198.** Your loss may be limited.	**32a** ☐ All investment is at risk. **32b** ☐ Some investment is not at risk.

For Paperwork Reduction Act Notice, see the separate instructions.   Cat. No. 11334P   Schedule C (Form 1040 or 1040-SR) 2019

Schedule C (Form 1040 or 1040-SR) 2019   Page **2**

Part III   **Cost of Goods Sold** (see instructions)

33   Method(s) used to
value closing inventory: **a** ☐ Cost   **b** ☐ Lower of cost or market   **c** ☐ Other (attach explanation)

34   Was there any change in determining quantities, costs, or valuations between opening and closing inventory?
If "Yes," attach explanation . . . . ☐ Yes   ☐ No

35   Inventory at beginning of year. If different from last year's closing inventory, attach explanation . . . | 35 |

36   Purchases less cost of items withdrawn for personal use . . . . | 36 |

37   Cost of labor. Do not include any amounts paid to yourself . . . . | 37 |

38   Materials and supplies . . . . | 38 |

39   Other costs . . . . | 39 |

40   Add lines 35 through 39 . . . . | 40 |

41   Inventory at end of year . . . . | 41 |

42   **Cost of goods sold.** Subtract line 41 from line 40. Enter the result here and on line 4 . . . . . | 42 |

Part IV   **Information on Your Vehicle.** Complete this part **only** if you are claiming car or truck expenses on line 9 and are not required to file Form 4562 for this business. See the instructions for line 13 to find out if you must file Form 4562.

43   When did you place your vehicle in service for business purposes? (month, day, year)   ▶ _____ / _____ / _____

44   Of the total number of miles you drove your vehicle during 2019, enter the number of miles you used your vehicle for:

a   Business _____   **b** Commuting (see instructions) _____   **c** Other _____

45   Was your vehicle available for personal use during off-duty hours? . . . . ☐ Yes   ☐ No

46   Do you (or your spouse) have another vehicle available for personal use?. . . . . ☐ Yes   ☐ No

47a   Do you have evidence to support your deduction? . . . . ☐ Yes   ☐ No

b   If "Yes," is the evidence written? . . . . ☐ Yes   ☐ No

Part V   **Other Expenses.** List below business expenses not included on lines 8–26 or line 30.

-- | |
-- | |
-- | |
-- | |
-- | |
-- | |
-- | |
-- | |

48   **Total other expenses.** Enter here and on line 27a . . . . | 48 |

Schedule C (Form 1040 or 1040-SR) 2019

DRAFT AS OF August 7, 2019 DO NOT FILE

SCHEDULE D
(Form 1040 or 1040-SR)

Department of the Treasury
Internal Revenue Service (99)

Capital Gains and Losses

▶ Attach to Form 1040, 1040-SR, or 1040-NR.
▶ Go to *www.irs.gov/ScheduleD* for instructions and the latest information.
▶ Use Form 8949 to list your transactions for lines 1b, 2, 3, 8b, 9, and 10.

OMB No. 1545-0074

2019

Attachment
Sequence No. **12**

Name(s) shown on return

Your social security number

Did you dispose of any investment(s) in a qualified opportunity fund during the tax year? ☐ **Yes** ☐ **No**
If "Yes," attach Form 8949 and see its instructions for additional requirements for reporting your gain or loss.

Part I   **Short-Term Capital Gains and Losses—Generally Assets Held One Year or Less** (see instructions)

See instructions for how to figure the amounts to enter on the lines below. This form may be easier to complete if you round off cents to whole dollars.	**(d)** Proceeds (sales price)	**(e)** Cost (or other basis)	**(g)** Adjustments to gain or loss from Form(s) 8949, Part I, line 2, column (g)	**(h) Gain or (loss)** Subtract column (e) from column (d) and combine the result with column (g)
1a Totals for all short-term transactions reported on Form 1099-B for which basis was reported to the IRS and for which you have no adjustments (see instructions). However, if you choose to report all these transactions on Form 8949, leave this line blank and go to line 1b				
1b Totals for all transactions reported on Form(s) 8949 with **Box A** checked				
2 Totals for all transactions reported on Form(s) 8949 with **Box B** checked				
3 Totals for all transactions reported on Form(s) 8949 with **Box C** checked				

4 Short-term gain from Form 6252 and short-term gain or (loss) from Forms 4684, 6781, and 8824 . .	**4**	
5 Net short-term gain or (loss) from partnerships, S corporations, estates, and trusts from Schedule(s) K-1	**5**	
6 Short-term capital loss carryover. Enter the amount, if any, from line 8 of your **Capital Loss Carryover Worksheet** in the instructions	**6**	( )
7 **Net short-term capital gain or (loss).** Combine lines 1a through 6 in column (h). If you have any long-term capital gains or losses, go to Part II below. Otherwise, go to Part III on the back	**7**	

Part II   **Long-Term Capital Gains and Losses—Generally Assets Held More Than One Year** (see instructions)

See instructions for how to figure the amounts to enter on the lines below. This form may be easier to complete if you round off cents to whole dollars.	**(d)** Proceeds (sales price)	**(e)** Cost (or other basis)	**(g)** Adjustments to gain or loss from Form(s) 8949, Part II, line 2, column (g)	**(h) Gain or (loss)** Subtract column (e) from column (d) and combine the result with column (g)
8a Totals for all long-term transactions reported on Form 1099-B for which basis was reported to the IRS and for which you have no adjustments (see instructions). However, if you choose to report all these transactions on Form 8949, leave this line blank and go to line 8b .				
8b Totals for all transactions reported on Form(s) 8949 with **Box D** checked				
9 Totals for all transactions reported on Form(s) 8949 with **Box E** checked				
10 Totals for all transactions reported on Form(s) 8949 with **Box F** checked.				

11 Gain from Form 4797, Part I; long-term gain from Forms 2439 and 6252; and long-term gain or (loss) from Forms 4684, 6781, and 8824	**11**	
12 Net long-term gain or (loss) from partnerships, S corporations, estates, and trusts from Schedule(s) K-1	**12**	
13 Capital gain distributions. See the instructions	**13**	
14 Long-term capital loss carryover. Enter the amount, if any, from line 13 of your **Capital Loss Carryover Worksheet** in the instructions	**14**	( )
15 **Net long-term capital gain or (loss).** Combine lines 8a through 14 in column (h). Then go to Part III on the back	**15**	

For Paperwork Reduction Act Notice, see your tax return instructions.   Cat. No. 11338H   Schedule D (Form 1040 or 1040-SR) 2019

Part III   **Summary**

16   Combine lines 7 and 15 and enter the result **16**

- If line 16 is a **gain,** enter the amount from line 16 on Form 1040 or 1040-SR, line 6; or Form 1040-NR, line 14. Then go to line 17 below.
- If line 16 is a **loss,** skip lines 17 through 20 below. Then go to line 21. Also be sure to complete line 22.
- If line 16 is **zero,** skip lines 17 through 21 below and enter -0- on Form 1040 or 1040-SR, line 6; or Form 1040-NR, line 14. Then go to line 22.

17   Are lines 15 and 16 **both** gains?
☐ **Yes.** Go to line 18.
☐ **No.** Skip lines 18 through 21, and go to line 22.

18   If you are required to complete the **28% Rate Gain Worksheet** (see instructions), enter the amount, if any, from line 7 of that worksheet   . . . . ▶   **18**

19   If you are required to complete the **Unrecaptured Section 1250 Gain Worksheet** (see instructions), enter the amount, if any, from line 18 of that worksheet   . . . . ▶   **19**

20   Are lines 18 and 19 **both** zero or blank?
☐ **Yes.** Complete the **Qualified Dividends and Capital Gain Tax Worksheet** in the instructions for Forms 1040 and 1040-SR, line 12a (or in the instructions for Form 1040-NR, line 42). **Don't** complete lines 21 and 22 below.

☐ **No.** Complete the **Schedule D Tax Worksheet** in the instructions. **Don't** complete lines 21 and 22 below.

21   If line 16 is a loss, enter here and on Form 1040 or 1040-SR, line 6; or Form 1040-NR, line 14, the **smaller** of:

- The loss on line 16; or
- ($3,000), or if married filing separately, ($1,500)   } . . . .   **21** (   )

Note: When figuring which amount is smaller, treat both amounts as positive numbers.

22   Do you have qualified dividends on Form 1040 or 1040-SR, line 3a; or Form 1040-NR, line 10b?

☐ **Yes.** Complete the **Qualified Dividends and Capital Gain Tax Worksheet** in the instructions for Forms 1040 and 1040-SR, line 12a (or in the instructions for Form 1040-NR, line 42).

☐ **No.** Complete the rest of Form 1040, 1040-SR, or 1040-NR.

SCHEDULE E
(Form 1040 or 1040-SR)

Department of the Treasury
Internal Revenue Service (99)

Supplemental Income and Loss

(From rental real estate, royalties, partnerships, S corporations, estates, trusts, REMICs, etc.)

▶ Attach to Form 1040, 1040-SR, 1040-NR, or 1041.

▶ Go to *www.irs.gov/ScheduleE* for instructions and the latest information.

OMB No. 1545-0074

2019

Attachment
Sequence No. **13**

Name(s) shown on return

Your social security number

| **Part I** | **Income or Loss From Rental Real Estate and Royalties** | **Note:** If you are in the business of renting personal property, use **Schedule C** (see instructions). If you are an individual, report farm rental income or loss from **Form 4835** on page 2, line 40. |

A Did you make any payments in 2019 that would require you to file Form(s) 1099? (see instructions) . . . . ☐ Yes ☐ No

B If "Yes," did you or will you file required Forms 1099? . . . . ☐ Yes ☐ No

1a Physical address of each property (street, city, state, ZIP code)

A

B

C

1b Type of Property (from list below)	**2** For each rental real estate property listed above, report the number of fair rental and personal use days. Check the **QJV** box only if you meet the requirements to file as a qualified joint venture. See instructions.		Fair Rental Days	Personal Use Days	QJV
A		A			☐
B		B			☐
C		C			☐

Type of Property:

1 Single Family Residence   3 Vacation/Short-Term Rental   5 Land   7 Self-Rental

2 Multi-Family Residence   4 Commercial   6 Royalties 8 Other (describe)

Income:	**Properties:**		A	B	C
3	Rents received	**3**			
4	Royalties received	**4**			
Expenses:					
5	Advertising	**5**			
6	Auto and travel (see instructions)	**6**			
7	Cleaning and maintenance	**7**			
8	Commissions.	**8**			
9	Insurance	**9**			
10	Legal and other professional fees	**10**			
11	Management fees	**11**			
12	Mortgage interest paid to banks, etc. (see instructions)	**12**			
13	Other interest.	**13**			
14	Repairs.	**14**			
15	Supplies	**15**			
16	Taxes	**16**			
17	Utilities	**17**			
18	Depreciation expense or depletion	**18**			
19	Other (list) ▶ _____	**19**			
20	Total expenses. Add lines 5 through 19	**20**			
21	Subtract line 20 from line 3 (rents) and/or 4 (royalties). If result is a (loss), see instructions to find out if you must file **Form 6198**	**21**			
22	Deductible rental real estate loss after limitation, if any, on **Form 8582** (see instructions)	**22**	( )( )( )

23a	Total of all amounts reported on line 3 for all rental properties	**23a**	
b	Total of all amounts reported on line 4 for all royalty properties	**23b**	
c	Total of all amounts reported on line 12 for all properties	**23c**	
d	Total of all amounts reported on line 18 for all properties	**23d**	
e	Total of all amounts reported on line 20 for all properties	**23e**	

24	**Income.** Add positive amounts shown on line 21. **Do not** include any losses	**24**	
25	**Losses.** Add royalty losses from line 21 and rental real estate losses from line 22. Enter total losses here .	**25**	( )
26	**Total rental real estate and royalty income or (loss).** Combine lines 24 and 25. Enter the result here. If Parts II, III, IV, and line 40 on page 2 do not apply to you, also enter this amount on Schedule 1 (Form 1040 or 1040-SR), line 5, or Form 1040-NR, line 18. Otherwise, include this amount in the total on line 41 on page 2	**26**	

For Paperwork Reduction Act Notice, see the separate instructions.   Cat. No. 11344L   Schedule E (Form 1040 or 1040-SR) 2019

Schedule E (Form 1040 or 1040-SR) 2019

Attachment Sequence No. **13**

Page **2**

Name(s) shown on return. Do not enter name and social security number if shown on other side.	Your social security number

Caution: The IRS compares amounts reported on your tax return with amounts shown on Schedule(s) K-1.

Part II **Income or Loss From Partnerships and S Corporations** — **Note:** If you report a loss, receive a distribution, dispose of stock, or receive a loan repayment from an S corporation, you **must** check the box in column **(e)** on line 28 and attach the required basis computation. If you report a loss from an at-risk activity for which **any** amount is **not** at risk, you **must** check the box in column **(f)** on line 28 and attach **Form 6198** (see instructions).

27   Are you reporting any loss not allowed in a prior year due to the at-risk or basis limitations, a prior year unallowed loss from a passive activity (if that loss was not reported on Form 8582), or unreimbursed partnership expenses? If you answered "Yes," see instructions before completing this section . . . .   ☐ **Yes**   ☐ **No**

28	(a) Name	(b) Enter **P** for partnership; **S** for S corporation	(c) Check if foreign partnership	(d) Employer identification number	(e) Check if basis computation is required	(f) Check if any amount is not at risk
A			☐		☐	☐
B			☐		☐	☐
C			☐		☐	☐
D			☐		☐	☐

	Passive Income and Loss		Nonpassive Income and Loss		
	(g) Passive loss allowed (attach **Form 8582** if required)	(h) Passive income from **Schedule K-1**	(i) Nonpassive loss allowed (see **Schedule K-1**)	(j) Section 179 expense deduction from **Form 4562**	(k) Nonpassive income from **Schedule K-1**
A					
B					
C					
D					
29a Totals					
b Totals					

30	Add columns (h) and (k) of line 29a.	30	
31	Add columns (g), (i), and (j) of line 29b.	31	( )
32	**Total partnership and S corporation income or (loss).** Combine lines 30 and 31	32	

Part III **Income or Loss From Estates and Trusts**

33	(a) Name	(b) Employer identification number
A		
B		

	Passive Income and Loss		Nonpassive Income and Loss	
	(c) Passive deduction or loss allowed (attach **Form 8582** if required)	(d) Passive income from **Schedule K-1**	(e) Deduction or loss from **Schedule K-1**	(f) Other income from **Schedule K-1**
A				
B				
34a Totals				
b Totals				

35	Add columns (d) and (f) of line 34a	35	
36	Add columns (c) and (e) of line 34b	36	( )
37	**Total estate and trust income or (loss).** Combine lines 35 and 36	37	

Part IV **Income or Loss From Real Estate Mortgage Investment Conduits (REMICs)—Residual Holder**

38	(a) Name	(b) Employer identification number	(c) Excess inclusion from **Schedules Q,** line 2c (see instructions)	(d) Taxable income (net loss) from **Schedules Q,** line 1b	(e) Income from **Schedules Q,** line 3b

39	Combine columns (d) and (e) only. Enter the result here and include in the total on line 41 below	39	

Part V **Summary**

40	Net farm rental income or (loss) from **Form 4835.** Also, complete line 42 below	40	
41	Total income or (loss). Combine lines 26, 32, 37, 39, and 40. Enter the result here and on Schedule 1 (Form 1040 or 1040-SR), line 5, or Form 1040-NR, line 18 ▶	41	

42   **Reconciliation of farming and fishing income.** Enter your **gross** farming and fishing income reported on Form 4835, line 7; Schedule K-1 (Form 1065), box 14, code B; Schedule K-1 (Form 1120-S), box 17, code AC; and Schedule K-1 (Form 1041), box 14, code F (see instructions) . | 42 |

43   **Reconciliation for real estate professionals.** If you were a real estate professional (see instructions), enter the net income or (loss) you reported anywhere on Form 1040, Form 1040-SR, or Form 1040-NR from all rental real estate activities in which you materially participated under the passive activity loss rules . . . . | 43 |

Schedule E (Form 1040 or 1040-SR) 2019

SCHEDULE SE
(Form 1040 or 1040-SR)

Department of the Treasury
Internal Revenue Service (99)

Self-Employment Tax

▶ Go to *www.irs.gov/ScheduleSE* for instructions and the latest information.
▶ Attach to Form 1040, 1040-SR, or 1040-NR.

OMB No. 1545-0074

2019

Attachment
Sequence No. **17**

Name of person with self-employment income (as shown on Form 1040, 1040-SR, or 1040-NR)

Social security number of person
with **self-employment** income ▶

Before you begin: To determine if you must file Schedule SE, see the instructions.

May I Use Short Schedule SE or Must I Use Long Schedule SE?

Note: Use this flowchart **only if** you must file Schedule SE. If unsure, see *Who Must File Schedule SE* in the instructions.

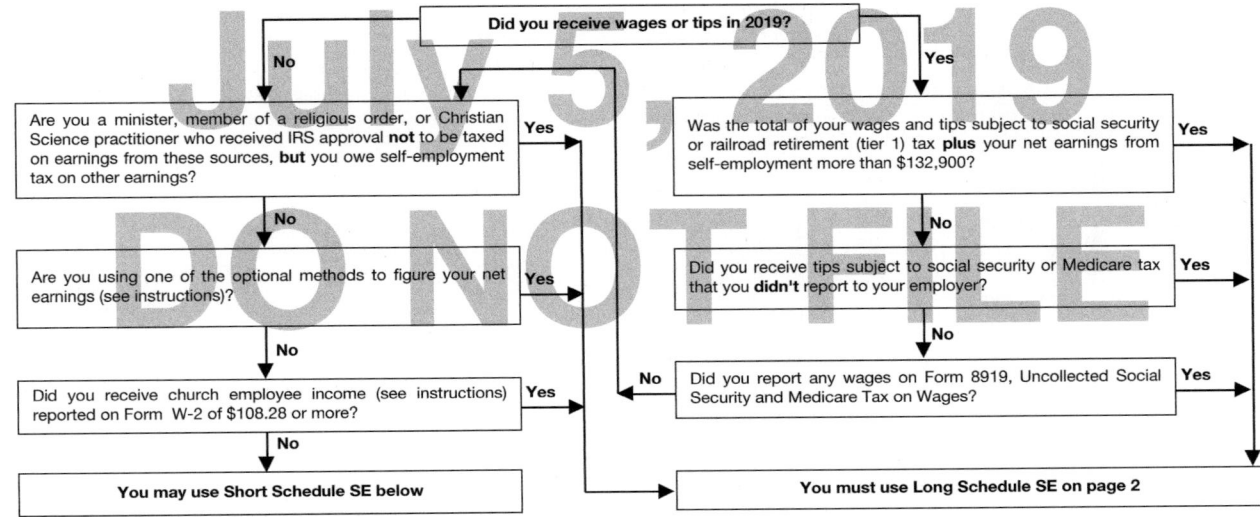

Section A—Short Schedule SE. Caution: Read above to see if you can use Short Schedule SE.

1a	Net farm profit or (loss) from Schedule F, line 34, and farm partnerships, Schedule K-1 (Form 1065), box 14, code A	**1a**
b	If you received social security retirement or disability benefits, enter the amount of Conservation Reserve Program payments included on Schedule F, line 4b, or listed on Schedule K-1 (Form 1065), box 20, code AH	**1b** ( )
2	Net profit or (loss) from Schedule C, line 31; and Schedule K-1 (Form 1065), box 14, code A (other than farming). Ministers and members of religious orders, see instructions for types of income to report on this line. See instructions for other income to report	**2**
3	Combine lines 1a, 1b, and 2	**3**
4	Multiply line 3 by 92.35% (0.9235). If less than $400, you don't owe self-employment tax; **don't** file this schedule unless you have an amount on line 1b . . . . ▶	**4**
	Note: If line 4 is less than $400 due to Conservation Reserve Program payments on line 1b, see instructions.	
5	**Self-employment tax.** If the amount on line 4 is:	
	• $132,900 or less, multiply line 4 by 15.3% (0.153). Enter the result here and on **Schedule 2 (Form 1040 or 1040-SR), line 4,** or **Form 1040-NR, line 55.**	
	• More than $132,900, multiply line 4 by 2.9% (0.029). Then, add $16,479.60 to the result. Enter the total here and on **Schedule 2 (Form 1040 or 1040-SR), line 4,** or **Form 1040-NR, line 55** .	**5**
6	**Deduction for one-half of self-employment tax.** Multiply line 5 by 50% (0.50). Enter the result here and on **Schedule 1 (Form 1040 or 1040-SR), line 14,** or **Form 1040-NR, line 27**	**6**

For Paperwork Reduction Act Notice, see your tax return instructions.   Cat. No. 11358Z   Schedule SE (Form 1040 or 1040-SR) 2019

Form **2441**

Child and Dependent Care Expenses

▶ Attach to Form 1040, 1040-SR, or 1040-NR.

▶ Go to *www.irs.gov/Form2441* for instructions and the latest information.

Department of the Treasury
Internal Revenue Service (99)

OMB No. 1545-0074

20**19**

Attachment Sequence No. **21**

Name(s) shown on return

Your social security number

You cannot claim a credit for child and dependent care expenses if your filing status is married filing separately unless you meet the requirements listed in the instructions under "Married Persons Filing Separately." If you meet these requirements, check this box. ☐

Part I **Persons or Organizations Who Provided the Care—**You **must** complete this part.
(If you have more than two care providers, see the instructions.)

1	(a) Care provider's name	(b) Address (number, street, apt. no., city, state, and ZIP code)	(c) Identifying number (SSN or EIN)	(d) Amount paid (see instructions)

Did you receive **dependent care benefits?**

No ——▶ Complete only Part II below.

Yes ——▶ Complete Part III on the back next.

Caution: If the care was provided in your home, you may owe employment taxes. For details, see the instructions for Schedule 2 (Form 1040 or 1040-SR), line 7a; or Form 1040-NR, line 59a.

Part II **Credit for Child and Dependent Care Expenses**

2 Information about your **qualifying person(s)**. If you have more than two qualifying persons, see the instructions.

(a) Qualifying person's name		(b) Qualifying person's social security number	(c) Qualified expenses you incurred and paid in 2019 for the person listed in column (a)
First	Last		

3	Add the amounts in column (c) of line 2. **Don't** enter more than $3,000 for one qualifying person or $6,000 for two or more persons. If you completed Part III, enter the amount from line 31 . .	**3**	
4	Enter your **earned income.** See instructions	**4**	
5	If married filing jointly, enter your spouse's earned income (if you or your spouse was a student or was disabled, see the instructions); **all others,** enter the amount from line 4	**5**	
6	Enter the **smallest** of line 3, 4, or 5	**6**	
7	Enter the amount from Form 1040 or 1040-SR, line 8b; or Form 1040-NR, line 35 . . . . **7**		
8	Enter on line 8 the decimal amount shown below that applies to the amount on line 7		

If line 7 is:			If line 7 is:		
Over	But not over	Decimal amount is	Over	But not over	Decimal amount is
$0—15,000		.35	$29,000—31,000		.27
15,000—17,000		.34	31,000—33,000		.26
17,000—19,000		.33	33,000—35,000		.25
19,000—21,000		.32	35,000—37,000		.24
21,000—23,000		.31	37,000—39,000		.23
23,000—25,000		.30	39,000—41,000		.22
25,000—27,000		.29	41,000—43,000		.21
27,000—29,000		.28	43,000—No limit		.20

8   X.

9	Multiply line 6 by the decimal amount on line 8. If you paid 2018 expenses in 2019, see the instructions	**9**	
10	Tax liability limit. Enter the amount from the Credit Limit Worksheet in the instructions **10**		
11	**Credit for child and dependent care expenses.** Enter the **smaller** of line 9 or line 10 here and on Schedule 3 (Form 1040 or 1040-SR), line 2; or Form 1040-NR, line 47	**11**	

For Paperwork Reduction Act Notice, see your tax return instructions.   Cat. No. 11862M   Form **2441** (2019)

DRAFT AS OF September 6, 2019 DO NOT FILE

Form **4562**	**Depreciation and Amortization**	OMB No. 1545-0172
	(Including Information on Listed Property)	**2019**
Department of the Treasury Internal Revenue Service (99)	▶ Attach to your tax return. ▶ Go to *www.irs.gov/Form4562* for instructions and the latest information.	Attachment Sequence No. **179**

Name(s) shown on return	Business or activity to which this form relates	Identifying number

Part I   **Election To Expense Certain Property Under Section 179**

Note: If you have any listed property, complete Part V before you complete Part I.

1	Maximum amount (see instructions)	1
2	Total cost of section 179 property placed in service (see instructions)	2
3	Threshold cost of section 179 property before reduction in limitation (see instructions)	3
4	Reduction in limitation. Subtract line 3 from line 2. If zero or less, enter -0-	4
5	Dollar limitation for tax year. Subtract line 4 from line 1. If zero or less, enter -0-. If married filing separately, see instructions	5

6	**(a)** Description of property	**(b)** Cost (business use only)	**(c)** Elected cost

7	Listed property. Enter the amount from line 29	**7**
8	Total elected cost of section 179 property. Add amounts in column (c), lines 6 and 7	8
9	Tentative deduction. Enter the **smaller** of line 5 or line 8	9
10	Carryover of disallowed deduction from line 13 of your 2018 Form 4562	10
11	Business income limitation. Enter the smaller of business income (not less than zero) or line 5. See instructions	11
12	Section 179 expense deduction. Add lines 9 and 10, but don't enter more than line 11	12
13	Carryover of disallowed deduction to 2020. Add lines 9 and 10, less line 12 ▶	**13**

Note: Don't use Part II or Part III below for listed property. Instead, use Part V.

Part II   **Special Depreciation Allowance and Other Depreciation (Don't** include listed property. See instructions.)

14	Special depreciation allowance for qualified property (other than listed property) placed in service during the tax year. See instructions	14
15	Property subject to section 168(f)(1) election	15
16	Other depreciation (including ACRS)	16

Part III   **MACRS Depreciation (Don't** include listed property. See instructions.)

Section A

17	MACRS deductions for assets placed in service in tax years beginning before 2019	**17**
18	If you are electing to group any assets placed in service during the tax year into one or more general asset accounts, check here . . . . ▶ ☐	

Section B—Assets Placed in Service During 2019 Tax Year Using the General Depreciation System

(a) Classification of property	(b) Month and year placed in service	(c) Basis for depreciation (business/investment use only—see instructions)	(d) Recovery period	(e) Convention	(f) Method	(g) Depreciation deduction
19a 3-year property						
b 5-year property						
c 7-year property						
d 10-year property						
e 15-year property						
f 20-year property						
g 25-year property			25 yrs.		S/L	
h Residential rental property			27.5 yrs.	MM	S/L	
			27.5 yrs.	MM	S/L	
i Nonresidential real property			39 yrs.	MM	S/L	
				MM	S/L	

Section C—Assets Placed in Service During 2019 Tax Year Using the Alternative Depreciation System

20a Class life					S/L	
b 12-year			12 yrs.		S/L	
c 30-year			30 yrs.	MM	S/L	
d 40-year			40 yrs.	MM	S/L	

Part IV   **Summary** (See instructions.)

21	Listed property. Enter amount from line 28	**21**
22	**Total.** Add amounts from line 12, lines 14 through 17, lines 19 and 20 in column (g), and line 21. Enter here and on the appropriate lines of your return. Partnerships and S corporations—see instructions .	**22**
23	For assets shown above and placed in service during the current year, enter the portion of the basis attributable to section 263A costs	**23**

For Paperwork Reduction Act Notice, see separate instructions.   Cat. No. 12906N   Form **4562** (2019)

Form 4562 (2019)   Page **2**

Part V   Listed Property   (Include automobiles, certain other vehicles, certain aircraft, and property used for entertainment, recreation, or amusement.)

Note: For any vehicle for which you are using the standard mileage rate or deducting lease expense, complete **only** 24a, 24b, columns (a) through (c) of Section A, all of Section B, and Section C if applicable.

Section A—Depreciation and Other Information (Caution: See the instructions for limits for passenger automobiles.)

24a Do you have evidence to support the business/investment use claimed? ☐ Yes ☐ No **24b** If "Yes," is the evidence written? ☐ Yes ☐ No

(a) Type of property (list vehicles first)	(b) Date placed in service	(c) Business/investment use percentage	(d) Cost or other basis	(e) Basis for depreciation (business/investment use only)	(f) Recovery period	(g) Method/ Convention	(h) Depreciation deduction	(i) Elected section 179 cost
25 Special depreciation allowance for qualified listed property placed in service during the tax year and used more than 50% in a qualified business use. See instructions . **25**								
26 Property used more than 50% in a qualified business use:								
		%						
		%						
		%						
27 Property used 50% or less in a qualified business use:								
		%				S/L –		
		%				S/L –		
		%				S/L –		
28 Add amounts in column (h), lines 25 through 27. Enter here and on line 21, page 1 . **28**								
29 Add amounts in column (i), line 26. Enter here and on line 7, page 1 . . . . **29**								

Section B—Information on Use of Vehicles

Complete this section for vehicles used by a sole proprietor, partner, or other "more than 5% owner," or related person. If you provided vehicles to your employees, first answer the questions in Section C to see if you meet an exception to completing this section for those vehicles.

	(a) Vehicle 1		(b) Vehicle 2		(c) Vehicle 3		(d) Vehicle 4		(e) Vehicle 5		(f) Vehicle 6	
30 Total business/investment miles driven during the year (**don't** include commuting miles) .												
31 Total commuting miles driven during the year												
32 Total other personal (noncommuting) miles driven												
33 Total miles driven during the year. Add lines 30 through 32												
34 Was the vehicle available for personal use during off-duty hours?	Yes	No	Yes	No	Yes	No	Yes	No	Yes	No	Yes	No
35 Was the vehicle used primarily by a more than 5% owner or related person? . . .												
36 Is another vehicle available for personal use?												

Section C—Questions for Employers Who Provide Vehicles for Use by Their Employees

Answer these questions to determine if you meet an exception to completing Section B for vehicles used by employees who **aren't** more than 5% owners or related persons. See instructions.

		Yes	No
37	Do you maintain a written policy statement that prohibits all personal use of vehicles, including commuting, by your employees?		
38	Do you maintain a written policy statement that prohibits personal use of vehicles, except commuting, by your employees? See the instructions for vehicles used by corporate officers, directors, or 1% or more owners . .		
39	Do you treat all use of vehicles by employees as personal use?		
40	Do you provide more than five vehicles to your employees, obtain information from your employees about the use of the vehicles, and retain the information received?		
41	Do you meet the requirements concerning qualified automobile demonstration use? See instructions.		

Note: If your answer to 37, 38, 39, 40, or 41 is "Yes," don't complete Section B for the covered vehicles.

Part VI   Amortization

(a) Description of costs	(b) Date amortization begins	(c) Amortizable amount	(d) Code section	(e) Amortization period or percentage	(f) Amortization for this year
42 Amortization of costs that begins during your 2019 tax year (see instructions):					
43 Amortization of costs that began before your 2019 tax year **43**					
44 **Total.** Add amounts in column (f). See the instructions for where to report **44**					

Form **4562** (2019)

SCHEDULE 8812	**Additional Child Tax Credit**		OMB No. 1545-0074
(Form 1040 or 1040-SR)	▶ Attach to Form 1040, 1040-SR, or 1040-NR.	1040 / 1040-SR / 8812	**2019**
Department of the Treasury Internal Revenue Service (99)	▶ Go to *www.irs.gov/Schedule8812* for instructions and the latest information.		Attachment Sequence No. **47**

Name(s) shown on return / Your social security number

Part I   All Filers

Caution: If you file Form 2555, **stop here;** you cannot claim the additional child tax credit.

1 If you are required to use the worksheet in Pub. 972, enter the amount from line 10 of the Child Tax Credit and Credit for Other Dependents Worksheet in the publication. Otherwise:

1040 and 1040-SR filers: Enter the amount from line 8 of your Child Tax Credit and Credit for Other Dependents Worksheet (see the instructions for Forms 1040 and 1040-SR, line 13a).

1040-NR filers: Enter the amount from line 8 of your Child Tax Credit and Credit for Other Dependents Worksheet (see the instructions for Form 1040-NR, line 49). ... **1**

2 Enter the amount from Form 1040, line 13a; Form 1040-SR, line 13a; or Form 1040-NR, line 49 ..... **2**

3 Subtract line 2 from line 1. If zero, **stop here;** you cannot claim this credit ... **3**

4 Number of qualifying children under 17 with the required social security number: _____ x $1,400.
Enter the result. If zero, **stop here;** you cannot claim this credit ... **4**

TIP: The number of children you use for this line is the same as the number of children you used for line 1 of the Child Tax Credit and Credit for Other Dependents Worksheet.

5 Enter the **smaller** of line 3 or line 4 ... **5**

6a Earned income (see instructions) ... **6a**

b Nontaxable combat pay (see instructions) ... **6b**

7 Is the amount on line 6a more than $2,500?
☐ **No.** Leave line 7 blank and enter -0- on line 8.
☐ **Yes.** Subtract $2,500 from the amount on line 6a. Enter the result ... **7**

8 Multiply the amount on line 7 by 15% (0.15) and enter the result ... **8**

Next. On line 4, is the amount $4,200 or more?
☐ **No.** If line 8 is zero, **stop here;** you cannot claim this credit. Otherwise, skip Part II and enter the **smaller** of line 5 or line 8 on line 15.
☐ **Yes.** If line 8 is equal to or more than line 5, skip Part II and enter the amount from line 5 on line 15. Otherwise, go to line 9.

Part II   Certain Filers Who Have Three or More Qualifying Children

9 Withheld social security, Medicare, and Additional Medicare taxes from Form(s) W-2, boxes 4 and 6. If married filing jointly, include your spouse's amounts with yours. If your employer withheld or you paid Additional Medicare Tax or tier 1 RRTA taxes, see instructions ... **9**

10 **1040 and 1040-SR filers:** Enter the total of the amounts from Schedule 1 (Form 1040 or 1040-SR), line 14, and Schedule 2 (Form 1040 or 1040-SR), line 5, plus any taxes that you identified using code "UT" and entered on Schedule 2 (Form 1040 or 1040-SR), line 8.

1040-NR filers: Enter the total of the amounts from Form 1040-NR, lines 27 and 56, plus any taxes that you identified using code "UT" and entered on line 60. **10**

11 Add lines 9 and 10 ... **11**

12 **1040 and 1040-SR filers:** Enter the total of the amounts from Form 1040 or 1040-SR, line 18a, and Schedule 3 (Form 1040 or 1040-SR), line 11.
1040-NR filers: Enter the amount from Form 1040-NR, line 67. **12**

13 Subtract line 12 from line 11. If zero or less, enter -0- ... **13**

14 Enter the **larger** of line 8 or line 13 ... **14**
Next, enter the **smaller** of line 5 or line 14 on line 15.

Part III   Additional Child Tax Credit

15 **This is your additional child tax credit** ... **15**

Enter this amount on
Form 1040, line 18b;
Form 1040-SR, line 18b; or
Form 1040-NR, line 64.

1040 / 1040-SR ◀

For Paperwork Reduction Act Notice, see your tax return instructions.   Cat. No. 59761M   Schedule 8812 (Form 1040 or 1040-SR) 2019

DRAFT AS OF July 17, 2019 DO NOT FILE

Form **8949**

Department of the Treasury
Internal Revenue Service

Sales and Other Dispositions of Capital Assets

▶ Go to *www.irs.gov/Form8949* for instructions and the latest information.
▶ File with your Schedule D to list your transactions for lines 1b, 2, 3, 8b, 9, and 10 of Schedule D.

OMB No. 1545-0074

2019

Attachment
Sequence No. **12A**

Name(s) shown on return

Social security number or taxpayer identification number

Before you check Box A, B, or C below, see whether you received any Form(s) 1099-B or substitute statement(s) from your broker. A substitute statement will have the same information as Form 1099-B. Either will show whether your basis (usually your cost) was reported to the IRS by your broker and may even tell you which box to check.

Part I **Short-Term.** Transactions involving capital assets you held 1 year or less are generally short-term (see instructions). For long-term transactions, see page 2.

Note: You may aggregate all short-term transactions reported on Form(s) 1099-B showing basis was reported to the IRS and for which no adjustments or codes are required. Enter the totals directly on Schedule D, line 1a; you aren't required to report these transactions on Form 8949 (see instructions).

You *must* check Box A, B, *or* C below. Check only one box. If more than one box applies for your short-term transactions, complete a separate Form 8949, page 1, for each applicable box. If you have more short-term transactions than will fit on this page for one or more of the boxes, complete as many forms with the same box checked as you need.

- ☐ **(A)** Short-term transactions reported on Form(s) 1099-B showing basis was reported to the IRS (see **Note** above)
- ☐ **(B)** Short-term transactions reported on Form(s) 1099-B showing basis **wasn't** reported to the IRS
- ☐ **(C)** Short-term transactions not reported to you on Form 1099-B

1 (a) Description of property (Example: 100 sh. XYZ Co.)	(b) Date acquired (Mo., day, yr.)	(c) Date sold or disposed of (Mo., day, yr.)	(d) Proceeds (sales price) (see instructions)	(e) Cost or other basis. See the **Note** below and see *Column (e)* in the separate instructions	Adjustment, if any, to gain or loss. If you enter an amount in column (g), enter a code in column (f). See the separate instructions.		(h) Gain or (loss). Subtract column (e) from column (d) and combine the result with column (g)
					(f) Code(s) from instructions	(g) Amount of adjustment	

2 Totals. Add the amounts in columns (d), (e), (g), and (h) (subtract negative amounts). Enter each total here and include on your Schedule D, **line 1b** (if **Box A** above is checked), **line 2** (if **Box B** above is checked), or **line 3** (if **Box C** above is checked) ▶

Note: If you checked Box A above but the basis reported to the IRS was incorrect, enter in column (e) the basis as reported to the IRS, and enter an adjustment in column (g) to correct the basis. See *Column (g)* in the separate instructions for how to figure the amount of the adjustment.

For Paperwork Reduction Act Notice, see your tax return instructions.   Cat. No. 37768Z   Form **8949** (2019)

Form 8949 (2019)   Attachment Sequence No. **12A**   Page **2**

Name(s) shown on return. Name and SSN or taxpayer identification no. not required if shown on other side	Social security number or taxpayer identification number

Before you check Box D, E, or F below, see whether you received any Form(s) 1099-B or substitute statement(s) from your broker. A substitute statement will have the same information as Form 1099-B. Either will show whether your basis (usually your cost) was reported to the IRS by your broker and may even tell you which box to check.

Part II   Long-Term. Transactions involving capital assets you held more than 1 year are generally long-term (see instructions). For short-term transactions, see page 1.

Note: You may aggregate all long-term transactions reported on Form(s) 1099-B showing basis was reported to the IRS and for which no adjustments or codes are required. Enter the totals directly on Schedule D, line 8a; you aren't required to report these transactions on Form 8949 (see instructions).

You *must* check Box D, E, *or* F below. Check only one box. If more than one box applies for your long-term transactions, complete a separate Form 8949, page 2, for each applicable box. If you have more long-term transactions than will fit on this page for one or more of the boxes, complete as many forms with the same box checked as you need.

☐ **(D)** Long-term transactions reported on Form(s) 1099-B showing basis was reported to the IRS (see **Note** above)

☐ **(E)** Long-term transactions reported on Form(s) 1099-B showing basis **wasn't** reported to the IRS

☐ **(F)** Long-term transactions not reported to you on Form 1099-B

1

(a) Description of property (Example: 100 sh. XYZ Co.)	(b) Date acquired (Mo., day, yr.)	(c) Date sold or disposed of (Mo., day, yr.)	(d) Proceeds (sales price) (see instructions)	(e) Cost or other basis. See the **Note** below and see *Column (e)* in the separate instructions	Adjustment, if any, to gain or loss. If you enter an amount in column (g), enter a code in column (f). See the separate instructions.		(h) Gain or (loss). Subtract column (e) from column (d) and combine the result with column (g)
					(f) Code(s) from instructions	(g) Amount of adjustment	
2 Totals. Add the amounts in columns (d), (e), (g), and (h) (subtract negative amounts). Enter each total here and include on your Schedule D, **line 8b** (if **Box D** above is checked), **line 9** (if **Box E** above is checked), or **line 10** (if **Box F** above is checked) ▶							

Note: If you checked Box D above but the basis reported to the IRS was incorrect, enter in column (e) the basis as reported to the IRS, and enter an adjustment in column (g) to correct the basis. See *Column (g)* in the separate instructions for how to figure the amount of the adjustment.

Form **8949** (2019)

Form **8962**

Department of the Treasury
Internal Revenue Service

Premium Tax Credit (PTC)

▶ Attach to Form 1040, 1040-SR, or 1040-NR.
▶ Go to *www.irs.gov/Form8962* for instructions and the latest information.

OMB No. 1545-0074

2019

Attachment
Sequence No. **73**

Name shown on your return

Your social security number

You cannot take the PTC if your filing status is married filing separately unless you qualify for an exception (see instructions). If you qualify, check the box   ▶ ☐

Part I	**Annual and Monthly Contribution Amount**	
1	Tax family size. Enter your tax family size (see instructions)	**1**
2a	Modified AGI. Enter your modified AGI (see instructions)	**2a**
b	Enter the total of your dependents' modified AGI (see instructions)	**2b**
3	Household income. Add the amounts on lines 2a and 2b (see instructions)	**3**
4	Federal poverty line. Enter the federal poverty line amount from Table 1-1, 1-2, or 1-3 (see instructions). Check the appropriate box for the federal poverty table used. **a** ☐ Alaska **b** ☐ Hawaii **c** ☐ Other 48 states and DC	**4**
5	Household income as a percentage of federal poverty line (see instructions)	**5** %
6	Did you enter 401% on line 5? (See instructions if you entered less than 100%.)	
	☐ **No.** Continue to line 7.	
	☐ **Yes.** You are not eligible to take the PTC. If advance payment of the PTC was made, see the instructions for how to report your excess advance PTC repayment amount.	
7	Applicable Figure. Using your line 5 percentage, locate your "applicable figure" on the table in the instructions . .	**7**
8a	Annual contribution amount. Multiply line 3 by line 7. Round to nearest whole dollar amount **8a**	**b** Monthly contribution amount. Divide line 8a by 12. Round to nearest whole dollar amount **8b**

Part II	**Premium Tax Credit Claim and Reconciliation of Advance Payment of Premium Tax Credit**	
9	Are you allocating policy amounts with another taxpayer or do you want to use the alternative calculation for year of marriage (see instructions)?	
	☐ **Yes.** Skip to Part IV, Allocation of Policy Amounts, or Part V, Alternative Calculation for Year of Marriage. ☐ **No.** Continue to line 10.	
10	See the instructions to determine if you can use line 11 or must complete lines 12 through 23.	
	☐ **Yes.** Continue to line 11. Compute your annual PTC. Then skip lines 12–23 and continue to line 24.	☐ **No.** Continue to lines 12–23. Compute your monthly PTC and continue to line 24.

Annual Calculation	**(a)** Annual enrollment premiums (Form(s) 1095-A, line 33A)	**(b)** Annual applicable SLCSP premium (Form(s) 1095-A, line 33B)	**(c)** Annual contribution amount (line 8a)	**(d)** Annual maximum premium assistance (subtract (c) from (b), if zero or less, enter -0-)	**(e)** Annual premium tax credit allowed (smaller of (a) or (d))	**(f)** Annual advance payment of PTC (Form(s) 1095-A, line 33C)
11 Annual Totals						
Monthly Calculation	**(a)** Monthly enrollment premiums (Form(s) 1095-A, lines 21–32, column A)	**(b)** Monthly applicable SLCSP premium (Form(s) 1095-A, lines 21–32, column B)	**(c)** Monthly contribution amount (amount from line 8b or alternative marriage monthly calculation)	**(d)** Monthly maximum premium assistance (subtract (c) from (b), if zero or less, enter -0-)	**(e)** Monthly premium tax credit allowed (smaller of (a) or (d))	**(f)** Monthly advance payment of PTC (Form(s) 1095-A, lines 21–32, column C)
12 January						
13 February						
14 March						
15 April						
16 May						
17 June						
18 July						
19 August						
20 September						
21 October						
22 November						
23 December						

24	Total premium tax credit. Enter the amount from line 11(e) or add lines 12(e) through 23(e) and enter the total here	**24**	
25	Advance payment of PTC. Enter the amount from line 11(f) or add lines 12(f) through 23(f) and enter the total here	**25**	
26	Net premium tax credit. If line 24 is greater than line 25, subtract line 25 from line 24. Enter the difference here and on Schedule 3 (Form 1040 or 1040-SR), line 9, or Form 1040-NR, line 65. If line 24 equals line 25, enter -0-. Stop here. If line 25 is greater than line 24, leave this line blank and continue to line 27	**26**	

Part III	**Repayment of Excess Advance Payment of the Premium Tax Credit**		
27	Excess advance payment of PTC. If line 25 is greater than line 24, subtract line 24 from line 25. Enter the difference here	**27**	
28	Repayment limitation (see instructions)	**28**	
29	Excess advance premium tax credit repayment. Enter the smaller of line 27 or line 28 here and on Schedule 2 (Form 1040 or 1040-SR), line 2, or Form 1040-NR, line 44	**29**	

For Paperwork Reduction Act Notice, see your tax return instructions.   Cat. No. 37784Z   Form **8962** (2019)

Form **8995**

Department of the Treasury
Internal Revenue Service

Qualified Business Income Deduction
Simplified Computation

▶ Attach to your tax return.
▶ Go to *www.irs.gov/Form8995* for instructions and the latest information.

OMB No. XXXX-XXXX

2019

Attachment
Sequence No. **55**

Name(s) shown on return

Your taxpayer identification number

1	(a) Trade, business, or aggregation name	(b) Taxpayer identification number	(c) Qualified business income or (loss)
i			
ii			
iii			
iv			
v			

2	Total qualified business income or (loss). Combine lines 1i through 1v, column (c)	2	
3	Qualified business net (loss) carryforward from the prior year	3 ( )	
4	Total qualified business income. Combine lines 2 and 3. If zero or less, enter -0-	4	
5	Qualified business income component. Multiply line 4 by 20% (0.20)		5
6	Qualified REIT dividends and publicly traded partnership (PTP) income or (loss) (see instructions)	6	
7	Qualified REIT dividends and qualified PTP (loss) carryforward from the prior year	7 ( )	
8	Total qualified REIT dividends and PTP income. Combine lines 6 and 7. If zero or less, enter -0-	8	
9	REIT and PTP component. Multiply line 8 by 20% (0.20)		9
10	Qualified business income deduction before the income limitation. Add lines 5 and 9		10
11	Taxable income before qualified business income deduction	11	
12	Net capital gain (see instructions)	12	
13	Subtract line 12 from line 11. If zero or less, enter -0-	13	
14	Income limitation. Multiply line 13 by 20% (0.20)		14
15	Qualified business income deduction. Enter the lesser of line 10 or line 14. Also enter this amount on the applicable line of your return . . . . ▶		15
16	Total qualified business (loss) carryforward. Combine lines 2 and 3. If greater than zero, enter -0- . .		16 ( )
17	Total qualified REIT dividends and PTP (loss) carryforward. Combine lines 6 and 7. If greater than zero, enter -0-		17 ( )

For Privacy Act and Paperwork Reduction Act Notice, see instructions.   Cat. No. 37806C   Form **8995** (2019)

2019 Child Tax Credit and Credit for Other Dependents
Worksheet—Line 13a

Keep for Your Records

1. To be a qualifying child for the child tax credit, the child must be your dependent, **under age 17** at the end of 2019, and meet all the conditions in Steps 1 through 3 under *Who Qualifies as Your Dependent*. Make sure you checked the "child tax credit" box in column (4) of the *Dependents* section on Form 1040 or 1040-SR for each qualifying child.

2. If you don't have a qualifying child, you can't claim the child tax credit; but you may be able to claim the credit for other dependents for that child. See Step 3 under *Who Qualifies as Your Dependent*.

3. To see if your qualifying relative qualifies you to take the credit for other dependents, see Step 5 under *Who Qualifies as Your Dependent*.

4. Be sure to see *Social security number* under *Who Qualifies as Your Dependent*.

5. Do **not** use this worksheet, but use Pub. 972 instead, if:

   a. You are claiming the adoption credit, mortgage interest credit, District of Columbia first-time homebuyer credit, or residential energy efficient property credit*;

   b. You are excluding income from Puerto Rico; or

   c. You are filing Form 2555 or 4563.

   * If applicable.

Part 1

1. Number of qualifying children under age 17 with the required social security number: _____ × $2,000. Enter the result. | **1** | |

2. Number of other dependents, including qualifying children without the required social security number: _____ × $500. Enter the result. | **2** | |

   Caution. Don't include yourself, your spouse, or anyone who is not a U.S. citizen, U.S. national, or U.S. resident alien. Also, don't include anyone you included on line 1.

3. Add lines 1 and 2. | **3** | |

4. Enter the amount from Form 1040 or 1040-SR, line 8b. | **4** | |

5. Enter the amount shown below for your filing status.

   ● Married filing jointly — $400,000

   ● All other filing statuses — $200,000 | **5** | |

6. Is the amount on line 4 more than the amount on line 5?

   ☐ **No.** Leave line 6 blank. Enter -0- on line 7, and go to line 8.

   ☐ **Yes.** Subtract line 5 from line 4.

   If the result isn't a multiple of $1,000, increase it to the next multiple of $1,000. For example, increase $425 to $1,000, increase $1,025 to $2,000, etc. | **6** | |

7. Multiply the amount on line 6 by 5% (0.05). Enter the result. | **7** | |

8. Is the amount on line 3 more than the amount on line 7?

   ☐ **No.** (STOP)

   You can't take the child tax credit on Form 1040 or 1040-SR, line 13a. You also can't take the additional child tax credit on Form 1040 or 1040-SR, line 18b. Complete the rest of your Form 1040 or 1040-SR.

   ☐ **Yes.** Subtract line 7 from line 3. Enter the result. *Go to Part 2.* | **8** | |

2019 Child Tax Credit and Credit for Other Dependents
Worksheet—*Continued*

Keep for Your Records

Before you begin Part 2: √ Figure the amount of any credits you are claiming on Schedule 3; Form 5695, Part II*; Form 8910; Form 8936; or Schedule R.

Part 2

9. Enter the amount from Form 1040 or 1040-SR, line 12b. **9** _____

10. Add any amounts from:

    Schedule 3, line 1 _____

    Schedule 3, line 2 + _____

    Schedule 3, line 3 + _____

    Schedule 3, line 4 + _____

    Form 5695, line 30* + _____

    Form 8910, line 15* + _____

    Form 8936, line 23 + _____

    Schedule R, line 22 + _____

    Enter the total. **10** _____

11. Are the amounts on lines 9 and 10 the same?

    ☐ **Yes.** (STOP)
    You can't take this credit because there is no tax to reduce.
    However, you may be able to take the **additional child tax
    credit** if line 1 is more than zero. See the **TIP** below.

    ☐ **No.** Subtract line 10 from line 9.   **11** _____

12. Is the amount on line 8 more than the amount on line 11?

    ☐ **Yes.** Enter the amount from line 11.
    Also, you may be able to take the
    additional child tax credit if line 1
    is more than zero. See the **TIP** below.

    ☐ **No.** Enter the amount from line 8.

    } This is your child tax
    credit and credit for
    other dependents.   **12** _____

    Enter this amount on
    Form 1040 or 1040-SR,
    line 13a.

TIP — *You may be able to take the **additional child tax credit**
on Form 1040 or 1040-SR, line 18b, if you answered "Yes" on
line 11 **or** line 12 above.*

- *First, complete your Form 1040 or 1040-SR through line
  18a (also complete Schedule 3, line 11).*
- *Then, use Schedule 8812 to figure any additional child tax
  credit.*

CAUTION — *If your child tax credit or additional child tax credit for a year after
2015 was reduced or disallowed, see* Form 8862, who must file *to
find out if you must file Form 8862 to take the credit for 2019.*

* If applicable.

DRAFT AS OF October 10, 2019

Qualified Dividends and Capital Gain Tax Worksheet—Line 12a

Before you begin:	✓ See the earlier instructions for line 12a to see if you can use this worksheet to figure your tax.
	✓ Before completing this worksheet, complete Form 1040 or 1040-SR through line 11b.
	✓ If you don't have to file Schedule D and you received capital gain distributions, be sure you checked the box on Form 1040 or 1040-SR, line 6.

1. Enter the amount from Form 1040 or 1040-SR, line 11b. However, if you are filing Form 2555 (relating to foreign earned income), enter the amount from line 3 of the Foreign Earned Income Tax Worksheet . . . . **1.** _____

2. Enter the amount from Form 1040 or 1040-SR, line 3a* . . . . **2.** _____

3. Are you filing Schedule D?*

   ☐ **Yes.** Enter the **smaller** of line 15 or 16 of Schedule D. If either line 15 or 16 is blank or a loss, enter -0-.

   ☐ **No.** Enter the amount from Form 1040 or 1040-SR, line 6.   **3.** _____

4. Add lines 2 and 3 . . . . **4.** _____

5. If filing Form 4952 (used to figure investment interest expense deduction), enter any amount from line 4g of that form. Otherwise, enter -0- . . . . **5.** _____

6. Subtract line 5 from line 4. If zero or less, enter -0- . . . . **6.** _____

7. Subtract line 6 from line 1. If zero or less, enter -0- . . . . **7.** _____

8. Enter:
   $39,375 if single or married filing separately,
   $78,750 if married filing jointly or qualifying widow(er),
   $52,750 if head of household.   . . . . **8.** _____

9. Enter the smaller of line 1 or line 8 . . . . **9.** _____

10. Enter the smaller of line 7 or line 9 . . . . **10.** _____

11. Subtract line 10 from line 9. This amount is taxed at 0% . . . . **11.** _____

12. Enter the smaller of line 1 or line 6 . . . . **12.** _____

13. Enter the amount from line 11 . . . . **13.** _____

14. Subtract line 13 from line 12 . . . . **14.** _____

15. Enter:
    $434,550 if single,
    $244,425 if married filing separately,
    $488,850 if married filing jointly or qualifying widow(er),
    $461,700 if head of household.   . . . . **15.** _____

16. Enter the smaller of line 1 or line 15 . . . . **16.** _____

17. Add lines 7 and 11 . . . . **17.** _____

18. Subtract line 17 from line 16. If zero or less, enter -0- . . . . **18.** _____

19. Enter the smaller of line 14 or line 18 . . . . **19.** _____

20. Multiply line 19 by 15% (0.15) . . . . **20.** _____

21. Add lines 11 and 19 . . . . **21.** _____

22. Subtract line 21 from line 12 . . . . **22.** _____

23. Multiply line 22 by 20% (0.20) . . . . **23.** _____

24. Figure the tax on the amount on line 7. If the amount on line 7 is less than $100,000, use the Tax Table to figure the tax. If the amount on line 7 is $100,000 or more, use the Tax Computation Worksheet . . . . **24.** _____

25. Add lines 20, 23, and 24 . . . . **25.** _____

26. Figure the tax on the amount on line 1. If the amount on line 1 is less than $100,000, use the Tax Table to figure the tax. If the amount on line 1 is $100,000 or more, use the Tax Computation Worksheet . . . . **26.** _____

27. **Tax on all taxable income.** Enter the **smaller** of line 25 or 26. Also include this amount on the entry space on Form 1040 or 1040-SR, line 12a. If you are filing Form 2555, don't enter this amount on the entry space on Form 1040 or 1040-SR, line 12a. Instead, enter it on line 4 of the Foreign Earned Income Tax Worksheet . . . . **27.** _____

* If you are filing Form 2555, see the footnote in the Foreign Earned Income Tax Worksheet before completing this line.

Solutions to Self-Study Problems

CHAPTER 1 THE INDIVIDUAL INCOME TAX RETURN

Self-Study Problem 1.1

Answer is d. Answers a, b, and c are goals of the U.S. income tax system.

Self-Study Problem 1.2

1. Schedule B, Forms 1040 and 1040-SR.
2. Schedule D, Forms 1040 and 1040-SR.
3. Schedule 1 and Schedule F, Forms 1040 and 1040-SR.
4. Form 1041 is used to report the income of estates and trusts.
5. Schedule K-1, Form 1065.
6. Form 1040.
7. Schedule 1 and Schedule C, Forms 1040 and 1040-SR.
8. Schedule 1 and Schedule E, Forms 1040 and 1040-SR.
9. Schedule B, Forms 1040 and 1040-SR.
10. Form 1120 or Form 1120S if making an S election.
11. Form 1065.
12. Schedule A, Forms 1040 and 1040-SR.
13. Form 1040-SR.

Self-Study Problem 1.3

1. Gross income = $29,000 + $1,500 = $30,500
2. Adjusted gross income = $30,500 − $2,200 = $28,300
3. Standard deduction = $12,200 (exceeds his itemized deduction amount of $6,500)
4. Taxable income = $28,300 − $12,200 = $16,100

Self-Study Problem 1.4

Refer to Figures 1.1, 1.2, and 1.3 in Chapter 1.

1. No   Income is below single under 65 threshold. See Figure 1.1.
2. No   Income is below MFJ with one spouse 65 or older limit. See Figure 1.1.
3. No   Standard deduction is earned income plus $350 up to $12,200 for single dependent. See Figure 1.2.
4. Yes Self-employment income is greater than $400. See Figure 1.3.

5. No   Income is below MFJ threshold; however, the taxpayers should file to obtain a refund. See Figure 1.1.
6. Yes   Social Security taxes are due. See Figure 1.3.
7. No   Income is below threshold for qualifying widow for under 65 with dependent. See Figure 1.1.

Self-Study Problem 1.5

1. B or C
2. D
3. A
4. C
5. D
6. E

Self-Study Problem 1.6

1. Yes. A baby born on or before December 31 may be a dependent.
2. No. The brother is not a qualifying child (he is older than Charlie) and fails the gross income test for qualifying relative.
3. Yes. The mother is a qualifying relative under the multiple support agreement rules.
4. Yes. The son qualifies as a qualifying child and the daughter-in-law is a qualifying relative.
5. Yes. The daughter is a full-time student under the age of 24 and Gary provides more than 50% of her support. Excluded scholarships do not count toward support.
6. Yes. The mother is a qualifying relative. Non-taxable Social Security benefits are not counted toward the gross income test.

Self-Study Problem 1.7

1. $12,200
2. $25,700 = $24,400 + $1,300
3. $15,500 = $12,200 + $1,650 + $1,650
4. $18,350
5. $1,100
6. $24,400

Self-Study Problem 1.8

1. $12,600 = $12,800 − $200
2. $8,750
3. $3,850 = $12,800 − $200 − $8,750
4. $3,850 = $12,800 − $200 − $8,750
5. Because the stock has been held for more than a year, the gain is a long-term capital gain. The long-term capital gain will be taxed at 0, 15, or 20 percent, depending on the taxpayer's income. A net investment income tax of 3.8% may also apply to certain high income taxpayers.

Self-Study Problem 1.9

1. True
2. True
3. True

Self-Study Problem 1.10

1. True
2. False
3. True
4. False

CHAPTER 2   GROSS INCOME AND EXCLUSIONS

Self-Study Problem 2.1

1. Included
2. Included
3. Excluded
4. Included and Excluded (the TCJA excludes alimony beginning in 2019)
5. Included
6. Excluded
7. Excluded
8. Excluded
9. Included
10. Included
11. Excluded
12. Included
13. Included
14. Included
15. Excluded
16. Excluded
17. Included
18. Included
19. Excluded

Self-Study Problem 2.2

a. $56,000
b. $3,456
c. $5,000

Self-Study Problem 2.3

None.   Neither the premiums nor the reimbursement are included in gross income.

Self-Study Problem 2.4

1. Excluded
2. Included
3. Excluded
4. Included
5. Excluded

Self-Study Problem 2.5

1. Excluded
2. Included (the excess discount over 15%)
3. Excluded
4. Excluded
5. Included
6. Included
7. Excluded

Self-Study Problem 2.6

1. $2,000
2. $10,000
3. $2,500
4. $5,000
5. $0. A service award less than $400 may be excluded from income.

Self-Study Problem 2.7

Part a

$14,645   The amount excluded from income will be $16,500 × [$42,500 ÷ ($1,500 × 12 months × 21 years)] = $1,855. Therefore, Phil will have taxable income of $14,645 ($16,500 − $1,855).

Part b

SIMPLIFIED METHOD WORKSHEET

1. Enter total amount received this year.	1.	$ 16,500.00
2. Enter cost in the plan at the annuity starting date.	2.	$ 42,500.00
3. Age at annuity starting date:		

	Enter	
55 or under	360	
56–60	310	
61–65	260	3. 260
66–70	210	
71 or older	160	

4. Divide line 2 by line 3.	4. $	163.46
5. Multiply line 4 by the number of monthly payments this year. If the annuity starting date was before 1987, also enter this amount on line 8; and skip lines 6 and 7. Otherwise, go to line 6.	5. $	1,798.06
6. Enter the amount, if any, recovered tax free in prior years.	6.	0.00
7. Subtract line 6 from line 2.	7. $	42,500.00
8. Enter the smaller of line 5 or 7.	8. $	1,798.06
9. Taxable amount this year: Subtract line 8 from line 1. Do not enter less than 0.	9. $	14,701.94

Self-Study Problem 2.8

Amount received	$ 13,250
Less: 1/10 of $100,000	(10,000)
Taxable interest	$ 3,250

Self-Study Problem 2.9

See Schedule B and the Qualifying Dividends and Capital Gain Tax Worksheet on Pages E-5 and E-6.

Self-Study Problem 2.10

1. $\dfrac{7\%}{1 - 0.24} = 9.21\%$

2. $\dfrac{6.5\%}{1 - 0.32} = 9.56\%$

Self-Study Problem 2.11

$40,000   Gifts in a business setting are taxable income, even if there was no obligation to make the payment. This problem is similar to the facts of a court case (*Duberstein*) in which the Supreme Court held that the value of the automobile was income, even where there was no legal obligation to make the gift.

Self-Study Problem 2.12

1. Excluded
2. Included
3. Included

4. Included
5. Included and Excluded. The $7,600 used for qualifying expenses is excluded but the excess scholarship of $2,400 in included in taxable income.
6. Included

Self-Study Problem 2.9

SCHEDULE B **(Form 1040 or 1040-SR)** Department of the Treasury Internal Revenue Service (99)	**Interest and Ordinary Dividends** ▶ Go to *www.irs.gov/ScheduleB* for instructions and the latest information. ▶ Attach to Form 1040 or 1040-SR.	OMB No. 1545-0074 20**19** Attachment Sequence No. **08**	

Name(s) shown on return	Your social security number
Victor and Grace Alito	313-44-5454

Part I

Interest

(See instructions and the instructions for Forms 1040 and 1040-SR, line 2b.)

Note: If you received a Form 1099-INT, Form 1099-OID, or substitute statement from a brokerage firm, list the firm's name as the payer and enter the total interest shown on that form.

			Amount
1	List name of payer. If any interest is from a seller-financed mortgage and the buyer used the property as a personal residence, see the instructions and list this interest first. Also, show that buyer's social security number and address ▶ Mango Savings and Loan	**1**	1,780
2	Add the amounts on line 1	**2**	1,780
3	Excludable interest on series EE and I U.S. savings bonds issued after 1989. Attach Form 8815	**3**	
4	Subtract line 3 from line 2. Enter the result here and on Form 1040 or 1040-SR, line 2b ▶	**4**	1,780

Note: If line 4 is over $1,500, you must complete Part III.

Part II

Ordinary Dividends

(See instructions and the instructions for Forms 1040 and 1040-SR, line 3b.)

Note: If you received a Form 1099-DIV or substitute statement from a brokerage firm, list the firm's name as the payer and enter the ordinary dividends shown on that form.

			Amount
5	List name of payer ▶ Grape Large Cap Index Fund	**5**	1,658
6	Add the amounts on line 5. Enter the total here and on Form 1040 or 1040-SR, line 3b ▶	**6**	1,658

Note: If line 6 is over $1,500, you must complete Part III.

Part III

Foreign Accounts and Trusts

Caution: If required, failure to file FinCEN Form 114 may result in substantial penalties. See instructions.

		Yes	No
	You must complete this part if you **(a)** had over $1,500 of taxable interest or ordinary dividends; **(b)** had a foreign account; or **(c)** received a distribution from, or were a grantor of, or a transferor to, a foreign trust.		
7a	At any time during 2019, did you have a financial interest in or signature authority over a financial account (such as a bank account, securities account, or brokerage account) located in a foreign country? See instructions		✓
	If "Yes," are you required to file FinCEN Form 114, Report of Foreign Bank and Financial Accounts (FBAR), to report that financial interest or signature authority? See FinCEN Form 114 and its instructions for filing requirements and exceptions to those requirements		✓
b	If you are required to file FinCEN Form 114, enter the name of the foreign country where the financial account is located ▶		
8	During 2019, did you receive a distribution from, or were you the grantor of, or transferor to, a foreign trust? If "Yes," you may have to file Form 3520. See instructions		✓

For Paperwork Reduction Act Notice, see your tax return instructions.	Cat. No. 17146N	Schedule B (Form 1040 or 1040-SR) 2019

Self-Study Problem 2.9

Qualified Dividends and Capital Gain Tax Worksheet—Line 12a

Before you begin:
✓ See the earlier instructions for line 12a to see if you can use this worksheet to figure your tax.
✓ Before completing this worksheet, complete Form 1040 or 1040-SR through line 11b.
✓ If you don't have to file Schedule D and you received capital gain distributions, be sure you checked the box on Form 1040 or 1040-SR, line 6.

1.	Enter the amount from Form 1040 or 1040-SR, line 11b. However, if you are filing Form 2555 (relating to foreign earned income), enter the amount from line 3 of the Foreign Earned Income Tax Worksheet ...... **1.**	42,000
2.	Enter the amount from Form 1040 or 1040-SR, line 3a* .... **2.**	1,600
3.	Are you filing Schedule D?* ☐ **Yes.** Enter the **smaller** of line 15 or 16 of Schedule D. If either line 15 or 16 is blank or a loss, enter -0-. ☒ **No.** Enter the amount from Form 1040 or 1040-SR, line 6. **3.**	200
4.	Add lines 2 and 3 .... **4.**	1,800
5.	If filing Form 4952 (used to figure investment interest expense deduction), enter any amount from line 4g of that form. Otherwise, enter -0- .... **5.**	
6.	Subtract line 5 from line 4. If zero or less, enter -0- .... **6.**	1,800
7.	Subtract line 6 from line 1. If zero or less, enter -0- .... **7.**	40,200
8.	Enter: $39,375 if single or married filing separately, $78,750 if married filing jointly or qualifying widow(er), $52,750 if head of household. **8.**	78,750
9.	Enter the smaller of line 1 or line 8 .... **9.**	42,000
10.	Enter the smaller of line 7 or line 9 .... **10.**	40,200
11.	Subtract line 10 from line 9. This amount is taxed at 0% .... **11.**	1,800
12.	Enter the smaller of line 1 or line 6 .... **12.**	1,800
13.	Enter the amount from line 11 .... **13.**	1,800
14.	Subtract line 13 from line 12 .... **14.**	0
15.	Enter: $434,550 if single, $244,425 if married filing separately, $488,850 if married filing jointly or qualifying widow(er), $461,700 if head of household. **15.**	488,850
16.	Enter the smaller of line 1 or line 15 .... **16.**	42,000
17.	Add lines 7 and 11 .... **17.**	42,000
18.	Subtract line 17 from line 16. If zero or less, enter -0- .... **18.**	0
19.	Enter the smaller of line 14 or line 18 .... **19.**	0
20.	Multiply line 19 by 15% (0.15) .... **20.**	0
21.	Add lines 11 and 19 .... **21.**	1,800
22.	Subtract line 21 from line 12 .... **22.**	0
23.	Multiply line 22 by 20% (0.20) .... **23.**	0
24.	Figure the tax on the amount on line 7. If the amount on line 7 is less than $100,000, use the Tax Table to figure the tax. If the amount on line 7 is $100,000 or more, use the Tax Computation Worksheet .... **24.**	4,439
25.	Add lines 20, 23, and 24 .... **25.**	4,439
26.	Figure the tax on the amount on line 1. If the amount on line 1 is less than $100,000, use the Tax Table to figure the tax. If the amount on line 1 is $100,000 or more, use the Tax Computation Worksheet .... **26.**	4,655
27.	**Tax on all taxable income.** Enter the **smaller** of line 25 or line 26. Also include this amount on the entry space on Form 1040 or 1040-SR, line 12a. If you are filing Form 2555, don't enter this amount on the entry space on Form 1040 or 1040-SR, line 12a. Instead, enter it on line 4 of the Foreign Earned Income Tax Worksheet .... **27.**	4,439

If you are filing Form 2555, see the footnote in the Foreign Earned Income Tax Worksheet before completing this line.

Self-Study Problem 2.13

Deductible by payer	Includable by recipient
a. $ 0	$ 0
b. 12,000	12,000
c. 0	0

Self-Study Problem 2.14

a. $0

b. $2,000. Henry's AGI is under $95,000 so there is no phase-out.

Self-Study Problem 2.15

$3,000 Unemployment compensation is fully taxable.

Self-Study Problem 2.16

Simplified Taxable Social Security Worksheet (for most people)

1. Enter the total amount of Social Security income.	1. $13,000
2. Enter one-half of line 1.	2. 6,500
3. Enter the total of taxable income items on Form 1040 except Social Security income.	3. 20,000
4. Enter the amount of tax-exempt interest income.	4. 30,000
5. Add lines 2, 3, and 4.	5. 56,500
6. Enter all adjustments for AGI except for student loan interest, the domestic production activities deduction, and the tuition and fees deduction.	6. 0
7. Subtract line 6 from line 5. If 0 or less, stop here, none of the Social Security benefits are taxable.	7. 56,500
8. Enter $25,000 ($32,000 if married filing jointly; $0 if married filing separately and living with spouse at any time during the year).	8. 32,000
9. Subtract line 8 from line 7. If 0 or less, enter -0-.	9. 24,500

Note: If line 9 is 0 or less, stop here; none of your benefits are taxable. Otherwise, go on to line 10.

10. Enter $9,000 ($12,000 if married filing jointly; $0 if married filing separately and living with spouse at any time during the year).	10. 12,000
11. Subtract line 10 from line 9. If 0 or less, enter -0-.	11. 12,500
12. Enter the **smaller of line 9 or line 10.**	12. 12,000
13. Enter one-half of line 12.	13. 6,000
14. Enter the **smaller of line 2 or line 13.**	14. 6,000
15. Multiply line 11 by 85% (.85). If line 11 is 0, enter -0-.	15. 10,625
16. Add lines 14 and 15.	16. 16,625
17. Multiply line 1 by 85% (.85).	17. 11,050
18. **Taxable benefits. Enter the smaller of line 16 or line 17.**	18. $11,050

Self-Study Problem 2.17

a.	Tom's salary (50 percent)	$20,000
	Rachel's salary (50 percent)	15,000
	Dividends, Rachel's property (100 percent)	3,000
	Interest (50 percent)	2,000
	Total	$40,000
b.	Tom's salary (50 percent)	$20,000
	Rachel's salary (50 percent)	15,000
	Dividends, Tom's property (50 percent)	2,500
	Dividends, Rachel's property (50 percent)	1,500
	Interest (50 percent)	2,000
	Total	$41,000

CHAPTER 3   BUSINESS INCOME AND EXPENSES

Self-Study Problem 3.1

See Schedule C on Pages E-9 and E-10.

Self-Study Problem 3.2

Part III	**Cost of Goods Sold** (see instructions)		
33	Method(s) used to value closing inventory: a ☑ Cost b ☐ Lower of cost or market c ☐ Other (attach explanation)		
34	Was there any change in determining quantities, costs, or valuations between opening and closing inventory? If "Yes," attach explanation . . . . ☐ Yes ☑ No		
35	Inventory at beginning of year. If different from last year's closing inventory, attach explanation . . .	35	62,500
36	Purchases less cost of items withdrawn for personal use	36	178,750
37	Cost of labor. Do not include any amounts paid to yourself	37	
38	Materials and supplies	38	
39	Other costs	39	
40	Add lines 35 through 39	40	241,250
41	Inventory at end of year	41	68,400
42	**Cost of goods sold.** Subtract line 41 from line 40. Enter the result here and on line 4	42	172,850

Self-Study Problem 3.3

Marc's transportation deduction is the greater of his actual costs or his deduction using the standard mileage method.

Actual Cost Calculation:

Cash Outlays	$ 4,028
Depreciation	4,000
	8,028
Business percentage (13,120/16,000)	×82%
Subtotal	6,583
Tolls & Fees	327
Actual Costs	$ 6,910

Self-Study Problem 3.1

SCHEDULE C		Profit or Loss From Business	OMB No. 1545-0074
(Form 1040 or 1040-SR)		(Sole Proprietorship)	**2019**
Department of the Treasury Internal Revenue Service (99)		▶ Go to *www.irs.gov/ScheduleC* for instructions and the latest information. ▶ **Attach to Form 1040, 1040-SR, 1040-NR, or 1041; partnerships generally must file Form 1065.**	Attachment Sequence No. **09**

Name of proprietor	Social security number (SSN)
Teri Kataoka	466-47-8833

A Principal business or profession, including product or service (see instructions)
Golf Instructor

B Enter code from instructions ▶ 8 1 2 9 9 0

C Business name. If no separate business name, leave blank.

D Employer ID number (EIN) (see instr.)

E Business address (including suite or room no.) ▶ 1234 Pinecrest Drive
City, town or post office, state, and ZIP code   Kennesaw, GA 30152

F Accounting method: **(1)** ☑ Cash **(2)** ☐ Accrual **(3)** ☐ Other (specify) ▶ ___

G Did you "materially participate" in the operation of this business during 2019? If "No," see instructions for limit on losses . ☑ **Yes** ☐ No

H If you started or acquired this business during 2019, check here . . . . ▶ ☐

I Did you make any payments in 2019 that would require you to file Form(s) 1099? (see instructions) . . . ☐ **Yes** ☑ No

J If "Yes," did you or will you file required Forms 1099? . . . . ☐ **Yes** ☐ No

Part I — Income

1	Gross receipts or sales. See instructions for line 1 and check the box if this income was reported to you on Form W-2 and the "Statutory employee" box on that form was checked . . . . ▶ ☐	**1**	40,125
2	Returns and allowances	**2**	
3	Subtract line 2 from line 1	**3**	40,125
4	Cost of goods sold (from line 42)	**4**	
5	**Gross profit.** Subtract line 4 from line 3	**5**	40,125
6	Other income, including federal and state gasoline or fuel tax credit or refund (see instructions) . . .	**6**	
7	**Gross income.** Add lines 5 and 6 . . . . ▶	**7**	40,125

Part II — Expenses. Enter expenses for business use of your home **only** on line 30.

8	Advertising	**8**		18	Office expense (see instructions)	**18**	660
9	Car and truck expenses (see instructions)	**9**	3,036	19	Pension and profit-sharing plans .	**19**	
10	Commissions and fees .	**10**		20	Rent or lease (see instructions):		
11	Contract labor (see instructions)	**11**		a	Vehicles, machinery, and equipment	**20a**	
12	Depletion	**12**		b	Other business property . . .	**20b**	2,700
13	Depreciation and section 179 expense deduction (not included in Part III) (see instructions)	**13**		21	Repairs and maintenance . .	**21**	
				22	Supplies (not included in Part III) .	**22**	
				23	Taxes and licenses	**23**	250
				24	Travel and meals:		
14	Employee benefit programs (other than on line 19) . .	**14**		a	Travel	**24a**	3,000
15	Insurance (other than health)	**15**	475	b	Deductible meals (see instructions)	**24b**	985
16	Interest (see instructions):			25	Utilities	**25**	1,015
a	Mortgage (paid to banks, etc.)	**16a**		26	Wages (less employment credits) .	**26**	
b	Other	**16b**		27a	Other expenses (from line 48) . .	**27a**	
17	Legal and professional services	**17**		b	**Reserved for future use** . .	**27b**	

28	**Total expenses** before expenses for business use of home. Add lines 8 through 27a . . . . ▶	**28**	12,121
29	Tentative profit or (loss). Subtract line 28 from line 7	**29**	28,004
30	Expenses for business use of your home. Do not report these expenses elsewhere. Attach Form 8829 unless using the simplified method (see instructions). **Simplified method filers only:** enter the total square footage of: (a) your home: _____ and (b) the part of your home used for business: _____. Use the Simplified Method Worksheet in the instructions to figure the amount to enter on line 30	**30**	
31	**Net profit or (loss).** Subtract line 30 from line 29. • If a profit, enter on both **Schedule 1 (Form 1040 or 1040-SR), line 3** (or **Form 1040-NR, line 13**) and on **Schedule SE, line 2.** (If you checked the box on line 1, see instructions). Estates and trusts, enter on **Form 1041, line 3.** • If a loss, you **must** go to line 32.	**31**	28,004
32	If you have a loss, check the box that describes your investment in this activity (see instructions). • If you checked 32a, enter the loss on both **Schedule 1 (Form 1040 or 1040-SR), line 3** (or **Form 1040-NR, line 13**) and on **Schedule SE, line 2.** (If you checked the box on line 1, see the line 31 instructions). Estates and trusts, enter on **Form 1041, line 3.** • If you checked 32b, you **must** attach **Form 6198.** Your loss may be limited.	**32a** ☐ All investment is at risk. **32b** ☐ Some investment is not at risk.	

For Paperwork Reduction Act Notice, see the separate instructions.   Cat. No. 11334P   Schedule C (Form 1040 or 1040-SR) 2019

DRAFT AS OF August 7, 2019 DO NOT FILE

Self-Study Problem 3.1

| **Part III** | **Cost of Goods Sold** (see instructions) |

33 Method(s) used to
   value closing inventory: **a** ☐ Cost   **b** ☐ Lower of cost or market   **c** ☐ Other (attach explanation)

34 Was there any change in determining quantities, costs, or valuations between opening and closing inventory?
   If "Yes," attach explanation . . . .   ☐ **Yes**   ☐ **No**

35 Inventory at beginning of year. If different from last year's closing inventory, attach explanation . . . | 35 |

36 Purchases less cost of items withdrawn for personal use . . . . | 36 |

37 Cost of labor. Do not include any amounts paid to yourself . . . . | 37 |

38 Materials and supplies . . . . | 38 |

39 Other costs . . . . | 39 |

40 Add lines 35 through 39 . . . . | 40 |

41 Inventory at end of year . . . . | 41 |

42 **Cost of goods sold.** Subtract line 41 from line 40. Enter the result here and on line 4 . . . . . | 42 |

| **Part IV** | **Information on Your Vehicle.** Complete this part **only** if you are claiming car or truck expenses on line 9 and are not required to file Form 4562 for this business. See the instructions for line 13 to find out if you must file Form 4562. |

43 When did you place your vehicle in service for business purposes? (month, day, year)   ▶   01 / 01 / 2019

44 Of the total number of miles you drove your vehicle during 2019, enter the number of miles you used your vehicle for:

   a Business _____ 5,234 _____   **b** Commuting (see instructions) _____ 1,200 _____   **c** Other _____ 5,000 _____

45 Was your vehicle available for personal use during off-duty hours? . . . .   ☑ **Yes**   ☐ **No**

46 Do you (or your spouse) have another vehicle available for personal use?. . . . .   ☐ **Yes**   ☑ **No**

47a Do you have evidence to support your deduction? . . . .   ☑ **Yes**   ☐ **No**

   b If "Yes," is the evidence written? . . . .   ☑ **Yes**   ☐ **No**

| **Part V** | **Other Expenses.** List below business expenses not included on lines 8–26 or line 30. |

----

48 **Total other expenses.** Enter here and on line 27a . . . . | 48 |

Standard Mileage Calculation:

13,120 miles @ 58¢	$ 7,610
Tolls & Fees	327
Marc's deduction for 2019 is	$ 7,937

Self-Study Problem 3.4

Deductible expenses:

Airfare	$ 480
Hotel while working on the audit	825
Meals while working on the audit	168
Laundry	22
Taxi	72
Total travel deduction	$1,567

Self-Study Problem 3.5

Business meals ($500 + $600) × 50% = $550. Entertainment, dues, and personal expenses are not generally deductible.

Self-Study Problem 3.6

Lodging	$1,200
Transportation	350
Meals (50% of $200)	100
Books	175
Tuition	550
Total Deduction	$2,375

The cost of the weekend trip to the Grand Canyon is not deductible.

Self-Study Problem 3.7

1. Deductible
2. Not Deductible
3. Not Deductible
4. Not Deductible
5. Not Deductible

Self-Study Problem 3.8

Safety shoes and orange vest	$ 650
Climbing equipment, etc.	275
Total special clothing deduction	$ 925

Self-Study Problem 3.9

1. Mr. Jones	$ 20
2. Mr. Brown	25
3/4. Mrs. and Mr. Green	25
5. Ms. Gray	0
6. Mr. Edwards	75
7. Various customers	140
Total business gift deduction	$ 285

Self-Study Problem 3.10

1. Business
2. Nonbusiness
3. Nonbusiness
4. Business
5. Nonbusiness

Self-Study Problem 3.11

Gross income	$ 2,900
Less: interest and taxes	(2,100)
Balance	$ 800
Less: maintenance, utilities, and cleaning ($1,400)	
limited to	(800)
Net income	$ 0

Note: The excess expenses of $600 may be carried forward.

Self-Study Problem 3.12

Income $250.   The hobby income must be recognized.
Deduction $0.   No deduction is permitted.

CHAPTER 4   ADDITIONAL INCOME AND THE QUALIFIED BUSINESS INCOME DEDUCTION

Self-Study Problem 4.1

1. No   Inventory is specifically excluded from the definition of a capital asset.
2. Yes
3. No   Property held by the creator is specifically excluded from the definition of a capital asset.
4. No   Accounts receivable are specifically excluded from the definition of a capital asset.
5. Yes
6. No   Section 1231 assets (depreciable property and real estate used in a trade or business) are specifically excluded from the definition of a capital asset.
7. Yes
8. Yes
9. Yes
10. Yes
11. No   Inventory is specifically excluded from the definition of a capital asset.
12. Yes

Self-Study Problem 4.2

1. Short-term
2. Long-term
3. Short-term
4. Long-term

Self-Study Problem 4.3

1. Adjusted basis = $11,000
2. Capital improvements = $2,000
3. Accumulated depreciation = $15,000
4. Original cost = $23,000

Self-Study Problem 4.4

Net long-term ($12,000 − $4,000) + ($14,000 − $17,500) =	$ 4,500
Net short-term	(1,800)
Net capital gains	2,700
Capital gains rate	× 15%
Tax	$ 405

Self-Study Problem 4.5

See Schedule D, Form 8949, and the Qualified Dividends and Capital Gain Tax Worksheet on Pages E-14 through E-18.

Self-Study Problem 4.6

a. Sales price	$350,000
Basis	(30,000)
Realized gain	320,000
Exclusion	(250,000)
Recognized gain	$ 70,000

b. $0. The $500,000 exclusion for joint filers exceeds the $320,000 realized gain.

c. $25,000 = ($350,000 − $200,000) − (½ × $250,000)

Self-Study Problem 4.7

See Schedule E on Page E-19.

Self-Study Problem 4.8

See Form 8582 on Page E-20.

Self-Study Problem 4.9

1. F NOLs generated after 2017 may only be carried forward. 2017 NOL deductions may be carried back 2 years and then forward 20 years.
2. F Generally, NOLs are only from the operation of a trade or business, casualty and theft losses, or confiscation losses.
3. F Individual NOLs require an analysis of business and nonbusiness income and deductions to determine the business portion that compose the NOL.
4. T
5. F NOLs generated after 2017 can only offset 80% of the taxable income in a future year. 2017 and prior NOLs may offset the entire income of a future year.

Self-Study Problem 4.5

SCHEDULE D	Capital Gains and Losses	OMB No. 1545-0074
(Form 1040 or 1040-SR)		**2019**
Department of the Treasury Internal Revenue Service (99)	▶ Attach to Form 1040, 1040-SR, or 1040-NR. ▶ Go to *www.irs.gov/ScheduleD* for instructions and the latest information. ▶ Use Form 8949 to list your transactions for lines 1b, 2, 3, 8b, 9, and 10.	Attachment Sequence No. **12**

Name(s) shown on return	Your social security number
Louis Winthrop	123-44-3214

Did you dispose of any investment(s) in a qualified opportunity fund during the tax year? ☐ **Yes** ☐ **No**
If "Yes," attach Form 8949 and see its instructions for additional requirements for reporting your gain or loss.

Part I Short-Term Capital Gains and Losses—Generally Assets Held One Year or Less (see instructions)

See instructions for how to figure the amounts to enter on the lines below. This form may be easier to complete if you round off cents to whole dollars.	(d) Proceeds (sales price)	(e) Cost (or other basis)	(g) Adjustments to gain or loss from Form(s) 8949, Part I, line 2, column (g)	(h) Gain or (loss) Subtract column (e) from column (d) and combine the result with column (g)
1a Totals for all short-term transactions reported on Form 1099-B for which basis was reported to the IRS and for which you have no adjustments (see instructions). However, if you choose to report all these transactions on Form 8949, leave this line blank and go to line 1b				
1b Totals for all transactions reported on Form(s) 8949 with **Box A** checked	12,000	19,200		(7,200)
2 Totals for all transactions reported on Form(s) 8949 with **Box B** checked				
3 Totals for all transactions reported on Form(s) 8949 with **Box C** checked				

4 Short-term gain from Form 6252 and short-term gain or (loss) from Forms 4684, 6781, and 8824	**4**	
5 Net short-term gain or (loss) from partnerships, S corporations, estates, and trusts from Schedule(s) K-1	**5**	
6 Short-term capital loss carryover. Enter the amount, if any, from line 8 of your **Capital Loss Carryover Worksheet** in the instructions	**6** (	)
7 **Net short-term capital gain or (loss).** Combine lines 1a through 6 in column (h). If you have any long-term capital gains or losses, go to Part II below. Otherwise, go to Part III on the back	**7**	(7,200)

Part II Long-Term Capital Gains and Losses—Generally Assets Held More Than One Year (see instructions)

See instructions for how to figure the amounts to enter on the lines below. This form may be easier to complete if you round off cents to whole dollars.	(d) Proceeds (sales price)	(e) Cost (or other basis)	(g) Adjustments to gain or loss from Form(s) 8949, Part II, line 2, column (g)	(h) Gain or (loss) Subtract column (e) from column (d) and combine the result with column (g)
8a Totals for all long-term transactions reported on Form 1099-B for which basis was reported to the IRS and for which you have no adjustments (see instructions). However, if you choose to report all these transactions on Form 8949, leave this line blank and go to line 8b				
8b Totals for all transactions reported on Form(s) 8949 with **Box D** checked	43,000	33,500		9,500
9 Totals for all transactions reported on Form(s) 8949 with **Box E** checked				
10 Totals for all transactions reported on Form(s) 8949 with **Box F** checked				

11 Gain from Form 4797, Part I; long-term gain from Forms 2439 and 6252; and long-term gain or (loss) from Forms 4684, 6781, and 8824	**11**	
12 Net long-term gain or (loss) from partnerships, S corporations, estates, and trusts from Schedule(s) K-1	**12**	
13 Capital gain distributions. See the instructions	**13**	
14 Long-term capital loss carryover. Enter the amount, if any, from line 13 of your **Capital Loss Carryover Worksheet** in the instructions	**14** (	)
15 **Net long-term capital gain or (loss).** Combine lines 8a through 14 in column (h). Then go to Part III on the back	**15**	9,500

For Paperwork Reduction Act Notice, see your tax return instructions.   Cat. No. 11338H   Schedule D (Form 1040 or 1040-SR) 2019

Self-Study Problem 4.5

Schedule D (Form 1040 or 1040-SR) 2019   Page **2**

Part III   **Summary**

16   Combine lines 7 and 15 and enter the result **16**   2,300

   • If line 16 is a **gain,** enter the amount from line 16 on Form 1040 or 1040-SR, line 6; or Form 1040-NR, line 14. Then go to line 17 below.
   • If line 16 is a **loss,** skip lines 17 through 20 below. Then go to line 21. Also be sure to complete line 22.
   • If line 16 is **zero,** skip lines 17 through 21 below and enter -0- on Form 1040 or 1040-SR, line 6; or Form 1040-NR, line 14. Then go to line 22.

17   Are lines 15 and 16 **both** gains?
   ☑ **Yes.** Go to line 18.
   ☐ **No.** Skip lines 18 through 21, and go to line 22.

18   If you are required to complete the **28% Rate Gain Worksheet** (see instructions), enter the amount, if any, from line 7 of that worksheet . . . . ▶ **18**   0

19   If you are required to complete the **Unrecaptured Section 1250 Gain Worksheet** (see instructions), enter the amount, if any, from line 18 of that worksheet . . . . ▶ **19**   0

20   Are lines 18 and 19 **both** zero or blank?
   ☑ **Yes.** Complete the **Qualified Dividends and Capital Gain Tax Worksheet** in the instructions for Forms 1040 and 1040-SR, line 12a (or in the instructions for Form 1040-NR, line 42). **Don't** complete lines 21 and 22 below.

   ☐ **No.** Complete the **Schedule D Tax Worksheet** in the instructions. **Don't** complete lines 21 and 22 below.

21   If line 16 is a loss, enter here and on Form 1040 or 1040-SR, line 6; or Form 1040-NR, line 14, the **smaller** of:

   • The loss on line 16; or
   • ($3,000), or if married filing separately, ($1,500)   } . . . . **21** (   )

   Note: When figuring which amount is smaller, treat both amounts as positive numbers.

22   Do you have qualified dividends on Form 1040 or 1040-SR, line 3a; or Form 1040-NR, line 10b?

   ☐ **Yes.** Complete the **Qualified Dividends and Capital Gain Tax Worksheet** in the instructions for Forms 1040 and 1040-SR, line 12a (or in the instructions for Form 1040-NR, line 42).

   ☐ **No.** Complete the rest of Form 1040, 1040-SR, or 1040-NR.

Schedule D (Form 1040 or 1040-SR) 2019

DRAFT AS OF August 30, 2019 DO NOT FILE

Self-Study Problem 4.5

Form **8949**

Department of the Treasury
Internal Revenue Service

Sales and Other Dispositions of Capital Assets

▶ Go to *www.irs.gov/Form8949* for instructions and the latest information.

▶ File with your Schedule D to list your transactions for lines 1b, 2, 3, 8b, 9, and 10 of Schedule D.

OMB No. 1545-0074

2019

Attachment
Sequence No. **12A**

Name(s) shown on return
Louis Winthorp

Social security number or taxpayer identification number
123-44-3214

Before you check Box A, B, or C below, see whether you received any Form(s) 1099-B or substitute statement(s) from your broker. A substitute statement will have the same information as Form 1099-B. Either will show whether your basis (usually your cost) was reported to the IRS by your broker and may even tell you which box to check.

Part I   **Short-Term.** Transactions involving capital assets you held 1 year or less are generally short-term (see instructions). For long-term transactions, see page 2.

Note: You may aggregate all short-term transactions reported on Form(s) 1099-B showing basis was reported to the IRS and for which no adjustments or codes are required. Enter the totals directly on Schedule D, line 1a; you aren't required to report these transactions on Form 8949 (see instructions).

You *must* check Box A, B, *or* C below. Check only one box. If more than one box applies for your short-term transactions, complete a separate Form 8949, page 1, for each applicable box. If you have more short-term transactions than will fit on this page for one or more of the boxes, complete as many forms with the same box checked as you need.

- ☑ **(A)** Short-term transactions reported on Form(s) 1099-B showing basis was reported to the IRS (see **Note** above)
- ☐ **(B)** Short-term transactions reported on Form(s) 1099-B showing basis **wasn't** reported to the IRS
- ☐ **(C)** Short-term transactions not reported to you on Form 1099-B

1 (a) Description of property (Example: 100 sh. XYZ Co.)	(b) Date acquired (Mo., day, yr.)	(c) Date sold or disposed of (Mo., day, yr.)	(d) Proceeds (sales price) (see instructions)	(e) Cost or other basis. See the **Note** below and see *Column (e)* in the separate instructions	(f) Code(s) from instructions	(g) Amount of adjustment	(h) Gain or (loss). Subtract column (e) from column (d) and combine the result with column (g)
100 shs Rose Corp	04/18/2019	12/07/2019	12,000	19,200			(7,200)
2 Totals. Add the amounts in columns (d), (e), (g), and (h) (subtract negative amounts). Enter each total here and include on your Schedule D, **line 1b** (if **Box A** above is checked), **line 2** (if **Box B** above is checked), or **line 3** (if **Box C** above is checked) ▶			12,000	19,200			(7,200)

Note: If you checked Box A above but the basis reported to the IRS was incorrect, enter in column (e) the basis as reported to the IRS, and enter an adjustment in column (g) to correct the basis. See *Column (g)* in the separate instructions for how to figure the amount of the adjustment.

For Paperwork Reduction Act Notice, see your tax return instructions.   Cat. No. 37768Z   Form **8949** (2019)

Self-Study Problem 4.5

Form 8949 (2019)   Attachment Sequence No. **12A**   Page **2**

Name(s) shown on return. Name and SSN or taxpayer identification no. not required if shown on other side	Social security number or taxpayer identification number
Louis Winthorp	123-44-3214

Before you check Box D, E, or F below, see whether you received any Form(s) 1099-B or substitute statement(s) from your broker. A substitute statement will have the same information as Form 1099-B. Either will show whether your basis (usually your cost) was reported to the IRS by your broker and may even tell you which box to check.

Part II   **Long-Term.** Transactions involving capital assets you held more than 1 year are generally long-term (see instructions). For short-term transactions, see page 1.

Note: You may aggregate all long-term transactions reported on Form(s) 1099-B showing basis was reported to the IRS and for which no adjustments or codes are required. Enter the totals directly on Schedule D, line 8a; you aren't required to report these transactions on Form 8949 (see instructions).

You *must* check Box D, E, or F below. Check only one box. If more than one box applies for your long-term transactions, complete a separate Form 8949, page 2, for each applicable box. If you have more long-term transactions than will fit on this page for one or more of the boxes, complete as many forms with the same box checked as you need.

- ☑ **(D)** Long-term transactions reported on Form(s) 1099-B showing basis was reported to the IRS (see **Note** above)
- ☐ **(E)** Long-term transactions reported on Form(s) 1099-B showing basis **wasn't** reported to the IRS
- ☐ **(F)** Long-term transactions not reported to you on Form 1099-B

1 (a) Description of property (Example: 100 sh. XYZ Co.)	(b) Date acquired (Mo., day, yr.)	(c) Date sold or disposed of (Mo., day, yr.)	(d) Proceeds (sales price) (see instructions)	(e) Cost or other basis. See the **Note** below and see *Column (e)* in the separate instructions	(f) Code(s) from instructions	(g) Amount of adjustment	(h) Gain or (loss). Subtract column (e) from column (d) and combine the result with column (g)
100 shs. Purple	6/21/2010	08/15/2019	18,000	12,500			5,500
50 shs. Blue	12/18/2011	10/02/2019	25,000	21,000			4,000
2 Totals. Add the amounts in columns (d), (e), (g), and (h) (subtract negative amounts). Enter each total here and include on your Schedule D, **line 8b** (if **Box D** above is checked), **line 9** (if **Box E** above is checked), or **line 10** (if **Box F** above is checked) ▶			43,000	33,500			9,500

Note: If you checked Box D above but the basis reported to the IRS was incorrect, enter in column (e) the basis as reported to the IRS, and enter an adjustment in column (g) to correct the basis. See *Column (g)* in the separate instructions for how to figure the amount of the adjustment.

Form **8949** (2019)

Self-Study Problem 4.5

Qualified Dividends and Capital Gain Tax Worksheet—Line 12a

Before you begin:	√ See the earlier instructions for line 12a to see if you can use this worksheet to figure your tax.	
	√ Before completing this worksheet, complete Form 1040 or 1040-SR through line 11b.	
	√ If you don't have to file Schedule D and you received capital gain distributions, be sure you checked the box on Form 1040 or 1040-SR, line 6.	

1. Enter the amount from Form 1040 or 1040-SR, line 11b. However, if you are filing Form 2555 (relating to foreign earned income), enter the amount from line 3 of the Foreign Earned Income Tax Worksheet 1. **59,000**

2. Enter the amount from Form 1040 or 1040-SR, line 3a* . . . . 2. _____

3. Are you filing Schedule D?*
   ☒ **Yes.** Enter the **smaller** of line 15 or 16 of Schedule D. If either line 15 or 16 is blank or a loss, enter -0-.
   ☐ **No.** Enter the amount from Form 1040 or 1040-SR, line 6.   3. **2,300**

4. Add lines 2 and 3 . . . . 4. **2,300**

5. If filing Form 4952 (used to figure investment interest expense deduction), enter any amount from line 4g of that form. Otherwise, enter -0- . . . . 5. _____

6. Subtract line 5 from line 4. If zero or less, enter -0- 6. **2,300**

7. Subtract line 6 from line 1. If zero or less, enter -0- 7. **56,700**

8. Enter:
   $39,375 if single or married filing separately,
   $78,750 if married filing jointly or qualifying widow(er),
   $52,750 if head of household. 8. **39,375**

9. Enter the smaller of line 1 or line 8 . . . . 9. **39,375**

10. Enter the smaller of line 7 or line 9 . . . . 10. **39,375**

11. Subtract line 10 from line 9. This amount is taxed at 0% 11. **0**

12. Enter the smaller of line 1 or line 6 . . . . 12. **2,300**

13. Enter the amount from line 11 . . . . 13. **0**

14. Subtract line 13 from line 12 . . . . 14. **2,300**

15. Enter:
    $434,550 if single,
    $244,425 if married filing separately,
    $488,850 if married filing jointly or qualifying widow(er),
    $461,700 if head of household. 15. **434,550**

16. Enter the smaller of line 1 or line 15 . . . . 16. **59,000**

17. Add lines 7 and 11 . . . . 17. **56,700**

18. Subtract line 17 from line 16. If zero or less, enter -0- 18. **2,300**

19. Enter the smaller of line 14 or line 18 . . . . 19. **2,300**

20. Multiply line 19 by 15% (0.15) 20. **345**

21. Add lines 11 and 19 . . . . 21. **2,300**

22. Subtract line 21 from line 12 . . . . 22. **0**

23. Multiply line 22 by 20% (0.20) 23. **0**

24. Figure the tax on the amount on line 7. If the amount on line 7 is less than $100,000, use the Tax Table to figure the tax. If the amount on line 7 is $100,000 or more, use the Tax Computation Worksheet 24. **8,338**

25. Add lines 20, 23, and 24 . . . . 25. **8,683**

26. Figure the tax on the amount on line 1. If the amount on line 1 is less than $100,000, use the Tax Table to figure the tax. If the amount on line 1 is $100,000 or more, use the Tax Computation Worksheet 26. **8,844**

27. **Tax on all taxable income.** Enter the **smaller** of line 25 or line 26. Also include this amount on the entry space on Form 1040 or 1040-SR, line 12a. If you are filing Form 2555, don't enter this amount on the entry space on Form 1040 or 1040-SR, line 12a. Instead, enter it on line 4 of the Foreign Earned Income Tax Worksheet 27. **8,683**

If you are filing Form 2555, see the footnote in the Foreign Earned Income Tax Worksheet before completing this line.

Self-Study Problem 4.7

SCHEDULE E (Form 1040 or 1040-SR) Department of the Treasury Internal Revenue Service (99)	**Supplemental Income and Loss** (From rental real estate, royalties, partnerships, S corporations, estates, trusts, REMICs, etc.) ▶ Attach to Form 1040, 1040-SR, 1040-NR, or 1041. ▶ Go to *www.irs.gov/ScheduleE* for instructions and the latest information.	OMB No. 1545-0074 2019 Attachment Sequence No. **13**

Name(s) shown on return	Your social security number
Janet Randolph	

Part I **Income or Loss From Rental Real Estate and Royalties**   Note: If you are in the business of renting personal property, use **Schedule C** (see instructions). If you are an individual, report farm rental income or loss from **Form 4835** on page 2, line 40.

A Did you make any payments in 2019 that would require you to file Form(s) 1099? (see instructions) . . . . ☐ Yes ☑ No
B If "Yes," did you or will you file required Forms 1099? . . . . ☐ Yes ☐ No

1a	Physical address of each property (street, city, state, ZIP code)
A	14 Lancaster Drive, Salem, OR 97305
B	
C	

1b	Type of Property (from list below)	2 For each rental real estate property listed above, report the number of fair rental and personal use days. Check the **QJV** box only if you meet the requirements to file as a qualified joint venture. See instructions.		Fair Rental Days	Personal Use Days	QJV
A	2		A	365		☐
B			B			☐
C			C			☐

Type of Property:
1 Single Family Residence   3 Vacation/Short-Term Rental 5 Land   7 Self-Rental
2 Multi-Family Residence   4 Commercial   6 Royalties   8 Other (describe)

Income:	Properties:		A	B	C
3 Rents received	**3**		6,000		
4 Royalties received	**4**				
Expenses:					
5 Advertising	**5**				
6 Auto and travel (see instructions)	**6**				
7 Cleaning and maintenance	**7**				
8 Commissions.	**8**				
9 Insurance	**9**		225		
10 Legal and other professional fees	**10**				
11 Management fees	**11**				
12 Mortgage interest paid to banks, etc. (see instructions)	**12**		1,700		
13 Other interest.	**13**				
14 Repairs.	**14**				
15 Supplies	**15**				
16 Taxes	**16**		600		
17 Utilities	**17**		900		
18 Depreciation expense or depletion	**18**		545		
19 Other (list) ▶ _____	**19**				
20 Total expenses. Add lines 5 through 19	**20**		3,970		
21 Subtract line 20 from line 3 (rents) and/or 4 (royalties). If result is a (loss), see instructions to find out if you must file **Form 6198**	**21**		2,030		
22 Deductible rental real estate loss after limitation, if any, on **Form 8582** (see instructions)	**22** (	) (	) (	) (	)

23a	Total of all amounts reported on line 3 for all rental properties	**23a**	6,000	
b	Total of all amounts reported on line 4 for all royalty properties	**23b**		
c	Total of all amounts reported on line 12 for all properties	**23c**	1,700	
d	Total of all amounts reported on line 18 for all properties	**23d**	545	
e	Total of all amounts reported on line 20 for all properties	**23e**	3,970	

24	**Income.** Add positive amounts shown on line 21. **Do not** include any losses	**24**	2,030
25	**Losses.** Add royalty losses from line 21 and rental real estate losses from line 22. Enter total losses here .	**25** (	)
26	**Total rental real estate and royalty income or (loss).** Combine lines 24 and 25. Enter the result here. If Parts II, III, IV, and line 40 on page 2 do not apply to you, also enter this amount on Schedule 1 (Form 1040 or 1040-SR), line 5, or Form 1040-NR, line 18. Otherwise, include this amount in the total on line 41 on page 2	**26**	2,030

For Paperwork Reduction Act Notice, see the separate instructions.   Cat. No. 11344L   Schedule E (Form 1040 or 1040-SR) 2019

Self-Study Problem 4.8

Form **8582**	**Passive Activity Loss Limitations**		OMB No. 1545-1008
Department of the Treasury Internal Revenue Service (99)	▶ See separate instructions. ▶ Attach to Form 1040, Form 1040-SR, or Form 1041. ▶ Go to *www.irs.gov/Form8582* for instructions and the latest information.		**2019** Attachment Sequence No. **88**

Name(s) shown on return | Identifying number
Sherry Moore |

Part I   2019 Passive Activity Loss

Caution: Complete Worksheets 1, 2, and 3 before completing Part I.

Rental Real Estate Activities With Active Participation (For the definition of active participation, see **Special Allowance for Rental Real Estate Activities** in the instructions.)

1a	Activities with net income (enter the amount from Worksheet 1, column (a)) .	1a			
b	Activities with net loss (enter the amount from Worksheet 1, column (b)) . .	1b	(21,000)		
c	Prior years' unallowed losses (enter the amount from Worksheet 1, column (c))	1c	( )		
d	Combine lines 1a, 1b, and 1c			1d	(21,000)

Commercial Revitalization Deductions From Rental Real Estate Activities

2a	Commercial revitalization deductions from Worksheet 2, column (a) . . .	2a	( )		
b	Prior year unallowed commercial revitalization deductions from Worksheet 2, column (b)	2b	( )		
c	Add lines 2a and 2b			2c	( )

All Other Passive Activities

3a	Activities with net income (enter the amount from Worksheet 3, column (a)) .	3a			
b	Activities with net loss (enter the amount from Worksheet 3, column (b)) . .	3b	(15,000)		
c	Prior years' unallowed losses (enter the amount from Worksheet 3, column (c))	3c	( )		
d	Combine lines 3a, 3b, and 3c			3d	(15,000)

4	Combine lines 1d, 2c, and 3d. If this line is zero or more, stop here and include this form with your return; all losses are allowed, including any prior year unallowed losses entered on line 1c, 2b, or 3c. Report the losses on the forms and schedules normally used	4	(36,000)

If line 4 is a loss and: • Line 1d is a loss, go to Part II.
  • Line 2c is a loss (and line 1d is zero or more), skip Part II and go to Part III.
  • Line 3d is a loss (and lines 1d and 2c are zero or more), skip Parts II and III and go to line 15.

Caution: If your filing status is married filing separately and you lived with your spouse at any time during the year, **do not** complete Part II or Part III. Instead, go to line 15.

Part II   Special Allowance for Rental Real Estate Activities With Active Participation

Note: Enter all numbers in Part II as positive amounts. See instructions for an example.

5	Enter the **smaller** of the loss on line 1d or the loss on line 4			5	21,000
6	Enter $150,000. If married filing separately, see instructions	6	150,000		
7	Enter modified adjusted gross income, but not less than zero. See instructions	7	102,000		
	Note: If line 7 is greater than or equal to line 6, skip lines 8 and 9, enter -0- on line 10. Otherwise, go to line 8.				
8	Subtract line 7 from line 6	8	48,000		
9	Multiply line 8 by 50% (0.50). **Do not** enter more than $25,000. If married filing separately, see instructions			9	24,000
10	Enter the **smaller** of line 5 or line 9			10	21,000
	If line 2c is a loss, go to Part III. Otherwise, go to line 15.				

Part III   Special Allowance for Commercial Revitalization Deductions From Rental Real Estate Activities

Note: Enter all numbers in Part III as positive amounts. See the example for Part II in the instructions.

11	Enter $25,000 reduced by the amount, if any, on line 10. If married filing separately, see instructions .	11	
12	Enter the loss from line 4	12	
13	Reduce line 12 by the amount on line 10	13	
14	Enter the **smallest** of line 2c (treated as a positive amount), line 11, or line 13	14	

Part IV   Total Losses Allowed

15	Add the income, if any, on lines 1a and 3a and enter the total	15	0
16	**Total losses allowed from all passive activities for 2019.** Add lines 10, 14, and 15. See instructions to find out how to report the losses on your tax return	16	21,000

For Paperwork Reduction Act Notice, see instructions.   Cat. No. 63704F   Form **8582** (2019)

Self-Study Problem 4.10

Taxpayer	Eligible for QBI deduction (Y/N)?	QBI deduction amount
a.	No. Corporations are not eligible for the QBI deduction and Aretha's dividend income from the corporation is not considered QBI income.	$0
b.	Yes. Barbara's business likely falls into the special services category that would subject her to the wage limitation; however, because Barbara's taxable income is below the threshold of $160,700, she is not subject to the wage or special service limits.	See Form 8995 below.
c.	Yes. Alice's restaurant business is not subject to the special service limitation; however, her joint taxable income exceeds the $321,400 threshold. As a result, her QBI deduction is subject to the wage limitation.	See Form 8995-A on Pages E-22 and E-23

Self-Study Problem 4.10b

Form 8995

Department of the Treasury
Internal Revenue Service

**Qualified Business Income Deduction
Simplified Computation**

▶ Attach to your tax return.

▶ Go to *www.irs.gov/Form8995* for instructions and the latest information.

OMB No. XXXX-XXXX

2019

Attachment
Sequence No. **55**

Name(s) shown on return
Barbara Jones

Your taxpayer identification number
317-65-4321

1	(a) Trade, business, or aggregation name	(b) Taxpayer identification number	(c) Qualified business income or (loss)
i	The Bee Hive	317-65-4321	120,000
ii			
iii			
iv			
v			

2	Total qualified business income or (loss). Combine lines 1i through 1v, column (c)	**2** 120,000	
3	Qualified business net (loss) carryforward from the prior year	**3** ( )	
4	Total qualified business income. Combine lines 2 and 3. If zero or less, enter -0-	**4** 120,000	
5	Qualified business income component. Multiply line 4 by 20% (0.20)		**5** 24,000
6	Qualified REIT dividends and publicly traded partnership (PTP) income or (loss) (see instructions)	**6**	
7	Qualified REIT dividends and qualified PTP (loss) carryforward from the prior year	**7** ( )	
8	Total qualified REIT dividends and PTP income. Combine lines 6 and 7. If zero or less, enter -0-	**8**	
9	REIT and PTP component. Multiply line 8 by 20% (0.20)		**9**
10	Qualified business income deduction before the income limitation. Add lines 5 and 9		**10** 24,000
11	Taxable income before qualified business income deduction	**11** 132,500	
12	Net capital gain (see instructions)	**12**	
13	Subtract line 12 from line 11. If zero or less, enter -0-	**13** 132,500	
14	Income limitation. Multiply line 13 by 20% (0.20)		**14** 26,500
15	Qualified business income deduction. Enter the lesser of line 10 or line 14. Also enter this amount on the applicable line of your return ▶		**15** 24,000
16	Total qualified business (loss) carryforward. Combine lines 2 and 3. If greater than zero, enter -0-		**16** (0)
17	Total qualified REIT dividends and PTP (loss) carryforward. Combine lines 6 and 7. If greater than zero, enter -0-		**17** ( )

For Privacy Act and Paperwork Reduction Act Notice, see instructions.   Cat. No. 37806C   Form **8995** (2019)

Self-Study Problem 4.10c

Form **8995-A**	**Qualified Business Income Deduction**	OMB No. XXXX-XXXX
Department of the Treasury Internal Revenue Service	▶ Attach to your tax return. ▶ Go to *www.irs.gov/Form8995A* for instructions and the latest information.	**2019** Attachment Sequence No. **55A**

Name(s) shown on return	Your taxpayer identification number
Alice Delvecchio	565-22-4321

Part I   Trade, Business, or Aggregation Information

Complete the schedules for Form 8995-A, (A, B, C, and/or D), as applicable, before starting Part I. Attach additional worksheets when needed. See instructions.

1	(a) Trade, business, or aggregation name	(b) Check if specified service	(c) Check if aggregation	(d) Taxpayer identification number	(e) Check if patron
A	D's Pizza	☐	☐	565-22-4321	☐
B		☐	☐		☐
C		☐	☐		☐

Part II   Determine Your Adjusted Qualified Business Income

			A	B	C
2	Qualified business income from the trade, business, or aggregation. See instructions	2	100,000		
3	Multiply line 2 by 20% (0.20). If your taxable income is $160,700 or less ($160,725 if married filing separately; $321,400 if married filing jointly), skip lines 4 through 12 and enter the amount from line 3 on line 13	3	20,000		
4	Allocable share of W-2 wages from the trade, business, or aggregation	4	36,000		
5	Multiply line 4 by 50% (0.50)	5	18,000		
6	Multiply line 4 by 25% (0.25)	6	9,000		
7	Allocable share of the unadjusted basis immediately after acquisition (UBIA) of all qualified property	7	67,000		
8	Multiply line 7 by 2.5% (0.025)	8	1,675		
9	Add lines 6 and 8	9	10,675		
10	Enter the greater of line 5 or line 9	10	18,000		
11	W-2 wage and qualified property limitation. Enter the smaller of line 3 or line 10	11	18,000		
12	Phased-in reduction. Enter amount from line 26, if any. See instructions	12	19,148		
13	Qualified business income deduction before patron reduction. Enter the greater of line 11 or line 12	13	19,148		
14	Patron reduction. Enter the amount from Schedule D (Form 8995-A), line 6, if any	14			
15	Qualified business income component. Subtract line 14 from line 13	15	19,148		
16	Total qualified business income component. Add all amounts reported on line 15 . . . . ▶	16	19,148		

For Privacy Act and Paperwork Reduction Act Notice, see separate instructions.   Cat. No. 71661B   Form **8995-A** (2019)

Part III   **Phased-in Reduction**

Complete Part III only if your taxable income is more than $160,700 but not $210,700 ($160,725 and $210,725 if married filing separately; $321,400 and $421,400 if married filing jointly) and line 10 is less than line 3. Otherwise, skip Part III.

			A	B	C
17	Enter amounts from line 3	**17**	20,000		
18	Enter the amounts from line 10	**18**	18,000		
19	Subtract line 18 from line 17	**19**	2,000		
20	Taxable income before qualified business income deduction **20** 364,000				
21	Threshold. Enter $160,700 ($160,725 if married filing separately; $321,400 if married filing jointly) **21** 321,400				
22	Subtract line 21 from line 20 **22** 42,600				
23	Phase-in range. Enter $50,000 ($100,000 if married filing jointly) **23** 100,000				
24	Phase-in percentage. Divide line 22 by line 23 **24** 42.6 %				
25	Total phase-in reduction. Multiply line 19 by line 24	**25**	852		
26	Qualified business income after phase-in reduction. Subtract line 25 from line 17. Enter this amount here and on line 12, for the corresponding trade or business	**26**	19,148		

Part IV   **Determine Your Qualified Business Income Deduction**

27	Total qualified business income component from all qualified trades, businesses, or aggregations. Enter the amount from line 16	**27**	19,148	
28	Qualified REIT dividends and publicly traded partnership (PTP) income or (loss). See instructions	**28**		
29	Qualified REIT dividends and PTP (loss) carryforward from prior years	**29**	( )	
30	Total qualified REIT dividends and PTP income. Combine lines 28 and 29. If less than zero, enter -0-	**30**		
31	REIT and PTP component. Multiply line 30 by 20% (0.20)	**31**		
32	Qualified business income deduction before the income limitation. Add lines 27 and 31 ▶	**32**		19,148
33	Taxable income before qualified business income deduction	**33**	364,000	
34	Net capital gain. See instructions	**34**	12,000	
35	Subtract line 34 from line 33. If zero or less, enter -0-	**35**		352,000
36	Income limitation. Multiply line 35 by 20% (0.20)	**36**		70,400
37	Qualified business income deduction before the domestic production activities deduction (DPAD) under section 199A(g). Enter the smaller of line 32 or line 36 ▶	**37**		19,148
38	DPAD under section 199A(g) allocated from an agricultural or horticultural cooperative. Don't enter more than line 33 minus line 37	**38**		
39	Total qualified business income deduction. Add lines 37 and 38 ▶	**39**		19,148
40	Total qualified REIT dividends and PTP (loss) carryforward. Combine lines 28 and 29. If zero or greater, enter -0-	**40**	( )	

Form **8995-A** (2019)

CHAPTER 5   DEDUCTIONS FOR AND FROM AGI

Self-Study Problem 5.1

a. 1. $7,000
   2. $0 A plan with no deductible does not qualify.
   3. $2,000
   4. $0 Individuals are not allowed to make contributions to an HSA after age 65 and qualify for Medicare.

b. HSA Deduction is $2,700 and taxable distribution is $0. See Form 8889 on Page E-25.

Self-Study Problem 5.2

$20,790 = $15,000 + $2,000 + $3,000 + $790 (limited by age)

Self-Study Problem 5.3

a. $5,400 = $6,000 \times \dfrac{\$74,000 - \$65,000}{\$10,000}$

b. $4,600 = \dfrac{\$137,000 - \$125,500}{\$15,000} \times \$6,000$

Self-Study Problem 5.4

a. $10,000, the lesser of (0.25/1.25) × $50,000 or $56,000
b. i. $10,000, lesser of 25% × $40,000 or $19,000 (annual dollar limit effective for 2019)
   ii. $19,000 (annual dollar limit effective for 2019)

Self-Study Problem 5.5

a. No. Professor Hill is not a K-12 educator.
b. Yes. Jackie worked for two employers, both of which paid her more than $200; her expenses exceeded 10% of the gross income from performing artist work ($1,100 > $8,000 × 10%); and her AGI was below $16,000.
c. Yes.

Self-Study Problems 5.6 through 5.10

See Schedule A and Form 4684 on Pages E-26 and E-27.
Line 1 of Schedule A is computed as follows:

Medical insurance	$ 425
Prescription medicines and drugs	364
Hospital bills	2,424
Doctor bills	725
Eyeglasses for Frank's dependent mother	75
Doctor bills for Betty's sister, who is claimed as a dependent by Frank and Betty	220
Medical transportation in personal vehicle (700 miles * $0.20)	140
Total	4,373
Less reimbursement	(1,420)
Medical and dental expenses	$2,953

Line 5 of Schedule A—The $225 refund is included on Line 1 of Schedule 1 of Form 1040 as gross income.
Line 11 of Schedule A—$11,075 is subject to the 60% limitation for cash donations and is deductible ($21,000 × 60% = $12,600). The clothing is subject to the 50% limit. Since $21,000 × 50% = $10,500, Eric has utilized all of his permitted deduction with his $11,075 60% deduction; thus the $150 must be carried over to 2020. The Mexican Red Cross is not a qualified organization and there is no deduction for sports tickets.
Line 16 of Schedule A—Only the gambling losses are deductible subject to the limit of gambling winnings.

Self-Study Problem 5.1

Form **8889**	**Health Savings Accounts (HSAs)**	OMB No. 1545-0074
Department of the Treasury Internal Revenue Service	▶ Attach to Form 1040, 1040-SR, or 1040-NR. ▶ Go to *www.irs.gov/Form8889* for instructions and the latest information.	**2019** Attachment Sequence No. **52**

Name(s) shown on Form 1040, 1040-SR, or 1040-NR	Social security number of HSA beneficiary. If both spouses have HSAs, see instructions ▶
Alex Morton	213-21-3121

Before you begin: Complete Form 8853, Archer MSAs and Long-Term Care Insurance Contracts, if required.

Part I   HSA Contributions and Deduction. See the instructions before completing this part. If you are filing jointly and both you and your spouse each have separate HSAs, complete a separate Part I for each spouse.

1	Check the box to indicate your coverage under a high-deductible health plan (HDHP) during 2019 (see instructions) . . . . ▶	☑ Self-only ☐ Family	
2	HSA contributions you made for 2019 (or those made on your behalf), including those made from January 1, 2020, through April 15, 2020, that were for 2019. **Do not** include employer contributions, contributions through a cafeteria plan, or rollovers (see instructions)	**2**	2,700
3	If you were under age 55 at the end of 2019 and, on the first day of **every** month during 2019, you were, or were considered, an eligible individual with the **same** coverage, enter $3,500 ($7,000 for family coverage). **All others,** see the instructions for the amount to enter	**3**	3,500
4	Enter the amount you and your employer contributed to your Archer MSAs for 2019 from Form 8853, lines 1 and 2. If you or your spouse had family coverage under an HDHP at any time during 2019, also include any amount contributed to your spouse's Archer MSAs	**4**	0
5	Subtract line 4 from line 3. If zero or less, enter -0-	**5**	3,500
6	Enter the amount from line 5. But if you and your spouse each have separate HSAs and had family coverage under an HDHP at any time during 2019, see the instructions for the amount to enter . .	**6**	3,500
7	If you were age 55 or older at the end of 2019, married, and you or your spouse had family coverage under an HDHP at any time during 2019, enter your additional contribution amount (see instructions)	**7**	
8	Add lines 6 and 7	**8**	3,500
9	Employer contributions made to your HSAs for 2019	**9** 300	
10	Qualified HSA funding distributions	**10**	
11	Add lines 9 and 10	**11**	300
12	Subtract line 11 from line 8. If zero or less, enter -0-	**12**	3,200
13	**HSA deduction.** Enter the **smaller** of line 2 or line 12 here and on Schedule 1 (Form 1040 or 1040-SR), line 12, or Form 1040-NR, line 25	**13**	2,700

Caution: If line 2 is more than line 13, you may have to pay an additional tax (see instructions).

Part II   HSA Distributions. If you are filing jointly and both you and your spouse each have separate HSAs, complete a separate Part II for each spouse.

14a	Total distributions you received in 2019 from all HSAs (see instructions)	**14a**	1,783
b	Distributions included on line 14a that you rolled over to another HSA. Also include any excess contributions (and the earnings on those excess contributions) included on line 14a that were withdrawn by the due date of your return (see instructions)	**14b**	0
c	Subtract line 14b from line 14a	**14c**	1,783
15	Qualified medical expenses paid using HSA distributions (see instructions)	**15**	1,783
16	**Taxable HSA distributions.** Subtract line 15 from line 14c. If zero or less, enter -0-. Also, include this amount in the total on Schedule 1 (Form 1040 or 1040-SR), line 8, or Form 1040-NR, line 21. Enter "HSA" and the amount on the line next to the box	**16**	0
17a	If any of the distributions included on line 16 meet any of the **Exceptions to the Additional 20% Tax** (see instructions), check here . . . . ▶ ☐		
b	**Additional 20% tax** (see instructions). Enter 20% (0.20) of the distributions included on line 16 that are subject to the additional 20% tax. Also include this amount in the total on Schedule 2 (Form 1040 or 1040-SR), line 8, or Form 1040-NR, line 60. Check box c on Schedule 2 (Form 1040 or 1040-SR), line 8, or box b on Form 1040-NR, line 60. Enter "HSA" and the amount on the line next to the box .	**17b**	

For Paperwork Reduction Act Notice, see your tax return instructions.   Cat. No. 37621P   Form **8889** (2019)

Self-Study Problems 5.6, 5.7, 5.8, 5.9, and 5.10

SCHEDULE A (Form 1040 or 1040-SR) Department of the Treasury Internal Revenue Service (99)	**Itemized Deductions** ▶ Go to *www.irs.gov/ScheduleA* for instructions and the latest information. ▶ Attach to Form 1040 or 1040-SR. **Caution:** If you are claiming a net qualified disaster loss on Form 4684, see the instructions for line 16.	OMB No. 1545-0074 20**19** Attachment Sequence No. **07**

Name(s) shown on Form 1040 or 1040-SR | Your social security number

Medical and Dental Expenses		**Caution: Do not include expenses reimbursed or paid by others.**		
	1	Medical and dental expenses (see instructions)	**1**	2,953
	2	Enter amount from Form 1040 or 1040-SR, line 8b	**2**	25,400
	3	Multiply line 2 by 10% (0.10)	**3**	2,540
	4	Subtract line 3 from line 1. If line 3 is more than line 1, enter -0-	**4**	413
Taxes You Paid	5	State and local taxes.		
	a	State and local income taxes or general sales taxes. You may include either income taxes or general sales taxes on line 5a, but not both. If you elect to include general sales taxes instead of income taxes, check this box ▶ ☐	**5a**	1,050
	b	State and local real estate taxes (see instructions)	**5b**	825
	c	State and local personal property taxes	**5c**	85
	d	Add lines 5a through 5c	**5d**	1,960
	e	Enter the smaller of line 5d or $10,000 ($5,000 if married filing separately)	**5e**	1,960
	6	Other taxes. List type and amount ▶ _____	**6**	
	7	Add lines 5e and 6	**7**	1,960
Interest You Paid **Caution:** Your mortgage interest deduction may be limited (see instructions).	8	Home mortgage interest and points. If you didn't use all of your home mortgage loan(s) to buy, build, or improve your home, see instructions and check this box ▶ ☐		
	a	Home mortgage interest and points reported to you on Form 1098. See instructions if limited	**8a**	9,250
	b	Home mortgage interest not reported to you on Form 1098. If paid to the person from whom you bought the home, see instructions and show that person's name, identifying no., and address ▶ _____	**8b**	
	c	Points not reported to you on Form 1098. See instructions for special rules	**8c**	
	d	Reserved	**8d**	
	e	Add lines 8a through 8c	**8e**	9,250
	9	Investment interest. Attach Form 4952 if required. See instructions	**9**	1,000
	10	Add lines 8e and 9	**10**	10,250
Gifts to Charity **Caution:** If you made a gift and got a benefit for it, see instructions.	11	Gifts by cash or check. If you made any gift of $250 or more, see instructions	**11**	11,075
	12	Other than by cash or check. If you made any gift of $250 or more, see instructions. You **must** attach Form 8283 if over $500.	**12**	0
	13	Carryover from prior year	**13**	
	14	Add lines 11 through 13	**14**	11,075
Casualty and Theft Losses	15	Casualty and theft loss(es) from a federally declared disaster (other than net qualified disaster losses). Attach Form 4684 and enter the amount from line 18 of that form. See instructions	**15**	5,400
Other Itemized Deductions	16	Other—from list in instructions. List type and amount ▶ _____ Gambling losses	**16**	1,400
Total Itemized Deductions	17	Add the amounts in the far right column for lines 4 through 16. Also, enter this amount on Form 1040 or 1040-SR, line 9	**17**	
	18	If you elect to itemize deductions even though they are less than your standard deduction, check this box ▶ ☐		

For Paperwork Reduction Act Notice, see the Instructions for Forms 1040 and 1040-SR.   Cat. No. 17145C   **Schedule A (Form 1040 or 1040-SR) 2019**

Self-Study Problem 5.10

Form **4684**	**Casualties and Thefts**	OMB No. 1545-0177
Department of the Treasury Internal Revenue Service	▶ Go to *www.irs.gov/Form4684* for instructions and the latest information. ▶ Attach to your tax return. ▶ Use a separate Form 4684 for each casualty or theft.	**20****19** Attachment Sequence No. **26**

Name(s) shown on tax return	Identifying number
Robert	

SECTION A—Personal Use Property (Use this section to report casualties and thefts of property **not** used in a trade or business or for income-producing purposes. You must use a separate Form 4684 (through line 12) for each casualty or theft event involving personal use property. **If reporting a qualified disaster loss, see the instructions for special rules that apply before completing this section.**)

If the casualty or theft loss is attributable to a federally declared disaster, check here ☑ and enter the FEMA disaster declaration number. (See instructions.) EM-5566

1 Description of properties (show type, location (city, state, and ZIP code), and date acquired for each property). Use a separate line for each property lost or damaged from the same casualty or theft. If you checked the box and entered the FEMA disaster declaration number above, enter the ZIP code for the property most affected on the line for Property **A**.

	Type of Property	City and State	ZIP Code	Date Acquired
Property **A**	Auto	Jupiter, FL	33477	July 2016
Property **B**				
Property **C**				
Property **D**				

			Properties			
			A	**B**	**C**	**D**
2	Cost or other basis of each property	2	18,500			
3	Insurance or other reimbursement (whether or not you filed a claim) (see instructions) **Note:** If line 2 is **more** than line 3, skip line 4.	3	5,000			
4	Gain from casualty or theft. If line 3 is **more** than line 2, enter the difference here and skip lines 5 through 9 for that column. See instructions if line 3 includes insurance or other reimbursement you did not claim, or you received payment for your loss in a later tax year	4				
5	Fair market value **before** casualty or theft	5	14,000			
6	Fair market value **after** casualty or theft	6	0			
7	Subtract line 6 from line 5	7	14,000			
8	Enter the **smaller** of line 2 or line 7	8	14,000			
9	Subtract line 3 from line 8. If zero or less, enter -0-	9	9,000			

10	Casualty or theft loss. Add the amounts on line 9 in columns A through D	10	9,000
11	Enter $100 ($500 if qualified disaster loss rules apply; see instructions)	11	100
12	Subtract line 11 from line 10. If zero or less, enter -0-	12	8,900

Caution: Use only one Form 4684 for lines 13 through 18.

13	Add the amounts on line 4 of all Forms 4684	13	
14	Add the amounts on line 12 of all Forms 4684. If you have losses not attributable to a federally declared disaster, see the instructions	14	8,900

Caution: See instructions before completing line 15.

15 • If line 13 is **more** than line 14, enter the difference here and on Schedule D. **Do not** complete the rest of this section.

• If line 13 is **equal** to line 14, enter -0- here. **Do not** complete the rest of this section.

• If line 13 is **less** than line 14, and you have no qualified disaster losses subject to the $500 reduction on line 11 on any Form(s) 4684, enter -0- here and go to line 16. If you have qualified disaster losses subject to the $500 reduction, subtract line 13 from line 14 and enter the smaller of this difference or the amount on line 12 of the Form(s) 4684 reporting those losses. Enter that result here and on Schedule A (Form 1040 or 1040-SR), line 16, or Form 1040-NR, Schedule A, line 7. If you claim the standard deduction, also include on Schedule A (Form 1040 or 1040-SR), line 16, the amount of your standard deduction (see the Instructions for Forms 1040 and 1040-SR). Do not complete the rest of this section if all of your casualty or theft losses are subject to the $500 reduction.

15		0

16	Add lines 13 and 15. Subtract the result from line 14	16	8,900
17	Enter 10% of your adjusted gross income from Form 1040 or 1040-SR, line 8b, or Form 1040-NR, line 35. Estates and trusts, see instructions	17	3,500
18	Subtract line 17 from line 16. If zero or less, enter -0-. Also, enter the result on Schedule A (Form 1040 or 1040-SR), line 15, or Form 1040-NR, Schedule A, line 6. Estates and trusts, enter the result on the "Other deductions" line of your tax return	18	5,400

For Paperwork Reduction Act Notice, see instructions.   Cat. No. 12997O   Form **4684** (2019)

Self-Study Problem 5.8

See Schedule A of Page E-26 for reporting of interest under part a.

	Total	Part a.	Part b.	Part c.
Interest on her home mortgage	$9,250	$ 9,250	$ 9,250	$ 9,250
Service charges on her checking account	48	0	0	0
Credit card interest	168	0	0	0
Auto loan interest	675	0	0	0
Interest from a home equity line of credit (HELOC)	2,300	0	2,300	0
Interest from a loan used to purchase stock	1,600	1,000	1,000	1,000
Credit investigation fee for loan	75	0	0	0
Deductible amount		$10,250	$12,550	$10,250

Dorothie's mortgage interest is from qualified mortgage debt (secured by residence, less than $1,000,000) and is deductible in parts a–c. Because Dorothie's mortgage originated prior to December 16, 2017, the $1 million threshold continues to apply in 2019. The home equity interest is deductible in part a under the pre-TCJA tax law. It is not deductible in part a in 2019 as generally home equity interest is not deductible under TCJA. In part b, the home equity debt is treated as acquisition debt which continues to qualify as deductible post-TCJA (subject to the $1 million limitation for grandfathered debt). The investment interest remains deductible after TCJA but also remains limited to net investment income ($1,000 in this example). The other forms of interest are nondeductible personal interest.

CHAPTER 6   ACCOUNTING PERIODS AND OTHER TAXES

Self-Study Problem 6.1

Taxpayer	Calendar year-end	Fiscal year-end	Fiscal year-end but some restrictions
1. Individual with no separate books and records	X		
2. Partnership for which all the partners are calendar year-end individuals			X
3. A corporation that keeps its book and records on a fiscal year ending June 30		X	
4. An S corporation for which all shareholders are calendar year-end individuals			X

Self-Study Problem 6.2A

Business income	$ 63,000
Less: business expenses	(42,000)
Operating income	21,000
Add: rent received	9,000
Add: prepaid interest received	12,000
Less: rent expense for one month ($7,200/6)	(1,200)
Net income	$ 40,800

Self-Study Problem 6.2B

1. Yes
2. Yes
3. No, annual receipts exceed $26 million
4. Yes, assuming this is a personal service corporation.

Self-Study Problem 6.3

1. 56%; 40% owned directly and 16% (80% × 20%) through X Corporation.
2. 40%; 20% owned directly plus 20% as Gene's brother.
3. 40%; 20% owned directly plus 20% as Frank's brother.
4. $0; since they are related parties, the loss would be disallowed.

Self-Study Problem 6.4

a. Taxable income = $1,900 ($3,000 − $1,100)
   NUI = $800 ($3,000 − $2,200)
   ETI = $1,100 ($1,900 − $800)
   Tax = $190 ($800 × 10% + $1,100 × 10%)
b. Taxable income = $1,900 ($3,000 − $1,100)
   Amount taxed at parent's rate = $800 ($3,000 − $2,200)
   Amount taxed at child's rate = $1,100
   Tax = $206 ($1,100 × 10%) + (800 × 12%)

Self-Study Problem 6.5

See Form 6251 on Page E-30.

Self-Study Problem 6.6

See Schedule SE on Page E-31.

Self-Study Problem 6.7

See Schedule H on Pages E-32 and E-33.

Self-Study Problem 6.8

See Form 8960 on Page E-34 and Form 8959 on Page E-35.

Self-Study Problem 6.5

Form **6251**	**Alternative Minimum Tax—Individuals**	OMB No. 1545-0074

Department of the Treasury
Internal Revenue Service (99)

▶ Go to *www.irs.gov/Form6251* for instructions and the latest information.
▶ Attach to Form 1040, 1040-SR, or 1040-NR.

2019

Attachment Sequence No. **32**

Name(s) shown on Form 1040, 1040-SR, or 1040-NR
Harold Brown

Your social security number

Part I — Alternative Minimum Taxable Income (See instructions for how to complete each line.)

1	Enter the amount from Form 1040 or 1040-SR, line 11b, if more than zero. If Form 1040 or 1040-SR, line 11b, is zero, subtract lines 9 and 10 of Form 1040 or 1040-SR from line 8b of Form 1040 or 1040-SR and enter the result here. (If less than zero, enter as a negative amount.)	1	556,000
2a	If filing Schedule A (Form 1040 or 1040-SR), enter the taxes from Schedule A, line 7; otherwise, enter the amount from Form 1040 or 1040-SR, line 9.	2a	10,000
b	Tax refund from Schedule 1 (Form 1040 or 1040-SR), line 1 or line 8	2b	( )
c	Investment interest expense (difference between regular tax and AMT)	2c	
d	Depletion (difference between regular tax and AMT)	2d	
e	Net operating loss deduction from Schedule 1 (Form 1040 or 1040-SR), line 8. Enter as a positive amount	2e	
f	Alternative tax net operating loss deduction	2f	( )
g	Interest from specified private activity bonds exempt from the regular tax	2g	100,000
h	Qualified small business stock, see instructions	2h	
i	Exercise of incentive stock options (excess of AMT income over regular tax income)	2i	
j	Estates and trusts (amount from Schedule K-1 (Form 1041), box 12, code A)	2j	
k	Disposition of property (difference between AMT and regular tax gain or loss)	2k	
l	Depreciation on assets placed in service after 1986 (difference between regular tax and AMT)	2l	
m	Passive activities (difference between AMT and regular tax income or loss)	2m	
n	Loss limitations (difference between AMT and regular tax income or loss)	2n	
o	Circulation costs (difference between regular tax and AMT)	2o	
p	Long-term contracts (difference between AMT and regular tax income)	2p	
q	Mining costs (difference between regular tax and AMT)	2q	
r	Research and experimental costs (difference between regular tax and AMT)	2r	
s	Income from certain installment sales before January 1, 1987	2s	( )
t	Intangible drilling costs preference	2t	
3	Other adjustments, including income-based related adjustments	3	
4	**Alternative minimum taxable income.** Combine lines 1 through 3. (If married filing separately and line 4 is more than $733,700, see instructions.)	4	666,000

Part II — Alternative Minimum Tax (AMT)

5	Exemption. (If you were under age 24 at the end of 2019, see instructions.)		

IF your filing status is . . .	AND line 4 is not over . . .	THEN enter on line 5 . . .		
Single or head of household	$ 510,300	$ 71,700		
Married filing jointly or qualifying widow(er)	1,020,600	111,700		
Married filing separately	510,300	55,850	5	32,775 (a)
If line 4 is **over** the amount shown above for your filing status, see instructions.				

6	Subtract line 5 from line 4. If more than zero, go to line 7. If zero or less, enter -0- here and on lines 7, 9, and 11, and go to line 10.	6	633,225
7	• If you are filing Form 2555, see instructions for the amount to enter. • If you reported capital gain distributions directly on Form 1040 or 1040-SR, line 6; you reported qualified dividends on Form 1040 or 1040-SR, line 3a; **or** you had a gain on both lines 15 and 16 of Schedule D (Form 1040 or 1040-SR) (as refigured for the AMT, if necessary), complete Part III on the back and enter the amount from line 40 here. • **All others:** If line 6 is $194,800 or less ($97,400 or less if married filing separately), multiply line 6 by 26% (0.26). Otherwise, multiply line 6 by 28% (0.28) and subtract $3,896 ($1,948 if married filing separately) from the result.	7	173,407
8	Alternative minimum tax foreign tax credit (see instructions)	8	
9	Tentative minimum tax. Subtract line 8 from line 7	9	173,407
10	Add Form 1040 or 1040-SR, line 12a (minus any tax from Form 4972), and Schedule 2 (Form 1040 or 1040-SR), line 2. Subtract from the result any foreign tax credit from Schedule 3 (Form 1040 or 1040-SR), line 1. If you used Schedule J to figure your tax on Form 1040 or 1040-SR, line 12a, refigure that tax without using Schedule J before completing this line (see instructions)	10	170,708
11	**AMT.** Subtract line 10 from line 9. If zero or less, enter -0-. Enter here and on Schedule 2 (Form 1040 or 1040-SR), line 1	11	2,699

For Paperwork Reduction Act Notice, see your tax return instructions.   Cat. No. 13600G   Form **6251** (2019)

(a) $32,775 = \$71,700 - [(\$666,000 - \$510,300) \times 25\%]$

Self-Study Problem 6.6

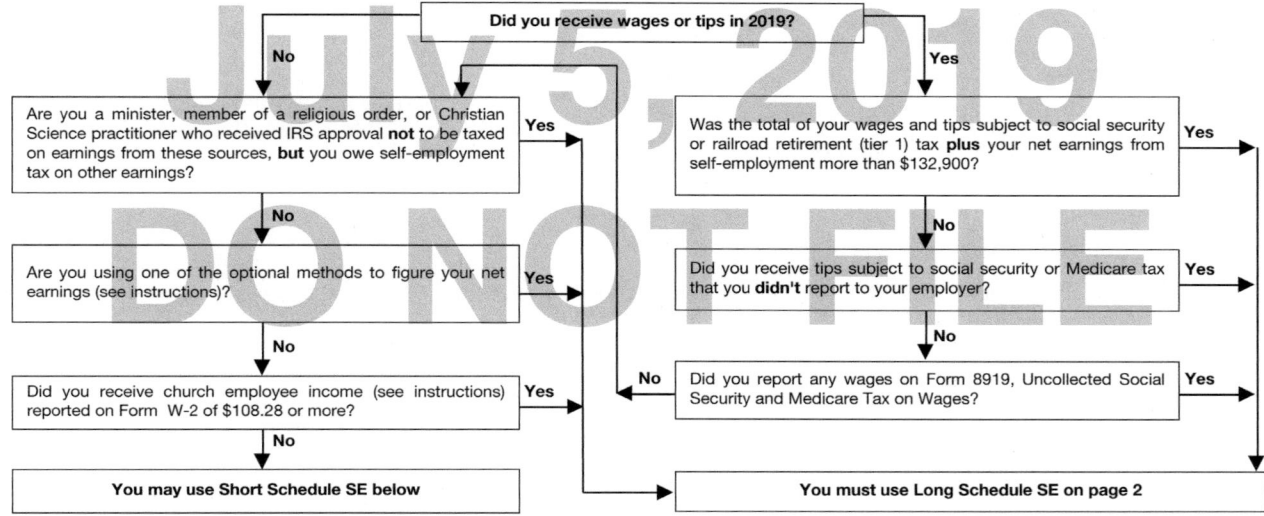

| SCHEDULE SE
(Form 1040 or
1040-SR)

Department of the Treasury
Internal Revenue Service (99) | **Self-Employment Tax**

▶ Go to *www.irs.gov/ScheduleSE* for instructions and the latest information.
▶ Attach to Form 1040, 1040-SR, or 1040-NR. | OMB No. 1545-0074

20**19**

Attachment
Sequence No. **17** |

Name of person with self-employment income (as shown on Form 1040, 1040-SR, or 1040-NR)
Joanne Plummer

Social security number of person
with **self-employment** income ▶

Before you begin: To determine if you must file Schedule SE, see the instructions.

May I Use Short Schedule SE or Must I Use Long Schedule SE?

Note: Use this flowchart **only if** you must file Schedule SE. If unsure, see *Who Must File Schedule SE* in the instructions.

Section A—Short Schedule SE. Caution: Read above to see if you can use Short Schedule SE.

1a	Net farm profit or (loss) from Schedule F, line 34, and farm partnerships, Schedule K-1 (Form 1065), box 14, code A	**1a**	
b	If you received social security retirement or disability benefits, enter the amount of Conservation Reserve Program payments included on Schedule F, line 4b, or listed on Schedule K-1 (Form 1065), box 20, code AH	**1b**	( )
2	Net profit or (loss) from Schedule C, line 31; and Schedule K-1 (Form 1065), box 14, code A (other than farming). Ministers and members of religious orders, see instructions for types of income to report on this line. See instructions for other income to report	**2**	36,600
3	Combine lines 1a, 1b, and 2	**3**	36,600
4	Multiply line 3 by 92.35% (0.9235). If less than $400, you don't owe self-employment tax; **don't** file this schedule unless you have an amount on line 1b . . . . ▶	**4**	33,800
	Note: If line 4 is less than $400 due to Conservation Reserve Program payments on line 1b, see instructions.		
5	**Self-employment tax.** If the amount on line 4 is: • $132,900 or less, multiply line 4 by 15.3% (0.153). Enter the result here and on **Schedule 2 (Form 1040 or 1040-SR), line 4,** or **Form 1040-NR, line 55.** • More than $132,900, multiply line 4 by 2.9% (0.029). Then, add $16,479.60 to the result. Enter the total here and on **Schedule 2 (Form 1040 or 1040-SR), line 4,** or **Form 1040-NR, line 55** .	**5**	5,171
6	**Deduction for one-half of self-employment tax.** Multiply line 5 by 50% (0.50). Enter the result here and on **Schedule 1 (Form 1040 or 1040-SR), line 14,** or **Form 1040-NR, line 27** **6**	2,586	

For Paperwork Reduction Act Notice, see your tax return instructions.   Cat. No. 11358Z   Schedule SE (Form 1040 or 1040-SR) 2019

Because Joanne's total wages plus self-employment income are less than $132,900, she may complete Short Schedule SE on page 1.

Self-Study Problem 6.7

SCHEDULE H	**Household Employment Taxes**	OMB No. 1545-1971
(Form 1040 or 1040-SR)	(For Social Security, Medicare, Withheld Income, and Federal Unemployment (FUTA) Taxes)	**2019**
Department of the Treasury Internal Revenue Service (99)	▶ Attach to Form 1040, 1040-SR, 1040-NR, 1040-SS, or 1041. ▶ Go to *www.irs.gov/ScheduleH* for instructions and the latest information.	Attachment Sequence No. **44**

Name of employer

Susan Green

Social security number

Employer identification number

Calendar year taxpayers having no household employees in 2019 don't have to complete this form for 2019.

A Did you pay **any one** household employee cash wages of $2,100 or more in 2019? (If any household employee was your spouse, your child under age 21, your parent, or anyone under age 18, see the line A instructions before you answer this question.)

☑ **Yes.** Skip lines B and C and go to line 1.
☐ **No.** Go to line B.

B Did you withhold federal income tax during 2019 for any household employee?

☐ **Yes.** Skip line C and go to line 7.
☐ **No.** Go to line C.

C Did you pay **total** cash wages of $1,000 or more in **any** calendar **quarter** of 2018 or 2019 to **all** household employees? (**Don't** count cash wages paid in 2018 or 2019 to your spouse, your child under age 21, or your parent.)

☐ **No.** **Stop.** Don't file this schedule.
☐ **Yes.** Skip lines 1–9 and go to line 10.

Part I	Social Security, Medicare, and Federal Income Taxes			
1	Total cash wages subject to social security tax	**1**	3,600	
2	Social security tax. Multiply line 1 by 12.4% (0.124)		**2**	446
3	Total cash wages subject to Medicare tax	**3**	3,600	
4	Medicare tax. Multiply line 3 by 2.9% (0.029)		**4**	104
5	Total cash wages subject to Additional Medicare Tax withholding	**5**		
6	Additional Medicare Tax withholding. Multiply line 5 by 0.9% (0.009)		**6**	
7	Federal income tax withheld, if any		**7**	
8	**Total social security, Medicare, and federal income taxes.** Add lines 2, 4, 6, and 7		**8**	550

9 Did you pay **total** cash wages of $1,000 or more in **any** calendar **quarter** of 2018 or 2019 to **all** household employees? (**Don't** count cash wages paid in 2018 or 2019 to your spouse, your child under age 21, or your parent.)

☐ **No.** **Stop.** Include the amount from line 8 above on Schedule 2 (Form 1040 or 1040-SR), line 7a. If you're not required to file Form 1040 or 1040-SR, see the line 9 instructions.

☑ **Yes.** Go to line 10.

For Privacy Act and Paperwork Reduction Act Notice, see the instructions.   Cat. No. 12187K   Schedule H (Form 1040 or 1040-SR) 2019

Self-Study Problem 6.7

Part II   Federal Unemployment (FUTA) Tax

		Yes	No
10	Did you pay unemployment contributions to only one state? If you paid contributions to a credit reduction state, see instructions and check **"No."** **10**	✓	
11	Did you pay all state unemployment contributions for 2019 by April 15, 2020? Fiscal year filers, see instructions **11**	✓	
12	Were all wages that are taxable for FUTA tax also taxable for your state's unemployment tax? **12**	✓	

Next: If you checked the **"Yes"** box on **all** the lines above, complete Section A.
    If you checked the **"No"** box on **any** of the lines above, skip Section A and complete Section B.

Section A

13	Name of the state where you paid unemployment contributions ▶ Virginia		
14	Contributions paid to your state unemployment fund **14** 194		
15	Total cash wages subject to FUTA tax **15**	3,600
16	**FUTA tax.** Multiply line 15 by 0.6% (0.006). Enter the result here, skip Section B, and go to line 25 . . **16**	22

Section B

17 Complete all columns below that apply (if you need more space, see instructions):

(a) Name of state	(b) Taxable wages (as defined in state act)	(c) State experience rate period		(d) State experience rate	(e) Multiply col. (b) by 0.054	(f) Multiply col. (b) by col. (d)	(g) Subtract col. (f) from col. (e). If zero or less, enter -0-.	(h) Contributions paid to state unemployment fund
		From	To					

18	Totals **18**		
19	Add columns (g) and (h) of line 18 . . . . **19**		
20	Total cash wages subject to FUTA tax (see the line 15 instructions)	**20**	
21	Multiply line 20 by 6.0% (0.060)	**21**	
22	Multiply line 20 by 5.4% (0.054) **22**		
23	Enter the **smaller** of line 19 or line 22		
	(If you paid state unemployment contributions late or you're in a credit reduction state, see instructions and check here) . . . . ☐	**23**	
24	**FUTA tax.** Subtract line 23 from line 21. Enter the result here and go to line 25	**24**	

Part III   Total Household Employment Taxes

25	Enter the amount from line 8. If you checked the **"Yes"** box on line C of page 1, enter -0-	**25**	550
26	Add line 16 (or line 24) and line 25	**26**	572
27	Are you required to file Form 1040 or 1040-SR?		

☑ **Yes. Stop.** Include the amount from line 26 above on Schedule 2 (Form 1040 or 1040-SR), line 7a. **Don't** complete Part IV below.

☐ **No.**   You may have to complete Part IV. See instructions for details.

Part IV   Address and Signature — Complete this part **only** if required. See the line 27 instructions.

Address (number and street) or P.O. box if mail isn't delivered to street address	Apt., room, or suite no.

City, town or post office, state, and ZIP code

Under penalties of perjury, I declare that I have examined this schedule, including accompanying statements, and to the best of my knowledge and belief, it is true, correct, and complete. No part of any payment made to a state unemployment fund claimed as a credit was, or is to be, deducted from the payments to employees. Declaration of preparer (other than taxpayer) is based on all information of which preparer has any knowledge.

▶ _____ Employer's signature	▶ _____ Date		
Paid Preparer Use Only	Print/Type preparer's name	Preparer's signature	Date	Check ☐ if self-employed	PTIN
	Firm's name ▶		Firm's EIN ▶
	Firm's address ▶		Phone no.

Self-Study Problem 6.8

Form **8960**	**Net Investment Income Tax—Individuals, Estates, and Trusts**	OMB No. 1545-2227
Department of the Treasury Internal Revenue Service (99)	▶ Attach to your tax return. ▶ Go to *www.irs.gov/Form8960* for instructions and the latest information.	**2019** Attachment Sequence No. **72**

Name(s) shown on your tax return	Your social security number or EIN
Ronald Trunk	

Part I   Investment Income

☐ Section 6013(g) election (see instructions)
☐ Section 6013(h) election (see instructions)
☐ Regulations section 1.1411-10(g) election (see instructions)

1	Taxable interest (see instructions)	**1**	110,000
2	Ordinary dividends (see instructions)	**2**	
3	Annuities (see instructions)	**3**	
4a	Rental real estate, royalties, partnerships, S corporations, trusts, etc. (see instructions)	**4a**	
b	Adjustment for net income or loss derived in the ordinary course of a non-section 1411 trade or business (see instructions)	**4b**	
c	Combine lines 4a and 4b	**4c**	
5a	Net gain or loss from disposition of property (see instructions)	**5a**	
b	Net gain or loss from disposition of property that is not subject to net investment income tax (see instructions)	**5b**	
c	Adjustment from disposition of partnership interest or S corporation stock (see instructions)	**5c**	
d	Combine lines 5a through 5c	**5d**	
6	Adjustments to investment income for certain CFCs and PFICs (see instructions)	**6**	
7	Other modifications to investment income (see instructions)	**7**	
8	Total investment income. Combine lines 1, 2, 3, 4c, 5d, 6, and 7	**8**	110,000

Part II   Investment Expenses Allocable to Investment Income and Modifications

9a	Investment interest expenses (see instructions)	**9a**	
b	State, local, and foreign income tax (see instructions)	**9b**	
c	Miscellaneous investment expenses (see instructions)	**9c**	
d	Add lines 9a, 9b, and 9c	**9d**	
10	Additional modifications (see instructions)	**10**	
11	Total deductions and modifications. Add lines 9d and 10	**11**	0

Part III   Tax Computation

12	Net investment income. Subtract Part II, line 11, from Part I, line 8. Individuals, complete lines 13–17. Estates and trusts, complete lines 18a–21. If zero or less, enter -0-	**12**	110,000

Individuals:

13	Modified adjusted gross income (see instructions)	**13**	380,000	
14	Threshold based on filing status (see instructions)	**14**	200,000	
15	Subtract line 14 from line 13. If zero or less, enter -0-	**15**	180,000	
16	Enter the smaller of line 12 or line 15		**16**	110,000
17	Net investment income tax for individuals. Multiply line 16 by 3.8% (0.038). **Enter here and include on your tax return** (see instructions)		**17**	4,180

Estates and Trusts:

18a	Net investment income (line 12 above)	**18a**	
b	Deductions for distributions of net investment income and deductions under section 642(c) (see instructions)	**18b**	
c	Undistributed net investment income. Subtract line 18b from 18a (see instructions). If zero or less, enter -0-	**18c**	
19a	Adjusted gross income (see instructions)	**19a**	
b	Highest tax bracket for estates and trusts for the year (see instructions)	**19b**	
c	Subtract line 19b from line 19a. If zero or less, enter -0-	**19c**	
20	Enter the smaller of line 18c or line 19c	**20**	
21	Net investment income tax for estates and trusts. Multiply line 20 by 3.8% (0.038). **Enter here and include on your tax return** (see instructions)	**21**	

For Paperwork Reduction Act Notice, see your tax return instructions.   Cat. No. 59474M   Form **8960** (2019)

Self-Study Problem 6.8

Form 8959

Department of the Treasury
Internal Revenue Service

Additional Medicare Tax

▶ If any line does not apply to you, leave it blank. See separate instructions.
▶ Attach to Form 1040, 1040-SR, 1040-NR, 1040-PR, or 1040-SS.
▶ Go to *www.irs.gov/Form8959* for instructions and the latest information.

OMB No. 1545-0074

2019

Attachment
Sequence No. **71**

Name(s) shown on return: Meng and Eang Ung

Your social security number

Part I   Additional Medicare Tax on Medicare Wages

1	Medicare wages and tips from Form W-2, box 5. If you have more than one Form W-2, enter the total of the amounts from box 5	**1**	265,000
2	Unreported tips from Form 4137, line 6	**2**	
3	Wages from Form 8919, line 6	**3**	
4	Add lines 1 through 3	**4**	265,000
5	Enter the following amount for your filing status: Married filing jointly . . . . $250,000 Married filing separately . . . . $125,000 Single, Head of household, or Qualifying widow(er) $200,000	**5**	250,000
6	Subtract line 5 from line 4. If zero or less, enter -0-	**6**	15,000
7	Additional Medicare Tax on Medicare wages. Multiply line 6 by 0.9% (0.009). Enter here and go to Part II	**7**	135

Part II   Additional Medicare Tax on Self-Employment Income

8	Self-employment income from Schedule SE (Form 1040 or 1040-SR), Section A, line 4, or Section B, line 6. If you had a loss, enter -0- (Form 1040-PR or 1040-SS filers, see instructions.)	**8**	130,000
9	Enter the following amount for your filing status: Married filing jointly . . . . $250,000 Married filing separately . . . . $125,000 Single, Head of household, or Qualifying widow(er) $200,000	**9**	150,000
10	Enter the amount from line 4	**10**	265,000
11	Subtract line 10 from line 9. If zero or less, enter -0-	**11**	0
12	Subtract line 11 from line 8. If zero or less, enter -0-	**12**	130,000
13	Additional Medicare Tax on self-employment income. Multiply line 12 by 0.9% (0.009). Enter here and go to Part III	**13**	1,170

Part III   Additional Medicare Tax on Railroad Retirement Tax Act (RRTA) Compensation

14	Railroad retirement (RRTA) compensation and tips from Form(s) W-2, box 14 (see instructions)	**14**	
15	Enter the following amount for your filing status: Married filing jointly . . . . $250,000 Married filing separately . . . . $125,000 Single, Head of household, or Qualifying widow(er) $200,000	**15**	
16	Subtract line 15 from line 14. If zero or less, enter -0-	**16**	
17	Additional Medicare Tax on railroad retirement (RRTA) compensation. Multiply line 16 by 0.9% (0.009). Enter here and go to Part IV	**17**	

Part IV   Total Additional Medicare Tax

18	Add lines 7, 13, and 17. Also include this amount on Schedule 2 (Form 1040 or 1040-SR), line 8 (check box a) (Form 1040-NR, 1040-PR, or 1040-SS filers, see instructions), and go to Part V	**18**	1,305

Part V   Withholding Reconciliation

19	Medicare tax withheld from Form W-2, box 6. If you have more than one Form W-2, enter the total of the amounts from box 6	**19**	4,428
20	Enter the amount from line 1	**20**	265,000
21	Multiply line 20 by 1.45% (0.0145). This is your regular Medicare tax withholding on Medicare wages	**21**	3,843
22	Subtract line 21 from line 19. If zero or less, enter -0-. This is your Additional Medicare Tax withholding on Medicare wages	**22**	585
23	Additional Medicare Tax withholding on railroad retirement (RRTA) compensation from Form W-2, box 14 (see instructions)	**23**	
24	**Total Additional Medicare Tax withholding.** Add lines 22 and 23. Also include this amount with federal income tax withholding on Form 1040 or 1040-SR, line 17 (Form 1040-NR, 1040-PR, or 1040-SS filers, see instructions)	**24**	585

For Paperwork Reduction Act Notice, see your tax return instructions.   Cat. No. 59475X   Form **8959** (2019)

CHAPTER 7 TAX CREDITS

Self-Study Problem 7.1

    a. $4,500. See Child Tax Credit Worksheet on Pages E-37 and E-38.
    b. $4,200. Total possible credit is $4,500. Income of $405,600 exceeds $400,000 threshold by $5,600 which is rounded up to $6,000. $6,000/$1,000 = 6. 6 × $50 = phase out of $300. $4,500 less $300 = $4,200
    c. Child tax credit = $383
       Additional child tax credit = $4,200. See Child Tax Credit Worksheet on Pages E-39 and E-40 and Schedule 8812 on Page E-41.

Self-Study Problem 7.2

$3,461. See Worksheet A—EIC Worksheet on Page E-42.

Self-Study Problem 7.3

$380. See Form 2441 on Pages E-43 and E-44.

Self-Study Problem 7.4

    1. $3,783
    2. Excess advance credit of $2,061.
    3. Repayment of $1,600.
    See Form 8962 on Page E-45.

Self-Study Problem 7.5

    a. $500. Refundable American Opportunity tax credit, Line 8 of Form 8863.
       $750. Nonrefundable American Opportunity tax credit, Line 19 of Form 8863. See Form 8863 on Pages E-46 and E-47.
    b. $1,040 = 20% × $5,200 ($10,000 maximum)

Self-Study Problem 7.6

Overall limitation:

$$\frac{\$1,500}{\$58,000} \times \$8,624 = \$223$$

The foreign tax credit is limited to $223. The remaining balance of $209 can be carried back one year or carried forward 10 years.

Self-Study Problem 7.7

See Form 8839 on Pages E-48 and E-49.

Self-Study Problem 7.1 part a

2019 Child Tax Credit and Credit for Other Dependents
Worksheet—Line 13a

Keep for Your Records

1. To be a qualifying child for the child tax credit, the child must be your dependent, **under age 17** at the end of 2019, and meet all the conditions in Steps 1 through 3 under *Who Qualifies as Your Dependent*. Make sure you checked the "child tax credit" box in column (4) of the *Dependents* section on Form 1040 or 1040-SR for each qualifying child.

2. If you don't have a qualifying child, you can't claim the child tax credit; but you may be able to claim the credit for other dependents for that child. See Step 3 under *Who Qualifies as Your Dependent*.

3. To see if your qualifying relative qualifies you to take the credit for other dependents, see Step 5 under *Who Qualifies as Your Dependent*.

4. Be sure to see *Social security number* under *Who Qualifies as Your Dependent*.

5. Do **not** use this worksheet, but use Pub. 972 instead, if:

   a. You are claiming the adoption credit, mortgage interest credit, District of Columbia first-time homebuyer credit, or residential energy efficient property credit*;

   b. You are excluding income from Puerto Rico; or

   c. You are filing Form 2555 or 4563.

   * If applicable.

Part 1

1.	Number of qualifying children under age 17 with the required social security number: __2__ × $2,000. Enter the result.	**1**	4,000
2.	Number of other dependents, including qualifying children without the required social security number: __1__ × $500. Enter the result.	**2**	500
	Caution. Don't include yourself, your spouse, or anyone who is not a U.S. citizen, U.S. national, or U.S. resident alien. Also, don't include anyone you included on line 1.		
3.	Add lines 1 and 2.	**3**	4,500
4.	Enter the amount from Form 1040 or 1040-SR, line 8b.	**4**	125,400
5.	Enter the amount shown below for your filing status. ● Married filing jointly — $400,000 ● All other filing statuses — $200,000	**5**	400,000
6.	Is the amount on line 4 more than the amount on line 5? [X] **No.** Leave line 6 blank. Enter -0- on line 7, and go to line 8. [ ] **Yes.** Subtract line 5 from line 4. If the result isn't a multiple of $1,000, increase it to the next multiple of $1,000. For example, increase $425 to $1,000, increase $1,025 to $2,000, etc.	**6**	
7.	Multiply the amount on line 6 by 5% (0.05). Enter the result.	**7**	0
8.	Is the amount on line 3 more than the amount on line 7? [ ] **No.** (STOP) You can't take the child tax credit on Form 1040 or 1040-SR, line 13a. You also can't take the additional child tax credit on Form 1040 or 1040-SR, line 18b. Complete the rest of your Form 1040 or 1040-SR. [X] **Yes.** Subtract line 7 from line 3. Enter the result. *Go to Part 2.*	**8**	4,500

Self-Study Problem 7.1 part a

2019 Child Tax Credit and Credit for Other Dependents Worksheet—*Continued*

Keep for Your Records

Before you begin Part 2: √ Figure the amount of any credits you are claiming on Schedule 3; Form 5695, Part II*; Form 8910; Form 8936; or Schedule R.

Part 2

9. Enter the amount from Form 1040 or 1040-SR, line 12b. **9** | 13,937

10. Add any amounts from:

Schedule 3, line 1 _____

Schedule 3, line 2 + _____

Schedule 3, line 3 + _____

Schedule 3, line 4 + _____

Form 5695, line 30* + _____

Form 8910, line 15* + _____

Form 8936, line 23 + _____

Schedule R, line 22 + _____

Enter the total.   **10** | 0

11. Are the amounts on lines 9 and 10 the same?

☐ **Yes.** (STOP)
You can't take this credit because there is no tax to reduce. However, you may be able to take the **additional child tax credit** if line 1 is more than zero. See the **TIP** below.

☒ **No.** Subtract line 10 from line 9.   **11** | 13,937

12. Is the amount on line 8 more than the amount on line 11?

☐ **Yes.** Enter the amount from line 11. Also, you may be able to take the **additional child tax credit** if line 1 is more than zero. See the **TIP** below.

This is your child tax credit and credit for other dependents.

12 | 4,500

Enter this amount on Form 1040 or 1040-SR, line 13a.

☒ **No.** Enter the amount from line 8.

TIP
*You may be able to take the **additional child tax credit** on Form 1040 or 1040-SR, line 18b, if you answered "Yes" on line 11 **or** line 12 above.*

- *First, complete your Form 1040 or 1040-SR through line 18a (also complete Schedule 3, line 11).*
- *Then, use Schedule 8812 to figure any additional child tax credit.*

CAUTION
If your child tax credit or additional child tax credit for a year after 2015 was reduced or disallowed, see Form 8862, who must file to find out if you must file Form 8862 to take the credit for 2019.

*If applicable.

Self-Study Problem 7.1 part c

2019 Child Tax Credit and Credit for Other Dependents Worksheet—Line 13a

Keep for Your Records

1. To be a qualifying child for the child tax credit, the child must be your dependent, **under age 17** at the end of 2019, and meet all the conditions in Steps 1 through 3 under *Who Qualifies as Your Dependent*. Make sure you checked the "child tax credit" box in column (4) of the *Dependents* section on Form 1040 or 1040-SR for each qualifying child.
2. If you don't have a qualifying child, you can't claim the child tax credit; but you may be able to claim the credit for other dependents for that child. See Step 3 under *Who Qualifies as Your Dependent*.
3. To see if your qualifying relative qualifies you to take the credit for other dependents, see Step 5 under *Who Qualifies as Your Dependent*.
4. Be sure to see *Social security number* under *Who Qualifies as Your Dependent*.
5. Do **not** use this worksheet, but use Pub. 972 instead, if:
   a. You are claiming the adoption credit, mortgage interest credit, District of Columbia first-time homebuyer credit, or residential energy efficient property credit*;
   b. You are excluding income from Puerto Rico; or
   c. You are filing Form 2555 or 4563.
   * If applicable.

Part 1

1.	Number of qualifying children under age 17 with the required social security number: ___3___ × \$2,000. Enter the result.	**1**	6,000
2.	Number of other dependents, including qualifying children without the required social security number: _____ × \$500. Enter the result.	**2**	0

Caution. Don't include yourself, your spouse, or anyone who is not a U.S. citizen, U.S. national, or U.S. resident alien. Also, don't include anyone you included on line 1.

3.	Add lines 1 and 2.	**3**	6,000
4.	Enter the amount from Form 1040 or 1040-SR, line 8b.	**4**	36,400

5. Enter the amount shown below for your filing status.
   - Married filing jointly — \$400,000
   - All other filing statuses — \$200,000

5	400,000

6. Is the amount on line 4 more than the amount on line 5?

   ☒ **No.** Leave line 6 blank. Enter -0- on line 7, and go to line 8.

   ☐ **Yes.** Subtract line 5 from line 4.
   If the result isn't a multiple of \$1,000, increase it to the next multiple of \$1,000. For example, increase \$425 to \$1,000, increase \$1,025 to \$2,000, etc.

6	

7.	Multiply the amount on line 6 by 5% (0.05). Enter the result.	**7**	0

8. Is the amount on line 3 more than the amount on line 7?

   ☐ **No.** (STOP)
   You can't take the child tax credit on Form 1040 or 1040-SR, line 13a. You also can't take the additional child tax credit on Form 1040 or 1040-SR, line 18b. Complete the rest of your Form 1040 or 1040-SR.

   ☒ **Yes.** Subtract line 7 from line 3. Enter the result.
   Go to Part 2.

8	6,000

Self-Study Problem 7.1 part c

**2019 Child Tax Credit and Credit for Other Dependents
Worksheet**—*Continued*

Keep for Your Records

Before you begin Part 2: √ Figure the amount of any credits you are claiming on Schedule 3; Form 5695, Part II*;
Form 8910; Form 8936; or Schedule R.

Part 2

9. Enter the amount from Form 1040 or 1040-SR, line 12b.

9	383

10. Add any amounts from:

Schedule 3, line 1 _____

Schedule 3, line 2 + _____

Schedule 3, line 3 + _____

Schedule 3, line 4 + _____

Form 5695, line 30* + _____

Form 8910, line 15* + _____

Form 8936, line 23 + _____

Schedule R, line 22 + _____

Enter the total.

10	0

11. Are the amounts on lines 9 and 10 the same?

☐ **Yes.** (STOP)
    You can't take this credit because there is no tax to reduce.
    However, you may be able to take the **additional child tax
    credit** if line 1 is more than zero. See the **TIP** below.

☒ **No.** Subtract line 10 from line 9.

11	383

12. Is the amount on line 8 more than the amount on line 11?

☒ **Yes.** Enter the amount from line 11.
    Also, you may be able to take the
    additional child tax credit if line 1
    is more than zero. See the **TIP** below.

    } **This is your child tax
    credit and credit for
    other dependents.**

12	383

Enter this amount on
Form 1040 or 1040-SR,
line 13a.

☐ **No.** Enter the amount from line 8.

TIP *You may be able to take the **additional child tax credit**
on Form 1040 or 1040-SR, line 18b, if you answered "Yes" on
line 11 **or** line 12 above.*

- *First, complete your Form 1040 or 1040-SR through line
  18a (also complete Schedule 3, line 11).*

- *Then, use Schedule 8812 to figure any additional child tax
  credit.*

CAUTION *If your child tax credit or additional child tax credit for a year after
2015 was reduced or disallowed, see Form 8862, who must file to
find out if you must file Form 8862 to take the credit for 2019.*

* If applicable.

Self-Study Problem 7.1 part c

SCHEDULE 8812 (Form 1040 or 1040-SR) Department of the Treasury Internal Revenue Service (99)	**Additional Child Tax Credit** ▶ **Attach to Form 1040, 1040-SR, or 1040-NR.** ▶ **Go to** *www.irs.gov/Schedule8812* **for instructions and the latest information.**

OMB No. 1545-0074

2019

Attachment Sequence No. **47**

Name(s) shown on return: Marie and Pierre Curry

Your social security number:

Part I　All Filers

Caution: If you file Form 2555, **stop here;** you cannot claim the additional child tax credit.

1	If you are required to use the worksheet in Pub. 972, enter the amount from line 10 of the Child Tax Credit and Credit for Other Dependents Worksheet in the publication. Otherwise: **1040 and**　　Enter the amount from line 8 of your Child Tax Credit and Credit for Other Dependents **1040-SR filers:**　Worksheet (see the instructions for Forms 1040 and 1040-SR, line 13a). **1040-NR filers:**　Enter the amount from line 8 of your Child Tax Credit and Credit for Other Dependents 　　　　　　　　Worksheet (see the instructions for Form 1040-NR, line 49).	**1**	6,000
2	Enter the amount from Form 1040, line 13a; Form 1040-SR, line 13a; or Form 1040-NR, line 49	**2**	383
3	Subtract line 2 from line 1. If zero, **stop here;** you cannot claim this credit	**3**	5,617
4	Number of qualifying children under 17 with the required social security number: ___3___ x $1,400. Enter the result. If zero, **stop here;** you cannot claim this credit **TIP:** The number of children you use for this line is the same as the number of children you used for line 1 of the Child Tax Credit and Credit for Other Dependents Worksheet.	**4**	4,200
5	Enter the **smaller** of line 3 or line 4	**5**	4,200

6a	Earned income (see instructions)		**6a**	36,400	
b	Nontaxable combat pay (see instructions)	**6b**			

7	Is the amount on line 6a more than $2,500? ☐ **No.** Leave line 7 blank and enter -0- on line 8. ☑ **Yes.** Subtract $2,500 from the amount on line 6a. Enter the result	**7**	33,900	
8	Multiply the amount on line 7 by 15% (0.15) and enter the result	**8**	5,085
	Next. On line 4, is the amount $4,200 or more? ☐ **No.** If line 8 is zero, **stop here;** you cannot claim this credit. Otherwise, skip Part II and enter the **smaller** of line 5 or line 8 on line 15. ☑ **Yes.** If line 8 is equal to or more than line 5, skip Part II and enter the amount from line 5 on line 15. Otherwise, go to line 9.		

Part II　Certain Filers Who Have Three or More Qualifying Children

9	Withheld social security, Medicare, and Additional Medicare taxes from Form(s) W-2, boxes 4 and 6. If married filing jointly, include your spouse's amounts with yours. If your employer withheld or you paid Additional Medicare Tax or tier 1 RRTA taxes, see instructions	**9**	
10	**1040 and**　Enter the total of the amounts from Schedule 1 (Form 1040 or 1040-SR), **1040-SR filers:**　line 14, and Schedule 2 (Form 1040 or 1040-SR), line 5, plus any taxes that you identified using code "UT" and entered on Schedule 2 (Form 1040 or 1040-SR), line 8. **1040-NR filers:**　Enter the total of the amounts from Form 1040-NR, lines 27 and 56, plus any taxes that you identified using code "UT" and entered on line 60.	**10**	
11	Add lines 9 and 10	**11**	
12	**1040 and**　Enter the total of the amounts from Form 1040 or 1040-SR, line **1040-SR filers:**　18a, and Schedule 3 (Form 1040 or 1040-SR), line 11. **1040-NR filers:**　Enter the amount from Form 1040-NR, line 67.	**12**	
13	Subtract line 12 from line 11. If zero or less, enter -0-	**13**	
14	Enter the **larger** of line 8 or line 13	**14**	
	Next, enter the **smaller** of line 5 or line 14 on line 15.		

Part III　Additional Child Tax Credit

15	**This is your additional child tax credit**	**15**	4,200

Enter this amount on Form 1040, line 18b; Form 1040-SR, line 18b; or Form 1040-NR, line 64.

For Paperwork Reduction Act Notice, see your tax return instructions.　　Cat. No. 59761M　　**Schedule 8812 (Form 1040 or 1040-SR) 2019**

DRAFT AS OF JULY 2019 DO NOT FILE

Self-Study Problem 7.2

Worksheet **A**—2019 EIC—Line 18a

Before you begin: √ Be sure you are using the correct worksheet. Use this worksheet only if you answered "No" to Step 5, question 2. Otherwise, use Worksheet B.

Part 1

All Filers Using Worksheet A

1. Enter your earned income from Step 5.
   Wages, salaries

   | 1 | 15,800 |

2. Look up the amount on line 1 above in the EIC Table (right after Worksheet B) to find the credit. Be sure you use the correct column for your filing status and the number of children you have. Enter the credit here.

   | 2 | 3,526 |

   If line 2 is zero, [STOP] You can't take the credit.
   Enter "No" on the dotted line next to Form 1040 or 1040-SR, line 18a.

3. Enter the amount from Form 1040 or 1040-SR, line 8b.
   Adjusted gross income

   | 3 | 15,900 |

4. Are the amounts on lines 3 and 1 the same?

   ☐ **Yes.** Skip line 5; enter the amount from line 2 on line 6.

   ☒ **No.** Go to line 5.

Part 2

Filers Who Answered "No" on Line 4

5. If you have:
   - No qualifying children, is the amount on line 3 less than $8,650 ($14,450 if married filing jointly)?
   - 1 or more qualifying children, is the amount on line 3 less than $19,050 ($24,850 if married filing jointly)?

   ☒ **Yes.** Leave line 5 blank; enter the amount from line 2 on line 6.

   ☐ **No.** Look up the amount on line 3 in the EIC Table to find the credit. Be sure you use the correct column for your filing status and the number of children you have. Enter the credit here.
   Look at the amounts on lines 5 and 2.
   Then, enter the **smaller** amount on line 6.

   | 5 | |

Part 3

Your Earned Income Credit

6. **This is your earned income credit.**

   | 6 | 3,526 |

   Enter this amount on Form 1040 or 1040-SR, line 18a.

   ### Reminder—

   √ If you have a qualifying child, complete and attach Schedule EIC.

⚠ CAUTION *If your EIC for a year after 1996 was reduced or disallowed, see Form 8862, who must file, earlier, to find out if you must file Form 8862 to take the credit for 2019.*

Self-Study Problem 7.3

Form **2441**	**Child and Dependent Care Expenses**			OMB No. 1545-0074

Form **2441**

Child and Dependent Care Expenses

▶ Attach to Form 1040, 1040-SR, or 1040-NR.

▶ Go to *www.irs.gov/Form2441* for instructions and the latest information.

Department of the Treasury
Internal Revenue Service (99)

1040 / 1040-SR / 1040-NR   2441

2019

Attachment Sequence No. **21**

Name(s) shown on return
Julie Brown

Your social security number
456-23-6543

You cannot claim a credit for child and dependent care expenses if your filing status is married filing separately unless you meet the requirements listed in the instructions under "Married Persons Filing Separately." If you meet these requirements, check this box. ☐

Part I   Persons or Organizations Who Provided the Care—You **must** complete this part.
(If you have more than two care providers, see the instructions.)

1	(a) Care provider's name	(b) Address (number, street, apt. no., city, state, and ZIP code)	(c) Identifying number (SSN or EIN)	(d) Amount paid (see instructions)
	Ivy Childcare	1 Sunflower Street Terre Haute, IN 47803	56-7654321	1,500
	De Anza Adult Care	13 Fort Harrison Rd. Dewey, IN 47805	43-1234567	2,400

Did you receive dependent care benefits?   No ▶ Complete only Part II below.
Yes ▶ Complete Part III on the back next.

Caution: If the care was provided in your home, you may owe employment taxes. For details, see the instructions for Schedule 2 (Form 1040 or 1040-SR), line 7a; or Form 1040-NR, line 59a.

Part II   Credit for Child and Dependent Care Expenses

2   Information about your **qualifying person(s)**. If you have more than two qualifying persons, see the instructions.

(a) Qualifying person's name		(b) Qualifying person's social security number	(c) Qualified expenses you incurred and paid in 2019 for the person listed in column (a)
First	Last		
Chuck	Brown	123-33-4444	0 *
Devona	Neuporte	214-55-6666	1,900 *

3	Add the amounts in column (c) of line 2. **Don't** enter more than $3,000 for one qualifying person or $6,000 for two or more persons. If you completed Part III, enter the amount from line 31 . .	**3**	1,900
4	Enter your **earned income**. See instructions	**4**	90,000
5	If married filing jointly, enter your spouse's earned income (if you or your spouse was a student or was disabled, see the instructions); **all others**, enter the amount from line 4	**5**	90,000
6	Enter the **smallest** of line 3, 4, or 5	**6**	1,900
7	Enter the amount from Form 1040 or 1040-SR, line 8b; or Form 1040-NR, line 35 . . . . **7** 90,000		
8	Enter on line 8 the decimal amount shown below that applies to the amount on line 7		

If line 7 is:				If line 7 is:		
Over	But not over	Decimal amount is		Over	But not over	Decimal amount is
$0—15,000		.35		$29,000—31,000		.27
15,000—17,000		.34		31,000—33,000		.26
17,000—19,000		.33		33,000—35,000		.25
19,000—21,000		.32		35,000—37,000		.24
21,000—23,000		.31		37,000—39,000		.23
23,000—25,000		.30		39,000—41,000		.22
25,000—27,000		.29		41,000—43,000		.21
27,000—29,000		.28		43,000—No limit		.20

8   X . 20

9	Multiply line 6 by the decimal amount on line 8. If you paid 2018 expenses in 2019, see the instructions	**9**	380
10	Tax liability limit. Enter the amount from the Credit Limit Worksheet in the instructions **10** 5,186		
11	**Credit for child and dependent care expenses.** Enter the **smaller** of line 9 or line 10 here and on Schedule 3 (Form 1040 or 1040-SR), line 2; or Form 1040-NR, line 47	**11**	380

For Paperwork Reduction Act Notice, see your tax return instructions.   Cat. No. 11862M   Form **2441** (2019)

*$2,000 of Dependent Care Flexible Spending Amount that is withheld from Julie's salary for the reimbursement of qualified dependent care expenses. $2,000 − $1,500 of son's care − $500 (limited) for mother's care.

Self-Study Problem 7.3

Part III   Dependent Care Benefits

12	Enter the total amount of **dependent care benefits** you received in 2019. Amounts you received as an employee should be shown in box 10 of your Form(s) W-2. **Don't** include amounts reported as wages in box 1 of Form(s) W-2. If you were self-employed or a partner, include amounts you received under a dependent care assistance program from your sole proprietorship or partnership.	**12**	2,000
13	Enter the amount, if any, you carried over from 2018 and used in 2019 during the grace period. See instructions	**13**	
14	Enter the amount, if any, you forfeited or carried forward to 2020. See instructions	**14** (	)
15	Combine lines 12 through 14. See instructions	**15**	2,000
16	Enter the total amount of **qualified expenses** incurred in 2019 for the care of the **qualifying person(s)** **16** 3,900		
17	Enter the **smaller** of line 15 or 16 **17** 2,000		
18	Enter your **earned income.** See instructions **18** 90,000		
19	Enter the amount shown below that applies to you.		
	• If married filing jointly, enter your spouse's earned income (if you or your spouse was a student or was disabled, see the instructions for line 5). **19** 90,000		
	• If married filing separately, see instructions.		
	• All others, enter the amount from line 18.		
20	Enter the **smallest** of line 17, 18, or 19 **20** 2,000		
21	Enter $5,000 ($2,500 if married filing separately **and** you were required to enter your spouse's earned income on line 19) **21** 5,000		
22	Is any amount on line 12 from your sole proprietorship or partnership? ☑ **No.** Enter -0-. ☐ **Yes.** Enter the amount here	**22**	0
23	Subtract line 22 from line 15 **23** 2,000		
24	**Deductible benefits.** Enter the **smallest** of line 20, 21, or 22. Also, include this amount on the appropriate line(s) of your return. See instructions	**24**	0
25	**Excluded benefits.** If you checked "No" on line 22, enter the smaller of line 20 or 21. Otherwise, subtract line 24 from the smaller of line 20 or line 21. If zero or less, enter -0-	**25**	2,000
26	**Taxable benefits.** Subtract line 25 from line 23. If zero or less, enter -0-. Also, include this amount on Form 1040 or 1040-SR, line 1; or Form 1040-NR, line 8. On the dotted line next to Form 1040 or 1040-SR, line 1; or Form 1040-NR, line 8, enter "DCB".	**26**	0

To claim the child and dependent care
credit, complete lines 27 through 31 below.

27	Enter $3,000 ($6,000 if two or more qualifying persons)	**27**	6,000
28	Add lines 24 and 25	**28**	2,000
29	Subtract line 28 from line 27. If zero or less, **stop.** You can't take the credit. **Exception.** If you paid 2018 expenses in 2019, see the instructions for line 9	**29**	4,000
30	Complete line 2 on the front of this form. **Don't** include in column (c) any benefits shown on line 28 above. Then, add the amounts in column (c) and enter the total here	**30**	1,900
31	Enter the **smaller** of line 29 or 30. Also, enter this amount on line 3 on the front of this form and complete lines 4 through 11	**31**	1,900

Form **2441** (2019)

Self-Study Problem 7.4

Form **8962**	**Premium Tax Credit (PTC)**	OMB No. 1545-0074
Department of the Treasury Internal Revenue Service	▶ Attach to Form 1040, 1040-SR, or 1040-NR ▶ Go to *www.irs.gov/Form8962* for instructions and the latest information.	**2019** Attachment Sequence No. **73**

Name shown on your return	Your social security number
Tracy and Marco Brigantine	123-44-5555

You cannot take the PTC if your filing status is married filing separately unless you qualify for an exception (see instructions). If you qualify, check the box . . . ▶ ☐

Part I   Annual and Monthly Contribution Amount

1	Tax family size. Enter your tax family size (see instructions)	**1**	4
2a	Modified AGI. Enter your modified AGI (see instructions) **2a** 68,040		
b	Enter the total of your dependents' modified AGI (see instructions) **2b** 0		
3	Household income. Add the amounts on lines 2a and 2b (see instructions)	**3**	68,040
4	Federal poverty line. Enter the federal poverty line amount from Table 1-1, 1-2, or 1-3 (see instructions). Check the appropriate box for the federal poverty table used. a ☐ Alaska b ☐ Hawaii c ☑ Other 48 states and DC	**4**	25,100
5	Household income as a percentage of federal poverty line (see instructions)	**5**	271 %*
6	Did you enter 401% on line 5? (See instructions if you entered less than 100%.) ☑ **No.** Continue to line 7. ☐ **Yes.** You are not eligible to take the PTC. If advance payment of the PTC was made, see the instructions for how to report your excess advance PTC repayment amount.		
7	Applicable Figure. Using your line 5 percentage, locate your "applicable figure" on the table in the instructions . .	**7**	.0899
8a	Annual contribution amount. Multiply line 3 by line 7. Round to nearest whole dollar amount **8a** 6,117	**b** Monthly contribution amount. Divide line 8a by 12. Round to nearest whole dollar amount	**8b** 510

Part II   Premium Tax Credit Claim and Reconciliation of Advance Payment of Premium Tax Credit

9 Are you allocating policy amounts with another taxpayer or do you want to use the alternative calculation for year of marriage (see instructions)?
☐ **Yes.** Skip to Part IV, Allocation of Policy Amounts, or Part V, Alternative Calculation for Year of Marriage.   ☑ **No.** Continue to line 10.

10 See the instructions to determine if you can use line 11 or must complete lines 12 through 23.
☑ **Yes.** Continue to line 11. Compute your annual PTC. Then skip lines 12–23 and continue to line 24.   ☐ **No.** Continue to lines 12–23. Compute your monthly PTC and continue to line 24.

Annual Calculation	(a) Annual enrollment premiums (Form(s) 1095-A, line 33A)	(b) Annual applicable SLCSP premium (Form(s) 1095-A, line 33B)	(c) Annual contribution amount (line 8a)	(d) Annual maximum premium assistance (subtract (c) from (b), if zero or less, enter -0-)	(e) Annual premium tax credit allowed (smaller of (a) or (d))	(f) Annual advance payment of PTC (Form(s) 1095-A, line 33C)
11 Annual Totals	11,484	9,900	6,117	3,783	3,783	5,844

Monthly Calculation	(a) Monthly enrollment premiums (Form(s) 1095-A, lines 21–32, column A)	(b) Monthly applicable SLCSP premium (Form(s) 1095-A, lines 21–32, column B)	(c) Monthly contribution amount (amount from line 8b or alternative marriage monthly calculation)	(d) Monthly maximum premium assistance (subtract (c) from (b), if zero or less, enter -0-)	(e) Monthly premium tax credit allowed (smaller of (a) or (d))	(f) Monthly advance payment of PTC (Form(s) 1095-A, lines 21–32, column C)
12 January						
13 February						
14 March						
15 April						
16 May						
17 June						
18 July						
19 August						
20 September						
21 October						
22 November						
23 December						

24	Total premium tax credit. Enter the amount from line 11(e) or add lines 12(e) through 23(e) and enter the total here	**24**	3,783
25	Advance payment of PTC. Enter the amount from line 11(f) or add lines 12(f) through 23(f) and enter the total here	**25**	5,844
26	Net premium tax credit. If line 24 is greater than line 25, subtract line 25 from line 24. Enter the difference here and on Schedule 3 (Form 1040 or 1040-SR), line 9, or 1040-NR, line 65. If line 24 equals line 25, enter -0-. Stop here. If line 25 is greater than line 24, leave this line blank and continue to line 27	**26**	

Part III   Repayment of Excess Advance Payment of the Premium Tax Credit

27	Excess advance payment of PTC. If line 25 is greater than line 24, subtract line 24 from line 25. Enter the difference here	**27**	2,061
28	Repayment limitation (see instructions)	**28**	1,600
29	Excess advance premium tax credit repayment. Enter the smaller of line 27 or line 28 here and on Schedule 2 (Form 1040 or 1040-SR), line 2, or Form 1040-NR, line 44	**29**	1,600

For Paperwork Reduction Act Notice, see your tax return instructions.   Cat. No. 37784Z   Form **8962** (2019)

*Per Form 8962 instructions, this amount is not rounded.

Self-Study Problem 7.5 part a

Form **8863** Department of the Treasury Internal Revenue Service (99)	**Education Credits** **(American Opportunity and Lifetime Learning Credits)** ▶ Attach to Form 1040 or 1040-SR. ▶ Go to *www.irs.gov/Form8863* for instructions and the latest information.	OMB No. 1545-0074 20**19** Attachment Sequence No. **50**

Name(s) shown on return	Your social security number
Santiago and Sophia Estudiante	

⚠️ **CAUTION** *Complete a separate Part III on page 2 for each student for whom you're claiming either credit before you complete Parts I and II.*

Part I — Refundable American Opportunity Credit

1	After completing Part III for each student, enter the total of all amounts from all Parts III, line 30	**1**	2,500
2	Enter: $180,000 if married filing jointly; $90,000 if single, head of household, or qualifying widow(er)	**2** 180,000	
3	Enter the amount from Form 1040 or 1040-SR, line 8b. If you're filing Form 2555 or 4563, or you're excluding income from Puerto Rico, see Pub. 970 for the amount to enter	**3** 170,000	
4	Subtract line 3 from line 2. If zero or less, **stop**; you can't take any education credit	**4** 10,000	
5	Enter: $20,000 if married filing jointly; $10,000 if single, head of household, or qualifying widow(er)	**5** 20,000	
6	If line 4 is: • Equal to or more than line 5, enter 1.000 on line 6 • Less than line 5, divide line 4 by line 5. Enter the result as a decimal (rounded to at least three places)	**6**	.500
7	Multiply line 1 by line 6. **Caution:** If you were under age 24 at the end of the year **and** meet the conditions described in the instructions, you **can't** take the refundable American opportunity credit; skip line 8, enter the amount from line 7 on line 9, and check this box ▶ ☐	**7**	1,250
8	**Refundable American opportunity credit.** Multiply line 7 by 40% (0.40). Enter the amount here and on Form 1040 or 1040-SR, line 18c. Then go to line 9 below	**8**	500

Part II — Nonrefundable Education Credits

9	Subtract line 8 from line 7. Enter here and on line 2 of the Credit Limit Worksheet (see instructions)	**9**	750
10	After completing Part III for each student, enter the total of all amounts from all Parts III, line 31. If zero, skip lines 11 through 17, enter -0- on line 18, and go to line 19	**10**	0
11	Enter the smaller of line 10 or $10,000	**11**	
12	Multiply line 11 by 20% (0.20)	**12**	
13	Enter: $136,000 if married filing jointly; $68,000 if single, head of household, or qualifying widow(er)	**13**	
14	Enter the amount from Form 1040 or 1040-SR, line 8b. If you're filing Form 2555 or 4563, or you're excluding income from Puerto Rico, see Pub. 970 for the amount to enter	**14**	
15	Subtract line 14 from line 13. If zero or less, skip lines 16 and 17, enter -0- on line 18, and go to line 19	**15**	
16	Enter: $20,000 if married filing jointly; $10,000 if single, head of household, or qualifying widow(er)	**16**	
17	If line 15 is: • Equal to or more than line 16, enter 1.000 on line 17 and go to line 18 • Less than line 16, divide line 15 by line 16. Enter the result as a decimal (rounded to at least three places)	**17**	.
18	Multiply line 12 by line 17. Enter here and on line 1 of the Credit Limit Worksheet (see instructions) ▶	**18**	0
19	**Nonrefundable education credits.** Enter the amount from line 7 of the Credit Limit Worksheet (see instructions) here and on Schedule 3 (Form 1040 or 1040-SR), line 3	**19**	750

For Paperwork Reduction Act Notice, see your tax return instructions.   Cat. No. 25379M   Form **8863** (2019)

Note: The taxpayers have a large tax liability relative to the AOTC. As a result, the nonrefundable AOTC will not be limited.

Self-Study Problem 7.5 part a

Form 8863 (2019)   Page **2**

Name(s) shown on return	Your social security number
Santiago and Sophia Estudiante	

> ⚠️ **CAUTION** **Complete Part III for each student for whom you're claiming either the American opportunity credit or lifetime learning credit. Use additional copies of page 2 as needed for each student.**

Part III **Student and Educational Institution Information.** See instructions.

20 Student name (as shown on page 1 of your tax return)	21 Student social security number (as shown on page 1 of your tax return)		
Judy Estudiante	434	11	7812

22 Educational institution information (see instructions)

a. Name of first educational institution	**b.** Name of second educational institution (if any)
Southwest University	
(1) Address. Number and street (or P.O. box). City, town or post office, state, and ZIP code. If a foreign address, see instructions.	**(1)** Address. Number and street (or P.O. box). City, town or post office, state, and ZIP code. If a foreign address, see instructions.
1234 Cleveland Ave. El Paso, TX 79925	
(2) Did the student receive Form 1098-T from this institution for 2019? ☑ Yes ☐ No	**(2)** Did the student receive Form 1098-T from this institution for 2019? ☐ Yes ☐ No
(3) Did the student receive Form 1098-T from this institution for 2018 with box 2 filled in and box 7 checked? ☐ Yes ☑ No	**(3)** Did the student receive Form 1098-T from this institution for 2018 with box 2 filled in and box 7 checked? ☐ Yes ☐ No
(4) Enter the institution's employer identification number (EIN) if you're claiming the American opportunity credit or if you checked "Yes" in **(2)** or **(3)**. You can get the EIN from Form 1098-T or from the institution. 1 2 – 7 6 5 2 3 1 1	**(4)** Enter the institution's employer identification number (EIN) if you're claiming the American opportunity credit or if you checked "Yes" in **(2)** or **(3)**. You can get the EIN from Form 1098-T or from the institution. __ __ – __ __ __ __ __ __ __

23	Has the Hope Scholarship Credit or American opportunity credit been claimed for this student for any 4 tax years before 2019?	☐ Yes — **Stop!** Go to line 31 for this student. ☑ No — Go to line 24.
24	Was the student enrolled at least half-time for at least one academic period that began or is treated as having begun in 2019 at an eligible educational institution in a program leading towards a postsecondary degree, certificate, or other recognized postsecondary educational credential? See instructions.	☑ Yes — Go to line 25. ☐ No — **Stop!** Go to line 31 for this student.
25	Did the student complete the first 4 years of postsecondary education before 2019? See instructions.	☐ Yes — **Stop!** Go to line 31 for this student. ☑ No — Go to line 26.
26	Was the student convicted, before the end of 2019, of a felony for possession or distribution of a controlled substance?	☐ Yes — **Stop!** Go to line 31 for this student. ☑ No — Complete lines 27 through 30 for this student.

> ⚠️ **CAUTION** *You **can't** take the American opportunity credit and the lifetime learning credit for the **same student** in the same year. If you complete lines 27 through 30 for this student, don't complete line 31.*

American Opportunity Credit

27	Adjusted qualified education expenses (see instructions). **Don't enter more than $4,000**	**27**	4,000
28	Subtract $2,000 from line 27. If zero or less, enter -0-	**28**	2,000
29	Multiply line 28 by 25% (0.25)	**29**	500
30	If line 28 is zero, enter the amount from line 27. Otherwise, add $2,000 to the amount on line 29 and enter the result. Skip line 31. Include the total of all amounts from all Parts III, line 30, on Part I, line 1 .	**30**	2,500

Lifetime Learning Credit

31	Adjusted qualified education expenses (see instructions). Include the total of all amounts from all Parts III, line 31, on Part II, line 10	**31**	

Form **8863** (2019)

Self-Study Problem 7.7

Form **8839**	**Qualified Adoption Expenses**	OMB No. 1545-0074
Department of the Treasury Internal Revenue Service (99)	▶ Attach to Form 1040, 1040-SR, or 1040-NR. ▶ Go to *www.irs.gov/Form8839* for instructions and the latest information.	**20**19 Attachment Sequence No. **38**

Name(s) shown on return: James and Michael Bass

Your social security number:

Part I — Information About Your Eligible Child or Children—You **must** complete this part. See instructions for details, including what to do if you need more space.

1	(a) Child's name — First / Last	(b) Child's year of birth	(c) born **before** 2002 and disabled	(d) a child with special needs	(e) a foreign child	(f) Child's identifying number	(g) Check if adoption became final in 2019 or earlier
Child 1	Allison / Bass	2019	☐	☐	☐	466-47-3311	✓
Child 2			☐	☐	☐		☐
Child 3			☐	☐	☐		☐

Caution: If the child was a foreign child, see **Special rules** in the instructions for line 1, column (e), before you complete Part II or Part III. If you received **employer-provided adoption benefits,** complete Part III on the back next.

Part II — Adoption Credit

			Child 1	Child 2	Child 3		
2	Maximum adoption credit per child. Enter $14,080 (see instructions)	**2**	14,080				
3	Did you file Form 8839 for a prior year for the same child? ✓ **No.** Enter -0-. ☐ **Yes.** See instructions for the amount to enter.	**3**	0				
4	Subtract line 3 from line 2	**4**	14,080				
5	**Qualified adoption expenses** (see instructions)	**5**	17,000				
	Caution: Your qualified adoption expenses may not be equal to the adoption expenses you paid in 2019.						
6	Enter the **smaller** of line 4 or line 5	**6**	14,080				
7	Enter modified adjusted gross income (see instructions)			**7**	219,160		
8	Is line 7 more than $211,160? ☐ **No.** Skip lines 8 and 9, and enter -0- on line 10. ✓ **Yes.** Subtract $211,160 from line 7			**8**	8,000		
9	Divide line 8 by $40,000. Enter the result as a decimal (rounded to at least three places). Do not enter more than 1.000					**9**	× .200
10	Multiply each amount on line 6 by line 9	**10**	2,816				
11	Subtract line 10 from line 6	**11**	11,264				
12	Add the amounts on line 11					**12**	11,264
13	Credit carryforward, if any, from prior years. See your Adoption Credit Carryforward Worksheet in the 2018 Form 8839 instructions					**13**	
14	Add lines 12 and 13					**14**	11,264
15	Enter the amount from line 5 of the Credit Limit Worksheet in the instructions					**15**	22,332
16	**Adoption Credit.** Enter the smaller of line 14 or line 15 here and on Schedule 3 (Form 1040 or 1040-SR), line 6, or Form 1040-NR, line 51. Check box **c** on that line and enter "**8839**" in the space next to box **c**. If line 15 is smaller than line 14, you may have a credit carryforward (see instructions)					**16**	11,264

For Paperwork Reduction Act Notice, see your tax return instructions.   Cat. No. 22843L   Form **8839** (2019)

Self-Study Problem 7.7

Form 8839 (2019)   Page **2**

Part III   Employer-Provided Adoption Benefits

		Child 1	Child 2	Child 3		
17	Maximum exclusion per child. Enter $14,080 (see instructions)	**17** 14,080				
18	Did you receive employer-provided adoption benefits for a prior year for the same child? ☑ **No.** Enter -0-. ☐ **Yes.** See instructions for the amount to enter.	**18**				
19	Subtract line 18 from line 17	**19** 14,080				
20	Employer-provided adoption benefits you received in 2019. This amount should be shown in box 12 of your 2019 Form(s) W-2 with code **T**	**20** 4,000				
21	Add the amounts on line 20				**21**	4,000
22	Enter the **smaller** of line 19 or line 20. But if the child was a child with special needs and the adoption became final in 2019, enter the amount from line 19	**22** 4,000				
23	Enter modified adjusted gross income (from the worksheet in the instructions)	**23** 219,160				
24	Is line 23 more than $211,160? ☐ **No.** Skip lines 24 and 25, and enter -0- on line 26. ☑ **Yes.** Subtract $211,160 from line 23	**24** 8,000				
25	Divide line 24 by $40,000. Enter the result as a decimal (rounded to at least three places). Do not enter more than 1.000		**25** × .200			
26	Multiply each amount on line 22 by line 25	**26** 800				
27	**Excluded benefits.** Subtract line 26 from line 22	**27** 3,200				
28	Add the amounts on line 27				**28**	3,200
29	**Taxable benefits.** Is line 28 more than line 21? ☑ **No.** Subtract line 28 from line 21. Also, include this amount, if more than zero, on line 1 of Form 1040 or 1040-SR or line 8 of Form 1040-NR. On the dotted line next to line 1 of Form 1040 or 1040-SR or line 8 of Form 1040-NR, enter "AB." ☐ **Yes.** Subtract line 21 from line 28. Enter the result as a negative number. Reduce the total you would enter on line 1 of Form 1040 or 1040-SR or line 8 of Form 1040-NR by the amount on Form 8839, line 29. Enter the result on line 1 of Form 1040 or 1040-SR or line 8 of Form 1040-NR. Enter "SNE" on the dotted line next to the entry line.				**29**	800

You may be able to claim the adoption credit in Part II on the front of this form if any of the following apply.

- You paid adoption expenses in 2018, those expenses were not fully reimbursed by your employer or otherwise, and the adoption was not final by the end of 2018.
- The total adoption expenses you paid in 2019 were not fully reimbursed by your employer or otherwise, and the adoption became final in 2019 or earlier.
- You adopted a child with special needs and the adoption became final in 2019.

Form **8839** (2019)

Self-Study Problem 7.8

    a. $7,500. The Nissan Leaf qualifies for the full $7,500 credit.

    b. $3,000 (30% × $10,000). The solar system for the hot tub is not an allowed cost
      for the credit.

Self-Study Problem 7.9

    See Form 8880 below.

Form 8880

Credit for Qualified Retirement Savings Contributions

OMB No. 1545-0074

2019

▶ Attach to Form 1040, 1040-SR, or 1040-NR.
▶ Go to *www.irs.gov/Form8880* for the latest information.

Department of the Treasury
Internal Revenue Service

Attachment Sequence No. **54**

Name(s) shown on return

Steve and Robin Harrington

Your social security number

You **cannot** take this credit if **either** of the following applies.

⊠ **CAUTION**

• The amount on Form 1040 or 1040-SR, line 8b; or Form 1040-NR, line 35, is more than $32,000 ($48,000 if head of household; $64,000 if married filing jointly).

• The person(s) who made the qualified contribution or elective deferral **(a)** was born after January 1, 2002; **(b)** is claimed as a dependent on someone else's 2019 tax return; or **(c)** was a **student** (see instructions).

			(a) You	(b) Your spouse
1	Traditional and Roth IRA contributions, and ABLE account contributions by the designated beneficiary for 2019. **Do not** include rollover contributions	1	6,000	6,000
2	Elective deferrals to a 401(k) or other qualified employer plan, voluntary employee contributions, and 501(c)(18)(D) plan contributions for 2019 (see instructions)	2		
3	Add lines 1 and 2	3	6,000	6,000
4	Certain distributions received **after** 2016 and **before** the due date (including extensions) of your 2019 tax return (see instructions). If married filing jointly, include **both** spouses' amounts in **both** columns. See instructions for an exception	4		
5	Subtract line 4 from line 3. If zero or less, enter -0-	5	6,000	6,000
6	In each column, enter the **smaller** of line 5 or $2,000	6	2,000	2,000
7	Add the amounts on line 6. If zero, **stop**; you can't take this credit	7		4,000
8	Enter the amount from Form 1040 or 1040-SR, line 8b;* or Form 1040-NR, line 35	8	39,500	
9	Enter the applicable decimal amount from the table below.			

If line 8 is—		And your filing status is—		
Over—	But not over—	Married filing jointly	Head of household	Single, Married filing separately, or Qualifying widow(er)
		Enter on line 9—		
---	$19,250	0.5	0.5	0.5
$19,250	$20,750	0.5	0.5	0.2
$20,750	$28,875	0.5	0.5	0.1
$28,875	$31,125	0.5	0.2	0.1
$31,125	$32,000	0.5	0.1	0.1
$32,000	$38,500	0.5	0.1	0.0
$38,500	$41,500	0.2	0.1	0.0
$41,500	$48,000	0.1	0.1	0.0
$48,000	$64,000	0.1	0.0	0.0
$64,000	---	0.0	0.0	0.0

Line 9: x 0.2

Note: If line 9 is zero, **stop**; you can't take this credit.

10	Multiply line 7 by line 9	10	800
11	Limitation based on tax liability. Enter the amount from the Credit Limit Worksheet in the instructions	11	1,510
12	**Credit for qualified retirement savings contributions.** Enter the **smaller** of line 10 or line 11 here and on Schedule 3 (Form 1040 or 1040-SR), line 4; or Form 1040-NR, line 48	12	800

* See Pub. 590-A for the amount to enter if you claim any exclusion or deduction for foreign earned income, foreign housing, or income from Puerto Rico or for bona fide residents of American Samoa.

For Paperwork Reduction Act Notice, see your tax return instructions.   Cat. No. 33394D   Form **8880** (2019)

DRAFT AS OF July 5, 2019 DO NOT FILE

Form 8880 (2019)   Page **2**

General Instructions

Section references are to the Internal Revenue Code.

Reminder

Contributions by a designated beneficiary to an Achieving a Better Life Experience (ABLE) account. A retirement savings contribution credit may be claimed for the amount of contributions you, as the designated beneficiary of an ABLE account, make before January 1, 2026, to the ABLE account. See Pub. 907, Tax Highlights for Persons With Disabilities, for more information.

Future Developments

For the latest information about developments related to Form 8880 and its instructions, such as legislation enacted after they were published, go to www.irs.gov/Form8880.

Purpose of Form

Use Form 8880 to figure the amount, if any, of your retirement savings contributions credit (also known as the saver's credit).

 This credit can be claimed in addition to any IRA deduction claimed on Schedule 1 (Form 1040 or 1040-SR), line 19; or Form 1040-NR, line 32.

Who Can Take This Credit

You may be able to take this credit if you, or your spouse if filing jointly, made (a) contributions (other than rollover contributions) to a traditional or Roth IRA; (b) elective deferrals to a 401(k), 403(b), governmental 457(b), SEP, or SIMPLE plan; (c) voluntary employee contributions to a qualified retirement plan, as defined in section 4974(c) (including the federal Thrift Savings Plan); (d) contributions to a 501(c)(18)(D) plan; or (e) contributions, as a designated beneficiary of an ABLE account, to the ABLE account, as defined in section 529A.

However, you can't take the credit if either of the following applies.

• The amount on Form 1040 or 1040-SR, line 8b; or Form 1040-NR, line 35, is more than $32,000 ($48,000 if head of household; $64,000 if married filing jointly).

• The person(s) who made the qualified contribution or elective deferral (a) was born after January 1, 2002; (b) is claimed as a dependent on someone else's 2019 tax return; or (c) was a student.

 You'll need to refigure the amount on Form 1040 or 1040-SR, line 8b, if you're filing Form 2555 or Form 4563 or you're excluding income from Puerto Rico. See Pub. 590-A at www.irs.gov/Pub590A for details.

You were a student if during any part of 5 calendar months of 2019 you:

• Were enrolled as a full-time student at a school; or

• Took a full-time, on-farm training course given by a school or a state, county, or local government agency.

A school includes technical, trade, and mechanical schools. It doesn't include on-the-job training courses, correspondence schools, or schools offering courses only through the Internet.

Specific Instructions

Column (b)

Complete column (b) only if you're filing a joint return.

Line 2

Include on line 2 any of the following amounts.

• Elective deferrals to a 401(k) or 403(b) plan (including designated Roth contributions under section 402A), or to a governmental 457(b), SEP, or SIMPLE plan.

• Voluntary employee contributions to a qualified retirement plan, as defined in section 4974(c) (including the federal Thrift Savings Plan).

• Contributions to a 501(c)(18)(D) plan.

These amounts may be shown in box 12 of your Form(s) W-2 for 2019.

Note: Contributions designated under section 414(h)(2) are treated as employer contributions and, as such, they aren't voluntary contributions made by the employee. They don't qualify for the credit and shouldn't be included on line 2.

Line 4

Enter the total amount of distributions you, and your spouse if filing jointly, received after 2016 and before the due date of your 2019 return (including extensions) from any of the following types of plans.

• Traditional or Roth IRAs (including *my*RAs), or ABLE accounts.

• 401(k), 403(b), governmental 457(b), 501(c)(18)(D), SEP, or SIMPLE plans.

• Qualified retirement plans, as defined in section 4974(c) (including the federal Thrift Savings Plan).

Don't include any of the following.

• Distributions not taxable as the result of a rollover or a trustee-to-trustee transfer.

• Distributions that are taxable as the result of an in-plan rollover to your designated Roth account.

• Distributions from your eligible retirement plan (other than a Roth IRA) rolled over or converted to your Roth IRA.

• Loans from a qualified employer plan treated as a distribution.

• Distributions of excess contributions or deferrals (and income allocable to such contributions or deferrals).

• Distributions of contributions made to an IRA during a tax year and returned (with any income allocable to such contributions) on or before the due date (including extensions) for that tax year.

• Distributions of dividends paid on stock held by an employee stock ownership plan under section 404(k).

• Distributions from a military retirement plan (other than the federal Thrift Savings Plan).

• Distributions from an inherited IRA by a nonspousal beneficiary.

If you're filing a joint return, include both spouses' amounts in both columns.

Exception. Don't include your spouse's distributions with yours when entering an amount on line 4 if you and your spouse didn't file a joint return for the year the distribution was received.

Example. You received a distribution of $5,000 from a qualified retirement plan in 2019. Your spouse received a distribution of $2,000 from a Roth IRA in 2017. You and your spouse file a joint return in 2019, but didn't file a joint return in 2017. You would include $5,000 in column (a) and $7,000 in column (b).

Line 7

Add the amounts from line 6, columns (a) and (b), and enter the total.

Line 11

Before you complete the following worksheet, figure the amount of any credit for the elderly or the disabled you're claiming on Schedule 3 (Form 1040 or 1040-SR), line 6. See Schedule R (Form 1040 or 1040-SR) to figure the credit.

Credit Limit Worksheet

Complete this worksheet to figure the amount to enter on line 11.

1. Enter the amount from Form 1040 or 1040-SR, line 12b; or Form 1040-NR, line 45 . . . . . **1.** _____1,510_____

2. **Form 1040 or 1040-SR filers:** Enter the total of your credits from Schedule 3, lines 1 through 3, and Schedule R, line 22.

   Form 1040-NR filers: Enter the total of your credits from lines 46 and 47 . . . . **2.** _____0_____

3. Subtract line 2 from line 1. Also enter this amount on Form 8880, line 11. But if zero or less, **stop;** you can't take the credit—don't file this form . **3.** _____1,510_____

CHAPTER 8 DEPRECIATION AND SALE OF BUSINESS PROPERTY

Self-Study Problem 8.1

Year	Depreciation Deduction
20X1	$ 583
20X2	700
20X3	700
20X4	700
20X5	700
20X6	117
Total	$3,500

Self-Study Problem 8.2

a. Bonus on 7-year property: $16,000 ($12,000 + $4,000)
   Real estate: $175,000 × 0.02033 = $3,558
   See Form 4562 on Page E-53.
b. MACRS: $12,000 × 0.1429 = $1,715
   MACRS: $4,000 × 0.1429 = $572
   Total 7-year property = $2,287
   Real estate: $175,000 × 0.02033 = $3,558
c. 7-year property: $0 (cost fully recovered through bonus depreciation in year 1)
   Real estate: $175,000 × 0.02564 = $4,487

Self-Study Problem 8.3

a. $405,407. $2,837,000 × 0.1429 (MACRS depreciation factor for the first year for 7-year property using the half-year convention).
b. $1,033,662. Chang's eligible §179 property exceeds the $2,550,000 threshold by $287,000; thus, she must reduce the 2019 Section 179 $1,020,000 annual limit to $733,000. The $2,104,000 remaining balance of the property ($2,837,000 − $733,000) is depreciated using the MACRS: $2,104,000 × 0.1429 = $300,662. The total cost recovery is $733,000 + $300,662 = $1,033,662.
c. $2,837,000. Chang is eligible for 100% bonus depreciation on the equipment and there are no taxable income limits or thresholds associated with bonus depreciation. Chang will generate a $337,000 net operating loss.

Self-Study Problem 8.4

1. No   Qualified business use is over 50 percent; therefore, Alvarez may use the accelerated method of depreciation.
2. No   Qualified business use is more than 50 percent; therefore, Laura may use the accelerated method of depreciation.

Self-Study Problem 8.5

	2019	2020	2021
Original cost	$56,000	$56,000	$56,000
Business use percentage	0.90	0.9	0.9
Basis for depreciation	$ 50,400	$ 50,400	$ 50,400
Depreciation factor	20%	32%	19.2%
MACRS depreciation	$10,080	$ 16,128	$ 9,677
Annual depreciation limit × 90%	$ 9,090	$14,490	$ 8,730

Self-Study Problem 8.2

Form **4562**	**Depreciation and Amortization**	OMB No. 1545-0172
Department of the Treasury Internal Revenue Service (99)	(Including Information on Listed Property) ▶ Attach to your tax return. ▶ Go to *www.irs.gov/Form4562* for instructions and the latest information.	20**19** Attachment Sequence No. **179**

Name(s) shown on return	Business or activity to which this form relates	Identifying number
Mary Moser		

Part I   Election To Expense Certain Property Under Section 179
Note: If you have any listed property, complete Part V before you complete Part I.

1	Maximum amount (see instructions)	**1**
2	Total cost of section 179 property placed in service (see instructions)	**2**
3	Threshold cost of section 179 property before reduction in limitation (see instructions)	**3**
4	Reduction in limitation. Subtract line 3 from line 2. If zero or less, enter -0-	**4**
5	Dollar limitation for tax year. Subtract line 4 from line 1. If zero or less, enter -0-. If married filing separately, see instructions	**5**

6	**(a)** Description of property	**(b)** Cost (business use only)	**(c)** Elected cost	

7	Listed property. Enter the amount from line 29	**7**
8	Total elected cost of section 179 property. Add amounts in column (c), lines 6 and 7	**8**
9	Tentative deduction. Enter the **smaller** of line 5 or line 8	**9**
10	Carryover of disallowed deduction from line 13 of your 2018 Form 4562	**10**
11	Business income limitation. Enter the smaller of business income (not less than zero) or line 5. See instructions	**11**
12	Section 179 expense deduction. Add lines 9 and 10, but don't enter more than line 11	**12**
13	Carryover of disallowed deduction to 2020. Add lines 9 and 10, less line 12 ▶	**13**

Note: Don't use Part II or Part III below for listed property. Instead, use Part V.

Part II   Special Depreciation Allowance and Other Depreciation (Don't include listed property. See instructions.)

14	Special depreciation allowance for qualified property (other than listed property) placed in service during the tax year. See instructions	**14**	16,000
15	Property subject to section 168(f)(1) election	**15**	
16	Other depreciation (including ACRS)	**16**	

Part III   MACRS Depreciation (Don't include listed property. See instructions.)

Section A

17	MACRS deductions for assets placed in service in tax years beginning before 2019	**17**
18	If you are electing to group any assets placed in service during the tax year into one or more general asset accounts, check here ▶ ☐	

Section B—Assets Placed in Service During 2019 Tax Year Using the General Depreciation System

(a) Classification of property	(b) Month and year placed in service	(c) Basis for depreciation (business/investment use only—see instructions)	(d) Recovery period	(e) Convention	(f) Method	(g) Depreciation deduction
19a 3-year property						
b 5-year property						
c 7-year property						
d 10-year property						
e 15-year property						
f 20-year property						
g 25-year property			25 yrs.		S/L	
h Residential rental property			27.5 yrs.	MM	S/L	
			27.5 yrs.	MM	S/L	
i Nonresidential real property	03/30/2019	175,000	39 yrs.	MM	S/L	3,558
				MM	S/L	

Section C—Assets Placed in Service During 2019 Tax Year Using the Alternative Depreciation System

20a Class life					S/L	
b 12-year			12 yrs.		S/L	
c 30-year			30 yrs.	MM	S/L	
d 40-year			40 yrs.	MM	S/L	

Part IV   Summary (See instructions.)

21	Listed property. Enter amount from line 28	**21**	
22	**Total.** Add amounts from line 12, lines 14 through 17, lines 19 and 20 in column (g), and line 21. Enter here and on the appropriate lines of your return. Partnerships and S corporations—see instructions	**22**	19,558
23	For assets shown above and placed in service during the current year, enter the portion of the basis attributable to section 263A costs	**23**	

For Paperwork Reduction Act Notice, see separate instructions.   Cat. No. 12906N   Form **4562** (2019)

DRAFT AS OF July 3, 2019 DO NOT FILE

Self-Study Problem 8.6

1. 15-year Amortization.   5. 15-year Amortization.
2. Useful Life.   6. Not Amortizable.
3. Useful Life.   7. 15-year Amortization.
4. 15-year Amortization.   8. Not Amortizable.

Self-Study Problem 8.7

	Land	Computer	Equipment
Proceeds	$ 37,000	$14,000	$16,000
Adjusted Basis:			
Cost	$24,000	$25,875	$25,000
Cost Recovery	0	5,175	4,300
Adjusted Basis	24,000	20,700	20,700
Selling Costs	500	0	1,600
Gain/(Loss)	$12,500	$ (6,700)	$ (6,300)

The land and the computer are both Section 1231 properties and thus the gain and loss is netted resulting in a $5,800 net Section 1231 gain. Thus both the gain on the land and the loss on the computer will be treated as long-term capital gains. The equipment was not held for more than one year and thus is an ordinary asset (depreciable business property is not a capital asset—see Chapter 4) and the loss will be treated as an ordinary loss.

Self-Study Problem 8.8

See Form 4797 on Pages E-55 and E-56.

Self-Study Problem 8.9

	Furniture	Machinery
Insurance proceeds	$ 0	$10,000
Adjusted basis	5,000	**14,000**
Decrease in FMV	4,000	15,000
Loss	$(5,000)	$ (4,000)

Since both result in a casualty loss, the losses are excluded from Section 1231 treatment and are treated as ordinary losses. The gain on the sale of the land would be treated as a Section 1231 long-term capital gain.

Self-Study Problem 8.8

Form **4797**		**Sales of Business Property**			OMB No. 1545-0184
		(Also Involuntary Conversions and Recapture Amounts Under Sections 179 and 280F(b)(2))			**20**19
Department of the Treasury Internal Revenue Service		▶ Attach to your tax return. ▶ Go to *www.irs.gov/Form4797* for instructions and the latest information.			Attachment Sequence No. **27**

Name(s) shown on return
Gary Farmer

Identifying number

1   Enter the gross proceeds from sales or exchanges reported to you for 2019 on Form(s) 1099-B or 1099-S (or substitute statement) that you are including on line 2, 10, or 20. See instructions **1**

Part I   Sales or Exchanges of Property Used in a Trade or Business and Involuntary Conversions From Other Than Casualty or Theft—Most Property Held More Than 1 Year (see instructions)

2 **(a)** Description of property	**(b)** Date acquired (mo., day, yr.)	**(c)** Date sold (mo., day, yr.)	**(d)** Gross sales price	**(e)** Depreciation allowed or allowable since acquisition	**(f)** Cost or other basis, plus improvements and expense of sale	**(g)** Gain or (loss) Subtract (f) from the sum of (d) and (e)
Land	12/03/2008	01/05/2019	37,000		24,500	12,500
Computer	04/05/2016	05/02/2019	14,000	5,175	25,875	(6,700)

3 Gain, if any, from Form 4684, line 39	**3**	
4 Section 1231 gain from installment sales from Form 6252, line 26 or 37	**4**	
5 Section 1231 gain or (loss) from like-kind exchanges from Form 8824	**5**	
6 Gain, if any, from line 32, from other than casualty or theft	**6**	146,050
7 Combine lines 2 through 6. Enter the gain or (loss) here and on the appropriate line as follows	**7**	151,850

Partnerships and S corporations. Report the gain or (loss) following the instructions for Form 1065, Schedule K, line 10, or Form 1120-S, Schedule K, line 9. Skip lines 8, 9, 11, and 12 below.

Individuals, partners, S corporation shareholders, and all others. If line 7 is zero or a loss, enter the amount from line 7 on line 11 below and skip lines 8 and 9. If line 7 is a gain and you didn't have any prior year section 1231 losses, or they were recaptured in an earlier year, enter the gain from line 7 as a long-term capital gain on the Schedule D filed with your return and skip lines 8, 9, 11, and 12 below.

8 Nonrecaptured net section 1231 losses from prior years. See instructions	**8**	
9 Subtract line 8 from line 7. If zero or less, enter -0-. If line 9 is zero, enter the gain from line 7 on line 12 below. If line 9 is more than zero, enter the amount from line 8 on line 12 below and enter the gain from line 9 as a long-term capital gain on the Schedule D filed with your return. See instructions	**9**	

Part II   Ordinary Gains and Losses (see instructions)

10   Ordinary gains and losses not included on lines 11 through 16 (include property held 1 year or less):

Equipment	10/21/2018	7/22/2019	16,000	4,300	26,600	(6,300)

11 Loss, if any, from line 7	**11** ( )	
12 Gain, if any, from line 7 or amount from line 8, if applicable	**12**	
13 Gain, if any, from line 31	**13**	7,600
14 Net gain or (loss) from Form 4684, lines 31 and 38a	**14**	
15 Ordinary gain from installment sales from Form 6252, line 25 or 36	**15**	
16 Ordinary gain or (loss) from like-kind exchanges from Form 8824	**16**	
17 Combine lines 10 through 16	**17**	1,300

18   For all except individual returns, enter the amount from line 17 on the appropriate line of your return and skip lines a and b below. For individual returns, complete lines a and b below.

a If the loss on line 11 includes a loss from Form 4684, line 35, column (b)(ii), enter that part of the loss here. Enter the loss from income-producing property on Schedule A (Form 1040 or Form 1040-SR), line 16. (Do not include any loss on property used as an employee.) Identify as from "Form 4797, line 18a." See instructions	**18a**	
b Redetermine the gain or (loss) on line 17 excluding the loss, if any, on line 18a. Enter here and on Schedule 1 (Form 1040 or Form 1040-SR), Part I, line 4	**18b**	1,300

For Paperwork Reduction Act Notice, see separate instructions.   Cat. No. 13086I   Form **4797** (2019)

Self-Study Problem 8.8

Part III Gain From Disposition of Property Under Sections 1245, 1250, 1252, 1254, and 1255
(see instructions)

19 (a) Description of section 1245, 1250, 1252, 1254, or 1255 property:	(b) Date acquired (mo., day, yr.)	(c) Date sold (mo., day, yr.)
A Building	12/3/2008	10/7/2019
B Furniture	12/3/2008	10/7/2019
C		
D		

These columns relate to the properties on lines 19A through 19D. ▶		Property A	Property B	Property C	Property D
20 Gross sales price (**Note:** *See line 1 before completing.*)	20	355,000	7,600		
21 Cost or other basis plus expense of sale	21	335,000	15,000		
22 Depreciation (or depletion) allowed or allowable	22	126,050	15,000		
23 Adjusted basis. Subtract line 22 from line 21	23	208,950	0		
24 Total gain. Subtract line 23 from line 20	24	146,050	7,600		
25 **If section 1245 property:**					
a Depreciation allowed or allowable from line 22	25a		15,000		
b Enter the **smaller** of line 24 or 25a	25b		7,600		
26 **If section 1250 property:** If straight line depreciation was used, enter -0- on line 26g, except for a corporation subject to section 291.					
a Additional depreciation after 1975. See instructions	26a				
b Applicable percentage multiplied by the **smaller** of line 24 or line 26a. See instructions.	26b				
c Subtract line 26a from line 24. If residential rental property **or** line 24 isn't more than line 26a, skip lines 26d and 26e	26c				
d Additional depreciation after 1969 and before 1976.	26d				
e Enter the **smaller** of line 26c or 26d	26e				
f Section 291 amount (corporations only)	26f				
g Add lines 26b, 26e, and 26f	26g				
27 **If section 1252 property:** Skip this section if you didn't dispose of farmland or if this form is being completed for a partnership.					
a Soil, water, and land clearing expenses	27a				
b Line 27a multiplied by applicable percentage. See instructions	27b				
c Enter the **smaller** of line 24 or 27b	27c				
28 **If section 1254 property:**					
a Intangible drilling and development costs, expenditures for development of mines and other natural deposits, mining exploration costs, and depletion. See instructions	28a				
b Enter the **smaller** of line 24 or 28a.	28b				
29 **If section 1255 property:**					
a Applicable percentage of payments excluded from income under section 126. See instructions	29a				
b Enter the **smaller** of line 24 or 29a. See instructions	29b				

Summary of Part III Gains. Complete property columns A through D through line 29b before going to line 30.

30 Total gains for all properties. Add property columns A through D, line 24	30	153,650
31 Add property columns A through D, lines 25b, 26g, 27c, 28b, and 29b. Enter here and on line 13	31	7,600
32 Subtract line 31 from line 30. Enter the portion from casualty or theft on Form 4684, line 33. Enter the portion from other than casualty or theft on Form 4797, line 6	32	146,050

Part IV Recapture Amounts Under Sections 179 and 280F(b)(2) When Business Use Drops to 50% or Less
(see instructions)

		(a) Section 179	(b) Section 280F(b)(2)
33 Section 179 expense deduction or depreciation allowable in prior years.	33		
34 Recomputed depreciation. See instructions	34		
35 Recapture amount. Subtract line 34 from line 33. See the instructions for where to report	35		

Form **4797** (2019)

Self-Study Problem 8.10

Cash	$ 20,000
Add: buyer's note	100,000
Selling price	120,000
Less: the adjusted basis ($80,000 − $26,000)	(54,000)
Total gain realized	$ 66,000
Contract price ($20,000 + $100,000)	$120,000
Taxable gain in 2019 = $66,000 / $120,000 × $20,000	$ 11,000

Self-Study Problem 8.11

Calculation of gain recognized:

Fair market value of new land	$ 22,000
Add: liability assumed by the buyer	8,000
Total amount realized	30,000
Less: the adjusted basis of the old land	(18,000)
Gain realized	$ 12,000
Boot received (liability assumed by the buyer)	$ 8,000
Gain recognized (the lesser of the gain realized or the boot received)	$ 8,000

Basis of the new land:

Basis of old land	$ 18,000
Less: boot received	(8,000)
Add: the gain recognized	8,000
Basis of the new land received	$ 18,000

Self-Study Problem 8.12

1. Insurance proceeds	$150,000
Less: the adjusted basis of the property	(70,000)
Gain realized	$ 80,000
Insurance proceeds	$150,000
Less: the cost of the replacement store	(135,000)
Proceeds not reinvested	$ 15,000
Gain recognized (the lesser of the gain realized or the proceeds not reinvested)	$ 15,000
2. Cost of the new store	$135,000
Less: the gain deferred ($80,000 − $15,000)	(65,000)
Basis of the new store	$ 70,000

CHAPTER 9   PAYROLL, ESTIMATED PAYMENTS, AND RETIREMENT PLANS

Self-Study Problem 9.1

1. Monthly salary	$2,500.00
Less: exemptions ($350.00 × 3)	1,050.00
Income subject to withholding	$ 1,450.00

Withholding:
$80.80 + [($1,450.00 − $1,125) × 12%] $ 119.80

2. From Appendix C, withholding = $121.00

Self-Study Problem 9.2

Form **1040-ES** Department of the Treasury Internal Revenue Service	20**19 Estimated Tax**	**Payment Voucher** **1** OMB No. 1545-0074

File only if you are making a payment of estimated tax by check or money order. Mail this voucher with your check or money order payable to **"United States Treasury."** Write your social security number and "2019 Form 1040-ES" on your check or money order. Do not send cash. Enclose, but do not staple or attach, your payment with this voucher.

Calendar year—Due April 15, 2019

Amount of estimated tax you are paying by check or money order.	Dollars	Cents
	1,670	00

Pay online at www.irs.gov/ etpay

Simple. Fast. Secure.

Print or type

Your first name and initial Ray	Your last name Adams	Your social security number 466-47-1131

If joint payment, complete for spouse

Spouse's first name and initial	Spouse's last name	Spouse's social security number

Address (number, street, and apt. no.)

City, state, and ZIP code. (If a foreign address, enter city, also complete spaces below.)

Foreign country name	Foreign province/county	Foreign postal code

For Privacy Act and Paperwork Reduction Act Notice, see instructions.   **Form 1040-ES (2019)**

*$1,670 = ($8,140/4) − $365

Self-Study Problem 9.3

Debbie:	Soc. Sec. — 6.2% × $132,900	$ 8,239.80
	Medicare — 1.45% × $137,000	1,986.50
	Total employee FICA tax	$10,226.30
Debbie's employer:	Soc. Sec. — 6.2% × $132,900	$ 8,239.80
	Medicare — 1.45% × $137,000	1,986.50
	Total employer FICA tax	$10,226.30
Total FICA tax		$20,452.60

Self-Study Problem 9.4

See Form 941 on Page E-59.

Self-Study Problem 9.4

Form 941 for 2019: Employer's QUARTERLY Federal Tax Return
(Rev. January 2019)   Department of the Treasury — Internal Revenue Service

950117

OMB No. 1545-0029

Employer identification number (EIN) ☐☐ – ☐☐☐☐☐☐☐

Name (not your trade name)   Charlotte York

Trade name (if any)

Address

Number	Street		Suite or room number
City		State	ZIP code
Foreign country name	Foreign province/county	Foreign postal code

Report for this Quarter of 2019
(Check one.)

- [X] **1:** January, February, March
- [ ] **2:** April, May, June
- [ ] **3:** July, August, September
- [ ] **4:** October, November, December

Go to *www.irs.gov/Form941* for instructions and the latest information.

Read the separate instructions before you complete Form 941. Type or print within the boxes.

Part 1:   Answer these questions for this quarter.

1	Number of employees who received wages, tips, or other compensation for the pay period including: *Mar. 12* (Quarter 1), *June 12* (Quarter 2), *Sept. 12* (Quarter 3), or *Dec. 12* (Quarter 4)	1	2
2	Wages, tips, and other compensation	2	9,600 . 00
3	Federal income tax withheld from wages, tips, and other compensation	3	995 . 00
4	If no wages, tips, and other compensation are subject to social security or Medicare tax	☐ Check and go to line 6.	

		Column 1		Column 2	
5a	Taxable social security wages	9,600 . 00	× 0.124 =	1,190 . 40	
5b	Taxable social security tips	.	× 0.124 =	.	
5c	Taxable Medicare wages & tips	9,600 . 00	× 0.029 =	278 . 40	
5d	Taxable wages & tips subject to Additional Medicare Tax withholding	.	× 0.009 =	.	

5e	Add Column 2 from lines 5a, 5b, 5c, and 5d	5e	1,468 . 80
5f	Section 3121(q) Notice and Demand—Tax due on unreported tips (see instructions)	5f	.
6	Total taxes before adjustments. Add lines 3, 5e, and 5f	6	2,463 . 80
7	Current quarter's adjustment for fractions of cents	7	.
8	Current quarter's adjustment for sick pay	8	.
9	Current quarter's adjustments for tips and group-term life insurance	9	.
10	Total taxes after adjustments. Combine lines 6 through 9	10	2,463 . 80
11	Qualified small business payroll tax credit for increasing research activities. Attach Form 8974	11	.
12	Total taxes after adjustments and credits. Subtract line 11 from line 10	12	2,463 . 80
13	Total deposits for this quarter, including overpayment applied from a prior quarter and overpayments applied from Form 941-X, 941-X (PR), 944-X, or 944-X (SP) filed in the current quarter	13	2,467 . 00
14	Balance due. If line 12 is more than line 13, enter the difference and see instructions	14	.
15	Overpayment. If line 13 is more than line 12, enter the difference 3 . 20 Check one: [X] Apply to next return. ☐ Send a refund.		

▶ **You MUST complete both pages of Form 941 and SIGN it.**

Next ▶

For Privacy Act and Paperwork Reduction Act Notice, see the back of the Payment Voucher.   Cat. No. 17001Z   Form **941** (Rev. 1-2019)

Self-Study Problem 9.5

a Employee's social security number 464-74-1132	OMB No. 1545-0008

Safe, accurate,
FAST! Use

IRS **e-file**

Visit the IRS website at
www.irs.gov/efile

b Employer identification number (EIN) 95-1234567	**1** Wages, tips, other compensation 16,150.00
	2 Federal income tax withheld 2,422.00

c Employer's name, address, and ZIP code	**3** Social security wages 16,150.00	**4** Social security tax withheld 1,001.30
Big Bank PO Box 12344 San Diego, CA 92101	**5** Medicare wages and tips 16,150.00	**6** Medicare tax withheld 234.18
	7 Social security tips	**8** Allocated tips

d Control number	**9**	**10** Dependent care benefits

e Employee's first name and initial Last name Suff.	**11** Nonqualified plans	**12a** See instructions for box 12
	13 Statutory employee ☐ Retirement plan ☐ Third-party sick pay ☐	**12b**
Mary Jones 6431 Gary Street San Diego, CA 92115	**14** Other	**12c**
		12d
f Employee's address and ZIP code		

15 State Employer's state ID number	**16** State wages, tips, etc.	**17** State income tax	**18** Local wages, tips, etc.	**19** Local income tax	**20** Locality name
CA 800 4039 250 092	16,150.00	969.00			

Form **W-2** Wage and Tax Statement   **2019**   Department of the Treasury—Internal Revenue Service

Copy B—To Be Filed With Employee's FEDERAL Tax Return.
This information is being furnished to the Internal Revenue Service.

☐ CORRECTED (if checked)

PAYER'S name, street address, city or town, state or province, country, ZIP or foreign postal code, and telephone no. Big Bank PO Box 12344 San Diego, CA 92101 800-555-1212	Payer's RTN (optional)	OMB No. 1545-0112	
	1 Interest income $ 461.00	**2019** Form **1099-INT**	**Interest Income**

PAYER'S TIN 95-1234567	RECIPIENT'S TIN 464-74-1132	**2** Early withdrawal penalty $	**Copy B**
		3 Interest on U.S. Savings Bonds and Treas. obligations $	**For Recipient**

RECIPIENT'S name Mary Jones	**4** Federal income tax withheld $	**5** Investment expenses $	
Street address (including apt. no.) 6431 Gary Street	**6** Foreign tax paid $	**7** Foreign country or U.S. possession	This is important tax information and is being furnished to the IRS. If you are required to file a return, a negligence penalty or other sanction may be imposed on you if this income is taxable and the IRS determines that it has not been reported.
	8 Tax-exempt interest $	**9** Specified private activity bond interest $	
City or town, state or province, country, and ZIP or foreign postal code San Diego, CA 92115	**10** Market discount $	**11** Bond premium $	
FATCA filing requirement ☐	**12** Bond premium on Treasury obligations $	**13** Bond premium on tax-exempt bond $	
Account number (see instructions)	**14** Tax-exempt and tax credit bond CUSIP no.	**15** State **16** State identification no. **17** State tax withheld $ $	

Form **1099-INT**   (keep for your records)   www.irs.gov/Form1099INT   Department of the Treasury - Internal Revenue Service

Self-Study Problem 9.6

See Form 940 on Pages E-61 and E-62.

Self-Study Problem 9.6

Form **940** for 2019:	Employer's Annual Federal Unemployment (FUTA) Tax Return	850113

Department of the Treasury — Internal Revenue Service

OMB No. 1545-0028

Employer identification number (EIN)   9 4 – 0 0 0 1 1 1 2

Name (not your trade name)   Rhus Company

Trade name (if any)

Address   400 8th Street N.
Number   Street   Suite or room number

La Crosse   WI   54601
City   State   ZIP code

Foreign country name   Foreign province/county   Foreign postal code

Type of Return
(Check all that apply.)

- [ ] **a.** Amended
- [ ] **b.** Successor employer
- [ ] **c.** No payments to employees in 2018
- [ ] **d.** Final: Business closed or stopped paying wages

Go to www.irs.gov/Form940 for instructions and the latest information.

Read the separate instructions before you complete this form. Please type or print within the boxes.

Part 1:   Tell us about your return. If any line does NOT apply, leave it blank. See instructions before completing Part 1.

1a If you had to pay state unemployment tax in one state only, enter the state abbreviation . **1a** W I

1b If you had to pay state unemployment tax in more than one state, you are a multi-state employer . . . . **1b** [ ] Check here. Complete Schedule A (Form 940).

2 If you paid wages in a state that is subject to **CREDIT REDUCTION** . . . . **2** [ ] Check here. Complete Schedule A (Form 940).

Part 2:   Determine your FUTA tax before adjustments. If any line does NOT apply, leave it blank.

3 Total payments to all employees . . . . **3** 113,000 . 00

4 Payments exempt from FUTA tax . . . . **4** .

Check all that apply: **4a** [ ] Fringe benefits   **4c** [ ] Retirement/Pension   **4e** [ ] Other
                        4b [ ] Group-term life insurance   **4d** [ ] Dependent care

5 Total of payments made to each employee in excess of $7,000 . . . . **5** 22,000 . 00

6 Subtotal (line 4 + line 5 = line 6) . . . . **6** 22,000 . 00

7 Total taxable FUTA wages (line 3 – line 6 = line 7). See instructions . **7** 91,000 . 00

8 FUTA tax before adjustments (line 7 x 0.006 = line 8) . . . . **8** 546 . 00

Part 3:   Determine your adjustments. If any line does NOT apply, leave it blank.

9 If ALL of the taxable FUTA wages you paid were excluded from state unemployment tax, multiply line 7 by 0.054 (line 7 × 0.054 = line 9). Go to line 12 . . . . **9** .

10 If SOME of the taxable FUTA wages you paid were excluded from state unemployment tax, OR you paid ANY state unemployment tax late (after the due date for filing Form 940), complete the worksheet in the instructions. Enter the amount from line 7 of the worksheet . . **10** .

11 If credit reduction applies, enter the total from Schedule A (Form 940) . . . . **11** .

Part 4:   Determine your FUTA tax and balance due or overpayment. If any line does NOT apply, leave it blank.

12 Total FUTA tax after adjustments (lines 8 + 9 + 10 + 11 = line 12) . . . . **12** 546 . 00

13 FUTA tax deposited for the year, including any overpayment applied from a prior year . **13** .

14 Balance due. If line 12 is more than line 13, enter the excess on line 14.
- If line 14 is more than $500, you must deposit your tax.
- If line 14 is $500 or less, you may pay with this return. See instructions . . . . **14** 546 . 00

15 Overpayment. If line 13 is more than line 12, enter the excess on line 15 and check a box below **15** 0 . 00
▶ You **MUST** complete both pages of this form and **SIGN** it.   Check one: [ ] Apply to next return. [ ] Send a refund.

Next ▶

For Privacy Act and Paperwork Reduction Act Notice, see the back of the Payment Voucher.   Cat. No. 11234O   Form **940** (2018)

Self-Study Problem 9.6

850212

Name (not your trade name)	Employer identification number (EIN)
Rhus Company	94-0001112

Part 5: Report your FUTA tax liability by quarter only if line 12 is more than $500. If not, go to Part 6.

16 Report the amount of your FUTA tax liability for each quarter; do NOT enter the amount you deposited. If you had no liability for a quarter, leave the line blank.

16a **1st quarter** (January 1 – March 31) . . . . 16a   150 . 00

16b **2nd quarter** (April 1 – June 30) . . . . 16b   156 . 00

16c **3rd quarter** (July 1 – September 30) . . . . 16c   96 . 00

16d **4th quarter** (October 1 – December 31) . . . . . 16d   144 . 00

17 **Total tax liability for the year** (lines 16a + 16b + 16c + 16d = line 17) 17   546 . 00   Total must equal line 12.

Part 6: May we speak with your third-party designee?

Do you want to allow an employee, a paid tax preparer, or another person to discuss this return with the IRS? See the instructions for details.

☐ **Yes.**   Designee's name and phone number

Select a 5-digit Personal Identification Number (PIN) to use when talking to IRS

☐ **No.**

Part 7: Sign here. You MUST complete both pages of this form and SIGN it.

Under penalties of perjury, I declare that I have examined this return, including accompanying schedules and statements, and to the best of my knowledge and belief, it is true, correct, and complete, and that no part of any payment made to a state unemployment fund claimed as a credit was, or is to be, deducted from the payments made to employees. Declaration of preparer (other than taxpayer) is based on all information of which preparer has any knowledge.

✗ Sign your name here

Print your name here

Print your title here

Date   /   /

Best daytime phone

Paid Preparer Use Only   Check if you are self-employed ☐

Preparer's name		PTIN	
Preparer's signature		Date	/ /
Firm's name (or yours if self-employed)		EIN	
Address		Phone	
City	State	ZIP code	

Form **940** (2019)

Self-Study Problem 9.7

    a. $12,500, lesser of 25% × $50,000 or $56,000 (annual limit effective for 2019)
    b. $56,000 (annual dollar limit effective for 2019)

Self-Study Problem 9.8

    a. $150,000
    b. $120,000 ($150,000 − 20% × $150,000)
    c. August 30, 20XX, which is the 60th day after the day the distribution was received, unless the hardship waiver provisions apply.
    d. $150,000

CHAPTER 10   PARTNERSHIP TAXATION

Self-Study Problem 10.1

1.	Yes	
2.	No	A corporation is not a partnership, but a separate type of entity.
3.	No	The mere joint ownership of property does not constitute a partnership; the owners must engage in some type of business activity.
4.	Yes	The marketing of oil qualifies the venture as a partnership.
5.	Yes and No	The married couple has the choice to operate as a qualified joint venture or as a partnership.

Self-Study Problem 10.2

1.	$0	
2.	$36,000	The amount of cash contributed.
3.	$0	
4.	$17,500	The same as Linda's basis in the equipment contributed to the partnership.
5.	$17,500	The same as Linda's basis in the equipment contributed.

Self-Study Problem 10.3

See Form 1065 and Schedule K-1 on Pages E-64 to E-69.

Self-Study Problem 10.4

1. Partnership income before guaranteed payments	$ 32,000
Less: guaranteed payments	(36,000)
Partnership loss after guaranteed payments	$ (4,000)
Jim's income:	
Guaranteed payments	$ 36,000
50% of the $4,000 partnership loss	(2,000)
Total income	$ 34,000
2. Jack's income (loss): 50% of the $4,000 partnership loss	$(2,000)

Self-Study Problem 10.5

12 months × $1,000 per month guaranteed payment	$12,000
Add: Robert's distributive share of income	21,000
Total income	$33,000

Self-Study Problem 10.3

Form **1065**		**U.S. Return of Partnership Income**			OMB No. 1545-0123

Department of the Treasury
Internal Revenue Service

For calendar year 2019, or tax year beginning _____ , 2019, ending _____ , 20 ____ .

► Go to *www.irs.gov/Form1065* for instructions and the latest information.

2019

A Principal business activity		Name of partnership	**D** Employer identification number
		Malus Valley Partnership	
B Principal product or service	**Type or Print**	Number, street, and room or suite no. If a P.O. box, see instructions.	**E** Date business started 2019
C Business code number		City or town, state or province, country, and ZIP or foreign postal code	**F** Total assets (see instructions) $ 257,750

G Check applicable boxes: **(1)** ☑ Initial return **(2)** ☐ Final return **(3)** ☐ Name change **(4)** ☐ Address change **(5)** ☐ Amended return

H Check accounting method: **(1)** ☐ Cash **(2)** ☑ Accrual **(3)** ☐ Other (specify) ► _____

I Number of Schedules K-1. Attach one for each person who was a partner at any time during the tax year ► 2

J Check if Schedules C and M-3 are attached . . . . ► ☐

K Check if partnership: **(1)** ☐ Aggregated activities for section 465 at-risk purposes **(2)** ☐ Grouped activities for section 469 passive activity purposes

Caution: Include **only** trade or business income and expenses on lines 1a through 22 below. See instructions for more information.

Income	**1a**	Gross receipts or sales	**1a**	255,600	
	b	Returns and allowances	**1b**		
	c	Balance. Subtract line 1b from line 1a		**1c**	255,600
	2	Cost of goods sold (attach Form 1125-A)		**2**	
	3	Gross profit. Subtract line 2 from line 1c		**3**	255,600
	4	Ordinary income (loss) from other partnerships, estates, and trusts (attach statement)		**4**	
	5	Net farm profit (loss) (attach Schedule F (Form 1040 or 1040-SR)) . . .		**5**	
	6	Net gain (loss) from Form 4797, Part II, line 17 (attach Form 4797) . . .		**6**	
	7	Other income (loss) (attach statement)		**7**	
	8	**Total income (loss).** Combine lines 3 through 7		**8**	255,600
Deductions (see instructions for limitations)	**9**	Salaries and wages (other than to partners) (less employment credits) . .		**9**	168,000
	10	Guaranteed payments to partners		**10**	
	11	Repairs and maintenance		**11**	
	12	Bad debts		**12**	
	13	Rent		**13**	12,000
	14	Taxes and licenses		**14**	6,100
	15	Interest (see instructions)		**15**	
	16a	Depreciation (if required, attach Form 4562)	**16a**	9,250	
	b	Less depreciation reported on Form 1125-A and elsewhere on return .	**16b**		**16c** 9,250
	17	Depletion **(Do not deduct oil and gas depletion.)**		**17**	
	18	Retirement plans, etc.		**18**	
	19	Employee benefit programs		**19**	
	20	Other deductions (attach statement)		**20**	
	21	**Total deductions.** Add the amounts shown in the far right column for lines 9 through 20 . . .		**21**	195,350
	22	**Ordinary business income (loss).** Subtract line 21 from line 8 . . .		**22**	60,250
Tax and Payment	**23**	Interest due under the look-back method—completed long-term contracts (attach Form 8697) .		**23**	
	24	Interest due under the look-back method—income forecast method (attach Form 8866) . . .		**24**	
	25	BBA AAR imputed underpayment (see instructions)		**25**	
	26	Other taxes (see instructions)		**26**	
	27	**Total balance due.** Add lines 23 through 26		**27**	
	28	Payment (see instructions)		**28**	
	29	**Amount owed.** If line 28 is smaller than line 27, enter amount owed . .		**29**	
	30	**Overpayment.** If line 28 is larger than line 27, enter overpayment . . .		**30**	

Sign Here

Under penalties of perjury, I declare that I have examined this return, including accompanying schedules and statements, and to the best of my knowledge and belief, it is true, correct, and complete. Declaration of preparer (other than partner or limited liability company member) is based on all information of which preparer has any knowledge.

► _____   ► _____
Signature of partner or limited liability company member   Date

May the IRS discuss this return with the preparer shown below? See instructions. ☐ Yes ☐ No

Paid Preparer Use Only

Print/Type preparer's name	Preparer's signature	Date	Check ☐ if self-employed	PTIN
Firm's name ►			Firm's EIN ►	
Firm's address ►			Phone no.	

For Paperwork Reduction Act Notice, see separate instructions.   Cat. No. 11390Z   Form **1065** (2019)

DRAFT AS OF September 26, 2019 DO NOT FILE

Self-Study Problem 10.3

Form 1065 (2019)   Page **2**

Schedule B	**Other Information**				

				Yes	No
1	What type of entity is filing this return? Check the applicable box:				
a	☑ Domestic general partnership	**b**	☐ Domestic limited partnership		
c	☐ Domestic limited liability company	**d**	☐ Domestic limited liability partnership		
e	☐ Foreign partnership	**f**	☐ Other ▶		
2	At the end of the tax year:				
a	Did any foreign or domestic corporation, partnership (including any entity treated as a partnership), trust, or tax-exempt organization, or any foreign government own, directly or indirectly, an interest of 50% or more in the profit, loss, or capital of the partnership? For rules of constructive ownership, see instructions. If "Yes," attach Schedule B-1, Information on Partners Owning 50% or More of the Partnership				✓
b	Did any individual or estate own, directly or indirectly, an interest of 50% or more in the profit, loss, or capital of the partnership? For rules of constructive ownership, see instructions. If "Yes," attach Schedule B-1, Information on Partners Owning 50% or More of the Partnership				✓
3	At the end of the tax year, did the partnership:				
a	Own directly 20% or more, or own, directly or indirectly, 50% or more of the total voting power of all classes of stock entitled to vote of any foreign or domestic corporation? For rules of constructive ownership, see instructions. If "Yes," complete (i) through (iv) below				✓

(i) Name of Corporation	(ii) Employer Identification Number (if any)	(iii) Country of Incorporation	(iv) Percentage Owned in Voting Stock

		Yes	No
b	Own directly an interest of 20% or more, or own, directly or indirectly, an interest of 50% or more in the profit, loss, or capital in any foreign or domestic partnership (including an entity treated as a partnership) or in the beneficial interest of a trust? For rules of constructive ownership, see instructions. If "Yes," complete (i) through (v) below . .		✓

(i) Name of Entity	(ii) Employer Identification Number (if any)	(iii) Type of Entity	(iv) Country of Organization	(v) Maximum Percentage Owned in Profit, Loss, or Capital

			Yes	No
4		Does the partnership satisfy **all four** of the following conditions?		
a		The partnership's total receipts for the tax year were less than $250,000.		
b		The partnership's total assets at the end of the tax year were less than $1 million.		
c		Schedules K-1 are filed with the return and furnished to the partners on or before the due date (including extensions) for the partnership return.		
d		The partnership is not filing and is not required to file Schedule M-3		✓
		If "Yes," the partnership is not required to complete Schedules L, M-1, and M-2; item F on page 1 of Form 1065; or item L on Schedule K-1.		
5		Is this partnership a publicly traded partnership, as defined in section 469(k)(2)?		✓
6		During the tax year, did the partnership have any debt that was canceled, was forgiven, or had the terms modified so as to reduce the principal amount of the debt?		✓
7		Has this partnership filed, or is it required to file, Form 8918, Material Advisor Disclosure Statement, to provide information on any reportable transaction?		✓
8		At any time during calendar year 2019, did the partnership have an interest in or a signature or other authority over a financial account in a foreign country (such as a bank account, securities account, or other financial account)? See instructions for exceptions and filing requirements for FinCEN Form 114, Report of Foreign Bank and Financial Accounts (FBAR). If "Yes," enter the name of the foreign country ▶		✓
9		At any time during the tax year, did the partnership receive a distribution from, or was it the grantor of, or transferor to, a foreign trust? If "Yes," the partnership may have to file Form 3520, Annual Return To Report Transactions With Foreign Trusts and Receipt of Certain Foreign Gifts. See instructions		✓
10a		Is the partnership making, or had it previously made (and not revoked), a section 754 election?		✓
		See instructions for details regarding a section 754 election.		
b		Did the partnership make for this tax year an optional basis adjustment under section 743(b) or 734(b)? If "Yes," attach a statement showing the computation and allocation of the basis adjustment. See instructions		✓

Form **1065** (2019)

Self-Study Problem 10.3

Form 1065 (2019)   Page **3**

Schedule B	Other Information *(continued)*	Yes	No
c	Is the partnership required to adjust the basis of partnership assets under section 743(b) or 734(b) because of a substantial built-in loss (as defined under section 743(d)) or substantial basis reduction (as defined under section 734(d))? If "Yes," attach a statement showing the computation and allocation of the basis adjustment. See instructions		✓
11	Check this box if, during the current or prior tax year, the partnership distributed any property received in a like-kind exchange or contributed such property to another entity (other than disregarded entities wholly owned by the partnership throughout the tax year) . . . . ▶ ☐		
12	At any time during the tax year, did the partnership distribute to any partner a tenancy-in-common or undivided interest in partnership property?		✓
13	If the partnership is required to file Form 8858, Information Return of U.S. Persons With Respect To Foreign Disregarded Entities (FDEs) and Foreign Branches (FBs), enter the number of Forms 8858 attached. See instructions . . . . ▶		
14	Does the partnership have any foreign partners? If "Yes," enter the number of Forms 8805, Foreign Partner's Information Statement of Section 1446 Withholding Tax, filed for this partnership . . . . . ▶		✓
15	Enter the number of Forms 8865, Return of U.S. Persons With Respect to Certain Foreign Partnerships, attached to this return . . . . ▶		
16a	Did you make any payments in 2019 that would require you to file Form(s) 1099? See instructions		✓
b	If "Yes," did you or will you file required Form(s) 1099?		
17	Enter the number of Forms 5471, Information Return of U.S. Persons With Respect To Certain Foreign Corporations, attached to this return . . . . ▶		
18	Enter the number of partners that are foreign governments under section 892 . . . . . ▶		
19	During the partnership's tax year, did the partnership make any payments that would require it to file Form 1042 and 1042-S under chapter 3 (sections 1441 through 1464) or chapter 4 (sections 1471 through 1474)?		✓
20	Was the partnership a specified domestic entity required to file Form 8938 for the tax year? See the Instructions for Form 8938		✓
21	Is the partnership a section 721(c) partnership, as defined in Regulations section 1.721(c)-1T(b)(14)?		✓
22	During the tax year, did the partnership pay or accrue any interest or royalty for which the deduction is not allowed under section 267A? See instructions If "Yes," enter the total amount of the disallowed deductions . . . . ▶ $		
23	Did the partnership have an election under section 163(j) for any real property trade or business or any farming business in effect during the tax year? See instructions		✓
24	Does the partnership satisfy one or more of the following? See instructions	✓	
a	The partnership owns a pass-through entity with current, or prior year carryover, excess business interest expense.		
b	The partnership's aggregate average annual gross receipts (determined under section 448(c)) for the 3 tax years preceding the current tax year are more than $26 million and the partnership has business interest.		
c	The partnership is a tax shelter (see instructions) and the partnership has business interest expense. If "Yes" to any, complete and attach Form 8990.		
25	Is the partnership electing out of the centralized partnership audit regime under section 6221(b)? See instructions. If "Yes," the partnership must complete Schedule B-2 (Form 1065). Enter the total from Schedule B-2, Part III, line 3 . . . . ▶ _____ If "No," complete Designation of Partnership Representative below.		✓

Designation of Partnership Representative (see instructions)

Enter below the information for the partnership representative (PR) for the tax year covered by this return.

Name of PR ▶

U.S. address of PR ▶ _____	U.S. phone number of ▶ PR

If the PR is an entity, name of the designated individual for the PR ▶

U.S. address of designated individual ▶ _____	U.S. phone number of ▶ designated individual

		Yes	No
26	Is the partnership attaching Form 8996 to certify as a Qualified Opportunity Fund? . . . . If "Yes," enter the amount from Form 8996, line 14 . . . . ▶ $		
27	Enter the number of foreign partners subject to section 864(c)(8) as a result of transferring all or a portion of an interest in the partnership or of receiving a distribution from the partnership . . . . . ▶		
28	At any time during the tax year, were there any transfers between the partnership and its partners subject to the disclosure requirements of Regulations section 1.707-8?		✓

Form **1065** (2019)

Self-Study Problem 10.3

Form 1065 (2019)   Page **4**

Schedule K		Partners' Distributive Share Items				Total amount
Income (Loss)	**1**	Ordinary business income (loss) (page 1, line 22)			**1**	60,250
	2	Net rental real estate income (loss) (attach Form 8825)			**2**	
	3a	Other gross rental income (loss)	**3a**			
	b	Expenses from other rental activities (attach statement)	**3b**			
	c	Other net rental income (loss). Subtract line 3b from line 3a			**3c**	
	4	Guaranteed payments: **a** Services **4a**		**b** Capital **4b**		
		c Total. Add lines 4a and 4b			**4c**	
	5	Interest income			**5**	
	6	Dividends and dividend equivalents: **a** Ordinary dividends			**6a**	
		b Qualified dividends **6b**		**c** Dividend equivalents **6c**		
	7	Royalties			**7**	
	8	Net short-term capital gain (loss) (attach Schedule D (Form 1065))			**8**	
	9a	Net long-term capital gain (loss) (attach Schedule D (Form 1065))			**9a**	
	b	Collectibles (28%) gain (loss)	**9b**			
	c	Unrecaptured section 1250 gain (attach statement)	**9c**			
	10	Net section 1231 gain (loss) (attach Form 4797)			**10**	
	11	Other income (loss) (see instructions) Type ▶			**11**	
Deductions	**12**	Section 179 deduction (attach Form 4562)			**12**	
	13a	Contributions			**13a**	1,500
	b	Investment interest expense			**13b**	
	c	Section 59(e)(2) expenditures: **(1)** Type ▶		**(2)** Amount ▶	**13c(2)**	
	d	Other deductions (see instructions) Type ▶			**13d**	
Self-Employ-ment	**14a**	Net earnings (loss) from self-employment			**14a**	60,250
	b	Gross farming or fishing income			**14b**	
	c	Gross nonfarm income			**14c**	
Credits	**15a**	Low-income housing credit (section 42(j)(5))			**15a**	
	b	Low-income housing credit (other)			**15b**	
	c	Qualified rehabilitation expenditures (rental real estate) (attach Form 3468, if applicable)			**15c**	
	d	Other rental real estate credits (see instructions) Type ▶			**15d**	
	e	Other rental credits (see instructions) Type ▶			**15e**	
	f	Other credits (see instructions) Type ▶			**15f**	
Foreign Transactions	**16a**	Name of country or U.S. possession ▶				
	b	Gross income from all sources			**16b**	
	c	Gross income sourced at partner level			**16c**	
		Foreign gross income sourced at partnership level				
	d	Reserved for future use ▶ **e** Foreign branch category ▶			**16e**	
	f	Passive category ▶ **g** General category ▶ **h** Other (attach statement) ▶			**16h**	
		Deductions allocated and apportioned at partner level				
	i	Interest expense ▶ **j** Other ▶			**16j**	
		Deductions allocated and apportioned at partnership level to foreign source income				
	k	Reserved for future use ▶ **l** Foreign branch category ▶			**16l**	
	m	Passive category ▶ **n** General category ▶ **o** Other (attach statement) ▶			**16o**	
	p	Total foreign taxes (check one): ▶ Paid ☐ Accrued ☐			**16p**	
	q	Reduction in taxes available for credit (attach statement)			**16q**	
	r	Other foreign tax information (attach statement)				
Alternative Minimum Tax (AMT) Items	**17a**	Post-1986 depreciation adjustment			**17a**	
	b	Adjusted gain or loss			**17b**	
	c	Depletion (other than oil and gas)			**17c**	
	d	Oil, gas, and geothermal properties—gross income			**17d**	
	e	Oil, gas, and geothermal properties—deductions			**17e**	
	f	Other AMT items (attach statement)			**17f**	
Other Information	**18a**	Tax-exempt interest income			**18a**	
	b	Other tax-exempt income			**18b**	
	c	Nondeductible expenses			**18c**	
	19a	Distributions of cash and marketable securities			**19a**	50,000
	b	Distributions of other property			**19b**	
	20a	Investment income			**20a**	
	b	Investment expenses			**20b**	
	c	Other items and amounts (attach statement)				

Form **1065** (2019)

Self-Study Problem 10.3

Form 1065 (2019)   Page **5**

Analysis of Net Income (Loss)

1	Net income (loss). Combine Schedule K, lines 1 through 11. From the result, subtract the sum of Schedule K, lines 12 through 13d, and 16p					**1**	58,750

2	Analysis by partner type:	(i) Corporate	(ii) Individual (active)	(iii) Individual (passive)	(iv) Partnership	(v) Exempt Organization	(vi) Nominee/Other
a	General partners		58,750				
b	Limited partners						

Schedule L   Balance Sheets per Books

	Assets	Beginning of tax year (a)	(b)	End of tax year (c)	(d)
1	Cash		Initial Return		27,000
2a	Trade notes and accounts receivable			10,000	
b	Less allowance for bad debts				10,000
3	Inventories				
4	U.S. government obligations				
5	Tax-exempt securities				
6	Other current assets (attach statement)				
7a	Loans to partners (or persons related to partners) .				
b	Mortgage and real estate loans				
8	Other investments (attach statement)				
9a	Buildings and other depreciable assets			115,000	
b	Less accumulated depreciation			9,250	105,750
10a	Depletable assets				
b	Less accumulated depletion				
11	Land (net of any amortization)				115,000
12a	Intangible assets (amortizable only)				
b	Less accumulated amortization				
13	Other assets (attach statement)				
14	Total assets				257,750

	Liabilities and Capital				
15	Accounts payable				29,750
16	Mortgages, notes, bonds payable in less than 1 year				
17	Other current liabilities (attach statement)				
18	All nonrecourse loans				
19a	Loans from partners (or persons related to partners) .				
b	Mortgages, notes, bonds payable in 1 year or more .				187,750
20	Other liabilities (attach statement)				
21	Partners' capital accounts				40,250
22	Total liabilities and capital				257,750

Schedule M-1   Reconciliation of Income (Loss) per Books With Income (Loss) per Return

Note: The partnership may be required to file Schedule M-3. See instructions.

1	Net income (loss) per books	58,750	6	Income recorded on books this year not included on Schedule K, lines 1 through 11 (itemize):	
2	Income included on Schedule K, lines 1, 2, 3c, 5, 6a, 7, 8, 9a, 10, and 11, not recorded on books this year (itemize): _____		a	Tax-exempt interest $ _____ _____	
3	Guaranteed payments (other than health insurance)		7	Deductions included on Schedule K, lines 1 through 13d, and 16p, not charged against book income this year (itemize):	
4	Expenses recorded on books this year not included on Schedule K, lines 1 through 13d, and 16p (itemize):		a	Depreciation $ _____	
a	Depreciation $ _____		8	Add lines 6 and 7	
b	Travel and entertainment $ _____		9	Income (loss) (Analysis of Net Income (Loss), line 1). Subtract line 8 from line 5	58,750
5	Add lines 1 through 4	58,750			

Schedule M-2   Analysis of Partners' Capital Accounts

1	Balance at beginning of year . . .	0	6	Distributions: a Cash	50,000
2	Capital contributed: a Cash . . .	31,500		b Property	
	b Property . .		7	Other decreases (itemize): _____	
3	Net income (loss) per books	58,750		_____	
4	Other increases (itemize): _____		8	Add lines 6 and 7	50,000
5	Add lines 1 through 4	90,250	9	Balance at end of year. Subtract line 8 from line 5	40,250

Form **1065** (2019)

Self-Study Problem 10.3

651119

☐ Final K-1	☐ Amended K-1	OMB No. 1545-0123

**Schedule K-1
(Form 1065)**
Department of the Treasury
Internal Revenue Service

2019

For calendar year 2019, or tax year

beginning   /   / 2019   ending   /   /

Partner's Share of Income, Deductions, Credits, etc. ▶ See back of form and separate instructions.

Part III   Partner's Share of Current Year Income, Deductions, Credits, and Other Items

#	Item	Amount	#	Item	Amount
1	Ordinary business income (loss)	30,125	15	Credits	
2	Net rental real estate income (loss)				
3	Other net rental income (loss)		16	Foreign transactions	
4a	Guaranteed payments for services				
4b	Guaranteed payments for capital				
4c	Total guaranteed payments				
5	Interest income				
6a	Ordinary dividends				
6b	Qualified dividends				
6c	Dividend equivalents		17	Alternative minimum tax (AMT) items	
7	Royalties				
8	Net short-term capital gain (loss)				
9a	Net long-term capital gain (loss)		18	Tax-exempt income and nondeductible expenses	
9b	Collectibles (28%) gain (loss)				
9c	Unrecaptured section 1250 gain				
10	Net section 1231 gain (loss)		19	Distributions	
11	Other income (loss)		A		25,000
12	Section 179 deduction		20	Other information	
			Z*		30,125
13	Other deductions		Z**		84,000
A		750			
14	Self-employment earnings (loss)				
A		30,125			

21 ☐ More than one activity for at-risk purposes*
22 ☐ More than one activity for passive activity purposes*
*See attached statement for additional information.

Part I   Information About the Partnership

A   Partnership's employer identification number

B   Partnership's name, address, city, state, and ZIP code
Malus Valley Partnership

C   IRS Center where partnership filed return ▶

D   ☐ Check if this is a publicly traded partnership (PTP)

Part II   Information About the Partner

E   Partner's identifying number (Do not use TIN of a disregarded entity. See instructions.)

F   Partner's name, address, city, state, and ZIP code
Robert Conrad

G   ☒ General partner or LLC member-manager   ☐ Limited partner or other LLC member

H   ☒ Domestic partner   ☐ Foreign partner
☐ Disregarded entity: Name of beneficial owner _____

I1   What type of entity is this partner?   Individual

I2   If this partner is a retirement plan (IRA/SEP/Keogh/etc.), check here ☐

J   Partner's share of profit, loss, and capital (see instructions):

	Beginning	Ending
Profit	%	50 %
Loss	%	50 %
Capital	%	50 %

Check if decrease is due to sale or exchange of partnership interest   ☐

K   Partner's share of liabilities:

	Beginning	Ending
Nonrecourse	$	$
Qualified nonrecourse financing	$	$
Recourse	$	$ 108,750

☐ Check this box if Item K includes liability amounts from lower tier partnerships.

L   **Partner's Capital Account Analysis**

	Tax Basis Capital
Beginning capital account	$ 0
Capital contributed during the year	$ 15,750
Current year net income (loss)	$ 29,375
Other increase (decrease) (attach explanation)	$
Withdrawals & distributions	$ (25,000)
Ending capital account	$ 20,125

M   Did the partner contribute property with a built-in gain or loss?
☐ Yes   ☒ No   If "Yes," attach statement. See instructions.

N   **Partner's Share of Net Unrecognized Section 704(c) Gain or (Loss)**
Beginning $ _____
Ending $ _____

For IRS Use Only

For Paperwork Reduction Act Notice, see Instructions for Form 1065.   www.irs.gov/Form1065   Cat. No. 11394R   **Schedule K-1 (Form 1065) 2019**

- At the time we go to print, the line 20 codes related to the QBI deduction have not been released. Z is qualified business income and Z** is allocated W-2 wages.

The $1,500 per month received in September, October, November, and December of 2019 will be reported on Robert's 2020 income tax return. The guaranteed payments received are reported for the partnership tax year that ends with or within the partner's tax year, in the same manner as a distributive share of the partnership income.

Self-Study Problem 10.6

1. Maxwell has a $5,000 realized loss ($70,000 − $75,000), but the loss is not recognized since he is a more-than-50 percent partner, 50 percent directly and 50 percent indirectly from his daughter.
2. The daughter has a $15,000 gain ($40,000 − $25,000). Since she is a more-than-50 percent partner (50 percent directly and 50 percent indirectly), and the car is not a capital asset to the partnership, the gain is ordinary income.

Self-Study Problem 10.7

a. Marla's QBI deduction with no limitation is $200,000 × 20% = $40,000.
The guaranteed payments and the capital gains are not part of QBI income. Because Marla's income exceeds the phase-out range for taxable income (starts at $160,700 and is completely phased out by $210,700 in 2019), the W-2 wage limitation applies.

    a. W-2 Wages allocated to Marla are $46,000 ($230,000 × 20% interest). Qualified property allocated to Marla is $240,000 ($1,200,000 × 20%). The limit is the greater of:
      i. $46,000 × 50% = $23,000
      ii. ($46,000 × 25%) + ($240,000 × 2.5%) = $17,500

The W-2 wages limit of $23,000 is less than $40,000; thus the QBI deduction is $23,000 (note that the taxable income limit of $155,200 ($776,000 × 20%) exceeds the QBI deduction).

b. If Salem is a service business, because Marla's income exceeds the phase-out range for taxable income (starts at $160,700 and completely phased out by $210,700 in 2019), she is not eligible for any QBI deduction.

Self-Study Problem 10.8

1. $45,000, his amount at risk in the activity.

2. Profit	$ 31,000
Less: carryover of disallowed loss from the prior year	
($60,000 − $45,000)	(15,000)
Taxable income for next year	$ 16,000

Self-Study Problem 10.9

1. False   An election must be made to be treated like a corporation for tax purposes.
2. False
3. True
4. True
5. False

CHAPTER 11   THE CORPORATE INCOME TAX

Self-Study Problem 11.1

$275,000 × 21% = $57,750

Self-Study Problem 11.2

a. $110,000 × 21% = $23,100

None of the capital losses may be used to offset current year ordinary income. The capital losses may be carried back 3 years and forward 5 years to offset capital gains, if any, recognized during those years.

b. Maxus may use the NOL to offset up to $36,000 ($45,000 × 80%) of the 2019 income leaving $4,000 ($40,000 − $36,000) of NOL to carryforward to 2020.

Self-Study Problem 11.3

a. The dividends received deduction is equal to the lesser of $45,500 = 65% × $70,000; or $39,000 = 65% × $60,000 ($90,000 + $70,000 − $100,000). Therefore, $39,000 is the amount of the deduction.

b. Organization costs of $5,222.22 can be deducted in 2019. Boyce is eligible to expense $5,000 organization costs. The balance of $8,000 ($13,000 − $5,000) is amortized over 180 months for 5 months of 2019 for a deduction of $222.22 ($8,000 ÷ 180 × 5 months). In 2020, Boyce will deduct $533.33 ($8,000 ÷ 180 × 12 months).

Start-up costs exceed $50,000, thus Boyce is not eligible to deduct $5,000 of start-up costs. The $5,000 is reduced by $2,000 (the start-up costs in excess of $50,000) to $3,000. The remaining balance of $49,000 ($52,000 − $3,000) is amortized over 180 months × 5 months in 2019 or $1,361.11 for a total 2019 deduction of $4,361.11. In 2020, Boyce will deduct $3,266.67 ($49,000 ÷ 180 × 12).

c. Gant's modified taxable income for purposes of the charitable contribution deduction limit of 10% is $95,000 ($70,000 + $15,000 + $10,000). Thus the charitable contribution limit is $9,500 ($95,000 × 10%). The remaining $500 can be carried forward for up to 5 years.

Self-Study Problem 11.4

	Schedule M-1 Reconciliation of Income (Loss) per Books With Income per Return				
	Note: The corporation may be required to file Schedule M-3. See instructions.				
1	Net income (loss) per books	115,600	7	Income recorded on books this year not included on this return (itemize):	
2	Federal income tax per books	29,400			
3	Excess of capital losses over capital gains .	9,100		Tax-exempt interest $ 4,700	
4	Income subject to tax not recorded on books this year (itemize):				
					4,700
			8	Deductions on this return not charged against book income this year (itemize):	
5	Expenses recorded on books this year not deducted on this return (itemize):				
			a	Depreciation . . $ 4,000	
a	Depreciation . . . . $		b	Charitable contributions $	
b	Charitable contributions . $				
c	Travel and entertainment . $				4,000
			9	Add lines 7 and 8	8,700
6	Add lines 1 through 5	154,100	10	Income (page 1, line 28)—line 6 less line 9	145,400

Self-Study Problem 11.5

See Form 1120 on Pages E-72 to E-77. The calculation of tax for Aspen Corporation is as follows: 21% × $14,000 = $2,940. Net income per the books is equal to $16,060, $19,000 net income before income tax expense − $2,940 income tax expense.

Self-Study Problem 11.6

See Form 1120S and Schedule K-1 on Pages E-78 to E-84.

Self-Study Problem 11.7

Tammy's realized gain is $125,000 + $34,000 − $75,000 = $84,000.
    Tammy's recognized gain is $0.
    Tammy's basis in her stock is $75,000 − $0 + $0 − $34,000 = $41,000.
    The corporation's basis in the real estate is $75,000 + $0 = $75,000.

Self-Study Problem 11.5

Form **1120**			U.S. Corporation Income Tax Return			OMB No. 1545-0123	
Department of the Treasury Internal Revenue Service			For calendar year 2019 or tax year beginning _____, 2019, ending _____, 20 ____ ▶ Go to *www.irs.gov/Form1120* for instructions and the latest information.			**2019**	

A Check if:

1a Consolidated return (attach Form 851)
b Life/nonlife consolidated return
2 Personal holding co. (attach Sch. PH)
3 Personal service corp. (see instructions)
4 Schedule M-3 attached

TYPE OR PRINT

Name: Aspen Corporation
Number, street, and room or suite no. If a P.O. box, see instructions.
City or town, state or province, country, and ZIP or foreign postal code

B Employer identification number

C Date incorporated 01/01/2019

D Total assets (see instructions) $ 183,000

E Check if: (1) Initial return (2) Final return (3) Name change (4) Address change

Income	1a	Gross receipts or sales		1a	285,000	
	b	Returns and allowances		1b		
	c	Balance. Subtract line 1b from line 1a		1c		285,000
	2	Cost of goods sold (attach Form 1125-A)		2		80,000
	3	Gross profit. Subtract line 2 from line 1c		3		205,000
	4	Dividends and inclusions (Schedule C, line 23)		4		10,000
	5	Interest		5		
	6	Gross rents		6		
	7	Gross royalties		7		
	8	Capital gain net income (attach Schedule D (Form 1120))		8		
	9	Net gain or (loss) from Form 4797, Part II, line 17 (attach Form 4797)		9		
	10	Other income (see instructions—attach statement)		10		
	11	**Total income.** Add lines 3 through 10 ▶		11		215,000
Deductions (See instructions for limitations on deductions.)	12	Compensation of officers (see instructions—attach Form 1125-E) ▶		12		90,000
	13	Salaries and wages (less employment credits)		13		82,000
	14	Repairs and maintenance		14		8,000
	15	Bad debts		15		
	16	Rents		16		
	17	Taxes and licenses		17		11,000
	18	Interest (see instructions)		18		
	19	Charitable contributions		19		
	20	Depreciation from Form 4562 not claimed on Form 1125-A or elsewhere on return (attach Form 4562)		20		5,000
	21	Depletion		21		
	22	Advertising		22		
	23	Pension, profit-sharing, etc., plans		23		
	24	Employee benefit programs		24		
	25	Reserved for future use		25		
	26	Other deductions (attach statement)		26		
	27	**Total deductions.** Add lines 12 through 26 ▶		27		196,000
	28	Taxable income before net operating loss deduction and special deductions. Subtract line 27 from line 11		28		19,000
	29a	Net operating loss deduction (see instructions)		29a		
	b	Special deductions (Schedule C, line 24)		29b	5,000	
	c	Add lines 29a and 29b		29c		5,000
Tax, Refundable Credits, and Payments	30	**Taxable income.** Subtract line 29c from line 28. See instructions		30		14,000
	31	Total tax (Schedule J, Part I, line 11)		31		2,940
	32	2019 net 965 tax liability paid (Schedule J, Part II, line 12)		32		
	33	Total payments, credits, and section 965 net tax liability (Schedule J, Part III, line 23)		33		3,000
	34	Estimated tax penalty. See instructions. Check if Form 2220 is attached ▶ ☐		34		
	35	**Amount owed.** If line 33 is smaller than the total of lines 31, 32, and 34, enter amount owed		35		
	36	**Overpayment.** If line 33 is larger than the total of lines 31, 32, and 34, enter amount overpaid		36		60
	37	Enter amount from line 36 you want: **Credited to 2020 estimated tax** ▶ 60 **Refunded** ▶		37		0

Sign Here ▶

Under penalties of perjury, I declare that I have examined this return, including accompanying schedules and statements, and to the best of my knowledge and belief, it is true, correct, and complete. Declaration of preparer (other than taxpayer) is based on all information of which preparer has any knowledge.

Signature of officer   Date   Title

May the IRS discuss this return with the preparer shown below? See instructions. ☐ Yes ☐ No

Paid Preparer Use Only

Print/Type preparer's name	Preparer's signature	Date	Check ☐ if self-employed	PTIN
Firm's name ▶			Firm's EIN ▶	
Firm's address ▶			Phone no.	

For Paperwork Reduction Act Notice, see separate instructions.   Cat. No. 11450Q   Form **1120** (2019)

Self-Study Problem 11.5

Form 1120 (2019)	Aspen Corporation		Page **2**

Schedule C	Dividends, Inclusions, and Special Deductions (see instructions)	(a) Dividends and inclusions	(b) %	(c) Special deductions (a) × (b)
1	Dividends from less-than-20%-owned domestic corporations (other than debt-financed stock)	10,000	50	5,000
2	Dividends from 20%-or-more-owned domestic corporations (other than debt-financed stock)		65	
3	Dividends on certain debt-financed stock of domestic and foreign corporations . .		see instructions	
4	Dividends on certain preferred stock of less-than-20%-owned public utilities . . .		23.3	
5	Dividends on certain preferred stock of 20%-or-more-owned public utilities		26.7	
6	Dividends from less-than-20%-owned foreign corporations and certain FSCs . . .		50	
7	Dividends from 20%-or-more-owned foreign corporations and certain FSCs . . .		65	
8	Dividends from wholly owned foreign subsidiaries		100	
9	**Subtotal.** Add lines 1 through 8. See instructions for limitations	10,000	see instructions	5,000
10	Dividends from domestic corporations received by a small business investment company operating under the Small Business Investment Act of 1958		100	
11	Dividends from affiliated group members		100	
12	Dividends from certain FSCs		100	
13	Foreign-source portion of dividends received from a specified 10%-owned foreign corporation (excluding hybrid dividends) (see instructions)		100	
14	Dividends from foreign corporations not included on line 3, 6, 7, 8, 11, 12, or 13 (including any hybrid dividends)			
15	Section 965(a) inclusion		see instructions	
16a	Subpart F inclusions derived from the sale by a controlled foreign corporation (CFC) of the stock of a lower-tier foreign corporation treated as a dividend (attach Form(s) 5471) (see instructions)		100	
b	Subpart F inclusions derived from hybrid dividends of tiered corporations (attach Form(s) 5471) (see instructions)			
c	Other inclusions from CFCs under subpart F not included on line 15, 16a, 16b, or 17 (attach Form(s) 5471) (see instructions)			
17	Global Intangible Low-Taxed Income (GILTI) (attach Form(s) 5471 and Form 8992) . .			
18	Gross-up for foreign taxes deemed paid			
19	IC-DISC and former DISC dividends not included on line 1, 2, or 3			
20	Other dividends			
21	Deduction for dividends paid on certain preferred stock of public utilities			
22	Section 250 deduction (attach Form 8993)			
23	**Total dividends and inclusions.** Add column (a), lines 9 through 20. Enter here and on page 1, line 4	10,000		
24	**Total special deductions.** Add column (c), lines 9 through 22. Enter here and on page 1, line 29b			5,000

Form **1120** (2019)

Self-Study Problem 11.5

Form 1120 (2019)   Aspen Corporation   Page **3**

Schedule J	**Tax Computation and Payment** (see instructions)		

Part I—Tax Computation

1	Check if the corporation is a member of a controlled group (attach Schedule O (Form 1120)). See instructions ▶ ☐		
2	Income tax. See instructions	**2**	2,940
3	Base erosion minimum tax amount (attach Form 8991)	**3**	
4	Add lines 2 and 3	**4**	2,940
5a	Foreign tax credit (attach Form 1118)	**5a**	
b	Credit from Form 8834 (see instructions)	**5b**	
c	General business credit (attach Form 3800)	**5c**	
d	Credit for prior year minimum tax (attach Form 8827) . .	**5d**	
e	Bond credits from Form 8912	**5e**	
6	**Total credits.** Add lines 5a through 5e	**6**	
7	Subtract line 6 from line 4	**7**	2,940
8	Personal holding company tax (attach Schedule PH (Form 1120))	**8**	
9a	Recapture of investment credit (attach Form 4255) . . .	**9a**	
b	Recapture of low-income housing credit (attach Form 8611) .	**9b**	
c	Interest due under the look-back method—completed long-term contracts (attach Form 8697)	**9c**	
d	Interest due under the look-back method—income forecast method (attach Form 8866)	**9d**	
e	Alternative tax on qualifying shipping activities (attach Form 8902)	**9e**	
f	Other (see instructions—attach statement)	**9f**	
10	**Total.** Add lines 9a through 9f	**10**	
11	**Total tax.** Add lines 7, 8, and 10. Enter here and on page 1, line 31	**11**	2,940

Part II—Section 965 Payments (see instructions)

12	2019 net 965 tax liability paid from Form 965-B, Part II, column (k), line 3. Enter here and on page 1, line 32 . .	**12**	

Part III—Payments, Refundable Credits, and Section 965 Net Tax Liability

13	2018 overpayment credited to 2019	**13**	
14	2019 estimated tax payments	**14**	3,000
15	2019 refund applied for on Form 4466	**15**	( )
16	Combine lines 13, 14, and 15	**16**	3,000
17	Tax deposited with Form 7004	**17**	
18	Withholding (see instructions)	**18**	
19	**Total payments.** Add lines 16, 17, and 18	**19**	3,000
20	Refundable credits from:		
a	Form 2439	**20a**	
b	Form 4136	**20b**	
c	Form 8827, line 5c	**20c**	
d	Other (attach statement—see instructions)	**20d**	
21	**Total credits.** Add lines 20a through 20d	**21**	
22	2019 net 965 tax liability from Form 965-B, Part I, column (d), line 3. See instructions	**22**	
23	**Total payments, credits, and section 965 net tax liability.** Add lines 19, 21, and 22. Enter here and on page 1, line 33	**23**	3,000

Form **1120** (2019)

Self-Study Problem 11.5

Schedule K	Other Information (see instructions)		Yes	No

1 Check accounting method: **a** ☐ Cash **b** ☑ Accrual **c** ☐ Other (specify) ▶ _____

2 See the instructions and enter the:

a Business activity code no. ▶ _____

b Business activity ▶ _____

c Product or service ▶ _____

3 Is the corporation a subsidiary in an affiliated group or a parent–subsidiary controlled group? . . . . | | | | ✓

If "Yes," enter name and EIN of the parent corporation ▶ _____

4 At the end of the tax year:

a Did any foreign or domestic corporation, partnership (including any entity treated as a partnership), trust, or tax-exempt organization own directly 20% or more, or own, directly or indirectly, 50% or more of the total voting power of all classes of the corporation's stock entitled to vote? If "Yes," complete Part I of Schedule G (Form 1120) (attach Schedule G) . . . . . | | | | ✓

b Did any individual or estate own directly 20% or more, or own, directly or indirectly, 50% or more of the total voting power of all classes of the corporation's stock entitled to vote? If "Yes," complete Part II of Schedule G (Form 1120) (attach Schedule G) . | | | | ✓

5 At the end of the tax year, did the corporation:

a Own directly 20% or more, or own, directly or indirectly, 50% or more of the total voting power of all classes of stock entitled to vote of any foreign or domestic corporation not included on **Form 851**, Affiliations Schedule? For rules of constructive ownership, see instructions. | | | | ✓

If "Yes," complete (i) through (iv) below.

(i) Name of Corporation	(ii) Employer Identification Number (if any)	(iii) Country of Incorporation	(iv) Percentage Owned in Voting Stock

b Own directly an interest of 20% or more, or own, directly or indirectly, an interest of 50% or more in any foreign or domestic partnership (including an entity treated as a partnership) or in the beneficial interest of a trust? For rules of constructive ownership, see instructions. | | | | ✓

If "Yes," complete (i) through (iv) below.

(i) Name of Entity	(ii) Employer Identification Number (if any)	(iii) Country of Organization	(iv) Maximum Percentage Owned in Profit, Loss, or Capital

6 During this tax year, did the corporation pay dividends (other than stock dividends and distributions in exchange for stock) in excess of the corporation's current and accumulated earnings and profits? See sections 301 and 316 . . . . | | | | ✓

If "Yes," file **Form 5452**, Corporate Report of Nondividend Distributions. See the instructions for Form 5452.

If this is a consolidated return, answer here for the parent corporation and on Form 851 for each subsidiary.

7 At any time during the tax year, did one foreign person own, directly or indirectly, at least 25% of the total voting power of all classes of the corporation's stock entitled to vote or at least 25% of the total value of all classes of the corporation's stock? . | | | | ✓

For rules of attribution, see section 318. If "Yes," enter:

(a) Percentage owned ▶ _____ and **(b)** Owner's country ▶ _____

(c) The corporation may have to file **Form 5472**, Information Return of a 25% Foreign-Owned U.S. Corporation or a Foreign Corporation Engaged in a U.S. Trade or Business. Enter the number of Forms 5472 attached ▶ _____

8 Check this box if the corporation issued publicly offered debt instruments with original issue discount . . . . . . ▶ ☐

If checked, the corporation may have to file **Form 8281**, Information Return for Publicly Offered Original Issue Discount Instruments.

9 Enter the amount of tax-exempt interest received or accrued during the tax year ▶ $ _____

10 Enter the number of shareholders at the end of the tax year (if 100 or fewer) ▶ _____

11 If the corporation has an NOL for the tax year and is electing to forego the carryback period, check here (see instructions) ▶ ☐

If the corporation is filing a consolidated return, the statement required by Regulations section 1.1502-21(b)(3) must be attached or the election will not be valid.

12 Enter the available NOL carryover from prior tax years (do not reduce it by any deduction reported on page 1, line 29a.) . . . . ▶ $ _____

Self-Study Problem 11.5

Schedule K	**Other Information** *(continued from page 4)*		Yes	No
13	Are the corporation's total receipts (page 1, line 1a, plus lines 4 through 10) for the tax year **and** its total assets at the end of the tax year less than $250,000?			✓
	If "Yes," the corporation is not required to complete Schedules L, M-1, and M-2. Instead, enter the total amount of cash distributions and the book value of property distributions (other than cash) made during the tax year ▶ $_____			
14	Is the corporation required to file Schedule UTP (Form 1120), Uncertain Tax Position Statement? See instructions			✓
	If "Yes," complete and attach Schedule UTP.			
15a	Did the corporation make any payments in 2019 that would require it to file Form(s) 1099?		✓	
b	If "Yes," did or will the corporation file required Form(s) 1099?		✓	
16	During this tax year, did the corporation have an 80%-or-more change in ownership, including a change due to redemption of its own stock?			✓
17	During or subsequent to this tax year, but before the filing of this return, did the corporation dispose of more than 65% (by value) of its assets in a taxable, non-taxable, or tax deferred transaction?			✓
18	Did the corporation receive assets in a section 351 transfer in which any of the transferred assets had a fair market basis or fair market value of more than $1 million?			✓
19	During the corporation's tax year, did the corporation make any payments that would require it to file Forms 1042 and 1042-S under chapter 3 (sections 1441 through 1464) or chapter 4 (sections 1471 through 1474) of the Code?			✓
20	Is the corporation operating on a cooperative basis?			✓
21	During the tax year, did the corporation pay or accrue any interest or royalty for which the deduction is not allowed under section 267A? See instructions			✓
	If "Yes," enter the total amount of the disallowed deductions ▶ $_____			
22	Does the corporation have gross receipts of at least $500 million in any of the 3 preceding tax years? (See sections 59A(e)(2) and (3))			✓
	If "Yes," complete and attach Form 8991.			
23	Did the corporation have an election under section 163(j) for any real property trade or business or any farming business in effect during the tax year? See instructions			✓
24	Does the corporation satisfy one or more of the following? See instructions			✓
a	The corporation owns a pass-through entity with current, or prior year carryover, excess business interest expense.			
b	The corporation's aggregate average annual gross receipts (determined under section 448(c)) for the 3 tax years preceding the current tax year are more than $26 million and the corporation has business interest expense.			
c	The corporation is a tax shelter and the corporation has business interest expense.			
	If "Yes," to any, complete and attach Form 8990.			
25	Is the corporation attaching Form 8996 to certify as a Qualified Opportunity Fund?			✓
	If "Yes," enter amount from Form 8996, line 14 ▶ $			

Form **1120** (2019)

Self-Study Problem 11.5

Form 1120 (2019)   Aspen Corporation   Page **6**

Schedule L — Balance Sheets per Books

		Beginning of tax year		End of tax year	
	Assets	**(a)**	**(b)**	**(c)**	**(d)**
1	Cash		Initial Return		35,000
2a	Trade notes and accounts receivable			10,000	
b	Less allowance for bad debts	( )		( )	
3	Inventories				10,000
4	U.S. government obligations				
5	Tax-exempt securities (see instructions)				
6	Other current assets (attach statement)				
7	Loans to shareholders				
8	Mortgage and real estate loans				
9	Other investments (attach statement)				
10a	Buildings and other depreciable assets			125,000	
b	Less accumulated depreciation	( )		(5,000)	120,000
11a	Depletable assets				
b	Less accumulated depletion	( )		( )	
12	Land (net of any amortization)				18,000
13a	Intangible assets (amortizable only)				
b	Less accumulated amortization	( )		( )	
14	Other assets (attach statement)				183,000
15	Total assets				
	Liabilities and Shareholders' Equity				
16	Accounts payable				
17	Mortgages, notes, bonds payable in less than 1 year				26,940
18	Other current liabilities (attach statement)				
19	Loans from shareholders				
20	Mortgages, notes, bonds payable in 1 year or more				
21	Other liabilities (attach statement)				
22	Capital stock: **a** Preferred stock				
	b Common stock			140,000	140,000
23	Additional paid-in capital				
24	Retained earnings—Appropriated (attach statement)				
25	Retained earnings—Unappropriated				16,060
26	Adjustments to shareholders' equity (attach statement)				
27	Less cost of treasury stock	( )		( )	
28	Total liabilities and shareholders' equity				183,000

Schedule M-1 — Reconciliation of Income (Loss) per Books With Income per Return

Note: The corporation may be required to file Schedule M-3. See instructions.

1	Net income (loss) per books	16,060	7	Income recorded on books this year not included on this return (itemize):		
2	Federal income tax per books	2,940		Tax-exempt interest $ _____		
3	Excess of capital losses over capital gains			_____		
4	Income subject to tax not recorded on books this year (itemize): _____			_____		
			8	Deductions on this return not charged against book income this year (itemize):		
5	Expenses recorded on books this year not deducted on this return (itemize):		a	Depreciation $ _____		
a	Depreciation $ _____		b	Charitable contributions $ _____		
b	Charitable contributions $ _____			_____		
c	Travel and entertainment $ _____			_____		
	_____		9	Add lines 7 and 8		0
6	Add lines 1 through 5	19,000	10	Income (page 1, line 28)—line 6 less line 9		19,000

Schedule M-2 — Analysis of Unappropriated Retained Earnings per Books (Line 25, Schedule L)

1	Balance at beginning of year	0	5	Distributions: **a** Cash		
2	Net income (loss) per books	16,060		**b** Stock		
3	Other increases (itemize): _____			**c** Property		
	_____		6	Other decreases (itemize): _____		
	_____		7	Add lines 5 and 6		0
4	Add lines 1, 2, and 3	16,060	8	Balance at end of year (line 4 less line 7)		16,060

Form **1120** (2019)

Self-Study Problem 11.6

Form **1120-S**	**U.S. Income Tax Return for an S Corporation**	OMB No. 1545-0123
Department of the Treasury Internal Revenue Service	▶ Do not file this form unless the corporation has filed or is attaching Form 2553 to elect to be an S corporation. ▶ Go to *www.irs.gov/Form1120S* for instructions and the latest information.	2019

For calendar year 2019 or tax year beginning _____, 2019, ending _____ , 20 ____

A S election effective date 01/01/2019	**TYPE OR PRINT**	Name Aspen Corporation	**D** Employer identification number
B Business activity code number (see instructions)		Number, street, and room or suite no. If a P.O. box, see instructions.	**E** Date incorporated 01/01/2019
C Check if Sch. M-3 attached ☐		City or town, state or province, country, and ZIP or foreign postal code	**F** Total assets (see instructions) $ 183,000

G Is the corporation electing to be an S corporation beginning with this tax year? ☑ Yes ☐ No   If "Yes," attach Form 2553 if not already filed

H Check if: **(1)** ☐ Final return **(2)** ☐ Name change **(3)** ☐ Address change **(4)** ☐ Amended return **(5)** ☐ S election termination or revocation

I Enter the number of shareholders who were shareholders during any part of the tax year . . . . ▶ _____

J Check if corporation: **(1)** ☐ Aggregated activities for section 465 at-risk purposes **(2)** ☐ Grouped activities for section 469 passive activity purposes

Caution: Include **only** trade or business income and expenses on lines 1a through 21. See the instructions for more information.

Income

1a	Gross receipts or sales	1a	285,000	
b	Returns and allowances	1b		
c	Balance. Subtract line 1b from line 1a			**1c** 285,000
2	Cost of goods sold (attach Form 1125-A)			**2** 80,000
3	Gross profit. Subtract line 2 from line 1c			**3** 205,000
4	Net gain (loss) from Form 4797, line 17 (attach Form 4797)			**4**
5	Other income (loss) (see instructions—attach statement)			**5**
6	**Total income (loss).** Add lines 3 through 5 . . . . ▶			**6** 205,000

Deductions (see instructions for limitations)

7	Compensation of officers (see instructions—attach Form 1125-E)	**7**	90,000
8	Salaries and wages (less employment credits)	**8**	82,000
9	Repairs and maintenance	**9**	8,000
10	Bad debts	**10**	
11	Rents	**11**	
12	Taxes and licenses	**12**	11,000
13	Interest (see instructions)	**13**	
14	Depreciation not claimed on Form 1125-A or elsewhere on return (attach Form 4562)	**14**	5,000
15	Depletion **(Do not deduct oil and gas depletion.)**	**15**	
16	Advertising	**16**	
17	Pension, profit-sharing, etc., plans	**17**	
18	Employee benefit programs	**18**	
19	Other deductions (attach statement)	**19**	
20	**Total deductions.** Add lines 7 through 19 . . . . ▶	**20**	196,000
21	**Ordinary business income (loss).** Subtract line 20 from line 6 . . .	**21**	9,000

Tax and Payments

22a	Excess net passive income or LIFO recapture tax (see instructions) . . .	22a		
b	Tax from Schedule D (Form 1120-S)	22b		
c	Add lines 22a and 22b (see instructions for additional taxes)		**22c**	0
23a	2019 estimated tax payments and 2018 overpayment credited to 2019 .	23a		
b	Tax deposited with Form 7004	23b		
c	Credit for federal tax paid on fuels (attach Form 4136)	23c		
d	Refundable credit from Form 8827, line 5c	23d		
e	Add lines 23a through 23d		**23e**	0
24	Estimated tax penalty (see instructions). Check if Form 2220 is attached . . . . . . ▶ ☐		**24**	
25	**Amount owed.** If line 23e is smaller than the total of lines 22c and 24, enter amount owed . . .		**25**	
26	**Overpayment.** If line 23e is larger than the total of lines 22c and 24, enter amount overpaid . . .		**26**	0
27	Enter amount from line 26: **Credited to 2020 estimated tax** ▶ _____ **Refunded** ▶		**27**	

Sign Here

Under penalties of perjury, I declare that I have examined this return, including accompanying schedules and statements, and to the best of my knowledge and belief, it is true, correct, and complete. Declaration of preparer (other than taxpayer) is based on all information of which preparer has any knowledge.

▶ Signature of officer	Date	▶ Title	May the IRS discuss this return with the preparer shown below? See instructions. ☐ Yes ☐ No

Paid Preparer Use Only

Print/Type preparer's name	Preparer's signature	Date	Check ☐ if self-employed	PTIN
Firm's name ▶			Firm's EIN ▶	
Firm's address ▶			Phone no.	

For Paperwork Reduction Act Notice, see separate instructions.   Cat. No. 11510H   Form **1120-S** (2019)

Self-Study Problem 11.6

Form 1120-S (2019)   Page **2**

Schedule B	Other Information (see instructions)		

		Yes	No
1	Check accounting method: **a** ☐ Cash **b** ☑ Accrual **c** ☐ Other (specify) ▶ _____		
2	See the instructions and enter the: **a** Business activity ▶ _____ **b** Product or service ▶ _____		
3	At any time during the tax year, was any shareholder of the corporation a disregarded entity, a trust, an estate, or a nominee or similar person? If "Yes," attach Schedule B-1, Information on Certain Shareholders of an S Corporation . .		✓
4	At the end of the tax year, did the corporation:		
a	Own directly 20% or more, or own, directly or indirectly, 50% or more of the total stock issued and outstanding of any foreign or domestic corporation? For rules of constructive ownership, see instructions. If "Yes," complete (i) through (v) below		✓

(i) Name of Corporation	(ii) Employer Identification Number (if any)	(iii) Country of Incorporation	(iv) Percentage of Stock Owned	(v) If Percentage in (iv) Is 100%, Enter the Date (if any) a Qualified Subchapter S Subsidiary Election Was Made

		Yes	No
b	Own directly an interest of 20% or more, or own, directly or indirectly, an interest of 50% or more in the profit, loss, or capital in any foreign or domestic partnership (including an entity treated as a partnership) or in the beneficial interest of a trust? For rules of constructive ownership, see instructions. If "Yes," complete (i) through (v) below		✓

(i) Name of Entity	(ii) Employer Identification Number (if any)	(iii) Type of Entity	(iv) Country of Organization	(v) Maximum Percentage Owned in Profit, Loss, or Capital

		Yes	No
5a	At the end of the tax year, did the corporation have any outstanding shares of restricted stock?		✓
	If "Yes," complete lines (i) and (ii) below.		
	(i) Total shares of restricted stock . . . . ▶ _____		
	(ii) Total shares of non-restricted stock . . . . ▶ _____		
b	At the end of the tax year, did the corporation have any outstanding stock options, warrants, or similar instruments? .		✓
	If "Yes," complete lines (i) and (ii) below.		
	(i) Total shares of stock outstanding at the end of the tax year . ▶ _____		
	(ii) Total shares of stock outstanding if all instruments were executed ▶ _____		
6	Has this corporation filed, or is it required to file, **Form 8918,** Material Advisor Disclosure Statement, to provide information on any reportable transaction?		✓
7	Check this box if the corporation issued publicly offered debt instruments with original issue discount . . . . ▶ ☐		
	If checked, the corporation may have to file **Form 8281,** Information Return for Publicly Offered Original Issue Discount Instruments.		
8	If the corporation **(a)** was a C corporation before it elected to be an S corporation **or** the corporation acquired an asset with a basis determined by reference to the basis of the asset (or the basis of any other property) in the hands of a C corporation **and (b)** has net unrealized built-in gain in excess of the net recognized built-in gain from prior years, enter the net unrealized built-in gain reduced by net recognized built-in gain from prior years. See instructions . . . . . . ▶ $ _____		
9	Did the corporation have an election under section 163(j) for any real property trade or business or any farming business in effect during the tax year? See instructions		✓
10	Does the corporation satisfy one or more of the following? See instructions		✓
a	The corporation owns a pass-through entity with current, or prior year carryover, excess business interest expense.		
b	The corporation's aggregate average annual gross receipts (determined under section 448(c)) for the 3 tax years preceding the current tax year are more than $26 million and the corporation has business interest expense.		
c	The corporation is a tax shelter and the corporation has business interest expense.		
	If "Yes," complete and attach Form 8990.		
11	Does the corporation satisfy **both** of the following conditions?		✓
a	The corporation's total receipts (see instructions) for the tax year were less than $250,000.		
b	The corporation's total assets at the end of the tax year were less than $250,000.		
	If "Yes," the corporation is not required to complete Schedules L and M-1.		

Form **1120-S** (2019)

Self-Study Problem 11.6

Schedule B	Other Information (see instructions) (continued)		Yes	No
12	During the tax year, did the corporation have any non-shareholder debt that was canceled, was forgiven, or had the terms modified so as to reduce the principal amount of the debt?			✓
	If "Yes," enter the amount of principal reduction ▶ $			
13	During the tax year, was a qualified subchapter S subsidiary election terminated or revoked? If "Yes," see instructions			✓
14a	Did the corporation make any payments in 2019 that would require it to file Form(s) 1099?		✓	
b	If "Yes," did the corporation file or will it file required Form(s) 1099?		✓	
15	Is the corporation attaching Form 8996 to certify as a Qualified Opportunity Fund?			✓
	If "Yes," enter the amount from Form 8996, line 14 ▶ $			

Schedule K		Shareholders' Pro Rata Share Items			Total amount
Income (Loss)	1	Ordinary business income (loss) (page 1, line 21)		1	9,000
	2	Net rental real estate income (loss) (attach Form 8825)		2	
	3a	Other gross rental income (loss)	3a		
	b	Expenses from other rental activities (attach statement)	3b		
	c	Other net rental income (loss). Subtract line 3b from line 3a		3c	
	4	Interest income		4	
	5	Dividends: a Ordinary dividends		5a	10,000
		b Qualified dividends	5b	10,000	
	6	Royalties		6	
	7	Net short-term capital gain (loss) (attach Schedule D (Form 1120-S))		7	
	8a	Net long-term capital gain (loss) (attach Schedule D (Form 1120-S))		8a	
	b	Collectibles (28%) gain (loss)	8b		
	c	Unrecaptured section 1250 gain (attach statement)	8c		
	9	Net section 1231 gain (loss) (attach Form 4797)		9	
	10	Other income (loss) (see instructions) Type ▶		10	
Deductions	11	Section 179 deduction (attach Form 4562)		11	
	12a	Charitable contributions		12a	
	b	Investment interest expense		12b	
	c	Section 59(e)(2) expenditures (1) Type ▶ _____ (2) Amount ▶		12c(2)	
	d	Other deductions (see instructions) Type ▶		12d	
Credits	13a	Low-income housing credit (section 42(j)(5))		13a	
	b	Low-income housing credit (other)		13b	
	c	Qualified rehabilitation expenditures (rental real estate) (attach Form 3468, if applicable)		13c	
	d	Other rental real estate credits (see instructions) Type ▶		13d	
	e	Other rental credits (see instructions) Type ▶		13e	
	f	Biofuel producer credit (attach Form 6478)		13f	
	g	Other credits (see instructions) Type ▶		13g	
Foreign Transactions	14a	Name of country or U.S. possession ▶			
	b	Gross income from all sources		14b	
	c	Gross income sourced at shareholder level		14c	
		Foreign gross income sourced at corporate level			
	d	Reserved for future use		14d	
	e	Foreign branch category		14e	
	f	Passive category		14f	
	g	General category		14g	
	h	Other (attach statement)		14h	
		Deductions allocated and apportioned at shareholder level			
	i	Interest expense		14i	
	j	Other		14j	
		Deductions allocated and apportioned at corporate level to foreign source income			
	k	Reserved for future use		14k	
	l	Foreign branch category		14l	
	m	Passive category		14m	
	n	General category		14n	
	o	Other (attach statement)		14o	
		Other information			
	p	Total foreign taxes (check one): ☐ Paid ☐ Accrued ▶		14p	
	q	Reduction in taxes available for credit (attach statement)		14q	
	r	Other foreign tax information (attach statement)			

Self-Study Problem 11.6

Form 1120-S (2019)   Page **4**

Schedule K	Shareholders' Pro Rata Share Items *(continued)*		Total amount

<table>
<tr><td rowspan="6">Alternative Minimum Tax (AMT) Items</td><td>15a</td><td>Post-1986 depreciation adjustment . . . .</td><td>15a</td><td></td></tr>
<tr><td>b</td><td>Adjusted gain or loss . . . .</td><td>15b</td><td></td></tr>
<tr><td>c</td><td>Depletion (other than oil and gas) . . . .</td><td>15c</td><td></td></tr>
<tr><td>d</td><td>Oil, gas, and geothermal properties—gross income . .</td><td>15d</td><td></td></tr>
<tr><td>e</td><td>Oil, gas, and geothermal properties—deductions . . .</td><td>15e</td><td></td></tr>
<tr><td>f</td><td>Other AMT items (attach statement) . . . .</td><td>15f</td><td></td></tr>
<tr><td rowspan="5">Items Affecting Shareholder Basis</td><td>16a</td><td>Tax-exempt interest income . . . .</td><td>16a</td><td></td></tr>
<tr><td>b</td><td>Other tax-exempt income . . . .</td><td>16b</td><td></td></tr>
<tr><td>c</td><td>Nondeductible expenses . . . .</td><td>16c</td><td></td></tr>
<tr><td>d</td><td>Distributions (attach statement if required) (see instructions) . .</td><td>16d</td><td></td></tr>
<tr><td>e</td><td>Repayment of loans from shareholders . . . .</td><td>16e</td><td></td></tr>
<tr><td rowspan="4">Other Information</td><td>17a</td><td>Investment income . . . .</td><td>17a</td><td></td></tr>
<tr><td>b</td><td>Investment expenses . . . .</td><td>17b</td><td></td></tr>
<tr><td>c</td><td>Dividend distributions paid from accumulated earnings and profits</td><td>17c</td><td></td></tr>
<tr><td>d</td><td>Other items and amounts (attach statement)</td><td></td><td></td></tr>
<tr><td>Recon- ciliation</td><td>18</td><td>**Income (loss) reconciliation.** Combine the amounts on lines 1 through 10 in the far right column. From the result, subtract the sum of the amounts on lines 11 through 12d and 14p .</td><td>18</td><td>19,000</td></tr>
</table>

Schedule L	Balance Sheets per Books	Beginning of tax year		End of tax year	
	Assets	(a)	(b)	(c)	(d)
1	Cash		Initial Return		35,000
2a	Trade notes and accounts receivable . .			10,000	
b	Less allowance for bad debts	(	)	(	) 10,000
3	Inventories				
4	U.S. government obligations				
5	Tax-exempt securities (see instructions) . .				
6	Other current assets (attach statement) . . .				
7	Loans to shareholders				
8	Mortgage and real estate loans				
9	Other investments (attach statement) . . .				
10a	Buildings and other depreciable assets . . .			125,000	
b	Less accumulated depreciation	(	)	(5,000)	120,000
11a	Depletable assets				
b	Less accumulated depletion	(	)	(	)
12	Land (net of any amortization)				18,000
13a	Intangible assets (amortizable only)				
b	Less accumulated amortization	(	)	(	)
14	Other assets (attach statement)				
15	Total assets				183,000
	Liabilities and Shareholders' Equity				
16	Accounts payable				24,000
17	Mortgages, notes, bonds payable in less than 1 year				
18	Other current liabilities (attach statement) . .				
19	Loans from shareholders				
20	Mortgages, notes, bonds payable in 1 year or more				
21	Other liabilities (attach statement)				
22	Capital stock				140,000
23	Additional paid-in capital				
24	Retained earnings				19,000
25	Adjustments to shareholders' equity (attach statement)				
26	Less cost of treasury stock		(	)	( )
27	Total liabilities and shareholders' equity . .				183,000

Form **1120-S** (2019)

Self-Study Problem 11.6

Schedule M-1	Reconciliation of Income (Loss) per Books With Income (Loss) per Return

Note: The corporation may be required to file Schedule M-3. See instructions.

1	Net income (loss) per books	19,000	**5**	Income recorded on books this year not included on Schedule K, lines 1 through 10 (itemize):	
2	Income included on Schedule K, lines 1, 2, 3c, 4, 5a, 6, 7, 8a, 9, and 10, not recorded on books this year (itemize)		**a**	Tax-exempt interest $	
3	Expenses recorded on books this year not included on Schedule K, lines 1 through 12 and 14p (itemize):		**6**	Deductions included on Schedule K, lines 1 through 12 and 14p, not charged against book income this year (itemize):	
a	Depreciation $		**a**	Depreciation $	
b	Travel and entertainment $		**7**	Add lines 5 and 6	0
			8	Income (loss) (Schedule K, line 18).	
4	Add lines 1 through 3	19,000		Subtract line 7 from line 4	19,000

Schedule M-2	Analysis of Accumulated Adjustments Account, Shareholders' Undistributed Taxable Income Previously Taxed, Accumulated Earnings and Profits, and Other Adjustments Account

(see instructions)

		(a) Accumulated adjustments account	(b) Shareholders' undistributed taxable income previously taxed	(c) Accumulated earnings and profits	(d) Other adjustments account
1	Balance at beginning of tax year	0			
2	Ordinary income from page 1, line 21 . . .	9,000			
3	Other additions	10,000			
4	Loss from page 1, line 21	( )			
5	Other reductions	( )			( )
6	Combine lines 1 through 5	19,000			
7	Distributions				
8	Balance at end of tax year. Subtract line 7 from line 6	19,000			

Form **1120-S** (2019)

Self-Study Problem 11.6

671117

☐ Final K-1	☐ Amended K-1	OMB No. 1545-0123

**Schedule K-1
(Form 1120-S)**
Department of the Treasury
Internal Revenue Service

2019

For calendar year 2019, or tax year

beginning __ / __ / 2019   ending __ / __ / __

Shareholder's Share of Income, Deductions, Credits, etc.   ► See back of form and separate instructions.

Part I Information About the Corporation

A Corporation's employer identification number

B Corporation's name, address, city, state, and ZIP code

Aspen Corporation

C IRS Center where corporation filed return

Part II Information About the Shareholder

D Shareholder's identifying number

E Shareholder's name, address, city, state, and ZIP code

Janet Nall

F Shareholder's percentage of stock ownership for tax year . . . . _____ 100 %

For IRS Use Only

Part III	Shareholder's Share of Current Year Income, Deductions, Credits, and Other Items

1	Ordinary business income (loss) **9,000**	13	Credits
2	Net rental real estate income (loss)		
3	Other net rental income (loss)		
4	Interest income		
5a	Ordinary dividends **10,000**		
5b	Qualified dividends **10,000**	14	Foreign transactions
6	Royalties		
7	Net short-term capital gain (loss)		
8a	Net long-term capital gain (loss)		
8b	Collectibles (28%) gain (loss)		
8c	Unrecaptured section 1250 gain		
9	Net section 1231 gain (loss)		
10	Other income (loss)	15	Alternative minimum tax (AMT) items
11	Section 179 deduction	16	Items affecting shareholder basis
12	Other deductions		
		17	Other information
		V	9,000
		V*	172,000
		V**	125,000
		A	10,000

* See attached statement for additional information.

For Paperwork Reduction Act Notice, see the Instructions for Form 1120-S.   www.irs.gov/Form1120S   Cat. No. 11520D   **Schedule K-1 (Form 1120-S) 2019**

- At the time we go to print, the Line 17 codes related to the QBI deduction have not been released. V is the qualified business income. V is allocated W-2 wages. V** is qualified property.

Schedule K-1 (Form 1120-S) 2019   Page **2**

This list identifies the codes used on Schedule K-1 for all shareholders and provides summarized reporting information for shareholders who file Form 1040 or 1040-SR. For detailed reporting and filing information, see the separate Shareholder's Instructions for Schedule K-1 and the instructions for your income tax return.

1. Ordinary business income (loss). Determine whether the income (loss) is passive or nonpassive and enter on your return as follows:

	Report on
Passive loss	See the Shareholder's Instructions
Passive income	Schedule E, line 28, column (h)
Nonpassive loss	See the Shareholder's Instructions
Nonpassive income	Schedule E, line 28, column (k)

2. Net rental real estate income (loss)   See the Shareholder's Instructions

3. Other net rental income (loss)

Net income	Schedule E, line 28, column (h)
Net loss	See the Shareholder's Instructions

4. Interest income   Form 1040 or 1040-SR, line 2b

5a. Ordinary dividends   Form 1040 or 1040-SR, line 3b

5b. Qualified dividends   Form 1040 or 1040-SR, line 3a

6. Royalties   Schedule E, line 4

7. Net short-term capital gain (loss)   Schedule D, line 5

8a. Net long-term capital gain (loss)   Schedule D, line 12

8b. Collectibles (28%) gain (loss)   28% Rate Gain Worksheet, line 4 (Schedule D instructions)

8c. Unrecaptured section 1250 gain   See the Shareholder's Instructions

9. Net section 1231 gain (loss)   See the Shareholder's Instructions

10. Other income (loss)

Code
A	Other portfolio income (loss)	See the Shareholder's Instructions
B	Involuntary conversions	See the Shareholder's Instructions
C	Sec. 1256 contracts & straddles	Form 6781, line 1
D	Mining exploration costs recapture	See Pub. 535
E	Global intangible low-taxed income (GILTI) under section 951A	
F	Section 965(a) inclusion	
G	Income under subpart F (other than inclusions under sections 951A and 965)	See the Shareholder's Instructions
H	Other income (loss)	

11. Section 179 deduction   See the Shareholder's Instructions

12. Other deductions

A	Cash contributions (60%)	
B	Cash contributions (30%)	
C	Noncash contributions (50%)	
D	Noncash contributions (30%)	
E	Capital gain property to a 50% organization (30%)	See the Shareholder's Instructions
F	Capital gain property (20%)	
G	Contributions (100%)	
H	Investment interest expense	Form 4952, line 1
I	Deductions—royalty income	Schedule E, line 19
J	Section 59(e)(2) expenditures	See the Shareholder's Instructions
K	Section 965(c) deduction	See the Shareholder's Instructions
L	Deductions—portfolio (other)	Schedule A, line 16
M	Preproductive period expenses	See the Shareholder's Instructions
N	Commercial revitalization deduction from rental real estate activities	See Form 8582 instructions
O	Reforestation expense deduction	See the Shareholder's Instructions
P	through **R**	Reserved for future use
S	Other deductions	See the Shareholder's Instructions

13. Credits

A	Low-income housing credit (section 42(j)(5)) from pre-2008 buildings	
B	Low-income housing credit (other) from pre-2008 buildings	
C	Low-income housing credit (section 42(j)(5)) from post-2007 buildings	
D	Low-income housing credit (other) from post-2007 buildings	See the Shareholder's Instructions
E	Qualified rehabilitation expenditures (rental real estate)	
F	Other rental real estate credits	
G	Other rental credits	
H	Undistributed capital gains credit	Schedule 3 (Form 1040 or 1040-SR), line 13, box a
I	Biofuel producer credit	
J	Work opportunity credit	
K	Disabled access credit	See the Shareholder's Instructions
L	Empowerment zone employment credit	
M	Credit for increasing research activities	

Code   *Report on*
N	Credit for employer social security and Medicare taxes	
O	Backup withholding	See the Shareholder's Instructions
P	Other credits	

14. Foreign transactions

A	Name of country or U.S. possession	
B	Gross income from all sources	Form 1116, Part I
C	Gross income sourced at shareholder level	

Foreign gross income sourced at corporate level
D	Section 951A category	
E	Foreign branch category	
F	Passive category	Form 1116, Part I
G	General category	
H	Other	

Deductions allocated and apportioned at shareholder level
I	Interest expense	Form 1116, Part I
J	Other	Form 1116, Part I

Deductions allocated and apportioned at corporate level to foreign source income
K	Section 951A category	
L	Foreign branch category	
M	Passive category	Form 1116, Part I
N	General category	
O	Other	

Other information
P	Total foreign taxes paid	Form 1116, Part II
Q	Total foreign taxes accrued	Form 1116, Part II
R	Reduction in taxes available for credit	Form 1116, line 12
S	Foreign trading gross receipts	Form 8873
T	Extraterritorial income exclusion	Form 8873
U	Section 965 information	See the Shareholder's Instructions
V	Other foreign transactions	See the Shareholder's Instructions

15. Alternative minimum tax (AMT) items

A	Post-1986 depreciation adjustment	
B	Adjusted gain or loss	
C	Depletion (other than oil & gas)	See the Shareholder's Instructions
D	Oil, gas, & geothermal—gross income	and the Instructions for Form 6251
E	Oil, gas, & geothermal—deductions	
F	Other AMT items	

16. Items affecting shareholder basis

A	Tax-exempt interest income	Form 1040 or 1040-SR, line 2a
B	Other tax-exempt income	
C	Nondeductible expenses	
D	Distributions	See the Shareholder's Instructions
E	Repayment of loans from shareholders	

17. Other information

A	Investment income	Form 4952, line 4a
B	Investment expenses	Form 4952, line 5
C	Qualified rehabilitation expenditures (other than rental real estate)	See the Shareholder's Instructions
D	Basis of energy property	See the Shareholder's Instructions
E	Recapture of low-income housing credit (section 42(j)(5))	Form 8611, line 8
F	Recapture of low-income housing credit (other)	Form 8611, line 8
G	Recapture of investment credit	See Form 4255
H	Recapture of other credits	See the Shareholder's Instructions
I	Look-back interest—completed long-term contracts	See Form 8697
J	Look-back interest—income forecast method	See Form 8866
K	Dispositions of property with section 179 deductions	
L	Recapture of section 179 deduction	See the Shareholder's Instructions
M	through **U**	
V	Section 199A information	
W	through **Z**	Reserved for future use
AA	Excess taxable income	
AB	Excess business interest income	See the Shareholder's Instructions
AC	Other information	

Self-Study Problem 11.8

20% × $190,000 = $38,000
Only $190,000 ($340,000 − $150,000) is subject to the accumulated earnings tax.

Self-Study Problem 11.9

Regular taxable income	$ 12,500
AMT Credit applied to 2019 tax	(12,500)
Regular tax liability for 2019	0
AMT Credits at start of 2019	20,000
AMT Credits used in 2019	(12,500)
AMT Credits remaining	7,500
Amount refundable (50%)	(3,750)
AMT credits carried forward	$ (3,750)

CHAPTER 12   TAX ADMINISTRATION AND TAX PLANNING

Self-Study Problem 12.1

1. True
2. True
3. False   The commissioner of internal revenue is appointed by the president of the United States.
4. False   The IRS is part of the Treasury Department.
5. True

Self-Study Problem 12.2

1. True
2. False   An office audit is conducted at the IRS office.
3. True
4. True
5. False   Audits can be appealed to an appellate agent.

Self-Study Problem 12.3

Part a.	Failure-to-pay penalty:		
	$3,000 × 0.5% × 2 months		$ 30
	Failure-to-file penalty:		
	$3,000 × 5% × 2 months	$ 300	
	Less: failure-to-pay penalty	(30)	
			270
	Total		$300
Part b.	20% × $10,000	$2,000	
Part c.	75% × $10,000	$7,500	

Self-Study Problem 12.4

1. True
2. False   For bad debts, the statute of limitations is 7 years.
3. False   There is no statute of limitations for fraudulent returns.
4. True
5. True

Self-Study Problem 12.5

1. False   Lawyers and enrolled agents may also represent taxpayers before the IRS.
2. False   A college degree is not required.
3. False   Anyone may prepare corporate tax returns.
4. True
5. False   The penalty is $530 for tax returns filed in 2020.
6. True
7. False   The burden of proof is on the IRS.
8. False   The burden of proof remains on the taxpayer.
9. True
10. True
11. True

Self-Study Problem 12.6

1. True
2. True
3. True   Publication 1 directs the reader to Publication 594.
4. True
5. True
6. True

Self-Study Problem 12.7

1. 17.46% = $15,541 / $89,000
2. 17.53% = $15,781 / $90,000
3. 24% = ($15,781 − $15,541) / ($90,000 − $89,000)

NOTE: The words and phrases appearing below have been defined to reflect their conventional use in the field of taxation. Such definitions may, therefore, be incomplete for other purposes.

0.9 percent Medicare tax

For tax years after 2012, the Affordable Care Act (ACA) imposed an additional Medicare tax on high-income taxpayers, at a rate of 0.9 percent applicable to wages, compensation, and self-employment income above an annual threshold amount.

Accelerated Cost Recovery System (ACRS)

For tax years after 1980, a rapid write-off of the cost of a capital asset is allowed by this system, which was later modified in 1986 and renamed Modified Accelerated Cost Recovery System (MACRS). The minimum number of years over which the asset may be depreciated and the applicable percentage of the asset's cost that may be deducted each year depend on the class of the property.

Accelerated death benefits

Early payouts of life insurance, also called accelerated death benefits or viatical settlements, are excluded from gross income for certain terminally or chronically ill taxpayers. The taxpayer may either collect an early payout from the insurance company or sell or assign the policy to a viatical settlement provider. See *Viatical settlements*.

Accident and health benefits

Employee fringe benefits provided by employers through the payment of health and accident insurance premiums, or the establishment of employer-funded medical reimbursement plans. Employers generally are entitled to a deduction for such payments, whereas employees generally exclude the fringe benefits from gross income.

Accrual method

A method of accounting that reflects expenses incurred and income earned for any one tax year. In contrast to the cash basis of accounting, expenses do not have to be paid to be deductible, nor does income have to be received to be taxable.

Adjusted basis

The cost or other basis of property reduced by depreciation allowed or allowable and increased by capital improvements. See *Basis*.

Adjusted gross income (AGI)

A determination unique to individual taxpayers used as the basis to calculate limitations on the amount of certain expenses which may be deductible, including medical expenses, charitable contributions, certain personal casualty losses, and certain other itemized deductions. Generally, AGI represents gross income minus specific deductions such as certain trade or business expenses (deductions *for* AGI) but before itemized deductions or the standard deduction (deductions *from* AGI).

Adoption expenses

Adoption fees, court costs, attorney fees, and other expenses directly related to the legal adoption of an eligible child.

Affordable Care Act (ACA)

Also referred to as Obamacare, ACA is a federal law providing for a fundamental reform of the U.S. healthcare and health insurance system, signed by President Barack Obama in 2010.

Alimony payments

Payments from one spouse or former spouse, to the other, required as a result of a divorce or separation agreement, which meet certain statutory requirements. Alimony and separate maintenance payments, but not child support payments, are included in the gross income of the recipient and are deducted by the payor for divorces occurring before 2019. The TCJA has repealed both the deduction of and inclusion of alimony for tax years beginning in 2019.

Alternative minimum tax (AMT)

Designed to prevent wealthy taxpayers (but now applicable to many taxpayers) from taking advantage of tax write-offs to pay little or no tax. Computed by calculating both regular tax and AMT and generally paying whichever tax is larger.

American Opportunity tax credit

Previously referred to as the Hope credit, a tax credit available for the first 4 years of postsecondary education expenses for students who meet specific requirements.

Amortization

The allocation (and charge to expense) of the cost or other basis of an intangible asset over its estimated useful life. Examples of amortizable intangibles include patents, copyrights, and goodwill.

Amount realized

The amount received by a taxpayer on the sale or exchange of property less the cost incurred to transfer the property. The measure of the amount received is the sum of the cash and the fair market value of any property or services plus any relieved liability of the taxpayer. Determining the amount realized is the starting point for arriving at a realized gain or loss.

AMT exemption allowance

Statutory deduction reducing AMT income for taxpayers with taxable income below an annually specified dollar amount.

AMT preferences

Items excluded from the computation of regular taxable income but required to be added to compute alternative minimum taxable income.

AMT tax rates

Tax rates that apply to alternative minimum taxable income.

Annuity

A fixed sum payable at specified intervals for a specific period of time or for life. Payments represent a partial return of capital and a return (e.g., interest income) on the capital investment. An exclusion ratio is generally used to compute the amounts of nontaxable and taxable income.

Automobile expenses

Automobile expenses are generally deductible only to the extent the automobile is used in business or for the production of income. Personal commuting expenses are not deductible. The taxpayer may deduct actual expenses (including depreciation and insurance), or choose to use the standard mileage rate.

Backup withholding

Certain situations in which the issuer of payment such as dividends or interest is required to withhold income tax at the time of payment. Designed to ensure that income tax is paid on payments to certain taxpayers (generally, non-U.S. tax residents).

Bad debts

An ordinary deduction is permitted if a business debt, such as an account receivable, subsequently becomes worthless (uncollectible), provided the income arising from the debt was previously included in taxable income. The deduction is allowed only in the year of worthlessness. A nonbusiness bad debt deduction is allowed as a short-term capital loss when a debt which did not arise in connection with the creditor's trade or business activities becomes worthless. Loans between related parties (family members) generally are classified as nonbusiness debts.

Basis

The amount assigned to an asset for income tax purposes. For assets acquired by purchase, the basis would be the cost of the asset plus any direct costs incidental to the purchase. Special rules govern the basis of property received as a result of another's death or by gift. See also *Adjusted basis*.

Bona fide

Authentic and genuine. In the context of tax law, serving a specific business purpose.

Bonus depreciation

The immediate deduction of all or some of the cost of otherwise slowly depreciated property.

Boot

Cash or property of a type other than that permitted to be received tax-free in a nontaxable like-kind exchange. The receipt of boot will cause an otherwise tax-free transfer to become taxable to the extent of the lesser of the fair market value of such boot or the realized gain on the transfer.

Business gifts

Business gifts are deductible only to the extent that each gift does not exceed $25 per person per year. Exceptions are made for promotional gifts and for certain employee awards.

Capital asset

All assets are capital assets except those specifically excluded by the tax law. Major categories of noncapital assets include property held for sale in the normal course of business (i.e., inventory), trade accounts and notes receivable, depreciable property, and real estate used in a trade or business.

Capital expenditure

An expenditure, the amount of which should be added to the basis of the property improved. For income tax purposes, this generally precludes a deduction for the full amount of the expenditure in the year paid or incurred. Any tax deduction has to come in the form of cost recovery or depreciation.

Capital gain

The gain from the sale or exchange of a capital asset. Gain from a property held 12 months or less is deemed to be a short-term capital gain. If the property is held more than 12 months, the gain is deemed to be long-term. See *Capital asset and Holding period*.

Capital loss

The loss from the sale or exchange of a capital asset. A loss from a property held 12 months or less is deemed to be a short-term capital loss. If the property is held more than 12 months, the loss is deemed to be long-term. See *Capital asset and Holding period*.

Capital loss carryovers

A net capital loss that is not deducted in the current tax year but is eligible to be carried forward into future taxable years.

Cash basis

A method of accounting under which income is reported when received and expenses are deductible when paid by the taxpayer. Prepaid rent and prepaid interest must be deducted using the accrual method.

Casualty loss

A casualty is defined as the complete or partial destruction of property resulting from an identifiable event of a sudden, unexpected or unusual nature (e.g., floods, shipwrecks, storms, fires, automobile accidents). Beginning in the 2018 tax year due to the TCJA, personal casualty losses are only eligible for deduction when resulting from a federally declared disaster area. Personal casualty losses are deductible as itemized deductions subject to a $100 nondeductible floor and only to the extent that the taxpayer's total losses from personal-use property (net of the $100 floor) exceed 10 percent of adjusted gross income. Special rules are provided for the combining (netting) of certain casualty gains and losses.

Change in accounting method

A change in the taxpayer's method of accounting (e.g., from the FIFO to the LIFO inventory method) generally requires prior approval from the IRS. In some instances, the permission for change will not be granted unless the taxpayer agrees to certain adjustments prescribed by the IRS.

Change in accounting period

A taxpayer must obtain the consent of the IRS before changing his or her tax year. Income for the short period created by the change must be annualized.

Charitable contributions

Contributions are deductible (subject to various restrictions and ceiling limitations) if made to qualified nonprofit charitable organizations. A cash-basis taxpayer is entitled to a deduction in the year of payment. Accrual-basis corporations may accrue contributions at year-end under certain circumstances.

Child and dependent care credit

This credit is available to individuals who are employed on a full-time basis and maintain a household for a dependent child or disabled spouse or dependent. The amount of the credit is equal to a percentage of the cost of employment-related child and dependent care expenses, up to a stated maximum amount.

Child support payments

Payments for child support do not constitute alimony, and are, therefore, not included in gross income by the recipient or deducted as alimony by the payor to the extent permitted otherwise. See also *Alimony*.

Child and other dependent tax credit

A direct reduction in tax liability granted for each qualifying child under age 17 and other qualifying dependents. The child and other dependent tax credit is phased out based on the level of modified adjusted gross income.

Community property

Community property is all property, other than separate property, owned by a married couple. The income from community property is generally split equally between spouses. The classification of property as community property is important in determining the separate taxable income of married taxpayers.

Consumer interest

Not deductible for tax purposes, consumer interest is interest expense generated from personal loans, credit cards or other debt used for personal purposes.

Cost of goods sold

The amount equal to the cost of inventory sold during the period. Generally, beginning inventory plus purchases of inventory (or the cost to create inventory) less ending inventory. Cost of goods sold is deducted from gross receipts on Schedule C.

Deferred compensation

Compensation which will be taxed when received or upon the removal of certain restrictions, not when earned. An example would be contributions by an employer to a qualified pension or profit-sharing plan on behalf of an employee. Such contributions will not be taxed to the employee until the funds are made available or distributed to the employee (e.g., upon retirement). See *Qualified pension or profit-sharing plan*.

Defined benefit plan

A type of pension plan in which the plan specifies the pension payment amounts payable to an employee upon retirement, based on the employee's earnings history, tenure of service and age.

Defined contribution plan

A type of pension plan in which the plan specifies the regular contributions made by the employer and employee in which the pension benefits are based on the contribution amounts and the returns of the plan's investments.

Depreciation recapture

The recharacterizing of gain on the sale of certain property used in a trade or business to ordinary income to the extent of depreciation previously allowed.

Discriminant Function System (DIF)

One process by which the IRS selects tax returns for audits. The DIF is a computerized statistical sampling technique.

Dividends received deduction

A special deduction for corporations that receive dividend income distributions from a domestic corporation that it has an ownership interest in. Generally designed to prevent double-taxation of corporate dividends paid by a corporate subsidiary to its parent.

Earned income

Income from personal services as distinguished from income generated by property.

Earned income credit

The earned income credit is a refundable credit available to qualifying individuals with income and AGI below certain levels.

Education expenses

Employees may deduct education expenses if such items are incurred either (1) to maintain or improve existing job-related skills or (2) to meet the express requirements of the employer or the requirements imposed by law to retain employment status. Such expenses are not deductible if the education is required to meet the minimum educational requirements for the taxpayer's job or the education qualifies the individual for a new trade or business.

Educational assistance program

A fringe benefit that provides that tax-free educational assistance may be paid to an employee or prior employee for a specific dollar amount provided annually. Requires a written plan to allow employees to receive tax-free payments for tuition, fees, books, course-related supplies and equipment, but not payments for meals, lodging or entertainment.

Election to expense (Section 179)

The tax code Section 179 allows a taxpayer to elect to immediately expense and deduct the cost of certain property when placed in service, up to a certain limit, rather than capitalizing and depreciating such property.

Employee Stock Ownership Plan (ESOP)

A type of defined contribution pension plan in which employers provide their employees with ownership in the employer's stock.

Entertainment expenses

Starting with the 2018 tax year, the TCJA has disallowed the deductibility of entertainment expenses.

Fair market value

The amount at which property would change hands between a willing buyer and a willing seller, neither being under any compulsion to buy or sell, and both having reasonable knowledge of the relevant facts.

Federal Insurance Contributions Act (FICA)

FICA imposes social taxes on forms of earned income to provide benefits for retired and disabled workers. Referred to as FICA taxes, Social Security and Medicare taxes are withheld for a specific percentage from an employee's wages. Both the employer, the employee, and the self-employed are responsible for the payment of FICA taxes.

First in, first out (FIFO)

An accounting method for determining the cost of inventories. Under this method, the first merchandise acquired is the first to be sold. Thus, the cost of inventory on hand is deemed to be the cost of the most recently acquired merchandise.

Fiscal year-end

An annual accounting period which does not end on December 31, a calendar year-end. An example of a fiscal year is July 1 through June 30.

Foreign tax credit or deduction

Both U.S. individual taxpayers and U.S. corporations may claim a foreign tax credit on income earned and subject to tax in a foreign country or U.S. possession. As an alternative to the credit, a deduction may be taken for the foreign taxes paid. The purpose of this credit is to eliminate double taxation on income earned in a foreign country.

Fringe benefits

Non-wage benefits or perquisites (perks) provided to employees in addition to their normal wages and salaries. Most fringe benefits are required to be included in the employee's gross income; however, certain *qualified* fringe benefits such as employee-paid health insurance premiums may be excluded from the employee's gross income but remain deductible by the business.

Gift

A transfer of property for less than adequate consideration. Gifts usually occur in a personal setting (such as between members of the same family) and are generally excluded from taxable income.

Goodwill

The ability of a business to generate income in excess of a normal rate on assets due to superior managerial skills, market position, new product technology, etc. In the purchase of a business, goodwill is the difference between the purchase price and the value of the net assets. Goodwill is an intangible asset which possesses an indefinite life; however, it is amortized over a 15-year period for federal income tax purposes.

Gross income

All income from whatever source derived except that which is specifically excluded by tax law. Gross income does not include income such as interest on municipal bonds. In the case of a manufacturing or merchandising business, gross income means gross profit (i.e., gross sales or gross receipts less cost of goods sold).

Guaranteed payments

Payments made to a partner for services rendered or for use of the partner's capital, that are made without regard to the income of the partnership (similar to wages). The payments are generally ordinary income to the partner and deductible by the partnership.

Head of household

An unmarried individual who maintains a household for another and satisfies certain conditions. Such status enables the taxpayer to use income tax rates lower than those applicable to other unmarried individuals (single) but higher than those applicable to surviving spouses (widow(er)) and married persons filing a joint return.

Health savings accounts (HSA)

A type of savings account established by an employer to pay unreimbursed medical expenses by taxpayers with certain high-deductible medical insurance. Contributions to HSAs are deductible for AGI and are subject to limitations.

Hobby loss

A nondeductible loss arising from a personal hobby as contrasted with an activity engaged in for profit. Generally, the law provides a presumption that an activity is engaged in for profit if profits are earned during any 3 or more years in a 5-year period.

Household workers

Employees hired to work at specific tasks within a household, including child care, cleaning, meal preparation, and household administration. The payment of household workers generally subjects the taxpayer to a requirement to withhold or pay related payroll taxes. See *Nanny tax.*

Holding period

The period of time that property has been held by a taxpayer. The holding period is of significance in determining whether gains or losses from the sale or exchange of capital assets are classified as long-term or short-term. See *capital asset.*

Hybrid method

A method of accounting that involves the use of both the cash and accrual methods of accounting. The tax law permits the use of a hybrid method, provided the taxpayer's income is clearly reflected by the method.

Installment method

A method of accounting enabling a taxpayer to spread the recognition of gain on the sale of property over the payment period. Under this procedure, the seller computes the gross profit percentage from the sale (i.e., the gain divided by the contract price) and applies the percentage to each payment received to arrive at the gain to be recognized for each accounting period.

Installment sales

A sale in which part of the proceeds will be received in a tax year or years following the year of sale and permits the partial deferral of gain to future tax years. See *Installment method.*

Intangible assets

An asset that does not have a physical presence but has value. Some examples of intangible assets include copyrights, goodwill, patents, trademarks, etc.

Internal Revenue Code

Sometimes referred to as the Tax Code or the Code, the comprehensive set of tax laws enacted as Title 26 of the United States Code of Congress. The Code is organized according to topic, and covers all relevant rules pertaining to income, gift, estate sales, payroll, and excise taxes. The IRS is the implementing agency of the Internal Revenue Code.

Internal Revenue Service (IRS)

A United States government agency that is responsible for the enforcement of the Internal Revenue Code and collection of taxes. The IRS was established in 1862 by President Lincoln and operates under the authority of the United States Department of the Treasury.

Inventory

The goods and raw materials used to produce goods, held for sale by a business, to be sold to produce a profit.

Involuntary conversion

The loss or destruction of property through theft, casualty, or condemnation. If the owner reinvests any proceeds received within a prescribed period of time in property that is similar or related in service or use, any gain realized on an involuntary conversion can, at the taxpayer's election, be deferred for federal income tax purposes.

Kiddie tax

The amount of tax on the unearned income of certain dependent children.

Last in, first out (LIFO)

An accounting method for determining the cost of inventories. Under this method, the most recently acquired goods are sold first and the cost of inventory on hand is deemed to consist of the earliest purchased merchandise (goods).

Life insurance proceeds

Generally, life insurance proceeds paid to a beneficiary upon the death of the insured are exempt from federal income tax. An exception exists when a life insurance contract has been transferred for valuable consideration to another individual who assumes ownership rights. In such a case, the proceeds are income to the assignee to the extent that the proceeds exceed the amount paid for the policy (cash surrender value at the time of transfer) plus any subsequent premiums paid.

Lifetime learning credit

The lifetime learning credit may be used in any tax year the American Opportunity tax credit is not used for expenses paid for education. Unlike the American Opportunity tax credit, the lifetime learning credit may be claimed for an unlimited number of tax years.

Like-kind exchange

An exchange of property held for productive use in a trade or business or for investment (except inventory and stocks and bonds) for property of the same type. Unless different property is received (i.e., "boot"), the exchange will be nontaxable.

Like-kind property

See *Like-kind exchange*.

Limited Liability Company (LLC)

Business organizations usually treated as partnerships for tax purposes but offering the limited liability of a corporate stockholder to all members.

Medical expenses

Medical expenses of an individual, spouse, and dependents are allowed as an itemized deduction to the extent that total medical expenses, less insurance reimbursements, exceed limitations based on the taxpayer's AGI.

Medical flexible spending account (FSA)

A medical flexible spending account is a fringe benefit that allows employees to be reimbursed for medical expenses tax-free up to a certain dollar limit when incurred and claimed within a specific time period. FSAs are usually funded through an employee's voluntary salary reduction agreement with their employer.

Moving expenses

A deduction in arriving at adjusted gross income available to employees and self-employed individuals provided certain tests are met (e.g., the taxpayer's new job must be at least 50 miles farther from the former residence than the former residence was from the former place of work). The TCJA has suspended the deduction of moving expenses for all taxpayers except members of the U.S. Armed Services beginning in the 2018 tax year and ending in 2025.

Nanny tax

Payroll taxes paid by a taxpayer that employs certain household workers. See *Household workers*.

Necessary

Appropriate and helpful in furthering the taxpayer's business or income-producing activity. See *Ordinary*.

Net investment income

Income such as dividends and interest from investment assets such as stocks, bonds, mutual funds and other investment assets, less investment expenses other than interest expense.

Net investment income tax

The ACA imposed a 3.8 percent Medicare tax on certain net investment income of individuals that have net investment income or modified adjusted gross income above the annual statutory threshold amounts.

Net operating loss

To mitigate the effect of the annual accounting period, taxpayers are allowed to use a net loss resulting from operations, as a deduction from net income in past or future years. A carryback period of 2 years and a carryforward period of 20 years are allowed.

Nonbusiness bad debts

A bad debt loss not incurred in connection with a taxpayer's trade or business. Such loss is deductible subject to annual limitations, as a short-term capital loss and will only be allowed in the year the debt becomes entirely worthless. Many investor losses fall into the classification of nonbusiness bad debts.

Nonrecourse debt

An obligation for which the endorser is not personally liable. An example of a nonrecourse debt is a mortgage on real estate acquired by a partnership without the assumption of any liability on the mortgage by the partnership or any of the partners. The acquired property generally is pledged as collateral for the loan.

Obamacare

See *Affordable Care Act*.

Office-in-the-home expenses

Business-related expenses attributable to the use of a residence (e.g., den or office) are allowed only if the portion of the residence is used exclusively and on a regular basis as the taxpayer's place of business or as a place of business which is used by patients, clients, or customers.

Ordinary

Common, accepted, and legitimate in the general industry or type of activity in which the taxpayer is engaged. It comprises one of the tests for the deductibility of expenses incurred or paid in connection with a trade or business: for the production or collection of income; for the management, conservation, or maintenance of property held for the production of income; or in connection with the determination, collection, or refund of any tax. See *Necessary*.

Organizational expenses

Organizational expenses (also known as organizational costs) are associated with the formation of a business prior to the beginning of operation. A corporation may amortize organizational expenses over a period of 180 months. Certain expenses related to starting a company do not qualify for amortization (e.g., expenses connected with issuing or selling stock or other securities).

Partnerships

Partnerships are conduit, reporting entities, that engage in some type of business or financial activity, and are not subject to taxation. Various items of partnership income, expenses, gains, and losses flow through to the partners and are reported on their respective individual income tax returns.

Passive losses

Passive losses are deductible only to the extent of passive income. Losses from actively managed rental real estate may be deducted up to $25,000 annually. Unused passive losses carry forward indefinitely (until the activity which generated the losses is disposed of) and can be used by taxpayers to offset passive income in future years.

Patents

A patent is an intangible asset which may be amortized over its life. The sale of a patent usually results in long-term capital gain treatment.

Per diem

An alternative to reporting actual expenses, a per diem allows for a daily allowance for travel expenses including lodging, meals, and incidentals to be reimbursed to employees. Per diem reporting is designed to eliminate the record keeping usually associated with travel expenses.

Personal expenses

Expenses of an individual incurred for personal reasons which are not deductible unless specifically allowed under the tax law.

Personal property

Generally, all property other than real estate. Personal property is sometimes designated as "personalty" while real estate is termed "realty." Personal property can also refer to property not used in a taxpayer's trade or business or held for the production or collection of income. When used in this sense, personal property could include both realty (e.g., a personal residence) and personalty (e.g., personal effects such as clothing and furniture).

Personal residence

The sale of a personal residence may result in the recognition of capital gain (but not loss). Taxpayers may permanently exclude $250,000 ($500,000 if married) of gain on the sale of their personal residence from income provided certain requirements are met, but generally not more than once every two years.

Points

Loan origination fees paid generally deductible as interest expense by a buyer of property.

Portfolio income

Portfolio income includes dividends, interest, royalties, annuities, and realized gains or losses on the sale of assets producing portfolio income.

Premium tax credit

Lower income individuals who obtain health insurance coverage may be eligible for the premium tax credit to assist in covering the cost of health care premiums. Eligible individuals can choose to receive the credit paid in advance or claim the total credit when filing their tax return. If an individual chooses to have the credit paid in advance, the individual will reconcile the amount paid in advance with the actual credit computed when filing their tax return.

Private mortgage insurance (PMI)

Mortgage insurance is an additional expense charged to a borrower that is often required when the borrower makes only a small investment (down payment) on their home at time of purchase.

Prizes and awards

The fair market value of a prize or award generally is included in gross income.

Qualified business income (QBI)

The income attributed to individual taxpayers by a pass-through entity such as a sole proprietorship, partnership, or S corporation that excludes capital gains, most dividends, interest, and other nonbusiness income.

Qualified business income (QBI) deduction

A deduction in the amount of 20 percent of the qualified business income, subject to certain limitations such as the taxable income limit, the wage limitation and the specified service business limitation. The limitations are computed before considering the QBI deduction.

Qualified business property

Tangible property subject to depreciation (i.e., not inventory or land) for which the depreciable period has not ended before the close of the taxable year, held by the business at year-end, and used at any point during the year in the production of QBI. Qualified business property is an element of the wage and capital limitation, which is a component of the wage limitation.

Qualified pension or profit-sharing plan

An employer-sponsored plan that meets certain requirements. If these requirements are met, none of the employer's contributions to the plan will be taxed to the employee until distributed to him or her. The employer will be allowed a deduction in the year the contributions are made.

Qualified tuition program

See *Section 529 tuition plan.*

Qualified trade or business

Any trade or business other than a specified service trade or business, or the trade or business of performing services as an employee.

Qualifying widow(er)

A tax filing status available to widows or widowers for two years after their spouse's death. To claim this status, the taxpayer must also have a dependent child who lives in the household and for which the taxpayer pays over half the cost of maintaining the household.

Realized gain or loss

The difference between the amount realized upon the sale or other disposition of property and the adjusted basis of such property.

Recognized gain or loss

The portion of realized gain or loss that is subject to income taxation. See *Realized gain or loss.*

Recovery period

The amount of time in which a business asset is depreciated and thereby creating a tax deduction, under the useful life requirements established by the Internal Revenue Service.

Rollover

Transfer of pension funds from one plan or trustee to another. The transfer may be a direct transfer or a rollover distribution.

Roth IRAs

The Roth IRA allows nondeductible contributions. Although the contributions to a Roth IRA are not deductible, earnings accumulate tax-free, and qualified distributions are generally not included in income when received.

S corporation

A small business corporation whose shareholders have filed an election permitting the corporation to be treated in a manner similar to partnerships for income tax purposes. Of major significance are the facts that S corporations usually avoid the corporate income tax and that corporate losses can be claimed by the shareholders, limited to individual shareholder's adjusted basis.

Saver's Credit

A tax credit designed to give low-to-moderate-income taxpayers a tax credit for part of a contribution to a qualified retirement plan.

Scholarships

Scholarships are generally taxable income to the recipient except for amounts received for tuition, fees, books, and course-required supplies and equipment.

Section 179

See *Election to Expense (Section 179)*

Section 401(k) plan

A Section 401(k) plan is a qualified retirement plan which grants employee participants a deferral of income for employer contributions to the plan. The plan allows taxpayers to elect to receive compensation or to have the employer make a contribution to the retirement plan. The plan may be structured as a salary reduction plan. There is a maximum annual dollar limitation, as well as a limitation based on the employee's compensation. Some employers match employee contributions up to a certain limit in order to encourage participation.

Section 1231 assets

Section 1231 assets include depreciable assets and real estate used in a trade or business, held for the long-term holding period. Under certain circumstances, the classification also includes timber, coal, domestic iron ore, livestock (held for draft, breeding, dairy, or sporting purposes), and unharvested crops. Gains may be treated as long-term capital gains while losses in some cases may be deducted as ordinary losses.

Section 1245 recapture

See *depreciation recapture*.

Section 1250 recapture

See *depreciation recapture*.

Self-employment income

Self-employment income is the taxpayer's net earnings from self-employment, which includes gross income from a taxpayer's trade or business, less trade or business deductions. Self-employment income also includes the taxpayer's share of income from a partnership trade or business.

SEP IRA

A form of qualified retirement plan for certain small businesses. See *Simplified Employee Pension (SEP)*.

Separate property

Separate property is property, other than community property, acquired by a spouse before marriage or after marriage as a gift or inheritance.

Simplified Employee Pension (SEP)

A retirement plan that any employer or self-employed individual can establish. SEPs are simple to set up and have flexible funding arrangements with contributions that are limited on an annual basis.

Simplified method

A specific calculation used by individual taxpayers to calculate the taxable amount of a payment from an annuity after November 18, 1996.

Social Security number

A unique 9-digit number provided by the U.S. Social Security Administration to identify each person and track Social Security benefits. Most taxpayers use the Social Security number as their taxpayer identification number. See *Taxpayer identification number*.

Social Security tax

A component of FICA (see *Federal Insurance Contributions Act (FICA)*), Social Security taxes refer to Old Age, Survivors, and Disability Insurance (OASDI) and are applied to all wages, up to an annual limitation.

Specified service trade or business

Used in the context of qualified business income as being excluded from a qualified trade or business, it involves the performance of services where the principal asset of such trade or business is based on the reputation or skill of one or more of its employees, such as accounting, actuarial science, consulting, financial and brokerage services, health, law, performing arts, and professional athletes.

Standard deduction

Taxpayers can deduct the larger of the standard deduction or their itemized deductions in calculating taxable income. An extra standard deduction amount is allowed for elderly and blind taxpayers. The standard deduction amounts are set by the IRS and may change annually.

Statute of limitations

A time period within which an action may be taken by the IRS or a taxpayer on a tax return. In general, the statute of limitations for a tax return runs for 3 years from the date the tax return was filed or the return extended due date, whichever is later.

Tax home

Since travel expenses of a taxpayer are deductible only if the taxpayer is away from home, the deductibility of such expenses rests upon the definition of "tax home." The IRS position is that the "tax home" is the business location, post, or station of the taxpayer. If the taxpayer is temporarily reassigned to a new post for a period of 1 year or less, the taxpayer's home should be his or her personal residence and the travel expenses should be deductible.

Taxpayer Bill of Rights

Passed by Congress in 1988 and amended several times, this set of provisions requires that the IRS informs taxpayers of their rights when dealing with the IRS and it expands taxpayers' rights and remedies when involved in disputes with the IRS. The provisions of the Taxpayer Bill of Rights are summarized in IRS Publication 1.

Taxpayer identification number

A unique number of a taxpayer used by the IRS in the administration of tax laws. For individuals, it is generally a Social Security number, but can also be an Individual Taxpayer Identification Number (ITIN) which is issued by the IRS to individuals who are not eligible to receive a Social Security number. For employers, it is an IRS-issued number known as an Employer Identification Number (EIN). See *Social Security number*.

TCJA

The Tax Cuts and Jobs Act (TCJA) of 2017 was signed into law resulting in the most dramatic change to the tax code since 1986.

Trade or business expenses

Deductions for AGI which are attributable to a taxpayer's business or profession. The expenses must be ordinary and necessary to that business.

Traditional IRA

An individual retirement account (IRA) for taxpayers. The traditional IRA often permits a deduction for contributions and deferred taxation of earnings until withdrawals.

Transportation expenses

Transportation expenses for a taxpayer include only the costs of transportation (taxi fares, automobile expenses, etc.) in the course of employment where the taxpayer is not "away from home" in a travel status. Commuting expenses are not deductible.

Travel expenses

Travel expenses include meals (50 percent deductible), lodging, and transportation expenses while away from home in the pursuit of a trade or business (including that as an employee).

Trustee-to-trustee transfer

When a trustee of a retirement plan transfers assets to the trustee of a different retirement plan, upon instruction from the taxpayer. There are no tax implications nor are there any restrictions on amounts or number of transfer occurrences in a given year.

Unearned income

For tax purposes, unearned income (e.g., rent) is taxable in the year of receipt. In certain cases involving advance payments for goods and services, income may be deferred.

Vacation home

The Internal Revenue Code places restrictions upon taxpayers who rent their residence or vacation home for part of the tax year. The restrictions may result in the limitation of certain expenses related to the vacation home.

Viatical settlements

An early payout resulting from the sale of a life insurance policy often due to the insured being terminally or chronically ill. A viatical settlement is a way to extract value from the policy while the policy holder is still alive. See *Accelerated death benefits*.

Wage and capital limitation

A limitation on the qualified business income deduction of 25 percent of wages and 2.5 percent of qualified business property.

Wage limitation

A limitation on the qualified business income deduction of 50 percent of wages.

Withholding

The amount of tax deducted (withheld) by a payer and ultimately remitted to the tax authority as a tax payment on behalf of the payment recipient. For example, income taxes are often withheld from an employee's wages and then remitted on behalf of the employee as a tax payment to the IRS.